HOW TO USE OCCUPATIONS v

DISABILITY AND CAREERS CHOICE vii

COLOUR VISION AND EMPLOYMENT ix

LIST OF OCCUPATIONAL ARTICLES IN CLCI ORDER xi

THE OCCUPATIONAL ARTICLES (BY GROUP)

A - SELF-EMPLOYMENT 1

B - ARMED FORCES 5

C - ADMINISTRATION, BUSINESS,
    CLERICAL AND MANAGEMENT 29

E - ART AND DESIGN 93

F - TEACHING AND CULTURAL ACTIVITIES 107

G - ENTERTAINMENT AND LEISURE 153

I - HOSPITALITY, CATERING AND OTHER SERVICES 204

J - HEALTH AND MEDICAL SERVICES 245

K - SOCIAL AND RELATED SERVICES 306

L - LAW AND RELATED WORK 331

M - SECURITY AND PROTECTIVE SERVICES 345

N - FINANCE AND RELATED WORK 361

O - BUYING, SELLING AND RELATED SERVICES 394

Q - SCIENCES, MATHEMATICS AND RELATED WORK 434

R - ENGINEERING 462

S - MANUFACTURING INDUSTRIES 493

U - CONSTRUCTION AND LAND SERVICES 552

W - ANIMALS, PLANTS AND NATURE 602

Y - TRANSPORT 646

ALPHABETICAL INDEX 689

ORDER FORM FOR CD-ROM VERSION

HOW TO USE OCCUPATIONS

Occupations '99 is a comprehensive reference book containing details of around 600 jobs and careers of all types, from unskilled to professional work.

The book contains: articles about disability and careers choice, and colour vision and employment; a list of the jobs included in Occupations '99 in Careers Library Classification Index (CLCI) order; the occupational articles; and the alphabetical index.

Occupations '99 is also now available on a CD-Rom. The price of this pilot version is £16.50 including VAT, postage and packing, and can be ordered using the order form which you will find after the Alphabetical Index.

Most careers advisers and teachers will be familiar with CLCI, a new edition of which was published in April 1998. It has 18 major occupational groups, each identified by an index letter. For example, group R is Engineering and group N is Finance and Related Work.

Each group is subdivided into smaller occupational areas identified by a further two- or three-letter classification, such as RAL: Electronic Engineering or NAD: Banking. As far as possible, we have used the CLCI. However, on occasion, we have departed from it for the sake of clarity. Hotel Receptionist, for example, is under Hospitality, Catering and Other Services in group I, rather than under its usual classification with clerical work, in group C.

Users of Occupations '99 can find information about occupations either by using the CLCI listing or through the alphabetical index.

The CLCI listing is useful because it groups jobs and careers with similar backgrounds together. Readers without a specific occupation in mind, but with a broad idea of their chosen career area (say, engineering or social work) are presented with a range of related careers.

However, if a reader wants information about a specific job, the relevant page can readily be found using the alphabetical index.

Each article contains the following details: background information, the work, work environment, skills and interests, entry requirements, training, late entry, opportunities, pay and conditions, prospects and related occupations. There is also a list of addresses and publications for further information. The address lists are of professional and other bodies which should be able to provide information over and above that contained in the relevant article.

Every effort is made to ensure that the information contained in Occupations '99 is accurate at the time of going to print.

However, if we have got something wrong then please let us know by writing to Peter Turvey (Editor), Occupations '99, COIC, Room West 4B, Moorfoot, Sheffield S1 4PQ.

DISABILITY AND CAREERS CHOICE: AWB

INTRODUCTION

Advice and practical help is readily available to people with disabilities. This article gives details of how they can be helped with making the right choice of employment opportunity, or choosing a training or further and/or higher education course.

People with disabilities have the right of equal access to jobs, goods and services. Recent legislation has removed many of the obstacles to equal access in the areas of employment and training opportunities.

THE DISABILITY DISCRIMINATION ACT

The Disability Discrimination Act (DDA) passed in November 1995 makes it unlawful to discriminate against people with disabilities in the areas of employment, the provision of goods and services and the buying or renting of land or property.

Employment provisions and those for goods and services covering refusal to serve a person or offer a different service or a service on different terms are now effective. Employers who currently employ 20 or more employees must comply with the Act, but with effect from 1 December 1998, the employment provisions of the DDA will be extended to employers employing 15 or more people.

A person will be considered to have a disability for the purpose of the Act if they have or have had a physical or mental impairment that has a substantial and long term adverse effect on their ability to carry out normal day to day activities. An employer would discriminate against a disabled person, 'if for a reason which relates to that person's disability, he/she treats them less favourably than he/she treats or would treat others to whom that reason does not or would not apply and he/she cannot show that the treatment in question is justified.' (DDA 1995 Part II 5(1)(a)&(b). An employer would be justified for example in refusing the job of a bus driver to a blind person because the central criteria to be able to do this work is being able to drive.

Discrimination has also been extended to cover all the terms and conditions of work for those employees who may have disabilities or those applying for vacancies as prospective employees. All should be treated equally and fairly in the areas of:
– recruitment
– pay and conditions of service
– training and development opportunities
– promotion and transfers, and
– unfair dismissal

Where any arrangements made by or on behalf of an employer or any physical feature of premises occupied by an employer place the disabled person at a substantial disadvantage in comparison with persons who are not disabled, it is the duty of employers to take such steps as it is reasonable, in all circumstances of the case, for the employer to have to take in order to prevent the arrangement having that effect - for example, where a wheelchair user is employed adaptations should be made to their premises to allow access for wheelchair employees.

Employers' interpretation of a 'reasonable adjustment' will be a key factor in the success of the Act eliminating the discrimination of people with disabilities. The booklet 'Guidelines for Policies on the Employment of Disabled People' (RADAR) gives positive advice to employers for formulating an equal opportunities policy towards employing people with disabilities.

Careers services are affected by the provisions covering employment and goods and services. As independent organizations they are responsible for ensuring that they comply with the provisions of the Act, both as employers, and as providers of goods and services (ie careers information and guidance). New provisions affecting service providers will be introduced in October 1999.

Government funded training provision is also covered by the Act. Through their contracts, Training and Enterprise Councils (TECs), Local Enterprise Companies (LECs) and other training providers must ensure that their policies and systems do not discriminate against people with disabilities, eg by limiting their training choices, restricting their access or denying them equality of opportunity for outcomes from training.

HELPING TO CHOOSE

People with disabilities are not a homogenous group. The extent and variety of disability is wide and can cover a broad range of physical, mental or sensory conditions; each person is different and the implications for job choice depend on each individual.

• Some jobs may aggravate health conditions or disabilities and make it difficult to perform tasks satisfactorily.

• Some occupations entail specified standards of health and fitness. Some, for example, such as airline pilots and train drivers cannot be undertaken by people with specific physical impairments.

• Those with defective colour vision cannot be electricians or signalling technicians where recognizing colour is essential to the high safety standards required. The Colour Vision and Employment article on page ix gives more information and help in this area.

Each condition, its nature and effects has to be taken into account in the particular circumstances. Some people would not necessarily be prevented from pursuing the job they had chosen. Medical conditions can be treated and specialist equipment can help with physical impairment enabling people to carry out tasks satisfactorily.

There are a number of organizations, educational establishments and Government agencies which can give help and advice to people with disabilities seeking employment, training or further education.

(i) **Careers services** play a critical role in facilitating the transition from education to the world of work. They have a particular responsibility for those of their clients who have disabilities and who remain in the client group until they are settled in their chosen career. Services are contractually required to work with the range of agencies to ensure that their clients are given information, guidance and assistance to enter appropriate further education, training and employment.

(ii) **The Employment Service** offers a comprehensive range of specialist services through Disability Employment Advisers (DEAs) who are usually based in Jobcentres. They work closely with employers,

DISABILITY AND CAREERS CHOICE: AWB

employees and people with disabilities seeking work. DEAs are supported by Placing, Assessment and Counselling Teams (PACTs) or Regional Business Centres. They can advise about the Access to Work programme (ATW) which helps disabled people in or entering work with specialist equipment, adaptations or human support to ensure that they can compete on equal terms in the workplace.

(iii) **The Royal Association for Disability and Rehabilitation (RADAR)** gives help and advice to people with disabilities on employment, education and welfare issues. RADAR provides information and advice to employers on the employment of disabled people.

(iv) **SKILL (National Bureau for Students with Disabilities)** helps young people and adults with any kind of disability to fulfil their potential. SKILL works in partnership with disabled people and service providers in further and higher education, training and employment. In post-16 education for example, advice will include college application, financial assistance whilst studying, disclosing a disability, seeking and finding work. A range of books, leaflets and information sheets are available. See **FURTHER READING**.

(v) **Colleges** are geared up to give help and advice about access to courses and learning facilities for students with disabilities.

(vi) **Training and Enterprise Councils (TECs)** in England and Wales and **Local Enterprise Companies (LECs)** in Scotland give help and advice and offer training opportunities through initiatives such as Modern Apprenticeships and National Traineeships (Skillseekers initiative in Scotland).

FURTHER INFORMATION

The following organizations will provide help and advice about employment, training, further and higher education opportunities. Leaflets/booklets are available from the addresses marked *.

Placing, Assessment and Counselling Teams (PACTs) with Disability Employment Advisers (DEAs) may be contacted through careers services or Jobcentres.

RADAR (the Royal Association for Disability and Rehabilitation)*, 12 City Forum, 250 City Road, London EC1V 8AF, 0171 250 3222.

SKILL - The National Bureau for Students with Disabilities*, 336 Brixton Road, London SW9 7AA, 0171 274 0565, Minicom: 0171 738 7722, E-mail: SkillNatBueDis@compuserve.com.

Lancaster University, Can Do Service (to disabled students and graduates), Careers Service, Lancaster LA1 4YW; tel: 01524 594370, http://cando.lancs.ac.uk/

Association of National Specialist Colleges, Lord Mayor Teloan College, Holybourne, Alton, Hampshire GU23 4EN.

The Post-16 Information Officer of the Royal National Institute for the Blind (RNIB) can refer you to an appropriate student adviser or employment consultant for your own area. Contact the RNIB at: RNIB Education and Employment Divisions, 224 Great Portland Street, London W1N 2AA. Phone the Helpline 0345 66 99 99, www.rnib.org.uk

The National Dyslexia Association has a helpline on 0118 966 8271.

The Royal National Institute for the Deaf represents the interests of the 8.7 million deaf and hard of hearing people in the UK. Contact them on 0870 60 50 123 or (Textphone only) 08870 60 33 007, http://www.rnid.org.uk

Local TECs/LECs, careers services. Their numbers are in the telephone directory.

FURTHER READING

Disability Discrimination Act Information Pack.

The DDA 1995 - What Services Providers Need to Know.

What employees and job applicants need to know - guidance on employment rights for disabled people under the DDA - DFEE [also available in braille and audio versions].

The DDA 1995 - What Employers Need to Know.

The above are available by telephoning the Disability Discrimination Act Information Line on 0345 622 633, or by writing to Freepost MID, Stratford-on-Avon CV37 9BR.

The Disability Discrimination Act 1995 [Employment] - RADAR - £1.00 inc p&p.

Make it Work - Employment Advice for People with Disabilities - The Employment Service.

Into Teaching - Positive Experiences of Disabled People in teaching - (SKILL).

Into Science & Engineering - Positive Experiences of Disabled People in science or engineering - (SKILL).

Able to Succeed - Disabilities, Health and Job Choice - Sara Bosley. Published by Cascaid. Gives help and advice for dealing with eleven health conditions and physical impairment (eg visual impairment, limited physical mobility).

COLOUR VISION AND EMPLOYMENT: AWB1.3

Normal colour vision is useful or important to a wide range of jobs that involve any kind of visual judgement.

In the case of a small number of occupations – notably those where colour recognition is critical to health and safety – perfect colour vision may be required as a condition for training or employment, eg transport, navigation and armed services.

Serious defects in colour vision are usually identified early on in childhood and those affected should seek detailed advice from their local careers service about the implications for them individually. For jobs or training in which perfect colour vision is essential, a sight test will normally form part of the selection procedure.

What is defective colour vision?

Defective colour vision (colour-blindness) occurs in about eight per cent of men and less than one per cent of women in Western Europe and America and is caused by a defect or abnormality in the light-sensitive pigments (photopigments) contained in the cone-shaped cells that form part of the retina (the layer of sensory cells at the back of the eye).

It is usually inherited, does not change with age and cannot be treated or corrected. Some colours that look different to people with normal colour vision look the same to people with colour deficiency. This leads to colour confusions and incorrect colour naming. Defects vary in type and severity. People with slight colour deficiency do not present any serious disability in terms of employment.

Types of defect

There are three main types of defective colour vision:

1. Total or partial loss of sensitivity to red light. This affects two per cent of men and four in every ten thousand women.

2. Total or partial loss of sensitivity to green light. This affects six per cent of men and 36 women in every ten thousand.

3. Total or partial loss of sensitivity to blue light affects about one person in every ten thousand. It occurs equally in men and women.

Only about three people in every hundred thousand are totally colour-blind and see the world exclusively in monochrome. In most cases these individuals have poor sight in general.

In addition there are some people who lose some degree of colour vision in later life due to injury, illness or adverse reaction to prescribed drugs. Their symptoms are different from those of people who have inherited defective colour vision and, according to individual circumstances, they may have other sight problems as well.

Testing for colour vision

Colour vision tests are usually carried out at school. In addition, the following university optometry departments can provide a diagnostic testing service (for which there may be a fee): Glasgow Caledonian, City (London), Bradford, and University of Manchester Institute of Science and Technology (UMIST), Wales (Cardiff), Aston (Birmingham).

Certain employers may also administer colour vision tests as part of the recruitment process.

A number of tests are available, including the Ishihara test (one of the most commonly used) and the City University test.

Tests check both the presence, type and degree of defective colour vision (eg whether different shades can be recognized).

Implications for career choice

Some occupations are not suitable for people with defective colour vision. For instance, people who lack sensitivity to red light may react slowly to red stop signals and would be unsuited to certain careers in transport. However, in some jobs, it is possible to predict where problems may occur and take steps to avoid them. It may also be possible to redesign a job so that a person with defective colour vision can do it satisfactorily.

Occupations where good colour vision is an entry requirement

Armed Forces – certain trades. Check with the appropriate Forces careers information office

Colour quality control in manufacturing industries – certain jobs. Check with your local careers office

Civil aviation – pilots, air traffic control, flight crew

Colour matcher – in dyeing, textiles, paints, inks, coloured paper, ceramics, cosmetics

Electrical/electronic technician/Engineer

Merchant Navy deck officer/Engineer

Police officer/Firefighter

Railway worker – train driver, signals/telecoms technician, track worker, station assistant

Radio and telecommunications – telecoms technician

Typical occupations where defective colour vision is a handicap, though not an absolute bar, to entry

Note: this is *not* an exhaustive list.

Cartography

Design

Horticulture

Pharmacy

There are many other occupations where normal colour vision may be helpful, but defective colour vision is not a serious handicap. If you have problems with your colour vision it is advisable to discuss your choice of occupation with your local careers service. The Health and Safety Executive's Employment Medical Advisory Service may advise on occupational placements and suggest agencies that can provide testing facilities.

Further information and further reading

NB: The following publication is primarily technical and aimed primarily at professionals in the field.

Diagnosis of Defective Colour Vision – Jennifer Birch – Butterworths (1998) – (Senior Lecturer in Clinical Optometry, City University), contains a checklist of occupations where normal colour vision is required or in which defective colour vision is a handicap.

COLOUR VISION AND EMPLOYMENT: AWB1.3

The Health and Safety Executive's (HSE) Employment Medical Advisory Service can offer advice. Contact your local HSE office listed under Health and Safety Executive in the phone book.

Thanks are due to the City University Optometry Department for their help in preparing this information.

LIST OF OCCUPATIONAL ARTICLES IN CLCI ORDER

GROUP A – SELF-EMPLOYMENT
Self-employment (AVD6) 1

GROUP B – ARMED FORCES

THE NAVAL SERVICE
1. RN/QARNNS Officer (BAB) 5
2. RN Rating (BAB) 8
3. Royal Marines Officer (BAB) 11
4. Royal Marines – Other Ranks (BAB) 13

THE ARMY
1. Army Officer (BAF) 15
2. Army Non-commissioned Officer/Private (BAF) 19

THE ROYAL AIR FORCE
1. RAF Officer (BAL) 22
2. RAF Airman/Airwoman (BAL) 25

GROUP C – ADMINISTRATION, BUSINESS, CLERICAL AND MANAGEMENT

CIVIL SERVICE
1. Administrative Staff (CAB) 30
2. Support Staff (CAB) 32
3. Specialist Staff (CAB) 33

LOCAL GOVERNMENT
1. Local Government Administrator (CAG) 39
2. Local Government Clerical/Administrative Assistant (CAG) 40

HEALTH SERVICE MANAGEMENT
1. Health Service Manager (CAL) 43
2. Medical Records Clerk (CAL) 45

INSTITUTE/BUSINESS ADMINISTRATION
Chartered Secretary (CAP) 48

HUMAN RESOURCES
1. Personnel/Human Resources Officer (CAS) 50
2. Training Officer (FAP) 52

SECRETARIAL WORK
1. Executive Secretary/Personal Assistant (CAT) 55
2. Specialist Secretary (CAT) 56

ADMINISTRATIVE/ CLERICAL WORK
1. Administrative/Clerical Staff (CAT) 61
2. Receptionist (CAT) 63

INFORMATION TECHNOLOGY
1. Systems Analyst/Designer (Systems Integrator) (CAV) 66
2. Software Engineer/Analyst Programmer (CAV) 68
3. Network Engineer (CAV) 70
4. Database Administrator (CAV) 72
5. Webmaster (CAV) 74
6. Multimedia Specialist (CAV) 76
7. Help Desk Operator (CAV) 78

MANAGEMENT SERVICES
1. Operational Researcher (COF) 81
2. Organization and Methods/Work Study Officer (COD) 83

CONSUMER PROTECTION
Trading Standards Officer (COP) 85

HEALTH AND SAFETY
1. Environmental Health Officer (COP) 87
2. Health and Safety Adviser (COT) 89
3. Health and Safety Inspector (COT) 91

GROUP E – ART AND DESIGN

ART AND DESIGN
1. Graphic Designer (ED) 93
2. Illustrator/Artist (ED) 95
3. Three-dimensional Designer (EG) 96
4. Fashion Designer (EJ) 98
5. Textile Designer (EP) 99
6. Interior Designer (ET) 100

PHOTOGRAPHY
1. Photographer (EV) 102
2. Photographic Technician (EV/SOZ) 105

GROUP F – TEACHING AND CULTURAL ACTIVITIES

TEACHING
1. School Teacher – England and Wales (FAB) 107
2. School Teacher – Scotland (FAB) 110
3. Special Educational Needs Teacher (FAB) 113
4. Further Education/Tertiary College Lecturer (FAB) 115
5. Higher Education Lecturer (FAB) 118

LIST OF OCCUPATIONAL ARTICLES IN CLCI ORDER

JOURNALISM AND TECHNICAL WRITING
1. Journalist (FAC) 121
2. Technical Author (FAC) 124

PUBLISHING
Editor (FAD) 127

MUSEUM AND ART GALLERY WORK
1. Museum Curator/Art Gallery Keeper (FAE)............129
2. Conservator/Restorer (EZ/FAE) 131

LIBRARY AND INFORMATION WORK
1. Librarian/Information Manager (FAF) 134
2. Library/Information Assistant (FAF) 136
3. Information Scientist (FAF) 138

ARCHAEOLOGY
Archaeologist (FAH) 141

LANGUAGES
1. Interpreter (FAL) 145
2. Translator (FAL) 147
3. Teacher of English as a Foreign or Second Language (FAL)..149

GROUP G – ENTERTAINMENT AND LEISURE

PERFORMING ARTS
1. Actor (GAB) 153
2. Musician (GAD) 156
3. Music Teacher (GAD/FAB) 159
4. Dancer (GAF) 162

SPORTS AND LEISURE
1. Sports Coach/Instructor (GAG)...................166
2. Professional Sportsman/woman (GAG) 169
3. Sports and Leisure Centre Manager (GAJ) 175
4. Sports and Leisure Centre Assistant (GAJ) 178

BROADCASTING/FILM/THEATRE
1. Production Assistant (GAL) 182
2. Researcher (GAL) 184
3. Floor/Stage Manager/Assistant Director (GAL) 186
4. Cameraman/woman/Camera Operator (GAL) 189
5. Sound Technician/Operator (GAL) 192

TRAVEL AND TOURISM
1. Tourist Information Centre Assistant (GAX)............196
2. Travel Consultant/Travel Agency Clerk (GAX)........197
3. Travel Courier (GAX) 199
4. Tour Manager (GAX) 200
5. Resort Representative (GAX) 201

GROUP I – HOSPITALITY, CATERING AND OTHER SERVICES

CATERING AND HOSPITALITY
1. Hotel Manager (IB) 204
2. Restaurant/Catering Manager (IB) 206
3. Housekeeper/Housekeeping Manager (IB) 208
4. Chef/Cook (IC) 210
5. Kitchen Assistant (IC) 212
6. Food Service Assistant (IC).....................213
7. Counter Service Assistant (IC) 215
8. Hotel Receptionist (IC/CAT) 217
9. Hotel Room Attendant (IC) 219
10. Hotel Porter (IC) 221

LICENSED RETAILING
1. Publican/Licensee (IB)..........................223
2. Barman/woman (IC) 224

HOME ECONOMICS
Home Economist (ID) 227

CLEANING SERVICES
1. Window Cleaner (IJ) 230
2. Refuse Collector (IJ) 231

BEAUTY
1. Beauty Therapist (IK) 234
2. Beauty Consultant (IK/OFM)...................236

HAIRDRESSING
Hairdresser (IL) 239

FUNERAL SERVICES
Funeral Director/Embalmer (IP) 242

GROUP J – HEALTH AND MEDICAL SERVICES

MEDICINE AND SURGERY
1. General Practitioner (JAB)......................245
2. Hospital Doctor (JAB) 247

NURSING AND AUXILIARY WORK
1. Registered Nurse (JAD) 250
2. Midwife (JAD) 252
3. District Nurse (JAD) 253
4. Health Visitor (JAD) 254
5. Occupational Health Nurse (JAD) 255
6. Health Care Assistant/Nursing Auxiliary (JAD) 256

DENTISTRY
1. Dentist (JAF) 260

LIST OF OCCUPATIONAL ARTICLES IN CLCI ORDER

2. Dental Nurse (JAF) 262
3. Dental Hygienist (JAF) 264
4. Dental Technician (JAF) 266

PHARMACY WORK
1. Pharmacist (JAG) 269
2. Pharmacy Technician (JAG) 271

OPHTHALMICS
1. Optometrist/Ophthalmic Optician (JAL) 273
2. Dispensing Optician (JAL) 274
3. Orthoptist (JAL) 276

THERAPY AND TREATMENT
1. Physiotherapist (JAN) 279
2. Radiographer (JAP) 280
3. Occupational Therapist (JAR) 282
4. Speech and Language Therapist (JAS) 283
5. Chiropodist/Podiatrist (JAT) 284
6. Dietitian (JAV) 286

MEDICAL TECHNOLOGY
Medical Technical Officer (JOB) 289

AMBULANCE WORK
Ambulance Person (JOC) 292

ALTERNATIVE/COMPLEMENTARY MEDICINE
1. Acupuncturist (JOD) 295
2. Aromatherapist (JOD) 295
3. Chiropractor (JOD) 295
4. Herbalist (JOD) 295
5. Homoeopath (JOD) 295
6. Naturopath (JOD) 296
7. Osteopath (JOD) 296
8. Reflexologist (JOD) 296

PROSTHETICS/ORTHOTICS
Prosthetist/Orthotist (JOL) 300

OTHER HEALTH WORK
1. Hospital Porter (JOZ) 302
2. Operating Department Practitioner (JOZ) 303

GROUP K – SOCIAL AND RELATED SERVICES

SOCIAL WORK
1. Field Social Worker (KEB) 306
2. Residential Social Worker (KEB) 308
3. Care Assistant (KEB) 309

PROBATION AND AFTERCARE
Probation Officer (KEB) 312

NURSERY WORK
Nursery Nurse (KEB) 315

CAREERS WORK
Careers Adviser (KED) 318

EMPLOYMENT AGENCY WORK
Employment Agency Consultant/Interviewer (KED)..321

YOUTH AND COMMUNITY WORK
Youth and Community Worker/Community Education Worker (KEG) 323

PSYCHOLOGY
Psychologist (KEL) 326

VOLUNTARY HELP MANAGEMENT WORK
Volunteer Manager (KEM) 329

GROUP L – LAW AND RELATED WORK

LAW AND RELATED WORK
1. Barrister/Advocate (LAB) 331
2. Solicitor (LAC) 334
3. Barristers' Clerk (LAZ) 337
4. Legal Executive (LAD) 339
5. Shorthand Writer (LAG) 341
6. Court Usher/Court Officer/Macer (LAG) 343

GROUP M – SECURITY AND PROTECTIVE SERVICES

POLICE AND RELATED WORK
1. Police Constable (MAB) 345
2. Traffic Warden (MAB) 347

PRISON SERVICE
1. Prison Governor (MAD) 349
2. Prison Officer (MAD) 351

FIRE SERVICE
Firefighter/Fire Officer (MAF) 354

SECURITY WORK
Security Officer (MAG) 357

COASTGUARD
Coastguard Officer (MAZ/YAL) 359

LIST OF OCCUPATIONAL ARTICLES IN CLCI ORDER

GROUP N – FINANCE AND RELATED WORK

ACCOUNTANCY
1. Private Practice Accountant (NAB)..........361
2. Industry and Commerce Accountant (NAB)..........363
3. Public Sector Accountant (NAB)..........364
4. Accounting Technician (NAB)..........366

BANKING AND BUILDING SOCIETY WORK
1. Manager (NAD/NAF)..........369
2. Bank Officer/Customer Service Assistant (NAD/NAF)..........371

INSURANCE WORK
1. Insurance Underwriter (NAG)..........374
2. Insurance Broker (NAG)..........376
3. Financial Adviser (NAG)..........378
4. Insurance Claims Official (NAG)..........379
5. Insurance Clerk (NAG)..........381
6. Insurance Surveyor (NAG)..........382
7. Insurance Loss Adjuster (NAG)..........383
8. Risk Manager (NAG)..........385

ACTUARIAL WORK
Actuary (NAJ)..........387

STOCK EXCHANGE WORK AND INVESTMENT ANALYSIS
1. Market Maker/Trader (NAL)..........389
2. Stockbroker/Equity Salesperson (NAL)..........390
3. Investment Analyst/Fund Manager (NAL)..........391

GROUP O – BUYING, SELLING AND RELATED SERVICES

MARKETING
1. Marketing Manager (OB)..........394
2. Market Research Executive (OB)..........396
3. Market Research Interviewer (OB)..........397

ADVERTISING
1. Account Executive (OD)..........400
2. Account Planner (OD)..........400
3. Media Executive (OD)..........400
4. Copywriter (OD)..........401

RETAIL DISTRIBUTION
1. Store Manager (OE)..........405
2. Store Assistant (OE)..........407
3. Store Demonstrator (OE/OFZ)..........408
4. Supermarket Worker (OE)..........410
5. Tyre/Exhaust Fitter (OFM/RAE)..........412
6. Forecourt Attendant (OFM)..........413
7. Retail Butcher (OFM)..........415
8. Florist (OFM)..........417
9. Display Person (OFM/ET)..........419
10. Shoe Repairer (OFZ)..........421

PUBLIC RELATIONS
Public Relations Officer (OG)..........423

SALES
Sales Representative/Manager (OM)..........425

BUYING
Buyer/Purchasing Officer (OP)..........428

FASHION MODELLING
Fashion Model (OT)..........431

GROUP Q – SCIENCES, MATHEMATICS AND RELATED WORK

SCIENCES
1. Scientist/Technician (QOB–QOM)..........434
2. Biomedical Scientist (QOB)..........437
3. Food Scientist/Technologist/Technician (QON)..........439
4. Materials Scientist/Technologist/Metallurgist (QOS)..........442

STATISTICS
Statistician (QOG)..........446

ECONOMICS
Economist (QOK)..........449

EARTH SCIENCES
1. Geologist (QOL)..........452
2. Meteorologist (QOL)..........454
3. Oceanographer (QOL)..........456

FORENSIC SCIENCE
Forensic Scientist (QOT)..........459

GROUP R – ENGINEERING

ENGINEERING
Engineer (RAB)..........462

VEHICLE MAINTENANCE
1. Motor Mechanic/Vehicle Technician (RAE)..........467
2. Vehicle Body Repairer (RON)..........469

ELECTRICAL WORK
Electrician (RAK)..........472

LIST OF OCCUPATIONAL ARTICLES IN CLCI ORDER

TELECOMMUNICATIONS WORK
Telecoms Technician (RAL) 475

OIL AND GAS PRODUCTION AND DRILLING
1. Roustabout (ROB) 478
2. Roughneck (ROB) 478
3. Derrickman (ROB) 478
4. Driller/Assistant Driller (ROB) 478
5. Toolpusher (ROB) 478
6. Production Staff (ROB) 479

ELECTRICAL AND MECHANICAL SERVICING
1. Maintenance Fitter (RAB) 481
2. Business Equipment Service Engineer (ROK) 483
3. Domestic Appliance/Gas Service Engineer (ROK) .. 485

FABRICATION ENGINEERING
1. Sheet Metal Worker/Plater/Fabricator (RON) 488
2. Welder (RON) 490

GROUP S – MANUFACTURING INDUSTRIES

MANUFACTURING
1. Production Manager (SAB) 493
2. Quality Controller/Tester (SAB) 496
3. Production Worker (SAB) 498
4. Assembler (Light Industry) (SAB) 500
5. Packer (SAB) 501

BAKING AND CONFECTIONERY
Baker (SAC) 503

MEAT INDUSTRY
Meat Process Worker (SAC) 506

BREWING
Technical Brewer (SAC) 508

GLASS
Glassmaker Craftsman/woman (SAD) 510

LEATHER GOODS
Leather Technologist (SAF) 513

TEXTILES
1. Textile Technician (SAG) 516
2. Textile Dyeing Technician (SAV/SAG) 517
3. Textile Operative (SAG) 519

CLOTHING
1. Tailor/Dressmaker (SAH) 521
2. Pattern Cutter/Grader (SAH) 522
3. Spreader/Cutter (SAH) 524
4. Sewing Machinist (SAH) 525
5. Clothing Presser (SAH) 526

FURNITURE CRAFTS
1. Cabinet Maker (SAJ) 528
2. Upholsterer (SAJ) 529
3. French Polisher (SAJ) 531

FOUNDRY INDUSTRY
1. Foundry Worker (SAM) 533
2. Patternmaker (SAM) 534
3. Moulder/Coremaker (SAM) 535

PLASTICS PROCESSING
Plastics Process Operative (SAN) 537

PAPER MANUFACTURE
Paper Manufacturing Worker (SAP) 539

PRINTING
1. Originator (SAR) 541
2. Machine Printer (SAR) 543
3. Print Finisher/Bookbinder (SAR) 544

CHEMICAL PLANT PROCESSING
Chemical Plant Process Operator (SAV) 547

BLACKSMITHING
Blacksmith (SAW/RAB) 549

GROUP U – CONSTRUCTION AND LAND SERVICES

ARCHITECTURE
1. Architect (UB) 552
2. Architectural Technologist (UB) 554

BUILDING TECHNOLOGY AND MANAGEMENT
Professional Builder/Technician (UD) 557

BUILDING AND CONSTRUCTION TRADES
1. Bricklayer (UF) 561
2. Carpenter/Joiner (UF) 562
3. Floor Layer (UF) 563
4. Glazier (UF) 565
5. Painter and Decorator (UF) 566
6. Plasterer (UF) 567
7. Plumber (UF) 568
8. Roofer (UF) 570
9. Scaffolder (UF) 571
10. Wall and Floor Tiler (UF) 573

LIST OF OCCUPATIONAL ARTICLES IN CLCI ORDER

OTHER CONSTRUCTION WORK
1. Construction Operative (UF) 575
2. Construction Plant Operator (UV) 577

HOUSING
Housing Officer/Manager (UH/CAG) 579

BUILDING SERVICES
1. Building Services Engineer/Technician (UJ) 582
2. Heating and Ventilating Fitter/Welder (UJ) 584

LANDSCAPE ARCHITECTURE
Landscape Architect (UL) 587

SURVEYING AND LAND MANAGEMENT
Surveyor (UM) 589

CIVIL ENGINEERING
Civil Engineer (UN) 594

TOWN PLANNING
1. Town Planner (US) 598
2. Town Planning Technician/Support Staff (US) 600

GROUP W – ANIMALS, PLANTS AND NATURE

FARM WORK
1. Farm Manager (WAB) 602
2. Farm Worker (WAB) 604
3. Fish Farmer (WAG) 605

HORTICULTURE
1. Horticultural Manager (WAD) 609
2. Horticultural Worker (WAD) 611

GROUNDSMANSHIP
Groundsman/woman (WAD) 614

FORESTRY
1. Forest Officer (WAF) 616
2. Forest Worker/Ranger (WAF) 618

VETERINARY WORK
1. Veterinary Surgeon (WAL) 621
2. Veterinary Nurse (WAL) 623

ANIMAL WELFARE
RSPCA/SSPCA Inspector (WAL) 626

OTHER WORK WITH ANIMALS
1. Guide Dog Trainer/Mobility Instructor (WAM) 628
2. Kennel Worker (WAM) 629
3. Dog Groomer (WAM) 631
4. Horse Groom (WAM) 632
5. Riding Instructor (WAM) 635
6. Zoo Keeper (WAM) 638

NATURE CONSERVATION
1. Countryside/Conservation Officer (WAR) 641
2. Countryside Ranger/Warden (WAR) 643

GROUP Y – TRANSPORT

CIVIL AVIATION
1. Airline Pilot (YAB) 646
2. Air Cabin Crew (YAB) 648
3. Aircraft Maintenance Engineer (YAB/RAC) 649
4. Air Traffic Controller (YAB) 651

ROAD TRANSPORT
1. Road Transport Manager (YAD) 654
2. Bus/Coach Driver (YAD) 655
3. Bus Conductor (YAD) 657
4. Taxi/Private Hire Vehicle Driver (YAD) 658
5. LGV Driver (YAD) 659
6. Car/Van Driver (YAD) 661
7. Driving Instructor (YAD) 662

RAIL TRANSPORT
1. Train Driver (YAF) 666
2. Station Assistant (YAF) 667
3. Track/Overhead Line Worker (YAF) 668
4. Signalling Technician (YAF/RAL) 670
5. Railway Fitter/Electrician (YAF/RAB/RAK) 671

MERCHANT NAVY
1. Merchant Navy Deck Officer (YAL) 673
2. Merchant Navy Engineering Officer (YAL) 675
3. Merchant Navy Dual Certificate Officer (YAL) 676
4. Merchant Navy Rating (YAL) 677

MATERIALS HANDLING AND DELIVERY
1. Warehouse Worker (YAT) 680
2. Lift Truck Operator (YAT) 681

POSTAL WORK
Postman/woman (YAT/CAM) 683

DIVING
Diver (YAZ) 685

GROUP A – SELF EMPLOYMENT

SELF-EMPLOYMENT

Britain is becoming an enterprise society with increasing numbers of people seeking self-employment. This is a career choice requiring appropriate skills like all others. As increasing numbers of companies 'downsize', their operations – making redundancies, taking on fewer experienced specialists and outsourcing their operations (putting work out to skilled contractors) – more and more people are opting to become self-employed. Many set up in business by using the skills they have gained through full-time employment or by turning a hobby into a commercial venture. A few people start up with no previous experience of the service or product they are selling, but they have generally invested a lot of time researching their business ideas.

The 1980s saw a huge increase in self-employment, as the Government introduced measures to assist the self-employed and owners of small businesses. However, the success rate of small businesses is very dependent on the economic climate; the recession of the early 1990s saw the failure of many new ventures and highlighted the risks of setting up on your own. However, recent figures suggest that the number of self-employed people is once again rising with the highest number of start-ups ever in 1997. There are now well over three million self-employed, the majority in one- and two-person businesses.

It is a sad fact that, even in times of recovery, around one in three new businesses fail to survive their first three years. So if you are thinking of 'going it alone', it is essential that you seek advice and undertake careful planning before committing yourself to spending any money or leaving the relative safety of full-time employment. The Small Firms Enterprise Development Initiative, which is a government sponsored organization but led by entrepreneurs, owner managers and representatives of all Britain's business support organizations, has shown that those setting up their business using the advice and training of their NVQ/SVQ Business Planning programmes have at least a twice better survival rate than the average.

Why choose self-employment?

Self-employment is open to anyone. Many of us probably consider the idea of becoming self-employed at some stage in our lives, but the number of people who dream about working for themselves far exceeds the number who actually start up on their own. Some people are born entrepreneurs, choosing to work for themselves from an early age. However, not everyone is an aspiring Richard Branson and the decision to start up in business is often triggered by external events, such as reduced employed positions available in the areas you wish to work. There are many different reasons why people want to become self-employed.

Becoming your own boss – you have a great degree of control over your own work and that of any employees. You can decide where to work, what type of work to do, what standards to achieve and at what pace. Any successes and achievements are your own. Working independently means that any failures are also your own and all business decisions rest fairly and squarely on your shoulders.

Choosing your own hours – some people see self-employment as an attractive alternative to a nine-to-five job. In theory you can work the hours you choose, but in reality you are likely to work much more than normal office hours. Setting up a business is hard work; its success, partially in the first most vulnerable years, may depend on you working ten-hour days with no holidays. Even an established business does not run itself – planning, book-keeping and re-stocking is often done in the evenings and at weekends.

Financial rewards – anyone who is considering self-employment purely for financial gain should think carefully – it is quite possible to make more money by working for yourself than for another employer, but there are just as many in self-employment who do not expect to earn any more or slightly less than they might do in an employed position.

Personality clashes at work – inability to get on with colleagues may seem like a good reason set up on your own, but to succeed in your own business you will probably come into contact with more people – customers, suppliers, advisers – than in a full-time job and the success of your business may well depend on your getting on with them. However many who are self-employed enjoy the freedom from 'politics' at work.

Unemployment or redundancy – many successful small businesses have set up as a result of unemployment, but unemployment is not in itself a reason to become self-employed. Think hard about your business ideas and take advice from business support organizations before parting with savings or your redundancy payment. Waiting for another full-time job suited to your skills and experience or waiting until a more viable business idea has been developed may be a better option.

Whatever your reasons for considering self-employment, it is essential to assess your suitability and to discuss the idea with family, friends and business advisers – their support improves the odds against failure.

Personal qualities

Do you have what it takes to be self-employed? The qualities and skills required depend to some extent on the type of business activity. For instance, someone involved in marketing or retail would need to be outgoing and confident, whereas freelance writing might suit a quieter, more reserved person. However, there are some general characteristics that successful self-employed people have in common. They can organize their business for sales and profit – able to plan ahead, motivate themselves and keep selling their products or services. They are good communicators. Always enthusiastic about work, they believe in what they are doing and are resilient to setbacks. Commitment is vital – a half-hearted approach to setting up in business is a recipe for disaster. There are likely to be periods of financial insecurity and extremely hard work so the ability to cope with stress is essential. A degree of flexibility is helpful too – things don't always run according to plan, and changes may have to be made in order to keep the business afloat. Above all, there must be a willingness to find and listen to advice.

Completing a self-assessment questionnaire (often included in books on self-employment) is a useful aid to deciding whether to go ahead.

Finding a business idea

Starting from scratch. Most of Britain's most successful entrepreneurs and those that succeed in self-employment have not succeeded with their first or even second business idea. The standard advice is to find a 'gap in the market' – a product or service that no one else is providing, either in the local area or nationally. The proposal need not

SELF EMPLOYMENT: AVD6

necessarily be original; for example, there may be no local desktop publisher, jobbing gardener or window cleaner – and it is worth investigating whether there is potential demand for such services. On the other hand, plenty of businesses are started up in direct competition with others, and competition may, in fact, stimulate trade. There still needs to be a good reason – high quality, for instance, or a particular line of speciality goods – to attract customers.

Buying an existing business. It is also possible to buy an existing business, although it is important to look at the reasons for its sale. For example, the owner may be selling because profits are falling. As with new businesses, professional advice and careful market research are essential.

Franchising. An alternative to starting a new business from scratch is to buy a franchise – in other words, a ready-made business format with a trading name and brand image. Well-known franchises include Kall-Kwik, Dyno-Rod and Pizza Express. However the majority of franchises require an investment of £10,000 to £60,000. In return for a fee, the company selling the franchise provides a blueprint for running the business, training and back-up support such as assistance with raising finance, national advertising and promotion, and management expertise. The franchisee (the person running the business) is not totally independent, but must follow guidelines laid down by the parent company. Franchising is a relatively safe way of starting up on your own. However, it is expensive and advice should always be sought from a bank before parting with any money.

Direct selling. A useful way to check out whether self-employment is for you is to join one of the many direct-selling companies on a part-time basis with the option, if successful, of becoming fully self-employed.

Market research

Having settled on a business idea, it is then necessary to devote some time to market research, in order to decide whether the proposed business is going to be viable. This could include:

– contacting potential customers, by phone or in person, to test out whether they would buy the proposed product or service, and if so, how much they would be prepared to spend;

– visiting the local library, to consult the specialist trade press and trade directories for information on potential customers, suppliers and competitors;

– discussing the proposal with your nearest Business Link or a Local Enterprise Agency;

– test marketing – if it is possible to sell a small number of items, or to provide a service to customers on a 'trial run' basis, then this can be a valuable way of assessing whether there is a market and whether the product or service satisfies customer needs.

Selling and pricing

Market research will establish whether anyone will buy the product or service. The next question is how to sell. There are a number of choices, including: direct selling – face-to-face or by telephone; advertisements; brochures and leaflets; or via an agent. Many businesses use a mixture of methods. If you have no sales experience, some training in direct selling skills may be beneficial.

Pricing is a complex question. If prices are too high, projected sales may not be achieved, but if prices are too low, little or no profit will be made. A price has to take into account a realistic rate for the work involved, as well as both fixed costs – like rent, heating and insurance – and variable costs, like materials or stock. Costing also has to take into account time spent on often quite time-consuming things like selling, quoting for work, keeping accounts and other business records. Some of the organisations and books listed below give advice on how to price a product or service.

Advice and information

It is very important to seek advice and training when the business is still an idea or plan rather than a reality. Sadly, the self-employed often fail to seek help until things go wrong, which is often too late. Positively those that seek help early and train for their new career do succeed. There is a lot of help available and much of it is free including many Business Start-up programmes that lead to an NVQ/SVQ in Business Planning. Start talking to people already in business – friends, relatives, members of the local small business club, for example – and by reading relevant books and newspaper articles. Contact the following organizations to see how they can help.

Business Links. There are over 200 Business Link outlets throughout the country. They provide local information and advice for small businesses. Part of a government initiative started in 1993, they are formed by partnerships between TECs, local enterprise agencies and chambers of commerce. The advice they offer covers a range of issues including: the availability of grants, financial planning and management, business start-up, business skills, marketing, and export services. Initial advice is usually free but there is normally a fee for specialized services. In Scotland they are called Business Shops; in Wales they are called Business Connect. Normally the Business Link provides start-up assistance through local enterprise agencies.

Training and Enterprise Councils (TECs). A network of offices throughout the country, the services offered by TECs and LECs (in Scotland) vary according to local needs, but all offer free information. They run business advice centres and arrange courses and programmes.

Local Enterprise Agencies/Trusts. These are supported by the government, local authorities and local businesses and banks. They encourage business start-ups and provide advice on a range of issues: planning, premises, marketing, accounting, tax, etc. Some provide start-up units and secretarial services and run small business clubs. Youth Enterprise Centres, which are sometimes part of Local Enterprise Agencies specialize in giving advice and providing starter premises, mainly for people under 26 years.

The Prince's Youth Business Trust and The Prince's Scottish Youth Business Trust. Helps 18–29-year-olds (30 for people with a disability) to set up and run their own business. They offer start-up capital and business support to those who have a sound business idea but can not obtain traditional bank finance. The Trust is particularly concerned to help people who are unemployed, and those from ethnic minorities.

Shell *Live*WIRE. The Shell *Live*WIRE Outreach programme encourages young people aged 16–30, and those whom they turn to for advice and guidance, to see starting a business as a viable and desirable career option. By contacting the national telephone hotline on **0345 573 252** enquirers will receive a free business start-up information pack tailored to their specific idea, and the opportunity to receive one to one advice on starting up and

SELF EMPLOYMENT: AVD6

running a business from a local business adviser.

Shell *Live*Wire also rewards and raises the profile of Britain's most promising young business entrepreneurs through its prestigious annual Business Start-Up Awards competition. Awards are also made to young businesses that have demonstrated considerable progress since starting up.

To get a FREE essential business kit, call the hotline or visit the website – please see FURTHER INFORMATION.

Instant Muscle. A national charity that specializes in helping unemployed people to set up in business. It provides counselling to individuals and helps people to produce a business plan with which they can approach relevant bodies for funding and premises.

Advice and information is also available from banks, many of which have small business advisers. Then there are specialist bodies, such as the Rural Development Commission, which assists businesses in rural counties in England. Some advisory bodies specialize in working with particular groups of people – the Ethnic Minority Career Development Unit is an example.

Specialist advice may also be necessary, depending on the size and scope of the intended business. Most will need the services of an accountant; in certain circumstances it will be necessary to consult a solicitor or an insurance broker. These advisers operate on a fee-paying basis (although an initial consultation may sometimes be free); it is important to shop around and choose an appropriate adviser – a one-person business, for instance, would probably be wasting money by going to a large, city-based firm of chartered accountants – a small practice or self-employed accountant would be cheaper and more suitable.

There are a number of small business organizations with yearly membership fees who provide information and support – Home Business Alliance, Forum for Private Business, Marketing Guild and the Federation of Small Businesses all have many thousands of members who receive help, ie support, business information, services, magazines,/news sheets; and a number have legal and debt-collecting support operations available through the membership fee.

Sources of finance

Even for a very simple idea for self-employment, with modest equipment costs, some capital is needed to get the business under way. Sales take a while to build up and in the meantime, stationery and other supplies need to be bought. Also, there is usually a gap between selling an item and being paid by the customer. If business premises or purchases of stock are required, then of course the start-up costs will be much greater. There are a number of sources of finance to start up a new enterprise:

– using one's own money – savings or redundancy payments, for example;

– borrowing from other family members – although this has its drawbacks, particularly if there are any problems about repaying the loan later on;

– borrowing from the bank – the most common source, usually in the form of an overdraft facility or a loan over a specified term of years. Bank managers are generally sympathetic to a well-thought-out case for borrowing, but do need written information on which to assess the business proposal. Remember to invest in yourself, in your own training – Career Development loans, Small Firms Loans and highly subsidized business planning training is available.

In order to borrow from the bank, it is necessary to draw up a written business plan. The length of the plan and the amount of detail it contains will vary according to the size of the business, but it should contain personal information about the owner, a clear description of the product or service being offered, the market and future prospects, backed up by detailed financial forecasts. Help with drawing up a business plan is available from the advice agencies described above.

Business Links can supply information about other sources of business finance such as local authority grants, private investors (often referred to as 'business angels') and the Government's Loan Guarantee Scheme for small businesses.

The business structure

Another choice to make before starting up is the form of business structure. Most self-employed people start off as sole traders, under their own name. This does not necessarily mean that they work alone, but they are solely responsible for the business and personally liable for any debts. There are few legal obligations involved in this type of business structure, other then keeping records for tax purposes.

A second option is to go into business with a partner or partners. Ideally, these should be individuals with complementary skills; for instance, someone whose skills are purely practical might seek out a partner with a liking for paperwork, to run the administrative side of the business. All members of a partnership are personally liable for the debts of the business, even if those debts are incurred without their knowledge.

A third possibility is to form a limited company, although this is not generally advisable for a very small new business. A limited company does have the advantage of limited liability – creditors' claims are limited to the assets of the company – but there are tax advantages in starting as a sole trader or partner.

The fourth possibility is a co-operative – a business owned and controlled by all the people who work in it. In a co-op, decisions are usually made by democratic majority vote. There are many examples of successful co-operatives, although there is always a danger of the democratic process involving too many meetings and unnecessary delay in making operational decisions.

Training, development and qualifications

The Small Firms Enterprise Development Initiative has developed a suite of National and Scottish Vocational Qualifications (NVQs/SVQs) based on the occupational standards for people starting up at the business planning stage – Business Planning (Level 3 NVQ/SVQ) and for owner managers in established businesses – Business Management and Development (Level 4 NVQ/SVQ).

Other matters

There are a number of other points to take into consideration before starting trading:

Where to work. Many people start by working from home, in order to save on costs. It may be necessary to check whether planning permission is required and whether the landlord or mortgagee will allow the premises to be used for business. An inexpensive alternative is to rent a 'starter unit' for small businesses – these are often available through Local Enterprise Agencies.

SELF EMPLOYMENT: AVD6

Income tax. The local Tax Office should be notified as soon as trading begins. Each year you are required to submit a tax return listing your income and expenditure, and you will be charged tax on your earnings. Information and help is available from Tax Offices – see in the phone book under 'Inland Revenue'.

National Insurance. The Contributions Agency also needs to be informed: the self-employed must pay a regular National Insurance contribution (the rates vary from year to year).

Financial records. Keeping clear and accurate records is very important. Accountants will advise on the most appropriate form of book-keeping for the business.

Insurance. It is important to check the insurance needs of the business and to make sure that existing insurers are notified where necessary (for example, if a car is to be used for business, the motor insurers should be informed).

FURTHER INFORMATION

British Franchise Association, Thames View, Newtown Road, Henley-on-Thames, Oxfordshire RG9 1HG, 01491 578050

Direct Selling Association, 29 Floral Street, Covent Garden, London WC2E 9DP, 0171 497 1234

DTI Small Firms Publications Orderline*, Admail 528, London SW1W 8YT, 0171 510 0169

The Ethnic Minority Career Development Unit, London Guildhall University, Calcutta House, Old Castle Street, London E1 7NT, 0171 320 1201

Federation of Small Businesses*, 32 Orchard Road, Lytham St Annes, Lancashire FY8 1NY, 01253 720911

Forum for Private Business, Ruskin Chambers, Drury Lane, Knutsford, Cheshire WA16 6HA 01565 634467

Home Business Alliance, The Firs, High Street, March, Cambridgeshire PE15 9LQ 01354 658 850, e-mail: homebusiness

Instant Muscle, Springside House, 84 North End Road, London W14 9ES, 0171 603 2604

Shell *Live*WIRE*, Hawthorn House, Forth Banks, Newcastle-upon-Tyne NE1 3SG, 0191 261 5584. Hotline 0345 573 252. www.shell-livewire.org

National Federation of Enterprise Agencies, Trinity Gardens, 9-11 Bromham Road, Bedford MK40 2UK, 01234 354055

The Prince's Youth Business Trust*, 18 Park Square East, London NW1 4LH, 0800 842 842

The Prince's Scottish Youth Business Trust*, Mercantile Chambers, 53 Bothwell Street, Glasgow, 0141 248 4999

Rural Development Commission, 141 Castle Street, Salisbury, Wiltshire SP1 3TP, 01722 336255

Small Business Bureau, Curzon House, Church Road, Windlesham, Surrey GU20 6BH, 01276 452010

Small Firms Enterprise Development Initiative, PO Box 393, Northampton, Northamptonshire NN1 4YG, 01604 234618

FURTHER READING

Leaflets/booklets are available from the addresses marked* and from Business Link (England) N- 0345 567765; Business Connect (Wales) N- 0345 969798; Business Shop (Scotland) - 0800 787878. The DTI produces a range of free booklets which are available at local TECs or Business Links, or from the DTI publications address above. See Yellow Pages for the address of your local TEC/LEC and Local Enterprise Agency.

A Guide to Help for Small Firms - DTI

Lloyds Bank Small Business Guide – Penguin

Taking up a Franchise – Kogan Page

The Which? Guide to Starting Your Own Business – Which? Books

Working for Yourself – The Daily Telegraph Guide to Self-Employment – Kogan Page

In the careers library classified under AVD6.

Please Note:

Self-employed people with disabilities are now eligible (from 1 October 1998) for 100% contribution from Access to Work programme (ATW), to the additional employment cost arising from disabilities.

GROUP B – ARMED FORCES

1. **RN/QARNNS OFFICER CLCI:BAB**
2. **RN RATING CLCI:BAB**
3. **ROYAL MARINES OFFICER CLCI:BAB**
4. **ROYAL MARINES – OTHER RANKS CLCI:BAB**

BACKGROUND INFORMATION

The Naval Service is made up of three branches: The Royal Navy (RN), The Royal Marines (RM), and Queen Alexandra"s Royal Naval Nursing Service (QARNNS). It provides Britain with a maritime defence force and plays an important role in NATO and world-wide.

The Royal Navy operates warships, submarines and ship-borne aircraft. The fleet at sea is supported by communications centres, training establishments and other installations ashore.

The Royal Navy is divided into six Branches: Warfare, Engineering, Supply, Medical, Fleet Air Arm and the Submarine Service. Women work alongside men in almost all jobs. The exception is jobs in submarines which are only available to men.

The Royal Marines is a specialist force of amphibious commandos. It operates from Royal Navy ships and assault/landing craft. Commando units may specialize as Air or Special Boat Squadrons, Ship"s Detachment, Embarked Force or in Jungle, Mountain and Arctic Warfare. The Royal Marines is not open to women with the exception of the Royal Marines Band Service.

Queeen Alexandra"s Royal Naval Nursing Service cares for Service personnel and their families in land-based Naval hospitals in Britain and abroad. QARNNS is open to men and women. All QARNNSS have a liability to serve at sea.

Entry to the Naval Service is as an officer or rating. All entrants undergo basic training as an officer or rating before beginning specialist training in one of the wide range of jobs. Some posts are open to those who have qualified in their specialization in civilian life (eg nursing officer).

1. RN/QARNNS OFFICER (BAB)

THE WORK

Officers manage and lead the many personnel who make up the Royal Navy. As well as specializing in a particular area, officers are responsible for looking after the welfare, career advancement and discipline of the ratings under their command.

Warfare officer

Warfare officers are responsible for 'working' and 'fighting' the ship; in other words, making sure the ship is handled safely and efficiently and to the best tactical advantage. Their first appointment is usually as officer of the watch, responsible for the safety of the ship and the ship's company during their watch on the bridge. This involves controlling the ship's course and speed, using information from charts, sensors, the weather and the sea. Most warfare officers then go on to a second watchkeeping job, but it is also possible to sub-specialize in a number of areas.

Aircraft Control. Air traffic control officers are responsible for the guidance and control of a wide variety of high-performance aircraft. They use some of the most sophisticated radar and communications equipment currently available. Air traffic control officers work in Naval Air Stations and afloat.

Fighter Control. Fighter controllers guide and control a variety of fixed wing fighter aircraft. They primarily control the Navy's own Sea Harriers operating from aircraft carriers. Fighter controllers guide fighter aircraft to carry out interception of enemy aircraft.

Aviation. Pilots fly naval helicopters or Sea Harrier 'jump jets' to locate and attack enemy vessels or to provide air defence. Observers co-ordinate warfare from the air. Aircrew officers (pilots and observers) also take part in amphibious warfare, search and rescue operations, casualty evacuation, communications work and reconnaissance.

Mine Warfare and Clearance Diving (MCD). MCD officers qualify as diving officers before learning how to handle and dispose of explosives, and the techniques of minehunting and minesweeping.

Submarines. Submariners are specially trained to serve in the Submarine Service and work similarly to Warfare Officers..

Hydrographic Surveying Service. Hydrographic surveyors carry out hydrographic and oceanographic surveying to obtain information for navigational charts.

Later, warfare officers can become principal warfare officers, specializing in Anti-Air Warfare or Anti-Submarine Warfare. They are responsible for 'fighting' the ship and working with the captain to direct fighting operations.

Engineer officer

The Royal Navy uses advanced technology in all areas, and engineer officers are responsible for monitoring the equipment and ensuring it works properly. Engineer officers specialize in one of five areas.

Weapon engineer officer (surface ships). Surface ship WEOs are responsible for the ship's weapon systems including gun, torpedo and missile systems. This work also covers all aspects of the weapons sensor and communications systems.

Weapon engineer officer (submarines). Submarines WEOs have similar responsibilities to WEOs on surface ships, but also act as control room watchkeepers.

Marine engineer officer (surface ships). Surface ships MEOs are responsible for everything that keeps the ship afloat, including the structure of the ship, the engines, electricity, air conditioning, heating, ventilation etc.

Marine engineer officer (submarines). In addition to the responsibilities of MEOs in surface ships, those in submarines are also concerned with nuclear reactors and the specialized submarine hull equipment.

Air engineer officer (mechanical and electrical). AEOs deal with the maintenance and repair of aircraft systems. They also look after the electrical systems and electronics associated with flight control radar and weapons systems.

Training management officer. Training management officers are responsible for the education and training of Navy personnel, from basic maths and English to science and engineering at postgraduate level.

Supply officer

Supply officers look after administration and the organization of equipment, food, money etc. They may serve at sea or on land. When at sea they must also perform operational duties. The work of a supply officer falls into four main areas.

THE NAVAL SERVICE: BAB

Captain's secretary. The Captain's secretary deals with official correspondence, administrative, welfare and personnel matters on land or at sea.

Naval stores. Supply officers in naval stores are responsible for ensuring that any piece of equipment is in the right place at the right time.

Catering. Supply officers in catering handle the long-term ordering of food and provisions, and supervise meal preparation on a daily basis.

Pay and cash. Officers deal with pay and with special allowances, foreign currency and accounts.

Specialist officer

Specialist officers carry out their profession within service life. They include:

Medical officers who care for Naval Service personnel and their families. They may also be involved in providing medical aid during crises or natural disasters. When serving at sea they have additional duties such as watchkeeping, organizing entertainments, acting as wardroom treasurer or secretary, publishing newsletters or public relations. They may also have responsibility for the welfare of a division of ten to fourteen staff.;

Dental officers look after the dental health of Naval Service personnel. On some postings they may also care for service families. Preventive dentistry is a large part of the work. Like medical officers they also carry out additional duties whilst at sea.

Nursing officers in The Queen Alexandra's Royal Naval Nursing Service care for service personnel and their families, and patients in both hospitals and medical centres. They have a liability to serve at sea both during peacetime and conflict.

Naval chaplains from many denominations, both male and female, serve ashore and afloat. They minister to service personnel and their families.

WORK ENVIRONMENT

RN officers serve at sea on a variety of ships (eg aircraft carriers, destroyers, frigates), or in a shore installation in Britain or abroad. Shore installations include training establishments, hospitals, air stations and base ports. RN (male) officers may also serve on submarines. Their immediate work environment depends on the job they do. Their social life, both at sea and ashore, revolves around the wardroom (officers' mess). They must be prepared to move abroad and within the UK.

SKILLS AND INTERESTS

Officers need leadership qualities and the ability to work effectively as part of a team. They must be able to think and react quickly. They must be ready to accept responsibility, make decisions and manage other personnel. They should be able to communicate with people of all abilities, explain ideas, give spoken and written instructions, and motivate others. Officers must be interested in the people they supervise, and be able to listen to, guide and discipline them. All officers must be physically fit and prepared to work in combat. An interest in science/technology is important in many of the jobs.

Each specialization has its own requirements. For example, air traffic control officers must be able to stay calm, think quickly and concentrate for long periods. Supply officers must be methodical and have a flair for organization.

Engineer officers need technological ability and the skills to find solutions to problems. Aviators must have initiative and the ability to react quickly.

ENTRY REQUIREMENTS

The minimum entry requirements for RN officers are two A levels/three H grades and three GCSEs/two S grades (A–C/1–3), including English and maths at either level. Applicants offering alternative qualifications, such as BTEC/SQA national awards or Advanced GNVQ/GSVQ Level III, are considered on their individual merits and should seek advice from any Armed Forces Careers Office. Entry is normally by Naval College Entry (NCE) or Direct Graduate Entry for those who have a degree. Naval college entrants begin as Midshipmen, graduates as Sub-Lieutenants.

Officers join the service on an initial commission which will be for a period of twelve years for Royal Navy Officers and eight years for Royal Marine Officers (except for Royal Marine Cadetships who will join for twelve years).

This will allow all Officer entrants, regardless of their entry route, an equal opportunity to demonstrate their future potential in productive employment, and aid selection for longer commissions.

From about two to three years after completion of initial training, selections for further Commissions will commence.

Medical officers can enter at all levels from student (on a bursary) to post-registration, initially on a short career commission (SCC), with the opportunity to apply for a full career commission (FCC) or medium career commission (MCC) after two years. Dental officers can join at any stage from obtaining 2nd BDS (Bachelor of Dental Surgery degree) or equivalent, to post-qualifications. They start on an SCC with the opportunity to apply for an MCC or FCC after two years. Nursing officers (QARNNS) must have proof of registration plus a minimum of two years' post-registration nursing experience in a hospital. They take an SCC, with the right to apply for an MCC, then an FCC. Chaplains must be ordained, be recommended by their church authorities and, normally, have had three or more years' experience of parish work.

There are a number of opportunities for sponsorship. The Scholarship and Reserved Place Scheme is available to those entering the RN as officers to enable them to study for A levels or H grades. Financial assistance may be given during the courses to the parents of those who are awarded scholarships. University cadetships provide a salary to students, whilst bursaries are available to those who wish to remain civilians during their studies. Those wishing to train as engineer officers may apply to read an appropriate degree at the University of Southampton under the RN's Engineering Sponsorship Scheme.

To become an RN officer, candidates must pass a series of selection tests held at the Admiralty Interview Board at HMS Sultan, Gosport. These last two days and include aptitude tests, practical initiative tests, gym tests and interviews.

The minimum height for an officer is 1.57 metres (5 feet 2 inches), and weight must be in proportion to height. There are strict eyesight standards, and all candidates must pass a medical.

All officers must meet the RN nationality and residence requirements. Armed Forces Careers Offices give guidance on eligibility.

THE NAVAL SERVICE: BAB

TRAINING

All new officers begin with Naval General Training at the Britannia Royal Naval College at Dartmouth. The length of this training varies from two to five terms, depending on qualifications and type of entry. It includes experience at sea. Specialist training for the officer's chosen branch begins at the end of this course.

Warfare officer

Warfare officers complete the last part of their Naval General Training with up to twelve months at sea before moving on to further professional training, such as the 16-week Officer of the Watch (OOW) course. Six months' satisfactory service leads to the Bridge Watchkeeping Certificate, and officers can take the Ocean Navigation Certificate at the same time. Those who wish to specialize then take appropriate courses:

Air traffic control officers take a five-month training course on the guidance and tactical control of a range of aircraft, using radar and computer systems.

Aviation trainee pilots combine practical training, initially in a dual-control Firefly, then in a Squirrel helicopter, with a theoretical course covering theory of flight, meteorology, navigation and air engineering. Observers have 100 hours flying in a Jetstream as well as learning the theory of airmanship, navigation, radar, navigation aids, air engineering, oceanography etc. Both pilots and observers then prepare for the aircraft they will operate on active duty. Sea Harrier pilots follow a 38-week Basic Flying Training course in Tuccanos, followed by 32 weeks on Advanced Flying Training in Hawks and a further 36 weeks on Tactical Weapons Training, before converting to Sea Harriers.

Mine warfare and clearance divers take a four-week course to qualify as ship's diving officer. They then serve as an SDO for at least one year, before following a seven-month course which includes diving to 180 feet, handling and disposing of explosives, and minehunting and minesweeping.

Submariners begin training immediately after they complete their Officer of the Watch course. They learn about the systems to be found on board a submarine, escape methods and the specific equipment carried on their first submarine. They then go to sea and gain the experience to qualify as an officer of the watch before either taking up a junior appointment, or undergoing further training in tactical operations.

Hydrographic surveyors spend six months on a surveying ship, followed by a 14-week course at the Royal Naval Hydrographic School. They are then appointed to a surveying ship.

Warfare officers may take a 42-week Principal Warfare Officer course. After serving as a PWO, specialists may return to their specialization.

Engineer officer

Engineer officers either join with a relevant degree acceptable to the Ministry of Defence, or are sponsored to take a degree in engineering at the University of Southampton. All engineer officers then take an application course appropriate to their sub-specialization. They may also undertake advanced courses in for example control engineering or guided weapons.

Training management officers receive a short period of teacher training after basic naval training. Those who go to sea also train in sub-specialist tasks required at sea.

Supply officer

After general naval training, supply officers follow supply courses to learn the organizational and administrative techniques required. Courses include specialist training, such as naval law. They may also take additional courses necessary to the operational role they will undertake at sea.

Medical and dental officers

Medical officers spend four weeks at Dartmouth before following a five-week post-registration course to become familiar with maritime medicine.

Dental officers also spend four weeks at Dartmouth, followed by a week's course to learn about the Naval Dental Services.

LATE ENTRY

Upper age limits vary according to the job (all ages apply to the first day of the month of entry):

Naval college entrants should be under 23 and direct graduate entrants under 26. University cadets must be under 22 and those on the Scholarship and Reserved Place Scheme may not have a break between GCSEs/S grades and A levels/H grades.

Training management direct graduate entrants, however, may be considered up to the age of 34.

Chaplains must be under 39, while engineers with experience may enter up to age 32. Medical and dental officers who are training should, preferably, be under 25, pre-registration medical officers under 33 and post-registration medical officers under 44. Post-qualification dental officers are preferred under 32. QARNNS nursing officers must be under 34.

There is normally a delay between being accepted for a commission and the start of training, so candidates are advised to apply at least a year in advance of age limits. Very rarely, upper age limits are waived for exceptional candidates.

OPPORTUNITIES

The number of officers recruited each year varies, but was 491 in 1998. Cutbacks in the Armed Forces are not expected to affect officer recruitment. Those not accepted can reapply, with a minimum of twelve months between applications. An individual can go before the Admiralty Interview Board up to three times.

PAY AND CONDITIONS

On entry a Midshipman would receive £10,471, rising to £13,015 after one year. Sub-Lieutenants are appointed on £14,921 and Lieutenants earn £25,512 to £29,240. Lieutenant-Commanders receive up to £38,208 and Commanders up to £49,731. Captains with more than six years' seniority earn £57,808. Additional flying pay and submarine pay are available for suitably qualified staff, and special allowances are paid to those serving at sea. An officer's point of entry would depend on the type of commission and, possibly, on professional or academic qualifications and past experience. Officers receive six weeks' paid leave a year, usually taken in periods of a fortnight.

Officers are on call 24 hours a day, but basically work eight-hour turns of duty. This can include shifts and irregular

THE NAVAL SERVICE: BAB

hours. During exercises, hours can be long and unpredictable. Whilst serving at sea, officers can be separated from their families for several months at a time.

PROSPECTS

RN officers can expect new appointments every two or three years.

Promotion is through a structured system from Midshipman (aged 17–26), through Sub-Lieutenant (aged 19–26), Lieutenant (aged 22–34), Lieutenant-Commander (aged 30–36) Commander (aged 33–40), Captain (aged around 45), to Admiral (aged around 52). Speed of promotion depends on a number of factors, including ability, qualifications and training.

RELATED OCCUPATIONS

Royal Marines officer, RN rating, Army officer, RAF officer, Merchant Navy officer, pilot, air traffic controller, training officer.

FURTHER INFORMATION AND READING

Please see article 4. ROYAL MARINES – OTHER RANKS.

2. RN RATING (BAB)

THE WORK

RN ratings work in a wide variety of jobs needed to run an efficient Naval Service. They may serve on a number of different kinds of ships or in shore establishments. Each has a skill or trade essential to the Navy, and they work closely in teams to keep ships, communications and weapons systems and other equipment ready for action. They work in one of six teams.

Warfare Branch

The Warfare Branch team comprises the people who operate and maintain ship and submarine weapon systems; they also carry out seamanship tasks to sustain operations at sea.

The Warfare Branch includes:

Above-water Warfare OM(AW)

The Above-water Warfare Team mans the sensors and weapons that protect the ship from air and surface threat. They compile the picture of surface vessels and aircraft to system range and beyond.

Underwater Warfare OM(UW)

Operator Mechanics(UW) support operations from the nerve centre of the ship – the Operations Room – detecting enemy submarines and torpedoes using powerful sonars. Thes transmit pulses of sound through the sea and analyse the returning echoes.

Electronic Warfare OM(EW)

The Electronic Warfare Team are the ears of the ship. They listen in to enemy electronic equipment and missiles in flight to provide early warning of danger.

Communications OM(C)

Heavily involved with the compilation and transfer of data and signal information via radio and terrestrial links.

Communications technicians are trained to receive and analyse radio communications, read morse code accurately at high speeds and operate sophisticated receiving, recording, direction-finding and analysis equipment.

Mine Warfare OM(MW)

The Royal Navy's Mine Counter Measures (MCM) capability is provided by ships mannd, in the main , by Mine Warfare Specialists. OM(MW)s are often required to work unsupervised in key roles but may also be employed as an integral part of a small team often in a potentially hazardous environment.

Survey Recorder OM(SR)

The Royal naval Hydrographic Service is a small specialization dedicated to surveying the seas and oceans of the world.Maintains the database of British Admiralty Charts, gathers navigational and oceanographic data for use in defence, commerce and development of scientific knowledge.

Communication Submarine OM(CSM)

Submarines need to remain invisible to the outside world for long periods. Mechanics (Communications Submarine) – OM(CMS)s – are the link with the outside world and the only channel of information beyond that provided by the sensors.

Weapons Submarine OM(WSM)

Weapons vary from torpedoes to hunt other submarines to anti-ship missiles which are fired when submerged. OM(WSM)s operate and assist with the maintenance of these weapons.

Tactical Submarine OM(TSM)

Operator Mechanics (Tactical Submarine) – OM(TSM)s – are central to the submarine's ability to hunt and hide. They plot its position and using information from its sensors the positions of enemies and friends.

Sensors Submarine OM(SSM)

OM(SSM)s are the submarine equivalent of the OM(UW)s in the surface fleet. Sonar plays a particularly important role in the 'silent service' and is often the only channel of information from the outside world.

Diver OM(D)

Divers are responsible for a wide range of underwater diving tasks. They man the diving elements of both Hunt and Sandown class mine countermeasure vessels and front-line diving units ashore. Diving is open only to male applicants.

Short Engagement (Seaman)

Carries out seamanship tasks under the supervision of the Chief Boatswain Mate and will include being part of a boats crew, acting as helmsman of a Frigate or Destroyer and assisting with Replenishment at Sea.

Engineering

The Engineering team is responsible for the maintenance and repair of the wide range of highly technical equipment used by the Royal Navy.

Engineering technicians (artificers) are highly skilled personnel, responsible for repairing and maintaining all types of equipment including flight systems (air), missiles (weapons) and propulsion plants (marine). They also manage teams of mechanics.

Air engineering mechanics help to service and repair the Navy's aircraft. They specialize in servicing the airframe, engine and major mechanical systems (mechanical), looking after avionic systems (radio) and weapons systems (electrical).

Marine engineering mechanics are concerned with the

THE NAVAL SERVICE: BAB

ship's power. MEMs look after the main propulsion and auxiliary systems, generators, power distribution systems, electrical switchgear and other heavy electrical plant.

Supply

The Supply team is responsible for the administrative side, including catering, office work and stores.

Stewards run the wardroom (the officers' mess), preparing and serving food, working the bar and looking after officers' accommodation.

Chefs produce food of all types, and maintain financial and stock control records.

Stores accountants ensure that all necessary equipment is available, properly controlled and accounted for.

Writers carry out a range of accounting and clerical duties in personnel, cash and administrative sections.

Medical

The Medical team is responsible for the health of the Navy's personnel.

Medical assistants are paramedics caring for patients either alone or as part of a team.

Dental surgery assistants' responsibilities include mixing fillings, preparing instruments, keeping appointments and record books and clerical and storekeeping jobs connected with the dental practice.

Dental hygienists carry out dental treatments such as scaling and polishing of teeth.

Fleet Air Arm

The Fleet Air Arm ensures that the Navy's aircraft are always ready for action.

The Aircraft Handler makes certain that the preparations for flying run as smoothly – and as safely – as possible. Ensures that each aircraft is in the right place, at the right time, from leaving the hangar to the moment of launch.

Naval airmen (survival equipment) keep all the life-saving equipment on the aircraft and ships in working order and ensure that it is correctly stored.

Naval airmen (meteorology and oceanography) observe and record the weather details to provide information for use by the whole ship.

Submarine Service

Men in the Submarine Service carry out their trade on submarines. The following jobs are available: sonar (submarine), tactical (submarine), weapon (submarine), communication (submarine), marine engineering artificer, weapon engineering artificer, marine engineering mechanic, cook, steward, stores accountant, writer, medical assistant.

At present, women do not serve on submarines.

WORK ENVIRONMENT

Please see article 1. RN OFFICER.

SKILLS AND INTERESTS

Ratings must be able to form part of a team, living and working closely with other people. Self-discipline and the ability to live in a small, closed environment are particularly important for those who serve on submarines. Ratings must be able to follow orders. The ability to accept responsibility, make decisions and react quickly under pressure is important. Physical fitness is essential. Ratings must be prepared to work anywhere in the world, and when serving at sea must be ready for long separations from their families. They must also be prepared to work in combat, if necessary.

Practical and technical skills are needed to deal with the advanced equipment used in the Navy, and an interest in science and technology is useful. Good communication skills are also important. In addition, each specialization has its own requirements. For example, some communications technicians must be fluent in another language, whilst stores accountants need to be methodical and have a good memory. Operator mechanics must have good co-ordination, common sense and the ability to stay calm.

ENTRY REQUIREMENTS

All candidates must pass a selection test (reasoning, English, numeracy and mechanical comprehension), interview and medical examination.

Applicants for a number of trades also need specified minimum qualifications: naval airmen (meteorology and oceanography) need one GCSE/S grade (A–C/1–3) in either maths, meteorology, geography or a science subject.

Communications technicians need two GCSEs/S grades (A–C/1–3), in English and maths. They must also pass aptitude tests. Artificer apprentices (the usual entry route for artificers) must either: pass aptitude tests, and have GCSEs/S grades (A–C/1–3) in physics or a physics-based science, maths and English, or have an appropriate BTEC/SQA national award or Intermediate GNVQ/GSVQ Level II and GCSE/S grade (A–C/1–3) English.

Dental surgery assistants need either: two GCSEs/S grades (A–C/1–3) including English, or NEBDN National Certificate achieved before 1 January 1989. Dental hygienists need the General Dental Council's Certificate of Proficiency in Oral Hygiene or Diploma in Dental Hygiene.

Probationary student nurses need either: a minimum of five GCSEs/S grades (A–C/1–3), including English, maths and a science subject (four of which must have been obtained in one sitting), or BTEC National Diploma in Health Studies, or Advanced GNVQ Health and Social Care/GSVQ Level III in Care. Registered nurses may apply for direct entry.

Entry to the Royal Navy is possible from age 16, except in the cases of medical assistants and dental surgery assistants (17), communications technicians and dental hygienists (18), student naval nurses (18_), and direct entry registered general nurses (21).

The minimum height for all entrants is 1.57 metres (5 feet 2 inches). Weight must be in proportion to height. There are strict eyesight standards and, for some jobs, normal colour vision is essential.

All entrants must meet the RN nationality and residence requirements. Armed Forces Careers Offices will give guidance on eligibility.

TRAINING

All new entrants spend eight weeks undergoing basic training at HMS Raleigh at Torpoint in Cornwall. This includes practical exercises, drill, PE, personal weapons test, swimming test, naval general training. Specialist training for the recruit's chosen trade begins at the end of

THE NAVAL SERVICE: BAB

this course. Some trade training involves working for nationally recognized qualifications, including BTEC, NVQ and City and Guilds certificates. Ratings may be encouraged to take other advanced qualifications as their careers progress.

The amount of time before a trainee is drafted to a ship varies according to the trade, but training often includes short periods at sea.

Warfare Branch

Above-water warfare training lasts eleven weeks, with the emphasis on the setting up and operating of operations room equipment, data processing, and practising the skills required on board ship.

Underwater warfare training lasts for nine weeks. This practical course involves learning how to operate sonar in realistic simulators.

Mine warfare training lasts for seven weeks and covers all aspects of mining (laying and recovery), minesweeping and minehunting.

Electronic warfare training lasts 13 weeks and covers audio and radar training, voice procedure and radar/platform/threat skills.

Communications training lasts for 18 weeks and covers work with a wide variety of modern equipment, including satellite communications.

Sensors submarine training lasts for twelve weeks. The course concentrates on the use of submarine sonar and the detection of both surface ships and submarines.

Weapons submarine training lasts for nine weeks. Training includes the operation and maintenance of submarine weapons, torpedoes, missiles and their launch systems.

Tactical submarine training lasts for eight weeks and includes the use of navigation equipment and computer-assisted plotting, and compiling the tactical picture from various sensors.

Communications submarine training lasts for 24 weeks and covers many types of communications including Morse code, radio, radio teletype, satellite and telex.

All submariners carry out additional special training to prepare them for life on board a submarine (including a simulated escape from 100 feet underwater in a training tank).

Communications technician training lasts for 150 weeks (including 52 weeks at sea). The linguist concentrates on voice communications, whilst the analyst is concerned with naval and air weaponry, radar and communications systems.

Survey recorders take a six-week course in the recording of data and the use and maintenance of survey instruments.

Divers undergo 20 weeks of professional training that includes mine countermeasure diving procedures, ship's bottom searches, open-water search techniques and underwater engineering skills.

Engineering

Engineering artificers follow a four-year training course to become skilled in air engineering, weapons engineering or marine engineering.

Engineering artificers follow a common 14-week course before training in their specialism.

Air engineering mechanics take a 20-week basic engineering course covering work on a wide range of airframes, hydraulics, flying controls, fuel systems, radio equipment, weapons and electrical systems.

Marine engineering mechanics have a nine-week course covering ship main propulsion, auxiliary systems, electrical principles, test equipment, various types of generators and power distribution systems, electrical switchgear and other heavy electrical plant.

Supply

Stewards spend five weeks learning the professional ways of serving food and drinks, some basic cookery, wardroom organization and the duties of a wine steward.

Chefs follow a 15-week course to learn basic culinary skills, accounting, field cookery and cooking for large numbers.

Stores accountants learn stores accounting, storekeeping, typing and keyboarding during an eight-week course.

Writers have a ten-week course which covers pay accounting, staff records, letter writing, office procedures and word processing.

Medical

Medical assistants' training lasts 50 weeks and includes a theory course covering anatomy, physiology, first aid, nursing, administration and storekeeping, followed by practical experience in the wards and medical departments.

Dental surgery assistants' training lasts for 23 weeks and includes the tasks required to assist dental surgeons in their treatment of patients and the administration of a dental practice.

Fleet Air Arm

All naval airmen take a ten-week course covering firefighting, first aid, air traffic control, flight safety and how a naval air station works. After this:

Naval airmen (aircraft handler) have a 15-week course on flight deck procedures, launching of aircraft and aircrew rescue. Rescue handlers are also responsible for firefighting duties.

Naval airmen (survival equipment) have a six-week introduction to aircraft engineering followed by an 18-week safety equipment course.

Naval airmen (meteorology and oceanography) spend 12 weeks learning how to use and maintain basic instruments, how to observe wind, weather, clouds and visibility, and how to code and plot these on weather charts.

Submarine Service

Everyone who serves on submarines undergoes specialist training to accustom them to the conditions and systems on submarines, the escape procedures etc.

LATE ENTRY

The upper age limit for communications technicians and artificer apprentices is 28. For all other trades it is 32.

There is normally a delay between being accepted and the start of the training, so candidates are advised to apply at least six months in advance of age limits. Very rarely, upper age limits will be waived for exceptional candidates.

OPPORTUNITIES

The number recruited into different jobs can vary. Cutbacks in the Armed Forces have caused some areas to be closed temporarily to new entrants. Individuals who are not accepted may apply a second time after a twelve-month gap.

THE NAVAL SERVICE: BAB

PAY AND CONDITIONS

RN ratings enter for a period of 22 years from age 18 years or date of entry, whichever is later. They can leave on 18 months' notice after two-and-a-half years' (technicians and student naval nurses three-and-a-half years') service or after completion of training, whichever is the later. Premature release is available under certain conditions to those who are not suited to Naval Service. Pregnant women have the choice of confinement leave and returning after a given period or of leaving the service. (If the option to remain is taken, the same conditions of service apply.)

Junior Ratings earn £479 a month under the age of 17 and £581 aged 17 to 17 years and 6 months. Ordinary ratings, aged over 17 years and 6 months, get £769 to £859, Able Ratings £1,000–1,247 and Leading Ratings £1,428 to £1,545. Petty Officers earn up to £1,726, Chief Petty Officers up to £1,927 and Warrant Officers up to £2,215. After training, artificers, communications technicians and medical technicians receive higher rates. Additional pay is available for those on submarines or in the Survey Service, divers and anyone required to fly. Ratings receive 36 days' paid leave each year.

Ratings work eight-hour turns of duty (but can be longer). This can include shifts and irregular hours. During exercises, hours can be long and unpredictable. Whilst serving at sea, ratings can be separated from their families for several months at a time.

PROSPECTS

Promotion is through a structured system. Those under 17 years and 6 months join as Junior Ratings and get automatic advancement to Ordinary Rating at 17 years and 6 months. New entrants over this age join as Ordinary Ratings. After this, promotion is to Able Rating, Leading Rating, Petty Officer, Chief Petty Officer and Warrant Officer. Promotion to Naval Officer rank is possible for those with the necessary qualifications and potential. Around 25 per cent of Naval Officers began their careers as an Ordinary Rating.

RELATED OCCUPATIONS

RN officer, Army NCO/private, RAF airman/woman, Merchant Navy rating, Royal Marines – other ranks.

FURTHER INFORMATION AND READING

Please see article 4. ROYAL MARINES – OTHER RANKS.

3. ROYAL MARINES OFFICER (BAB)

THE WORK

The Royal Marines go wherever they are required around the globe, both within and outside NATO. This is illustrated by 3 Commando Brigade's (3 Cdo Bde) integral role in the make-up of the Joint Rapid Deployment Force, whose tri-service lead elements are ready to deploy anywhere at 24 hours notice.

The varied commitments, including , Jungle, Mountain and Artic Warfare and Temperate training give 3 Cdo Bde RM an unparalled flexibility of role as shown by recent deployments to such places as Africa, the Baltic States and the Mediterranean.

As the UK's amphibious forces, the Royal Marines are trained to land and secure footholds on all types of coastline. Fast manoeuvrable Rigid Raiders and various other landing craft capable of carrying troops and vehicles are used to transport the marines ashore. With the introduction of the Landing Platform Helicopter (LPH), HMS Ocean, the Royal Marines have the capability to air-lift two companies ashore simultaneously, in addition to the sea-borne capability which will be provided by the two Landing Platform Dock Replacement (LPD(R)) which are due for future production.

The Royal Marines also fulfil a number of other roles such as disaster relief and the Fleet Standby Rifle Troop, dedicated to supporting the Royal Navy at short notice.

After basic training, Royal Marines officers choose, in negotiation with their trainers, to work in one of ten specializations:

Landing craft officers plan and lead beach assaults and supervise the maintenance and development of all landing craft and raiding boats. Landing craft officers are appointed to an Assault Squadron or to an Assault Ship, and are involved in navigation, seamanship and operational planning.

Signals officers plan and oversee all radio communications across the Corps.

Heavy weapons officers work in the support company of a commando with responsibility for up to 80 men. Officers work with weapons such as anti-tank missiles or mortars and are also responsible for transporting and installing weapons and for the men in their command.

Weapons training officers advise on the use of small arms and snipers. Officers are responsible for training men in the use of these arms; they also supervise firing ranges.

Special boat services officers supervise and organize special reconnaissance projects from both ships and aircraft.

Mountain leaders advise and instruct companies on mountain exercises and lead the reconnaissance troops in a commando. All aspects of mountaineering are involved in the work, including route finding and low-temperature survival.

Intelligence officers collect and co-ordinate information and circulate it to the appropriate people. Analysis and interpretation are important aspects of this job.

Helicopter pilots fly the full range of helicopters used by the Royal Navy and Marines, after initial work on fixed wing aircraft.

Physical training and sports officers are responsible for the development and supervision of all physical training, and work either within a commando or at a training centre.

Staff duties officers cover a wide range of specialist areas and could be located at the Ministry of Defence, in a commando unit or one of the larger headquarters. Jobs include training, personnel and logistics work.

WORK ENVIRONMENT

Royal Marines officers have to work in a very wide range of conditions, from jungle heat to arctic mountains. They are engaged in action in Northern Ireland, and have to be prepared to move at short notice to any areas in the world where crises occur. As specialist leaders, they operate from air or sea craft as well as on the land, and are required to undergo some of the most physically demanding tasks of any armed force.

THE NAVAL SERVICE: BAB

SKILLS AND INTERESTS
Please see article 1. RN OFFICER.

ENTRY REQUIREMENTS
The minimum entry requirements are two A levels/three H grades and three GCSEs/two S grades (A–C/1–3), including English and maths at either level. Applicants offering alternative qualifications, such as BTEC/SQA national awards or Advanced GNVQ/GSVQ Level III, are considered on their individual merits.

Entrants should be between 17 years and 22 years on the first day of the month of their entry.

Direct graduate entrants must have a UK degree or equivalent and English and maths at GCSE/S grade (A–C/1–3). They should be under 26 on the first day of the month of their entry.

Details of scholarships and bursaries are available from Armed Forces Careers Offices, as are nationality and residence requirements.

All applicants must pass the three stages in the recruitment process as well as a medical screening.

1. Potential officers course. This is a three-day course held at the Commando Training Centre at Lympstone in Devon. Candidates are tested on physical ability, mental aptitude and leadership potential.

2. Admiralty interview board. This takes place over three days at HMS Sultan in Gosport, Hampshire, and is designed to assess motives, personality and suitability for training.

3. Final selection board. The Ministry of Defence makes a final decision based on the first two stages and the number of places available.

Successful candidates are normally notified about a month before their start date. Those not accepted may reapply after one year. Three applications are allowed.

TRAINING
The first 12 months of Young Officer training is based at CTCRM, Lympstone. This training phase is similar to that taken by commando trainees, but officers are expected to receive a higher standard than other ranks. About 40 per cent of the course is classroom based.

There are five parts to the training:

1. Initial training consists of nine weeks of general basic instruction. Among the areas covered are general fitness, drill and weapon handling, and the role and history of the Royal Marines.

2. Military training takes 13 weeks and for this, trainees work in sections of eight men, and then troops of 28 men. The physical tempo speeds up from working in the gym to tackling the Assault Course.

Weapon training progresses to include the use of more advanced weapons. Classroom work includes military law and its application, current affairs, information technology, and nuclear, biological and chemical defence.

3. Amphibious training consists of a week spent at RM Poole introducing trainees to amphibious warfare. Practical exercises take place on raiding and landing craft and a day's familiarization is spent with the Special Boat Service.

4. Commando course consists of four weeks' preparation for the Commando Test Week which includes a speed march, a 30-miler with full kit and the Assault Course. Much of the preparation concentrates on amphibious training as well as survival techniques and unarmed combat. There is an emphasis on long-distance endurance work.

5. Advanced military training is the last phase of training and includes Resource and Initiative training, instructional and supervision techniques based on a live-firing range package, culminating in a ten-day final exercise. Much of this part covers management technique, particularly leadership skills.

After this twelve-month phase, trainee officers are given command of a troop or other sub-unit, consisting of up to 28 men, including a sergeant and three corporals. After twelve months working in one of the specialist activity areas of the Royal Marines, they are fully qualified.

Officers can expect their education and training to continue throughout their careers. Courses, which may be taken with the Navy or the Army, can be in preparation for standard promotion examinations or to enhance ability in their own specialist area.

OPPORTUNITIES
The number of officers recruited each year varies. The Royal Marines is a relatively small force, but suitable applicants are in demand.

PAY AND CONDITIONS
Pay rates on appointment vary according to an officer's type of commission, experience, and in some cases, academic or professional qualifications. A Royal Marines Second Lieutenant is appointed at £13,015 for example, and an Acting Lieutenant entering the Corps as a graduate would earn £14,921.

Men who are married and work away from their families for any length of time are given extra daily payments. Travel warrants are available to cover the cost of visits home, and officers normally take six weeks' paid holiday annually (often longer).

Officers are on call at all times, but usually work eight-hour shifts. During exercises, hours are long and irregular.

PROSPECTS
Royal Marines officers can expect new appointments on a frequent basis.

Promotion is through a clearly structured system. After seven years' development as a Lieutenant, officers can expect promotion to Captain. Subsequent promotion is awarded by selection based on performance record, qualifications and aptitude. It is possible to become a Major by the age of 35, a Lieutenant-Colonel by 45, and opportunities exist to achieve the rank of Colonel and higher.

RELATED OCCUPATIONS
Royal Navy officer, Army officer, RAF officer, Royal Marines – other ranks, police officer, physical education teacher.

FURTHER INFORMATION AND READING
Please see article 4. ROYAL MARINES – OTHER RANKS.

THE NAVAL SERVICE: BAB

4. ROYAL MARINES – OTHER RANKS (BAB)

THE WORK

All Royal Marines have some specialization in their work, as in other parts of the Navy. Commando troops, however, are all primarily trained for combat and their daily duties and the operations and exercises in which they take part all reflect this. The only exceptions are those who join as musicians or buglers – these men and women serve only with the Royal Marines Band Service.

After training, Royal Marines can enter the same six areas of work as officers: **Ships Detachment, Air Squadron, Special Boat Squadron, Jungle Warfare, Mountain and Arctic Warfare** and the **Embarked Force**. Please see article 3. ROYAL MARINES OFFICER.

The majority of Royal Marines work as riflemen in one of the above areas, but specialist trades are available for men to enter after commando training, or after spending some time as riflemen.

Armourers are responsible for inspecting and repairing all weapons and optical instruments.

Assault engineers provide immediate engineering support in a range of areas which may include mine warfare or demolition work.

Physical training instructors work on all areas of fitness training and sports coaching.

Landing craft specialists pilot, navigate and maintain all types of water-borne assault vessels.

Heavy weapons specialists are expert in all large weapons, such as mortars and anti-tank missiles.

Platoon weapons specialists train troops to use personal weapons.

Chefs provide troops with vital nutrition in battle conditions and in extreme weather conditions.

Clerks provide an efficient administrative system, so that all areas function smoothly.

Mountain leaders are expert in long-range patrols and reconnaissance work in mountainous country.

Signallers use all forms of communications equipment.

Telecoms technicians maintain and keep radio equipment working.

Drivers drive, service and administer all motor vehicles, including large goods vehicles.

Vehicle mechanics work on vehicle body repairs including panel beating and welding.

Illustrators work on all graphics, map making, aerial photography interpretation and making briefing models.

WORK ENVIRONMENT

Please see article 3. ROYAL MARINES OFFICER.

SKILLS AND INTERESTS

All Royal Marines must be able to work as part of a team, living and working closely with other people. They must be able to follow orders and supervise others. The ability to accept responsibility, make decisions and react quickly is important.

Practical and technical skills are important, as a wide range of equipment and advanced weaponry is used in all areas of the work.

Physical fitness and stamina are crucial. Marines must be prepared to work anywhere in the world at short notice and be separated from their families for long periods of time. All must be prepared to work in combat.

Each specialism has its own requirements. For example, those involved in the Special Boat Squadron must be strong swimmers, while those who work in Mountain and Arctic Warfare must be skilled at skiing and rock climbing. Fluency in foreign languages is useful for those who wish to work in communications and telecommunications.

ENTRY REQUIREMENTS

All candidates must pass a selection test involving reasoning, English language, numeracy and mechanical comprehension. An interview and medical check are also given. The minimum height requirement for all Royal Marines is 1.65 metres (5 feet 5 inches), and weight must be in proportion to height.

Those entering as musicians and junior musicians will have to audition and take a musical aptitude test.

Junior Marines and Junior Musicians must be aged between 16 and 17 years and 6 months. Others must be aged between 17 years and 6 months and 28 years.

All entrants must meet the RN nationality and residence requirements. Armed Forces Careers Offices will give guidance on eligibility.

All non-musicians must pass the Potential Royal Marine Course, which consists of three days of written tests, physical exercises and a personal interview.

TRAINING

For commandos, initial training lasts for 30 weeks and is based at the Commando Training Centre, Royal Marines at Lympstone in Devon.

The first 15 weeks of training includes care of equipment, drill, assault courses, survival training, weapons training and one week spent gaining amphibious warfare skills at Royal Marines Poole, in Dorset. This part of training concentrates mainly on individual fitness and skills.

Part two of training is spent working in small groups consolidating team work. Work includes endurance tests, heavy weapons training and the use of live ammunition. Classroom studies are also an important part of Stage Two training, as all men must understand, for example, how weapons work and the strategies and techniques of modern warfare.

All aspects of training are used in the final three-day exercise on Dartmoor, after which trainees become full commandos and are entitled to wear the green beret.

Those who have completed this training period may choose to train further for one of the specialist trades, and are encouraged to take City and Guilds, NVQ or BTEC certificates appropriate to their trade and their qualifications on entry.

Musicians and buglers train at the Royal Marines School of Music in Portsmouth.

LATE ENTRY

The upper age limit for entrants is their 28th birthday.

THE NAVAL SERVICE: BAB

OPPORTUNITIES
The Royal Marines is a comparatively small force but suitable applicants are in demand.

PAY AND CONDITIONS
Please see article 2. ROYAL NAVY RATING – pay and service requirements are the same as for Navy entrants, both for Junior Marines and those who enter later.

PROSPECTS
People who do well in training and exercises have good prospects for promotion. The rank of Corporal can be reached after five years, and Sergeant after seven or eight years. It is possible to gain commissions from the ranks.

Commandos who wish to find civilian work may attend Naval vocational training centres for six months in order to train for a new trade, or to study supervisory and management techniques. Many Royal Marines, however, have obtained qualifications and experience as part of their work that are acceptable to civilian employers.

RELATED OCCUPATIONS
Royal Marines officer, Royal Navy rating, Army NCO/private, RAF airman/woman, Merchant Navy rating, police officer.

FURTHER INFORMATION
Free leaflets and advice are available from all local Armed Forces Careers Offices. The addresses of these can be found in telephone directories (listed under Naval Establishment).

FURTHER READING
Working in The Armed Services – COIC

In the careers library classified under BAB.

THE ARMY: BAF

1. ARMY OFFICER CLCI:BAF
2. ARMY NON-COMMISSIONED OFFICER/PRIVATE CLCI:BAF

BACKGROUND INFORMATION

The British Army defends Britain and its allies both in this country and abroad, and plays an important part in NATO. It provides the commander and much of the headquarters of NATO's new Allied Command Europe Rapid Reaction Corps (ARRC), as well as 1st UK Armoured Division, 3 UK Division and 24 Airmobile Brigade, together with their support elements.

The Army is made up of regiments and corps, each of which has a specific military function. New recruits join a regiment or corps which will train them in the skills necessary to carry out their chosen employment trade, as well as encouraging them to develop their particular interests and abilities.

Regiments and corps are either an Arm or a Service. The Arms are actively involved in fighting, or providing close support to those fighting (eg engineering, communications, flying). The Services provide a range of essential support services to the Arms (eg transport, catering, medical care).

Entry to the Army is by joining a specific regiment or corps. Both men and women can join all corps except the Household Cavalry, the Royal Armoured Corps and the Infantry, which are open to men only. Entrants go through basic training at officer or soldier level before going on to train with their chosen regiment or corps. Some jobs are open to those who have trained in their specialism in civilian life, eg registered general nurses, doctors, dentists and lawyers, who meet the eligibility requirements.

1. ARMY OFFICER (BAF)

THE WORK

Officers lead and manage teams of trained soldiers. They are responsible for both personnel and equipment, and for making decisions about their deployment. They must understand how weapons and equipment work, as well as the skills and tactics necessary in battle. All officers follow two alternating career development paths – regimental duty and staff administration – and must, therefore, develop administrative as well as leadership skills. In addition, they are responsible for the training and welfare of the men and women under their command.

Officers develop their expertise according to the regiment or corps they are in.

Household Cavalry

The Household Cavalry consists of the two senior regiments of the British Army – the Life Guards and the Blues and Royals. Between them they provide an armoured reconnaissance regiment and the Mounted Regiment, which is well known for its ceremonial duties.

Royal Armoured Corps (RAC)

The RAC consists of armoured regiments equipped with the main battle tank, and armoured reconnaissance regiments equipped with light but fast armoured reconnaissance vehicles. The role of the armoured regiments is to fight the armoured battle, whilst the reconnaissance regiments obtain information about the ground and the enemy, as well as guarding the flanks and countering any enemy air or heli-borne assaults.

Royal Artillery

The Royal Artillery provides both ground fire support and air defence for the Army. In the ground fire support role, the Royal Artillery has a number of indirect fire weapons. In the air defence role there is a variety of surface-to-air missile systems. In both roles the Royal Artillery works closely with the other combat arms, and provides forward observation officers to RAC and Infantry units.

Corps of Royal Engineers

The Royal Engineers have a wide range of responsibilities. In combat they build bridges, lay minefields, create obstacles, and destroy enemy bridges, minefields and obstacles. Behind the combat area they build bridges, roads and airfields, construct camps, ports and bulk fuel installations, and generate and distribute electric power. They also provide support for the Royal Air Force by constructing airstrips and helicopter pads, repairing airfields and maintaining essential services. They carry out military survey work and explosive ordnance disposal of enemy delivered munitions for all three Armed Forces.

Royal Corps of Signals

The Royal Corps of Signals is responsible for providing, operating and maintaining the field communication system of the Army, using both voice and data transmissions. It also provides satellite communications to facilitate world-wide contact between the UK and elements of the Armed Forces wherever they are deployed. In addition, it is responsible for electronic warfare.

Infantry

The Infantry is made up of a large number of regiments and forms around 25 per cent of the Army. It takes a major role in the Army's peace-keeping tasks. It is also responsible for closing with and fighting the enemy, using machine guns, rifles, anti-tank weapons and mortars. Dependent on role, they may also be equipped with the modern Warrior armoured fighting vehicle.

Special Air Service Regiment (SAS)

The SAS undertakes special, often top secret, operations. It consists of highly skilled personnel who have proved themselves in other regiments and corps. They volunteer for the SAS and, if selected, are seconded to it.

Army Air Corps (AAC)

The AAC has a variety of helicopter borne roles, including reconnaissance, directing artillery fire, controlling ground attack aircraft, evacuating casualties, and their main task of launching missile attacks on enemy armour. They may also transport troops, stores or equipment or act as an airborne command post. Officers in the AAC are all qualified helicopter pilots.

Intelligence Corps

The Intelligence Corps collects, analyses and interprets information to form a picture of the enemy and what it is likely to do. In addition to providing combat intelligence, the Corps is responsible for providing security intelligence and protective security to counter espionage, subversion and sabotage; signal intelligence; specialist intelligence; and photographic interpretation. Languages are an important part of the Corps' activities.

The Services

Royal Army Chaplains' Department (RAChD)

The Department is responsible for the spiritual and moral needs of the Army. It has chaplains of a number of denominations who minister to both soldiers and their

THE ARMY: BAF

families.

Royal Logistics Corps (RLC)

The RLC is responsible for providing, storing and distributing all stores and equipment used by the Army; for the transportation of men and freight by rail, road, sea and air; for all catering and food supplies; and for providing postal and courier facilities for all three Services. These operations are world-wide.

Officers will specialize in one particular area to start with, but will broaden their knowledge of the Corps' activities as they progress up the promotion ladder. Specializations include transport, supply, ammunition, petroleum, catering, postal, and civil labour.

Royal Army Medical Corps (RAMC)

The RAMC provides a medical health care service to the Army, in both peace and war, ranging from general practice to consultancy and specialist facilities within military hospitals.

Royal Electrical and Mechanical Engineers (REME)

REME is the Equipment Support Corps of the Army. It is concerned with the maintenance and availability of all technical equipment including vehicles, weapons, radio etc. It is divided into three categories: Mechanical, Electrical/Electronic and Aeronautical, and makes up around ten per cent of the Army.

Adjutant General's Corps

The Adjutant General's Corps consists of four Branches, through which it provides a range of administrative services to the Army:

Education Training Services Branch (ETS)

The ETS is an all-officer branch that provides education for all Army personnel. It prepares candidates for promotional examinations, carries out language training (including English as a foreign language) and advises on the Army's training systems. It also provides guidance for those about to leave the Army.

Provost Branch (Royal Military Police) (RMP)

In peacetime the RMP is responsible for preventing and detecting crime and helping to maintain discipline. In war, it additionally controls traffic moving to and from the battle area. It has a separate detective force, the Special Investigation Branch (SIB), and also has specially trained personnel who protect Royalty and diplomatic/military VIPs abroad.

Army Legal Services Branch (ALS)

The ALS is an all-officer branch consisting of barristers, advocates and solicitors who advise on military law, prepare for and prosecute at courts martial, lecture in military law, and provide legal aid for Army personnel and their families.

Staff and Personnel Support Branch (SPS)

The SPS Branch is responsible for providing all the personnel administration in the Army, including pay and allowances. SPS officers specialize in personnel management, management accountancy and information technology.

Royal Army Veterinary Corps (RAVC)

The RAVC is responsible for the provision, care and training of the Army's animals – mainly dogs and horses.

Small Arms School Corps (SASC)

The SASC is responsible for training those who train others in the use of small arms.

Military Provost Staff Corps (MPSC)

The MPSC runs corrective training at the Military Corrective Training Centre at Colchester for soldiers who are deemed to need such training,

Royal Army Dental Corps (RADC)

The RADC is responsible for the dental health of Army personnel. It also looks after Service families abroad.

Army Physical Training Corps (APTC)

The APTC is responsible for all fitness training in the Army, including the oversight of fitness training by other staff.

Queen Alexandra's Royal Army Nursing Corps (QARANC)

The QARANC provides a complete nursing service to the Army, and works closely with the RAMC.

WORK ENVIRONMENT

Army officers are likely to be stationed in the United Kingdom (including Northern Ireland) or Germany but there are also forces elsewhere. There are officers stationed in other parts of Europe (including Bosnia), the Falkland Islands, Brunei, Cyprus, Gibraltar and Belize. Exercise locations include Australasia, North America, the Middle East and several African countries. Officers may be expected to work in climates from desert to arctic, but their immediate work environment depends on the job they do.

SKILLS AND INTERESTS

Officers need leadership qualities and the ability to work effectively as part of a team. They must be able to think and react quickly. They must be ready to accept responsibility, make decisions and manage other personnel. Officers must be able to lead their soldiers and earn their respect. They should be able to communicate with people of all abilities, explain ideas, give spoken and written instructions and motivate others. Officers must be interested in the people they supervise, and be able to listen to, guide and discipline them when necessary. All officers must be physically fit and prepared to work in combat. An interest and ability in science/technology is important for many of the jobs.

As well as having the general leadership and management qualities required of an Army Officer, officers in particular corps and regiments need to have the skills and attributes required by that corps or regiment.

ENTRY REQUIREMENTS

Officer candidates must first decide which regiment or corps they wish to join, and then apply to that regiment or corps for sponsorship through the selection process. (The final choice of regiment or corps – and subsequent acceptance – is made during the latter stage of the Sandhurst commissioning course.)

To become an officer, candidates must pass a medical board and a series of selection tests at the Regular Commissions Board (RCB). These last three-and-a-half days, and include computer tests, written tests, outdoor tasks and interviews.

There are two main types of commission in the Army:

The Regular Commission (REG C) is for men and women over the age of 17 years and 9 months but under the age of 25, who wish to make the Army their career. Applicants

THE ARMY: BAF

should have a minimum of five GCSEs/S grades (A–C/1–3) with two A levels/three H grades. These qualifications should be in approved subjects, and must include English and maths, and either a science subject or a foreign language. Applicants with alternative qualifications, such as BTEC/SQA national awards or Advanced GNVQ/GSVQ Level III, are considered on their individual merits and should seek advice from any Armed Forces Careers Office.

Graduates should have a recognized UK degree, although some BTEC/SQA higher national diploma or DipHE qualifications may also be acceptable, as may membership of certain professional institutions. REME and the ETS Branch of the Adjutant General's Corps only accept graduates with appropriate degrees. The RAMC, RADC, RAChD, RAVC, ALS Branch of the AG Corps and QARANC only accept those who are professionally qualified. Some of these corps accept candidates of a higher age.

The Short Service Commission (SSC) is for three years after completing the Sandhurst course, and is extendible, if mutually agreed, to eight years. Non-graduates require five GCSEs/S grades (A–C/1–3), normally including English and mathematics, though some corps require much higher qualifications. Applicants with alternative qualifications, such as BTEC/SQA national awards or Advanced GNVQ/GSVQ Level III, are considered on their individual merits and should seek advice from any Armed Forces Careers Office.

Graduates should have a recognized UK degree, although some BTEC/SQA higher national diploma or DipHE qualifications may also be acceptable, as may membership of certain professional institutions. REME and the ETS Branch of the Adjutant General's Corps only accept graduates with appropriate degrees. The RAMC, RADC, RAChD, RAVC, ALS Branch of the AG Corps and QARANC only accept those who are professionally qualified.

Candidates must be at least 17 years and 9 months and under the age of 25. Some of the technical/professional corps accept candidates of a higher age. After two years' service an SSC officer may apply for a REG C provided they are recommended and a vacancy is confirmed. (NB: SSCs are not available in the Intelligence Corps.)

A third type of commission:

The Short Service Limited Commission (SSLC) is available to people aged between 18 and 20 who have a firm place at a UK university for a first degree. In effect it is a Gap Year Commission. They must be recommended by their headteacher, be unmarried, pass an Army Medical Board and pass the Regular Commissions Board with a special recommendation for SSLC. (NB: not all corps accept SSLC officers.)

Certain corps require appropriate qualifications:

Graduate clergy applying for a commission in the Royal Army Chaplains' Department should ideally be under 34 and have served at least one curacy, or equivalent.

Candidates for the Royal Army Medical Corps can join as fully qualified medical practitioners, as qualified doctors in their pre-registration year, or as Medical Cadets if they have passed the second MB and are within three years of qualifying.

Entry to the Royal Army Dental Corps is open to qualified dental practitioners or to those within two years of completing their studies, who may be awarded Dental Cadetships.

The Royal Army Veterinary Corps requires applicants to be qualified veterinary graduates.

The Army Legal Services employs qualified barristers, advocates and solicitors who are aged at least 24. Those who have reached the final year of a law degree and have at least one year's full professional training to complete may apply for an Army Legal Cadetship or Bursary.

Queen Alexandra's Royal Army Nursing Corps is open to qualified Registered General Nurses aged over 21 with at least one year's post-registration experience.

Those who are already professionally qualified may apply to the corps which is appropriate to their qualifications.

Sponsorship. Various forms of sponsorship are available for undergraduates and A level/H grade students. There are two types of undergraduate awards: Cadetship and Bursary. The Cadetship is designed for young men and women who decide, before entering university or early in their degree course, to make a career as an Army officer. Cadetship officers serve for a minimum of five years after completing their training at the Royal Military Academy Sandhurst (RMAS) (42 weeks). While at university they receive a special rate of pay. The Bursary is for men and women who wish to commit themselves to a minimum of three years' service after the end of their training at RMAS. Bursary holders receive financial support which supplements the local education authority grant.

The Army Scholarship Scheme is for the last years at school when A levels/H grades are being studied and assures entry to Sandhurst with a commitment to serve a minimum of three years after commissioning, on a REG C (providing that at least two A levels/three H grades were achieved). Candidates should have the GCSE/S grade academic requirements for a REG C, and be aged between 16 and 16 years 6 months. Financial assistance during the A level/H grade course is given to the parents or guardians of those who are awarded scholarships.

Welbeck College, the Army's sixth-form college, provides a residential sixth-form education. Candidates should have at least five GCSEs/S grades (A–C/1–3), including English, maths, physics (or a subject involving physics). All students take A levels in maths and a science subject (usually physics), a third subject (science or arts) and, often, general studies. Candidates must be under 17 years and 6 months on entry. After the A level course, students may go on to a degree course at the Royal Military College of Science at Shrivenham or at a civilian university, or may go straight to the Commissioning Course at Sandhurst.

Officers must be physically fit and capable of strenuous work and of working long hours. Height and weight should be within the limits for the candidate's age and build. There are strict hearing and visual standards, and candidates must be able to distinguish accurately white, signal red and signal green.

All candidates must meet the Army nationality and residence requirements. Further guidance is available from Army careers advisers. Contact the appropriate careers adviser through your university or school careers staff; contact can also be made with local Armed Forces Careers Offices.

TRAINING

All officers, except those listed below, follow a 44-week (three-term) Commissioning Course (CC) at Royal

THE ARMY: BAF

Military Academy Sandhurst (RMAS). The aim of the course is to develop qualities of leadership and to provide the basic knowledge required by an officer, regardless of their corps. The CC includes tactics and weapon training, Army organization and administration, lessons from military history, leadership, military law, physical fitness and adventure training (eg climbing, parachuting, sailing).

Professionally qualified officers joining the Royal Army Chaplains' Department, the Royal Army Medical Corps, the Royal Army Dental Corps, the Royal Army Veterinary Corps and the Army Legal Services Branch follow a four-week course of basic training and general information about the Army. Professionally qualified officers joining the QARANC follow a nine-week course at the Army Medical Services Training Centre. The Short Service Limited Commission officers follow a three-week course of basic training at Sandhurst before joining the regiment or corps for SSLC commission. Undergraduate Cadets also attend a two-week course at Sandhurst before taking up Cadetship and proceeding to university.

After leaving Sandhurst at the end of the commissioning course, officers join their regiments or corps to learn their necessary skills, putting into practice the leadership and management skills that they learnt at Sandhurst. Many then complete the Young Officers course run by their regiment or corps; others carry out a short tour of regimental duty before attending the course.

Throughout their career, REG C officers attend a variety of courses which may be specific to their own particular cap badge or common across the Army. Many of these courses are associated with preparation for promotion to the next higher rank.

LATE ENTRY

Army officers on either a REG C or SSC must be at least age 17 years 9 months and under 25 on entry to the Royal Military Academy Sandhurst. There are some exceptions: graduate candidates for the Royal Engineers, Royal Signals, REME and the Educational Training Services Branch of the Adjutant General's Corps who hold a degree in a relevant discipline may be considered up to age 27; graduate clergy for the RAChD up to age 34; veterinary surgeons for the RAVC up to age 42; qualified solicitors and barristers for the Army Legal Services Branch up to age 30. Professionally qualified officers for the RAMC, RADC and QARANC who are over the age of 25 need to apply to the appropriate corps headquarters for consideration.

As the selection procedure can take some time, candidates are advised to apply well before they reach the upper age limit.

OPPORTUNITIES

There are approximately 13,000 officers in the Army. Around 750 are recruited each year for the CC.

Approximately 60 per cent of candidates pass the Regular Commissions Board. Those not accepted may be able to reapply, depending on the recommendations made by the RCB. If the recommendation is that the candidate should reapply, the RCB will also state when this should be. An RCB pass remains valid for four years.

PAY AND CONDITIONS

Those who join the Army on REG C can reasonably expect a career to age 55. They must serve three years after completion of their officer training at RMAS. They may then apply to leave at any time (unless there are exceptional circumstances such as a national emergency), giving seven months' notice. There are certain time bars of between two and five years from the completion of some courses. On retirement they must transfer to the Regular Army Reserve of Officers. SSC is for a period of three years (six years for Army Air Corps) from the date of leaving RMAS, extendible to a maximum of eight years. SSC officers may apply for a REG C after completing two years. On leaving they have a reserve liability until eight years after their commissioning. SSLC officers serve for between four and eighteen months and must give six weeks' notice prior to leaving. (SSLCs are only available to individuals from 18 to 20 between school and university.)

On entry, Second Lieutenants earn £15,177. Lieutenants receive £20,068 to £22,170, Captains £25,583 to £29,744 and Majors £32,441 to £38,865. Lieutenant-Colonels are paid £45,767 to £50,585 and Colonels £53,195 to £58,802. Brigadiers receive £65,291. Those on SSLC are paid £11,377 to £12,155 and Cadetship Officers £8,702 to £12,242. Bursary holders receive £1,500 (£500 a term). Doctors' and dentists' pay is allied to NHS pay scales.

NB – the above pay rates are as at December 1998 (and will be revised for April 1999).

Officers can be called upon to work 24 hours a day, but in barracks usually work a normal office hours day and five-day week. However, they remain on call and will be required to work the occasional weekend. On exercises and operations they work throughout, taking breaks for sleep and meals when conditions permit.

Female officers who become pregnant are granted maternity leave at the end of which they may resume their commissions. Those who have completed the minimum service for their commission may leave; those who have not will need to negotiate with the appropriate department on how their commission may be either fulfilled or terminated.

PROSPECTS

Promotion is through a structured system from Second Lieutenant through Lieutenant, Captain, Major, Lieutenant-Colonel and beyond. Promotion exams have to be passed for promotion from Lieutenant to Captain, and from Captain to Major. Promotion beyond Major is on selection and merit. All officers start as Second Lieutenants, though professionally qualified officers (eg for the RAChD, RAMC, RADC, RAVC, ALS and QARANC) are commissioned as Lieutenants or Captains, depending on their qualifications and experience. Graduate officer entrants on commissioning are given an antedate of seniority for their degree which usually results in promotion to Lieutenant. All candidates attend the commissioning course at Sandhurst as officer cadets.

Before being promoted, officers are trained for the next level of responsibility. Successful candidates can expect to become Captains at about age 26, and Majors at about age 33. Promotion beyond Major is on selection and merit, and is subject to vacancies. Majors will be considered for promotion to Lieutenant-Colonel between the ages of 36 and 45 years.

THE ARMY: BAF

RELATED OCCUPATIONS

Army NCO/private, Royal Navy officer, Royal Marines officer, RAF officer, police officer.

FURTHER INFORMATION AND READING

Please see article 2. ARMY NON-COMMISSIONED OFFICER/PRIVATE.

2. ARMY NON-COMMISSIONED OFFICER/PRIVATE (BAF)

THE WORK

All soldiers are trained firstly for combat. This means that each person in the Army must keep very fit, maintain a high level of combat skills and awareness of battle strategy, and be able to use an increasingly sophisticated range of weapons and equipment. They must also go on exercises from time to time, both near to their base and in other countries, so that they can test out their battle skills in a realistic, simulated situation.

There are over 100 different employments available in the Army. They range from pure soldiering as an infantryman to a skilled technician or craftsman/woman.

The regiments and corps that make up the Army are either an Arm or a Service. The Combat Arms and Combat Support Arms are those actively involved in the fighting, and the Services provide the necessary support, both administrative and logistical.

Although women may not be enlisted into the Household Cavalry, Royal Armoured Corps and the Infantry, and are therefore unlikely to be involved in front-line fighting, they may join any other part of the Army, and could find themselves deployed in a combat zone. Seventy per cent of occupations are open to women; the other 30% are constantly under review.

The Combat Arms

The Household Cavalry – (male only) provides an armoured reconnaissance regiment and the mounted regiment for ceremonial tours of duty. Jobs include armoured vehicle crewman and mounted dutyman.

The Royal Armoured Corps – (male only) consists of armoured regiments equipped with the main battle tank, and armoured reconnaissance vehicles. The role of the armoured regiments is to fight the armoured battle; whilst the reconnaissance regiments obtain information about the ground and the enemy, as well as guarding the flanks and countering any enemy air or heli-borne assaults. Everyone starts by learning to drive an armoured vehicle before progressing to crewman.

The Infantry – (male only) forms about 25 per cent of the Army. The role of the Infantry is to close with and defeat the enemy. They are trained to operate principally on their feet but dependent on role may operate from armoured fighting vehicles or helicopters. The Infantry usually take a major role in the Army's peace-keeping task. The Foot Guards and Parachute Regiment are part of the Infantry.

The Army Air Corps – operates the Army's fleet of helicopters which are tasked with carrying out reconnaissance, attacking enemy armour with air-to-surface missiles, or with lifting troops, casualties, equipment or stores. Soldiers in the AAC carry out a variety of ground crew duties but may progress to aircrew, including pilot.

The Combat Support Arms

The Royal Artillery – provides ground fire support and air defence for the Army. In both roles the Royal Artillery works closely with the Infantry and Royal Armoured Corps. Jobs include gunner technical (covering surveyor, meteorologist, command post assistant and artillery intelligence operator, radar operator and range assistant), gunner, signaller/driver, mounted gunner and gunner weapons. There are also units serving with commando and parachute forces.

The Corps of Royal Engineers – provides engineering support to the Army and particularly to the Combat Arms. Engineers carry out construction work such as making bridges, roads and airfields. They also create obstacles and carry out demolitions. The Corps also produces the maps for the Army, the Royal Navy and the Royal Air Force. Jobs include a variety of engineering trades such as surveyor, draughtsman, plant operator, carpenter and blacksmith.

The Royal Corps of Signals – is responsible for all communications and electronic warfare. Jobs include telecoms technician, telecoms mechanic, and telecoms operator.

The Intelligence Corps – collects and analyses information about the enemy so that successful operations can be carried out. It is responsible for security and counter-intelligence. Jobs include intelligence and security operator and special intelligence operator (analyst or linguist).

The Services

The Royal Logistics Corps – is responsible for providing, storing and distributing all stores equipment used by the Army; for the transportation of men and freight by rail, road, sea and air; for all catering and food supplies; and for providing postal and courier facilities for all three Services. Jobs include movement controller, railwayman/woman, seaman/woman, driver, supply controller, supply specialist, chef, postal and courier operator, pioneer, ammunition technician, air despatcher, seaman, marine fitter and petroleum operator.

The Corps of Royal Electrical and Mechanical Engineers – organizes the maintenance, repair and recovery of all technical equipment. The Corps divides into three sections: mechanical, electrical/electronic and aeronautical. Jobs include aircraft technician, avionics technician, telecoms technician, radar technician, control equipment technician, instrument technician, armourer, gun fitter, metalsmith, vehicle electrician, vehicle mechanic, technical storeperson, recovery mechanic and shipwright.

The Adjutant General's Corps – provides a range of administrative services for the Army. Branches of this corps that soldiers may join are:

Provost Branch (RMP) – prevent and detect crime, maintain discipline and control the traffic on operations and training. All soldiers in this group are known as military policemen/women.

Staff and Personnel Support Branch (SPS) – is responsible for providing all the personnel administration in the Army, including pay and allowances. All soldiers in this Branch are military clerks but may specialize further in the clerical aspects, including accountancy and information technology.

The Royal Army Medical Corps – provides a medical health care service to the Army, in both peace and war, ranging from general practice to consultancy. Jobs in this

THE ARMY: BAF

corps include radiographer, laboratory technician, physiological measurement technician, pharmacy technician, physiotherapist, operating theatre technician, environmental health technician, and combat medical technician.

The Queen Alexandra's Royal Army Nursing Corps – provides a nursing service to the Army and works closely with the RAMC. Jobs include registered general nurse, registered mental nurse and health care assistant.

The Royal Army Dental Corps – is responsible for the dental health of the Army. Jobs include dental support specialist, dental hygienist and dental technician.

The Royal Army Veterinary Corps – provides, trains and cares for the Army's animals – mainly horses and dogs. Soldiers join the corps as animal technical assistants.

The Corps of Army Music – provides the Army's State and Staff Bands. In addition to their musical skills, musicians also have an operational role, usually as medical assistants. Soldiers join this corps as musicians.

WORK ENVIRONMENT

Please see article 1. ARMY OFFICER.

SKILLS AND INTERESTS

All soldiers must be able to form part of a team, living and working closely with their colleagues. They must be able to follow orders without question on some occasions, while at other times be able to accept responsibility, make decisions quickly and use their initiative.

The ability to act promptly and remain calm under pressure is important.

Practical and technical skills are essential, as all soldiers are expected to use a wide range of equipment, advanced weaponry and vehicles.

Physical fitness and stamina are vital as soldiers could be required to work in extremes of climate after strenuous physical exertion, when tired and when under stress. Army staff must be prepared to be sent anywhere in the world at short notice, and be separated from their families for long periods of time. Every soldier may be called upon to work in hostile combat conditions when necessary.

Each specialism has its own additional requirements. For example, fluency in foreign languages is useful for those wishing to work in telecommunications and intelligence, and a methodical approach to paperwork is required for administrative posts. Those involved in particularly dangerous jobs such as bomb disposal must be absolutely calm and steady at all times and have very high levels of manual dexterity. Absence of such skills, however, is not a bar to application. The Army seeks volunteers and selects those with the potential aptitude who can be trained to fulfil these specialist roles.

ENTRY REQUIREMENTS

All candidates must pass the Army Entrance Test and do well at interview to be sent to the Recruit Selection Centre. Here candidates must pass a medical examination, a physical assessment test and an interview with an Army personnel selection officer.

For the majority of jobs, no particular academic qualifications are needed, but those who have taken some GCSEs/S grades and have a good school report have a better chance of being selected. In general, personal qualities and good motivation are more important than exam passes. The minimum age on entry (except for apprentices) is 16 years 9½ months.

Entry to technical trades as an apprentice requires GCSEs/S grades (A–C/1–3) in maths, English and science. Applicants with alternative qualifications, such as BTEC/SQA awards or Intermediate GNVQ/GSVQ Level II, are considered on their individual merits and should seek advice from any Armed Forces Careers Office.

Apprentices must be between 16 and 17 years and 6 months on entry.

Those entering the Corps of Army Music will have to undertake a two-day audition.

All entrants must meet Army nationality and residence requirements. Those not accepted at their first attempt will be advised about further applications. The possibility and timing of subsequent applications will depend on the reasons for an individual's rejection.

TRAINING

All new entrants to the Army take an initial eleven-week training course, known as the Common Military Syllabus for Recruits.

The first few days of the course are taken up with administration, documentation, a full medical examination and a general introduction. The course continues with instruction in drill, weapon training, fieldcraft, map reading, first aid, defensive measures in nuclear, biological and chemical warfare, military history and physical fitness. The training is also designed to develop self-discipline, teamwork and fitness.

The course ends with a passing out parade. Recruits then leave the Army Training Regiment and move to their Arm or Service for training in their chosen employment.

Army apprentices – are encouraged in those technical corps where a lengthy employment training is involved. These are:

The Royal Engineers; The Royal Signals; The Royal Logistic Corps (Chefs and Marine Engineers); The Royal Electrical and Mechanical Engineers.

Apprentices join the Apprentice Training establishment of their corps (except for RLC Marine Engineers who join in with Royal Engineer Apprentices) for a foundation course which includes the eleven-week Common Military Syllabus for Recruits, as well as character and leadership training, and instruction in the theory principles of their chosen trade.

Apprentices then move on to the appropriate Army School for training in their specific trade up to Class 2 standard. This is then followed by on-the-job experience in an operational unit before returning to further training at the appropriate Army School up to Class 1 standard. Depending on their chosen trade, apprentices work towards BTEC/SQA, NVQ/SVQ or City and Guilds qualifications at an early stage of their career.

An Army apprenticeship is a fast-track sandwich course designed both to produce Class 1 tradespeople at an early age, and to prepare suitable candidates for early promotion to middle management.

Apprentices may join the Army at the age of 16 (the upper limit is 17 years 6 months), and may apply to Armed Forces Careers Offices from the age of 15. These offices can give

THE ARMY: BAF

up-to-date details of the apprenticeships available.

LATE ENTRY

The upper age limit for the majority of trades is 26. Some sections will take recruits aged up to 31, and for certain employments in RAMC, RADC and QARANC the upper age limit is 33.

Armed Forces Careers Offices will give precise details of age limits. The Army normally prefers candidates at the lower end of the age ranges.

OPPORTUNITIES

There is a constant need for new recruits to the Army, despite the current restructuring. To maintain staff levels, approximately 15,000 adult entrants are taken each year of which about 1,100 are Apprentices. Information on the present situation is available from Army Careers Information Offices.

PAY AND CONDITIONS

All recruits are enlisted on an Open Engagement, which is for a period of 22 years' service from the age of 18 or the date of entry, whichever is later. All soldiers have the right to leave on completion of three years' service from the age of 18. One year's notice is required. The exception to this is in the case of pregnancy, when women may choose either to resign or take maternity leave.

A recruit who is under the age of 17 years 6 months on enlistment may leave at any time after the end of 28 days and before the end of six months. A recruit who is enlisted between 17 years 6 months and 18 years may also leave, but with repayment, and, for those aged 18 or over, on payment, at an early stage of their training.

Salaries are reviewed every year, and pay depends on age, profession and qualifications and rank held. An entrant aged 16 to 17 will earn a minimum of £113.82 a week, while an untrained Private aged over 17 years 6 months on entry will initially earn a minimum of £182.70 a week. Rates of pay are the same for men and women.

NB – pay as at December 1998.

Additions to pay are made in certain circumstances. For example, extra money is given to those serving overseas, and a separation allowance can be made to those living away from their families. Certain specialists, such as parachutists, receive additional pay.

Charges are made for accommodation and where appropriate, for meals.

Soldiers are on call at all times, but usually work a normal office hours day and five-day week. However, they remain on call and will be required to work the occasional evening and weekend.

Four weeks' annual holiday is normal, but this rises to six weeks when serving overseas.

PROSPECTS

Those who do well in training and exercises have good prospects of promotion, and a planned promotional structure exists. The route is from Private to Lance-Corporal, to Corporal to Sergeant, then Staff Sergeant. Warrant Officer Class 2 and Class 1 are the following ranks and at this level, soldiers may be considered for a commission. In some trades, soldiers may become non-commissioned officers as soon as they qualify.

About five per cent of those entering Sandhurst for officer training are taken from the ranks.

RELATED OCCUPATIONS

Army officer, Royal Navy rating, Royal Air Force airman/air woman, police officer.

FURTHER INFORMATION

Free leaflets and advice are available from the Army's university and schools liaison officers (details available from university or school careers staff), from an Armed Forces Careers Office, or by phoning 0345 300111, or by visiting the Army Website www.mod.uk

FURTHER READING

Working in The Armed Services – COIC

In the careers library classified under BAF.

THE ROYAL AIR FORCE: BAL

1. RAF OFFICER CLCI:BAL
2. RAF AIRMAN/AIRWOMAN CLCI:BAL

BACKGROUND INFORMATION

The Royal Air Force patrols and defends the United Kingdom from the air, and plays an important role in NATO.

It has a force of around 55,000 men and women, comprising more than 70 branches, trades and specializations, and is organized into three commands: Strike Command, Logistics Command, and Personnel and Training Command. Strike Command is directly concerned with flying and operating missile systems. Logistics Command is responsible for supply and maintenance. Personnel and Training Command looks after careers and training. Organizational changes and force reductions will continue to take place until 1999 in order to reduce RAF strength to around 52,500.

The commands are made up of stations which are divided into wings. The number of wings depends on the size and role of the station, but is likely to include operations, engineering and administrative wings. The wings are divided into squadrons and the squadrons into flights. Stations are communities made up of RAF personnel and their families.

Entry to the Royal Air Force is either at officer, sergeant aircrew or airman/airwoman level. All entrants undergo initial training before beginning specialist or trade training.

Some posts are open to those who have qualified in their speciality in civilian life, such as legal officer, nursing officer, chaplain or dentist. All specializations are open to both sexes, except that women cannot join the Royal Air Force Regiment.

1. RAF OFFICER (BAL)

THE WORK

Officers manage and lead the many personnel who make up the RAF. Their specific roles vary according to the branch in which they work. In addition to their primary duty, officers can have secondary duties to contribute to the welfare of the RAF community. This may mean organizing such things as sports teams or a station social club.

Pilots and Navigators

They are employed almost exclusively in flying during the early part of their careers, although later they may combine flying with ground duties.

Pilots usually specialize in one type of aircraft – fast jets, multi-engine aircraft or helicopters. All pilots plan flights and fly training exercises. Fast jet pilots learn many techniques, including battle formation flying and low-level fighting formations. Pilots flying multi-engine aircraft carry out maritime patrol, transport duties and air-to-air refuelling. Helicopter pilots supply support for Army exercises and may specialize in search and rescue services.

Navigators guide pilots by map reading and operating radar and navigational equipment. They are involved in planning routes and sorties. Additionally, they watch for enemy action and co-ordinate evasive activity.

Fighter Controllers

There are two types of fighter controllers: systems controllers who keep a constant watch on the airspace using radar, and report and identify objects within it, and interception controllers who use radar to detect aircraft. They direct RAF fighters to intercept suspect aircraft, giving them information about the direction, speed and height of the possible intruder aircraft. Some fighter controllers now fly as mission crew on airborne early-warning aircraft. In war, fighter controllers co-ordinate the air battles.

Air traffic Controllers

Air traffic controllers work in one of two areas. Terminal controllers are responsible for aircraft on the ground and within about 30 miles of the airfield. They use radar equipment and radio contact to help aircraft take off and land safely. Area controllers cover hundreds of square miles, providing pilots with flight information, navigational assistance and a position-fixing service to help them fly safely through airspace.

RAF Regiment Officers

RAF Regiment officers lead teams of men who defend RAF airfields and other installations from ground and low-level air attacks, using specialist ground defence units and surface-to-air missiles.

Flight Operations Officers

Flight Operations officers look after the planning and management of the operational support functions for the RAF's flying tasks.

Intelligence

Intelligence officers use a variety of photographic and electronic equipment to analyse defence-related and civil installations. They interpret images received from reconnaissance aircraft and advise other staff on the development and implementation of plans.

Engineers

Engineer officers work in one of two areas. Aerosystems engineers are concerned with keeping as many aircraft in operation as possible – this includes looking after aircraft, weapons and air-to-ground communications systems.

Communications/electronics engineers work with computer networks, defence radar systems and radio and air security systems – they are involved with planning, operating and maintaining battle management systems.

Suppliers

Suppliers are responsible for providing equipment, using a large automated stock control system. They deal with all goods ranging from complete aircraft, weapons, fuel and gases to clothing and furniture. Technical supply officers liaise with engineer and other officers, and set up supply systems in the field. Movements officers specialize in moving freight, mail and people, usually by air but often by land and sea. Other specialisms include fuels, explosives, data processing and systems design.

Administrators

The administrative branch is responsible for the smooth running of RAF bases and includes a wide range of jobs.

Catering officers have similar duties to civilian catering managers – food purchase and accounting, food preparation and service, bar service and accommodation, and personnel management. They may organize catering for a banquet or a disco or arrange in-flight meals for aircrew and meals for those on exercise.

Secretarial officers may work in accounts dealing with pay

instructions, budget forecasts and fund administration. They may also be estates officers, responsible for organizing the construction and maintenance of all RAF buildings from hangars to housing. Other secretarial officers work in personnel and may have responsibility for over 1,000 people, helping with their work and personal problems, advising on RAF careers and attending courts martial.

Training officers advise on the implementation and development of training schemes for RAF personnel.

Physical education officers administer and manage a wide variety of sports, promote a healthy lifestyle and assess fitness, as well as providing specialist training in military parachuting, survival techniques, leadership and adventurous activities.

Provost officers manage the RAF police force that protects personnel, aircraft and other equipment as well as investigating criminal and security offences. They may also maintain discipline.

Specialist officers

They carry out their profession within service life.

Medical officers provide medical care for RAF personnel and their families, advise on occupational and community medicine and assist in the aeromedical evacuation of patients.

Nursing officers in the Princess Mary's Royal Air Force Nursing Service care for patients whilst helping to manage a ward. They nurse service personnel and their families.

Dental officers work in dental centres on RAF stations, looking after the dental health of RAF personnel. Those abroad also take care of the families of service personnel.

Legal officers advise on evidence for courts martial, drafting charges and conducting prosecutions. They also provide general legal advice to staff.

Chaplains from a number of denominations work in RAF stations to minister to service personnel and their families.

WORK ENVIRONMENT

An RAF station usually consists of around 1,000 staff, including 100 to 150 officers. Officers can be posted to RAF bases in the UK or abroad; they may also go on exercises anywhere in the world. Their social life focuses around the officers' mess but their immediate work environment depends on the job they do.

SKILLS AND INTERESTS

Officers need leadership qualities and the ability to work as part of a team. They must be able to accept responsibility, make decisions and manage large groups of personnel. Officers should be able to communicate with people of all abilities, explain ideas, give spoken and written instructions and motivate others. They must be interested in the people they supervise, able to listen, guide and discipline them. All officers must be physically fit and prepared for combat.

Each branch has its own requirements. The ability to think and react quickly is particularly important for pilots, navigators, fighter controllers and air traffic controllers, as are skills and aptitude for operating advanced equipment.

Ground intelligence officers need analytical skills and a wide general knowledge to understand what an image represents. Engineer officers must be logical, analytical and practically minded. Supply officers need to be methodical and have a flair for organization. Regiment officers must enjoy being outdoors and active; they should be able to think and react quickly to situations.

ENTRY REQUIREMENTS

Basic entry

Candidates for entry to branches that do not require specialist qualifications should possess, as a minimum, two A levels/three H grades, plus five GCSEs/S grades (A–C/1–3), including English language and maths or equivalent qualifications, such as a BTEC/SQA national award or Advanced GNVQ/GSVQ Level III. Basic entry is not available in all branches.

Qualified entry

Candidates should hold acceptable professional qualifications (contact RAF Careers Information Offices for details). For example, a candidate for the administrative secretarial branch who holds a BTEC/SQA Higher National Certificate in Business Studies would meet the qualified entry standard for that branch and would enjoy special terms of entry. Qualified entry is available in all branches.

Graduate entry

Special enhanced terms of service are available for those with recognized degrees.

Nationality

All candidates must meet nationality requirements. RAF Careers Information Offices will give guidance on eligibility.

Sponsorship

The RAF operates a number of sponsorship schemes, most of which require individuals to commit themselves to some future form of RAF service. Contact an RAF Careers Information Office for details.

TRAINING

All new officer recruits begin with an intensive 24-week training course which includes physical fitness, classroom learning and practical exercises to develop operational and leadership skills. Specialist training in the chosen branch begins at the end of this course.

Pilots

Entrants with no flying experience spend time on elementary flying training. Those with university air squadron flying experience begin with six weeks at ground school, covering aerodynamics, radar, air traffic control and cockpit training. This is then followed by basic flying training with an instructor before pilots are streamed as fast jet, multi-engine or helicopter pilots. They then receive training according to the type of aircraft they may be flying. Pilot training takes around three years.

Navigators

Basic navigator training is lengthy and includes study at ground school covering subjects such as maths, meteorology, radar and basic navigational techniques. Trainees also experience flight simulations and sorties in various aircraft. They are then trained in fast-jet, multi-engined aircraft or support helicopters.

Fighter Controllers

Fighter controllers begin training with an Air Defence

THE ROYAL AIR FORCE: BAL

Foundation course in which their speed, reactions and technical abilities are tested. Simulators are used to allow fighter controllers to talk 'pilots' into contact positions.

Systems controllers then undertake an Identification and Recognition course, whilst interception controllers take an Interception Control course followed by further training at a front-line unit.

Air Traffic Controllers

Student air traffic controllers attend a course covering division of airspace, meteorology, navigation and air traffic regulation, as well as practical training in a variety of simulators. Further training in the relevant control positions follows.

Ground intelligence

Ground intelligence officers follow a course at the Joint School of Photographic Interpretation. Here they are trained to analyse what photographic and electronic images represent and to use this information to advise on strategies. Training involves many aspects of intelligence and security and it is important that ground intelligence officers keep up to date with changes in technology.

Flight operations

Flight operations officers are trained in the planning, management and maintenance of all aspects of ground support operations and the application of aircraft and their allocated roles.

RAF Regiment officers complete a course that concentrates on command skills, weapon training and field combat exercises. Depending on the squadron to which they are posted, officers then receive further instruction about the specific equipment used by that squadron. Additional training on specialist courses usually follows.

Engineers

All engineer officers undergo Engineering Officer Training – Phase 1 which involves management training as well as practical experience of technical problems. After a brief pre-employment course on the aircraft or equipment, a first tour of duty is normally followed by the Phase 2 course. The first part is completed by all engineer officers and covers the work of engineering staff and the applications of computers. Students are then streamed to follow aerosystems or communications and electronics modules. There are further courses, if the work requires it, on weapons, computers, propulsion etc.

Suppliers

Suppliers follow a Supply Training course during which they learn about the RAF's computerized supply system. They may undertake further specialist training in areas such as movements, storing fuels and explosives, or advanced data processing systems.

Administrative

Secretarial officers follow a course covering office management, personnel management, Service accountancy, military law, estate management and welfare matters.

Catering officers follow a course that introduces them to the RAF's catering management and accounting systems.

Physical education officers attend a course to familiarize them with the RAF's physical education requirements, followed by a parachute course.

Training officers have a four-week introductory course at the Training Development Support Unit, and other specialist training is given as required by new postings.

Provost officers attend a course at the RAF Police School where they learn about criminal law, security and counter intelligence. Later they may be selected for specialist training in criminal detection or computer security. There are opportunities to attend the civil police staff college at Bramshill. After some 18 months' service all officers follow an advanced course, leading to opportunities with the RAF's specialist criminal and investigation and counter intelligence service.

Medical

Fully registered medical practitioners undertake general service training and courses in community and occupational and aviation medicine. Provisionally registered house officers attend the RAF Institute of Community and Occupational Medicine for a short stay and then follow the RAF medical training described above.

LATE ENTRY

Upper age limits on entry vary according to the job:

The upper age limit is 24 for pilots, 26 for navigators and RAF Regiment candidates.

Fighter controllers, air traffic controllers, flight operations, ground intelligence, provost, engineer, supply, secretarial, legal and training officers should be under 30.

Physical education officers should be under 27 on entry, catering officers under 39 and chaplains under 39.

Medical officers should be under 39 if fully registered and under 38 if house officers. Dental officers should be under 33 on entry and nursing officers under 35.

There is normally a delay between being accepted for a commission and the start of training, so candidates are advised to apply at least a year in advance of age limits.

NB: Age limits are subject to continual review.

OPPORTUNITIES

The numbers of officers recruited varies from year to year. About 40 per cent are graduates. Competition is fierce. Candidates not accepted may be able to reapply. The RAF may recommend a one- or two-year gap between applications, depending on the reason for non-selection.

PAY AND CONDITIONS

Salaries are subject to annual independent review. The annual salary for a Pilot Officer is approximately £15,000. A Flying Officer earns between £19,728 and £21,797. The maximum for a Flight Lieutenant is £29,240 and for a Squadron Leader £38,208. Wing Commanders can earn up to £49,731. Aircrew are entitled to flying pay in addition to their basic salary. Various allowances can also be paid. Starting ranks and salaries depend on the type of entry and relevant qualifications. Officers are available for duty at all times but usually work an 8-hour day. However, some officers can be expected to work shifts and irregular hours. In particular, hours during exercises and detachments can be long and unpredictable.

Officers enter the RAF on either permanent or short service commission. A permanent commission means serving as an officer either to the age of 38 years, or for 16 years in total, whichever is the later. A short service commission is usually six years, but this period can vary in specialist branches. All pilots and navigators are required to serve for a minimum of twelve years. Women can be released early from their commission if pregnant or they can choose to take maternity leave.

PROSPECTS

Non-graduate entrants may spend about a year as an Acting Pilot Officer followed by a year as a Pilot Officer and up to four years as a Flying Officer before being promoted to Flight Lieutenant, subject to satisfactory service. Graduates are normally eligible for a faster promotion system up to the rank of Flight Lieutenant.

Promotion beyond Flight Lieutenant to Squadron Leader, Wing Commander, Group Captain and above is usually competitive and depends on merit, performance and quotas.

RELATED OCCUPATIONS

Royal Navy officer, Royal Marines officer, Army officer, RAF airman/woman, airline pilot, air traffic control officer, police officer, engineer, aircraft engineer.

FURTHER INFORMATION AND READING

Please see article 2. RAF AIRMAN/AIRWOMAN.

2. RAF AIRMAN/AIRWOMAN (BAL)

THE WORK

All non-commissioned staff who join the RAF are referred to as airmen or airwomen.

Airmen and airwomen are employed in a wide range of trades. They are all expected to carry out other essential duties, such as taking part in military exercises and training sessions.

All trades are open to both sexes except for the RAF Regiment.

The RAF divides the work into two areas: non-commissioned officer airmen (aircrew) and specialist ground trades. Over 50 separate job categories are available.

Airmen (aircrew) fly on multi-engined aircraft and helicopters. They consist of: air engineers, who are responsible for the operation of all aircraft systems; air electronics operators, who use electronic communications equipment such as radar or underwater detection systems on air–sea rescue missions and on-water and below-water surveillance; and air loadmasters, who supervise the despatch of parachute troops, aircraft loading and cabin services in passenger aircraft, together with tasks on air–sea rescue helicopters.

The majority of airmen and airwomen are employed in the ground trades, which are:

Aircraft Engineering

Airmen/airwomen in this group maintain and repair RAF aircraft, armament and propulsion systems. They carry out checks on RAF aircraft before and after flight, and do regular routine services. They also work in specialist maintenance units making major repairs, or on restructuring work.

Avionics

Personnel in this group maintain all airborne electrical, electronic, radar, navigation and flight systems, aircraft cameras, and communications and recording equipment in aircraft and airborne missiles.

Ground Electronic Engineering

Staff in this specialization are responsible for ground-based telecommunications, air defence radar and airfield navigation systems.

General Engineering

This group looks after aircraft ground support equipment, and ground electrical equipment, including aerials. It involves machine tool work, metalworking and welding. Work done by this section is divided into four areas: ground support equipment, workshops, electrical work and aerial erecting.

Mechanical Transport

This group comprises drivers who drive and operate the vehicles, and mechanics and technicians who maintain vehicles in an operational and roadworthy condition.

Air Traffic Control

Staff in air traffic control monitor aircraft transmissions, help plan flights and control aircraft access to runways from airfield control towers. They may also be employed at area radar units, where they may work alongside civilian controllers. Duties for airmen and airwomen in this group include updating essential information displays, setting up airfield signals, recording aircraft movement, operation of switchboards.

Telecommunications

The telecommunications section operate and control all land and radio communications, often using computerized systems. This is a 24-hour operation. Employed in this group are: telecommunications operators – who send and receive messages – and systems analysts – who work with both telegraphic and voice communications.

Aerospace Operations

Using advanced radar systems, aerospace systems operators help monitor and report the air situation. They provide warning of aircraft and missile attack using information from radars. They help to provide a recognized air picture for the United Kingdom airspace and its approaches.

Aerospace systems operators also man mobile radar convoys, and suitably qualified operators form part of the E3D airborne early-warning mission crews.

Safety Equipment

This trade group consists of survival equipment fitters who maintain and repair equipment such as parachutes, ejection seats, life-rafts and life-preservers.

Photography

The Photographic Trade Group currently comprises three elements: Photographer, Air Cartographer and Intelligence (Imagery). Photographers take photographs, operate and service ground cameras, carry out film processing work, and print and copy photographs. Air Cartographers prepare air navigation charts and maps for world-wide operations. Intelligence (Imagery) staff assist in the interpretation and production of imagery based reports from aerial reconnaissance missions.

Medical

The medical trade group is concerned with providing an essential medical service to the RAF at home and

THE ROYAL AIR FORCE: BAL

overseas. Highly trained staff are engaged in the technical, diagnostic and administrative support elements to the medical services (lab technician, environmental health technician, radiographer and medical assistant/administrator).

This group includes personnel of the Princess Mary's Royal Air Force Nursing Service which provides all staff nurses in the Royal Air Force medical service.

Dental

A dental service is provided to all RAF personnel. Jobs include dental surgery assistants, and dental technicians.

Personnel Administration

This group provides the accounting, personnel administration, administrative, computer and statistical support for the RAF.

Supply and Movements

Staff in this group are responsible for the storage of all sorts of RAF materials, as well as organizing the transportation of passengers, equipment, supplies and vehicles.

Catering

This trade group orders, prepares and serves food for all RAF institutions, including hospitals, temporary bases, and officers', sergeants' and airmen's messes.

Musician

Work is in established bands, ranging from marching and concert bands to the RAF salon orchestras and wind ensembles. Selected airmen and airwomen may also work as music instructors.

Security

This group is made up of three separate specialisms:

The RAF police carries out criminal investigations and counter-intelligence work, and is responsible for base security and dog handling.

The RAF Regiment provides a wide variety of jobs, all closely related to the support of flying operations. The Regiment provides field squadrons and Rapier squadrons. The Regiment also includes instructors for training all RAF personnel in all aspects of ground defence.

The RAF Fire Service is responsible for aircraft crash rescue.

WORK ENVIRONMENT

An RAF station may consist of from 300 to over 1,500 staff. Airmen/airwomen can be posted to RAF bases in the UK or abroad; they may also go on exercises anywhere in the world. Communal living and close team work are an important part of RAF life.

SKILLS AND INTERESTS

All airmen/airwomen require initiative, good communication skills and the ability to work as part of a team. They must be prepared to spend much of their free time with colleagues and, in most cases, live in RAF accommodation. It is important to be able to follow orders, and all personnel must appreciate the main function of the RAF and be prepared to work in combat. Airmen/airwomen must be prepared to work under pressure and maintain security at all times.

Each trade has its own particular requirements, but the ability to organize work and pay attention to detail are important in all trades.

Airmen (aircrew) and those working in engineering and transport need practical and technical aptitudes.

Clear speech and verbal skills are necessary in aerospace and telecommunications, and the ability to speak foreign languages is also an asset in any communications-based trade.

Trades involved in the interpretation of data (eg photographic interpretation, ground electronics and data analysis) require the ability to write clear reports.

ENTRY REQUIREMENTS

There are no minimum educational qualifications needed for many jobs. Applicants for the trades listed below, though, require academic qualifications. Entry is described mainly in terms of GCSEs/S grades but technical or vocational qualifications, such as BTEC/SQA national awards or Intermediate GNVQ/GSVQ Level II may be considered. Where entry requirements refer to a specific science subject, such as physics, chemistry or biology, in most cases combined science or dual science that includes the required subject is acceptable.

RAF Technician Apprenticeships – (Engineering Trades). Qualified entry: a minimum of three GCSEs/S grades (A–C/1–3) in English language, maths and physics or a physics-based science. Acceptance gives guaranteed access to learning facilities to complete a BTEC NC which is currently a prerequisite for promotion to corporal in the aircraft engineering trades.

Unqualified applicants may be considered who would be granted access to the BTEC NC learning package providing they show sufficient academic ability during basic trade training.

Air Engineer, Air Loadmaster and Air Electronics Operator: aged under 31, GCSEs/S grades (A–C/1–3) in English language, maths and one other subject, which for air engineer and air electronics operator would normally be physics-based.

Laboratory Technician: five academic GCSEs/S grades (A–C/1–3) minimum including English language, maths, biology (or human biology), physics (or approved physics-based science) and chemistry (or approved chemistry-based science), together with one A level in biology, chemistry or physics..

Environmental Health Technician: five GCSEs/S grades (A–C/1–3) including English language, maths, physics (or approved physics-based science) and chemistry (or approved chemistry-based subject) and physics (or a physics-based subject).

Mental Nurse: civilian qualified UKCC Register, Registered Mental Nurse (RMN).

Radiographer: five GCSEs/S grades (A–C/1–3) minimum including English language, maths and a science. Two subjects must be at A level (Passes in 2 subjects at AS level may in most cases be regarded as equivalent to one A level pass) or

a BTEC Certificate or Diploma in a subject appropriate to the degree with merit passes in at least 3 Level III units.

Staff Nurse: RGN/UKCC registration.

Student Staff Nurse: five GCSEs/S grades minimum (C/3) including English language, maths, one science and two further academic subjects. Applicants must be at least 1.58 metres (5 feet 2 inches) tall.

Dental Surgery Assistant: No qualifications are necessary.

However, those who wish to be considered for further training as Dental Hygienists must posess five GCSE/S grades minimum (C/3) including English language and one science subject.

Dental Technician: City and Guilds Dental Technician Certificate (Final) or BTEC/SQA National Diploma in Dental Technology.

Musician: Grade 8 of the Associated Board or a Degree/Diploma in Music and passing an audition.

The minimum age for entry varies according to the trade.

All candidates must meet the RAF's nationality and residence requirements, and must sit aptitude tests in arithmetic, English vocabulary and general knowledge, as well as mechanical and electrical aptitude, where appropriate.

A complete medical check has to be passed before applicants can go on to the interview stage.

Good colour vision is needed by photography staff, movements operators, most security workers, engineers and those in safety and surface and aerospace systems. Perfect vision is a requirement for firefighters but, in other security services, glasses for reading are allowed.

Good hearing is necessary for firefighters, gunners and all staff in the telecommunications group.

TRAINING

All entrants to ground trades, with the exception of the RAF Regiment Gunners who undertake basic recruit training at RAF Honington, attend a seven week recruit training course at RAF Halton, which includes physical fitness and military weapons training for all staff. An increasing proportion of trades training now involves working for nationally recognized qualifications, such as NVQ/SVQ, BTEC/SQA or City and Guilds qualifications, and the RAF encourages airmen and airwomen to take advanced vocational qualifications as their careers progress.

Most entrants receive specialist training, for example:

Engineering Mechanics (Technicians stream) and Mechanics take courses in different engineering skills, which are a combination of theory and practical work. Initial engineering training takes place at RAF stations Cosford, Locking and St Athan.

Air Engineers, Air Loadmasters and Air Electronics Operators take a 12-week basic training course followed by a specialist training course. Trainees then do more detailed training to develop their expertise on particular aircraft.

Motor Transport Drivers are taught to drive light vehicles, and after experience can be selected for PSV and LGV training.

Policemen/women are given a three-week driving course if necessary. This is followed by a six-week basic police course, covering activities such as crowd control and vehicle search procedures. Further training can lead to dog handling, security services work or counter-intelligence duty.

Gunners take a seven-week basic training course, followed by a 13-week specialist training course. This includes weapons training, survival, navigation and fieldcraft. The course is practical training done outdoors. Most gunners then take specialist courses in either light armour or Rapiers.

Assistant Air Traffic Controllers are trained at the Central Air Traffic Control school at RAF Shawbury. Tests are taken in signalling, meteorology, navigation, air traffic procedures and aircraft control regulations.

Physical Training Instructors require specialist training and take a 23-week course at RAF Cosford.

Telecommunications Operators are taught typing, message handling, and how to work by computer, radio, telegraph and facsimile. Morse code is taught at a later stage.

Communications Systems Analysts are initially trained in a combination of relevant computer/technology skills and languages. This is followed by operational techniques and RAF aircraft operations theory. Training is usually consolidated by work in an operational unit.

Aerospace Systems Operators are trained on a 8-week induction course at the RAF School of Fighter Control at RAF Boulmer. This includes keyboard skills training, basic radio principles, radar and computer systems, radar interpretation, meteorology and navigation.

Survival Equipment Fitters train in parachute maintenance and packing as well as learning about life-rafts, flying clothing and all types of aircrew safety equipment.

Photographic Trades – photographers, photographic interpreters' assistants and air cartographers all have separate courses.

Medical Trades for which recruits can receive full training from the RAF include radiographer, laboratory technician, and environmental health technician. Courses are similar to those available in civilian life.

Dental Hygienists' training lasts two years, and includes the study of anatomy, physiology and pathology, as well as practical work on model mouths for the first stage of the training.

Personnel and Administrative clerks' training includes work on typing, filing and data transmission and postal procedures, as well as personnel management skills such as disciplinary procedures and document administration.

Suppliers take an 8-week initial course followed by on-the-job training at an RAF Unit. Training covers both administration, which includes computerized accounting techniques, and practical work. Further specialist courses are available for work within, for example, explosives and fuels.

Movements Operators – training lasts for 16 weeks and is a combination of practical and theoretical work, covering air, road, rail and sea transport.

Caterers take a general catering course lasting four months, before returning to RAF bases where they may choose to take advanced or specialist training.

Musicians train at the RAF School of Music, studying the theory of music and band drill, and developing their playing ability in two musical instruments. The initial training course lasts up to a year, and is followed by more specialized work with one of the RAF bands.

Command and management training is provided for those who show potential, so that they may be promoted to non-commissioned status.

LATE ENTRY

The upper age limit for entry to the RAF is 30. Some trades, however, specify different limits: motor transport drivers, chefs and stewards should be under 24 on entry, staff nurses under 33 and student staff nurses under 26.

THE ROYAL AIR FORCE: BAL

Airmen (aircrew) should be under 31.

NB: Age limits are subject to continual review.

OPPORTUNITIES

The number of vacancies available depends on particular trades, some of which are more competitive than others.

PAY AND CONDITIONS

Pay is reviewed annually. All non-commissioned aircrew are paid £9,365 per annum during initial training. Air Electronics Operators and Air Engineers are paid £18,669 after twelve months and Air Loadmasters receive £18,669 on completion of Phase 1 training. Eighteen months after award of flying brevet, pay increases to £22,648 for Air Electronic Operators and Air Engineers, and to £20,637 for Air Loadmasters. Various allowances can also be paid.

All non-commissioned aircrew are required to enlist for twelve years service. Opportunities exist to serve for 22 years total service and to ages 47 and 55. All aircrew categories are open to women, who can be granted early discharge if they are pregnant or they can choose to take maternity leave.

For Airmen/airwomen in ground trades, rates vary according to rank and trade. Pay on completion of training ranges from £9,365 to £10,763. After tweve months satisfactory service, pay increases to between £13,026 and £16,592. Promotion to Corporal and above, up to Warrant Officer rank, is by selection based on annual reports. Salaries range from £16,979 to £20,830 for a Corporal up to between £22,604 and £29,433 for a Warrant officer. In addition, increments are paid after nine, twelve, 15, 18 and 22 years service; these range from an additional £317 per annum for a Senior Aircraftman/woman or Corporal who has completed nine years service, to £1,200 per annum for a Warrant Officer after 22 years service. Various allowances can also be paid.

All airmen and airwomen in ground trades enlist initially for nine years. Recruits have a right to claim discharge within a maximum period of six months from enlistment, depending on age; in some cases discharge is free, but payment can be required. Although airmen/airwomen are expected to be available for duty 24 hours a day, most trades work standard hours except when on exercises or detachments. People in a few trades work regular shifts. Airwomen can be released early if they are pregnant or they can choose to take maternity leave.

Most trades have fairly standard working hours, except when on exercises. Some workers, such as those involved in telecommunications, aerospace systems and security services, need to take part in 24-hour watch, which means that shift work is a regular feature. Catering staff and aircrew often work flexible hours and shifts, while medical and dental staff are on call as normal routine.

PROSPECTS

Promotion for all airmen and airwomen is generally awarded for good individual performance. Examination results and Trade Ability Test marks are used to assess trade knowledge and skills. A high standard of personal conduct is also needed.

Some non-commissioned officer positions are reached only after prescribed training courses have been completed.

Airmen/women are promoted to Leading Aircraftmen/women on completion of basic training, and to Senior Aircraftmen/women after a minimum of one year's service.

The ranks of Corporal and Sergeant are normally achieved by selection to fill vacancies, apart from some medical and dental trades, where time and qualifications are the criteria. Warrant Officer is the highest rank a non-commissioned officer can achieve.

Commissions and cadetships are available to airmen/airwomen who satisfy the various conditions of eligibility – most types of commission are open to serving personnel.

RELATED OCCUPATIONS

Army non-commissioned officer, Royal Navy rating, Royal Marines - other ranks, aircraft maintenance engineer, RAF officer, police constable.

FURTHER INFORMATION

Free leaflets and advice are available from all Armed Forces Careers Offices. The addresses of these offices can be found in telephone directories.

FURTHER READING

Working in The Armed Services – COIC

In the careers library classified under BAL.

GROUP C – ADMIN, BUSINESS, CLERICAL AND MANAGEMENT

1. ADMINISTRATIVE STAFF CLCI:CAB
2. SUPPORT STAFF CLCI:CAB
3. SPECIALIST STAFF CLCI:CAB

BACKGROUND INFORMATION

Civil servants work directly for the Crown and put the policies of the elected government into practice.

The Civil Service is non-political, and civil servants are expected to remain impartial, working for successive governments formed by different political parties.

The Civil Service is amongst the largest employers in the UK with more than 60 departments and over 100 executive agencies throughout the country. The departments are responsible for developing government policies while the agencies are the executive arm which carry out the policies. The work of each department and agency differs widely and the diversity of posts available is enormous. Civil servants are employed to help formulate policy on all aspects of life from nursery education to food production. They also pay benefits totalling over £80 billion and supply 30 million citizens with driving licences.

There are approximately 500,000 civil servants. Although the headquarters of some departments are in London, others are based throughout the UK and many departments and agencies have networks of regional offices.

The main government departments and agencies, and their responsibilities, are:

Advisory, Conciliation and Arbitration Service: industrial relations, conciliation in industrial disputes and arbitration.

Army Base Repair Organisation: repair, refurbishment of army equipment.

Audit Commission for Local Authorities and the National Health Service in England and Wales: auditing and advisory services; value for money.

Benefits Agency: administration and handling of social security benefits.

Cabinet Office: includes Cabinet Secretariat which supports Cabinet business and the Office of Public Service which exercises central oversight of the Civil Service.

Central Office of Information: information and publicity services – a procurement agency for government departments, agencies and other public sector clients.

Charity Commission: registering, advising and monitoring charities.

Child Support Agency: assessing and collecting child maintenance.

Contributions Agency: collection and recording of national insurance contributions.

Department of Culture, Media and Sport: the arts, sport, heritage and the media.

Commission for Racial Equality: elimination of racial discrimination; promotion of good race relations.

Crown Prosecution Service: prosecution of offenders on behalf of the police in England and Wales.

HM Customs and Excise: collection of VAT and duties on tobacco, drink and petrol.

Office of Data Protection Registrar: establish register of data users and computer bureaux and enforce data protection principles.

Ministry of Defence: Navy, Army and Air Services policy and support, procurement research and development.

Defence Evaluation and Research Agency: research organization supporting ministry of defence and private industry.

Department for Education and Employment: primary, secondary, further and higher education; employment and training.

Department of the Environment, Transport and the Regions and Highways Agency: local government; housing and construction, aviation, shipping, roads and railways.

Driver and Vehicle Licencing Agency: registering and licensing vehicles, issuing driving licences.

Equal Opportunities Commission: elimination at work of sexual and racial discrimination and other areas such as disability and sexual orientation – a fringe body of the Civil Service.

Export Credit Guarantee Department: insuring businesses against non-payment by overseas customers.

Office of Fair Trading: protecting the public and businesses from unfair trading practices.

Farming and Rural Conservation Agency: farming, fishing and food production.

Foreign and Commonwealth Office: foreign policy; representing business interests overseas.

Forensic Science Service: providing scientific support to crime investigation.

Forestry Commission: regulating and managing forest areas.

Government Actuaries Department: independent actuarial consultancy.

Government Communications Headquarters: communications intelligence.

Government Economic Service: providing expert economic advice to other government departments.

Government Legal Service: providing legal advice to other government departments.

Department of Health: administration of the National Health Service.

Health and Safety Executive: advice and enforcement of health and safety legislation – an executive agency of the Department of the Environment, Transport and the Regions.

Home Office: law and order administration; immigration.

Inland Revenue: collection of income, capital gains and corporation tax; valuation of properties.

Lord Chancellor's Department: government court services.

Meteorological Office: weather forecasting and information services.

Office for National Statistics: government statistical services, including registration of births, marriages and deaths, population census and national surveys.

Northern Ireland Office: policy and legislation relevant to Northern Ireland.

Ordnance Survey: mapping, charting and surveying.

Overseas Development Administration: overseas aid to developing countries.

Scottish Office: policy and legislation relevant to Scotland.

Department of Social Security: social security benefits and welfare services.

The Stationery Office: publisher for government and

CIVIL SERVICE: CAB

Parliament – an executive agency of the Office of Public Service.

Department of Trade and Industry: international trade policy, industrial liaison, consumer protection, insurance, radio and patent regulations.

HM Treasury: economic policy and public spending.

Valuation Office Agency: Valuing land and property for local and central government.

War Pensions Agency: delivering war pensions to war disablement pensioners.

Welsh Office: policy and legislation relevant to Wales.

It is possible to start work in the Civil Service at a number of different levels, depending on qualifications and experience. There are opportunities to develop a successful career in general administrative, strategic and managerial roles as well as in many different specialisms. There are certain special schemes of entry for those who show exceptional ability and the potential to progress quickly.

It is also possible for civil servants to work on secondment for statutory bodies such as English Nature, the Rural Development Commission or the Arts Council as well as in private industry and local government.

1. ADMINISTRATIVE STAFF (CAB)

THE WORK

There is a massive range of employment opportunities for administrators in hundreds of different fields, from developing policy for the National Health Service to running a Jobcentre or helping to calculate war pensions.

Administrative assistants are basically junior clerks. Their work can include keeping records, either manually or on computer, sorting and filing papers, simple figure work, writing basic letters and dealing with enquiries. Administrative assistants usually support more senior staff.

Administrative officers work with administrative assistants, but have a higher level of responsibility. Their work can include handling incoming correspondence, writing or drafting letters, assessing charges or grants, checking accounts, maintaining records, either manually or on computer, and assisting the public either face to face or on the telephone.

Junior managers (formerly called executive officers) usually fill first line management roles although some personal performance and policy work may be available. They may be responsible for managing a section of administrative officers and assistants in a local office. They have responsibility for organizing and controlling the work of their group as well as responsibility for motivating and training staff. They may be assisting a senior civil servant with policy work, external liaison or general administration. They may also deal with case work where they are required to apply complex rules, laws and procedures and report their findings to senior colleagues. There are opportunities for personnel work, financial management, estate management and report writing. About a third of executive officers take up specialized work in areas such as customs and excise or immigration.

Higher executive and senior executive officers are more senior management posts available to experienced staff. Success in these posts can lead to promotion to the most senior posts – from grade 7 to grade 1, a permanent secretary.

Fast-stream and development programme administrators and managers take part in an accelerated promotion scheme for high-calibre graduate entrants. The work could include working in a minister's office, providing support to an agency chief executive, or as part of a management team on a special project or inquiry. The work could involve researching and analysing policy options, working with specialists transforming policy objectives into the delivery of services, dealing with parliamentary business or in the many current international or national political issues. The Government Communications Headquarters also operates a graduate management training scheme. This fast-track scheme provides work experience and development training to prepare those involved for early promotion. Some of the work is technical, some administrative. There is a special scheme for those wishing to work in Europe which provides work experience and language training to help prepare for EU recruitment competitions. Other departments also operate management development schemes for graduates.

WORK ENVIRONMENT

Administrative staff are normally office-based. Some staff work in offices that are open to the public while others may be required to spend a great deal of time visiting the public in their own homes or visiting other establishments to check facilities or discuss issues.

The work of many civil servants – particularly those in more senior grades – involves travel to external meetings, conferences or exhibitions. This can involve long days and periods spent away from home. The growing importance of the EU is resulting in more European travel for some administrative staff.

Some jobs may involve an extensive amount of driving.

SKILLS AND INTERESTS

The Civil Service is dependent on team work, and staff at all levels must be able to work well with others. Effective communication – in writing, face-to-face and on the telephone – is essential to the smooth running of government departments, and civil servants are therefore expected to be able to communicate well with their colleagues, representatives of external organizations and members of the public.

Good organizational abilities and a methodical and accurate approach to work are important at all levels. A responsible and sensitive approach to confidential information is necessary for many civil servants. A high standard of numeracy is required for some posts.

Those recruited at junior manager level and above require the potential to lead and motivate other staff. They require an ability to act on their own initiative, to work without close supervision and to deliver results within agreed deadlines. They have to be forward thinking with good analytical skills with the ability to plan and prioritize their work and the work of others. Some positions require the ability to absorb and follow complex rules and procedures.

Fast-stream entrants must be able to work quickly and under pressure, to think creatively, to exercise sound judgement and achieve results. They need to identify salient points when confronted with a vast amount of facts and information. They may need consultation and negotiating skills. Those wishing to enter the Diplomatic Service or participate in the European fast-stream

CIVIL SERVICE: CAB

programme must also have an interest in international affairs.

Many specialist posts require specific abilities. For example, a high level of mathematical ability is essential for government actuaries and statisticians.

ENTRY REQUIREMENTS

To join the Civil Service, candidates must be British citizens, Commonwealth citizens or citizens of the Republic of Ireland. For posts in the Cabinet Office (or its agencies) and the Ministry of Defence, at least one parent must also have been born a citizen of a Commonwealth country or the Republic of Ireland. Applicants must have close affiliations with the UK in terms of upbringing and residence. All members of the Diplomatic Service, the Government Communications Headquarters and in potentially sensitive jobs must undergo enquiries, known as developed vetting, to ensure that they have the right temperament and attitudes to handle confidential work. A medical or vision test may be required. Some positions require a clean current driving licence.

Those wishing to work in the Welsh Office or in a department or agency with offices in Wales may be required to speak Welsh.

It is possible to enter the Civil Service at a number of different levels, depending on qualifications and previous experience. There are no longer any nationally applied educational requirements and precise requirements and job titles vary between departments.

Administrative assistant/officer

Selection for administrative assistant/officer posts is by competitive interview. Candidates for administrative assistant posts must normally possess a minimum of two GCSEs/S grades (A–C/1–3) including English or equivalent. NVQs/SVQs may also be accepted. Administrative officers usually require five GCSEs/S grades (A–C/1–3) including English or equivalent. Departments may also recruit clerical staff by means of written tests for which no specific educational qualifications are required, or on the basis of previous relevant experience. Some departments and agencies recruit via competencies and not educational qualifications. Applicants are required to show evidence of previous work or educational experience of competence in some of the following areas: getting on with people, prioritizing work, making decisions, working in a team., written and oral communication, numeracy. Disabled people who do not possess qualifications may take written tests instead.

Modern Apprenticeships (part of the Skillseekers Initiative in Scotland) may be available leading to at least an NVQ/SVQ Level 3. Contact your local careers office, Jobcentre, TEC/LEC for details.

Junior managers

The minimum qualifications for entry as a junior manager (executive officer/grade 9) are normally two A levels/three H grades and three GCSEs/S grades (A–C/1–3).

Equivalent qualifications including BTEC/SQA awards and GNVQs/GSVQs may also be acceptable. However, competition for entry to the Civil Service at junior manager level is fierce, and half of all recruits are graduates. Selection processes vary from department to department but usually involve competitive tests and an interview.

Fast-stream administrators

Around 100 graduate entrants are accepted each year to the Administrative fast-stream, after a rigorous selection procedure that is designed to test both intellectual and other abilities including personal and leadership qualities. The tests consist of an initial qualifying test followed up by two days of written tests. Successful candidates then attend an interview and take part in management exercises which are then evaluated. It is also possible to enter the Diplomatic Service fast-stream. There is now a European fast-stream, which offers a route to a career in the European Union. It is specifically designed to help British candidates compete for administrative posts in EU institutions. A first- or upper-second-class honours degree or equivalent in any discipline is usually required for fast-stream entry. The Inland Revenue and the Security Service also run their own fast-stream entry scheme

TRAINING

Training opportunities are available throughout the Civil Service including day release for those under 18 years, block release, college and university sponsorship, distance learning, in-house and on-the-job training, assistance with study for professional qualifications and attachment to external organizations.

There is a well-structured system for regular staff appraisal; identifying training needs and development opportunities is a key element of this. Fully structured management training development programmes ensure that staff with potential are encouraged to enhance their knowledge and skills.

The Civil Service College provides residential training both in specialist subjects, such as accountancy, personnel and finance, and in general management skills such as communication and negotiation. Its courses are available to all civil servants.

Administrative officers and assistants

Training is provided to develop knowledge and skills and to prepare administrative staff for promotion. NVQs/SVQs may be available. These vary depending on the post held and the employing department or agency. Those who are under the age of 18 years can apply for day release to attend further education courses.

Junior managers

Most departments organize a management development programme aimed at improving the effectiveness of middle management. Specialist training is given for specific positions. Managers are encouraged to take mainstream qualifications that complement the work they do and financial assistance and study leave may be available. Specialist training is given to accountancy trainees, those in the automatic data processing field, to tax officers and examiners in insolvency.

A range of NVQs/SVQs are available – these vary depending on the post held.

For mainstream entrants to the Diplomatic Service, training in the first two years includes professional, developmental and management courses. Training for a first posting can include both specific skills and foreign languages.

Fast-stream administrators

Fast-stream administrators and managers are provided with extensive training opportunities, demanding work and early responsibility to develop their skills.

CIVIL SERVICE: CAB

European fast-stream administrators receive additional training to prepare them for Europe, including language tuition, courses and tutorials on European issues and coaching to prepare them for the EC competitions.

LATE ENTRY

It is possible for mature entrants to take up careers in the Civil Service and to return to work after a career break. There are no age limits for administrative assistants and officers or junior managers except for the European fast-stream.

OPPORTUNITIES

Departments and agencies are now responsible for recruiting all their own personnel, excluding some senior appointments. They either undertake this recruitment themselves or via a recruitment company or organization, often the Recruitment and Assessment Services Agency. Many applicants contact their preferred department or agency direct.

There is no longer any service-wide vacancy information. Vacancies are advertised in Jobcentres and sometimes in the national or local press. It is also possible to write directly to the department or agency in which applicants are interested in working.

Recruitment to the Civil Service is now far more limited than in the past, and competition for entry in many areas is highly intense.

PAY AND CONDITIONS

There are variations in pay and conditions between different jobs, grades and locations, although there are many common factors. Starting salaries are linked to skills and experience, and there is a system of annual increments.

Most civil servants work normal office hours from Monday to Friday. However, longer hours and weekend work may be required during busy periods and in more senior posts. Shift work may be required for a limited number of posts where it is essential for services to be provided on a 24-hour basis, for example, in the Government Information Service or in the Immigration Service.

Civil Servants have between 22 and 30 days' holiday according to grade and length of service.

Employees working at junior manager level and above are appointed as mobile staff and must be prepared to work anywhere in the country.

Salary scales are no longer set for the Civil Service as a whole, but by individual departments. Performance-related pay has been introduced in most areas and there may be additional allowances for those working in London and outer London.

Part-time work and job-share opportunities may be available. The Civil Service has a good record as an equal opportunities employer.

PROSPECTS

Promotion for staff throughout the Civil Service is based on merit, regardless of level or method of entry. All employees are set targets, and performance is assessed against these goals. Some employees may take professional qualifications which enable them to move into the private sector, others gain specific experience which may enable them to transfer to the private sector or local government.

Promotion to the highest grades is very competitive and only the most talented staff could expect to reach these positions.

There are many opportunities to widen experience by working in different departments and agencies.

RELATED OCCUPATIONS

Local authority administrator, local authority clerk, Health Service manager, medical records clerk, clerk.

FURTHER INFORMATION AND FURTHER READING

Please see article 3. SPECIALIST STAFF.

2. SUPPORT STAFF (CAB)

THE WORK

The Civil Service requires many different types of support staff to function effectively. These include personal secretaries, typists, telephonists, reprographics and photocopier operators, paperkeepers, messengers, cleaners, car drivers and security officers. The work varies considerably but usually involves supporting administrative staff in the day-to-day running of each department and agency.

WORK ENVIRONMENT

Support staff are normally office-based. They may work in offices that are open to the public.

Telephonists and typists may spend much of the time sitting while security staff and messengers may spend the majority of their time walking.

Some security staff may work outside.

Cleaners may be required to work after normal office hours in large empty buildings.

SKILLS AND INTERESTS

Please see article 1. ADMINISTRATIVE STAFF

ENTRY REQUIREMENTS

All civil servants must be British citizens. Please see article 1. ADMINISTRATIVE STAFF.

Typists recruited without a recognized typing qualification are usually required to pass a 30 wpm test. Personal secretaries, who are normally promoted from the typing grades, should have the same skill, and be capable of 100 wpm shorthand or 360-word audio transcription in 20 minutes. Secretaries may also need three GCSEs/S grades (A–C/1–3) including English or the equivalent. Many departments test applicants typing ability including ability with specific computer packages and spreadsheets if appropriate to the work to be undertaken.

Entry requirements for other support staff vary depending on the nature of the post and may include academic qualifications or previous relevant experience. Security

CIVIL SERVICE: CAB

staff should have no current convictions; police checks may be undertaken.

TRAINING

Relevant training is provided for support staff to equip them with the knowledge and skills to perform effectively. This can range from secretarial skills courses to programmes on the use of office equipment. Most receive an initial induction programme which is followed up by on-the-job training.

NVQs and SVQs may be available and staff are encouraged to undertake other training which may help them to perform their tasks. Financial help may be available to undertake courses and time off may be allowed for examinations at the discretion of managers.

LATE ENTRY

There is no upper age limit for entry and many support staff are mature entrants with previous relevant experience.

OPPORTUNITIES

Vacancies for support staff exist throughout the UK and are usually advertised locally in Jobcentres or the local press. Please see article 1. ADMINISTRATIVE STAFF.

PAY AND CONDITIONS

See article 1. ADMINISTRATIVE STAFF. Many support staff work part-time or on short-term contracts.

PROSPECTS

Promotion for all support staff is based on merit. All Civil Service staff are given regular staff appraisals. Support staff may be promoted to supervisory posts or transfer to the administrative stream.

Many private companies recognize the specials skills and responsibilities that support staff gain in the Civil Service and opportunities may exist in the private sector.

RELATED OCCUPATIONS

Typist, secretary, security guard, messenger, driver, personal assistant, telephonist, cleaner.

FURTHER INFORMATION

Please see article 3. SPECIALIST STAFF.

FURTHER READING

Please see article 3. SPECIALIST STAFF.

3. SPECIALIST STAFF (CAB)

THE WORK

The Civil Service recruits a variety of specialists.

Accountants are employed throughout the Civil Service to audit, analyse and verify their department's accounts. They also pay creditors' invoices, collect debts, provide financial accounts, and supply financial advice and information to managers.

Actuaries are employed by the Government Actuary's Department. The work involves acting as a financial services consultant to the public sector in the areas of social security, pensions and insurance. This could include costing of benefit provision, developing national pensions policy or monitoring insurance companies.

Architects are employed in very limited numbers by the Department of the Environment, Transport and the Regions and the Building Research Establishment, primarily on policy work.

Cartographic staff are employed by the Ordnance Survey and several other departments to carry out mapping and charting work. As well as the traditional geographic maps, air and sea charts, many map production techniques and processes are now automated and mapping information is frequently provided in digital form. Mapping and charting officers work in jobs requiring specialist knowledge in a particular aspect of cartography, hydrography, topographic surveying, map and chart production or an associated function.

Computing staff work in a wide range of government departments and agencies in a variety of information technology roles, from data processing to systems analysis. The work centres on developing and updating hardware and software systems and providing administrative support. Computer scientists, normally entering as assistant scientific officers, are employed by government research establishments, laboratories and organizations such as the Meteorological Office. Much of the work involves very advanced technology.

Diplomatic Service Staff are employed to protect and promote British interests abroad, and advise and support ministers as they formulate Britain's foreign policy. The work is divided between the Foreign and Commonwealth Office in London and diplomatic missions overseas. In Commonwealth countries these missions are known as High Commissions and in other countries as Embassies. In addition, Britain maintains missions to a number of international organizations, including the United Nations and the European Commission. The work of diplomatic missions is divided into five sections: political, commercial, information, consular/immigration and management.

Those starting in mainstream Diplomatic Service posts at grade 9 can expect to spend their first two years in London. A first overseas post is likely to involve consular, immigration or management work in a mission. With experience, it is possible to progress to more senior posts.

The Diplomatic Service also operates a fast-stream programme for high-calibre graduates.

Economists are employed in the Government Economic Service to provide ministers and senior administrators in all major departments with expert advice on economic matters. The work includes the analysis of current trends, the development of forecasting models and the preparation of forecasts, the development and evaluation of economic policy, and application of economic principles and techniques to industrial, social and institutional problems. There are also opportunities for research. It is possible to join as an economic assistant or senior economic assistant and to progress to economic adviser.

Engineers and *engineering technicians* work on a wide variety of different projects, from costing a new weapons system to advising on field drainage, from investigating aircraft accidents to developing computer systems. The main areas of employment are in the Ministry of Defence,

CIVIL SERVICE: CAB

the Government Communications Headquarters, the Department of the Environment, Transport and the Regions and the Radiocommunications Agency. Much of the work involves the most advanced technologies, and there are opportunities for engineers to be attached to industry and research establishments. There is a science and engineering fast-stream scheme for high-calibre graduates.

Inspectors of Health and Safety are responsible for the well-being of the UK's workforce and those who may be affected by its activities. Most of their time is spent visiting workplaces to ensure that conditions, machinery and safeguards comply with health and safety legislation. They also advise employers, staff and suppliers, and investigate accidents at work. Inspectors work in all industrial sectors and agricultural inspectors work mainly in farming, horticulture and forestry. Please see article HEALTH AND SAFETY INSPECTOR (COT).

Immigration Service staff are employed by the Home Office. Those who are recruited at junior manager level can choose to specialize in this area of activity. The work includes office-based activities, such as processing immigration applications and dealing with appeals, as well as work at airports and seaports, which includes checking passports and visas.

Information officers are employed by the Government Information Service to explain government policy and action. They work in every department. Press officers keep the media informed and may accompany ministers on official visits.

Publicity officers are responsible for marketing and the organization of publicity campaigns, conferences and exhibitions. Information specialists provide the creative input and include graphic and exhibition designers, journalists, writers, illustrators and film producers.

Lawyers are employed by both the Government Legal Service(GLS) and the Crown Prosecution Service (CPS). Within the Government Legal Service, lawyers work in all departments and some agencies, covering virtually every aspect of the law dealt with by private practice. They also have additional responsibilities for drafting legislation, advising ministers and, increasingly, with EU law. The Crown Prosecution Service prosecutes criminal cases instituted by the police in magistrates' courts and the Crown Court in England and Wales. It is possible to specialize in areas, such as juvenile law or fraud investigation.

Librarians work in all major government departments and agencies. Areas of work include cataloguing, classifying and indexing, database and computer systems, editorial work, literature searches, supervision of readers' services and clerical staff, and general library duties.

Linguists work for the Joint Technical Language Service, which is part of the Government Communications Headquarters, on transcription, translation and linguistic research for a number of government departments. The Ministry of Defence also employs linguists who initially carry out written translation, largely of a technical nature, and research into publications in a foreign language. More senior staff can work on advanced and specialized translation, foreign document research and simultaneous translation at conferences.

Museum staff are responsible for the vast and richly varied collections housed in Britain's museums and galleries. As well as having the opportunity to pursue studies in a particular area of interest, graduate curators are occupied in organizing exhibitions, managing technical staff, assisting with administrative work, helping to prepare publications and answering enquiries from the public. The type of work varies as greatly as the collections themselves – from computerizing records to supervising the care of antiquities. Some posts have a significant research element and some a requirement for public speaking.

Patent staff blend scientific, technical and legal work in the field of patents and designs, technical information and other intellectual property rights. Patent examiners work in the Patent Office to evaluate patent applications, to check that the requirements of patent law are met and that the public interest and the rights of other inventors are protected. Patent officers are employed by either the Ministry of Defence or the Defence Research Agency and are involved in all aspects of intellectual property rights related to research, development and production.

Photographers can work on a wide variety of projects from taking black-and-white news shots of a government press conference to shooting a series of transparencies of equipment for use in an information booklet. The work frequently involves working away from the office.

Psychologists in the Civil Service are involved in both research and casework. Those working for the Department for Education and Employment may work across a broad range of occupational psychology, assessing, guiding and counselling special-needs clients in order to help them into employment. Psychologists are also employed in the Prison Service, the Research and Planning Unit of the Home Office, and by the Ministry of Defence and the Defence Research Agency.

Research officers study the impact of government policies and provide information on which future policy decisions will be based. The Resource and Planning Research Group deals with policies relating to resource allocation and the environment. Staff normally have a degree in geography, economics, agricultural economics or economic history. The Social Sciences Research Group looks at patterns of behaviour among people in contemporary society, with staff usually having a social science degree.

Scientists and *technicians* are employed in various government departments and agencies, including the Meteorological Office, the National Physical Laboratory, and the Forensic Science Service. Their work covers a broad range, including fundamental research, technical administration, operational research, providing advisory services and contributing to the development of government policy. Half of the scientists in the Civil Service are engaged in research and development, the rest in advisory, management and policy activities. There is a science and engineering fast-stream scheme for high-calibre graduates.

Statisticians collect and process data of national importance and interest. The Government Statistical Service is the UK's largest employer of statisticians. Areas of work include the economy, population, labour market, transport, environment, crime, education and health. They manage the collection of data and analyse and interpret it. It is possible to join as a fast-stream assistant statistician or a temporary statistical officer.

Surveyors are employed in a number of departments, including the Valuation Office Agency, the Ministry of Defence, the Ministry of Agriculture, Fisheries and Food, and by the Mapping and Charting Group. Areas of work

CIVIL SERVICE: CAB

include general practice, rural practice, quantity, building, land and mineral surveying.

Tax inspectors are concerned with determining the tax liability of individuals and companies. The work includes assessing whether accounts submitted are accurate, further investigation when this is considered necessary, reaching fair settlements and, on occasions, defending judgements at an independent tribunal. District inspectors, who head local offices, must also be managers. It is possible to specialize in areas such as serious fraud, tax avoidance, international taxation and oil taxation.

WORK ENVIRONMENT

Specialist staff – such as scientists, engineers and graphic designers – may work in research laboratories, test centres or design studios. Engineers, surveyors and architects may be involved in outdoor site visits.

The work of many specialist civil servants, particularly those in more senior grades, involves travel to external meetings, conferences or exhibitions. This can involve long days and periods spent away from home. The growing importance of the EU is resulting in more European travel for some administrative staff.

Members of the Diplomatic Service must be prepared to work anywhere in the world. Postings can include locations in tropical climates or in cities where living conditions are difficult. In the course of a full career, those working in the Diplomatic Service are likely to spend up to two-thirds of their time abroad.

SKILLS AND INTERESTS

Please see article 1. ADMINISTRATIVE STAFF.

Most specialist posts require specific abilities. For example, a high level of mathematical ability is essential for government actuaries and statisticians.

ENTRY REQUIREMENTS

All civil servants must be British citizens; please see article 1. ADMINISTRATIVE STAFF.

Accountants
Accountancy trainees require five GCSEs/S grades (A–C/1–3) and two A levels/three H grades or equivalent, including English and maths.

Actuaries
The Government Actuary's Department requires trainee actuaries to possess a first- or upper-second-class honours degree, and a good A level/H grade in maths, statistics or economics.

Architects
Architects require a recognized diploma in architecture. However, as the Civil Service employs very few architects and numbers are expected to fall in the near future, opportunities for new recruits are extremely limited.

Cartographic staff
Entrants as mapping and charting technicians grade 2 must have two GCSEs/S grades (A–C/1–3) in relevant subjects. Entry at grade 1 requires three GCSEs/S grades (A–C/1–3) or a BTEC national award in a relevant subject. NVQs/SVQs at the appropriate level in a relevant subject may also be accepted. Mapping and charting officer trainees require five GCSEs/S grades (A–C/1–3), including English and maths, and two A levels/three H grades.

Computing staff
Computing staff are recruited at a number of different levels. Junior managers normally require a minimum of two A levels, although many are graduates. Qualified and experienced staff are also recruited for many senior posts in systems development and administrative support. Research establishments and government laboratories also recruit graduates with relevant degrees, such as computer studies or maths, for assistant scientific officer posts.

Diplomatic staff
Mainstream Diplomatic Service officers require a minimum of two A levels, but many are graduates. Entry to the Diplomatic fast-stream requires entrants to hold at least a second-class honours degree in any subject. An aptitude for languages is an asset but not a prerequisite. For posts in HM Diplomatic Service, at least one parent must have been a Commonwealth citizen or a citizen of the Republic of Ireland from a date 30 years or more before appointment. If they have died, they should have been a Commonwealth citizen or citizen of the Irish Republic continuously from a date 30 years or more before appointment.

Economists
A first- or good second-class honours degree or a postgraduate degree in economics or in a related subject with around 50 per cent economics content is required for entry as an economist. Cadet economists require a first- or good second-class honours degree, plus the ability to complete a master's degree in economics.

Engineers and engineering technicians
Technician apprentices require four GCSEs/S grades (A–C/1–3) including maths, an appropriate science subject and, preferably, English. Engineers entering the Defence Engineering Service require an honours degree in a relevant engineering discipline. GCHQ or the Radiocommunications Agency require entrants to hold a first- or second-class degree in electrical/electronic engineering, physics or computing. Entry to the Department of the Environment, Transport and the Regions and Highways Agency requires a first- or second-class honours degree and an appropriate engineering qualification accredited by a professional engineering body.

Inspectors of Health and Safety
Trainee Inspectors of Health and Safety normally require an honours degree or equivalent in any subject and they must hold a valid driving licence.

Immigration service staff
Entry at junior manager level requires a minimum of two A levels/three H grades and three GCSEs (A–C) or two S grades (1–3). However, many recruits are graduates.

Information specialists
For press and publicity officer posts, a high standard of education and excellent communication skills are required. Entry is with a relevant professional qualification or appropriate experience.

Lawyers
Although the majority of government lawyers enter after completing their training contract or pupillage, both the Government Legal Service and the Crown Prosecution Service offer salaried training contracts and pupillage. Applicants must have passed the Legal Practice Course (LPC) or Bar Vocational Course (BVC). The Government

CIVIL SERVICE: CAB

Legal Service offers sponsorship to potential trainees and pupils for both the LPC and BVC.

Librarians
Assistant librarians require professional qualifications and some practical experience of librarianship.

Linguists
The Joint Technical Language Service requires entrants to possess a first- or second-class honours degree or a substantial working knowledge of a foreign language. Linguist officers require a degree or equivalent in at least one modern foreign language. Translators require a degree or equivalent in a modern foreign language with a sound knowledge of at least one other language.

Museum staff
Minimum entry requirements for curatorial staff are four GCSEs/S grades (A–C/1–3) including English. Conservation staff require two GCSEs/S grades (A–C/1–3) including English. Graduate entry requires a degree in an appropriate subject or equivalent qualification. However, competition for curatorial posts is intense; many entrants have postgraduate qualifications and research or other relevant experience.

Patent examiner
Patent examiners require a first- or second-class honours degree or equivalent qualification in engineering, science or maths, or an equivalent qualification, such as corporate membership of one of the major professional institutions.

Photographers
Photographers are recruited with a relevant qualification or experience.

Psychologists
Psychologists require a first- or second-class honours degree in psychology or an equivalent qualification that is acceptable for registration with the British Psychological Society. A postgraduate qualification is desirable, and experience in a relevant field is valued.

Research officers
Entry as a research officer requires a first- or second-class degree or equivalent in an appropriate subject, such as geography, economics, agricultural economics or economic history.

Scientists and technicians
Assistant scientific offers require at least four GCSEs/S grades (A–C/1–3) including English, maths and a science subject. Scientific officers require a relevant degree or equivalent. Higher scientific officers require a relevant first - or upper-second-class degree plus at least two years' postgraduate experience. Senior scientific officers require a relevant first- or upper-second-class degree and at least four years' postgraduate experience. More specialized qualifications or abilities may be desirable for some posts.

Entry to the science and engineering fast-stream and most research posts require a first- or upper-second-class honours degree in an engineering or science-related subject.

Statisticians
Entry as an assistant statistician requires a first- or second-class honours degree in a numerate discipline (eg statistics, mathematics, business studies etc). Temporary statistical officers require at least a second-class honours degree with a minimum of 25% formal training in statistical theory, or equivalent.

Surveyors
Surveyors must have passed or gained exemption from the written examinations of the Royal Institution of Chartered Surveyors or the Incorporated Society for Valuers and Auctioneers. Some training posts are open to graduates in other disciplines.

Tax inspectors
Entry to the Tax Inspectorate requires a first- or second-class degree or equivalent in any subject.

Fast-stream scientists and engineers
There is a fast stream for scientist and engineers wishing to make the most of their technical training while at the same time receiving in-depth management training. Candidates need a first- or good second-class degree in a technical discipline as well as interpersonal skills. Candidates must undergo a rigorous testing system which measures management potential as well as technical ability.

TRAINING
Please see article 1. ADMINISTRATIVE STAFF.

Accountants
Accountancy trainees are trained under sponsored schemes for a professional accountancy qualification (eg the Chartered Association of Certified Accountants, The Institute of Cost and Management Accountants, The Institute of Chartered Accountants and the Chartered Institute of Public Finance and Accountancy). Trainees have time off on full pay for block or day release tuition, pre-examination study and attendance at examinations.

Actuaries
Trainees are given the opportunity to gain experience in all three main areas of work in the Government Actuary's Department (social security, pensions and insurance). They are prepared for the professional examinations of the Institute of Actuaries.

Cartographic staff
Training is provided in a particular aspect of cartography, hydrography, topographic surveying or map and chart production.

Computing staff
Junior managers specializing in automatic data processing receive training to equip them for their first post in computing, followed by further training which may lead to qualifications for membership of the British Computer Society.

Diplomatic Service staff
For mainstream and fast-stream entrants to the Diplomatic Service, training in the first two years includes professional, developmental and management courses. Recruits are also expected to acquire information technology and keyboard skills. Training for a first overseas posting can include both specific skills and foreign languages.

Some posts in the Diplomatic Service carry a language requirement and, if necessary, training to the required standard is provided. Certain postings carry with them a language requirement, such as Russian, Japanese or Arabic. For these languages, two years' intensive tuition is provided, split between London and living with a family in the host country. For overseas posts that do not have a language requirement, 100 hours' tuition is available to officers and their spouses.

Economists

Economists receive both professional and administrative training, as all staff are encouraged to develop their economic skills and managerial abilities. This includes courses at the Civil Service College and other external seminars. Cadet economists undertake a postgraduate university course in economics.

Engineers and engineering technicians

GCHQ provides special project manager training schemes which lead to Institution of Electrical Engineers chartered status (Graduate Electronic Engineer scheme). The Radiocommunications Agency offers a two-year Institution of Electrical Engineers accredited training programme, followed by opportunities to gain experience for corporate membership.

The Highways Agency's graduate training scheme for civil engineers provides experience throughout the highways engineering industry and enables young graduates to gain early chartered status with the Institution of Civil Engineers.

A range of training opportunities is provided by the Defence Evaluation Research Agency (DERA).

Inspectors of Health and Safety

There is a two-year training period of which the first year is a formal probationary period. During this time the trainee inspector will be involved in hands-on inspection work in the company of more senior inspectors, combined with training. Trainees also undertake a modular, residential postgraduate diploma course.

Immigration service staff

Training is provided both to develop management skills and in specific skills related to the Immigration Service.

Information specialists

Assistant information officers receive training in various information subjects in each of their first two years, with additional training thereafter. Information officers are offered a similar but slightly reduced training package.

Lawyers

Pupil barristers with the GLS spend their first six months in chambers, followed by their second six months within two GLS departments.

Trainee solicitors within the GLS complete their four study topics over the required two-year period. Areas of law covered include contentious and non-contentious. All four topics can be completed within a GLS department, although there are opportunities for one topic to be completed in private practice or another GLS department.

Librarians

Qualified librarians may undertake both management development and specialist training programmes.

Linguists

Graduate entrants may be given additional linguistic training, which may involve full-time study of a new language. Further training is provided for those moving on to advanced and specialized translation, foreign document research or simultaneous interpretation at conferences.

Museum staff

A range of NVQs for curatorial and conservation staff has been developed by the Museums Training Institute, and junior staff are encouraged to undertake training leading to these qualifications.

Graduate entrants are given the opportunity both to develop specialist research interests relevant to the collections with which they are working, as well as undertaking management development programmes.

Patent examiner

Newly appointed patent examiners are assigned to an experienced examiner for a period of training – up to two years. They receive instructions and gain experience in all aspects of Patent Law and the various skills required of an examiner. Many documents searched by examiners are published in French or German and training is given in these languages.

Psychologists

Psychologists receive professional training leading to chartered status. Those joining the Prison Service receive two years' part-time training leading to an MSc in Applied Criminological Psychology.

Research officers

Training is provided in areas such as research techniques and project management as well as more general topics such as communication skills and staff management.

Scientists and technicians

Training is provided in specialist scientific disciplines and recruits are encouraged to develop their professional and management skills. Scientists are encouraged to publish and present reports and papers related to their research activities.

Statisticians

Assistant statisticians join a fast-stream development programme and will be expected to develop their technical, statistical, communications, administrative and managerial skills. To complement their training they will move through a number of training postings probably in different departments and sometimes overseas.

Surveyors

Training is given in general practice, rural practice, quantity, building, land and mineral surveying, and to qualify for full membership of the Royal Institution of Chartered Surveyors or the Incorporated Society of Valuers and Auctioneers.

Tax inspectors

Entrants receive two to three years' training, leading to two sets of examinations comparable to those of other professions. In addition to one day a week spent at a training centre, ten hours a week of office time are set aside for this training.

Fast-Stream scientists and engineers

An individually tailored programme of training and development is devised for each trainee comprising a range of placements and a series of courses.

LATE ENTRY

Many specialist staff are recruited after gaining experience and qualifications in their chosen field. Trainees posts are usually only available to school/college leavers.

OPPORTUNITIES

Please see article 1. ADMINISTRATIVE STAFF.

Specialist posts may be advertised in trade or professional publications. For example, vacancies for librarians are advertised in the *Library Association Record* and for psychologists in the *British Psychological Society Appointment Memorandum*.

CIVIL SERVICE: CAB

PAY AND CONDITIONS

Please see article 1. ADMINISTRATIVE STAFF.

Those working in the Diplomatic Service overseas receive allowances to ensure that their standard of living is maintained wherever they are serving in the world. These include cost-of-living allowances based on local living conditions, family size and grade, hardship allowances in posts where living conditions are difficult, rent-free accommodation overseas, free removal of personal effects, an education allowance for dependent children and fare-paid journeys for children at school in the UK, and overseas additions to basic leave with one or more fare-paid journeys to and from the UK.

PROSPECTS

Please see article 1. ADMINISTRATIVE STAFF.

Most specialist staff gain professional qualifications and experience which allows them to work in the private sector.

Some specialists may become self-employed consultants.

RELATED OCCUPATIONS

Local government specialist and other specialist professional occupations in the private sector – Private Practice and Industry and Commerce accountant, actuary, architect, economist, librarian, information scientist, psychologist, translator, interpreter, chartered surveyor.

FURTHER INFORMATION

Civil Service Careers*, Ship Shape Promotional Handling Ltd, Units 2–4 Lescren Way, Avonmouth, Bristol BS11 8DG, 0117 982 1171

Office of Public Service*, Fast-Stream and European Staffing Division, Graduate and Schools Liaison Branch, Horse Guards Road, London SW1P 3AL, 0171 270 5697. (Can supply leaflets and list of current addresses for all departments and agencies.)

Capita RAS, (Application helpdesk/general enquiries), Innovation Court, New Street, Basingstoke, Hampshire RG21 7DP, 01256 846466

FURTHER READING

Leaflets/booklets are available from the addresses marked*.

In the careers library classified under CAB.

LOCAL GOVERNMENT: CAG

1. **LOCAL GOVERNMENT ADMINISTRATOR CLCI:CAG**
2. **LOCAL GOVERNMENT CLERICAL/ADMINISTRATIVE ASSISTANT CLCI:CAG**

BACKGROUND INFORMATION

Local government is one of the UK's largest employers, with a multi-million pound budget. It directly employs about two and a half million people working in local authorities. Thousands more are indirectly employed through contracts. Local authorities vary in structure. In England there is a mixture of district, county, metropolitan district and unitary councils plus London boroughs. Wales and Scotland have unitary authorities. Their exact responsibilities vary according to type but between them they provide a full range of services to the community. These include architecture, art galleries and museums, building control, education, the emergency services, engineering, finance, housing, legal, leisure and recreation, libraries, planning, social services, tourism, environmental health, trading standards, transport co-ordination, waste collection and disposal.

1. LOCAL GOVERNMENT ADMINISTRATOR (CAG)

THE WORK

Every department of a local authority employs specialist staff such as lawyers, social workers, planners (whose work is described in other relevant articles) and a number of administrators who are responsible for putting into practice decisions made by committees of elected councillors and for making sure that departments function smoothly. Administrators plan, control, organize and maintain systems and procedures in order to implement councillors' decisions, and ensure that specialist staff are able to do their jobs effectively.

Administrative work includes managing staff; servicing committees (preparing agendas and minutes of meetings); dealing with enquiries and providing advice; handling data – collecting, storing and retrieving information; processing statistics; dealing with finance – budgeting, purchasing and supply and processing invoices; and research. Administrators may also recruit, select and train the junior administrative staff in their departments. The particular combination of duties depends largely on the level of job and the department in which the administrator is employed.

Wherever they work, administrators usually work in close contact with other people. These include colleagues from the same and different departments, elected councillors and often, members of the public. An administrator working in a housing department could for instance, prepare reports on the availability of council-owned housing and land at the request of councillors or of another council department such as planning. This would involve information retrieval and processing of statistics (for instance numbers and types of housing available by ward), liaison with colleagues from different departments, councillors and tenants.

Recent changes to the way in which local government is organized have led to many services being contracted out, so that for instance, private contractors may provide catering services, collect refuse or run leisure centres. This has changed the emphasis of administrators' work. They are now responsible for drawing up service specifications, managing relationships with contractors and monitoring their performance to ensure it is of a high enough quality and provides value for money.

WORK ENVIRONMENT

Administrators work mainly in offices. Those working at a senior level may be required to travel to attend conferences and meetings in other regions.

SKILLS AND INTERESTS

Local government administration suits people who have good organizational skills. They should be methodical and pay close attention to detail. Administrators should be adaptable and flexible. They must be able to work with elected councillors from all political parties and be able to implement the policy they decide whether or not they personally agree with the decisions taken.

A numerical aptitude is useful in some types of administrative work. An ability to analyse figures is vital when producing statistical reports. It is also useful for checking invoices and setting, implementing and monitoring budgets.

As a large part of any administrative role involves liaison with other people, it is essential to get on with people from a wide variety of backgrounds. This is particularly true for administrators who have any personnel or management responsibilities. Good communications skills are essential both verbally and in writing. Administrators should enjoy teamwork. They must be able to elicit information from other people and provide clear advice that is easily understood.

They should have an interest in providing a service to the community and enjoy ensuring that council tax payers' money is spent efficiently. 'Value for money' is the aim of all departments.

ENTRY REQUIREMENTS

Normal entry requirements for junior administrators are one A level or equivalent; an Advanced GNVQ/GSVQ Level III in Business; an NVQ/SVQ in Administration at Levels 2, 3 or 4. An increasing number of councils recruit graduates to administrative posts, and some require non-graduate entrants to have a BTEC/SQA higher national certificate/diploma. Other councils may place as much emphasis on skills as formal qualifications.

An alternative route to becoming an administrator is to start as a clerical/administrative assistant. With experience and/or training such as NVQ/SVQs it is possible to be promoted to administrative level.

TRAINING

New administrators are given induction training in the role of their authority and work of their own department plus extensive on-the-job training in their particular duties. Some councils offer in-house training courses in key skills such as computer applications. In addition, administrators may study and train for additional qualifications. Most local authorities are firmly committed to training, so release for study to specific qualifications as well as actual job training is not unusual. Many councils offer day or

LOCAL GOVERNMENT: CAG

block release. Alternatively, evening or distance learning courses may be possible.

Increasingly, training for local government administrators is leading to the award of NVQ/SVQs Level 3. These awards are usually in Administration, showing competence in such areas as researching and retrieving information, preparing and administering meetings, maintenance of health and safety standards, banking procedures and a wide range of office duties. Other awards that a local government administrator can train towards include: Higher National Diplomas/Certificates in Public Administration; the professional qualification of the Institute of Chartered Secretaries and Administrators (ICSA); and the Certificate or Diploma in Management Studies (CMS or DMS).

LATE ENTRY

Age is no barrier to starting work as a local government administrator.

Adults can gain recognition of their skills and experience by working towards NVQ/SVQs. There is open access to NVQ/SVQs. No academic qualifications are required, and there are no age limits. NVQ/SVQs are based on competence – which may have been gained through experience, in-house training programmes, college courses or open learning. Past experience can be put forward as evidence of competence, via Accreditation of Prior Learning (APL).

There may be specific training opportunities directed at adults in some areas for this type of work. Candidates may have to satisfy certain conditions to be eligible. Contact your local Jobcentre, careers office or TEC/LEC for details.

OPPORTUNITIES

Opportunities for administrators are available in every department of a local authority. A large number of local government jobs have an administrative element, and it has been estimated that nearly half the workforce employed by local government work in administrative jobs of one type or another.

Administrative jobs are equally widespread geographically. Local government operates in every area of the UK, so opportunities are fairly evenly distributed around the country. There are offices in most towns, even small ones. However, competition for these posts can be fierce. Both part-time and temporary work opportunities for local government administrators are available.

PAY AND CONDITIONS

Exact salaries are determined locally by each council, but most administrative staff are paid in a salary range within a national pay framework negotiated by the National Joint Council for Administrative, Professional, Technical and Clerical Staffs. The range is usually revised in April each year. The current range is £7,644 to £17,319. Salaries reflect differences between jobs, local grading policies, labour market forces and size of council. They are usually higher in London and South East England – London locations and those adjoining London attract an additional allowance (£360 and £522 for outer and inner fringes, and £1,052 and £2,163 for outer and inner London). More senior managers (such as chief executives and chief officers) have different agreements.

Administrators usually work office hours. Salary scales are based on a 37-hour week, although some authorities operate a 35-hour week. Flexitime working is normally available. At more senior levels administrators may have to attend some evening meetings.

Several local authorities have introduced extremely flexible working patterns, which include part-time working, job sharing, term-time working (with taking of additional unpaid leave permitted during school holidays) and annual hours contracts – under which the number of hours worked is calculated over the whole year with employees working more hours at particularly busy times.

Career breaks of up to three years are often on offer. During the period away from work employee and employer keep in touch and the employee's skills and knowledge are kept up to date with a view to their returning to full-time employment.

PROSPECTS

Ambitious, motivated administrators can progress all the way up the local government hierarchy. Promotion will depend on the administrator having the right experience, particularly in managing other staff. Administrators wishing to progress to the upper levels of management will find it advantageous to acquire further qualifications, such as NVQ/SVQs in Management at Levels 4 and 5. Other options might include a general management qualification, such as a Master of Business Administration (MBA).

For those with ambitions to move out of local government, the experience and skills gained in the work of administrators are highly transferable to management positions in the private sector.

RELATED OCCUPATIONS

Civil service executive officer, company secretary, health service manager, personnel/human resources officer, local government clerical/administrative assistant.

FURTHER INFORMATION AND READING

Please see article 2. LOCAL GOVERNMENT CLERICAL/ADMINISTRATIVE ASSISTANT.

2. LOCAL GOVERNMENT CLERICAL/ADMINISTRATIVE ASSISTANT(CAG)

THE WORK

There is a wide variety of clerical/administrative work available in most departments in a local authority.

Clerical/administrative work is essential to local government. Clerical/administrative assistants work wherever administrators are employed, helping them to do their jobs by undertaking some of the more routine administrative work under their direction. Much of the work is concerned with paperwork, correspondence and dealing with telephone and personal enquiries. Some are given more responsibility, including supervisory duties, where more personal initiative is required.

Clerical/administrative assistants work for supervisors and administrators in virtually every type of local government work. Their duties usually include opening, sorting and distributing mail, filing documents and retrieving

LOCAL GOVERNMENT: CAG

information as required. They may write letters in response to enquiries from other departments, organizations and the public. Some process statistical and financial information, inputting data for invoices, budgets, rents, council tax etc.

Some of the work involves dealing with enquiries. These may come from colleagues, outside bodies or the public. Often, these are dealt with on the telephone, but they can be written requests. Clerical/administrative assistants either respond to these themselves, finding out the information if necessary, or refer the query on to an administrator or other colleague. They may use standard format letters or draft their own.

They use a range of office equipment, such as word processors, telephones and switchboards, fax and telex machines, calculators and photocopiers. Increasingly, they use computers.

Their precise duties vary according to the work of the department in which they are employed. In a housing department for instance they may be responsible for collecting rents, issuing receipts and keeping accurate records of payments and arrears. In a planning department they might answer requests for information on planning permission and in a legal department, file and process legal documents. If working in a department which is open to personal enquirers, such as education, social services or housing, they might spend a part of their day working behind a reception desk, answering questions or finding someone with a more specialized knowledge to do so.

WORK ENVIRONMENT

Clerical/administrative assistants generally work in an office environment. They could be based in a large county headquarters, a medium sized department or in a small building where they work with only two or three other people.

SKILLS AND INTERESTS

Clerical/administrative assistants need a certain amount of initiative, in that if they do not know the answer to a particular query they need to know where to find it out, or to whom they should refer it. They should therefore, be capable of working without constant supervision.

They need good written and spoken communication skills. They need to be able to understand and follow instructions They must also be able to convey information back to an enquirer clearly.

Clerical/administrative assistants who work on telephones and in reception are often the first point of contact for the public, so it is very important that they are helpful and can provide the correct information or directions. A smart appearance is also a requirement.

They need to be able to get on well with other people, because their job includes a great deal of contact with colleagues and possibly with the public. They should enjoy working in a team.

Numeracy is important in many jobs.

They should have an interest in providing a service to the community.

ENTRY REQUIREMENTS

A good general education is required, although for many local authorities, skills and interests are just as important as more formal qualifications. Many local authorities prefer candidates with three GCSEs/S grades (A–C/1–3). English and maths and keyboard skills are useful. Specific requirements vary, so individual authorities should be contacted for exact details.

A few authorities offer trainee posts for people with few or no qualifications, where they can learn the necessary skills on the job.

People with keyboard skills, who are applying for clerical/administrative work with a typing element, will need to demonstrate speed and accuracy. Specific speeds and/or knowledge of one or more of the common word-processing packages may be stipulated.

Entry may be possible for young people through a Modern Apprenticeship (part of the Skillseekers Initiative in Scotland) leading to at least an NVQ/SVQ in Business Administration at Level 3. Contact your local careers office, Jobcentre, TEC/LEC for details.

TRAINING

Most local government clerical/administrative assistants receive induction training in the role of their authority and work of their own department plus extensive on-the-job training in their particular duties. In addition, clerical/administrative assistants can often study and train for further qualifications. Many local authorities offer day or block release. Alternatively, evening courses or distance learning may be possible. Most local authorities are firmly committed to training, so release to study for specific qualifications as well as actual job training is not unusual. Increasingly, training in local government is leading to the award of NVQs/SVQs at Level 2 and 3, which for clerical/administrative assistants would usually be in administration, covering subjects such as the operation and maintenance of office equipment, processing and retrieving information, organizing office supplies, and travel and accommodation. For those who wish to add keyboard qualifications to their skills, opportunities to study for RSA, Pitman, LCCI or BTEC/ SQA awards may be available.

It is possible to start work as a local government clerical/administrative assistant through a training scheme for young people. This may be done either by obtaining day release from an existing employer to go to college, or by going directly to a college to study and being sent to employers for work experience. Contact your local careers office, Jobcentre TEC/LEC for details.

LATE ENTRY

There are no barriers for mature applicants to start work as a local government clerical/administrative assistant.

Previous experience in administrative work or in dealing with the public would be an advantage.

Adults can gain recognition of their skills and experience by working towards NVQs/SVQs. No previous academic qualifications are required for access to NVQs/SVQs which are based on competence and it does not matter how that competence has been gained. Past experience can be put forward as evidence of competence, via Accreditation of Prior Learning (APL). Relevant competence may have been gained through experience, company training programmes, college courses or open learning.

In some parts of the country there may be specific training opportunities directed at adults for this type of work. Candidates may have to satisfy certain conditions to be

LOCAL GOVERNMENT: CAG

eligible. Contact your local Jobcentre, careers office or TEC/LEC for details.

OPPORTUNITIES

Opportunities for clerical/administrative assistants are available in almost every department in a local authority. It has been estimated that about half of the workforce employed by local government work in administrative roles.

Jobs are equally widespread geographically. Local government operates in every area of the UK, so opportunities are fairly evenly distributed around the country.

PAY AND CONDITIONS

Exact salaries are determined locally by each authority but most clerical/administrative staff are paid in a salary range within a national pay framework negotiated by the National Joint Council for Administrative, Professional, Technical and Clerical Staffs. Please see article 1. LOCAL GOVERNMENT ADMINISTRATOR for details.

Clerical/administrative assistants usually work office hours. Salary scales are based on a 37-hour week, although some authorities operate a 35-hour week. There are plenty of opportunities for flexible working. Please see article 1. LOCAL GOVERNMENT ADMINISTRATOR for details.

PROSPECTS

With motivation and experience, clerical/administrative assistants can move to more responsible and supervisory posts. It is possible to be promoted to administrator and beyond, though it is likely that further qualifications would be required, such as BTEC/SQA national awards, NVQs/SVQs, in Administration at Level 3 or in other subjects relevant to the employing department.

The experience and skills gained as a local government clerical/administrative assistant are easily transferred into other areas. Similar work is available for example in the civil service and the National Health Service. It is also possible to move out of the public sector altogether, and move into private industry and commerce. Clerical/administrative assistants whose work has included a good deal of keyboarding or typing work and who have good typing speeds and the necessary organizational aptitude could look for secretarial work. They may wish to add a secretarial certificate or diploma to their qualifications if they choose this route, such as those of the Royal Society of Arts (RSA) or the London Chamber of Commerce and Industry (LCCI).

RELATED OCCUPATIONS

Accountancy technician, civil service administrative assistant/officer, administrative/clerical staff, local government administrator, medical records clerk, secretary.

FURTHER INFORMATION

Edexcel Foundation (incorporating BTEC)*, Stewart House, 32 Russell Square, London WC1B 5DN, 0171 393 4444

Convention of Scottish Local Authorities (COSLA), Rosebery House, 9 Haymarket Terrace, Edinburgh EH12 5XZ, 0131 474 9200, www.cosla.gov.uk

Institute of Administrative Management*, 40 Chatsworth Parade, Petts Wood, Orpington, Kent BR5 1RW, 01689 875555, http://www.electranet.com.iam

Institute of Chartered Secretaries and Administrators (ICSA), 16 Park Crescent, London W1N 4AH, 0171 580 4741, http://www.icsa.org.uk/icsa/

Local Government Opportunities (LGO)*, Local Government Management Board*, Layden House, 76–86 Turnmill Street, Farringdon, London EC1M 5QU, 0171 296 6503, http://www.datalake.com/lgo/jobsearch

LCCI Examinations Board*, Athena House, 112 Station Road, Sidcup, Kent DA15 7BJ, 0181 302 0261, www.iccieb.org.uk

Qualifications and Curriculum Authority (QCA), 29 Bolton Street, London W1Y 7PD, 0171 509 5555, http://www.open.gov.uk/qca/

Pitman Qualifications*, 1 Giltspur Street, London EC1A 9DD, 0171 294 2471

RSA Examinations Board*, Westwood Way, Coventry CV4 8HS, 01203 470033

Scottish Qualifications Authority (SQA)*, Hanover House, 24 Douglas Street, Glasgow G2 7NQ, 0141 248 7900

FURTHER READING

Leaflets/booklets are available from the addresses marked*.

Careers and Training in Local Government (CATLOG)

Working In Local Government – COIC

In the careers library classified under CAG.

HEALTH SERVICE MANAGEMENT: CAL

1. HEALTH SERVICE MANAGER CLCI:CAL
2. MEDICAL RECORDS CLERK CLCI:CAL

1. HEALTH SERVICE MANAGER (CAL)

BACKGROUND INFORMATION

The National Health Service is the largest organization in the UK, with over a million staff. NHS reforms have been introduced in recent years, with the aim of providing patients with better health care and a greater choice of service.

There is now a clear distinction between 'purchasers' and 'providers' of health care services. 'Purchasers' of health care are health authorities (health boards in Scotland and Northern Ireland) and GP fundholders, who have opted to take responsibility for buying services for their own patients.

'Providers' of health care include hospitals, health service units (for example, community services such as day centres for the mentally ill), social services departments and the voluntary and private sectors. Providers agree contracts with both local and more distant purchaser organizations, to provide healthcare to the public.

A related development has been the creation of self-governing trusts within the NHS. These organizations (which include almost all hospitals) employ their own staff and set their own rates of pay for managers. Trust status allows them to decide which services to offer, to seek out new opportunities and to organize their services to respond to local health needs.

Health service managers, who are employed both by purchasers and providers, face major challenges in terms of implementing and coping with change, in an environment that is continually affected by social trends, political decisions and advances in technology.

THE WORK

Most general managers are involved in the provision or purchasing of services, and concern for quality and cost is a major focus of their work. Increasingly, managerial roles in the health service involve decision making on matters such as marketing, provision of services, resources and budgeting.

However, the work varies considerably in different settings. Broadly, a general manager may be responsible for some or all of the following.

Staff management: of clerical and secretarial staff, and often clinical/professional staff. Responsibilities include recruitment, selection and appraisal.

Operational management: day-to-day management of a unit or a service within a unit.

Financial management: maintaining cash limits, setting budgets, working with health care professionals to decide on the best use of resources, staying within budgets.

Planning: setting objectives and deciding, with health care professionals, on the resources that will be needed to meet those objectives. Planning the implementation of changes.

Working with people: creating effective working relationships with teams of health professionals, eg medical staff within a particular clinical speciality.

Information management: using information collected by medical records departments to make informed decisions, for instance on the provision of a specific service or the recruitment of staff, and determining the costs of providing or purchasing health care.

Most jobs involve negotiating with health care staff, attending committee meetings, using computers, analysing numerical data and writing reports, job descriptions, etc. Some managers liaise with the press.

There are also several specialist areas, and it is quite common for a managerial career to start in one of the specialist areas, with transfer to general management later on. The main specialisms are:

Finance: the work is broadly similar to that of other public finance accountants, and involves the management of financial systems, auditing, responsibility for proposing and assessing cost-effective projects, issuing and paying invoices, paying salaries, etc. Financial specialists usually study for accountancy qualifications.

Human resources: human resource managers are responsible for recruitment, selection and training of staff, for industrial relations, manpower planning and associated functions.

Purchasing and supply: this involves the organization and management of stores (except drugs), purchase of equipment, and advice to other departments on supply matters.

Hotel services: managing services such as catering, cleaning, linen and laundry, portering, security, telephones and hairdressing.

There are also opportunities for IT specialists and for statisticians. The management of information, and its use to identify health care costs and future demand for services, is growing in importance.

WORK ENVIRONMENT

The work is office-based. At junior levels, managers usually share offices; more-senior managers normally have their own private offices.

The amount of travel involved in the work varies according to the manager's seniority. Most jobs involve some travel – for instance, to different sites, and to attend training courses. The more responsible posts are likely to involve more extensive travel. For some positions, a driving licence is an advantage.

Most health service management posts involve a considerable degree of contact with medical, nursing and clerical staff and with representatives of other organizations.

SKILLS AND INTERESTS

Although the main objective of the work is the provision of health care, the manager's contribution is to run the organization efficiently. Management skills, rather than medical knowledge or an interest in helping people, are the main requirement. Managers need adaptability, drive and determination, with the ability to lead others and to implement and manage change. It is essential that they should be capable of working under pressure.

Excellent spoken and written communication skills are required. Managers need to persuade and influence others and to convince people of their case. It is also important to listen to other people's views.

Intellectual ability – including the capacity to analyse complex issues and to understand numerical data – is

HEALTH SERVICE MANAGEMENT: CAL

important. Managers need to be resourceful and creative, able to innovate and find imaginative solutions to problems.

ENTRY REQUIREMENTS

Applicants from outside the Health Service, applying for management training schemes, need a degree in any subject or an equivalent qualification, or a professional qualification in a health or management-related discipline.

Although there are no specific requirements in terms of first degree discipline, there are first degree courses available in relevant subjects – a list of these is available from the Institute of Health Services Management.

Applicants without these qualifications may enter the NHS at clerical or secretarial level and can apply for management training after gaining relevant experience and qualifications within the service. Nurses and other health service staff may also move into management posts, after gaining appropriate experience and qualifications.

For the Management Education Scheme by Open Learning (MESOL) Scheme there are no specific academic entry requirements, but people learning about management through MESOL need to be employed by the NHS, social services or a voluntary/charitable organization.

TRAINING

There are two main entry and training routes: (1) via national training schemes, (2) via entry into other branches of the health service, followed by in-service training.

1. National training schemes

England: The NHS Management Training Scheme combines work experience with formal management training, projects and attachments. Most trainees complete the scheme in 22 months. The scheme is delivered through eight NHS regional offices, and applicants are able to select the region in which they wish to take their training.

The pattern of training varies somewhat in different regions, but it usually comprises:

Stage 1 – health service orientation (an introduction to all aspects of the NHS), lasting up to three months;

Stage 2 – first management post, nine to twelve months;

Stage 3 – management elective(s) – these may involve attachments to organizations concerned with health care, secondment to major UK companies, or a piece of research;

Stage 4 – second management post, four to eight months.

Successful completion of the scheme results in a postgraduate diploma in management and an NVQ in Management at Level 4.

Training schemes for specialists in personnel etc are run, according to need, by regional offices. A national Financial Management Training Scheme recruits on an annual basis.

Scotland: The NHS in Scotland co-ordinates and administers its own management training schemes. These are in:

– Finance: a 40-month scheme, leading to a CIPFA qualification (See ACCOUNTANT: PUBLIC SERVICE article);

– Business and Operations Management: a 24-month scheme, leading to an MSc in Healthcare Management;

– Human Resources: a 24-month scheme, leading to a MSc in Healthcare Management.

Wales: The Health Service in Wales offers a graduate-entry management programme, the Management Development Scheme.

Northern Ireland: Training in Northern Ireland is via the Health and Social Services Management Scheme.

For further details, contact the addresses at the end of the article.

2. In-service training

Individuals who are already employed by the NHS – for instance, in clerical, secretarial or clinical roles – may apply for management training, which may be available through in-house training programmes and/or open learning.

The MESOL (Management Education Scheme by Open Learning) scheme is a flexible programme open to staff working in the NHS who want to gain management qualifications. It can provide access to NVQs/SVQs in Management at Levels 4 and 5, Institute of Health Services Management qualifications, university post-experience certificates or diplomas in management, and credit towards higher education awards such as the MBA.

LATE ENTRY

There is no upper age limit for entry to health service management. Applicants with previous experience in the NHS (in any capacity) are particularly welcome. The MESOL scheme is appropriate pre-entry training for mature applicants who are employed in the NHS, social services or similar fields.

Individuals who have obtained professional qualifications outside the NHS may apply for management posts. Appropriate qualifications may be in professions such as accountancy, personnel, purchasing and supply, information technology or general management.

OPPORTUNITIES

The vast majority of health service managers are employed by the NHS. Small numbers work for private hospitals and HM Forces. Experienced managers with Institute of Health Services Management qualifications can work abroad; one of the main areas in which health service managers work is the Middle East.

Entry to the Management Training Scheme is highly competitive.

PAY AND CONDITIONS

The salary for the NHS Management Training Scheme is around £14,750. General management posts command salaries from around £15,000 up to £50,000 and above, depending on the level of seniority.

Managers work a basic 37-hour week, Monday to Friday. However, more-senior managers work longer hours when necessary. There is an annual holiday entitlement of 20 working days, plus public holidays. This entitlement increases with length of employment. The NHS runs a contributory pension scheme.

PROSPECTS

After training, it is usual to gain experience in operational management. There are opportunities to reach the most senior posts. Willingness to relocate to different areas of the country is likely to improve promotion prospects.

HEALTH SERVICE MANAGEMENT: CAL

There are opportunities for experienced managers to study for qualifications such as the Master of Business Administration (MBA) or the Diploma in Management Studies (DMS). Such qualifications may be particularly useful for specialists who wish to move into general management.

RELATED OCCUPATIONS

Civil Service junior manager/administration trainee, local government administrator, social services/voluntary sector manager, public finance accountant, personnel officer, purchasing officer, medical records clerk.

FURTHER INFORMATION

The Institute of Health Services Management, Registry, 7–10 Chandos Street, London W1M 9DE, 0171 388 2626, www.ihsm.co.uk

Management Training Schemes

England:

NHS Management Training Scheme, 29 Lodge Moor Complex, Redmires Road, Sheffield S10 4NA (Information about MESOL is also available from this address.)

NHS Financial Management Training Scheme, Financial Development Unit, Room IW29, Quarry House, Quarry Hill, Leeds LS2 7UE

Scotland:

The Management Development Group, Scottish Health Services Centre, Crewe Road South, Edinburgh EH4 2LF

Wales:

The Programme Team, NHS Staff College Wales, Hensol Castle Conference Centre, Pontyclun, Mid Glamorgan CF72 8YS

Northern Ireland:

Provider Support Unit, Personnel Department, Central Services Agency, 25 Adelaide Street, Belfast BT2 8FH

FURTHER READING

Working in Hospitals – COIC

In the careers library classified under CAL.

2. MEDICAL RECORDS CLERK (CAL)

BACKGROUND INFORMATION

Medical records clerks play an essential role in the management of the NHS. They provide a reception service for the public, maintain links between GPs and consultants and provide administrative support for the treatment and care of patients. They also process statistical information that is vital for the Health Service's effective management.

THE WORK

The work involves initiating, filing, maintaining and compiling all the documents relating to hospital patients, making sure medical records are available to hospital staff, receiving patients, arranging appointments and directing patients to wards or clinics.

There are several areas of work – clerks may rotate between these different areas, or may be concerned with only one aspect. The specialist areas are:

Filing and administration. Every hospital has a Master Patient Index (this may be computerized), with details of every patient who has had contact with the hospital – either as an inpatient or outpatient – at any time. When a patient registers with the hospital, clerks check the Master Patient Index to see if that person has previously attended – if not, they allocate a unit number to the patient and start a new case record containing details of treatment, operations etc.

Clerks are also responsible for filing and retrieving case records. For outpatient clinics, they work from a list of patients due to attend, pulling out the case records, checking them off against clinic lists, making sure the records are ready for use in clinics and the results of tests have been correctly filed.

Other duties include retrieving case records for waiting lists and admissions, compiling and updating waiting lists, and tracing any files or documents that go missing.

Outpatient reception and admissions clerks. These jobs involve contact with patients, as well as administration and telephone work.

Outpatient receptionists deal with correspondence from GPs, book appointments, receive patients and direct them to clinics, arrange follow-up appointments and, where necessary, book ambulance transport.

Admissions clerks may work either in planned admissions or in accident/emergency departments; in smaller hospitals, these functions may be combined in a single department. Clerks dealing with planned admissions keep records of all patients to be admitted to the hospital, direct patients to wards, maintain a register of patients who have been admitted, and circulate patient details to telephonists, ward staff and hospital chaplains. They also keep records of patient transfers, discharges and deaths. Emergency admissions work involves taking patient details, recording attendances, and keeping records of children attending the hospital and of patients who have been in specific types of accidents (eg road traffic accidents).

Clinical coding. This type of work involves adding a distinguishing code, which shows the type of disease the patient is suffering from and any operation or procedure performed. Clinical coding clerks use doctors' notes and medical reference books to select the correct codes. The coded data is then input on to the computer and sent to a central point where it is used for contracting, planning, statistical analysis etc.

Clinical coding has become increasingly important since the NHS reforms because, with the current emphasis on best use of resources, accurate information about the diagnosis, length of stay and cost of treating each patient is essential.

The information processed by clinical coding clerks is also important for the collection of statistics for epidemiology, for research purposes and for the Department of Health's statistical records.

Other statistical work. Clerks are also involved in gathering statistics for various other purposes. For example, each day they check the number of beds available; this involves keeping a record of the patients admitted and discharged from each ward within the previous 24 hours. They also gather information about the number of referrals to the hospital and the number of patients attending clinics. On a monthly basis, they complete forms showing the pattern of activity in the

HEALTH SERVICE MANAGEMENT: CAL

hospital – including outpatient attendances, admissions, discharges, and the number of patients on the waiting list.

Most jobs now involve the use of computers.

WORK ENVIRONMENT

Filing clerks generally work in the medical records library, which can be the size of a hospital ward. Records are stored on metal or wooden racks, or mobile filing units. Clerks need reasonable agility, they may have to bend to reach lower racks, or climb on ladders or kickstools (running on castors) to reach the upper tiers. The passages between the racks may be narrow, and some agility is required for manoeuvring. Occasionally, when clerks need to retrieve older records from secondary storage areas (eg in basements), the work environment may be dusty.

Outpatient and admissions receptionists work at reception desks in outpatient clinics, admissions departments or accident/emergency departments. Admissions work may also take place in separate offices.

Statistical clerks are office-based. Coding clerks are based in separate offices within the medical records department, or sometimes on wards or adjacent to doctor's offices.

Most jobs involve some movement in and around the hospital – fetching and delivering case records, messages and other documents.

SKILLS AND INTERESTS

A methodical and efficient approach to administrative tasks is essential.

Clerks who deal directly with patients need good spoken communication skills, together with a pleasant, reassuring manner. They have to be able to cope tactfully with patients and relatives who are anxious or apprehensive.

Flexibility about tackling a range of tasks is an important requirement. Clerks also need to be able to work well with others, as members of a team.

It is essential to respect the confidentiality of patient records, and not to mention details of patients or their treatment to outsiders, or to colleagues within the hospital (unless the colleagues are involved in the patient's treatment or care).

Clerks specializing in statistical work need an aptitude for figures. Clinical coding clerks need some knowledge of human anatomy and physiology and an understanding of medical terminology.

ENTRY REQUIREMENTS

There are no minimum educational entry requirements. However, those who wish to take the Institute of Health Record Information and Management (IHRIM) Certificate need five GCSEs/S grades (A–C/1–3), including English language and one of the following: arithmetic, maths or statistics. Candidates for the IHRIM Diploma need either the IHRIM Certificate or an equivalent qualification which grants exemption from the Certificate (such as associateship of the Institute of Health Services Management).

Keyboard skills are an advantage for most posts.

TRAINING

Training varies in different hospitals, but is mainly on-the-job.

One-day induction courses, introducing new staff to the NHS, are usually available. Additionally, there may be an introduction to medical records work, lasting one week to one month, typically involving short attachments to each department within medical records. Trainees learn how to use computers, and how the hospital's administrative systems operate. Further on-the-job training, under supervision, continues until clerks are fully proficient – this can take about six months.

There are no NVQs/SVQs specific to health records practice, but the IHRIM has introduced Certificates of Technical Competence (CTCs) in Basic Medical Records Practice, which are assessed in the workplace. These certificates are awarded for demonstrable knowledge and skills in health records practice.

Career prospects are improved for those who take the IHRIM Certificate and Diploma qualifications. Training for the Certificate and Diploma exams may be via:

– courses at local colleges (full-time, day release or evening);

– courses run by regional branches of the IHRIM (usually at weekends);

– a reading course for the Certificate exam, provided by IHRIM. This may be used in addition to other study methods or as a 'stand alone' course.

The qualifying letters CHRIM for Certificate exam success or AHRIM (associate) for Diploma success are awarded.

For clerks who wish to specialize in diagnostic coding, a specialist IHRIM diagnostic coding qualification is available. Training is usually provided in-house, and study notes are available from IHRIM.

Training opportunities for young people may be available. Contact your local careers office, TEC/LEC or Jobcentres for details.

LATE ENTRY

There are good opportunities for adult entrants. Maturity is an advantage, particularly for clerks who deal directly with patients. Previous experience in clerical, reception or related work is useful.

The academic entrance qualifications for the IHRIM Certificate exams may be waived for mature students, depending on age and experience. Contact IHRIM for details.

OPPORTUNITIES

Opportunities are increasing because NHS reforms have created more administrative/information processing work and therefore a greater need for clerical staff.

Every hospital employs medical records clerks. The availability of vacancies, and the degree of competition for jobs, varies in different parts of the country. There is more competition for vacancies in areas of high unemployment.

The principal employer is the NHS, but there are also opportunities in private hospitals and HM Forces. Trained coding clerks are employed by insurance companies.

Local hospital personnel departments may give advice about vacancies.

Medical records clerks with IHRIM qualifications may work abroad; one of the main countries in which medical records clerks work is Saudi Arabia.

HEALTH SERVICE MANAGEMENT: CAL

PAY AND CONDITIONS

In the basic clerical Grade 2, 16-year-olds start on about £5,544 rising to £6,596 at 17 years. At the age of 18 years and over, the basic salary range is from £7,687 to £8,815. Full-time staff work a basic 37-hour week; for any additional hours, paid overtime or time off in lieu is available. Some hospitals now operate flexitime systems.

In the supervisory grades, salaries range from Grade 3 £8,815 to Grade 6 £15,104. Managers' salaries depend on the size of the hospital and range of duties.

Most medical records clerks work days. Some filing clerks and receptionists in accident and emergency departments work shifts, including nights, weekends and bank holidays.

Part-time work is widely available, and opportunities for job sharing are increasing.

PROSPECTS

Experienced medical records clerks may progress to supervisory and management posts. Supervisors are typically responsible for between four and ten staff, for instance in the medical records library. Assistant managers are responsible for the work of supervisors; managers oversee the whole medical records department, and in a large hospital this means taking responsibility for several hundred staff. There are further opportunities to move into general NHS management.

Staff who are aiming for promotion usually take the IHRIM qualifications (see TRAINING). Good interpersonal skills are also required for promotion, as supervisory and managerial posts in medical records are very much orientated towards the management of people.

There are opportunities for clerks to move into other types of clerical/administrative/information technology work, for instance in banking, insurance or solicitors' offices. Some clerks train as medical secretaries.

RELATED OCCUPATIONS

Medical secretary, receptionist, Civil Service administrative officer/assistant, local government clerk, health service manager.

FURTHER INFORMATION

Institute of Health Record Information and Management (IHRIM-UK) Headquarters*, c/o Warrington Community Healthcare NHS Trust, Winwick Hospital, Warrington, Cheshire WA2 8RR, 01925 639772

FURTHER READING

Leaflets/booklets are available from the address marked*.

Working in Hospitals – COIC

In the careers library classified under CAL.

INSTITUTE/BUSINESS ADMINISTRATION: CAP

CHARTERED SECRETARY CLCI:CAP

BACKGROUND INFORMATION

Chartered secretaries are professional administrators. Their job is to make sure that their organization runs efficiently and economically within the law.

This calls for understanding and judgement. In order to improve efficiency it is necessary to understand how every part of the organization works and integrates – its finances, business activities, the people who work there and what they do.

Chartered secretaries may perform a variety of administrative roles, such as legal adviser, financial administrator or office manager. They are ideally qualified to work as company secretaries, the chief administrative officers of their organization. Associateship of the Chartered Institute of Secretaries is recognized in company law as a suitable professional qualification for this job.

THE WORK

A chartered secretary working as a company secretary has a very wide range of responsibilities. Some of these are defined by law.

Secretaries maintain the statutory company records – its Memorandum and Articles of Association, lists of directors and shareholders, annual accounts – and send annual returns based on these to the Company Registry. This involves making sure that the company reports and accounts are produced and distributed on time each year. They also keep records of acquisitions and dispersals, which can range from car fleets and office blocks to shares in other companies. Secretaries of public companies – those in which members of the public can buy shares – are required to supply details about their company to the Stock Exchange.

The memorandum and articles define how a company is governed and financed and the nature of its business. The company secretary makes sure that none of the company's activities infringes either its own memorandum and articles or the Companies Act, and advises the directors on what they can legally do within these terms.

The company secretary is the company's named representative on legal documents and has charge of the company seal, authorizing and signing the official stamp on share certificates and other documents.

Company secretaries organize board and general meetings. At the meetings they take minutes and advise the directors on legal points. They act as a link between shareholders and directors, monitoring share ownership, keeping shareholders and the public informed about new issues and keeping the directors informed about the take-up of shares.

Besides these statutory duties, company secretaries may have a range of other administrative duties: many are involved in accounting and finance, including responsibility for the payroll, the annual budget, internal audit, credit control and financial or management accounting.

Other responsibilities may include personnel management, pension schemes, office management, insurance or computer systems. They may also assist the general management team in planning and in liaising with professional advisers.

WORK ENVIRONMENT

The work is office-based, with some travelling to meetings. There may be frequent discussions and meetings with departmental managers and other members of staff throughout the organization, and also with bankers, accountants, lawyers and other professional advisers.

SKILLS AND INTERESTS

Chartered secretaries need the ability to understand the details and implications of complex legal and financial affairs. As there are often several matters in hand at once, they should be quick to assess priorities and methodical in dealing with them.

They work alongside managers and policymakers, and must be familiar with all that goes on in the organization. Chartered secretaries require tact and good powers of judgement in solving problems. Tact, discretion and absolute integrity are vital.

Chartered secretaries require an excellent command of written and spoken English. They have to write up the minutes of board and other meetings, so have to be able to express themselves accurately. They have to explain complex business and technical matters to experts and non-experts in a clear, balanced way. They are involved in negotiations with lawyers, auditors and other professional advisers. As they deal with accounts, insurance and other financial matters, competence with figures is essential.

ENTRY REQUIREMENTS

To achieve membership of the Institute of Chartered Secretaries and Administrators, it is necessary to:

– successfully complete the ICSA Qualifying Examination;

– gain appropriate work experience, normally three years for graduates, six years for others;

– be recognized as a fit and proper person by two referees.

The Qualifying Examination Scheme has three stages: Foundation, Pre-professional, Professional. The minimum age for entry is 17 years. Through the ICSA's open access policy, there are no formal academic requirements for the Foundation programme.

Graduates who already hold recognized first degrees or postgraduate diplomas are normally exempt from the Foundation and Pre-professional stages and register directly onto the Professional programme. Students holding BTEC/SQA higher national awards or certain professional qualifications may be exempt from at least the Foundation stage.

TRAINING

The ICSA scheme of study is based on the themes of administration, management, corporate law and corporate finance. It also aims to qualify students for a wide range of careers in administration and management across both public and private sectors.

The Foundation stage introduces business subjects: business economics, information systems, organization and the human resource, quantitative techniques, introduction to English and European Union law.

The Pre-professional stage prepares for positions of responsibility: managing information systems, management principles, business law, introduction to accounting.

INSTITUTE/BUSINESS ADMINISTRATION: CAP

The Professional stage covers the eight modules: management accounting; financial accounting; company secretarial practice; professional administration; corporate finance and taxation; management practice; corporate law; administration of corporate affairs.

Success in the qualifying examinations confers graduateship for the ICSA. To become an associate member (ACIS) it is also necessary to gain six years' appropriate work experience. This may be reduced by up to three years for time spent in full-time study. Associates should be at least 21 years. Fellows of the Institute (FCIS) should be at least 25 years with a minimum of eight years' experience, of which some should be in a position of seniority.

The courses may be studied full-time, part-time in the evening, or by distance learning. On average it takes three to four years to complete the three programmes by part-time study. Several universities and colleges offer collaborative qualifying programmes developed and assessed jointly with the ICSA. These lead to graduate membership of the ICSA as well as postgraduate award. Full details are available from the ICSA.

LATE ENTRY

The ICSA's open access policy enables anyone over 17 years, with or without formal academic qualifications, to register on the Foundation Programme. There is no upper age limit.

Access courses for adults who wish to qualify for a degree but do not have the necessary qualifications are available in many parts of the country.

A chartered secretary's job carries a high level of responsibility and demands such organizational skill that maturity and experience can be an advantage.

It is usual to spend several years gaining experience in different kinds of administrative work before becoming a company secretary. Up to six years' relevant experience is in any case required for full associate membership of the ICSA.

OPPORTUNITIES

Every company in the UK is required by law to have a company secretary, who should hold a suitable professional qualification either in law or accountancy, or as a member of the ICSA. Besides company secretarial work, chartered secretaries are well qualified for a wide variety of administrative jobs in all sectors of the economy. Their roles range from financial or personnel management to computing services or corporate planning. They may work in public or private companies, financial services, utilities such as gas or water supply, central and local government, health service, trade and professional associations, charities and educational administration.

The ICSA internationally has about 45,000 members and 28,000 students in the United Kingdom and around 100 other countries. The ICSA qualification is recognized under the European Community Professional Qualifications Directive, enabling chartered secretaries to work in all EU states.

Vacancies are advertised in the national and local press and in *Chartered Secretary,* the journal of the ICSA.

PAY AND CONDITIONS

Salaries vary widely. A typical starting figure for a newly qualified associate member might be £20,000 rising to over £60,000 with experience.

Chartered secretaries generally work 36 to 40 hours a week, Monday to Friday. Hours may vary, according to the demands of the job. They may have to attend evening meetings. Part-time work may be available in some companies.

PROSPECTS

Most company secretarial departments are small and offer limited prospects for internal promotion. It is usual to change jobs and change companies in order to gain experience and responsibility. Some chartered secretaries specialize in, for example, pensions, office administration, financial management or personnel management.

Experience as a company secretary can lead to positions in general management, or to partnerships in other firms.

Administrators in the Civil Service or local government have a more structured career ladder than in industry, but it is increasingly common to move from one sector to another.

RELATED OCCUPATIONS

Accountant, solicitor, advocate/barrister, Civil Service administrator, local government administrator, health service manager, personnel officer, bank manager, stockbroker, office manager.

FURTHER INFORMATION

Education Help Desk, The Institute of Chartered Secretaries and Administrators (ICSA)*, 16 Park Crescent, London W1N 4AH, 0171 580 4741, http://www/isca.org.uk

FURTHER READING

Leaflets/booklets are available from the address marked*.

Information pack available from the ICSA.

In the careers library classified under CAP.

HUMAN RESOURCES: CAS/FAP

1. PERSONNEL/HUMAN RESOURCES OFFICER CLCI:CAS
2. TRAINING OFFICER CLCI:FAP

BACKGROUND INFORMATION

An organization's workforce is extremely important in determining whether it is successful. Personnel/human resources officers are specialist members of the management team who help to make the most effective use of the workforce. They help to recruit suitable people, arrange for training and help to keep the people the organization require. They also make sure an organization deals with its employees consistently, fairly and within employment law.

Training of staff is vital as it helps people to acquire the knowledge and skills needed to do their jobs successfully. Developing staff helps to prepare them for more responsibility in the future. Specialist training officers are employed in many organizations for this important area of work, although an increasing number of posts combine personnel and training responsibilities.

1. PERSONNEL/HUMAN RESOURCES OFFICER (CAS)

THE WORK

Personnel officers, often called human resources officers, are responsible for selecting the right people for an organization and helping to make sure they are managed effectively.

The work of personnel/human resources officers can differ considerably from organization to organization but the following are the main areas of work:

Recruitment and selection, which includes drawing up job descriptions and personnel specifications, preparing advertisements, checking application forms, interviewing and sometimes testing applicants, obtaining references and selecting or rejecting candidates. Personnel/human resources officers work closely with other departments of the organization and with Jobcentres and careers offices.

Training and development is concerned with providing training programmes for employees, including induction and skills training for new employees. Personnel/human resources officers consult line managers (those with direct authority over some people in a work area) to analyse training needs. They may deliver some training themselves and arrange training by other staff and with outside training organizations, such as local colleges. They also monitor the effectiveness of training.

Industrial and employee relations includes meeting trade union representatives to negotiate pay and conditions or advising the managers who conduct these negotiations. Personnel/human resources officers also deal with disciplinary matters and disputes, grievances and redundancy procedures. This area can include responsibility for equal opportunities policy, recruitment literature, employee handbooks and house magazines.

Employee services work is concerned with matters of health and safety. It can include responsibility for medical, sports and social facilities, maintaining staff records, personal counselling, community relations and other welfare related activities.

Reward management involves setting up and running a pay policy that is appropriate to the staff, meets legal requirements and can be afforded by the employer. It also includes reviewing, introducing and administering company benefits, such as share ownership and incentive schemes.

Human resource planning is about assessing an organization's future staffing needs and measuring them against current availability. A human resources plan indicates how much an organization needs to recruit, train, re-train, transfer or reduce staff.

Personnel/human resources officers in some organizations are responsible for just one of the above areas, while in other organizations they are responsible for all areas of work for one type of staff, eg production workers. Personnel/human resources officers are increasingly becoming an important part of management groups as organizations recognize the value of human resources.

WORK ENVIRONMENT

Personnel/human resources officers spend most of their time working in an office but are mobile within their place of work to attend meetings and to see individual members of staff.

They may travel locally, eg to visit a local college. They also travel to other sites for which they are responsible, such as branch offices.

SKILLS AND INTERESTS

Personnel/human resources officers should like working with people. They must be able to get on well with many different people and have good social skills including tact, patience, understanding and persuasiveness.

Communication skills are important, both written and spoken: personnel/human resources officers should be able to write reports accurately; listening and spoken skills are essential for interviewing, discussions with staff, negotiations and delivery of training.

It is essential that personnel/human resources officers have a commercial awareness and see things from the employer's as well as the employee's perspective.

Ability with figures is necessary, as work involves making financial calculations and producing statistics on, for example, labour turnover, absence rates and salary budgets.

Personnel/human resources officers need analytical and problem-solving skills to help them create policies, plan and forecast future staffing needs. Good organizational ability is required, for example, when planning and arranging recruitment interviews.

Personnel/human resources officers should be able to work in a team, as they work closely with other personnel and management staff, line managers, training personnel and employees.

ENTRY REQUIREMENTS

There are no minimum entry requirements. In practice, however, the majority of personnel/human resources officers enter with degrees or higher national diplomas. The minimum entry requirement for degree courses is two A levels/three H grades plus five GCSEs/S grades (A–C/1–3), or equivalent, eg Advanced GNVQ/GSVQ Level III or a BTEC/SQA national award.

HUMAN RESOURCES: CAS/FAP

Entry to a higher national diploma course is normally with a minimum of one A level/two H grades plus three GCSEs/S grades (A–C/1–3), or equivalent, eg Advanced GNVQ/GSVQ Level III or a BTEC/SQA national award.

It is possible to become a personnel/human resources officer following experience in a personnel department in a clerical or secretarial post. Entry to such posts often needs several GCSEs/S grades (A–C/1–3), an Intermediate GNVQ/GSVQ Level II, a BTEC first or national award or a SQA national award. Progression to personnel/human resources officer is normally only possible if part-time study has led to the Institute of Personnel and Development's (IPD) Certificate in Personnel Practice (CPP) or to an NVQ/SVQ in Personnel Support at Level 3. There are no specific entry requirements for either the CPP or for NVQs/SVQs.

The IPD's Professional Qualification Scheme has no specific entry requirement but candidates should be aware that it involves study at degree level.

There are some postgraduate personnel management courses. They require a degree for entry.

Many personnel/human resources officers have had experience of other work before entering personnel.

TRAINING

Pre-entry

BTEC/SQA Higher National Diplomas in Business and Finance (two years full-time or three years sandwich) and degrees (three years full-time or four years sandwich) in such subjects as economics, business studies, law, industrial psychology or sociology and public administration are useful preparation for personnel work.

Some BA Business Studies and similar degrees, eg in human resources management, have been approved by the IPD as giving exemption from the Professional Qualifying Scheme (PQS). There are also a number of one-year full-time postgraduate courses in personnel management that fully exempt students from the PQS and others that give accreditation for particular modules. A list of such courses is available from the IPD.

On entry

Training for personnel/human resources officers is provided in-house but many employers expect staff to become professionally qualified by working for IPD qualifications.

The IPD's Certificate in Personnel Practice (CPP) is designed for candidates from a variety of backgrounds, eg line managers, secretarial/personal assistants and clerical staff. The course includes interpersonal and interviewing skills, employment law, personnel records and optional subjects. Courses normally last for one year and are offered at over 100 colleges, universities and private training providers on a day release or evening class basis. Those who successfully complete the CPP are eligible for associate membership of the IPD.

The IPD's Professional Qualification Scheme (PQS) has three parts – Core Management, Core Personnel and Development, and Specialist and Generalist Personnel and Development. Successful completion of any one part leads to licentiate membership of the IPD, while graduate membership is achieved on successful completion of all three parts.

Core Management includes: corporate environment, management information systems, managing processes and functions, and managing human resources.

Core Personnel and Development provides an overview of how each aspect of the management and development of people in organizations affects others and the organization as a whole.

Specialist and Generalist Personnel and Development – candidates study four modules from 22 as follows: employee resourcing, selection and assessment centres, human resource planning, career management, employee development, management development, vocational education and training, managing learning processes, managing training operations, organizational consultancy, employee reward, pensions, performance management, employee relations, employment law, international employee relations, health and safety, employee involvement and communications, employee counselling support and welfare, international personnel and development, strategic human resource management/development, equality management. Candidates can either follow a personnel management route, a training and development route or can 'mix and match' modules.

Many universities, colleges and other training providers throughout the UK offer courses to study for the PQS on a part-time and flexible learning basis. Part-time courses last from two to three years. PQS candidates are required to join the IPD as studying affiliates while undertaking the programme.

Personnel/human resources officers may work towards NVQs/SVQs in Personnel Support Level 3, Personnel Management Level 4 and Personnel Strategy Level 5. Achieving these gives holders eligibility for IPD associate, licentiate and graduate membership respectively.

LATE ENTRY

There are no age restrictions on entry to personnel work. Many personnel/human resources officers have had experience of other work such as marketing, production, sales or public administration.

Mature applicants may be accepted for entry to relevant higher education courses without the usual entry requirements. They may prepare for application by successfully completing an Access course.

People seeking entry to personnel work should be willing to study for IPD qualifications. Those who already hold a relevant qualification or have significant experience in a relevant area may be eligible for accreditation of prior learning. That can lead to IPD membership at associate, licentiate or graduate grade, depending on the assessed equivalence of their prior learning.

OPPORTUNITIES

Personnel/human resources officers are employed throughout the UK by all but the smallest organizations. Employers include manufacturers, retailers, banks, insurance companies and other commercial companies, transport companies, local authorities, the Civil Service, the National Health Service, educational institutions, and those in the leisure and hotel catering industries.

Competition for vacancies is very keen. Vacancies may be advertised in the local and national press and in specialist journals such as *People Management*.

Increasingly, organizations are seeking to recruit graduates with IPD qualifications. Relatively few organizations,

HUMAN RESOURCES: CAS/FAP

however, recruit graduates direct into personnel work. Instead, they tend to recruit them into general management training schemes that include personnel experience and that may later lead to specialization in personnel work.

Opportunities for those in clerical and secretarial posts to move into professional personnel work are decreasing.

PAY AND CONDITIONS

Starting salaries paid to graduates entering personnel traineeships immediately after a first degree are very similar to those entering other trainee posts.

Personnel/human resources officers earn between £12,716 and £23,790. Personnel directors earn between £35,000 and £82,200. Salaries paid by local authorities and smaller retailers tend to be lower than those paid by large manufacturing firms and public authorities.

Personnel/human resources officers work standard office hours, Monday to Friday, with pressure of work leading, on occasion, to work outside those hours.

PROSPECTS

Promotion is dependent largely on achievement and potential, although it is helpful to have IPD qualifications. Promotion possibilities are greater in larger organizations, where there may be a structure that includes a personnel manager and personnel director. It is common for personnel staff to move from employer to employer in order to progress.

It is possible for those who have specialized in one area of personnel work to achieve promotion, although it is perhaps easier for those who have had experience of several areas.

Some experienced personnel/human resources officers set up their own consultancies offering specialist services, such as recruitment.

There are some opportunities to work abroad for multinational organizations.

RELATED OCCUPATIONS

Careers adviser, retail manager, training officer, employment agency consultant/interviewer, occupational psychologist, Civil Service junior manager.

FURTHER INFORMATION AND READING

Please see article 2. TRAINING OFFICER.

2. TRAINING OFFICER (FAP)

THE WORK

Training officers identify the training needs of employees, then plan and organize appropriate training programmes for them.

The work of individual training officers can differ greatly between organizations but the following are the main activities:

Analysing training needs. Training officers seek to identify the training gap (the difference between what employees can do and what they need to be capable of in order to perform their jobs successfully). This involves discussions with line managers and personnel/human resources officers, and reference to job descriptions.

Meeting training needs. Training officers have to advise on the most effective methods of training to meet the identified needs, eg in-house courses, on-the-job instruction, coaching, distance learning, external courses. An important consideration is the cost of training.

Clarifying learning objectives. Before recommending a training activity, training officers need to clarify with the line manager exactly what is required. A clear statement is agreed on what skills people should be able to perform after training and within what time-scale.

Designing training programmes. Training officers need a good knowledge of available training provision. Cost of training is important and they must be aware of any government financial assistance that may be available. If it is decided to use external training, eg at colleges, universities or by using consultancies, the training officer makes the necessary arrangements. In-house training may be delivered by training officers or they may negotiate with other staff to deliver it. Training officers choose or recommend appropriate methods of training delivery, eg lectures, discussion groups, role playing, videos.

Evaluating effectiveness. Training must be evaluated to make sure it has achieved what was required. Training officers use questionnaires, interviews and discussions with line managers to achieve this.

In some organizations a training officer is responsible for all these tasks, either for the whole staff or for a particular category, eg technical staff. In others, responsibilities are divided laterally so that training officers are responsible for different activities, eg designing training courses, delivering training, liaison with external training providers and associated administration.

WORK ENVIRONMENT

Training officers spend most of their time working indoors in an office or training centre. They are mobile within their place of work to attend meetings and to liaise with line managers, personnel/human resources officers and employees. They may travel to visit training providers and employees in training.

SKILLS AND INTERESTS

Training officers must be interested in people as individuals and in their development.

They need a good standard of English and strong communication skills, both spoken and written. Verbal skills are necessary in discussions with line managers, training providers and others and for presenting training sessions. Written skills are needed for writing reports and keeping records.

Social skills are important. Training officers must be able to work well with a variety of people – which needs tact, patience and understanding. Negotiation skills are required in their contacts with line managers, employees, training providers and others. Identifying training needs and designing training programmes requires the ability to analyse problems and consider possible solutions.

Organizational ability is necessary. Training officers have to plan ahead, meet deadlines and keep accurate records. They work within a training budget so need numerical ability to control the budget. Judgement is required to weigh the cost-effectiveness of different methods of training available.

HUMAN RESOURCES: CAS/FAP

Commitment to training is essential. Training officers have to keep up to date with changes in vocational training, financial assistance and legal requirements affecting training. They do this by reading and by attending meetings and courses.

ENTRY REQUIREMENTS

No formal educational qualifications are required for entry as a training officer, but numeracy and a high standard of written and spoken English are necessary.

Although most entrants have qualified in another area of work before entering training, some begin as trainees in a personnel or training department. There is no standard entry requirement for trainees but such posts often need several GCSEs/S grades (A–C/1–3), a BTEC first award, BTEC/SQA national award or Intermediate GNVQ/GSVQ Level II.

The Institute of Personnel and Development's (IPD) Certificate in Training Practice has no specific entry requirements. The IPD's Professional Qualification Scheme has no specific entry requirements but candidates should be aware that it involves study at degree level.

NVQs/SVQs have no specific entry requirements.

TRAINING

Training officers may receive in-house training from their employers. Some attend short external introductory courses and/or seminars and courses on particular topics. Such courses rarely last longer than a few days and are run by private training organizations.

There are professional qualifications available through the Institute of Personnel and Development (IPD). The IPD's Certificate in Training Practice (CTP) provides a first step for those seeking to develop as proficient trainers in training officer, training adviser, line manager and similar roles. The CTP programme covers core training and development topics and the identification and analysis of training needs. Successful completion of the programme leads to eligibility for Associate membership of the IPD. Around 80 local colleges and private training providers, and four universities, offer CTP courses. Courses usually last for one year on a day release or block release basis or through open learning.

The IPD's Professional Qualification Scheme (PQS) allows candidates to follow a training development route – please see article 1. PERSONNEL/HUMAN RESOURCES OFFICER for details of the PQS, including courses that allow partial and total exemption.

Training officers may work towards NVQs/SVQs in Training and Development at Level 3, Training and Development (Human Resource Development) at Level 4, Training and Development (Learning Development) at Level 4, and Training and Development Strategy at Level 5. Achieving Level 3 leads to eligibility for IPD Associate membership, Level 4 to Licentiate membership and Level 5 to Graduate membership.

LATE ENTRY

There is no upper age limit for entry, and the maturity that late entrants bring to the training role is valuable. Most training officers come to training following experience in another area of work, eg personnel, teaching, supervisory and management posts.

Those who already hold a relevant qualification or have significant experience in a relevant area may be eligible for accreditation of prior learning which can lead to IPD membership at Associate, Licentiate or Graduate grade, depending on the assessed equivalence of their prior learning.

OPPORTUNITIES

Training officers are employed throughout the UK by many different kinds of organizations including commercial firms, eg banks and building societies, retailers, manufacturers, voluntary bodies, local authorities and other public sector organizations, and by local and national training agencies. The number of training consultancies is increasing, as is the number of trainers working freelance.

The number of training officers employed was increasing until the late 1980s. That growth has since stopped and the number is now stable.

Competition is keen when vacancies arise. Some vacancies are advertised in *People Management, Personnel Today* and in the local and national press.

PAY AND CONDITIONS

There are no set salary scales but a training officer may expect to earn between £13,653 and £24,195 depending on experience, responsibilities and the type of employing organization. A training manager may expect to earn between £20,225 and £38,214 and a training director between £29,850 and £53,040.

Training officers normally work standard office hours, Monday to Friday. Pressure of work can involve additional hours. Some training officers with organizations that have shift work may have to work outside normal office hours to liaise with staff and to conduct training. Some part-time work is available, particularly with training consultancies.

PROSPECTS

It may be possible in a large organization to gain promotion from training officer to training manager and training director. Small organizations do not offer that possibility. It is common for training officers to move from employer to employer for advancement.

Some training officers regard training as just one of a number of management skills they wish to acquire. They may seek promotion into personnel or general management.

It is possible for British-trained training officers to work abroad. It is particularly helpful if they have previous experience of the country in which they wish to work.

Experienced training officers may join training consultancies or set up a consultancy themselves.

RELATED OCCUPATIONS

Personnel/human resources officer, careers adviser, employment agency consultant/interviewer, safety officer, further education/tertiary college lecturer, teacher, training manager, training instructor.

FURTHER INFORMATION

Institute of Personnel and Development*, IPD House, 35 Camp Road, London SW19 4UX, 0181 971 9000, www.ipd.co.uk

HUMAN RESOURCES: CAS/FAP

FURTHER READING

Leaflets/booklets are available from the address marked*.

Careers in Personnel and Development – IPD

Personnel – The Department at Work – IPD

Personnel Work – AGCAS

In the careers library classified under CAS; FAP.

SECRETARIAL WORK: CAT

1. EXECUTIVE SECRETARY/PERSONAL ASSISTANT CLCI:CAT
2. SPECIALIST SECRETARY CLCI:CAT

BACKGROUND INFORMATION

Businesses of every type employ secretaries to undertake administrative work. Secretarial roles are called by a variety of job titles, sometimes reflecting work of different levels, but sometimes as an anomaly of the particular business or sector providing the employment. Job titles include secretary, senior secretary, administrative assistant, personal assistant and executive secretary. While PA and executive secretary are viewed as the most senior of these job titles, job titles vary between employers.

1. EXECUTIVE SECRETARY/PERSONAL ASSISTANT (CAT)

THE WORK

Secretaries/PAs take care of many administrative tasks for executives. They follow office procedures as laid down by superiors, or at a more senior level may decide upon and implement them themselves. Key duties include the efficient flow in and out of documents, and being the first point of contact for their manager with colleagues and people from outside organizations. The main tools of secretarial work are: word processor or networked/personal computer, dictaphone for audio work, telephone, fax.

At more junior levels, a secretary spends time doing general word processing for one or more managers. Word processing may be done from handwritten notes, shorthand or audio (when the secretary listens to a dictated tape). Word processing is likely to include documents such as invoices, business forms and correspondence. Other duties at this level may include sorting and opening incoming mail, franking outgoing mail, photocopying, filing, maintaining stationery and other supplies, and providing refreshments. Another key element of the job is answering the telephone, routing calls and taking messages. Some diary management skills may be needed at this level, to organize internal or external meetings.

Senior secretaries usually work for only one executive. They may have a junior for the photocopying, filing and some of the word processing or they may do all of the duties themselves. Senior secretaries may type and file confidential documents. Filing procedures and other systems for record management are often set up and arranged by senior secretaries. They open all the manager's and their own mail and deal with or respond to routine mail without consultation, but would not be involved in franking of outgoing mail. Senior secretaries also organize all aspects of functions, conferences, meetings and travel arrangements without supervision. This work can include the preparation of agendas, taking of minutes and distribution to participants. They are often required to attend and minute meetings with their manager.

At the most senior level of personal assistant or executive secretary, a great deal of personal initiative is required. Indeed, in some jobs, there is a certain amount of job crossover between the executive or director and the personal assistant. While some PAs may do all of the above duties, many supervise more junior secretaries and only perform confidential word processing or filing. They may be responsible for recruiting and training these staff. PAs often screen their executive's incoming telephone calls and mail, dealing with it themselves if they do not consider it necessary to pass on to their manager. They collate, organize and edit material for inclusion in reports to be written by their executive, and research and précis information and other materials for meetings. Many PAs are responsible for preparing budget or other financial or statistical records, and may be responsible for purchasing equipment and supplies. The most senior PAs stand in for their managers – greeting or having preliminary meetings with clients or suppliers, liaising with clients and senior management, delegating tasks to appropriate departments or making decisions in the absence of their manager. PAs also have a responsibility for ensuring office procedures are updated in line with new equipment and personnel, and to keep abreast of developments in office automation. They should be aware of new legislation, such as Health and Safety or Data Protection laws, and ensure their requirements are implemented.

WORK ENVIRONMENT

Secretarial work is sedentary. Secretaries of every level work mainly in offices, whatever the nature of business of their employer. The more senior they become, the more likely they are to have their own office. At senior levels, secretaries/PAs may be expected to travel on business with their manager.

SKILLS AND INTERESTS

Secretarial work requires a well-organized and orderly approach. Attention to detail, accuracy and a conscientious attitude are needed for this type of work. Clear speaking and writing, as well as a good grasp of the English language – spelling, grammar, punctuation and sentence construction – are essential. Employers also look for people who are well-presented and smart.

It is a career for people who enjoy working closely with others – both colleagues and a wide variety of other people. It is essential to enjoy contact with people from different backgrounds and to have the communications skills this requires. Tact and diplomacy may be called for when putting off would-be callers whom the secretary knows their manager does not wish to speak to or see. At more senior levels, good judgement is required, both for recruitment purposes and deciding whether to put through calls or arrange meetings for the executive or director.

ENTRY REQUIREMENTS

There are a variety of ways to start work as an executive secretary/personal assistant. The Royal Society of Arts (RSA) offers a Higher Diploma in Administrative and Secretarial Procedures (HDASP) at Advanced level, or the Diploma in Administrative and Secretarial Procedures (DASP) at Intermediate level, while the London Chamber of Commerce and Industry (LCCI) offers a Private and Executive Secretary's Diploma (PESD) at Advanced level and a Private Secretary's Certificate (PSC) at Intermediate level. Pitman Qualifications offer an Advanced Diploma in Administration and Secretarial Procedures.

The advanced diplomas are equivalent to NVQ/SVQ in Administration at Level 4, and the intermediate awards to NVQ/SVQ Level 3. NVQs/SVQs can be obtained in part

SECRETARIAL WORK: CAT

or in full prior to entry to employment. Formal entrance requirements for these courses are not stipulated, but the intermediate awards are intended as post-GCSE/S grade qualifications and the advanced awards as post-A level/H grade qualifications. Individual colleges should be contacted directly, as they may have specific entry requirements, such as four GCSEs/S grades, including English. GNVQs/GSVQs in Business are useful backgrounds for these courses. An equivalent level qualification is a BTEC/SQA HNC/D in Business and Finance combined with RSA, LCCI or Pitman shorthand, audio and word processing awards, or the SQA HNC/D in Administration and Information Management.

An alternative entry route is to get basic RSA, Pitman, SQA or LCCI qualifications in word processing, audio or shorthand and to start work at a more junior level. With the right experience and motivation, promotion may be possible. This may require additional study or attaining NVQs/SVQs in Administration while at work. Some larger employers offer in-house training courses for staff development.

TRAINING

The courses mentioned above last one to two years on a full-time basis or may be studied on a modular scheme whilst working. They cover shorthand, word processing, audio, general office procedures, communication, business structures, finance and human resource management. Once qualified, secretaries are most likely to receive additional training that is specific to their work. Training may include the office procedures of the particular business, or additional computing applications, such as the spreadsheet or word processing packages used by the company. Secretaries with the LCCI certificate may be encouraged to study for the diploma. Those without NVQs/SVQs may be encouraged to train for NVQ/SVQ in Administration at Level 3 and 4. Senior secretaries and PAs may be encouraged to do specific short courses such as time management or budget control. With appropriate skills and qualifications, they can join a professional body such as the Institute of Qualified Private Secretaries (IQPS).

It may be possible to enter secretarial work via training schemes for young people, for example via a Modern Apprenticeship in Business Administration. Contact your local career office, Jobcentre, TEC/LEC for details.

LATE ENTRY

Age is not a barrier for starting secretarial work. Some employers prefer more mature secretaries. Training schemes are available for suitably qualified unemployed adults in some areas. Contact TECs/LECs for more information.

Adults can gain recognition of their skills and experience by working towards NVQs/SVQs. Past experience can be put forward as evidence of competence.

OPPORTUNITIES

As every type of business and industry needs people to work in secretarial roles, opportunities for secretaries tend to reflect the general economic mix and state of the particular region or times. Opportunities are immensely varied, reflecting the whole range of businesses. Particularly in demand are people with a range of qualifications and skills, such as in desktop publishing, spreadsheets and databases. While vacancies are reasonably plentiful, competition can be fierce, so extra skills, such as foreign languages, can improve employment prospects.

Self-employment is possible for those who wish to concentrate on the word processing side. Work can be done with a home computer, or more ambitious secretaries could set up word processing bureaux employing several people.

PAY AND CONDITIONS

According to the IQPS, a typical starting salary for a secretary is about £8,713. For more senior secretaries £15,000 is typical, while for top PAs in London £20,000 to £25,000 is the accepted range. Salaries vary according to company, business sector and region, with those in central London usually being higher than elsewhere.

Most secretaries work a five-day week for office hours only (usually 9/9.30am to 5/5.30pm). More senior secretaries and PAs are expected to be flexible about their working hours, especially if travelling on business. Part-time work and temping opportunities are usually plentiful, especially for holiday cover.

PROSPECTS

The most direct route up the career ladder for a secretary is to work for increasingly senior executives, managers and directors. A managing director's PA is often an extremely senior and responsible job. For those who wish to go into more general administration, it is possible to be promoted to office or operations manager and possibly eventually operations director. For secretaries in the right type of department, it is possible to cross over to executive work in the same department. This type of move occurs most often in sales, marketing and personnel departments, although it may also be possible in market research and customer training. Further training specific to the department may be needed.

RELATED OCCUPATIONS

Administrative assistant, specialist secretary, telephonist/receptionist, customer care officer, hotel receptionist, office manager, operations manager/director.

FURTHER INFORMATION AND READING

Please see article 2. SPECIALIST SECRETARY.

2. SPECIALIST SECRETARY (CAT)

THE WORK

Medical

The medical secretary practises secretarial duties in a variety of medical places of work, including general practice (GP) surgeries, a wide variety of departments in hospitals (general, teaching, psychiatry etc) and research laboratories. Much of the work is similar to that of general secretaries, except that correspondence and documents are about medical matters and are full of medical terminology.

In general practice, medical secretaries work a great deal on their own initiative. They make patient appointments and arrange home visits, establish priorities and emergencies, keep records and deal with telephone

SECRETARIAL WORK: CAT

enquiries. The administration of a practice, including financial affairs, may be run by the secretary. Medical secretaries in private consultant practice often work on their own for much of the time, acting as receptionist too.

Legal

Legal secretaries work in solicitors' offices as well as in the legal departments of a wide range of other businesses, such as local government, manufacturers, financial services companies and estate agents. Their work is similar to that of general secretaries, but they must use and understand the use of legal terminology and abbreviations. In addition, they must know what type of documents are required in different types of cases. In particular, legal secretaries must be especially accurate in their work, as the exact wording of contracts can make all the difference to their legal interpretation.

Bi/multilingual

In addition to the duties of a general secretary (see article 1. EXECUTIVE SECRETARY/PERSONAL ASSISTANT), bi/multilingual secretaries also translate documents. Their duties often involve a great deal of client liaison as well: the bi/multilingual secretary communicates with overseas clients and suppliers, both in writing and on the telephone; may participate in social or cultural occasions for overseas visitors; and may serve as interpreter at business meetings.

Farm

Farm secretaries are responsible for the administrative work of farms. Their duties include keeping the farm accounts (manual and computerized), maintaining livestock and crop records, and preparing and completing forms required by the Ministry of Agriculture. They are also responsible for the farm's payroll and contracts of employment. For this work, an understanding of the technical side of farming and law relating to rural business is needed, such as food and environment protection and hazardous substances laws. Experienced secretaries form part of the farm's management team, providing budgets and draft accounts, as well as researching new enterprises. This side of the work can involve a good deal of liaison with bank managers, accountants and consultants.

THE WORK ENVIRONMENT

Specialist secretaries still tend to work in offices, mainly sitting at office equipment, whatever the general location (hospital department, GP practice, solicitors' offices, import/export office). Farm secretaries are the exception. As well as working in farm offices, they may work outdoors or in farm buildings during stocktaking and may spend time travelling between farms and bank managers and other advisers. Mobile farm and farm bureaux secretaries operate their own offices/office equipment.

SKILLS AND INTERESTS

Apart from the skills and interests mentioned in article 1. EXECUTIVE SECRETARY/PERSONAL ASSISTANT, specialist secretaries require in addition:

Medical

A demonstrable keen interest in medicine, medical matters and people in general is essential. The ability to be sympathetic and helpful to patients who may be distressed is vital, to inspire confidence and allay anxiety. Employers look for people who are well organized and can deal with a large number of tasks simultaneously, keeping calm through numerous interruptions and possible emergencies. Medical secretaries need to be confident enough to work on their own initiative.

They also need tact, to serve the needs of patients as well as doctors, even if these may sometimes be in conflict.

Legal

An interest in legal matters and a careful, conscientious approach are important. People who wish to be legal secretaries need to take pride in the end product of their work and be perfectionist in terms of accuracy. Flexibility is required to adapt to different companies' systems and facilities.

Bi/multilingual

An aptitude for languages and excellent communications skills are a prerequisite for this job. Since it tends to involve an unusual amount of client, supplier and overseas colleagues contact, a particularly good ability to get on with other people is needed.

Farm

Self-motivation and an ability to work alone, with the confidence to work on one's own initiative, are essential for this job. However, getting on with other people is important, as the farm secretary is often the liaison point between the farm and outside organizations such as the Inland Revenue. The work is varied and calls for an investigative approach. An organized mind helps to run the administrative and financial systems. Common sense, hard work and a sense of humour are needed too.

ENTRY REQUIREMENTS

Medical

The qualifying body for medical secretaries is the Association of Medical Secretaries, Practice Managers, Administrators and Receptionists (AMSPAR). The entry requirements for AMSPAR medical secretarial qualifications are four GCSEs/S grades (A–C/1–3). An Intermediate GNVQ/GSVQ Level II in Business is an acceptable alternative. A good standard of English is essential.

Students with A levels/H grades may be able to take shortened courses. Mature students are accepted at the discretion of each college.

Legal

There are no set academic entry requirements. However, for entry to training courses, GCSE/S grade (A–C/1–3) in English may be required, and in some cases it is necessary to have four GCSEs/S grades (A–C/1–3), or equivalent.

Entry routes are varied and depend both on the policies of individual employers and local availability of legal secretarial courses. It is an advantage to start by taking a legal secretaries' course leading to one of the awards listed under TRAINING, but it is also possible to find work in a legal practice after taking a general secretarial course.

Bi/multilingual

Good secretarial skills and a high level of fluency in at least one foreign language are needed. There are no set academic entry requirements, but many entrants have A levels/H grades or degrees in languages. GCSE/S grade (A–C/1–3) in English is usually required.

Farm

There are no set entry requirements, although competence

SECRETARIAL WORK: CAT

in maths and English is required. Some colleges specify two to four GCSEs/S grades (A–C/1–3) or equivalent. Contact individual colleges for details.

TRAINING

Medical

Courses for the AMSPAR Diploma/Certificate in Medical Secretarial Studies are available at a large number of colleges throughout the UK. Courses last one to two years and may be full- or part-time. There are two alternative methods of qualifying: a traditional programme, assessed by examination, or a competence-based programme, assessed by portfolio. The syllabus includes the administrative and legal aspects of the NHS and social services, effective communications, medical secretarial practices, finance and medical aspects such as anatomy, first aid, medical ethics and patients' rights.

For the Diploma, candidates must gain RSA/Pitman Certificates in two of the following: medical shorthand, medical audio transcription, medical word processing. The Certificate is awarded if only one skill is achieved.

Some centres offer a dual award scheme which enables students to achieve an NVQ in Administration at Level 3, in addition to an AMSPAR qualification.

In Scotland, colleges offer the AMPSAR qualifications or SQA national certificate courses with medical modules. SVQ in Administration at Level 3 may be obtained in employment.

Legal

There are a number of college courses, often one or two years full-time, leading to legal secretarial qualifications. They include:

– ILEX (Paralegal Training) Ltd – Legal Secretaries' Certificate (Level 2), Diploma in Legal Secretarial Studies (Level 3). These awards are similar to, and based on, NVQs;

– Institute of Paralegal Training (incorporating the former Association of Legal Secretaries) – Legal Secretaries' Certificate and Diploma;

– London Chamber of Commerce and Industry;

– First and Second Certificates for Legal Secretaries;

– RSA legal text processing awards and legal option in the Diploma in Administrative and Secretarial Procedures;

– SQA – national certificate modules in specialist legal text processing, audio and shorthand, Higher National Certificate/Diploma in Legal Services.

Distance learning and part-time courses are also available. These may be combined with on-the-job training in the particular procedures of the employer.

Bi/multilingual

Bi/multilingual secretarial courses cover English secretarial syllabuses, plus tuition in the second (or more) language(s), including word processing, audio and perhaps shorthand. Commercial terminology and business studies in the foreign language are often included too. Most colleges offer work experience either in the UK or abroad. NVQ/SVQ language units can be taken separately or as part of an NVQ/SVQ or GNVQ/GSVQ.

The RSA, LCCI, City & Guilds, BTEC and the SQA award qualifications in secretarial/business subjects and languages.

Once bi/multilingual secretaries have started work, they receive on-the-job induction training on employer procedures and on new computer packages.

Farm

Courses specifically for farm secretaries are run at some agricultural colleges – a list of these is available from the Institute of Agricultural Secretaries and Administrators Ltd.

Courses lead to the City and Guilds National Certificate in Farm Secretarial Studies (C+G 0330) or to other awards in agriculture and/or business administration, eg BTEC national certificates/diplomas, intermediate/advanced GNVQs. In Scotland there is no specific SQA award for farm secretaries, but general secretarial awards may be adapted to take account of the specific duties of a farm secretary.

The nature of the work means that the learning process is continuous. Although farm secretaries are fully qualified when they start work, they need to keep updating their knowledge, particularly with the legal and technical aspects of the job. New computer applications for agriculture are just one example of the constant updating that a farm secretary requires. Keeping up to date can involve reading, questioning other secretaries, farmers and advisers, and attending meetings of the Institute of Agricultural Secretaries and Administrators. The Institute has introduced a programme of professional development to help raise standards.

NVQs/SVQs

Specialist secretaries may take NVQs/SVQs in Administration, available at Levels 1,2,3 and 4.

Training opportunities for young people

It may be possible to enter medical, legal or farm secretarial work via training opportunities for young people, including National Traineeships or Modern Apprenticeships (part of the Skillseekers Initiative in Scotland). Contact your local careers office, Jobcentre, TEC/LEC for details.

LATE ENTRY

There is no age limit for starting work as a specialist secretary. For medical and farm secretaries, some employers actually prefer more mature candidates. Mature candidates for legal secretarial work often enter by cross-training on the legal side. Training schemes for specialist secretarial work are available for suitably qualified unemployed adults in some areas. Contact local TECs/LECs for more information.

OPPORTUNITIES

Medical

Opportunities exist in numerous specialities, such as general medicine, general surgery, paediatrics, dermatology, psychiatry, cardiology, ophthalmics, X-ray department, and research. Other options include the World Health Organization (WHO), the medical corps of the Armed Forces, and pharmaceutical companies. Competition for vacancies is often fierce.

Legal

There are opportunities in companies with legal departments and in private legal practices. Competition for vacancies can be quite intense. Most openings are in large cities, with competition being fiercest in London.

SECRETARIAL WORK: CAT

Opportunities for temporary work are quite good and part-time work may be available.

Bi/multilingual

The number of jobs available in the UK is usually greater than the number of students qualified to fill them. Opportunities are found mainly in large cities. In addition, bi/multilingual secretaries can pursue openings abroad.

In the UK, the languages most in demand are French and German, with Spanish and Italian having some importance too. Other European languages and those of more geographically remote countries are not in much demand.

Farm

Opportunities are available for resident farm secretaries, who work on one farm or estate, for mobile farm secretaries who work for a number of businesses, and in farm secretarial bureaux, which also work for several farms. Mobile farm secretaries are usually self-employed, and may have their own offices, while farm secretarial bureaux offer part-time and temporary opportunities as well as full-time work. Bureaux sometimes offer work for secretaries in agricultural accountants and consultants. Changes in agricultural technology and legislation have increased the demand for trained agricultural administrators. Competition for the relatively scarce full-time jobs for college leavers can be fierce, and so newly qualified applicants often start at bureaux or in administrative jobs at accountants or land agents specializing in agriculture.

PAY AND CONDITIONS

Medical

Starting salaries for newly qualified medical secretaries in the NHS are in the region of £9,261 and for those working in the London area, a weighting allowance of between £1,225 and £2,060 is available.

Salaries are based on a 36-hour week in the London area and 37 hours elsewhere. Normal office hours are usually worked, although flexibility may be required to fit in with clinic hours, such as evenings and Saturday mornings.

Legal

The average salary for a legal secretary in London is around £16,000, although pay is generally lower outside the capital. Legal secretaries normally work office hours, but they are expected to be flexible if work occurs late in the day.

Bi/multilingual

Starting salaries for bi/multilingual secretaries are in the region of £11,000 to £12,000 in London. Pay varies by company, business sector and region, with salaries normally being higher in London than elsewhere. Office hours are normally worked, though at more senior levels secretaries are expected to work longer hours.

Farm

Typical starting salaries for full-time farm secretaries are £8,500 to £9,000 although many farm secretaries work only part-time. Office hours are usually worked, although flexibility is necessary. For a resident farm secretary, accommodation is sometimes provided, which may be reflected in the salary.

PROSPECTS

Medical

Medical secretaries with the right motivation and experience can gain promotion in the health service. Within general practice, this could lead to practice management, but managerial and further financial training will be required. AMSPAR offers both a Diploma and Certificate in Practice Management. Secretaries wishing to leave the medical profession find their skills and experience can be translated into other business contexts.

Legal

Legal secretaries can work their way up the company, perhaps aiming for the job of personal assistant to the most senior partner. Alternatively, they can become legal executives, with a more managerial role, running the office. For this move, they will require additional paralegal qualifications.

Bi/multilingual

Bi/multilingual secretaries often use their job as an entry point to a particular industry or type of work in which they are interested. With the right motivation and ability, it is not uncommon for them to move into an executive role, such as in sales, personnel or even stockbroking. To pursue the language element of the work, it is possible to become a translator, especially if a secretary has a particular expertise, for instance in computer terminology.

Farm

Farm secretaries can move into larger farms or from bureaux to farms, or set up as self-employed mobile farm secretaries or open a bureau. Areas other than farm estate management, into which farm secretaries move, include forestry, land agency, agricultural marketing, food processing and retailing, veterinary practice management, conservation and countryside management, rural tourism, and auctioneering. Some farm secretaries take further accountancy qualifications to work in these and other areas.

RELATED OCCUPATIONS

Executive Secretary/PA, hotel receptionist, dental/medical receptionist, translator, legal executive, medical practice manager, farm manager, agricultural accountant.

FURTHER INFORMATION

AMSPAR*, Tavistock House North, Tavistock Square, London WC1H 9LN, 0171 387 6005

ILEX (Paralegal Training) Ltd*, Kempston Manor, Kempston, Bedford MK42 7AB, 01234 841000, www.ilex.org.uk

Institute of Qualified Private Secretaries Ltd (IQPS)*, First Floor, 6 Bridge Avenue, Maidenhead, Berkshire SL6 1RR, 01628 625007

Institute of Paralegal Training*, The Mill, Clymping Street, Clymping, Littlehampton, West Sussex BN17 5RN, 01903 714276

Institute of Agricultural Secretaries and Administrators Ltd*, NAC, Stoneleigh, Kenilworth, Warwickshire CV8 2LZ, 01203 696592

London Chamber of Commerce and Industry (LCCI)*, Athena House, Station Road, Sidcup DA15 7BJ, 0181 302 0261, www.lccieb.org.uk

SECRETARIAL WORK: CAT

Pitman Qualifications*, 1 Giltspur Street, London EC1A 9DD, 0171 294 2471

RSA Examinations Board, Westwood Way, Coventry CV4 8HS, 01203 470033

Scottish Qualifications Authority (SQA)*, Hanover House, 24 Douglas Street, Glasgow G2 7NQ, 0141 248 7900

FURTHER READING

Leaflets/booklets are available from the addresses marked*.

Working in Medicine and Dentistry – COIC

Working in Hospitals – COIC

Working in Law – COIC

Working in Languages – COIC

Working in Agriculture and Horticulture – COIC

In the careers library classified under CAT.

ADMINISTRATIVE/CLERICAL WORK: CAT

1. **ADMINISTRATIVE/CLERICAL STAFF CLCI: CAT**
2. **RECEPTIONIST CLCI: CAT**

1. ADMINISTRATIVE/CLERICAL STAFF (CAT)

BACKGROUND INFORMATION

Almost every kind of organization – from schools and hospitals, insurance companies and banks, shops and factories to solicitors' offices, accountancy firms, estate agencies, airlines, hotels and travel companies – needs administrative/clerical staff to organize its information. They record, update, amend and store information relating to their employer's business. They could work with factual, scientific, technical, financial or other specialist information or deal mainly with correspondence. The work could include word processing.

In addition to their general duties, many administrative/clerical staff have specialist tasks, which vary according to where they work.

THE WORK

Administrative/clerical staff manage all the information that is produced in their organizations and the additional information that comes into the company from other sources. Their main duties are:

Communicating information. Administrative/clerical staff open all the incoming mail and distribute it to the appropriate staff. At the end of the day they ensure that outgoing mail is collected for the post. They are usually responsible for photocopying documents and addressing envelopes and sending all these to the relevant people. They may also answer telephones, take messages and produce standard letters using word processors.

The fact that so many administrative/clerical staff are now able to key information directly into VDUs sited on their desks has, in many companies, reduced the number of people employed solely as typists, and the 'typing pool' has virtually disappeared. However, in some organizations that generate a lot of written material – such as legal firms and local government departments –some employees retain similar job roles. The place where they work may be known as a word processing centre.

Word processor operators type reports, memos, notes, minutes and legal documents for a number of different people. They may receive the work written in longhand or it may have been dictated on to audio tape. Sometimes they are allocated the work by a supervisor; sometimes each operator works for a certain number of people and does all the work that they produce; or they may all share the work, taking the next tape or piece of work from a central tray where all incoming work is placed, as they become free. If audio typing they use headphones and control the tape by foot controls which enable them to stop and replay it if necessary.

Word processor operators use their employer's approved form of layout for the work. They may correct spelling and grammatical errors as they work. When they have finished producing a piece of work they may have to make a back-up copy but often this is done automatically by their machine and saved on to a database.

In some jobs, administrative/clerical staff spend some of their time working directly with members of the public. If they work for an organization that receives enquirers in person they may have to leave their office to go to the reception or information desk and answer the query.

Recording information. This may be done manually, either by filling in forms or by writing notes, or increasingly, by keying it into a computer. If any information is missing or is incorrect, the administrative/clerical worker searches files and records and may have to telephone other departments or external customers to obtain the correct facts. These are then recorded and notes are made cross-referring to other files and sources of information where necessary.

Storing information. Administrative/clerical staff are responsible for making sure that all information can be easily found. It may be stored on computer or in filing cabinets. Specialist filing administrative/clerical staff may have total responsibility for this aspect of the work. General administrative/clerical staff may do certain amounts of filing among their duties. Filing is also a duty often given to the newest entrants or trainees. This helps them to learn about the company, its organization and its products. Some examples of the specialist tasks undertaken by clerical/administrative workers follow.

Accounts and finance. In the accounts office of a company or business, accounts clerks calculate the cost of orders placed by customers, check figures, prepare invoices and keep accurate records of them and keep records of each day's financial transactions. They use calculators and computers but do not do the more complex auditing and accounting tasks that belong to accountancy technicians. In wages offices they calculate the amount of pay due to every employee, using records showing the number of hours worked and the number of these worked at overtime rates, deducting income tax and contributions for national insurance, pension funds, medical insurance etc. They then produce a pay slip itemizing all these facts and either send one of these to all staff, showing that the salary has been paid into their bank accounts or put cash into pay packets and issue these to employees.

Export departments. Clerical/administrative staff's duties include processing documents for goods to be exported, recording the fact that customs clearance and insurance cover have been obtained and making transport arrangements with shipping or airline companies.

Hospitality and travel. In the central reservations office of a hotel chain or travel company administrative/clerical staff make bookings for clients, checking availability of seats or rooms, quoting a price and taking credit card details for payment or sending an invoice to the client. They then send written confirmation of the reservation.

Personnel/human resources departments. Here, clerical/administrative staff look after employee records, send out application forms and subsequently letters inviting applicants for interview, and update records showing staff absences, holidays taken and contributions to pension schemes.

Sales departments. In a sales office they keep records of sales made by individual salesmen/women, record details of items ordered, and make out and send invoices to customers.

WORK ENVIRONMENT

Offices vary in size and age but are usually clean and comfortable. Small companies tend to have older furniture

ADMINISTRATIVE/CLERICAL WORK: CAT

and equipment but nearly all of them now make use of word processors and computers. Some administrative/clerical staff work in small offices of two or three people; others work in large open-plan offices.

Most administrative/clerical staff work in sections managed by a supervisor who allocates work. They may or may not have contact with other employees and with managers, depending on the size of their firm and the nature of the work. Many administrative/clerical staff remain seated all day. Those dealing with the post or responsible for distributing documents around the building, however, may be on their feet for a large part of the day. Word processor operators spend most of their working day seated but in some organizations they return the work in person to the executive who generated it – which involves them in moving around the building from time to time.

With the exception of those who deal with enquirers in person most administrative/clerical staff normally have contact with people outside their immediate working environment only by telephone.

SKILLS AND INTERESTS

Administrative/clerical staff should be well organized and able to work accurately and neatly. Some of the tasks may be repetitive, but must all be completed to the same standard. They need to be able to spell and have a knowledge of grammar. In many jobs clear handwriting is essential; in others a liking for basic arithmetic is needed, as is the ability to work with figures.

Increasingly they use computers and word processors. In some jobs they are also expected to use calculators or adding machines.

Some administrative/clerical staff need a good telephone manner; others may need to deal with personal enquirers helpfully and efficiently. Although they work under the general direction of a supervisor or office manager, they should be capable of using their initiative and of working without constant supervision.

Word processor operators should be able to plan the presentation of a piece of work. They should know when to correct grammatical mistakes in the original work. If typing from an audio tape they need to be good at spelling.

Administrative/clerical staff should normally be willing to wear smart and conventional clothes since most employers expect this.

They must respect the confidentiality of any correspondence and information they handle.

ENTRY REQUIREMENTS

There are no minimum entry requirements to administrative/clerical work but many employers expect new entrants to have three or four GCSEs/S grades (A–C/1–3). The most useful subjects are English and maths. Other useful subjects are business studies, accounts and, sometimes, languages.

Equivalent qualifications such as NVQs/SVQs in Administration at Levels 1 and 2, and Intermediate GNVQ/GSVQ Level II awards in Business, are usually acceptable.

Word processor operators are normally expected to have obtained minimum typing speeds and hold certificates from one of the nationally recognized examining bodies. Minimum speeds required vary with different employers but are usually 40–50 words per minute (wpm) or the ability to transcribe a tape in a given amount of time, often 350 words in 30 minutes.

Entry may be possible through training opportunities for young people, including National Traineeships. Contact your local careers office, Jobcentre, TEC/LEC for details.

TRAINING

Most training for administrative and clerical work is given by employers on the job. They may learn by watching and working with experienced colleagues or may be given initial training by their supervisors. Many begin by working as office juniors and do the more routine tasks such as opening and distributing the post, simple filing and operating fax, franking and photocopying machines.

Employers may expect administrative/clerical staff to obtain work-based NVQs/SVQs – up to Levels 1 or 2. Modules are available in audio typing plus transcription, communicating, data processing, filing, information processing, keyboarding, liaising with customers and colleagues, mail handling, maintaining financial records, preparing and producing documents, processing business documents, processing payments, processing payroll, reception, reprographics, servicing meetings, stock handling, storing and supplying information and telecommunications. (Not all modules are available at all levels.)

There is no set time limit for obtaining NVQs/SVQs. Employees may work at their own pace and take modules as and when appropriate.

Some employers may give their staff day release to a college of further education to study for single subject examinations in typing, word processing and information technology. Others encourage them to attend evening classes and pay for them to do so.

Some may give day release for an Intermediate/Advanced GNVQ/GSVQ Level II/III in Business.

The above contain core units in general business procedures and optional or additional units that are chosen according to the employee's duties. Examples include business law, business within Europe, financial planning and control, human resources and marketing.

These methods are less likely however, since the above awards were designed to be and are more normally studied on a full-time basis. Length of courses varies – from one to three years.

BTEC/SQA higher national diplomas and certificates may also be taken. These are useful for administrative/clerical staff with management potential. Courses usually take two years of part-time study. NVQs/SVQs at Levels 3 and 4 would also be useful for anyone aiming at higher level work.

Word processor operators need to be competent typists. They may have learned to type through day release or evening classes while employed as general administrative/clerical workers or may have completed a full-time course at a college of further education.

The main examining bodies offering relevant examinations are Pitman Qualifications, the London Chamber of Commerce and Industry Examinations Board, and the Royal Society of Arts Examinations Board (typing, audio transcription, information technology, word processing and office practice). They also offer Group Awards that

ADMINISTRATIVE/CLERICAL WORK: CAT

combine several of the subjects.

(Units in keyboarding, office practice and preparing and producing documents are also included in NVQs in Administration, described above.)

Training for word processor operators is also provided by private training organizations and by equipment manufacturers who offer cross-training in different word processing packages.

LATE ENTRY

There is no upper age limit for entering administrative/clerical work. If an adult entrant decides to work towards an NVQ/SVQ past experience may be put forward as evidence of competence through Accreditation of Prior Learning. In many areas colleges run refresher courses for adults who have been away from employment for some time. Other training opportunities specifically geared to adults may be available. Certain eligibility conditions may have to be met. TECs/LECS and Jobcentres have details.

OPPORTUNITIES

There are openings for administrative/clerical staff in all parts of the country and in almost every type of organization in industry, commerce and the public sector. Examples of places of employment include educational establishments, factories, insurance companies, financial companies, the Civil Service, health service and local government departments. Although the number of jobs has decreased due to office technology, there is still a steady demand, particularly for those with, or prepared to gain, qualifications, usually in keyboarding and IT.

Smaller companies usually employ general administrative/clerical staff who are expected to carry out a range of clerical tasks. In the bigger companies it is more usual to specialize.

PAY AND CONDITIONS

Salaries vary considerably according to employer and location. They could be anywhere between £7,000 and £16,000 with the highest salaries being paid in London and the South East. Most administrative/clerical staff work 35 to 37 hours a week, Monday to Friday, with opportunities for paid overtime. Some companies work from 9am to 5pm or 8.30am to 5.30pm. Others operate a flexitime system with staff being permitted to choose their hours outside core time (stipulated hours, during which all staff must be present).

There are often opportunities for part-time work and job sharing. Some word processor operators work as temps.

Some firms give a range of benefits such as subsidized canteens, pension schemes and life assurance.

All administrative and clerical staff who use VDUs must be given eye tests by their employers. There are health and safety regulations regarding the positioning of screens and height and position of chairs which must be observed by employers.

PROSPECTS

There may be opportunities to change departments within a company and move to a different type of administrative/clerical work, or to gain promotion to section head, supervisor or office manager.

People who have studied for recognized qualifications in business studies or office administration are most likely to gain promotion. It is also possible to obtain promotion or higher salaries by changing employer. Staff who have specialized in word processing work may sometimes progress to become secretaries, although this normally involves gaining further qualifications.

RELATED OCCUPATIONS

Accounting technician, bank officer, building society staff, Civil Service administrative assistant/officer, insurance clerk, local government administrative/clerical staff, medical records clerk, receptionist, secretary, travel consultant/travel agency clerk.

FURTHER INFORMATION AND READING

Please see article 2. RECEPTIONIST.

2. RECEPTIONIST (CAT)

BACKGROUND INFORMATION

Organizations that receive frequent callers require a receptionist to greet them and record their visit. In addition to dealing with callers from outside the organization, they may deal with fellow employees visiting from other departments.

The receptionist is frequently the first person to greet a visitor and therefore creates the initial impression of the organization. Similarly, when a visitor leaves the building it is often the receptionist who shows the person out and so creates the lasting impression.

Receptionists work in a wide range of organizations, both large and small. They are employed throughout industry and commerce, and in both the public and private sectors.

THE WORK

When a caller arrives it is the receptionist's job to ask the nature of their business and check to see if they have an appointment. Therefore, receptionists need to be aware of all meetings taking place and the location in which they are to be held. If an appointment has been arranged, the receptionist advises the appropriate department and confirm that it is all right to direct the visitor to the office, or wait for an escort. If any delay is anticipated, the receptionist is responsible for directing the person to a waiting area, and often, providing them with refreshment and/or reading material. For visitors arriving without an appointment, the receptionist may try to arrange an immediate or alternative appointment.

Visitors may require a variety of information ranging from who does what in the organization, to details of local accommodation, restaurants, directions and so on. The receptionist is expected to provide the information, or at least know how to quickly obtain it. Receptionists often maintain address/telephone number lists to answer such requests.

In small organizations the receptionist may be responsible for the overall running of the reception area and work largely on their own. In addition to greeting visitors, their duties may include operating a switchboard, answering telephones, taking messages for others, maintaining a

ADMINISTRATIVE/CLERICAL WORK: CAT

visitor's book (which records caller's names and addresses – useful to ascertain who is in the building in case of emergencies such as a fire), issuing security passes and car parking permits, and receiving deliveries and signing for them on behalf of their organization. They may also be required to carry out general clerical tasks such as keeping an appointments diary, typing letters, sorting correspondence, franking mail, sending fax messages and photocopying documents. In some jobs, receptionists may be required to issue receipts for sales, assist in simple payroll duties, and account for petty cash disbursements.

In large organizations, receptionists are more likely to work as part of a team under the supervision of a manager. Here, their duties may be restricted to purely reception tasks. Alternatively, they may specialize in a particular aspect of their organization's business, for example, law, or medicine, and therefore require specialist knowledge and skills to carry out their duties. (See article HOTEL RECEPTIONIST CLCI: IC).

WORK ENVIRONMENT

Reception areas vary depending on the organization. They are often located in light, airy, offices, though sometimes office environments can be small or cramped. Where the reception area is situated near a main entrance, doors may be frequently in use, which can make the area draughty and noisy. Most of the work is carried out sitting down at a desk or counter, although at busy times receptionists may be constantly on their feet

SKILLS AND INTERESTS

Receptionists should enjoy meeting people and caring for visitors' needs. They need to be confident individuals with a personable manner, clear speech and of neat appearance. Good interpersonal skills such as listening to people and understanding their requests are essential. A good memory for faces and names is an asset, so that returning visitors can be personally greeted by name. Receptionists need the ability to accurately remember and record verbal or written messages. They should have a methodical and efficient approach to their work. At times they need to be able to work under pressure, for example, when several people are demanding their attention at the same time. In these situations the receptionist needs the ability to remain calm. Receptionists sometimes need to be polite but firm when dealing with visitors/telephone callers who are angry or impatient.

ENTRY REQUIREMENTS

No formal academic qualifications are required although a good standard of general education is expected. A GCSE/S grade (A–E/1–5) pass in English (or equivalent subject) is desirable. However, the personal qualities of common sense, confidence, politeness and an ability to put people at their ease, are often regarded by employers as more important than specific qualifications.

Employers may require typing ability and familiarity with a word processor/computer. Qualifications in these skills are an advantage. Experience of using a telephone, and office equipment such as fax machines and photocopiers is useful. Proficiency in a foreign language may be required in some organizations.

TRAINING

Various employment-based training leading to certificates, diplomas and NVQs/SVQs are available. The Customer Service Lead Body (CSLB) is responsible for developing NVQ/SVQ standards. Awarding bodies include RSA, City & Guilds, BTEC, SQA and AMSPAR (Association of Medical Secretaries, Practice Managers, Administrators and Receptionists). Those who wish to follow any course of study should contact their local careers office, TEC/LEC, and/or local colleges of further education.

Training opportunities for young people including National Traineeships leading to NVQ/SVQ awards at Levels 1 and 2 may be available. Contact your local careers office, Jobcentre TEC/LEC for details. The type of training varies according to the employer, but normally includes business administration and word processing. Training is normally carried out in the workplace with day release at a local college.

Intermediate GNVQ/GSVQs in Business at Level II are available. These comprise four core units: business organization and employment, consumers and customers, financial and administrative support, and people in business organizations.

RSA offer a Certificate in Reception which is awarded on the successful completion of four units: reception – receive and direct visitors; visitor and staff liaison – provide support services for visitors; reception servicing – maintain service of reception; telephone services – using a variety of telephone services and paging systems. The Certificate in Reception can then form part of the work towards the Diploma in Reception which comprises a further eight units. The eight units are taken directly from the NVQ in Administration at Level 2. Candidates can opt to go on to achieve a full NVQ at Level 2, or take the Diploma as an integral part of an Administration NVQ programme.

NVQ/SVQs in Customer Service are available at Level 2 and 3. Level 2 covers the following units: operate service and delivery systems for customers; store, retrieve and supply information; develop and maintain positive working relationships with customers; solve problems for customers; improve service reliability for customers. Level 3 covers: maintain reliable customer service; communicate with customers; develop positive working relationships with customers; solve problems on behalf of customers; initiate and evaluate change to improve service to customers.

For details of qualifications in the catering and hospitality industry see article HOTEL RECEPTIONIST CLCI: IC.

AMSPAR offer two methods of achieving the Diploma in Health Service Reception. The traditional programme involves a written examination of 2_ hours with papers covering health and social services, communications/office practice and medical aspects and oral communication assessment plus two written assignments, first aid certificate and work placements.

NVQ Level 2 includes 14 units of competence – nine core units in Administration at Level 2, plus five AMSPAR specialist medical units covering health, safety and security in a clinical environment; patient care and support; maintain and operate appointment systems; ethical and legal requirements; medical terminology; first aid and work placements. For those working in the medical field and already employed as a general practice receptionist, AMSPAR offer short courses that are suitable as preparation for the first level Certificates in General

ADMINISTRATIVE/CLERICAL WORK: CAT

Practice Reception. AMSPAR also offer other related certificate and diploma courses.

SQA offer National Certificates in the following: Working in a Reception Area – which introduces students to the routine tasks that normally form part of the duties of reception personnel; Medical Reception and Records – designed for those wishing to prepare for employment as a medical receptionist in general medical practice; Reception Skills – for those dealing with callers and visitors to the workplace, which includes helping to route enquiries and maintain the reception area, and sending information using electronic equipment.

LATE ENTRY

There is no upper age limit. Employers sometimes prefer to recruit mature applicants with appropriate skills and experience gained in either clerical/administrative work, or jobs that involve work with the public.

OPPORTUNITIES

Opportunities occur for receptionists in all parts of the country and jobs are usually plentiful. Receptionists work in a wide range of organizations throughout industry and commerce, with most growth in the service industries. Employers include those in the public and private sectors: in businesses of all types, medical services, education, the health service and in local authorities. Opportunities exist for full-time and part-time work, job sharing and sometimes temporary work.

PAY AND CONDITIONS

Rates of pay vary depending on the employer and the location. Average salaries can start from £5,000 and rise to £12,500. Higher salaries are available in London and the South East.

Working hours are normally 9am to 5pm, Monday to Friday. In certain industries receptionists may be required to work shifts or at weekends, in which case, time off during the week is usually given. Benefits such as a pension scheme or subsidized meals may be offered. Some organizations provide a uniform, and a very few firms offer a dress or grooming allowance.

PROSPECTS

In general, opportunities for promotion, other than to head receptionist or supervisor, are few and only occur in large organizations. However, for those who are ambitious and prepared to undertake further training in related skills, such as information technology, there may be opportunities to move into other administrative areas. In addition, knowledge, experience and contacts gained in reception work can be useful to career development within an organization. It may also be possible to obtain greater responsibility/higher salary by changing employer.

RELATED OCCUPATIONS

Hotel receptionist, clerical assistant, personnel assistant, medical secretary, computer operator.

FURTHER INFORMATION

The Administration Standards Council*, 20 Bedfordbury, London WC2N 4LB, 0171 379 5080

Association of Medical Secretaries, Practice Managers, Administrators and Receptionists Limited*, Tavistock House North, Tavistock Square, London WC1H 9LN, 0171 387 6005

City and Guilds (C+G)*, I Giltspur Street, London EC1A 9DD, 0171 294 2468, http://www.city-and-guilds.co.uk

Customer Service Lead Body, The Brackens, London Road, Ascot, Berks SL5 8BJ, 01344 886223

Edexcel Foundation (incorporating BTEC)*, Stewart House, 32 Russell Square, London WC1B 5DN, 0171 393 4500, http://www.edexcel.org.uk

London Chamber of Commerce and Industry Examination Board*, Athena House, Station Road, Sidcup, Kent DA15 7BJ, 0181 302 0261, www.iccieb.org.uk

Pitman Qualifications*, 1 Giltspur Street, London EC1A 9DD, 0171 294 2471

RSA Examinations Board*, Westwood Way, Coventry CV4 8HS, 01203 470033

Scottish Qualifications Authority*, Hanover House, 24 Douglas Street, Glasgow G2 7NQ, 0141 248 7900

FURTHER READING

Leaflets are available from addresses marked*.

In the Careers Library classified under CAT.

INFORMATION TECHNOLOGY: CAV

1. **SYSTEMS ANALYST/DESIGNER (SYSTEMS INTEGRATOR) CLCI:CAV**
2. **SOFTWARE ENGINEER/ANALYST PROGRAMMER CLCI:CAV**
3. **NETWORK ENGINEER CLCI:CAV**
4. **DATABASE ADMINISTRATOR CLCI:CAV**
5. **WEBMASTER CLCI:CAV**
6. **MULTIMEDIA SPECIALIST CLCI:CAV**
7. **HELP DESK OPERATOR CLCI:CAV**

BACKGROUND INFORMATION

Information technology (IT) is increasingly important in all our lives, not least in the world of work. Modern businesses increasingly use IT for a wide range of activity, including financial management, design, stock control, sales, marketing, project management and communication. This expansion in the use of IT has led to a rapid growth in the opportunities for IT specialists. In 1997 it was estimated that over £40 billion was spent on IT in the UK. Approximately 26% of that was spent on staff costs.

The main employers of specialist IT staff are the organizations that use IT and have their own computing departments, that is, most sizeable organizations. Not all large organizations, though, wish to manage their own IT systems. A recent trend has been for some organizations to contract out the running of their IT systems to 'facilities management' companies, which are specialist IT companies that run other companies' computer departments. Some specialist IT staff are also employed by companies that manufacture hardware, software and other IT equipment. Some work for companies that offer a consultancy service. Yet others work for bureaux, which are companies that undertake IT work for clients outside the clients' premises. Self-employment also attracts a number of experienced IT personnel.

The computer industry is constantly developing and the rate of change is increasingly rapid. Such is the pace of change that it is impossible to predict future developments in job terms but it seems clear that there will be increasing career opportunities within IT. Many of these opportunities, though, will need more than just technical IT expertise. They will also need effective communication skills and an appreciation of business.

NB: When reading these articles it should be noted that there are no standard definitions for jobs in the IT industry and many job titles are used interchangeably.

1. SYSTEMS ANALYST/DESIGNER (SYSTEMS INTEGRATOR) (CAV)

THE WORK

Systems analysts/designers investigate and analyse a business problem, design a suitable computer system to deal with the problem, then set up and test the system. This process is known as systems integration, and systems analysts and designers may be known as systems integrators. Systems analysis and systems design may be the responsibility of one person or the roles may be separated.

Systems analysts begin by conducting a feasibility study, that is, they investigate whether an existing IT system can be modified or if a new system will be needed. An important consideration is whether the benefits to the client will outweigh the costs.

If the feasibility study is favourable, the analyst then spends time talking to relevant staff. They observe how things are done within the organization and develop an understanding of the client's business and information requirements.

The analyst draws up outline proposals for the client's approval. If they are agreed, the analyst then draws up more specific proposals, including detailed costs, benefits to the client, staffing implications and training needs. When the client gives final approval the next step is to design and create in detail the recommended system. A systems analyst may do this if a project or system is small, otherwise this is the responsibility of a system designer. Whether or not a designer is involved, the analyst continues to oversee the project, liaising between the client and the designer, programmers and other IT specialists concerned. This involvement continues until the project has been successfully completed..

Systems designers are responsible for providing a detailed plan for implementing the agreed system. An important consideration for the designer is the cost of installing and running the new system. The designer oversees the installation of the system and its testing. The designer may write a manual for the new system and be involved in training staff in the use of the system.

WORK ENVIRONMENT

Systems analysts and designers work in an office environment, in clean, light surroundings. Although some of their work is carried out at their own offices, much of their time is spent on clients' premises. This may involve local travel or being away from home for lengthy periods of time. The ability to drive may be essential for some jobs.

SKILLS AND INTERESTS

Systems analysts and designers should have a high level of information technology knowledge and skill, as they need to be expert in both hardware and software. It is essential that they keep up to date with technological changes in both hardware and software and are prepared to re-train when necessary.

The ability to get on with people easily and well is essential. They need good communication skills, both spoken and written. They ought to be able to listen carefully to clients to be able to understand their requirements. They must be willing to gain an understanding of the user's business and be able to see things from the user's perspective. They should be able to explain their proposals in a way that users can easily understand.

A persuasive manner is helpful, as are good negotiation skills. It is important that they can express themselves clearly, both to people who are IT specialists and to those who have little knowledge of computers. Writing skills are necessary when presenting proposals to a client and writing instructions for users.

Systems analysts and designers need to be capable of working in a team, as well as able to work independently. They should be capable of logical, analytical thought and

INFORMATION TECHNOLOGY: CAV

enjoy solving problems. They must be able to meet agreed deadlines and, if working on several projects, have the ability to prioritize their work. They must be willing to undertake any travel that their job involves.

ENTRY REQUIREMENTS

Entrants to systems analyst posts have usually had a few years' experience of programming. Most have a degree or higher national award, though not necessarily in a computer related discipline. Systems designers usually enter with a degree in computer science, electronics, maths or physics. Some entrants to systems analysis and design have a postgraduate computing qualification.

The computer industry is flexible in the qualifications it accepts from people it considers suitable. For the more technical, scientific areas of IT, employers usually require computer science, electronics, maths or physics qualifications. For other types of work, such as programming, it will accept applicants whose degrees and higher national awards are computer related as well as those whose qualifications are unrelated to computing.

Entry to degree courses is with a minimum of two A levels/three H grades plus three GCSEs/S grades (A–C/1–3) in other subjects, although three A levels/four H grades are required for some courses. English and maths are usually required at GCSE/S grade (A–C/1–3) for computing related degree courses. A level/H grade maths is often required or preferred for entry to the more theoretical degree courses, such as computer science and software engineering. A level/H grade maths is usually required for entry to electronics, maths and physics degrees, while A level/H grade physics is usually required for physics degrees and preferred for electronics degrees. Alternative qualifications are accepted for entry to degree courses, such as a BTEC/SQA national award and Advanced GNVQ/GSVQ Level III.

BTEC/SQA higher national awards require a minimum of one A level/two H grades and three GCSEs/S grades (A–C/1–3) in other subjects, usually including English and maths. Alternative qualifications are accepted for entry, such as a BTEC/SQA national award and Advanced GNVQ/GSVQ Level III.

Entry to postgraduate computing courses is with a good class first degree. The first degree can be in a computing related discipline or in a discipline unrelated to computing.

The IT industry is more flexible than most other industries. It can be possible to enter computing work at a basic level and work towards more responsible posts, including those in different areas of IT. A first step for some can be a full-time college course:

– BTEC national diploma in such as computer studies or information technology. Entry is usually with four GCSEs (A–C), or a BTEC first award, or Intermediate GNVQ; or

– SQA national certificate modules in information technology. There are no set entry requirements. Applicants should check with individual colleges, which may set their own requirements, as they wish to be satisfied that students are able to benefit from the courses; or

– Advanced GNVQ/GSVQ Level III in Information Technology. Entry requirements vary but are often a minimum of four GCSEs/S grades (A–C/1–3) or Intermediate GNVQ/GSVQ Level II.

Some young people may seek to enter computing work through Modern Apprenticeships and National Traineeships (part of the Skillseekers Initiative in Scotland). There are no set entry requirements but employers will want to be sure that applicants can benefit from the training.

TRAINING

Degree courses in computer science, electronics, maths and physics are offered at many colleges and most universities throughout the UK. They last three years full-time or four years on a sandwich basis, where one year is spent on placement with an employer. (In Scotland, degree courses usually last three or four years full-time and four or five years on a sandwich basis.) Some universities offer MEng degree courses which take an additional year. These courses involve study in more depth and breadth. Degree courses can also be studied part-time.

It is possible to study a degree in computer science, electronics, maths or physics on its own or to combine it with study of another of those subjects, or of an unrelated subject such as a modern foreign language or business studies.

Many universities and colleges throughout the UK offer BTEC/SQA higher national diploma (HND) and higher national certificate (HNC) courses relevant to computing, such as computer studies, computing, information systems, information technology and software engineering. Most HND courses last two years full-time, while some last three years on a sandwich basis. HNC courses are offered on a part-time basis, usually over two years. Successful completion of an HND or HNC can lead to the second year of a degree course.

Many universities offer postgraduate courses concerned with systems analysis and design. Courses usually last one year full-time or two years part-time. Some courses are designed for graduates with a degree in computing or a related discipline. Other courses are known as conversion courses and enable graduates in disciplines unrelated to computing to train in systems analysis and design.

BTEC national diploma courses in computer studies and information technology are offered by many local colleges and usually last two years.

SQA national certificate courses in information technology are offered by a number of local colleges and usually last one year full-time.

Advanced GNVQ/GSVQ Level III courses in information technology are offered by some schools and many local colleges and usually last two years.

Modern Apprenticeships involve work-based training leading to a relevant NVQ/SVQ at Level 3. There is no set length of time for Modern Apprenticeship training but it is likely to be at least three years. National Trainees are trained in a similar way to Modern Apprentices but to NVQ/SVQ Level 2. Training normally takes around two years. Contact local careers offices, Jobcentres, or TECs/LECs for information on Modern Apprenticeships and National Traineeships.

There are a number of professional qualifications that systems analysts and designers can work towards, including those of The British Computer Society (BCS), the Institute for the Management of Information Systems (IMIS) and National Computing Centre Ltd. They may also work towards NVQs/SVQs at Levels 2 to 4.

INFORMATION TECHNOLOGY: CAV

LATE ENTRY

There is no set upper age limit for entry to this work but attitudes to mature entrants vary between employers.

Mature applicants may be accepted onto university and college courses without the usual entry requirements, particularly if they have relevant experience and/or qualifications.

Many local colleges offer Access courses for adults who wish to study for a degree or higher national award but who do not have the necessary qualifications. Courses usually last one year full-time or one to two years part-time with day and/or evening attendance.

OPPORTUNITIES

Systems analysts and designers are employed by computer manufacturers and software houses. They are also employed by companies specializing in systems integration. Some work for consultancy companies.

There is growing demand for systems analysts and designers. Opportunities arise throughout the UK but there is a concentration in London and the south east of England. Vacancies are advertised in the local and national press, in *Computing* and *Computer Weekly*, and increasingly through the Internet.

It may be possible to work abroad for a UK company that has overseas facilities or works on projects abroad. There are also opportunities to work for companies based in Europe, the Middle East, USA and Australia.

PAY AND CONDITIONS

The standard working week for most systems analysts and designers is 37 to 40 hours, Monday to Friday. Evening and/or weekend work may be necessary to meet deadlines or to deal with problems that have arisen. Some systems analysts and designers also have their working days extended by travel to and from clients' premises.

There are no set pay-scales for systems analysts and designers. Salaries tend to range from £20,000 to £40,000 a year.

PROSPECTS

Systems analysts and designers may progress within their organizations to more senior posts, such as senior or principal analyst or designer, then on to project manager. They may eventually manage the IT systems for an employer.

Movement between employers is common in IT and some systems analysts and designers take this route to gain more experience, responsibility and reward.

Experienced systems analysts and designers can become self-employed and offer their services on a contract or consultancy basis. There are opportunities for working in IT training and in journalism and technical writing.

RELATED OCCUPATIONS

Software engineer, analyst programmer, database administrator, network engineer, webmaster, multimedia programmer, help desk operator.

FURTHER INFORMATION AND READING

Please see article 7. HELP DESK OPERATOR.

2. SOFTWARE ENGINEER/ANALYST PROGRAMMER (CAV)

THE WORK

Software engineers/analyst programmers are responsible for designing software (computer programs).

Traditionally software engineers worked on the most complex software, such as computer operating systems or software used to control complicated technological equipment, eg automated engineering equipment, while analyst programmers worked on business software. The distinction is less clear now and the term 'software engineer' is increasingly used to describe both types of work.

Software engineers discuss with users wanting a new or improved system or program to find out exactly what they want from it. To do this successfully they must develop a thorough understanding of the user's business and information requirements and analyse existing systems to see how far they may be modified.

Software engineers prepare a specification for the user's approval. This details the proposals, including the computers and other hardware that are required, the proposed program, costs and time-scales. When the specification has been approved, the software engineer writes the program, often using computer-aided software engineering tools. On sizeable programs a team may work together on the programming. Software engineers test the program, install it, retest it and deal with any bugs (problems in the program) that may arise.

They write up details of the program, write instructions for users and may train staff in the use of the program.

Some software engineers may be responsible for all the tasks outlined above. Others may specialize in programming, systems analysis or systems design, or act in a support role.

WORK ENVIRONMENT

Software engineers work in an office environment, in clean, light surroundings. Those working for large users are usually based at one site but those working for consultancy companies visit clients. This may involve local travel or being away from home for variable periods of time. The ability to drive may be essential for some jobs.

SKILLS AND INTERESTS

Software engineers should have a high level of information technology knowledge and skill, as they need to be expert in both hardware and software. It is essential that they keep up to date with technological changes in both hardware and software and are prepared to re-train when necessary.

They need good communication skills, both spoken and written. They must be able to listen carefully to users and be able to understand their requirements. They must be willing to gain an understanding of the user's business and be able to see things from the user's perspective. They must be capable of explaining their proposals clearly to users. Clarity is also important when expressing themselves to people who may have little knowledge of computer hardware and software. Writing skills are necessary when presenting proposals to a client and writing instructions for users.

INFORMATION TECHNOLOGY: CAV

Software engineers need to be capable of working in a team, as well as being able to work independently. They should be capable of logical, analytical thought and enjoy solving problems. They must be able to meet agreed deadlines and, if working on several projects, have the ability to prioritize their work. They must be willing to undertake any travel their job involves.

ENTRY REQUIREMENTS

Entry to software engineering is usually with a degree in software engineering, electronics or computer science. Entry to such degrees is with a minimum of two A levels/three H grades plus three GCSEs/S grades (A–C/1–3) in other subjects, usually including English and maths. Three A levels/four H grades are required for some courses. A level/H grade maths is often required or preferred, as is A level/H grade physics, for entry to electronics degrees. Alternative qualifications are accepted for entry to degree courses, such as a relevant BTEC/SQA national award and Advanced GNVQ/GSVQ Level III.

NB: where the term software engineering is used loosely to describe systems programming, entry is usually with a computing related degree or with experience as an applications programmer. Where software engineering is used to describe applications programming, entry can be with a degree or higher national award in any discipline.

Entry to software engineering can also be with a higher national award. BTEC/SQA higher national awards require a minimum of one A level/two H grades and three GCSEs/S grades (A–C/1–3), usually including English and maths. Alternative qualifications are accepted for entry, such as a BTEC/SQA national award and Advanced GNVQ/GSVQ Level III.

Some entrants to this work have a postgraduate computing qualification. Entry to postgraduate courses is with a good class first degree. The first degree can be in a computing related discipline or in a discipline unrelated to computing.

The computer industry is more flexible than most other industries. It can be possible to enter computing work at a basic level and work towards more responsible posts, including those in different areas of IT. A first step for some can be a full-time college course:

– BTEC national award in such as computer studies or information technology. Entry is usually with four GCSEs (A–C), or a BTEC first award, or Intermediate GNVQ; or

– SQA national certificate modules in information technology. There are no set entry requirements. Applicants should check with individual colleges, which may set their own requirements, as they wish to be satisfied that students are able to benefit from the courses; or

– Advanced GNVQ/GSVQ Level III in Information Technology. Entry requirements vary but are often a minimum of four GCSEs/S grades (A–C/1–3) or Intermediate GNVQ/GSVQ Level II.

Some young people may seek to enter computing work through Modern Apprenticeships and National Traineeships (part of the Skillseekers Initiative in Scotland). There are no set entry requirements but employers will want to be sure that applicants can benefit from the training.

TRAINING

Degree courses in software engineering, electronics and computer science are offered at many colleges and universities throughout the UK. They last three years full-time or four years on a sandwich basis, where one year is spent on placement with an employer. In Scotland, degree courses usually last three or four years full-time and four or five years on a sandwich basis. Some universities offer MEng degree courses which take an additional year. These courses involve study in more depth and breadth. Degree courses are also offered part-time.

It is possible to study a degree in software engineering or computer science on its own or to combine it with study of another subject, such as a modern foreign language, business studies or electronics. Similarly, electronics may be studied on its own or in combination with another subject.

Many universities and colleges throughout the UK offer BTEC/SQA higher national diploma (HND) and higher national certificate (HNC) courses in software engineering but few offer computer science. Most HND courses last two years full-time, while some last three years on a sandwich basis. HNC courses are offered on a part-time basis, usually over two years. Successful completion of an HND or HNC can lead to the second year of a degree course.

Many universities offer postgraduate courses in software engineering. Courses usually last one year full-time or two years part-time. Some courses are designed for graduates with a degree in computing or a related discipline. Other courses are known as conversion courses and enable graduates in disciplines unrelated to computing to train in software engineering.

BTEC national diploma courses in computer studies and information technology are offered by many local colleges and usually last two years.

SQA national certificate courses in information technology are offered by a number of local colleges and usually last one year full-time.

Advanced GNVQ/GSVQ Level III courses are offered by some schools and many local colleges and usually last two years.

Modern Apprenticeships involve work-based training leading to a relevant NVQ/SVQ at Level 3. There is no set length of time for Modern Apprenticeship training but it is likely to be at least three years. National Trainees are trained in a similar way to Modern Apprentices but to NVQ/SVQ Level 2. Training normally takes around two years. Contact local careers offices, Jobcentres, or TECs/LECs for information on Modern Apprenticeships and National Traineeships.

There are a number of professional qualifications that software engineers can work towards, including those of The British Computer Society (BCS), the Institute for the Management of Information Systems (IMIS) and National Computing Centre Ltd. They may also work towards NVQs/SVQs at Levels 2 to 4.

LATE ENTRY

There is no set upper age limit for entry to this work but attitudes to mature entrants vary between employers.

Mature applicants may be accepted onto university and college courses without the usual entry requirements, particularly if they have relevant experience and/or qualifications.

Many local colleges offer Access courses for adults who wish to study for a degree or higher national award but

INFORMATION TECHNOLOGY: CAV

who do not have the necessary qualifications. Courses usually last one year full-time or one to two years part-time with day and/or evening attendance.

OPPORTUNITIES

Software engineers are employed by a wide range of large organizations that are computer users; this includes a wide variety of manufacturing companies, retailers, gas, electricity and oil companies, financial organizations – such as banks, building societies and insurance companies – hospitals, educational institutions, transport companies, the Armed Forces, the Civil Service, local government and the media industry, including newspapers, television and radio companies.

They are also employed by computer manufacturers and software houses. Some work for consultancy companies.

There is continuing demand for software engineers. Opportunities arise throughout the UK but there is a concentration in London and the south east of England. Vacancies are advertised in the local and national press, in Computing and *Computer Weekly,* and increasingly through the Internet.

It may be possible to work abroad for a UK company that has overseas facilities or works on projects abroad. There are also opportunities with companies based in Europe, the Middle East, USA and Australia.

PAY AND CONDITIONS

The standard working week for most software engineers is 37 to 40 hours, Monday to Friday. Evening and/or weekend work may be necessary to meet deadlines or to deal with problems that have arisen. Some software engineers may also have their working days extended by travel to and from clients' premises.

There are no set pay-scales for software engineers. They tend to receive at least £16,000 a year on entry. Most software engineers earn between £22,000 and £35,000 a year

PROSPECTS

Software engineers may progress within their organization to senior, team leader and project manager. They may eventually manage the IT systems for an employer.

Movement between employers is common in IT and some software engineers take this route to gain more experience, responsibility and reward.

Experienced software engineers can become self-employed and offer their services on a contract or consultancy basis. There are opportunities for working in IT training and in journalism and technical writing.

RELATED OCCUPATIONS

Systems analyst, systems designer, systems integrator, network engineer, database administrator, webmaster, multimedia programmer, help desk operator.

FURTHER INFORMATION AND READING

Please see article 7. HELP DESK OPERATOR.

3. NETWORK ENGINEER (CAV)

THE WORK

Network engineers are responsible for installing and maintaining networks. In some companies they are known as network managers, controllers or administrators.

A network is a system of computers and other communications equipment that is linked to exchange information. Networks are either local area networks (LANs), which link offices in one building or branches of a company, or wide area networks (WANs), which connect different premises across a region, a country or internationally.

The importance of networks is that they enable staff of an organization to have access to common information, transfer files electronically, communicate by electronic mail (e-mail) and have access to the Internet and the World Wide Web.

Network engineers are responsible initially for designing a network system, which includes both mainframe computers and PCs, other hardware, software and the communication systems for linking the computers. This needs an understanding of hardware, software and electronics. Network engineers have discussions with users to find out their requirements. They advise on the potential uses and benefits of a network system and the costs involved in installing a system and running it. When the user has given approval, the network engineer may select the appropriate equipment, install it and test it.

Security is essential in network systems. Network engineers may write programs that include passwords to make sure only authorised users are allowed access to the network. Network engineers usually train staff in the use of the network. Some engineers work in a support role, diagnosing the cause of faults reported by network users and correcting them; this can involve faults arising in hardware, software or cabling systems.

WORK ENVIRONMENT

Network engineers work in an office environment, in clean, light surroundings.

Those working for large users may be based at one site or have to travel between sites. Those working for manufacturers and specialist computer network companies visit clients. This may involve local travel or being away from home for variable periods of time. The ability to drive may be essential for some jobs.

SKILLS AND INTERESTS

Network engineers should enjoy working with computers and have a high level of knowledge and skill in hardware, software and electronics. It is essential that they keep up to date with developments in these areas and are prepared to re-train when necessary.

They need good communication skills. They must be able to understand the user's requirements. This includes the ability to gain an awareness of the user's business in order to suggest how best a network system can be used to benefit the user. It is important that network engineers can express themselves clearly both to IT specialists and to those who may know little about computers.

They should be capable of logical, analytical thought and enjoy solving problems. They must be able to prioritize their work. They need to be willing to undertake any travel that their job involves.

ENTRY REQUIREMENTS

There is no set entry requirement but a computer science and/or electronic engineering degree or higher national award is excellent preparation. Entry to such degrees is with a minimum of two A levels/three H grades plus three GCSEs/S grades (A–C/1–3) in other subjects, usually including English and maths. Three A levels/four H grades are required for some courses. A level/H grade maths is often required or preferred for computer science degrees while A level/H grade maths is required and physics required or preferred for entry to electronics degrees. Alternative qualifications are accepted for entry to degree courses, such as a relevant BTEC/SQA national award and Advanced GNVQ/GSVQ Level III.

BTEC/SQA higher national awards require a minimum of one A level/two H grades and three GCSEs/S grades (A–C/1–3) in other subjects, usually including English and maths. A level/H grade maths or physics is usually preferred for electronic engineering courses. Alternative qualifications are accepted for entry, such as a relevant BTEC/SQA national award and Advanced GNVQ/GSVQ Level III.

Some entrants have a postgraduate computing qualification. Entry to postgraduate courses is with a good class first degree. The first degree can be in a computing or related discipline or in a discipline unrelated to computing.

Those seeking to enter this type of work may take short courses offered by netware manufacturers such as Novell or Microsoft.

The computer industry is more flexible than most other industries. It can be possible to enter computing work at a basic level and work towards more responsible posts, including those in different areas of IT. A first step for some can be a full-time college course:

– BTEC national award in such as computer studies or information technology. Entry is usually with four GCSEs (A–C), or a BTEC first award, or Intermediate GNVQ; or

– SQA national certificate modules in information technology. There are no set entry requirements. Applicants should check with individual colleges, which may set their own requirements, as they wish to be satisfied that students are able to benefit from the courses.

Some young people may seek to enter computing work through Modern Apprenticeships and National Traineeships (part of the Skillseekers Initiative in Scotland). There are no set entry requirements but employers will want to be sure that applicants can benefit from the training.

TRAINING

Degree courses in computer science and electronic engineering are offered at many colleges and universities throughout the UK. They last three years full-time or four years on a sandwich basis, where one year is spent on placement with an employer. (Degree courses in Scotland usually last three or four years full-time and four or five years on a sandwich basis.) Some universities offer MEng degree courses which take an additional year. These courses involve study in more depth and breadth. Degree courses can also be studied part-time.

It is possible to study computer science or electronic engineering on their own or to combine them with each other or with study of another subject, such as a modern foreign language or business studies.

Many universities and colleges throughout the UK offer BTEC/SQA higher national diploma (HND) and higher national certificate (HNC) courses in electronic engineering but few offer computer science. Most HND courses last two years full-time, while some last three years on a sandwich basis. HNC courses are offered on a part-time basis, usually over two years. Successful completion of an HND or HNC can lead to the second year of a degree course.

Some universities offer postgraduate courses relevant to network engineering. Courses usually last one year full-time or two years part-time. Some courses are designed for graduates with a degree in computing or a related discipline. Other courses are known as conversion courses and enable graduates in disciplines unrelated to computing to train for work related to network engineering.

BTEC national diploma courses in computer studies and information technology are offered by many local colleges and usually last two years.

SQA national certificate courses in information technology are offered by a number of local colleges and usually last one year full-time.

Advanced GNVQ/GSVQ Level III courses in information technology and engineering are offered by some schools and many local colleges and usually last two years.

Modern Apprenticeships involve work based training working towards a relevant NVQ/SVQ at Level 3. There is no set length of time for Modern Apprenticeship training but it is likely to be at least three years. National Trainees are trained in a similar way to Modern Apprentices but to NVQ/SVQ Level 2. Training normally takes around two years. Contact local careers offices, Jobcentres or TECs/LECs for information on Modern Apprenticeships and National Traineeships.

There are a number of professional qualifications that network engineers can work towards, including those of The British Computer Society (BCS) and National Computing Centre Ltd. They can also work towards NVQs/SVQs at Levels 2 to 4.

LATE ENTRY

There is no set upper age limit for entry to this work but attitudes to mature entrants vary between employers.

Mature applicants may be accepted onto university and college courses without the usual entry requirements, particularly if they have relevant experience and/or qualifications.

Many local colleges offer Access courses for adults who wish to study for a degree or higher national award but who do not have the necessary qualifications. Courses usually last one year full-time or one to two years part-time with day and/or evening attendance.

OPPORTUNITIES

Network engineers are employed by a wide range of large organizations that are computer users; this includes a wide variety of manufacturing companies, retailers, gas, electricity and oil companies, financial organizations – such as banks, building societies and insurance companies – hospitals, educational institutions, transport companies, the

INFORMATION TECHNOLOGY: CAV

Armed Forces, the Civil Service, local government and the media industry, including newspapers, television and radio companies.

They are also employed by manufacturers of computers and associated equipment and by companies that specialize in the supply, installation and servicing of computer networks.

The use of computer networks is growing and there is currently a shortage of skilled network engineers. Opportunities arise throughout the UK, although there is a concentration in London and the south east of England. Vacancies are advertised in the local and national press, in Computing, *Computer Weekly* and *Electronics Weekly*, and increasingly through the Internet.

It may be possible to work abroad for a UK company that has overseas facilities or works on projects abroad. There are also opportunities with companies based in Europe, the Middle East, USA and Australia.

PAY AND CONDITIONS

Most network engineers work standard office hours (37 to 40), Monday to Friday. They may have to work outside these hours when installing systems in order to cause least disruption to the user. They may be on call if breakdowns occur outside their normal hours. Those working for specialist computer network companies may have their working days lengthened by travel to and from clients' premises.

There are no set pay-scales for network engineers. They tend to receive at least £16,000 a year on entry and can earn in excess of £30,000 a year.

PROSPECTS

Network engineers may progress within their organization to more senior posts, such as project leader and departmental manager. Movement between employers is common in IT and some network engineers take this route to gain more experience, responsibility and reward.

Experienced network engineers can become self-employed and offer their services on a contract or consultancy basis. There are opportunities for working in IT training and in journalism and technical writing.

RELATED OCCUPATIONS

Software engineer, systems analyst, systems designer, systems integrator, database administrator, electronics engineer (incorporated), electronics engineer (chartered), help desk operator.

FURTHER INFORMATION AND READING

Please see article 7. HELP DESK OPERATOR.

4. DATABASE ADMINISTRATOR (CAV)

THE WORK

Database administrators are responsible for managing and supervising computer databases. Databases are large stores of information that are made easily accessible through the use of computers. Databases are used by many organizations to store information on, such as, customers, stock or accounts. Database administrators may be known in some organizations as database administration managers, database controllers or information centre managers.

Database administrators make sure a database is complete, accurate and kept up to date; this involves ensuring staff load information accurately and on schedule. They are responsible for having reliable back-up systems in place, in case of breakdown or loss of data.

Security of information is important. It must be accessible only to authorized people, so administrators have to make sure appropriate access control facilities are built into the system.

Administrators provide training to staff using the database. This includes instruction on how to access the database, input information, conduct searches, maintain security, report problems and on the need to comply with the Data Protection Act.

An important part of administrators' work is solving problems that may arise, whether from breakdown, loss of data or problems experienced by users of the database.

Administrators are responsible for recommending when a database system needs altering or expanding. This involves close liaison with the user and working with database programmers and IT project managers.

WORK ENVIRONMENT

Database administrators work in an office environment, in clean, light surroundings.

Those working for specialist information technology bureaux that run database services for a number of clients, visit clients. This may involve local travel or being away from home for variable periods of time. The ability to drive may be essential for some jobs.

SKILLS AND INTERESTS

Database administrators should have a high level of information technology knowledge and skill, as they need to be expert in both the hardware and software used for their databases. They must keep up to date with technological changes in both hardware and software and be prepared to re-train when necessary.

Database administrators should enjoy supporting others in their work, as users rely on that support to make the best use of their databases. Administrators need good communication skills, both spoken and written. They must be able to listen carefully to users to understand what is required of the database. They need to gain a thorough understanding of the user's business and be able to see things from the user's perspective. They should be capable of explaining the system to users clearly and patiently and dealing with their queries and problems. They should also be able to advise analysts who design new systems.

Problem solving is a major part of a database administrator's job, so they must like tackling technical problems and solving them.

ENTRY REQUIREMENTS

There is no set entry requirement for database administrators. Some administrators progress into this work from the business side of an organization. Most, though, have experience in systems programming or systems design and often have a degree or higher national award.

INFORMATION TECHNOLOGY: CAV

Degree entry is with a minimum of two A levels/three H grades plus three GCSEs/S grades (A–C/1–3) in other subjects, although three A levels/four H grades are required for some courses. English and maths are usually required at GCSE/S grade (A–C/1–3) for computing related degree courses. A level/H grade maths is often required or preferred for entry to the more theoretical degree courses, such as computer science and software engineering. Alternative qualifications are accepted for entry to degree courses, such as a BTEC/SQA national award and Advanced GNVQ/GSVQ Level III.

BTEC/SQA higher national awards require a minimum of one A level/two H grades and three GCSEs/S grades (A–C/1–3) in other subjects, usually including English and maths. Alternative qualifications are accepted for entry, such as a BTEC/SQA national award and Advanced GNVQ/GSVQ Level III.

Some entrants to this type of work have a postgraduate computing qualification. Entry to postgraduate courses is with a good class first degree. The degree can be in a computing related discipline or in a discipline unrelated to computing.

The computer industry is more flexible than most other industries. It can be possible to enter computing work at a basic level and work towards more responsible posts, including those in different areas of IT. A first step for some can be a full-time college course:

– BTEC national award in such as computer studies or information technology. Entry is usually with four GCSEs (A–C), or a BTEC first award, or Intermediate GNVQ; or

– SQA national certificate modules in information technology. There are no set entry requirements. Applicants should check with individual colleges, which may set their own requirements, as they wish to be satisfied that students are able to benefit from the courses; or

– Advanced GNVQ/GSVQ Level III in Information Technology. Entry requirements vary but are often a minimum of four GCSEs/S grades (A–C/1–3) or Intermediate GNVQ/GSVQ Level II.

Some young people may seek to enter computing work through Modern Apprenticeships and National Traineeships (part of the Skillseekers Initiative in Scotland). There are no set entry requirements but employers will want to be sure that applicants can benefit from the training.

TRAINING

Degree courses relating to computing are offered at many colleges and universities throughout the UK. There are many different titles for these degree courses, including computing science, computing, systems analysis, software engineering and information technology. They have many similarities but there are marked differences between courses, so it is important to check course content carefully.

It is possible to study a computer related degree on its own or to combine it with study of another subject, such as a modern foreign language, business studies or electronics.

Most degree courses last three years full-time (four in Scotland) or four years (five years in Scotland) if taken on a sandwich basis, where one year is spent on placement with an employer. Some universities offer MEng degree courses which take an additional year. These courses involve study in more depth and breadth. Some degree courses can be studied part-time.

Many universities and colleges throughout the UK offer BTEC/SQA higher national diploma (HND) and higher national certificate (HNC) courses relevant to computing, such as computer studies, computing, information systems, information technology and software engineering. Most HND courses last two years full-time, while some last three years on a sandwich basis. HNC courses are offered on a part-time basis, usually over two years. Successful completion of an HND or HNC can lead to the second year of a degree course.

Many universities offer postgraduate courses relevant to computing. Courses usually last one year full-time or two years part-time. Some courses are designed for graduates with a degree in computing or a related discipline. Other courses are known as conversion courses and enable graduates in disciplines unrelated to computing to train for work related to network engineering.

BTEC national diploma courses in computer studies and information technology are offered by many local colleges and usually last two years.

SQA national certificate courses in information technology are offered by a number of local colleges and usually last one year full-time.

Advanced GNVQ/GSVQ Level III courses in Information Technology are offered by some schools and many local colleges and usually last two years.

Modern Apprenticeships involve work-based training leading to a relevant NVQ/SVQ at Level 3. There is no set length of time for Modern Apprenticeship training but it is likely to be at least three years. National Trainees are trained in a similar way to Modern Apprentices but to NVQ/SVQ Level 2. Training normally takes around two years. Contact local careers offices, Jobcentres or TECs/LECs for information on Modern Apprenticeships and National Traineeships.

There are a number of professional qualifications that database administrators can work towards, including those of The British Computer Society (BCS), the Institute for the Management of Information Systems and National Computing Centre Ltd. They may also work towards NVQs/SVQs at Levels 2 to 4.

LATE ENTRY

There is no set upper age limit for entry to this work but attitudes to mature entrants vary between employers.

Mature applicants may be accepted onto university and college courses without the usual entry requirements, particularly if they have relevant experience and/or qualifications.

Many local colleges offer Access courses for adults who wish to study for a degree or higher national award but who do not have the necessary qualifications. Courses usually last one year full-time or one to two years part-time with day and/or evening attendance.

OPPORTUNITIES

Database administrators work for a wide range of employers, including manufacturing companies, retailers, gas, electricity and oil companies, financial organizations – such as banks, building societies and insurance companies – hospitals, educational institutions, transport companies, the Armed Forces, the Civil Service, local government and the media industry, including newspapers, television and radio companies.

INFORMATION TECHNOLOGY: CAV

Some database administrators work for specialist information technology bureaux, which provide a database service to clients.

The demand for database administrators is increasing. Opportunities arise throughout the UK, although there is a concentration in London and the south east of England. Vacancies are advertised in the local and national press, in *Computing* and *Computer Weekly,* and increasingly through the Internet.

It may be possible to work abroad, either for UK companies or for companies based overseas.

PAY AND CONDITIONS

Most database administrators work standard office hours (37 to 40), Monday to Friday. They may be on call if breakdowns occur outside their normal hours. Those working for bureaux may have their working days lengthened by travel to and from clients' premises.

There is no set pay-scale for database administrators. Salaries vary between employers but they may earn between £25,000 and £40,000 a year.

PROSPECTS

Movement between employers is common in IT and some database administrators take this route to gain more experience, responsibility and reward.

Some administrators transfer to other areas of computing work, such as systems analysis. Others seek to progress into IT management or general management. Experienced database administrators may use their expertise to work on a contract basis. There are opportunities for working in IT training and in journalism and technical writing.

RELATED OCCUPATIONS

Systems analyst, systems designer, systems integrator, software engineer, information scientist, help desk operator.

FURTHER INFORMATION AND READING

Please see article 7. HELP DESK OPERATOR.

5. WEBMASTER (CAV)

THE WORK

Webmasters set up and run web sites on the Internet.

The Internet is a world-wide network that links over 50 million computers by telephone and cable. The World Wide Web, often known simply as the 'web', is a collection of on-line documents accessible to users of the Internet. Web sites are used by organizations for various purposes. An increasing number of commercial organizations are using the web to advertise their goods and services, some also enabling people to buy those goods and services via the Internet. Other organizations, such as professional bodies, universities and colleges and charitable bodies use the web to promote their area of activity.

Webmasters begin by having discussions with a client. They advise on linking existing systems into the Internet and on how the Internet may be used to the client's benefit. They advise on what could be included on the web site, including possible use of text, pictures, sound, video clips and potential links to other sites. They provide details of the set-up costs and ongoing costs.

Webmasters may supervise web authors who design and program the pages that make up the web site, or they may themselves do the designing and programming. They test the pages, then seek the client's approval for them. When the client has given approval, the webmaster uploads the pages to a server – a computer that holds pages of information on the web – and installs the Internet software onto the client's computers. They train the client in the use of the system.

It is important that web sites are kept up to date. Webmasters liaise with clients to check when updating is necessary and then program changes into the site. They deal with any problems that may arise from the site.

Some webmasters do this work full-time for one employer. Others work full-time for one employer but have other computing duties in addition to their work with the web. Yet others are contracted by a number of organizations to set up sites and maintain them. These independent webmasters may also offer their expertise to organizations for training and consultancy purposes.

WORK ENVIRONMENT

Webmasters work indoors in an office environment, in clean, light surroundings.

Those working for large users are usually based at one site but those working freelance or for consultancy companies visit clients. This may involve local travel or, occasionally, time away from home. The ability to drive may be essential for some jobs.

SKILLS AND INTERESTS

Webmasters should enjoy working with computers, have a high level of programming skill and a thorough appreciation of how the web operates. It is essential that they keep up to date with technological changes and are prepared to re-train when necessary.

It is important that webmasters are able to get on easily and well with people. They need good communication skills, both spoken and written. They should be able to listen carefully to users to understand their requirements. They must be willing to gain an understanding of a users' business and be able to see things from the users' perspective. They need to be able to explain clearly what benefits the user may get from having a web site. A persuasive manner is very helpful.

It is important that webmasters can express themselves clearly to people who may have little knowledge of computers. Writing skills are necessary for presenting proposals to a client and writing pages for sites. Ability with figures is needed to calculate the set-up and ongoing costs of a site.

Webmasters should be capable of logical, analytical thought and enjoy solving problems. They must be able to meet agreed deadlines and, if working on several projects, have the ability to prioritize their work. They must be willing to undertake any travel their job involves.

ENTRY REQUIREMENTS

There is no set route into this work. Most webmasters have had experience in other areas of computing. Some have undertaken training courses in web authoring.

INFORMATION TECHNOLOGY: CAV

As with any work in computing, anyone interested is well advised to undertake training, such as a course leading to a degree or a higher national award.

The computer industry is flexible in the qualifications it accepts from people it considers suitable. For the more technical, scientific areas of IT employers usually require computer science, electronics, maths or physics qualifications. For other types of work, though, such as programming, it will accept applicants whose degrees and higher national awards are computer related and those whose qualifications are unrelated to computing.

Entry to a degree course is with a minimum of two A levels/three H grades plus three GCSEs/S grades (A–C/1–3) in other subjects. English and maths are usually required at GCSE/S grade (A–C/1–3) for computing related degree courses. A level/H grade maths is often required or preferred for entry to the more theoretical degree courses, such as computer science and software engineering. A level/H grade maths is usually required for entry to electronics, maths and physics degrees, while A level/H grade physics is usually required for a physics degree and preferred for electronics degrees. Alternative qualifications are accepted for entry to degree courses, such as a BTEC/SQA national award and Advanced GNVQ/GSVQ Level III.

BTEC/SQA higher national awards require a minimum of one A level/two H grades and three GCSEs/S grades (A–C/1–3) in other subjects, usually including English and maths. Alternative qualifications are accepted for entry, such as a relevant BTEC/SQA national award and Advanced GNVQ/GSVQ Level III.

Some entrants to this type of work have a postgraduate computing qualification. Entry to postgraduate courses is with a good class first degree. The first degree can be in a computing related discipline or in a discipline unrelated to computing.

The computer industry is more flexible than most other industries. It can be possible to enter computing work at a basic level and work towards more responsible posts, including those in different areas of IT. A first step for some can be a full-time college course:

– BTEC national award in such as computer studies or information technology. Entry is usually with four GCSEs (A–C), or a BTEC first award, or Intermediate GNVQ; or

– SQA national certificate modules in information technology. There are no set entry requirements. Applicants should check with individual colleges, which may set their own requirements, as they wish to be satisfied that students are able to benefit from the courses; or

– Advanced GNVQ/GSVQ Level III in Information Technology. Entry requirements vary but are often a minimum of four GCSEs/S grades (A–C/1–3) or Intermediate GNVQ/GSVQ Level II.

Some young people may seek to enter computing work through Modern Apprenticeships and National Traineeships (part of the Skillseekers Initiative in Scotland). There are no set entry requirements but employers will want to be sure that applicants can benefit from the training.

TRAINING

Many colleges and universities throughout the UK offer degree courses relating to computing. There are many different titles for these degree courses, including computing science, computing, systems analysis, software engineering and information technology. They have many similarities but there are marked differences between courses, so it is important to check course content carefully.

It is possible to study a computer related degree on its own or to combine it with study of another subject, such as a modern foreign language, business studies or electronics.

Most degree courses last three years full-time (four in Scotland) or four years (five years in Scotland) if taken on a sandwich basis, where one year is spent on placement with an employer. Some universities offer MEng degree courses which take an additional year. These courses involve study in more depth and breadth. Some degree courses can be studied part-time.

Many universities and colleges throughout the UK offer BTEC/SQA higher national diploma (HND) and higher national certificate (HNC) courses relevant to computing, such as computer studies, computing, information systems, information technology and software engineering. Most HND courses last two years full-time, while some last three years on a sandwich basis. HNC courses are offered on a part-time basis, usually over two years. Successful completion of an HND or HNC can lead to the second year of a degree course.

Many universities offer postgraduate courses relevant to computing. Courses usually last one year full-time or two years part-time. Some courses are designed for graduates with a degree in computing or a related discipline. Other courses are known as conversion courses and enable graduates in disciplines unrelated to computing to train for work related to computer work.

BTEC national diploma courses in computer studies and information technology are offered by many local colleges and usually last two years.

SQA national certificate courses in information technology are offered by a number of local colleges and usually last one year full-time.

Advanced GNVQ/GSVQ Level III courses in information technology are offered by many schools and local colleges and usually last two years.

Modern Apprenticeships involve work-based training leading to a relevant NVQ/SVQ at Level 3. There is no set length of time for Modern Apprenticeship training but it is likely to be at least three years. National Trainees are trained in a similar way to Modern Apprentices but to NVQ/SVQ Level 2. Training normally takes around two years. Contact local careers offices, Jobcentres or TECs/LECs for information on Modern Apprenticeships and National Traineeships.

There are a number of professional qualifications that webmasters can work towards, including those of The British Computer Society (BCS) and National Computing Centre Ltd. They may also work towards NVQs/SVQs at Levels 2 to 4.

LATE ENTRY

There is no set upper age limit for entry to this work but attitudes to mature entrants vary between employers.

Mature applicants may be accepted onto university and college courses without the usual entry requirements, particularly if they have relevant experience and/or qualifications.

Many local colleges offer Access courses for adults who wish to study for a degree or higher national award but

INFORMATION TECHNOLOGY: CAV

who do not have the necessary qualifications. Courses usually last one year full-time or one to two years part-time with day and/or evening attendance.

OPPORTUNITIES

Some webmasters are employed in the IT departments of large organizations. Others work on a freelance basis or work for companies that contract their services to a number of clients.

The demand for webmasters is increasing rapidly. Opportunities arise throughout the UK but there is a concentration in London and the south east of England. Vacancies are advertised in the local and national press, in *Computing* and *Computer Weekly*, and increasingly through the Internet.

It may be possible to work abroad.

PAY AND CONDITIONS

The standard working week for most webmasters is 37 to 40 hours, Monday to Friday. Evening and/or weekend work may be necessary to meet deadlines or to deal with problems that have arisen. Some webmasters also have their working days extended by travel to and from clients' premises.

Self-employed webmasters' working hours depend on their workload. They too may have to work evenings and weekends to meet deadlines.

There are no set pay-scales for webmasters. They may earn between £25,000 and £30,000 a year, while the earnings of self-employed webmasters depend on the success of their business.

PROSPECTS

Progression for webmasters varies. Those who are employed by a user and who have other IT responsibilities may progress by specializing in one of those other areas, such as systems analysis, and seeking advancement in that field. Alternatively, they may seek to move to an employer where they can work solely on work with the web.

Movement between employers is common in IT and some webmasters may take this route to gain more experience, responsibility and reward.

Experienced webmasters can become self-employed and offer their services on a contract or consultancy basis. There are opportunities for working in IT training and in journalism and technical writing.

RELATED OCCUPATIONS

Software engineer, systems analyst, systems designer, systems integrator, network engineer, database administrator, multimedia programmer, help desk operator.

FURTHER INFORMATION AND READING

Please see article 7. HELP DESK OPERATOR.

6. MULTIMEDIA SPECIALIST (CAV)

THE WORK

Multimedia programs can be described as those that combine at least three from: text, data, graphics, sound, still pictures, animation and moving pictures. Multimedia programs are produced as CD-ROMs for many purposes, such as teaching and learning programs, computer games and publications such as encyclopaedias. They are also increasingly being used on web sites.

Most computer work involves IT specialists working with non-computer specialists. This is particularly the case in multimedia, as multimedia production is the result of people with different skills combining to produce the finished product. They include writers, artists and graphic designers, animators and sound engineers.

It is the job of IT specialists to convert the combined efforts of all those concerned into a complete program. This can only be achieved with close liaison. **Multimedia systems designers** are responsible for designing whole multimedia systems, including the hardware and software aspects. **Software engineers/programmers** work closely with others to organize the material that is to make up the program, including sound and animation. They take on the complex programming tasks, using 'object-orientated' computer programming languages such as C++ and JAVA. When the program has been written, they test it, re-test it and deal with any bugs (problems in the program) that may arise.

WORK ENVIRONMENT

IT specialists working on multimedia programs work in an office or studio environment, in clean, light surroundings.

Those working as consultants may often visit clients. This may involve local travel or being away from home for variable periods of time. The ability to drive may be essential for some jobs.

SKILLS AND INTERESTS

IT specialists working on multimedia should enjoy working with computers and have a high level of IT knowledge and skill. They must be prepared to expand their existing skills in order to learn the skills involved in such as sound and animation. It is essential that they keep up to date with developments in both hardware and software and are willing to re-train when necessary.

IT specialists must be able to work well in a team that includes specialists from other disciplines. This needs a thorough appreciation of the other specialists' contribution to projects. Good communication skills are essential, as they deal both with people who are IT specialists and with those who have little knowledge of computers.

They should be capable of logical, analytical thought and enjoy solving problems. They must be able to meet agreed deadlines, and, if working on several projects, be capable of prioritising their work. They ought to be willing to undertake any travel that their job involves.

ENTRY REQUIREMENTS

There is no set entry requirement but a computer related degree or higher national award is good preparation. Entry to such degrees is with a minimum of two A levels/three H grades plus three GCSEs/S grades (A–C/1–3) in other subjects, usually including English and maths. Three A levels/four H grades are required for some courses. A level/H grade maths is often required or preferred for the more theoretical degree courses, such as computer science

INFORMATION TECHNOLOGY: CAV

and software engineering. Alternative qualifications are accepted for entry to degree courses, such as a BTEC/SQA national award and Advanced GNVQ/GSVQ Level III.

BTEC/SQA higher national awards require a minimum of one A level/two H grades and three GCSEs/S grades (A–C/1–3) in other subjects, usually including English and maths. Alternative qualifications are accepted for entry, such as a BTEC/SQA national award and Advanced GNVQ/GSVQ Level III.

Some entrants to this type of work have a postgraduate computing qualification. Entry to postgraduate courses is with a good class first degree. The first degree can be in a computing related discipline or in a discipline unrelated to computing.

The computer industry is more flexible than other industries. It can be possible to enter computing work at a basic level and work towards more responsible posts, including those in different areas of IT. A first step for some can be a full-time college course:

– BTEC national award in such as computer studies or information technology. Entry is usually with four GCSEs (A–C), or a BTEC first award, or Intermediate GNVQ; or

– SQA national certificate modules in information technology. There are no set entry requirements. Applicants should check with individual colleges, which may set their own requirements, as they wish to be satisfied that students are able to benefit from the courses; or

– Advanced GNVQ/GSVQ Level III in Information Technology. Entry requirements vary but are often a minimum of four GCSEs/S grades (A–C/1–3) or Intermediate GNVQ/GSVQ Level II.

Some young people may seek to enter computing work through Modern Apprenticeships and National Traineeships (part of the Skillseekers Initiative in Scotland). There are no set entry requirements but employers will want to be sure that applicants can benefit from the training.

TRAINING

Degree courses in computer related subjects are offered at many colleges and most universities throughout the UK. They last three years full-time or four years on a sandwich basis, where one year is spent on placement with an employer. In Scotland, degree courses usually last three or four years full-time and four or five years on a sandwich basis. Some universities offer MEng degree courses which take an additional year. These courses involve study in more depth and breadth. Some degree courses can be studied part-time.

Many computing degrees include multimedia technology but there are an increasing number of courses that specialize in multimedia studies and technology.

It is possible to study a computing subject on its own or to combine it with study of another subject, such as a modern foreign language or business studies.

Many universities and colleges throughout the UK offer higher national diploma (HND) and higher national certificate (HNC) courses in computer related subjects and a few offer specialist multimedia courses. Most HND courses last two years full-time, while some last three years on a sandwich basis. HNC courses last two years part-time. Successful completion of an HND or HNC can lead to the second year of a degree course.

A number of universities offer postgraduate multimedia courses. Courses usually last one year full-time or two years part-time. Some courses are designed for graduates with a degree in computing or a related discipline. Other courses are known as conversion courses and enable graduates in disciplines unrelated to computing to train in multimedia.

BTEC national diploma courses in computer studies and information technology are offered by many local colleges and usually last two years.

SQA national certificate courses in information technology are offered by a number of local colleges and usually last one year full-time.

Advanced GNVQ/GSVQ Level III in Information Technology are offered by some schools and many local colleges and usually last two years.

Modern Apprenticeships involve work-based training leading to a relevant NVQ/SVQ at Level 3. There is no set length of time for Modern Apprenticeship training but it is likely to be at least three years. National Trainees are trained in a similar way to Modern Apprentices but to NVQ/SVQ Level 2. Training normally takes around two years. Contact local careers offices, Jobcentres or TECs/LECs for information on Modern Apprenticeships and National Traineeships.

There are a number of professional qualifications that multimedia specialists can work towards, including those of The British Computer Society (BCS), the Institute for the Management of Information Systems and National Computing Centre Ltd. They may also work towards NVQs/SVQs at Levels 2 to 4.

LATE ENTRY

There is no set upper age limit for entry to this work but attitudes to mature entrants vary between employers.

Mature applicants may be accepted onto university and college courses without the usual entry requirements, particularly if they have relevant experience and/or qualifications.

Many local colleges offer Access courses for adults who wish to study for a degree or higher national award but who do not have the necessary qualifications. Courses usually last one year full-time or one to two years part-time with day and/or evening attendance.

OPPORTUNITIES

There are opportunities for computer specialists in multimedia with companies that produce software, as well as with publishers and companies in the entertainment, television, cable and film industries. Some multimedia specialists work as consultants.

Opportunities arise throughout the UK but there is a concentration in London and the south east of England. Vacancies are advertised in the local and national press, in *Computing* and *Computer Weekly*, and increasingly through the Internet.

It may be possible to work abroad.

The multimedia industry is growing rapidly and there are an increasing number of opportunities for employment in this field. It seems likely that multimedia will be increasingly used on web sites, possibly at the expense of CD-ROMs, which could further increase opportunities in this field.

INFORMATION TECHNOLOGY: CAV

PAY AND CONDITIONS

The standard working week for most multimedia specialists is 37 to 40 hours, Monday to Friday. Evening and/or weekend work may be necessary to meet deadlines or to deal with problems that have arisen. Those working on a consultancy basis may also have their working days extended by travel to and from clients' premises.

There are no set pay-scales for IT specialists in multimedia. They tend to receive at least £16,000 a year on entry, while experienced staff can earn between £22,000 and £35,000 a year.

PROSPECTS

Movement between employers is common in IT and some staff in multimedia work take this route to gain more experience, responsibility and reward. They may progress to project management.

Experienced multimedia specialists can become self-employed and offer their services on a contract or consultancy basis. Alternatively they may use their skills to transfer to IT work outside the multimedia field. There are opportunities for working in IT training and in journalism and technical writing.

RELATED OCCUPATIONS

Software engineer, systems analyst, systems designer, systems integrator, designer, sound engineer, help desk operator.

FURTHER INFORMATION AND READING

Please see article 7. HELP DESK OPERATOR.

7. HELP DESK OPERATOR (CAV)

THE WORK

Help desk operators are responsible for diagnosing the causes of hardware or software problems experienced by users and for helping to remedy them.

Some help desk operators work for a hardware or software company and are responsible only for providing support for that company's products. Others work for an organization that uses computers and are responsible for any hardware or software problems that arise within that organization.

Help desk operators answer telephone calls from users with problems. They talk over the problem with the user and ask questions to try to locate the cause. The problem may be easily diagnosed, such as a user misunderstanding a simple procedure, or may be complex and take much time. The help desk operator aims to diagnose the cause of the problem and talk through the solution with the user. If the problem appears to be caused by a hardware or software fault, the operator may offer to arrange for a support person or field engineer to call on the user. Alternatively they may ask the user to return the faulty item for inspection and repair.

Help desk operators working for a user may visit the person with the problem to see the problem first hand and try to remedy it.

Operators normally keep a record of calls received, action taken and the outcome.

WORK ENVIRONMENT

Help desk operators work in an office environment, in clean, light surroundings. They usually spend much of their time seated at a desk answering telephone calls.

Those working for large users may be mobile on site or have to travel between sites to visit staff who have problems that cannot be remedied by telephone help. The ability to drive may be essential for such jobs.

SKILLS AND INTERESTS

Help desk operators should be thoroughly familiar with the hardware and software for which they are providing support.

They must enjoy tackling problems and solving them. Excellent communication skills are essential, in particular, the ability to communicate with users who may have little or no computer knowledge. Good listening skills are important as a first step towards understanding the users' problem. They need the ability to ask clear questions and explain procedures in an understandable way. Operators need to be able to get on easily and well with people, some of whom may be anxious or annoyed at the problems they are experiencing. Patience is essential.

As they usually solve problems by telephone rather than first hand, help desk operators must be capable of logical thought; this needs the ability to work methodically through possible causes of a problem. Having located the cause they must be capable of advising the user of the exact sequence of actions to remedy the problem.

Help desk operators must be capable of keeping records of calls received, action taken and the outcomes. They must be prepared to update their skills and knowledge as developments in hardware and software are introduced.

ENTRY REQUIREMENTS

People entering help desk work have usually had experience of the computer system and the particular business area of the employer. Some employers require a degree or higher national qualification, while others prefer to recruit staff with lesser qualifications and provide training themselves. Some employers require applicants to have a certificate in one of the main software systems.

Degree entry is with a minimum of two A levels/three H grades plus three GCSEs/S grades (A–C/1–3) in other subjects. English and maths are usually required at GCSE/S grade (A–C/1–3) for computing related degree courses. A level/H grade maths is often required or preferred for entry to the more theoretical degree courses, such as computer science and software engineering. Alternative qualifications are accepted for entry to degree courses, such as a BTEC/SQA national award and Advanced GNVQ/GSVQ Level III.

BTEC/SQA higher national awards require a minimum of one A level/two H grades and three GCSEs/S grades (A–C/1–3) in other subjects, usually including English and maths. Alternative qualifications are accepted for entry, such as a BTEC/SQA national award and Advanced GNVQ/GSVQ Level III.

Some entrants to this type of work have a postgraduate computing qualification. Entry to postgraduate courses is with a good class first degree. The degree can be in a computing related discipline or in a discipline unrelated to computing.

INFORMATION TECHNOLOGY: CAV

There are some full-time college courses that are useful preparation for this work:

– BTEC national award in such subjects as computer studies or information technology. Entry is usually with four GCSEs (A–C), or a BTEC first award, or Intermediate GNVQ; or

– SQA national certificate modules in information technology. There are no set entry requirements. Applicants should check with individual colleges, which may set their own requirements, as they wish to be satisfied that students are able to benefit from the courses; or

– Advanced GNVQ/GSVQ Level III in Information Technology. Entry requirements vary but are often a minimum of four GCSEs/S grades (A–C/1–3) or Intermediate GNVQ/GSVQ Level II.

Some young people may enter this work through Modern Apprenticeships and National Traineeships (part of the Skillseekers Initiative in Scotland). There are no set entry requirements but employers will want to be sure applicants can benefit from the training.

TRAINING

Degree courses relating to computing are offered at many colleges and universities throughout the UK. There are many different titles for these degree courses, including computing science, computing, systems analysis, software engineering and information technology. They have many similarities but there are marked differences between courses, so it is important to check course content carefully.

It is possible to study a computer related degree on its own or to combine it with study of another subject, such as a modern foreign language, business studies or electronics.

Most degree courses last three years full-time (four in Scotland) or four years (five years in Scotland) if taken on a sandwich basis, where one year is spent on placement with an employer. Some universities offer MEng degree courses which take an additional year. These courses involve study in more depth and breadth. Some degree courses can be studied part-time.

Many universities and colleges throughout the UK offer BTEC/SQA higher national diploma (HND) and higher national certificate (HNC) courses relevant to computing, such as computer studies, computing, information systems, information technology and software engineering. Most HND courses last two years full-time, while some last three years on a sandwich basis. HNC courses usually last two years part-time. Successful completion of an HND or HNC can lead to the second year of a degree course.

Many universities offer postgraduate courses relating to computing. Courses usually last one year full-time or two years part-time. Some courses are designed for graduates with a degree in computing or a related discipline. Other courses are known as conversion courses and enable graduates in unrelated disciplines to train for computing.

BTEC national diploma courses in computer studies and information technology are offered by many local colleges and usually last two years.

SQA national certificate courses in information technology are offered by a number of local colleges and usually last one year full-time.

Advanced GNVQ/GSVQ Level III courses in information technology are offered by some schools and many local colleges and usually last two years.

Modern Apprenticeships in this area of work involves work-based training working towards NVQ/SVQ Support Users of Information Technology Level 3. There is no set length of time for Modern Apprenticeship training but it is likely to be at least three years. National Trainees are trained in a similar way to Modern Apprentices but to NVQ/SVQ Level 2. Training normally takes around two years. Contact local careers offices, Jobcentres or TECs/LECs for information on Modern Apprenticeships and National Traineeships.

On starting work, help desk operators are usually trained by experienced staff. Some employers provide training for a certificate in the relevant software system. Operators may work towards NVQ/SVQ Support Users of Information Technology Levels 2 and 3.

LATE ENTRY

There is no set upper age limit for entry to this work but attitudes to mature entrants vary between employers

Mature applicants may be accepted onto university and college courses without the usual entry requirements, particularly if they have relevant experience and/or qualifications.

Many local colleges offer Access courses for adults who wish to study for a degree or higher national award but who do not have the necessary qualifications. Courses usually last one year full-time or one to two years part-time with day and/or evening attendance.

OPPORTUNITIES

Help desk operators are employed throughout the UK by a wide range of large organizations that are computer users; this includes a wide variety of manufacturing companies, retailers, gas, electricity and oil companies, financial organizations – such as banks, building societies and insurance companies – hospitals, educational institutions, transport companies, the Armed Forces, the Civil Service, local government and the media industry, including newspapers, television and radio companies. They are also employed by computer manufacturers, software houses and Internet service providers.

The demand for help desk operators is growing. Vacancies are advertised in the local and national press, in *Computing* and *Computer Weekly,* and increasingly through the Internet.

It may be possible to work abroad.

PAY AND CONDITIONS

Most help desk operators work a standard 37 to 40 hour week. The pattern of work varies between employers and can involve shifts that include weekends and evenings.

There are no set pay-scales but salaries tend to range between £14,000 to £30,000 a year.

PROSPECTS

Help desk operators can progress to more senior positions within their organization, such as team leader, section leader or departmental manager. Movement between employers is common in IT and some support staff take this route to gain more experience, responsibility and reward.

Help desk work is often regarded as a good stepping stone

INFORMATION TECHNOLOGY: CAV

towards other work within IT and some staff progress to such as programming or systems administration.

There are opportunities for working in IT training.

RELATED OCCUPATIONS

Computer service engineer, software engineer, systems analyst, network engineer, database administrator, multimedia programmer, computer sales person.

FURTHER INFORMATION

The British Computer Society*, 1 Sanford Street, Swindon SN1 1HJ, 01793 417417, http:/www.bcs.org.uk/

The National Training Organisation for Information Technology*, 16 Berners Street, London W1P 3DD, 0171 580 6677. http://www.itno.org.uk

The National Computing Centre Ltd*, Oxford House, Oxford Road, Manchester M1 7ED, 0161 228 6333, http://www.ncc.co.uk

Institute for the Management of Information Systems*, IMIS House, Edgington Way, Ruxley Corner, Sidcup, Kent DA1 5HR, 0181 308 0747

Institute of Electrical Engineering, Savoy Place, London WC2R 0BL, 0171 240 1871

FURTHER READING

Leaflets/booklets are available from the addresses marked*.

Working In Information Technology – COIC

Degree Course Guide – Computer Science and Computing – Hobsons

Ivanhoe Career Guide – Information Systems – CMI

Information Technology – AGCAS

In the careers library classified under CAV.

MANAGEMENT SERVICES: COF/COD

1. **OPERATIONAL RESEARCHER**
   CLCI:COF
2. **ORGANIZATION AND METHODS/WORK STUDY OFFICER**
   CLCI:COD

BACKGROUND INFORMATION

Industry, commerce and the public sector are able to call on the services of a range of professionals whose specialist skills are used to advise managers and executives on how to make the best use of the resources available to them.

Such experts – sometimes known under the umbrella title of management services consultants – advise on problems of resource allocation and use (finance, staff and equipment) and on the effectiveness of methods and procedures, recommend and design new systems, and advise on long-term strategy.

Historically, work study or industrial engineering was the first management service. It developed from time-and-motion study techniques originating in the USA at the beginning of the century and was based firmly in factory and other manual workplaces, measuring work output. Organization and methods (O&M) came next. Similar techniques for measuring the efficiency of clerical workers began to be applied in the 1920s.

Strictly speaking, work study is still concerned with work measurement: observing and assessing tasks in order to set standard times and skill levels to complete them – information that can be used in determining staffing levels and pay structures – and method study: examining the stages of a manufacturing process and the mechanical and technical equipment used, in order to suggest more efficient ways of carrying out the process.

O&M uses a similar process of analysis and review in relation to clerical and administrative work. It examines working structures, systems, procedures and tasks in order to advise more effective or efficient working practices through the reorganization, rescheduling and reshaping of a system or job, including the introduction of appropriate information and communication technologies.

Since they use similar and overlapping techniques, O&M and work study have to all intents and purposes become a single profession.

Operational research (OR) was used during the Second World War, when it began as part of the UK defence effort. Government scientists started to analyse the campaign against U-boats to establish why it was proving less successful than hoped, and to use mathematical modelling techniques ultimately to plan better air and sea defences. After the war, experts returned to peacetime employment and began to apply their techniques to analysing all types of work-related problems. OR became established in manufacturing industry and, for a while, remained linked with that. Today it is used throughout industry and commerce.

OR originally used computational, statistical and mathematical techniques. These are still an important part of the work, but other techniques are now used. Hard OR makes much use of mathematical modelling, including visually interactive models, on which, for example, the effects of altering the speed of machinery or substituting pieces of equipment can be simulated on a computer screen. Soft OR refers to various techniques (usually of a graphical nature, using diagrams, flip charts etc though computer-based methods are emerging) that help people understand or structure problems, rather than necessarily pointing towards a solution. Visual models built for managers to experiment with as decision support systems come under the heading of soft OR.

Operational research is commonly concerned with more complex situations than are work study/O&M. It is used in all kinds of situations, but particularly where large-scale problems of logistics are concerned – in oil extraction, defence planning or large-scale manufacturing.

1. OPERATIONAL RESEARCHER (COF)

THE WORK

Operational researchers work alongside the managers and executives who take the key decisions in an organization by using a broadly based scientific or logical approach to examine managerial problems.

They may be consulted about decisions as varied as where to build a new factory, how to estimate the profitability of a new crop on a typical farm, how to lay out shelves to maximize profit in a supermarket, how to improve economy and efficiency in health authorities or local councils, or where to re-route a local bus service. They may be concerned with strategic or immediate problems.

Working alone or as part of a small team, operational researchers first establish what the problem is and what solution is hoped for. They then gather information, finding out how the present system works, what inefficiencies must be changed and what is worth retaining.

They often interview a wide range of people, for example directors, managers and workers at all levels, about the nature of the problem.

When they have completed the initial research they may be able to represent the system being examined with a model. Models can produce erroneous outputs, since assumptions have to be made. To guard against this possibility, accuracy is tested against already known data (known as validating the model). The model is used to compare various solutions.

Finally they present the results, often suggesting several different solutions and their recommendations to the managers who asked for their assistance. Often they produce a computer 'decision support' system, designed to help managers in making decisions in similar future situations.

WORK ENVIRONMENT

Operational researchers are based in offices, but the work involves interacting with people at their places of work. Depending on the projects they are engaged on, they visit different business and industrial environments: factories, offices, shops, and building sites and processing plants. Some projects require a considerable amount of travel, long periods away from home and possibly travel overseas.

SKILLS AND INTERESTS

Operational researchers must be capable of analysing technical and complex problems, handling large amounts of data and using computers. They need the ability to use the data they have acquired to get to the core of the problem, and they need logical and creative minds to produce potential solutions. They must be accurate and

MANAGEMENT SERVICES: COF/COD

attentive to detail. While a solid grounding in maths is essential, not all problems require a high level of mathematical techniques. Many require a greater emphasis on numerical ability.

Communication skills are equally important, as operational researchers spend approximately one third of their time in analysing problems, and two thirds in discussing, interviewing, writing reports and giving verbal presentations to clients in meetings.

They must be able to talk easily to a variety of people when conducting the early stages of research during a project, and discuss the results confidently with senior managers and directors.

The ability to write clear, concise reports and explain technical matters to non-experts in easily understood language is essential.

Persuasive skills are important, since they are, in effect, selling their solutions.

Operational researchers should also be flexible – able to work on very different types of project according to the needs of their clients.

ENTRY REQUIREMENTS

Most entrants are graduates and hold a master's degree in Operational Research. Although entry with A levels or equivalent qualifications is possible in theory, in practice it is almost impossible to find a traineeship.

Minimum entry requirements to a degree course are five GCSEs/S grades (A–C/1–3) plus two A level/three H grades or equivalent. Normal requirements are three A levels at grade C and above/four to five H grades at grade B.

There are some first degrees that include OR, although it is not necessary to have taken one. Other preferred subjects are maths, statistics, sciences, economics, business studies or computer studies.

An A level/H grade standard in a maths-related subject is the usual minimum requirement for those whose degree is not in a similar subject. Most people with a degree in a non-related subject may choose to take a one- or two-year full-time postgraduate course in Operational Research, Management Science or Management Systems. A list is available from the Operational Research Society.

TRAINING

Training is on-the-job, usually supplemented by postgraduate training for entrants at first-degree level. Employers with large OR departments run graduate training programmes which assign new entrants to OR teams and permit them to work on projects under supervision, gradually giving them more responsibility. These programmes often include the opportunity to take a part-time MSc course.

Most employers also provide training in communication, presentation, business and management skills.

LATE ENTRY

Although late entry is by no means impossible, the majority of entrants come straight from university.

OPPORTUNITIES

There are opportunities throughout industry, commerce, local and central government, in the health service and in independent management consultancies. The Operational Research Society estimates that over 250 organizations employ OR staff.

Major employers include manufacturers, the oil industry, large retailers, banks, building societies, local authorities and central government departments including the Treasury, Ministry of Defence, the Inland Revenue, Customs and Excise, the Department of Health and the Home Office.

There are also increasing opportunities to work in consultancies, which are retained on a fee-paying basis by organizations that do not have their own departments, or sometimes by those that do have their own OR staff, to work on specialized assignments. It is quite possible, during the course of an OR career, to work for several different types of employer. Opportunities for self-employment and part-time work are good.

Vacancies appear in the national press and in the OR newsletter, supplied to members of the OR Society. The Society can also provide a list of organizations that intend to recruit new people to work in OR in the current year.

PAY AND CONDITIONS

Newly qualified operational researchers can expect to earn from £14,000 to £18,000. Those entering with an MSc can expect £15,000 to £22,000. With experience, high salaries can be expected. OR managers earn at least £40,000, but salaries can exceed £70,000.

Hours of work vary with the project being undertaken. It is often necessary to work in the evenings or to take work home, particularly when the deadline for the end of the project and the presentation of a report is approaching.

PROSPECTS

Prospects for promotion or advancement are very good. Within OR departments there are prospects of promotion to project and team leader, then to department manager.

There are opportunities to set up one's own consultancy business.

Promotion into general management within a company is becoming very usual. Operational researchers gain a thorough knowledge and overview of the workings of their organizations and are therefore well placed to move into management in other departments, such as marketing or production. Many senior managers and company directors have OR backgrounds.

RELATED OCCUPATIONS

Computer systems programmer, actuary, organization and methods officer, statistician, systems analyst, operations manager.

FURTHER INFORMATION

Operational Research Society*, Seymour House, 12 Edward Street, Birmingham B1 2RX, 0121 233 9300, www.orsoc.org.uk

FURTHER READING

Leaflets/booklets are available from the address marked*.

In the careers library classified under COF.

MANAGEMENT SERVICES: COF/COD

2. ORGANIZATION AND METHODS/WORK STUDY OFFICER (COD)

THE WORK

O&M/work study takes place in almost all large organizations, which normally have their own work study/O&M teams.

Like operational researchers, O&M/work study officers are often called in by managers and requested to solve a problem. Alternatively, the management services department or section may have a brief to monitor performance levels and identify problems or opportunities for investigation. The need is usually to improve working practices in order to achieve greater productivity, efficiency or economy, to improve quality or to improve workers' health and safety.

They record (using a variety of charts and other recording techniques), examine and critically analyse the way in which a series of tasks is performed, in order to identify parts of the work that can be eliminated, combined, simplified or made more efficient by the introduction of new tools or equipment.

The projects they work on could range from reorganizing a company's post room – by such simple tasks as restructuring the work, changing the work flow, redesigning workstations or rescheduling activities to reduce the amount of walking, sorting and carrying – to investigating the implications of closing a local authority's public enquiry office in a small town and moving the workload to an office in another.

O&M officers/work study officers visit employees at their workplace to interview them in depth about their work. They observe them and possibly use work measurement to obtain times for the completion of certain tasks. Such observation and measurement sometimes makes use of sampling techniques to obtain data quickly, reliably and economically. Their observations may include the tasks that are performed, the persons doing the work, the sequence of the work, the physical layout, the tools and equipment and the conditions. Each of these are then examined to see if improvement can be made. O&M officers/workstudy officers usually write a detailed report showing their observations and making recommendations for the change.

WORK ENVIRONMENT

Please see article 1. OPERATIONAL RESEARCHER.

SKILLS AND INTERESTS

Personal qualities are very important in work study/O&M work. Employees are often anxious or hostile, since they may be worried about the implications for their jobs. Good communication and interview skills are necessary to put people at ease, reassure them about the purpose of a survey and win their co-operation. Persuasive powers are needed to convince managers of the need for a survey and to sell the recommendations when the investigation is completed.

Work study/O&M officers must also be able to liaise with other experts, who explain to them some of the technical features of the production processes being investigated.

A logical and orderly mind is essential, with the ability to grasp the core of a problem, research it, discard irrelevant material and produce a solution.

Work study/O&M officers must also be able to express themselves clearly in writing, since the end result of a survey is usually a written report.

Most of their work is carried out in teams. The ability to work well with colleagues is important.

ENTRY REQUIREMENTS

There are no formal entry requirements but an increasing number of practitioners have degrees.

Although employers consider personal qualities more important than degree subject, some may give preference to entrants with degrees in business studies, computing, engineering or economics.

The minimum qualifications required for entry to a degree course, or to take the examinations of the Institute of Management Services (which is the professional body for work study/O&M officers), are five GCSEs/S grades (A–C/1–3) plus two at A level/three at H grade or equivalent.

School-leavers with A levels/H grades either join an organization as work study/O&M or general management trainees, study part-time for qualifications of the Institute of Management Services and move into O&M/work study later.

Graduates/higher national diploma holders may be recruited to O&M/work study directly or join companies' general graduate trainee management programmes.

TRAINING

Most organizations put trainees through a planned training programme which involves working on real projects under the guidance of senior staff.

Some companies give graduate entrants the opportunity to study for an MBA.

Most employers expect trainees to obtain membership of the Institute of Management Services by obtaining appropriate qualifications from the Institute, or qualifications recognized by the Institute as equivalent.

The Institute offers a Certificate in Management Services which may be studied on a part-time basis over one year or through distance learning. The certificate may be followed by study for the Institute's diploma.

People with suitable qualifications may be given subject-for-subject exemptions at diploma level.

LATE ENTRY

This is frequently a second career, often not entered before the mid-twenties. People with relevant experience in commerce or industry are particularly welcome.

OPPORTUNITIES

The Institute of Management Services has approximately 5,000 members, the majority of whom are engaged in the promotion and development of productivity and quality through techniques such as workstudy, O&M and similar analytical methodologies. The incorporation of such approaches into mainstream management education and practice means the demand for specialist practitioners is decreasing slightly.

MANAGEMENT SERVICES: COF/COD

Most practitioners work in teams within organizations, but some are employed by management consultancies that work on a freelance basis for employers who do not have their own in-house teams.

There are opportunities nationwide in large commercial companies, with banks, retailers and in manufacturing industry. There are also some in local authorities, central government departments and the health service, although these organizations now tend to use outside consultancies as and when necessary.

Job vacancies are advertised in the national and local press and in *Management Services,* the journal of the Institute of Management Services.

PAY AND CONDITIONS

Salaries vary between employers, but a new entrant could expect a salary of approximately £12,000. Experienced practitioners may earn between £16,000 and £25,000, while senior posts carry salaries of up to £40,000.

Hours are normally 9am to 5pm, Monday to Friday, but will vary according to the job being studied.

PROSPECTS

There are prospects of promotion to team leader and on to department head within the profession itself. Many practitioners use the experience and skills they have gained to move into general management.

RELATED OCCUPATIONS

Please see article 1. OPERATIONAL RESEARCHER.

FURTHER INFORMATION

Institute of Management Services*, 1 Cecil Court, London Road, Enfield, Middlesex EN2 6DD, 0181 363 7452, http://www.imgtserv.co.uk/imgerserv/

FURTHER READING

Leaflets/booklets are available from the address marked*.

In the careers library classified under COD.

CONSUMER PROTECTION: COP

TRADING STANDARDS OFFICER
CLCI:COP

BACKGROUND INFORMATION

Local authorities have a statutory duty to enforce standards of fairness and safety that are laid down by law for the protection of consumers and traders. The Trading Standards Service puts into effect the large and growing range of legislation on consumer affairs.

Important measures include the Trade Descriptions Act, Weights and Measures Act, Food Safety Act, Consumer Protection Act and the Consumer Credit Act. Other legislation includes animal health and welfare, certain aspects of road traffic law and price legislation.

To assess the potential need to visit the premises (other than those visits caused by complaints from the public or trade), the service seeks to risk assess the premises in each local authority area and produce a plan to routinely inspect premises to check that controls are being correctly and fully applied.

Trading standards officers (TSOs) have the right to enter trade premises and seize and retain, for evidential purposes, documents and goods.

THE WORK

Trading standards officers visit traders in their area to check equipment, trading practices, advertising etc. Many are routine inspections, but others are made in response to complaints.

All sorts of businesses are covered: shops, street markets, garages, factories, dairies, night clubs, finance companies and many others. Officers test and verify the weighing machines in shops and the petrol pumps at filling stations. They take samples of goods such as bread, meat pies, paint or fabric for analysis in the laboratory. TSOs check that information on labels is accurate and that advertisements do not mislead. Cases of fraud can involve them in long, complex investigations.

Duties vary to some extent from one place to another. In rural areas, TSOs may spend time ensuring transmittable animal disease is fully controlled whereas in urban areas counterfeiting may be a major problem. TSOs work with other law enforcement officials including the police, fire service, customs and excise, health and safety etc.

In the more serious of cases, action in the criminal courts becomes appropriate. In such cases, the TSO may be required to present the case or it may be conducted by a lawyer. In any event, it will be the evidence compiled by the TSO that forms the basis of any charge and, of course, the likelihood of conviction.

In the office, TSOs may take turns as duty officers, receiving complaints and enquiries and advising people on their legal position.

To gain the co-operation of business and industry and to educate the public on their rights as consumers, trading standards officers give talks to trade associations, schools and other community groups.

Officers write reports on all cases and keep statistics on the problems they encounter. They plan their own work, in liaison with the police, environmental health officers, laboratory scientists and others. They attend meetings and may supervise assistants and trainees who help with scientific, technical or legal work.

WORK ENVIRONMENT

Trading standards officers are usually based at an office, but spend much of their time out visiting traders and suppliers. Usually, they go out alone, sometimes taking an assistant, but a major investigation would involve a team of officers. Court attendance is regularly required. Officers enter all sorts of premises, some dirty and smelly. Protective clothing is provided.

SKILLS AND INTERESTS

Initiative, determination and resilience are demanded in organizing and carrying out inspections and investigations. Trading standards officers need the ability to take a clear, impartial view of a situation, and should be able to justify their decisions.

Good communication skills are essential. They have to talk to people from a variety of backgrounds – interviewing, advising or persuading. Trading standards officers should be good listeners and very observant. A firm but tactful manner is required. They also need the ability to write clear, concise reports and have the confidence to present them in court. Team work is important, as they work in co-operation with colleagues and other professionals.

The job demands interest and aptitude in both technology and law.

ENTRY REQUIREMENTS

The minimum requirements for trainee TSOs are five GCSEs/S grades (A–C/1–3) and two A levels/three H grades, including English, maths and physics at either level, or equivalent qualifications. Most new entrants hold a degree. Maths, science, law, technology and business subjects are all relevant to some extent, but a wide range of degrees is acceptable.

The statutory qualification is currently the Diploma in Trading Standards (DTS) although discussions are advanced in the review of this qualification which may well lead to the establishment of the DTS as a postgraduate qualification by the end of 1998.

A driving licence is generally required after qualification.

An alternative means of qualification is the BA (Hons) Degree in Consumer Protection at Glasgow Caledonian, Manchester Metropolitan or Teesside universities. Entry requirements are five GCSEs/S grades (A–C/1–3) in English language, maths and a science, and two A levels/three H grades, or equivalent.

A Diploma in Consumer Affairs is also available. This is a professional qualification run by the Institute of Trading Standards Administration and is aimed at consumer advisers and enforcement specialists who do not need all the training provided by the DTS.

TRAINING

The Diploma in Trading Standards (DTS) is administered by the Local Government Management Board.

The degree course in Consumer Protection lasts three years full-time and is followed by the taking of the practical subjects and project work. Candidates who achieve at least a 2:2 honours degree will gain exemptions from certain papers in the DTS exam.

CONSUMER PROTECTION: COP

LATE ENTRY

There are no upper age limits. Applications are welcome from adults with relevant work experience, for example in health and safety, food hygiene, laboratory work or citizens' advice.

However, there are no exemptions from the DTS course, except for some degree holders, and all applicants are expected to hold the minimum entry qualifications of five GCSEs/S grades and two A levels/three H grades.

OPPORTUNITIES

The Trading Standards Service is provided by local authorities. The service may stand alone or be merged with a range of regulatory services such as environmental health or building control.

There are about 1,500 trading standards officers in the UK, and a shortage of qualified staff. However, it can be difficult to find training places and competition is fierce.

There is an increasing demand for qualified TSOs in private industry. They work in businesses such as retailing or food manufacture, as advisers on consumer law or in quality control and management.

PAY AND CONDITIONS

Salary scales vary widely. Newly qualified TSOs normally earn between £18,000 and £20,000.

It is usual to work a 37 hours a week although employers expect that some unsociable working hours will be necessary in order to deal with those aspects of trade such as Sunday markets or public houses which are normally operated outside the normal office hours. Increasingly, retail activities are seven days a week and longer opening hours.

PROSPECTS

The promotion structure leads through the grades of senior officer, section head or divisional officer to assistant, deputy and chief TSO. There are usually good opportunities for advancement, although it often means relocation. An increasing number of TSOs join the private sector.

It is possible to specialize in particular aspects of the job, such as legal metrology, consumer credit, product safety, animal health and food safety. Post-professional training courses are run by the Institute of Trading Standards Administration (ITSA), the professional organization for trading standards officers. Part-time management courses, such as the Diploma in Management Studies or Master in Business Administration, may be available for senior staff.

The ITSA offers various grades of membership from studentship to retirement.

RELATED OCCUPATIONS

Environmental health officer, consumer adviser, HM factory inspector, quality controller, police officer, scientist/technician.

FURTHER INFORMATION

The Institute of Trading Standards Administration*, 3–5 Hadleigh Business Centre, 351 London Road, Hadleigh, Essex SS7 2BT, 01702 559922

Local Government Opportunities (LGO), Local Government Management Board, 76–86 Turnmill Street, London EC1M 5QU, 0171 296 6600. Website: datalake.com/lgo/jobsearch

Anyone wishing to find out more about this work is advised to contact their local trading standards department.

FURTHER READING

Leaflets/booklets are available from the address marked*.

Working in Local Government – COIC

In the careers library classified under COP.

HEALTH AND SAFETY: COP/COT

1. **ENVIRONMENTAL HEALTH OFFICER**
   CLCI:COP
2. **HEALTH AND SAFETY ADVISER**
   CLCI:COT
3. **HEALTH AND SAFETY INSPECTOR**
   CLCI: COT.

1. ENVIRONMENTAL HEALTH OFFICER (COP)

BACKGROUND INFORMATION

Environmental health officers have a common goal to reduce the risks and eliminate the dangers to human health associated with the living and working environment. Legislation covers many aspects of their work including food safety, noise, industrial waste, housing, occupational health and safety, pollution control and control of infectious disease. Environmental health officers' work involves educating and advising but also using their statutory powers to enforce regulations.

THE WORK

Environmental health officers have a wide range of responsibilities. These include food safety, public health, the control and notification of infectious disease, housing and occupational health and safety. Much of their daily work involves inspecting premises, identifying problems and defects with the fabric of the building or with the equipment or the processes being carried out within the building. They are also involved in monitoring conditions and carrying out lengthy and involved investigations by collecting and evaluating evidence. Typical incidents include occurrences of pollution and outbreaks of infections like typhoid, salmonella and hepatitis.

Environmental health officers visit homes, shops, food premises, factories, refuse disposal sites, air and sea ports and other places in order to check food safety, hygiene, living and working conditions, pollution emissions etc. They collect samples and specimens for laboratory testing and take account of the results in decision making. This part of the work involves close liaison with other experts like scientists, microbiologists and building surveyors, who can offer specialized support.

Environmental health officers carefully and impartially consider the facts of every case they investigate before deciding on the most appropriate action. They base their decisions on a good understanding and working knowledge of relevant legislation. Action may be formal, possibly leading to prosecution, or it may take the form of educating and advising those who have broken the law, so as to avoid the problem in the future.

Environmental health officers must take detailed notes and write reports on every aspect of their work. They are required to give evidence in courts of law.

WORK ENVIRONMENT

Officers may spend time working alone outside the office and may be required to visit unpleasant, dirty and sometimes potentially dangerous places. Where appropriate they may wear protective clothing including hats, masks, boots and overalls.

SKILLS AND INTERESTS

The work requires investigative and decision-making abilities. It suits those who are interested in the quality of life and the well-being of other people and who enjoy solving problems. An interest in social problems and helping others to solve them is useful. Environmental health officers need a methodical, careful approach to gathering facts and assessing evidence.

A very high standard of written and spoken communication skills is required, because environmental health officers deal with a wide range of people and prepare reports. It is important to be able to discuss problems with the public and colleagues. Negotiating skills and a patient, diplomatic manner are assets. Environmental health officers must remain polite at all times, although some visits can be confrontational.

A high level of scientific and technical understanding is necessary when checking pollution, safety and industrial processes, and interpreting rules like building regulations. Officers must be able to use their own judgement when examining and assessing hazards and to apply scientific principles.

It is important to be thorough, persistent and self-confident in order to make enquiries successfully; some of the people they meet may resent their work. Some site visits require a certain amount of physical agility and occasionally involve working at heights and in confined spaces.

ENTRY REQUIREMENTS

The minimum recommended entry requirements to Chartered Institute of Environmental Health (CIEH) accredited degree courses in England, Wales and Northern Ireland are five GCSEs (A–C) with two A levels. One A level must be in a science subject and the GCSEs must include English, maths and another science.

Those who enter by studying a postgraduate course need a pure science degree, such as biology, physics, chemistry or biochemistry, although other science-based degrees may be acceptable. Entry to a degree course requires a minimum of five GCSEs (A–C), with two A levels.

Entry requirements may vary at different universities and candidates with non-standard qualifications should consult individual universities.

In Scotland, entrants must complete a four-year BSc in Environmental Health at either the University of Edinburgh or the University of Strathclyde. Entry to Edinburgh is with either: four H grades (BBBC) including chemistry (at B grade) and two from biology, maths and physics (with a B grade in at least one of them), plus S grade (1 or 2) in maths; or three A levels (CCC) including chemistry and one from biology, maths or physics, plus GCSE maths at grade A or B.

Entry to the University of Strathclyde is with four H grades (minimum ABBC or BBBB) including maths and chemistry and either physics or biology. S grade (1–3) physics is desirable if not held at H grade. Three A levels (CCC or BCD) including maths, chemistry and physics or biology are also acceptable.

Alternative qualifications to A levels/H grades are acceptable for all courses, such as relevant BTEC/SQA national awards and Advanced GNVQ/GSVQ Level III, eg science.

Many students are sponsored by local authorities but it is

HEALTH AND SAFETY: COP/COT

possible to train without sponsorship.

A driving licence is usually required.

TRAINING

England and Wales

There are four main routes leading to the award of the Certificate of Registration of the Environmental Health Officers Registration Board (EHORB). All require the candidate to obtain a degree or an MSc from a CIEH accredited course and all require candidates to obtain 48 weeks of practical training of which at least 24 weeks must be with a UK local authority. Candidates must register with EHORB prior to beginning their practical training and complete the CIEH Practical Training logbook including obtaining 50 or 200 hours of meat inspection training in a slaughter house. Following their practical training the logbook must be assessed as satisfactory by the CIEH.

After sitting the final exams of their degree or MSc, candidates are required to sit the CIEH Professional Examination which consists of three elements – five written papers in each of the main areas of environmental health (food, health and safety, housing environmental protection, and public health), a risk audit paper and an interview.

The main academic routes are:

1. Four-year sandwich degree in Environmental Health/Science approved by the Chartered Institute of Environmental Health. This is the most common training route. Courses are offered at the following universities: Nottingham Trent, Leeds Metropolitan, Greenwich, Kings College London, Middlesex, Manchester Metropolitan, Salford, Ulster, Wales Institute (Cardiff), West of England and Edinburgh. Students spend the third year of the course on practical placement with an employer.

2. Students who are unable to find a placement for their practical training may complete a degree in three years and then complete their 48 weeks of practical training, complete the logbook and the professional examinations before obtaining their Certificate of Registration. This route is available for part-time students also.

Some courses – those at Nottingham Trent, Greenwich, Middlesex, West of England and Edinburgh – allow them to complete a three-year degree course. Most universities that offer the four-year degree course have now applied also to offer it on a three-year basis. Norwich City College hopes to offer such a three-year degree course from 1998.

3. Two-year MSc course in Environmental Health. Courses are offered at University of West of England and at the University of Birmingham. Courses include at least 48 weeks' practical experience.

4. Part-time study of an environmental health/science degree while working as an environmental health technician or technical officer. This route normally takes five or six years on a day release basis. Part-time courses are offered at the following universities: Leeds Metropolitan, Greenwich, Kings College London, Manchester Metropolitan, and at North East Surrey College of Technology and Norwich City College. Students must have at least 48 weeks' practical training at professional level during the course or two years' work experience following it.

The Institute maintains a list of all approved first degree and postgraduate courses that lead to the award of the Certificate of Registration of the Environmental Health Officers Registration Board.

Scotland

The recognized qualification for environmental health officers in Scotland is the Diploma in Environmental Health of the Royal Environmental Health Institute of Scotland. Candidates for the Diploma must hold an honours degree in Environmental Health.

Most trainees are appointed as student environmental health officers with a district council before starting a degree course. To gain the Diploma in Environmental Health, students are required to undertake 48 weeks of practical training, followed by a professional interview aimed at assessing their practical skills.

All courses include chemistry, microbiology, food science and hygiene, statistics, law, housing, public health, occupational health and safety, and pollution. There is a high scientific content, as much of the work relates to the identification and control of problems that can often only be identified in the laboratory.

LATE ENTRY

There are no age restrictions on entry to this occupation. Mature applicants may be accepted on to a degree course without the usual entry requirements, particularly if they have relevant work experience. Adults may prepare for application to a degree course by first studying a science Access course, which most universities accept for entry.

OPPORTUNITIES

Environmental health services are provided at district levels of local government. There are around 6,000 qualified environmental health officers employed by local authorities throughout the country.

There is a steady demand for qualified staff, though applicants may have to move to find a suitable vacancy. Cutbacks in local authority spending have led to a decline in the number of training places available. This has led to fierce competition for trainee posts. The situation may change, depending on local and national government policy and funding.

A growing number of environmental health officers are employed by hotel and retail companies and food manufacturers. Others work as self-employed consultants to industry and commerce.

PAY AND CONDITIONS

Salaries vary between individual local authorities. Newly qualified environmental health officers may earn from £16,000 to £18,000. Those working in the London area are paid additional allowances. Highest-level managers may earn from £25,000 to £40,000.

Environmental health officers work 35 to 39 hours a week, with a rota covering occasional weekend and night duties. It may be necessary to make visits outside the normal hours, in the early mornings and evenings. Flexitime and part-time work may be available.

In Scotland, newly qualified environmental health officers enter on a salary scale starting at £17,000 rising to £21,000.

PROSPECTS

There is a clear promotion path into management, becoming a chief environmental health officer, or section

HEALTH AND SAFETY: COP/COT

leader, after gaining experience and proving managerial ability. It is usual to obtain further qualifications and specialize in certain aspects of the work.

RELATED OCCUPATIONS

Trading standards officer, health and safety inspector, quality controller, safety officer, forensic scientist, meat inspector.

FURTHER INFORMATION

Chartered Institute of Environmental Health*, Chadwick Court, 15 Hatfields, London SE1 8DJ, 0171 928 6006

The Royal Environmental Health Institute of Scotland*, 3 Manor Place, Edinburgh EH3 7DH, 0131 225 6999. www.ed.ac.uk/~tbell/rehis.html

LGMB Layden Hse, 76–86 Turnmill Street, London, EC1M 5QV, 0171 296 6600, http://www.lgmb.gov.uk

FURTHER READING

Leaflets/booklets are available from the addresses marked*.

Working in Local Government – COIC

Careers in Local Government – Kogan Page

In the careers library classified under COP.

2. HEALTH AND SAFETY ADVISER (COT)

BACKGROUND INFORMATION

Health and safety advisers are also called health and safety managers/officers/practitioners/specialists. They are concerned with safe and trouble free operations in industrial and commercial premises including those used by service industries and local and national government, as well as in educational establishments and hospitals.

In some organizations, especially large ones, health and safety officers work with specialists such as qualified medical practitioners or nurses who look after employee health as part of the human resources or personnel department.

THE WORK

Health and safety advisers work in conjunction with line managers, employees, safety groups and trade unions to ensure safety policy and practices are adopted to minimize operational losses, occupational health problems and accidents.

They formulate occupational health and safety strategies and ensure that best working practice is implemented which includes providing practical advice and specific training for improved safety.

Duties include liasing with the appropriate official to ensure that the organization is complying with mandatory health and safety, fire and environmental regulations.

Health and safety advisers concentrate on risk assessment and hazard management, throughout the whole organization. This means identifying unsafe work practices and assessing potential dangers and problems so that they may be eliminated. It also involves carrying out accident investigations and developing preventive and remedial programmes. The work involves encouraging employees to take care of their health and safety, assessing the need for, and advising on wearing personal protective equipment.

Explaining and often enforcing fire regulations is also usually part of the work as is ensuring the safe storage and use of inflammable liquids and gases.

When working in organizations where foodstuffs are being produced or processed, the work involves maintaining high standards of occupational hygiene and complying with food safety regulations.

In addition, the work may involve monitoring and developing means of controlling liquid or gaseous discharges or the disposal of solid wastes as part of the organization's responsibilities under environmental legislation and regulation.

In cases of accidents, it also involves liaison with legal and insurance departments and regulatory bodies such as the Health and Safety Executive or the local authority environmental health officer.

WORK ENVIRONMENT

Although office-based, the health and safety adviser spends much time in the factory, plant or working premises. In large-scale processing plants, on offshore platforms, on construction sites and on transportation systems it means work outdoors – sometimes in extreme weather conditions. It may involve work at heights.

SKILLS AND INTERESTS

As the work involves promoting and ensuring implementation of health and safety policy and practice at every level within the workplace, health and safety advisers require good communication and presentation skills which they need to employ with assertiveness, diplomacy and tact. To overcome frustration at any resistance they encounter, the health and safety adviser also needs to be self-motivated, enthusiastic and committed.

The work is also becoming more technically based so a practical understanding is required as much of the work now involves appreciating the operational processes as well as the use of instruments and electronic monitoring, especially of hazardous conditions.

Knowledge of computer-based word processing, database and spreadsheet systems is important to prepare reports and record and analyse statistics as the basis of analysing trends. Understanding of multi-media systems (due to the advent of CD-ROM and other advanced technology training systems) is also becoming useful.

Physical fitness is needed, especially for operating in large-scale plants or outdoor sites.

An interest in the law and the ability to understand regulations and codes of practices is needed.

ENTRY REQUIREMENTS

A key professional qualification for those seeking to work in health and safety is either the NVQ/SVQ Level 4 in Occupational Health and Safety Practice, or the two-part national diploma awarded by the National Examination Board in Occupational Safety and Health (NEBOSH). Entry to Part Two requires the completion of Part One, an equivalent vocational qualification or others that may be approved by NEBOSH.

Holders of the NEBOSH Diploma, or the NVQ/SVQ

HEALTH AND SAFETY: COP/COT

Level 4 with three years' relevant experience, can apply for corporate membership of the Institution of Occupational Safety and Health (IOSH) and after a year as a member and three years' post-Diploma experience they can apply to be included on the IOSH Register of Safety Practitioners.

Entrants can obtain first degrees offered by a number of universities and colleges in occupational health and safety or health and safety management. Entry to degree courses is with a minimum of five GCSEs/S grades (A–C/1–3) with three A levels/four H grades or two A levels/three H grades and two A/S levels. Equivalent Advanced GNVQs/GSVQ Level III and BTEC national certificates in technical or scientific subjects are also acceptable.

TRAINING

Training is mostly on the job with various short courses in the organization's operations (training alongside managers or operatives) or at some colleges of further education or via specialist training providers. Amongst these is the Institution of Occupational Safety and Health (IOSH) which also provides a programme of continuing professional development with a series of courses for health and safety advisers.

In addition, knowledge for the NVQ/SVQ in Occupational Safety and Health Practice at Levels 3 and 4 can be underpinned by the NEBOSH Diploma.

Study for the NEBOSH Diploma may be full-time, part-time or on a distance learning basis. Part One requires 170 hours of tuition and Part Two needs about 200 hours with private study in both cases. The course comprises of five modules: the management of risk, legal and organizational factors, the workplace and work equipment, safety agencies.

Those with responsibility for health and safety but not employed full-time as a safety adviser (eg managers, supervisors and site agents) may complete the short courses and examinations for the NEBOSH General Certificate or the Certificate in Construction Safety.

NEBOSH also awards the Specialist Diploma in Environmental Management for health and safety advisers to increase knowledge and understanding of the environmental impact in work activities.

In addition, the British Safety Council awards the Diploma in Safety Management.

LATE ENTRY

Graduates in science, engineering or a technical discipline can take postgraduate degrees in occupational health and safety management/technology or risk assessment and management. Students with experience or an equivalent qualification (such as membership or chartered status of a professional body) may be considered for a postgraduate degree.

Adults can gain recognition of any relevant skills and experience by working towards an NVQ/SVQ in Occupational Health and Safety Practice at Level 3 or 4.

Assessment is usually carried out in the workplace and previous experience is taken into account. Study areas range from how to form health and safety policy through to means of implementing it within the legal and moral responsibilities that an organization has for the health and safety of its employees.

NEBOSH will consider experienced health and safety officers as candidates for the Diploma and Certificate.

OPPORTUNITIES

Though traditionally associated with industrial, processing and manufacturing sites, health and safety advisers can be employed in food processing and packaging plants as well as in hotel and restaurant chains.

Health and safety advisers also work in hospitals, local authority and national government organizations and establishments.

Jobs for Health and Safety Officers are advertised in *The Safety and Health Practitioner, Hazards, Health and Safety at Work, Health and Safety Europe, Health and Safety in Industry and Commerce, Occupational Health, Occupational Health Review, Occupational Safety* and *Health and Safety Management*.

PAY AND CONDITIONS

Salaries start at about £9,000 for health and safety advisers working part-time but mid-range practitioners earn between £15,000 to £18,000.

At the top end of the scale, health and safety managers and directors devising policy and managing specialist teams implementing the practice in the oil, gas, petrochemical and nuclear power and processing industries can expect to earn £60,000 to £70,000. Similar salaries are earned in the pharmaceuticals industry. Health and safety advisers, implementing the tactical programmes, can expect to earn up to £30,000 plus shift allowances and payments for unsociable hours.

Those supervising the implementation of health and safety in other production and operational environments would earn up between £25,000 and £34,000.

Other benefits usually include occupational pension contributions, and private health plans.

PROSPECTS

With the future involvement of the health and safety adviser in production and operations, a distinctive career pattern is developing whereby a fully trained and qualified health and safety adviser can rise to a key management position with business, administrative and relevant technical skills. This trend is underlined by recent mandatory requirements (formed in Westminster and Brussels) as well as increased litigation by accident victims in the workplace.

In particularly hazardous environments (such as nuclear power and processing, oil, gas and petrochemicals), health and safety advisers with high-level technical qualifications can expect to progress to well-paid employment.

RELATED OCCUPATIONS

Health and safety consultant, occupational health nurse, occupational hygienist.

FURTHER INFORMATION

Institution of Occupational Health and Safety (IOSH)*, The Grange, Highfield Drive, Wigston, Leicestershire LE18 1NN, 0116 257 3100, www.iosh.co.uk

The National Examination Board in Occupational Safety

HEALTH AND SAFETY: COP/COT

and Health (NEBOSH)*, NEBOSH House, The Grange, Highfield Drive, Wigston, Leicestershire LE18 1PP, 0116 288 8858

The Occupational Health and Safety Lead Body (OHSLB)*, 8th Floor, Rose Court, 2 Southwark Bridge, London SE1 9HS, 0171 717 6000

FURTHER READING

Leaflets/Booklets available from the addresses marked*.

Courses in Occupational Health and Safety leading to NEBOSH Examinations – NEBOSH

Safety and Health – Part of Everybody's Working Life – IOSH

In the careers library classified under COT.

3. HEALTH AND SAFETY INSPECTOR (COT)

BACKGROUND INFORMATION

Health and Safety inspectors are civil servants, employed by the Health and Safety Executive (HSE), a part of the Department of the Environment, Transport and the Regions. The Executive is responsible for ensuring the health and safety of workers and members of the public who may be affected by work activities, and for minimizing injuries caused by unsafe working practices. Through its inspectors it is responsible for enforcing health and safety legislation and may prosecute offenders where necessary.

The Executive is divided into a number of Directorates and Divisions, the largest of which is the Field Operations Directorate. This is made up of Factory, Agricultural and Quarries Inspectors, Regional Specialist Groups and which include doctors and specialist inspectors who are all supported by administrative teams.

Inspectors visit industrial premises as well as hospitals, docks, construction sites, sports grounds, fairgrounds and commercial premises other than shops, which are the responsibility of the Local Authority Environmental Health Officers. Specialist inspectors in the Regional Specialist Groups cover technical aspects, such as mechanical engineering, chemicals, construction, electrical matters and explosives. Other Inspectorates deal with Railways, Offshore Safety, Mines, Nuclear Installations, and Chemicals and Explosives.

This article deals mainly with the more general work and training of the Field Operations Directorate inspectors.

THE WORK

Health and safety inspectors work from offices within one of seven regions and are responsible for the inspection of workplaces that fall within HSE's remit. They work in groups of six or eight inspectors, reporting to a principal inspector. National Interest Groups within the Sectors have responsibility for the policy relating to different sectors of industry. Within limitations, inspectors have much freedom in planning their own work. Headquarters provides guidelines on planning and work targets, but much is left to the discretion of Regional Directors who know the needs of their own Regions.

A principal inspector may allocate a number of premises to each inspector, who must then draw up their own plans for the year's work. Not all premises can be visited annually, but inspectors must know which are 'high risk' or have proved unsatisfactory on previous visits, as against those which can safely be inspected less regularly.

Inspectors usually give no advance warning of their visits. They are mainly concerned with the management's or employer's strategies for controlling risks to health and safety. On arrival, they ask to see the person in charge and are taken on a tour of the premises. They check machinery, management systems, equipment, substances and working methods. Among the things they are looking for might be unguarded machinery, toxic or inflammable materials not stored correctly, workers taking short cuts to increase speed but ignoring safety regulations, and excessive levels of dust or fumes. If they see any evidence of unsafe practices, they first try to persuade the owner or manager to remedy the situation. If verbal advice is ignored they may take several legal steps, from issuing a written 'improvement' notice – which gives an employer a certain period of time to put matters right; a 'prohibition' order – ordering work to cease until the required improvement is made; to taking a prosecution. Inspectors use prosecution as a last resort and prefer to achieve their objectives by persuasion and diplomacy. After each visit, inspectors type a full report.

About 35 per cent of inspections are routine assessments. Inspectors carry out the rest in response to complaints, accidents or disasters.

If inspectors feel in need of more technical help, they can obtain this by calling in an expert from a regional team of specialist inspectors. They may also use the services of the Health and Safety Executive's own research and analytical laboratories.

Inspectors in England and Wales conduct their own prosecutions in the magistrates' courts or, if a case goes to a higher court, they provide the necessary information for lawyers conducting the case and appear as witnesses. In Scotland, inspectors refer cases for prosecution to the Procurator Fiscal. If a case goes to trial the inspector may be called as a witness.

WORK ENVIRONMENT

Inspectors are based in offices, but spend at least 50 per cent of their time visiting a wide variety of workplaces, both indoors and outside. Conditions may be noisy, dirty, smelly or dangerous. They may have to work outdoors in all weathers, at height or in confined spaces, for example crawling under road tunnels to examine air ducts. When necessary, they wear protective clothing.

SKILLS AND INTERESTS

Health and safety inspectors need to be observant, able to pay attention to detail, and make accurate assessments of potential safety hazards. They must be capable of absorbing a large amount of information, continually updating their knowledge, keeping abreast both of new technology in the various work places, and changes to health and safety legislation.

They must enjoy working on their own, be willing to make their own decisions and accept responsibility for them. However, they must also know when to ask colleagues for advice, or when to call on the expertise of a specialist inspector for technical help.

They must be able to plan their own work, and be sufficiently flexible to change their plans in response to a

HEALTH AND SAFETY: COP/COT

sudden emergency that requires an immediate visit.

Inspectors must be good communicators, as they need to establish relationships with a wide range of people: employers, managers, workers and those in other government departments. Since they rely heavily on advice and persuasion in their work they must be tactful and diplomatic, yet assertive when necessary.

Public speaking skills are important. If they do decide to bring a prosecution they must be able to present facts clearly when presenting the case in court. Senior inspectors sometimes have to give press and television interviews, either following an incident or as part of a particular publicity campaign.

Written communication skills are also important, since inspectors have to write reports on investigations and inspections they carry out.

ENTRY REQUIREMENTS

Inspectors should normally have a degree or an equivalent qualification. Exceptionally, applications will be considered from those without a degree who can demonstrate clearly the intellectual qualities required. In addition, applicants will need to offer at least two years work experience, which could be either paid or voluntary employment.

Entry requirements for degree and higher diploma courses vary according to the subject of study and the university or college chosen.

Minimum entry requirements for a degree course are usually: two A levels/three H grades plus five GCSEs/S grades (A–C/1–3); or Advanced GNVQ/GSVQ Level III; or a BTEC/SQA national award; or equivalent.

All entrants must meet Civil Service nationality requirements and possess a full UK driving licence.

TRAINING

Inspectors have a two-year training period, the first year of which is probationary.

Practical training is conducted on-the-job. Trainees usually work in two different industry groups during the training period. At first they accompany and observe experienced inspectors, then gradually carry out site visits under supervision as they gain in confidence, writing reports which they discuss with a senior inspector.

They also attend a number of short, in-house specialist courses, including a one-week course in communication skills.

Once they have successfully completed the probationary year, they will study for a mandatory post graduate Diploma in Occupational Health and Safety. This course is run at Aston University over a period of 21 weeks. The course is a combination of residential modules at the University and some distance learning. There are a series of course examinations which they are required to pass in order to continue their career as an inspector.

Throughout their training, they will be developing the knowledge and competence, through practical and formal training, to achieve an NVQ/SVQ Level 4 in Health and Safety Regulation. It is normally expected that this be completed in the first three years.

LATE ENTRY

As well as having the normal entry requirements, applicants can offer life and work experience to the role of health and safety inspector.

OPPORTUNITIES

There are approximately 660 inspectors, working in 20 offices across the seven Regions. Numbers of specialist inspectors are much smaller.

There are opportunities to work in different industry groups as an individual inspector's interests develop, to move to the head office on Merseyside and to work in branches concerned with policy-making in London.

PAY AND CONDITIONS

Entrants start on £16,000 (national scale) or £16,600 plus London Weighting (in London). On promotion, the next post carries a salary up to £31,368. Annual increments are dependent on performance in the job.

Health and safety inspectors normally work a standard five-day week, Monday to Friday, of 37 hours nationally excluding lunch and 36 hours in London, but must be prepared to make some visits at unsociable hours or at weekends in the case of emergencies.

In order to run its business flexibly, HSE needs to be able to move staff according to need. Inspectors must therefore be prepared to move on appointment, if necessary, and to any part of the UK in the future.

PROSPECTS

Inspectors are recruited at Band 4 (Higher Executive Officer equivalent). They should gain promotion to Band 3 after two years, subject to satisfactory performance and the attainment of the post graduate diploma.

RELATED OCCUPATIONS

Environmental health officer, health and safety consultant, occupational hygienist, safety officer, trading standards officer.

FURTHER INFORMATION

Health and Safety Executive*, St Hugh's House, Stanley Precinct, Bootle L20 3QY, 0151 951 3366

Office of Public Service and Science (OPSS)*, Cabinet Office, Fast-Stream and European Staffing Division, Room 127/2, Horse Guards Road, London SW1P 3AL, 0171 270 5697

FURTHER READING

Leaflets/booklets are available from the addresses marked*

In the careers library classified under COT.

GROUP E – ART AND DESIGN

1. GRAPHIC DESIGNER CLCI:ED
2. ILLUSTRATOR/ARTIST CLCI:ED
3. THREE-DIMENSIONAL DESIGNER CLCI:EG
4. FASHION DESIGNER CLCI:EJ
5. TEXTILE DESIGNER CLCI:EP
6. INTERIOR DESIGNER CLCI:ET

BACKGROUND INFORMATION

There are very few areas of modern living that are not influenced by the work of artists and designers. Every item in the sitting room of a house is produced using art and design skills – furniture, carpets, wall coverings, curtains, television sets, telephones, ornaments and paintings have all been professionally designed or painted. Design techniques also extend to every other room from kitchen to bathroom, and in the wider environment to advertisements, books, exhibitions, buildings like schools, hospitals, shops, offices and factories, and transport systems.

The distinction between art and design is not clear-cut, but in general it is accepted that artists are concerned purely with self-expression. They create pieces of work that people will eventually buy because they like them. Designers could be described as applied artists. They use a combination of creativity and technical knowledge to produce designs for products that serve a specific purpose while at the same time are pleasing to look at.

Designers have to accept limits on their creativity, since articles have to be produced within set time limits and to stipulated budgets; the clients commissioning the work will usually have their own ideas and requirements. Depending on their specialism, they may produce a design for selling and promotional purposes that must have a sharp impact on consumers, as in advertising and marketing. Alternatively, they may design a product or a piece of equipment that has to be reliable and safe to use.

Whilst some design work is concerned with totally new products, the majority is concerned with modifications or improvements to existing ones.

Two-dimensional design communicates ideas through illustration, colour and, often, words, on flat surfaces. It includes graphic, textile and surface pattern design (for furnishing fabrics, china and pottery).

Three-dimensional design is concerned with the effective use of form and space and embraces many specialisms: fashion, glass, ceramics, furniture, interior exhibition, industrial, theatre design, and jewellery and silversmithing.

Graphic design is part of the communications industry. Graphic designers have to know how to put across a message for information or publicity purposes, using illustration, line and colour. They work closely with copy writers or advertising writers who produce the text of an advertisement, leaflet etc. Graphic designers can also be involved in designing advertisements and educational information that use multi-media, sound and visuals, to convey the message and which are produced as a CD-ROM.

Illustration is concerned with the visual image that stands alongside written text, eg representing a scene from a novel or illustrating a technical process that the author has described. (Computer Aided Design – CAD – is now used a lot by illustrators.)

Three-dimensional (3D) design is the broadest category of design. 3D designers work with a range of materials including metal, plastics, wood and glass. They design the exterior of a product, which may or may not contain moving parts. (Strictly speaking, design for products containing working parts forms another subdivision – **manufacturing** or **engineering design**.)

Fashion designers design garments and accessories while **textile designers** produce both print and weave and knitted, embroidered, embellished designs for the fabrics from which clothes, household linens and furnishings are made.

Interior or **spatial design** is another broad area, which contains its own subdivisions of exhibition/display/retail design and theatre/set/stage design. Interior designers are responsible for effective and attractive use of space – whether it is a small stage set for a production or a large national exhibition centre.

Whatever their specialism, all designers share similar working practices. If working on a project, designers first receive a brief, or detailed specification, from the client or person/company paying for the work, discuss this with the client, study the requirements, carry out research, and present ideas to the client – which are often modified several times – before producing the final design. If they work as freelances, they assess the market for different types of work, make up sample designs and are then responsible for finding buyers through their own efforts.

1. GRAPHIC DESIGNER (ED)

THE WORK

Graphic designers convey ideas and information through the appropriate use of images and words.

Designers receive the brief for the project together with the results of any market research already completed on the target audience and discuss it thoroughly with the client, clarifying the aim of the project and the media to be used. They are also given a time-scale to work to and are informed of the limit on cost.

Examples of graphic design projects include: a promotional cover for a book jacket or record sleeve; stationery for a company selling a particular product or service, which is to be suggested by the letter heading; designs for a retailer, which will be used on labels, carrier bags and signs throughout the store and which will have a common logo and colour scheme; a coloured signing scheme for a hospital which could include carpet stripes and wall designs in the same colour to lead patients easily to one department; brochures for a small company to be mailed out, promoting its services; a major advertising campaign incorporating posters, leaflets, brochures and TV advertisements; an encyclopaedia produced on multi-media CD-ROM which uses sounds, photographs, animations, video and film clips and text to bring the information to life.

After discussing the brief with the client, graphic designers do any necessary research, including looking at previous related projects and comparing costs of using different processes. They also consult the copywriter, if any new text is to be written, and make sure that both understand the aims of the project.

They next make rough sketches as a base for a series of visuals, or mock-ups, that they produce to show to the

ART AND DESIGN: E

client. Depending on where they are employed, or whether they are self-employed, they may liaise directly with the client. In large studios, a senior designer or design manager is responsible for all liaison work with clients, attending all necessary meetings and then briefing the design team.

Visuals may be rough or simple sketches and sample black-and-white or colour layouts showing the spacing of the text, size of illustrations, type of lettering and headings, or they may be highly finished, closely resembling the intended finished design.

After discussion with clients, designs often have to be changed and re-submitted. Later, when the words are incorporated, the graphic designer may have to make further alterations if the text is now longer than at first proposed.

When the final layout is approved, the designer prepares detailed instructions for the printer, specifying typefaces and sizes, and produces either a full-colour layout, or one in black and white, with every colour to be used at each point clearly indicated with marker pen.

Much design work can now be created and manipulated via electronic systems, the whole page being designed using desktop publishing, altering wording and layout on the computer screen. In some cases the disk is sent direct to the printer. Hand skills are still used, however, at least in the early sketching stages. Graphic designers therefore work with a range of equipment – computer or drawing board and layout paper, using pencils, crayons, water colours and marker pens in the exact shade of the printer's ink colours.

WORK ENVIRONMENT

Graphic designers spend most of their time working in studios. They also, however, visit clients at their premises, and travel to see printers and possibly to visit exhibitions or libraries when doing research. Some stages of their work are done alone, but many work in teams. In addition, they work closely with colleagues such as account executives, copywriters and marketing or public relations professionals.

SKILLS AND INTERESTS

Graphic designers must possess creative talent and imagination and be able to visualize the end result of a project. At the same time they must understand the technical processes through which their work will be put. They must also be able to analyse problems and suggest solutions.

All need a thorough understanding of the technicalities of printing processes, surfaces, inks and colours. Some use hand drawing skills more than others, but the following skills are still essential.

They must be able to use computers. A basic understanding of photography techniques is also important.

They must be able to manage their time well and accept the discipline of working to tight deadlines, very often putting in long hours, if necessary, in order to finish a project on schedule.

As they work with colour, defective colour vision could present a handicap in this career.

Communication skills are necessary, when working with clients, in order to put forward their own ideas and explain why a certain idea might not work. Teamwork is important.

They need an understanding of business skills, budgets and costing.

They also need to be able to accept criticism and rejection of work on which they may have spent considerable time.

ENTRY REQUIREMENTS

These vary according to the level of training course chosen. (It is very difficult now to get a job as a junior in a studio and work up, although it may be possible in some parts of the country; day release courses still exist.)

Most graphic designers have completed one or more of the full-time courses listed below. There are no minimum entry requirements; students may be accepted on the basis of a good portfolio of work and interview. However, most colleges expect academic qualifications in addition. Requirements vary from college to college and must always be checked individually. The most usual entry requirements are given below.

Foundation course: two years for students aged 16 years with five GCSEs/S grades (A–C/1–3) or one year for students aged 17 years with the same qualifications. However, colleges may ask for higher qualifications for the one-year route, including A levels or H grades.

A Foundation course for students aged 18 years plus in England and Wales requires a minimum of one A level Art/CDT and five GCSEs (A–C/1–3).

An Advanced GNVQ/GSVQ Level III in Art and Design (General) can be an alternative to a foundation course and normally takes two years. (GNVQs in Art and Design are also available at Foundation and Intermediate levels; GSVQs in Design at Levels II and III.) When students begin a specialist Design course (in this case for graphic design) they take one of the following:

BTEC/SQA national diploma or certificate. Entry is usually with a minimum of four GCSEs/S grades (A–C/1–3).

BTEC/SQA higher national diploma or certificate. These normally require successful completion of a national-level programme, a foundation course or, exceptionally, four GCSEs/S grades (A–C/1–3) plus one A level/two H grades.

There are: a BTEC Higher National award in Design; SQA national awards in Graphic Reproduction, and in Graphics and Illustration, and SQA Higher National awards in Graphic Design, and in Graphics and Illustration.

Degree course. In England and Wales the entry requirements are usually a minimum of five GCSEs/S grades (A–C/1–3) plus two A levels and, often, successful completion of a foundation course.

In Scotland, completion of a foundation course is not required, but entry requirements are higher. Applicants must have: five S grades (1–3) plus three H grades including English; or five GCSEs (A–C) plus two A levels with English being included at either level; or a BTEC national award plus A level English/SQA national award plus H grade English.

An NVQ/SVQ in Graphic Design is available at Level 2.

TRAINING

Foundation and general art and design courses act as a preparation for a higher-level specialist course. Students are introduced to a wide range of techniques and specialisms and are helped by tutors to decide on the branch of design in which they wish to specialize.

Students who are sure of their career intentions and are able to convince admissions staff, through their portfolio of work and by interview, that they are ready for a specialized course, may apply for direct entry to a relevant higher diploma or degree course. (It is, however, rare to gain admission without having completed a foundation course.)

Some students choose to take a postgraduate course of one to three years before entering employment.

Intermediate GNVQ/GSVQ Level II diploma courses last one year; Advanced GNVQ/GSVQ Level III/national diploma courses, two years; higher national courses take two years full-time. Degrees in Scotland take four years, with the first year acting as a diagnostic year similar to a foundation course. In England and Wales most degree courses take three years. (Four-year sandwich courses are occasionally available.) Recently introduced are some four-year design 'pathways' which include a 'year zero' diagnostic course which is similar to a one year 18 plus Foundation course in Art and Design.

The content of graphic design courses varies with different aspects being given greater emphasis by different institutions, so syllabuses must be carefully checked.

After completing a course, many designers join a company or agency, where they must carry out routine tasks or work on small parts of projects before being assigned greater responsibility. At this stage they may work for higher qualifications through part-time study or open learning.

LATE ENTRY

Mature students may be accepted on to courses with fewer than usual, or no qualifications, if they possess a good portfolio of work.

OPPORTUNITIES

There are more openings in graphic design than in many other areas. More than 50 per cent of designers working in commerce and industry are in graphics. It is still a very competitive field, however, with new designers leaving colleges each year, and it can be difficult to find a first job or to become established as a freelance designer.

Many graphic designers opt for freelance work, which means they must constantly promote themselves to prospective clients by showing their portfolios or sending samples of work. When established, they may gain commissions from previous clients. Their reputation always depends on the quality of the last project they completed for a client.

Salaried graphic designers work for particular employers, such as advertising agencies, TV companies, publishers, or for design groups and consultancies that gain commissions from a wide variety of clients.

PAY AND CONDITIONS

Salaries vary according to ability, experience and the type of employer. Salaried designers could expect a starting salary of £11,500 to £13,000. Experienced designers could expect to earn an average of £22,000, with design managers earning from £20,000 to £35,000 (more in London).

The salary of freelance graphic designers depends very much on their reputation, the effort put into marketing their work and seeking out new clients, and the number of hours they choose to work. Successful designers could earn over £30,000 and very well-established designers might earn up to £60,000, but initially work may be slow to come in and earnings low in a competitive environment.

Graphic designers often work normal office hours, five days a week, with considerable overtime required when working to deadlines. Freelance designers choose their own hours. There are opportunities for part-time employment and to work from home.

PROSPECTS

Salaried graphic designers often work for agencies or companies that have a promotion structure. Progress to senior designer or design manager – who direct the work of teams – is possible, or to art director – who is responsible for creating new ideas, liaising with clients and bringing in new work. Alternatively, designers change employers in order to achieve higher salaries. It is, in fact, quite acceptable to change employers frequently in order to acquire a range of experience.

RELATED OCCUPATIONS

Art director, advertising account executive, copywriter, marketing manager, photographer, signwriter.

FURTHER INFORMATION AND READING

Please see article 6. INTERIOR DESIGNER.

2. ILLUSTRATOR/ARTIST (ED)

THE WORK

Illustrators

Illustrators combine elements of fine art and graphic design in their work, producing drawings and paintings for illustrations to accompany text in books and magazines. They also provide images for use in brochures, leaflets, advertising companies/corporate literature – posters, packaging (food, drink, household goods), retail display and exhibition design.

They discuss a brief with an editor or designer who describes the editorial content and the style required. They may read the whole text in order to get the 'feel' of it and may also consult the author.

First, designs are prepared and shown to the client. Following discussion, designs may have to be changed, and later, when the words are incorporated and the page layout finalized, the illustrator may have to make more alterations if the text is longer than at first intended.

General illustration includes all types of pictorial material but, in practice, many illustrators specialize and receive commissions from art editors who know of their work and its appropriateness for the publication in question.

Scientific, medical and technical illustration are three particular specialisms that cover the illustration of buildings, products, processes, illustrations for scientific textbooks, and, in the case of medical illustration, can include illustrating the stages of a new surgical technique.

Artists

Artists have very similar skills to those of the illustrator, in that they draw and paint. However, their work is not produced with any commercial constraints but for purely aesthetic reasons. They have usually studied fine art.

Since they rely on selling their work for a living, they must be able to promote their art, approaching managers of galleries and exhibitions to persuade them to display

ART AND DESIGN: E

pieces. They must also develop business skills and be able to price work realistically. They may sell paintings for anything from a few pounds to several thousand pounds.

Very few artists make a living from selling work alone. Many combine it with teaching while others undertake some commercial art commissions – eg illustration work, signwriting or occasionally, scenic artist work, painting the 'flats' or backgrounds for theatre sets.

WORK ENVIRONMENT

Illustrators spend most of their time working in studios. Many work from home. They also spend considerable time taking their portfolios to commissioning clients in editorial, publishing, design, advertising and the gift industry in order to get work, and may travel to see printers and visit libraries when doing research.

SKILLS AND INTERESTS

Illustrators must possess creative talent and imagination. Communication skills are also necessary. They must be able to grasp exactly what it is a client has in mind so as to make their own suggestions for suitable illustrations to accompany text.

Like graphic designers, they must understand the technicalities of printing processes. Some illustrators use computer-aided design (CAD) to make illustrations, some scan in drawing-based work and enhance it with the use of computers. Some continue drawing and painting by hand.

Most illustrators are freelance. Therefore, they need self discipline and time-management ability plus business and marketing skills. They must be prepared to take their portfolios to potential clients and negotiate contracts and fees.

They must be able to accept criticism and rejection of work on which they have spent considerable time.

As they work with colour, defective colour vision could cause difficulties.

ENTRY REQUIREMENTS

See article 1. GRAPHIC DESIGNER.

TRAINING

This is largely described under article 1. GRAPHIC DESIGNER.

SQA National Awards are available in Fine Art and in Graphics and Illustration; and SQA Higher National Awards are available in Graphics and Illustration.

There are some courses in general illustration and others in the specialist branches: technical illustration; scientific and technical graphics; and industrial, scientific and technical illustration. There is one evening course in wildlife technical illustration (Bournemouth and Poole College).

Illustration may also be studied jointly with graphic design and, at some colleges, with animation.

LATE ENTRY

Mature entrants may be accepted onto courses with fewer than usual, or no qualifications, if they possess a good portfolio of work.

OPPORTUNITIES

Most illustrators are self-employed. It can be very difficult to become established. They must constantly market their work by showing their portfolios to possible clients. When established they may get commissions from previous clients or by word of mouth.

A very few work for design consultancies or in-house design departments.

PAY AND CONDITIONS

Please see article 1. GRAPHIC DESIGNER.

Salaries vary according to ability, experience, the effort put into marketing their work and seeking out new clients, and the number of hours they choose to work.

PROSPECTS

Salaried illustrators could become design managers.

RELATED OCCUPATIONS

Art director, advertising account executive, copywriter, graphic designer, marketing manager, photographer, signwriter.

FURTHER INFORMATION AND READING

Please see article 6. INTERIOR DESIGNER.

3. THREE-DIMENSIONAL DESIGNER (EG)

THE WORK

Three-dimensional (3D) designers are concerned with making a product look attractive and at the same time functional, and easy to use and maintain.

3D designers usually choose to specialize in either industrial or craft-based design and follow appropriate training courses.

Since many products contain internal working parts, industrial designers work closely with the engineers who design these and must themselves have an understanding of engineering principles.

Craft-based designers mainly design static objects – such as ornaments, pieces of jewellery and furniture. Their designs may be for mass-production in factories or for production by individual craftworkers, using traditional methods. Some produce their own designs and are more properly called designer/craftworkers.

The work of 3D designers has similarities wherever they work, but varies in detail in different industries, companies and in self-employment.

Designers examine their brief carefully and make notes of any problems they can foresee. They then discuss it thoroughly with everyone who will be involved in production and sales – production managers, design engineers and marketing staff – taking into account factors like safety, availability of materials, and whether the product can be manufactured using available machinery and equipment.

The next stage is to produce the design. Designers begin by selecting materials, colours and possible shapes for the product, bearing in mind the intended market.

Technical or price constraints often change designers' first

ART AND DESIGN: E

ideas. Often, they are working to a tight schedule – and on several products simultaneously – and must produce new ideas within a specified time.

When a design has been approved, designers prepare detailed working designs. They may do this themselves, or it may be done by specialist draughtsmen/women. In either case, much of the design is likely to be done using a computer.

A full-size working test model or prototype of the product may then be made and if this is seen to work satisfactorily, full-scale production begins. The designer is normally expected to be available to help to solve any problems that might arise during manufacture.

WORK ENVIRONMENT

This is similar to that of the graphic designer with the exception that 3D designers' colleagues include engineers, production managers and technical experts, in addition to marketing managers. Please see article 1. GRAPHIC DESIGNER.

SKILLS AND INTERESTS

3D designers should be creative and imaginative, and possess the ability to think logically and solve problems. They must also be able to visualize and think in three dimensions.

They must be able to sketch, in order to demonstrate their ideas, and to produce very detailed drawings and specifications for production workers to follow. Increasingly, they must be able to make use of computer-aided design.

They need some mathematical ability and scientific knowledge (usually of physics and engineering principles, although some chemistry may also be necessary when working with different materials and their properties).

Craft-based designers need less engineering knowledge, but must understand all the hand processes involved in manufacturing the objects they design: carving, decorating, firing, glazing, engraving etc.

3D designers should be good communicators. They must be capable of presenting their ideas and justifying a point of view when necessary. Persuasive skills are often useful.

They need an understanding of business skills, budgets and costing.

Poor colour vision could be a handicap.

Like all designers, they must be willing to accept criticism and rejection of work on which they may have spent considerable time.

ENTRY REQUIREMENTS

Please see article 1. GRAPHIC DESIGNER.

Some colleges specify passes in maths, technology or science.

TRAINING

Please see article 1.GRAPHIC DESIGNER.

NVQs are available in Ceramic Design; Product Design and Furniture Design, all at Level 2, and Design at Levels 3 and 4.

NB New BTEC (Edexcel) national diplomas are to be launched which will include Three-Dimensional design as a generic title with various pathways. Please contact Edexcel Foundation.

BTEC higher national awards in Ceramics; Crafts; Industrial Design; Jewellery and Packaging.

Numerous universities throughout the UK offer degree courses in 3D design. These courses may be broad-based or specialize in either industrial or craft-based design. Students are usually required to attend a foundation course in art and design prior to acceptance onto a degree course. There are also a number of postgraduate MA courses available for students who have successfully completed a first degree.

Industrial design courses often have titles such as product design, industrial design or 3D design. They are predominantly available at higher diploma and degree level, with a small number offered at national diploma level. National diploma courses are available at: Bournemouth and Poole College of Art and Design; Cardonald College, Glasgow; Coventry Technical College; Dunstable College and increasingly GNVQ/GSVQ Advanced and Foundation courses have Three-Dimensional pathways.

Craft-based design courses are available at all levels and may also be known as 3D design or as design crafts. There is usually the opportunity to specialize, for example, in wood, metals and plastics.

Competition for places on 3D design courses is not as severe as in other branches of art and design.

LATE ENTRY

Please see article 1. GRAPHIC DESIGNER.

OPPORTUNITIES

Traditionally, engineers designed the exterior of a product in addition to its internal components. In some companies this is still the case. However, there has been a growing awareness of the need for designers with creative skills who can combine these with an understanding of technology. The openings for 3D designers are therefore increasing.

Industrial designers may be employed as staff designers by manufacturers, or work for design consultancies, or in partnerships of consulting design engineers.

Some craft-based designers work for manufacturers. Others are self-employed, either as freelance designers, submitting their designs to manufacturers, or making the products they have designed. Opportunities for this type of employment depend on the market for their work and how easily they can afford the equipment required.

PAY AND CONDITIONS

Please see article 1. GRAPHIC DESIGNER.

PROSPECTS

Newly qualified 3D designers may begin work in a design team in either a manufacturing company or in a design consultancy. Promotion to senior designer or design manager is possible.

Prospects in self-employment depend on the designer's ability to find outlets for work and also on business skills.

Some 3D designers move into marketing, sales or technical writing.

ART AND DESIGN: E

RELATED OCCUPATIONS

Architect, engineering craftsman/woman, engineer, interior designer, model maker, packaging designer, potter.

FURTHER INFORMATION AND READING

Please see article 6. INTERIOR DESIGNER.

4. FASHION DESIGNER (EJ)

THE WORK

Designers usually work in one of three main fields: couture; designer ready-to-wear; or high-street fashion. They may also specialize in various types of clothing: outerwear, lingerie, swimwear, knitwear or theatrical costumes. The majority work in clothing, but some specialize in hats and other accessories.

Couture involves the design of garments for individual customers, who pay for original clothes and attend the designer's workroom for fittings.

Most designers also design ready-to-wear clothes. These are produced in fairly small numbers and sold under the designer's label.

Mass market work involves the design of clothes and accessories that will be sold in large quantities through shops.

Ranges are designed and produced by wholesale manufacturers who sell them to retailers for resale.

Designs are produced well in advance of clothes appearing in the shops – often a year ahead. Designers do not work alone on this, but in close co-operation with fashion buyers from retail companies and fashion forecasters, whose job is to predict what customers will want two seasons ahead.

The first design stage takes the form of sketches, done by hand or using a computer. Fabrics and trimmings are then selected. At this stage, designers usually try out their ideas by pinning fabrics on to a dummy.

Then comes the making-up stage. Designers and their assistants make a pattern and cut sample garments, noting the number of different operations needed to make the garment and taking steps to reduce these, if necessary, to keep in line with budgeted costs.

Some designers cut the patterns themselves and make up the samples. Large manufacturers normally employ specialist pattern cutters and sample machinists. When the garment goes into production, the designer remains on hand to assist with any problems that arise.

WORK ENVIRONMENT

Fashion designers spend some of their time working alone, or with one or two other people in studios. They also attend meetings with textile designers, fashion buyers, production managers and individual clients. Most also have to work closely with sample machinists and pattern cutters.

They may travel extensively in this country and abroad to attend shows and sell their work and keep up-to-date with international trends.

SKILLS AND INTERESTS

Fashion designers must be artistic, creative and know how to use textiles effectively. They need an eye for tone and colour. Poor colour vision could be a handicap.

They should be able to explain their ideas through sketches, but do not need outstanding drawing ability. In developing a design, computer-aided design techniques may be used.

Communication and persuasive skills are important. Much of their time may be spent in persuading buyers from large retailers to accept their ideas.

Designers need a thorough understanding of how garments are made and should have a sound training in hand and machine sewing and in pattern cutting. They must be able to calculate the costs of producing garments.

Freelance designers need business and marketing skills. They must be prepared to take their portfolios to potential clients and negotiate contracts and fees.

Last, they need to be able to accept criticism and rejection of their ideas.

ENTRY REQUIREMENTS

Please also see article 1. GRAPHIC DESIGNER.

TRAINING

This is largely described in article 1. GRAPHIC DESIGNER.

Most designers have some formal design training. Although, in theory, it is possible to train in a designer's studio, openings are almost non-existent.

NB BTEC (Edexcel) national diplomas are also being launched. Please contact Edexcel Foundation.

BTEC Higher National awards are available in Fashion/Surface Pattern, and in Fashion/Textiles. There are SQA National awards available in Fashion and Clothing; Fashion with Business Administration; Fashion – Design and Production with Retail.

BTEC Higher National Diploma and National Diploma courses in Design (Footwear/Accessories) are available at Cordwainers College, London.

Numerous universities throughout the UK offer degree courses and postgraduate courses in fashion.

Fashion design courses may concentrate solely on design, or may combine this with management, marketing or technology. (A certain amount of technology is included on all courses.) A growing number of courses include tuition in a European language.

Many have specialist options such as knitwear, footwear or accessory design.

Courses in clothing technology concentrate on garment production and management, but if they include design, they can be a suitable preparation for work in mass-market design.

LATE ENTRY

Please see article 1. GRAPHIC DESIGNER.

OPPORTUNITIES

Very few designers become well-known names. The largest number work in the mass-market sector with very few finding openings as assistants to couture designers.

New graduates from British higher education institutions often spend a period working abroad, particularly in Italy and France, to gain further experience in an international environment before looking for a job at home.

ART AND DESIGN: E

There are opportunities to work in design studios within manufacturing companies. A new graduate is likely to begin here as the junior in the design team and must be prepared to do the more routine tasks, initially. Some begin as pattern cutters.

Other fashion designers work in specialist design studios that produce designs for a number of manufacturers, and others opt for self-employment.

Designers who have specialized in costume design are sometimes employed by theatrical costumiers, or more usually work on a contract basis with film and TV companies.

PAY AND CONDITIONS

Please see article 1. GRAPHIC DESIGNER.

PROSPECTS

In a manufacturer's design studio there are prospects of promotion to senior designer or to move into design management, which is less concerned with producing designs and more with acting as the link between designers, production managers and workers in mass-market production companies.

Alternatively, designers change employers in order to achieve higher salaries.

There are possibilities to move into associated jobs such as marketing, buying, production management and, occasionally, into fashion forecasting.

RELATED OCCUPATIONS

Clothing production manager, fashion buyer, pattern cutter, quality controller, sample machinist, tailor, textile designer, fashion trend forecaster.

FURTHER INFORMATION AND READING

Please see article 6. INTERIOR DESIGNER.

5. TEXTILE DESIGNER (EP)

THE WORK

Designers usually specialize in printed, woven or knitted textiles. They may also specialize in designs for one particular type of product, for example furnishing fabrics, men's or women's clothing, or in designs for other surface patterns – not strictly textiles, but those decorated with a pattern repeat – like wallpaper or wrapping paper.

Before starting work on a design, textile designers research the market. They must be aware of fashions in colour, design trends and the popularity of different fabrics. They may analyse previous sales figures, and work with fashion designers and buyers in anticipating trends.

Every design must take into account the way in which the fabric is produced and the eventual cost. If the design is to be woven in, the designer has to consider the quality of the yarn and the dyes and colours available. If it is to be printed, the number of different colours each requiring a separate screen for printing will affect the final cost.

The first rough sketches are produced on paper. Next the designer works out the construction of the design to very accurate measurements, using squared paper or computer, and specifying the colours of different parts of the thread and the position of the design on the fabric.

The sample stage involves the designer in working with technicians to produce a sample of cloth. Samples are then chosen by the marketing staff of a design company, or used by the designer in person to present to clients.

When the design goes into production the designer is expected to assist with any problems that arise during manufacture, or modify the design according to customers' requirements, which may involve extensive liaison with customers' buying, merchandising and in-house design departments.

WORK ENVIRONMENT

Textile designers employed by manufacturers for the mass market often work in studios attached to the factories where the cloth is produced. Those who produce designs for printed fabrics or other surfaces sometimes work in design studios – the designs are then printed in a factory at another site.

They frequently work in small teams of no more than five designers, but also attend meetings with fashion designers, buyers, production managers and individual clients. This can involve them in a considerable amount of travel.

Self-employed textile designers have to travel to see agents and manufacturers and attend exhibitions, sometimes abroad, in order to get commissions and keep up-to-date with international trends.

SKILLS AND INTERESTS

Textile designers must be artistic and creative with a good eye for colour. Poor colour vision could be a handicap. They must also be capable of working in fine detail.

The amount of creativity required depends very much on where they work. Many popular designs are reproductions of traditional patterns or repeats of designs that have sold well in the past. Designers may be asked to reproduce a pattern making slight modifications, or to reproduce it using different colourways, rather than always create an original.

An understanding of the technical processes involved is essential. Weave designers must know what dyeing and weaving processes are used and what can be done on looms or knitting machines. Printed pattern designers need to know about printing processes. Their skills are similar to those of a graphic designer.

Communication and persuasive skills are important. They must be able to sell their ideas and must spend time getting feedback from customers. Freelance designers, in particular, need business and marketing skills. They must be prepared to take their portfolios to potential clients and negotiate contracts and fees.

ENTRY REQUIREMENTS

Please see article 1. GRAPHIC DESIGNER.

TRAINING

This is largely described in article 1. GRAPHIC DESIGNER.

NVQs/SVQs in Constructed Textile Design, and in Surface Pattern Textile Design, are available at Level 2. There is an SQA National award available in Art and Design, and a BTEC Higher National award in Textiles.

ART AND DESIGN: E

Some courses are joint courses in fashion and textile design. On such courses, students normally eventually specialize in one or the other. A number of courses exist in surface pattern design. These include training for design on fabrics, paper, china, plastic, laminate and other materials.

LATE ENTRY
Please see article 1. GRAPHIC DESIGNER.

OPPORTUNITIES
This is a very competitive area in which to find work. There are some openings for trained junior designers with in-house design units at textile manufacturers' premises and in specialist studios that work for a number of manufacturers, but opportunities for newcomers are limited with both.

Some designers work on a freelance basis, from home or sharing a studio with other designers, and many find more success if they also produce their own work and sell it at craft fairs or direct to shops.

There are frequently more opportunities to sell designs to foreign markets than in Britain.

PAY AND CONDITIONS
Please see article 1. GRAPHIC DESIGNER.

PROSPECTS
In a design studio there are prospects of promotion to senior designer but, since studios are small, these opportunities are limited.

Alternatively, designers change employers in order to achieve higher salaries, and it is quite usual to do so.

Some designers change employers frequently, in order to acquire a range of experience before setting up their own businesses.

There are possibilities to move out of design work and into associated jobs such as marketing, buying, sales, and, occasionally, into textile conservation and museum work.

RELATED OCCUPATIONS
Fashion buyer, graphic designer, photographer, production manager, quality controller, textile technician.

FURTHER INFORMATION AND READING
Please see article 6. INTERIOR DESIGNER.

6. INTERIOR DESIGNER (ET)

THE WORK
Interior designers are concerned with the organization of space and the decoration of the interiors of many kinds of structures: buildings (shops, hotels, office blocks and private houses), ships and aircraft.

Like other designers, they are initially briefed by a client, then work through the brief thoroughly to ensure that they understand all the requirements.

They then produce their first sketches and turn these into designs that are presented to the client. They normally produce several sets of designs for the client to compare.

Interior designers work bearing several factors in mind. They have to consider what image the client wishes to convey. If it is a hotel for example, the owners may want it to follow the style of a particular period. They must also consider the purpose of the building – the number of people who will be working in an office for instance, and limitations imposed by fittings and equipment. Shops need storage space as well as counters and display areas; aircraft interiors are particularly small, yet sufficient space must be allowed for passengers, luggage and working quarters for cabin crew.

Every interior has to include services, like electricity, plumbing and heating. The designer has to incorporate radiators, lighting and power points into the design.

Interior designers also design or recommend furniture, fittings etc. and recommend (specify) materials, fabrics, wallcoverings etc. They also plan colour schemes. (Some interior designers who specialize in advising on furnishings and colour schemes only, are known as interior decorators.)

Interior designers prepare detailed working drawings for the workmen/women who will be carrying out the work. This may be done using a computer. Some designers do this themselves; others employ draughtsmen/women.

Interior designers are expected to make frequent visits to the site while work is in progress, to check that everything is being done according to plan, and are responsible for contracting out the work and choosing the firm of carpenters/joiners, decorators, shopfitters etc.

Theatre/set design
This is a specialist branch of interior design. The work is very similar, with the client being a theatre, television or film director. Designers are responsible for everything on the set from scenery to furniture. They have to read the script, know how many changes of set there will be and, if it is a period play or film, do some historical research in order to make all the details accurate.

If designing a stage set, they must design sets that can be moved without difficulty by scene-shifters between acts. Television sets may be in small studios and allowances must be made for camera positions and angles. If working on a film or a television programme that requires outside shots, they are responsible for finding suitable locations.

Exhibition or display design
This is another specialism. Designers may plan a whole exhibition or one or more stands inside it for a client. They have limited space in which to work and must be able to plan the display around available power points and sometimes water supply. They need to make a stand look attractive, contain all the information an exhibitor wishes to display, and allow sufficient space within the area of floor space rented for customers to circulate.

WORK ENVIRONMENT
Interior designers are based in studios, but spend considerable time visiting sites. They also spend time travelling to meet prospective clients and making presentations in order to win contracts.

In order to keep abreast of the latest trends in materials and furnishings they may travel abroad to visit trade fairs and exhibitions.

ART AND DESIGN: E

SKILLS AND INTERESTS

Interior designers need creative talent and imagination and must be able to think three-dimensionally. They must also be capable of understanding building and safety regulations.

Drawing ability is important, from being able to convey their ideas in sketches to producing detailed working drawings. Increasingly, they need to work with computers.

Communication skills are extremely important. They may be working for clients who know exactly what they require or who have only a hazy idea. In both cases, they must translate those ideas into workable designs, and often explain why modifications are necessary. As they work with colour, defective colour vision could cause a problem.

They need an understanding of business skills, budgets, costing, and charging as well as contract and insurance requirements.

Selling skills are important. They spend much time in presenting ideas to prospective clients and bidding for business.

Willingness to work in a team is important. Interior designers work very closely throughout with architects, while the later stages of a project require them to liaise with contractors and, sometimes, directly supervise craftsmen/women.

They need to be able to accept criticism and rejection of work on which they may have spent considerable time.

ENTRY REQUIREMENTS

Please see article 1. GRAPHIC DESIGNER.

TRAINING

This is largely described in article 1. GRAPHIC DESIGNER.

NVQs/SVQs in Interior Design are available at Level 2. There are also BTEC higher national awards, and SQA National and Higher National awards are available in Interior Design.

It is also possible to train for interior design through private distance learning tuition. Courses are offered by Rhodec International and the Regent Academy.

LATE ENTRY

Please see article 1. GRAPHIC DESIGNER.

OPPORTUNITIES

This is not an easy branch of art and design in which to find employment. There are some openings with large organizations, like retail chains or hotel groups, but most interior designers work in interior design consultancies. Some are employed in architects' practices and others work on a freelance basis.

Theatre design is a particularly competitive area and there is very little salaried employment here, especially since the BBC, which used to employ its own designers, has now changed largely to using freelances.

PAY AND CONDITIONS

Please see article 1. GRAPHIC DESIGNER.

PROSPECTS

Most qualified interior designers first work assisting experienced designers. If they are in salaried positions they may then become designers. There are limited opportunities for promotion to the job of design manager, supervising the work of a number of designers and dealing with clients.

Many aim to become self-employed and may become partners in design consultancies.

RELATED OCCUPATIONS

Textile designer, graphic designer, fashion designer, illustrator/artist.

FURTHER INFORMATION

The Chartered Society of Designers*, 32–38 Saffron Hill, London EC1N 8FH, 0171 831 9777

The Association of Illustrators, 1st Floor, 32–38 Saffron Hill, London EC1N 8FH, 0171 531 7377, www.aoi.co.uk

The Crafts Council, 44A Pentonville Road, Islington, London N1 9BY, 0171 278 7700, www.craftscouncil.org.uk

Institute of Packaging*, Sysonby Lodge, Nottingham Road, Melton Mowbray, Leicestershire LE13 0NU, 01664 500055, http://www.op.co.uk

Institute of Printing*, 8A Lonsdale Gardens, Tunbridge Wells, Kent TN1 1NU, 01892 538118, globalprint.com/uk/iop

Interior Decorators & Designers Association Ltd*, 1/4 Chelsea Harbour Design Centre, Lots Road, London SW10 0XE, 0171 349 0800, www.IDDA.co.uk

National Society for Education in Art and Design (NSEAD)*, The Gatehouse, Corsham Court, Corsham, Wiltshire SN13 0BZ, 01249 714825

Regent Academy of Fine Arts*, 153-155 Regent Street, London W1R 8PX, 0800 378281

Rhodec International College of Interior Design*, 35 East Street, Brighton, East Sussex BN1 1HL, 01273 327476, www.rhodec com.

University and Colleges Admissions Service, UCAS*, Fulton House, Jessop Avenue, Cheltenham, Glos GL50 3SH, 01242 544867, http://www.ucas.ac.uk

FURTHER READING

Leaflets/booklets are available from the addresses marked*.

Guide to Courses and Careers in Art, Craft and Design – NSEAD

Working in Art and Design – COIC

Working in Fashion – COIC

In the careers library classified under ED; EG; EJ; EP; ET.

PHOTOGRAPHY: EV

1. **PHOTOGRAPHER CLCI:EV**
2. **PHOTOGRAPHIC TECHNICIAN CLCI:EV/SOZ**

BACKGROUND INFORMATION

Photography is a highly competitive career and is not always as glamorous as it might appear. Photography students are often attracted to areas like fashion and advertising, which offer relatively few jobs; there are far greater opportunities in the more mundane areas, such as wedding photography, portraiture and industrial or scientific work.

Many college courses in photography are available, but there is no clear progression from formal training to employment. Most industry sources agree that there is an oversupply of photography graduates, relative to the number of jobs available.

Job opportunities in professional photography may be affected in future by the growing use of electronic imaging. With a computer, a designer can now manipulate photographs, merging them and adding special effects to create new images. The extent to which these techniques will affect the demand for original photographs is not yet clear, but they will certainly have an increasing impact on professional photography.

It is much easier to find a job as a photographic technician than as a professional photographer. However, working as a photographic technician should be seen as an interesting career in its own right, and not a second-best option for failed photographers.

Technicians work in photographic laboratories, which fall into two main categories:

Photofinishing laboratories provide developing and printing services for amateur photographers. Some are very large processing plants, with hundreds of employees; others are 'mini-labs', generally found in town centres, which provide a quick processing service.

Professional processing laboratories provide a range of services to professional photographers.

1. PHOTOGRAPHER (EV)

THE WORK

Professional photographers make permanent records of visual images – which may be of anything, from new-born babies to scientific processes.

Photography involves choosing and preparing locations, setting up lighting, selecting appropriate cameras, film, lenses and accessories, and composition of pictures.

A professional photographer usually works to a brief, set by the client or employer. The brief may be very detailed, or it may allow the photographer scope for creative interpretation of the client's ideas, after appropriate discussion and negotiation.

It is usual to specialize in one particular area of work. The main specializations are:

General practice photographers provide a service for the local community. The majority of their work is social photography – mainly portraits and weddings. They may also work for local businesses and advertising agencies, producing shots for brochures, posters and other promotional material. Some general practice photographers freelance for local newspapers.

Advertising, fashion and editorial photography. Advertising photographers tend to specialize in a particular area, such as cars or food, although some do a variety of work. Fashion photographers are also concerned with advertising, but of clothes, make-up and fashion accessories. Editorial photographers produce illustrations for magazine articles. Photographers in these fields often work with a team, including models, stylists, lighting technicians and photographers' assistants.

Most **press photographers** work for provincial or local newspapers, and much of their work involves recording local events and news stories. On the national newspapers they often specialize, for instance, in sports photography or political coverage. Photo-journalists provide words as well as pictures, and they generally work for magazines rather than newspapers.

Medical photographers make records used in hospitals for educational, diagnostic and scientific purposes. They use specialized techniques such as microphotography (photographing images of very small objects). Medical work may involve taking photographs on the wards, in theatres, research laboratories or post-mortem rooms.

Industrial photographers record industrial processes and similar subjects. They may also take photographs for company brochures and publicity material.

Scientific photographers are concerned with recording experiments or providing research data, often for purposes of measurement. They use special techniques, such as ultraviolet light or high-speed photography.

Police photographers may be concerned with forensic work – photographing scenes of crime – or with other types of police photography, including press and public relations, training material, or photographing accident victims.

The majority of photographers are self-employed and have to cope with all the problems of running a small business. Typically, they devote far more time – perhaps 85 per cent of their working hours – to running their businesses, rather than taking photographs.

Many photographers also make videos – for instance, of weddings or promotional events.

WORK ENVIRONMENT

Some photographers are studio-based, particularly those working in advertising and portraiture. Others work in a variety of locations, both indoors and out.

Location work involves travel and spending periods away from home.

SKILLS AND INTERESTS

Photographers have to be well-organized and practical, as well as creative. Business skills are essential. Strong motivation and self-confidence are needed to find work and survive in a competitive and overcrowded profession.

Artistic ability, with an understanding of the principles of composition and an appreciation of shape, form, colour and tone are required. It is also important to be able to master different techniques and to understand technical processes.

Photographers need to be able to deal with people – for instance, when taking wedding pictures or working with professional models. They also need negotiating skills for dealing with clients. Patience is important – in press photography they may wait for hours to get the right shot, or any kind of outdoor work may depend on waiting for the right weather conditions.

Medical and scientific photographers should have an interest in science and be capable of working to a high degree of accuracy.

ENTRY REQUIREMENTS

No set academic qualifications are required to work as a photographer or photographer's assistant. It is not always necessary to take a formal training course in photography. However, a keen amateur interest in the subject is absolutely essential. Employers and colleges assume a considerable knowledge of the subject prior to entry.

A portfolio of the candidate's photographic work is essential for applying for jobs and courses. The portfolio should be relevant, neatly presented and not too long – between ten and fifteen photographs is sufficient.

A driving licence is a great advantage for those applying for posts as photographers' assistants.

College courses: there are no set entry requirements for courses leading to C+G, NVQ/SVQ or SQA national awards.

Entry to BTEC national certificate/diploma courses is with four GCSEs/S grades (A–C/1–3). Entry to BTEC/SQA higher national certificate/diploma courses is with one or two A levels/H grades and supporting GCSEs/S grades (A–C/1–3) or a national certificate/ diploma, Advanced GNVQ/GSVQ Level III or completion of a foundation course in Art and Design.

Entry to courses leading to the BIPP professional qualifying examinations is with a higher national diploma.

Entry to degree courses is with five GCSEs/S grades (A–C/1–3) with two A levels/three H grades, a BTEC/SQA national award, foundation course in Art and Design or equivalent.

Some specialist areas have particular requirements:

Press photographers: minimum educational requirements for direct entry to a newspaper as a trainee are: five GCSEs/S grades (A–C/1–3) including English; or two years' relevant experience in photography; or a further education course in photography. For the full-time pre-entry course at Sheffield College, minimum entry requirements are one A level/H grade and four other subjects at GCSE/S grade (A–C/1–3).

Medical photographers: for trainee posts, employers tend to prefer candidates with five GCSEs/S grades (A–C/1–3) including English, maths and a science subject. Some entrants have photography qualifications.

TRAINING

There is no set training pattern for most types of professional photography. Many training courses are available, but there is no direct link between formal training and employment, and it is possible to become a successful photographer by learning on the job.

In fields such as general practice, advertising, fashion and editorial photography, entrants usually start as a photographer's assistant. Assistants help with shoots, making sure that the set or location is prepared, loading film, setting up lighting. They organize transport of people and equipment, check supplies and deal with paperwork. They are also responsible for the day-to-day running of the studio, dealing with all the necessary mundane tasks, like making coffee, answering the telephone, making deliveries and cleaning.

It is not always necessary to have a formal qualification in photography to find a post as a photographer's assistant, and some photographers prefer to take untrained staff with a keen interest in photography, rather than college leavers.

Assistants may be granted day release to take college courses – until recently, the most usual course for assistants and trainees has been City & Guilds 747, Photography Competencies. This qualification is still currently available, but may have been replaced by NVQs or SVQs in Photography. Colleges may run courses leading to NVQs/SVQs; employers and other training providers may also be able to act as assessment centres.

NVQs/SVQs in Photography accredited to date are at Levels 2, 3 and 4.

Other qualifications include:

BTEC/SQA national awards or GNVQs/GSVQs in Art and Design are mainly full-time courses, lasting two years, although a few part-time courses are available. Higher national diploma courses normally last two years, full-time.

Degree courses in photography normally last three years. There are specialist degree and higher national diploma courses in areas such as medical, industrial, scientific and advertising photography.

The Professional Qualifying Examination (PQE) of the British Institute of Professional Photography is a qualification with a good reputation with employers. Some colleges link the PQE to their higher national diploma courses, enabling students to take a third year of study and obtain both a PQE and a degree.

There is no guarantee that a formal qualification will lead to employment as a photographer or assistant. However, a photography course does provide a technical grounding and the opportunity for students to test their commitment to photography and make contacts in the industry – particularly if the course includes a period of industrial release. It is important to research courses thoroughly, finding out about their equipment, contacts in the industry and the record of past students in finding appropriate employment.

Two specialist areas of photography have a more standard pattern of training.

Press photography. There are two main schemes of training:

1. Direct entry to a training contract with a local or provincial newspaper. Direct entrants receive on-the-job training, supplemented by block release courses at Sheffield College.

2. A one-year full-time pre-entry course in Photo-Journalism/Press Photography at Sheffield College, followed by on-the-job training with a newspaper.

Both routes lead to qualifications of the National Council for the Training of Journalists (NCTJ), from whom further details are available.

It is not necessary to gain NCTJ qualifications to work as a freelance press photographer.

An NVQ in Newspaper Journalism (Press Photography) is available at Level 4.

Medical photography. Trainees in hospitals gain experience on the job and usually study for the medical

PHOTOGRAPHY: EV

photography examinations of the British Institute of Professional Photography or the Institute of Medical Illustrators. It is also possible to enter after taking a specialist full-time course.

LATE ENTRY

There are no upper age limits and adults with a strong amateur interest in photography may be able to sell their work and develop a freelance business or small studio. They are most likely to succeed in general practice, taking wedding photographs and portraits – maturity can be an asset for this type of photography.

People in their twenties may have an advantage over school-leavers when applying for work as photographer's assistants. However, starting pay is likely to be low – this may be a deterrent.

Colleges may waive their normal academic entry requirements for mature applicants.

OPPORTUNITIES

Photography is a very competitive area, and considerable determination is needed to find work.

In fields like advertising, fashion and general practice photography, posts for assistants are sometimes advertised in the photographic press, but they are often found through word-of-mouth – informal contacts are important in photography. Would-be assistants can make speculative approaches to individual photographers or studios – probably the best way is to send a letter and CV, followed up by a telephone call. It is important that applicants can be easily contacted. A home telephone number is essential, and an answering machine, mobile phone or pager is an advantage.

Assistants may work full-time for one photographer or (in London and other large cities) as freelances, working for many different photographers as and when required. There is no set career pattern, although the work of a full-time assistant is more straightforward and therefore easier for a beginner. After gaining sufficient experience they usually leave to set up their own photographic practices.

Advice on finding employment in advertising, fashion and editorial photography is available from the Association of Photographers, who hold regular careers talks and supply details of current vacancies.

Entry to press photography is also highly competitive. Applicants can approach local or regional newspapers or apply to the full-time course at Sheffield College. The national newspapers only employ experienced photographers.

Entry to other areas, such as medical or police photography, is slightly less competitive and advertisements may be found in the local press, Jobcentres and the British Journal of Photography.

According to the Photography and Photographic Processing Industry Training Organization, there are about 17,000 people employed in professional photography.

About half of all professional photographers work in general practice. They are usually self-employed, although some larger practices employ photographers.

Most photographers working in advertising, fashion and editorial photography are also self-employed.

Full-time employment is the norm in police and medical photography. Some police photographers are uniformed officers, but the trend is towards employment of civilians for this type of work.

The Civil Service employs photographers in a number of departments, particularly in the Ministry of Defence, Central Office of Information (COI) and Department of the Environment, Transport and the Regions (DETR). There are also opportunities in HM Forces. Some large industrial firms have their own photographic departments. There are also opportunities for stills photographers with television and film companies.

PAY AND CONDITIONS

Because many photographers are self-employed, there is a great variation in earnings. Those with a good reputation in the more creative areas, such as advertising, fashion or press photography, can earn high incomes, but this is unusual. A more realistic figure for experienced photographers would be about £12,000 plus, with assistants or trainees earning from about £5,500 to £7,000.

Those on a fixed salary scale, such as medical photographers, may earn more during training and the early years of their careers, but do not have the opportunity of reaching the level of income sometimes achieved in the more creative areas.

Most self-employed photographers work long hours, including evenings and weekends. Wedding photography always involves weekend work.

Press photographers often work very irregular hours, to cover news stories and other events.

Police photographers should be prepared to work shifts.

PROSPECTS

Success for a self-employed photographer consists of building up a business and steadily gaining more prestige and higher fees.

Organizations that employ photographers, such as the police or Civil Service, have a formal promotion structure, but prospects are likely to be limited, as photographic departments are usually quite small.

RELATED OCCUPATIONS

Illustrator/artist, graphic designer, fashion designer, stage/set designer, camera operator, picture editor, photographic technician.

FURTHER INFORMATION

British Institute of Professional Photography*, Fox Talbot House, 2 Amwell End, Ware, Herts SG12 9HN, 01920 464011 (Please send A4 sae, with 38p stamp)

The Association of Photographers*, 9–10 Domingo Street, London EC1Y 0TA, 0171 608 0598, www.aophoto.co.uk

National Council for the Training of Journalists*, Latton Bush Centre, Southern Way, Harlow, Essex CM18 7BL, 01279 430009 (please include sae), http://www.itecharlow.co.uk

The Royal Photographic Society*, The Octagon, Milsom Street, Bath BA1 1DN, 01225 462841, http://www.rps.org.uk

Photography and Photographic Processing Industry Training Organization*, PO Box 2270, Reading RG1 4YG, 01189 590816

PHOTOGRAPHY: EV

FURTHER READING

Leaflets/booklets are available from the addresses marked*.

Working in Photography – COIC

Where to Study – Photography, film, video and television – The British Journal of Photography

Beyond the Lens – Rights, Ethics and Business in Professional Photography – The Association of Photographers

Working in Photography – Arthur Henry Lewes – Published by How To Books

Periodicals: The British Journal of Photography

In the careers library classified under EV.

2. PHOTOGRAPHIC TECHNICIAN (EV/SOZ)

THE WORK

There is a wide range of different types of work, both in photofinishing and professional laboratories. Technicians may specialize in one area, or carry out a variety of different tasks. Some jobs are routine, involving machine operating; others are highly skilled.

All laboratories work to highly accurate, controlled standards, with fast turn-around times. However, targets vary in different parts of the processing industry. In labs processing films for the amateur market, the aim is to produce prints in large quantities, whereas the professional laboratories cater for more specialist needs. In terms of tasks, however, there is considerable overlap between the different types of lab.

Technicians' work can include:

Chemical mixing: photographic laboratories use large quantities of chemicals and these have to be combined in the correct order, following manufacturers' instructions and health and safety procedures.

Processing: is automatically controlled, although technicians are responsible for setting and adjusting the machines. Films are loaded into the machines, processed in total darkness and inspected as they emerge. Quality control is extremely important and test films are checked against control standards set by the manufacturers.

Negatives can be graded on a video analyser or by a colour-and-density scanner, to adjust colour and density.

Printing: mainly by machine, but also by hand. Most amateur prints, and many professional ones, are printed by sophisticated electronic machinery. The technician is responsible for setting up the machine, making adjustments and fault-finding.

Hand printing: is used when the photographer has specific requirements – for instance, for an unusual size, or for enlargement of part of the picture.

Finishing: prints can be mounted on hardboard, card or canvas. They can be laminated or given a variety of different surface textures.

Other specialist techniques include:

Re-touching: removing blemishes on prints and transparencies by hand, using a brush and dye;

Copying photographs or artwork, when no negative is available, by photographing them and producing a negative or transparency;

Duplicating or 'duping' – copying transparencies and negatives;

Reverse printing: making prints from transparencies;

Electronic imaging: mainly used for manipulating images, for instance merging two photographs, or re-touching. A print, transparency or negative is converted into a computer image, which can be manipulated on screen. The new image is then converted back into photographic form.

Electronic imaging is developing rapidly, and is likely to replace some of the traditional skills – particularly re-touching – in the next few years.

WORK ENVIRONMENT

Technicians spend most of their time in the laboratory, in clean and comfortable conditions. With modern technology, very little time is spent in total darkness.

When dealing with chemicals, technicians wear rubber gloves, goggles and laboratory coats.

SKILLS AND INTERESTS

Photographic technicians need patience, meticulous accuracy and must pay close attention to detail. An eye for colour, shade and tone is important. Re-touching work requires some artistic aptitude.

A responsible attitude is important, as technicians may be handling valuable negatives and transparencies. If they are processing film in large quantities, a small error in machine setting could cost thousands of pounds.

They may work under pressure to meet deadlines.

Manual dexterity and some mechanical aptitude, for operating machinery, are necessary.

ENTRY REQUIREMENTS

There are no set entry requirements for employment as a photographic technician. GCSEs/S grades, particularly in sciences, are useful.

Entry to the BTEC National Diploma in Photography and Photographic Laboratory Practice course at Kingsway College, London, is with four GCSEs/S grades (A–C/1–3) or equivalent, and a portfolio of photographic work.

TRAINING

The usual method of training is on-the-job. Entrants start as juniors or trainees, usually starting on the more routine and repetitive work, such as machine operating. Depending on the employer, they may be able to gain experience in different departments and attend short courses run by equipment manufacturers.

It is likely that trainees will work towards full NVQs/SVQs (or individual units of competence), which are expected to become available through companies, colleges and other training providers.

An NVQ/SVQ in Photographic Processing is available at Level 3.

There is no fixed training period, but it is likely to take two to three years to become proficient as a technician. Technicians will need to take further training courses throughout their careers (eg equipment manufacturers' courses) to keep pace with new technology.

It is also possible to enter after taking the following full-time course:

PHOTOGRAPHY: EV

The BTEC National Diploma in Photography and Photographic Laboratory Practice at Kingsway College, London. The course includes training in professional laboratory work and photography. It lasts two years, full-time, and can also be taken part-time over a longer period.

There is a considerable demand from employers for more training facilities for photographic processing skills, and it is likely that more courses will be established in the future.

LATE ENTRY

Adult entry is possible, although it tends to be school-leavers or young people aged about 18–21 years who are trained by employers in a range of skills. Older entrants are more likely to be taken on by the very large photofinishing laboratories to carry out less-skilled work.

OPPORTUNITIES

Laboratories have expanded rapidly in the past 15–20 years and there is a shortage of qualified staff.

Photofinishing laboratories include a small number of very large firms and several hundred 'mini-labs'. Professional photographic laboratories number about 600 and are found in every major town or city. Many professional labs specialize.

Some photographic technicians are employed by hospitals and colleges.

About 12,000 people are employed in photographic laboratories, according to estimates by the Photography and Photographic Processing Industry Training Organization.

It is possible for experienced technicians to become self-employed, running their own photographic labs.

PAY AND CONDITIONS

Most technicians work a five-day week, Monday to Friday. In a few large laboratories they work shifts. Overtime may be available. It is possible to work part-time.

Pay varies with different employers and in different parts of the country. Young people, carrying out basic tasks, are likely to earn between £7,000 and £10,000. Top rates for the most skilled and experienced technicians can be up to £25,000.

PROSPECTS

Promotion prospects vary according to the size of the firm. It is possible to progress to senior technician level, and then into management.

It may be necessary to move to another firm to gain experience or improve chances of promotion.

RELATED OCCUPATIONS

Photographer, laboratory technician, textile dyeing technician, sound technician/operator, cameraman/woman/camera operator, cinema projectionist

FURTHER INFORMATION

Professional Photographic Laboratories Association, 35 Chine Walk, West Parley, Ferndown, Dorset BH22 8PR

British Institute of Professional Photography*, Fox Talbot House, 2 Amwell End, Ware, Herts SG12 9HN, 01920 464011 (Please send A4 size sae, with 38p stamp)

Photography and Photographic Processing Industry Training Organization*, PO Box 2270, Reading RG1 4YG, 01189 590816

Blackpool and the Fylde College*, Ashfield Road, Bispham, Blackpool, Lancashire FY2 0HB, 01253 352352

Kingsway College, The Gray's Inn Centre, Sidmouth Street, London WC1H 8JB, 0171 306 5700

FURTHER READING

Leaflets/booklets are available from the address marked*.

Working in Photography–COIC

In the careers library classified under EV; SOZ.

GROUP F – TEACHING AND CULTURAL ACTIVITIES

1. **SCHOOL TEACHER – ENGLAND AND WALES CLCI:FAB**
2. **SCHOOL TEACHER – SCOTLAND CLCI:FAB**
3. **SPECIAL EDUCATIONAL NEEDS TEACHER CLCI:FAB**
4. **FURTHER EDUCATION/TERTIARY COLLEGE LECTURER CLCI:FAB**
5. **HIGHER EDUCATION LECTURER CLCI:FAB**

1. SCHOOL TEACHER – ENGLAND AND WALES (FAB)

BACKGROUND INFORMATION

Most schools are run by local authorities or are grant-maintained, though increasing numbers of children are being educated in independent schools. In the state system, children attend primary school from four or five to eleven or twelve years, and secondary school until 16 or 18 years. Some primary schools have a nursery unit or nursery school attached for three- to five-year-olds. Provision for 16- to 19-year-olds includes school sixth-form and further education and tertiary colleges.

The 1988 Education Reform Act and Education Acts of 1993 and 1996 are having a major effect. The most radical measure is the introduction of a prescribed National Curriculum made up of core and foundation subjects. Children's work is assessed continuously and tested at key stages.

There is now an increased variety of educational institutions, including grant-maintained schools, City Technology Colleges, colleges of technology or languages, and schools specializing in arts and sport are being developed.

Another potential major force for change is the single European market, which is broadening educational perspectives and offering teachers new challenges and openings.

THE WORK

Teachers aim to build a relationship with their pupils that brings out the best in them and makes them receptive to ideas and knowledge.

Teachers use a variety of methods, including whole-class, group and individual teaching. Lessons may be given based on information technology, textbooks, materials teachers have devised themselves, or may take the form of a demonstration, an experiment, a discussion, a field trip or a workplace visit. Pupils are encouraged to take an active role in their learning, sometimes discovering facts for themselves rather than relying on teachers to present them; teachers direct pupils' research, provide resources, arrange group projects and periods of practical experience, and help pupils collate information, as well as giving formal instruction.

Teachers must devise balanced learning programmes that develop pupils' academic, practical, creative, social and life skills. Teachers draw up a syllabus related to the National Curriculum, when appropriate, for the 39-week school year, frequently working in teams to plan work with colleagues.

Outside the classroom, teachers spend necessary time preparing lessons. This could entail practical preparation, from drawing letter shapes for first-year primary writing practice to setting up complicated apparatus for an A level chemistry class. Teachers are also expected to set and mark homework appropriate to the age and ability of their pupils, which could cover a range of supplementary exercises and activities, such as essays, mathematical problems or project research. They are required to assess pupils' work continuously in National Curriculum subjects at ages seven, eleven and 14. Further evaluation takes place in other tests and examinations, which must also be set and marked. At the end of each year, subject and general progress reports are written.

Teachers' resources vary, but a wide range of materials and teaching aids is available. In nursery and primary schools, where children engage in a range of practical activities, resources may include children's literature, paints and pens, scissors and glue, modelling clay, sewing materials, musical instruments, building blocks, dressing-up clothes, simple woodworking tools, water and sand, and gardening tools.

Technology teachers train young pupils to handle simple tools, such as chisels and soldering irons, and older ones to use precision tools. Information technology teachers show pupils how to use sophisticated design software. Language and music tapes and video cassettes are widely used, and computer skills are taught from the early primary years.

Teachers have extra administrative duties, managing resources, taking registers etc. They also attend different types of meeting, such as departmental and staff meetings and parents' evenings.

Teachers have a pastoral or caring role, guiding pupils and advising them on personal problems. They have a role in promoting pupils' spiritual and moral development on such matters as drugs, bullying and truancy. Year or form tutors have special responsibilities of this kind, and boarding school teachers can expect responsibility for pupils outside school hours. Many teachers organize extra-curricular activities such as concerts, outings and adventure holidays; there is a particular emphasis on these in residential independent schools.

As well as working closely with colleagues, teachers come into contact with parents, social workers, education welfare officers, police officers, counsellors and many other members of the community.

Nursery/primary school teacher

Teachers specializing in the 'early years' (three to seven or eight years) work in nursery, infant or first schools. Those opting for the later years work in junior and middle schools. Most primary teachers cover every curriculum subject but have a specialism – for example, science, maths, technology, language development, special educational needs, personal and social education – which they help develop through the school as curriculum leaders and advisers to other members of staff. Unless the school is very small, they teach children of a particular age group, taking sole charge of a class or working with several other teachers and classroom assistants. A small but growing number of schools are employing specialist teachers to teach their own subject to a number of classes across an age group, particularly in the upper years of primary school.

Primary teachers are responsible for teaching the basic skills of literacy and numeracy. They also teach science and

TEACHING: FAB

design technology, information technology, history, geography, drama, music, dance, art, religious education, physical education and, in some case, modern foreign languages. Primary teachers teach and assess children in a variety of contexts, including whole class and when they are working on a structured group or individual basis.

Secondary school teacher

Teachers specialize in one or two subjects, but commonly teach them to all age groups and abilities. They may only see each class for 40 minutes a day. Pupils are prepared for GCSE, Advanced Supplementary (AS) and A level examinations, GNVQs and other qualifications.

Secondary schools have introduced Records of Achievement prepared jointly by teachers and pupils to give prospective employers a profile of the student's attainments, such as positions of responsibility, yearly reports, extra-curricular and sporting activities etc. Trials of a new record of achievement (under the name Progress File) have taken place. Subject to evaluation the new materials will be launched nationwide in early 1999. Progressive introduction into schools, colleges and elsewhere will commence in September 1999.

Teachers make contacts in local industry and arrange work experience for their pupils.

WORK ENVIRONMENT

Teachers may work in many different types of school of varying sizes, from large comprehensives with more than 1,000 pupils, to village schools with 20 children and two teachers. Large urban schools, particularly, often cater for children from many different ethnic cultures. Most state schools are co-educational, and many independent schools are also becoming co-educational.

Most teachers work in classrooms, but they may teach in workshops, laboratories, and gyms. They are on their feet much of the day and must be fit and able to move around the school. Teachers may work outside, or away from, the school when involved in walks, games and playground duty, the school farm or garden, sports matches, school journeys, adventure holidays, and outings.

Boarding school teachers may live on the premises or nearby, working in residential and recreational areas as well as in classrooms. Other teachers tutor children in their homes, in hospitals, in centres for young offenders, and on film sets.

SKILLS AND INTERESTS

Teachers have to be caring and fair. They must respect, as well as like, children and want to help them realize their potential. They must be able to build trusting relationships with children, parents and colleagues.

Teachers need detailed knowledge of and enthusiasm for their subjects. All teachers need the confidence and imagination to hold pupils' attention, stimulate their interest and creativity, and maintain order.

They must be able to explain ideas clearly, adapting their teaching methods to the requirements of different age groups and abilities. It is essential that teachers are competent with information technology.

Teachers have to be good listeners and must be able to encourage pupils to express themselves. Patience and a sense of humour are essential.

Teachers need the flexibility to adapt to new approaches and keep up to date with educational developments, engage in research and contribute to initial teacher training.

Teachers have to be highly motivated and able to organize their time properly and do much of their work on their own. They must be effective managers of time, people and resources.

The work requires a sense of responsibility and dedication from which is derived the satisfaction of promoting children's academic, social, spiritual and moral development. It is often stressful and requires mental and physical stamina and resilience to meet the varied daily challenges.

Teachers must accept that developments such as the assessment of pupils, external inspection of schools and publication of results have led to their being increasingly accountable for their work.

ENTRY REQUIREMENTS

Teachers in state-maintained schools in England and Wales must have Qualified Teacher Status (QTS). Independent schools also prefer their staff to be qualified.

QTS is obtained by taking an approved course of initial teacher training (ITT), which can be through either a first degree or a postgraduate course.

The minimum requirements for entry are GCSEs (A–C) in English language and maths, and , for entrants to primary courses who were born after 1 September 1979, GCSE Science (A–C). An A level or equivalent in the main subject of study is also required. Higher Education Institutions specify their own academic entry requirements to degree courses. Entry to degree courses is usually with a minimum of five GCSEs (A–C) plus two A levels.

Postgraduate course leading to the Postgraduate Certificate in Education (PGCE). The entry requirement is a degree plus GCSEs (A–C) in English language and maths. GCSE (A–C) in a science subject is also required for entrants to primary teaching courses born after 1 September 1979, and is encouraged for those entering secondary teaching courses. Some institutions require at least 50% of the degree to be in a National Curriculum subject (see above) or in religious education or have a high content of study relevant to such subjects, eg biochemistry or engineering. Minority subjects, such as sociology, economics and the classics, are however, also taught in secondary schools.

Alternative qualifications, such as Advanced GNVQ and BTEC national awards, are acceptable in some subjects, eg science, performing arts and art. Other GNVQs and BTEC national awards, though – such as health and social care, and leisure and tourism – lack the required National Curriculum subject content. Applicants with these qualifications may be accepted onto early years general degrees with QTS and onto some biology and PE courses, although teacher training institutions may also require evidence of subject strength. Applications are stronger if they have very good course assessments, some additional extension units, a good set of GCSEs and relevant work experience.

Preference is usually given to applicants who have experience working with children through work experience in a school and, perhaps, through a holiday play scheme or local church. Students usually have to be 18 years old in the year they start a degree course and must be

TEACHING: FAB

mentally and physically fit to teach. Any previous criminal convictions must be declared.

Applicants with disabilities are encouraged to enter teaching, providing the disability does not inhibit the ability to teach, and they are fit and able to move around the school. (For further information refer to teacher training institutions or DfEE Circular 13/93.)

TRAINING

Undergraduate courses

The undergraduate route is more common for primary teaching. Secondary-level courses are available, but mainly in maths, the sciences, craft, design and technology, business studies, home economics and PE. Some institutions may offer other subjects.

BEd, and BA/BSc with QTS courses usually last three or four years and are offered at universities and colleges and institutes of higher education.

Courses include the study of specialist subjects (usually one main and one subsidiary subject, although an increasing number of courses for primary teaching are modular and allow for higher level of study in six subjects) and their application to teaching; training in the teaching and assessment of National Curriculum subjects; educational and professional studies – teaching methods, classroom discipline, information technology, pastoral responsibilities etc, and school experience. Teaching practice accounts for a minimum of 32 weeks in school for four-year courses, 24 weeks for three-year courses and 18 weeks for part-time courses. Early years teachers can take advanced study in early years as their specialist subject.

Postgraduate courses

The postgraduate route is more common for secondary teaching, although primary level courses are offered and are popular.

Postgraduate courses are offered at universities, colleges and institutes of higher education, and consortia of schools. Most courses lead to a Postgraduate Certificate of Education (PGCE).

These full-time courses last about 36 weeks and concentrate on educational and professional studies rather than graduate studies in a subject. They include at least 24 weeks of school experience for secondary and 18 weeks for primary, during which trainee teachers watch others at work, teach individuals and small groups under supervision, plan class work and undertake at least one placement requiring them to demonstrate capability at teaching, managing and assessing a whole class. A few postgraduate courses include additional options, such as special needs or youth work.

An 18-month distance learning PGCE is also offered by the Open University for primary teaching and selected secondary subjects.

Religious education teaching

Catholic school teachers – particularly those teaching RE – may need the Catholic Certificate in Religious Studies. They can qualify for this while taking a postgraduate course at a Catholic college or on a part-time in-service course. Details are available from diocesan religious education advisers.

Anglican colleges of higher education offer the Church Colleges' Certificate in Religious Studies course for teachers of RE in Church of England schools. This can be studied either as part of an initial teacher training course or by experienced teachers on a part-time basis.

In-service training

Schools, teacher training institutions, LEAs and HMI run day release, evening and intensive full-time courses through which teachers may keep up with developments in their field, learn about new initiatives and teaching methods, and develop technical or management skills. There are also courses to help teachers to return to teaching after a career break. In-service training at present includes five days a year for school-based continuing professional development.

The National Association of Teachers in Further and Higher Education (NATFHE) publishes a handbook listing all initial teacher training courses in England and Wales (see FURTHER READING). Detailed course prospectuses are available from individual institutions. Course guides and handbooks are also available from the application clearing houses: the Universities and Colleges Admissions Service (UCAS) for undergraduates, or the Graduate Teacher Training Registry (GTTR) for graduates.

LATE ENTRY

There is no upper age limit for entry to teacher training. Older entrants are encouraged and advised to consult teacher trainers about course details.

Many local colleges offer Access courses to adults over 21 years without conventional qualifications, to prepare them for entry to higher education. Many include GCSEs in English, maths and science and some school experience. Part-time PGCE courses are also offered over two years.

A few institutions offer two-year BEd courses for mature students who have successfully completed a minimum of one year of full-time study beyond A level, such as higher national diploma or equivalent, or who have been trained overseas.

Employment-based routes

School governing bodies may apply to the Teacher Training Agency (TTA) for a teaching licence for suitable applicants. They must have GCSEs (A–C) or equivalent in maths and English language (and, from 1998, for primary entrants born after 1 September 1979, GCSE science (A–C)). They must also have successfully completed two years in higher education (or part-time equivalent), be graduates or have qualified overseas. The school must devise a suitable training plan, which may run from one term to two years, depending on the trainee's previous teaching experience, following which the trainee may be recommended for QTS.

OPPORTUNITIES

About 400,000 teachers work in state schools in England and Wales. There are 4,200 secondary schools and 19,000 primaries, catering for more than seven million pupils. The independent sector has about 2,500 schools.

There are shortages of teachers in some parts of the country. Secondary schools are particularly short of teachers in maths, science, music, modern languages, information technology and design and technology. In Wales there is a demand for Welsh-language teachers and those who can teach in the Welsh language.

Opportunities arise in the City Technology Colleges,

TEACHING: FAB

funded by the Government and industry. These follow the National Curriculum, but have a technological bias, offering a broad education across the ability range.

There are also openings in HM Forces schools, in young offender institutions, in private tuition, affiliated schools and in hospitals.

The lifting of EU controls on professional qualifications offers prospects for language teachers. It also opens up the field for teachers with linguistic skills to work in Europe. Teachers without foreign languages may still find work abroad in company-run and other British schools, and in those run by missionary and other religious or charitable organizations. Details are available from the British Council or Voluntary Service Overseas.

Teaching posts are advertised in internal newsletters carrying details of posts available with the authorities, *The Times Educational Supplement; The Teacher*, local papers, Jobcentres and national daily newspapers such as *The Guardian, The Times, The Independent*, and *The Daily Telegraph* each week on their education days.

PAY AND CONDITIONS

Teachers with QTS are paid according to a nationally agreed pay spine that is reviewed annually. Salaries for good honours graduates currently start from £14,751 (£15,012 from 1/12/98). Teachers progress up the scale to a designated limit. Additional points may be awarded for excellent performance, recruitment and retention, and special educational needs. Head teachers and deputy head teachers are paid on a pay spine ranging from £25881 to £58,548 (£26,337 to £59,580 from 1/12/98). Their salaries depend on the size of the school and the ages of the pupils. Teaching in the London area attracts London weighting.

Salaries vary enormously in independent schools. Many independent schools link their scales to the state scale, while others pay higher or lower salaries. Boarding schools may have a separate scale for those living in school accommodation.

State school teachers work 195 days (39 weeks) in the year. They must be available to work under the direction of the head teacher for 1,265 hours during those days – roughly six-and-a-half hours a day. In addition, they plan and prepare courses and lessons, prepare and mark tests and assignments, and attend meetings, sometimes having to work for three or four hours after school.

Opportunities also exist for part-time work, job share and supply teaching.

PROSPECTS

In most schools, there are opportunities for promotion to positions of responsibility. In primary schools, there is a strong demand for head teachers, deputy head teachers and curriculum leaders. Secondary teachers may become head of a subject department or head of year. The new pay structure also encourages those who wish to pursue a career as an expert classroom teacher.

In-service training, geographical mobility, and a willingness to take added responsibility – helping with timetabling or curriculum development, tutoring new teachers, becoming a mentor in training new teachers, becoming a teacher governor etc – increase prospects of promotion.

Some teachers branch into special needs, teacher training or educational administration, become education advisers for local authorities, or work for OFSTED (the national school inspectorate service).

RELATED OCCUPATIONS

Social worker, educational welfare officer, youth and community worker, nursery nurse, careers officer, educational psychologist, outdoor education leader, specialist teacher assistant.

FURTHER INFORMATION AND READING

Please see article 5. HIGHER EDUCATION LECTURER.

2. SCHOOL TEACHER – SCOTLAND (FAB)

BACKGROUND INFORMATION

Most Scottish schools belong to the state system – only four per cent are grant-aided or independent. The Scottish Office Education and Industry Department (SOEID) and the 32 unitary authorities are responsible for state education, and most authorities have both non-denominational and Roman Catholic state schools. Children attend state primaries from five to twelve years, then move without selection to a comprehensive, where they stay for four to six years. There is nursery provision for some three- to five-year-olds. Scotland has its own curriculum guidelines (5–14 programme) and national assessment of primary children in English and maths.

THE WORK

Teachers aim to build a relationship with their pupils that brings out the best in them and makes them receptive to ideas and knowledge.

Teaching methods vary enormously. Lessons may be delivered from a prepared text or may take the form of a demonstration, an experiment, a discussion, a field trip or a workplace visit. Pupils are encouraged to take an active role in their learning, discovering facts for themselves rather than relying on teachers to present them; teachers direct pupils' research, provide resources, arrange group projects and periods of practical experience, and help pupils collate information.

Whether teachers structure lessons informally or formally, they must devise balanced learning programmes that develop pupils' academic, practical, creative, and social skills. Teachers draw up a syllabus for the 38-week school year, liaising with colleagues when themes are chosen for cross-curriculum study.

Outside the classroom, many hours are spent preparing lessons. This could entail drawing letter shapes for infants' writing practice, or setting up complicated apparatus for an H grade chemistry class. Teachers also set and mark homework, which takes many forms, including essays, lists of questions, mathematical problems etc. They make continuous assessments of pupils' work and evaluate it through tests and examinations, which must also be set and marked. At the end of each year, subject and general progress reports are written.

Teachers' resources vary, but a wide range of materials and teaching aids is available. In nursery and primary schools, for instance, these may include paints and pens, scissors and glue, modelling clay, sewing materials, musical instruments, building blocks, dressing-up clothes, simple woodworking tools, water and sand, and gardening tools.

Technological education teachers educate young pupils to handle simple tools such as chisels and soldering irons, older ones to use precision tools and sophisticated design software. Language and music tapes and video cassettes are widely used, and computer skills are taught from the early primary years.

All teachers have administrative duties, such as recording attendance. They may also become involved in more general administration and have to attend departmental, curriculum, and parent–teacher meetings.

Teachers have a pastoral or caring role, guiding pupils and advising them on personal problems. Guidance teachers have special responsibilities of this kind and boarding school teachers often care for pupils outside school hours. Many teachers organize extra-curricular activities such as concerts, outings, and adventure holidays.

As well as working closely with colleagues, teachers come into contact with parents, social workers, counsellors and many other members of the community.

Nursery/primary school teacher

Nursery/primary teachers usually have opportunities to teach all ages from three to twelve years, perhaps teaching one age group for a year and another the next. They teach all subjects in the 5–14 curriculum at primary level including maths, language, environmental studies (science, technology, information technology, social subjects and health education), expressive arts (drama, music, art and design, and physical education), religious and moral education and personal and social development. Specialist help may be available in a number of areas.

Secondary school teacher

Secondary school teachers work with children of different age groups and levels of ability, and specialize in teaching one or two subjects.

In the first and second years, subject study is broad. In years three and four teachers prepare pupils for Scottish Certificate of Education (SCE) Standard Grade Examinations (S grades), taken at the end of the fourth year. Pupils may also study a wide range of SCE short courses and SQA national certificate modules in S3 and S4. A variety of courses may be followed in the fifth and sixth years. SCE Higher Grades and, in S6 the Certificate of Sixth Year Studies, may be combined with further short courses and SQA modules. A new curriculum and assessment system for the upper secondary, called Higher Still, will be introduced in 1998.

Guidance teachers help pupils choose SCE subjects and give them advice on careers and personal problems. They work as part of a team and may have fewer teaching duties.

WORK ENVIRONMENT

Most primary schools have 100–400 pupils, though in remote districts there may be only 20 pupils and one or two teachers. Most secondary schools have 600–1,000 pupils. All Scottish state schools are co-educational.

Most teachers work in classrooms, but they may teach in workshops, laboratories, and gyms. They are on their feet much of the day and must be fit and mobile. They may walk long distances between classes or between sites, and often carry heavy loads of books and other equipment. Teachers may work outside, or away from, the school when involved in walks, games and playground duty, the school farm or garden, sports matches, field trips, and outings.

Boarding school teachers may live on the premises or nearby, working in residential and recreational areas as well as in classrooms. Other teachers tutor children in their homes or in hospital.

SKILLS AND INTERESTS

Please see article 1. SCHOOL TEACHER – ENGLAND AND WALES.

ENTRY REQUIREMENTS

Teachers in state and grant-aided schools, and some independent schools, have to register with the General Teaching Council for Scotland (GTC). To be eligible they must have a teaching qualification. Primary teachers need a BEd degree in teaching or a Postgraduate Certificate in Education (PGCE). Secondary teachers need a Postgraduate Certificate in Education or a BEd degree in Music, Technological Education or PE, or a concurrent degree.

Primary – minimum entry requirements are:

1. BEd in Primary Education – three H grades (A–C), including English and two S grades (1–3) in other subjects, including maths if not offered as an H grade, or equivalent.

2. Postgraduate Certificate in Education – degree plus H grade English and S grade (1–3) maths, or equivalent.

NB: Applicants for entry to both primary teacher training routes from academic session 2000/2001 will need S grade credit-level (1–2) maths.

For primary school teacher training Teacher Education Institutions (TEIs) must be satisfied that applicants' previous education, including their degree, provides the necessary foundation for work as a primary teacher. They will, therefore, normally be looking for evidence of prior learning in at least two of the following areas (in addition to English and maths): science, social studies, expressive arts, religious and moral education, technology or modern foreign languages.

Secondary – minimum entry requirements are:

1. Postgraduate Certificate in Education – degree plus H grade English, or equivalent. The degree should normally contain passes in at least two Teacher Subject Qualifying Courses (TSQCs) in the subject or subjects to be taught, one of which must be at second year level. (A TSQC is the part of an applicant's degree that relates to the subject as taught in Scottish secondary schools and will represent approximately one third of the total study in one academic year.)

Entry to all one-year PGCE secondary courses from academic session 2000/2001 will require a degree with passes in at least three TSQCs in each subject to be taught. One TSQC will have to be at second year level and one at third year level.

Some secondary subjects have more specific individual degree requirements. Details are available from the teacher education institutions, the SOEID or the GTC.

2. BEd in Music, Technological Education or PE and combined/concurrent degrees. TEIs assess applicants in terms of their own entry requirements but applicants for BEd courses must have H grade English, or equivalent. Students on combined/concurrent degrees must have H grade English, or equivalent, when starting the teacher education component of the course.

A broad range of qualifications may be acceptable in place of SCE qualifications, eg SQA modules, GNVQs/GSVQs, higher national certificates/diplomas, A levels and GCSEs.

TEACHING: FAB

Individual TEIs are responsible for assessing equivalence of such qualifications and any enquiries should be directed to them.

Applications for entry to the postgraduate course are dealt with centrally by the Teacher Education Admissions Clearing House (TEACH) and the undergraduate courses by the Universities and Colleges Admissions Service (UCAS). All entrants must pass a medical examination before starting a course.

TRAINING
Primary

1. BEd in Primary Education – four-year courses are run at all the Scottish teacher education institutions: University of Paisley Craigie Campus (Ayr), University of Strathclyde Jordanhill Campus (Glasgow), Moray House Institute (Edinburgh), Northern College (Aberdeen/Dundee), and St Andrew's College (Glasgow) – Scotland's national Catholic college. Students increase their knowledge of curriculum subjects and study the theory and practice of teaching. Topics include child development, teaching methods, and learning resources. Day and block placements allow students to watch teachers at work and gain classroom experience at nursery and all primary stages.

2. Postgraduate Certificate in Primary Education – one-year courses are run at all the TEIs (but at the Dundee campus at Northern College, rather than at Aberdeen). The course includes the theory and practice of teaching, curriculum study and analysis, and school placements.

Secondary

1. Postgraduate Certificate in Secondary Education – one-year courses are run at: University of Paisley (Craigie Campus), University of Strathclyde (Jordanhill Campus), Moray House Institute, Northern College (Aberdeen), and St Andrew's College. Applicants are advised to choose courses in two subjects if possible. Courses include subject study, studies in education, psychology, sociology, and educational administration. Half the course is spent on school placement.

2. BEd in Music – four-year courses are run at: University of Strathclyde (Jordanhill), St Andrew's College, and at Northern College (Aberdeen). Courses combine specialist musical studies with a thorough grounding in teaching and practical experience in schools.

3. BEd in Technological Education – four-year courses are run at the University of Glasgow, the University of Strathclyde (Jordanhill) and Moray House Institute/Napier University (Edinburgh). These qualify graduates to teach craft and design, technological studies and graphic communication. Courses combine acquisition of technological skills with problem solving, theoretical studies, and placements in schools, colleges and industry.

4. BEd in PE – four-year course run at Moray House Institute. It includes study of teaching and learning and of the nature and practice of physical activities, plus four school placements.

5. Combined/concurrent degrees – The University of Stirling offers a course that leads to a secondary school teaching qualification and a degree in any one of a number of secondary teaching subjects. Courses last four and a half years (five and a half for modern foreign languages, because of a year spent abroad). Other combined/concurrent courses that include a secondary school teaching qualification are offered at The University of Strathclyde (maths), Northern College (Aberdeen) (maths and computing) and St Andrew's College (theology). Northern College's course lasts four years, the other courses four and a half years. An increasing number of courses are being offered and those interested should consult the current UCAS handbook.

Registration

Once qualified, it is necessary to register with the General Teaching Council for Scotland (GTC) before teaching in an education authority school. New teachers undertake a two-year probationary period, before being eligible for full registration.

Students undertaking their probationary period outwith Scotland should consult the GTC regarding probation arrangements. Teachers educated outwith Scotland should write to the GTC to ensure that they qualify for 'exceptional' admission to the register. The GTC welcomes applications from qualified teachers from outwith Scotland.

In-service training, staff development and appraisal

All education authorities are introducing staff development and appraisal schemes on a phased basis. These provide opportunities to review teachers and identify staff development needs. These needs are met through a combination of school-based and externally provided in-service training.

LATE ENTRY

There is no upper age limit for entry to teacher training. Teacher education institutions run Access courses for mature students who lack conventional qualifications.

OPPORTUNITIES

The state system employs more than 22,000 nursery/primary school teachers and nearly 24,000 secondary school teachers.

There may be opportunities for employment in all 32 education authorities.

There is a continuing demand for teachers who are Gaelic speakers, particularly at primary level. At secondary level, there are opportunities for teachers in maths, physics, computing, technological education, religious education, modern languages and music.

Part-time work is available and job-sharing schemes are run in some areas.

There are openings outwith the state education sector for teachers to work in independent schools, to give one-to-one tuition, to teach Forces children overseas, to teach in hospitals and community homes, and to work voluntarily on short-term contracts overseas.

Teaching posts are advertised in *The Times Educational Supplement* (Scottish edition), *The Scotsman* (Wednesdays) and *The Herald* (Tuesdays). Lists of vacancies should be available from the 32 education authorities and from governing bodies of independent schools.

PAY AND CONDITIONS

Salaries are paid on an incremental scale ranging from £13,305 to £21,315. The scale entry point for ordinary graduates and equivalents is £13,305; for honours

TEACHING: FAB

graduates, £13,944. Additional allowances are paid to teachers in remote schools and distant islands. Late entrants may be paid half a scale point extra for every year over 24, up to a maximum of eight increments (subject to certain adjustments).

Head teachers' salaries vary according to number of pupils. They range from £27,036 to £36,420 in primary schools; £31,455 to £50,079 in secondary schools.

Independent school salaries are generally comparable or higher than those in the state sector.

State school teachers work 195 days a year, five of which are pupil-free (190 are within the 39-week school year). The school day is usually 9am to 3.30pm or 4pm. Teachers work 27 hours in school with maximum class contact of 25 hours in primary schools, and 23 hours in secondary schools. In addition, up to 30 hours a year may be required for a maximum of six parents' meetings, along with an annual maximum of 50 hours for planned activities (eg staff meetings, professional development).

PROSPECTS

Large primary schools may have one or more assistant head teachers, as well as a head. Assistant heads are responsible for an area such as early-stage education or curriculum development.

More than 50% of secondary teachers are in promoted posts.

Promotion to senior teacher depends on expertise and experience. A senior teacher might, for instance, be responsible for helping probationer teachers. Other promoted posts include principal teacher – in charge of a subject department or working in guidance – and assistant principal teacher, assistant head, deputy head and head (rector).

There are opportunities for experienced teachers to move into special needs, work as advisers or administrators for an education authority, or join the schools inspectorate. Overseas work is possible, particularly for experienced teachers.

RELATED OCCUPATIONS

Please see article 1. SCHOOL TEACHER – ENGLAND AND WALES.

FURTHER INFORMATION AND READING

Please see article 5. HIGHER EDUCATION LECTURER.

3. SPECIAL EDUCATIONAL NEEDS TEACHER (FAB)

BACKGROUND INFORMATION

About 20% of school-age children and young people have special educational needs at some time during their school career, although only around two per cent have a long-term need requiring special provision to be made for them. It is this two per cent of children that have statements of special educational needs (records of needs in Scotland), and that make up the majority of the special school population. The trend is for mainstream schools to have an increasing number of pupils with statements of special educational needs or records of needs. All children with impairments are entitled to an appropriate education, regardless of the nature or severity of their difficulty. Most go to ordinary schools. Others attend special schools or units for all or part of their school days, sometimes moving in and out of mainstream schooling as their needs change.

In common with all pupils in the state sector, children with special educational needs are taught a broad and balanced curriculum.

Over the past decade, increasing numbers of children with severe learning difficulties have been integrated successfully into mainstream schools. Integration policies vary from authority to authority and from school to school.

THE WORK

Teaching methods and curricula vary according to the children's individual requirements. Some pupils are taught mainstream curriculum subjects with the help of special equipment and resources. Teachers may also devise individual learning programmes or follow programmes designed for children with a particular impairment.

Helping children become more confident and independent is an important part of the work. Children with profound impairments may have to be taught to speak or sign, and to dress themselves. Many children with communication impairments have individual curriculum programmes or adapted programmes that bring out their strengths, helping them, for example, to understand the written and spoken word. Pupils with emotional and behavioural problems are taught to cope with stress and to manage feelings of anger, fear or frustration. The teacher's work includes helping children to gain self-confidence, which will enable them to make the best of their abilities.

Pupils with moderate learning difficulties may be taught in special schools or classes or given extra help in an ordinary class. Some need special assistance across the curriculum, while others receive additional help in only one or two subjects.

Teachers of pupils who are deaf or have hearing impairment may use a sign language, finger spelling and other methods to communicate.

Children who are blind or partially-sighted are taught to make the maximum use of residual vision and their other senses. Teaching aids include closed-circuit television, Braille and Moon (methods of reading by touch), cassettes, light-rooms, and computer touch screens.

Children and young people in special schools may require medical care and teachers consult with doctors, nurses, and therapists in primary educational programmes. Teachers also liaise with educational psychologists, social workers, advisers and parents.

In residential schools, staff help care for and counsel the children, run hobbies and clubs, and organize games and outings. These extra-curricular activities are used to improve skills and social training, as well as provide recreation.

Advisory and peripatetic teachers provide specialist services for schools and units. They teach and provide learning support, ensuring children have the correct lighting, seating position, equipment and resources etc.

Special educational needs teachers have to carry out administrative duties, write detailed assessments and evaluations, prepare lessons, correct assignments, and attend meetings. Lesson preparation may involve the production of special resources, such as Braille copy.

TEACHING: FAB

An increasing number of pupils with special educational needs attend mainstream schools. Teachers designated as special educational needs co-ordinators are responsible for working with these children and for co-ordinating the work of other teachers with them.

WORK ENVIRONMENT

Teachers work with small groups of children and occasionally with individuals.

Mainstream schools may have a special unit attached, which draws pupils from a wide radius. Some schools have a classroom, or a quiet room, where teachers give one-to-one assistance. Advisory and peripatetic teachers travel extensively, seeing children at many schools and units. They also visit pre-school children in their homes. Special schools are smaller than most mainstream schools. Many take residential pupils, who are accommodated in family-style units.

SKILLS AND INTERESTS

The work is physically and emotionally demanding, requiring exceptional maturity and resilience and the ability to remain calm under stress.

Some pupils and students with special educational needs have a wide range of impairments and behavioural problems. It may take a long time to win their confidence and build individual relationships. They must be treated firmly, but always fairly.

Teachers have to be enthusiastic, sympathetic, patient and persistent. They must remain encouraging and positive, despite setbacks or apparent lack of progress. They need to be able to communicate well by whatever means is most suitable, and have a cheerful and optimistic nature and a good sense of humour. Certain impairments require certain qualities in the teacher. Teachers of the deaf, for instance, need an interest in communication and an open mind on the method used, eg sign language and oral communication.

All special educational needs teachers require the organizational skills to allocate their time effectively and make full use of equipment and resources. They work as part of a broad-based team and must relate well to other professionals and support staff. It is also particularly important for special educational needs teachers to build good relationships with parents.

Teachers must be committed to continuing professional development.

ENTRY REQUIREMENTS

Only qualified school teachers may teach children with special educational needs. Please see articles 1. and 2. SCHOOL TEACHER – ENGLAND AND WALES/SCOTLAND for initial teacher training entry requirements. Candidates for specialist training courses must have qualified as a school teacher (via a teaching degree or a subject degree and Postgraduate Certificate in Education) and normally have had at least two years' teaching experience.

TRAINING

In England and Wales, specialist training is compulsory for those wishing to teach children with impaired vision or hearing.

In Scotland, teachers of children and young persons with special educational needs are expected to undertake specialist in-service training.

Training to teach pupils/students who are deaf or hearing impaired. In England and Wales it is possible to teach pupils who are deaf during the two years following initial teacher training, providing the teacher is being supervised by a qualified teacher of the deaf. It is also possible to apply for a position that requires a Teaching of the Deaf Diploma before qualifying but training must be completed within two years of taking up the position. In Scotland it is not mandatory for teachers of deaf pupils to have the relevant specialist qualification.

One-year full-time diploma and advanced certificate courses are run at Birmingham University, Manchester University and the University of Hertfordshire. Two-year part-time in-service diploma courses are run at Birmingham University, the University of Hertfordshire, Leeds University, Northumbria University, University College, Wales and Moray House Institute (Edinburgh).

Qualified, hearing impaired teachers wishing to train to teach deaf pupils may obtain information on the most suitable institutions from the Co-ordinator, The Hearing Impaired Teacher's Group, c/o RNID, the Director, The National Deaf Children's Society and the Scottish Sensory Centre, Moray House Institute (Edinburgh).

Training to teach pupils/students who are blind or visually impaired. In England and Wales teachers planning to work in a special school for children who are blind or visually impaired normally first undertake specialist training, although, in principle, they may take up an appointment and complete a specialist training course within three years. In Scotland teachers working with such pupils are expected to undertake specialist in-service training.

One-year full-time diploma courses are run at: Birmingham University, Gwent College of Higher Education, London University (Institute of Education), Manchester Metropolitan University and University College Swansea. Two-year part-time diploma courses are run at: Birmingham University (distance learning), the Cambridge Institute of Education, London University and Moray House Institute (Edinburgh).

Training to teach others with special educational needs. Specialist training is recommended for all teachers wishing to teach young people with special educational needs. Some teachers may prepare by training before moving into special needs work.

Others may begin work in special needs and then seek training. Teachers should consult their local education authority about the availability of special needs training.

In-service training courses are run at higher education institutions throughout the UK on a day release, block release, evening, distance learning and outreach basis. The opportunity for teachers to be seconded to full-time training has greatly decreased.

Some courses consider issues common to the whole range of special needs work. Others allow specialization in such areas as: social, emotional and behavioural difficulties; severe, profound and multiple difficulties; language and communication difficulties. Many courses are modular and enable teachers to consider their specialist interests.

Local authorities also organize short courses, conferences and other training activities.

The Open University offers an Advanced Diploma in

TEACHING: FAB

Special Needs in Education that is designed both for teachers in mainstream and in special schools.

LATE ENTRY

Please see articles 1. and 2. SCHOOL TEACHER – ENGLAND AND WALES/SCOTLAND. The work may be suitable for someone returning to teaching after a career break or for someone who, before qualifying as a school teacher, has experience in an area related to special educational needs.

OPPORTUNITIES

Most special educational needs teachers work for local education authorities in special schools and units, in peripatetic services, in mainstream schools, in community homes, and in youth custody centres. Some are employed by the Royal National Institute for the Blind, Barnardo's, National Children's Homes and other voluntary organizations. They work in NHS hospitals and in clinics providing audiological and advisory services.

There are 1,234 local authority special schools in the UK, employing 15,688 full-time equivalent teachers in England, 590 in Wales, and 1,582 in Scotland.

The number of special schools is declining, partly because more children are being taught in mainstream schools. Vacant posts tend to be filled by those already employed in special schools. More posts may be created to cope with the increasing number of special educational needs children attending mainstream schools.

There are seven grant-aided residential schools in Scotland, run by charities, which cater for sensory impaired and physically impaired children.

In England and Wales demand is increasing for teachers to work with children who are language impaired, with children who have mild learning difficulties, and with children who have social and behavioural difficulties. In Scotland demand is stable.

Teachers may need to move location in order to obtain work, particularly those who specialize in a certain impairment. There are limited opportunities for part-time and supply teaching.

Vacancies are advertised in *The Times Educational Supplement, The Scottish Educational Journal, The Glasgow Herald, The Scotsman, The Guardian* and *The Journal of the British Association of Teachers of the Deaf.*

PAY AND CONDITIONS

Most special educational needs teachers in England and Wales are paid on a national 18-point pay spine. (Please see articles 1 and 2. SCHOOL TEACHER – ENGLAND AND WALES/SCOTLAND). Pupils have regular school hours, but teachers work extra hours for lesson and resource preparation, assessments etc.

In England and Wales an additional spine point is paid to teachers in special schools and to teachers in mainstream schools who teach pupils with statements of special educational needs. Teachers will also be entitled to an additional point if they take charge of the classes for the hearing impaired or visually impaired, even if these children do not have statements.

PROSPECTS

Special schools offer limited prospects for promotion because of their declining number. Teachers with relevant experience are sometimes able to move into special schools from other areas of special educational needs. In-service training is widely available to provide advanced specialist qualifications.

There are opportunities for experienced special educational needs teachers to become local education authority advisers, join the inspectorate or move into teacher training.

RELATED OCCUPATIONS

Special support assistant, child care assistant, speech and language therapist, occupational therapist, youth leader, teacher, social worker.

FURTHER INFORMATION AND READING

Please see article 5. HIGHER EDUCATION LECTURER.

4. FURTHER EDUCATION/TERTIARY COLLEGE LECTURER (FAB)

BACKGROUND INFORMATION

Further education is provided in a wide range of colleges, adult education institutes and other institutions.

The further education sector has close links with commerce and industry, and course provision reflects local and national needs. Increasing emphasis is placed on meeting the educational and personal development requirements of whole communities. Many institutions provide a balanced and comprehensive range of vocational, non-vocational, and academic courses for young people and adults of all ages. Others specialize in an area such as art and design, agriculture and horticulture or hotel and catering, but still ensure that course provision remains broad. A growing number of tertiary colleges offer full-time academic and vocational courses for 16- to 19-year-olds, plus part-time courses for young people and adults. (Post-16 education is also provided in schools and sixth-form colleges.)

THE WORK

Further education/tertiary college lecturers may teach vocational or academic subjects. A growing number teach recreational or hobby interest subjects. Teaching methods include lectures, seminars, tutorials, demonstrations and practical sessions. Lecturers give advice on background reading and other methods of research, and stimulate analysis and discussion.

Many courses equip students for a particular occupation, trade or profession such as farming, horticulture, light engineering, building, social care, catering, hairdressing or business. Courses often have a high practical content, requiring the lecturer to demonstrate skills, operate equipment and supervise workshop practice. Lecturers may also have to arrange and monitor students' work projects and industrial or commercial placements.

Lecturers teach full-time, sandwich, part-time, and short courses. They prepare students for City and Guilds, Royal Society of Arts, BTEC and SQA qualifications,

TEACHING: FAB

GNVQs/GSVQs and NVQs/SVQs, and for A levels/H grades in academic subjects. They also teach Access to Higher Education courses. Lecturers in private tutorial colleges coach students for A levels and university entrance. In some colleges of further education, lecturers also prepare students for degrees and higher national certificates and diplomas. Increasingly, lecturers are providing courses on an outreach basis at the workplace or in the community.

Recent school-leavers and unemployed young people are taught skills to help them obtain work, eg job application and interview techniques, and information technology skills.

Lecturers' duties also include designing the curriculum, preparing lectures and practical sessions, setting and marking assignments, tests and examinations, carrying out continuous assessments, and performing administrative duties associated with the planning and delivery of courses. Many agricultural and horticultural colleges are residential and lecturers may be involved in sports and other extra-curricular activities.

When vocational courses are linked to local employment needs, lecturers spend a substantial amount of time making and maintaining contacts in industry and commerce. They may have to determine the training requirements of individual employers and design appropriate courses.

Lecturers have to keep up with the latest developments in their subjects, through extensive reading or other research.

Some lecturers teach evening and other classes in subjects or skills that do not lead to a particular qualification, eg painting or sculpture as a hobby, or a language for holiday or business purposes. These classes are sometimes referred to as 'informal further education' (as opposed to 'formal further education' that leads to a qualification). Lecturers have to make their subjects accessible to students of widely differing abilities.

WORK ENVIRONMENT

Further education colleges vary greatly in size. A small college may have 50 or fewer staff, while larger establishments could have up to 500 full-time staff.

Lecturers work in classrooms, laboratories, demonstration rooms, kitchens, studios, workshops etc. These may be purpose-built or consist of facilities shared with a school or other centre.

Specialist colleges – those teaching agriculture and horticulture, for instance – have land and buildings attached where practical work is supervised.

SKILLS AND INTERESTS

Lecturers in further/tertiary education must have an interest in their subject and like teaching and training others. They must be able to deliver an appropriate curriculum, based on particular course requirements.

They have to express themselves concisely, and to present and explain ideas clearly to people of differing levels of ability and understanding. They need tact and patience and should be able to gain the respect of others. They must be able to lead and motivate others to develop high standards of work and study.

Lecturers in vocational subjects must have relevant skills and work experience to enable them to run demonstrations and practical workshops and laboratory classes efficiently and safely.

Lecturers need to be able to manage their workloads efficiently.

ENTRY REQUIREMENTS

England and Wales

Further education (FE) lecturers are usually expected to have a professional or academic qualification in the subject they intend to teach, plus relevant professional, industrial or business experience.

Currently there is no legal requirement for FE lecturers to have a professional teaching qualification. In practice, however, an increasing number of FE employers require a teaching qualification and over 60% of those teaching in FE have a teaching qualification.

Part-time lecturers, particularly in adult education classes, may be accepted on the basis of their work experience alone.

1. Full-time Certificate in Education (Further Education) courses require a qualification in the subject to be taught, such as a degree, BTEC/SQA higher national award, membership of a professional institution, full Technological Certificate or where this is not awarded a Final Certificate of the City and Guilds Institute, or Advanced RSA Certificate. Applicants should also have relevant industrial or business experience. Non-graduates must normally be age 24 or over.

2. Part-time Certificate in Education (Further Education) courses require applicants to be in relevant FE teaching.

3. Postgraduate Certificate in Education (PGCE) courses need a degree relevant to the subject to be taught and relevant work experience of around two to three years. While GCSEs (A–C) in English language and maths are essential for teaching in schools they are not a requirement for FE teaching.

4. City and Guilds Further and Adult Education Teacher's Certificate (7306 and 7307) courses require relevant qualifications and/or work experience, plus the opportunity for teaching practice.

5. Other courses usually require experience or qualifications relevant to the area of study.

Scotland

To be eligible for permanent appointments in further education, candidates need one of the following: UK degree, associateship or diploma of a Scottish college of education or other central institution (or equivalent), SQA/BTEC higher national award, full City and Guilds Technological Certificate.

Candidates must also have reached an appropriate level in communication and numeracy (usually SQA Communication 3 and Maths 3 or equivalent). Applicants under age 23 require H grade English or equivalent. In addition to formal qualifications applicants normally need industrial, commercial or other relevant experience.

A teaching qualification is not compulsory but is highly desirable. About 80% of lecturers have a teaching qualification and promotion within the further education service is difficult without one. Most lecturers, however, enter the service without a teaching qualification and are seconded by their employers for professional training to the Scottish School of Further Education (University of Strathclyde). Courses are open to lecturers in further and higher education who are in permanent employment.

A medical examination may be requested for full-time posts.

TEACHING: FAB

TRAINING

England and Wales

1. One-year full-time pre-service or in-service courses leading to the Certificate in Education (Further Education) are offered at Bolton Institute of Higher Education, The University of Huddersfield, University of Greenwich, The Nottingham Trent University and University of Wolverhampton. Courses are offered in many subjects including business studies, engineering, general studies, maths, science, social science, humanities, languages, health and social care, hairdressing and beauty therapy, art and design, computing and building. Courses include study of teaching theory and methods, and eleven weeks' teaching practice.

2. Part-time and day release pre-service or in-service courses, leading to a Certificate in Education (Further Education) are offered at around 40 universities and colleges.

3. Some one-year, full-time Postgraduate Certificate in Education (PGCE) initial teacher training courses have further education options. Courses are offered at 15 universities and colleges.

4. City and Guilds Further and Adult Education Teacher's Certificate (7307) is designed mainly for those new to teaching or those who wish to work through a set programme of tuition.

City and Guilds Further and Adult Education Teacher's Certificate (7306) is designed to lead to NVQ in Training and Development at Levels 3 and 4. Candidates do not have to follow a formal programme of study but must prove competence in the required NVQ units.

Both Certificate courses (7307 and 7306) are offered at over 250 colleges in England and Wales, mainly on a day release or evening basis. They are generally recognized as equivalent to the first year of a two-year Certificate in Education (Further Education) programme.

5. Other courses include the RSA Teachers' Certificate in Office Studies, which is offered at over 50 colleges, mainly on a day release or evening basis over varying lengths of time.

FE teachers wanting to train for work with special needs students can study for City and Guilds Continuing Professional Development (Special Needs) (7401). It is offered at over 40 colleges on a day release or evening basis over varying lengths of time.

Further details are in *The NATFHE Handbook of Initial Teacher Training*, NATFHE's *Training to Teach in Further Education* and *The Directory of Further Education*, published by the Careers Research Advisory Centre.

Scotland

The Scottish School of Further Education (SSFE) Certificate in Education (Further Education) and Postgraduate Certificate in Education (Higher and Further Education) courses span two years and consist of two four-week and two one-week periods of block release, combined with distance learning between the blocks. These courses are only available to lecturers in employment in further and higher education. There is no pre-service training in Scotland for teaching in post-school education.

From late in 1998 the SSFE will be offering a Certificate in Education (Tertiary Education). This fully modular provision will be available in a variety of flexible modes including day release and evening classes as well as distance learning provision of certain modules. The course will be suitable for those already employed, either full-time or part-time, as lecturers in further or higher education. It will also be available to those wishing to acquire the Teaching Qualification (Further Education) on a pre-service self-funded basis.

The SSFE also offers post-experience courses for career development purposes to lecturers employed in post-16 education. These are part-time courses that lead to certificate, diploma, first and higher degree awards of the University of Strathclyde. They are open to those who already have a recognized teaching qualification.

LATE ENTRY

There is no upper age limit to teaching in further/tertiary education, though the need to be up to date in developments and current working practice in a given field may preclude entrants who have had a lengthy career break.

Further education teaching is often a second career, and the mature entrant with appropriate experience is more likely to obtain a lectureship than a young graduate. Qualified adults often start by teaching evening classes. These also provide openings for adults without formal qualifications to teach in a wide range of art and leisure-based subjects.

OPPORTUNITIES

There are about 400 further education colleges in England and Wales and about 55 tertiary colleges, employing a total of about 55,000 full-time and at least 100,000 part-time teachers. There are about 43 further education colleges in Scotland offering further/higher education and employing about 6,000 full-time and 1,500 part-time lecturers.

The majority of openings arise in local colleges and adult education centres. Colleges may specialize in a particular field, or offer a variety of vocational and academic subjects and general interest courses.

Opportunities arise in tutorial colleges and in private industrial/commercial training establishments. There are also openings in the Prison Service. The Armed Forces employ lecturers (details from Armed Forces Careers Offices), and organizations such as the British Council recruit lecturers to work in developing countries.

Demand varies locally, but competition is intense for many posts. In vocational subjects, appointments depend largely on work experience, while in more academic subjects, a teaching qualification and secondary school teaching experience may be an advantage.

There are widespread opportunities for part-time lecturing. Full-time lectureships often go to those who have worked part-time for the same local college, though many lecturers prefer to retain their original career and continue to teach part-time.

Positions are advertised in the national press, including *The Times Educational Supplement*, *The Times Higher Education Supplement*, *The Guardian*, *The Herald* and *The Scotsman*, in trade and professional magazines, and locally.

PAY AND CONDITIONS

In England and Wales, local authority incremental pay scales pay within the following ranges: lecturers £12,573 to £24,354, senior lecturers £21,999 to £29,073, management spine £22,845 to £54,189. Teaching in the London area attracts London weighting.

TEACHING: FAB

Rates of pay are similar in Scotland.

NB: Pay and conditions of service in England, Wales and Scotland are under review.

PROSPECTS

In England and Wales, highly qualified candidates are sometimes appointed directly to the post of senior lecturer, but it is usually a promoted position that carries a fair amount of managerial responsibility.

Prospects of promotion to senior lecturer, head of department etc, are enhanced for those who have teaching qualifications and experience, keep up with developments in their field, have management skills, and are willing to move location. To gain promotion in Scotland, a teaching qualification is essential.

Many colleges run their own in-service training courses and many have staff development officers who advise other colleges and individuals. Management training is available at the Further Education Development Agency (FEDA), Bristol, and elsewhere. In Scotland, the national centre for such courses is the Scottish School of Further Education at the University of Strathclyde.

RELATED OCCUPATIONS

School teacher, youth and community worker, training officer, higher education lecturer.

FURTHER INFORMATION AND READING

Please see article 5. HIGHER EDUCATION LECTURER.

5. HIGHER EDUCATION LECTURER (FAB)

BACKGROUND INFORMATION

In Britain, higher education is provided in a variety of establishments – universities, colleges of education etc. Lecturers prepare students for a wide range of first and higher degrees, professional and other qualifications. Courses may be purely academic, or may provide pre-employment training, or specialist training for professionals already in employment.

THE WORK

Lecturers spend many hours researching and preparing for lectures and practicals, setting and marking assignments and exams, carrying out continuous assessment, evaluating research, and monitoring work projects and placements.

Much of the teaching takes the form of lectures on a particular topic or course option. As well as providing information and suggesting areas for further research, lecturers aim to develop students' powers of interpretation, analysis and original thought.

Lectures last for about 50 minutes and may be attended by up to 400 students. Less formal teaching takes place in seminars or tutorials for small groups of students; lecturers may deliver prepared material, but also lead discussions and give comments on students' essays or other work.

In subjects such as science and engineering, lecturers supervise sessions of practical work or experiments lasting up to three hours. Lecturers also lead field trips and arrange work projects and placements.

Increasing numbers of higher education institutions are adapting curricula and teaching methods so that students can take more responsibility for their learning. Lecturers help students plan learning programmes based on their interests and talents, and encourage them to acquire skills, such as word processing, communication, presentation, management techniques etc. They may arrange work experience for students who would normally require it, and link courses more closely to regional and community needs.

Many full-time lecturers act as personal tutors to individual students, advising them on their study, careers and personal problems. They may specialize in student counselling, or become wardens of residential halls.

They also have many administrative duties, whether helping with student admissions, serving on curriculum development and departmental committees, or acting as external examiners for other colleges.

Lecturers have to keep up to date with their subject, through extensive reading and through following developments outside higher education. Most university staff are required to undertake research. They aim to publish their findings or contribute them to relevant companies or associations. The proportion of time devoted to teaching and to research varies between posts and institutions.

WORK ENVIRONMENT

Higher education institutions vary greatly in size and may have over 1,000 full- and part-time academic staff, plus a greater number of other staff.

Depending on their subject, teachers work in lecture halls, seminar and tutorial rooms, laboratories and workshops, hospital wards and clinics. Field trips, work project placements, and visits to employer contacts, all take lecturers off campus.

Research takes place in libraries, laboratories, and in the field. Many science and technical projects are team efforts, but research in the arts, for instance, may be undertaken alone.

SKILLS AND INTERESTS

Lecturers need an extensive knowledge of their subject. They are likely to specialize within their field, and must be able to produce a well-balanced programme of lectures based on course requirements.

They must be interested in teaching and be able to explain facts and theories clearly and imaginatively. This requires self-confidence and good written and spoken communication skills.

Lecturers should be able to encourage the development of intellectual skills in others and motivate them to achieve course objectives and deadlines. It is important to be flexible and to be able to work both with large numbers of students and in one-to-one situations. Lecturers, especially those who are personal tutors, must be interested in the welfare of their students. Tact, patience, and the ability to get on with all kinds of people are essential.

Lecturers in vocational subjects must have relevant work experience and be able to set their teaching in an appropriate professional or industrial context.

All higher education teachers need to manage their work schedules efficiently.

TEACHING: FAB

ENTRY REQUIREMENTS

Entry is usually with a good honours first degree (a first-class or upper second), together with a postgraduate qualification, such as an MA, MSc or PhD, or an equivalent professional qualification.

Applicants to full-time posts in universities usually need to have, or be working towards, a PhD and have a record of research and publication. A PhD is desirable but not essential for posts in colleges of higher education.

Those teaching applied or vocational subjects may also need several years' professional or industrial experience, as well as academic qualifications, particularly in fields such as engineering, management, journalism, art and design or teaching.

When making appointments, universities and colleges usually recruit lecturers whose specialist research and/or training corresponds with the needs of the department concerned and the syllabus to be taught. Many posts are offered on a fixed- term contract.

A medical is usually needed for permanent full-time positions.

TRAINING

There is, as yet, no specific training for lecturing in higher education. Most institutions of higher education have their own induction and training schemes for newly appointed lecturers and there is increasing provision both for new and existing staff through staff development programmes. A new institute is being set up which will, in future, oversee training for new staff.

LATE ENTRY

People are usually at least 24 years old before they are sufficiently qualified to consider lecturing in higher education. There is no upper age limit and late entry is common. Mature applicants may be accepted for entry to first degree courses without the usual entry requirements.

OPPORTUNITIES

There are over 100 institutions of higher education, employing around 60,000 lecturers on a part-time or full-time basis.

The institutions include universities, colleges, institutes of education and higher education. These are found throughout the United Kingdom, and are based in most major towns and cities.

Posts in higher education are generally scarce and go to those who have excellent academic or professional qualifications, plus substantial work experience, where applicable. In the universities, there are openings for young researchers, particularly in the sciences.

Competition is intense, although vacancies may be easier to find in shortage subjects, such as maths and science, predominantly on a fixed-term, externally funded basis. The availability of vacancies also depends on student numbers and funding.

Some lecturers work abroad, teaching in English-speaking colleges or universities, or training teachers in developing countries. American universities have openings for highly qualified and experienced lecturers. The Overseas Development Administration and Voluntary Service Overseas recruit teacher-training staff.

Positions are advertised in *The Times Higher Education Supplement* and in national newspapers.

PAY AND CONDITIONS

Old universities in England, Wales and Scotland

The pay scales are: lecturer A, £16,655 to £21,815; lecturer B, £22,726 to £29,048 (discretionary to £32,457); senior lecturer, £30,496 to £34,464 (discretionary to £37,257). There is no nationally agreed salary scale for professors, although the minimum is £35,170. Professorial salaries are normally negotiated individually and initial appointments are likely to be made above the minimum. There is no maximum. Clinical academic staff are paid higher salaries, which mirror salaries paid to NHS hospital doctors.

New universities in England and Wales

The revised incremental pay scale for new universities and colleges: lecturer, £14,398 to £24,002; senior lecturer, £23,199 to £29,600; principal lecturer, £27,998 to £35,204; head of department, minimum £27,304.

Scotland

The incremental pay scale for centrally funded institutions: lecturer, £15,406 to £27,650; senior lecturer, £25,360 to £32,782; department head, £32,782 to £45,110. Salaries of principals and other senior management staff are determined by individual governing boards.

Lecturers employed by local authorities are paid on the same scale as further education lecturers. Please see article 4. FURTHER EDUCATION/TERTIARY COLLEGE LECTURER.

Universities and colleges have ten- to twelve-week terms, but working hours vary enormously according to subject, research commitments etc.

PROSPECTS

In the old universities, academic ability is usually considered more important than teaching skill. This is less true in new universities and colleges. Promotion prospects are enhanced by published research and scholarship, and through evidence of administrative skill. In recent years, promotional prospects have declined because of reduced funding.

In other higher education institutions, publication of work, acquisition of specialist professional qualifications, and proof of management ability enhance promotion prospects. Promotion usually leads to more consultancy work and more administration.

Specialists and recognized scholars are frequently offered work outside the institution where they teach. They may act as consultants, edit or annotate texts, contribute to magazines and newspapers, take part in radio and television broadcasts, and run or address conferences.

RELATED OCCUPATIONS

Training manager, further education/tertiary college lecturer, training officer, management consultant.

FURTHER INFORMATION

Association of University Teachers (AUT), Egmont House, 25 Tavistock Place, London WC1H 9UT, 0171 670 9700, http://www.aut.org.uk

The British Council*, Corporate Personnel (Recruitment),

TEACHING: FAB

10 Spring Gardens, London SW1A 2BN.

General Teaching Council for Scotland*, Clerwood House, 96 Clermiston Road, Edinburgh EH12 6UT, 0131 314 6000, www.gtcs.org.uk

Graduate Teacher Training Registry*, Fulton House, Jessop Avenue, Cheltenham, Glos GL50 3SH, 01242 544788

The National Deaf Children's Society, 15 Dufferin Street, London EC1Y 8PD, 0171 250 0123

The Open University, Walton Hall, Milton Keynes MK7 6AA, 01908 653231

University and College Lecturers' Union*, 27 Britannia Street, London WC1X 9JP, 0171 837 3636, www.natfhe.org.uk

Universities and Colleges Staff Development Agency (UCOSDA), Level 6, University House, Sheffield University, Sheffield S10 2TN, 0114 222 1335

Physical Education Association of the United Kingdom*, Suite 5, 10 Churchill Square, Kings Hill, West Malling, Kent ME19 4DU, 01732 875888, www.teleschool.org.uk/pea

Royal National Institute for the Blind*, Physiotherapy Support Service, 224 Great Portland Street, London W1A 6AA, 0171 388 1266 (please send sae)

Royal National Institute for Deaf People*, 19–23 Featherstone Street, London EC1Y 8SL, 0171 296 8000 (please send sae)

The Scottish School of Further Education*, University of Strathclyde, 76 Southbrae Drive, Glasgow G13 1PP, 0141 950 3143

Further Education Development Agency (FEDA), Dumbarton House, 68 Oxford Street, London W1N 0DA, 0171 436 0020

The Teacher Training Agency (TTA)*, Communication Centre, PO Box 3210, Chelmsford, Essex CM1 3WA, 01245 454454, www.teach.org

Teacher Education Admissions Clearing House (TEACH)*, PO Box 165, Edinburgh EH12 6YA, 0131 588 6169/70

Universities and Colleges Admissions Service, UCAS*, Fulton House, Jessop Avenue, Cheltenham, Glos GL50 3SH, 01242 544867, www.ucas.ac.uk

The Welsh Office*, Education Department, Cathays Park, Cardiff CF1 3NQ

FURTHER READING

Leaflets/booklets are available from the addresses marked* above, including a wide selection of literature from TTA, and videos from TEACH and GTC.

Working in Teaching – COIC

NATFHE Handbook of Initial Teacher Training available in libraries and careers advisory departments. Or buy from Linneys (NATFHE), 121 Newgate Lane, Mansfield, Notts NG18 2PA.

In the careers library classified under FAB.

JOURNALISM AND TECHNICAL WRITING: FAC

1. JOURNALIST CLCI:FAC
2. TECHNICAL AUTHOR CLCI:FAC

1. JOURNALIST (FAC)

BACKGROUND INFORMATION

Journalists keep people informed about events around them by researching, writing and presenting news stories and feature articles in newspapers, magazines, on radio and television and in other media.

THE WORK

Newspaper journalists may work for local and regional newspapers, where everyday activities form much of the reported news. Their reporters gather news of fêtes, council meetings, court sittings and local crime. Stories reported in the larger national newspapers may be very different, but the work of all journalists brings them into contact with people, events and places.

Research methods, often aided by shorthand notes, include face-to-face and telephone interviews (with or without sophisticated recording equipment), visits and library research. The news story, or 'copy' is then written and typed by the journalist, often using a word processor or computer terminal in a newspaper newsroom. The completed copy, together with a carefully worded introduction and headline, then passes to a sub-editor who edits the work, and possibly returns some of the work for rewriting.

Magazine journalists may work for consumer magazines, or for business and trade magazines. There are many similarities with newspaper journalism – research, interviews, checking facts, writing up copy and sub-editing – but magazines are usually produced to weekly or monthly deadlines. Business magazines often have strong news sections, which require high quality investigative reporting. Many magazine publishers employ specialist freelance writers in addition to staff journalists. There are three main branches to magazine journalism: news writing, feature writing (both functions are carried out by one person) and sub-editing (editing copy, writing headlines and preparing the magazines for printing).

Broadcast journalists work for national and independent radio and television companies. Many experienced press journalists hoping to move into this type of work start by working as a local radio reporter, preparing scripts for presentation and interviewing people. The radio industry is not extensive and the BBC is its largest employer. All BBC journalists are now trained in 'bi-media' techniques so that they can report for both television and radio. Broadcast journalists, in addition to writing and other skills, need a good knowledge of broadcast law, in order to avoid expensive legal action should something be wrongly worded.

When employed as programme assistants, journalists may have to operate broadcast studio equipment as well as reading the news or presenting programmes. Most television newsreaders are also experienced journalists. Journalists also work on documentary programmes as researchers.

Press agency journalists supply news stories, features and photographs to newspaper and magazine publishers. Some press agencies, such as Reuters, specialize in supplying international news. Other journalists work as press or public relations officers for major companies and other commercial organizations. They prepare press releases of information about the organization, and provide information to their press and broadcasting colleagues.

WORK ENVIRONMENT

Many journalists are office-based, in conditions that vary considerably. Some offices are modern and well equipped, but others may be small and cramped. Working on an assignment may involve anything from interviewing on location and in the street to using the full range of facilities provided in the press room at a major event.

While some reporters use the latest satellite links for the instant transmission of a news story back to a distant newsroom, others are still using a traditional notebook and pencil.

There are opportunities to travel locally while covering news stories. Journalists working on national newspapers may be expected to travel widely in the UK, often staying overnight in hotels. A small number of press and broadcast journalists travel abroad. The work environment may be pressured and hectic, particularly when publication deadlines are close.

SKILLS AND INTERESTS

Successful journalists need to be interested and inquisitive communicators: they must be interested in local and current affairs, able to discover the relevant facts of any story and to have the ability to communicate their interest and enthusiasm in clear and concise writing, or through broadcasting. Journalists interested in broadcasting journalism are also likely to need a clear and distinct voice for broadcasting.

Some journalists have a detailed knowledge of one particular technical field, and work closely with people sharing the specialization. Information technology skills can be important, and include the ability to use different computer software systems and a knowledge of how information can be transferred electronically.

Self confidence, attention to detail, the ability to face criticism, the ability to work in a team and a willingness to work unsocial hours are important. A driving licence is an asset.

ENTRY REQUIREMENTS

Although this is an occupation without standard formal entry requirements, the majority of journalists now enter as graduates – but not necessarily with degrees in journalism – and many of the others have achieved a minimum of two A Levels or equivalent. A GNVQ in Media: Communication and Production may be a useful indicator of a student's skills and interests in journalism. Good communication skills are essential and appropriate technical knowledge of computer systems may be required.

Entry to degree courses – minimum entry requirements to a degree course are usually two A levels/three H grades plus five GCSEs/S grades (A–C/1–3), or equivalent. English is an essential requirement at GCSE/S grade level, but may not be required at A level/H grade. Appropriate work experience is essential for entry to some degree courses.

Entry requirements for a postgraduate diploma are usually a BTEC/SQA higher award, or a first degree. A good first

JOURNALISM AND TECHNICAL WRITING: FAC

degree, or a postgraduate diploma, is usually required for entry to a higher degree.

Entry to BTEC and SQA higher awards – usual entry requirements are usually one pass at A level/H grade, plus five GCSEs/S grades (A–C/1–3). Appropriate industrial experience, or alternative qualifications, may also be acceptable.

Direct entry: minimum entry qualifications are five GCSEs/S grades (A–C/1–3) including English, or an equivalent. The majority of entrants have at least two A levels/three H grades. More than half of all recruits to training schemes now enter as graduates.

Entry to City and Guilds courses – no specific academic qualifications are required for entry to the 7790 Certificate in Media Techniques (Broadcast), although this course is often provided with appropriate A level courses to create a full-time two-year course, for which entry requirements may be at least four GCSEs/S grades (A–C/1–3).

Entry to pre-entry courses – although five GCSEs/S grades (A–C/1–3) are the minimum NCTJ requirements, most colleges expect applicants to have at least two A levels/three H grades, or equivalent qualifications.

Entry to fashion journalism – relevant journalism qualifications are useful but not essential, whereas a degree in fashion journalism and promotion is considered ideal for work in this area.

Entry to broadcast journalism – direct entry as an experienced journalist is possible (maybe transferring from newspaper or periodicals journalism). A first degree in a specialist subject such as politics, economics, social affairs or the environment, followed by a postgraduate broadcast journalism course, is generally required. It is also possible to enter via a television or radio company training scheme (see TRAINING). Again, a first degree is generally necessary to gain a place, as the competition is fierce.

TRAINING

There are many ways of training for a career in journalism. Degree courses in Journalism recognized by the NCTJ are available at Bournemouth University, University of Central Lancashire, Darlington College/Teesside University, Napier University and the University of Sheffield. These courses usually last for three years.

Full-time postgraduate courses in various aspects of journalism recognized by the NCTJ are available at City of Liverpool Community College, University of Central Lancashire, City University, De Montfort University, Lambeth College, Strathclyde University/Glasgow Caledonian University, Trinity and All Saints College, University of Wales – Cardiff, University of Ulster. These courses usually last for one academic year.

BTEC and SQA Higher National courses in Journalism recognized by the NCTJ are available at Bell College of Technology and the London College of Printing. These courses usually last for two years.

A small number of school and college leavers, and some graduates, are recruited directly by newspaper groups as journalist trainees. Most training schemes are linked to the National Council for the Training of Journalists (NCTJ). Trainees usually sit NCTJ examinations after two years, but may be entered for other qualifications. Some of the larger groups operate their own in-house training schemes.

Pre-entry and other certificate courses in journalism are available at Brighton College of Technology, City of Liverpool Community College, Cornwall College, Crawley College, Darlington College, Gloucestershire College of Arts and Technology, Greenhill College, Harrow, Gwent Tertiary College, Harlow College, Highbury College, Lambeth College, Sheffield College (Norton), Sutton Coldfield College and South East Essex College of Art and Technology. These courses usually last for up to one year. Some courses start in January and run for one calendar year.

City and Guilds certificate courses in journalism are available at some colleges of further education. These one-year part-time courses lead to a Level 2 C+G Certificate in Media Techniques – Journalism and Radio (7790). The course may be combined with A level courses as a full-time two-year foundation course in journalism that may be taken as preparation for direct-entry schemes or for further training and degree courses.

Sheffield College (Norton) offers a journalism-based course with photography as its foundation.

NVQs/SVQs in Journalism and Broadcast Journalism are available at Level 4, and at Levels 3 and 4 in Periodical Journalism.

Fast-track courses for graduates are run at Harlow College (20 weeks), Sheffield College (18 weeks) and Cornwall College (20 weeks) and Highbury College, Portsmouth.

There are generally two ways of training for a career in magazine journalism: by direct entry on to a formal training scheme with a magazine company in a junior position, or by attending one of the periodical journalism courses accredited by the Periodicals Training Council at City University (postgraduate diploma), Highbury College (college diploma and NVQ units), Journalism Training Centre (NVQ foundation skills certificate), PMA Training (postgraduate course), London College of Printing (graduate diploma or Higher National Diploma), University of Wales – Cardiff (postgraduate diploma) and University of Westminster (postgraduate diploma).

There are various training schemes for broadcast journalism run by the television companies. However, they are directly linked to operational needs, so are not always available. All courses are usually advertised in the press. Previous experience, such as working in hospital radio or writing for school or college magazines, is an advantage.

Although courses recognized by the Broadcast Journalism Training Council (BJTC) have a television element, they tend to concentrate on teaching radio journalism. This is because almost everyone entering broadcast journalism starts out in local radio, after such a course, and moves on to regional or national radio on to television as their careers progress. Most BJTC-recognized courses are one-year, full-time postgraduate courses, although there are some exceptions. Contact the BJTC for a current list, as the type of courses available is likely to increase in variety and number in the future.

For further details about training in journalism contact NCTJ Training Ltd or the BJTC.

LATE ENTRY

There are no formal upper age limits for entry to this occupation, but some newspaper groups may restrict training scheme entry to applicants under 25 years. Many adults develop a career in freelance journalism after previous career experience in another field. Some postgraduate courses in broadcast journalism will accept

JOURNALISM AND TECHNICAL WRITING: FAC

mature applicants without a first degree who have relevant work experience and/or who can demonstrate a commitment to a career in broadcasting. Contact individual institutions for details (list from the BJTC).

Access-to-journalism courses are available at Lambeth College, Handsworth Technical College, Sheffield College, Highbury College, Swansea College and City of Liverpool Community College.

OPPORTUNITIES

With the large numbers of national and regional newspapers, consumer and business magazines, local and national broadcasting stations and news agencies, the range of opportunities in journalism is broad. More than 130 daily and Sunday newspapers are published in the UK, plus almost 800 weekly newspapers and more than 1,000 local free papers. More than 2,000 consumer magazine titles are currently in publication, plus a further 4,500 business and professional titles. There has been considerable recent growth in the number of business and professional magazines, with the total number of magazines increasing by 33% in the past ten years. The expansion of satellite broadcasting may offer further opportunities in the future.

Approximately 800 places are taken by trainee journalists each year. More than half of these are direct entrants, who attend block release courses at college. The remainder train through one-year pre-entry or postgraduate courses. Opportunities are available throughout the country, but there is a concentration of national newspaper and magazines publishers in London and South East England. There is also a concentration of broadcasting and press agency opportunities in London, and many regional newspapers have London offices.

Freelance journalists work on a self-employed basis, often for a variety of newspaper or magazine publishers. Estimates of the total number of journalists vary. The largest organization, the National Union of Journalists, currently has approximately 26,000 members. Some of these work as press or information officers. Job advertisements are found in the *UK Press Gazette, Media Week* and *The Guardian*.

PAY AND CONDITIONS

The basic rates for trainee journalists can start at between £6,000 and £10,000 for those working in provincial newspapers, or more than £10,000 for those working in radio or television journalism. The pay and working conditions of more experienced journalists vary considerably. Salaries are usually higher in national newspapers and in television journalism: experienced reporters can earn up to £40,000, but a small number of senior journalists earn considerably more.

Freelance journalists usually negotiate and agree a set fee for each piece of work. These rates vary considerably, according to the newspaper or magazine publisher. Some publishers pay freelance journalists at a rate for every 1,000 words.

Many journalists work on a freelance basis for a number of publishers. Very few journalists work a routine 9am–5pm day and Monday to Friday week.

Newspaper journalists can be expected to work long and irregular hours, including some evenings and weekends spent reporting on events or writing up copy in time to reach a deadline.

Magazine journalists may work more regular hours, although they usually work long days as publication deadlines approach. Fashion journalists may have to work long and unsocial hours, particularly when on location.

National newspaper and broadcast journalists may work shifts, perhaps of eight hours, and be on call to cover any major news stories.

PROSPECTS

Promotion is based solely on merit. Many newspaper journalists spend at least two or three years working on a local paper, perhaps then progressing to a regional morning or evening daily.

Competition for national newspapers, magazines and broadcasting work is severe. There are far fewer trainee posts on magazines than on newspapers; many gain the necessary experience by working 'shifts' on a freelance basis. In this way, journalists become known for their style of work, and improve their chances of finding a permanent or 'staff' job. Experienced staff may have the opportunity to become specialist correspondents, providing regular contributions, for example, on arts, sports or education topics.

Examples of more senior jobs include: sub-editor, with responsibility for copy accuracy, headlines and page layout; news editor; features editor; editor; and chief editor (of a group of newspapers).

Each post involves an increasing level of responsibility for the nature of the editorial items included in the publication. Some journalists, often with a specialist background, move from newspapers to magazine journalism, with occasional opportunities for promotion to editor, publisher and director posts. Other experienced journalists move into broadcast journalism, news agency work and public relations.

Many large companies employ experienced journalists as press officers, with the responsibility for all communications between that company and the media.

RELATED OCCUPATIONS

Public relations officer, press officer, information officer, editor, advertising copywriter, writer, photojournalist, researcher.

FURTHER INFORMATION

British Broadcasting Corporation*, PO Box 7000, London W5 2WY, 0181 752 5252

Broadcast Journalism Training Council, 188 Litchfield Court, Sheen Road, Richmond, TW9 1BB

National Council for the Training of Journalists*, Latton Bush Centre, Southern Way, Harlow, Essex CM18 7BL, 01279 430009 (please include sae), www.itecharlow.co.uk/nctj/

National Union of Journalists, 314–320 Gray's Inn Road, London WC1X 8DP, 0171 278 7916 (please send sae)

Newspaper Society*, Bloomsbury House, Bloomsbury Square, 74–77 Great Russell Street, London WC1B 3DA, 0171 636 7014, www.newspapersoc.org.uk

Periodicals Training Council, Queen's House, 55–56 Lincoln's Inn Fields, London WC2A 3LJ, 0171 404 4168, www.ppa.co.uk

JOURNALISM AND TECHNICAL WRITING: FAC

Scottish Newspaper Publishers' Association*, 48 Palmerston Place, Edinburgh EH12 5DE, 0131 220 4353

FURTHER READING

Leaflets/booklets are available from the addresses marked*.

Working in Journalism – COIC

Working in TV, Film and Radio – COIC

Careers in Journalism – Kogan Page

Benn's UK Media Directory (Annual) – Benn Business Ltd

In the careers library classified under FAC.

2. TECHNICAL AUTHOR (FAC)

BACKGROUND INFORMATION

As technological equipment and commercial processes have become increasingly complex, and the demand for published information has continued to expand, this occupation has developed to deal with the preparation of technical documents, reports and instruction manuals.

There are various fields of technical authorship: writing manuals and user guides for computer software systems; writing technical reports for scientific, engineering and various commercial operations; preparing technical documents for publication; preparing technical catalogues and indexes; producing 'executive summaries' from longer documents and reports; writing instruction manuals for those using or maintaining technical equipment – from consumer products to large-scale manufacturing plant; writing sales literature and technical articles for trade journals.

THE WORK

The list of organizations producing technical publications is very long, and includes engineering companies, software publishers, computer manufacturers, scientific research organizations, financial companies and other commercial firms.

Technical authors have to plan each new project to find out what information is needed, who will be using the publication and how the information will need to be presented. They collect necessary information by a variety of research methods, including tape-recorded interviews, 'on-site' visits, frequent meetings, telephone interviews, library work and using computer databases.

Much of the information needs to be carefully checked before it can be used. Once all the data is collected and prepared, the publication can be written in the most appropriate style for the intended readers. An instruction manual for someone without technical knowledge is written in a completely different way to a technical report intended only for experts in that field.

If illustrations are required, the technical author may need to work with a technical illustrator or a photographer. Before any technical publication can be published, the first draft version has to be carefully studied by other experts in that particular field. A second draft version is produced once everything has been checked and all corrections and alterations made.

The text is then produced in a style ready for publication. This may be done by the technical author, using word processing or desktop publishing software, by a professional typesetter, or by the printing company. The final responsibility of a technical author is to check and correct the printer's proof copy before printing and final publication.

Writers frequently have to work on several projects at once, with each at a different stage of production. Most projects have to be completed and checked by a particular deadline. Freelance authors have to spend some of their time finding new projects.

WORK ENVIRONMENT

Technical authors employed directly by industrial or research organizations may be based in offices close to production or laboratory areas; alternatively they may work in well-lit and well-equipped offices. Freelance technical authors may work at home, or from their own small office, but often make visits to the organizations for whom they are doing a particular project.

SKILLS AND INTERESTS

All technical authors must be able to write clearly and concisely. Those involved in the production of instruction manuals or summaries of detailed reports must be able to explain technical terms in straightforward language.

The work involves a great deal of research, cataloguing, cross-referencing and filing; technical authors need an enquiring mind and the ability to work methodically. They frequently have a detailed knowledge of one particular technical field, and work closely with people sharing the specialization.

They also need the ability to work with a wide variety of other people, including publishers and editors, technical specialists from other fields, and those who do not share their technical background.

Information technology skills are important for most technical authors. These include the ability to use different personal computer software systems, and a knowledge of how information can be transferred between computer systems. They also need to know about print production processes to be able to prepare text for publication.

ENTRY REQUIREMENTS

There are no standard formal entry requirements, but the majority of technical authors have previous qualifications and experience in specialist scientific, engineering, technical or commercial fields; many technical authors are graduates.

Good communication skills and appropriate technical knowledge are essential. It is possible for a school- or college-leaver to train specifically in technical authorship, but the majority of students taking City and Guilds training courses are studying by day release or by distance learning, and are already employed in an engineering or other technical field.

Entry to City and Guilds courses – no specific academic qualifications are required for entry to the Level 1 course in Technical Communication. Applicants are usually expected to have technical qualifications and experience appropriate to their particular specialization. Applicants for the Level 2 course in Technical Authorship are usually expected to have a pass in the Level 1 course.

Entry to BTEC/SQA higher awards – minimum entry

JOURNALISM AND TECHNICAL WRITING: FAC

requirements are one A level/two H grades plus five GCSEs/S grades (A–C/1–3). Preferred examination subjects include English language, maths, and science or technical subjects. Appropriate industrial experience, or alternative qualifications, may also be acceptable.

Entry to postgraduate courses – usual entry requirements for a postgraduate diploma are a BTEC/SQA higher award, or a first degree, together with appropriate employment experience, such as working experience as a practising engineer for at least three years. A good first degree, or a postgraduate diploma, is usually required for entry to a higher degree.

TRAINING

City and Guilds courses in The Communication of Technical Information are available at Chippenham Technical College and Cleveland College of Further Education. These one- and two-year part-time evening or day release courses lead to a Level 1 C+G Certificate in Technical Communications Techniques (5361) and to a Level 2 C+G Certificate in Technical Authorship (5362).

On completion of C+G 5361, students should be able to have an outline appreciation of the communication process, match information to different users' needs, collect and sort information, prepare and present information, understand special factors in international communication, understand methods of communicating. On completion of C+G 5362, students should be able to appreciate the role of the technical author, plan an assignment, gather information, establish the technical content, prepare draft information, commission technical illustrators, prepare work for reproduction and distribution, understand supporting equipment and processes.

Commercial training organizations, such as Tutortex Services, offer tuition programmes by distance learning leading to certificate qualifications, and to the City and Guilds awards. These distance learning courses are available to individuals working as freelance technical authors, and to companies that offer them as in-house training provision for their employed technical authors.

BTEC/SQA Higher National courses in Communication Studies are available for students with an appropriate BTEC/SQA national diploma or with A level/H grade qualifications. The Higher National Diploma in Publications at Blackpool and the Fylde College is specifically related to technical authorship. This two-year course includes a practical project, and is suitable for people with a technical background.

There is currently one degree course in Technical Communication at Coventry University and a three-year MA or two-year postgraduate diploma in Technical Authorship is available, part-time and distance learning, at Sheffield Hallam University and is suitable for people with a degree, higher national certificate/diploma or relevant work experience, eg an engineer with at least three years' experience.

Full-time postgraduate diploma courses in Technical Authorship and Technical Communication are available at Humberside University, Northumbria University at Newcastle and Sheffield Hallam University. These courses usually last for one academic year. Postgraduate higher degrees in Multilingual Professional Communication and Science Communication can be studied at Aston University and Imperial College of Science and Technology.

Other training opportunities for adults are available in some areas for this type of work. Contact your local Jobcentre, careers office or TEC/LEC for details.

LATE ENTRY

There are no formal upper age limits for entry to this occupation. Many technical authors undertake the work after previous technical career experience.

OPPORTUNITIES

The principal opportunities for technical authors are working as salaried employees of a company, or working as self-employed freelance writers. Employed technical writers typically work for the publications departments of major engineering and scientific companies, or for computer software publishers, where they produce a wide range of technical literature. There are also employed opportunities with professional bodies, research organizations and government departments.

Some technical authors are employed by technical publications contractors. These companies specialize in technical writing, and provide services for smaller companies that do not have their own publications departments.

There are full-time and part-time opportunities for employed technical authors. Freelance technical authors work on a self-employed basis. They often have considerable experience of technical authorship within a company or other organization, before setting up their own business. Some freelance writers work on projects for one main company, or for a technical publications contractor, while others work for a variety of clients.

Opportunities are available throughout the country. There is currently a shortage of skilled and experienced technical authors with an appropriate technical background.

PAY AND CONDITIONS

There are no standard pay scales for this occupation. Actual rates of pay within companies vary considerably, according to the level of previous technical experience, writing experience, qualifications, complexity of the project and the type of employer. Technical authors in training may earn less than £10,000; those with experience may earn in excess of £30,000.

Freelance technical authors either charge for their services at an hourly rate, or negotiate and agree a set fee for each piece of work. There are no standard fees; rates vary considerably according to the company involved and the degree of complexity of the particular project. Some freelance technical authors may charge £25 an hour or more, but others are paid considerably less. Employed technical authors usually work normal daytime office hours. Those who are self-employed are often expected to complete projects by a certain deadline, and therefore frequently work longer hours – sometimes including evenings and weekends.

PROSPECTS

There are few formal promotion routes with this type of work, although there are limited editorial and managerial opportunities in the publications departments of larger companies. With experience, many technical authors choose to set up their own business and work on a

JOURNALISM AND TECHNICAL WRITING: FAC

freelance basis.

RELATED OCCUPATIONS

Engineer, scientist, journalist, editor, technical illustrator, computer programmer.

FURTHER INFORMATION

City and Guilds (C+G)*, 1 Giltspur Street, London EC1A 9DD, 0171 294 2468

Institute of Scientific and Technical Communicators*, Kings Court, 2–16 Goodge Street, London W1P 1FF, 0171 436 4425 (please include sae)

Eston Training*, PO Box 20, Glossop, Derbyshire SK13 9JU, 01457 855875

Tutortex Services, 55 Lightburn Avenue, Ulverston, Cumbria LA12 0DL, 01229 586333

College of Technical Authorship, PO Box 7, Cheadle, Cheshire, SK8 3BY, 0161 437 4235

FURTHER READING

Leaflets/booklets are available from the addresses marked*.

In the careers library classified under FAC.

PUBLISHING: FAD

EDITOR CLCI:FAD

THE WORK

Editors control the process of newspaper, book and magazine publishing by deciding what to publish, finding the right person to research and write the copy, checking and making any necessary amendments to the completed copy, deciding the final page layout to be used, working with production staff and checking final proof copies immediately before printing. The work varies considerably with the type of publication, and with the type of editing to be done. Many different job titles are in use.

Newspaper publishing

Sub-editors receive items submitted by journalists and then check thoroughly for any spelling, grammatical or style errors that require amendment. Their work may also involve selection of suitable illustrations, liaison with production staff and a responsibility for checking the legality of printing particular items. Senior editors – with job titles such as features editor, political editor or sports editor – look after different sections of a national newspaper. Art editors, or picture editors, are responsible for the photographs and other illustrations used in each issue.

Book and magazine publishing

Copy-editors or desk-editors see each project through from first proposals and draft outline to final proofs. Once a completed manuscript has been submitted they have to check it carefully for any grammatical or factual errors. They may also need to amend the text to match a particular 'house-style', or sometimes request the author to make some alterations to style or length. Commissioning editors decide which titles will eventually be published. They gradually build-up a 'list' of titles by considering proposals or completed manuscripts submitted by authors, by suggesting topics to authors with whom they have worked previously, or by buying titles previously published by other publishing houses. They negotiate terms for payment with the author and produce some form of contract, usually a standard publishing agreement, and regularly discuss progress with the author.

Other jobs in editing

Some publishers employ specialist proofreaders to check manuscripts, and indexers to create the index to a technical book. Proofreaders and indexers, when required, are increasingly employed on a freelance basis for particular projects. Larger publishing houses may have senior posts, such as editorial managers or editorial directors, with overall responsibility for a team of editors, or for developing the list of that company.

WORK ENVIRONMENT

Many editors are office-based, in conditions that vary considerably. Some offices are modern and well equipped, but others may be small and cramped. Many editors work 'on-screen' using word processing computer software to edit the work of journalists or writers. Some editors produce final page layouts on-screen by using desktop publishing software. Book and magazine editors frequently attend meetings with writers, designers and production specialists, and with suppliers. The work environment is frequently pressured and hectic, particularly when publication deadlines are close.

SKILLS AND INTERESTS

Successful editors must have a good command of grammar and spelling, in order to locate and correct errors, and make essential checks for accuracy before final printing. They may also have to rewrite sections of copy. A knowledge of proof-correction marks, typography, in-house style guides and the requirements of various printing processes are all essential. Some book and technical magazine editors have a detailed knowledge of one particular field, and work closely with people sharing the specialization. Information technology skills can be important, including the ability to use different computer software systems and a knowledge of how information can be transferred electronically. Self-confidence, attention to detail, the ability to face criticism, the ability to work in a team and a willingness to work unsocial hours, are important. A driving licence is an asset.

ENTRY REQUIREMENTS

There are no standard formal entry requirements, but a large proportion of editors are graduates. The majority of editors working in newspaper publishing and in broadcasting enter as experienced journalists. Most editors working for publishing houses enter as graduates, although people are increasingly entering with degrees specifically related to publishing.

Entry to degree courses is usually with a minimum of two A levels/three H grades, plus five GCSEs/S grades (A–C/1–3), or a BTEC/SQA national or higher award, or equivalent. Some courses may require additional examination passes at specific grades. Usual entry requirements for a postgraduate diploma are either a BTEC/SQA higher award, a first degree, or appropriate professional experience. A good first degree, or a postgraduate diploma is usually required for entry to a higher degree.

Entry to BTEC and SQA higher awards – usual entry requirements are one A level/two H grades, plus three GCSEs/S grades (A–C/1–3). Appropriate industrial experience, or alternative qualifications, may also be acceptable.

Publishers of specialist titles may recruit entrants with previous qualifications and experience in a particular field, perhaps legal, commercial scientific or teaching. Typing ability and word processing experience are often essential. Some editors are recruited with experience of particular desktop publishing computer systems, or with previous experience of preparation for various printing processes.

Entry to City and Guilds courses requires no specific academic qualifications, but applicants are usually already employed as editors.

TRAINING

Degree courses in aspects of publishing are available at Loughborough University of Technology, Napier University, Robert Gordon University, and Thames Valley University. Degree courses in Graphic Media Studies, including publishing options, are available at Hertfordshire University and West Hertfordshire College. Multidisciplinary degree courses, including options in publishing, are available at Middlesex University, Oxford Brookes University and Swansea Institute of Higher Education. Postgraduate diplomas in aspects of publishing are available at London College of Printing, Middlesex

PUBLISHING: FAD

University, Plymouth University, Stirling University and West Hertfordshire College. Postgraduate higher degrees in aspects of publishing are available at Leeds University, Middlesex University, Plymouth University and Stirling University.

Short courses in a wide range of relevant topics, including copy-editing, production skills, proofreading, on-screen editing, computer skills, layout and print buying, are provided by various colleges, and by organizations such as the Publishing Training Centre at Book House (the ITO for book and journal publishing – also offers distance learning courses in editing, copywriting and proofreading). Participants are usually already employed in publishing companies. These courses are often provided 'in-house' by the larger publishing companies, who may use them as part of a training scheme. City and Guilds courses in information technology are available at many colleges. These part-time day release or one-year full-time courses lead to the C+G 7261 award, which is available at Levels 1,2,3 and 4. This is a modular scheme with a wide variety of topics, but certain colleges offer particular modules to provide a qualification in desktop publishing. Other college courses lead to RSA awards in desktop publishing. (BTEC and SQA higher national courses in various aspects of publishing are available at Farnborough College of Technology, Glasgow College of Building and Printing, London College of Printing and West Hertfordshire College.)

NVQs/SVQs in various aspects of magazine publishing are available at Levels 3 and 4.

LATE ENTRY

There are no formal upper age limits for entry to these occupations. Editors working in newspaper publishing usually undertake the work after previous career experience in journalism. Editors working in book or magazine publishing frequently have previous career experience in the specialist fields covered by the publications, or in journalism.

OPPORTUNITIES

Competition for the limited number of vacancies in all editing occupations can be intense. Newspaper reporters may progress to sub-editing and editing posts, but promotion is not automatic.

Recent mergers and take-overs in book publishing have led to some redundancies. Many magazine publishers employ freelance editors, often with knowledge of a specialist field. A small number of the larger publishing houses have graduate recruitment schemes. There are magazine and book publishing houses in many major cities, but they are concentrated in London and South East England. Newspapers are published throughout the UK.

PAY AND CONDITIONS

Initial salaries for copy-editors and sub-editors may start at between £11,000 and £12,000 – even less on provincial newspapers. There are few agreed pay scales for these occupations. Experienced national newspaper sub-editors may earn up to £40,000 and book or magazine commissioning editors up to £30,000. Salaries for more senior editors in large publishing companies can be higher.

Freelance editors usually negotiate a set fee for each commission, but may be paid at a daily rate. Fees for freelance editors vary considerably. Editors in all types of publishing rarely work a routine 9am to 5pm day and Monday to Friday week. As publishing deadlines approach, working days can become longer, often including evening and occasional weekend work.

PROSPECTS

Experience is essential for promotion within these occupations. With some exceptions, newspaper publishers usually recruit only experienced journalists to editorial posts, and magazine and book publishers increasingly recruit those with previous experience. A first post in editing is frequently the most difficult to find.

Promotion prospects in all types of publishing are usually greater within the larger publishing houses. Experienced editors may move into senior management posts within larger publishing companies.

RELATED OCCUPATIONS

Journalist, proofreader, indexer, layout artist, publishing production controller, print buyer, researcher, bookseller.

FURTHER INFORMATION

Book House Training Centre*, 45 East Hill, Wandsworth, London SW18 2QZ, 0181 874 2718

IPC Magazines, Training and Development Department*, King's Reach Tower, Stamford Street, London SE1 9LS, 0171 261 7096

London College of Printing*, Elephant and Castle, London SE1 6SB, 0171 514 6514, www.linst.ac.uk

National Council for the Training of Journalists*, Latton Bush Centre, Southern Way, Harlow, Essex CM18 7BL, 01279 430009 (please include sae), www.itecharlow.co.uk

Newspaper Society*, Bloomsbury House, Bloomsbury Square, 74–77 Great Russell Street, London WC1B 3DA, 0171 636 7014, www.newspapersoc.org.uk

Periodicals Training Council*, Quenn's House, 55–56 Lincoln's Inn Fields, London WC2A 3LJ, 0171 404 4168, www.ppa.co.uk

Publishers' Association*, 1 Kingsway, London WC2B 6XF, 0171 565 7474 (please include sae), www.publisher.org.uk

Society of Freelance Editors and Proofreaders, 1 Mermaid Court, London SE1 1HR, 0171 403 5141, www.sfep.demon.co.uk

Society of Indexers, Mermaid House, 1 Mermaid Court, London SE1 1HR, 0171 403 4947

FURTHER READING

Leaflets/booklets are available from the addresses marked*.

Working in Journalism – COIC

Working in Publishing – COIC

Careers in Journalism – Kogan Page

Inside Book Publishing – Blueprint/Book House

The Bookseller – weekly

In the careers library classified under FAD.

MUSEUM AND ART GALLERY WORK: FAE

1. **MUSEUM CURATOR/ART GALLERY KEEPER CLCI:FAE**
2. **CONSERVATOR/RESTORER CLCI:EZ/FAE**

BACKGROUND INFORMATION

The world of museums and art galleries has changed considerably in recent years. The more traditional national and local government museums and art galleries have witnessed the rapid growth of heritage centres and independent, commercial museums. All museums and art galleries are now part of the leisure industry, increasingly concerned to entertain and inform the public and market themselves to attract increasing numbers of visitors. They have moved towards positive presentation of their objects and have developed educational and other services.

Many objects are seen as worth preserving because of their historical interest, or because they are collectors' items. However, objects are subject to long-term deterioration caused by exposure to humidity, heat, light, dirt or micro-organisms. They may also be damaged by fire, flood, accident and vandalism etc.

Conservation has the aim of arresting decay in such objects and preventing further deterioration. Restoration shares that aim, but goes further by treating objects to restore them to their original appearance. Restoration is also concerned with making something work that has broken.

1. MUSEUM CURATOR/ART GALLERY KEEPER (FAE)

THE WORK

Museum curators and art gallery keepers manage collections of objects of artistic, archaeological, scientific, historical and general interest.

The work involved varies considerably, depending on the size and nature of the museum or art gallery. Curators tend to specialize if employed either by a specialist museum, eg natural history, or by a large general museum. In small general museums, curators tend not to specialize.

In smaller museums and art galleries, curators plan and mount displays and exhibitions. This involves choosing exhibits from the museum's or art gallery's stock, or buying or borrowing items. They label and arrange the exhibits, having designed the layout of the display. They arrange publicity and write the catalogue.

Curators and keepers are responsible for identifying objects, recording details (often using a computer), planning the cleaning and care of the objects, and arranging for restoration or conservation work if necessary.

Many curators and keepers are available to be consulted by visitors about the collection and to give talks to groups of visitors, including school parties. They may examine items brought in for identification.

Curators and keepers liaise with, and consult, colleagues in their own and other museums and art galleries, and with restorers and conservation experts.

Some curators and keepers in large national museums and art galleries are concerned solely with the management of collections, while others specialize in administration. Many combine both responsibilities. In smaller museums and art galleries, collection management and administration tend to be combined. Administration involves supervising staff – assistant curators, technicians and attendants – attending meetings, dealing with budgeting and fund raising.

Some curators and keepers research their specialist area and write books and articles for publication.

While the work of art gallery keeper is very similar to that of museum curator, in private galleries an important aspect of the work is selling art work to the public.

WORK ENVIRONMENT

Working conditions depend on the institution concerned. Exhibits must be kept in controlled conditions to preserve them, so most museums and art galleries tend to be warm and reasonably well lit. Some museums, eg working farms and industrial sites, are based outdoors, so working conditions depend on the weather.

Jobs vary in the amount of heavy lifting and carrying involved.

SKILLS AND INTERESTS

The varied aspects of their work means that curators and keepers have to be versatile. They should have expertise and a keen interest in the subject matter they deal with. They need the ability to assess objects, to describe and record them accurately and in detail. They should understand the environmental conditions that exhibits need to prevent their deterioration.

Creative flair is important, together with the visual imagination to create exhibitions and displays that will attract the public. Many museums aim for visitor participation in their exhibitions, and curators need a good imagination to make that possible.

Good communication skills are important – curators should be able to explain facts and ideas to visitors, give lectures and discuss matters with colleagues. Writing skills are necessary for the accurate recording of information and for writing catalogues, articles and papers.

A polite, pleasant manner is necessary, as contact with the public has become increasingly important.

Administration skills are essential for most curators. They should be capable of organizing staff and running a department or institution. Commercial interest is necessary too, as many curators are responsible for managing their department or institution within a fixed budget. Those working in private art galleries must have good selling ability.

In all but the smallest museums and art galleries, curators must be capable of working within a team, which may include other curators, restorers, conservation experts and attendants.

ENTRY REQUIREMENTS

Although there are no formal qualifications required for entry to curatorial work, in practice over 85% of curators and keepers have degrees and higher degrees. Large or specialist museums, however, may employ on the strength of an applicant's school record alone.

The minimum entry requirement for degree courses is five GCSEs/S grades (A–C/1–3) with two/three A levels or three/four/five H grades, or equivalent. Degrees relevant to museum work include history, fine art, biology, botany, chemistry, anthropology, engineering, ceramics, textiles and

MUSEUM AND ART GALLERY WORK: FAE

any degree relevant to a specialist field of museum work. Degrees relevant to art gallery work include fine art, art history and applied art. Applicants for degrees at art colleges are usually required to have completed a foundation art and design course.

Entry to postgraduate courses is with a relevant degree, plus some evidence of commitment to the work, eg through voluntary work in a museum or art gallery. The National Association of Decorative and Fine Arts Societies (NADFAS) runs a volunteers scheme that offers such experience, or museums and art galleries may be approached direct.

Given the competition for vacancies in museum and art gallery work, it is recommended that applicants gain some relevant voluntary experience.

TRAINING

Pre-entry training

While there are no first degrees concerned solely with museum and art gallery studies, there are some that include museum studies and/or a period of study in museums, galleries or collections. They include the University of London/Courtauld Institute of Art's History of Art (three years full-time), the University of Leeds' History of Fine and Decorative Arts (four years full-time), the University of East Anglia's Art History (three years full-time) and De Montfort University's History of Art and Design (three years full-time).

Some first degrees include museum and heritage management, eg Heritage Conservation at Bournemouth University (three years full-time), Museum and Heritage Studies at University of Central Lancashire (three years full-time), Heritage Management at Cumbria College of Art and Design (three years full-time) and Social History and Heritage studies at the University of Kent (three years full-time).

There are a number of one-year full-time postgraduate courses that specifically train for museum or art gallery work. The University of Leicester offers a Diploma, MA or MSc, in Museum Studies, while the University of East Anglia offers an MA in Museology/Museum Studies. The MA in Gallery Studies at Essex University emphasizes art gallery work. The Courtauld Institute of Art offers an MA in Art Museum Studies, City University has an MA in Museums and Gallery Management, the University of St Andrews an MPhil or Diploma in Museum/Gallery Studies, while University College London and The University of Newcastle-upon-Tyne both offer an MA in Museum Studies. Nottingham Trent University has an MA and Diploma in Heritage Studies. The Museum Training Institute has approved courses at Leicester, University College London, Essex, Newcastle, St Andrews, Nottingham Trent, the Heritage Management MA at the Ironbridge Institute, City University, and the MA in Museology at the Reinwardt Academy in Amsterdam.

Other relevant courses include MA in Museums and Galleries in Education at the Institute of Education, Sotheby's Works of Art course (nine months full-time), Christie's Fine Arts course (nine months full-time) and The Study Centre for the History of the Fine and Decorative Arts (one year full-time).

Post-entry training

Most training in museums and art galleries is on-the-job, with some organizations having formal training schemes.

There are a number of postgraduate courses that can be undertaken part-time while working, eg at University College London and at the universities of Leicester, St. Andrews and Newcastle-upon-Tyne.

The Museum Training Institute has introduced NVQs/SVQs at Levels 3, 4 and 5 in Curatorial and Conservation Skills. Similarly, The Arts and Entertainment Training Council is working towards the introduction of NVQs/SVQs at Levels 2, 3 and 4 that have relevance for art gallery staff. NVQs/SVQs are based on demonstrating competence in the practical skills of a job. Modern Apprenticeship training places are also available in some museums.

LATE ENTRY

There is no upper age limit for entry to work as a museum curator or art gallery keeper.

Mature applicants need the same qualifications as described in ENTRY REQUIREMENTS. Experience of voluntary work in a museum or art gallery is extremely helpful.

There is a growing trend for museums and art galleries to recruit managers from outside the profession. This could provide some openings for those with experience in marketing, accountancy or administration, who may be looking for a change.

OPPORTUNITIES

There are just over 3,000 museums in the UK, employing approximately 13,000 curators and managers. There are far fewer art galleries. Opportunities differ according to the type of museum or art gallery.

National museums and art galleries offer particular scope for specialist curators and keepers. While many of these institutions are based in London, there are around 35 throughout the rest of the UK.

Local authority museums and art galleries are to be found in most cities and towns in the UK and vary considerably. There are some large city museums and galleries that can offer specialist curatorial work. There are many more small local museums, including some that include a display of art, and opportunities in these tend to be for general curatorial work.

Independent museums are extremely varied, both in size and degree of specialization. There are many throughout the UK and they tend to offer general, rather than specialist, work to curators.

Opportunities in museums and art galleries grew in the 1980s, particularly as a considerable number of new independent museums opened. That growth has stopped. Turnover of staff is low and vacancies for museum curators and art gallery keepers are scarce. When vacancies arise, competition is very keen and applicants should be prepared to move to another location to find a job.

There are opportunities to work overseas, particularly in Australia, New Zealand and other Commonwealth countries. A small number of British curators work in Europe and the USA.

Vacancies for museum and art gallery work are advertised in *Museums Journal* (published by the Museums Association), the bi-monthly journal of the Association of Independent Museums (AIM), in the quality national newspapers and in the local press.

MUSEUM AND ART GALLERY WORK: FAE

PAY AND CONDITIONS

Pay scales vary. The national museums and art galleries have similar terms of pay and conditions to the Civil Service. Many entrants start on trainee grade, with a starting salary of £7,623, or on curator grade G, with a salary scale from £8,679 to £11,766. Some graduates of 26 years or over start on curator grade F, with a salary scale from £11,138 to £16,813. A curator grade D is paid on a scale £16,813 to £24,167. Those working in London are paid extra. High standards of work performance can lead to considerable increases beyond these scales.

Local authority museums and art galleries pay local authority salary scales, which may be between £10,080 and £15,288, according to responsibilities and length of service. There are senior posts that attract over £17,500.

Independent museums have no standard salary scales, but they tend to pay similar salaries to local authorities.

Private art galleries often pay a basic salary with commission on sales.

Curators and art gallery keepers tend to work 36 to 37 hours a week, with a rota to include weekend opening times. Part-time work is possible.

PROSPECTS

Most entrants start as assistant curators or keepers and can move to curator or keeper posts. Beyond that level, advancement is difficult, as there are comparatively few posts.

In the national museums and art galleries there is a promotion structure from assistant curator to curator, department head and director. Many curators in these institutions tend to seek advancement within their department, rather than move elsewhere.

Promotion within individual local authority and independent museums and art galleries depends on the size of the institution. Many are too small for there to be a promotion structure and it is usual for curators and keepers to move for advancement.

There is some movement from the national museums and art galleries into academic posts in universities, and from local authority organizations into the leisure management field.

RELATED OCCUPATIONS

Conservator/restorer, information officer/scientist, archivist, archaeologist, leisure manager, antiques and fine arts dealer, teacher, further education/tertiary college lecturer, higher education lecturer, museum attendant/art gallery assistant.

FURTHER INFORMATION AND READING

Please see article 2. CONSERVATOR/RESTORER.

2. CONSERVATOR/RESTORER (EZ/FAE)

THE WORK

Conservators and restorers clean, repair and maintain works of art, objects of historic interest and buildings.

Many objects are the subject of conservation and restoration including easel paintings, wall paintings, prints, ceramics, textiles, fossils, statues, monuments, buildings, arms and armour, natural history objects, furniture, machinery, metalwork and paper items. Conservators and restorers may work on a range of objects, although many specialize in one type. They take account of the context and location of the object as part of this process.

Conservators and restorers first examine objects to assess the materials used in their creation. They diagnose the causes of damage or deterioration and decide on appropriate treatment. Conservators aim to arrest decay, whereas restorers may seek to restore the objects to their original condition. Both may need to estimate the time it will take to treat objects and the cost of treatment.

Having decided on treatment, conservators and restorers clean and treat objects appropriately. This may include cleaning, support, repair, restoration, protection, or a combination of these. Tools used depend on the work involved and can include microscopes, magnifying glasses, swabs, x-rays, scalpels, small brushes and carpentry hand-tools. Materials used include solvents and adhesives.

Treatment can involve undoing previous repair and restoration work. All modern treatment is designed to be reversible as far as possible. The work is very painstaking, and work on one object can take months. Careful recording of all treatment is important, both written and photographic.

An important part of the work of conservators and restorers is to survey collections and advise on the correct conditions needed to maintain the condition of objects, taking into account temperature, light and humidity. Those employed by museums and art galleries may help to set up exhibitions.

WORK ENVIRONMENT

Much conservation and restoration work takes place in laboratories or workshops, usually at a workbench or an easel. Much is done in laboratory conditions, which are clean, light and airy, but some work involves the use of chemicals, which can be inflammable or toxic. Some conservation and restoration work has to be undertaken on site, eg architectural stonemasonry. Conservators dealing with buildings or building elements are frequently required to spend much of that time on site.

Time is often spent in museums, art galleries and private homes advising on correct storage and monitoring environmental conditions.

Work involves much sitting or standing, depending on the subject of the work.

SKILLS AND INTERESTS

Conservators and restorers need a high level of hand skills for work that can be very intricate and painstaking. Good powers of concentration and infinite patience are required to work in detail on objects, possibly for weeks or months. Excellent colour vision is essential.

Conservators and restorers should have a scientific knowledge and understanding of materials used to create objects. This is necessary to determine when items were created, which materials were used, the causes of deterioration and the effect treatment may have. Aptitude for chemistry, artistic appreciation and interest in history are important in making those assessments. A strong regard for health and safety is important, as some processes are hazardous.

Conservators must be able to work as part of a team with

MUSEUM AND ART GALLERY WORK: FAE

other conservators, historians, museum and gallery staff, and have good communication skills in order to explain their work. Self-employed conservators need to communicate well with clients, who may include private collectors, museum and art gallery staff. Numerical skills are important in calculating the time and cost of treatment and for monitoring costs as projects progress.

Self-employed conservators and restorers need good commercial skills to run their businesses successfully.

Techniques of conservation are constantly improving and conservators need to keep up to date with such developments.

ENTRY REQUIREMENTS

There are no strict minimum entry qualifications for conservation and restoration work. Most entrants, though, have had full-time training before entering the work, many at degree and postgraduate level. Courses are available at different levels.

BTEC national diploma courses require – a minimum of four GCSEs/S grades (A–C/1–3), or a relevant BTEC first diploma, or appropriate SQA modules, or equivalent.

BTEC higher national diploma courses require – five GCSEs/S grades (A–C/1–3) with one A level/two H grades, or a relevant BTEC national diploma, or appropriate SQA modules, or equivalent.

Degree courses require – five GCSEs/S grades (A–C/1–3) with two or three A levels/three or four H grades, or a relevant BTEC national diploma, or appropriate SQA modules, or equivalent.

Most conservation degree courses require A level chemistry or an equivalent qualification.

Some courses require applicants to have completed a foundation art and design course.

Postgraduate courses require a relevant degree. Science, fine art and art history are extremely useful first degrees, while architecture, graphic art and archives studies degrees are accepted for some postgraduate courses.

There are some courses leading to certificates and diplomas awarded by individual colleges. Entry requirements for these vary.

It can be very helpful to have some voluntary experience before applying for entry to a course. This can be gained by joining the volunteers system organized by NADFAS – the National Association of Decorative and Fine Arts Societies.

TRAINING

Nearly all conservators and restorers undergo full-time training before entering work. There are many full-time conservation and restoration courses offered at universities, colleges and private institutions. Details of the courses are available from The Museum Training Institute. The *Conservation Training Index* is available from the Scottish Conservation Bureau.

Most courses specialize in one type of object or material, eg sculpture, furniture, paintings, metalwork, archaeological objects, ceramics, textiles, stained and architectural glass, clocks, stonework, wood and paper objects. Not all subject areas have courses at all levels. Some courses are geared to the needs of the antiques and fine arts trades, while others are concerned more with museums' prime aim of preservation

There are some broad-based courses that allow students to follow a variety of career paths. De Montfort University offers a BA(Hons) course in Conservation (three years full-time, which includes the treatment of a wide range of historical materials).

The City and Guilds of London Art School offers a Diploma/Graduateship in Restoration and Conservation Studies (three years full-time) that allows students to train as general object conservators, or to specialize, eg in ceramics or gilding.

Archaeological conservation degree courses are offered by University College London and University of Wales, Cardiff. They are concerned with training to conserve a broad range of archaeological materials.

The Area Museums Councils organize short post-entry training courses in aspects of preventive conservation. The Museum Training Institute (MTI) has introduced NVQs/SVQs in Conservation Skills at Levels 4 and 5. NVQs/SVQs are based on demonstrating competence in the practical skills of a job.

The few who obtain apprenticeships in conservation and restoration are trained by their employer, or may have opportunities to study part-time for a relevant qualification. Many conservation professional bodies are currently devising a profession-wide accreditation scheme which will help guarantee standards of competence in this field.

LATE ENTRY

There is no upper age limit for entry to conservation or restoration work. Adults with relevant craft qualifications and experience may be able to enter the work, eg a cabinet maker into furniture restoration, or a stonemason into architectural stonework conservation. Adults seeking entry into full-time training courses may find that usual entry requirements are relaxed, particularly if they can offer relevant experience.

It can be helpful to have had some relevant voluntary experience.

OPPORTUNITIES

The majority of conservators and restorers work in the private sector for small firms, in partnerships or are self-employed. They take on work contracted out by museums and art galleries and work for private collectors, antiques dealers, auction houses, the National Trust and similar organizations.

There are a small number of apprenticeships or traineeships in the private sector, mainly concerned with furniture, textiles, and stone and wood carving.

About a third of conservators and restorers work in the public sector. They work in national and local museums and art galleries, laboratories and studios run by the nine Area Museums Councils, English Heritage and their Scottish and Welsh equivalents, Historic Scotland and Cadw. Some are employed by universities, archaeological units and government bodies. Some national museums have large conservation departments with sections for different kinds of materials, eg ceramics and prints.

The conservation and restoration field is small. Numbers employed in the private sector have grown over the past few years, while the number in the public sector appear to have remained steady. Vacancies appear in the national press, *Museums Journal, Conservation News* and *Paper*

MUSEUM AND ART GALLERY WORK: FAE

Conservation News.

There are openings for trained conservators and restorers overseas, particularly in Canada, Australia and the USA.

PAY AND CONDITIONS

Conservators and restorers in the public sector tend to be paid similar salaries to museum curators, either based on Civil Service or local government pay scales. Salaries in national museums and art galleries range from £11,138 to £16,813, with more senior staff earning from £16,813 to £24,167. Those working in London are paid extra.

Those working for local authorities may earn between £10,080 and £15,288, with some senior staff earning over £17,500.

There are no set salary scales for conservators and restorers working in the private sector, particularly as many are self-employed. Salaries tend to range widely, some being below those in the public sector, others being above. Senior posts may offer salaries up to £45,000.

Those in the public sector work 36 to 37 hours a week, Monday to Friday, while hours worked in the private sector vary according to pressure of work.

PROSPECTS

Opportunities for promotion in conservation and restoration work are few. Only large national or regional museums and art galleries have a promotion structure – assistant conservation officer to conservation officer to senior keeper (conservation). These organizations may also have senior administrative and managerial posts. Small organizations are unlikely to have a career structure, so conservators and restorers seeking advancement in the public sector need to be willing to move to compete for scarce vacancies elsewhere.

In the private sector, organizations tend to be too small to have a career structure. Self-employment or entry into partnership is normal. Success is then measured in terms of expanding business and profit.

There are some opportunities for conservators and restorers to enter teaching, or become conservation scientists, seeking to develop new conservation techniques.

RELATED OCCUPATIONS

Fine artist, museum curator/art gallery keeper, archivist, taxidermist, archaeologist, cabinet maker.

FURTHER INFORMATION

Metier (Arts and Entertainment NTO), Glyde House, Glydegate, Bradford BD5 0BQ, 01274 738800

Association of British Picture Restorers*, Station Avenue, Kew, Surrey TW9 3QA, 0181 948 5644

Association of Independent Museums (AIM)*, c/o LT Transport Museums, Covent Gardens, London WC3 7BB, 0171 379 6344

Institute of Field Archaeologists, University of Reading, 2 Earley Gate, PO Box 239, Reading RG6 6AU, 0118 931 6446

The Institute of Archaeology*, University College London, 31–34 Gordon Square, London WC1H 0PY, 0171 387 7050

Institute of Paper Conservation, Leigh Lodge, Leigh, Worcestershire WR6 5LB, 01886 832323

Museums and Galleries Commission, 16 Queen Anne's Gate, London SW1H 9AA, 0171 233 4200

Museum Training Institute*, Glyde House, Glydegate, Bradford BD5 0UP, 01274 391 056

The Museums Association*, 42 Clerkenwell Close, London EC1R 0PA, 0171 250 2933 (please include sae), www.museumass

National Association of Decorative and Fine Arts Societies (NADFAS), NADFAS House, 8 Guilford Street, London WC1N 1DT, 0171 430 0730

Recruitment and Assessment Services*, Alençon Link, Basingstoke, Hampshire RG21 1JB, 01256 846205

Scottish Conservation Bureau*, Historic Scotland, Longmore House, Salisbury Place, Edinburgh EH9 1SH, 0131 668 8668

The United Kingdom Institute for Conservation of Historic and Artistic Works (UKIC), 6 Whitehorse Mews, London SE1 7QD, 0171 620 3371

Scottish Society for Conservation and Restoration, The Glasite Meeting House, 33 Barary Street, Edinburgh EH3 6NX, 0131 556 8417

FURTHER READING

Leaflets/booklets are available from the addresses marked*.

Working In – Art and Design – COIC

Working In – History – COIC

Museums Yearbook – Museums Association

Heritage Management and Museum Work – AGCAS

In the careers library classified under EZ; FAE.

LIBRARY AND INFORMATION WORK: FAF

1. **LIBRARIAN/INFORMATION MANAGER CLCI:FAF**
2. **LIBRARY/INFORMATION ASSISTANT CLCI:FAF**
3. **INFORMATION SCIENTIST CLCI:FAF**

BACKGROUND INFORMATION

Information is vitally important in all aspects of life, which makes information work very varied. Distinctions between librarians, information managers and information scientists are increasingly blurred, with the difference often being one of emphasis in their work, rather than one of their role.

In general terms librarians, information managers and information scientists acquire, organize and exploit information in printed form and other media. They have professional and managerial skills and either a broad-based general knowledge, or an in-depth subject knowledge, depending on where they work. Information technology (IT) developments have led to new ways of obtaining, storing, retrieving, exploiting and manipulating information, and everyone involved in this work must be familiar with computerized systems and on-line services.

Librarians, information managers and information scientists may work alone or as part of a team. They are supported in their professional and managerial roles by library/information assistants.

1. LIBRARIAN/INFORMATION MANAGER (FAF)

THE WORK

Librarians/information managers handle information in a variety of media – books, journals, newspapers, leaflets, video, audio cassette, microfiche, multi-media CDs, computer databases, the Internet etc. The emphasis of their work depends on their particular job but, in general, they are responsible for:

– being aware of new publications and materials and information sources, and deciding what to add to the library and which existing stock to update. This includes which remote on-line services to subscribe to and which Internet resources are appropriate for sourcing information;

– cataloguing, classifying and indexing new material acquired for stock to make it available to library users;

– helping people access the information.

This may mean directing users to particular sources, or researching material, sometimes in depth, to answer enquiries. They may display new acquisitions or materials on a particular theme and produce bulletins listing new items, possibly with summaries of their contents as a current-awareness service. They can also obtain information held in other libraries by arranging inter-library loans or document retrieval.

Other tasks include budgeting and accounting, managing staff, stock, computer systems, buildings and fittings, and developing policy. Computers are heavily used both for internal management (keeping details of clients, stock, catalogues etc) and to access information held elsewhere through on-line systems and on the Internet. Other equipment that is used may include microfiche readers, video recorders and photocopiers.

In all areas of professional practice, in all kinds of employment, even increasingly in public and school libraries, computer databases and management systems, on-line services, email, and the Worl-Wide Web are very much part of daily life. Library and information professionals are expert at sourcing and evaluating information which is now exploding in quantity. They are the navigators through what is now a jungle of information and are therefore key players in shaping this new world using new technologies to the full.

In a small library or information unit, the librarian/information manager may be responsible for all aspects of the work. In a larger organization, tasks are divided and one person may be responsible for a specific area, eg acquisitions (buying stock), cataloguing, on-line database enquiry work.

Other work is available in different types of library. For example, in a public library, where a wide range of services is provided, a librarian can specialize in working with a particular group such as the disabled, prisoners, the mentally ill, ethnic minorities, the elderly or children. Work with children involves organizing story readings or puppet shows and liaising with local schools. Some librarians/information managers are responsible for a particular collection, such as music, visual images, European Union information, local studies, foreign language materials. Public libraries usually have mobile facilities to take services to people who are housebound, or do not live near a library.

Librarians in academic libraries and learning resource centres (colleges, universities) may be in charge of a particular subject, and be involved in planning courses in that subject. They also provide information and research skills teaching to help students and lecturers make the most of library facilities. School librarians provide teachers with appropriate books and other teaching aids, encourage pupils to use libraries, assist with student-centred learning and help with curriculum development.

Librarians/information managers in industry, commerce, the NHS, local government, government departments, professional bodies and voluntary organizations provide information primarily for colleagues, but may also offer services to people outside the organization. Their work may involve research, information analysis, translating, report-writing etc. There is the greatest overlap with information science work in this area. (Please see article 3. INFORMATION SCIENTIST.) In other kinds of special libraries, librarians/information managers may work only with media such as photographs, pictures, videos, philatelic collections, newspapers etc.

WORK ENVIRONMENT

Librarians/information managers work indoors (except for the mobile service), often by artificial light. Some areas can be dusty. Libraries may be purpose-built or converted from other buildings. Some are very old, others new; some spacious and some cramped (eg a small room in a firm's offices).

Libraries that are open to the public are sometimes noisy. In busy libraries, continual enquiries can cause pressure on staff. Some librarians/information managers are responsible for more than one library and must travel regularly between them.

LIBRARY AND INFORMATION WORK: FAF

SKILLS AND INTERESTS

Librarians/information managers must be able to work with people of all ages and from a variety of backgrounds. They should have an outgoing personality, patience, tact, courtesy and stamina. They need good spoken and written communication skills. An interest in working with computers is essential, as information technology is widely used. Librarians/information managers should be methodical, organized and accurate. They need a good memory, an enquiring mind and the initiative to research information.

The job requires the ability to handle complex tasks, possibly with interruptions and whilst under pressure. Deadlines often have to be met. Flexibility is important, particularly as librarians/information managers often have to change roles (eg cataloguer to researcher to teacher to writer).

A willingness to take on responsibility and develop management skills is needed. Staff working in small units are often isolated from other colleagues and should be independent and resourceful.

Some jobs require specific skills. For example, some librarians/information managers need specialized subject knowledge; others need skills in a foreign language to deal with materials in that language. Those working with children must be able to relate to them, and librarians in academic and school libraries may need teaching ability.

ENTRY REQUIREMENTS

Entry to professional librarianship and information management is by a Library Association-accredited first degree or postgraduate qualification. Either route is acceptable, although some academic libraries prefer applicants with postgraduate qualifications.

Entry to degree courses usually requires a minimum of two A levels/three H grades plus five GCSEs/S grades (A–C/1–3), or equivalent, such as a BTEC/SQA national diploma/certificate, or Advanced GNVQs/GSVQs Level III. Some courses specify particular subjects. Contact individual institutions for details. Entrants to full-time first degree courses do not need pre-course experience, although it can be required for part-time and distance learning courses.

Entry to postgraduate courses generally requires a degree in any subject or equivalent. Most postgraduate courses require applicants to have had between three and twelve months' appropriate work experience. This can be difficult to obtain, and students often have to apply to a good number of libraries or information services in both the public and private sectors. The Library Association publishes an annual directory of graduate training opportunities offering fixed-term pre-postgraduate work experience. Other vacancies are advertised in the professional press or quality daily newspapers or placed with specialist recruitment agencies. Some graduates take posts as library/information assistants to gain the necessary experience.

Candidates should check with individual departments of library and information studies before making decisions.

TRAINING

First degree courses

First degree courses accredited by The Library Association are offered by eleven universities. They last three to four years full-time. Some are also available on a part-time basis over four to eight years.

Subjects studied include management; training in information technology skills; information technology applications; on-line services; the Internet; organization and promotion of library and information services; what information is, where it comes from and who uses it; acquisition, organization, storage, retrieval and dissemination of information; information analysis; and the information needs of society. Optional subjects may include literature, archives, a foreign language or a specialist/technical subject.

Postgraduate courses

A number of courses are accredited by The Library Association and lead to postgraduate diplomas or Masters' degrees, are offered by 16 universities. They usually last one year full-time or two to three years part-time. Subjects studied at postgraduate level include the same core subjects offered at first degree level, but some provide greater emphasis on information technology applications or specialist training, such as health information. It is important to check prospectuses, as course titles are not a complete guide to their content.

All departments of library and information studies offer research degrees leading to PhD or MPhil and a number also offer post-experience Masters' degrees aimed at professionals who are mid-career and seeking a higher qualification.

Professional qualifications

The Library Association, which is the chartered professional body for librarians and information managers, maintains a register of chartered members. It awards professional qualifications to graduates who have met its requirements (by admitting members to the Register as Associates). Most candidates complete a Library Association-accredited course, followed by a minimum of a year's work experience and professional training. Candidates must submit an application that demonstrates their professional development and competence.

After at least five years as an Associate, candidates who demonstrate appropriate continuing professional development may apply for the award of Fellowship of The Library Association.

The Institute of Information Scientists also offers professional qualifications. Please see article 3. INFORMATION SCIENTIST.

NVQs/SVQs in Information and Library Services are available at Levels 2, 3 and 4. There is no prescribed training route, though training and open learning is available at a number of colleges and some universities. At the present time a degree or postgraduate Library Association accredited qualification is required for professional entry and NVQs/SVQs therefore represent opportunities for continuing professional development once in post.

LATE ENTRY

Mature entrants can develop successful careers in library and information work, but must still obtain professional qualifications (see ENTRY and TRAINING). Normal academic course entry requirements may be waived at the discretion of the academic institution. People with experience as library/information assistants, plus

LIBRARY AND INFORMATION WORK: FAF

vocational qualifications, are often admitted to degree courses in librarianship/information studies. Successful completion of a one-year Access course is also an acceptable entry route to many degree courses in librarianship and information studies. Candidates with degree, or equivalent qualifications, and/or experiential learning and, if required, appropriate pre-course experience, can enter a postgraduate course. Prospects for mature entrants depend on age, previous experience, knowledge and skills.

OPPORTUNITIES

Posts for librarians/information managers are found all over the country, primarily in towns and cities, with a majority of specialized posts in South East England. They are employed in the public sector in public libraries, academic libraries, government departments, the NHS, schools, museums, the four large national libraries, and in the private sector by, for example, banks, professional practices (accountants, engineers, surveyors, architects etc), legal firms, the media, professional bodies, learned societies, publishers and the voluntary sector. There are some opportunities for work abroad, and both the British Council and Voluntary Service Overseas occasionally recruit for work overseas.

The largest number of Library Association members in the UK is found in public libraries (25.1 %), followed by further and higher education libraries (17.37 %), government, national, health, industry and commerce (15.31 %) and school libraries (5.56 %). Opportunities in the private sector are increasing, whereas those in the public sector are more static. Some qualified graduate librarians/information managers may take paraprofessional (library/information assistant) posts in order to make a start in the profession.

Librarians/information managers with a first degree in scientific/technical, business-related or computing subjects are particularly sought after.

Vacancy information is published by The Library Association, the Institute of Information Scientists and Aslib for their members, and vacancies are advertised in *Times Educational Supplement, Times Higher Education Supplement, New Scientist,* quality national dailies and local or university/college careers offices. Vacancy information also appears on the Library Association's website and is available to anyone. There are also specialist recruitment agencies, such as INFOmatch (The Library Association), Aslib, TFPL, Instant Library, Informed Business Services and Access Information Recruitment.

PAY AND CONDITIONS

Salaries vary depending on the employer and the duties and responsibilities of the post. The Library Association publishes a series of salary guides. In local authority public libraries in England and Wales salaries for the main professional grades range from £12,171 to £20,313. Chartered members of The Library Association may start at £17,481. (Figures do not include London weighting.) Senior librarians/information managers with considerable responsibility for staff or departments receive higher salaries.

Salaries in other types of library (eg academic, industry, commerce) are broadly similar, ranging for example in specialist libraries and information services from £13,000 to £33,000 upwards for professional staff. They are sometimes lower in sectors such as schools and the NHS.

In many libraries, especially public and academic, librarians/information managers work shifts, including evenings and weekends. In other library and information services, staff usually work office hours.

PROSPECTS

Larger libraries and information services often have a clearly defined structure for promotion to management positions, with responsibility for a specific subject, service or branch/site library. Promotion can be internal, but staff may have to change employers to progress in their career.

In small libraries and information units, an individual may be in charge very quickly, and will have to move for greater experience or promotion.

Some chartered librarians, who qualified before a degree was necessary, may now need an academic qualification for promotion in the current highly competitive job market.

It may be possible to become self-employed after several years of professional practice and take on consultancy work.

RELATED OCCUPATIONS

Museum/art gallery curator/keeper, archivist, public records officer, information scientist, library/information assistant.

FURTHER INFORMATION AND READING

Please see article 3. INFORMATION SCIENTIST.

2. LIBRARY/INFORMATION ASSISTANT (FAF)

THE WORK

Library/information assistants (often referred to as paraprofessionals) carry out work to support professionally qualified librarians/information managers and information scientists. The work is a mixture of routine administrative and library duties.

Assistants issue and take back materials (books, cassettes, journals etc) and answer initial enquiries. They help people to find books and information and to use equipment such as photocopiers, microfiche readers, CD-ROM and computer terminals. They check returned materials for damage and arrange for repair. They replace books and other items that have been returned and or used to their correct places and keep the library tidy. Assistants send out routine letters, and search computer databases to find out the numbers of photocopies made, inter-library loans, fines, book reservations etc. They use computers to issue books, to update catalogues, to order new items and follow up orders, and to input and retrieve data.

Assistants also arrange for the purchase of new materials selected by professional staff. They check that materials have arrived and process them by recording their details in the catalogue and adding library details and classification codes where necessary. In public libraries, they may help librarians with story readings for children or community events. They may work in a mobile library, providing a service for people who cannot get to a library.

Senior assistants supervise junior staff and may liaise with caretakers, cleaners and maintenance staff and may take

LIBRARY AND INFORMATION WORK: FAF

day-to-day responsibility for running a library.

WORK ENVIRONMENT

Library/information assistants share the work environment of librarians/information managers. Please see article 1. LIBRARIAN/INFORMATION MANAGER. As they are responsible for replacing materials on shelves, the work can include a lot of bending, lifting, carrying and walking.

SKILLS AND INTERESTS

Library/information assistants often have regular contact with the public and should enjoy helping people of all ages and backgrounds. They need an outgoing personality, patience, tact, courtesy and stamina. They should have good communication skills. Assistants should be methodical and organized and have a good memory. An enquiring mind and initiative are essential to find information for people. An aptitude for work with computers is essential.

Some jobs require specific skills. For example, work with young children may make special demands on patience and ingenuity, and work with a collection of foreign language materials makes some knowledge of the language necessary.

ENTRY REQUIREMENTS

Although there are no minimum academic entry requirements, the majority of employers look for five GCSEs/S grades (A–C/1–3), including English. Some posts (for example, in academic or specialist libraries) require applicants to have A level or equivalent qualifications, such as BTEC/SQA national certificates/diplomas or Advanced GNVQs/GSVQs Level III. Specialist knowledge (a foreign language or technical expertise, including word processing, for example) is necessary for many posts. Senior library/information assistant posts are likely to require vocational qualifications (see TRAINING).

Four GCSEs/S grades (A–C/1–3) are required to study for BTEC national awards. GCSE/S grade (A–C/1–3) in English is desirable for entry to the SQA national certificate. Colleges will usually only accept students who are in appropriate full-time or part-time employment onto these vocational courses.

TRAINING

Training is largely in the workplace, with supervision from a senior library/information assistant and/or a professional librarian/information manager. Trainees may study for the following qualifications, usually by day release to college, or through distance learning:

The City and Guilds 737 in Library and Information Assistants Certificate is a one-year part-time or distance learning programme for those who are employed in library or information services. It is offered by a number of centres around the country on a day release basis, and by Sandwell College (West Midlands), Somerset College (Taunton) and Telford College (Edinburgh) through distance learning. Competences are assessed through practical coursework and examination.

The SQA National Certificate in Library and Information Science is available at Aberdeen College of Further Education (day release or evening classes), Central College of Commerce, Glasgow (day release) and Telford College of Further Education, Edinburgh (day release, full-time or distance learning). The SQA Higher National Certificate in Library and Information Science is offered by Bell College, Hamilton (full or part-time), Napier University (distance learning) and Telford College, Edinburgh (full or part-time). The courses last one year full-time or two years part-time/distance learning.

Training opportunities, such as National Traineeships or Modern Apprenticeships (Skillseekers initiative in Scotland) are available for young people. Contact the Information and Library Services Lead Body or your local careers office, Jobcentre, TEC/LEC for details.

NVQs/SVQs in Information and Library Services are available at Levels 2 and 3.

NB Information and Library Services Lead body are revising all their qualifications with new versions available in January 1999. Modern Apprenticeships, Skillseekers and National Traineeships will be revised later to incorporate the new qualifications.

LATE ENTRY

There are no age limits for entry. Specialist knowledge can be useful for some posts (eg in a technical library).

Many libraries are open in the evenings and at weekends. This can provide opportunities for flexible hours and part-time work. Some libraries employ assistants on a casual basis.

There may be specific training opportunities, directed at adults, available in some areas for this type of work. Candidates may have to satisfy certain conditions to be eligible. Contact your local Jobcentre, careers office, or TEC/LEC for details.

OPPORTUNITIES

Please see article 1. LIBRARIAN/INFORMATION MANAGER. Overall, there are far more library/information assistants than librarians/information managers, although some very small units do not employ any paraprofessional staff.

Some assistant posts are taken by graduates looking for pre-postgraduate course experience. Others are filled by graduates with library and information qualifications because of a shortage of professional posts in their area.

Vacancies are mainly advertised in local and national newspapers and in job bulletins published by local authorities, colleges and universities.

PAY AND CONDITIONS

Salaries vary depending on the employer and the duties and responsibilities of the post and, in public libraries in England and Wales, can range from £7,008 to £11,937. Senior library assistants receive from £11,157 to £15,264, and those with considerable responsibility receive up to £16,815. (Figures do not include London weighting.) Holders of vocational qualifications may start at £12,171.

Salaries in other types of library (eg academic, industrial, commercial) are broadly similar. For example in specialist libraries and information services paraprofessional staff can earn between £11,000 and £17,000. Salaries are sometimes lower in sectors such as schools and the NHS. The Library Association publishes a series of salary guides.

LIBRARY AND INFORMATION WORK: FAF

In many libraries, especially public and academic, library/information assistants work shifts, including evenings and weekends. In other libraries, library and information services staff usually work office hours.

PROSPECTS

Larger libraries and information units may have several paraprofessional grades, and assistants can progress to senior assistant posts. Some senior posts require vocational qualifications (see TRAINING). Organizations with a less formal structure may promote assistants by giving them more responsibility.

Library/information assistants cannot move into professional posts without taking professional qualifications, but experience in a post of this type may be acceptable for entry to university courses in library and information work. Please see article 1. LIBRARIAN/INFORMATION MANAGER.

RELATED OCCUPATIONS

Museum/art gallery assistant, tourist information assistant, research assistant, record keeper, librarian/information manager, information scientist, clerk.

FURTHER INFORMATION AND READING

Please see article 3. INFORMATION SCIENTIST.

3. INFORMATION SCIENTIST (FAF)

THE WORK

Information scientists research, obtain, produce, evaluate, organize and disseminate information. There is a lot of overlap with the work of librarians/information managers (please see article 1. LIBRARIAN/INFORMATION MANAGER), but information scientists' work often has a different emphasis. For example, information scientists frequently have a scientific or technical background and may be experts in a particular field (eg engineering, law, pharmaceuticals). They are often concerned with current information, rather than building a large collection of material for long-term use. They may also be involved in more retrieval and evaluation work than librarians/information managers (except those librarians/information managers employed in specialist and technical libraries), and tend to research information in greater depth. Some information scientists provide a service only to their colleagues. Others have regular contact with the public, either in person or by telephone or computer.

There are many jobs involved in information science work, but the most common tasks include:

– assessing the types of user and their information needs and providing appropriate materials and services;

– setting up and maintaining manual and computerized systems for efficient handling and storage of information;

– identifying relevant and useful information, which may involve searching on-line or CD-ROM databases, or printed versions of newspapers, abstracts, reports and other documents, and presenting the results to an enquirer;

– writing reports, abstracts of documents, information bulletins and so on.

Some information scientists are involved in press and publicity work and prepare and edit material for enquirers outside the organization. They may also arrange specialist displays or exhibitions, translate (or arrange for the translation of) material, produce technical manuals, participate in training, or be responsible for budgeting and accounting. Some supervise other staff.

WORK ENVIRONMENT

Information scientists work indoors in a wide range of organizations. Their immediate surroundings can vary from a spacious, purpose-built, highly computerized information base to a cramped back room. In larger organizations there may be a team of information professionals and support staff; in others, information scientists work alone.

The work is often done by artificial light, and conditions may be dusty, particularly where there are many paper-based resources.

SKILLS AND INTERESTS

Information scientists need good interpersonal skills. They have to be able to clarify exactly what users want from the information service and use imagination and initiative to develop it. They must be good communicators, and be able to write reports, abstracts and other documents. An ability and willingness to work with information technology is essential.

Information scientists should be organized, methodical and adaptable. A good memory is essential. They should display resourcefulness in researching information, and be able to evaluate the results to ensure they are appropriate to the needs of the user.

The job requires the ability to handle complex tasks, possibly with interruptions and whilst under pressure. Deadlines often have to be met. Information scientists must be able both to work closely with colleagues, and to motivate themselves when working alone. A willingness to take on responsibility and develop management skills is often needed.

Some jobs require specific skills. For example, those who work in specialized services may need subject knowledge, both to communicate with experts in the field and to evaluate technical information. Foreign language skills may also be useful for translating and abstracting (producing a summary of an article or book).

ENTRY REQUIREMENTS

Most professionally qualified information scientists are graduates and the most common routes into the profession are by relevant first degree or postgraduate qualification. Other pathways would be considered, including an NVQ/SVQ in Information and Library Services at Level 4. Please see article 1. LIBRARIAN/INFORMATION MANAGER for entry to degree and postgraduate courses.

TRAINING

First degree courses

First degree courses approved by the Institute of Information Scientists are offered at 14 universities. They last three to four years full-time. Some are also available on a part-time basis over four to eight years. Subjects studied include what information is; providers and users of information; sources, storage, retrieval and dissemination of information; information analysis; information management and information technology.

Postgraduate courses

Courses approved by the Institute of Information Scientists, leading to postgraduate diplomas or Masters' degrees, are offered by 16 universities. The Library Association accredited postgraduate courses are offered at 17 universities. They usually last one year full-time or two to three years part-time. Some are available through distance learning. Subjects studied include the same core subjects offered at first degree level. All departments of library and information studies also offer research degrees for qualified professionals and many offer post-experience Masters' degrees as higher qualifications for professionals who are mid-career.

Professional qualifications

Information scientists who hold a degree can apply for full professional membership of the Institute of Information Scientists after a period of relevant experience. They must complete a detailed form demonstrating their experience and skills in information science. Exemptions from the period of work experience of one to three years may apply if the candidate has a first degree or postgraduate qualification approved by the Institute.

Graduate information scientists can also gain professional qualifications awarding chartered status through The Library Association. Please see article 1. LIBRARIAN/INFORMATION MANAGER.

NVQs/SVQs in Information and Library Services are available at Levels 2, 3 and 4.

LATE ENTRY

Mature entrants can develop successful careers as information scientists. Normal entry requirements for courses approved by the Institute of Information Scientists may be waived at the discretion of the academic institution. Successful completion of a one-year Access route is an acceptable entry route to degrees in information studies. Prospects for mature entrants depend on age, previous experience, knowledge and skills. Those with scientific/technical backgrounds or computing/management skills are most likely to find late entry possible.

OPPORTUNITIES

Information scientist posts occur all over the country, although the majority are found in the South East. There are jobs in industry (especially the pharmaceutical, energy, construction and chemical industries), libraries (particularly academic libraries), central and local government departments, business and finance, research associations etc. Information posts are increasing in the private sector, although the public sector is static.

Twenty per cent of members of the Institute of Information Scientists work in industry, with more than twelve per cent employed in the information industry (including information technology, publishing etc). Another eleven per cent work in academic libraries. There are some opportunities to work abroad, and the British Council occasionally recruits for overseas posts. Some information scientists work as self-employed brokers and consultants, designing and setting up information services.

Vacancy information is published by the Institute of Information Scientists, Aslib and The Library Association for their members, and vacancies are also advertised in *New Scientist,* quality national dailies, specialist computing, business or scientific journals, and local or university/college careers offices.

PAY AND CONDITIONS

Salaries vary depending on the employer and the duties and responsibilities of the post. In industry, the range starts at under £12,000, with the average being £23,236. Other averages range from £18,000 in local government to £32,000 in intergovernmental organizations. The salary for those aged under 25 ranges between £9,852 and £36,500 with an average of £14,687. (Source IIS Remuneration Survey 1996)

In many information offices, staff work five days a week from 9am to 5pm. Where offices are open longer hours and at weekends, information scientists are likely to work shifts.

PROSPECTS

Most information departments are small and an individual may be in charge very quickly. Career progression is normally by changing job. Some organizations employ a number of information scientists and may have a formal promotion structure. Experienced information scientists may become consultants.

RELATED OCCUPATIONS

Museum/art gallery curator/keeper, technical author, computer database manager, researcher, patent agent, librarian/information manager, library/information assistant.

FURTHER INFORMATION

Aslib, The Association for Information Management*, Information House, 20–24 Old Street, London EC1V 9AP, 0171 253 4488, www.aslib.co.uk

Information and Library Services Lead Body*, c/o The Library Association, 7 Ridgmount Street, London WC1E 7AE, 0171 242 2244, www.ilsnvq.org.uk/ilsnvq/

The Institute of Information Scientists (IIS)*, 44–45 Museum Street, London WC1A 1LY, 0171 831 8003, www.iis.org.uk

The Library Association*, Information Services, 7 Ridgmount Street, London WC1E 7AE, 0171 636 7543, www.la-hq.org.uk

Local Government Opportunities (LGO)*, Local Government Management Board*, 76–86 Turnmill Street, Farringdon, London EC1M 5QU, 0171 296 6600

Specialist recruitment agencies for library and information work:

Access Information Recruitment, 13–14 Upper Street, London N1 0PQ, 0171 704 1333

Aslib Professional Recruitment Ltd, Staple Hall, Stone House Court, London EC3A 7PB, 0171 903 0000

Glen Recruitment, Glen House, 200 Tottenham Court Road, London W1P 9LA, 0171 255 1139

INFOmatch, c/o The Library Association, 7 Ridgmount Street, London WC1E 7AE, 0171 636 7543/0171 436 5843 (answerphone) Email: infomatch@la-hq.org.uk

LIBRARY AND INFORMATION WORK: FAF

Informed Recruitment Services, 25 Old Street, London EC1V 9HL, 0171 490 2811

Instant Library Ltd, 22 Frederick Street, Loughborough, Leicestershire, LE11 1UW, 01509 232748

Sue Hill Recruitment & Services Ltd, 71 Montpelier Road, London SE15 2HD, 0171 732 6718

TFPL, 17–18 Britton Street, London EC1M 5NQ, 0171 251 5522, www.tfpl.com

FURTHER READING

Leaflets/booklets are available from the addresses marked*.

Working in Natural Sciences – COIC

In the careers library classified under FAF.

ARCHAEOLOGY: FAH

ARCHAEOLOGIST CLCI:FAH

BACKGROUND INFORMATION

Archaeology is the study of the human past through material remains. Evidence can range from buried cities to microscopic organisms. It provides us with the only source of information about many aspects of our development. Milestones such as the beginning of agriculture, the origins of towns, or the discovery of metals can only be understood through the examination of physical evidence. Archaeology links with many subjects, including anthropology, geography, history, social sciences, maths, physics, biology, chemistry, art, religion and technology.

Most professional archaeologists have an archaeology degree or postgraduate qualification.

THE WORK

Although its popular image is of site excavation, archaeology embraces many different kinds of work. Most jobs require a broad knowledge of archaeology, but most archaeologists specialize either geographically (Egypt, Britain, Europe etc), chronologically (pre-history, Roman, Anglo-Saxon etc), technically (excavation, field survey, standing buildings, artefact study etc), or, more usually, in a combination of these.

Field archaeology. Most excavation work is carried out by archaeological trusts or units, many of which operate over a wide geographical area. Archaeology units vary in size, the largest employing a director, field officers for excavation, field survey staff, conservators, finds researchers, environmental specialists, an editorial assistant, archivist, illustrators and graphic designers, a photographer and a team of professional excavators. Small units tend to employ specialist staff on a short-term or consultancy basis.

Field officers supervise the evaluation of a site to assess its archaeological potential. Evaluation often begins with a desktop assessment of a site. If it is to proceed, decisions are made on methods of further evaluation, such as geophysical survey or trial trenching. Preservation of an archaeological site is preferable to excavation, but is not always possible where a site is to be developed. On-site earth moving is sometimes initially done by machine, but excavators use all kinds of equipment, ranging from pick and shovel to compressed air, trowel or toothpick, depending on circumstances.

The main objective of excavation is recovery of information. Although retrieval of objects is important, the recording of all kinds of accompanying features is of equal relevance. Such features may range from simple discoloration in the soil, to wells, burials, waterlogged timbers, deposits of seeds, pottery kilns and a huge range of traces of past activities.

Much work in archaeology takes place away from an excavation site and often takes much more time than the excavation. All finds from excavations are cleaned and catalogued, some are conserved. All information is recorded to form an archive for the site.

Archaeological science. A wide range of scientists is involved in the study of excavated materials. Specialisms include radio-carbon dating of objects; the study of excavated environmental material, such as bones, teeth, wood, charcoal, seeds and grain, insect skeletons and pollen; the examination of excavated artefacts (man-made objects) to determine how they were made, the processes used and the exact composition of the materials; statistical study of the finds on-site; conservation of archaeological objects.

Geophysical survey of sites is increasingly important in field archaeology. All archaeological sites are built up from the accumulation of sediments. These may be naturally deposited or a deliberate part of the site structure. They may result from the decay of buildings, or the development of soils and vegetation over parts of the site. Using the techniques of geology and soil science, study of these sediments forms a vital part of the unravelling of a site's history.

National agencies. Some archaeologists work for government agencies, principally English Heritage, Historic Scotland, Cadw (Welsh Historic Monuments) and the Environment and Heritage Service (Northern Ireland). Inspectors of Ancient Monuments are responsible for the preservation and protection of sites and monuments, monitoring fieldwork projects and recommending grant aid. Historic Building Inspectors have a similar responsibility for buildings. Inspectors are assisted by a wide range of specialists, including architects, conservators, photographers, draughtsmen/women, illustrators and research assistants.

Archaeologists also work for The Royal Commissions on Ancient and Historical Monuments of England, Scotland and Wales. They are responsible for recording all ancient buildings and visible features of historical importance by carrying out detailed surveys (including aerial surveys) and publishing the results. A knowledge of surveying is essential for this work.

Archaeologists are employed by other national organizations, eg the National Trust, the National Trust for Scotland and the National Parks to record, survey and, occasionally, excavate sites in their care. They also manage the archaeological resource and ensure its continued survival for future generations.

Local authorities. All English counties, some of the unitary authorities and districts in England and Wales, and many Scottish local authorities, have an archaeologist and/or a sites monuments office. They are responsible for acting as curator for the area's archaeology and maintaining the Sites and Monuments Record (SMR) – a database of the historic environment. They help the local authority to monitor the archaeological implications of proposed developments.

Museums. Some archaeologists work in museums as keepers or assistant keepers of archaeology. Their responsibilities include management, conservation and care of collections, preparing exhibitions and dealing with enquiries from the public. The recent growth of heritage interpretation centres has led to the employment of some archaeologists, often for work that includes design and marketing. For further information please see the article on MUSEUM CURATOR.

Education. Some archaeologists are concerned mainly with education. Archaeology lecturers or technicians work in universities and colleges of higher education, while some archaeologists provide an education and information service on the archaeological concerns of museums and archaeology units, and organizations such as English Heritage and Cadw.

ARCHAEOLOGY: FAH

WORK ENVIRONMENT

As the jobs within archaeology vary, so do the types of workplace and working conditions.

Excavation work takes place outdoors at all times of the year in any weather. Work can be dirty and cold and involve bending, kneeling and working in cramped conditions. Fieldwork and surveying involve travel over short or long distances to visit sites and attend meetings. The work may also include administration in offices.

Those in scientific archaeology may work outdoors on-site, but also in laboratory conditions that are clean, light and comfortable. Most work in museums is in warm, reasonably lit surroundings, although some museums are based outdoors and working conditions then depend on the weather. Some archaeological conservation work may take place outdoors on-site, but most is in laboratories or workshops, which are clean and light. Work involves much sitting.

Archaeologists in education spend most of their time indoors, except when taking students on field trips or carrying out fieldwork in vacation periods.

Computer specialists, eg those responsible for keeping excavation records or national monuments records, work in clean, light and airy conditions and spend much time sitting.

SKILLS AND INTERESTS

Different jobs in archaeology demand different skills and interests, although some are common to all. Archaeologists should have a keen sense of curiosity about the past. Most archaeological activities involve team work, and individuals must be able to work as team members. Good communication skills are important in most jobs. Written skills are needed for recording purposes, while spoken communication is required when dealing with colleagues or members of other organizations. All archaeological work demands a methodical approach.

Those involved in excavation need to be capable of working fast to meet deadlines and prepared to work in all weather conditions. In common with archaeologists involved in conservation, they also need good practical ability to be able to use tools and instruments skilfully, as well as patience and an eye for detail.

Archaeologists concerned with field investigation should be physically fit. Archaeologists in museums and heritage centres need some artistic ability to design exhibitions. Tact is a requirement for inspectors and others who liaise with landowners, planners and other agencies.

Archaeologists involved in scientific investigation need to be capable of clear, logical thought, able to implement practical experiments and draw logical conclusions from their findings.

The use of computers in archaeology is widespread. Some organizations employ specialist computer officers, while others have many staff using computers in their work. It is desirable, therefore, that archaeologists should have a knowledge of computers.

Many archaeologists need management skills, as their work includes staff organization and financial planning.

ENTRY REQUIREMENTS

It is usual for entrants to archaeology to have a degree that includes archaeology, although there is scope for graduates in other disciplines to enter following relevant postgraduate training.

Entry to degree courses is usually with a minimum of five GCSEs/S grades (A–C/1–3) and two A levels/three H grades, or equivalent. Competition for entry to archaeology degrees is such that applicants normally need three A levels/three or four H grades, often with high grades. Science-related and conservation courses often require science subjects at A level/H grade, particularly chemistry. Useful subjects at GCSE/S grade include English, maths, geology, history, geography and foreign languages, plus sciences for archaeology courses with a scientific emphasis.

Given the competition for entry to degrees that include archaeology, it is desirable to have evidence of prior interest. That can be shown through membership of an archaeology society, and having helped voluntarily in a dig or in a museum. A supplement to *British Archaeology*, published by the Council for British Archaeology, gives information on excavations and fieldwork that volunteers can join and details of how young people (aged 9–16) can join the Young Archaeologists' Club. Archaeology itself is taught at GCSE/S grade and A level/H grade in over 100 schools.

The Higher National Diploma in Practical Archaeology requires one A level/two H grades, preferably in archaeology, history, geography, physical sciences or classical civilization, with GCSEs/S grades (A–C/1–3) in English and maths, or a science (not biology alone), or equivalent. Applicants are expected to have four weeks' excavation experience.

Those seeking to enter academic work in archaeology normally need a postgraduate research degree. Postgraduate training is also necessary for museum work and environmental archaeology. Entry to postgraduate courses is with a first degree.

TRAINING

Archaeology can be studied at first degree level as a single subject or combined with a wide range of other subjects such as ancient or medieval history, geography, art or anthropology. Most courses are full-time for three years. Approximately 25 universities also offer diploma or certificate courses in archaeology, through their Continuing Education departments. They are studied part-time over one to three years and can be a method of entry to full-time undergraduate study.

The archaeological emphasis varies considerably between courses. Some courses offer a general approach with the opportunity to specialize as the course progresses. Some are concerned with particular periods or regions, while others specialize in conservation or archaeological science.

Courses include practical experience of excavations and field surveys, sometimes abroad. Methods and techniques, such as surveying, photography and conservation of finds are featured in most courses, particularly those with a scientific emphasis.

The Higher National Diploma in Practical Archaeology is offered by Bournemouth University as a franchise at Yeovil College. It lasts for two years and includes archaeological skills and knowledge, non-destructive archaeological investigation, practical fieldwork, excavation, a field survey project and five weeks' archaeological experience. On completion of the course the majority of students transfer to a degree course in archaeology.

ARCHAEOLOGY: FAH

As with first degrees there are a wide range of postgraduate archaeology courses, eg archaeological sciences, aerial photography, conservation, heritage management, museum studies and period-based studies. Some courses are taught, others involve research.

LATE ENTRY

It is possible and common for late entrants to enter archaeology, but they need the qualifications described in ENTRY REQUIREMENTS. Those with relevant experience, eg in computing or science, may be more successful in entering the work.

Mature applicants may be accepted for the higher education courses without the normal entry requirements. As with applicants of any age, it is helpful to have evidence of interest in archaeology, eg membership of an archaeological society and practical experience of fieldwork.

Many certificate and diploma courses in archaeology can be used as an entry qualification for mature students for degree courses.

OPPORTUNITIES

There are approximately 4,500 archaeologists in the UK, an estimated 2,000 of them working on short-term contracts.

Fieldwork opportunities are found mainly with archaeology units, some of which are independent trusts or charities, others being attached to museums, local authorities and universities. English Heritage also employs some archaeologists for fieldwork. Most fieldwork vacancies are short-term for the duration of a project, although employment may be extended as other projects are taken on.

Some archaeologists are employed as Inspectors of Ancient Monuments and Historic Buildings Inspectors by English Heritage, Historic Scotland, Cadw (Welsh Historic Monuments) and the Environment and Heritage Service (Northern Ireland).

Local authorities employ archaeologists in their planning departments, while some archaeologists are employed by organizations such as the National Trust, the Forestry Commission, British Gas and Thames Water.

Some archaeologists work for national and local museums as curators or keepers. Archaeologists specializing in conservation are employed by museums, as well as by university departments and national agencies, such as English Heritage.

Jobs in science-based archaeology are found in university research projects, in laboratories – such as in the British Museum and English Heritage – in various dating services, and in environmental archaeology units.

Universities and colleges of higher education employ some archaeologists as lecturers and technicians, while some work as education officers for museums, archaeology units and the national agencies.

Organizations such as the Council for British Archaeology and Council for Scottish Archaeology employ some archaeologists. They act as a bridge between amateur and professional archaeologists, promoting the subject with emphases on information, education, conservation and publication. Competition for all vacancies in archaeology is fierce and applicants should be prepared to move to find a job. Vacancies are advertised in *The Guardian, The Independent* and *Museums Journal*. The Institute of Field Archaeologists runs a jobs information service.

Work abroad is possible, usually on a temporary basis. Information on overseas openings is given in *Archaeology Abroad*, published three times a year.

Freelance work is common in archaeology, particularly for site supervisors, post-excavation analysts, conservators, illustrators and computing officers. Working freelance is often undertaken by experienced specialists who wish to work on a consultancy or self-employed basis. It is also undertaken by the inexperienced as a means of gaining sufficient experience to apply for a permanent post.

PAY AND CONDITIONS

Salaries vary according to the employing organization and position held. The average starting salary for a graduate archaeologist is approximately between £10,000 and £13,000. Those in senior posts may earn between £14,000 and £22,000, while some archaeologists with substantial managerial responsibility, and some involved in higher education lecturing, earn considerably more.

Hours and patterns of work vary between employing organizations. Field archaeologists working on excavations often work variable hours depending on the location of the site and urgency of the project.

Archaeologists working for local authorities and national agencies, and those involved in laboratory work, usually work standard office hours, Monday to Friday, but may work outside normal hours because of pressure of work.

Those working in museums tend to work 36 to 37 hours a week, with a rota to include weekend opening times.

Part-time work is possible in many areas of archaeology.

PROSPECTS

Promotion in archaeology is difficult and usually very slow because of intense competition. Those with management and financial experience and ability may find it easier to progress. Moving geographically for promotion is often necessary.

Some archaeologists in fieldwork aim initially for permanent employment with a unit. Progression may then be from site assistant to site supervisor, then site director.

Some experienced archaeologists become self-employed. Progress is then measured in terms of expanding business and profit.

RELATED OCCUPATIONS

Museum/art gallery curator, conservator, archaeological surveyor, librarian/information officer, archivist, countryside/conservation officer, scientist, research assistant.

FURTHER INFORMATION

Council for British Archaeology*, Bowes Morrell House, 111 Walmgate, York YO1 2UA, 01904 671417, email 100271.456@compuserve.com

Institute of Archaelogy*, University College London, 31 – 34 Gordon Square, London WC1H 0PY, 0171 3877050

Institute of Field Archaeologists, University of Reading, 2

ARCHAEOLOGY: FAH

Earley Gate, PO Box 239, Reading RG6 6AU, 0118 931 6446

Museums Association*, 42 Clerkenwell Close, London EC1R 0PA, 0171 250 2933

FURTHER READING

Leaflets/booklets are available from the addresses marked*.

Working in History – COIC

In the careers library classified under FAH.

1. INTERPRETER CLCI: FAL
2. TRANSLATOR CLCI: FAL
3. TEACHER OF ENGLISH AS A FOREIGN OR SECOND LANGUAGE CLCI:FAL

BACKGROUND INFORMATION

There are a number of jobs where linguistic skills are an advantage and even an important attribute. However, in many of them, knowledge of foreign languages is secondary to other abilities, even though, for some, it may be a requirement. This is true of travel couriers and resort representatives, bilingual managers and secretaries, and diplomats.

The two occupations where linguistic skills are the dominant ones are interpreter and translator. Interpreters work with the spoken word, translating spoken statements in one (or more) language(s) into another language (or languages) (or vice versa) so that people who understand only the mother tongue can follow what is being said. Translators work with the written or printed word, converting documents originated in one language into the language of those who need to read them. Both jobs require detailed knowledge of foreign languages, but they call for very different skills and have different work situations, as the following articles show. They usually also demand a knowledge of specialist terms in both languages, such as legal, business or medical.

Jobs where linguistic skills are essential to obtaining employment but where other skills or knowledge are equally important, include foreign language teacher, information scientist and tour guide. Teaching skills are as vital to the foreign language teacher as knowledge of science and engineering is to the information scientist, and knowledge of tourist sites and history is to the tour guide.

There are many jobs where conversational ability in a foreign language is useful, for instance travel couriers, resort representatives, hotel receptionists, and crew of ships or airlines. Languages are important in the diplomatic service, or for administrative posts with international organizations. Combined with knowledge of business expressions and practices, skills in a foreign language are a vital tool of bilingual managers and secretaries, and of sales and marketing staff selling to overseas customers. In these jobs, the work may involve an element of translating and interpreting, though the amount will vary.

In general, the increase in trade and tourism with other countries, and especially with other countries within the European Union, is making ability to converse in other languages a valuable asset in a whole range of occupations. It also opens up the possibility of employment abroad, whatever the occupation.

1. INTERPRETER (FAL)

THE WORK

Interpreting concerns the spoken word. The normal rule is that interpreters convert spoken statements from one or more languages into another (other) language(s). There are several forms of interpreting.

Simultaneous interpreting is used at multi-language international conferences and meetings, at which the interpreter sits in a soundproof booth (one for each conference language). They listen via headphones to speeches in t... the interpretat... feeding headph... speak that langua... target language i... interpret for peri... because the wor... Simultaneous interp... **conference interpreti**... booth situation.

Consecutive interpreting ...ings where simultaneous inter... ...ed. Instead of interpreting at the same ... ...preter waits until the speaker has finished so... ...tences and with the aid of notes and memory, repeats what has been said in another language. Consecutive interpretation is usually provided for a maximum of three languages. Consecutive interpreting is often referred to loosely as **business interpreting**.

Liaison interpreting is for conversations between two or more politicians, engineers etc who speak different languages. Here the interpreter works into and out of each language after each person speaks.

Community interpreting is used to enable officials to talk with non-English speakers or ethnic minority citizens, again with the interpreter working both ways.

Public service interpreting is the new title intended to cover both community interpreting and sections of liaison interpreting. It includes the interpreting needs of local authorities, police services, immigration authorities, hospitals etc.

Court interpreting is the term applied to interpreting for witnesses and defendants in court. It has much in common with business (consecutive) interpreting and liaison interpreting but qualified and experienced practitioners will have an excellent knowledge of court procedure and will tend to specialize in this area.

WORK ENVIRONMENT

Places of work vary greatly. Simultaneous interpreting involves periods in the confines of a booth looking out on a conference or meeting through a glass partition. Consecutive interpreting puts the interpreter in the conference room with the speaker performing his/her address in another language. Conference interpreting usually involves a great deal of travelling and meeting a variety of people in working and social institutions. Liaison and public service interpreting may involve work in local government offices, hospitals, immigration centres, law courts, prisons, factories, and industrial and commercial premises.

SKILLS AND INTERESTS

Interpreters have to present in their mother tongue, or target language, the equivalent of what was spoken in the source language, including tone of voice, jokes, ambiguities, colloquialisms. This calls for a sound command of the mother tongue, together with a comparable understanding of the way the other language is used by a native speaker, including its cultural background. An ability to manipulate language in skilful ways is needed where exact equivalents are not available. It also demands a clear, non-hesitant speaking voice and, in certain contexts, a knowledge of the appropriate specialist vocabulary of politics, economics,

...llingness to research a topic ...re a conference or meeting. ...shy of performing in public. ...ld have stamina, a good memory and ...th. They need the ability to maintain intense ...tion and to think rapidly. Coping with the ...ures of speed and accuracy in close contact with ...lleagues and clients can be stressful. Integrity and a sense of responsibility is essential in interpreting.

ENTRY REQUIREMENTS

These vary from organization to organization. Most international organizations require two other languages besides English. Different organizations have different official languages. For the European Commission it is the languages of the EU member countries; for the UN it is Arabic, Chinese, English, French, Russian and Spanish.

Most interpreters hold a degree in languages or in translation and interpreting, or a combined degree of languages with business, law, engineering etc. Normal entry for degree courses is five GCSEs/S grades (A–C/1–3) with two A levels/three H grades. A levels/H grades in a relevant foreign language and English may be required. Most interpreters hold postgraduate interpreting qualifications, and many live and work in the language's country to obtain normal usage and awareness of the culture.

Applicants for permanent posts with international organizations normally have to take a highly competitive entry test and interview. International organizations generally require formal qualifications and prior experience.

Successful conference interpreters are very often members of the International Association of Conference Interpreters (AIIC). Entrance to the Association and to other organizations, such as the Institute of Translation and Interpreting (ITI), is not automatic and candidates must have completed at least 200 days' work, which can take several years to achieve. AIIC and ITI both have freelance and permanently-employed interpreters among its members. ITI also accepts interpreters who practise forms of interpreting other than conference interpreting. Interpreters wishing to work for the EU must speak one of the fourteen EU languages as their native language and have a thorough understanding of three other EU languages.

The Institute of Linguists (IOL) offers exams at several levels, for qualifications that validate language skills in a range of languages and may offer an alternative to a degree course or postgraduate qualification. These involve language tasks normally encountered in work situations. Its higher-level exams relate more to aspects of public service interpreting and to translating, ie Intermediate Diploma (covering guided research, interviewing, summarizing and report-writing), and Diploma in Languages for International Communication (this tests language skills at degree-level in negotiating, translating, translation editing, and interpreting) plus the skills test at Intermediate Diploma Level.

Many candidates take IOL exams on the basis of work or life experience plus self-study, while many others attend part-time continuing education classes leading to the exams at FE colleges, universities or one of the few private language schools. Courses are usually one evening a week for one or two years. As the external examining body, the IOL asks for no formal qualifications to sit these exams but makes the required level of language competence very clear. Some local colleges may ask for a GCSE/S grade in a language for entry to a course.

Postgraduate courses at universities are usually aimed at conference interpreters and can be up to two years' duration.

Familiarity with English and a widely used ethnic minority language or one of the languages of the EU, one of which is of mother tongue standard, is a good basis for public service interpreting. The IOL's Diploma in Public Service Interpreting is recognized by the DfEE and widely accepted as the required qualification. It is the highest public service interpreting qualification in the UK. The exams for this are usually taken by people following short courses run by some local adult education institutes, FE colleges or universities. Exceptionally, people with the appropriate skills from past experience may take the examination without attending a course. The exams are at approximately first degree level in terms of language skills, but not in the breadth, and will be the equivalent NVQ/SVQ Level 5 for Interpreting. The exams are in three parts, including sight translation, written translation from and into English, as well as simultaneous and consecutive (liaison) interpreting from and into English. Candidates choose one area from public health, legal or local government.

The National Standards for Translation and Interpreting (NSTI) were developed by the Languages Lead Body and have a requirement to achieve four professional (mandatory) units plus three (Interpreting) or two (Translation) level 5 language units, plus two more specialized, including MCI/Managerial (optional)units. Practitioners are able to achieve the NVQ by completing a portfolio compiled from actual professional examples.

TRAINING

Specific training in interpreting skills is provided on specialist interpreting degree and postgraduate courses. Postgraduate courses for conference interpreters cover the techniques of simultaneous interpreting (with practice in a language laboratory) and consecutive interpreting (including memory exercises and note-taking techniques). They also cover liaison interpreting. Some experience of specialist vocabularies – such as legal, financial, medical – may also be included. Some courses leading to the exams of the IOL may provide interpreting practice, as do public service interpreting courses leading to the IOL Diploma in Public Service Interpreting.

Some training is provided in Civil Service linguist posts, where duties may cover translating as well as interpreting. Other organizations recruiting trainees offer mainly on-the-job training.

Most conference interpreters undertake postgraduate training at university. Many local adult education institutes and FE colleges run short courses, often in conjunction with local authorities and community organizations, for people who work in a bilingual environment which lead to the IOL Bilingual Skills Certificate.

LATE ENTRY

It is rare for people to enter interpreting later in life because of the special techniques and skills involved, though a few enter from language teaching or bilingual posts in industry. The exception is community interpreting, where life experience, ability in spoken English and an ethnic minority language are important factors. However, mature students can also take degree and postgraduate courses to qualify. The exams offered by the IOL test language ability and interpreting skills and enable those who have acquired these from life or work experience to obtain a qualification proving professional competence.

OPPORTUNITIES

There are about 500 conference interpreters in full-time posts with international organizations in all countries covering all official language combinations, and about 50–60 posts are advertised every year. Many of these are on short-term contracts. Membership of the AIIC is 2,000, including 120 members in Britain. On average about 50–60 new members qualify to join the AIIC each year. There are no figures available for public service and liaison interpreters, though the potential demand is quite high. The small number of openings and the stiff competition make this a difficult profession to succeed in.

The European Commission is the largest employer of interpreters, with each of its institutions recruiting separately and regularly, followed by the United Nations and its agencies. Other international organizations, such as NATO and trade organizations, employ a small number of each.

Interpreting and translating agencies normally fill the needs of their clients by hiring freelance interpreters. Due to the limited opportunities available, interpreters often do other work, such as translating or teaching, from which they can take days off to interpret when the opportunities arise.

Liaison and public service interpreters gradually build up contacts with clients. The National Register of Public Service Interpreters and the ITI's (Institute of Translation and Interpreting) Directory of Translators & Interpreters provide details of qualified and experienced public service interpreters to enable health or local authorities, police etc to find a suitable interpreter easily.

PAY AND CONDITIONS

The starting salary for recently qualified graduate interpreters at the European Commission is 1,641,216 Belgian francs (over £32,000) rising by increments and on promotion to a higher grade. The annual income of freelance interpreters depends on the rate (per day or hour) they agree with the clients and agencies who engage their services, and the number of engagements they get. For freelance conference interpreters, daily rates range from £220 to £350; for liaison interpreters, the rate is about £200 a day, though some areas pay much less, eg law courts.

Staff interpreters normally work a 35-hour week plus overtime but, like freelancers, they have to be available for conferences, meetings or interviews, and may be expected to travel in their own time. This work can be in the evenings and at weekends. It may include emergency meetings at short notice.

PROSPECTS

In the interpreting departments of international organizations there may be the possibility of promotion to senior interpreter or head of department. For freelance interpreters, advancement involves increasing the number of clients and the frequency of engagements, and commanding higher fees relating to increasing skill and experience. Even well-established interpreters sometimes have a second earning activity, such as translating or language teaching. A small number move into teaching full-time on degree or postgraduate courses, or into administrative posts with international organizations.

Many interpreters add to their skills during their careers by learning additional languages and studying for extra qualifications. The ITI runs in-career training sessions for its members and offers professional development courses in conjunction with a number of new universities.

RELATED OCCUPATIONS

Translator, journalist/foreign correspondent, tourist guide, travel courier, resort representative, specialist secretary (bi/multilingual), teacher (languages).

FURTHER INFORMATION

Institute of Linguists (IOL)*, Saxon House, 48 Southwark Street, London SE1 1UN, 0171 940 3100

Institute of Translation and Interpreting (ITI)*, 377 City Road, London EC1V 1NA, 0171 713 7600. www.ITI.org.uk

International Association of Conference Interpreters (AIIC), 10 Avenue de Secheron, CH-1202, Geneva, Switzerland

Languages National Training Organisation (LNTO)*, 20 Bedfordbury, London WC2N 4LB, 0171 379 5134

National Business Language Information Service (NatBLIS) c/o LNTO (address above), 0171 379 5131

European Commission Information Office, Commission of the European Communities, Rue de la Loi 200, B-1049 Brussels, Belgium

United Nations Information Centre, 21st Floor, Millbank Tower, London SW1P 4QH, 0171 630 1981, www.un.org

FURTHER READING

Leaflets/booklets are available from the addresses marked*.

Working in Languages – COIC

Careers Using Languages – Kogan Page

Languages and Your Career – IOL

Interpreters... What do they do? – ITI

National Standards for Translation and Interpreting – available from LNTO

The Guide to Languages & Careers – Centre for Information on Language Teaching & Research (CILT) – available from LNTO

In the careers library classified under FAL.

2. TRANSLATOR (FAL)

THE WORK

Translators work with the written word. They convert documents from the original or source language into the language of the people who need to know the content (the target language) and who will read the translation. Normally, they work into their mother tongue, or language of habitual use, from one or more other languages. The translated document should read as though originated in

LANGUAGES: FAL

the target language.

The majority are concerned with scientific, technical or commercial material. Documents may include business letters, financial reports, legal communications, sales brochures, technical manuals etc. Knowledge of fields such as finance, medicine, law or engineering and the technical terms they use can be important, and translators often specialize in one or more of these. In the course of translating, they refer to specialist dictionaries and reference books, type up translations on a word processor or personal computer, or dictate into a tape-recorder for later typing. A few large companies use computer programs to create a rough 'machine' translation which the translator then revises and edits.

Literary translation requires the translator to recreate the literary effects the original novelist, playwright or poet intended in another language.

WORK ENVIRONMENT

Translators normally work with a word processor and with reference books and specialist dictionaries to hand. They may visit clients, experts or specialist organizations, though most contact is by phone or mail, fax or modem.

SKILLS AND INTERESTS

Translators need ability in one or more foreign languages and also the skill of writing clearly and appropriately in their target language, as the translated text should read as though written originally in English. They should be self-motivated and able to work at speed. Freelance translators have to cope with being on their own most of the time. A meticulous mind is needed to search for the correct word or phrase and to ensure they are themselves clear on complicated or ambiguous aspects. This may involve an element of problem solving.

Wide education and interests are important, as is sufficient interest in their specialist fields to keep up to date by reading magazines and books. Translators have to be discreet and trustworthy in translating secret and confidential documents. They must be neutral and free of bias, even if translating statements they disapprove of. Ability to use a word processor is important, though some translators speak their translation into a Dictaphone and pay someone else to type it up.

ENTRY REQUIREMENTS

Most translators firstly obtain a degree in

– one or more modern foreign languages (preferably an applied language studies course, which offers some practice in translation);

– a foreign language combined with a specialist subject, such as business, law, engineering, computer studies or European studies;

– translation and/or interpreting (including basic study of some specialist subjects and vocabulary).

It is increasingly common for translators to take a postgraduate diploma in translation by full-time or part-time study, or a Master's degree. If not, they often take the Institute of Linguists' (IOL) Diploma in Translation.

Degree courses normally require a minimum of five GCSEs/S grades (A–C/1–3) with two A levels/three H grades. They may specify at least one relevant foreign language and English at A level/H grade for language and translation degrees. An appropriate specialist subject may be needed for a combined degree.

The Institute of Linguists (IOL) offers exams at several levels, for qualifications that validate language skills in a range of languages and may offer an alternative to a degree course.

Specifically for translators, a main qualification is the IOL's Diploma in Translation (DipTrans IOL). Entry for this requires linguistic ability in the source language, at least equivalent to a good honours degree in languages, or appropriate professional experience. Membership of the Institute of Translation and Interpreting is generally also accepted as recognition of status as a translator or interpreter. Candidates can join as Associates on the basis of academic qualifications and experience, and as full members by assessment of work or examination.

Many candidates take IOL exams on the basis of work or life experience plus self-study, while others attend part-time adult education classes leading to the exams at colleges, universities and a few private language schools. Usually they are one evening a week for one or two years. The IOL asks intending applicants to be able to meet one of the entry requirements listed in the DipTrans syllabus, and sets out the required level of language competence. Content of these courses, as of degree courses, varies considerably.

TRAINING

Training is normally obtained during degree and postgraduate courses or by taking evening courses at colleges or universities, leading to qualifications of the IOL.

All IOL courses are based on practical language tasks normally encountered in work situations. At higher levels they cover translation and interviewing tasks, ie the Intermediate Diploma (covering guided research, interviewing, summarizing and report-writing), and the Diploma in Languages for International Communication (this tests language skills at professional level in negotiating, translating, translation editing, and interpreting). The Diploma in Translation is set at postgraduate level and involves a written exam with three papers covering general translation plus annotation of difficult points, and semi-specialized translation in one of the areas of technology, business, literature, and one of science or humanities. A pass in all three papers is required. Dip'Trans courses are available at a number of universities and HE colleges. A distance learning course leading to the DipTrans is offered by the National Extension College etc.

Those recruited to trainee posts with international organizations, government departments or commercial companies have a period of training during which they learn the specialist practices and vocabulary involved and pick up accuracy and speed by doing increasingly more complex tasks.

Freelance translators have to practise to achieve a fast speed, together with accuracy of content and style.

LATE ENTRY

Because of the importance of detailed knowledge in a specialist field, people who have worked as lawyers, accountants, engineers etc who also have a second language and experience of reading and writing foreign texts may become a translator with no further training, or by taking the IOL's DipTrans. This, and other courses and exams, test language ability and translating skills and provide proof of professional competence. Mature students can also take degrees and postgraduate courses in languages and in translating.

Familiarity with an ethnic minority language, as well as good English, enables some mature people to obtain translation work at local level, sometimes starting as an unpaid volunteer. They go on to take training courses and aim for a relevant qualification.

OPPORTUNITIES

Full-time posts are few, so there is strong competition. Principal employers are international organizations, government departments, multinational companies and some large translation agencies. Some industrial and commercial companies with regular trade with other countries have staff translators to translate documents, such as technical manuals, about their products.

Recruitment to United Nations organizations, EU institutions and government departments is by competitive examination and interview. Some vacancies are for trainee positions, but others require two years' experience. UN and EU jobs are based in New York, Brussels and other cities overseas.

However, many translators work on a freelance basis. They obtain individual translating tasks through translation agencies, or from personal contacts and mailings to companies, offering their services.

It is possible to make a full-time living from freelance translating, but some find it necessary to do teaching or interpreting work as well. Some freelance engagements are to work for a period in the offices of the employing organization.

Literary translation is a wholly freelance activity and few people rely on it solely for a living.

PAY AND CONDITIONS

The starting salary for a recently qualified graduate at the European Commission is about 1,641,216 Belgian francs (over £32,000), rising by increments and on promotion to a higher grade. Salaries in the UK range from £17,000 for full-time translators in smaller organizations to £30,000–£35,000 for senior, experienced staff in large ones. The annual income of freelance translators depends on the rate (per job or per thousand words) they agree with the clients and agencies who engage their services, the number of engagements they get, and the speed and accuracy with which they work. Rates can range from £55 per thousand words for translating into English from French, Spanish or Italian to £100 per thousand characters from Chinese. Translating from English into another language usually adds about 25 to 30 per cent to these fees, more for Japanese and Chinese. Additional charges are made for urgency and for areas of specialist knowledge.

Staff translators work normal office hours, around 35 hours a week, with occasional overtime for urgent tasks. Freelance translators working from home choose their own hours, but may have to work weekends to meet deadlines.

PROSPECTS

Promotion is to senior translator and to head of department for those employed in large translation departments or agencies. This may occasionally offer a route into management. Freelance translators who are successful sometimes start their own translation agency. Progress for freelance translators usually takes the form of more jobs and clients, and higher fees. The European single market and the freeing of trade with Eastern Europe have increased the opportunities for translation work in other countries.

A small number of translators move into teaching full-time, or into administrative posts with international organizations.

Many translators add to their skills during their careers by learning additional languages and studying for extra qualifications, often through the IOL. In addition, the ITI runs in-career training sessions for its members and offers professional development courses in conjunction with a number of new universities.

RELATED OCCUPATIONS

Interpreter, teacher (foreign languages), journalist/foreign correspondent, specialist secretary (bi/multilingual), information scientist.

FURTHER INFORMATION

Institute of Linguists (IOL)*, Saxon House, 48 Southwark Street, London SE1 1UN 0171 940 3100

Institute of Translation and Interpreting (ITI)*, 377 City Road, London EC1V 1NA, 0171 713 7600. www.ITI.org.uk

Languages National Training Organisation (LNTO), 20 Bedfordbury, London WC2N 4LB 0171 379 5134

National Business Language Information Service (NatBLIS) c/o LNTO (address above), 0171 379 5131

European Commission Information Office, Commission of the European Communities, Rue de la Loi 200, B-1049 Brussels, Belgium

United Nations Information Centre, 21st Floor, Millbank Tower, London SW1P 4QH, 0171 630 1981

FURTHER READING

Leaflets/booklets are available from the addresses marked*.

Working in Languages – COIC

Careers Using Languages – Kogan Page

National Standards for Translation and Interpreting – available from LNTO

The Guide to Languages & Careers – The Centre for Information on Language Teaching & Research (CILT) – available from LNTO

In the careers library classified under FAL.

3. TEACHER OF ENGLISH AS A FOREIGN OR SECOND LANGUAGE (FAL)

THE WORK

Teaching English as a Foreign Language, known as TEFL, is often used as an umbrella title to cover several activities with somewhat different methods and requirements,

LANGUAGES: FAL

though increasingly the title Teaching English to Speakers of Other Languages (TESOL) is used for this purpose.

Teaching English as a Foreign Language (TEFL), strictly speaking, involves teaching people in or from non-English-speaking countries how to understand, speak, read and write English. The students could be school pupils or adults in other countries, or foreigners (whether pupils, students or adults) visiting Britain to study. The emphasis in teaching is normally on spoken English, so teacher and pupils are expected to conduct classes in English. However, knowledge of the students' language may be useful, at times, to identify learner problems.

Teachers may follow a coursebook that ensures students gain practice in a balance of skills; they may use games, tasks and grammar exercises learnt on training courses, or prepare their own teaching materials, such as articles and photographs cut from newspapers and magazines, or pre-recorded audio-tapes. Teaching methods range from 'chalk and talk' using black/whiteboards, question-and-answer sessions and group conversation, to flash cards, videos and computers. Teachers plan and prepare lessons in advance, using textbooks and published materials, but also create their own teaching materials and exercises. They also mark tests, essays and exercises in non-teaching hours.

Teaching English as a Second Language (TESL or, sometimes, TE2L) is concerned primarily with teaching groups of students who do not have English as their mother tongue and who have settled, or intend to settle, in the UK. TESL also takes place in multilingual countries, such as Kenya or Singapore, which use English for administrative purposes and in the education system. Students learn how to use English for everyday life, to shop, to get a job and to be able to successfully study other subjects at school or college in English.

All TESL teaching in UK schools, and much in colleges, is through giving language support to students' work on the National Curriculum, rather than in ESL classes. This may involve co-teaching with specialist teachers, or acting as an adviser to other teachers, running workshops with small groups, or teaching on a one-to-one basis. TESL teachers are likely to have a pastoral, as well as a teaching, role.

They use a range of teaching techniques – textbooks may be used but many classroom activities are based on materials prepared by the teacher, with topics often related to everyday life in the UK. Students may study for examinations such as C+G Communication Skills or GNVQ Core Skills in Communication.

Teaching English for Specific Purposes (TESP) consists of showing foreign managers, civil servants, lawyers etc how to use English to do business, negotiate, or conduct themselves at special events. It includes courses to enable foreign students to study for degrees at British universities or colleges, ie English for Academic Purposes (EAP), and others to enable foreign nationals to teach English. Normally, the students know enough English already to be taught further in English only, so knowing the students' language is not an essential requirement.

Role-play simulations, possibly videotaped, of social or business situations can be an important part of the teaching, though, for some topics, formal explanation and learning of specialist vocabularies may predominate.

Some courses lead to exams for a certificate awarded by a range of bodies.

In different contexts, teaching aids may include black/whiteboards, wallcharts, slide projectors, video players and cameras, tape recorders, and language laboratories.

WORK ENVIRONMENT

The normal place of work is a classroom in a school, college or private language school, though for TESL it may sometimes be a room in a community centre or evening institute. For TESP it may be a training centre attached to a large company's premises in another country. For many, the work involves living abroad, with wide variations in social environment and living/working conditions. It may involve travelling to several locations. Classes for adults are often in the evening.

In commercial language schools, a maximum class size of about twelve students is normal and in some contexts, eg English for executives, the numbers may be even fewer. Some commercial schools in the UK offer individual tuition.

SKILLS AND INTERESTS

Teachers need enthusiasm and energy. They have to be experienced and skilled in the way English is used in a wide range of situations. The ability to speak one or more foreign languages can be important in some areas, but not in all, and is not essential.

Clarity of diction is important. Ability to devise teaching exercises and activities to suit the level of the students and the course is needed. The teacher must be patient when pupils find it difficult to grasp a point and able to stay calm and think out other ways of getting the concept across.

A pleasant personality and the ability to get on with a wide range of people of different ages, abilities and cultures, are useful in the close relationships of small classes.

ENTRY REQUIREMENTS

To teach in schools within the state system in Britain requires a degree plus qualified teacher status (QTS). In England and Wales this is a Postgraduate Certificate in Education (PGCE) and in Scotland a one-year college of education course. A BEd degree also gives QTS. TEFL and TESL are no longer available as main subjects, though they may be a subsidiary option when taking Modern Languages as the main subject. Those hoping to teach TESL in schools should, therefore, aim for an additional specialist qualification, or go on to a specialist MA in TESL or Applied Linguistics.

Minimum entry requirements for degree courses are normally five GCSEs/S grades (A–C/1–3) with two A levels/three H grades, including at least GCSE/S grade English. An A level/H grade in the language to be studied may be needed, especially for French or German. For other languages, A levels/H grades should include a foreign language and English.

An appropriate degree gives entry to postgraduate courses leading to QTS. Prospective teachers in England and Wales must have GCSEs/S grades (A–C/1–3) in English and maths. In Scotland, they require H grade English and S grade maths.

No formal teaching qualifications are needed to teach in FE colleges and universities, but the usual minimum entry requirements are a degree plus a TEFL or TESL certificate.

Recognized commercial language schools in Britain (and

most reputable commercial schools abroad) employing EFL teachers ask for graduates with at least the Royal Society of Arts/University of Cambridge Local Examinations Syndicate (RSA/UCLES) Certificate in the Teaching of English as a Foreign Language to Adults (CTEFLA) or the Trinity College London Certificate in Teaching English to Speakers of Other Languages (CTESOL). Though there is no standard international qualification, these are recognized in many countries. Although each institution sets its own entry requirements, in some cases graduate level education is expected or at least evidence of a good standard of education, for example A levels/H grades, and minimum age of 20. Application forms for some schools also set pre-interview tasks to demonstrate language awareness. Most people take these courses after a degree, or after teaching experience in another discipline.

The British Council and larger language education organizations expect higher qualifications – usually a degree and an RSA/UCLES Diploma (DTEFLA), or a Trinity Licentiate Diploma in Teaching English to Speakers of Other Languages (TESOL), or a Master's degree in Applied Linguistics or TEFL. Enrolling for most of these requires a minimum of two years' experience of teaching EFL or ESL and, for some, a TEFL or TESL qualification and/or a degree.

For TESL, the most widely accepted qualifications are the RSA Certificate of Initial Training in English as a Second Language for Adults (CITESLA) and the RSA Diploma in ESL in Further, Adult and Continuing Education (FACE). For school-level teaching there is the RSA Diploma in Teaching of English across the Curriculum in Multilingual Schools, which is especially valuable for language support work.

Some universities offer their own postgraduate certificates and diplomas in TEFL and TESL and diplomas in linguistics or language education. These are not necessarily regarded as the equivalent of the RSA/UCLES and Trinity qualifications, because few have a practical teaching component.

A number of universities and independent colleges offer courses in TESP at Introductory, Certificate or Diploma levels, and in Business English. There is no course specifically in EAP, but ESP courses will normally cover this area. For entry, some colleges ask for a degree, most require two or three years' experience and a few want CTEFLA or CTESOL, so normally people take these courses after work in EFL, or part-time while working in it. Some people enter ESP from experience of working in business, engineering, the law, medicine etc, with or without an ESP course.

Requirements for teaching English in overseas countries vary considerably and some are stringent. A detailed listing appears in the *EFL Guide*.

TRAINING

Modern-language degree courses are normally four years, with one year spent in the country of the language. An English degree is three years. PGCE and other courses leading to QTS are one year. Specialist TEFL and TESL certificate courses vary from four weeks full-time to twelve months part-time. Diploma courses are from eight weeks full-time to one year part-time. Fees vary for these courses. A list of training courses is issued by The British Council and details also appear in the *EFL Guide*.

The RSA Cambridge certificate (known as the RSA CTEFLA certificate) course is part of the new revised Cambridge Integrated Language Teaching Scheme, introduced in all course centres from January 1997. The course is very practical and is for students without experience of TEFL but who have a good standard of education, normally a minimum of two A levels or equivalent.

The Trinity certificate course is similar, but varies from college to college within a set of syllabus requirements, so suitability should be checked. It includes techniques and practice of teaching children, an area that is not in the RSA course.

Courses are available at a wide range of universities, FE colleges and independent language schools around the country. To test one's aptitude for this field, it is possible to take a short introduction to EFL courses, one week full-time to ten weeks part-time. These do not count as qualifications, though two institutions regard their own introductory courses as stage one of certificate courses.

It is important to check that courses have a significant element of teaching practice and that this is with students, not fellow trainees. Some courses offer an element of distance learning but, because of the importance of practical aspects, none are wholly distance learning.

The ability to teach both EFL and ESL, or to teach other subjects as well as one of them, is likely to increase the chances of obtaining a post in further or adult education.

LATE ENTRY

As life experience is a distinct advantage, many people obtain TEFL/TESL qualifications and/or teaching qualifications and enter after work in teaching, training, or other industries, or after living and working abroad. Experience of business, for instance, is an asset for teaching in the ESP area.

OPPORTUNITIES

Employers for work in TEFL in Britain are mainly commercial language schools and FE colleges and, for TESL, local education authorities and FE colleges or adult education institutes. Some education authorities with high proportions of ethnic minority pupils employ specialist TESL teachers. Permanent full-time posts in TESL in FE colleges and adult education are few and teachers may be expected to act as 'language support' in classes in, for example, science, business studies or engineering taught by other lecturers. The easiest time to obtain initial TEFL engagements at commercial schools is the summer vacation, when parties of foreign schoolchildren come over.

For work abroad in TEFL and TESP, employers include The British Council, local education authorities, private schools and language schools, large industrial concerns and government departments. A freelance teacher may obtain short-term engagements from some of these plus, in Britain, foreign embassies, cultural institutes, and branches of foreign companies situated in Britain. Some other regular employers are the Overseas Development Administration (ODA), Voluntary Service Overseas (VSO), and International House. There are a number of agencies that locate teachers for overseas posts.

In TESL, employment is possible with state education authorities and private language schools in other English-

LANGUAGES: FAL

speaking countries, such as the USA, Australia and New Zealand, or countries that use English for administration and communication.

Private tuition may also be a possibility. Some schools in Europe and Japan have posts of language assistant, who support the teacher and provide conversation opportunities for pupils.

Advertisements for vacancies appear in national newspapers and, especially, the *Times Educational Supplement,* and in the *EL Gazette.* There is increasing competition for places, particularly in year-round jobs.

With English increasingly the dominant language of international trade and culture, there is growing demand for people equipped to teach it. The single European market and the EC's encouragement of languages, and the opening up of Eastern Europe and, to some extent, China have increased this demand. The increased training of their own nationals to teach English counters this trend somewhat. Continuing restrictions on immigration into Britain could mean the need for ESL teachers will decline.

PAY AND CONDITIONS

Salaries for posts within the UK state education system start at £12,500 with a degree and QTS. In the state education systems of other countries, pay is in line with normal levels for those countries, or with levels agreed by those countries with The British Council. Hours of work and other conditions also vary. Contracts for engagements overseas with The British Council and other British organizations are normally for one or two years; salaries are at the top end of local rates, and air fares and medical insurance are paid as well.

A full-time EFL teacher in a recognized commercial language school in the UK could expect anything from £10,000 to £17,000 for teaching 21 to 27 hours a week. Rates of £6 to £18 an hour apply to part-time and casual staff. Unrecognized schools pay less and are less likely to offer long-term contracts or paid holidays, and other conditions may be unfavourable. Similar variations apply to commercial language schools in other countries.

In Britain, most of the schools that are recognized by The British Council are members of the Association of Recognized English Language Services (ARELS), which insists on contracts, or of First Quality English Language Services (FIRST), which has charters regulating high standards for staff and students.

Fees paid by commercial language schools in other countries vary drastically depending on their status and financial soundness. In all situations, higher qualifications should win higher remuneration.

Teaching hours vary, but to these should be added time for preparation of teaching materials and lessons and marking of exercises. Teachers working with young people, especially on summer courses, may be expected to take parties sightseeing and oversee them in sporting and social activities outside teaching hours.

PROSPECTS

In Britain, some commercial schools and FE colleges may offer some promotion to senior or managerial posts, as may some overseas centres to staff on long-term contracts. However, the majority of teachers cannot expect this, though long experience and continued work for one establishment should bring increases in salaries or fees. A successful teacher may open their own private language school. A successful freelance should be able to demand higher fees as their reputation grows. Some teachers move into teacher training and others into writing books and articles about EFL. Experienced teachers add to their skills by taking additional courses, eg in ESP, or go on to an MA in TEFL, TESL, or linguistics in Britain or another country.

RELATED OCCUPATIONS

Teacher (foreign languages), teacher (English), community interpreter, resort representative, tour guide, bilingual secretary, bilingual manager.

FURTHER INFORMATION

Association of Recognized English Language Services (ARELS)*, 2 Pontypool Place, Valentine Place, London SE1 8QF, 0171 242 3136

The British Council, English Language Information Section*, 1 Bridgewater House, 58 Whitworth Street, Manchester M1 6BB, 0161 957 7755

National Association for Teaching English and other Community Languages to Adults (NATECLA)*, South Birmingham College, 524 Stratford Road, Birmingham B11 4AJ, 0121 694 5070

International Association for Teachers of EFL (IATEFL), 3 Kingsdown Chambers, Kingsdown Park, Tankerton, Whitstable, Kent CT5 2DJ, 01227 276 528

FURTHER READING

Leaflets/booklets are available from the addresses marked*.

Working in Languages – COIC

Careers Using Languages – Kogan Page

Languages and Your Career – IOL

Teaching English as a Foreign Language and Teaching Abroad – AGCAS

EFL Guide – EFL Ltd

How to Become a Teacher of English as a Foreign Language – The British Council

In the careers library classified under FAL.

GROUP G – ENTERTAINMENT AND LEISURE

1. ACTOR CLCI:GAB
2. MUSICIAN CLCI:GAD
3. MUSIC TEACHER CLCI:GAD/FAB
4. DANCER CLCI:GAF

1. ACTOR (GAB)

BACKGROUND INFORMATION

In this article the word 'actor' refers to both men and women. The title 'actress' is becoming less and less used in the profession.

Some people are attracted to the acting profession, believing it to be glamorous and well paid. The reality is that, at any one time, an estimated four out of five actors are without acting work, or 'resting'. During this time, they may have to rely for income on state benefits, or money from casual work, such as temping.

Actors may work either in live stage performances, or in recorded media, such as films, radio, television and video. Some actors prefer one of these to the other, and the techniques used differ. Most actors cover both in order to gain experience, improve their chances of obtaining regular work and reduce the risk of becoming 'type-cast'. Although film and television is often better paid, many actors find live theatre more challenging and stimulating.

When they are working, most actors work long, hard hours for relatively little pay. Even well-known names have periods when they are without work, and very few make a fortune from acting.

For many people, acting remains a pastime, which can be satisfied at any number of amateur theatre groups around the country.

THE WORK

Acting is a performance art, alongside music and dance. An actor's job is to assume a character created by a playwright or author, and communicate this to an audience, usually under the guidance of a director. The production may be anything from Shakespeare to street theatre, but, in each case, the actor must understand and interpret what the writer is trying to convey.

Actors use their own experience and emotions to help them portray characters. Communication is achieved through imaginative and creative use of the body and voice.

Much of an actor's time is spent learning parts and rehearsing plays. Acting is very much a group activity, in which each player is dependent upon others, including the director. Individual characters are developed by close co-operation between the actors and the director. The performance is the culmination of all the hard work, although it occupies only a small proportion of an actor's time.

The range and scope of acting is considerable. Some actors work mainly in the classical theatre, performing plays by Shakespeare and others; some specialize in more 'mainstream' theatre, including old and new plays; others work on comedy, musicals, community theatre, puppetry, mime etc.

When they are out of work, actors spend as much time as possible auditioning for parts.

WORK ENVIRONMENT

Actors work mainly indoors in theatres and studios, though for films and TV, some scenes may be recorded on location. Actors taking part in open air and street theatre obviously work outside, though rehearsals may take place under cover.

The temperatures in which actors work can vary widely, from cold and draughty rehearsal rooms to warm theatres and studios, where spotlights and (perhaps) heavy costumes may add to the overall heat.

Actors in the theatre have to work more or less continuously during the duration of the show, while in films and, to a lesser extent, television, there may be long breaks as sets are changed, lights and cameras re-angled etc. There can be a good deal of sitting around waiting for the next scene to be recorded.

While taking part in a show, actors may have to live away from their homes, in lodgings with other actors. If the show goes on tour, or a film or TV programme on location, they can spend lengthy periods away from home, perhaps even abroad.

SKILLS AND INTERESTS

Actors need to understand and interpret the roles they are given, and have a good memory, both for their lines and their moves. A clear speaking voice is important, and they also need empathy and imagination to understand and express the emotions of the characters they are asked to portray.

Actors must be mentally and physically tough, to cope with the demands of the job. They must be resilient and able to cope with the uncertainty of working in a profession where, at the end of a run or series, unemployment is always a prospect. Good general health is also important; actors are expected to turn up for rehearsals and performances even when unwell.

ENTRY REQUIREMENTS

There are no formal entry requirements for becoming an actor, and it is still possible for untrained people with talent and determination to enter the profession, perhaps via fringe or amateur theatre. The majority of actors today, however, have been through stage and/or drama school.

Drama schools take students from the age of 18 years for two- and three-year courses, 21 for one-year courses. Many do not set minimum academic entry requirements for performance courses, preferring to assess potential by audition and interview. Others specify five GCSEs/S grades (A–C/1–3), and a few require two A levels or three H grades. Competition is extremely intense, with some schools auditioning 20 or more people for each place.

Auditions vary, but often follow a two-tier system. For the first stage, candidates may be asked to prepare two contrasting pieces, one modern and one by Shakespeare, and perform them in front of a selection panel. They may then be required to read a piece at sight, improvise on a given subject, or sing. Those who succeed at this stage are invited back for a longer, more detailed, final audition. Selection panels are looking for evidence of talent, combined with absolute commitment to an acting career.

Degree courses in drama or theatre arts/studies usually ask for a minimum of five GCSEs/S grades (A–C/1–3) and two A levels or three H grades, or equivalent. The application

PERFORMING ARTS: GAB/GAF

procedure may include auditions and/or participation in workshops.

Stage schools are part of the private (fee-paying) education sector. They take children from the age of five upwards, and offer the usual National Curriculum subjects, but with extra training in drama, voice production, dance, mime, singing and so on. Nowadays, only a minority of new entrants to the acting profession have been through stage school. Young people who have not followed this path can gain acting experience in other ways, for example by taking part in school productions and/or joining a youth theatre group.

TRAINING

Although it is still possible to enter the acting profession without formal training, nowadays the National Council for Drama Training (NCDT) recommends that all intending actors should complete a course of recognized training. Courses are listed in *The Official UK Guide to Drama Training*.

Professional acting courses

Twenty drama schools throughout the UK run professional acting courses that have been accredited by the NCDT. Courses vary widely, and students are recommended to read schools' prospectuses carefully before applying. Some courses are classically orientated, and concentrate on teaching students a range of skills in acting, movement, stage combat etc. Other courses start from the student's own experience, emphasizing self-discovery and self-development, then move on to acquiring the necessary skills. At some colleges, students form a repertory company, performing a series of plays or musicals, and possibly touring. Professional acting courses are intensive. Most last three years, and often they involve working from early in the morning until late at night.

Although there is some variation between courses, the first year usually concentrates on the development of the actor's body and voice. Students learn how to breathe, project their voices and, move; they may also study singing, mask work, stage fighting, improvisation, different styles of dance, and stage make-up. As students' skills develop, they spend more time working on set texts and rehearsing plays, culminating in public performances. Students also study social history and the history of drama and the visual arts.

Other courses

There are other drama schools throughout the country, but graduates from non-accredited courses are likely to have more difficulty in obtaining an Equity card and beginning a career as an actor when they leave.

Many other courses, at all levels, include drama as part, or all, of their content. Colleges may offer A level drama or theatre studies, Foundation, Intermediate and Advanced GNVQ/GSVQ Level I, II and III in Performing Arts and Entertainment, BTEC/SQA National Certificate/Diploma and/or Higher National Certificate/Diploma in Performing Arts. These courses may be accepted as the academic part of the entry requirements for an acting course. The GNVQs/GSVQs and BTEC courses are vocationally based and provide practical experience in drama, music, dance and stagecraft, through workshops and performance. This experience can be invaluable when preparing for auditions. A level Theatre Studies tends to be preferred to the BTEC/SQA qualifications for entry to drama schools.

A degree course in drama or performance arts is another option, and there are many courses to choose from. Some are academic, concentrating on the theoretical aspects of theatre, sometimes combining drama with an academic subject, such as English. Others offer a more practical training, perhaps alongside music and dance. The emphasis on most courses is not on training actors, though undoubtedly some graduates do go into the profession, perhaps after postgraduate training at drama school. An increasing number of drama schools are now themselves offering degree courses with NCDT accreditation.

Drama graduates can go into any field where a degree is a prerequisite, giving them an opportunity to pursue alternative careers should acting not work out.

Grants

Most professional acting courses do not attract mandatory grants. Students needing financial assistance with drama school fees and living expenses are often dependent on discretionary awards. Check with your local education authority on the funding status of the various courses concerned, and, if appropriate, the availability of discretionary awards.

LATE ENTRY

Experience of life outside the theatre can be of great benefit to an actor, and many drama schools are prepared to accept mature students. The average age of students on three-year courses is 20–21 years, but there are often mature students on one-year courses. Some schools set an upper age limit of 25 or 26 years. Others accept students up to the age of 30, and, very occasionally, even older. Academic entry requirements, where specified, may be relaxed for mature students over a certain age; this varies between 21 and 25 years.

Once over the age of 30, opportunities to enter the acting profession are very limited.

OPPORTUNITIES

It is sometimes thought that opportunities for actors depend on their being accepted into Equity, the actors' trade union, and obtaining an Equity card. However, this is only true to a very limited extent. Equity negotiates pay and conditions for actors, but entry to acting jobs is dependent on selection by casting directors. This depends on the ability of an actor to impress at audition, which in turn depends on the talent of the actor.

Once an actor has been given a professional acting job in theatre, television, film or radio, they are eligible to join Equity. Newcomers receive provisional membership, and can apply for a full Equity card after completing 30 weeks of approved work (not necessarily consecutive). Actors who have successfully completed a drama school course accredited by the National Council for Drama Training can join Equity immediately as registered graduate members.

In films, radio and television, there are no restrictions on who can be employed. Within the theatre, Equity has agreements with employers limiting the number of newcomers to the profession who can be engaged in any one year. Even here, however, the requirement is not that the majority of people taken on should be Equity members, but rather that they should be 'people with previous professional experience', or registered graduates. Most experienced actors are members of Equity, but possession of an Equity card is, in itself, no guarantee of employment.

As already mentioned, even experienced actors face intense competition for jobs. Actors must therefore take every opportunity to bring themselves to the notice of producers and casting directors. Many advertise with a photograph in the actors' annual directory *Spotlight*.

Opportunities for actors are sometimes advertised in *The Stage and Television Today*, the weekly newspaper of the acting profession. Personal contacts and word-of-mouth are also important. Actors can find out who is currently casting for productions through publications such as *Production and Casting Report* and *Repertory Report*.

Many actors obtain work through agents, who negotiate their contracts and take a percentage of their earnings. Good agents can greatly assist their clients' careers. Having an agent is not, however, essential.

Actors may work in the following areas:

Repertory companies

There are around 70 regional repertory companies, which may offer a starting point for newly trained actors. Actors are engaged for a whole season, performing a different play on average every three weeks. Young actors are usually advised to gain varied experience in rep, before attempting to specialize in film, television or theatre work.

Commercial theatre companies

Several prominent commercial producers tour shows with a view to bringing them to the West End. Sometimes companies are set up to perform one particular play or show. Productions normally run for a specified period of weeks or months, though they may finish early if unsuccessful. Leading roles in such productions almost invariably go to experienced actors, but young actors may be taken on for juvenile or smaller parts.

Films

Actors are hired for a particular film. Although the whole production may take months, most are taken on for only a few days or weeks. Few films are made in Britain today, so opportunities for film actors in this country are limited.

Television

Television offers a growing number of opportunities, though starting work can be difficult. Actors are usually employed for one particular programme, though some may appear in long-running serials. Television work requires special skills for working to a camera.

Radio

Most radio work is on a one-off basis, although there are serials, and actors may also specialize in radio plays. Most work is with the BBC, and opportunities exist at both national and regional levels.

Commercials

Many actors work in commercials to boost their income, and such jobs can be well paid. Actors either appear in person in the commercials, or do 'voice-overs'.

Promotional and training videos

An increasing number of companies specialize in producing videos for commercial purposes. These may be to promote an organization and its products or services, or for staff training. Such companies offer a range of opportunities for actors.

Stunt work

Stunt performers need to have a range of skills, as well as acting. These might include driving, parachuting, riding, fencing, gymnastics, martial arts and diving. Equity operates a stunt register that film and television producers use. New applicants must be Equity members between 18 and 30 years and have recent qualifications in a range of skills.

Summer shows and pantomimes

Some actors specialize in this area, moving from one to the other, and thereby achieving regular work throughout the year.

Fringe theatre

There are many fringe theatre companies throughout the UK, whose aims are to put on productions that might not be viable in the commercial theatre, and to bring theatre to a wider than usual audience. They may perform in pubs, clubs, community centres, church halls, old people's homes etc. Some try to raise awareness of issues, such as the environment or the role of women in society. Many have only a few members and operate on a low budget. Often, they are run as co-operatives with payment on a profit (or loss) sharing basis, rather than Equity rates. Occasionally, groups of out-of-work actors form themselves into a company, financing their own performances.

Community theatre

Community theatre companies aim to involve local people in productions reflecting local issues and concerns. Like fringe theatre, many such groups are unable to pay their members a living wage. However, working in a fringe or community theatre company provides valuable experience, and may give actors the chance of being 'spotted' by an agent or casting director.

Children's theatre

These companies perform work for children. A few large companies have their own theatre, but many smaller ones tour venues such as schools, parks and playgrounds. Many of the programmes demand a variety of skills, such as juggling, mime and puppetry, and often the children themselves are encouraged to participate.

Theatre-in-education

Like children's theatre companies, these companies bring theatre to children and young people. Working primarily in schools, they put on productions related to the curriculum, such as current set books and topics in history or science, as well as dramatizations of social issues. Theatre-in-education and children's theatre are most likely to appeal to actors who have an interest in the educational potential of drama.

Clubs and variety

Some actors perform speciality acts (for example, comedy, mime, conjuring), obtaining bookings in clubs, cabaret and variety shows, and perhaps going on to television, radio or films.

PAY AND CONDITIONS

The British Actors' Equity Association, or Equity, negotiates minimum wages and conditions for its members. Actors in the theatre may be employed on a once-nightly or, twice-daily/nightly rate. An actor on a once-nightly contract can be asked to perform a show on no more than six days a week (a total of eight performances). The basic minimum for an actor on a once-nightly contract at a West End theatre venue is £275.00 a week. In a provincial repertory theatre, the once-nightly minimum is £212.50 a week. If actors have to work away from home, they receive an additional allowance for lodgings.

PERFORMING ARTS: GAB/GAF

The above are the minimum rates that would be paid to a newcomer to the profession. Agents can normally negotiate higher salaries for their clients. However, this must be set against the fact that many actors experience long periods of unemployment. Actors have to pay their Equity subscription whether or not they are working (although they pay less when they are not earning) and they often have to pay travelling expenses to auditions. Only a small minority of actors earn anything approaching a comfortable living from their profession.

While in employment, most actors work very long hours. Much of the work, particularly in live theatre, is performed in the evenings and at weekends, when most other people are at leisure. In addition, a considerable amount of time is spent rehearsing parts and learning lines. Actors working in television and film often start early in the morning, and may spend long periods waiting for their scenes to be shot.

PROSPECTS

An actor's prospects depend upon talent, good fortune and being in the right place at the right time. Many actors wait for as much as six months to a year after leaving college, before finding their first job. A tiny minority are 'spotted' by an agent or casting director while at college. Considerable numbers of actors leave the profession because of the insecurity and lack of a steady income. Some actors move into directing, while others become teachers. A number have found success as playwrights or novelists.

RELATED OCCUPATIONS

Dancer, musician, teacher, drama therapist, stage manager, director, theatre technician.

FURTHER INFORMATION

The Arts Council of Great Britain*, 14 Great Peter Street, London SW1P 3NQ, 0171 973 6450

British Actors' Equity Association*, Guild House, Upper St Martin's Lane, London WC2 9EG, 0171 379 6000, www.equity.org.uk

Community Dance and Mime Foundation*, 13–15 Belvoir Street, Leicester LE1 6SL, 0116 275 5058

National Association of Youth Theatres, Unit 1304, The Custard Factory, Digbeth, Birmingham B9 4AA, 0121 608 2111

National Council for Drama Training*, 5 Tavistock Place, London WC1H 9SS, 0171 387 3650

Production and Casting Report, PO Box 100, Broadstairs, Kent 01843 860885

The Spotlight, 1st Floor, Charles House, 7 Leicester Place, London WC2H 7BP

Westlake Publishing*, 17 Sturton Street, Cambridge CB1 2SN, www.drama.ac

FURTHER READING

Leaflets/booklets are available from the addresses marked*.

Working in The Performing Arts – COIC

The Official UK Guide to Drama Training – Westlake Publishing

Acting Skills – A and C Black Ltd

Careers in the Theatre – Kogan Page

In the careers library classified under GAB.

2. MUSICIAN (GAD)

BACKGROUND INFORMATION

Many people are drawn to the idea of making music their profession, but few ever achieve that ambition. For those who do, the work is rarely glamorous or highly paid. When starting out, musicians have to take any work they can get while they build a reputation. They may also have to take work outside music, but must all the time keep on practising in case a music job arises.

Musicians produce music using an instrument, or, in the case of singers, their own voice. Musical instruments can be broadly divided into five main categories: keyboard, such as the organ or piano; woodwind, such as the flute or clarinet; brass, such as the trumpet or saxophone; strings, such as the guitar or violin; and percussion, such as the xylophone or drums. Some musicians play a number of instruments, but most concentrate their efforts on mastering just one. Performing music to a professional standard requires considerable talent allied with constant practice.

THE WORK

Music as a performing art can be divided into two main areas: classical and popular.

Classical music

Most classical musicians play in orchestras, ensembles or chamber groups, although they may also work as soloists. Singers may be part of a professional choir, and/or work as soloists or opera singers.

Classical music is probably more demanding, in terms of what is required of the performer, than other areas of music. Live performances occupy only a very small proportion of the musician's time, and are the culmination of many hours spent practising and rehearsing. Touring is also time-consuming and tiring. The highly developed skills of a violinist or classical pianist soon deteriorate without practice. Singers must take care of their voices, avoiding strain or overwork.

Classical musicians often make a living by working in several groups or orchestras. Some musicians feel that they can make more of an individual contribution in smaller groups. Some, especially soloists, may have agents, who help them get work.

Popular music

This includes rock and pop, jazz, blues, country and western, folk, light and brass band music. Some pop musicians combine playing an instrument, such as the guitar or piano, with singing. Pop or rock musicians either work as part of a group or band, or as solo artists. They usually work closely with a manager. Like classical musicians, their time is spent practising, rehearsing and performing.

In all areas of music, musicians sometimes make recordings, although it is far more common in the field of pop music. Some pop musicians rarely perform live to an audience, becoming well-known through recordings and videos. A tour often follows the release of an album, to ensure wide publicity. Some musicians, mainly in the popular field, write and perform their own music, and may also arrange musical scores for others to perform.

PERFORMING ARTS: GAB/GAF

WORK ENVIRONMENT

Performance venues vary widely, from concert halls, theatres and arts centres to pubs, clubs, restaurants, schools, parks, sports grounds and street corners. They may be spacious and comfortable, or crowded and shabby. Pubs and clubs may be smoky and dark and, when full of people, hot and humid. Most recording studios have little natural light, and may be cramped. Classical musicians usually perform in more comfortable conditions, although premises such as church halls can be draughty and uncomfortable.

Rehearsal rooms can also be draughty and uncomfortable, with poor acoustics. Some rehearsal time is usually spent waiting, while other musicians work on their parts.

Musicians usually work indoors, although they may occasionally perform an outdoor concert. They often work as part of a team in a group or orchestra, although they also work at home while practising.

Classical concerts usually last for about two hours, during which time the musicians must remain fully alert.

Most musicians travel long distances and spend lengthy periods away from home, either for performances or while touring, in the UK or abroad. Although they usually work with a group of people, it can be a very lonely life.

SKILLS AND INTERESTS

Musicians must be talented and completely dedicated to a career as a performer. A high degree of self-discipline and motivation is essential to practise as much as required. Patience is also important while acquiring the necessary skills. For pop musicians, an attractive or striking appearance can be an asset.

Musicians must be prepared to work as part of a team, and be willing to accept constructive criticism and disappointment. They must be able to cope with insecurity and a variable income. Good general health is important, as is self-confidence.

ENTRY REQUIREMENTS

It is possible to become a musician without formal qualifications, although this is particularly unlikely in classical music. (Most rock/pop musicians have little or no relevant training, currently.) The usual requirements for full-time music courses are as follows:

Performers' diploma courses

Entry requirements for these courses vary, and some do not specify traditional academic qualifications. Others look for five GCSEs/S grades (A–C/1–3), and possibly A level/H grade music. A high standard of musicianship is looked for, usually to grade 8 on the principal instrument, and grade 5 or 6 on the second. (Graded examinations are provided by organizations such as the Associated Board, Guildhall School of Music and Drama etc.) Entry is by audition, which may include playing a number of pieces on first and second instruments, sight reading, written and aural tests, and an interview. Competition for places is intense, and experience gained playing in a school or local orchestra is an advantage.

Graduate diploma courses

These courses are equivalent to degrees. Entry requirements vary between schools of music, but most ask for five GCSEs/S grades (A–C/1–3) and two A levels or 3 H grades, usually including music. Most look for grade 8 on the principal instrument and grade 6 on the second, tested at audition. Most courses also require a reasonable standard of keyboard skills (at least grade 3–5).

Degree courses

Five GCSEs/S grades (A–C/1–3) are needed, together with two A levels or three H grades, usually including music, or equivalent BTEC/national certificate course (music specific) pass. Auditions and interviews normally form part of the selection procedure.

Military bands

The Armed Forces (Royal Marines, Army and Royal Air Force) offer bursaries to students who have a place on a music course at a college of further or higher education, a university or a conservatoire, to study for three or four years for a nationally recognized diploma or degree. On completion of the training there is the possibility of a career in one of the Services' bands and orchestras. The Royal Marines and Army require most musicians to play both a wind and a stringed instrument. For more information, including minimum standards required, contact the local Armed Forces Careers Office.

TRAINING

In the field of classical music, most people start learning an instrument during childhood, by taking lessons either at school or privately. There are also a few specialist music schools that take musically gifted children, usually from around the age of eleven; they combine musical training with a traditional academic education. Choir schools take boys from the age of eight or nine years to train as choristers.

There are now many further and higher education courses available offering training in popular music. *The Music Education Yearbook* has detailed information on all courses, and the *Music Education Directory '97* available free from The British Phonographic Industry provides a list of courses in the contemporary music industry.

Musicians in the Armed Forces will be required to complete basic military and medical training after completion of their music course, to enable them to work as a serviceman/woman as required.

Performers' diploma courses

These courses are primarily aimed at training performers, and have limited academic content. They are run through specialist schools of music or conservatoires. Courses emphasize the development of performing skills, and students are expected to spend many hours practising. These courses usually lead to licentiate or associate qualifications, eg LRAM (Licentiate of the Royal Academy of Music).

Graduate diploma courses

These courses are also run through specialist schools of music or conservatoires, and are regarded as equivalent to degrees. They combine training for performance with academic study. Most such courses lead to qualifications with the word Graduate in their titles, eg GRSM (Graduate of the Royal Schools of Music).

Performers' courses last for three or four years. Although most time is devoted to a first study instrument, in most courses a second instrument must also be learned. Courses offer many opportunities to practise and perform in student groups and orchestras, and take classes with visiting professionals. There are many differences between

PERFORMING ARTS: GAB/GAF

courses, and applicants should check prospectuses carefully and visit institutions where possible.

Degree courses

Degree courses in music are also available at various colleges and universities. Many of these are academic, rather than strongly practical, and are not particularly aimed at training performers. Subjects studied may include history of music, musicology, methods of composition, musical analysis etc. All degree courses in music do, however, offer some opportunities for performance. It is possible to complete a degree in music, then go on to a specialist music school to train for performance.

Grants

All students on degree and graduate diploma courses are normally eligible for mandatory awards. Performers' diploma courses at schools of music rate only discretionary awards. The availability of discretionary awards varies across the country, and students should contact their local education authority for more information.

LATE ENTRY

It is very difficult for adults to train as musicians. Most adults who become professional musicians have already had considerable experience as amateurs. Most late opportunities are for singers, whose voices mature at a later age, and for those in the light music field, especially jazz, folk, country and western etc. The usual upper age limits for entry to the Armed Forces' Music Service are as follows: RAF – 27 years, Royal Marines – 28 years, and Army – 30 years.

OPPORTUNITIES

Music is probably the most overcrowded of all the performing arts, and competition for jobs is therefore intense. The number of permanent full-time jobs is very small, and mainly in the classical field. Most musicians take whatever work they can find, trying to make a living from several sources, while building up a reputation. They are often self-employed. Opportunities exist in the following areas:

Orchestral players

Around 1,500 full-time jobs exist in British orchestras, with only a small number of new openings coming up each year. Many of these are in London with orchestras such as the London Symphony Orchestra (LSO). The remainder are in other major cities, such as Glasgow and Birmingham. The BBC has its own orchestras based in London, Manchester, Wales and Scotland. Vacancies are advertised in the press, with selection based on interview and audition.

Some orchestras offer occasional freelance work, which can sometimes lead into more regular jobs. A high standard of sight-reading is required. Opportunities also exist within smaller ensembles; these also use musicians on a freelance basis. Occasionally, groups of enterprising students from music colleges set up their own self-financing ensemble, which provides valuable experience and sometimes leads on to paid bookings.

Soloists

There are even fewer opportunities for soloists than orchestral players, so it is even harder for them to make a living. Solo performers are generally engaged for a particular event or performance, and must have acquired a considerable reputation to be assured of regular work. Many soloists engage an agent who finds work and negotiates terms for them, in exchange for a percentage of their earnings.

Singers

A few opportunities exist for trained singers in opera, oratorio, sacred music, solo recitals and a variety of concert work, including light music and cabaret. Young singers often begin in a chorus, and can gain valuable experience with small touring companies. Many singers nowadays undergo training for musical theatre. Professional choirs, such as the BBC Singers, also recruit singers occasionally. Competition is fierce.

Pianists

Only the most outstanding performer can hope to make a career in solo recitals and concerts, and orchestras rarely use a full-time pianist. Some pianists find work in chamber groups or jazz ensembles, while others accompany dancers during rehearsals. A number are engaged by opera companies as repetiteurs, coaching singers and accompanying them on the piano during rehearsals.

Conductors

This is another extremely competitive field. In the past, conductors were usually also experienced performers, but nowadays some opportunities exist for younger people to enter this occupation directly. Regular competitions are held for young conductors (details in *Music Journal*), and some orchestras offer trainee conductorships with the chance to understudy experienced conductors.

Composers

Only a very few musicians make a full-time living from composing, and most are obliged to supplement their income by other work such as teaching. A fortunate few earn a living writing music for film, television, theatre, dance or TV commercials, but getting established is not easy, and luck, as well as talent, is needed. The Arts Council and regional arts associations provide some funds to commission new works.

Church music

Full-time paid opportunities are extremely limited, although the cathedrals employ organists and musical directors. Occasional work may be available with choral societies or by giving recitals.

Military bands

The Armed Forces (the Army, the RAF and the Royal Marines) offer musicians excellent training through their own schools of music. Military bandsmen and women travel overseas regularly. They perform all types of music from pop to classical. String and woodwind players are in particular demand.

Session work

Experienced musicians may be able to supplement their income by working sessions in a studio. They record music for films, television programmes, commercials and jingles, or backing tracks for singles and albums. Sessions are often held in the morning to allow performers time to do other work. Much of the work is in London.

Pop music

Many successful bands start as a group of friends playing together, perhaps at school or college, and first building a reputation locally. Most bands have a manager to deal with their business affairs and negotiate bookings and recording deals. Only a tiny number ever achieve fame and fortune,

PERFORMING ARTS: GAB/GAF

and the great majority, after brief success, quickly slip back into obscurity. Many bands are part-time ventures, with the members also doing other jobs, often unrelated to music.

Vacancies for orchestral players and singers are advertised in *Classical Music, Church Music Quarterly, Melody Maker, The Stage and Television Today, The Daily Telegraph* and *Music Journal*.

PAY AND CONDITIONS

Musicians receive payment for recorded work, either through royalties (whereby the artist receives a percentage payment for each record sold), or in a single payment. Musicians' pay, particularly at the start of their careers, may be very low.

For orchestral players in a 'continuing contract' orchestra such as the CBSO, Halle and RLPO, there are standard salary scales. Other symphony and chamber orchestras pay musicians on an ad hoc per-concert basis. The payments vary from £65 to £75. Musicians' Union casual engagement (gig) rates are a minimum of about £6 per half hour, with a minimum payment of about £30 for engagements up to two hours.

Rates for TV, radio and film performances are governed by often complex agreements. They depend on the length of time worked, and also on factors such as whether the performance is live. For example, rates for one hour of incidental music are around £140 per musician for a single episode or programme. Additional fees may be payable if the music is repeated over several episodes, or the programme repeated, or sold overseas.

Musicians in the Armed Forces generally enjoy greater job security than their civilian colleagues, and have a clear-cut career path that they can follow. An Army musician starts on a salary of around £10,000.

Most musicians work long, irregular hours. Performances are generally held during the evening and at weekends. While recording in a studio, musicians work very long hours; with pop musicians, in particular, this may be until midnight or later. Many musicians, particularly at the start of their careers, combine music with other jobs.

PROSPECTS

A musician's prospects depend on talent, good fortune and offering the public what they want. Being seen by the right people, and being in the right place at the right time, are also important. Competitions and prizes, such as those offered by the schools of music and the BBC, can greatly assist the winners' careers.

After further training, musicians can move into related fields, such as music therapy, teaching, or arts administration. Many people, having taken a degree in music, decide not to pursue a performing career.

Musicians in the Armed Forces may seek promotion within the service, or may elect to leave and further their career as civilians. According to the service, those wishing to leave early may be required to purchase their discharge at a price related to the length of time they have served. Musicians who have been on advanced training courses may be required to go on serving for a fixed period after completing the course to justify the expenditure that has been made on their musical education.

RELATED OCCUPATIONS

Music teacher, music therapist, dancer, actor, musical instrument tuner/technician, TV/radio producer, roadie.

FURTHER INFORMATION AND READING

Please see article 3. MUSIC TEACHER.

3. MUSIC TEACHER (GAD/FAB)

BACKGROUND INFORMATION

Music is increasingly recognized as having an important place in a well-rounded education. In schools, the availability of new technology, such as synthesizers, has contributed to a shift in music teaching away from traditional history and theory of music to practical music making and composition. School music teachers aim to foster children's creativity, as well as developing skills in areas such as communication and working as part of a team. They aim to develop in pupils greater discrimination in their appraisal of music, and introduce them to music of different times and cultures. Music is a foundation subject in the National Curriculum, which means it is taught to all children between the ages of 5 and 14 years.

Instrumental teachers are more concerned with developing performing skills on individual instruments to a high level. Many gain great satisfaction from passing on their skills and knowledge to a new generation of musicians.

THE WORK

Music teachers work in a variety of settings. They include the following:

School teaching

In nursery, infant and junior classes, music is often taught by the classroom teacher, but co-ordinated and led by a teacher responsible for music in the curriculum. Teachers (and particularly music co-ordinators) may also be involved in arranging school concerts, assemblies, recorder clubs etc.

Secondary schools usually have one or more full-time specialist music teachers who, as well as teaching in the classroom, organize and encourage the musical life of the school. Their work may include conducting choirs and orchestras, supervising school concerts and productions, and organizing schedules for visiting instrumental teachers. Classroom duties include teaching National Curriculum to age 14, GCSEs/S grades to age 16, and in some schools A level/H grade examinations.

Some teachers work on a part-time basis in schools, youth and specialist music centres, adult education institutes and further education colleges. Instrumental teachers may work in a number of schools, teaching individuals or groups of pupils, and occasionally organizing orchestras.

Private teaching

Private teachers work with people of all ages and abilities. They give lessons individually, or in small groups, and generally charge by the hour for their services. Some have national reputations and take on only the most talented students; others take anyone who is interested. They may combine this work with part-time teaching in a school, performing or composing.

PERFORMING ARTS: GAB/GAF

Other teaching

Teachers in music schools and colleges tend to be highly experienced and specialized, either in instrumental work or in the theoretical and historical aspects of music. Many are also accomplished performers and composers. Music is also taught at various levels in colleges and higher education institutions.

WORK ENVIRONMENT

Teachers work indoors in a variety of settings, including schools, colleges, higher education institutions, adult education institutes, youth clubs, arts centres, and many other places. The conditions are often, though not always, warm and comfortable. Since music teachers rarely work in purpose-designed accommodation, the acoustics are often poor. Many part-time and private teachers spend a lot of time travelling between pupils and schools.

SKILLS AND INTERESTS

A wish to share a love of music with other people is essential, combined with the desire to develop pupils' musical potential to the full. Patience is important to any teacher, and a broad appreciation of music in all its forms – popular and classical, European and other traditions – is essential. Because of their wide range of responsibilities, music teachers need to be well organized and good at managing their time. Good verbal communication skills are needed to work effectively with individual students and groups. Some music teachers are also performers, which gives a useful added dimension to their work.

Private teachers need to be self-motivated and resourceful, since they usually work alone. As most are self-employed, they need good business skills in areas such as budgeting, pricing and marketing their services.

ENTRY REQUIREMENTS

Music teachers working within state schools must have Qualified Teacher Status (QTS). Teachers in Scotland must be registered with the General Teaching Council for Scotland. In practice, peripatetic instrumental teachers may not be required to have QTS/Registered status.

Private teachers working independently are not legally required to possess qualifications in teaching or music, although they are advised to have appropriate qualifications. The standard qualifications are the teaching diplomas awarded by the music colleges, though performers' diplomas, graduate diplomas and music degrees may be acceptable. (Please see article 2. MUSICIAN.) The Incorporated Society of Musicians accepts only professionally qualified and experienced teachers for its Register of Professional Private Music Teachers.

Intending school teachers in England and Wales normally require a minimum of five GCSEs/S grades (A–C/1–3) with two A levels or three H grades for entry to a first degree course (for exact details see SCHOOL TEACHER CLCI:FAB). Music teachers in England and Wales are normally expected to have an A level or equivalent in music. In Scotland, H grade English, or equivalent, is required, and the Teaching Subject Qualifying Course (TSQC) requirements for music, which are degree level, include the study of music over at least three years, including study of a) theory elements, b) keyboard and c) an instrument or voice to an advanced standard.

Music teachers in higher education are usually required to hold a second degree, such as an MA or PhD in music. Requirements for applicants to further education teaching are variable, but similar to secondary teaching. A high standard of instrumental or vocal performance is normally required.

TRAINING

Full-time music teachers in state schools normally have followed a course of initial teacher training (ITT) leading to Qualified Teacher Status (QTS), or, in Scotland, Registration. The two most common ways of qualifying are as follows:

1. Completion of a three- or four-year graduate diploma or degree in Music at a conservatoire or university (please see article 2. MUSICIAN for more information). This must be followed by a Postgraduate Certificate of Education (PGCE), which usually lasts about 36 weeks, and 18 months part-time through the Open University. PGCE courses are offered at a large number of universities and colleges in England and Wales and two institutions in Scotland.

2. Completion of a four-year teaching degree course, either Bachelor of Education (BEd) or Bachelor of Arts (BA), with Qualified Teacher Status. Study of music at an advanced level is combined with the theory and practice of teaching. Courses such as these are generally seen as more suitable for people intending to make a career in primary school teaching. There are few institutions in the UK offering secondary school teacher training with music. At primary level, music is normally offered alongside other subjects.

The situation in Scotland differs from that above in a number of ways. Rather than QTS, intending teachers must gain a recognized Teaching Qualification (TQ). They must then complete two years' satisfactory service as probationary teachers before being granted full registration with the General Teaching Council for Scotland. Both one-year PGCE and four- year BEd courses are available in Scotland, but they are designated as qualifying the student to teach specifically in primary or secondary education. It is generally harder for teachers in Scotland to switch between primary and secondary school teaching. Further information is available from the Teacher Education Institutions or the Education and Industry Department of The Scottish Office.

Employment-based teacher training

From September 1997 the Graduate Teacher Programme provides one-year training for graduates who do not want to follow traditional routes. The Registered Teacher Scheme in England and Wales continues to provide two-years training for people aged 24 or over, with two years' successful full-time higher education experience and GCSEs (grade A–C) in maths and English (and science for primary teachers born on or after 1st September 1979). Not all employers operate work-based training, and many of those who do may only have a limited number of places available. A similar programme operates for registered teachers in City Technology Colleges. In Scotland, acceptance of teachers who have successfully completed the work-based route will depend on an evaluation of the individual's training scheme.

Teacher training courses are listed in the *British Music Education Yearbook,* published by Rhinegold Publishing.

Music teachers in independent schools may not require QTS.

PERFORMING ARTS: GAB/GAF

Instrumental and private teaching.

The usual qualification for an instrumental teacher is a teaching diploma awarded by a conservatoire. These courses are similar to the performers' diploma courses described in article 2. MUSICIAN, but include modules in teaching, rather than performance. Most such teachers work as part-time instrumental teachers in schools, or as private teachers, and will have had a performance-biased main training.

LATE ENTRY

Some music schools and conservatoires are reluctant to take instrumentalists over the age of 20 years, while singers are often preferred between the ages of 20 and 24, as the voice matures later. Musical talent, apart from singing, often emerges early. Most institutions offering BEd or BA with QTS courses are willing to consider applications from adults without the normal entry requirements, since maturity is a definite asset in teaching. Some colleges offer a specially shortened two-year BEd course in music for people with substantial experience and advanced qualifications in music, or a related subject.

Colleges look for evidence of considerable musical ability, and may request graded examination passes. They also like to see evidence of recent study, which may be gained via an Access course. These provide a bridge to higher education for people without the normal academic entry qualifications.

OPPORTUNITIES

Opportunities for school music teachers exist within both the state and independent sectors. A few posts are available for working with people with special needs, both in schools and other institutions. There is currently an acute shortage of music teachers in state schools. Vacancies are advertised in the *Times Educational Supplement* and other national newspapers, and the monthly magazines *Music Teacher* and *Music Journal*.

There are a small number of opportunities for music teachers in universities, colleges and music schools. As well as teaching, some research may be required. Competition for such vacancies is intense.

Anyone may set themselves up as a private music teacher, although those registered with the Incorporated Society of Musicians (ISM) are required to meet certain professional standards.

PAY AND CONDITIONS

Rates of pay for full-time music teachers in schools and part-time instrumental teachers are generally governed by national regulations and recommendations, based on qualifications and types of employment. Visiting instrumental and singing teachers working in maintained and independent schools earn around £14 to £20 an hour, according to experience. The ISM recommends its newly qualified registered private teachers charge £15.90 to £16.80 an hour for individual tuition. A shared lesson, with four pupils, earns a minimum fee of one-and-a-half times the individual rate. Private teachers set their own rates, and some charge considerably more than those quoted.

Teachers in maintained schools in England and Wales are paid on a nationally agreed spine. Salaries for good honours graduates start from £15,012. In Scotland, a new teacher earns a minimum starting salary of £13,305. Salaries within the private sector vary between schools.

Music teachers in schools work normal school hours, although they regularly give up time during lunch-breaks and after school to organize additional musical activities. In addition, they have to spend some time at evenings and weekends marking work, preparing lessons and writing arrangements. Private teachers often work during the evenings and weekends (outside normal school/working hours).

PROSPECTS

School music departments are generally small, so there are good prospects of promotion to head of department. More senior jobs may involve a greater proportion of administration, with less time devoted solely to teaching. While continuing their work in school, some teachers develop their careers by conducting a local choir or orchestra. Experienced music teachers may become examiners for one of the main boards, or adjudicators in musical competitions. Others go on to become school headteachers and deputy heads – these are predominantly management posts, and may involve little actual teaching.

RELATED OCCUPATIONS

Teacher, musician, music therapist, actor, dancer, musical instrument technician, arts administrator.

FURTHER INFORMATION

Arts Council of Great Britain*, 14 Great Peter Street, London SW1P 3NQ, 0171 973 6450

British Actors' Equity Association*, Guild House, Upper St Martin's Lane, London WC2 9EG, 0171 379 6000, www.equity.org.uk

British Phonographic Industry Ltd (BPI)*, 25 Savile Row, London W1X 1AA, 0171 287 4422, www.bpi.co.uk

British Broadcasting Corporation*, PO Box 7000, London W5 2WY, 0181 752 5252

Department for Education and Employment*, Sanctuary Buildings, Great Smith Street, Westminster, London SW1P 3BT, 0171 925 5000, www.dfee.gov.uk

Directorate of Naval Recruiting*, Royal Marines School of Music, HMS Nelson, Portsmouth, Hampshire PO1 3LS, 01705 727753

Education and Industry Department, The Scottish Office, Floor 3G West, Victoria Quay, Edinburgh EH6 6QQ, 0131 244 0964, www.scotland.gov.uk

Incorporated Society of Musicians*, 10 Stratford Place, London W1N 9AE, 0171 629 4413, http://www.ism.org

Musicians' Union*, 60–64 Clapham Road, London SW9 0JJ, 0171 582 5566 (please send sae)

National Music and Disability Information Service (Sound Sense)*, Riverside House, Rattlesden, Bury St Edmunds IP30 0SF, 01449 736287 (please include sae), ourworld.compuserve.com/homepages/soundsens

RAF School of Music*, Royal Air Force, Uxbridge, Middlesex UB10 0RZ, 01895 237144 ext 6345/6478

Rhinegold Publishing Ltd, 241 Shaftesbury Avenue, London WC2H 8EH, 0171 333 1736

Royal Military School of Music*, Cleveland Lodge, Westhumble, Dorking, Surrey RH5 6BW, 01306 877676

PERFORMING ARTS: GAB/GAF

The Teacher Training Agency, Communication Centre*, PO Box 3210, Chelmsford, Essex, CM1 3WA, 01245 454454, http://www.teach.org

FURTHER READING

Leaflets/booklets are available from the addresses marked*.

Working in Music – COIC

Working in Performing Arts – COIC

British Music Yearbook – Rhinegold

Music Teachers' Yearbook – Rhinegold

Degree Course Guide – Music – CRAC

Periodicals: Music Journal; Music Teacher.

In the careers library classified under GAD.

4. DANCER (GAF)

BACKGROUND INFORMATION

The life of a dancer can seem glamorous and exciting. While this may be true for a minority, the reality of gruelling daily exercise, combined with evening performances, is somewhat different. Although trained dancers may find it easier to get work than actors or musicians, the field is still highly competitive, and many dancers face periods of unemployment during their careers. At all times, however, dancers must keep their bodies in peak condition, exercising regularly and following a healthy eating plan. Few dancers make a fortune, and most face financial uncertainty throughout their lives. A dancer's working life is short: most retire from performing at around 35, or earlier if they suffer injury. Dancers need talent, stamina and a complete dedication to their art.

THE WORK

Dance is a performing art; dancers use their bodies to communicate creatively with an audience. The movements are usually directed by a choreographer, although they are occasionally devised by the dancers themselves. Dancers use their movements to portray a role without using words. In classical dance, the story is often obvious; in more modern work the story (if one exists) may not be immediately recognizable to an audience. Dancers spend only a small amount of their time actually performing; much more time is spent practising, exercising, taking classes and rehearsing. Even if they are unemployed, dancers must keep up with their exercise regime.

Classical ballet is one of the most demanding and precise forms of dance, and training generally begins at an early age, before the body is fully developed. Contemporary, or modern, dance is less formal and more experimental, with a wide and varying repertoire; it is often performed barefoot. Modern stage dance covers a wide range of dance styles, including tap. It originally developed in the variety theatre and stage musicals, and can also be seen today in television and films. Disco dancing is a more recent development, associated with modern pop music. A growing number of opportunities exist in night-clubs, films, promotional videos etc, though mostly on part-time or short-term contracts. Social dance is performed mainly for the pleasure of those taking part, rather than for an audience. It includes the many forms of ballroom dancing, as well as folk and country dance.

Opportunities in social dance are mainly confined to teaching. Finally, non-western dance is an area of growing importance in the UK. It includes South Asian and African dance. South Asian dance, in particular, is very demanding, involving a wide range of formalized movements, which may take many years to learn and master.

The majority of dancers work in a group or company, such as a *corps de ballet*, chorus line or dance troupe. Members of the company support and depend on each other, and may enjoy a greater degree of stability in their working lives than their colleagues in the other performing arts. There are some opportunities to become a solo dancer, especially in non-western forms of dance.

Music is important in all forms of dance, and most dance is performed to it. In some areas, such as musical theatre, performers sing and act, as well as dance.

WORK ENVIRONMENT

Dancers work in a variety of settings, including theatres, film and TV studios, night-clubs, restaurants and hotels, summer shows at holiday resorts, circuses and Christmas pantomimes. The increase in community arts has extended dance beyond traditional venues, to places that offer access to a wider audience, including church and community halls, arts centres, art galleries, parks and schools.

Venues are usually warm, but dancers spend much of their time in rehearsal rooms, which may be cold and draughty. Dancers must make sure that cold conditions do not cause muscle strain, so they wear layers of clothing which may be discarded as they warm up.

Dancing places tremendous demands on the body, and these are probably greatest in ballet. Many dancers have painful feet from dancing on points, and they may also suffer from orthopaedic problems.

Dancers work away from home when on tour, and the working hours may be longer than usual. While working, dancers' social lives can suffer, as performances are normally held in the evenings.

SKILLS AND INTERESTS

Talent is essential to succeed in a profession where competition is intense. In addition, dancers must have a well-proportioned body, strong legs and back, good general health and a high standard of physical fitness. They need stamina and resilience to cope with the mental and physical stresses of dancing, and a high degree of commitment and motivation.

Dancers must be tough, persistent and hard working, quick to learn, creative, intelligent and imaginative. They also need a retentive memory to learn and memorize complex sequences of movements, together with good powers of concentration. A good sense of rhythm and timing is important. Dancers with musical or acting skills may have improved job prospects. Those wishing to teach dance need patience and good verbal communication skills.

ENTRY REQUIREMENTS

There are no minimum academic entry requirements for most performers' courses in dance, though some require specific passes in relevant dance examinations. Entry to most courses is via audition, which normally involves participation in one or more classes, and sometimes the presentation of a solo piece. Some colleges give a music aural test, and may ask for a written explanation of why the student wants to dance. Candidates are given a medical examination.

Ballet dancers must be well-proportioned, with a good line, attractive appearance and a very high standard of fitness. Women should be from 1.52 metres to 1.65 metres (5 feet to 5 feet 5 inches), and men from 1.6 metres to 1.78 metres (5 feet 3 inches to 5 feet 10 inches). A background in ballet is useful for all dancers, although it is not essential for contemporary dance. Some contemporary schools look for potential and suitability for dancing, if the candidate has not had much chance to take lessons.

Teaching courses for the private sector do not generally require specific academic entry qualifications (though these are welcomed and encouraged, and will be introduced over the next couple of years). Candidates are expected to have achieved a high standard of performance, with passes in graded examinations in the case of theatre dance, or medals up to the third gold bar in the case of social dance.

Degree courses often ask for previous practical experience in dance, along with minimum educational requirements of five GCSEs/S grades (A–C/1–3) with two A levels or three H grades, or equivalent. The BTEC National Diploma in Performing Arts is not widely acceptable as an alternative to A levels or H grades, and prospective students should check this with individual institutions. Applicants for degrees leading to Qualified Teacher Status (BEd or BA with QTS) must also have maths and English at GCSE/S grade (A–C/1–3). Maths at GCSE/S grade (A–C/1–3) and H grade English or equivalent is required for applicants to BEd degree courses in Scotland. There is intense competition for most courses. Foundation, Intermediate and Advanced GNVQs/GSVQs Levels I, II and III in Performing Arts and Entertainment Industries are available.

Most of the leading examining bodies in dance-teaching operate registration schemes. In order to be registered, dance teachers must be qualified, with passes in specific examinations covering practical, theoretical and historical aspects of dance. Only registered teachers are allowed to enter candidates for some of the major examination societies – these include the Royal Academy of Dancing, the Imperial Society of Teachers of Dancing, the British Ballet Organization, The British Theatre Dance Association and the Cecchetti Society.

The Council for Dance Education and Training (CDET) has set up a national register and a directory of dance teachers. As this becomes established, it will become increasingly difficult for unqualified dance teachers to find work in theatre dance. In the private sector, teachers normally require a qualification from an organization that is a member of either CDET, the Stage Dance Council or the British Council of Ballroom Dancing.

TRAINING

Formal full-time training in dance is essential for anyone wishing to work as a performer, and is preferable for a teacher. Many dancers start their training by attending part-time classes as children, often taking a series of graded examinations. The ideal age to begin ballet training is around eight to ten years, since at this age the bones and joints are still flexible. Ballet dancers must normally have started to train by the age of twelve at the latest, for girls, and 14 for boys.

Several schools accept pupils from around the age of eleven, offering them a dance training alongside traditional academic subjects. It is also possible to learn dance at a stage or theatre school, often as part of a general theatre training that includes acting and music. Standards vary between schools, and it is advisable to check a school's standing with the Council for Dance Education and Training.

Most professional training for dancers takes place after leaving school. Performers' courses at independent vocational schools typically last three years, though a few are shorter. The Council for Dance Education and Training recognizes various courses as being of a suitably high standard for performers, and will supply a list of accredited courses on receipt of an SAE. Most courses lead to a diploma or certificate awarded by the school, but five vocational schools offer degree courses in dance: the Laban Centre for Movement and Dance (BA Honours Degree in Dance Theatre), the Northern School of Contemporary Dance (Bachelor of Performing Arts (Dance) Degree), the London Contemporary Dance School (BA Honours Degrees in Contemporary Dance), London Studio Centre (Theatre Dance (BA Hons)), and Doreen Bird College (Dance and Theatre Performance (BA Hons)). These courses are validated by universities and accredited by CDET.

Course content varies between schools, but often includes ballet, modern theatre dance, jazz and contemporary dance, other dance forms from countries such as Greece, Spain, Africa and India, tap dance and choreography. Practical classes are supplemented by the theoretical study of anatomy, dance history and dance notation, as well as make-up and stagecraft. Music, drama and singing feature in many courses.

Courses specializing in contemporary dance often include choreography. In many schools, students stage a production at the end of the course, giving them experience in all aspects of dance administration and stage management, as well as the actual performing.

Degree courses, including dance, are available at over 30 colleges, institutions of higher education and universities across the UK (again, a list is available from CDET). Many courses lead to a BA honours degree, but they vary considerably in emphasis. This is reflected in the course names, which include dance, performing arts, human movement studies, creative arts, and others. Courses vary in the balance between practical work and academic study, though all include some practical dance. They are not, however, primarily aimed at training performers, and do not provide the intensive vocational training offered by the independent schools. There is now a SQA Higher National Certificate in Dance (Community) at Edinburgh's Telford College, and SQA National Certificate courses are also available in Scotland in Performing Arts – Dance, and Dance and Exercise Studies.

Those intending to teach dance in schools or colleges can study for a BEd degree or PGCE, specializing in dance, at a number of colleges, institutions of higher education and universities. The College of the Royal Academy of Dancing also offers a specialist accredited dance teacher training course – BA (Hons) The Art and Teaching of Ballet.

Grants

Students on degree courses at universities receive mandatory grants, but those on non-degree and degree performers' courses are eligible only for discretionary

PERFORMING ARTS: GAB/GAF

awards. The two exceptions to this are students on the degree course at the Northern School of Contemporary Dance, and those students under 19 years of age at the Rambert School. In some cases LEAs may agree to pay tuition fees only, leaving the student to fund day-to-day expenses from other sources. It is advisable to contact your LEA early on to find out their position on discretionary awards for dance courses.

From October 1997 Lottery funding has been available for independent, self-financing dance and drama schools that offer two- and three-year dance and drama courses, and two-year stage management courses accredited by either the Council for Dance Education and Training (CDET) or the National Council for Drama Training (NCDT).

It is a temporary, interim solution, covering the entire course of two intakes of students – those who started their training in Autumn 1997 and those who start their training in Autumn 1998. It has been developed by the Arts Council of England in partnership with the Council of Local Education Authorities, the Department for Education and Employment and others, with the expectation that central Government will implement a permanent solution.

Please note: *Grants are not available to individual students but to colleges only.*

Dance and drama students should discuss with their college the possibility of reduced fees. To qualify, students will need to have secured a place at an accredited college and have been awarded a discretionary grant by their local education authority.

Funding in Scotland is also available for higher national certificate/diploma courses.

LATE ENTRY

Opportunities for mature students to train as professional dancers are almost non-existent, since dance training normally starts in the teens (and earlier for ballet). Adults up to the age of 30 may occasionally be accepted for contemporary dance training. It is possible for adults with some dance experience to train in dance therapy or community dance.

OPPORTUNITIES

Dance teaching offers more employment opportunities than performing. Dance teachers working in state primary and secondary schools are qualified teachers who specialize in dance; most teach other subjects as well. Dance is now included as part of physical education within the National Curriculum, which may lead to some growth in demand for dance teachers in schools. Outside the state sector there are numerous dance schools and studios in the UK offering recreational classes as well as more-formal training. Some teachers with sufficient financial resources set up their own schools, while others work in several locations, including adult education institutes and youth centres.

Ballet is a highly competitive area, with jobs in the Birmingham Royal Ballet and the Royal Ballet normally going to former students of the Royal Ballet Upper School. Opportunities also exist with the English National Ballet and Northern Ballet Theatre. There are a handful of other smaller ballet companies in the UK, and British-trained dancers may find work abroad, especially in continental Europe.

Contemporary dance is an expanding area, due partly to the recent growth in community dance. Because of the intense competition for jobs in established companies, dance schools encourage students to use their initiative and set up their own dance groups, either self-financing or occasionally grant-aided by the Arts Council or Regional Arts Boards. Such groups usually work for short seasons, after which the dancers must either find other work, or face periods of unemployment.

Musical theatre and cabaret is a major source of employment for dancers. Opportunities include working in night-clubs, on cruise ships, in circuses, in pantomimes and in West End musicals.

Non-western dance, including South Asian and African dance, is an area where opportunities are increasing. Employment is mainly in dance groups, though in South Asian dance, in particular, there are also opportunities for solo performers.

Ballroom dancing provides a few couples with the opportunity to make a living by giving dance demonstrations and appearing in cabaret. The majority of opportunities in this area, however, are in teaching.

Opera often employs choreographers and dancers, for example at the Royal Opera House, English National Opera and Scottish Opera. Employment is usually for one particular production.

Ice dancing combines dance with ice skating. In recent years it has become a popular form of mass entertainment. Ice dancing is a competitive amateur sport, and many competitors, once their competing days are over, make the move to ice dancing professionally. Ice dancers are sometimes required to perform in costume.

Dance-in-education involves visits to schools and colleges by dance companies to encourage students to enjoy watching and performing dance. As well as dancers, some larger companies also employ education officers.

Community dance is a growing field: dancers are employed, usually by local authorities, to encourage the development of dance in specific areas. They sometimes teach classes themselves, and also organize workshops and classes for a variety of groups in the community, including children, adults, elderly people, and those with special needs.

Choreography is a difficult area to break into. Traditionally, it was the preserve of older, experienced dancers, but there are now younger choreographers who may combine this with an active performing career. There are several choreographer-led companies successfully touring the UK.

Notators/reconstructors use one of the two established systems of notation, Benesh or Labanotation, to record the movements of a dance so that it can be reconstructed by other dancers.

Dance/movement therapy is still relatively new to the UK. The therapeutic effects of dance are used to help people in need, due to physical disability, emotional disturbance etc.

PAY AND CONDITIONS

Minimum salaries for dancers are negotiated by Equity and depend on the type, length and location of the job. For example, a member of the *corps de ballet* at The Royal Ballet earns about £267.20 a week in the first year, rising to £334.17 in the fifth year. A soloist earns £440.89 a week, and a principal £584.48. All grades receive an additional £16.65 for classes. Salaries for most other companies are below Royal Ballet rates. Most contemporary dancers in subsidized productions earn £200-£300 a week.

Dancers in their own groups may be paid on a profit-share basis. Dancers with non-Equity jobs, such as working in some night-clubs, may have to live on a very low income. Dance teachers in schools and adult education are paid at standard teaching rates. Teachers at private dance schools may receive a low basic salary supplemented by commission on lessons taken.

Working hours are long and hard for dancers, and regularly include evenings and weekends. Dancers at The Royal Ballet spend at least 33 hours a week in rehearsals and performances, with a minimum of four additional hours in classes.

PROSPECTS

Even if dancers are fortunate enough to obtain a job with a top ballet company, they start at the bottom of the ladder and face keen competition for promotion. Most ballet dancers remain members of the *corps de ballet*. Only a minority go on to become soloists or principals. There are only a very few permanent ballet companies, and a number of ballet dancers move on to contemporary dance, which is a growth area.

The life of a performer in dance is a short one. Few go on beyond the age of 35, and only in very exceptional cases is there much chance of working as a performer after 40 years of age. Ex-dancers often move on to careers in teaching, lecturing, choreography, or arts administration. Performers and teachers can improve their prospects by further study, perhaps for a degree, or for a specialist diploma in choreography, notation, special education, teaching, community dance or dance therapy.

RELATED OCCUPATIONS

Choreographer, dance teacher, actor, singer, musician, dance therapist, health and fitness instructor.

FURTHER INFORMATION

ADiTi, The National Organization of South Asian Dance*, 3rd floor, Oldbourne House, 46–47 Chancery Lane, London WC2A 1JB, 0171 831 5288

Arts Council of Great Britain*, 14 Great Peter Street, London SW1P 3NQ, 0171 973 6450

British Actors' Equity Association, Guild House, Upper St Martin's Lane, London WC2 9EG, 0171 379 6000, www.equity.org.uk

British Ballet Organization*, Woolborough House, 39 Lonsdale Road, Barnes, London SW13 9JP, 0181 748 1241

British Council of Ballroom Dancing, 240 Merton Road, South Wimbledon, London SW19 1EQ, 0181 545 0085

Council for Dance Education and Training (UK)*, Riverside Studios, Crisp Road, London W6 9RL, 0181 741 5084 (please include sae)

Dance UK, 23 Crisp Road, London W6 9RL, 0181 741 1932

Imperial Society of Teachers of Dancing*, Imperial House, 22–26 Paul Street, London EC2A 4QE, 0171 377 1577

International Dance Teachers Association*, 76 Bennett Road, Brighton BN2 5JL, 01273 685652

National Resource Centre for Dance*, University of Surrey, Guildford, Surrey GU2 5XH, 01483 259316

Royal Academy of Dancing*, 36 Battersea Square, London SW11 3RA, 0171 223 0091

Stage Dance Council International, 113 Braemar Road, Fallowfield, Manchester M14 6PQ, 0161 224 5231

FURTHER READING

Leaflets/booklets are available from the addresses marked*.

Working In Performing Arts – COIC

Periodicals: Ballroom Dancing Times; Dance and Dancers; Dance News; Dance Theatre Journal; Dancing Times.

A wide range of resource packs, videos, catalogues and directories is available from the National Resource Centre for Dance.

In the careers library classified under GAF.

SPORTS AND LEISURE: GAG/GAJ

1. **SPORTS COACH/INSTRUCTOR CLCI:GAG**
2. **PROFESSIONAL SPORTSMAN/WOMAN CLCI:GAG**
3. **SPORTS AND LEISURE CENTRE MANAGER CLCI:GAJ**
4. **SPORTS AND LEISURE CENTRE ASSISTANT CLCI:GAJ**

BACKGROUND INFORMATION

Leisure is a growth industry. In Britain it now employs over 400,000 people, making it a larger source of employment than many traditional industries, such as chemicals or agriculture.

The leisure industry caters for the entire population, offering a wide range of sports and other forms of recreation. In recent years there has been a big increase in the demand for leisure facilities.

Sport is part of the leisure industry, but professional sportsmen/women make up only a tiny proportion of those working in leisure. Many more work as sports coaches/instructors, or as assistants and managers at sports and leisure centres. These have undergone a boom over the last 20 years or so. Many centres are operated by local councils as a service for the community; many others have been opened as commercial enterprises. All these centres need managers and assistants to run them, and coaches and instructors to take classes and supervise activities.

Millions of people take part regularly in sport. Some are professionals who are paid for what they do, but many more are amateurs who are involved in sport purely as a recreation. Whether amateur or professional, most participants need the help of coaches and instructors to learn the sport, improve their skills and perform to the best of their ability.

1. SPORTS COACH/INSTRUCTOR (GAG)

THE WORK

Large numbers of coaches and instructors are needed to assist the millions of people who regularly participate in sport. Everyone taking up a sport needs someone to show them the skills and techniques, and, if they prove to have an aptitude, to help them develop their talents. Even in professional sport, however, full-time jobs are scarce. Many coaches are self-employed or employed part-time, and may combine coaching with another part-time or full-time job. Many others are amateurs, working in their spare time for love of their sport. Coaches and instructors teach the skills and techniques of one particular sport, or a few related ones, to a wide range of people, from beginners to experts.

Coaches in professional sport

Coaches who work with professional sportsmen/women have to devise a training programme that develops individuals to the full and gets them in peak condition at the right moment. They monitor performance and technique carefully, and point out where and how further improvements may be made. Coaches may also become involved on the administrative side, sorting out problems with equipment, and arranging accommodation, transport etc.

Team coaches have to mould their players into an effective team by developing individual skills to the full and teaching team tactics. They use videos to explain techniques and strategies, and to analyse the performance of the team and their opponents. They may also use blackboards or overhead projectors to illustrate points. Team coaches work closely with managers, for example in selecting the members of a team for a particular match or contest.

Coaches/instructors in amateur sport

Coaches and instructors in amateur sport may work with anyone, from a complete beginner to an Olympic athlete. It is very important that beginners, even those who see sport primarily as a form of recreation, are taught the right techniques from the start; bad habits are hard to break, and bad techniques can lead to injury. Coaches have to see that sportsmen/women train safely and know their own capabilities.

It is part of a coach's job to motivate sportsmen/women, and this can involve thinking up interesting and varied ways of practising the same activity over and over again. Those who coach top-level performers must devise training programmes that will have their sportsmen/women in top mental and physical condition on the right day. Sometimes they have to be prepared to pass their trainees on to another coach who can do more for them.

Every sport, amateur or professional, has its governing body and its own rules and regulations. Coaches must be familiar with these, so that they can teach them to competitors and ensure that they stay within the rules.

Health and fitness instructors

Health and fitness instructors deliver training in aerobics, keep fit, weight training and other forms of exercise at privately run health and fitness centres and local authority sports centres. Their work includes assessing clients' levels of fitness when they arrive at the centre, and devising a programme of training that is neither too easy for them nor too demanding. They must be aware of the health and safety aspects of different forms of exercise, and prevent clients from injuring themselves by working too hard or using faulty techniques.

A few health and fitness instructors work with clients on a one-to-one basis, visiting them in their homes and workplaces, and planning and monitoring a personal fitness schedule for them.

WORK ENVIRONMENT

Coaches and instructors may work in gymnasiums, sports centres, sports clubs, health clubs, outdoor pursuits centres, on playing fields etc. They may have to work outside in all weathers and spend long hours at matches and training sessions. They are likely to have to stand for long periods, and may expend considerable amounts of energy when taking part in training sessions. Those involved in professional, or serious amateur sport, are likely to have to travel a great deal to specialist training facilities, competitions and matches all over the UK and abroad.

SKILLS AND INTERESTS

Coaches and instructors must be enthusiastic about their sport, and have an in-depth knowledge and understanding of it. They must want to help people achieve their full potential, and this means finding the right approach for each individual. They must understand how to motivate people and encourage them to persevere – not always easy when things are not going well. They need patience and tact when teaching new skills and techniques. Good verbal communication skills are required, for example, when explaining where a performer may be going wrong and how they can improve.

Coaches and instructors must be able to teach, but they need not be exceptional at the sport themselves. They should inspire confidence, so need considerable expertise in their speciality and should set a good example in their appearance and behaviour. Good organizational skills are also desirable, for example, when arranging visits to sporting events in other parts of the UK or the world.

ENTRY REQUIREMENTS

No formal academic qualifications are required, but individuals must have experience in their sport and the relevant governing body coaching qualifications.

Applicants to go on coaching courses must normally be at least 18 years, and may be required to hold a first aid certificate.

It is also possible to obtain coaching qualifications as part of a broader programme of study. The options here include NEBSM (National Examining Board for Supervisory Management) courses, BTEC/SQA Higher National Certificate/Diploma courses in Leisure Studies, or the Diploma in Youth and Community work, and degree courses in subjects such as sports or movement science.

There are no specific academic entry requirements for NEBSM, though applicants are expected to show some evidence of previous academic achievement. For the BTEC/SQA Higher National Certificate/Diploma in Leisure Studies, applicants must hold four GCSEs/S grades (A–C/1–3), including one A level/two H grades, or equivalent.

Minimum entry requirements for a degree course are five GCSEs/S grades (A–C/1–3) with two A levels/three H grades, or equivalent. For a BEd or BA with Qualified Teacher Status, GCSEs/S grades (A–C/1–3) in English and maths are also required.

Entry requirements for a Diploma in Youth and Community Work (England and Wales) are age 23+, relevant experience and five GCSEs/S grades (A–C/1–3) or equivalent.

Entry requirements for a Diploma in Youth and Community Work (Scotland) are age 18+, four S grades (1–3) and two H grades, including English.

Modern Apprenticeships (part of the Skillseekers Initiative in Scotland) may be available for young people leading to at least an NVQ/SVQ Level 3. Contact your local careers office, Jobcentre, TEC/LEC for details.

TRAINING

To become a qualified coach or instructor in a particular sport it is necessary to take the coaching awards offered in that sport. These are administered by the national governing body of the sport, and are usually achieved through part-time study. Alternatively, it is possible to gain suitable qualifications by completing a college or university course, in which coaching awards have been incorporated within a broader programme of studies. Such courses include some NEBSM and BTEC/SQA Higher National Certificate and Diploma courses in Leisure Studies, and degree courses in sports science, movement studies or physical education. The National Coaching Foundation (NCF) also runs a programme of generic coaching courses and workshops, at all levels from introductory to advanced, including a Diploma in Sports Coaching.

A number of new qualifications in sports coaching are currently being offered. These include The National Coaching Foundation Introductory Coach Education Award and the Certificate in Coach Education. These qualifications are being offered at a limited number of colleges and institutes of further and higher education – further advice is available from the NCF.

The Introductory Coach Education Award incorporates an NGB (National Governing Body) Leader's Award, and the Certificate in Coach Education is an award at NVQ/SVQ Level 2.

NVQs/SVQs are available in Sport, Recreation and Allied Industries, including Coaching, Teaching and Instructing at Levels 1, 2 and 3. NVQs/SVQs are only available in the context of certain sports/activities. Information on which contexts are available can be obtained from the NCF. A Modern Apprenticeship is available in Sports and Recreation, and for further details you should contact your local TEC/LEC or careers office.

Universities throughout the UK offer both BA degree courses in Sport and Recreation Studies, and BSc in Exercise and Sports Sciences, some of which include coaching studies elements.

The training for sports coaches and instructors varies widely from sport to sport, and according to the type of client worked with.

Professional golf

Professional golfers usually coach for a club or are full-time competitors. Those who have been registered for three years with the Professional Golfers' Association (PGA) may follow a residential course and, on passing the PGA's tests, become members and apply for professional jobs.

Swimming

The Swimming Teachers' Association and Amateur Swimming Association (ASA) offer teaching and coaching qualifications. Student membership of the Swimming Teachers' Association requires a pass in the student examination for young people aged 16 to 18 years. Associate membership requires a pass in the Swimming Teachers' Certificate, and a Royal Life Saving Society bronze medallion. Candidates for this must be 18 years or over. There are further exams leading to qualified member and diploma member status. The ASA offers a Preliminary Teachers' Certificate, Teachers' Certificate for Swimming and Advanced Teachers' Certificate for Swimming.

Mountain leaders

Applicants to the certificate course must be over 18 years and hold a first aid certificate. To obtain the certificate, applicants must keep an expedition logbook, assist a qualified mountain leader and pass practical and written tests in map reading, rescue work and equipment selection. Certificate holders can go on to take the instructors' certificate or the advanced certificate.

Health and fitness instructors

Health and fitness instructors must hold recognized qualifications, such as the RSA/Sports Council-validated Basic Certificate in the Teaching of Exercise to Music, or the British Amateur Weightlifters' Association Instructors'

SPORTS AND LEISURE: GAG/GAJ

Certificate. Qualifications in more traditional types of exercise are offered by The Keep Fit Association. The Physical Education Association offers a Certificate in Exercise and Health Studies, and the YMCA a variety of modular courses in exercise and fitness.

Outdoor pursuits instructors

Outdoor pursuits instructors must have gained instructor awards in a range of sports such as climbing, canoeing and mountaineering. They must also have considerable practical experience.

Youth and community workers

Some coaches and instructors are qualified youth and community workers. In England and Wales, courses take two years; in Scotland they take three, though exemption from the first year is granted to those with relevant experience. Such courses may include the opportunity to take coaching qualifications – these include the Community Sports Leaders Award (CSLA), and the CCPR's Hanson Leadership Award and Basic Expedition Training Award.

PE teachers

Some BEd courses offer specialization in outdoor pursuits, or youth and community work.

Armed Forces

The awards offered by the Armed Forces are the same as those recognized by civilian sporting bodies. Only the RAF takes recruits to train as PT instructors. The Army and Royal Navy recruit instructors from their serving members.

LATE ENTRY

Most people who go into coaching are older entrants from professional or serious amateur sport. Maturity is usually an asset in coaching and most sports bodies have a minimum age limit of 18 years or more. Opportunities depend on physical fitness and abilities, rather than academic qualifications. Entry requirements for the Diploma in Youth and Community Work course may be waived for mature applicants with relevant experience.

OPPORTUNITIES

Full-time paid jobs are very scarce. Professional sport is extremely competitive, and coaches tend to be judged by results. Many coaches and instructors also do administrative and other work. Many are self-employed, giving private lessons to individuals; many others are volunteers who work in sports clubs, with local and national teams, in amateur sports etc. There are openings for paid part-timers who coach and instruct in the evenings and weekends. If they have several such jobs and build up a reputation, they may then become self-employed, or they may get full-time jobs, either just coaching, or doing other management or administrative work, for example in sports centres.

There are paid jobs as national coaches with the governing bodies of various sports, with professional football clubs, golf clubs and local authorities. The six national sports centres employ coaches who, in addition to their practical work, are often involved in management and administration. Holiday camps, private hotels, leisure centres, outward bound schools and large sports and leisure centres employ instructors and coaches to run sporting/fitness events and classes, and give private tuition to individuals.

Instructors are needed by organizations such as the security services to give training in areas such as personal fitness and self-defence. There is also an increasing demand for outdoor pursuits instructors to cater for the growing number of people who are choosing to spend some of their leisure time in the countryside. There are outdoor pursuit or activity holiday centres in coastal and rural areas across the UK, offering a range of activities such as mountaineering, climbing, walking, canoeing, skiing, orienteering and sailing.

Some sports goods manufacturers employ instructors and coaches for publicity and public relations work. All three of the Armed Forces have physical training instructors, but not all take on recruits to train specifically for these posts.

Opportunities vary between sports. Professional sports, like soccer and cricket, have a long tradition of employing coaches; among the recreational sports, coaches and instructors have for many years been employed to teach ice skating, riding and golf. More recently, there have been openings for coaches and instructors in swimming, squash, tennis, water sports, horse-riding, table tennis, badminton and the martial arts.

Vacancies for sports coaches and instructors appear in *The Times Educational Supplement*. Vacancies for coaching jobs for different sports appear in specialist magazines devoted to the sports concerned, and are advertised by sports associations. A lot of vacancy information is passed on by word of mouth, and, not infrequently, employers with vacancies will directly approach the candidate they want.

PAY AND CONDITIONS

National governing bodies of sports employ coaches on fixed contracts and for fixed salaries. In professional sport, pay often depends on how much prize money is earned, how well a particular team or individual is doing, how popular a sport is with spectators, how much television coverage it gets etc. Coaches are likely to get a basic salary, with bonuses for good results. Earnings for the self-employed depend on how many people they coach or teach, at what level, and how successful their students are. Self-employed people normally charge by the hour, and coaches and instructors with good reputations can charge more.

Work in holiday resorts, leisure centres and the like, which is usually seasonal, is not particularly well paid, but there may be extra money from tips, and accommodation is often included. Most of the coaches and instructors in this area are young people.

Work in local authority sports centres and outdoor pursuits centres, among others, is paid on nationally agreed scales for instructors. Full-time recreational assistants' rates are around £5 an hour. Many youth club leaders are unpaid volunteers, but there are some paid posts and scales that are nationally agreed. Most coaches work on a voluntary basis.

Coaches and instructors tend to work unsocial hours, since most sports competitions and matches take place in the evenings and weekends. They may also have to work during the day, as training for professional and high-level amateur sport is virtually full-time. Coaches attend training sessions, competitions and matches and can therefore work very long hours during the season. They also work during the off-season, when much of the preparatory training is done. A lot of coaches and instructors work part-time and do another job during the day. In amateur sport, they may

SPORTS AND LEISURE: GAG/GAJ

have to work with participants very early in the morning, or late at night. In outdoor sports, the amount of time spent training on site varies with the season, but where floodlights and all-weather surfaces have been installed, only very severe conditions bring training to a halt. Some coaching and instruction is only seasonal, so those who coach a summer or winter sport may have to find other work in the off-season.

PROSPECTS

Coaches' and instructors' prospects usually depend on their results. Successful coaches in professional sport may be rewarded by higher fees and earnings. In amateur sport, success may be judged not merely by the number of medals won, but by the progress and the level of enjoyment of the participants. Most sports coaches and instructors are in their 20s and 30s. As they grow older, they may move into less physically demanding jobs in management or administration.

RELATED OCCUPATIONS

Professional sportsman/woman, PE teacher, sports physiotherapist, sports/leisure centre manager, sports/leisure centre assistant.

FURTHER INFORMATION

British Amateur Weight Lifters' Association, 131 Hurst Street, Oxford OX4 1HE, 01865 200339 (please include sae)

Central Council of Physical Recreation (CCPR)*, Francis House, Francis Street, London SW1P 1DE, 0171 828 3163/4

Institute of Sport and Recreation Management (ISRM)*, Giffard House, 36–38 Sherrard Street, Melton Mowbray, Leicestershire LE13 1XJ 01664 565531, www.isrm.co.uk

Institute of Leisure and Amenity Management (ILAM), Education and Training Unit, ILAM House, Lower Basildon, Reading, Berkshire RG8 9NE, 01491 874800

The Keep Fit Association*, Francis House, Francis Street, London SW1P 1DE, 0171 233 8898

Local Government Opportunities (LGO), Local Government Management Board*, 76–86 Turnmill Street, Farringdon, London EC1M 5QU, 0171 296 6600

The National Coaching Foundation (NCF)*, 114 Cardigan Road, Headingley, Leeds LS6 3BJ, 0113 274 4802

The Physical Education Association of the United Kingdom*, Francis House, Francis Street, London SW1P 1DE, 0171 828 9229

The Exercise Association of England, Unit 4, Angel Gate, City Road, London EC1V 2PT, 0171 278 0811

Recreation Managers Association of Great Britain*, Recreation House, 7 Burkinshaw Avenue, Rawmarsh, Rotherham, South Yorkshire S62 7QZ, 01709 522463

Scottish Sports Council*, Caledonia House, South Gyle, Edinburgh EH12 9DQ, 0131 317 7200

The English Sports Council*, 16 Upper Woburn Place, London WC1H 0QP, 0171 273 1500, http://www.english.s

The Sports Council for Northern Ireland, House of Sport, Upper Malone Road, Belfast BT9 5LA, 01232 381222

The Sports Council for Wales, Information Centre*, Welsh Institute of Sport, Sophia Gardens, Cardiff CF1 9SW, 01222 300500

SPRITO (The Specialist Industry Training Organisation for Sport, Recreation, Playwork, Outdoor Education and Development Training, Fitness and Exercise), Euston House, 81–103 Euston Street, London NW1 2ET, 0171 388 3111

London and Central YMCA, Training and Development Department, 112 Great Russell Street, London WC1B 3NQ, 0171 343 1850, www.central-ymca.demon.co.uk

The UK Sports Council, Walkden House, 10 Melton Street, London NW1 2EB, 0171 380 8000

FURTHER READING

Leaflets/booklets are available from the addresses marked*.

Working in Leisure – COIC

Working in Outdoor Jobs – COIC

Careers in Sport and Recreation – CCPR

Careers in Sport – Kogan Page

In the careers library classified under GAG.

2. PROFESSIONAL SPORTSMAN/WOMAN (GAG)

BACKGROUND INFORMATION

While most people take part in sport as amateurs, professional sportsmen and women get paid for their efforts. Amateurs may take their sport very seriously and compete at the highest level. In general, however, they take part for their own pleasure, and pay all their own costs and expenses. They do not make any money from the sport itself.

Historically, the distinction between amateur and professional has been an important one, and even today turning professional can have wide-ranging implications. Some events (eg the Olympic Games) are, in theory at least, open only to amateurs. In many sports, however, the old distinctions between amateur and professional are breaking down. In tennis, for instance, no official distinction is now drawn between amateurs and professionals, and highly paid tennis stars have been allowed to compete at the Olympics.

This article covers sportsmen/women who get paid for competing in their chosen sport. Comparatively few are able to make a living from sport alone, and only a tiny number earn large sums. Most sportsmen/women have to take other full or part-time jobs, and play professional sport at the weekends or in the evenings. They may have to take time off work, perhaps unpaid, to attend tournaments and competitions, and may depend on the goodwill of a sympathetic employer.

There are two types of sport: team games and sports for individuals. Among the most popular team games in this country are soccer, cricket, rugby, cycling (also an individual sport) and basketball. Among individual sports, the best known are golf, tennis, boxing, horse racing and other equestrian sports, motor sports, darts and snooker. This article deals briefly with all of these.

Soccer. This is organized into clubs, with players also having the chance to join their national squads. There are several leagues and other competitions, and the clubs are placed in divisions according to their success. There are around 90 Football League clubs in England and Wales,

SPORTS AND LEISURE: GAG/GAJ

and 40 in Scotland. Matches are played mid-week and at weekends (mostly Saturday afternoons). Professional footballers spend the rest of their working week in running, fitness and weight-training, practising skills such as ball control and tackling, planning and rehearsing moves and tactics, and generally building their stamina, skill and strength.

There are eleven players in a football team, together with three nominated substitutes, of which at most two may actually play. Even taking into account second teams, this means each club can offer only a limited number of opportunities for full-time professionals. In England and Wales there are an estimated 2,000 full-time footballers, with 1,000 part-timers and 250 youth trainees. The corresponding figures in Scotland are around 450 full-time and 550 part-time players.

The governing bodies in soccer are the Football Association, the Football League, the Scottish Football Association and the Scottish Football League. The Professional Footballers Association (PFA) looks after the interests of professional footballers. Although many women now play the game, there are as yet no opportunities for women to play professionally in this country.

Cricket. There are 18 county sides which play in a championship league and other competitions such as the Sunday league. There is also an English national side run from the England and Wales Cricket Board at Lord's. Members of the England team are selected on merit from the county sides.

There are eleven players on a cricket team, and a twelfth man who may substitute in certain situations, eg if one of the players is unwell. Each county club retains a squad of around 20 to 25 professionals, creating opportunities for around 450 full-time players. Minor Counties cricket, Scottish and local county leagues (eg the Lancashire League) offer some opportunities for part-time professionals, who may supplement their playing fees with coaching and instructing.

Cricket is played in the summer months between April and September, in matches lasting between one and four days. During the winter most full-time professionals play or coach abroad or have other jobs.

Most cricketers specialize in either batting or bowling, though it is useful if they can do both. The other specialist, the wicket-keeper, benefits from being able to bat. When they are not playing, they train for fitness and stamina, and practise fielding or batting/bowling in the nets. Cricketers must keep fit and agile, as they may spend long hours on the field. Teams are tactically picked, depending on the type of game, the weather and the state of the pitch.

Cricket is regulated by the English Cricket Board and the International Cricket Conference.

Rugby League. There are some 1,600 professional rugby league players. They play in 36 professional clubs, most of which are based in Yorkshire, Lancashire or Cumbria.

There are 13 players, plus two substitutes in a rugby league team. Many teams are sponsored by breweries or tobacco companies, and the sport is regulated by the Rugby Football League. While the players are paid professionals, only a minority receive enough to make a full-time living from it. Many have a full-time job as well, and fit in playing and training at evenings and weekends.

Basketball. There is a national league, with over 60 clubs competing in men's, women's and junior men's divisions. There are also cup competitions. Each team has ten players, though only five are on the court at any one time. Matches are played indoors according to three basic rules: no contact, no running with the ball, and one continuous dribble. Basketball matches are played in two 20-minute halves with a 10-minute interval, although most matches last around an hour-and-a-quarter, as the clock is stopped every time the referee blows his or her whistle. There are only a handful of full-time paid professionals, and most players do other jobs to support themselves. The best players may be invited to study at American universities.

Cycling. There are some 70 full-time professional cyclists, most of whom have worked their way up from the amateur ranks. Professional cycle racing is a tough and highly competitive world. The sport divides into four broad categories: road racing, time trials, track racing and cyclo-cross (cross-country cycle racing). Except for major international races such as the Tour de France, the financial rewards in cycling are small. Only the very top names can support themselves entirely through the sport, and the great majority have other part or full-time jobs. Cycling in Britain is regulated by the British Cycling Federation and the Professional Cycling Association. Cycling is both a team and an individual sport.

Speedway. There are around 300 professional speedway riders who are contracted to one of the 26 clubs currently operating. Teams of seven riders contest home and away matches in a league with two divisions. Top riders also ride for clubs abroad, and hence have considerable earning power. New riders, in contrast, are likely to have to supplement their income by other work. The British governing body is the Speedway Control Board Limited. The riders' interests are protected by the Speedway Riders' Association, while the British Speedway Promoters' Association represents the promoters.

Golf. There are two types of professional. The first is the player on the national and international tournament circuit, whose income derives mainly from prize money and sponsorship. There are currently around 250 men and 100 women. Golfers wishing to become tournament players must first obtain a qualifying card, competition for which is intense.

The other type of golfer is the club professional, attached to a golf club. Club professionals' duties include teaching players at all levels, organizing competitions, and selling and repairing golf equipment. Club professionals also take part in competitions and tournaments. There are around 2,200 club professionals in the UK, of whom 31 are female.

Professional golfers need to become members of the Professional Golfers Association (PGA). This requires considerable talent and dedication, and the ability to pass a set of rigorous examinations. Golf is currently undergoing a boom in Britain, and opportunities for club professionals, in particular, are increasing with a number of new courses being opened.

Tennis. Tennis is now played on four main types of surface: grass, clay, cement and indoor. Players compete on all types of surface, though many find their game better suited to some surfaces than others. In Britain, no distinctions are drawn between professional and amateur status, but only a very small number of players are able to make any sort of living from the game.

Tennis players are ranked world-wide according to their successes. High-ranking players gain direct entry to top tournaments such as Wimbledon, and may even be 'seeded', so that they do not meet other top players until the later stages. Those with more modest rankings, by contrast, play in less prestigious 'satellite' tournaments to raise their rankings. They may also gain entry to top tournaments by playing well in preliminary, qualifying events.

Professionals play singles and, to a lesser extent, doubles matches. The most successful players can make a great deal of money on the circuit, as they move from tournament to tournament. All tennis players spend a lot of time travelling and living away from home.

Boxing. Boxing is a popular sport with spectators, with huge audiences watching televised bouts. Rewards for top boxers can be correspondingly large, but those lower down the scale may need to supplement their purses (payments received per bout) with other work.

Matches take place at night or weekends, or at special times suited to world-wide television coverage. They last for a prescribed number of two or three-minute rounds (up to a maximum of twelve) or until one contestant is counted out, or until the referee or the contestant's seconds judge that one man has reached the limits of his endurance. The main regulatory body in this country is the British Boxing Board of Control (BBBC). The BBBC licenses professional boxers, who are required to show a high level of skill and to undergo rigorous medical tests to prove their fitness for the professional ring.

Horse racing. Some 35,000 people work full and part-time in the horse racing industry; around 7,000 at the stables where the horses are kept and trained. Although many of those joining a stable hope to become jockeys, competition is intense and only a tiny proportion can be successful.

Jockeys ride for racehorse owners and trainers. They get rides depending on their past performance and their weight. There are two types of horse racing: flat (March to November) and National Hunt, over jumps (throughout the year). Jockeys are paid a riding fee and a percentage of any winnings, and most make a steady living rather than a fortune. There are, however, a fair number of established jockeys who earn a good income from the industry. The top jockeys are usually contracted to ride for wealthy owners and can command very high fees.

Equestrian sports. Apart from horse racing, there are a number of other equestrian sports. They include horse trials, endurance riding, dressage and horse-driving trials. Riders' income comes from sponsorship and prize money. They travel from event to event and, when not competing, spend most of their time caring for and schooling their horses. The horses are graded A, B or C, and move into the higher categories as they improve their placings. Most equestrian sports are under the control of the British Horse Society.

Motor racing. This includes car and motorbike racing. Motor racing and speedway take place on purpose-built circuits. Rallying, motocross and motorcycle road racing take place on the open road or in country areas on trails and tracks. Although the top drivers can earn large sums, earnings fall away sharply further down the scale. The Royal Automobile Club (RAC) has overall responsibility for the standards in some of these sports.

Darts. This is a sport sponsored mainly by the brewing industry. Many of the players have a high level of showmanship as well as considerable individual skills. Accuracy and a steady hand are more important than all-round physical fitness, but darts players still need to spend many hours practising.

Professional darts players compete in national and international competitions and championships. When not competing, they give exhibitions in clubs, holiday camps, hotels etc. They spend a great deal of time travelling between venues and generally work in the evenings in pubs and clubs. The national governing body is the British Darts Organization.

Snooker. In recent years, with the help of widespread television coverage, snooker has become a very popular sport, and top players can earn large sums in sponsorship and prize money. Players also give exhibitions and visit clubs, where they are challenged by the best players. There are around 600 snooker professionals, but only a minority can support themselves entirely by playing, and most have other jobs elsewhere. Professional snooker is controlled by the World Professional Billiards and Snooker Association.

THE WORK

Professional sports people spend a great deal of time practising their event, exercising and looking after their bodies. It is important for them to stay at peak skill and fitness, even when not playing, as there are always promising adults and youngsters waiting to fill any vacancy. It is common to train twice or more a day, building strength and stamina as well as sporting prowess. Physical fitness also helps protect against injury.

They have to look after their clothing and equipment, mending it and keeping it clean. For most professional sportsmen/women, actual competing takes up only a small proportion of their time. Much more is spent preparing, practising and training.

Some sports, such as horse racing and boxing, require competitors to maintain certain weights. Jockeys have to pay a great deal of attention to weight, as, if they get too heavy, they may not get rides in races. Boxers are divided into weight divisions according to their size. Matches are made at a particular weight, and if a boxer is above the prescribed limit on the morning of a fight he may have to attempt to lose weight quickly by strenuous exercise.

In sports that rely on a partnership with a horse, the riders or jockeys spend a great deal of time schooling, exercising and caring for their animals.

In most cases sportsmen/women do not work on their own. They rely on coaches and trainers to improve their skills, physiotherapists and doctors to care for their injuries, and agents or managers (if they have them) to look after travel, competition bookings and other administrative matters. Tournament golfers normally employ a caddie, who carries their clubs for them and may assist them in judging distances, deciding which club to use and so on.

In darts and snooker, the competitors are sometimes considered to be entertainers, rather than athletes, but they still have to practise regularly to maintain their consistency.

WORK ENVIRONMENT

Professional sportsmen/women provide entertainment for spectators and fans when they compete. They therefore perform in venues that allow spectators to attend and watch the action. Many sports take place in the open air at

SPORTS AND LEISURE: GAG/GAJ

venues including stadia, sports grounds, race courses and so on. Professionals in sports such as soccer and rugby are expected to perform in almost all weathers; other sports, such as cricket, may only be practicable when conditions are fine.

Some sports, such as boxing and basketball, are performed indoors in halls, clubs and arenas. Even in indoor sports, conditions are normally light and well ventilated. The exceptions may be snooker and darts, which traditionally take place in pubs, clubs and theatres.

Professional sportsmen/women often have to travel long distances between competitions, perhaps driving themselves, going on team coaches or using public transport. This can necessitate overnight stays in hotels or bed and breakfasts. Those competing in international events overseas may spend lengthy periods away from home.

SKILLS AND INTERESTS

The two main characteristics required by a professional sportsman/woman are ability and commitment. At the highest level, talent on its own is not sufficient. Players must be committed to winning, and prepared to put in all the hard work required to achieve that.

Most professional sportsmen/women have good all-round sporting ability. They need to be physically fit and strong, well balanced and sure-footed, have good hand–eye co-ordination, and be quick-thinking and decisive.

With coaching and constant practice, they build their skills until they are at the peak of skill and stamina. They must look after their bodies, using the help of doctors and physiotherapists to correct injuries, and eating and resting properly. They have to follow a regular, demanding daily routine that often leaves no time for a social life and which requires them to go to bed early when not competing. They must accept the advice of coaches, and practise single-mindedly to correct any weaknesses.

Professional sportsmen and women must also be able to cope with the enormous pressures placed on them. These may come from colleagues and opponents, parents and managers, and, not least, the paying public who watch them perform. They must have faith in themselves and their talents, and when they lose must have the resilience and self-discipline to go on training.

They must have a competitive nature and want to win, or at least improve their personal best performance. While they must be committed to winning, they must also play fairly.

Those in team sports need to be friendly and able to get on with other team members. Apart from the importance of co-operating during matches, players also spend lengthy periods together, training, travelling to matches, and staying overnight in hotels.

ENTRY REQUIREMENTS

There are no academic requirements for most sports, though a good standard of education is useful, bearing in mind that sporting careers are generally short. The Professional Golfers' Association, however, requires candidates to hold a minimum of four GCSEs which show ability in literacy and numeracy, have a handicap of four or better and pass a playing ability test.

Sportsmen/women must have talent which, in the opinion of coaches or talent scouts, can be developed into a top-level skill. Age of entry varies from sport to sport, from as young as 14 in football's Associated Schoolboy Scheme, while entry to cricket is common in the early twenties. The one thing all sports have in common is that most professionals started playing them at a very early age.

Certain sports have very specific entry requirements. Boxing has divisions according to weight. It also runs regular checks on participants, including eye tests and brain scans, which boxers must pass to be allowed to go on competing. Horse racing requires boys and girls weighing no more than 57 kilograms (nine stone). Professional basketball players are usually well over 1.83 metres (six feet) tall.

Most sports professionals have well-proportioned bodies, and 100% vision, with or without glasses/contact lenses.

TRAINING

Some sports may have training opportunities for young people. Contact your local careers office, Jobcentre, TEC/LEC for details. In others, one progresses through school into clubs, county and national events until reaching a standard that allows one to join the professional circuit. Progress after that depends on achieving good results in competition. Most clubs have coaches or senior members who coach and train club members.

Football. Most professional footballers begin at the age of 14 as Associated Schoolboys at a professional club, having been 'spotted' by one of the club's talent scouts. They attend evening training sessions at the club two or three nights a week. At 16 they may be invited to become full-time trainees on the club's training programme. As well as playing and practising, trainees undertake a variety of chores within the club, such as cleaning and checking kit. They are also required to attend college part-time to gain further academic qualifications. At 17 or 18 years they are either offered full-time professional terms, or not retained. Even if they are not retained, there is still a chance they may be taken on by another club. Even so, only a minority of trainees make it into the ranks of full-time professionals.

A small number of 14- and 15-year-old boys identified as having exceptional talent are selected each year to attend the Football Association's School of Excellence at Lilleshall in Shropshire. Here they have the chance to develop their skills with the country's top coaches and facilities, while attending local schools to continue their academic studies. The boys are signed to clubs in the normal way, and with this 'fast-track' approach have a good chance of going on to achieve success at the highest level.

Cricket. In cricket, all the counties have selectors who watch school and club matches and invite young players with ability to attend trials. Players may also be recommended by teachers or club coaches. The best such players may be invited to play a few matches for the county 2nd XI. At this stage they play part-time until they are offered a summer season contract and a place on the playing staff. Counties use the 2nd XI as a means of discovering whether players have the ability to perform at the highest level, and only a very few get regular second-team places, let alone a place in the first.

The MCC operate a scheme offering three summer seasons of cricket, together with study for an Advanced GNVQ in Leisure and Tourism.

Rugby League. Players often begin by playing in school teams. All professional clubs have scouts who go to school and amateur matches seeking new talent. Many clubs run training schemes for apprentices, and it is possible to take up a professional contract from the age of 17. Training usually consists of intensive sessions two or three nights a week. Players are also required to maintain a strict personal fitness programme in their own time.

Basketball. Players also frequently begin playing at school. Many clubs operate junior or 'cadet' teams that provide a training ground for the best players to go on to join senior teams. In training, players practise individual skills, such as dribbling, shooting, passing, pivoting and protecting the ball, and also team tactics for attack and defence. Basketball players often train in pairs or in groups.

Tennis. Players who perform well in school or club competitions may be invited to join county and regional training courses. The best young players in each of three age groups (under-12, under-14 and under-16) are invited to join the national training squad and attend training weekends or summer school at the Bisham Abbey National Sports Centre in Buckinghamshire. This is run by the Lawn Tennis Association as a national tennis centre. Trainees here practise and play tennis under the guidance of top national coaches. At 16, tennis players are classed as adults, and can expect to find themselves matched in competition against older and much more experienced players.

Golf. Professionals begin as assistant professionals in golf clubs. They are contracted to the club professional, and work in the club shop, selling and repairing equipment, and helping with the paperwork and administration. They may also coach club members, and have to fit in their own playing and practice in their spare time. The PGA offer a training scheme which involves a minimum three-year training period. The subjects covered include, amongst others, physiology, biomechanics and psychology and the scheme combines distance learning and residential courses which are held at the PGA Training Academy at The Belfry, Sutton Coldfield. At the end of this, PGA final examinations are taken, which, if passed, allow election as a full member of the PGA.

Golfers wishing to compete in professional tournaments must first obtain a 'player's ticket'. This is obtained by achieving good results in local competitions, and applicants must also have a handicap of less than two. This allows entry to one of the two pre-qualifying events. From here, about 130 players go on to a larger tournament of 250 players in Spain; and from this, about 50 go on to the European circuit with their 'card'.

Horse racing. Training for the horse racing industry is supervised by the Racing and Thoroughbred Breeding Training Board (RTBTB). The Board offers three separate NVQs/SVQs: in Horse Care at Level 1, Racehorse Care at Level 2, and Racehorse Care and Management at Level 3. Anyone joining the racing industry between the ages of 16 and 18 is registered on the industry's youth training programme. Most new entrants begin working in stables as 'lads' (a term used for both sexes), where their responsibilities include riding and caring for the horses, and cleaning and maintaining the stables and equipment. All new entrants to the industry who are under age 19 have to attend one of the two racing schools at Newmarket and Doncaster. The job of the racing schools is to train stable staff. The best riders may have the chance to become trainee jockeys (known as apprentice jockeys in flat racing, conditional jockeys in jump racing). Apprenticeship as a jockey in flat racing finishes at the age of 25, or when 95 winners have been ridden. The equivalent for jump jockeys is age 26, or 65 winners.

Other equestrian sports. Training in other equestrian sports varies. Physical fitness is always very important, and riders have to exercise regularly for strength and suppleness. They also have to learn the correct posture for riding. Riders in sports that involve jumping need regular practice at this. They start with low obstacles, and gradually, as horse and rider become more experienced, work up to full competition height. Plenty of practice helps develop a good understanding between horse and rider, and also helps riders learn to judge pace.

Cycling. Most cyclists begin by joining a local club. Clubs may be based in sports and leisure centres, or in parks with suitable facilities. Cycling in itself promotes fitness, but professional cyclists regularly exercise out of the saddle as well. Exercise such as running improves stamina, while weight training helps build physical strength. A professional cyclist may prepare for a long road race by means of a series of shorter rides. With the aid of a coach or trainer, they aim to reach peak physical condition for the start of the race.

Motor sports. They require strength and stamina, as events often take place over a long period. In most such sports, a licence grading system operates. Drivers have to compete in a specified number of events to achieve each grade, not necessarily winning every time but driving well and safely. It is not possible to become a professional driver without an International Rally and Racing Licence. Successful drivers may be invited to join teams run by manufacturers on a professional or semi-professional (part-time) basis. Apart from racing skills and techniques, they learn how to maintain their vehicles and how to get the best out of them. Speedway riders over 16 have to hold an Auto-Cycle Union licence.

Boxing. Boxers have to join a club that can provide proper training to the high safety standards required. They can compete in youth matches from the age of twelve, but seniors must be at least 17. All boxers have to train regularly. They may go on runs for stamina, and do weight and circuit training to build up their physical strength. Boxers practise punching on a punch-ball. They also spend some time practising in the ring with a sparring partner.

Darts and snooker. Players are traditionally self-taught. Players work their way up from local pub and club teams by performing well in competitions and defeating highly rated players. Here they combine practising their sport with general duties such as cleaning and brushing the tables. Both sports require long hours of practice to reach the top and to remain there. Some coaching schemes to assist young players are being set up under the auspices of the World Professional Billiards and Snooker Association.

LATE ENTRY

Most professional sportsmen/women have been playing and training seriously in their sport from an early age. In many sports it would be unlikely for someone taking up the sport as an adult to be able to achieve the required standard to compete professionally. Those who are successful as amateurs may, however, decide to turn professional at any point.

Some sports offer more opportunities for late entrants than others. Some cricketers, for example, do not become full-time professionals until their twenties, having first completed a university degree or a training in some other profession. Golf and snooker are two sports that can be

SPORTS AND LEISURE: GAG/GAJ

performed at a high level until well into middle age.

Nevertheless, the average length of time a professional sportsman/woman can expect to stay at the top is around eight years, and many careers are over by the age of 35. In many sports, therefore, the opportunities for anyone to become a professional diminish rapidly from about the mid-twenties.

OPPORTUNITIES

Most of the sports mentioned have amateur associations and clubs, where promising newcomers can receive instruction and coaching, and compete against more experienced opponents. The most successful may be spotted by managers or scouts and invited to try out for teams. Playing as an amateur in county, national or international competitions improves the chances of gaining recognition. There is a list of the main sports governing bodies in FURTHER INFORMATION.

There are clubs all over the country covering most sports, but anyone wishing to join a professional circuit or team is likely to have to move away from home.

In the main, opportunities are governed by the number of competitions or tournaments, and by the popularity of the sport with the paying public and the mass media. Sports that attract large crowds and receive regular television coverage can attract business sponsors and advertisers keen to promote their products to the viewing public. This, in turn, brings money into the sport, which can provide prize money, finance for sporting venues, and support for the sport in general.

Many professional sportsmen/women are self-employed in their sporting capacities, though they may have other jobs to support themselves. Others have contracts that are reviewed annually – this can mean a pattern of short-term employment with a succession of different employers. For instance, footballers may be asked to go on the transfer list and may have to change team and location, and move home and family.

PAY AND CONDITIONS

In most professional sports – apart from football, cricket, cycling and a few others – players support themselves on appearance fees, prize money and income from advertising and product endorsements.

Prize money varies greatly between sports. In high-profile sports, such as tennis, boxing and golf, the prize for a win in a major competition can easily run into six figures. Most players, however, never have a major win. They make a steady living rather than a fortune. After they have paid for insurance, travel, accommodation, tournament entry fees and training expenses they may have only a small balance and may need part or full-time jobs to support themselves. Many, in sports such as cricket, speedway, cycling and so on, work on annual or fixed-term contracts.

Most professional sports take place in front of an audience, which means sportsmen/women have to work when spectators are free to watch, usually at evenings and weekends. They may have to practise when the public, who use the facilities for leisure or recreation, have finished. This often means using running tracks, gymnasiums and so on late at night or very early in the morning.

PROSPECTS

There is no promotional ladder as such, except for the captaincy in team sports. Status is measured by success in competition and income, including sponsorships. Professional sportsmen/women must be seen to succeed at national and international level, to enhance their status and increase their earning potential.

Most sporting careers are short. Many competitors, because of the wear and tear on their bodies, finish by the age of 35, or earlier still if they suffer a serious injury. In less physically demanding sports, it may be possible to go on playing longer. However, as professional careers are, in general, so short, it is important for sportsmen/women to make the most of their earning potential while they can, and to plan and prepare for their later careers. In football, the PFA provides finance for all its members to continue vocational training for their post-playing careers.

It is not uncommon for sportsmen/women to move into coaching or team management. Some find jobs in sports and leisure centres, or with national sporting organizations such as The Sports Council. Modelling, public relations and promotional work are other possibilities. Many sports people make contacts during their years as competitors, which they follow up when they leave. They may also become radio or television sports commentators or journalists. Some move into officiating in their sports (eg most cricket umpires in first-class matches are former players). Some join firms that develop and design sports clothing, footwear and equipment; some even design ranges of goods themselves; others open their own sports equipment shops. Many move away from sport, creating new careers for themselves while keeping up their sporting interests.

RELATED OCCUPATIONS

Sports coach/instructor, PE teacher, sports physiotherapist, sports administrator, sports journalist/photographer, groundsman, sports and leisure centre manager, sports and leisure centre assistant.

FURTHER INFORMATION

In the first instance contact the local or regional organizer of the sport that is of interest. The national governing bodies below can give you details of local clubs, and will also advise on the best way to progress in your chosen sport.

Sports national governing bodies

The British Boxing Board of Control*, Jack Peterson House, 52a Borough High Street, London SE1 1XW (please include sae), 0171 403 5879

British Cycling Federation, c/o National Cycling Centre, Stuart Street, Manchester M11 4DQ, 0161 230 2301

British Darts Organization, 2 Pages Lane, Muswell Hill, London N10 1PS, 0181 883 5544

The British Horse Society, British Equestrian Centre, Stoneleigh Park, Kenilworth, Warwickshire CV8 2XZ, 01926 707700 (please include sae), http://www.equiweb.co.uk

English Basketball Association, 48 Bradford Road, Stanningley, Pudsey, West Yorkshire LS28 6DF, 0113 2361166

Football Association*, 16 Lancaster Gate, London W2 3LW, 0171 262 7151

SPORTS AND LEISURE: GAG/GAJ

Lawn Tennis Association*, The Queens Club, Barons Court, Palliser Road, West Kensington, London W14 9EG, 0171 381 7111

Professional Golfers Association National Training Academy*, Ping House, The Belfry, Sutton Coldfield, West Midlands B76 9PW, 01675 470333

Racing and Thoroughbred Breeding Training Board (RTBTB)*, Suite 16, Unit 8, Kings Court, Willie Snaith Road, Newmarket, Suffolk CB8 7SG, 01638 560743

RAC Motor Sports Association, Motor Sports House, Riverside Park, Colnbrook, Berkshire SL3 0HG, 01753 681736

Rugby Football League, Redhall House, Redhall Lane, Leeds LS17 8NB

Speedway Control Board Limited, ACU House, Wood Street, Rugby CV21 2YX, 01788 540096

World Professional Billiards and Snooker Association, 27 Oakfield Road, Clifton, Bristol BS8 2AT, 0117 974 4491

Other organizations

The Institute of Professional Sport, Francis House, Francis Street, London SW1P 1DE, 0171 630 7486

The English Sports Council*, 16 Upper Woburn Place, London WC1H 0QP, 0171 273 1500

English Sports Council Publications*, PO Box 255, Wetherby, Yorks LS23 7LZ, 0990 210 255

Scottish Sports Council*, Caledonia House, South Gyle, Edinburgh EH12 9DQ, 0131 317 7200

The Sports Council for Northern Ireland, House of Sport, Upper Malone Road, Belfast BT9 5LA, 01232 381222

The Sports Council for Wales, Information Centre, Welsh Institute of Sport, Sophia Gardens, Cardiff CF1 9SW, 01222 300500

FURTHER READING

Leaflets/booklets are available from the addresses marked*.

Working in Leisure – COIC

Careers in Sport – Kogan Page

Numerous specialized books and periodicals cover every sport, including Wisden Cricket Monthly, Footballers World, Tennis World, Golf World, Rally Sport, Cycling Weekly, Sporting Life, Horse and Hound, Motor Sport, Match, Snooker Scene and Darts World.

In the careers library classified under GAG.

3. SPORTS AND LEISURE CENTRE MANAGER (GAJ)

THE WORK

Sports and leisure centre managers are responsible for the smooth and efficient running of the centres in which they work. Centres vary widely, but a typical one might include a gymnasium, swimming pool, weights room, dance studios, squash courts, sauna, solarium, bar and cafe.

Managers' duties are wide-ranging. They include financial planning and record-keeping; organizing events and tournaments; timetabling facilities for use by schools, clubs and the general public; arranging for specialist coaches such as aerobics and swimming instructors to work at the centre; ensuring health and safety requirements are met; and dealing with any complaints. They have a team of office staff who assist them in this work, and coaches, instructors and assistants who are responsible for the day-to-day activities of the centre. Managers must handle personnel matters, such as recruitment and staff training. In addition, as most centres are open long hours, they may have to arrange shift rotas for themselves and their staff. Although their role is primarily one of organizing other people, they may also spend some time coaching and instructing, checking and maintaining equipment, and helping out at reception.

Managers may promote their centres by giving talks at schools, colleges, clubs and so on, and may be involved in preparing brochures and other publicity materials. Publicizing the centre and increasing the use of its facilities is an important part of a manager's job. Centres operated by commercial organizations are run as money-making operations, and high on the list of managers' responsibilities is maintaining and improving profitability. Local authority and other centres, while not primarily profit-making, must still be run as efficiently as possible and be seen to provide value for money.

Centres cover a wide range of interests and activities. They may include popular sports and pastimes such as swimming and keep fit, as well as more specialized ones like judo, archery, gymnastics or canoeing. Depending on the facilities, managers and their staff have to ensure that fuel for warming the premises, chemicals for the pool and equipment, such as badminton nets, mats and trampolines, are available and in good order.

Often the interests of the various user groups – eg schools, clubs and the public – may be in conflict, especially in a small centre. The manager has to balance all interests and try to arrive at a solution acceptable to everyone. Although managers have an executive role and are primarily responsible for organizing others, they must also be prepared to step in themselves when required – for example, to cover at reception or to take over a class when a coach or instructor fails to arrive.

Sports and leisure centres are also used for craft fairs, exhibitions, conferences and sports tournaments. These involve a great deal of work for managers and their staff. Competitive quotations for use of facilities and meals have to be provided and then, once accepted, everything has to be prepared. Managers must arrange for part-time security staff and stewards to be hired if necessary, and ensure that sufficient tables and chairs, and any other equipment required, are available. They must also be there on the day to handle any problems if and when they arise.

WORK ENVIRONMENT

Centres vary considerably, but all managers spend a good deal of time working in an office. They may visit schools and clubs to give talks, and local council offices for meetings. This is likely to involve driving.

Most of a centre manager's work is carried out indoors, though at centres with outdoor facilities some time may be spent outside, coaching or instructing. They may also be involved with some water sports.

SKILLS AND INTERESTS

Self-motivation, administrative ability and management skills are essential.

Attention to detail and the ability to plan one's own work

SPORTS AND LEISURE: GAG/GAJ

and the work of others is important. Numeracy is required to cope with the financial aspects of the job, such as book-keeping and budgeting.

Managers need business acumen and flair, to develop ideas for attracting new customers, and for increasing the use of facilities by existing ones. Interpersonal skills are also important. Managers must be able to relate well with their staff, colleagues in other organizations and departments, centre management committees and the general public. They need sufficient authority to tell staff what to do and to take charge when necessary (eg in an emergency). On the other hand, they must also be able to deal with any personnel problems fairly and sympathetically. They must be good team workers, capable of delegating responsibility where possible, and able to enthuse staff and motivate them to perform at their best.

Managers need good verbal skills for giving instructions, talking to people (in groups or individually) and expressing their views and recommendations at meetings. They must be capable of tact and diplomacy when required, for example when handling complaints from the public. Good written skills are needed for preparing reports and letters.

They must be enthusiastic about sport and recreation, and, as this is a service business, enjoy working with and helping people. They must be able to see a task through, analyse statistics and plan a budget. They are responsible for the efficient day-to-day running of their centre, and for the health and safety of visitors and those working there.

ENTRY REQUIREMENTS

Employers increasingly require an applicant for sports and leisure centre management to have a recognized qualification. This can mean one of a number of awards, as there is no single clear-cut route to becoming a sports and leisure centre manager. Practical experience is also essential in applicants for senior posts. Those with purely academic qualifications may start at middle management level (eg assistant manager).

BA and BSc degree courses are available, leading to qualifications in Sports and Recreation, Leisure Management, Exercise and Sports Sciences or Recreation Management. It is also possible to study for a first degree in another subject, then take a postgraduate course. An MPhil is available in Leisure Management, and in Strategic Leisure Management. The minimum qualifications needed for admission to a degree course are five GCSEs/S grades (A–C/1–3) with two A levels/three H grades, or equivalent.

BTEC/SQA Higher National courses in Leisure Studies are available. Entry to a BTEC/SQA higher national course requires five GCSEs/S grades (A–C/1–3) with one A level/two H grades, or equivalent.

There are also GNVQs in Business and in Leisure and Tourism at Foundation, Intermediate and Advanced levels. GSVQs are available in Business and in Leisure and Tourism at Levels 2 and 3, as are NVQs/SVQs in Sports and Recreation – Development, and Sports and Recreation – Supervision, both at Level 3; Sports and Recreation Management – Facilities, and Sports and Recreation Management – Sports Development, are available at Level 4. In addition, there are SVQs in Management at Levels 4 and 5, and NVQs in Sports Administration at Levels 3 and 4, and Management at Levels 3, 4 and 5.

A Modern Apprenticeship in sports and recreation is available, and details can be obtained from your TEC/LEC or careers office.

Entry is also possible by entering as a sports and leisure centre assistant and, with experience and qualifications such as NVQs/SVQs, progressing to management.

The Recreation Managers Association of Great Britain runs a correspondence course aimed at people recently employed within clubs or leisure centres. There is also a Certificate (Recreation) course run by the National Examining Board for Supervisory Management (NEBSM).

Whatever educational standards are reached, anyone entering sports and leisure centre management would normally study toward the Institute of Leisure and Amenity Management (ILAM) or the Institute of Sport and Recreation Management (ISRM) qualifications and membership.

In many cases, sports and leisure centre managers need to be able to drive.

Where work at a centre involves looking after a swimming pool, a manager is expected to hold, or be capable of gaining, the Pool Lifeguard Bronze Medallion Award of the Royal Life Saving Society. Some employers ask for Red Cross or St John's Ambulance first aid qualifications. In some cases, ability in one or more sports can be a big advantage, as can coaching or instructing qualifications.

Modern Apprenticeships (part of the Skillseekers Initiative in Scotland) may be available for young people leading to at least an NVQ/SVQ Level 3. Contact your local careers office, Jobcentre, TEC/LEC for details.

TRAINING

Training to become a sports and leisure centre manager can be done by either part-time or full-time study. It can also be a combination of both.

One way is to take a degree course in Leisure Studies or Recreation Management and then look for a job in a sports/leisure centre. There are now numerous courses run at colleges and universities throughout the country. They last three years, and lead to either a BA or BSc honours degree. Courses have varying emphases. Courses may concentrate on business management, sports or movement science, physical education, sociology etc. It is therefore important to study individual prospectuses carefully before making any application. Many courses include the opportunity to gain coaching qualifications in one or more sports, and this can be particularly useful for jobs in centres where managers are expected to be able to take coaching sessions.

It is also possible to take a first degree in another subject and follow this up with a postgraduate qualification in sport or recreation. Most commonly these are MA or MSc or the Diploma in Management Studies (DMS) with an emphasis on leisure and recreation. Courses are available at many colleges and universities, including Bangor, Birmingham, Cardiff, Loughborough, Sheffield, Southampton and the Moray House Institute at Heriot-Watt University. Courses usually last for one or two years. They are well regarded by employers, and competition for places is intense.

BTEC Higher National Diplomas (full-time) and Certificates (part-time) in Leisure Studies and related subjects are available at colleges throughout England, Wales and Northern Ireland. SQA higher national certificate/higher national diplomas are available at

SPORTS AND LEISURE: GAG/GAJ

Aberdeen, Falkirk, Fife, Motherwell and Stow. Courses last two years full-time or three years part-time, a higher national diploma two years full-time or three years part-time.

It is unlikely that a holder of a degree, higher national diploma or even a postgraduate qualification would obtain a manager's job without experience. They would be most likely to start as a trainee or assistant manager and work their way up as they gain experience and further qualifications. During this stage of their careers, trainee managers would normally study for vocational qualifications, such as those offered by the Institute of Leisure and Amenity Management (ILAM) or the Institute of Sport and Recreation Management (ISRM).

ILAM operates a Qualification Scheme based on the completion of work-based projects. The ILAM Scheme is at four levels; it is not course-based and does not require attendance at college. For the ILAM First Award, candidates must complete a project of 1,500-2,000 words. For the ILAM Certificate in Leisure Operations, 3,000-4,000 words are required. For the ILAM Certificate in Leisure Management, the project must be 5,000-7,000 words, and for the ILAM Diploma in Leisure Management, 8,000-10,000 words. Projects are related to real practical issues and problems in the candidate's own place of work.

To enter the ILAM Awards at each level, candidates must have attained NVQs/SVQs in leisure-related competencies, or have completed an appropriate college-based award in a leisure-related area. People working in the industry, but without such qualifications, may apply to have their experience recognized under the Institute's Recognition of Prior Experience Scheme. Holders of the ILAM Certificate in Leisure Management are entitled to apply for full membership MILAM (Cert) and the Diploma MILAM (Dip).

Courses for the Institute of Sport and Recreation Management's examinations are held in colleges across the country on a day release and evening basis, and a correspondence course is also available. The main qualification for managers is the ISRM Sport and Recreation Management Certificate. The examination for this consists of four modules: operational management; resource management and administration; sport and recreation facility planning, design and technology; and sport and recreation environment. Candidates with other qualifications recognized by the ISRM may be given exemptions from up to three of the modules. Holders of the Certificate are entitled to apply for full membership of the Institute (MInstSRM).

The ISRM also offers a Diploma Examination for experienced managers who already possess the Certificate. This is designed to provide sports and leisure centre managers with the knowledge and understanding to progress to senior management levels, and/or to manage major facilities. The ISRM Diploma consists of two modules: the management of people, finance, and information; and the management of recreation technology. Qualification at this level is recognized by diploma membership of the Institute (MInstSRM Dip).

Other categories of ISRM membership are available for those without the qualifications above. For example, candidates studying for the Sport and Recreation Management Certificate may become registered students. Associate membership is open to people with various qualifications, including the ISRM's own Sport and Recreation Technician's Certificate and Sport and Facility Supervisor's Certificate, NVQ in Sport and Recreation Facility Operation at Level 2, and NVQ in Sport and Facility Supervision at Level 3. Applicants for associate membership must also have suitable experience in the industry.

Associate membership of the ISRM is also open to those who have a recognized qualification and relevant experience in an area associated with recreation facilities or management, for example architects, engineers, or managers with other professional qualifications.

Sports and leisure centre management is increasingly becoming a graduate profession. It is, however, possible to become a manager without having a degree or higher national certificate/higher national diplomas, perhaps by starting at operative or technician level and working one's way up. (Please see article 4. SPORTS AND LEISURE CENTRE ASSISTANT.) One common approach is to do a part-time college course, then go on to study for ILAM or ISRM awards. Anyone considering a college course needs to check carefully whether it will suit their needs and whether the qualifications are acceptable to gain admission on to a vocational training course. To study for ILAM or ISRM management qualifications, for instance, candidates are recommended to have an NVQ/SVQ at Level 3 or 4, four GCSEs/S grades (A–C/1–3), including one A level or two H grades, an Advanced GNVQ/GSVQ Level III in Leisure and Tourism, or equivalent qualifications.

LATE ENTRY

Sports and leisure centre management is an area where employers do take on adults. Athletes, former athletes, coaches, and semi-professional or ex-professional sportsmen/women may have an advantage. Some colleges are prepared to relax their normal entry requirements in the case of adult students with relevant interests and/or experience.

Both the ILAM and ISRM are prepared to relax their normal academic entry requirements for management courses for candidates over the age of 23. They must have had at least three years' management or supervisory experience, or have worked for at least five years in the industry.

OPPORTUNITIES

Sports and leisure centre management is an area where opportunities have increased greatly in recent years, as people have had more time for leisure pursuits, and a growing awareness of the importance of physical fitness. As a luxury industry, however, leisure is also vulnerable to downturns in the economy.

Opportunities occur throughout the country, in rural as well as urban areas. Many centres are run by councils as a service to the local community, but an increasing number are being opened by commercial operators. Large employers, such as the health service and police, provide centres for the benefit of their staff. Educational institutions, such as universities, also run centres for staff and students, and there are some centres run by voluntary groups or trusts.

Five national centres are operated by The Sports Council. These are: Bisham Abbey, Lilleshall, Holme Pierrepont (water sports), Plas y Brenin (mountain activities) and Crystal Palace. There are a number of major sports centres

SPORTS AND LEISURE: GAG/GAJ

in Scotland, including Inverclyde, Glenmore Lodge and Aviemore. Opportunities also exist to work in sports and leisure centres overseas.

PAY AND CONDITIONS

Salaries vary according to location, experience and responsibilities. Junior managers can expect to earn up to £12,000, middle managers from £15,000 to £20,000, and senior managers from £20,000 upwards. In local authority centres, payment is based on nationally or locally agreed scales; in commercial centres, payment may be negotiable, based on performance and the profitability of the centre.

Managers at local authority centres work a 37-hour, five-day week. Many centres are open from 7am until 10pm, making some unsocial hours necessary. Senior managers may have to work longer hours.

Managers employed by local authorities may be required to attend council meetings in the evenings. Evening and weekend work is usually done on a rota basis and shared between the manager and deputies or assistants.

PROSPECTS

Promotion prospects for sports and leisure centre managers are to more senior management positions in large centres, though to get such jobs, managers have to be prepared to move to another location. For managers who work in local authorities, there are also prospects of moving into administrative positions in the recreation department. Many authorities prefer sports and leisure administrators who have had experience of managing a centre.

RELATED OCCUPATIONS

Sports coach/instructor, professional sportsman/woman, retail manager, countryside/conservation officer, local authority administrator, sports and leisure centre assistant.

FURTHER INFORMATION AND READING

Please see article 4. SPORTS AND LEISURE CENTRE ASSISTANT.

4. SPORTS AND LEISURE CENTRE ASSISTANT (GAJ)

THE WORK

Sports and leisure centre assistants carry out a range of duties concerned with sport and recreation.

Their work varies according to the type of centre and the exact nature of their job. Many assistants spend some or all of their time working at reception. This may involve selling tickets and taking bookings or reservations, eg for use of squash courts; accepting payments and giving receipts; responding to personal and telephone enquiries; general clerical and administrative work; handling complaints.

Other responsibilities may include keeping sports areas clean and tidy; looking after sports equipment; setting up equipment, such as badminton nets or table tennis tables; setting out tables and chairs for public events and generally assisting other staff and users of the centre.

In centres with a swimming pool, assistants who are suitably qualified may work as swimming pool attendants. This involves keeping a close watch on people using the pool, especially children and beginners. The attendant usually sits in an elevated observation chair giving a good view across the pool. The attendant may have to rescue a swimmer in difficulty. In the event of an accident the attendant provides first aid, including resuscitation if required. Some attendants also give swimming instruction.

Some assistants have specific responsibility for the safe and hygienic operation of the pool and associated facilities, such as spa pools, jacuzzis and showers. They ensure that heating, ventilation and filtration equipment is working correctly; treatment chemicals are maintained at the correct levels; and electrical equipment, such as pumps, is regularly maintained and operating safely and efficiently.

Assistants with coaching qualifications may run classes and give personal tuition and instruction in a wide range of sports and activities. These could include aerobics, keep fit, dance, yoga, t'ai chi, squash, tennis, judo, weightlifting and many more. (Please see article 1. SPORTS COACH/INSTRUCTOR.)

Some assistants work in catering facilities or bars. Their duties include assisting customers, preparing and serving food and drinks, taking payments and giving change, washing up, and generally keeping the facilities clean and tidy.

Experienced sports and leisure centre assistants may have supervisory responsibilities, for example organizing duty rotas and arranging cover if other staff are off sick.

WORK ENVIRONMENT

Sports and leisure centre assistants work mainly indoors. Many centres do have some outdoor facilities, however, and assistants may spend some time working outside, coaching or supervising sports such as tennis or football.

Sports and leisure centres are mainly clean, light and airy. In swimming pools, however, the chlorine-based chemicals used to treat the water can cause breathing irritation in some people. Newer forms of water treatment are less likely to have this effect.

For assistants whose jobs include coaching or instructing, the work may require considerable personal mobility. Catering and bar assistants may spend much of the time on their feet. Pool attendants, on the other hand, spend lengthy periods sitting in one place. Reception assistants may spend much of their time either sitting or standing.

Most assistants work on one site only, and they are rarely required to travel. They do, however, often have to work unsocial hours, including evenings and weekends. Many sports and leisure centre assistants work shifts.

SKILLS AND INTERESTS

Sports and leisure centre assistants must have an interest in sport. Some sporting ability is helpful, and essential if the job involves coaching or instructing.

Assistants need to be cheerful and outgoing and enjoy working with the public. They should be courteous and helpful and able to work as members of a team. Flexibility and adaptability are often required, for example in changing shifts to cover for a colleague who is off sick.

They must be conscientious and reliable. Assistants working as pool attendants need good powers of concentration, as they must watch events in the pool over a lengthy period and be prepared to intervene at a

SPORTS AND LEISURE: GAG/GAJ

moment's notice if a swimmer appears to be getting into difficulties.

Good verbal communication skills are important, for example when coaching or giving classes. Sometimes assistants must be assertive, for example if some pool users are being rowdy or otherwise endangering the comfort and safety of other swimmers. They must also be tactful and diplomatic, for example when dealing with complaints from members of the public.

Assistants whose work involves handling money – such as reception and catering staff – must be trustworthy. They must be capable of adding up a bill and giving the correct change.

Assistants must have good general health and stamina to cope with the demands of the work and the variable, sometimes long, hours.

ENTRY REQUIREMENTS

No formal academic qualifications are required to become a sports and leisure centre assistant. Personal qualities, such as self-motivation and a pleasant personality, are generally seen as more important. Some employers look for good GCSEs/S grades in English and maths. A good standard of general education is helpful, especially for those who hope to move on to supervisory and management positions.

GNVQs are available in Leisure and Tourism at Foundation, Intermediate and Advanced Levels, and GSVQs are available in Leisure and Recreation at Levels 2 and 3. NVQs/SVQs in Sports and Recreation are available at Level 1; Coaching and Activity Delivery – Adults, Coaching and Activity Delivery – Children, and Sports and Recreation – Facility Operations, are available at Level 2; and Sports Administration at Levels 3 and 4. A Modern Apprenticeship (part of the Skillseekers Initiative in Scotland) is available leading to at least an NVQ/SVQ Level 3. Contact your local careers office, Jobcentre, TEC/LEC for details.

According to the exact nature of the job, some specific qualifications may be required. Assistants whose work involves coaching or instructing require coaching qualifications in the sport concerned. These are normally acquired through part-time study, either in the candidate's own time or as part of a full-time course. For further information, please see article 1. SPORTS COACH/INSTRUCTOR.

Swimming pool attendants must be good swimmers and are usually required to obtain life-saving qualifications, such as the Royal Life Saving Society's Pool Lifeguard Bronze Medallion.

Candidates for an Advanced GNVQ/GSVQ Level III in Leisure and Tourism need to prove that they can successfully undertake courses. Colleges may set their own requirements.

Candidates for a BTEC/SQA Higher National Diploma/Certificate in Leisure Studies require one A level or two H grades, with supporting GCSEs/S grades (A–C/1–3), or equivalent.

Assistants working in a licensed bar must be 18 years or over.

TRAINING

New assistants joining the industry may study for NVQs/SVQs in Sports and Recreation.

Full-time GNVQs/GSVQs are also being introduced for those who wish to study at school or college for a vocational qualification. GNVQs/GSVQs in Leisure and Tourism are available at three levels: Foundation, Intermediate and Advanced/Level I, II and III.

Assistants may also study for BTEC/SQA qualifications in Leisure Studies. The national certificate takes two years part-time and the national diploma three years part-time or two years full-time. Courses are available at colleges and institutes across the country.

Both ILAM and ISRM offer a wide range of short courses for sports and leisure centre assistants. The ILAM offers a Certificate in Technical Operations (approved by SPRITO) which is aimed at all those involved in the maintenance of swimming pool plant and water quality. The ISRM Sport and Recreation Technician's Scheme provides opportunities for staff to register with ISRM as Candidate Sport and Recreation Technicians. They may acquire modular qualifications over an open period of learning, and join the ISRM as associate members (AInstSRM). Training modules, normally studied over two or three days, include core skills, pool plant operations, customer care, reception work, operation of health and fitness suites and health/fitness skills.

LATE ENTRY

Some opportunities exist for adults to enter this occupation, but they would normally have relevant qualifications or experience, eg in coaching.

Adults can gain recognition of their skills and experience by working towards NVQs/SVQs. There is open access to NVQs/SVQs – no academic qualifications are required, and there are no age limits. NVQs/SVQs are based on competence, and it does not matter how that competence has been gained – through experience, company training programmes, college courses or open learning. Past experience can be put forward as evidence of competence, via Accreditation of Prior Learning (APL).

OPPORTUNITIES

The last 20 years have seen a growth in interest in sports and leisure, and many new centres have been built. Opportunities occur throughout the country, in rural as well as urban areas.

Many centres are run by local councils as a service to the community, but an increasing number are being opened by commercial companies. These include private health clubs, gymnasiums, health and fitness centres etc. There are also sports and leisure facilities in many hotels and holiday centres. Educational institutions, such as colleges and universities, often run sports centres for staff and students. Large employers, such as the health service and police, also run centres for the benefit of their employees.

Competition to work in sports and leisure centres is intense, and those with relevant qualifications or experience have an advantage. As a luxury industry, leisure is vulnerable to downturns in the economy. In addition, many sports and leisure pursuits fluctuate in popularity.

PAY AND CONDITIONS

Salaries vary according to the job and the location. Assistants can expect to start on a salary of £7,000 to

SPORTS AND LEISURE: GAG/GAJ

£9,000. Assistants gaining qualifications may receive increments, and it may also be possible to augment income through part-time teaching and/or coaching work. Assistants at some centres may receive commission for enrolling new members.

Many centres are open from early in the morning until late at night, six or seven days a week, making some unsocial hours necessary. Many assistants are required to work shifts, for example 7am to 2.30pm one week, 2.30pm to 10pm the next. They also have to work some weekends.

Some part-time work may be available, especially for those with relevant experience.

PROSPECTS

Prospects exist for promotion initially to supervisory level. Pool attendants may be promoted to baths supervisor, where their responsibilities may include arranging duty rotas and organizing cover if a member of staff is off sick. Alternatively, they may be promoted to sports hall supervisor, with a wide range of duties and responsibilities. Courses for supervisors are run by a variety of organizations, including NEBSM, ILAM and ISRM.

For those with the ability and aptitude, there are also prospects for progression to sports and leisure centre management. To make the move to this level, a management qualification such as the Diploma of Management Studies (DMS) – available at many colleges and institutes – is a necessity. This normally requires two years' part-time study. The ladder of promotion varies from centre to centre; it is likely to involve progressing from the post of assistant manager, responsible for some specific area of operations, such as the gymnasium, to deputy manager and finally to manager.

RELATED OCCUPATIONS

Sports coach/instructor, professional sportsman/woman, retail assistant, receptionist, counter service assistant, tourist information centre assistant, groundsman/woman, sports and leisure centre manager

FURTHER INFORMATION

Central Council of Physical Recreation (CCPR)*, Francis House, Francis Street, London SW1P 1DE, 0171 828 3163/4

Institute of Sport and Recreation Management (ISRM)*, Giffard House, 36–38 Sherrard Street, Melton Mowbray, Leicestershire LE13 1XJ, 01664 565531, www.isrm.co.uk

Institute of Leisure and Amenity Management (ILAM), ILAM House, Lower Basildon, Reading, Berkshire RG8 9NE, 01491 874800

Local Government Management Board*, 76–86 Turnmill Street, Farringdon, London EC1M 5QU, 0171 296 6600

National Coaching Foundation*, Information Centre, 114 Cardigan Road, Headingley, Leeds LS6 3BJ, 0113 274 4802

Recreation Managers Association of Great Britain*, Recreation House, 7 Burkinshaw Avenue, Rawmarsh, Rotherham, South Yorkshire S62 7QZ, 01709 522463

Scottish Sports Council*, Caledonia House, South Gyle, Edinburgh EH12 9DQ, 0131 317 7200

The English Sports Council*, 16 Upper Woburn Place, London WC1H 0QP, 0171 273 1500

SPRITO – The NTO for Sport, Recreation and Allied Occupations, 24-32 Stephenson Way, London NW1 2HD 0171 388 7755, www.sprito.org.uk

FURTHER READING

Leaflets/booklets are available from the addresses marked*.

Working in Tourism and Leisure – COIC

Careers in Sport and Recreation – CCPR

Careers in Sport – Kogan Page

Periodicals: Recreation; The Leisure Manager.

In the careers library classified under GAJ.

BROADCASTING/FILM/THEATRE: GAL

1. **PRODUCTION ASSISTANT CLCI:GAL**
2. **RESEARCHER CLCI:GAL**
3. **FLOOR/STAGE MANAGER/ASSISTANT DIRECTOR CLCI:GAL**
4. **CAMERAMAN/WOMAN/CAMERA OPERATOR CLCI:GAL**
5. **SOUND TECHNICIAN/OPERATOR CLCI:GAL**

BACKGROUND INFORMATION

This is a very complex industry with a range of jobs involved. On major projects, for example a feature film or TV drama, the structure would be roughly as follows:

Producers have overall responsibility for completion on time and within budget – they may make many early decisions on writer/script, the choice of director and performers and generally oversee the organizational and financial side. The director makes most of the creative decisions, directing the actors, and briefing the designers, camera team, sound crew, editors etc on the effect they want to achieve. The producer may be assisted by a production manager who deals with the day-to-day organization, and a production accountant who keeps track of the financial aspects. In TV, a production assistant acts as the director's personal assistant. A set designer (or production designer/art director) and a costume designer design settings and costumes. During filming, an assistant director (in film) or floor manager (in TV) is responsible for ensuring that all the practical things needed are present and ready, either in the studio ('sound stage') or on location, and has a key role in shooting. After shooting/recording, especially if film is being used, a picture editor and sound editor assemble the material to make the finished product, and post-production may involve recording sound effects and specially composed music and mixing or dubbing the various soundtracks together (voice, music, sound effects). Many other people are involved, from carpenters and electricians to stuntmen/women and drivers.

For documentary or news TV, the team is much smaller and many tasks are doubled up. A researcher gathers information on the subject, finds suitable people to be interviewed and places to be filmed, and writes a script or treatment. An independent video production company may have as few as four people on a shoot – director, camera operator, sound recordist and a camera assistant (or general assistant/runner).

Most feature films, many commercials, some pop promos and some films and dramas for TV are made on celluloid film that is processed and printed by a film laboratory. Other TV programmes and most corporate and non-broadcast videos are created on videotape using electronic cameras. The period of scripting and planning before filming is called 'pre-production'; the actual filming or recording is 'production'; and the process of editing the picture and soundtrack is known as 'post-production'.

A big theatre production (eg a West End play) will have a structure that is similar in many ways, though the stage manager takes the place of the floor manager and, to some extent, the production assistant, and the company manager that of the production manager. There are no camera people involved but there may be a sound technician/designer and a lighting designer. In theatre, the term 'company' often means the team of people brought together to mount a specific play or show.

Structure of the industry

Feature film production companies. Basically, these may be just a producer and a secretary, or producers, secretaries and management people in a larger company. Other staff are employed for their particular specialism on a freelance basis.

Broadcast TV companies. These include BBC TV at national and regional levels and the ITV network companies. They have their own studios and equipment, edit suites etc. They employ some staff in all categories for the programmes they make themselves, though increasingly these are on fairly short-term (eg one-year) renewable contracts, and they take on additional freelances as required. They also buy ready-made programmes from other countries and commission independent production companies to make at least 25% of their programmes for them. Channel 4 and S4C operate entirely on a commissioned-programme basis.

Satellite and cable TV companies. These put out mainly programmes and films bought from other sources, but create linking and promotional material and some programmes themselves. For example, cable companies broadcast local news; for this, they employ some production staff plus freelances.

Independent production companies. There are more than 1,000 of these, the vast majority with only a few permanent staff. They make commissioned TV programmes and TV films and/or corporate videos, commercials, pop promos, educational or training videos – including interactive videos – and videos for sale in bookshops. The larger ones have their own studio and post-production facilities and employ some production staff full-time but most hire in freelances or the services of facilities houses, as needed for each project.

In-house film/video/audio-visual units. Some major industrial and commercial concerns and non-business organizations have their own units or departments to create promotional and training videos for the company's own use. Some of these employ production technicians full-time, though many have a producer who hires in freelances and facilities for each project. The technicians may also look after closed-circuit TV and audio-visual aspects of sales and training activities. Some universities and colleges also employ multiskilled technicians to provide audio-visual services.

Facilities houses and suppliers. These range from film studios to post-production facilities, such as video editing suites and sound mixing (dubbing) studios, but also include companies that hire out camera, sound and lighting equipment, costumes and props, build scenery, search for suitable locations, create computer graphics sequences etc. Some employ full-time staff to operate equipment and resources provided to clients; others have a list of technicians they call in to meet demand. Some of them also service theatre and radio/recording.

West End and touring theatre production companies. Some touring companies are subsidized and create a full company for at least a season. Commercial companies are more likely to put together a new company from freelance performers and technicians for each show they produce, though they may have some staff on retainers, moving them from show to show if they have a continuing programme of productions. Length of employment may depend on the success of a show in attracting audiences,

BROADCASTING/FILM/THEATRE: GAL

determining the length of a West End run. Some fringe and small-scale touring companies are very small and performers and stage managers may act as technicians, too.

Subsidized national and regional repertory theatres. Companies like the National Theatre, Royal Opera House, and Bristol Old Vic maintain a permanent staff of technicians, including stage management, lighting and sound. Some performers will be under contract for a long period. Other staff may be recruited for specific productions or a season.

Theatrical venues. West End theatres in London and touring theatres in other cities are hired by theatre production companies wanting to present their show. The venues usually have front-of-house and technical staff that include technicians capable of setting up and operating the lighting and sound, though big productions may take their own people for these tasks. The same applies to small-scale and fringe touring venues, down to the cabaret circuit in pub rooms, though in some cases the venue manager may act as the technician.

Network radio. Network radio includes BBC Radios 1, 2, 3, 4 and 5 and the two independent channels. At both national and regional levels these have their own studio facilities and make many of their own news, drama, documentary etc programmes for transmission. They are similar to BBC TV and ITV in their employment policies – most staff are on fixed-term or 'rolling' contracts.

Local radio stations. These include BBC local stations and Independent Local Radio (about 120 companies), which broadcast to specific geographic areas and/or ethnic/cultural communities. All employ multiskilled technicians to maintain and operate their equipment, though radio journalists, presenters and disc jockeys may prepare news items and programmes and do an element of operating themselves. Average staff of an ILR station is about twelve.

Independent radio/audio production companies operate much like independent TV/video production companies, offering ideas to radio stations and making commissioned drama or documentary programmes, but may also create audio tapes on special topics, eg car maintenance or readings of novels for sale in newsagents and record shops, or make training tapes, audio-magazines or recordings of conferences for industrial and commercial concerns.

Closely associated with this field is the music and recording industry.

The film and TV industry has changed a lot in recent years and is still changing. Pressures from new technology, deregulation, the ending of the union closed shop, and the drive to cut costs are resulting in, for instance, multiskilling, which in effect means the merging of several jobs into one, whereby a camera operator may handle lighting and sound and even some editing tasks. However, it is still not clear how these changes will work out. They also tend to mean that working hours are longer for less remuneration and with less favourable conditions. A much smaller proportion of the industry's workers are long-term employees; most are now freelance and 'casualized'. However, entry is more open, though this means that the competition for places in employment and on relevant education and training courses has intensified.

1. PRODUCTION ASSISTANT (GAL)

THE WORK

TV

The production assistant (PA) functions as personal assistant to the director or producer, giving organizational and secretarial support. In the planning stage of drama programmes, the director has meetings with the designers, lighting, camera, sound experts and leading performers to discuss how the play or show is going to be done. The PA attends, takes notes of any decisions and follows up with minutes or memos and phone calls to make sure everyone knows what they have to do, checks that it has been done, and receives messages back for the director. It may be possible to pass some of the typing work to a production secretary. The PA may arrange meetings, book rehearsal rooms and hotel accommodation, book or hire equipment, crews, catering facilities and other services, and type up and circulate the script, rehearsal schedule, shooting schedule and shotlist. They may also arrange the permission-to-film and copyright on, for example, the music used.

During rehearsals, often held in rooms outside the studios, or meetings with the scriptwriter or researcher, changes may be made to the script that have to be typed up and circulated. This can happen repeatedly. Other changes may be made, or requirements realized, that call for modifications of set, costumes, type of camera equipment needed etc, and these have to be passed on to the relevant department for action. During the final camera rehearsal and actual recording in the studio, the PA sits with the director in the control room. They call out cues over 'talkback' systems to the camera operators and other technicians, pass messages to the floor manager, time each sequence with a stopwatch to make sure the finished programme will be the correct length (critical with TV to fit standard time-slots), advise the presenter to speed up or slow down, and take notes of any comments by the director that require action. During post-production, the PA's notes and timings are important to the picture and sound editors and they may refer to the PA to answer queries that arise. On completion, the PA makes sure the finished videotape reaches the transmission point on time.

On location, filming with a single camera, the PA also handles the functions of the continuity person in films, carefully noting the position of everything, especially actors' hands, to ensure everything matches up when the camera is moved to shoot from a different angle. In short, the PA is the main co-ordinator of a programme or series and a key figure in bringing it in on time, to length and within budget.

Radio

PAs here do similar work in assisting the producer/director, booking studio space and facilities, keeping track of programme expenditure etc. They may also make arrangements for guests and interviewees, and look after them.

Film

There is no directly comparable role. The production manager, or sometimes on feature films a production co-ordinator, does the work of arranging transport for crews and equipment, making location arrangements, booking facilities, catering, accommodation etc.

Theatre

Some large theatre and opera companies have a

production assistant who helps with administrative/organizational tasks, but it is not a clearly defined occupation, as in TV and radio.

WORK ENVIRONMENT

Much of the work is in a production office, but the PA also attends meetings in a variety of offices and meeting rooms; may have cause to visit the camera, sound, lighting, set construction and wardrobe departments; sits with the director and vision mixer in the enclosed control room; checks that everything is ready on the studio floor; and goes on location to whatever places are involved. Location work may involve travel to other parts of Britain or foreign countries, working in buildings, city streets, the depths of wild country, and being away from home for short or long periods.

SKILLS AND INTERESTS

Social and communication skills are needed to relate tactfully and confidently to technicians and professionals inside the company and suppliers and contacts outside. PAs must be able to work quickly and calmly under pressure but still need to be accurate, to analyse, organize and assess priorities, and to interpret instructions correctly. They should be able to split their attention, keeping an eye or ear on one activity while doing something else themselves. A methodical and orderly mind is needed to keep track of the different versions of the script and amendments, as well as of matters that await resolution.

Some financial awareness is important in handling budgets and spreadsheets. Stamina, a cheerful personality and sense of humour help the PA to cope with the pressure and long hours, and to get on easily with others in the production team. They also need initiative and self-reliance, normal eyesight and hearing, good colour vision (in TV) and a clear speaking voice. They need keyboard skills, and shorthand is an advantage.

ENTRY REQUIREMENTS

Basic educational requirements are a broad general education with three/four GCSEs/S grades (A–C/1–3) including English, but many PAs have A levels/H grades and some have degrees – usually in an arts subject, sometimes in media-related studies. Advanced and Intermediate GNVQs are available in Media, Communication and Production, and GSVQs Levels II and III in Communication and Media. Other basics are speedy and accurate typing (about 40 wpm), reliable shorthand or speedwriting (about 100 wpm), and secretarial skills. Also required are previous secretarial and/or organizing experience and familiarity with word processors/computers, gained in another job. Ability to talk knowledgeably about television, current affairs, theatre, music, films is an advantage, and experience in amateur dramatics, radio or film-making is useful.

TRAINING

After an initial short course, a trainee production assistant in TV or radio learns mainly on the job by working alongside and helping an experienced PA, usually with periods on different types of programme, and possibly with short courses to understand the more technical aspects. They are then given responsibility for segments or aspects of programmes, before handling PA duties on a programme on their own. However, they will be expected to have acquired some of their skills in earlier training and employment in secretarial or administrative work before becoming a trainee PA.

There are few pre-entry training courses aimed specifically at this occupation. Film and Television Freelance Training (ft2) includes production assistant as one of the training areas within its national new-entrant training programme. Applicants should already have an NVQ in Administration at Level 2/3 or experience in the use of IT, particularly word processing, and be able to type at 40-60 wpm. ft2 is the UK film and television industry's only national provider of new-entrant training in the junior technical and production grades for the freelance market. (Please see TRAINING in article 4. CAMERAMAN/WOMAN/CAMERA OPERATOR.) A number of FE and HE courses will give an understanding of the production processes and techniques, so may be helpful (see course directories listed in FURTHER READING), but gaining secretarial skills may be more so. There are also a variety of short courses available in different aspects of film/TV/radio.

The BBC offers a two-year training in programme making, providing the skills and knowledge to compete for a career in TV. A degree or equivalent and relevant experience are the minimum requirements for entry.

LATE ENTRY

This occupation is normally entered as an adult after experience in at least one job, often from within the TV or radio organization, with most PAs starting in their twenties. Later entry may be possible.

OPPORTUNITIES

The starting point with large TV companies is as a trainee production assistant. However, these posts are normally only advertised internally and are filled by people working in the company as a secretary, or in a clerical or administrative job. Competition for these posts is intense.

Independent production companies are likely to look for people with experience as a PA with a large TV company, though they may occasionally consider someone who has been a personal secretary or personal assistant in another industry, where organizing and co-ordinating was a significant part of the job.

When advertised publicly, job vacancies appear in *The Guardian, Broadcast, Screen International, The Stage* and *Television Today*, ethnic newspapers, some local newspapers. BBC external vacancies appear on CEEFAX page 696. Most smaller companies do not advertise, but appoint from people who contact them speculatively.

PAY AND CONDITIONS

A trainee with a regional TV company could expect a salary of about £12,000 and an experienced PA about £15,000. Senior PAs could earn up to £20,000. Salaries in radio and in independent production companies are lower.

Working hours are unlikely to be regular, with early morning starts and late nights during busy periods being common. Some PAs work shifts. Overtime may be paid in some situations. PAs are more likely to be on permanent or renewable contracts, rather than freelance.

BROADCASTING/FILM/THEATRE: GAL

PROSPECTS

PAs progress from relatively straightforward programmes, eg local news and current affairs, to more complex and costly ones, and ultimately drama. The promotion line in major TV organizations is to senior PA, principal PA, senior principal PA, up to head of production assistants. These posts may give responsibility for all the PAs on a major series, in a department or in charge of all the PAs in a TV production company. The job gives a thorough understanding of the whole process of television production and transmission, with a knowledge of the different personnel and activities involved. This makes it a good training ground for future producers or production managers. PAs also move into positions as floor manager, vision mixer or researcher.

RELATED OCCUPATIONS

Production secretary, floor/stage manager/assistant director, assistant/associate producer, production manager, producer, director, continuity person, film/video editor.

FURTHER INFORMATION AND READING

Please see article 5. SOUND TECHNICIAN/OPERATOR.

2. RESEARCHER (GAL)

THE WORK

TV

The work varies according to the nature of the programme involved. On a chat show, where a host interviews famous guests, the researcher provides the host with background notes on the life and career of each guest, suggestions for questions that may result in interesting anecdotes and possibly also photographs and film coverage of the guest when younger, for use in the programme. They may also put forward names of possible guests for the show's producer to decide on, research their availability and make the initial contacts with guests or their agent. On a quiz programme, the researcher has to find suitable people to take part, possibly selecting from hundreds of applicants responding to advertisements, provide information and opinions about them to enable the producer to select, and notes about amusing incidents in their lives and questions for the presenter.

On a current affairs programme, especially a local one, the researcher has to find suitable topics, incidents and people, possibly going out with a camera crew to film material for inserts or doing actual location interviews, either on- or off-camera, themselves, and writing either a script or a treatment for the on-screen presenter in the studio. On a network current affairs programme, serious investigative journalism is involved, often on sensitive and controversial issues, which may incur personal risk.

On documentaries or arts programmes, the researcher may do library research into the subject, or interview visits to provide the producer, editor, director or scriptwriter with the information needed to compile the programme. This may also include finding suitable places and people to film, which could be in other countries, and locating and negotiating the use of old prints, paintings, photographs, newsreel/archive clips and appropriate music. They may write a script. When interviewees or participants come to the studio, the researcher may look after them, see that they are comfortable and at ease, explain what clothes they should wear etc. The researcher would be expected to suggest ideas/topics for future programmes.

So the actual work may be reading or writing, looking through files of old photographs or screening old newsreels, phoning or writing to, or advertising for, potential subjects, dealing with agents or copyright holders of visual or audio material, going out to visit and assess possible locations and people, interviewing informally to gather information and provide cassette or photographic evidence of the suitability of a potential interviewee, typing up their findings, so the producer and director can make decisions, discussing these with them, setting up a schedule of visits/locations for reconnaissance or filming, or conducting filmed/recorded interviews. There will also be meetings and discussions with producer, director, editor, scriptwriter, presenter depending on the type of programme. Some researchers specialize, for example, in science, religion, or nature.

Radio

Broadly similar to TV, except that the title 'research assistant' is often used and the emphasis is more on research in books, newspapers and sound archives. Many producers do their own research.

Film

Employment of researchers is not common and then mainly in pre-production. When it occurs, it is likely to be to provide information for historical movies (on costumes, customs, practices) or for scientific/technical plausibility on science fiction movies or those with a specialist basis, eg medical or legal. For these, people with specialist knowledge may be preferred to general researchers. Researchers may also be engaged for film documentaries, working in the same way as for TV documentaries.

Theatre

A researcher may be engaged occasionally (but very rarely) by the larger permanent theatres to research visual and textual material that will help designers, director and performers to achieve historical accuracy and/or to provide pictures and text for a programme booklet.

WORK ENVIRONMENT

Much is office-based – reading, at the keyboard, writing, or making phone calls. As many researchers are self-employed, freelances may work from home. Considerable time is spent in archives and libraries, and looking at possible locations, talking to possible subjects, taking notes, or recording on a pocket tape recorder. This could involve travel to many parts of the country or TV region and to other countries. During preparation for filming/recording, the researcher is present in the studio, dressing rooms and entertainment facilities, ensuring that subjects are briefed.

SKILLS AND INTERESTS

Communication and social skills are of prime importance. Researchers have to understand, and be understood by, a wide range of people, in different occupations and social classes, as well as communicating with their producer/director/editor. They have to be able to get on friendly terms quickly and inspire trust, in order to draw out the information and co-operation required. They work alone and carry responsibility for their own work, so they need to be self-motivated, but also capable of relating and contributing as part of the production team. They should be open-minded and investigative, determined and resourceful. Resilience is needed – carefully researched ideas can suddenly be dropped.

Researchers should be logical and methodical in their approach and presentations, well organized, able to think quickly and flexibly and to make decisions/recommendations. Intense concentration may be needed to sort out the essentials of a story that will make a good programme or item, plus the ability to switch immediately to a totally different topic. For magazine and news programmes, they may have to follow leads on several topics at the same time. They work under time pressure. Some programme series may have more than one researcher.

They need a clear speaking voice. Also important are keyboard skills, a good telephone manner, knowledge of reference/archive sources and production processes (to be able to reject subjects for filming/recording that cannot work for technical or logistical reasons). A driving licence and car may be essential for some projects.

ENTRY REQUIREMENTS

There are no minimum educational requirements, though about 75% of researchers have a degree which, for many specialist researchers, is in their specialist subject. However, staff vacancies tend to go to people already working in the organization, eg as production secretary or production assistant, or to applicants with experience in journalism. Their chances are increased if they have film, TV or radio experience as well. Those offering their skills as a freelance researcher also need a track record, usually in journalism, and knowledge of a specialist area helps. Fluency in one or more foreign languages opens up work on programmes about other countries, or possibly for production companies in other countries. As the vast majority of researcher posts are not advertised, it is essential to make direct contact and build up a network.

TRAINING

Most researchers have either gained experience in the research aspects of another job, as a journalist or editorial assistant on a newspaper or magazine, or production assistant in TV, or start on local current affairs programmes, learning on the job, and go on to more complex and specialist programmes.

An NVQ in Production Research is available at Level 3.

LATE ENTRY

Most researchers enter as adults after work in journalism, TV, radio or a specialist field. There is no maximum age limit.

OPPORTUNITIES

The BBC employs a few full-time researchers on a permanent basis, though, even here, limited-term renewable contracts are becoming more usual. More common is a 'run-of-series' contract basis, though, in some cases, this can be quite long. Most researchers are employed on short fixed-term contracts for the pre-production and production period of, for example, a documentary series or quiz show. This may lead to a more established post, or they may find they go from contract to contract, but there are likely to be gaps. The work is usually on a freelance basis. In the corporate video and independent TV production area, contracts may be for only a few weeks, or even days, and may be on a daily-rate basis. They and film/theatre production companies engage researchers when a project requires one.

Local current affairs programmes sometimes provide a useful starting point with a local journalist suggesting topics to the producer or editor at a local radio or regional TV station, possibly topics the journalist has covered for a newspaper. Similarly, a national newspaper or magazine journalist, staff or freelance, may offer ideas in the special area they cover and be asked to follow through and so gain the necessary experience to become a regular freelance or contract researcher.

Many freelance researchers may do work in other fields, eg for magazine or book publishers, either as researchers or as writer/researchers.

Most companies and regional TV/radio stations that employ researchers are based in large cities. The majority of employers are in London and South East England, though there are centres in Edinburgh/Glasgow, Cardiff/Swansea and Manchester/Liverpool. Some independent production companies operate from a small town or rural situation.

Research posts on, for example, a major new documentary series are sometimes advertised externally. Job advertisements appear in *The Guardian* (Monday), *Broadcast, Screen International,* ethnic newspapers and some local newspapers. BBC external vacancies appear on CEEFAX page 696.

PAY AND CONDITIONS

Salaries for full-time posts for an experienced researcher may be from about £15,000 to £20,000 in TV, depending on size of the company, or £13,000 to £19,000 in radio. A researcher with an independent production company may receive a minimum recommended weekly rate of £368 and daily rate of £92, although many are paid much less. Freelance work could be based on a daily rate of from £100 to £400, depending on status of the project, experience and specialism, or, more usually, on an agreed fee for the whole project. Travel, accommodation and subsistence expenses will normally be paid for research visits away from base or home, and incidental expenses (eg phone and postage costs) when the production company's resources cannot be used. Overtime may be paid in some situations.

Some programmes may have a regular 9-to-5 work pattern, but most researchers work long irregular hours that vary with the type of programme. It often involves evening and weekend work, as these are the times when people doing other jobs can be contacted, or because deadlines have to be met.

Freelancers may provide their own office space and equipment (eg word processor, tape recorder, camera).

PROSPECTS

There is no formal promotion ladder, though some companies promote to senior researcher and even associate producer, especially if they have management and budget control skills. Researchers may move on to writing or journalism, to programme editor of documentary series, or to director or producer, for which the experience they gain of organizing the content of

BROADCASTING/FILM/THEATRE: GAL

programmes is a good basis. Some join with one or more colleagues to start their own independent production companies. A few become presenters or newsreaders.

RELATED OCCUPATIONS

Journalist, screenwriter, production assistant, assistant producer, floor/stage manager, presenter.

FURTHER INFORMATION AND READING

Please see article 5. SOUND TECHNICIAN/OPERATOR.

3. FLOOR/STAGE MANAGER/ASSISTANT DIRECTOR (GAL)

THE WORK

These jobs relate to similar roles in different industries, but there are distinct differences.

Film

The assistant director (AD), or first assistant director on a feature film, acts as the general foreman of the unit during filming in the studio or on location. On features, commercials and drama series created on film, this is a team activity with a first assistant director, second assistant director and third or even fourth assistant director. On documentaries, there may be one assistant director plus possibly a runner.

The first assistant director analyses the script with the producer, director and production manager to break it down into scenes and arrive at a shooting schedule that will be most economical on time, both on different sets in the studio and on location, and can be divided into amounts of filming that can be achieved in a day's shoot (or a night in some cases). They make sure that the necessary equipment and props are ready and on site, and that the appropriate performers, crowd artists, hairdressers, make-up artists and stuntpeople have been called. Having learnt from the director what the next camera position will be ('set-up') and the content of the picture (close-up, wide-shot, two-shot etc), the first assistant director informs the camera and sound teams, so that they can get their equipment and lighting ready. The first assistant director also tells the carpenters, painters, set-dressers etc to, for example, remove or replace a wall of a set if necessary, retouch paintwork or age a wall, or rearrange the props to suit the new camera angle.

When everyone is ready, the first assistant director calls a rehearsal, and performers and technicians practise to shoot the scene. Problems are spotted and adjustments may be made. When all is ready, the first assistant director calls for the studio doors to be shut, the red light switched on forbidding entry and everyone in the studio to be silent, for the lights to be switched on, for the camera motor to be started, and then tells the director all is ready for filming.

Because the first assistant director is tied to the shooting area, the second assistant director liaises with the producer and production manager off the set and with the design and technical departments, and prepares the call-sheet for the following day. The third and fourth assistant directors (sometimes called runners) call performers from their dressing rooms, run messages and fetch refreshments for leading technicians and performers and the director. The third assistant director usually gets the call-sheet copied and circulates it to everyone present – performers and technicians. This tells them if they are needed the following day and at what time. On location, the assistant directors could all be involved in cueing (eg a distant car not visible to the first assistant director to start and move into shot) by arm signals from one to another, or in requesting pedestrians or vehicles to stay out of an area where a shot is in progress. On a big crowd scene, they may each be involved in directing the action of the crowd artists ('extras') in sections of the set or location. If, for some reason, the first assistant director has to be away from the camera for a time, the second assistant director takes over, and so on down the line.

On documentary crews, there may be only one assistant director and a runner, or, on small video shoots, no assistant directors at all, with the director and possibly a researcher doing all the organizing and co-ordinating.

TV

The floor manager (FM) co-ordinates activity on the studio floor. The team includes assistant floor managers (much like the second assistant director, above) – who liaise between the production office and other departments and work out call times – and floor assistants – who call performers to make-up and set, run errands, deliver scripts etc. With the director in the control room, the FM passes on instructions (relayed by the production assistant over headphones) to the performers, presenters, newscasters, celebrities and members of the public taking part in the programme. With studio audiences, safety and ready access to fire exits are major considerations of the FM. They may brief guests and audience on what is happening and how to relate to the cameras, microphones etc. The FM thinks ahead to make sure everything is ready and everyone is in the right place at the right time. They may also book rehearsal rooms, mark out floor plans of the set (scenery) and act like a stage manager during rehearsals, though some TV companies have stage managers who handle this part of the production process. Floor management staff play similar roles on outside broadcasts (eg recording a pop concert) but, when film is used on location for a TV drama or programme, a film crew is used including assistant directors.

Theatre

The stage manager (SM) also co-ordinates during rehearsals and performances but, in this case, the director is not present during most of the performances, so that the SM carries full responsibility for ensuring that the show goes on at the right time and in the form and quality intended, with especial regard to safety.

Again, this is a team job, with a deputy stage manager (DSM) and one or more assistant stage managers (ASM). Tasks delegated to them vary from company to company, but often it is the DSM who runs performances from the prompt corner at the side of the stage and the ASM who has responsibility for obtaining and looking after hand props, arranging costume fittings, calling performers when needed, running messages to technical departments. Some tasks may be carried out in rotation.

With the director, the stage manager may prepare a rehearsal schedule and a production schedule for the main events: the design of sets and costumes, their construction and painting, the casting auditions if needed, the 'get in' (when the set is put up on stage and lighting and sound equipment are rigged/adjusted/focused), technical rehearsal, dress rehearsal, opening night, and the 'get out' if it is a short run (when the set and technical equipment are removed). They liaise with the technical departments to make sure everything is ready on time. They book rehearsal rooms and get them ready by marking out on the floor, with chalk or tape, the positions of the elements of scenery and furniture. They get together 'substitute props' to stand in for the furniture and for hand props such as guns, books, teacups, until these are obtained by the ASM or, in large companies, by the props department.

One of the team, usually the DSM, is present at all rehearsals, where they 'hold the book'. This is the prompt book, a specially pasted-up version of the acting script, with dialogue on one side and ruled-up sheets for notes on the other. They prompt the performers with any forgotten lines, but also note any changes to the dialogue, draw small sketches of the positions of the performers at key points and their moves, and note any special requirements of scenery, props, sound effects, and lighting changes as they are realized. The SM handles liaison and makes sure the relevant departments are informed.

When rehearsals are nearly complete, a final version of the prompt book is prepared, which becomes the company bible and contains all the sound and lighting cues and points to call performers from their dressing room in time for their entrance on stage. During performances, this is in the prompt corner at the side of the stage, as the guide for the DSM to call the performers and cue the lighting and sound operators either over headphones or by push buttons which operate red and green cue lights (though in large theatres the lighting is controlled by a computer program). From here they prompt performers with any forgotten lines. They also supervise the stage-hands in any scene changes and may cue the fly gallery to raise or lower backcloths, or direct the person operating the revolving stage.

During a run, the SM is responsible for company discipline and, when the director has gone, if they feel aspects of the performance are slipping, they may call an extra rehearsal to get them right. If a performer is ill, they alert the stand-in/understudy and possibly rehearse them. If there is no stand-in, they may have to 'read-in' the part, going on stage and walking through the character's moves but reading the lines from a script. ASMs quite often do 'walk-on' and 'one-line' acting parts themselves.

In a small touring company, where there is no company manager, the SM may be responsible for organizing transport and accommodation, liaising with the management of the theatres they visit over get-ins, get-outs and rehearsals, briefing the resident technicians at these theatres, and even paying the performers at the end of each week.

Radio

The studio manager fills this role as well as some duties of a sound technician or recordist. Please see article 5. SOUND TECHNICIAN/OPERATOR for more details.

WORK ENVIRONMENT

Film and TV studios are specially built to ensure that everything needed is to hand and within reach of workshops and equipment stores. They are usually big enclosed spaces, with smooth floors and many lights suspended above or on scaffolding, and capable of being made completely soundproof and lightproof when the doors are closed. Many TV programmes involve a studio audience, who can watch the crew as they work.

Outside broadcasts could be in concert halls or cathedrals. Location filming, whether for feature films, TV dramas or documentaries, may be in city streets, on mountains, in caves, factories, dockyards, offices, or people's homes, with all the complications of being away from full resources, variable weather and sometimes very cramped working conditions. Facilities (including catering), equipment and personnel may all have to be brought to the location. On location (or touring for theatre), travel to other parts of Britain and to other countries is involved, which may mean short or long periods away from home.

Radio studios are generally smaller than film or TV studios and are enclosed, with artificial light. Normally the soundproof studio with table, chair and microphones where presenter, guests, and performers sit or stand is separated by a glass partition from the control room where the director/producer sits, which contains tape decks, record turntables, CD players, sound mixing desk etc.

In theatre, stage managers spend time in rehearsal rooms, on stage, in the theatre auditorium, and in offices and also visit backstage dressing rooms and departments (eg wardrobe) and workshops where scenery is built.

SKILLS AND INTERESTS

The ability to handle people tactfully but firmly is the main requirement. There are a lot of people working under pressure and depending on one another to achieve results. Assistant directors/floor managers/stage managers have to be able to resolve differences, smooth things over and keep the show on the road. They need a strong personality, a clear analytical mind to spot the real basis of a problem and devise a solution, and a methodical one to plan and organize very complex work processes, as well as calmness in a crisis, an ability to get on with everybody and to accept decisions made by the producer or director.

Leadership qualities, ability to work in a team, a commanding voice and manner and the ability to deal tactfully with the conflicting interests of different personalities and departments – all help. Though often not technically expert themselves, they need to understand the technical aspects, because they have to relate to skilled technicians on a knowledgeable basis that wins respect. They need to be alert and keep a clear mind despite the high level of stress and long hours.

In film work, a driving licence is useful and a knowledge of one or more languages opens up employment on films being shot in other countries, possibly using some foreign technicians.

ENTRY REQUIREMENTS

Film

There are no minimum requirements, but some entrants now have C+G or BTEC/SQA certificates or diplomas and/or degrees in media-related subjects, although the majority get their first job through contacts, regardless of academic background. Traditionally, many start as third or fourth AD (runner) and work their way up. Gaining experience as a runner or in a junior position within another area of the industry, eg post-production facilities house or film laboratory, may make it easier to obtain work as a third AD on a film production. Evidence of good work in an organizing capacity on student or amateur films/videos/theatre can help a lot, as well as indicating knowledge of the production process. It is possible for

BROADCASTING/FILM/THEATRE: GAL

applicants with experience in student productions to be taken on as first or second AD on an independent feature or pop promo.

TV

Entry is usually post-experience, either from other jobs in TV, such as production assistant or camera assistant (from which they may be seconded for a period to discover aptitude), as a stage manager in theatre, or an assistant director in films. Floor assistants may be recruited from secretarial, clerical or administrative staff in the same TV company.

Theatre

Entry is usually as an ASM, for which there are no minimum requirements, but many applicants have done a drama school course in stage management or have a degree in drama or theatre studies. Practical experience in a stage management role on student or amateur theatre productions is advisable. Casual work in a local theatre, as, for example, stage-hand or front-of-house manager is useful. For details of courses, refer to Association of British Theatre Technicians (ABTT) or Conference of Drama Schools directories listed in FURTHER READING in article 5. SOUND TECHNICIAN/OPERATOR.

Radio

Please see article 5. SOUND TECHNICIAN/OPERATOR.

Entry requirements for C+G courses vary, so check locally. For national certificate/diploma courses they are four GCSEs/S grades (A–C/1–3); for higher national courses one/two A levels/H grades and four GCSEs/S grades (A–C/1–3); for degree courses five GCSEs/S grades and two/three A levels/H grades. However, competition for places on media courses is high, so a keen interest in the arts, entertainment and current affairs, and evidence of having gained some understanding of film/TV/theatre from work on school or amateur plays/films/videos, may be vital.

TRAINING

Trainee floor managers learn mainly by working on the job alongside an experienced floor manager, possibly with short off-the-job courses. Otherwise, entrants in the most junior grade (floor assistant/third assistant director/assistant stage manager) learn the higher-level jobs by observing as they handle their own duties.

Many people obtain training before entry by doing a BTEC/SQA national certificate/diploma or higher national certificate/diploma course or a degree or postgraduate course at an FE/HE college. Some people take short courses or evening classes in film/video/TV techniques or drama. Many employers rate 'real' practical experience higher than courses.

For suitable courses, consult the course directories listed in FURTHER INFORMATION AND READING in article 5. SOUND TECHNICIAN/OPERATOR. Courses with a higher practical content may be most useful when applying for jobs. Check with potential employers before embarking on courses.

The NVQ in Production at Level 3 includes units relevant to floor managers and assistant directors.

LATE ENTRY

There is no upper age limit; FE and degree courses are open to mature students (sometimes on the basis of life experience and/or an Access course). However, most adult entrants to these jobs are moving from other jobs in film/TV/theatre, eg as a junior technician or stage-hand.

OPPORTUNITIES

Generally, competition for work is very intense and deregulation has resulted in a lot more experienced technicians (previously staff in TV and broadcasting studios) working on a freelance basis, making entry for newcomers extremely difficult.

Film

Assistant director is, in the main, a freelance occupation with production companies engaging individuals as needed. Work at any level is on a project basis – a few days for a commercial or pop promo, several months for a major feature film. The film industry fluctuates drastically and there are times when very few films are being made, and so there are few opportunities.

TV

BBC TV, ITV companies and the larger independent TV/video production companies employ full-time floor managers. A common entry route is as holiday relief during the summer, which may lead to further engagements or a staff job.

Theatre

All producing theatres and most theatrical production companies need SMs, DSMs and ASMs (small touring companies may just have an SM), but the number of permanent theatres and touring companies has been reducing, which cuts opportunities and increases competition for jobs.

Most studios, production companies and theatres are in major towns and cities, with the bulk of them in London and the South East of England.

When advertised externally, job vacancy advertisements appear in *The Guardian, Broadcast, Screen International, The Stage* and *Television Today,* ethnic newspapers and some local newspapers. BBC external vacancies are on CEEFAX page 696.

PAY AND CONDITIONS

In major TV studios, salaries vary from about £10,000 for a floor assistant to about £20,000 for an experienced or supervisory FM, with significant variations between companies. Minimum weekly rate for an ASM in a major repertory theatre is £158 and for a SM on a West End production £315 (but on a big musical it would be much more). Minimum weekly salary for a first AD on a feature film is £368.50 and £313 for a second AD. A freelance third AD earns £207.50 minimum a week with a daily rate of £51.87.

Hours are often irregular. In films, early starts and late finishes are common. In TV, shift-working enables maximum use to be made of studios. In repertory theatre, rehearsals may take place for a future production during the day, while the current one is performed in the theatre during the evenings, and the same stage management team may handle both, though they may rotate some duties to provide some days or evenings off. In major subsidized and West End theatres, when working on performances, SMs would start late afternoon to prepare, and finish after the show when all performers have left the theatre. Because of the importance of the senior positions, they may take work home to prepare for the next day, reading and analysing scripts, preparing shotlists, schedules etc. In TV, theatre and major feature films, overtime working may be paid at overtime rates but, in independent production, it is increasingly common to sign a contract that includes a percentage of overtime within the agreed fee.

PROSPECTS

The job structures listed in THE WORK traditionally serve as promotion ladders with TV companies, going up to senior and supervisory grades of FM. On documentary films, TV programmes or videos made by small production companies, or in fringe theatre companies, there may be only one assistant director or stage manager. By being in on the start of such a company with, perhaps, other ex-students, employment and increasing experience can sometimes be assured.

The logical next step is to production manager in films and TV, and company manager or production manager in theatre, but some go on to director or producer.

Some people use an ASM post as a stepping stone to an acting career.

RELATED OCCUPATIONS

Road manager, production assistant, production manager/co-ordinator, assistant producer, producer, director, company manager.

FURTHER INFORMATION AND READING

Please see article 5. SOUND TECHNICIAN/OPERATOR.

4. CAMERAMAN/WOMAN/CAMERA OPERATOR (GAL)

Feature films, documentaries, commercials and non-broadcast videos are normally filmed with one camera and one camera crew, whether created on film or videotape. TV shows made inside a studio, and also TV outside broadcasts (OBs), such as sporting events, are created on several cameras at once, each with its own operator, with the director in a control room selecting from the available pictures to broadcast live or to record on tape for future broadcasting, while a vision mixer ensures a neat flow from camera to camera. The film or videotape from one-camera shoots goes to a film editor or video editor for editing, or 'cutting', to assemble shots in the final sequence, working with the director.

There are different standards of film (70mm for widescreen, 35mm for feature films and many commercials, and 16mm for documentaries and some independent features) and videotape (from one-inch for TV studio work and Beta SP for TV documentaries and quality corporate videos, to VHS for recording weddings). These call for different sizes and complexities of camera and any one cameraman/woman or camera operator may have experience of, or specialize in, only a limited range of these, though many of the skills involved are similar.

THE WORK

Film

In feature films, and in TV when shooting drama or commercials on celluloid film, rather than videotape, the senior member of the camera team is the lighting cameraman/woman (called director of photography or DP on major feature film productions). Other members are the camera operator, focus puller and clapper-loader. The DP discusses with the director and the production designer/art director the effect required, decides on the filmstock and lenses to be used, instructs the gaffer (who controls the electricians) on how to place the lights, their intensity and colour, agrees with the director and camera operator the positioning of the camera, any camera or lens movement, and the framing of the picture. The DP also instructs the laboratories in any special treatment required during processing, assesses the results of each day's filming and decides if anything needs to be shot again for lighting or camera reasons, and plans ahead to the next day's shoot. The DP is responsible for the photography, creating the right mood with light, shade and colour, eliminating unwanted shadows, making sure all that should be visible is, to create a pleasing or striking picture on the screen.

Some aspects of this may be delegated to the camera operator. As well as operating the camera while looking through the viewfinder during filming, they usually decide the precise framing and composition of shots, and may settle the pace of camera movement, such as pans (sideways movement), tracks (forward and backward moving the whole camera) and zooms (forward and backward using only the lens). They also instruct the focus puller on lens and camera movement, the key grip on the laying of tracks or mounting the camera on dolly or crane, and the clapper-loader on assisting generally.

During shooting (and rehearsals to shoot) the focus puller turns the lens and/or the camera on its mount at the agreed speed and time, and otherwise assists the camera operator with preparing the camera with any special lenses, filters or mounts, and generally cleans and looks after the camera and accessories.

The clapper-loader is a camera assistant who writes up and operates the clapperboard to mark the beginning of each take, loads film into magazines and unloads used film and labels and packs it for sending to the laboratories for processing.

The key grip, though working closely with the camera crew, is regarded as leader of a separate team of grips or riggers who, as well as preparing tracks, cranes and dollies, erect scaffolding and platforms for the camera and lighting. On a modest feature, drama or documentary, this might be a grip and assistant grip.

On a small documentary unit using film, the cameraman/woman could be responsible for the lighting as well as camera aspects and have just a camera assistant to help with all tasks.

TV

In the TV studio, there are from three to six electronic cameras, each with its own electronic camera operator and one or more camera assistants or trainee camera operators. The most junior moves the cables out of the way as the camera moves around ('cable bashing'). If the camera is mounted on a motorized crane, one assistant is responsible for swinging the counterbalanced arm or jib and another drives the crane to positions marked on the studio floor. But most cameras are on pedestals on mobile mountings

BROADCASTING/FILM/THEATRE: GAL

that the camera operator moves or drives into position. This is not always easy when other cameras, the sound boom and performers have to be avoided. During camera rehearsals, these movements are practised to a shotlist fixed to the camera and, during shooting, the production assistant reminds the camera operator over headphones of what is coming next.

The director decides most aspects of camera position, size of shot etc, possibly consulting with the lighting director, but the operator may offer up on the studio monitor the framing and composition they feel the director is after. On current affairs, quiz shows and other programmes which cannot be rehearsed in detail, the director will depend much more on the operator to obtain good shots, passing general instructions on position and size of shot over headphones via the production assistant. During shooting/recording, the director sits in a control room and selects from the pictures seen by different cameras displayed on a bank of monitors. For dramas and other rehearsed programmes, this selection may be decided in advance; for others, the director decides on the spot.

On outside broadcasts (sporting events, ceremonial occasions), the operator may have more say in the positioning of the camera and choice of picture (though still connected by a talkback system to the control room in a van). The camera may be supported on their shoulder or set up on a tripod or a specially installed mount (eg at a sports stadium) or on top of a moving vehicle (eg at a racetrack).

In the studio, lighting is controlled by a lighting director, who may have been a camera operator previously, but may also have come in by another route.

TV dramas, or the sections of them made on location, are often created with film rather than electronic cameras. In this case, a lighting camera operator functions like a lighting cameraman/woman in films, supervising lighting and camera teams.

Electronic news gathering (ENG) is increasingly done, using an electronic camera, by a lone camera operator, or a team of two who handle all aspects of camera, sound, lighting and basic maintenance of equipment, and use communications links to play their material back to base. They may work closely with a reporter/presenter or researcher, who goes with them.

Documentary filming may be handled by an exterior camera operator working with a camera assistant, handling all lighting and camera aspects.

Video

Independent production companies creating corporate videos or TV programmes on videotape may use large or small crews, depending on the video or programme and the size of the budget. However, in many cases, the cameraman/woman is likely to operate the camera as well as setting the lighting, with the aid of one or more camera assistants. Speed may be essential because of a limited shooting schedule and the short time people being filmed can spare from their normal duties or are prepared to give.

Theatre

There are no cameras in theatre, but lighting designers/technicians design and control the lighting aspects of the stage show, as the director of photography or lighting director does in films/TV. On a major West End show or pop concert, they choose the types of lighting equipment to achieve the effects they and the director envisage, design how it will be rigged in the theatre, decide on colours of 'gels' in front of each light at different points, intensities and changes, and may prepare a lighting plot with diagrams, for use by technicians and operator, or for programming into a computer.

On pop concerts and some stage and promotional shows, lighting aspects may include laser beams and projected images, strobes and flashing/moving lights or reflectors, and dry ice for smoke effects. In smaller theatres, the chief electrician may design and operate the lighting. Touring pop groups may have a technical road manager who handles both lighting and sound aspects. Lighting designers/technicians may work on fashion shows, exhibitions, conferences and multi-media presentations for advertising/PR agencies and industrial clients to, for example, launch (promote) a new car, as well as on theatrical productions.

WORK ENVIRONMENT

See this section in article 3. FLOOR/STAGE MANAGER/ASSISTANT DIRECTOR for general characteristics of film, TV and radio studios and location work.

News gathering may involve competing with other camera crews and photographers for a position to catch an adequate view of a celebrity or event, and may involve personal danger and rough conditions when covering war, riot and natural disasters. Outside broadcasts could mean being in uncomfortable positions in the cold and rain. Travel to other parts of Britain and to other countries is often involved, which may mean short or long periods away from home.

SKILLS AND INTERESTS

A strong interest in photography, film and video, both artistically and technically, is important, as are a good sense of colour and composition and some knowledge of optics and electronics. All this implies creativity in interpreting the scriptwriter's/playwright's and director's ideas into visual form. Physical fitness and stamina are essential in coping with working long hours, carrying heavy equipment, and sometimes the camera, on the shoulder.

Normal eyesight and colour vision, a good head for heights, and the ability to react quickly, are all attributes of a good cameraman/woman. Verbal cueing from actors' dialogue, or over headphones from the control room, calls for good hearing. In some situations, such as news gathering, personal initiative and the ability to work alone may be more important than the ability to work in a team. Ability to work at speed, take quick decisions and keep calm under pressure are all valuable.

A driving licence is essential for news gatherers and useful in many other types of camera work, as studios and locations are not always easily accessible.

ENTRY REQUIREMENTS

For direct entry to training posts with the BBC TV and ITV companies, whether on the electronic or film sides, the minimum requirement is normally GCSEs/S grades (A–C/1–3) in English, maths and physics. But these openings are relatively rare, competition is fierce and successful applicants often have some A levels/H grades and have done a film/TV or photography course at FE or HE college leading to a City and Guilds (C+G),

BTEC/SQA national certificate/diploma, or higher national certificate/diploma, or degree (see TRAINING below). Practical evidence of interest and ability in photography (a portfolio of still photographs or a videotape of film/video work) is important. An involvement in amateur dramatics, knowledge of lighting/optics/electronics, and an interest in current affairs, TV, film or theatre all help. Some applicants have experience in the industry, or in professional photography. Others join appropriate trade associations and attend relevant events to make contacts. Some senior camerapeople look for ability to compose a picture and to be able to draw.

Entry as a freelance is difficult even with a BTEC/SQA qualification and usually requires significant experience on student/amateur films.

Entry requirements for C+G courses vary so check locally. For national certificate/diploma courses they are four GCSEs/S grades (A–C/1–3); for higher national courses one/two A levels/H grades and four GCSEs/S grades (A–C/1–3); for degree courses, five GCSEs/S grades and two/three A levels/H grades. However, competition for places on media courses is high, and interests and knowledge, such as those cited above for entry to traineeships, may prove important.

Most entrants to theatre lighting have GCSEs/S grades, A levels/H grades and a college or drama school course to higher national diploma level, possibly entering as electrician or assistant electrician.

TRAINING

The number of traineeships offered by employers (BBC TV, ITV companies), which carry the likelihood of a job at the end, is very small and competition for them is fierce.

Traditionally, the BBC TV and ITV companies have had an annual intake of trainees, with most training on the job over a number of years, together with periods off the job and/or in training centres. However, they are now tailoring training to meet specific requirements as they arise, covering shorter time-scales and, increasingly, training multiskilled technicians over a range of equipment and aspects (eg camera, sound, some editing techniques) rather than specialists.

Faced with the need to train technicians for a freelance career, the whole industry has developed the following schemes:

– ft2 (Film and Television Freelance Training) is the UK film and television industry's national provider of new-entrant training. It takes about 20 trainees (aged over 18 years and unemployed) each year for a two-year scheme. In the first year, trainees are seconded to a range of different film and TV production situations to experience a variety of departments in feature films, drama series, commercials and documentaries. In the second year, their attachments relate to one discipline. Job areas offered currently include camera assistant/clapper-loader, sound assistant, production assistant, research assistant, art department assistant, grips assistant and assistant editor/videotape operations/post-production. This on-the-job training is backed up by practical and theoretical courses at colleges and training centres. Applications are accepted throughout the year, but the closing date is 1 April of each year. Competition is tough as ft2 receives on average 70 applications per place. Completion brings eligibility for union membership (BECTU) and all trainees work towards achieving the relevant SKILLSET NVQs/SVQs at Levels 2/3. A training allowance is paid and also travel expenses to location shoots. This is seen as similar to an apprenticeship.

– CYFLE offers six to eight places on a full-time one- or two-year course to train Welsh-speaking technicians.

– Gaelic Television Training Trust offers up to nine places each year on a two-year training programme to enable Gaelic speakers to train with Scottish Television (STV), BBC Scotland or Grampian TV on extended attachments.

– Scottish Broadcast and Film co-ordinates and provides training in Scotland. It offers training in selected skill areas.

– Channel 4 finances a training scheme, called 4FIT, every two years for people from ethnic backgrounds, which is managed by ft2 and runs in parallel with its new-entrant scheme.

Most traineeships are advertised.

Many people organize their own training by taking media-related diploma, degree and postgraduate courses at colleges and universities. Some of these offer students the possibility of hands-on experience and of gaining credits on student films, and can possibly be used in a showtape (a videotape of excerpts). However, it is important to analyse prospectuses carefully, as some courses in this area of study are primarily theoretical, with very little practical content. It is also useful to ask about help with work placements and to find out about industry contacts, the backgrounds of lecturers and the destinations of previous graduates. Another possibility is the many short courses available. Consult the course directories listed in FURTHER READING for details of courses.

NVQs/SVQs in Camera Assistance at Level 2, Camera Operation at Level 3 and Camera Direction at Level 4 are available.

Drama school stage management courses include theatre lighting and sound (stage electrics). City of Westminster College offers one-year courses in lighting and in sound, evolved with the ABTT. Oldham College has two-year national diploma courses. Some degree courses in drama and theatre studies offer a chance to gain practical experience. Some larger theatres provide part-time college training for assistant electricians.

LATE ENTRY

There is no upper age limit, but most of the training schemes are intended primarily for people in their late teens or early twenties. Degree and diploma courses are open to mature students. However, most mature people moving into camerawork have experience in other jobs in the industry, such as lighting electrician/gaffer, or in professional photography.

OPPORTUNITIES

This is a very competitive industry, with more qualified people than jobs. The larger TV organizations sometimes advertise trainee camera posts in videotape or film. Nowadays, this is usually to meet specific needs, rather than an annual intake, and the vacancies may be filled internally from people already working in secretarial, clerical or general assistant/runner jobs. Some cameramen/women are employed full-time on long or short contracts by BBC TV and ITV companies. The more successful independent production companies and facilities houses that provide crews, as well as equipment, employ cameramen/women or have a contractual or retainer relationship with them.

Most camera crew members are freelance and are hired on a fee-basis or daily/weekly rate for each film, or project, by film, TV or video production companies. Freelance cameramen/women may obtain work through specialist agencies or facilities houses, by entries in directories, advertising in the trade press, mailings to production companies or (more effective) personal phone calls and visits. In order to obtain enough bookings to earn a living it is essential to establish and maintain contacts with a number of producers, production managers and lighting cameramen/women or DPs. Some ex-students of film/TV courses join with others to form an independent production company of their own and try to set up film, TV or video projects together.

The number of theatres and theatre companies has been reducing, so there are few openings for theatre lighting specialists. Even if entry as an assistant electrician or electrician is achieved, it may be a long time before an opportunity to design the lighting for a show arrives.

PAY AND CONDITIONS

In the regional TV companies, on completion of training, a cameraman/woman can earn from £11,500 to £16,500, with news and features camera operators earning significantly more than studio-based ones. Senior cameramen/women may earn around £20,000 or more. A freelance lighting cameraman/woman on feature films has a minimum weekly rate of £839 and a daily rate of about £210. A well-known director of photography on major feature films would expect a very much higher fee, as one of the most important technicians involved. The recommended camera operator weekly minimum is £470, and for a focus puller £345. Some freelance camera operators supply their own camera equipment.

To work in the industry or gain essential experience, existing freelance technicians and new entrants find themselves working on 'deferred payment' on low-budget feature films, on the understanding that they will be paid at professional rates retrospectively if and when the film is sold and makes a profit. Normally expenses and sometimes daily payments are made.

In full-time posts, overtime is normally paid at overtime rates. This applies also for work in feature films/commercials and the independent sector but, increasingly, agreements are reached allowing an extended working day or an agreed amount of overtime per week within the agreed fee. Shift work may be involved in TV.

PROSPECTS

The crew structures described in THE WORK for film and TV serve as promotion ladders from junior to more senior jobs. This works reasonably effectively in organizations that are producing regularly with established crews, like TV companies, where the ladder may include senior and supervisory posts up to, for example, head of production operation services.

Deregulation, multiskilling and the ending of the trade union closed shop mean that entry is, in theory, easier, but that crews are smaller and more skills may have to be acquired so that a cameraman/woman, with or without an assistant, may handle lighting, camera and sound. This trend is likely to continue. Another development has been the opening up of television to independent production companies, which has increased the number of potential employers. But, at the same time, many companies that once hired permanent staff have switched to hiring freelances on short-term contracts and, as a result, there are now many more experienced cameramen/women competing for freelance work.

Some lighting cameramen/directors, DPs and editors move on to become directors.

In theatre, the promotion route is: assistant electrician, electrician, chief electrician, lighting designer. Achieving this may involve moving from smaller to larger theatre companies as opportunity arises. A small number of expert lighting designers have set up their own companies providing lighting design services for theatres, pop concerts, fashion shows etc.

When externally advertised, job vacancy advertisements, including traineeships, appear in *The Guardian, Broadcast, Screen International, Televisual, The Stage* and *Television Today,* ethnic newspapers and some local newspapers. BBC external vacancies appear on CEEFAX page 696.

RELATED OCCUPATIONS

Photographer, vision mixer, sound technician/operator, film/TV director, film/video editor, lighting electrician/technician, telecine operator.

FURTHER INFORMATION AND READING

Please see article 5. SOUND TECHNICIAN/OPERATOR.

5. SOUND TECHNICIAN/OPERATOR (GAL)

THE WORK

Film

On feature films, the sound crew is headed by the sound mixer, who sits at a mobile mixing desk, or console, and adjusts the level, tone etc, of the sound of the actors' speech coming through his headphones. Other crew members are the boom operator and sound assistant. Sound reaches the sound mixer from fixed microphones within the set and/or radio microphones on the actor's person, but primarily from the movable microphone on the mechanical boom operated by the boom operator. The sound assistant helps them both and prepares blank audio tapes, labels recorded tapes to go for transfer to sprocketed magnetic tape for use by the sound editor or dialogue editor, and may keep a log of takes, noting any problem areas. Guided by the sound mixer, the boom operator sets up the microphones in the best positions available (so that they are not visible and do not cast a shadow) and runs cables to them.

During shooting, the boom operator's task is to swivel and move/raise/lower the microphone to catch the best possible speech from each of the performers. The sound mixer may switch between microphones, as performers move within the set, and adjust controls rapidly to compensate for any drop in level as a performer turns their head. The sound mixer usually has the power to end a take if they hear a distant sound that could affect the recording, perhaps an aeroplane or train, or to declare sound quality unusable and requiring replacement dialogue recording during post-production. The overall aim is to achieve 'perspective' sound, so that the performers' voices sound as though they are the distances from one another that the camera sees. The sound crew also record an 'atmos track' (ie the background sound when no-one is speaking) for use by the sound editor to fill any gaps in the edited soundtrack. They may record sound effects as well, such as vehicles braking or starting up, or may be sent out separately to obtain these for the sound editor.

On documentaries, all these tasks may be handled by one sound recordist who, when appropriate, holds the microphone on a boom (usually a long metal rod) while keeping an eye on the dials on a portable recorder or, for some video systems, a control panel slung round the neck and attached to the video camera by cable. They may mix between several microphones and control tone, volume etc. On other units, a sound assistant or general assistant (to camera and sound) may assist with, for example, boom operation.

In post-production, specialist sound technicians and mixers work in sound studios on, for example, recording the narrator's voice for documentaries, sound effects, the music or replacement dialogue for feature films etc. Re-recording mixers (or dubbing mixers) and their assistants handle the tasks of 'cleaning up', 'equalizing' and 'levelling out' of all the dialogue, music and sound effects tracks to create the final balanced soundtrack.

TV

A similar structure applies in TV, but there could be more than one boom operator to allow for reaching other sets or distant areas of a large set, when performers move. In the studio, the sound mixer sits in the control room with the mixing console, in direct touch with the director and vision mixer, and communicates with boom operators over headphones (talkback). Microphones may also be suspended from the studio ceiling. On rehearsed shows, the boom operators work to a sound script that tells them when to move the mechanical boom to new positions etc. On others, they work on their own initiative and guidance from the control room. In a studio discussion, possibly with audience participation, a lot can depend on their catching each speaker in turn and adequately receiving any interruptions.

On outside broadcasts, the control room is in a van and microphones and cables have to be rigged for the occasion (sports fixture, royal wedding, pop concert) and taken down afterwards. The sound crew also handles communications back to the studio.

Other sound jobs in TV include the grams operator. On cue from the director via the production assistant, they play music or sound effects chosen from a collection of audiotapes and CDs that the sound mixer mixes into the soundtrack.

Theatre

In large theatres and on West End and major touring productions, a sound designer, or technician or engineer, designs the sound aspects. For some productions and companies, this may mean only discussing with the director and stage manager the sound effects and music needed, obtaining these (sometimes recording them specially) and editing them onto one audiotape.

For a major musical, it could involve positioning microphones for instruments in the orchestra, as well as on stage for the performers (which could include radio microphones on individuals) and the loudspeakers for best coverage of the audience. During performances, a sound operator sits at a complex mixing console, switching between microphones and adjusting levels to get the required balance between singers and different instruments, working to a complex sound plot as the live sound is fed through the speakers.

In smaller theatres, the sound technician may design and operate, or the chief electrician may set up the sound, as well as the lights, and operate both from the lighting box, or the stage manager may operate the sound during performances from the prompt corner.

Radio

The studio manager (SM) runs each studio, handling bookings of studio time (received from producers or production assistants) for the succession of programmes that may use it during each day or week. The SM prepares for each user programme by setting up chairs, tables, stands to hold music and/or scripts, and microphones, which is more complex for a panel discussion or musical ensemble than for a talk, newscast or one-to-one interview. During recording, the studio manager operates tape recorders, mixing between microphones and adjusting volume, tone etc to their own creative/technical feeling and to instructions from the producer/director, who sits in the control room with them. They may mix in music, sound effects and previously recorded elements from tape, disc and CD players, which they also operate. Some sound effects may be created manually.

During rehearsals and run-throughs, the SM tests presenters, guests and performers for level, advises them on the use of microphones and adjusts the positions of microphones, and they mark up their own copy of the script with cues for effects, music etc. Some elements of a documentary, arts, news or current affairs programme may be recorded in advance during another studio session, or by a radio journalist on location. The studio manager may edit these tapes, extracting selected statements from an interview and cutting out unnecessary words and pauses. All elements may be pre-mixed for broadcast from one tape, or mixed during broadcast.

Some studio managers go on location to set up equipment and microphones to record or broadcast, for example, sports fixtures, concerts, travelling discussion programmes, with all the problems of coping with extraneous sounds, wind, variable acoustics, and audience/crowd participation.

Increasingly the work of a studio manager is carried out by sound recordists, presenters and producers working together with easy-to-operate but sophisticated electronic desks.

WORK ENVIRONMENT

See this section in article 3. FLOOR/STAGE MANAGER/ASSISTANT DIRECTOR for general characteristics of film, TV and radio studios and location work.

News gathering may involve competing with other sound recordists, camera crews and photographers for a position to best catch the statements of a celebrity, or the live sounds of an event, and may involve personal danger and rough conditions when covering war, riot and natural disasters. Outside broadcasts could mean being in uncomfortable positions in the cold and rain. Travel to other parts of Britain and to other countries is often involved, which may mean short or long periods away from home.

BROADCASTING/FILM/THEATRE: GAL

Theatre sound technicians rig equipment on stage, in the orchestra pit and in the auditorium. They may have a workroom and equipment store backstage or outside the actual theatre building. During dress rehearsal and performances, they usually sit in a control box or open area at the back of the auditorium.

SKILLS AND INTERESTS

Sharp hearing is needed to catch faint sounds and to differentiate an unwanted sound from the intended sounds coming through the headphones. Good hand and ear/eye co-ordination and speedy reactions are important in responding to performer moves and changes of voice level. Sound technicians must be able to concentrate, hold one physical position for lengthy periods, and have steady arms and stamina. A methodical mind and close attention to detail will also help. They should be able to read music, and may possibly have studied it and be able to play a musical instrument, gaining a sense of timing and rhythm. They have knowledge of and interest in IT, electronics and computers and a strong interest in film, television, radio or recording and the current music scene. They need to be able to get on well with people, fit easily into a team and have good communication skills. In some situations they need to be able to take initiative and work alone. Physical fitness is required for moving and setting up equipment.

For freelance work and work on location, a driving licence is important.

ENTRY REQUIREMENTS

For direct entry to training posts with the BBC and ITV companies, the minimum requirement is GCSEs/S grades (A–C/1–3) in English, maths and physics, but competition for these places is fierce, and successful applicants often have some A levels/H grades and have done a film/TV or electronics course at FE college leading to a BTEC/SQA certificate or diploma (see TRAINING, below). These courses also require the exam results mentioned above. Practical evidence of interest and ability in sound, recording and music is important. Having your own hi-fi rig and doing mixes (of which you should offer a tape as a portfolio), or helping out on a local, hospital, or university radio station, or with a pop group (amateur or professional) or disco, or working on student productions during a college course, provides this evidence. An involvement in amateur dramatics, playing a musical instrument, knowledge of electronics, and an interest in current affairs, TV, radio, film or theatre all help. Some applicants have experience in the industry or in recording in junior or ancillary roles, for example, as a runner, clerical assistant or secretary.

Entry as a freelance is the most common route but difficult, even with a BTEC/SQA qualification, and usually requires significant experience on student/amateur films or radio, on hospital radio or in DJ mixing, constituting a list of credits and providing an impressive showtape (and hopefully a few contacts with potential employers). Marketing skills are useful in this highly competitive area and interpersonal skills, reliability and organization will influence 'rehire' decisions.

TRAINING

Please see TRAINING in article 4. CAMERAMAN/WOMAN/CAMERA OPERATOR.

In addition, NVQs/SVQs are available in Sound Assistance at Level 2, Sound Operation at Level 3 and Sound Direction at Level 4.

LATE ENTRY

There is no upper age limit, but most of the training schemes are intended primarily for people in their late teens or early twenties. Degree and diploma courses are open to mature students. However, most mature people moving into sound work have experience in other jobs in the industry, or related industries.

OPPORTUNITIES

This is a very competitive industry, with more qualified people than jobs. The larger TV and radio organizations occasionally advertise for trainee sound operators, or audio assistants, or trainee studio managers, but there is no longer an annual intake, and these posts may be filled internally from people in secretarial, clerical or assistant jobs. Some sound technicians/operators are employed full-time on long or short contracts by BBC TV and ITV companies, post-production houses and established theatres. The more-successful independent production companies and facilities houses that provide crews, as well as equipment, employ small numbers of sound technicians/operators, or have a contractual, or retainer relationship with them that amounts to regular or near-regular employment. Most sound crew members are freelance and are hired on a fee-basis or daily/weekly rate for each film or project, by film, TV or video production companies. Freelance sound technicians/operators may obtain work through specialist agencies or facilities houses, by entries in directories, advertising in the trade press, mailings to production companies or (more effective) personal phone calls and visits.

The number of theatres and theatre companies has been declining, so openings are few. It may be easier to start in theatre as an electrician or assistant stage manager.

When advertised externally, job vacancy advertisements, including traineeships, appear in *The Guardian, Broadcast, Screen International, Televisual, The Stage* and *Television Today*, ethnic newspapers and some local newspapers. BBC external vacancies are on CEEFAX page 696.

PAY AND CONDITIONS

In a regional TV company, a trainee sound technician earns about £9,000, and, after training, goes onto a scale rising to over £17,000. An experienced electronic recordist could receive over £25,000. Union (BECTU) freelance weekly rates for feature film work are: sound assistant around £450, boom operator around £660, sound mixer around £770.

A trainee studio manager in radio at the BBC would earn about £10,000, while an experienced studio manager could receive over £30,000.

Some freelance sound recordists supply their own sound equipment.

To work in the industry or gain essential experience, existing freelance technicians and new entrants may work on low-budget feature films on the understanding that they will be paid at professional rates retrospectively if and when the film is sold and makes a profit. Normally expenses and sometimes daily payments are made.

In full-time posts, overtime is normally paid at overtime rates. This applies also for work in feature films/commercials and the independent sector, but, increasingly, agreements are reached allowing an extended working day or an agreed amount of overtime per week within the agreed fee.

PROSPECTS

The crew structures described in THE WORK section for film and TV traditionally serve as promotion ladders from junior to more senior jobs. The heavily practical training courses and funding sometimes found for student films/audio projects have made it possible for some individuals to demonstrate their technical and creative abilities early and so jump a few rungs.

In large TV and radio organizations, there may be progress to senior sound mixer or senior sound technician, or to sound engineer in charge of sound staff in a specific area or concern. The largest theatres have a sound department with a promotion structure to head of sound or head of post-production sound services.

Deregulation, multiskilling and the ending of the trade union closed shop mean that entry is, in theory, easier, but that crews are smaller and more skills may have to be acquired so that a cameraman/woman may handle lighting, camera and sound, eliminating the need for a sound recordist. Another development has been the opening up of television to independent production, cable and satellite companies, which has increased the number of potential employers. However, at the same time, areas that once had permanent staff now use freelances or people on short-term contracts.

Some sound mixers/recordists/technicians move on to become sound/dialogue/effects editors, or move into the recording or pop music industries. Some radio studio managers graduate to producer or director, as do some senior sound staff in TV. Some sound technicians set up their own small company as a facilities house, servicing production or post-production. Work on pop concerts as a technical road manager is a related field that may offer openings, though it may be necessary to start as a non-technical roadie (humper) with a pop group.

RELATED OCCUPATIONS

Recording technician, audio/visual technician, sound maintenance engineer, sound editor, broadcasting engineer, electrical/electronics technician.

FURTHER INFORMATION

Association of British Theatre Technicians* (ABTT), 47 Bermondsey Street, London SE1 3XF, 0171 403 3778 (please enclose a large sae), www.abtt.org.uk

Association of Independent Commercial Radio Companies Association*, 77 Shaftsbury Avenue, London W1V 7AD, 0171 306 2603 (sae required)

British Broadcasting Corporation*, PO Box 7000, London W5 2WY, 0181 752 5252

British Film Institute (BFI), BFI Publications, 21 Stephen Street, London W1P 2LN, 0171 255 1444

BKSTS – The Moving Image Society*, 63–71 Victoria House, Vernon Place, London WC1B 4DA, 0171 242 8400

Conference of Drama Schools, Honorary Secretary*, c/o Central School of Speech and Drama, Embassy Theatre, Eton Avenue, London NW3 3HY

CYFLE*, Gronant, Penrallt Isaf, Caernarfon, Gwynedd LL55 1NW, 01286 671000, //www.cyfle-cyf.demon.co.uk

ft2 – Film and Television Freelance Training*, The Administrator, ft2, Fourth Floor, Warwick House, Warwick Street, London W1R 5RA, 0171 734 5141 (A4 sae required)

Gaelic Television Training Trust, Sabhal Mor Ostaig College, An Teanga, Isle of Skye IV44 8RQ, 01471 844373

North East Media Training Centre (NEMTC), Stonehills Studios, Stonehills, Shields Road, Pelaw, Gateshead, Tyne and Wear NE10 0HW, 0191 438 4044

Television and Radio Training Unit*, GWR Group plc, Granville House, Granville Road, Leicester LE1 7RW, 0116 255 1616

Scottish Film Council*, 212 Broomielaw, Glasgow G1, 0141 334 4445

SKILLSET* (The Industry Training Organization for Broadcast, Film and Video), 91–101 Oxford Street, London W1R 1RA, 0171 534 5300

Stage Management Association* (SMA), Southbank House, Black Prince Road, London SE1 7SJ, 0171 587 1514

FURTHER READING

Leaflets/booklets are available from the addresses marked*.

Working in Performing Arts – COIC

Working in TV, Film and Radio – COIC

Careers in the Theatre – Kogan Page

Careers in Television and Radio (Fifth Edition) – Kogan Page

Media Courses UK 1996 (Third Edition) – BFI

A Guide to Short Courses – BFI

So You Want to Work in Theatre – ABTT

Directory of Drama and Theatre Courses – ABTT

Guide to Courses – Conference of Drama Schools Stage

Changing Channels – A Guide to Working in Television, Film and Radio – BBC

I Want to Work in Television – RTS

In the careers library classified under GAL; RAL

TRAVEL AND TOURISM: GAX

1. **TOURIST INFORMATION CENTRE ASSISTANT CLCI:GAX**
2. **TRAVEL CONSULTANT/TRAVEL AGENCY CLERK CLCI:GAX**
3. **TRAVEL COURIER CLCI:GAX**
4. **TOUR MANAGER CLCI:GAX**
5. **RESORT REPRESENTATIVE CLCI:GAX**

BACKGROUND INFORMATION

Travel and tourism is big business in the UK and very important to the economy. It employs 1.7 million people and is Britain's fastest growing industry.

Overseas visitors are attracted to Britain by its heritage, cultural attractions and beautiful countryside. It is very important that these visitors have help in identifying places of interest and in booking travel and accommodation. Tourist Information Centres (TICs) provide that help.

TICs also have an important job in relation to British tourists. An increasing number of people in Britain have short-break holidays. By attracting those people and helping them, TICs bring money into their localities and help provide jobs.

There have been a number of trends that have led to more Britons taking holidays abroad more frequently – increased leisure time, greater wealth, improved transport facilities and longer life expectancy. A large industry has developed to cater for travel abroad, particularly using package holidays. Travel agents are vital in selling package holidays and travel (both holiday and business) to the public. Travel couriers and resort representatives play an important part in ensuring the smooth running of these holidays.

1. TOURIST INFORMATION CENTRE ASSISTANT (GAX)

THE WORK

Tourist Information Centre (TIC) assistants aim to encourage people to spend time and money in a local area by providing information and help and promoting local facilities. The range of services offered by TICs varies according to their location and size, but many activities are common to them all.

The main task of assistants is to deal with enquiries by post, by telephone and from personal callers. They give information on places of local interest, eg museums, leisure parks, stately homes and country houses. This includes opening times, admission prices etc.

They also provide information on local transport facilities, including bus and train timetables, and on local entertainments and facilities, eg theatres, cinemas, nightclubs, restaurants and sporting events. In addition to local information, TICs are required to hold detailed information for a 50-mile radius and less detailed information for the rest of the UK.

TIC assistants liaise with local guesthouses and hotels to keep a record of good quality accommodation. Most TICs offer callers an accommodation booking service both locally and nationally, known as the BABA (book-a-bed-ahead) Service. This involves working closely with other TICs to book accommodation in other parts of the UK. In some TICs, assistants use computers for information storage and for making reservations.

Assistants can also make reservations for sightseeing tours, theatres, sporting events and transport.

TIC assistants gather information by sending for leaflets, brochures, guidebooks and timetables, both for their own use and to give to customers. They regularly reorder and update stock, and display free material.

TIC staff also sell a range of retail goods, for example guidebooks, maps and souvenirs. Assistants have to order these items, display them, handle cash and keep accounts.

At times of the year when there are few callers, assistants often try to improve their knowledge of local attractions by making familiarization visits.

WORK ENVIRONMENT

TICs are located in a variety of premises, at council offices, in bus and railway stations, airports, libraries and museums. Other TICs occupy purpose-built shops or kiosks.

TIC assistants work indoors, usually in comfortable, pleasant conditions. Their work involves standing and sitting and occasional travel in the locality.

SKILLS AND INTERESTS

Much of TIC assistants' work is in direct contact with other people, in person or by telephone. It is important, therefore, that they enjoy dealing with people and can do so in a pleasant and friendly way. They need to be keen to help and have tact and patience.

Communication skills are important. Assistants should be good listeners, to find out what an enquiry is about and be able to answer enquiries clearly and accurately. Accuracy is also important when making reservations. Since much work is conducted by telephone, a good telephone manner is necessary.

In high season, TICs can be very busy, so assistants should be able to keep calm and work well under pressure. They need to be able to work well in a team.

Assistants should have an interest in, and good knowledge of, their local area – its history, geography and places of interest. The greater their knowledge, the more they are able to help clients.

As computers are used increasingly for information storage in TICs, keyboard skills are usually required and an interest in information technology is important.

The ability to communicate in one or more foreign languages is useful and, in some TICs, it is essential.

A smart, tidy appearance is required.

ENTRY REQUIREMENTS

Entry requirements vary, but employers usually prefer applicants with at least four GCSEs/S grades (A–C/1–3) or equivalent.

The ability to communicate in one or more foreign languages may be required for some posts. This is particularly the case in major tourist areas, such as London, and at sites frequented by many overseas visitors. In areas that tend to have few overseas visitors, a foreign language may not be required.

Many entrants are over 21 years.

TRAINING

There are no pre-entry courses to prepare specifically for

TRAVEL AND TOURISM: GAX

TIC work, although some entrants have taken a travel and tourism college course – see article 2. TRAVEL CONSULTANT/TRAVEL AGENCY CLERK.

All TIC assistants receive training from their employers and regional tourist boards, and may also have the opportunity of going on familiarization visits within the UK.

Most TIC assistants are expected to study for NVQs/SVQs in Tourist Information at Levels 2 and 3. Candidates must study a number of mandatory units and a further selection of optional units that are applicable to their work. Common units include providing an accommodation information and booking service, identifying and providing tourist information, and maintaining a tourist information centre information system.

LATE ENTRY

Previous experience of work in dealing with people is useful, as is experience of clerical work. It can also be helpful to have lived in the TIC locality for some years and to have good local knowledge.

The part-time and/or seasonal nature of the work in some TICs may make the work attractive to adult entrants.

Adults may be able to enter travel and tourism courses without the usual educational qualifications.

OPPORTUNITIES

TIC assistants are employed by local authorities and regional tourist boards. They are employed in approximately 560 TICs in England, 170 in Scotland, 80 in Wales, 30 in Northern Ireland, six in the Isle of Man and six in the Channel Islands. TICs are located wherever tourism is actively encouraged. In England there are about 2,500 staff.

About one fifth of TICs in England open only from Easter to September, as do most TICs in other regions. Other TICs are open all year round.

Although a few TICs employ up to 20 staff, many have just one or two employees. Full-time permanent vacancies occur infrequently and, when they arise, competition for them is strong. Part-time and seasonal vacancies are more plentiful, but entry to them is also competitive.

PAY AND CONDITIONS

There are no nationally agreed rates of pay for TIC assistants. Salaries vary according to age, geographical location and employer. Some TIC assistants are on a salary scale that starts at about £8,000 and rises to about £13,000. In London, salaries are considerably higher.

TICs in major cities and towns, and at particularly busy sites, are open seven days a week. Other TICs open from 9am to 5pm, Monday to Friday, but also open at weekends during the summer season and extend their opening hours to meet local requirements.

Assistants may work full-time or part-time, and some work in the summer season only. Some assistants work shifts.

PROSPECTS

TIC assistants who work part-time, or on a temporary basis, may seek full-time or permanent posts. Promotion possibilities with TICs are limited. All TICs have a manager and some larger employers have a structure of senior information assistant, supervisor and manager, but there are relatively few staff in TICs above assistant level.

There are some opportunities for TIC assistants to seek promotion with local authority tourism departments and regional tourist boards. TIC assistants may use their experience to enter the travel agency or tour operating fields.

RELATED OCCUPATIONS

Hotel receptionist, travel consultant/travel agency clerk, air passenger service assistant, reservations clerk, tourist guide, retail assistant, local authority tourism officer.

FURTHER INFORMATION AND READING

Please see article 5. RESORT REPRESENTATIVE.

2. TRAVEL CONSULTANT/TRAVEL AGENCY CLERK (GAX)

THE WORK

Travel agencies act as a link between travellers and companies selling holidays, transport and accommodation.

Much of a travel consultant/travel agency clerk's work takes place at the counter, dealing with clients wanting package holidays. Travel consultants talk to clients to find out what they require, then show them brochures containing suitable packages. If a client is interested in a particular holiday, the travel consultant checks its availability by telephone or computer. If the holiday is not available, the clerk suggests alternative holidays, usually using a computer to identify them. When the client chooses an available holiday, the travel consultant collects a deposit and makes a booking with the tour operator.

Travel consultants also advise clients about health requirements, visas, insurance and foreign currency, and arrange holiday excursions, passports and car hire and/or airport parking.

Travel consultants book holidays on a computerized system linked directly to tour operators. Tour operators usually send tickets and transport details to the travel agency, where they are checked and then passed to the client prior to departure.

When first working in a travel agency, a travel consultant normally stamps travel brochures and displays them, as well as undertaking administrative duties, such as writing out late availability cards and opening and sorting incoming mail.

Travel agencies also provide a service for independent travellers, who do not wish to use package holidays. Travel consultants may help the client work out an itinerary by consulting travel timetables, booking rail, sea or air tickets and accommodation.

Some travel agencies specialize in business travel. This involves making arrangements for travel abroad, often to very tight schedules. Nearly all business travel work is conducted with the client by telephone.

At least two large travel agency groups provide foreign exchange facilities. The work involves providing clients with foreign currency and travellers cheques, and arranging for money to be transferred abroad. Foreign exchange work is dealt with by specially trained travel consultants.

TRAVEL AND TOURISM: GAX

A large part of the travel consultant's work is spent dealing with clients and others in person and by telephone. Travel consultants are sales people and have to meet sales targets. They also complete forms, use computers, photocopiers and calculators and handle cash, debit and credit card payments.

WORK ENVIRONMENT

Travel consultants spend most of their time working indoors in comfortable surroundings. Travel agencies tend to be in modern shop premises.

Travel consultants spend most of their working day sitting behind a counter. They may go on one 'educational' visit a year, spending time at a resort, usually abroad, to learn about the accommodation and facilities at the resort. They may occasionally travel to short training courses in the UK. Some business travel clerks work in offices within large companies.

SKILLS AND INTERESTS

Travel consultants should like dealing with people and be polite and friendly. Communication skills are important. They should be good listeners, able to find out what clients require and able to give information clearly and accurately. A good telephone manner is important, as much work is conducted by telephone.

A knowledge of travel geography is essential for discussing travel and holiday resorts.

Travel agencies can be very busy, particularly at lunchtimes and on Saturdays. Travel consultants should therefore be able to work under pressure, which includes being able to organize work to make sure that priorities are met.

Travel consultants need a smart and tidy appearance. As computers are used increasingly in travel agencies, both for information and for booking purposes, keyboard skills are required, and an interest in information technology is very useful.

Numeracy is important, as travel agency work includes some figure work, such as calculating holiday or travel costs and deposits.

ENTRY REQUIREMENTS

There are no set entry requirements, although a good standard of secondary education is necessary. Many employers prefer applicants with some GCSEs/S grades (A–C/1–3), particularly in English, maths and geography.

Most young people enter the work via The Travel Training Programme.

A number of entrants to travel agency work have previously taken a course relevant to travel and tourism. NVQs/SVQs in Travel Services are available at a number of colleges of further education. (Contact The Travel Training Company for a list of approved centres.) In addition, Intermediate and Advanced GNVQs/GSVQs Levels II and III in Leisure and Tourism are available.

While NVQs/SVQs and GNVQ/GSVQ courses do not necessarily need particular entry qualifications, educational institutes may specify entry requirements for such courses.

NVQs/SVQs are also available through The Travel Training Company's Approved Centre, and many large companies run NVQ/SVQ training programmes.

BTEC/SQA Higher National Certificate/Diploma in Tourism or Travel and Tourism, or Business and Finance or Business Studies with travel and tourism options, require a minimum of one A level/two H grades and three other subjects at GCSE/S grade (A–C/1–3), including English and maths, or equivalent.

Degree courses in Travel and Tourism or in Business Studies with travel and tourism options, require a minimum of two A levels/three H grades and three other subjects at GCSE/S grade (A–C/1–3), usually including English and maths or equivalent.

Postgraduate courses in tourism usually need a degree for entry.

TRAINING

All entrants to travel agencies start as a junior travel consultant and receive on-the-job training from their employers. Some clerks may be sent on short courses for telephone techniques and selling skills. They may also attend 'educational' visits to hotels and resorts, organized by tour operators, and short courses in airline ticketing, held by airlines.

The Travel Training Programme. Most young people who enter travel agency work do so through The Travel Training Programme, organized by The Travel Training Company. The Travel Training Programme involves work experience and travel training lasting about 24 months, which leads to NVQs/SVQs Level 2 and 3 in Travel Services.

Modern Apprenticeships (part of the Skillseekers Initiative in Scotland) in Travel Services includes on- and off-the-job training, leading to an NVQ/SVQ in Travel Services at Level 3. Contact your local careers office, Jobcentre, TEC/LEC or The Travel Training Company for details.

BTEC Higher National Diploma in Tourism or Travel and Tourism – two years full-time.

SQA Higher National Diploma in Tourism – two years full-time.

Degree courses relating to travel and tourism are either three-year full-time or four-year sandwich courses. Sandwich courses include one year away from college, or university, gaining experience in one part of the travel and tourism industry.

Postgraduate courses last one year full-time.

ABTAC ABTA Travel Agents Council offer ABTAC at Primary and Advanced Levels. This qualification is relevant to the work of a retail travel agent and provides evidence of underpinning knowledge for NVQ/SVQ candidates.

LATE ENTRY

There is no maximum age limit for entry to travel agency work, although entry beyond age 35 is likely to be difficult.

Some agencies prefer mature adults, particularly if they have relevant experience, such as work with people, or in travel and tourism.

The increase in part-time work in travel agencies may be particularly helpful to adult applicants with family commitments.

It may be possible for adults to be accepted onto courses in travel and tourism without the usual minimum entry

TRAVEL AND TOURISM: GAX

requirements.

There may be specific training opportunities directed at adults, in some areas, for this type of work. Candidates may have to satisfy certain conditions to be eligible. Contact your local Jobcentre, careers office or TEC/LEC for details.

OPPORTUNITIES

There are just over 7,300 travel agencies in the UK. They range from small, independent agencies to large agencies with branches in most cities and towns. Some specialize in arranging travel and holidays for one area, such as Australia, but most offer a more general service. An average travel agency is staffed by five or six people.

The number of staff employed in travel agencies expanded until the late 1980s. This growth has stopped and the number employed is now stable. Entry to travel agency work is always competitive.

The main route into the work for young people is The Travel Training Programme. The percentage of trainees that progress into full-time work in travel agencies is very high (approximately 98%).

PAY AND CONDITIONS

Trainees on The Travel Training Programme are paid a training allowance plus travelling expenses.

Rates of pay for trained travel consultants vary between approximately £10,000 and £13,000. Experienced travel consultants dealing with foreign exchange work, or business travel, earn up to £15,000 or more. Clerks may receive a discount on the cost of their own holidays.

Travel agencies normally open shop hours Monday to Saturday. Travel consultants usually work between 35 and 37½ hours a week over five days. Part-time work is available in some agencies and is increasingly used to cover busier periods, eg lunch-times and Saturdays.

PROSPECTS

Moving between agencies for promotion is common. Many small travel agencies have little or no promotion possibilities. Opportunities for progression are much greater in large agencies and can be from travel consultant to senior travel consultant, assistant manager, manager and area manager.

It may be possible to transfer to other branches of travel and tourism, such as tourist information centres and tour operators, including work as a travel courier or resort representative.

RELATED OCCUPATIONS

Tourist information centre assistant, tourist guide, tour operator, foreign exchange clerk, travel courier, resort representative, travel agency manager, retail assistant.

FURTHER INFORMATION AND READING

Please see article 5. RESORT REPRESENTATIVE.

3. TRAVEL COURIER (GAX)

THE WORK

Travel couriers represent tour operators and are responsible for ensuring that travel arrangements made for parties of holiday-makers run smoothly and as enjoyably as possible. This they do by accompanying holiday parties on their journey. Most couriers work with holiday-makers travelling by coach.

Couriers join the party at the start of a journey, welcome clients, check tickets and seat allocation, and announce details of the travel arrangements and stopover points. They commentate on places of interest during the journey and liaise with the coach driver to stop at appropriate times and places. Couriers also liaise with hotel staff, on arrival at stopover points, concerning meals and accommodation.

Couriers make sure, during changes of transport, that the full party and all luggage is successfully transferred. They are responsible for answering enquiries and helping their party with any problems they may have, such as illness or mislaid luggage.

There are different kinds of courier work:

Coach couriers escort parties from the UK to the continent, ensuring passengers and luggage all arrive safely via coach and ferry or channel tunnel. They may then meet a similar party returning from holiday and escort them from the continent to the starting point of their holiday in the UK.

Transfer couriers meet flights at airports and accompany a party to their hotel by coach. They give any help needed in passing through customs and immigration, making sure that the entire party and all luggage are aboard the coach. They make announcements about the holiday and resort. At the end of the holiday they escort the party from the hotel onto their flight home.

WORK ENVIRONMENT

Most travel couriers are concerned with travel overseas with British tourists, although some work in the UK with incoming tourists.

Coach couriers spend the majority of their time travelling – mostly by coach; sometimes by cross-channel ferry. Much of their time is spent sitting. Overnight stops are usually spent in hotels.

Transfer couriers work at airports and on coaches between airports and holiday resorts.

SKILLS AND INTERESTS

Couriers work in very close contact with their party of holiday-makers. They should, therefore, like dealing with people. They need to be outgoing, self-confident, polite and tolerant of others.

Couriers have to cope with any problems that may arise during a journey, such as lost luggage, travel delays and illness. This requires them to be adaptable, flexible and able to make decisions.

They are responsible for ensuring that travel arrangements run as smoothly as possible, without delays caused by any of the party. To achieve this, couriers have to be able to organize others in a tactful manner. Couriers must be well-organized and self-reliant as they work with little or no supervision.

TRAVEL AND TOURISM: GAX

Communication skills are important, since couriers deal with holiday-makers, coach drivers, customs and immigration officials etc. Communication often needs to be in a foreign language, so fluency in one or more foreign languages is important.

Travel couriers must be in good health to cope with the long hours and physical demands of the job.

Travel couriers need a smart and tidy appearance.

ENTRY REQUIREMENTS

No formal educational qualifications are required, but a good general education is necessary. Some employers prefer couriers to have some GCSEs/S grades (A–C/1–3). English, maths, geography and languages are useful. A background in travel agency work can also be useful.

Regardless of qualifications, a good working knowledge of foreign languages is important, except if working solely in the UK.

The minimum age of entry for most companies is 20–21 years, although most entrants are in their mid-twenties. Good health is essential.

Employers look for applicants who have previous experience of working with people. Experience of working abroad is particularly valuable.

Some entrants have previously taken a course relevant to travel and tourism – please see article 2. TRAVEL CONSULTANT/TRAVEL AGENCY CLERK.

TRAINING

Employers usually provide a short induction course for couriers, to familiarize them with the company and the work. Couriers must learn about the route they are to take and the places of interest they will pass through, so they can describe them to holiday-makers.

The main qualifications for couriers are NVQs/SVQs in Travel Services (Tour Operations or Commentaries and Interpretation for Tourism) at Levels 2 and 3.

LATE ENTRY

Entry after 35 years tends to be restricted largely to companies specializing in holidays for retired people.

Any kind of work that involves working with the public is valuable experience, with previous work abroad particularly useful.

OPPORTUNITIES

Travel couriers are mainly employed by tour operators that organize package holidays, particularly holidays that include coach transport. Employing companies range from large, international organizations to small specialist companies. The majority of couriers are freelance and work on fixed-term contracts.

The work is seasonal, and couriers are employed on a short-term basis. Vacancies arise every year, but competition for them is very strong. Vacancies are sometimes advertised, but many companies find that they do not need to advertise, as they receive a large number of speculative enquiries. Applications for summer season jobs should be made in the preceding autumn. For jobs in the winter season, applications are made in the preceding summer. When advertisements are used, they appear in the quality newspapers and in *Overseas Jobs Express*, *Travel Trade Gazette* and *Travel Weekly*.

PAY AND CONDITIONS

Pay varies from company to company, but is within a range between £70 to £130 a week plus free board and lodgings, and expenses.

Hours of work depend on the job concerned.

Coach couriers have no set hours, as they are responsible for their party from the time they join the coach until the end of the journey.

Transfer couriers tend to work shifts, including nights, but travel delays can prolong their hours.

PROSPECTS

Inexperienced staff in some companies begin as transfer couriers and progress to coach couriers or tour managers.

It is possible for couriers employed by large companies to progress to supervising a team of couriers.

Couriers rarely see their work as a long-term career. Typically, they work as couriers for two or three years, although some work for much longer. If they wish to work abroad they may seek to become overseas resort representatives for tour operators. Those wishing to settle in the UK may seek permanent work with a travel company in administration, or promotions work. Some become tourist guides in the UK on a self-employed basis.

RELATED OCCUPATIONS

Tourist guide, air cabin crew, resort representative, travel consultant/travel agency clerk, travel agency manager, tourist information centre assistant, holiday centre worker, tour operator.

FURTHER INFORMATION AND READING

Please see article 5. RESORT REPRESENTATIVE.

4. TOUR MANAGER (GAX)

THE WORK

Tour managers represent tour operators and are responsible for ensuring that travel arrangements made for groups of tourists run according to the published itinerary. They also ensure that the standards and quality of all services are maintained, and care for the well-being of each individual in their group. This they do by accompanying the tour group throughout their entire journey. Most tour managers work with tourists travelling by coach. The duration of a tour can be as short as two or three nights, up to one month, or even longer.

Tour managers meet their group at the beginning of the tour, welcome clients and announce details of travel arrangements, stopover points, safety requirements, border procedures etc. They provide background information on places of interest during the journey and liaise with the coach driver to organize stops at appropriate times and places. Tour managers also liaise with hotel staff on arrival, concerning meals and accommodation. They may organize optional excursions to shops, restaurants or places of entertainment.

Tour managers are responsible for answering enquiries and helping the group with any problems they may

TRAVEL AND TOURISM: GAX

encounter, such as mislaid baggage, theft, local regulations, hospitalization etc.

WORK ENVIRONMENT

Most tour managers accompany groups of clients on cross-border itineraries throughout Europe, though some work in the UK with incoming tourists.

SKILLS AND INTERESTS

Tour managers work in very close contact with their groups. They should, therefore, genuinely like people and be able to relate to people of all kinds and nationalities. They need to be outgoing, self-confident, polite and tolerant of others.

Tour managers have to be able to cope with any problems or emergencies that may arise during the tour, such as lost luggage, travel delays and illness. This requires them to be adaptable, flexible and able to make decisions.

They are responsible for ensuring that all arrangements run as published in the tour operator's brochure, without delays caused by any of the group. To achieve this, tour managers must be well-organized themselves and able to organize others in a tactful manner. Tour managers must be self-reliant as they work with little or no supervision.

Communication skills are important, both in dealing with tourists and with coach drivers, hoteliers, customs and immigration officials. A tour manager must be articulate and able to convey information and instruction clearly and confidently. Most communication needs to be in a foreign language, so a good working knowledge of one or more foreign languages is important.

Tour managers must be in good health to cope with the long hours and physical demands of the job.

Tour managers need a smart and tidy appearance.

ENTRY REQUIREMENTS

No formal educational qualifications are required, but a good general education is essential. Proficiency in English, and a sound knowledge of geography and history are important.

Regardless of qualifications, a good working knowledge of foreign languages is important, except if working solely in the UK.

Most tour operators prefer tour managers to be in their mid-twenties or older. Good health is essential.

As well as a good educational standard, employers look for applicants who are mature and caring. Personality and the ability to inspire confidence are major factors in the selection process.

TRAINING

Tour operators usually provide a short induction course for tour managers to familiarize them with the company and the work. Tour managers must learn about the routes they are to take and the countries they will pass through, so they can describe them to tourists.

A number of NVQs/SVQs in Travel Services are available at Levels 2 and 3.

LATE ENTRY

The vast majority of tour managers are in their mid-twenties or older. Due to the long hours on duty, all tour managers need to be physically fit and in excellent health.

Any kind of work that involves working with the public is valuable, with previous experience of working abroad particularly useful, but personality and the ability to inspire confidence are equally important.

OPPORTUNITIES

Tour managers are employed by tour operators that organize group package holidays, usually by coach. Employing companies range from large, international organizations to small specialist companies. The majority of tour managers are freelance and are hired from tour to tour.

The work is seasonal, and many tour operators invite tour managers they have used before to work successive seasons. Vacancies do arise each year, but competition for them is very strong. Vacancies are sometimes advertised, but most companies find they do not need to advertise as they receive a large number of speculative enquiries. Applications for work in the summer season should be made in the preceding autumn. When advertisements are used, they appear in the quality newspapers and in *Overseas Job Express*, *Travel Trade Gazette* and *Travel Weekly*.

PAY AND CONDITIONS

Pay, and the means of payment, varies from company to company, but is usually based on a daily allowance and free board and lodgings for the duration of the tour, plus expenses.

Tour managers do not work set hours and are usually active from early morning until late evening.

PROSPECTS

Some tour managers are also tourist guides and may prefer to confine themselves to local tour guiding. Those wishing to settle in an office environment may sometimes be offered a position by their tour operator in a planning or quality control department.

RELATED OCCUPATIONS

Tourist guide, tour operator, travel agency manager.

FURTHER INFORMATION AND READING

Please see article 5. RESORT REPRESENTATIVE.

5. RESORT REPRESENTATIVE (GAX)

THE WORK

Resort representatives are responsible for representing a tour operator at a holiday resort, usually abroad, although some work in the UK. They normally spend a whole holiday season in the resort.

Representatives meet a party of holiday-makers on their arrival at a resort and help them settle into their accommodation. A common way for representatives to welcome holiday-makers and give them information is to host a party. They give details about the resort and its facilities and information on sightseeing trips. They may sell tickets for trips.

TRAVEL AND TOURISM: GAX

Representatives usually meet holiday-makers regularly to make announcements and are always on hand to answer enquiries, give advice and help with any problems. Problems may be minor, concerning difficulties about accommodation, lost passports or money, or may be more serious, for example dealing with holiday-makers who are ill, injured or who may have been arrested. This may involve representatives contacting the police or medical personnel.

Representatives liaise with staff in hotels, restaurants and coach companies and with tourist guides. They also keep any necessary records, including accounts.

Whilst most representatives are responsible for normal package tours, some are concerned with more specialist holidays. Winter sports representatives have similar responsibilities to those of other representatives, but also act as guides to ski trips and organize *après-ski* activities.

Representatives can spend much of their time organizing and participating in entertainments for their holiday-makers.

Children's representatives are responsible particularly for looking after younger children and organizing activities and entertainment for them. Some may also provide evening patrols to allow parents to leave their children during the evenings.

There are other specialist representatives employed by some travel companies, for example, for caravan and tent campsites and for sports.

WORK ENVIRONMENT

Resort representatives work in holiday resorts, usually abroad, with conditions varying according to location and climate. Work is both indoors and outdoors. It involves travel within the locality to deal with holiday-makers and to liaise with local people and officials.

Representatives in summer resorts typically are based abroad from April to October, while winter holiday representatives may be abroad from December to April.

Representatives usually live in hotels, villas or apartments. Those working for specialist camping holiday organizers live in tents.

SKILLS AND INTERESTS

Resort representatives should like dealing with a wide variety of people, including holiday-makers and local people and officials. They must be polite and tolerant of others.

It is essential that representatives are flexible and adaptable, as they must deal effectively with any problems or crises that arise. They must be able to organize their own work with little or no supervision.

Communication skills are important: advice and information must be given clearly and accurately. Listening skills are necessary, if representatives are to understand the exact nature of holiday-makers' queries and problems.

Good conversational ability in the language of the country concerned is necessary, as representatives have to liaise with local hoteliers, officials, police, medical personnel and others in their own language.

Good health, energy and great stamina are required, as representatives are on call at all times and the work can be very demanding.

Basic literacy is needed for dealing with necessary paperwork. Numeracy is required, as money is collected for excursions, and simple accounts have to be kept.

ENTRY REQUIREMENTS

No formal educational qualifications are required, but most employers prefer applicants with some GCSEs/S grades (A–C/1–3). English, maths, geography and foreign languages are useful.

Applicants should have a good working knowledge of one or more foreign languages and it is useful to have lived abroad. Employers usually expect resort representatives to be at least 20 to 21 years old; some companies require them to be single. Good health is essential.

Applicants' previous work experience is important, with experience of working with people being an asset. Specialist knowledge is required for specialist holidays, such as photography skills. Winter sports representatives must be able to ski to an advanced level.

Children's representatives may be accepted from age 18 or 19 years. They are usually expected to have a qualification in nursery nursing, nursing or teaching. Some companies require them to be single.

Some entrants have previously taken a course relevant to travel and tourism – see article 2. TRAVEL CONSULTANT/TRAVEL AGENCY CLERK.

TRAINING

There is no set pattern of training for resort representatives. Employers usually provide a few days' induction training in the UK. Experienced staff in the resort concerned then support newly appointed representatives. Some large tour operators have overseas offices where they provide additional training.

The main qualifications for resort representatives are NVQs/SVQs. These are available in Travel Services (Tour Operations) at Levels 2 and 3.

LATE ENTRY

Most entrants are over 19 years. Opportunities are limited for adults over 35 years, except for companies that specialize in holidays for mature clients.

Many different kinds of experience are valuable, such as retail, nursing, teaching, reception and other work within travel and tourism. Previous experience of working abroad is particularly useful.

OPPORTUNITIES

Resort representatives are employed by tour operators, which range from large, international organizations to small, specialist firms. The travel industry expanded until the late 1980s, with a consequent increase in the number of representatives employed. This growth has stopped and the number employed is now stable.

As the jobs are short-term, vacancies arise regularly. Competition for vacancies is very strong, although children's representatives posts tend to be less competitive.

Vacancies are sometimes advertised, but many companies find that they do not need to advertise, as they receive a large number of speculative enquiries. Applications for work as a representative during a summer season should be made in the preceding autumn. For winter season vacancies, applications should be made in the previous summer. When advertisements are used, they appear in the quality newspapers and in *Overseas Jobs Express; Travel Trade Gazette* and *Travel Weekly*.

PAY AND CONDITIONS

Pay varies considerably according to the employer and the responsibility a job involves. One national company pays its representatives between £86 and £145 a week, depending on experience. Another company pays between £95 and £125 a week. Representatives are provided with free accommodation, insurance and uniform, and can earn commission by selling excursions and arranging car hire.

Representatives have no set working hours. They are usually on call 24 hours a day and are often active from early morning to late in the evening. It is usual for representatives to have free time each day and one day a week free, but they may lose part, or all, of this if they are needed.

Work is seasonal for a fixed term, although some representatives manage to work approximately ten months a year, with summer work being followed by winter sports or winter sun work.

PROSPECTS

Some resort representatives do not consider the work as a long-term career, but in large companies there is a promotion structure abroad. Typically this may be to senior representative, head representative or resort controller, area manager and regional manager.

Those wanting to settle in the UK may seek permanent work with a tour operator in personnel, marketing or brochure production work. Experience of resort representative work is excellent preparation for entry to other branches of travel and tourism, such as local government, national and regional tourist boards and travel agencies. Some become tourist guides in the UK on a self-employed basis.

RELATED OCCUPATIONS

Tourist guide, hotel manager, travel courier, tourist information centre assistant, travel representative/travel agency clerk, travel agency manager, holiday centre worker.

FURTHER INFORMATION

The Travel Training Company*, The Cornerstone, The Broadway, Woking, Surrey GU21 5AR, 01483 727321 (please include sae)

British Tourist Authority/English Tourist Board*, TIC Networking Unit, Thames Tower, Blacks Road, Hammersmith, London W6 9EL, 0181 563 3219 (please include sae)

Institute of Travel and Tourism*, 113 Victoria Street, St Albans, Hertfordshire AL1 3TJ, 01727 854395 (Please enclose £3 for a careers information pack)

Local Government Opportunities (LGO)*, Local Government Management Board*, 76–86 Turnmill Street, Faringdon, London EC1M 5QU, 0171 296 6600

Northern Ireland Tourist Board, St Anne's Court, 59 North Street, Belfast BT1 1NB, 01232 231221, www.ni-tourism.com

Scottish Tourist Board, 23 Ravelston Terrace, Edinburgh EH4 3EU, 0131 332 2433, www.holiday.scotland.net

Wales Tourist Board, Brunel House, 2 Fitzallan Road, Cardiff CF2 1UY, 01222 499909

FURTHER READING

Leaflets/booklets are available from the addresses marked*.

Working in Tourism and Leisure – COIC

Working in Languages – COIC

Jobs in Travel and Tourism – Kogan Page

Careers in the Travel Industry – Kogan Page

How To Get a Job in Travel and Tourism – How To Books

ABTA's guide to working in travel – The Travel Training Company

In the careers library classified under GAX.

GROUP I – HOSPITALITY, CATERING AND OTHER SERVICES

1. HOTEL MANAGER CLCI:IB
2. RESTAURANT/CATERING MANAGER CLCI:IB
3. HOUSEKEEPER/HOUSEKEEPING MANAGER CLCI:IB
4. CHEF/COOK CLCI:IC
5. KITCHEN ASSISTANT CLCI:IC
6. FOOD SERVICE ASSISTANT CLCI:IC
7. COUNTER SERVICE ASSISTANT CLCI:IC
8. HOTEL RECEPTIONIST CLCI:IC/CAT
9. HOTEL ROOM ATTENDANT CLCI:IC
10. HOTEL PORTER CLCI:IC

BACKGROUND INFORMATION

The hotel and catering industry is one of Britain's largest growth industries, with the fastest growth in restaurants and contract catering. Seven per cent of the UK workforce (or just over two million people) is employed in this sector.

Employment opportunities are split between the commercial sector and the catering services sector. The commercial sector includes hotels, restaurants, holiday camps, leisure centres, pubs, wine bars, motorway services, take-away restaurants, and clubs, as well as contract catering to a wide range of establishments, from businesses in the City of London to sports stadia. The catering services sector covers schools and colleges, rail, airlines and cruises, hospitals, nursing homes, residential hostels and the Armed Forces.

The hospitality industry spans large international groups, competing in a world market, to small family-owned restaurants and guesthouses. This range can make a great difference to the nature of the work within the same job title, with small businesses often requiring involvement in all aspects of the operation.

1. HOTEL MANAGER (IB)

THE WORK

Hotel managers are responsible for the efficient provision of all hotel services for guests, that is, food, drink and accommodation. In large hotels, services may also include entertainment and conference facilities. Hotel managers have the final responsibility for customer satisfaction, ensuring guests enjoy their visit. If guests have any complaints, it is the manager's responsibility to rectify them and make amends to the guest.

The type of work depends, to an extent, on the size of the hotel and the number of its staff. Large hotels have departmental managers, such as food and beverage manager and housekeeping manager, each of whom is responsible for their own department and who reports to the hotel manager. The hotel manager's job is more to analyse financial and statistical data, set business targets and plan marketing and investment strategies to meet those targets. Hotel managers prepare budgets, control expenditure and keep accounts. They supervise hotel security and plan all aspects of the hotel's operation, from building work to daily operations, such as the time of staff shift changes or of meals provision. Managers spend a lot of time in meetings and dealing with key staff and VIP customers. In a smaller hotel, the manager is much more involved in the practical day-to-day running of the hotel's services, sometimes including making beds and serving drinks, and solving any problems that arise, which could include minor repairs.

A major responsibility for hotel managers is management of staff, and monitoring their performance to ensure guests have a good impression of the hotel's services. Managers set the standard for hotel services provision, and it is their job to ensure other staff meet that standard. In addition, the manager is responsible for selling and marketing the hotel's services to new and previous customers, and ensuring the hotel is well run and makes a profit.

WORK ENVIRONMENT

The work environment of a hotel manager depends, again, on the size of hotel. Generally, in smaller establishments, a manager could be working in the dining room or bar, as well as doing the administrative tasks at the end of the day in the reception area or a back room. In a larger establishment, the manager would spend more time at a desk in an office, and in meetings. Managers with sales responsibilities may visit other businesses, such as tour operators, to sell their facilities. However, in larger establishments, the sales department would generally have this responsibility.

SKILLS AND INTERESTS

Hotel managers need a wide range of knowledge and skills, not just those of managing food, drink and accommodation services, but also in finance, marketing and staff management. They need leadership skills, such as the ability to make decisions and take action quickly. An ability to think quickly, come up with creative solutions to problems and have plenty of ideas, energy and enthusiasm are all qualities the hotel manager needs.

Hotel managers need an outgoing personality and a natural flair for dealing with people, both staff and customers. Good communication skills are vital for all aspects of this job. To deal with the financial, statistical and marketing side, a numerical aptitude is important. Good organizational skills are essential, whether dealing with few staff in a small establishment, or with dozens of staff in several different departments in a large hotel.

A smart appearance is an asset, and a knowledge of foreign languages is useful, especially in areas popular with overseas visitors.

ENTRY REQUIREMENTS

The larger hotels and hotel chains offer management trainee schemes, which may lead to hotel manager or departmental manager posts. Entry to these is after a university/college course with a degree (not necessarily in a hospitality-related subject but it helps) or a BTEC/SQA higher national diploma/certificate. Entry to most degrees requires at least two A levels/three H grades plus five GCSEs/S grades (A–C/1–3), or equivalent, such as Advanced GNVQ in Hospitality and Catering or GSVQ Level III in Hospitality or NVQ/SVQ Level 3. Higher National Diplomas require one A level/two H grades plus four GCSEs/S grades (A–C/1–3), or equivalent. Graduates in subjects other than hospitality management may take a one-year postgraduate hospitality conversion course, either through a university or college.

CATERING AND HOSPITALITY: IB/IC

Another route is to enter employment in another capacity and gain promotion (which can be rapid in this industry) to a supervisory position in a section or department – see other articles for entry requirements to other posts. Promotion to hotel general manager or assistant manager may then be on the basis of proven ability and acquired qualifications eg NVQ/SVQ Level 3 or 4, or via a management trainee scheme. Entry to a scheme from here may require an Hotel and Catering International Management Association (HCIMA) Professional Diploma or Certificate. Entry requirements for HCIMA Certificate are to be working at supervisory level with two years experience in the industry plus GNVQ Intermediate, GSVQ Level II, NVQ/SVQ Level 2, City & Guilds qualifications, BTEC National Diploma, SQA National Certificate, or four GCSEs/S grades (A–C/1–3). Normal entry requirements for the HCIMA Professional Diploma on a part-time basis is to be working full time in a position with section or departmental responsibility plus at least one of the following: HCIMA Certificate, BTEC National Diploma or Continuing Education Certificate in Hospitality Management, SQA National Certificate (Hospitality), appropriate NVQ/SVQs or equivalent. For the one-year full-time Professional Diploma course, access is possible with one year's full-time employment in the industry or 48 weeks planned and supervised work experience plus at least one of the qualifications listed above.

It may be possible to do the full-time one-year HCIMA Professional Diploma course as a bridging course for holders of non-catering degrees or BTEC/SQA HND in Business Studies (or, exceptionally, another qualification at this level acceptable to HCIMA) without work experience in the industry.

Modern Apprenticeships (part of the Skillseekers Initiative in Scotland) may be available for young people. Contact your local careers office, Jobcentre or TEC/LEC for details. These allow entry without set requirements (though employers will look for evidence of ability to benefit from the apprenticeship) to a training/work experience ladder leading to at least NVQ/SVQ Level 3 and possibly Level 4. These levels imply individuals handling supervisory duties by that point, which could open up direct promotion to manager or entry to a management trainee scheme. Modern Apprenticeships normally relate to one department and are available as Accommodation Apprentice (Reception/Front Office or Housekeeping), Chef Apprentice, Restaurant Apprentice and Pub Apprentice.

TRAINING

Pre-entry

Most of the pre-entry training options listed above take between two and four years to complete. The HCIMA Professional Diploma can be taken full-time in a year for those with substantial experience in the industry, but it is usually completed part-time in three years, or as a two-year sandwich course. Degrees and higher national diplomas are available in hospitality management. Studies cover subjects such as management accounting, the industry's role in the economy, sales and marketing, food and operations management, accommodation management, interior furnishings and fittings, customer care, and the management of staff and plant and premises in accommodation operations.

Post-entry

Management trainee schemes provide on-the-job training, giving trainees experience in a wide variety of departments, such as the kitchens, banqueting, reception, accommodation or bar and restaurant, so that they understand the whole hotel operation. In hotel chains, this can include working in departments that deal with taking over new hotels. A management trainee programme may include day release to complete the HCIMA Professional Diploma or Certificate, short courses (lasting one or more days) in such areas as the Craft Trainer Award (so that the manager is qualified to train craft-level staff), or interviewing skills. Entrants may train towards NVQs/SVQs at Level 3 in Supervision and Level 4 in Management relating to Multiskilled Hospitality or a specific department. NVQ/SVQs may take two to three years to complete at each level.

Modern Apprenticeships are normally served in one department and completed in three years. They include: an induction phase to provide a grounding in the industry, information about the employing organization, and development of basic skills; an intermediate phase of learning practical skills leading to NVQ/SVQ Level 2 plus a number of additional units in key skills (core skills in Scotland); and a final phase leading to at least NVQ/SVQ Level 3.

For further information – please see article 10. HOTEL PORTER.

LATE ENTRY

Promotion from a managerial or supervisory post in a hotel department to assistant general manager or general manager or successful application for such a post in another hotel may happen at any age.

However, for entry to a typical hotel management training scheme, an upper age limit of 25 or 30 years may apply. Contact individual hotel groups for details. Colleges/universities may waive entry requirements for mature applicants.

Small to medium hotels may recruit from managers in other industries, especially those dealing with the public such as travel and tourism and where special skills are required, eg marketing.

Adults can gain recognition of their skills and experience by working towards NVQs/SVQs. Past experience can be put forward as evidence of competence, via Accreditation of Prior Learning (APL).

OPPORTUNITIES

Competition for entry to training schemes with hotel chains varies depending on the state of the industry. While there are more openings in London, there are correspondingly more applicants. Most trainees are moved all around the country during their training.

Hotel managers are employed in every type of establishment, whether it is a large luxury hotel, in one of a chain of mid-market hotels, a country house hotel, a small privately owned hotel or a budget-priced lodge. There are about 35,000 hotels and guesthouses in the UK, over half of which are small and are proprietor- or partnership-run, and another 20 per cent or so employ ten staff or less. There are, therefore, plenty of opportunities for self-employment.

CATERING AND HOSPITALITY: IB/IC

Competition for hotel manager positions is fierce. The hotel industry is quite mature, so opportunities are limited, as little growth is expected. The largest number of hotels (about 23%) are located in South East England, with Scotland and South West England coming next. The three regions together account for 50% of the total. However, hotels are spread over the whole of the UK. Some hotel chains provide opportunities to travel and work abroad.

Opportunities for similar work exist in catering management in the 70,000 catering establishments in the UK, and in contract catering. Please see article 2. RESTAURANT/CATERING MANAGER.

PAY AND CONDITIONS

The average salary for a hotel manager in a three-star hotel in central London is £32,000. The salary range for duty managers is £12,500 to £15,000 and for trainee managers £7,500 to £8,500. Salaries vary according to type and size of hotel and the location. Salaries in central London are normally higher than elsewhere.

Hotel managers work long hours, although they may arrange a shift system with deputy or assistant managers in larger hotels. Some hotel chains do not like their managers to live on the premises. In smaller establishments, the manager will often live on or very near the premises, and will always be on call in an emergency.

PROSPECTS

Promotion from management trainee to hotel manager requires successful experience in departmental management positions. Depending on the size of hotel, a typical route could be: assistant front-of-house manager, assistant conference and banqueting manager, food and beverage manager, deputy general manager, manager. This progression could easily take five to ten years.

It is then possible to be promoted to larger or more prestigious hotels. Within a chain, it is also possible to move into the corporate management side, perhaps working in acquisition departments, looking at possible new hotels to add to a chain, or working in a corporate sales or marketing department. Other possible developments could be in corporate training or personnel departments. To progress into these other fields, it may be necessary to gain additional qualifications, such as a Master of Business Administration (MBA), an Institute of Personnel and Development (IPD) qualification, or a marketing qualification. General management experience and training is also transferable to completely different areas in business, industry or public services.

RELATED OCCUPATIONS

Restaurant/catering manager, publican/licensee, holiday centre manager, personnel/training manager.

FURTHER INFORMATION AND READING.

Please see article 10. HOTEL PORTER.

2. RESTAURANT/CATERING MANAGER (IB)

THE WORK

Restaurant and catering managers are responsible for ensuring their customers are satisfied with the quality of food and service and that the restaurant or catering services operate efficiently and profitably. Restaurant managers are found in restaurants, hotels and fast-food outlets, while catering manager is the term often used for managers who provide catering for businesses, educational and welfare establishments, and the Armed Forces.

The restaurant manager's job involves dealing with people – both staff and customers. Managers often welcome guests and see them to their table, and organize table reservations. Catering managers may have less direct contact with their customers. For both, staff management duties include recruitment, training and motivating, as well as organizing and supervising shifts. Ultimate responsibility for quality control, hygiene, and health and safety falls to managers too, as it is their job to ensure high standards are kept. This includes the quality of the raw materials of the food, how staff handle it, and the state of the equipment used to store and prepare it. Ensuring this side of the operation works smoothly is an essential part of providing a service that will satisfy customers, whether they are guests, hospital patients or factory workers. If a customer is not satisfied with any aspect of the catering service, it is the manager's job to deal with complaints.

The restaurant manager also sets budgets, or agrees them with more senior management, and then implements them. It is the manager's job to keep costs down and profits up, while maintaining standards. Planning the efficient provision of supplies can be an important part of this. Some managers are responsible for planning and co-ordinating menus and ordering supplies, but others delegate this work to the head chef. This side of the job involves a certain amount of paperwork, especially for stock and cash control.

WORK ENVIRONMENT

Restaurant/catering managers are required in all styles of restaurants, fast-food outlets, hotels, sports and entertainment establishments, businesses, factories, schools, hospitals, department stores, yachts, airlines etc. In small restaurants, the proprietor may act as manager. Managers are often on duty in the dining area as well as in the kitchen, if they are responsible for the whole operation. Some managers have use of an office for paperwork and meetings.

SKILLS AND INTERESTS

Leadership and management skills are important qualities for restaurant/catering managers, as it is their job to keep staff motivated so as to provide a quality service that attracts new, and retains existing, customers. Enjoying working with other people as part of a team is as important as being a leader. Good communication skills and an outgoing personality are assets, both in relation to staff and to customers. Managers are often in a dining area welcoming customers, or near at hand to deal with problems or complaints.

Organizational and planning skills are necessary, as is an ability to keep calm under pressure when things are very

CATERING AND HOSPITALITY: IB/IC

busy. The fast pace of the catering business means problems can arise at any time, so a calm and creative mind helps the manager to find workable solutions.

Contract catering managers can work regular hours, though their counterparts in restaurants, fast-food outlets and hotels may work unsocial shifts. In both cases, a willingness to work beyond the set hours is often needed.

ENTRY REQUIREMENTS

The larger restaurants and restaurant chains, fast-food chains, contract catering companies, offer management trainee schemes leading to these posts. The general management trainee schemes of large hotels and hotel chains may also lead to restaurant/catering manager posts within hotels – please see article 1. HOTEL MANAGER.

Post-education entry to these is normally after a university/college course with a degree (not necessarily in hospitality or food management but it helps) or a BTEC/SQA higher national diploma/certificate. Entry to most degrees requires at least two A levels/three H grades plus five GCSEs/S grades (A–C/1–3), or equivalent, such as Advanced GNVQ /GSVQ Level III in Hospitality and Catering or NVQ/SVQ Level 3. Higher national diplomas require one A level/two H grades plus four GCSEs/S grades (A–C/1–3), or equivalent.

Graduates in subjects other than hospitality management may take a one-year postgraduate hospitality conversion course, either through a university or college. A few employers make a point of opening their training schemes to those without high-level educational qualifications or straight from school.

However, a common route in restaurants/pubs is to enter employment as a chef/cook or waiter/bar assistant and gain promotion to a supervisory position – please see articles 4. CHEF/COOK and 6. FOOD SERVICE ASSISTANT for entry requirements. In fast-food chains, contract catering companies and institutional catering the starting point may be as a cook, counter assistant or kitchen assistant – see relevant articles. Promotion to restaurant/catering manager or assistant/deputy manager may then be direct on the basis of proven ability and acquired qualifications eg NVQ/SVQ Level 3 or 4 or via a management trainee scheme.

Entry to a scheme may require an Hotel and Catering International Management Association (HCIMA) Professional Diploma or Certificate. Entry requirements for HCIMA Certificate are to be working at supervisory level with two years' experience in the industry plus GNVQ Intermediate, GSVQ Level II, NVQ/SVQ Level 2, City and Guilds qualifications, BTEC First Certificate or Diploma (for those who already have one), SQA National Certificate, or four GCSEs (A–C)/S grades (1–3). Normal entry requirements for the HCIMA Professional Diploma on a part-time basis is to be working full time in a position with section or departmental responsibility plus at least one of: HCIMA Certificate, BTEC National Diploma or Continuing Education Certificate in Hospitality Management, SQA National Certificate (Hospitality), appropriate NVQ/SVQs or equivalent. For the one-year full-time Professional Diploma course, access is possible with one year's full-time employment in the industry or 48 weeks' planned and supervised work experience plus at least one of the qualifications listed above.

It may be possible to do the full-time one-year HCIMA Professional Diploma course as a bridging course for holders of non-catering degrees or BTEC/SQA HND in business studies (or, exceptionally, another qualification at this level acceptable to HCIMA) without work experience in the industry. City & Guilds Progression Awards in food and beverage service may be available at some colleges as a bridge between GNVQ and the more practical NVQ qualifications.

Modern Apprenticeships (part of the Skillseekers Initiative in Scotland) as a Restaurant Apprentice, Chef Apprentice, Fast Food Apprentice or Pub Apprentice may be available for young people. Contact your local careers office, Jobcentre or TEC/LEC for details. These allow entry without set requirements (though employers will look for evidence of ability to benefit from the apprenticeship) to a training/work experience ladder leading to at least NVQ/SVQ Level 3 and possibly Level 4. These levels imply individuals handling supervisory duties by that point which could open up direct promotion to manager or entry to a management trainee scheme.

TRAINING

Most of the pre-entry training options listed above take between two and four years to complete. Degrees and higher national diplomas are available in hospitality, hotel and catering management, and catering technology. Studies cover subjects such as catering technology, the industry's role in the economy, sales and marketing, gastronomy, customer care, and the management of staff and equipment in food and beverage operations. The HCIMA Professional Diploma can be taken full-time in a year for those with experience in the industry, but it is usually completed part-time in three years, or as a two-year sandwich course.

Modern Apprenticeships are normally completed in three years. They include: an induction phase to provide a grounding in the industry, information about the employing organization, and development of basic skills; an intermediate phase of learning practical skills leading to NVQ/SVQ Level 2 plus a number of additional units in key skills (core skills in Scotland); and a final phase leading to at least NVQ/SVQ Level 3 either in advanced skills or in supervision.

Entrants without high-level qualifications, who have progressed within the industry, may wish to train for NVQs/SVQs in Catering and Hospitality at Levels 3 (Restaurant Supervision or Kitchen Supervision or Multiskilled Supervision) and 4 (Restaurant Management or Kitchen Management or Multiskilled Management).

A number of restaurant chains, fast-food chains, theme restaurants etc recruit applicants with suitable personalities straight from school, and then train them for management positions. These employers provide on-the-job training, moving trainees through the different operations of the restaurant (the kitchen, the bar, waiting at tables etc), promoting them on the way until they are judged to have adequate experience and skills to become managers. Some chains provide training towards NVQ/SVQ qualifications. Employers are increasingly using the Modern Apprenticeship mechanism for this purpose.

For further information, please see article 10. HOTEL PORTER.

CATERING AND HOSPITALITY: IB/IC

LATE ENTRY

The flexibility of entry routes to the job of restaurant/catering manager means there are no formal set age limits to start training for the job or to enter it from another post in catering. However, it should be remembered that catering is a young industry that depends on personality, to a large extent. For entry to a typical management training scheme, an upper age limit of 25 or 30 years may apply. Contact individual hotel groups and restaurant chains for details.

Colleges may waive entry requirements for adult candidates with experience in the industry – check with individual colleges for details.

People with and without catering experience may become their own catering managers by opening or buying a café, small restaurant or take-away or by purchasing a fast-food franchise, with or without taking a catering management training course first. Normally fast-food companies would provide new franchisees with appropriate training.

Mature entrants, including owner managers, may also achieve NVQ/SVQs. Relevant prior experience can be taken into account.

OPPORTUNITIES

There are around 70,000 restaurants, cafés and snack bars in the UK, with a proprietor or manager in charge, while a significant proportion of the 35,000 hotels also have a restaurant requiring management. The mid-price sector of restaurants is a growth area, while the fast-food sector is increasing most rapidly. The licensed retailing sector has become increasingly important in recent years, with a very large number of pubs and wine bars offering restaurant facilities.

Contract catering remains fairly buoyant, with the greatest number of opportunities in industry and commerce, private education, the Ministry of Defence and health care. Recent privatization programmes have opened up new opportunities in the National Health Service, local government, schools and the Civil Service.

Self-employment opportunities are good – more than half of the UK's restaurants are proprietor- or partnership-run. Contract catering attracts former managers who wish to set up on their own. As food and drink is often prepared on customers' own sites, large investment in property is often unnecessary.

Although catering opportunities are spread throughout the UK, South East England dominates, with 36% of restaurants and 37% of contract catering companies. The next largest number of opportunities are in the North West of England (11% of restaurants and 9% of contract catering companies) and Yorkshire (10% of restaurants).

PAY AND CONDITIONS

Salaries range from £15,000 to £35,000 for a restaurant or catering manager, as an average for three-star, four-star and five-star hotels in central London. Clearly, salaries vary according to the type of restaurant or establishment, and will tend to be higher in central London than elsewhere. In contract catering, average salaries would be at the lower end of these scales.

Restaurant and catering managers usually work long hours, although shifts can be arranged with deputies or assistants in large restaurants and hotels. Contract catering managers for commerce and industry often work regular hours, as lunch is usually the main focus of the day.

PROSPECTS

There are a number of routes by which to progress from the role of restaurant/catering manager. Opportunities to progress to regional/area management exist for managers in restaurant chains or large contract caterers. Managers wishing to run their own business often decide to open their own restaurant or catering company. Restaurant managers at hotels could be promoted to hotel manager. Another option would be to move into pub management.

RELATED OCCUPATIONS

Hotel manager, publican/licensee, room service manager, banqueting and conference manager, head chef, head food service assistant.

FURTHER INFORMATION AND READING

Please see article 10. HOTEL PORTER.

3. HOUSEKEEPER/HOUSEKEEPING MANAGER (IB)

THE WORK

Housekeepers, or housekeeping managers, are responsible for the provision of accommodation services and sometimes for choosing furnishings and fittings in hotels. It is the housekeeper's responsibility to ensure that the bedrooms, bathrooms and public rooms look clean, tidy and attractive, creating a good impression with the hotel's customers. Housekeepers work in hotels and similar establishments, while domestic services managers and bursars are responsible for the catering and accommodation services at colleges, universities, hospitals and residential homes.

Housekeepers/housekeeping managers (sometimes called head housekeeper or executive housekeeper) supervise other staff, such as room attendants, cleaners, linen and laundry staff. They allocate daily cleaning duties, issue keys, linen and cleaning materials to the staff, and inspect rooms to check they have been thoroughly cleaned. It is their duty to ensure that every detail is attended to, and whether cleaning or repairs are required. They are responsible for replacing damaged items and, in some hotels, for arranging maintenance work. They liaise with other hotel departments, such as reception, to check availability of rooms or to ensure guests' requests are met quickly and efficiently. Housekeepers may be responsible for their own budget, preparing and implementing it and keeping records of expenditure. They may be responsible for buying supplies, and getting them at the best possible price.

In a large hotel, the housekeeping manager may manage several floor housekeepers, who all supervise room attendants on their floor. In smaller establishments there may be just one housekeeper/housekeeping manager in charge. In either case, the job involves team work, motivating and managing staff, and sometimes stepping in to do the actual cleaning and tidying work. In very small establishments, there may be only one or two people involved in cleaning duties, reporting directly to the manager or proprietor.

CATERING AND HOSPITALITY: IB/IC

Domestic services managers and bursars are more concerned with organizing the provision of catering and accommodation services for students, tourists and conference delegates. They are responsible for the daily supervision of dining rooms and the allocation of rooms. They are usually responsible for their own budgets, often using contract caterers and cleaners rather than permanent staff.

WORK ENVIRONMENT

Housekeepers are required in every type of hospitality establishment, from bed and breakfasts to holiday centres and five-star hotels. In smaller establishments, the housekeeper is more often involved in the physically demanding work of cleaning and tidying rooms. In larger hotels, the housekeeper may spend more time liaising with management and suppliers, and checking that high standards of cleanliness are maintained.

Domestic services managers and bursars work in a wide variety of establishments, from private residential homes to large student halls of residence. Much of their work is office-based, especially when they are involved in letting accommodation for other uses, such as conferences.

SKILLS AND INTERESTS

Like any management position, the job of housekeeper/housekeeping manager requires leadership skills. The ability to recruit, train, motivate and lead staff is essential. Good communications are necessary for dealing with guests, management and staff, as well as liaising with other departments, such as maintenance and reception. Strong organizational skills are needed, both for arranging staff duties and keeping supplies well stocked. A practical approach and an eye for detail help the housekeeper provide a consistent environment for the hotel's guests. Housekeepers must be able to make decisions and to keep calm in a crisis.

As well as being a leader, though, housekeepers/housekeeping managers need to be part of a team. They are not only in the housekeeping team, but are also a key member of the team that runs the hotel, working with a variety of departments and other managers. Being a member of the housekeeping team means doing the actual cleaning sometimes, so it is essential to be physically fit and prepared to work hard.

The job of housekeeper entails unsocial hours, as accommodation needs to be available 24 hours a day. While people with day jobs sleep at night, airline crew for instance may require a clean room to check into and go to bed in at 11am after flying all night. Housekeepers must be prepared to start work early in the morning, and often have to work shifts. It is an active job, suitable for people who do not want to be tied to a desk or work from nine to five.

As well as leadership and organizational skills, housekeeping managers need skills to handle budgets. For domestic services managers and bursars, these can be in the order of several million pounds a year.

ENTRY REQUIREMENTS

Entry to housekeeper/housekeeping manager posts in large hotels and hotel chains may be via general management trainee schemes – please see article 1. HOTEL MANAGER. These may require a degree or BTEC/SQA higher national diploma or certificate. Occasionally establishments specifically recruit trainee housekeepers.

More-modestly sized hotels and hospitals, colleges etc may recruit to trainee housekeeper positions. A formal qualification such as Advanced/Intermediate GNVQ/GSVQ Level II/III in Hospitality and Catering may be sufficient for successful application for a floor housekeeper or assistant housekeeper post, especially with previous experience in holiday jobs or placements as a room attendant. Four GCSEs (A–C)/S grades (1–3) or equivalent may be required for entry to GNVQ/GSVQ courses.

A common route is to start straight from school as a room attendant (please see article 9. HOTEL ROOM ATTENDANT), cleaner or similar and get promotion to assistant or floor housekeeper or assistant housekeeping manager on the basis of proven enthusiasm and ability and acquired qualifications, eg NVQ/SVQ Level 2 in Catering and Hospitality (Housekeeping).

Entry to a Modern Apprenticeship (part of the Skillseekers Initiative in Scotland) as an Accommodation Apprentice may in future be a useful route for young people without formal qualifications. This leads to at least NVQ/SVQ Level 3 in Accommodation Supervision. Contact your local careers office, Jobcentre or TEC/LEC for details.

For domestic service managers or bursars, experience in managing budgets, catering or accommodation services is usually required. This could be gained during work, for example, as an assistant housekeeping manager.

TRAINING

The Advanced GNVQ in Hospitality and Catering gives students an introduction to accounting and finance as well as cleaning programmes and accommodation operations. Students learn subjects such as the safe use of hazardous cleaning substances and how to make beds properly. Housekeepers training towards NVQ/SVQ Level 2 learn similar subjects, as well as about the materials of different floorings and their appropriate cleaning agents, organizing cleaning systems and rotas, and training other staff. In Scotland, there is a specialist GSVQ Level III in Hospitality: Rooms Division Operations.

Once in post, housekeepers/housekeeping managers may wish to train for NVQ/SVQ Level 3 in Accommodation Supervision or Level 4 Accommodation Management. A housekeeper without relevant qualifications in the personnel or training side of the job may wish to pursue further relevant training, such as with the Institute of Personnel and Development (IPD) or via organizations such as the Hospitality Training Foundation (HTF) or the Hotel and Catering International Management Association (HCIMA). This study could be done part-time or by distance learning. Some hotel chains may be able to organize relevant training via their own in-house training.

A Modern Apprenticeship would be served mainly in the accommodation areas and completed in three years. The apprenticeship includes: an induction phase to provide a grounding in the industry, information about the employing organization, and development of basic skills; an intermediate phase of learning practical skills leading to NVQ/SVQ Level 2 plus a number of additional units in key skills (core skills in Scotland); and a final phase leading to at least NVQ/SVQ Level 3.

CATERING AND HOSPITALITY: IB/IC

For further information, please see article 10. HOTEL PORTER.

LATE ENTRY

Age is not a barrier for housekeeper/housekeeping management posts. Well-motivated and qualified people can be appointed to the post of assistant housekeeper or housekeeper/housekeeping manager from as young as 20 to late middle age. As promotion is often on the basis of experience as a room attendant or supervisor or in a supervisory capacity in another department, it is perfectly possible to move into the job aged over 40 years.

Adults can gain recognition of their skills and experience by working towards NVQs/SVQs. Past experience can also be taken into account.

OPPORTUNITIES

Housekeeper/housekeeping managers tend to stay in the job for extended periods once started, so opportunities at this level do not come up regularly. Opportunities at more-junior housekeeping levels are more frequent, but competition is fairly strong. There are about 35,000 hotels and guest-houses spread across the UK, although many are small and do not employ housekeepers. The largest number of hotels (about 23%) are located in South East England, with Scotland and South West England coming next. The three regions together account for 50% of the total.

Openings for domestic services work at hospitals are spread across the country according to the density of population. Competition for similar work at residential homes is fiercer, and opportunities for bursars at colleges and universities are almost exclusively for the more mature person, who already has industry experience. Few colleges have openings for younger staff at more-junior levels, as they tend to use students or contracted-in services.

PAY AND CONDITIONS

The average salary for a head housekeeper in hotels in central London is £14,000 to £21,000. The range for assistant head housekeeper and floor housekeeper is £8,250 to £17,000. Salaries vary according to type and size of hotel and the location. Salaries in central London are normally higher than elsewhere.

Housekeepers usually work shift systems, often covering evenings and weekends as well as early mornings, to ensure every day of the week is covered, and every part of every day.

PROSPECTS

Housekeepers/housekeeping managers often move into similar areas in other establishments, such as head of domestic services at a hospital, or facilities manager in businesses or schools. As the post involves all the management skills of other managerial posts, housekeepers have transferable skills. So if, for example, a housekeeper joined a contract cleaning company, it would be quite possible to progress to area manager.

Staying within the hotel world, possibilities include managing the front of house in a hotel, or pursuing personnel or training management positions, perhaps by taking additional qualifications, such as those of the Institute of Personnel and Development (IPD). In some cases, it might be possible to progress to hotel manager, or to open their own guesthouse or hotel.

RELATED OCCUPATIONS

Domestic/school bursar, hospital domestic services manager, facilities manager, contract cleaning manager, front-of-house manager, room attendant/cleaner, head linen keeper, hotel manager.

FURTHER INFORMATION AND READING

Please see article 10. HOTEL PORTER.

4. CHEF/COOK (IC)

THE WORK

Chefs or cooks are responsible for preparing and cooking attractive food that is enjoyable and safe to eat, at a huge variety of restaurants and other eating establishments. Chef is the term normally used in kitchens at restaurants or hotels; cook is the word used in hospitals and schools. The same job is called short order cook or call order cook in some snack bars, cafés and fast-food outlets.

There are a number of different types of chef. Large kitchens in restaurants and hotels are divided into departments, each responsible for specific preparation and cooking activities, such as the pastry section, which makes all the desserts, pastries and breads. Trainee chefs, or *commis chefs,* work for three to six months in each section to gain experience in every area of the kitchen. They learn, for instance, how to prepare and cook vegetables or make sauces, as well as doing general cleaning and washing up (although there may be kitchen porters or assistants to help with this). Hygiene is essential for the safe preparation of food, so this side of the work is very important. Each different section of the kitchen is run by a *chef de partie*. The next step up is *sous chef or under-chef,* who is skilled and experienced enough to run any section, and to take charge of the whole kitchen in the absence of the head chef. The head chef (sometimes called executive chef or *maitre chef de cuisine*) runs the whole kitchen, including planning menus, ordering supplies, managing staff and budgets, and ensuring food of a consistently high standard is produced.

In smaller establishments, the cook or chef could be doing everything: food preparation and cooking, cleaning up and even helping serve customers. In fast-food restaurants, staff often work on a rota system, sometimes serving, sometimes cooking.

Chefs/cooks use a wide variety of cooking utensils and equipment, and must learn the safe handling of sharp knives and hot apparatus. Protective uniforms and head coverings are worn. Some employers provide uniforms, but other chefs buy their own. For hygiene reasons, chefs/cooks are not allowed to wear jewellery (except for a plain wedding ring).

WORK ENVIRONMENT

Whether in a coffee shop, carvery, French or Japanese restaurant, the kitchen is likely to be hot, steamy and noisy. Cooking smells tend to get into clothes and hair. The kitchen atmosphere reflects the style of the head chef – some kitchens are calm, low key and quiet; others are noisy and buzzing. Chefs/cooks spend most of their working day

CATERING AND HOSPITALITY: IB/IC

in this hot environment, and are on their feet for a good deal of the time.

SKILLS AND INTERESTS

Working as a chef/cook is very demanding, with a lot of pressure at service time. Kitchens can get very hectic, especially when many dishes must be produced at the same time. So it is important to be able to deal with pressure and cope with several tasks at once. Equally important is the ability to get on with others in the kitchen and enjoy working in a team.

An interest in food preparation is a prerequisite. Those with creative flair and imagination, and who enjoy learning a wide variety of skills, find the work rewarding. But organizational skills are vital too, to ensure correct timing of different dishes and to have the right ingredients and equipment available in the right quantities at the right time. A practical approach and an ability to plan methodically are useful qualities for this side of the work. The ability to stay calm in a crisis and to think of a practical solution can avert a potential problem.

Chefs need good communication, management and leadership skills to manage and train kitchen staff under them. Some chefs are responsible for budgets and negotiating with suppliers, so a head for figures helps.

ENTRY REQUIREMENTS

For entry to more prestigious restaurants and hotel restaurants, a full-time one- or two-year college-based course to gain NVQ/SVQ Levels 1 and 2 in Catering and Hospitality (Food Preparation and Cooking) is advisable. Starting point is as a trainee or commis chef. Some contract caterers, hospital kitchens etc expect similar qualifications. Other employers, such as fast-food chains, smaller restaurants, cafés, school caterers etc, may be prepared to take on cooks or trainee cooks on the basis of enthusiasm and provide appropriate training. Experience of holiday or part-time work in catering can be an advantage. A GNVQ/GSVQ qualification in Hospitality and Catering may be valuable for entry to full-time college courses. City & Guilds Progression Awards in Food Preparation may be available at some colleges as a bridge between GNVQs and the more practically based NVQs.

Various employers offer chef training schemes, usually for 16- to 19-year-olds. These include a number of the luxury hotels and hotel chains, and some contract caterers. Entry requirements vary.

A number of private cookery schools offer a wide variety of short courses for fee-paying students. Courses usually last between a few weeks and a year, and lead to the school's own certificate. Students sometimes go into business catering (such as directors' dining rooms) or private dinner parties. Success there may lead to a career in the mainstream catering industry.

A popular route to work in a kitchen is via training opportunities for young people, eg a National Traineeship (Skillseekers in Scotland). This can be done either by getting day release from an existing employer to go to a college or training centre, or by getting a traineeship at an organization such as the Hotel and Catering Training Company (HCTC) and for them to send trainees to employers for work experience. For details of schemes, contact local careers office, Jobcentre, TEC/LEC, HTF or Springboard.

Entry for young people may be possible through a Modern Apprenticeship (part of the Skillseekers Initiative in Scotland) as a Chef Apprentice or Fast-Food Apprentice. Contact your local careers office, Jobcentre, TEC/LEC for details. These allow entry without set requirements (though employers will look for evidence of ability to benefit from the apprenticeship) to a training/work experience ladder leading to at least NVQ/SVQ Level 3 and possibly Level 4. These levels imply individuals handling advanced skills or supervisory duties by that point which could open up direct promotion to chef de partie, head chef/cook, chef manager posts or entry to a management trainee scheme.

TRAINING

Working in a kitchen involves a great deal of on-the-job training and often off-the-job college study as well. To become a chef, it is necessary to learn different methods of food preparation and cooking. Training usually begins with the simpler (but often repetitive) preparation and cooking tasks. Hygiene and safety, including the safe handling of knives, are very important.

Increasingly, employers provide training, both on and off the job, and assessment support, enabling chefs to qualify with NVQs/SVQs in Catering and Hospitality (Food Preparation and Cooking) at Levels 1 and 2 for the basic skills, at Level 3 in Food Preparation and Cooking – Patisserie and Confectionery, or Food Preparation and Cooking – Kitchen and Larder Work, or Vegetarian Preparation and Cooking or possibly in Kitchen Supervision, and at Level 4 in Kitchen and Larder Specialist or Patisserie and Confectionery Specialist or Kitchen Management.

A Modern Apprenticeship would normally be served in different sections of the kitchen and completed in three years. The apprenticeship includes: an induction phase to provide a grounding in the industry, information about the employing organization, and development of basic skills; an intermediate phase of learning practical skills leading to NVQ/SVQ Level 2 plus a number of additional units in key skills (core skills in Scotland); and a final phase leading to at least NVQ/SVQ Level 3 either in advanced skills or in supervision.

Different cooking skills, such as carving or decorating, can be learned on the job. Some large employers let chefs experiment too, for example trying out new recipes or styles, such as Mexican or Japanese cooking. Differences between service styles are learned too – for instance, producing food to be presented on platters and trays for banquets and on individual plates, which must be done very quickly.

Entrants to chef/cook jobs in fast-food outlets or restaurants with a limited range of dishes, eg pizzas, may be trained by short courses on company premises.

For further information, please see article 10. HOTEL PORTER.

LATE ENTRY

Although there are few age limits on entering kitchen work, many employers in hotels and restaurants prefer to train chefs while they are young and adaptable. So applicants beyond their mid- to late-twenties may find it easier to enter hospital or educational or contract catering.

There may be specific training opportunities, directed at

CATERING AND HOSPITALITY: IB/IC

adults, available in some areas for this type of work. Candidates may have to satisfy certain conditions to be eligible. Contact your local Jobcentre, careers office or TEC/LEC for details.

Some individuals, with or without experience in catering, start or buy their own restaurant or café, fast-food outlet or take-away, preparing and cooking the food themselves, and becoming their own chef/cook as well as manager.

Mature entrants may also be assessed for NVQ/SVQs. Relevant prior experience can be taken into account.

OPPORTUNITIES

Opportunities are far greater for qualified chefs than for trainees. Please see article 2. RESTAURANT/CATERING MANAGER for more details on distribution of restaurants, catering companies and hotels.

PAY AND CONDITIONS

Salaries range from £7,000 to £8,500 for a *commis chef* and £16,750 to £37,500 for a head chef as an average for three-star, four-star and five-star hotels in central London. Salaries vary according to the type of establishment and are usually higher in central London than elsewhere.

Chefs/cooks usually work long and hectic hours. In restaurants and hotels, shift work covering evenings and weekends is normal to cover all the hours the restaurant is open. Contract catering chefs for commerce and industry, and school cooks, often work regular hours, as lunch is usually the main focus of the day. However, for residential schools, colleges and hospitals, shifts are required.

PROSPECTS

With NVQs/SVQs at Levels 3 or 4, or the equivalent in work experience, a chef can be promoted to head chef. For those at smaller establishments, it is always possible to move to larger and more prestigious ones. From there it is possible to move towards management as a catering or food and beverages manager in a hotel, employing their own kitchen staff. Some chefs may open their own restaurant, often with a partner who focuses on service aspects. The management experience of running a busy kitchen could also lead to contract catering management, pub management or hotel management. Other opportunities lie in lecturing, becoming a nutritionist, or moving into food product development for commercial producers of tinned, chilled, frozen or other packaged foodstuffs.

RELATED OCCUPATIONS

Restaurant/catering manager, head chef, food and beverage manager, kitchen assistant, contract caterer, chef manager, food product development manager.

FURTHER INFORMATION AND READING

Please see article 10. HOTEL PORTER.

5. KITCHEN ASSISTANT (IC)

THE WORK

Kitchen assistants work for chefs in hotels, restaurants and other catering establishments and organizations. A large part of their job can be cleaning, but they also perform basic food preparation tasks. Some assistants get involved in organizing storerooms, and may help with unloading deliveries.

Kitchen assistants who help with the preparation of meals perform tasks related to the kitchen department in which they work (such as larder or pastry). Their work could include cleaning, peeling or slicing vegetables, dicing or chopping meat or skinning fish. Sometimes they may be responsible for simple cooking jobs, such as grilling bacon, making toast or tea and coffee. Using automatic equipment, such as chipping machines, can be part of the job too.

High standards of cleanliness and hygiene are essential in kitchens, so that food is safe to eat, as well as enjoyable. Keeping the kitchen clean is often the kitchen assistant's major responsibility. Washing up is needed, even if there is a dishwasher for crockery and cutlery, as pots and pans may need to be scoured by hand. Equipment must be kept clean and shining too (fridges, ovens and so on) while surfaces, floors and walls must be kept free from grease and dirt. However, cleaning contractors may be used to do the heavier jobs.

Kitchen assistants use a variety of cleaning equipment and materials, many of which are hazardous or corrosive, as well as kitchen utensils. Protective uniforms, head coverings and, when appropriate, gloves are normally provided.

WORK ENVIRONMENT

Kitchen assistants spend most of their working day on their feet, in a hot and often steamy and noisy kitchen. Cooking smells may get into their clothes and hair. Assistants may need to reach into awkward spaces to clean them or stretch up to the top part of a wall to keep it clean. Handling heavy loads may also be required – such as carrying and unpacking deliveries of supplies.

SKILLS AND INTERESTS

A great deal of stamina and enthusiasm is needed for this job, as the kitchen assistant has to do a variety of jobs that keep them on their feet in a hot, and sometimes pressured, environment all day. They must be flexible and prepared to tackle a range of tasks – not always directly related to food preparation – including doing some fairly dirty jobs. It is a job for practical people, who can work quickly and efficiently under the direction of other people. It is important to be able to complete a number of different tasks in the time allocated, according to the chef's needs.

Kitchens are very much team-based environments, and it is essential that a kitchen assistant gets on well with people and enjoys working as part of a team. They should be able to communicate clearly with chefs and other kitchen staff and may need to do so with suppliers too. It is essential for assistants to understand the pressure that chefs come under at service time and to learn the protocol for when and how to ask questions so that they do not disturb the chef's concentration at a vital moment.

CATERING AND HOSPITALITY: IB/IC

ENTRY REQUIREMENTS

Formal academic qualifications are not needed to start a job as a kitchen assistant. Employers are more interested in a basic interest in food preparation and a willingness to learn. A demonstrable ability to communicate well, and to participate in a team, helps. Employers are also looking for people who are prepared to work hard, take a pride in their work and start at the bottom. Experience of holiday work or a work experience placement in catering is an advantage.

A kitchen assistant's job is a fairly active one, so a reasonable level of fitness is required. This is particularly true for jobs where lifting and carrying are involved. Even if a kitchen assistant does not help with unloading deliveries, they are likely to be asked to carry supplies in the kitchen and storeroom and in between.

TRAINING

Kitchen assistants learn a great deal on the job. They also get on-the-job training, both in how to clean different materials and what to use, and in different food-preparation techniques. They are trained in hygiene, health and safety, the safe handling of dangerous equipment, such as sharp knives, as well as the safe use of hazardous cleaning substances. Off-the-job training may be available too, in basic food-preparation skills. This can be done at catering colleges or through organizations such as the Hotel and Catering Training Company (HCTC) or Edexcel. Kitchen assistants may train towards NVQs/SVQs in Catering and Hospitality Level 1 (Preparing and Serving Food) or (Kitchen Portering) or Level 2 (Preparing and Serving Food – Quick Service).

It may be possible to start working in a kitchen via training opportunities for young people, for example a National Traineeship (Skillseekers in Scotland) leading to an NVQ/SVQ qualification. For details, contact your local careers office, Jobcentre, TEC/LEC, the HTF or Springboard.

Entry to a Modern Apprenticeship (part of the Skillseekers Initiative in Scotland) as a Fast-Food Apprentice or Kitchen Apprentice may be possible, where kitchen assistant work forms the first part of the apprenticeship before moving on to more advanced duties. Please see article 4. CHEF/COOK.

For further information, please see article 10. HOTEL PORTER.

LATE ENTRY

There are no age restrictions on entering kitchen work, although those with ambition for promotion may find opportunities limited if they start too late. The physical fitness, lifting and carrying element should also be remembered. Some employers favour more mature applicants in the belief that their standards may be higher.

There may be specific training opportunities, directed at adults, available in some areas for this type of work. Candidates may have to satisfy certain conditions to be eligible. Contact your local Jobcentre, careers office or TEC/LEC for details.

Mature entrants may also be assessed for NVQ/SVQs. Relevant prior experience can be taken into account.

OPPORTUNITIES

Vacancies for kitchen assistants are usually fairly plentiful. Please see article 2. RESTAURANT/CATERING MANAGER for more details on the distribution of restaurants, catering companies and hotels.

PAY AND CONDITIONS

A kitchen assistant's salary ranges from £6,500 to £8,250 as an average for three-star, four-star and five-star hotels in central London. Salaries vary according to the type of establishment and are usually higher in central London than elsewhere.

In restaurants and hotels, kitchen assistants work shifts in the evenings and at weekends to cover all the hours the restaurant is open. Assistants with contract catering companies for commerce, industry and school often work regular hours, as lunch is usually the main focus of the day. However, for residential schools, colleges and hospitals, shifts are required.

PROSPECTS

Kitchen assistants with the right motivation may aim to become chefs. After gaining an NVQ/SVQ in Catering and Hospitality (Food Preparation and Cooking) at Level 1, or equivalent experience, they could be appointed trainee or *commis chef*. This move may be easier in smaller operations, where the kitchen assistant's job involves more food preparation. The employer may offer in-house training, or college study, or a combination. With further experience and qualifications, they could then work their way up the kitchen career ladder (please see article 4. CHEF/COOK. Alternatively, they may prefer to move into food service, fast-food provision, banqueting provision, or to bar work, portering work or other cleaning work, such as a hotel room attendant, and then up the career ladder from any of those areas.

RELATED OCCUPATIONS

Hotel room attendant, contract cleaner, steward (cruise liners and trains), food service assistant, catering assistant, storeperson, *commis chef*.

FURTHER INFORMATION AND READING

Please see article 10. HOTEL PORTER.

6. FOOD SERVICE ASSISTANT (IC)

THE WORK

Food service assistants may also be known as waiters or waitresses. The duties of individual food service assistants differ according to their place of work, but generally the work includes three elements: preparation, serving and clearing away.

Preparation. Before a restaurant or dining room opens to the public, it must be made ready. Food service assistants may clean floors, dust, set tables with clean cloths (if cloths are used), cutlery and condiments, and generally make sure that the area is clean and tidy.

Serving. Assistants greet customers on arrival and show them to their tables. They discuss the menu and answer questions about the dishes on offer. In doing so, they may encourage customers to increase their spending. Orders

CATERING AND HOSPITALITY: IB/IC

are written down on a pad and taken to the kitchen for preparing. In some restaurants, orders for drinks are taken by specialist wine waiters/waitresses. In other outlets, the same food service assistants take orders for food and drink.

While food is being prepared in the kitchens, assistants set any additional cutlery that will be needed and bring items such as sauces to the table. They then serve the food. The main types of food service are plate service and silver service.

The majority of organizations now use plate service, where meals are put onto plates by kitchen staff and carried to tables in the dining area by food service assistants. In silver service, food is placed into dishes or tureens in the kitchen. Food service assistants then serve the food onto plates at the table by using a spoon and fork.

Other kinds of service include: guèridon service, where food service assistants cook dishes at the table; carvery/buffet service, used especially for breakfasts, where guests help themselves to food, although a food service assistant may serve main dishes and carve meat and poultry.

Clearing away. When they see that diners have finished a course, food service assistants clear the table and take orders for the next course. At the end of the meal they may prepare the bill and take payment, using a cash register and dealing with credit cards. When diners have left, assistants clear the table and prepare it for the next customers.

In many catering outlets, food service assistants are responsible for all the activities described above. In more formal outlets, food service may be a team responsibility. A head waiter, who may be restaurant manager, oversees *chefs de rang*. These are senior waiters, responsible for a specific number of tables. They advise on menus, take orders and serve food. There are also *commis waiters*, who are learning the skills involved and, at this stage, are mostly involved in preparation work, fetching and carrying dishes and clearing away.

WORK ENVIRONMENT

Food service assistants work in the dining rooms of restaurants and other catering establishments, which tend to be clean, warm and comfortable. Some time is spent in kitchens, which can be hot, steamy and noisy. They are on their feet all day and may carry heavy loads.

SKILLS AND INTERESTS

The reputation of restaurants and other catering establishments is based as much on the quality of service as of the food. Food service assistants are the main contact with diners and need, therefore, to be interested in providing a service, and they need to be pleasant, polite and tactful. It is also important that they are neat and tidy in appearance, with high standards of personal hygiene and cleanliness.

Food service work can be very busy, so the ability to work well and remain calm under pressure is desirable. Good memory is needed to remember which diners at a table ordered which dishes. Good spoken English is required for dealing with customers, as is clear handwriting for noting orders. Ability with figures is necessary for making up bills and giving change.

Food service assistants need good knowledge of the food on the menu so they can answer diners' questions and advise them on their choices. A knowledge of wine and other drinks is also necessary, unless there is a specialist wine waiter.

Selling skills are required to advise diners of the range of products on offer, with the aim of increasing sales.

The work requires good dexterity when serving food.

Food service assistants work as part of a team, with kitchen staff and other food service staff, and should be capable of operating as team members.

Most food service assistants must be willing to work unsocial hours. Good health and fitness are essential, as food service is physically active and demanding.

ENTRY REQUIREMENTS

No formal qualifications are required for entry to food service, although a good standard of education is desirable. In particular, GCSEs/S grades in English and maths are useful. Foreign languages may be helpful. Experience of catering from holiday jobs or placements is an advantage.

The more prestigious restaurants and hotel restaurants recruiting waiters/waitresses or trainees are more likely to look for educational qualifications eg GNVQ/GSVQ in Hospitality and Catering or NVQ/SVQ in Catering and Hospitality (Serving Food and Drink – Table). Other restaurants may be prepared to train on the job from scratch.

Entry to many full-time courses leading to GNVQ/GSVQ and NVQ/SVQ qualifications does not demand specific qualifications, but schools and colleges wish to be satisfied that students can benefit from the courses.

A training opportunity for young people such as a National Traineeship (Skillseekers in Scotland) leading to NVQ/SVQ Level 2 or a Modern Apprenticeship (part of the Skillseekers Initiative in Scotland) as a Restaurant Apprentice may be available. Contact your local careers office, Jobcentre or TEC/LEC for details. Modern Apprenticeships allow entry without set requirements (though employers will look for evidence of ability to benefit from the apprenticeship) to a training/work experience ladder leading to at least NVQ/SVQ Level 3 and possibly Level 4. Pub Apprenticeships may also be available in some areas.

TRAINING

Pre-entry

GNVQs/GSVQs in Hospitality and Catering can provide useful preparation for entry to a wide range of work in the hotel and catering industry, including food service. GNVQ Foundation and Intermediate courses and GSVQ Level I and II courses, and Scottish national certificate courses, are offered by many schools and colleges of further education, mostly one year full-time. They do not provide specific training for jobs, but aim to give students knowledge and understanding of the industry and develop their communication, numeracy and information technology skills. They can lead to direct entry to work, or to further courses.

Full-time training

Many colleges of further education throughout the UK offer one-year or two-year full-time courses leading to Catering and Hospitality NVQ/SVQ qualifications in serving food and drink. Courses include a large amount of practical work experience in colleges' own training kitchens and restaurants, and often in industry.

CATERING AND HOSPITALITY: IB/IC

NVQ/SVQ qualifications are based on demonstrating competence (adequate ability) in the practical skills of the work as well as knowledge and understanding. In food service, the relevant NVQs/SVQs are Level 1 Serving Food and Drink – Table or Counter/Take-away or Bar and Level 2 Serving Food and Drink – Table or Serving Food and Drink – Function or Serving Food and Drink – Bar.

Post-entry training

An increasing number of employers offer training leading to NVQs/SVQs. In some cases, this is provided with the help of a local college.

Training opportunities for young people

It may be possible to start work via training opportunities for young people such as a Modern Apprenticeship or a National Traineeship (successful completion of which may allow entry to a Modern Apprenticeship). For details of opportunities, contact your local careers office, Jobcentre, TEC/LEC, HTF or Springboard. National Traineeships leads to an NVQ qualification at Level 1 or 2. Modern Apprenticeships lead to at least NVQ/SVQ Level 3 in Food Service Advanced Craft or Drink Service Advanced Craft or Restaurant Supervision. Pub apprentices work towards NVQ/SVQs in Serving Food and Drink – Bar and On-Licensed Premises Supervision.

A Modern Apprenticeship would normally be completed in three years. The apprenticeship includes: an induction phase to provide a grounding in the industry, information about the employing organization, and development of basic skills; an intermediate phase of learning practical skills leading to NVQ/SVQ Level 2 plus a number of additional units in key skills (core skills in Scotland); and a final phase leading to at least NVQ/SVQ Level 3 either in advanced skills or in supervision.

For further information, please see article 10. HOTEL PORTER.

LATE ENTRY

There is no upper age limit for entry to food service. Recruitment policy differs from company to company. Previous experience of work in hotel and catering is an advantage, as is experience of other work providing service to the public and handling cash/credit cards.

There may be specific training opportunities, directed at adults, available in some areas for this type of work. Candidates may have to satisfy certain conditions to be eligible. Contact your local Jobcentre, careers office or TEC/LEC for details.

Mature entrants may also be assessed for NVQs/SVQs. Relevant prior experience can be taken into account.

OPPORTUNITIES

The number of food service assistants is increasing and there are approximately 100,000 employed throughout the UK. They work in hotels, restaurants, public houses, contract catering and industrial catering organizations, cafés, fast-food outlets, transport companies and roadside and motorway outlets.

Vacancies arise frequently as staff turnover in food service is high. Vacancies are advertised in *Caterer and Hotelkeeper, Catering, Scottish Licensed Trade News* and in local newspapers.

Work overseas is possible, both in the EU and elsewhere, providing the language of the country is spoken.

PAY AND CONDITIONS

Wages vary according to location and employer. For a 39-hour week, food service assistants may earn between £110 and £220 plus tips. Overtime may be available at enhanced rates.

Employers often provide a uniform or clothing.

Full-time work is usually 38 to 40 hours a week, but patterns of work vary. Some work split shifts, ie working at lunch-times and evenings with a rest period during the afternoons. Weekend work is usual. Where restaurants are open for very long hours, shift work is normal. Those working for contract caterers providing lunch-time service may work Mondays to Fridays only.

There are many opportunities for part-time work. Casual work, for special events, is also common, as is temporary or seasonal work – over the Christmas and summer holiday seasons, for instance.

PROSPECTS

Prospects for promotion depend to some extent on the size of organization. Most food service assistants work for small organizations that do not have a career structure, so those seeking advancement have to change employers. Large organizations often have a career structure allowing promotion to supervisory and management positions. Head waiters/waitresses often also act as restaurant managers, organizing and supervising restaurant staff.

Those aiming to advance to management positions can work towards NVQs/SVQs at Levels 3 and 4.

The turnover of staff in food service tends to be high, which means that prospects for promotion are good and rapid advancement is possible.

RELATED OCCUPATIONS

Barman/woman, sales assistant, airline steward/stewardess, merchant navy steward/stewardess, counter service assistant, cook, restaurant/catering manager, kitchen assistant.

FURTHER INFORMATION AND READING

Please see article 10. HOTEL PORTER.

7. COUNTER SERVICE ASSISTANT (IC)

THE WORK

Counter service assistants serve food to customers at catering establishments, where customers collect food from a counter or bar, rather than being served at their tables. Examples include: snack bars, canteens, cafés, coffee shops and self-service restaurants. Many work in fast-food outlets, where they are known as food service assistants.

In fast-food restaurants, staff rotate duties. In other organizations, duties differ according to the place of work but may include:

Preparation. Assistants make sure that the counter area is clean and tidy, and well stocked with crockery, cutlery, glasses and trays. They may fill hot and cold drinks machines.

Food is usually prepared by chefs or cooks, but counter service assistants may help with some tasks, such as preparing salads and mixing sauces. In smaller

CATERING AND HOSPITALITY: IB/IC

establishments, like snack bars, assistants may prepare all the food and drinks – make sandwiches and tea and coffee, for example. They may set out food in display cabinets.

Serving customers. In some establishments, such as canteens and self-service restaurants, assistants serve hot dishes selected by customers. That can involve cutting dishes, such as pies, into portions and serving a set amount of each dish on to plates, taking care to arrange the food attractively. They may use knives, ladles and scoops.

Assistants keep a watch for items of food and drink that are running low, and reorder them from the kitchen, or prepare more themselves.

Those working in snack bars and fast-food restaurants may also cook certain food items – eg pies, pizzas, hamburgers, chicken portions and chips – that can involve using ovens, microwave cookers, grills or deep fat fryers. The cookery skills required are fairly easy to master.

In take-away restaurants, assistants may also cook food, or use food that has already been cooked and kept hot. They pack the food into trays or cartons for the customers to take away. With large chains of fast-food take-aways, there are carefully worked out set procedures for serving each customer.

One of the duties for assistants is taking customers' money. Each item bought is entered on a cash register that gives a total to be charged. Assistants take cash and may also process credit cards and/or luncheon vouchers. Some assistants cash up at the end of a work session, checking that the takings and cash register records agree.

Cleaning. Assistants keep the counter area clean and tidy throughout the serving session, which includes mopping up spilt food and drink and wiping over counter surfaces. They may clear tables, collect used crockery and cutlery, empty ashtrays and wipe tables. They may have to wash up, although most establishments have dishwashing machines, which the assistants stack and unload.

At the end of a session, assistants may sweep and wash the floor, clean out drinks machines, wash equipment and leave everything clean and tidy in readiness for the next session.

WORK ENVIRONMENT

Counter service assistants work in warm and light conditions. Some spend time in preparing food in kitchens or washing up, which can be hot and steamy. Clearing away used crockery and cutlery and cleaning food dishes can be messy. The work involves standing much of the time, with some bending and carrying.

SKILLS AND INTERESTS

Counter service assistants need to get on well with people. They should be able to cope with any difficult customers, and deal with complaints. With counter service, customers usually have to be served quickly, so assistants should be capable of working under pressure.

Assistants have to be able to work well in a team with other staff, cooks or supervisors.

Counter service work can be physically demanding, so it is necessary to be fit and capable of standing for long periods of time.

Appearance is important. Assistants should be clean and tidy and concerned with high standards of hygiene, health and safety. Assistants must be prepared to follow their employers' rules restricting the wearing of cosmetics and jewellery.

Practical skills are required for basic food preparation, such as sandwich making. An eye for presentation is useful for displaying and serving food attractively. Accuracy is important for portion control.

Assistants responsible for taking money and giving change should have the ability to use tills and deal with cash accurately.

ENTRY REQUIREMENTS

No formal qualifications are required for entry, although a good standard of education is desirable. A qualification that shows interest in the industry such as GNVQ/GSVQ in Hospitality and Catering may be an advantage as is experience of catering gained from holiday jobs or work experience placements. Employers are more concerned with personal qualities, but look for some ability with figures if handling cash is involved.

Entry to GNVQ/GSVQ courses does not demand specific qualifications, but schools and colleges wish to be satisfied that students can benefit from the courses.

TRAINING

Pre-entry

Full-time or part-time college courses are available leading to NVQs/SVQs in Catering and Hospitality (Serving Food and Drink) at Levels 1 and 2. GNVQs/GSVQs in Hospitality and Catering can provide useful preparation for entry to a wide range of work in the hotel and catering industry, including counter service. GNVQ Foundation and Intermediate courses and GSVQ Level I and II courses are offered by many schools and colleges of further education, mostly one year full-time. They do not provide specific training for jobs, but aim to give students knowledge and understanding of the industry and develop their communication, numeracy and information technology skills. They can lead to direct entry to work or to further courses.

Post-entry

Training for counter service work usually takes place on entry to a job. It varies between organizations, although assistants are usually trained by experienced assistants or supervisors on the job.

Assistants may begin by learning simple jobs, such as preparing the counter and keeping cutlery containers filled, before progressing to serving food. Large organizations, especially the fast-food companies, have formal training programmes. These may be off the job on company premises in simulated situations. New recruits learn about the company and its policies, conditions of employment and staff welfare matters. They are also instructed on matters such as health and safety, using the cash register and presenting food.

Assistants may be helped by their employer to work towards NVQ/SVQ qualifications, which are based on demonstrating competence (adequate ability) in the practical skills, knowledge and understanding of the job. Counter service assistants can work for an NVQ/SVQ in Catering and Hospitality Level 1 (Serving Food and Drink – Counter/Take Away) or Level 2 (Preparing and Serving Food – Quick Service), which include dealing with customers, effective working relationships, dealing with payments, preparing and cleaning areas for counter service, providing a counter service, plus hygiene, health and safety.

Training opportunities for young people

There may be opportunities for 16- and 17-year-olds to train for counter service via a National Traineeship (Skillseekers in Scotland) leading to an NVQ/SVQ Level 1 or 2 qualification as above. Contact your local careers office, Jobcentre, TEC/LEC for details.

Entry to a Modern Apprenticeship (part of the Skillseekers Initiative in Scotland) as a Fast-Food Apprentice may be possible, where counter service assistant work forms an early part of the apprenticeship which may also include kitchen work before moving on to more advanced supervisory duties. Please see article 6. FOOD SERVICE ASSISTANT. Contact your local careers office, Jobcentre, TEC/LEC for details.

For further information, please see article 10. HOTEL PORTER.

LATE ENTRY

There is no upper age limit for entry to counter service work. Some fast-food outlets mainly employ people in their teens and twenties, but most catering organizations are happy to employ adults of varying ages.

The large amount of part-time work available may particularly attract adults with family commitments. However, starting rates of pay and shift-working may be a disincentive in some cases.

For this type of work, specific training opportunities, directed at adults, may be available. Candidates may have to satisfy certain conditions to be eligible. Contact your local Jobcentre, careers office or TEC/LEC for details.

Mature entrants may also be assessed for NVQ/SVQs. Relevant prior experience can be taken into account.

OPPORTUNITIES

Counter service assistants work in a variety of catering establishments throughout the UK. They include cafés, self-service restaurants, coffee shops, fast-food outlets, snack bars, cafeterias, pubs, motorway service areas, staff restaurants in factories, schools, colleges and hospitals, and outside caterers specializing in functions.

The number employed in this work is increasing, particularly as more fast-food outlets are opening, and vacancies arise frequently. Vacancies may be advertised in local newspapers, Jobcentres, careers offices, or may be found by direct approach to local catering establishments.

There are no opportunities for self-employment.

PAY AND CONDITIONS

Wages vary according to location and employer. For a 39-hour week, counter service assistants may earn between £111 and £175, with extra for overtime.

Full-time work is usually between 38 and 40 hours a week, but patterns of work vary according to the place of work. Weekend work may be required, especially in fast-food restaurants. Where outlets are open for very long hours, shift work is normal. There are opportunities for permanent day and permanent night work in some outlets that open 24 hours a day, such as motorway service areas.

Seasonal work is common – eg working during the summer season in a tourist area – and there are many opportunities for part-time work.

PROSPECTS

Some organizations have a career structure that allows promotion from counter service work to supervisor and then to manager. Assistants working for organizations where that possibility does not exist need to move to another employer for advancement. Capable workers can find that advancement in the catering industry is rapid. Prospects for promotion, particularly with large catering organizations, may be improved by achieving further NVQs/SVQs, for example, in Catering and Hospitality (Food Preparation and Cookery) or (Food Service) at Level 2 or above.

RELATED OCCUPATIONS

Fast-food cook, retail assistant, cash till/checkout operator, barman/woman, food service assistant, chef/cook, kitchen assistant.

FURTHER INFORMATION AND READING

Please see article 10. HOTEL PORTER.

8. HOTEL RECEPTIONIST (IC/CAT)

THE WORK

Hotel receptionists provide the first impression guests have of a hotel, and often the last one too, when they check out. The first impression may come across the telephone, when a booking is made, or face-to-face when guests first arrive at the beginning of their visit.

The job is not just about greeting and helping guests, though a large part of reception work involves administration. This can include taking reservations and cancellations, allocating rooms, record-keeping (for instance use of the telephone or delivery of newspapers), taking and passing on messages, compiling bills and handling money (including foreign exchange), ordering room service and organizing the fulfilment of any special requirements guests have. In all but the smallest hotels, reservations will be handled by a computer system, on which the receptionist must update and check information. Receptionists often use word processors to write letters confirming reservations, as well as fax and telex machines and telephone switchboards.

Apart from checking guests in and out of the hotel, the receptionist has a great deal of other contact with guests. Questions about the local area and its amenities must be answered, valuables taken for safe keeping, and requests for taxis or theatre tickets must be dealt with. These queries and requests often provide constant interruptions to the routine administrative tasks. Sometimes guests' requests must be referred on to other hotel departments, such as porters or restaurant staff. Receptionists must liaise constantly with the housekeeping department too, so that they know which rooms are occupied and which are not.

CATERING AND HOSPITALITY: IB/IC

In large hotels, specialist teams may deal with certain aspects of reception work, for instance there may be an advance reservations telephone team and/or one handling guest accounts. In smaller hotels, the receptionist may handle a very large range of tasks, including carrying luggage or helping in the bar or restaurant.

WORK ENVIRONMENT

The nature of reception areas depends, to an extent, on the size and nature of hotel, but in general they are situated near the main hotel entrance behind a counter, often with office equipment. Receptionists work both standing at the counter and sitting at computer terminals and telephone switchboards. In smaller establishments, receptionists may also work in bars, restaurants and elsewhere.

SKILLS AND INTERESTS

This is a job where personality is of the utmost importance. Hotel reception work suits people who are friendly, outgoing and cheerful. It is essential to enjoy interacting with other people, guests and colleagues alike, and to have the good communications skills this entails. These skills include verbal and written communications, as well as body language. Receptionists must be willing to please and serve customers, and so the work suits people who enjoy a lot of contact with people and helping them to enjoy their visit. Sometimes receptionists find themselves being constantly interrupted, so they need to be patient and helpful, even with the occasional difficult guest.

Receptionists also need to be able to think on their feet, come up with creative solutions to problems, or be able to direct guests to another department or person who can. They need to be able to handle a wide variety of tasks at the same time and remain calm under the pressure this situation can cause.

Hotel reception work involves a good deal of administration too, so it suits people who are well organized and have an administrative flair. An aptitude for using office equipment is useful too.

ENTRY REQUIREMENTS

Personal qualities tend to be regarded by employers as more important requirements than specific qualifications. A good general education, good handwriting and reasonable levels of numeracy and literacy to deal with billing, record-keeping and letter writing all help. So, for example, GCSEs/S grades in English and maths are useful, as are keyboard skills. Alternatively, a GNVQ in Hospitality and Catering at Foundation, Intermediate or Advanced level or GSVQ Level I, II or III demonstrates an interest in, and understanding of, the industry. Experience of hotels or catering gained from holiday work or a placement may go some way to serving the same function. The more prestigious the hotel or hotel chain the higher the level of qualifications they are likely to look for.

Conversational ability in one or more foreign languages is helpful for dealing with overseas guests and will enhance opportunities for working abroad. A demonstrable ability to communicate well with a wide variety of people and to enjoy helping them is sought by employers. Problem-solving skills and experience are of interest too. Employers look for people who have a smart appearance and pleasant personality and who can keep calm when under pressure.

TRAINING

Pre-entry

Those who wish to study before starting full-time work can go on a full-time or part-time college course for one or two years, gaining NVQs/SVQs in Hospitality and Catering (Reception) at Levels 1 and 2. Alternatively, with four GCSEs/S grades (A–C/1–3), or equivalent, and the two-year Advanced GNVQ/GSVQ Level III in Hospitality and Catering is an option. From that route, work would still be started at the level of trainee receptionist, but promotion would be quicker. Training includes either realistic simulated work environments, or work experience, or both, and covers subjects such as reservations systems, telephone answering techniques, customer care, credit control, accounting and invoicing. In Scotland, the SQA National Certificate and Higher National Certificate in Reception is offered at some colleges.

Post-entry

Trainee reception staff receive extensive on-the-job training in the technical side of the work, such as making and cancelling reservations and allocating rooms, how to calculate bills, and how to use computers and the office equipment. They are also trained on information about the local area, places of interest and transport facilities. Training is provided in the all-important area of customer care too. Trainees without relevant qualifications are often given the opportunity to train towards NVQs/SVQs in Catering and Hospitality (Reception) at Levels 1 and 2. These qualifications are normally offered through in-house training, although some employers provide the opportunity to attend a part-time college course. Those with qualifications may also be assessed for NVQ/SVQs.

It is possible to start or develop work as a hotel receptionist via a training opportunity for young people, for example a National Traineeship (Skillseekers in Scotland) leading to NVQ/SVQ Level 2 in Catering and Hospitality (Reception). This can be done either by getting day release from an existing employer to go to college, or by going on a traineeship at a centre such as the Hotel and Catering Training Company (HCTC) and being sent by them to employers for work experience. For details of opportunities, contact your local careers office, Jobcentre, TEC/LEC, HCTC or Springboard.

Similarly, entry and training via a Modern Apprenticeship (part of the Skillseekers Initiative in Scotland) as an Accommodation Apprentice may be possible, leading to at least NVQ/SVQ Level 3 in Front Office Supervision. This would normally be intended to train for supervisory positions, so, though there are no set entry requirements, employers may look for higher-calibre applicants.

A Modern Apprenticeship would normally be completed in three years. The apprenticeship includes: an induction phase to provide a grounding in the industry, information about the employing organization, and development of basic skills; an intermediate phase of learning practical skills leading to NVQ/SVQ Level 2 plus a number of additional units in key skills (core skills in Scotland); and a final phase acquiring NVQ/SVQ Level 3 skills and further key/core skills.

For further information, please see article 10. HOTEL PORTER.

CATERING AND HOSPITALITY: IB/IC

LATE ENTRY

It can be harder to start work as a hotel receptionist over the age of 30, although some employers prefer more mature applicants, especially with good secretarial skills.

Experience in jobs relating to the public, especially those involving the handling of money, and in secretarial or reception jobs in other industries may be an advantage.

Mature entrants may also be assessed for NVQ/SVQs and relevant prior experience can be taken into account.

OPPORTUNITIES

Vacancies for reception staff are usually plentiful, but competition is fierce. For further details on the numbers and distribution of hotels and other accommodation establishments, please see article 1. HOTEL MANAGER.

PAY AND CONDITIONS

Salaries range from £7,500 to £9,750 for a receptionist and £6,500 to £10,250 for hotel reservations clerks, cashiers and telephonists, as an average for three-star, four-star and five-star hotels in central London. Salaries vary according to the type of establishment and are usually higher in central London than elsewhere.

Reception desks operate from early morning to late at night, many for 24 hours a day, so receptionist staff usually work shifts, including evenings, overnight and weekends. Some hotels compensate for this by providing accommodation; others help with transport to and from home.

PROSPECTS

For receptionists at smaller establishments, it is always possible to move to larger and more prestigious hotels. From there, with appropriate experience and qualifications, such as an NVQ/SVQ in Catering and Hospitality (Hotel Reception Supervisory Management) at Level 3, receptionists can be promoted to shift leader or supervisor, and then on to head receptionist. Those with the right management potential and skills could be promoted to front office manager. For this level, further qualifications may be desired, such as an NVQ/SVQ in Catering and Hospitality (Reception Management) at Level 4, or more general hotel management qualifications, such as membership of the Hotel Catering and International Management Association (HCIMA).

Alternatively, hotel receptionists may choose to try out other departments of the hotel, such as the bar, restaurant or banqueting services. Many large hotels operate schemes encouraging employees to work in different departments to develop their skills and so increase promotion prospects. Many receptionists choose to move into the sales or accounts departments, which, in turn, can lead up the management path. Some move into personnel or training, where a qualification from the Institute of Personnel and Development (IPD) is useful. Those who wish to try other environments, could take their skills to commerce and industry to take office jobs. Other options include customer care, administration, sales and marketing roles in the travel or leisure industry.

RELATED OCCUPATIONS

Secretary, book-keeper, administrative assistant, air steward/hostess, information officer, hotel porter, reservations clerk, front office manager.

FURTHER INFORMATION AND READING

Please see article 10. HOTEL PORTER.

9. HOTEL ROOM ATTENDANT (IC)

THE WORK

Hotel room attendants are responsible for keeping bedrooms, bathrooms and public rooms in hotels clean, tidy and pleasant. It is their job to ensure the hotel's appearance is clean, tidy, attractive and welcoming to guests.

Hotel room attendants are often allocated between six and fifteen rooms to clean. The number depends on the type and size of hotel, the type and size of room and its furnishings, the number of cleaning staff available, and the standards expected. This work involves replacing used towels and linen, making the beds, emptying bins, dusting, vacuuming the floor and so on. Apart from cleaning the bedroom and bathroom, the attendant also tidies up and replenishes stocks of guest supplies, such as soap and shampoo, drinks in the mini-bar or coffee, tea and biscuits. Room attendants may also turn down beds before guests retire, and leave a good night message and chocolate on the pillow. Room attendants must take care not to disturb guests' possessions in occupied rooms, and to check vacated ones for left property.

Room attendants clean, polish and tidy public rooms too, and may arrange flowers or displays of tourist information and hotel sales leaflets and brochures. It is their job to make sure every detail of how a room looks is just right. If an item is damaged and needs to be repaired or replaced, the room attendant notifies the housekeeper, who will arrange for its repair or replacement.

Room attendants routinely use a vacuum cleaner, mop or both, and a variety of cleaning materials and substances. They learn to care for different types of surfaces, including wood, glass and fabrics. Some cleaning substances are hazardous or corrosive, and protective gloves and aprons, or overalls, should be worn.

Room attendants often work on their own as they perform the actual cleaning and tidying duties, but also work in a team. In large hotels, room attendants report to a floor housekeeper or assistant housekeeper. In smaller ones, they report directly to the housekeeper or housekeeping manager. In the smallest establishments, the room attendant may report directly to the manager or proprietor.

WORK ENVIRONMENT

Room attendants work in bedrooms, bathrooms, public rooms and supplies rooms (such as the linen room). They may need to access awkward spaces to clean, either bending down (for instance in bathrooms) or stretching up (perhaps to polish to the top of a mirror). The work can involve handling heavy loads of linen, turning mattresses, or using equipment such as vacuum cleaners.

CATERING AND HOSPITALITY: IB/IC

SKILLS AND INTERESTS

Hotel room attendants need to be strong and physically fit. People with back or other physical problems would not be suitable for this work. Apart from moving heavy loads, and bending and stretching while making beds and cleaning bathrooms, they have to work hard, efficiently and quickly to complete all their rooms in the time allocated.

Attention to detail is very important in this job. The right number of towels should be left, the correct display of menus and stationery should be available and the flowers replaced if they are no longer fresh. It is the room attendant's job to notice these details (although, in most establishments, work is checked by supervisors or housekeepers). The work suits careful, practical people with an eye for detail, who like to see results quickly.

Hotel room attendants must be prepared to work on their own a lot of the time as they clean and tidy rooms. An ability to work on their own initiative is important, although equally important is working within the housekeeping team. This may involve liaising with supervisors, letting them know if items are damaged, or requesting replacement cleaning materials or fresh linen and reporting anything unusual or suspicious. So good communications and an ability to get on well with people are necessary. These characteristics will help with dealing with customers too. Hotel guests quite often ask room attendants for information or bring them problems or complaints.

ENTRY REQUIREMENTS

Formal qualifications are not usually required to start this job. Employers are looking for people who are reasonably strong and fit, to cope with the physical demands of the job. They also require people who are prepared to work hard and for unsocial hours – hotel room attendants must fit in their work around guests, which usually means starting early in the morning and can involve working shifts in the evenings and weekends, so that services are provided seven days a week, whenever guests require them.

Applicants need to demonstrate an ability to work on their own initiative and in a team, and to get on with other people.

Entry at 16/17 may be to a National Traineeship (Skillseekers in Scotland) with no set entry requirements.

TRAINING

Hotel room attendants often start straight from school, or later in life, with few formal qualifications. Most employers offer them on-the-job training, combined with in-house training or sometimes part-time study at a college or commercial training centre, which would normally lead towards NVQs/SVQs in Catering and Hospitality (Housekeeping) at Levels 1 and 2. This may be via a National Traineeship (Skillseekers in Scotland). This can be done either by getting day release from an existing employer to go to college, or by going on a traineeship at a centre such as the Hotel and Catering Training Company (HCTC) and being sent by them to employers for work experience. For details of opportunities, contact your local careers office, Jobcentre, TEC/LEC, HCTC or Springboard.

Essential training for hotel room attendants includes the safe handling of hazardous substances for cleaning, which may be provided by the suppliers of the materials. Room attendants are also trained on the safe use of equipment, such as industrial vacuum cleaners and presses. Training on security issues, and general health and safety procedures is provided too. In addition, many employers offer hotel room attendants training in customer care to help them deal with guests.

Completion of a National Traineeship may bring the choice of progressing to a Modern Apprenticeship (part of the Skillseekers Initiative in Scotland) – please see article 3. HOUSEKEEPER/HOUSEKEEEPING MANAGER.

For further information, please see article 10. HOTEL PORTER.

LATE ENTRY

There are no age restrictions on entering the job of hotel room attendant, but it should be remembered that physical fitness, stamina and a degree of strength are needed for it. Room attendants with ambition for promotion may find opportunities limited if they start too late.

Mature entrants may also be assessed for NVQ/SVQs and relevant prior experience can be taken into account.

OPPORTUNITIES

Apart from the opportunities available in-house in hotels, guesthouses, holiday centres and the like, hotel room attendants can also work for agencies and contract cleaning companies. Those working for agencies can work in a variety of establishments, gaining experience in different systems. Many hotels use such agencies to vary their staff numbers, according to the different needs they have on different days. Generally, there are plenty of vacancies available.

For the numbers and distribution of hotels and accommodation establishments, please see article 1. HOTEL MANAGER.

PAY AND CONDITIONS

Average salaries for a hotel room attendant range from £7,300 to £9,000 in hotels in central London. Salaries vary according to type and size of hotel and the location. Salaries in central London are normally higher than elsewhere.

Hotel room attendants usually work shift systems, covering early mornings, evenings and weekends.

PROSPECTS

Hotel room attendants who demonstrate ability and management potential, and who are physically fit and well-motivated, can progress to supervisory posts such as floor housekeeper. Increasingly, employers are offering the opportunity and training support to gain an NVQ/SVQ in Catering and Hospitality (Housekeeping) at Level 2.

RELATED OCCUPATIONS

Contract (or other) cleaner, linen porter, hospital domestic services assistant, room steward (cruise liners and trains), head linen keeper, floor housekeeper, housekeeping manager.

FURTHER INFORMATION AND READING

Please see article 10. HOTEL PORTER.

CATERING AND HOSPITALITY: IB/IC

10. HOTEL PORTER (IC)

THE WORK

Porters are often the first people guests meet when they arrive at a hotel, so they can make an enormous impact on the guests' first impression. Porters have a great deal of contact with people, and helping guests is their main function.

Apart from greeting guests, porters' duties include carrying luggage, directing people through the hotel, advising on hotel facilities (such as how to work the TV, when the restaurant serves dinner and where the fire exits are) and those of the local area, looking after keys, post and messages, calling or booking taxis, parking cars, arranging restaurant, theatre and travel reservations and running any other errands that guests require. Hotels with conference facilities may involve porters in organizing conference equipment, carrying it and setting it up in the right place. Porters on duty overnight may become involved in an even wider range of tasks, including checking guests in and out if no receptionist is on duty, preparing and serving snacks, drinks and breakfast trays and distributing morning newspapers.

In larger hotels, these tasks may be split among the different porters (or uniformed staff as they are also known). For instance, the doorman/woman is responsible for greeting guests, opening and closing car doors and hailing taxis; the luggage porter helps guests with carrying their bags; the hall porter answers queries and passes on post; while the bell hops locate guests and deliver messages. The head porter, or concierge, manages the team and arranges its shifts, recommends and books restaurants, shows and travel facilities. In smaller establishments, there may be only one or two porters to provide all these services.

WORK ENVIRONMENT

Whatever the size and nature of hotel, porters work mainly on their feet, standing or walking around the hotel. Depending on the particular job, a porter may stand near the hotel main entrance, or at the porter's desk, usually a counter in the main reception area, or be engaged in lifting and carrying luggage, laundry, linen, housekeeping supplies, furniture or conference equipment all around the hotel.

SKILLS AND INTERESTS

As a porter's main function is to help guests, a friendly, pleasant and helpful personality will be a great asset in this job. It is a job for people who enjoy meeting and helping others. Good communications skills help with this side of the work. As part of the package of helping create a good impression with guests, porters are required to look their best, so employers look for people who have a smart appearance. People suited to portering work have an interest in the local area, for instance the different types of show available at different theatres and concert halls, the relative merits and prices of different restaurants, and the fastest, cheapest or most comfortable way to travel from one place to another.

Porters' jobs are active ones, so a reasonable degree of physical fitness helps. There is a lot of lifting and carrying work to be done, especially for new trainees, and so it is not a job for someone with a bad back. Even if a specific porter's job does not include much lifting and carrying, porters need to be comfortable with being on their feet most of the working day.

ENTRY REQUIREMENTS

Formal or academic qualifications are not usually required. A personality that is demonstrably friendly, cheerful and helpful is generally considered more important. Good communication skills are required, with employers often stipulating that porters have good spoken English, or are well spoken. An aptitude for and/or knowledge of other languages is useful too, for helping guests from overseas. Employers look for candidates with a smart appearance, and some ask for them to be over the age of 18, while others are prepared to take 16- or 17-year-olds.

Employers look for a reasonable degree of physical fitness too, particularly for those being considered for luggage or linen portering. Good local knowledge is important, especially for those working on the hall porter's desk, or at reception.

TRAINING

Training for porters is generally provided on the job, including training in hotel services and local amenities. Security and fire procedures are covered, as well as health and safety and, often, first aid. Customer care training is provided too.

Porters who work overnight shifts are trained on procedures for checking guests in and out if they arrive late or depart early, and on preparing and serving refreshments. Occasionally, employers support this with off-the-job training, either through an in-house school (available in some hotel chains) or external providers. In this way, porters can work towards gaining an NVQ/SVQ in Catering and Hospitality (Portering) at Level 1, learning subjects such as customer care, room service and making continental breakfasts. For those involved in a range of activities in the hotel, Catering and Hospitality (Guest Service) at Levels 1 and 2 may be appropriate.

It may be possible to start or develop work as a hotel porter via a training opportunity for young people such as a National Traineeship (Skillseekers in Scotland) leading to an NVQ/SVQ qualification. This can be done, either by getting day release from an existing employer to go to college or training centre, or by entering a traineeship with an organization such as the Hospitality Training Foundation (HTF) and being sent by them to employers for work experience. For details of opportunities, contact your local careers office, Jobcentre, TEC/LEC, the HTF or Springboard.

LATE ENTRY

Age is not a barrier to starting work as a hotel porter, but obviously the need for a degree of physical fitness and the ability to carry heavy loads should be borne in mind.

There may be specific training opportunities, directed at adults, available in some areas for this type of work. Candidates may have to satisfy certain conditions to be eligible. Contact your local Jobcentre, careers office or TEC/LEC for details.

Mature entrants may also be assessed for NVQ/SVQs. Relevant prior experience can be taken into account.

CATERING AND HOSPITALITY: IB/IC

OPPORTUNITIES

Vacancies for hotel porters are usually plentiful, but competition is quite strong. For further details of the number and distribution of hotels and other accommodation establishments, please see article 1. HOTEL MANAGER.

PAY AND CONDITIONS

Salaries range from £6,500 to £8,000 for a luggage porter, £7,250 to £9,250 for hall porters and £7,500 to £8,750 for doormen/women as an average for three-star, four-star and five-star hotels in central London. Salaries vary according to the type of establishment and are usually higher in central London than elsewhere. Generous tips can add to the salary. For head concierges in luxury city hotels, perks can include theatre tickets, restaurant meals and sightseeing tours, so that they can make informed recommendations to guests.

Portering services are usually available 18 to 24 hours a day, so porters work shifts, including evenings, overnight and weekends.

Porters are normally required to wear a uniform provided by the employer.

PROSPECTS

For porters at small establishments, it is always possible to move to larger and more prestigious hotels. From there, with further experience and qualifications, such as NVQs/SVQs, porters can proceed up the career ladder to head porter – managing the team – or concierge. It is sometimes possible to proceed to jobs such as front-of-house manager.

Porters may choose to move across the hotel to the nearest department, reception, or some may prefer to try out other departments, such as working in the bar or food service in the restaurant, and proceed up the career ladders there.

RELATED OCCUPATIONS

Security officer, hospital porter, receptionist, bartender, food service assistant, air steward/hostess, linen porter, front-of-house manager.

FURTHER INFORMATION

Edexcel Foundation (incorporating BTEC)*, Stewart House, 32 Russell Square, London WC1B 5DN, 0171 393 4500, www.edexcel.org.uk

City & Guilds (C+G)*, 1 Giltspur Street, London EC1A 9DD, 0171 294 2468, http://www.city-and-guilds.co.uk

Hotel and Catering International Management Association (HCIMA)*, 191 Trinity Road, London SW17 7HN, 0181 672 4251

Hospitality Training Foundation (HTF), 3rd Floor, International House, High Street, Ealing, London W5 5DB, 0891 443322, www.htf.org.uk

Hotel and Catering Training Company (HCTC) – address as above

Qualifications and Curriculum Authority (QCA), 29 Bolton Street, London W1Y 7PD, 0171 509 5555, http://www.open.gov.uk/qca/

Scottish Qualifications Authority (SQA)*, Hanover House, 24 Douglas Street, Glasgow G2 7NQ, 0141 248 7900; Helpdesk 0141 242 2214; www.sqa.org.uk

Springboard*, 3 Denmark Street, London WC2H 8LP, 0171 497 8654 (please include sae)

FURTHER READING

Leaflets/booklets are available from the addresses marked*.

Working in Hotels and Catering – COIC

Working in Tourism and Leisure – COIC

Careers and Training in Hotels, Catering and Tourism – Butterworth Heinemann

The Handbook of Tourism and Leisure – CRAC

Careers in Catering and Hospitality – HCTC

How To... Get a Job in Hotels and Catering – How To Books

Periodical: Caterer and Hotelkeeper (also publishes annual careers guide, available from HTF)

In the careers library classified under IB; IC

LICENSED RETAILING: IB/IC

1. PUBLICAN/LICENSEE CLCI:IB
2. BARMAN/WOMAN CLCI:IC

BACKGROUND INFORMATION

The on-licensed retail sector is a large and important part of the hospitality and catering industry. There are around 60,000 pubs in Britain employing about 500,000 staff.

The majority of British adults visit a pub on a regular basis and their demands, together with changes in legislation, have led to pubs changing considerably over the past few years. Many offer a much wider range of drinks, both alcoholic and non-alcoholic. The provision of food has become a very important part of pub business and an increasing number of pubs now offer food, ranging from bar snacks to full meals. Some pubs offer accommodation and, to compete with other leisure activities, many pubs offer a variety of types of entertainment.

1. PUBLICAN/LICENSEE (IB)

THE WORK

Publicans/licensees run pubs and other premises licensed to sell alcohol for consumption on the premises. They are concerned with running the business profitably, which involves buying in drink, food and other goods and pricing them to sell for a profit, as well as stock control and keeping accounts. Publicans/licensees must observe the laws governing the retail sale of intoxicating drink in the operation of licensed premises.

Many publicans/licensees employ bar staff, and they recruit, train and supervise those staff. They may also employ cellar and catering staff. Publicans/licensees often work alongside bar staff, making sure the pub is well stocked and prepared for opening, serving customers, re-stocking, collecting and washing glasses and keeping the bar areas clean. If pubs serve food, publicans/licensees supervise the catering operations; any entertainment is their responsibility too. After closing time publicans/licensees help to clean up.

Publicans/licensees are responsible for the health and safety of staff and customers and for maintaining hygienic conditions for food and drink service. They must deal with security, due to the large amounts of cash that go through the tills and the high value of alcoholic drinks. The success of pubs is largely due to the publicans/licensees. They must make sure that their pub has a welcoming atmosphere and that the quality of service, food, drink and entertainment encourages customers to return.

WORK ENVIRONMENT

Pubs vary considerably in size and type but, when busy, most can be noisy and smoky. The work is physical, involving lifting and carrying crates and handling barrels. The hours are long and publicans/licensees spend most of their time standing.

SKILLS AND INTERESTS

Publicans/licensees must be able to get on well with people of all kinds. They should be polite and outgoing with good conversational and listening skills, so they can talk easily to customers, whether regulars or occasional visitors. They must, though, be capable of dealing with any trouble that may arise in the pub.

Publicans/licensees need managerial skills to be able to recruit, train and motivate staff, in order that they can work efficiently and well, while maintaining a friendly, welcoming atmosphere in the pub.

Good numeracy skills are needed for cash handling, costing and the keeping of accounts. Good business sense is vital. They need to be capable of controlling spending, buying effectively, pricing goods realistically and operating careful stock control. New ways of attracting business need to be tried, which may involve trying different menus or different forms of entertainment.

Publicans/licensees must be able to learn and observe the legal aspects of their business relating to licensing, food provision and health and safety.

ENTRY REQUIREMENTS

No formal academic qualifications are required to become a publican/licensee, but personal qualities are considered important.

Previous business experience is very desirable, although not essential, and some experience of bar work is helpful.

Relevant qualifications include NVQs/SVQs in Catering and Hospitality (Serving Food and Drink – Bar) at Levels 1 and 2, On-Licensed Premises Supervisory Management at Level 3 and On-Licensed Premises Management at Level 4. Also relevant are the British Institute of Innkeeping's Certificate of Induction and Qualifying Examinations, the Degree in Licensed Retail Management awarded by the University of Wolverhampton, and higher diplomas or degrees including licensed retailing modules and catering management.

Running a pub is often seen as a job for a couple, but there are an increasing number of openings for individuals. There is no legal minimum age to become a publican/licensee, other than the requirement to be at least 18 years to serve behind a bar. However, 25 years is considered to be a realistic lower age limit for a publican/licensee, with the occasional exception, and, increasingly, publicans/licensees require the National Licensee's Certificate awarded by the British Institute of Innkeeping (BII).

In Scotland, some licensing boards insist on experience and/or qualifications to prove candidates are a 'fit and proper person' to hold a licence to sell alcohol. Others make it a condition of granting a licence that the holder should attend a training course after receiving the license.

Anyone considering becoming a publican/licensee ought to be in good health and be physically fit. A driving licence, while not essential, is useful.

TRAINING

Publicans/licensees can be managers, tenants or free traders (owners). Please see OPPORTUNITIES for the differences.

Managers can receive training from the employing brewer or pub owner, which can last from a few weeks to several months. Trainee managers may be sent to a training pub, followed by periods of relief management at different pubs, before being sent to manage their own. Many trainees take the BII Qualifying Examination, which covers all aspects of running a public house.

Publicans/licensees may gain NVQs/SVQs, in On-Licensed Premises Supervisory Management at Level 3 and On-

LICENSED RETAILING: IB/IC

Licensed Premises Management at Level 4.

Many pub owners provide training for potential tenants, which may lead to a BII qualification. Those considering becoming tenants or free traders can undertake a fee-paying five-day course run by the colleges and training companies. The course includes business planning and finances, cellar management, stock control, menu planning, food hygiene, health and safety, staff selection and recruitment, legislation, marketing and security. On completion of the course, the BII Qualifying Examination may be taken. The BII has also developed a new qualification aimed at those wishing to obtain a justice's licence for the first time. The exam –The National Licensee's Certificate – covers all aspects of licensing legislation and the social responsibilities of the licensee.

The Hospitality Training Foundation also offers some one-day courses suitable for publicans/licensees.

The BII admits those who have attained specific units of NVQs/SVQs in On-Licensed Premises Management, or its own qualifications, in the various grades of membership. It also offers advanced qualifications in areas such as catering management, wine retailing and customer services. Additionally the BII has introduced the Scottish License Certificate qualification which takes into account the legal differences between England and Scotland.

A number of HND/degree courses are available in Hotel and Catering Management which contain modules in licensed retailing. Graduates may then attend fast-track training courses run by the bigger companies, including a mixture of class-room based training and placements.

Modern Apprenticeships are also available. Please see article 2. BARMAN/WOMAN.

LATE ENTRY

Pub owners tend to select trainee managers who are between 25 to 45 or 50 years. Their tenants tend to be selected between 25 to 50 or 55 years. People of any age can buy a free house, providing they have the necessary capital.

There may be specific training opportunities, directed at adults, available in some areas for this type of work. Candidates may have to satisfy certain conditions to be eligible. Contact your local Jobcentre, careers office or TEC/LEC for details.

OPPORTUNITIES

There are opportunities for publicans/licensees throughout the UK, either as managers, tenants or free traders. Entry is very competitive.

Managers are employed by a company that owns the pub; they are salaried staff. Applicants do not need to have capital to become managers.

Tenants (sometimes known as lessees) run pubs leased to them by a landlord – usually a brewer, a licensed retailer or a property company. They effectively operate their business independently although, if the pub is owned by a brewer, they may have to sell the beer of the brewer concerned. Tenants have to buy fixtures and fittings, and furnishings and stock, the cost of which varies according to the pub in question.

Free traders run pubs they have bought themselves and are independent of brewers. The cost of buying a pub varies, but averages over £250,000.

There are approximately 13,500 managed houses in Britain, 29,800 tenancies and over 22,000 free traders. The proportion of managed free houses is growing, while that of tenancies is declining. A feature of Scotland is that a larger proportion of pubs are privately owned, and managed pubs outnumber tenancies.

PAY AND CONDITIONS

Managers are paid a salary, either individually or as a couple, and may be able to earn bonuses, or participate in a profit-sharing scheme. They usually have accommodation provided on the premises. There are no set earnings for tenants or managed free traders. Earnings vary considerably from pub to pub, according to turnover. Publicans'/licensees' annual earnings range from under £5,000 to over £40,000. Additional benefits may include profit-related pay, qualifications-related pay and bonus schemes.

Pubs are able to serve alcohol between 11am and 11pm Monday to Saturday and 12 noon to 10.30pm on Sundays. In Scotland, Sunday hours are 12.30 to 2.30pm and 6.30 to 11pm, although application can be made to open between 2.30 and 6.30pm.

Preparation takes place before opening time and clearing up after closing. While not necessarily working all those hours, publicans/licensees work very long hours, often seven days a week, with few holidays.

PROSPECTS

Successful managers may get promoted to run a larger pub, with an increased salary and larger bonuses.

There is no promotion as such for tenants or free traders. Success for them is measured in increased earnings through increased and more profitable business. Successful tenants may buy the tenancy of a larger pub or buy a free house. Free traders may buy larger free houses.

RELATED OCCUPATIONS

Hotel manager, catering/restaurant manager, off-licence manager, club steward, retail manager, barman/woman.

FURTHER INFORMATION AND READING

Please see article 2. BARMAN/WOMAN

2. BARMAN/WOMAN (IC)

THE WORK

Bar staff work in licensed premises. They are responsible for selling drinks of all kinds, tobacco products like cigarettes and cigars, and food. Depending where they work, the food can range from crisps and peanuts to bar snacks and full meals.

An important part of the work is to talk to customers and to provide a welcoming, friendly atmosphere. They must, though, keep alert for any trouble that may develop and try to prevent it.

Duties begin before the bar opens. Bar staff prepare the bar by stocking it with bottles, putting out fresh beer mats and ashtrays and any small snacks, like bowls of peanuts and crisps. They stock up with ice and sundries, like sliced lemons and cherries. Bar staff may help to organize the cellar, where beer barrels and bottles of all kinds are

LICENSED RETAILING: IB/IC

stored. They may clean the beer pipes.

During opening time, they mix and serve a whole range of drinks, both alcoholic and non-alcoholic. They calculate customers' bills, collect the money and give change. This involves using cash registers. Some also deal with payments by cheque and credit card.

Apart from serving customers, bar staff collect empty glasses and wash them – often using a glass-washing machine – collect bottles, empty ashtrays, and keep the bar and tables clean. When beer barrels are empty they may attach fresh barrels to the pumps. They stock up on any bottle shortages as they occur and change the optics on empty spirits bottles.

When the bar closes, bar staff make sure all glasses are washed and that the premises are left clean and tidy.

WORK ENVIRONMENT

Licensed premises can differ greatly. They can be old or modern. Some are large, some quite small. When busy, most can be noisy and smoky.

Bar staff spend most of their time standing. Their work can be physically demanding as it involves lifting and carrying crates and handling barrels, bending and stretching to reach glasses and goods for sale.

SKILLS AND INTERESTS

It is important that bar staff get on well with people of all kinds. They should be cheerful and outgoing, polite and tactful.

Communication skills are important, to gauge which customers wish to talk and which do not. Those skills are needed too when coping with difficult situations, like refusing to serve a customer who has had too much to drink or in asking a troublesome customer to leave.

Entrants to bar work must be able to gain a knowledge of the range of products sold, and of the licensing laws.

Bar work can be hectic, so an ability to work under pressure is desirable. A good memory is helpful for keeping track of orders and prices. Mental arithmetic ability is useful, as bills are often calculated in the head rather than on a till. As bar staff handle money, they must be honest and reliable.

Bar staff should have a clean and tidy appearance. Some may wear a uniform or standard clothing.

ENTRY REQUIREMENTS

No formal educational qualifications are required to enter bar work although some employers now require a recognized food hygiene qualification. Personal qualities are more important. Employers have a preference for entrants with some ability in mental arithmetic. The minimum age for bar work is, by law, 18 years. However, 16- and 17-year-olds are allowed to carry out such work if they are on an accredited training scheme.

TRAINING

Most bar staff are trained on the job by the publican/licensee, bar manager or experienced bar staff, although some employers run formal training programmes. They learn the skills needed to dispense and serve drinks, serve food, stock the bar, clean glasses, handle cash and use the cash register. Staff are taught the legal aspects of work in licensed premises and their employer's policies concerning the running of the business.

Bar staff can work towards NVQs/SVQs in Catering and Hospitality (Serving Food and Drink – Bar) at Levels 1 and 2. To register for an NVQ/SVQ candidates normally need to be employed within the industry although in some areas local colleges, training companies and TEC/LECs may be able to provide alternative access.

The Pub Apprenticeship is one of five designed for young people of between 16 and 24 years. Candidates must be employed full-time within the industry; training leads to NVQ Level 3. The apprenticeship normally takes 2–3 years to complete.

LATE ENTRY

There is no upper age limit. Providing the applicant is suitable, maturity can be a distinct advantage in bar work. The part-time nature of much bar work can be particularly suitable for adults with family responsibilities.

OPPORTUNITIES

Bar staff are employed at numerous licensed premises throughout the UK. There are many different kinds of public houses, including city centre, town, country, theme, disco, those offering accommodation and many specializing in food service. There are wine bars, hotels, restaurants, private clubs, holiday centres, leisure and sports centres, workplace social centres, and bars at airports, stations, on board trains and ships and in Armed Forces establishments.

The number of people employed in bar work has grown over the past few years.

It is comparatively easy for a suitable applicant to find work in a bar, as the turnover of bar staff is high. There are few opportunities to become self-employed. There are some possibilities of working abroad.

PAY AND CONDITIONS

Earnings vary according to the type of bar and its location. Hourly rates vary regionally and range between £3.00 and £6.00.

Pubs can serve alcohol from 11am to 11pm Monday to Saturday and 12 noon to 10.30pm on Sundays (12.30 to 2.30pm and 6.30 to 11pm on Sundays in Scotland, although application can be made to open between 2.30 and 6.30pm). Bar work can be full-time or part-time, with part-time work often used to cover the busiest times of evenings and weekends. In some areas, like holiday resorts, bar work can be seasonal. Full-time staff may work a 40-hour week on a shift basis, usually including lunch-times and evenings. Paid overtime may be available to full-time and part-time staff.

PROSPECTS

Bar staff can become bar managers or club stewards. They may become pub managers or, with capital, buy a tenancy or the freehold of a pub.

RELATED OCCUPATIONS

Food service assistant, counter service assistant, retail assistant, publican/licensee.

LICENSED RETAILING: IB/IC

FURTHER INFORMATION

Brewers and Licensed Retailers Association*, 42 Portman Square, London W1H 0BB, 0171 486 4831; website: www.blra.co.uk

The British Institute of Innkeeping*, Park House, 22–24 Park Street, Camberley, Surrey GU15 3PL, 01276 684449

Leisure Careers UK: www.barzone.co.uk (operated by the BII)

Hospitality Training Foundation (HTF)*, International House, High Street, Ealing, London W5 5DB, 0181 579 2400; Training Hotline: 0891 443322

The Scottish Licensed Trade Association*, 95a Clerk Street, Loanhead, Midlothian EH20 9RE, 0131 440 4544

FURTHER READING

Leaflets/booklets are available from the addresses marked*

Working in Hotels and Catering – COIC.

New Innkeeper – a business monthly solely for members of the British Institute of Innkeeping. See address above.

Publican (Quantum Publishing – 0181 565 4200)

Licensee & Morning Advertiser (01753 811911)

Caterer & Hotelkeeper (01444 475633)

In the careers library classified under IB; IC.

HOME ECONOMICS: ID

HOME ECONOMISTCLCI:ID

BACKGROUND INFORMATION

Home economists are professional advisers concerned with food, clothing, home management and design, household services and research related to the home and community. They act as a link between consumers and producers, advising consumers on the use of products and services and representing the consumer's point of view to manufacturers.

With increased public awareness of consumer issues, such as food safety, the role of the home economist is important. However, courses and jobs are changing, and new titles are tending to replace the term 'home economics'. Courses increasingly have titles such as applied consumer science, consumer studies, food and consumer studies. Job titles are very varied and could include training adviser, journalist, home care organizer, consumer adviser or customer service adviser.

THE WORK

Food industry. This is one of the main employers of home economists. Within the food industry there are several areas of work:

– product development. This involves taking food products (such as ready-prepared meals) from the original concept through to commercial, large-scale production. It includes testing recipes, and working with other specialists to make sure that products can be commercially manufactured;

– writing instructions on products, preparing educational material and promotional literature, giving presentations or demonstrations of new products;

– quality assessment – for instance, running a 'taste panel' of consumers, who check the quality of products;

– advising consumers, eg by replying to correspondence. Consumers often want to know, for instance, whether certain products are suitable for vegetarians, or whether they include specific allergens, such as peanuts;

– liaising with other departments, particularly marketing, PR and research and development.

Home economists may move into other areas of work in the food industry, such as analytical work in the laboratory, supervision of production, or marketing.

Food retailing. There are opportunities for home economists with the large supermarket chains. Their work can be similar to that in the food industry; alternatively, they may be involved in store management.

Domestic equipment manufacturers. Companies that manufacture electrical goods or gas appliances employ people with a home economics background to work in an advisory capacity, representing the interests of consumers. In some companies they train sales and service repair staff to demonstrate the use of electrical goods, such as cookers and washing machines, to consumers.

Fuel and energy industries. The fuel and energy industries employ staff, usually called customer service advisers, who visit elderly and disabled customers in their homes to advise on the safe and efficient use of appliances. There are also some opportunities for educational/community liaison work, eg giving talks to local groups, developing educational resources.

Media and communications. A number of home economists work for magazines, and a few work for radio and television. They write reports, for instance on domestic equipment or issues relevant to consumers. They may create and test recipes, and write feature articles.

Some home economists specialize in food photography or food styling. Food styling involves preparing food for photographic sessions or filming, and is a specialist area in its own right. Various techniques are employed, eg the use of cardboard to stabilize the food, or glycerine to give a glazed finish.

Education. Teachers train in design and technology, rather than home economics, but in secondary schools they are able to specialize in areas such as food or textiles technology. They can also contribute to courses in health and social care, hospitality and catering.

In further and higher education there are opportunities to teach subjects such as consumer science or hospitality and catering.

Caring services. As increasing numbers of elderly, ill and disabled people are now cared for in their own homes, rather than in institutions, opportunities have arisen for care work within clients' homes. For example, *home care organizers* supervise and train *home care assistants,* who go into clients' homes to help with practical tasks such as washing and dressing.

Other areas related to caring work that attract people with an interest or training in home economics include housing work and health promotion.

Consumer affairs. Home economics is linked to the study of consumer affairs, and some home economists work in areas where they protect consumer interests. They may, for instance, train to become *trading standards officers,* who put into effect the large and growing range of legislation on consumer affairs. Alternatively, they may work in local authority consumer advice centres, providing help and information for the public.

WORK ENVIRONMENT

The work environment varies with different jobs – it could be an office, kitchen, laboratory, school, college, retail store or an individual's home.

Some jobs involve travel, for instance to give talks, lectures or demonstrations, or attend exhibitions in the UK, Europe or further afield. A driving licence is useful.

SKILLS AND INTERESTS

It is essential to be able to communicate with people from different backgrounds. Most jobs related to home economics involve interaction with people, and it is often part of the home economist's role to liaise between technical specialists and consumers.

A confident, outgoing personality, with a strong interest in people, is required. A good standard of dress and personal appearance is needed in jobs that involve meeting the public.

Writing skills are required in some areas, such as journalism, liaison roles and education. Home economists need to be methodical, with an eye for detail. Some jobs – particularly in the food industry – require scientific skills.

ENTRY REQUIREMENTS

A wide range of courses is available in areas related to home economics, such as consumer studies, cookery,

HOME ECONOMICS: ID

business studies, hospitality, leisure and catering. Formal academic entry qualifications are not always necessary, but it is useful to have GCSEs/S grades in home economics, maths, English and science, and/or Foundation or Intermediate GNVQs/GSVQs Level II/III in leisure, hospitality and catering or business.

BTEC/SQA higher national certificate/diploma courses: entry is with one A level/two H grades and three other GCSEs/S grades (A–C/1–3), or equivalent.

Degree courses: minimum entry requirements are two A levels/three H grades with five GCSEs/S grades (A–C/1–3), or equivalent. Useful subjects at A level/H grade include home economics, sciences and social sciences, but in most cases there are no set requirements. For entry to courses leading to teaching qualifications, GCSEs/S grades (A–C/1–3) in English and maths are essential.

Other courses: entry to BTEC National Diploma courses is with four GCSEs (A–C) or equivalent. For SQA national certificate clusters, there are no set entry requirements, although guidance is available for entry to specific units.

TRAINING

Only a few courses with the title 'Home Economics' remain. There are, however, many courses at all levels that are related to this field.

Degrees. These courses and closely related subjects are available at several universities. Applied consumer science or consumer studies cover the development and management of consumer products and services. These courses include the study of subjects such as food, textiles and clothing, design, development, manufacturing, psychology, marketing and business studies, consumer education and social policy.

There are also degree courses allowing greater specialization in particular areas related to home economics, such as:

– food science, food technology, food and nutrition, food marketing management;

– textiles, textile design, fashion management, clothing design and manufacture;

– hotel management, catering management, hospitality management;

– retail management, retail design management, food retail management.

There are degree courses in consumer protection/consumer and trading standards, which can lead to employment as a trading standards officer or to related work in consumer advice.

Postgraduate qualifications. Many graduates in home economics and consumer science/studies go on to take higher degrees or postgraduate diplomas in subjects such as food technology, textile technology or marketing. Some take professional qualifications to train as social workers or dietitians.

Teaching qualifications. It is possible to take a BEd course in Design and Technology, leading to a degree and a teaching qualification. Alternatively, postgraduate certificate in education (PGCE) courses are available for graduates with first degrees.

BTEC higher national diploma courses in Home Economics or related subjects (Consumer Studies, Food and Consumer Studies) are run at a small number of institutions. They normally last two years. Some students progress to degree courses.

SQA higher national certificate/diploma courses are available in Home Economics and Applied Consumer Studies.

Other courses. A small number of colleges run BTEC national diploma courses in Home Economics, lasting two years. In Scotland, it is possible to take National Certificate Clusters in Home Economics at Levels 1, 2 and 3.

LATE ENTRY

Home economics/consumer science is a field that attracts a high proportion of mature entrants.

Candidates over 21, applying for degree courses, may be accepted with non-standard qualifications. Many enter after taking Access courses. Other qualifications, such as professional examinations in another field, may also be acceptable. Check with the individual institution.

After training, it may be necessary to move to another geographical area to find suitable employment.

OPPORTUNITIES

Whilst the number of people who use the job title 'home economist' is declining, there are many jobs in related areas, and those who complete relevant training courses stand a good chance of finding employment, particularly if they are prepared to move to another location.

An increasing number of home economists work on a freelance basis. It is of some advantage for freelances to be based in or near London; those living elsewhere must be willing to travel.

There are opportunities to work abroad – most likely for staff working for multinational companies.

PAY AND CONDITIONS

Home economists with higher national diploma/degree qualifications start in industry on £13,000 to £16,000. After two to six years' work experience, typical salaries rise to between £15,500 and £23,500. Those in senior positions earn more.

Additional benefits can include a car, car allowance or mileage, allowances for meals and overnight expenses, a uniform or clothes allowance. Increasingly, companies are offering profit-sharing bonus schemes.

Teachers of design and technology/home economics are paid on the same scale as teachers of other subjects. Local authority staff are paid on local government scales.

Freelance fees vary enormously, depending on the individual's reputation and experience. A guide to freelance fees, and to salaries, is published annually by the Institute of Home Economics.

The majority of jobs involve office hours, but home economists need to be flexible and prepared to work long hours when there are deadlines to be met.

PROSPECTS

Home economists are employed in a wide variety of different fields, and therefore promotion prospects vary considerably. However, because home economics is a specialist area, it is likely that promotion will involve

HOME ECONOMICS: ID

moving into other areas of work within a company, such as marketing management.

Sideways moves to different industries are possible.

RELATED OCCUPATIONS

Food scientist / technologist / technician, chef / cook, restaurant / catering manager, dietitian, trading standards officer, health promotion officer, environmental health officer, store demonstrator.

FURTHER INFORMATION

Institute of Home Economics*, 21 Portland Place, London W1N 3AF, 0171 436 5677, sae (C5 size) required

National Association of Teachers of Home Economics and Technology*, Hamilton House, Mabledon Place, London WC1H 9BJ, 0171 387 1441

FURTHER READING

Leaflets/booklets are available from the address marked*.

MODUS College Courses Guide – National Association of Teachers of Home Economics and Technology.

In the careers library classified under ID.

CLEANING SERVICES: IJ

1. WINDOW CLEANER CLCI:IJ
2. REFUSE COLLECTOR CLCI:IJ

1. WINDOW CLEANER (IJ)

THE WORK

When cleaning domestic or ground floor shop windows, the window cleaner usually works alone. On domestic rounds, window cleaners are able to arrange their working days to suit themselves. This type of window cleaning has the greatest amount of customer contact. Domestic and shop window cleaners usually work from ladders at low levels. Some companies may provide a barrow or a car/van to transport materials.

In addition to cleaning windows, larger companies clean and polish the glass in fanlights, skylights and glass partitions, both indoors and outdoors in domestic, commercial and industrial buildings. They also clean windows that are too high to be reached by ladder. This involves working from a cradle – a working platform operated by ropes and pulleys – or from a bosun's chair or scaffolding. Although the actual cleaning techniques are the same, this type of work carries greater responsibilities. All window cleaners involved in high-risk work must be familiar with the rigging of these devices and how to operate them, including the fixing and knotting of the ropes. When working on scaffolding, or from a cradle, it may be necessary to wear a safety harness.

Larger-contract window cleaners tend to work in gangs and are paid on a piece-rate basis. It is therefore important to be able to work quickly and efficiently, so as to keep up production without taking any safety risks.

These gangs of window cleaners usually move from job to job in a van. Very few gang-working window cleaners have any contact with the customer. One of them, usually the foreman/woman, must ensure that the gang's worksheet is signed to say that the work has been satisfactorily completed. There is not usually any cash handling involved in larger contract cleaning jobs.

WORK ENVIRONMENT

The major part of the work is outdoors in both cold and hot weather, though work may stop during rain. Cradle work on office and tower blocks can be particularly cold and windy. Contract window cleaners may also work indoors, cleaning the interior faces of windows.

SKILLS AND INTERESTS

Window cleaning is a job suited to someone interested in working outdoors in all weathers. Much of the work is carried out at heights, requiring a good sense of balance. The amount of carrying and climbing varies according to the type of building being cleaned, but it is an advantage to be physically fit and reasonably strong. Safety is an important aspect of the job, particularly when working at heights or dealing with the winching machinery for a cradle/bosun's chair containing other workers. Window cleaners must follow workplace health, safety and welfare regulations. When working they must also respect and care for other people's property. The self-employed window cleaner, or one working for a small company, must enjoy working alone. When cleaning domestic windows they may also collect money, and need a pleasant manner when dealing with customers. They should also be completely trustworthy.

Larger contract cleaning companies often send out their window cleaners in gangs. Gang workers must work effectively as a team and co-operate with each other.

ENTRY REQUIREMENTS

Window cleaners are seldom required to have any formal educational qualifications. Some employers may test basic literacy and numeracy to ensure that applicants are able to understand their worksheets.

Some companies may prefer applicants who hold a full UK driving licence. This tends to be desirable, rather than essential.

TRAINING

It is possible to set up as a self-employed window cleaner without any training at all, and many smaller companies do not offer any structured training programme.

Larger organizations usually insist that a trainee works alongside an experienced window cleaner or as a member of a gang. Initially they work on interior glass and partitions, possibly using a short ladder. They then progress to outside and long-ladder work, receiving instructions on the correct angle of ladders, footing and lashing them. They also learn how to clean outside glass from the inside of the building without taking unnecessary risks. Safety is always a vital component in training.

Becoming a 'cradle hand' is usually the final part of the training. The trainee must become familiar with the principles of cradle rigging, traversing the cradle, operating winches and electrical gear, tying off and generally handling the equipment in the correct and safe manner. The length of training varies according to the policy of the employer and how quickly the trainee is able to progress and accept increasing responsibility.

An NVQ/SVQ in Cleaning: Windows, Glass and Facade Surfaces is available at Level 2. A Modern Apprenticeship in Cleaning is available leading to an NVQ in Supervisory Management Skills at Level 3 plus three cleaning industry technical units and the Cleaning Support Services Association (CSSA) Cleaning Management Apprentice Certificate. Contact your local careers office or TEC/LEC for details.

LATE ENTRY

Window cleaning is a responsible job and some employers prefer to recruit candidates with a more mature approach. The work can, however, be physically demanding, and older applicants must demonstrate that they are sufficiently agile to cope with the climbing and carrying that window cleaning involves.

OPPORTUNITIES

It is very difficult to be precise about the numbers of people employed as window cleaners.

There are two main types of employer offering opportunities to window cleaners: the small local concern dealing mainly with domestic windows, and the large commercial cleaning companies who deal with industrial and commercial buildings. Some small window cleaning companies also get contracts for cleaning local low-rise buildings where ladders give sufficient height. Larger

CLEANING SERVICES: IJ

organizations often obtain the contracts for cleaning the windows of high-rise multi-storey industrial and commercial buildings. In addition to providing window cleaners, these larger concerns are often able to provide a whole range of contract cleaning services.

PAY AND CONDITIONS

Self-employed window cleaners set their own rates of charges, often related to the numbers and size of windows to be cleaned. They therefore control their earnings by working additional hours as and when necessary. Window cleaning rates vary and range from around £3 to £6 for a house of average size. Contract window cleaners operate on a piecework basis, and earnings vary according to the type of work being done. Those working on high-rise buildings, using sophisticated equipment, earn more than those cleaning ground floor or interior windows only. Most experienced contract window cleaners can expect to earn about £120 to £180 a week. However, this varies from area to area.

Small businesses dealing with the windows of high street stores often need to work regular hours; many stores like to have their windows cleaned on the same day(s) of the week. This type of work often calls for an early start. Contract window cleaners usually work a 37½-hour, five-day week. Starting and finishing times can be variable. Paid overtime may be available.

PROSPECTS

Window cleaning is a job with limited promotion prospects. When working for a large contract cleaning company it may be possible to progress from low-rise building work to multi-storey work. This requires the use of more equipment and the acceptance of increasing responsibility for safety. Multi-storey work usually attracts higher salaries. Opportunities also occur for promotion to foreman/woman responsible for a gang of workers. Many window cleaners leave contract cleaning companies in order to become self-employed.

Those working in small businesses may be offered partnerships.

RELATED OCCUPATIONS

Road sweeper, cleaner, forecourt attendant, carpet cleaner.

FURTHER INFORMATION

British Institute of Cleaning Science, Whitworth Chambers, George Row, Northampton NN1 1DF, 01604 230075

Cleaning and Support Services Association Industry Training Organization (ITO), CSSA Suite 3.01, New Loom House, 101 Back Church Lane, London EL1 1LU, 0171 481 0881

Cleaning Industry Lead Body (CILB), 6 Grange Meadows, Elmswell, Bury St. Edmonds, Suffolk IP30 9GE, 01359 244014

National Federation of Master Window and General Cleaners, Summerfield House, Harrogate Road, Reddish, Stockport, Cheshire SK5 6HQ, 0161 432 8754

FURTHER READING

Working in Outdoor Jobs – COIC
In the careers library classified under IJ.

2. REFUSE COLLECTOR (IJ)

THE WORK

The job involves emptying dustbins and large containers of rubbish, and taking it in a specially built vehicle (a dust cart or refuse wagon) to an official refuse tip or incinerator. Refuse collectors work in small teams, usually of two to five loaders and a driver. Covering a specified area each day and following a planned route, the team collect refuse from a variety of premises – household, commercial and industrial.

The bins, containers and plastic sacks are taken, either by hand or on a trolley, to the refuse vehicle. Refuse collectors may work ahead of the lorry, moving the rubbish to a point that is easily accessible. They empty the rubbish into the back of the vehicle by hand, or by attaching the bins to a mechanical or electrical lift and operating a tipping device. The team may return to the depot or dumping site several times with a full lorry, which they may help to unload.

Most vehicles are equipped with an automatic device for crushing and compressing the refuse, enabling large quantities to be collected and transported. The team follows safety regulations while this is in operation.

They return the empty bins, ensuring there is no spilt rubbish left on the road or pavement. They may also supply new bins to houses and provide plastic sacks for the following week's collection.

Refuse collectors can reject large items, such as furniture or excess garden rubbish, unless a special collection has been arranged. Private firms often undertake the removal of such items.

Some local authorities offer a service to collect waste material from large office buildings or industrial sites and they loan out containers or skips that are emptied at regular intervals. If waste or dust from industrial processes is a potential health hazard, employers provide special protective clothing, and washing facilities are usually provided for the refuse collectors at the depot.

WORK ENVIRONMENT

Refuse collection is an outdoor job. Daily schedules must be completed, regardless of weather conditions. Although a job in the open air has pleasant aspects, it also involves work in cold and wet conditions. A refuse collector is considerably hampered when it is icy, or if there is snow on the ground, making it hazardous underfoot.

The work is generally dirty, and in hot weather may also be smelly and dusty.

Specific working environments vary, depending on the location of an employer, or the route allocated to a team. They may work in city, suburban or rural areas. A lot of work is undertaken on busy roads; refuse collectors must remain aware of traffic.

Their work base is the depot, from where they receive instructions and route details, and to which they return each day. It is usually equipped with basic facilities for the convenience of staff, such as a cafeteria and showers.

The job involves being constantly mobile, both by lorry

CLEANING SERVICES: IJ

from district to district and by foot from house to house. Continual bending, lifting, carrying and walking is unavoidable.

SKILLS AND INTERESTS

Refuse collection is a manual job suited to someone who enjoys working outdoors regardless of weather conditions. The work is demanding, very active and may involve emptying around 1,100 dustbins a day, so good health and physical strength are essential. Applicants should not suffer from bad backs, chest complaints or allergies.

Refuse collectors need to be able to work quickly and for long periods without a break. They must not mind dirt, unpleasant smells or occasionally encountering vermin.

The ability to work and co-operate as part of a team is important, and all workers must be reliable and able to carry out instructions.

Extreme care must be taken not to drop litter or damage people's property; the public should be treated with respect and courtesy.

Refuse collectors must also be aware of safety precautions at work. Slippery paths, steps and busy roads are all potentially dangerous and particular attention should be paid to safety regulations regarding the refuse vehicle.

ENTRY REQUIREMENTS

No formal educational qualifications are necessary, although some employers may prefer a good general education. Basic literacy and numeracy are needed, in order that instructions may be followed correctly and the work quota completed satisfactorily.

Applicants must be at least 18 years; older applicants are sometimes preferred. They must be fit and reasonably strong. A full UK driving licence may be an advantage, but is not essential.

TRAINING

Training is often provided by the employer and carried out on the job, alongside, and under the supervision, of experienced workers.

An introduction to the job may include being offered, or asked to attend short courses lasting one or two days, covering subjects like health and safety at work.

NVQs/SVQs relating to waste collection are under development by the Waste Management Industry Training and Advisory Board (WAMITAB) and are to be introduced at the end of 1998.

LATE ENTRY

The work requires a mature, reliable and responsible attitude. Employers often prefer to recruit older candidates, providing they are able to meet the physical demands of the job.

OPPORTUNITIES

Refuse collectors are employed by local authority cleansing departments and private contract firms and they deal mainly with domestic refuse collection.

There is usually competition for jobs and few advertised vacancies. Private contract firms may operate in an area where a local authority has contracted out the work. Hired by a variety of individuals or bodies, they undertake daily domestic collections and/or specialize in collecting bulky items and large quantities of waste material, for instance, after demolition processes or house clearances. Similar work may be offered by waste disposal or food disposal firms and waste paper merchants. The job is open to both men and women.

PAY AND CONDITIONS

Refuse collectors employed by local authorities are paid according to manual worker grades that are set on an hourly scale. Basic wages are around £167 a week. Additional bonus payments are payable.

Refuse collectors in London are paid an additional allowance.

Contract refuse collectors may be paid on a piece-rate basis, so earnings may vary according to the number of hours they work, or collections they complete.

Most refuse collectors work eight-hour shifts, five days a week. Work normally begins early in the morning, between 6 and 7am. Some employers operate a task-and-finish system, which enables workers to go home once their allocation of work has been completed; this may be by 1 or 2pm. Other employers require the team to return to the depot, where they must remain until the official clocking-off time, rarely later than 4pm.

At Christmas and Easter periods, workloads are heavier and hours are therefore longer.

Hours vary for refuse collectors employed by private contractors, depending on workloads. They may start and finish work at relatively later times.

Paid overtime may be available.

PROSPECTS

Promotion prospects for refuse collectors depend on ability. It may be possible to progress to being in charge of a team of collectors, with responsibility for their work, ensuring that daily tasks are completed and that the streets are left litter free.

Opportunities may exist for suitably qualified workers to become drivers, although drivers are generally recruited specifically for the job and are LGV licence holders.

Those with proven ability and suitable experience may move to a higher-level job, such as a depot superintendent or an inspector, but such openings are limited. After gaining experience working for a small, private firm, there may be an opportunity to move into management or partnership. Setting up a contract firm requires considerable business sense, management skills, and a lot of capital.

RELATED OCCUPATIONS

Industrial cleaner, road sweeper, building/construction operative, water/sewage worker, removal man/woman, groundsman/woman.

FURTHER INFORMATION

Job information and details of vacancies are available from the cleansing department of local authorities. The addresses and telephone numbers of private contractors are listed in Yellow Pages.

FURTHER READING
Working in Outdoor Jobs – COIC
In the careers library classified under IJ.

BEAUTY: IK

1. **BEAUTY THERAPIST CLCI:IK**
2. **BEAUTY CONSULTANT CLCI:IK/OFM**

BACKGROUND INFORMATION

Beauty consultants and beauty therapists are concerned with improving people's physical appearance and well-being, either through offering treatments for the face and body, or by recommending special products. Beauty therapists and beauticians are primarily concerned with offering treatments in salons. A beauty therapist (sometimes called an aesthetician) is trained to be able to offer more extensive treatments than a beautician, who will have had a more basic training. In this context, the term beauty therapist is used to cover all beauty professions offering treatment in salons and similar environments.

Beauty consultants sell and demonstrate products in stores and do not offer treatments, although they may do make-up demonstrations and advise customers on skin care.

Most beauty therapist and beauty consultants are women. Most clients are also women, although there is a growing interest amongst males for skin and body care treatments and cosmetics.

Beauty salons can claim exemption from the Sex Discrimination Act, which normally requires all jobs to be open to both men and women applicants.

1. BEAUTY THERAPIST (IK)

THE WORK

Beauty therapists are trained to be able to offer a wide range of treatments for the face and body, including the hands and feet. Some of these treatments are designed to improve the texture and appearance of the skin; others are concerned with body shaping and fat reduction. All therapists must be able to perform facials, wax treatments, eye lash tinting, manicures and pedicures, and apply make-up. Some of these treatments involve the use of special machines. Some salons offer ear piercing.

Facials

A beauty therapist needs to be able to analyse a client's skin condition and offer appropriate treatment. The purpose of a facial differs according to the needs of each client. Some may need special treatment for acne; older clients and those with drier skins may need treatments that hydrate and nourish the skin. The classic facial starts with thorough cleansing of the skin. This may be followed by a steam treatment, which helps to bring impurities to the surface of the skin, then by facial massage with creams or oils and, finally, a face mask.

There are also a number of specialist facial treatments. Some involve the use of aromatherapy oils or other special products and techniques. Other treatments work by stimulating the facial muscles or the application of high frequency currents through vacuum electrodes, resulting in a 'mini face lift'. Separate training is needed before a therapist can administer some of these treatments, which all involve the use of special machines. Other facial treatments include eyebrow plucking and eyelash and eyebrow tinting.

Make-up

All beauty therapists administer make-up to clients. This is often called a makeover. It may include make-up for photographic sessions, corrective make-up for blemishes, or make-up for special occasions, such as weddings.

Manicure and nail extensions

This involves filing and shaping fingernails, removal of cuticles and hard skin, the application of creams to make the hands more supple and the application of nail polish. Many salons now offer nail extensions and other special treatments.

Pedicure

This is similar to the manicure, but is concerned with the feet. The therapist may also offer foot massage.

Body treatments

A beauty therapist may be expected to carry out a number of body treatments. Body massage is normally carried out manually, although there are some treatments that use machines.

Special creams or oils (such as aromatherapy oils) are often used. The therapist needs to have a good understanding of anatomy and physiology and of the effect of massage on clients with high blood pressure or back problems. Some massage treatments are concerned with lymph drainage, which helps remove wastes and toxins from the body. Massage therapists are people who specialize in massage.

A range of slimming treatments, which use different types of machinery, are offered in many salons. These include faradic treatments, where pads are applied to areas of muscle to give physical contractions, and toning tables and vibro belts, which help to remove stubborn fat. There are also treatments for cellulite (a condition that affects many women and makes the skin look dimpled like orange peel). These include galvanic machines and other electrical slimming machines that give a vigorous massage; machines with a vacuum suction device to help break down fat and various treatments using products containing seaweed or mud.

Hair removal

Depilation (temporary hair removal) involves the use of wax or sugaring to remove hair, most frequently from the legs. It is also used for other parts of the body, including the face and bikini line. Epilation involves the insertion of a needle, through which an electric current is sent, into the hair follicle, destroying it progressively over a number of treatments.

Other treatments

Some salons and health spas may offer hydrotherapy treatments (literally, any treatment using water) with whirlpool baths, spa pools or air baths, where jets of air are passed through water to massage the body. Many beauty salons also offer saunas and steam treatments, as well as tanning treatments, usually from a sun bed. These can be used by clients with minimal supervision. However, therapists must be able to advise clients on correct usage.

Other duties

Beauty therapists may also be required to book appointments, take telephone calls, work in reception, handle money, order new supplies and generally keep the salon clean and tidy. Beauty therapists may also be required to take down details of clients' medical history and advise on exercise, slimming and healthy eating. Beauty therapists should also be able to recognize situations when a client ought to be referred to a medical practitioner.

WORK ENVIRONMENT

Most beauticians and beauty therapists work in high street salons, or in salons within department stores. Some work in health and fitness clubs, hotels, in holiday centres or on cruise ships; some self-employed beauty therapists visit clients in their homes or work from a room within their own homes.

Salons are usually divided up into small cubicles where the treatments take place. Beauty therapists spend most of the day on their feet in these cubicles, which are sometimes cramped, carrying out treatments on clients. There may not be a great deal of contact with other staff during the working day.

SKILLS AND INTERESTS

Clients may be nervous and shy about undergoing treatments. Beauty therapists must be sympathetic and able to put clients at their ease. They are dealing with the public in a most intimate sense. Beauty therapists should also be knowledgeable enough to be able to diagnose a client's skin condition, advise on treatments and recommend the best products. They may sometimes have to deal with difficult clients, or have to cope when things go wrong, such as when an eyelash tint may not have taken properly. Patience and knowledge of corrective treatments are important in these situations.

Beauty therapists must be clean, well groomed, wear suitable make-up and pay attention to personal hygiene. A perfect skin is not essential, but they must take care with their appearance. Stamina is also important, as the work involves long periods of standing. Massage, in particular, can be very tiring. There may be little time to rest or take breaks between clients.

An interest in science, particularly anatomy and physiology, and the way that treatments affect the skin, is important. Therapists must be aware of the effect of treatments on the client and be able to answer probing questions.

ENTRY REQUIREMENTS

Most people train for beauty therapy by taking a full-time course and gaining a qualification. Entry requirements for the principal qualifications and qualifying bodies are:

NVQs/SVQs: there are no specific entry requirements, although colleges offering full-time courses may require three GCSEs/S grades (A–C/1–3). They may specify subjects they require or prefer, such as a science. They will usually accept equivalent qualifications, such as Intermediate GNVQ/GSVQ Level II.

City and Guilds: there are no set requirements but colleges may require three GCSEs/S grades (A–C/1–3), including biology or dual science, or equivalent, such as Intermediate GNVQ/GSVQ Level II.

SQA national certificate modules: there are no set entry requirements.

BTEC national diploma/certificate: the minimum entry requirements are four GCSEs/S grades (A–C/1–3), including biology or dual science, or equivalent, such as Intermediate GNVQ/GSVQ Level II.

BTEC higher national diploma/certificate and SQA higher national diploma: the minimum entry requirements are one A level/two H grades and supporting GCSEs/S grades, including English and a science subject, or equivalent, such as a BTEC/SQA national award or Advanced GNVQ/GSVQ Level III. Entry to SQA higher national certificate courses is similar except that one H grade is acceptable.

Confederation of International Beauty Therapy and Cosmetology (CIBTAC): minimum entry requirements are three GCSEs/S grades (A–C/1–3), including English and preferably human biology or other science subject, or equivalent, such as Intermediate GNVQ/GSVQ Level II.

Vocational Awards International (VAI) incorporating the International Health and Beauty Council (IHBC): there are no specific entry requirements but some colleges may require at least three GCSEs/S grades (A–C/1–3).

International Therapy Examination Council (ITEC): students under age 30 need at least five GCSEs/S grades (A–C/1–3) including English, or, at the discretion of individual colleges, equivalent qualifications, such as Intermediate GNVQ/GSVQ Level II.

Comitè International d'Esthètique et de Cosmètologie (CIDESCO): there are no specific entry requirements.

Entry may also be possible through training opportunities for young people, for example a Modern Apprenticeship. There are no set entry requirements but training providers may require specific GCSE/S grade subjects and levels. Four GCSEs/S grades (A–C/1–3), and A levels /H grades or GSVQs/SVQs would be an advantage.

TRAINING

The most usual method of training is a full-time course at a further education college or at a private beauty school. Courses in further education colleges usually last one to two years. Courses in private training schools are shorter, more intensive and require the payment of course fees.

Courses should cover all the essential treatments (facials, make-up, eyebrow and eyelash tinting, waxing, manicure, pedicure and some body treatments), plus some or all of the following: anatomy and physiology of the head, face and neck; the structure of the skin (including skin diseases and disorders, skin types and skin care); the structure of nails; cosmetic science; chemistry; electricity; hygiene, health and safety; first aid; salon procedure; business skills; communication skills; and professional ethics.

There are a number of qualifications in beauty therapy, the principal ones of which are listed below. Courses are available full-time and part-time. Full-time courses often lead to more than one of these qualifications. In particular, NVQs/SVQs have increasingly been built into beauty therapy courses.

NVQs/SVQs: full-time courses usually last for two years. Part-time courses are offered by day release and evening classes over varying lengths of time. NVQs/SVQs in Beauty Therapy are currently available at Levels 1, 2 and 3. Level 1 is appropriate for trainees and other salon staff working as assistant beauty therapists. Level 2 includes the essential facial, nail and wax treatments, together with basic sales skills. Level 3 goes into greater depth and involves more skills, including manual and electrical body treatments plus management and supervisory skills. There are also two further NVQs/SVQs at Level 3 in Epilation and Aromatherapy Massage.

City and Guilds: most courses last one to two years full-time, or two or more years part-time. They include: Beauty Therapy Certificate, Electrical Epilation Certificate, Cosmetic Make-Up, Manicure, and Salon Management.

BEAUTY: IK

BTEC National Diploma/National Certificate in Beauty Therapy courses normally last two years. National Diploma courses are full-time, National Certificate part-time.

SQA national certificate modules are available in beauty care and associated subjects full-time and by day release and evening class. Full-time courses usually last one year and part-time courses two years.

BTEC Higher National Diploma (HND)/Certificate (HNC) courses usually last for two years. HND courses are full-time, HNC courses part-time. SQA Higher National Diploma (HND)/Certificate (HNC) Beauty Therapy courses are both full-time. The HND lasts two years, the HNC one year.

Confederation of International Beauty Therapy and Cosmetology (CIBTAC) is the examining body of the British Association of Beauty Therapists and Cosmetologists (BABTAC). To become a fully qualified beauty therapist with CIBTAC qualifications normally takes up to one year full-time or two years part-time.

Vocational Awards International (VAI) incorporating the International Health and Beauty Council (IHBC) – a number of courses and qualifications are available through IHBC, including the International Beauty Therapy Diploma. Courses are available full-time and part-time over varying lengths of time.

International Therapy Examination Council (ITEC) – major course is Beauty Therapy. Courses are usually full-time for one year or part-time for two or three years.

Comitè International d'Esthètique et de Cosmètologie (CIDESCO) – the CIDESCO International Diploma is an internationally recognized qualification. Training is offered full-time and part-time over varying lengths of time.

Training opportunities for young people involve work experience in a salon and day release to college or a training centre. Trainees work towards NVQs/SVQs in Beauty Therapy to Levels 2 and/or 3. Contact your local careers office, Jobcentre, TEC/LEC for details.

LATE ENTRY

There is no upper age limit for entry to this work. There are good opportunities for late entrants, as maturity is a desirable quality for beauty work. Most mature entrants take part-time courses in colleges of further education or private schools.

OPPORTUNITIES

Newly qualified beauticians or beauty therapists usually start by working in a high street salon. There is no shortage of qualified therapists and there is usually considerable competition for jobs. Jobs are advertised in the beauty press, eg *Health and Beauty Salon, Professional Beauty, International Therapist*, in the magazines issued by the organizations awarding qualifications, in the local press, and through specialist recruitment agencies and Jobcentres.

There are also opportunities to work on cruise ships, in hotels, at health farms, fitness centres and spas. Many beauty therapists are self-employed and work either by visiting clients in their homes, or through fitness centres. Opportunities for make-up artists exist in photographic studios, theatres, films and on television, although entry to the work is highly competitive and mostly freelance. There are also opportunities to work abroad.

PAY AND CONDITIONS

There are no nationally agreed rates of pay – it varies from employer to employer. Salaries start at around £130 a week, rising to around £200 a week.

Most therapists can expect to earn more through commission. Perks may include free treatments, discounts on products, or free use of facilities on cruise ships and also at health farms, where accommodation may also be included. Working hours are normally 9am to 5pm, although some salons stay open until about 8pm on some days. Beauty therapists normally work on Saturdays and receive one day off in lieu during the week.

PROSPECTS

Opportunities for promotion to managing a salon within about five years of qualifying are good. Many beauty therapists eventually open their own salons or become self-employed. Others move into teaching or training; into professional make-up work (sometimes working in photographic studios, theatres, films or television); or into image consultancy work. Many go on to train in the field of complementary therapies, such as aromatherapy, reflexology, shiatsu and Indian head massage.

RELATED OCCUPATIONS

Hairdresser, make-up artist, massage therapist, image consultant, health and fitness instructor, aromatherapist.

FURTHER INFORMATION AND READING

Please see article 2. BEAUTY CONSULTANT.

2. BEAUTY CONSULTANT (IK/OFM)

THE WORK

Beauty consultants sell cosmetics and advise customers on choosing and using cosmetic products. These include skin creams and lotions, make-up and cosmetics. They may also include perfumes and hair care products as well.

The work is essentially that of a salesperson: the job is to sell products. Beauty consultants must also be able to diagnose a customer's skin condition and advise on the appropriate type of product. In most cases, beauty consultants are employed by a particular cosmetics company (Revlon, Clarins, Clinique, Elizabeth Arden, Estèe Lauder, Lançome and Max Factor are some of the best known) rather than by the store, although in smaller shops and high street chemists, some beauty consultants may be employed directly by the shop to sell a range of products.

Consultants advise customers on the best combination of products to suit a range of different skin types and faces. They are also responsible for product displays, and may be involved in ordering stock. Some beauty consultants may be involved in doing demonstration makeovers. Experienced consultants may find opportunities organizing special sales campaigns and promotions, demonstrating the products, training staff and in area management.

Consultants normally wear the uniform of the cosmetic company they are representing and are expected to use the company's products.

BEAUTY: IK

WORK ENVIRONMENT

Beauty consultants work behind counters in department stores or shops. Most of the working day is spent standing behind a sales counter. Occasionally, a consultant may be involved in demonstrating products or giving a customer a makeover. A small amount of time may be spent in the stock-room.

SKILLS AND INTERESTS

Beauty consultants are essentially salespeople. They must be confident and used to dealing with the public. An outgoing personality, a friendly manner, a clear voice and a certain amount of persistence are important. Beauty consultants are also required to maintain a high standard of personal appearance. They must be well groomed and appropriately made up, using the company's products. Good health is important: firstly, because it affects physical appearance, and secondly, because the work can be strenuous and tiring.

Consultants must be familiar with the products they are selling and be able to advise customers on the best range of products for their particular skin type.

Beauty consultants usually work as members of a small team and need to be able to co-operate and get on well with colleagues.

Numeracy is required for the cash-handling aspect of the work.

ENTRY REQUIREMENTS

There are no set entry qualifications other than a good general education, although some GCSE/S grades are helpful. Applicants are assessed on their general physical appearance, presentation skills, and interest in and knowledge of cosmetics. Sales or other customer service experience is very useful but not essential. Some applicants have previously had beauty therapy training.

Most cosmetics companies prefer applicants to be over 18 years. The preferred age of applicants, though, varies according to the policy of the store the consultant works in and on the age range for whom the product range is intended.

No particular qualifications are required for entry to the International Therapy Examination Council's (ITEC) Beauty Consultant Certificate course, the International Health and Beauty Council's (IHBC) Beauty Consultant Diploma course, nor to NVQ/SVQs.

TRAINING

Pre-entry

It is possible, but certainly not essential, to train full-time to prepare for application for beauty consultant work.

ITEC's Beauty Consultant Certificate course is offered at a number of local and private colleges. It includes cleansing and toning, the composition and functions of the skin, skin types, allergy testing, different types of make-up, cosmetic product ranges and selling techniques. Full-time courses normally last two or three months.

IHBC's Beauty Consultant Diploma is offered at a few local and private colleges. It is designed to give a comprehensive knowledge of make-up and manicure, together with the marketing of cosmetics and perfumes, stock handling and stock control. Courses involve 350 hours of training and are offered over varying lengths of time.

On entry

The individual cosmetic companies normally offer residential training courses for their consultants, usually lasting between three and five days. Training includes the history and philosophy of the company, product knowledge, the structure of the skin, skin care, make-up techniques, dealing with the public, stock-taking and sales techniques. Some cosmetic companies have their own examinations and diplomas.

Some smaller shops and high street chemists, such as Boots, recruit beauty consultants to sell a range of cosmetics. Consultants are trained by their employer and may, in some cases, undertake a residential training course similar to that provided by cosmetic companies.

Some beauty consultants may study for ITEC's Beauty Consultant Certificate. Part-time courses lasting a year are offered at a number of local and private colleges. Some may study for IHBC's Beauty Consultant Diploma. Part-time courses are offered at a number of local and private colleges and last for varying lengths of time.

There are no NVQs/SVQs specifically relating to beauty consultancy, although beauty consultants may work towards retail NVQs/SVQs at Levels 2, 3 and 4.

LATE ENTRY

There is no particular upper age limit for entry to this work. Older applicants may be preferred if they are thought to be suitable for the cosmetic range to be sold and the age range of the customer target group.

OPPORTUNITIES

Beauty consultants generally work in department stores, where they are usually employed by one particular cosmetics company to sell their products, or in large high street chemists. Most of the opportunities are in towns and cities. There are also opportunities in the duty-free shops at airports, on cruise ships or ferries, in hotels and occasionally in health farms. Although many beauty consultants are employed by individual cosmetic companies to sell only their branded products, there is a trend towards stores employing staff to sell a number of different products. There is considerable competition for jobs in the large stores. Opportunities exist for temporary employment during busy times such as Christmas. A number of agencies supply the beauty houses with temporary staff at these times and give two- to three-day courses on the products of different cosmetic companies.

PAY AND CONDITIONS

Starting salaries are usually between £5,000 and £7,500 plus commission, rising to about £9,000. Rates of pay are higher in most of the London stores. Most consultants are paid commission on everything they sell and are expected to reach sales targets.

They normally work the same hours as any other retail sales staff and are expected to work on Saturdays. Temporary and part-time work is possible. Staff are usually required to wear a special uniform. Discounts on products and allowances for make-up are normally available.

BEAUTY: IK

PROSPECTS
There are prospects of promotion from junior consultant to senior consultant and then to supervisor and regional manager. Experienced beauty consultants may also have the opportunity to give make-up demonstrations, or move into training. There are also some senior posts in organizing special sales campaigns and promotions.

RELATED OCCUPATIONS
Make-up artist, beauty therapist, image consultant, retail manager, sales assistant, sales representative.

FURTHER INFORMATION
CIDESCO*, c/o The Ray Cochrane Beauty School, 118 Baker Street, London W1M 1LB, 0171 4866291

City and Guilds* ,1 Giltspur Street, London EC1A 9DD, 0171 2942468, http://www.city-and-guilds,co.uk

Confederation of International Beauty Therapy and Cosmetology (CIBTAC)*, Parabola House, Parabola Road, Cheltenham, Gloucestershire GL50 3AH, 01242 570284 (please send sae)

Federation of Recruitment and Employment Services, 10 Belgrave Square, London SW1X 8PH (for advice on agencies that find temporary work for beauty consultants)

Hairdressing and Beauty Industry Authority (NTO), 3 Chequer Road, Doncaster DN1 2AA, 01302 342837, http://www.htb.org

International Therapy Examination Council*, James House, Oakelbrook Mill, Newent, Gloucestershire GL18 1HD, 01531 821875

Vocational Training Charitable Trust/Vocational Awards International*, 46 Aldwick Road, Bognor Regis, West Sussex PO21 2PN, 01243 842064

FURTHER READING
Leaflets/booklets are available from the addresses marked*.

Working in Beauty and Hairdressing – COIC

Getting Jobs in Beauty – Cassell

Careers in Hairdressing and Beauty Therapy – Kogan Page

In the careers library classified under IK; OFM.

HAIRDRESSING: IL

HAIRDRESSER CLCI:IL

BACKGROUND INFORMATION

In recent years, hairdressing has become increasingly linked with fashion. As fashions in clothes change, so do hair fashions. The development of new hairdressing techniques and treatments now allows a greater range of styles to be created than ever before.

Hairdressers play an important part in helping both males and females to make the most of their appearance. Many males now demand treatments that were once associated just with females – tinting, perming and styling. Some salons no longer specialize in men's or women's hairdressing, but offer a service to both sexes.

THE WORK

Hairdressers cut and style hair. They begin by giving client consultations, in which they discuss what clients require, and may make recommendations on style or hair treatment. They may diagnose any basic problems clients may have with their hair or scalp, and suggest how improvements can be made.

Stylists (trained hairdressers) shampoo, condition and rinse hair, cut it wet or dry and may perm, colour, tint or bleach hair. They then style clients' hair, either by setting, blow-drying, or using other techniques, and may apply hairspray or gel. They may recommend hair-care products stocked by the salon and sell them to clients. Some hairdressers also fit wigs, which is a specialized area of work, requiring careful and painstaking handiwork.

Some tasks may be undertaken by a junior or apprentice – tasks such as washing and rinsing clients' hair and applying conditioner. Juniors also assist stylists and are trained to take on increasingly skilled tasks, such as blow drying and colouring.

Stylists use a variety of equipment, including scissors, clippers, combs, razors, pins, curlers, tongs, straightening irons, hot brushes, heated rollers, highlighting materials and dryers. They use shampoos and conditioners, lotions for perming, colouring, bleaching, blow-drying and setting and products such as mousse, gel, polish, wax and sprays. Some of the chemicals used are powerful and hairdressers wear thin protective gloves while working with them.

An important part of hairdressing is customer contact. Hairdressers talk to clients to build up a good relationship. Some of their discussions with clients concern hairdressing, eg styles and hair products, such as shampoos and conditioners, but much is social. Hairdressers gauge whether clients want to chat or whether they prefer to relax quietly.

Hairdressers may be responsible for other tasks – reception, answering the telephone, making appointments, stock control, sorting towels and gowns, keeping the salon well supplied with clean linen, sweeping up, cleaning basins, helping clients with their coats and bags and making tea and coffee for staff and clients. These tasks are normally done by an apprentice or junior in a salon.

Some hairdressers specialize in ladies' hairdressing. Others specialize in barbering (men's hairdressing), which can include all the treatments offered in ladies' hairdressing, but also beard and moustache trimming. Most hairdressers, however, cut and style both men's and women's hair.

Some hairdressers specialize in Afro-Caribbean styling.

WORK ENVIRONMENT

Hairdressers work indoors. Most of them work in salons, although some work in private homes. Salons are usually clean and light, but some may become warm and humid in summer.

Hairdressers spend much of their time standing and bending.

Most hairdressers work in local salons. Some work on a mobile basis and travel locally to clients' homes. A driving licence is necessary for mobile work. A few hairdressers work on cruise ships and are away from home for much of the time.

SKILLS AND INTERESTS

Hairdressers should have good hand skills for cutting and styling hair. An interest in art and fashion is useful, to be able to appreciate different styles and keep up to date with changing styles. An interest in science is desirable, to understand the use of chemical products in hairdressing.

Hairdressers need a friendly manner and should be capable of getting on well with people of all kinds. They must be good listeners and be able to talk easily to clients.

Hairdressers need patience and concentration for their work. A careful approach is required, particularly when working with scissors, razors and chemical products.

Fitness and stamina are important, as hairdressers stand all day. They ought to be free from skin complaints, such as eczema, as the chemical products used tend to aggravate these conditions.

Hairdressers should be clean and well groomed, with a general appearance that gives their clients confidence.

Hair styles change with fashion. Hairdressers must keep up to date with new styles and hairdressing products and be willing to put them into practice.

ENTRY REQUIREMENTS

There are no minimum qualifications for entry to hairdressing, but GCSEs/S grades in English, science, maths and art are useful.

Although no education qualifications are necessary to work towards NVQs/SVQs, some colleges offering full-time courses leading to NVQs/SVQs may ask for specific subjects and/or grades at GCSE/S grade.

BTEC National Diploma in Design Fashion Styling for Hair and Make-up requires: four GCSEs/S grades (A–C/1–3), or Intermediate GNVQ Art and Design/GSVQ Level II Design. Candidates also need a portfolio of art and design work that includes several life and fashion images.

BTEC Higher National Diploma in Design Fashion Styling for Hair and Make-up requires: one A level/two H grades, normally including art, and four GCSEs/S grades (A–C/1–3); or a relevant BTEC national diploma; or Advanced GNVQ Art and Design/GSVQ Level III Design. Candidates also need a portfolio of art and design work that includes several life and fashion images.

Modern Apprenticeships (part of the Skillseekers Initiative in Scotland) may be available for young people leading to at least an NVQ/SVQ Level 3. Contact your local careers office, Jobcentre, TEC/LEC for details. Experience of salon work with a Saturday or holiday job can be an advantage.

HAIRDRESSING: IL

TRAINING

The traditionally recognized qualifications in hairdressing are NVQs/SVQs.

NVQ/SVQ in Hairdressing at Level 1 is concerned with reception, stock control, health and safety, personal presentation, working with others and the first steps of hairdressing.

NVQ/SVQ in Hairdressing at Level 2 includes working as part of a team, reception, client consultation, conditioning hair and scalp, shampooing, cutting, blow-drying, setting, perming and neutralizing, and colouring.

NVQ/SVQ in Hairdressing at Level 3 involves higher technical skills, such as perming, colouring, cutting and long hair work, and also includes training, supervisory skills, improving systems and procedures and organizing promotional activities for the salon.

There are several routes into hairdressing, most of which involve working towards NVQ/SVQ qualifications.

Training opportunities for young people. The majority of 16- and 17-year-olds entering hairdressing do so via training opportunities. Trainees combine on-the-job training at a salon with day release to college or a training centre. They work towards NVQ/SVQ Hairdressing at Level 2, which normally takes around two years.

Modern Apprenticeships (part of the Skillseekers Initiative in Scotland) in hairdressing are available for young people. Apprenticeships may take up to three years and combine training in a salon with day release to college to work towards at least an NVQ/SVQ in Hairdressing at Level 3. Contact your local careers office, Jobcentre, TEC/LEC, the Hairdressing Training Board or HTB Scotland for details.

Full-time college courses. Many local colleges throughout the UK offer full-time courses that lead to NVQs/SVQs in Hairdressing at Levels 2 or 3. Some offer qualifications such as the National Diploma of Hairdressing, which is awarded by the Guild of Hairdressers.

Courses usually last for two years and combine theory and practice. Practical work may include working with members of the public in a training salon at the college, and regular work experience within salons.

The London College of Fashion offers a BTEC National Diploma and a Higher National Diploma in Design Fashion Styling for Hair and Make-up (both two years full-time). These courses are designed to prepare students for work as a make-up and hair artist in the fashion-related fields of beauty, editorial, catwalk and advertising.

Apprenticeships. Some salons offer three-year apprenticeships. Apprentices assist qualified hairdressers and are trained by them. They may gain additional experience with customers on 'model evenings' and usually attend a local college or training centre to work towards an NVQ/SVQ in Hairdressing at Level 2.

Private hairdressing schools. There are many privately run hairdressing schools that offer full-time courses, where students pay their own tuition and examination fees. The courses are usually shorter and more intensive than courses offered by local colleges or training centres.

Students at some private hairdressing schools work towards NVQs/SVQs, while some work towards other hairdressing qualifications. Students are advised to check how far other qualifications are recognized by the hairdressing industry, before deciding on a course at a private hairdressing school. Check with local careers offices.

After training, hairdressers are expected to work for at least one year as an improver, before being considered experienced. Those with an NVQ/SVQ in Hairdressing at Level 2 may apply to the Hairdressing Council to become state registered hairdressers.

LATE ENTRY

There is no strict upper age limit for entry to hairdressing, but most entrants are school-leavers. Adults who enter hairdressing often do so after a full-time course.

There may be specific training opportunities, directed at adults, in some areas for this type of work. Candidates may have to satisfy certain conditions to be eligible. Contact your local Jobcentre, careers office or TEC/LEC for details.

OPPORTUNITIES

There are approximately 170,000 hairdressers, most of whom work in the 36,000 salons throughout the UK. Most salons are unisex, with a minority for males or females only.

Salons range from one-person businesses to large national chains of salons. Most hairdressers work in high street salons, while others work in department store salons, beauty salons, health farms, hotels and clubs, the Armed Forces and in hospitals. There are a few opportunities for hairdressers to work on cruise ships, in film and television work and with fashion photographers.

Self-employment is possible in a number of ways. Some hairdressers rent a chair from a salon owner and work with their own customers. Others offer hairdressing at their own homes, while some operate on a mobile basis, travelling to customers' homes. Many hairdressers open their own salon. It is also possible for hairdressers to open their own salon by entering a franchise arrangement with a regional or national hairdressing company.

Work abroad is possible, particularly at European holiday resorts that are popular with English-speaking tourists.

PAY AND CONDITIONS

The suggested wage scales in hairdressing are: Trainee – £43.50 a week plus £3.50 per unit of NVQ/SVQ Level 2 passed. Trainee with NVQ/SVQ Level 1 – £46.60 a week plus £3.60 per unit of NVQ/SVQ Level 2 passed. Stylist with NVQ/SVQ Level 2 or three years' salon experience – £88 a week plus £4.30 per unit of NVQ/SVQ Level 3 passed. Senior stylist with NVQ/SVQ Level 3, or Level 2 plus two years' salon experience, or five years' salon experience – £157.50 a week. These exclude commission and are suggested wage scales. Some salons pay more than these, while others pay less.

Hairdressers usually work a 39-hour week over five days, including Saturdays. They may work one late evening a week. Part-time work is common.

PROSPECTS

In most small salons there is no scope for promotion. In large salons it may be possible to specialize, perhaps as a perming technician or colour technician. Salons that are part of a large group can offer promotion to salon manager and further management positions within the organization.

HAIRDRESSING: IL

Hairdressers with an NVQ/SVQ in Hairdressing at Level 3 may train for management by working towards an NVQ/SVQ in Management at Level 4. An NVQ/SVQ in Hairdressing at Level 4 is being developed and will be concerned with management, rather than additional hairdressing skills.

There are opportunities for experienced hairdressers to teach hairdressing in a local college, or at a private hairdressing school. Colleges usually require applicants to have a further education teaching qualification.

In Scotland, hairdressers with SVQ Level 2 or 3 may study for the SQA Higher National Certificate in Hairdressing and Salon Organization. Courses are offered at a number of Scottish colleges, full-time for one year or on a day release basis for two years. It can be used to prepare for salon management. It is also useful with further qualifications in assessing NVQs/SVQs for those wishing to teach hairdressing in colleges or with private training providers.

A few hairdressers become technical consultants for hair product companies and teach hairdressers the most effective ways of using hairdressing products.

RELATED OCCUPATIONS

Beauty therapist, beautician beauty consultant, receptionist, fashion model, trichologist, retail assistant, retail manager.

FURTHER INFORMATION

Hairdressing and Beauty Industry Authority (NTO) 3 Chequer Road, Doncaster DN1 2AA, 01302 342837 (please include sae), http://www.htb.org

Hairdressing Training Board (HTB) Scotland, PO Box 8805, Carluke ML8 4ET, 01555 773095 (please enclose sae)

FURTHER READING

Leaflets/booklets available from the address marked*.

Working in Beauty and Hairdressing – COIC

Careers in Hairdressing and Beauty Therapy – Kogan Page

In the careers library classified under IL.

FUNERAL SERVICES: IP

FUNERAL DIRECTOR/EMBALMER
CLCI:IP

BACKGROUND INFORMATION

Funerals, which are ceremonies organized for the disposal of the bodies of the deceased, take the form of burials or cremations. In Great Britain there are strict regulations governing the procedures to be followed from the time a death occurs to the actual burial or cremation. Funeral directors or undertakers are responsible for preparing the deceased for burial or cremation and for arranging and supervising funerals. This involves a variety of duties. In large organizations, the tasks may be divided between employees – different workers may be responsible for driving, pall bearing, administration etc. The majority of funeral directors, however, are small family firms, with one person having responsibility for the broad range of tasks. Extra staff may be hired, for example, as bearers or drivers, when required.

Many funeral directors also carry out embalming, which is concerned with preserving bodies until they are buried or cremated. Embalming, however, is a separate profession and may be carried out by fully qualified embalmers who are not concerned with the other aspects of undertaking.

THE WORK

Funeral director

Funeral directors are usually contracted by the relatives or friends of a deceased person to arrange a funeral. Having received notification of a death, the funeral director arranges to collect the remains, and establishes basic information about the deceased, such as the name and age and date of death.

Arrangements are made for further visits to the clients so that detailed preparations can be made for the funeral. Funeral directors offer advice and make all the practical arrangements for families. This includes organizing transport, flowers, catering, accommodation and obituary notices. Having decided upon a burial or cremation, funeral directors arrange times and dates with the officials involved – clergy, cemetery staff, crematorium officials etc on their clients' behalf. Funeral directors may deal with all the financial arrangements and transactions. In addition, they ensure that all the legal requirements are satisfied. They assist their clients in obtaining the necessary paperwork, such as the death certificate, and clients may also need advice about claiming death grants.

The body must be prepared for burial or cremation. This may include embalming, and general preparations such as washing/setting hair, shaving men, and applying cosmetics discreetly to faces. Pads are inserted under the eyelids and the mouth is sutured to stop the jaw opening.

The prepared body is placed into a coffin which will have been fitted with a lining and handles chosen by the clients. On the day of the funeral, funeral directors are responsible for ensuring that everything runs smoothly and according to the agreed routine and timetable. They usually ride in the hearse and precede the cortège to the ceremony. All legal aspects, such as handing over certificates to the crematorium officials, are also dealt with.

Embalmer

Embalming is linked to funeral directing and is carried out by a professional embalmer. The process is concerned with the disinfection and preservation of bodies until burial/cremation. Embalming is not a legal requirement in this country, but it is increasingly carried out for reasons of hygiene. The main objectives of modern embalming are to: prevent deterioration prior to the funeral; remove obvious and distressing signs of death; restore as normal an appearance as possible; and ensure that there is no health risk to those who come into contact with the deceased.

The treatment of deceased people, to arrest or retard the process of decay, involves washing the body with germicidal soap, and injecting the body with sterilizing fluid. The process may be more complicated when the embalmer is dealing with severely injured persons, and after post-mortem investigations have taken place complete embalmment may be necessary. It may be necessary to restore normal appearance to parts of the body, particularly visible aspects such as faces, which have become misshapen or disfigured.

Embalmers use materials such as wax and plaster of Paris for this purpose, and apply cosmetics to provide colour.

WORK ENVIRONMENT

The premises of a funeral director are often fairly large and comprise warm, pleasant, comfortable reception rooms, offices, storerooms, and an embalming area. Although based inside and working in fairly comfortable conditions for much of the time, undertakers are required to work outside in all weathers when attending funerals. The work also involves quite a lot of travelling, which usually entails driving – to collect the remains, visit clients, attend funerals etc. Funeral directing and embalming work can be heavy, as it entails lifting and carrying.

Embalmers work in a clinically clean environment, often part of the funeral director's premises. The temperature of the work area is usually slightly lower than normal room temperature. They may spend long periods standing in one position with few opportunities to sit whilst working. Those who do not combine the work with funeral directing have little contact with the public. The vast majority of embalmers are required to drive and travel a fair amount during the day to provide services for different funeral directors, or carry out undertaking duties.

SKILLS AND INTERESTS

Funeral directors must have good communication skills and be able to deal with people of all ages and from a variety of social backgrounds. They should be well spoken, tactful and understanding. They have to be able to cope with people in a very unhappy and distressed condition. Genuine sympathy and sensitivity are necessary, but funeral directors must not allow themselves to become too deeply and emotionally involved. Smart and conventional dress is required, and individuals must be prepared to conduct themselves in a serious and dignified manner.

Administrative and organizational ability is required for carrying out the office work and to co-ordinate funeral arrangements. It is essential that funerals proceed without problems. Attention to detail, therefore, is vital, so that nothing is forgotten or mistimed. Management skills are also necessary, in order to negotiate with representatives of other organizations, organize and control staff, make financial arrangements etc. Familiarity with religious rituals is useful; however, it is not essential, in general, that individuals are religious or are of any particular religious persuasion. It is essential that individuals are not squeamish, do not mind handling corpses and are able to

FUNERAL SERVICES: IP

endure unpleasant sights and smells. They should be able to adopt a professional, mature and responsible attitude to the duties involved. Embalmers are required to have an interest in science, particularly anatomy and chemistry. Manual dexterity is also necessary for handling surgical instruments and tools. Cleanliness and neatness are essential.

ENTRY REQUIREMENTS

No formal educational qualifications are required for entry into funeral directing or embalming work. Some employers, however, prefer new recruits to have GCSEs/S grades (A–C/1–3), including English.

Candidates may find the study of subjects such as English, maths, chemistry, biology and religious studies useful. A background of business and secretarial studies may also be advantageous for carrying out the administrative and office-keeping tasks.

Funeral directors and embalmers are often required to drive, so a full driving licence is desirable and often essential.

TRAINING

Undertaking

There may be opportunities for those entering jobs as drivers or pall bearers to learn all aspects of funeral directing work and to become funeral directors. Individuals interested in becoming funeral directors should check with employers as to the possibility and availability of training. In some companies, employees start and remain in the same jobs.

Training is on-the-job and new entrants usually begin in operative jobs, such as driving, cleaning the vehicles and carrying out routine maintenance. Other routine duties include cleaning out the embalming room and collecting the deceased from homes and hospitals. Supervision is by the funeral director or an experienced worker. Trainees may move on to finishing coffins – fitting handles, linings, plaques etc – and placing bodies into them. They will gradually be introduced to tasks of increased responsibility, such as bearing at funerals, driving the hearse and assisting with the office work.

Having gained experience of all the different aspects of funeral directing, individuals may firstly assist the funeral director and then arrange and conduct funerals alone. Those who express an interest may be trained in embalming.

The British Institute of Funeral Directors runs, through its qualified tutors, part-time training courses leading to the Diploma of Funeral Directing – the recognized professional qualification. Students must be already in employment with a firm of undertakers. Candidates must pass a preliminary examination set by the National Association of Funeral Directors or hold other acceptable qualifications, such as two GCSEs/S grades (A–C/1–3) in English and maths. Exemption is also given to those who hold the Certificate of the British Institute of Embalmers, or the Registered General Nurse qualification, or the Certificate and Diploma in Mortuary Hygiene and Technology. Training is usually over one year and is mainly on the job with part-time tuition from an approved tutor during weekends and evenings, at a training centre or by correspondence course. Students must successfully complete theoretical and practical examinations, and candidates may then be considered for membership of the Institute.

Embalming

Many funeral directors train as professional embalmers, although individuals may train solely in embalming. Trainees are normally in full-time employment, although this is not essential. The British Institute of Embalmers is the professional body and members are normally required to pass theoretical and practical examinations set by the National Examinations Board of Embalmers.

Contact the Institute for a list of schools and accredited tutors.

Training is by the modular system of education, comprising a foundation module, followed by five further modules in preparation for the final theory and practical examinations. Candidates must pass the foundation module examination before they are allowed to commence the course. There are no educational requirements to join a study course for the foundation module.

Candidates are required to sit an end-of-module test under exam conditions, and obtain a minimum pass mark of 60% in each of the five modules before they are permitted to sit the theory examination. Marks gained from the five end-of-modules tests account for up to 60% of the total marks awarded for the final theory examination requirement.

The majority of courses are run on a part-time basis for those in work, although a small number are full-time. Practical training is mainly on the job, with part-time tuition from a registered tutor during weekends or evenings, or via a correspondence course. Home study will be required if candidates are to reach the standard required to pass the examinations.

Successful candidates may apply to be considered for membership of the Institute.

LATE ENTRY

The opportunities for mature candidates to enter funeral directing or embalming work are favourable, as compared to those for school-leavers. Many employers look for candidates with a full driving licence and some driving experience. Skills and interests are very important, and a mature attitude to the work is essential. Entry is usually into operative posts, for example as drivers or pall bearers. There may be opportunities to train in undertaking or embalming, depending on the employer. Training for adult entrants is as described in TRAINING.

OPPORTUNITIES

Funeral directors and embalmers may be employed by large or small firms throughout the country. Many funeral directors are self-employed and run their own businesses. This type of business is often kept as a small family concern and consequently may be difficult to get into.

Individuals may run other types of business, such as building or cabinet making, in conjunction with funeral directing. This is particularly the case in the smaller towns and villages. There is, however, no specific link between undertaking and carpentry/joinery, as most coffins are now bought in from specialist manufacturers. Larger organizations (such as the Co-operative Society) specialize in providing funeral directing services, and employ staff to carry out funeral directing. Embalmers may work for the larger organizations or become self-employed – serving

FUNERAL SERVICES: IP

local funeral directors within an area, as required. Many individuals will provide both funeral directing and embalming services.

Work is available for funeral directors and embalmers throughout the UK. Some entrants to the work find themselves unsuitable and the work distasteful, but many find it a satisfactory, steady job and there is a low turnover of staff. Funeral directing is generally difficult to get into unless the business is in the family. Recruitment by the larger organizations is at a fairly low level. There are few opportunities for school-leavers and openings are mainly for drivers and/or bearers. There may then, however, be a chance to learn the other aspects of the work.

Individuals may set up in business on their own, providing they can raise the capital – a substantial amount may be required. In addition, it will be necessary to have learned the trade with an established funeral director. There may be slightly better opportunities to enter embalming work and, depending on demand in local areas, embalmers may become self-employed.

Vacancies for qualified embalmers are advertised in the publication *The Embalmer* (British Institute of Embalmers).

PAY AND CONDITIONS

It is difficult to give figures. Earnings depend on duties, and may be supplemented by a series of bonuses, for example for attending funerals, working unsocial hours and being on call during unsocial hours. Generally, funeral directors earn slightly more than bearers/drivers, and may receive additional payments for embalming.

Salaries for funeral directors and embalmers working on a self-employed basis vary according to the amount of work they are able to obtain. Earnings are generally favourable, compared to the wages of employees of larger companies.

Funeral directors may have very irregular hours and are required to be on call 24 hours a day for seven days a week. Most of the administration and organizing is carried out during office hours but they must be prepared to turn out at any hour when notified of deaths. Visits to relatives often take place in the evenings. The demand for services may also be irregular and may provide work on a part-time basis only. Those concerned solely with embalming may be able to work more normal office hours – Monday to Friday, for 37 hours a week. However, demand for their services is also variable.

PROSPECTS

Promotion prospects are generally very limited for funeral directors and embalmers. Those working for large organizations as employees may have opportunity to train in embalming, and there may be a formal career structure that provides opportunities of progression into management. Similar opportunities may be available for embalmers. Those funeral directors and embalmers working as employees for large or small businesses may aim to become self-employed owners of their own businesses, or partners of existing firms.

RELATED OCCUPATIONS

Hospital porter, grave digger, crematorium technician, mortuary attendant, pathology technician, car/van driver.

FURTHER INFORMATION

British Institute of Embalmers*, 21c Station Road, Knowle, Solihull B93 0HL, 01564 778991

British Institute of Funeral Directors*, 140 Leamington Road, Coventry, CV3 6JY (please include sae)

National Association of Funeral Directors*, 618 Warwick Road, Solihull, West Midlands B91 1AA, 0121 711 1343

FURTHER READING

Leaflets/booklets are available from the addresses marked*.

In the careers library classified under IP.

GROUP J – HEALTH AND MEDICAL SERVICES

1. GENERAL PRACTITIONER CLCI:JAB
2. HOSPITAL DOCTOR CLCI:JAB

1. GENERAL PRACTITIONER (JAB)

THE WORK

GPs (general practitioners), or family doctors, play an important part in the life of a community. Their job is to listen to patients, perform examinations if necessary and, using their extensive knowledge of medicine, provide a diagnosis of the illness. The illness may not be apparent at first, or one set of symptoms may be masking the real problem. GPs advise patients on how to manage the illness, disability or problem, and prescribe appropriate medicines. They may also perform minor surgery. When appropriate, GPs refer patients to a hospital specialist, or for x-ray examinations, or other tests. GPs may also refer patients to a social worker, psychologist, psychiatrist, or speech therapist, if appropriate.

After surgery, doctors have telephone calls to make to patients, specialists or colleagues, as well as referral letters to write to hospitals. Notes on patients must also be completed, and GPs must keep fully up to date with changes in medical practice, law, ethics, drugs etc. There is a great deal of paperwork; GPs are called upon to certify a patient's state of health for social security, insurance or employment purposes, and to sign death certificates.

Preventing illness is an increasingly important aspect of the work of GPs; they are involved in immunizations, developmental checks on babies and young children, and health education during consultations.

GPs have the chance to get to know their patients and their families, as they often treat them over a period of many years. A relationship of trust is built up which puts the GP in a position of great responsibility. GPs usually work as partners in group practices, or at health centres provided by the local health authority, but may be single handed. Reception and secretarial services are often shared. There is an increasing trend towards large practices; nurses, health visitors, midwives, and physiotherapists may also be employed, ensuring a full service to patients.

WORK ENVIRONMENT

Although doctors in a practice are part of a team, much of their working day is spent on a one-to-one basis with patients. The average consultation lasts seven minutes, with the result that the work is extremely busy. Surgeries are normally pleasant environments. Home visits in rural areas may involve driving long distances. Modern, purpose-built health centres now provide professional accommodation for an increasing number of doctors.

SKILLS AND INTERESTS

GPs must be good listeners. Patients often find it difficult to explain what is wrong with them, and the GP needs to ask the right questions, and often look beyond the presenting symptoms.

GPs need to be responsible and trustworthy, with the ability to remain calm in a crisis. Practical ability and a steady hand are necessary for examining patients. GPs need the ability to absorb large amounts of information, normally of a scientific or technical nature. Good written skills are required for letters, reports etc. There is an increasing need for GPs to have some computer literacy.

ENTRY REQUIREMENTS

A qualified doctor in the UK must hold a degree in medicine awarded by a university medical school recognized by the General Medical Council. The degree course lasts five years for candidates who have taken science subjects at A level or H grade, or six years for candidates with non-science subjects who study a pre-medical year.

The minimum entry requirements for a degree in medicine are three A levels/five H grades plus five GCSE/S grades (A–C/1–3), including English, and, if not held at A level/H grade, maths, biology and physics (or dual science).

For the five-year course, candidates should have A level chemistry or physical science, and at least one of physics, biology and maths. (See below for Scottish requirements.) Most medical schools prefer A level biology, as students not offering biology may find parts of the course particularly difficult. An increasing number of medical schools now accept an arts subject as a third A level.

The grades required at A level vary from three grade As to three grade Bs. Many universities accept two AS levels in place of one A level. Applicants should consult admissions tutors about acceptable combinations of subjects and grade requirements.

Most medical schools in Scotland require candidates to obtain five H grades, typically AAAAB. They must usually include chemistry and two from physics, biology and maths. English and another language may be requested at S grade (1–3), maths sometimes at S grade (1–2) if not held at H grade.

The pre-medical year for those without science A levels/H grades is offered only by a few medical schools. Candidates must offer excellent grades in sciences and maths at GCSE/S grade or equivalent.

Most successful applicants to medical schools have A levels/H grades. That is likely to continue to be the case, although a small number of schools may consider applicants with a distinction in a relevant Advanced GNVQ, such as science, plus an A level/H grade in a science subject.

The competition for places at all medical schools is intense, and in most years less than half the applicants are successful in being offered a place. Academic ability is not the only prerequisite for a career in medicine. Commitment, perseverance, determination, initiative, originality, concern for others, and the ability to communicate are essential. High grades at A level/H grade are normally demanded because the course is long and intellectually demanding.

TRAINING

The total training period for doctors varies. All medical students spend five or six years as undergraduates and obtain a bachelor of medicine and surgery – MB BS, MB ChB, or a diploma from a non-university licensing body.

Medical schools do not offer identical courses. They differ in the way they organize and teach their courses and in their systems of assessment. It is important to research courses carefully; consult books listed in FURTHER READING.

The one-year **pre-medical course** is offered by a few medical schools and provides a preliminary course in chemistry, physics and biology, lasting 30 weeks. It is designed for students who have taken mainly arts subjects

MEDICINE AND SURGERY: JAB

at A level or H grade, not for those who have performed poorly in sciences.

Medical schools traditionally had a two-year pre-clinical course which involved a study of the basic medical sciences, including anatomy (the structure of the human body), physiology, biochemistry, psychology, medical sociology, pathology and pharmacology. Some schools still organize their courses in this way but, as a result of recommendations of the General Medical Council (GMC) which were published in 1993 entitled "Tomorrow's Doctors", most have reorganized their courses.

As a result of the GMC's recommendations, there is now more integration of the teaching of science with that of clinical medicine. Many medical schools centre their teaching on body systems, eg the cardiovascular and respiratory systems and the nervous system. Some courses place emphasis on a problem-solving approach to learning. Most schools now devote more time to communication skills, practical clinical tasks and in-depth study of modules chosen by the student. Some courses have also introduced an increasing element of continuous assessment.

However their courses are organized, students may have the opportunity for a **one-year intercalated degree course**. This allows medical students to take a degree in a science subject, usually related to medicine, before progressing to the next part of a doctor's training. It is a built-in feature of some courses, while at other medical schools the opportunity is only offered to the most successful students. This opportunity usually arises at the end of the second year of a five-year course (later in some medical schools).

Traditional courses followed the two-year pre-clinical course with a three-year clinical course, which, for many students was their first real contact with patients. Most medical schools now integrate the non-clinical and clinical parts of their courses more closely. The result is that the majority of courses have incorporated a number of weeks clinical experience in the first two years and extended non-clinical work into the later years of the course. Some medical schools, for example, give students a family attachment, which allows them to have regular contact throughout the course with a particular family with health problems, in order to understand perceptions of contact with the health service. Some other courses include attachment to a family doctor.

The aim of clinical experience is to help students develop practical skills and acquire knowledge, while taking responsibility for their own decisions. In some schools the clinical training starts with a nursing attachment and continues with training on the ward. Student doctors are attached to a 'firm', comprising a small group of consultants and senior and junior doctors, who are responsible for a number of patients. Student doctors assist in theatre, help deliver babies, and take blood.

Clinical training involves working hospital hours and taking a share of night duties. The training takes place on ward rounds, in outpatient clinics and during seminars. Various specialities are taught via the firms, including pathology, haematology, obstetrics, paediatrics and psychiatry. There may be an attachment to the accident and emergency unit, as well as placements in general practice and community medicine.

On successful completion of their degree course doctors hold a bachelor of medicine and surgery degree. They only have provisional registration, though, until they have completed a year as a pre-registration house officer. House officers work long hours, with many nights spent on call. At present, the twelve months of full-time training must include four months in medicine and four months in surgery, and may include four months in general practice.

Postgraduate training

About half of all medical students eventually become GPs, for which the training lasts at least three years. On completion of postgraduate training for general practice doctors apply to Joint Committee on Postgraduate Training for General Practice (JCPTGP) for a certificate of prescribed or equivalent experience. This is the certificate they must have in order to work as a principal in the NHS.

The training programme consists of at least 12 months and up to two years as a GP registrar in an NHS training practice under the supervision of an approved GP trainer. In reality funding for GP registrar posts is usually only available for a maximum of 12 months – these posts are supernumerary and directly funded by the government. GPs in training must also, by law, spend at least six months training in two of the following specialities:

– general medicine;

– geriatic medicine;

– paediatrics;

– psychiatry;

– one of: accident and emergency medicine; or general surgery; or accident and emergency medicine together with either general surgery or orthopaedic surgery;

– one of: obstetrics; or gynaecology; or obstetrics and gynaecology.

Most in fact undertake at least two years training in these specialities and sometimes ask for periods of training in specialities such as orthopaedics, anaesthetics, and ENT (ear, nose and throat), for example, to be taken into consideration when applying for certification to become a GP.

A typical structured VTS (vocational training scheme) for a GP will be

– six months as a GP registrar;

– six months in obstetrics and gynaecology;

– six months in paediatrics;

– six months in general surgery;

– six months in psychiatry;

– six months as a GP registrar.

All GPs must pass a test of competence known as summative assessment in order to be eligible for their JCPTGP certificate. There are four parts to summative assessment: a multiple choice questionnaire; assessments of consultation skills as recorded on a two-hour video tape; a 3,000 word (maximum) written submission of practical work; and a trainer's report.

Many GPs in training also choose to study for the examination leading to membership of the Royal College of General Practitioners. Most undertake this exam during their GP registrar year.

LATE ENTRY

Medical schools have different policies regarding entry for mature students. Thirty years is generally considered to be the upper age to start training, although many schools are reluctant to take people beyond the age of 25. Entrance requirements are not normally relaxed.

MEDICINE AND SURGERY: JAB

About ten per cent of entrants to medical training have first taken a degree in another subject. They may have to finance themselves for all or part of the course. Even if the first degree was taken in a relevant subject, the length of training will not normally be shortened, although exemptions may be given from certain parts of the course. An upper-second-class degree is the minimum entry requirement for graduates, and some schools will only consider candidates with relevant degrees.

OPPORTUNITIES

There are about 34,000 GPs in the UK. They are contracted by the NHS and receive fees and allowances for the work they do.

A very small number work in the Armed Forces. Doctors wishing to work abroad may find opportunities in the EU; there are very few openings in Australia, Canada, New Zealand and the USA. Voluntary organizations provide jobs in poorer countries, although remuneration is small.

PAY AND CONDITIONS

GPs and their partners should be available to their patients for not less than 26, 19 or 13 hours a week (depending on their contract) for consultations and home visits (this includes travelling time to the home visits). In practice, most GPs work 50–60 hours a week, including administration, reading etc. Two-and-a-half hours are normally spent in the surgery, seeing patients each morning and afternoon or early evening. Visits are usually offered during late mornings and afternoons. A Saturday morning surgery is usually required. All GPs are expected to be on call for emergencies, but the frequency depends on the number of partners in the practice, and whether a deputizing service or co-operative is used.

General practice offers a higher income at an earlier stage (and a lower income at a later stage) than a career in hospitals. The average income of a GP is about £47,540 but this can vary, depending on the area and the number of services offered by the GP. Terms and conditions of service are negotiated with the National Health Service, although GPs are self-employed, being independent contractors to the NHS. A minority of GPs have a small number of private patients.

The money GPs receive has to pay the salaries of nurses, receptionists and other staff, as well as overheads for premises, rates and rents, although health authorities provide some reimbursement. Some partners buy a share in the premises, although they never 'buy in' to the goodwill of the partnership.

PROSPECTS

A minority of GPs combine their work as a general practitioner with part-time work in a hospital, or as a journalist writing medical articles for magazines or newspapers.

A GP might also work as a medical adviser to a pharmaceutical company, to the occupational health service, or the Benefits Agency, or work as a police surgeon or part-time prison medical officer. Some are employed to work in postgraduate training.

RELATED OCCUPATIONS

Dentist, optometrist/ophthalmic optician, psychologist, social worker, pharmacist.

FURTHER INFORMATION AND READING

Please see article 2. HOSPITAL DOCTOR.

2. HOSPITAL DOCTOR (JAB)

THE WORK

Hospital doctors work in various specialities, and the nature of the work they do depends on their grade. The junior grades of hospital medical staff are training posts, and are known as house officer, senior house officer, and specialist registrar. At the top of the hospital ladder is the consultant, who has the ultimate responsibility for patient welfare.

The first training grade is **pre-registration house officer,** which all doctors must undertake for one year before they can be fully registered with the General Medical Council (GMC). In April 1996 the GMC published its recommendations for this period of training entitled "The New Doctor". House officers examine patients as they arrive, take notes, and organize the initial investigations and treatment. They prescribe drugs for minor symptoms, and ensure that any intravenous infusions are working. They undertake most work under direct supervision.

Senior house officers gain increasing responsibility for patient care and develop the necessary wide range of general and specialist skills.

Specialist registrars supervise the work of house officers and usually examine and treat patients who have the diseases in which they have specialized whilst undergoing structured higher specialist training.

Consultants are the career grade of hospital doctor. They are fully trained and capable of acting independently. Consultants are personally responsible for the treatments they prescribe, and supervise the work and training of all doctors in training grades.

There are over 50 specialities in hospital medicine, which can be divided into four main types:

Medicine. There are various specialities in medicine, although many doctors are experienced in a variety of areas; general medical emergencies may demand a varied knowledge. Doctors examine patients, diagnose their condition and decide upon a suitable treatment. Specialities within medicine include paediatrics, cardiology, dermatology, geriatrics, neurology and tropical medicine. Doctors work in teams and co-operate with nurses and other staff.

Surgery. Surgeons are concerned with patients who need operations, and they are responsible for each patient before, during, and after the operation. Many surgeons are general surgeons, but most have a special area of expertise. Neurosurgeons diagnose disorders and injuries of the brain and nervous system, performing lengthy operations. Orthopaedic surgeons diagnose and treat injuries and diseases affecting the bones, tendons, joints and ligaments. Plastic surgery involves the delicate surgical repair of deformities, either those present since birth, or those caused by injuries or burns in later life. Surgeons liaise closely with anaesthetists before performing operations.

MEDICINE AND SURGERY: JAB

Pathology. Pathologists investigate the causes and effects of disease. They work in laboratories, supervising the work of other laboratory staff, and often have little contact with patients. Histopathologists diagnose disease from changes in tissue structure, whilst the chemical pathologist looks at the biochemical nature of disease. Other specialities within pathology include blood transfusion and medical microbiology.

Psychiatry. Psychiatrists work with people suffering mental illness, and with those with mental disabilities. They often work within a team of professionals, including social workers, psychologists, and occupational therapists. Psychotherapy is a speciality within psychiatry, although not all psychotherapists are qualified doctors.

Other specialized fields include: **anaesthetics** – the provision of pain relief or anaesthesia during surgical operations, childbirth and diagnostic procedures; **obstetrics** – the care of pregnant women; **gynaecology** – the speciality dealing with diseases confined to women; **radiology** – taking x-rays and other scanning techniques used to make a diagnosis; and **oncology** – the treatment of cancer patients using radiation and drugs.

WORK ENVIRONMENT

Hospital doctors work as part of a team with other doctors, health professionals such as nurses, radiographers, and physiotherapists, and administrative staff. They deal with patients and their families on a day-to-day basis. Hospital doctors work in a number of hospital settings, eg in accident and emergency, in maternity, in wards and in operating theatres. Pathologists are based in laboratories.

SKILLS AND INTERESTS

Please see article 1. GENERAL PRACTITIONER. In addition, surgeons need a high level of manual dexterity and practical ability.

ENTRY REQUIREMENTS

Please see article 1. GENERAL PRACTITIONER.

TRAINING

Pre-registration training. This is as for GENERAL PRACTITIONER; please see previous article.

Postgraduate training. Once the pre-registration period has been completed, doctors choose a speciality, such as general practice, hospital medicine, public health medicine, or one of the less usual areas, such as occupational medicine, pharmaceutical medicine, research, or working for the Armed Forces.

Doctors opting for National Health Service hospital work begin with a period of general professional/basic specialist training as a senior house officer. During this time, which lasts for about two years, doctors develop a wide range of general skills and basic specialist skills. They gain increasing responsibility for patient care under the supervision of one or more consultants.

Doctors then seek appointment to a higher specialist training post at specialist registrar grade. They enrol with the Specialist Advisory Committee (SAC) relevant to their field, eg surgical, medical, psychiatric, obstetric and gynaecological. On successful completion of training, which is likely to take four or five years, the doctor is awarded the Certificate of Completion of Specialist Training (CCST). The CSST enables the doctor to be put on the General Medical Council's Specialist Register, which makes them eligible for appointment to an NHS consultant post.

In practice, doctors normally need a diploma for membership (or fellowship in surgery) of a royal college or faculty before they can be awarded the CSST. This is obtained either at the end of basic specialist training or at the beginning of higher specialist training, depending on the speciality.

LATE ENTRY

Please see article 1. GENERAL PRACTITIONER.

OPPORTUNITIES

There are some 43,700 hospital doctors in the NHS. Opportunities for hospital doctors vary considerably according to the chosen speciality. Surgery, general medicine, and paediatrics have traditionally been very competitive, whereas promotion in fields such as anaesthetics and geriatric medicine may be a little easier to obtain. Hospital doctors may have to move to different parts of the country several times during their career, as jobs can arise anywhere.

Some consultants working in the NHS also see private patients. The NHS is going through a number of changes, which may affect opportunities for doctors.

Doctors in the Army may have the opportunity of working in hospitals overseas, in places such as Hong Kong, Cyprus, and Gibraltar.

PAY AND CONDITIONS

Salaries for hospital doctors within the NHS are as follows: house officer – £15,800 to £17,840, senior house officer – £19,715 to £26,340, specialist registrar – £22,040 to £32,135, registrar –£22,040 to £26,735, senior registrar –£25,385 to £32,135, consultant – £44,780 to £57,800. Additional payments are made for extra hours for doctors in training. Consultants may receive additional merit payments and staff in London receive London weighting allowances.

The hours for hospital doctors are long and irregular, but junior doctors must not work more than 72 hours a week.

Hospital doctors work two types of shift system, full or partial, or an on-call rota system.

Terms and conditions of service may differ for consultants working in NHS Trust hospitals, although doctors in the training grades work on a national model contract.

PROSPECTS

There are four grades of hospital doctor: pre-registration house officer, senior house officer, specialist registrar, and consultant. There is keen competition for promotion, and hospital doctors have to take a series of examinations in their chosen speciality if they want to progress.

Doctors, in the past, may have had to wait many years for a suitable post. However, there have been changes that will shorten the training period and ensure a more structured approach.

RELATED OCCUPATIONS

Please see article 1. GENERAL PRACTITIONER.

MEDICINE AND SURGERY: JAB

FURTHER INFORMATION

British Medical Association (BMA)*, BMA House, Tavistock Square, London WC1H 9JP, 0171 387 4499 (please include A5 sae)

General Medical Council*, 178 Great Portland Street, London W1N 6JE, 0171 580 7642

FURTHER READING

Leaflets/booklets are available from the address marked*.

Working in Medicine and Dentistry – COIC

Careers in Medicine, Dentistry, and Mental Health – Kogan Page

Learning Medicine – British Medical Association

Medical Careers – A General Guide – British Medical Association

Thinking of a Career in Medicine? – Peter Richards – BMJ Publishing Group

In the careers library classified under JAB.

NURSING AND AUXILIARY WORK: JAD

1. **REGISTERED NURSE CLCI:JAD**
2. **MIDWIFE CLCI:JAD**
3. **DISTRICT NURSE CLCI:JAD**
4. **HEALTH VISITOR CLCI:JAD**
5. **OCCUPATIONAL HEALTH NURSE CLCI:JAD**
6. **HEALTH CARE ASSISTANT/NURSING AUXILIARY CLCI:JAD**

BACKGROUND INFORMATION

This section covers the work of those concerned with health care both in hospitals and in the community. Nurses are members of the primary health care team – which may include doctors, other relevant health care professionals and, sometimes, social workers. They work with and in collaboration with dietitians, psychologists, social workers, therapists etc who provide other forms of treatment and services.

Those interested in nursing should read all the articles in this section, as qualified nurses with additional training can move into midwifery, health visiting (ie public health nursing), district nursing, and occupational health nursing.

1. REGISTERED NURSE (JAD)

THE WORK

Nurses are responsible for the care of patients in hospital or in the community. They assess their patients' physical, emotional, spiritual and social needs prior to developing a plan of care. The plan is developed in partnership with the patient where possible and may also involve the patient's family and friends. Nurses regularly evaluate the care they give and the effect it has on the patient, adapting the plan as necessary to remain responsive to the patient's needs.

They familiarize themselves with the patient's medical history and circumstances, keep careful records of treatment and response, and work collaboratively and in co-operation with doctors and other health care professionals. They take into account both the psychological and the physical needs of the patient, and the needs of their relatives.

Nurses work as part of a team and participate in all aspects of care. There are four major branches for registered nurses: adult; children's; mental health; and learning disability.

There are many settings in which **adult nurses** may work. In hospitals, they work in general medical and surgical wards as well as more specialized areas such as intensive care, accident and emergency, and care of the elderly. In the community, they may be attached to a general practice or community health centre, for example. Nurses can take post-registration courses so that they are able to deal confidently with particular aspects of specialist areas of nursing care.

Nurses plan and learn to manage the areas of care on the ward. At the practical level, nursing care may include: taking temperature, blood pressure and respiration rates; giving injections; administering medications; cleaning and dressing wounds; applying lotions; draining wounds and ulcers; bandaging and splinting; administering blood transfusions and drips; as well as the more routine tasks of physical care. Nurses are involved in any actions that contribute to the direct comfort and ease of their patients, and they provide psychological, emotional and spiritual support.

In other situations, nurses may work in theatre, preparing the appropriate instruments for use by the surgeons. In intensive care, in theatre and in other wards, they use sophisticated technological equipment, such as life-support systems, renal dialysis equipment for kidney malfunction etc.

Children's nurses carry out similar duties to adult nurses, but apply their specialist knowledge of the particular needs and problems of children, from birth to adolescence. The work involves a more flexible approach to routines, and anticipation of the needs of children, who are not always able to communicate as easily as adults, and their families.

Mental health nurses aim to provide care appropriate to the individual, so that they may achieve the highest possible level of independence.

Nursing mentally ill people may involve providing practical care, as in adult nursing, although much more time may be spent in counselling and exploring ways of helping patients overcome or come to terms with their illness.

Learning disability nursing involves helping and encouraging patients to develop to their full potential, and providing support to people with learning difficulties and their families. Nurses help adults and children with learning disabilities to gain everyday skills and so increase confidence. The aim is to enable people to achieve as much independence and quality of life as possible.

There are very many sources of satisfaction and success in nursing, but nurses also have to cope with failures of treatment. The work may be at times messy and distressing, although experienced nurses generally come to terms with this. Occasionally, nurses have to comfort grieving relatives when a patient dies.

WORK ENVIRONMENT

Hospitals Types of hospital vary widely from large general hospitals with numbers of specialized departments and wards, outpatients and accident and emergency departments, to much smaller specialist units treating patients with particular health problems, eg orthopaedic units. There are also psychiatric hospitals, some of which are 'secure' in that they are custodial, as well as therapeutic, units. Most hospitals are modern, light, airy, and very clean. Some of the older buildings, however, are dark and comparatively dismal. Most hospital nurses are based on one particular ward at a time but may quite regularly move around to other departments.

Community Community settings vary widely – they include health centres, GP practices and projects such as half-way houses for the mentally ill. In some cases nurses spend a lot of time visiting patients in their own homes. In others they may work in a community setting such as a school, college or work place.

SKILLS AND INTERESTS

Nursing is very demanding work and calls for a great deal of personal commitment. An interest in, and an ability to get on well with, a wide variety of people is essential. Nurses need both physical and mental stamina. They must be alert, observant, show initiative and be able to act decisively. Tact, patience and sensitivity are called for, as are maturity and a sense of humour. Both as individuals in all nursing activities and as part of a team, they should be able to get on with and work with others effectively. Communication skills are very important for dealing with patients, their relatives and members of staff.

Increasingly complex technology and sophisticated systems, along with in-depth psychological care, make greater demands today on the skills of nurses. An interest in science is useful. Common sense and a down-to-earth approach are highly valued.

ENTRY REQUIREMENTS

Applicants for pre-registration (RN) nurse education may take either a diploma or degree course.

Minimum entry requirements for a diploma course are five GCSEs/S grades (A–C/1–3) or equivalent. Acceptable alternative qualifications include NVQ/SVQ Level 3 or Advanced GNVQ (but not Intermediate GNVQ) or a BTEC National or Higher National Diploma. Those without these qualifications may be able to sit an entrance test (DC test). Schools of nursing or colleges often ask for higher than minimum qualifications, including A levels or H grades, and may require specific subjects, such as English and/or science.

Entry into degree courses is with a minimum of two A levels/three H grades plus supporting GCSEs/S grades (A–C/1–3). Science or Social Science subjects may be required, as are maths and English, at least at GCSE/S grade (A–C/1–3).

Graduates can train by taking either the three-year RN course or a shortened postgraduate RN course. Relevant degrees are required for most of the shortened courses, usually in a physical, biological or behavioural science.

Pre-nursing – some colleges of further education offer full-time and/or part-time access to higher education courses.

The minimum age of entry to nurse training is $17\frac{1}{2}$ years (17 in Scotland). The minimum age for applications to nurse training is $16\frac{1}{2}$ years (16 in Scotland).

A confidential occupational health examination is an essential part of the screening process for entry.

TRAINING

Diploma courses last three years. The course is made up of an 18-month common foundation programme, which provides a general introduction to nursing, and an 18-month branch programme in one of the four branches – adult, children, mental health or learning disability. The branch must be chosen before entering the course.

The common foundation programme provides a comprehensive introduction to the principles of modern nursing, along with the study of disciplines that underpin nursing, such as biological sciences, psychology, sociology and social policy. There is a strong emphasis on health promotion and preventive care. Theory and practice are integrated by means of varied placements in hospitals and in the community.

Branch programmes prepare students for nursing in one of the four branches, and include theoretical study and practical experience.

Degrees in nursing

Courses lead to a degree, either in nursing plus registration, or to a degree in the social or natural sciences as well as registration. Length of courses varies, although they usually last three or four years. Some degree courses offer opportunities for specialization, for example it is possible to take a course leading to registered nurse and health visitor qualifications.

Postgraduate qualification

Those with relevant degrees, which normally means a degree including physical, behavioural or natural sciences (depending on individual nursing schools/colleges) may take a shortened course lasting around two to two-and-a-half years, and leading to nurse registration. Graduates in non-related subjects may be accepted onto a three-year postgraduate course. Those with a degree in a non-relevant subject and A level/H grade in physics, chemistry or biology may be accepted onto shortened courses. Competition for postgraduate courses is intense.

Registration

Successful completion of training allows registration to be sought with the professional and regulatory body, the United Kingdom Central Council for Nursing, Midwifery and Health Visiting (UKCC).

Further training

There is an increasingly wide range of further training possibilities for nurses after registration. Courses are available in a wide range of clinical specialisms, such as care of older people, coronary care and orthopaedics. Further training courses are available for qualified nurses for specialized work, such as district nursing, midwifery or school nursing.

There are also some part-time, day and block release degrees offered for qualified nurses.

LATE ENTRY

Nursing is an area where mature entry is possible. There is no statutory upper age limit for entry to nurse training and higher education institutions may use discretion in accepting older applicants. Some schools of nursing may set an upper age limit of 45 years. Health will also be considered.

Mature applicants may be offered the opportunity of taking the DC educational test if they do not hold the academic entry qualifications of a minimum five GCSEs/S grades (A–C/1–3), or equivalent.

Access courses may be available at local colleges of further education.

NVQ/SVQ Level 3 is accepted as an entry qualification for nurse training or a BTEC National or Higher National Diploma.

Some part-time training programmes are available, suitable for students with family commitments.

OPPORTUNITIES

The NHS is by far the largest employer of nurses, although there are opportunities for work in non-NHS hospitals, nursing homes, self-employment and agency nursing work and private nursing.

The number of nursing and midwifery staff in the NHS is over 400,000.

The Armed Forces also provide nursing opportunities.

Qualified nurses are employed in prisons and young offender institutions.

NURSING AND AUXILIARY WORK: JAD

British nursing qualifications are acceptable in many countries abroad, including those in Europe, the Middle East and Australasia.

Advertisements for posts in the NHS, private hospitals and nursing homes, and for positions overseas appear in the nursing journals. Vacancies for qualified nurses also appear from time to time in local newspapers. Large Jobcentres will offer their specialized service.

PAY AND CONDITIONS

Salaries vary according to skills, responsibilities, experience and local conditions. In general, staff nurse basic salaries range from £12,855 to £19,985. Sisters/charge nurses earn basic salaries of £16,310 to £24,580.

Nurses in psychiatric and chronic-illness departments receive extra allowances. The NHS also provides free uniforms and subsidized meals, and pays inner and outer London weighting allowances.

Nurses in private hospitals and nursing homes receive similar, and sometimes higher, wages.

In the National Health Service, the agreed working hours are 75 over a two-week period. Hospital nursing is likely to involve shift, weekend and bank holiday duties. Nurses working on the wards have a three-shift system, but arrangements can vary between different hospitals and areas. Part-time work is available for qualified staff.

Nurses in nursing education and management positions usually work around normal office hours, and those in outpatient units work straight shifts that do not involve overnight cover.

Night duty may be required. Some nurses work permanent nights.

PROSPECTS

Promotion for registered nurses is usually to charge nurse/sister – in charge of the ward or clinic. There are also opportunities for registered nurses to move into health service management, research, nurse education, or one of the statutory nursing bodies developing training or giving careers advice. There are opportunities to specialize in clinical nursing, or to undertake further training for midwifery or community nursing jobs.

Qualified and experienced nurses can move into fields such as social and counselling work. Good academic qualifications are essential for research, teaching and working for statutory bodies.

RELATED OCCUPATIONS, FURTHER INFORMATION AND READING

Please see article 6. HEALTH CARE ASSISTANT/NURSING AUXILIARY.

2. MIDWIFE (JAD)

THE WORK

Midwives give supervision, care and advice to women during pregnancy, labour and after birth. They deliver babies on their own responsibility and care for the newborn in the days following birth. This care includes preventive measures, the detection of abnormal conditions in mother and child, calling for medical assistance when necessary and carrying out emergency measures in the absence of medical help. They also offer guidance and counselling, and promote woman-centred care.

During pregnancy, midwives monitor the health of the mother and development of the baby. They take the mother's blood pressure, as well as making other physical examinations.

Midwives assist women to give birth. After the birth, they continue to monitor the health of the mother and baby, weighing and examining the baby, providing support and advice and promoting breastfeeding.

They also have an important role in health counselling and education. This includes antenatal education, preparation for parenthood and family planning advice.

Midwives may work both in hospitals and in the community.

In hospital, midwives are involved in providing antenatal, intranatal and postnatal care and with education for parenthood. In the majority of cases the mother goes into hospital when she begins labour, and the midwife looks after her during labour and assists the woman to give birth.

Midwives working in the community, provide antenatal and postnatal care, either in the home or at health centres and GPs' surgeries. They also provide care and support during home births, which are increasing in number, and during 'domino' deliveries, where they accompany the mother to hospital or a GP unit to deliver the baby.

In carrying out all their duties, midwives take into account the psychological and emotional needs of mothers and their families and the economic and environmental factors that affect them.

WORK ENVIRONMENT

Hospital-based midwives work in the maternity units of general hospitals, or in maternity hospitals. Community midwives make home visits and work in hospitals, antenatal clinics, community health centres and GPs' surgeries. In an integrated service, midwives work in both the hospital and community.

Community midwives can do quite a lot of travelling, particularly in rural areas.

SKILLS AND INTERESTS

As described in article 1. REGISTERED NURSE. In midwifery, enthusiasm and commitment are essential. Stamina, good physical health and robustness are also particularly important, as the work can be physically demanding.

A driving licence is useful, especially where the midwife practises in the community.

ENTRY REQUIREMENTS

There are two methods of training as a midwife.

Three-year pre-registration training: minimum educational requirements for entry into training for registration as a midwife are five GCSEs/S grades (A–C/1–3), including English and a science subject, or approved educational equivalents. This is very much the minimum requirement; places are limited and competition for entry is intense. It is an advantage to have at least one A level/H grade. For degree programmes, two A levels/three H grades are required. Science subjects may be preferred. Student midwives beginning three-year training in England and Wales must be at least 17½ years old (17 in Scotland).

Pre-registration –shortened training – 18 months: Many trainee midwives are already registered nurses (on parts 1 or 12 of the UKCC Register). Appropriately qualified registered nurses may apply for 18-month courses (minimum). No additional qualifications are laid down, though colleges may expect GCSEs/S grades (A–C/1–3).

TRAINING

Three-year pre-registration training. Applicants who are not registered nurses are required to take the full course of midwifery training. Programmes are based in colleges or faculties of midwifery that have links with colleges of higher education. The programmes lead to a midwifery qualification and a higher education diploma (three years) or a midwifery qualification and a degree (three or four years). Contact the National Boards for Nursing, Midwifery and Health Visiting for details.

Pre-registration shortened training. Many midwives begin training after completing training as registered adult nurses. Midwifery training lasts a minimum of 18 months.

Training courses take place in colleges or faculties of midwifery, and include theoretical and clinical instruction and practical experience in the care of pregnant mothers and babies. The courses cover all aspects of midwifery, the care of newly born infants, the principles and practice of health education, the social and psychological aspects of child bearing, the complications that may occur during childbirth, neonatal paediatrics, the use of analgesics and obstetrics. The emphasis today is on promoting woman-centred care.

The successful completion of training, at either entry stage, leads to eligibility to register with the United Kingdom Central Council for Nursing, Midwifery and Health Visiting (UKCC). Registration is a statutory requirement to practise as a midwife. Midwives must notify their intention to practise annually, and take refresher courses every five years (every three years after 2001).

LATE ENTRY

The majority of midwives begin their training after qualifying as registered nurses, so most entrants are over 21. There are return-to-practice programmes for qualified midwives who return to work after a career break. It may be difficult to enter training after the age of 50.

Mature applicants who are not registered nurses may enter via direct entry pre-registration programmes. They may qualify for entry by taking a relevant Access (to higher education) course.

OPPORTUNITIES

Around 34,000 midwives work in the UK, the vast majority of whom are employed by the National Health Service. There are a few opportunities in private nursing homes and clinics, and other miscellaneous organizations.

This occupation is equally open to men and women, although, so far, few men have trained.

United Kingdom midwifery qualifications are accepted in the EU and Commonwealth countries but sometimes only alongside a registered nursing qualification so there may be possibilities for work abroad. There can be opportunities, too, for voluntary or paid work in the developing world – this is particularly true for midwifery teachers. The Armed Forces also have opportunities for midwives to train and practise. Midwives may also be self-employed and practise independently.

Advertisements for vacancies appear in the nursing and midwifery journals. Some private employment agencies deal with this type of work, while others actually specialize in this field.

PAY AND CONDITIONS

Salaries for NHS midwives range from £12,855 to £26,965, with or without London weighting and dependent on local conditions. Salaries in the private sector vary.

Community midwives receive car mileage and telephone allowances. Pension schemes are available within the NHS.

Hospital-based midwives work shift systems, which are broadly the same as those worked by general nursing staff in hospitals.

Community midwives normally work days on an office-hours basis, although they have periods when they are on call.

PROSPECTS

Post-basic courses enable midwives to specialize in various clinical areas, such as special care baby units, maternal and neonatal emergencies and obstetric ultrasound. Some midwives specialize in teaching. There are other opportunities and also appropriate courses for those who wish to pursue a management career in the National Health Service.

RELATED OCCUPATIONS, FURTHER INFORMATION AND READING

Please see article 6. HEALTH CARE ASSISTANT/ NURSING AUXILIARY.

3. DISTRICT NURSE (JAD)

THE WORK

District nurses provide skilled nursing care for patients in the community –either in their own homes or in residential care homes. They care for those released from hospital after acute illness, the chronically ill before and after hospitalization, the dying and the bereaved. Their patients can be any age, but usually include a large number of older people.

They assess and deliver skilled nursing care. They are concerned with both the physical and psychological well-being of their patients and teach care skills to their families. At the same time, they give support to patients and encourage as much independence as possible. They may visit some patients several times a day to give care, support and treatment. This is particularly the case when patients are terminally ill.

District nurses liaise with other agencies within the community, such as social workers, occupational therapists, and voluntary agencies, as well as with hospital colleagues and other members of the primary health team.

They work in a team that includes GPs, health visitors and community midwives. Methods and programmes of treatment of individual patients are discussed and drawn up, and a careful record kept of decisions, action and

NURSING AND AUXILIARY WORK: JAD

progress. In some areas, particularly thinly populated rural areas, one person takes on the triple responsibilities of district nurse, midwife and health visitor (see relevant articles). In urban areas duties may include giving advice and treatment in a community health centre or GP's practice.

WORK ENVIRONMENT

District nurses work primarily in patients' homes, residential care homes, GPs' surgeries and community health clinics. Those in rural areas may have to travel considerable distances.

SKILLS AND INTERESTS

These are similar to the skills and interests for a registered nurse (see article 1. REGISTERED NURSE). In addition, it is important that they are good listeners, can give advice tactfully and are tolerant. A mature attitude is important, as well as the ability to work responsibly and independently.

Stamina is very important as the work is usually very demanding. District nurses are sometimes the main contact for people who are socially isolated, frightened, in pain, or dying.

A driving licence is necessary in most cases.

ENTRY REQUIREMENTS

To enter training in district and community nursing, candidates must be qualified as registered nurses (see article 1. REGISTERED NURSE), have an appropriate level of education and meet the requirements of the institution to which application is being made. An entrance test may also be required.

TRAINING

Training programmes are at degree level and last for at least 32 weeks full-time or the equivalent part-time. They include a period of supervised clinical practice (50% of programme). Courses are held at higher education institutions. Subjects include psychology, physiology, sociology and epidemiology. Skills in communication are taught, as well as counselling and teaching.

Students are normally sponsored by their employers.

On qualification, in order to practise, district nurses must be registered with the United Kingdom Central Council for Nursing, Midwifery and Health Visiting.

LATE ENTRY

There are good opportunities for adult entry. Many take up training after a career break or after working abroad, though they may in these cases have to take an entrance test set by the individual institution. A period of hospital-based nursing may also be required before secondment for training.

There is no official upper age limit.

OPPORTUNITIES

District nurses are employed in the UK only in the NHS, but there are also opportunities for work overseas, particularly in the developing countries.

Vacancies are advertised in the nursing journals.

PAY AND CONDITIONS

Salaries range from £19,240 to £26,965, with or without London weighting and dependent on local conditions. Some qualified district nurses commence on £16,029.

Telephone and car mileage allowances are paid.

Hours of duty vary depending on the area. In some areas shifts are worked; in others a rota system for being on call during nights is used, coupled with day work between 9am and 6pm. Some unsocial hours can be expected. Opportunities exist for part-time work, particularly for evening and night duties.

PROSPECTS

There are further courses in specialist aspects of district nursing, and district nurses with a minimum of two years' full-time experience can take a fieldwork teacher course and go on to help training student district nurses. There are also appropriate courses for those who wish to pursue a management career in the NHS.

RELATED OCCUPATIONS, FURTHER INFORMATION AND READING

Please see article 6. HEALTH CARE ASSISTANT/NURSING AUXILIARY.

4. HEALTH VISITOR (JAD)

THE WORK

Health visitors promote health and help prevent illness through health education and promotion. They also help chronically ill and disabled people to learn to cope with their disabilities.

Health visitors are primarily concerned with health needs assessment and public health. There is less emphasis on clinical care than in other nursing specialisms, and more emphasis on giving advice and monitoring the public's health.

The work involves giving advice on health matters, promoting healthy lifestyles and preventing illness. Health visitors monitor people's health, particularly that of young children and elderly people. They identify problems – mental, physical and social – by working with, and talking to, individuals and families. They may run clinics for mothers and babies and give talks to groups in schools and health centres. They offer a service to monitor babies' health and provide parents with support and advice about feeding, safety, normal child development etc. In rural areas, those qualified may combine the role of midwife, district nurse and health visitor.

Health visitors are responsible for organizing their own work within the framework of their Trust's policies and work much more independently than other nurses.

WORK ENVIRONMENT

Health visitors are usually attached to work with a group of GPs, or alternatively work in a defined geographical area. They may be based at clinics, health centres or GP group practices.

NURSING AND AUXILIARY WORK: JAD

The work involves visiting people in their own homes, health and community centres, schools, playgroups, day centres, and special schools and centres for the disabled, GPs' surgeries and old people's homes. In some rural areas mobile health clinics are used.

SKILLS AND INTERESTS

As described in article 1. REGISTERED NURSE.

In addition, health visitors need the ability to communicate effectively with a wide range of people and should have tact and understanding. They need to be able to write clear reports, liaise with other members of the primary health care team and other agencies, and teach and counsel patients. When dealing with people from a variety of social backgrounds, health visitors must have both an understanding of social pressures and sympathy with people.

The capability to observe, evaluate and anticipate potential health problems in individuals, families and groups is essential.

Health visitors must be able to work independently, as they spend much of the time working alone, and should have the stamina to be out and about a good deal.

A driving licence is useful and/or required.

ENTRY REQUIREMENTS

Most candidates entering training in health visiting are qualified as registered nurses (see article 1. REGISTERED NURSE). They must have an appropriate level of education and meet the requirements of the institution to which application is being made. An entrance test may also be required.

It is also possible to train by taking an integrated degree course leading to qualification as a registered nurse and health visitor. Entry to degree courses is with a minimum of two A levels/three H grades plus supporting GCSEs/S grades (A–C/1–3). Science subjects are usually required, as are maths and English, at least at GCSE/S grade (A–C/1–3).

TRAINING

Training programmes are at degree level and last for at least 32 weeks full-time or the equivalent part-time. They include a period of supervised clinical practice (50% of programme). Courses are held at higher education institutions. Subjects include psychology, sociology, social policy and epidemiology. Skills in communication are taught, as well as counselling and teaching.

Students are normally sponsored by their employers.

Integrated degree courses

Nursing degrees are available at a number of institutions of higher education. Courses last for around four years and combine practical nursing with theoretical instruction usually in science or social sciences. Courses most often lead to a registered nursing qualification and some provide options for candidates to qualify as a registered health visitor. These include courses available at Southampton, Manchester, Liverpool and King's College London.

The content of the training for the health visiting certificate in these courses covers the study of human growth (psychological, physiological and social), social policy and administration, and social aspects of health and disease. The skills taught include those of observation, developing relationships with, and teaching, both individuals and groups, and planning and organization. The courses include practical field work experience and involve a period of supervised practice with a small case-load.

Registration

On qualification, in order to practise, health visitors must be registered with the United Kingdom Central Council for Nursing, Midwifery and Health Visiting.

LATE ENTRY

The majority of health visitors enter the profession having qualified as registered nurses. Adult entry is therefore an important feature of the work.

OPPORTUNITIES

In the UK there are around 30,000 health visitors. The work is nation-wide and covers rural, urban and inner-city communities.

Advertisements appear in the nursing journals.

PAY AND CONDITIONS

Salaries for health visitors are between £19,204 and £26,965, with or without London weighting and dependent on local conditions.

Health visitors usually work office hours, Monday to Friday. However, hours are dictated by the nature of the work and can involve evening work (giving talks or lectures on health care matters) and occasional weekend work.

There are sometimes opportunities for part-time working and job share.

PROSPECTS

There are further courses in specialist aspects of health visiting, and health visitors with a minimum of two years' full-time experience can take a field-work teacher course and go on to help train student health visitors. There are also appropriate courses for those who wish to pursue a management career within the NHS.

RELATED OCCUPATIONS, FURTHER INFORMATION AND READING

Please see article 6. HEALTH CARE ASSISTANT/ NURSING AUXILIARY.

5. OCCUPATIONAL HEALTH NURSE (JAD)

THE WORK

There are three main aspects of occupational health (OH) nursing.

The first is concerned with identifying potential health hazards in the workplace, using a risk management approach. This means being aware of possibly dangerous materials, substances, plant and machinery, and can involve environmental surveillance and biological monitoring.

NURSING AND AUXILIARY WORK: JAD

The second is the promotion and maintenance of health and the prevention of ill-health. OH nurses have an educational role, both in promoting the personal health of individual employees, and health and hygiene related to work.

The third aspect (in some occupational health services) is the organization of emergency treatment of people who are injured at work, and the treatment of minor illnesses and injuries people may suffer while at their workplace. OH nurses may have to give initial care to people who have suffered heart attacks, experienced injury involving broken bones, burns etc and may administer medicines.

Added to these core functions can be rehabilitation work with employees who have been ill, counselling, and referral work.

OH nurses may make assessment of previously ill or injured employees and make recommendations as to their suitability for the same or different work. They also maintain confidential records.

In providing a nursing service, OH nurses have an administrative role and may have responsibilities for organizing the service in the workplace, liaising with management, formulating nursing and occupational health policy, providing advice to management on nursing salaries and conditions of service, preparing and working within budgets, and appointing personnel.

WORK ENVIRONMENT

OH nursing posts may be found in industry, commercial and public sector organizations. In all these various areas, nurses have to be familiar with the whole working environment and have to spend some time visiting workers in their work environment.

In some posts, the nurse needs to travel between the different sites of the organization. A driving licence is useful for this type of work.

SKILLS AND INTERESTS

As described for REGISTERED NURSE, but, in addition, OH nurses require business-like efficiency because of the environment in which they work. Skills include writing and implementing policy, and negotiation and management of change with both the employer and employee.

ENTRY REQUIREMENTS

Occupational health work is open to registered nurses who are trained in the adult or mental health branches (not children's or learning disability nursing).

TRAINING

It is not a statutory requirement for nurses to have specialist occupational health nursing education for an occupational health nurse job. However, it is the policy of the Royal College of Nursing Society of Occupational Health Nursing that all nurses should be trained for the work.

The number of training programmes for OH nurses varies across the country.

Training programmes are at degree level and last for at least 32 weeks full-time; part-time and distance learning modes of study are also available. They include a period of supervised clinical practice (50% of programme). Courses are held at higher education institutions.

Core subjects for OH nurse education include management skills, health assessment, epidemiology, ergonomics, risk management, organizational behaviour, psychology and sociology of health, health promotion, research, occupational hygiene and safety.

LATE ENTRY

People who move into occupational health nursing are already qualified nurses, so adult entry is the norm.

Although many nurses have a range of hospital experience before moving into occupational health nursing, it is possible to study for OH nursing qualifications following first qualification. It is desirable, however, to have at least two years' post-registration experience. There is no official upper age limit for training, but colleges may apply their own age limits on entrants to courses.

OPPORTUNITIES

Employers include industry, commerce and public sector organizations. There are many jobs in universities, hospitals, large department stores, food shops, banks and industry. Increasingly, OH nurses are employed in a consultative capacity.

PAY AND CONDITIONS

Salaries are negotiated with individual employers. They range from about £13,751 to £29,585. Senior occupational nurses can earn in excess of £30,000.

Working patterns vary. In a large plant involved in continuous-process production, there may be a team of nurses (and doctors) who work shifts to provide total cover. In other organizations, the pattern may be normal office hours. There are opportunities for part-time work.

PROSPECTS

In large occupational health departments, there can be opportunities to move into nursing management positions.

There can be prospects in the development and administration of occupational health services in some NHS districts/areas, and other public sector employment.

RELATED OCCUPATIONS, FURTHER INFORMATION AND READING

Please see article 6. HEALTH CARE ASSISTANT/ NURSING AUXILIARY.

6. HEALTH CARE ASSISTANT/NURSING AUXILIARY (JAD)

THE WORK

Health care assistants (who have sometimes been known as nursing auxiliaries and may still be referred to by that title in some areas) work in hospitals, homes and in the wider community. They support professionally trained staff – nurses, midwives, health visitors, occupational therapists, physiotherapists, speech therapists and chiropodists – in caring for patients. In psychiatric hospitals, they are usually known as nursing assistants. They often work as part of a nursing or care team made up, for example, of a sister or

NURSING AND AUXILIARY WORK: JAD

staff nurse, registered nurse, student nurse and health care assistant.

Duties may vary according to the level of training, local policy and place of work. All tasks are performed under the supervision of a qualified professional and, on **wards**, may involve:

Treatment – take and chart patient's temperature and pulse; take urine and sputum samples; perform urine tests; weigh patients; put on simple dressings; take patients to theatre and for x-rays; help with treatments – set up trolleys, assist professionals during treatments; and clear up afterwards. Health care assistants do not give drugs or injections.

Nutrition – help patients feed themselves; feed incapacitated patients; encourage children to eat; make snacks and hot drinks.

Hygiene and cleanliness - give out and empty bed-pans and urinals; help patients use the toilet; change incontinence pads/sanitary towels/nappies; give bed-baths; help patients wash themselves; accompany patients to bathroom or shower; bathe children and babies.

Mobility – help patients dress and undress; support patients who are unsteady on their feet; help patients carry out therapists' instructions.

Comfort and emotional support – turn bed-bound patients to prevent pressure sores developing; change soiled linen and clothing, provide extra blankets, pillows etc; help patients with radio headphones, position of television, contents of locker etc; talk or read to patients; comfort anxious or frightened patients; play with children; help patients make the most of recreational facilities.

Death of patients – help with last offices; help with related paperwork.

General duties – health care assistants/nursing auxiliaries also have duties such as escorting patients to other departments, making beds and tidying the ward, checking and sorting stock such as linen, and helping with the department's paperwork.

In **psychiatric hospitals**, many activities centre on helping patients build confidence and independence, perhaps in preparation for their return home, or a move into the community after a long stay in hospital. Nursing assistants may help patients learn/re-earn basic skills such as dressing themselves or – when professional supervision is not required – may accompany them on trips to, for example, libraries, theatres or restaurants, which will help them adjust to life in the community.

In **hospital clinics and outpatient departments**, duties may include taking clients from one area to another, weighing and measuring, helping with treatments, taking and testing urine samples, and ensuring medical staff have correct files.

Community health care assistants visit clients in their homes. They provide nursing support, such as giving baths, renewing simple dressings etc, or provide social care to clients who might otherwise have to stay in hospital.

Health care assistants are provided with a uniform. Uniforms are not worn in a psychiatric setting.

WORK ENVIRONMENT

Health care assistants work in wards and clinics in general hospitals, nursing and residential homes, and in clients' homes. They are active for much of the day and at night during shift work and may have to do a lot of manual handling, for which they are trained. Training and updating in all aspects of health and safety at work are given. On some wards, they deal regularly with blood, vomit, excreta etc.

SKILLS AND INTERESTS

Health care assistants need to be practical and well organized. They must be able to work well under supervision and as part of a team, and to follow instructions clearly. They must be reliable, hard-working and able to remain calm in an emergency. The work is often stressful, because suffering, and perhaps death, are involved, so resilience is needed to cope.

As the work is physically demanding, they must be fit and healthy. Stamina is needed; health care assistants work on their feet most of the time. They have to be prepared to do unpleasant jobs. Health care assistants work in an environment where hygiene and safety are particularly important.

Health care assistants care for patients from many different backgrounds. They need to be sympathetic and tactful, and discreet with confidential information. They must be firm when necessary, but always treat patients as human beings and with respect, however dependent they may have become. They need a pleasant and courteous manner and a good sense of humour.

Illness, anxiety or senility can make patients awkward or angry, and health care assistants must respond with understanding and patience.

ENTRY REQUIREMENTS

No formal academic qualifications are needed, but candidates must be literate and numerate. Some employers may require GCSEs/S grades, GNVQs, NVQs or equivalent. Applicants need to be at least 17 to 18 years old.

Candidates may have to complete a medical questionnaire and may have to undergo a medical examination. References will be vetted.

There are a number of courses relevant to work as a health care assistant. In most cases, no particular entry requirements are laid down, although individual schools and colleges may specify their own requirements.

Modern Apprenticeships (part of the Skillseekers Initiative in Scotland) may be available for young people leading to at least an NVQ/SVQ Level 3. Contact your local careers office, Jobcentre, TEC/LEC for details.

TRAINING

Pre-entry courses

The following courses are a useful preparation for those wanting to enter this type of work:

A levels/H grades – in social subjects.

GNVQ in Health and Social Care/GSVQ in Care – some schools and many colleges now offer GNVQ in Health and Social Care at Foundation, Intermediate or Advanced level (one year). A number offer GSVQ in Care Level II (one year).

NURSING AND AUXILIARY WORK: JAD

NVQs/SVQs in Care – a number of colleges offer care courses that provide students with a basis of knowledge and work experience to prepare them for relevant NVQs/SVQs at Level 2. Some also offer training to Level 3.

SQA National Certificate – a number of colleges offer one-year or two-year courses that lead to national certificate modules in care.

BTEC First Diploma in Care – just a few colleges now offer this one-year course.

Voluntary work in a hospital or community home could be useful.

On entry

Local employers take different approaches to training. Applicants seeking vocational qualifications should ensure training allows for assessment towards NVQs/SVQs.

Health care assistants may register for assessment for NVQs/SVQs in Care at Levels 2 and 3.

Training may be on the job, or a combination of on-the-job training and time spent in a school of nursing or local college. Basic skills, such as bed-making and lifting, are taught; lectures are given on such subjects as first aid, infection control, and health and safety.

Details of local training opportunities are available from NHS/private hospital personnel departments, FE colleges and Jobcentres. In-house training is available. Also see local newspapers.

LATE ENTRY

There is no upper age limit and no formal qualifications are needed. Because of the demands of the work, mature entrants may be particularly well suited to it, provided they meet the physical and emotional requirements.

Adults can gain recognition of their skills and experience by working towards NVQs/SVQs. There is open access to NVQs/SVQs – no academic qualifications are required, and there are no age limits. NVQs/SVQs are based on competence, and it does not matter how that competence has been gained – through experience, company training programmes, college courses or open learning. Past experience can be put forward as evidence of competence, via Accreditation of Prior Learning (APL).

OPPORTUNITIES

Health care assistants are employed by NHS Trusts, local authorities and the private sector.

They work in general and psychiatric hospitals, hospitals for those with enduring mental illness, specialist hospitals and in the community. Openings also arise in private hospitals, residential nursing homes and clinics and private homes for the elderly, or the physically or mentally impaired.

Opportunities are related to local recruitment policies and vary from area to area. It may be necessary to move to find a job.

Openings are advertised at Jobcentres and in local papers. Details of vacancies are also available from hospital personnel departments.

PAY AND CONDITIONS

In England and Wales, local agreements are made for health care assistants. In Scotland, health care assistants are paid the same as nursing auxiliaries.

There may be the possibility of moving to another post at a higher grade with experience and NVQ qualifications.

Allowances may be paid to health care assistants for shifts worked at night and on Saturday or Sunday.

Full-time NHS health care assistants work 37_ hours per week. There are often three shifts: early, evening afternoon, late or night. Many hospitals have flexible working hours and there are many opportunities for part-time work.

Staff employed by local authorities or the private sector are paid on Whitley Council scales, or on the hospital/home/clinic's own scale.

PROSPECTS

There are opportunities for those nursing auxiliaries prepared to take extra responsibility, to move from supervised work in hospitals to less directly supervised work in the community.

NVQs/SVQs (e.g NVQ/SVQ Level 3) will offer health care assistants the opportunity to use their experience to count towards an application for other health careers such as nursing and physiotherapy.

RELATED OCCUPATIONS

Care assistant, home help, special needs teaching auxiliary, ward clerk, hospital porter, operating department assistant, nurse, social worker, occupational therapist, dietitian, physiotherapist.

FURTHER INFORMATION

English National Board for Nursing, Midwifery and Health Visiting*, Careers Service, PO Box 2EN, London W1A 2EN, 0171 291 6200/5, www.enb.org.uk

National Board for Nursing, Midwifery and Health Visiting for Northern Ireland*, RAC House, 79 Chichester Street, Belfast BT1 4JE, 01232 333298

National Board for Nursing, Midwifery and Health Visiting for Scotland*, 22 Queen Street, Edinburgh EH2 1NT, 0131 225 2096, www.nbs.org.uk

NBS Centralised Application to Nurse Training Clearing House, PO Box 21, Edinburgh EH2 INT.

Welsh National Board for Nursing, Midwifery and Health Visiting*, 2nd Floor, Golgate House, 101 St Mary Street, Cardiff CF1 1DX, 01222 261400

Nursing and Midwifery Admissions Service (NMAS)*, Fulton House, Jessop Avenue, Cheltenham, Gloucestershire GL50 3SH, 01242 544949

The United Kingdom Central Council for Nursing, Midwifery and Health Visiting, 23 Portland Place, London W1N 4JT

NURSING AND AUXILIARY WORK: JAD

FURTHER READING

Leaflets/booklets are available from the addresses marked*.

Working in Nursing and Midwifery –COIC

Working in Work with Children – COIC

A Career in Nursing or Midwifery

Midwifery – Meet Someone New Every Day

Both of the above publications are available from English National Board for Nursing, Midwifery and Health Visiting –see above.

In the careers library classified under JAD.

DENTISTRY: JAF

1. **DENTIST CLCI:JAF**
2. **DENTAL NURSE CLCI:JAF**
3. **DENTAL HYGIENIST CLCI:JAF**
4. **DENTAL TECHNICIAN CLCI:JAF**

BACKGROUND INFORMATION

Dentistry is the branch of medical science concerned with the diagnosis and treatment of diseases and disorders of the teeth, gums and surrounding tissue.

Dentists, dental nurses, dental technicians and dental hygienists are employed in private or NHS general practice, in the community dental service or in hospitals. They also work in the Armed Forces and in the health centres of large organizations.

1. DENTIST (JAF)

THE WORK

There are several different branches of dentistry, and the work varies in each area.

General practice

Dentists in general practice are responsible for the dental health of their patients, using a variety of preventive and restorative measures.

They start their work with patients by taking a medical history and examining their teeth and mouth. They often have to reassure patients that the treatment will be conducted as painlessly and quickly as possible. X-rays may be taken to reveal any areas of decay undetected by examination.

The dentist may administer a local anaesthetic to reduce any discomfort experienced by the patient. Dentists restore teeth by filling them with silver-coloured amalgam and white composite materials. They restore gaps in the mouth by fitting bridges and dentures, which are made by a dental technician. Badly decayed teeth may be removed, although they are often saved nowadays by root fillings.

Dentists are helped by a dental nurse, who assists in (four-handed) dentistry, passing instruments and other materials to the dentist as required. Dentists also scale, polish, and clean teeth, unless a dental hygienist is employed to perform those tasks. Dentists also apply fissure sealants, formed from an acrylic-like substance that bonds to the surface of the tooth, helping to prevent decay.

Prevention of dental decay and disease is becoming increasingly important, with many dentists employing hygienists to help them in this role. With the advent of fluoride toothpaste and fluoridated water in some parts of the UK, dental decay is becoming far less common. Dentists encourage their patients to return for further treatment where necessary, and to attend for regular check-ups.

Dentists in general practice may work single-handed, or as part of a group of several professionals. A dentist in general practice may concentrate on orthodontics, which involves straightening teeth using braces, and is used mainly with children who have overcrowded mouths. Other dentists may have a special interest in restorative work for damaged or missing teeth, which includes crowning teeth and fitting bridges. Others may be specially trained and qualified in anaesthesia, although anaesthetics at the local dental surgery are much less common than in the past.

Hospital work

Hospitals offer dentists the opportunity to carry out treatments that may not be possible within general practice. Dentists may work in a specialized dental hospital, or in the dental department of a general hospital. Much of the work is concerned with outpatients, with only a minority staying in hospital for any length of time.

In a dental hospital, patients are often treated by student dentists, closely supervised by senior members of staff. Patients may be referred to a dental hospital for complex bridgework, or periodontal surgery, where the dentist performs surgical procedures to the gums. The dentist may remodel a patient's gums by trimming diseased tissue and applying stitches.

The hierarchy for dentists in hospital is similar to that for doctors, starting at the house officer grade, and progressing to the rank of consultant. All grades other than consultant are considered to be training grades. Hospital dentists seeking promotion normally take a series of higher qualifications. Dentists wishing to make a career in hospital work normally specialize in one of the following areas:

Orthodontics. Dentists in general practice work on straightening teeth by the use of mechanical appliances, but more complex cases are frequently referred to a hospital. The dentist in general practice may ask the hospital orthodontist for specialist advice, although the actual treatment may be performed in the general practice.

Oral and maxillo-facial surgery. Oral and maxillo-facial surgeons treat people who have been born with facial defects, such as a cleft palate, as well as those who have been damaged by accidents and cancers of the jaw and face. This is highly skilled and demanding work, requiring co-operation with other members of the medical team, including ear, nose and throat specialists. Many oral and maxillo-facial surgeons are qualified in medicine, as well as dentistry.

Community dental service

Community dentists work in clinics, providing a service to young children, expectant mothers, and people with special needs, such as those with physical or mental disabilities. State school children are required by law to receive dental checks, and community dentists visit schools to ensure these take place. The community dental service is also involved in surveys and research into dental disease and health education.

Industrial dentistry

Some large companies employ dentists to provide dental services for their employees. The work is similar to that performed in general practice.

Armed Forces

The Armed Forces offer some cadetships, similar to sponsorships, during training. After training, dentists can serve for a short commission of five years, or may sign up as a regular officer.

University teaching

Highly qualified and experienced dentists may be able to teach undergraduate and postgraduate students within a dental school or hospital. They also publish the results of any research they are engaged in.

WORK ENVIRONMENT

Dentists in general practice work in a surgery, which may

DENTISTRY: JAF

be in their own house or elsewhere. Dentists may work in a company dental surgery, or in community health clinics and schools, which can involve some travelling. Within a hospital, the dentist may work in a surgery, in a clinic, and in the operating theatre. The working conditions are clean, hygienic, and well lit.

SKILLS AND INTERESTS

Dentists need an interest in their patients as people. Many patients are anxious and worried about dental treatment. A friendly manner helps to put patients at their ease, whilst a sense of humour helps both the dentist and the patient. Good verbal communication skills are important in order to relate well, both to patients and other members of the dental team. Manual dexterity and an interest in science are also essential. Dentists must be hard-working and, in general practice, possess good business sense, because they have to manage the financial and administrative side of the practice. Dentists are increasingly required to market their services in an attractive and imaginative way.

ENTRY REQUIREMENTS

Before dentists can practise, they should be registered by the General Dental Council. To qualify for registration, students take the Bachelor of Dental Surgery (BDS).

Dental schools normally ask for three good A levels for the BDS – chemistry and two from biology, maths, and physics. Occasionally an arts subject may be offered as the third A level – requirements vary between dental schools. Students are normally asked to obtain grades between AAA and ABB at A level. Two AS levels can sometimes be substituted for one A level. Between five and six H grades are normally requested, to include chemistry and other science subjects, at grades between A and B. Candidates normally need a GCSE/S grade (A–C/1–3) in English language, and many schools ask for physics, maths and biology at this level also. Some dental schools offer candidates with non-science A levels/H grades the opportunity of taking a pre-dental year, which is a conversion course to science A levels/H grades. Competition for all courses is intense, with admissions staff looking for evidence of a candidate's suitability for dentistry as well as academic strength. All prospective candidates should visit a dentist for work shadowing, to find out whether they might be suited to dentistry.

TRAINING

Training for the BDS degree lasts five years. A further preliminary year is involved if non-science A levels are held.

Pre-dental course

This course is only available at some of the dental schools, and covers the study of physics, chemistry, and biology for candidates without A levels/H grades in these subjects. Candidates already holding sciences at A level/H grade are exempt.

Five-year dental course

The first part of the course introduces student dentists to the study of anatomy (the study of parts of the body), dental anatomy, physiology (the study of body function), biochemistry and histology (which is the microscopic study of parts of the body). These subjects are taught via lectures, practicals, tutorials, and clinical demonstrations, and are normally examined during the first two years of the course. As the course progresses, students learn how to examine, diagnose and care for patients. Practical skills are learnt, initially in the laboratory, and, later in the course, students work with patients under supervision. Courses also include theoretical and practical teaching in general medicine – to enhance the student's knowledge and all-round experience – as well as visits to general dental practices, community dental services etc.

A wide variety of subjects are studied, which include: preventive dentistry; children's dentistry and orthodontics; anaesthetics; oral surgery; periodontics, which is the study of gum disease; radiology; drugs or pharmacology; oral pathology, or the study of diseases of the mouth; public health dentistry; restorative dentistry including crown and bridge work; the construction of dentures and associated laboratory work, known as dental prosthetics; dental materials science. After the final examination has been passed, the dentist can apply for admission to the Dentists Register to begin practising.

It is sometimes possible for suitable students to take an *intercalated degree,* after the first two or three years of the dental course, and obtain a Bachelor of Science (BSc) qualification. This entails an extra one to two years of study. In addition, it is usual to take an *elective*, which gives the opportunity to gain work experience in the UK or abroad.

Postgraduate training

New graduates can join a practice on a one-year vocational training scheme, under the supervision of trained and experienced dentists. This supplements their existing knowledge of general practice, with lectures and demonstrations attended outside the surgery. Vocational training is mandatory for those wishing to work as a principal in NHS general dental practice.

Various postgraduate courses are provided by the university dental schools and the Royal Surgical Colleges (contact the Royal College of Surgeons of England, the Royal College of Surgeons of Edinburgh or the Royal College of Physicians and Surgeons of Glasgow for further details). Community dental officers spend two years on a special training course, which emphasizes health education and the prevention of oral and dental disease. It is possible to take the Diploma in Dental Public Health of the Royal College of Surgeons, after which community dentists may apply for promotion to more senior posts.

LATE ENTRY

It is possible to enter dental school training up to the age of 30 years, although individual schools have different policies regarding the admission of mature students. It is unlikely that dental schools will relax entry requirements for mature students.

OPPORTUNITIES

There are approximately 27,000 dentists in the UK, with about 800 new graduates each year. Over half of all dentists work in general dental practice. Only about five per cent work in hospitals, with a similar percentage working in the Community Dental Service. Many dentists spend a short spell working in a hospital to improve their all-round experience. It may be possible to work in Australia and New Zealand, with the necessary work permits, and in countries of the European Union without

DENTISTRY: JAF

restrictions. In America, British dental qualifications are not fully recognized, and State Board examinations must be sat, which are similar to dental school final examinations. Voluntary organizations employ dentists to work in developing countries.

PAY AND CONDITIONS

Most dentists in general practice work within the NHS. Income is dependent upon a scale of fees and therefore the amount that each dentist earns depends upon the amount and type of work they do, as each piece of work attracts a fee laid down by the NHS. The fees for NHS dental treatment are calculated to include both an earnings element and an expenses element. Fees for private work vary considerably between dentists. Dentists in general practice have to meet all their own overheads for premises and so on, and usually have to buy into the 'goodwill' of the practice if they wish to become partners. This can be very expensive.

For children's routine dental treatment, dentists receive a fixed monthly fee, which varies according to the age of the child, plus a fee per item charged. For adults, they receive a small per capita payment, but most of the dentists' fees for treating adults come from set fees for different items of treatment.

Salaries for dental officers in the Community Dental Service range from £22,145 to £32,245. Senior dental officers earn from £32,245 to £46,180. Assistant district and district dental officers earn salaries which vary according to the population of the area. These salaries range from around £35,490 to £54,860. In the hospital service, a house officer starts at about £15,800, while consultants can earn up to £57,795.

Dentists in general practice can arrange their own working hours to fit in with the needs of their patients. Most dentists in general practice start work between 8.30am and 9am and finish between 5.30pm and 6pm, and may work some evenings and Saturday mornings. Dentists in NHS general practice have to provide emergency cover, often on a rota basis. The community dental service offers more regular hours. Some hospital dentists can expect to work more irregular hours, with those in oral and maxillo-facial surgery, where emergencies are most likely to occur, working at night and during weekends on occasions. They are also be expected to be on call during some periods.

Dentistry, particularly in general practice, provides opportunities for part-time work.

PROSPECTS

The use of fluoride toothpaste and fluoridated water has greatly reduced the need for fillings. This means that the type of treatment performed by dentists is changing, and many are more involved in preventive work. Competition for places at some dental schools is now severe, because fewer dentists are being trained, although this means that there will be fewer people applying for jobs after qualifying. Within the hospital service, there are often more people applying for senior posts than there are vacancies, and dentists may have to move to another area of the country for a suitable job.

RELATED OCCUPATIONS

Doctor, pharmacist, medical laboratory scientist, dental therapist, dental hygienist.

FURTHER INFORMATION

The British Dental Association*, 64 Wimpole Street, London W1M 8AL, 0171 935 0875, www.bda-dentistry.org.uk

Faculty of General Dental Practitioners (UK), The Royal College of Surgeons of England, 35/43 Lincoln's Inn Fields, London WC2A 3PN, 0171 405 3474 ext 3534

National Advice Centre for Postgraduate Education, Faculty of Dental Surgery, Royal College of Surgeons of England, 35 Lincoln's Inn Fields, London WC2A 3PN, 0171 312 6671, www.rcseng.ac.uk/fdgp/

FURTHER READING

Careers in Medicine, Dentistry, and Mental Health – Kogan Page

In the careers library classified under JAF.

2. DENTAL NURSE (JAF)

THE WORK

Dental nurses perform an important job in the dental team by providing support to dentists, hygienists, and therapists. Their work can combine administrative and clerical duties with practical work in the surgery, thus ensuring the patients receive a good service.

Dental nurses prepare the dental surgery before patients arrive, making sure all the equipment is ready, and clear up the surgery throughout the working session and at the end of a day's work. They may also make sure the waiting area is a clean and welcoming place. Sterilizing dental equipment is an important part of the dental nurse's job, and is something that continues throughout the day. Dental nurses play an important part in helping to make patients feel comfortable and relaxed, by being friendly and interested in them.

During a check-up, the dental nurse may amend a patient's records, noting down details dictated by the dentist on a specially designed chart. Dental nurses work quickly, mixing fillings and materials for impressions, and pass these to the dentist as required, along with any necessary instruments. They sometimes hold suction instruments to remove saliva from a patient's mouth. All the work is done under the direction of the dentist, and can vary according to the preferences of individual dentists. Dental nurses may also process and mount x-ray films.

Patients may undergo treatment with general anaesthesia in dental surgeries and dental hospitals. Appropriately qualified dental nurses look after patients while they are unconscious and help care for them during recovery. This involves checks on their pulse and breathing rates, appearance, and colour. Patients are carefully monitored at all times by the dental team, with the dental nurse assisting the dentist as a nurse would a surgeon.

In a smaller practice the dental nurse may act as a receptionist – answering the phone, greeting patients and making appointments, as well as dealing with all the NHS paperwork needed for the proper payments to be received. Dental nurses often organize and file record cards, as well as maintaining supplies of stationery and materials. Reminder cards may be sent out to inform patients of the need to make regular appointments. Dental nurses keep patient records up to date, noting information on the state of their teeth and a history of the work that has been done.

DENTISTRY: JAF

In larger practices and hospitals, a receptionist may be employed.

Dental nurses wear a uniform or white coat and, when assisting the dentist, a protective mask and rubber gloves should always be worn during clinical procedures.

WORK ENVIRONMENT

Dental nurses work in dental surgeries, or in company surgeries, community health clinics, or dental or general hospitals. They may work alone with the dentist in a very small practice, or may be part of a much larger team. They work with people from a variety of different backgrounds, and in community health centres their work is mainly with children. The environment is always clean and well lit, and many dentists make their surgeries even more attractive places, with music playing to help patients feel relaxed. Much of the work is done standing up, which can be physically tiring.

SKILLS AND INTERESTS

Dental nurses need a warm, friendly, willing personality and a liking for people. They need to be understanding and sympathetic, since many people are very anxious about visits to the dentist. They need to be able to communicate clearly, both verbally and in writing. A sense of humour is an asset, along with the ability to remain calm under pressure.

An interest in health, oral hygiene, and biology is important. Dental nurses should be fit and healthy since the work can involve standing for long periods. They should be clean and neat with healthy-looking teeth. Practical ability, or manual dexterity, is important in order to handle instruments and prepare fillings.

Dental nurses need to be well organized and methodical to cope with the administrative aspects of the work.

ENTRY REQUIREMENTS

Many dentists in general practice are willing to train dental nurses who do not have any experience and may not have any academic qualifications. A good general education is normally requested, and GCSE/S grade qualifications, perhaps in English and biology, would be an asset. There are no formal entry requirements for the National Certificate of Dental Nurses examination.

Entry requirements for the full-time course for dental nurses vary according to the dental hospital, school or college attended. Between two and four GCSEs/S grades (A–C/1–3) are normally requested at present, preferably including English language and biology or human biology, although personal qualities and a suitability for the work are also important. The minimum age for entry varies between dental schools, but is usually 16 or 17 years. Applicants should be physically fit.

TRAINING

Many dental nurses train on the job within a general dental practice, where they receive instruction from the dentist. It is advisable for young people training in this way to study for the National Certificate for Dental Nurses, available on a part-time evening basis at colleges of further education.

An alternative method of training is to take a full-time, national certificate, one- or two-year course for dental nurses at a dental school or hospital, or college of further education for which a salary at the appropriate rate is paid. The course combines practical work with theory, and includes lectures, small group seminars, and individual tuition. A wide variety of relevant topics are studied, including anatomy and physiology, the use of dental instruments and materials, prevention of cross-infection and sterilization, the use and storage of drugs, anaesthesia and sedation, elementary orthodontics, oral surgery, the care of patients, the causes of decay and gum disease, the maintenance of dental records and charting, the preparation of fillings, general principles of dental radiography, dental health, law and health safety. The final examination consists of a written paper, an oral examination, and practical tests.

LATE ENTRY

There is no upper age limit for the full-time and part-time national certificate courses for dental nurses (as described in TRAINING). Some dental schools expect mature candidates to possess the normal academic entry requirements, whilst others may offer an entrance test to applicants over the age of 23 years who do not hold formal qualifications. The test examines written communication skills and ability in English. Evidence of practical ability is assessed at interview, along with a suitable personality for the work. As an alternative to the full-time college course, mature students may find employers willing to train them on-the-job, providing they are prepared to accept the low salaries generally offered during training.

OPPORTUNITIES

There are about 25,000 dental nurses in the UK. Job prospects are good in most areas of the country, with a shortage of experienced staff in some areas, such as the South East of England. Dental nurses work in several areas: in general practice, both private and NHS, or a combination of the two; in dental hospitals and the dental departments of some general hospitals; in community dental services; in the Royal Navy, Army and RAF; and in private industry and commerce.

Opportunities for working abroad are limited, although possibilities exist, particularly in the Middle East.

Jobs may be advertised in the careers office, or Jobcentre, as well as in local newspapers.

PAY AND CONDITIONS

The British Dental Association (BDA) and the British Association of Dental Nurses (BADN) make annual recommendations on minimum pay for dental nurses and take account of years of experience and whether a nurse is registered. From 1 April 1998 they recommend that dental nurses should not be paid less than the following:

Unregistered–£2.85 per hour in the first year rising to £4.95 per hour after eight year's experience.

Registered–£4.45 per hour after three years rising to £5.65 per hour after eight year's experience.

They also recommend a loyalty bonus of £0.15 per hour after five years service with the same practice, and £0.40 per hour and an extra week's holiday after ten years service; and an additional payment of up to £0.65 per hour for those who hold post-qualification certificates in oral health education, radiography or simple sedation, according to the extent that the extra qualifications are used in the practice. .

DENTISTRY: JAF

For nurses who are qualified but not registered, the unregistered rates apply. The BDA and BADN encourage all nurses to qualify and register. Nurses can register on the basis of :
- The national Examining Board for Dental Nurses National Certificate;
- The BTEC National Certificate in Science (Dental Assisting);
- A Certificate of Proficiency from a dental hospital recognised by the Association of Dental Hospitals of the UK, following a full-time course of at least one year;
- The SQA National Certificate in Dental Surgery Assisting; or other equivalent qualifications acceptable to the Registration committee of the Voluntary National Register for Dental Nurses. (See TRAINING above).

However these are recommendations only, not statutory rates, and apply to basic working hours (excluding lunch breaks). It is for nurses and practices to agree basic hours per week and a way of paying for any work outside those hours.

Dental nurses in general practice rarely work a 9am to 5pm day. They may start at 8am or 8.30am and finish at 5.30pm, or later. Many dentists work one or more late nights, and some Saturday mornings, when the dental nurse is also expected to work, although in a large practice these duties may be shared on a rota basis. During busy periods they may work through lunch hours. The hours are more regular in a community health centre, perhaps 8.30am to 4.30pm, or 9am to 5pm. Hospital work may involve working unsocial hours. Part-time work is sometimes possible.

PROSPECTS

There is no set pattern of promotion for dental nurses within general practice. However, in larger practices there may be scope for more senior dental nurses to train new recruits, or to move into practice management and administration, after management and financial training.

In dental hospitals and in community dental services, career progression is more obvious. After one or two years' training within a hospital, student dental nurses become qualified dental nurses. After three years' experience they can then become senior dental nurses, with responsibility perhaps for a specialized department within the hospital. Dental nurses can also progress by taking various other qualifications, such as specialist certificates in oral health education, dental radiography and conscious sedation, which may enhance promotion prospects.

Within hospitals there is also the possibility of moving into teaching, after taking the Further and Adult Education Adult Teacher's Certificate. Most dental hospitals have posts for a principal of a school for dental nurses.

Many dental nurses undertake further training to become dental hygienists, which is possible after two years' experience. There is also a combined course in dental hygiene and dental therapy at the Dental Auxiliary School of the London Hospital Medical College, for which experienced dental nurses may apply.

RELATED OCCUPATIONS

Dental hygienist, dental therapist, dental technician, nurse, nursing auxiliary/health care assistant, receptionist, medical secretary.

FURTHER INFORMATION

British Association of Dental Nurses (BADN), 11 Pharos Street, Fleetwood, Lancashire FY7 6BG, 01253 778631 (please include sae)

National Examining Board For Dental Nurses, 110 London Street, Fleetwood, Lancashire FY7 6EU, 01253 778417

FURTHER READING

In the careers library classified under JAF.

3. DENTAL HYGIENIST (JAF)

THE WORK

Dental hygienists are involved in preventing tooth decay and gum disease, enabling people to keep their own teeth in a healthy condition for as long as possible. They work under the direction of dentists, who devise and prescribe treatment plans.

Dental hygienists scale, clean, and polish teeth, remove stains, and apply fluorides and fissure sealants to reduce decay and deterioration, using a variety of special instruments. Hygienists perform post-operative hygiene work on the mouth after gum surgery, and in hospitals they look after patients' mouths before and after oral surgery of any kind. In a small minority of cases they are assisted by a dental nurse. They do not do fillings or remove teeth.

Preventive dentistry is an important part of dental hygienists' work. They advise adults and children on the proper care of teeth and gums. Detailed instruction is given on the correct use of toothbrushes and how to remove plaque, along with advice on diet. Hygienists may talk to groups of children or adults in schools, clinics, and community centres, as well as giving advice to individual patients. One of the most satisfying aspects of the work is when patients follow the advice of their dental hygienist and thus improve the condition of their teeth, mouth, and gums. Hygienists often see the direct results of their work.

WORK ENVIRONMENT

Dental hygienists work in dental surgeries, as well as visiting clinics and community centres. They may travel to two or three places in the course of a week, although about half of dental hygienists are employed in one place. Hygienists work with people of all ages. Their work environment is clean and well lit. Hygienists wear protective clothing, such as a white coat, a mask and gloves to reduce the risk of infection.

SKILLS AND INTERESTS

Dental hygienists need good communication skills to explain to patients, both individually and in groups, about the importance of caring for the mouth and teeth. The hygienist must gain the confidence and co-operation of patients. Dental hygienists also need to establish a good working relationship with the dentist. They need good eyesight and concentration, along with practical ability. Hygienists need an ability and interest in science, whilst a sense of humour helps to put anxious patients at their ease. Dental hygienists should also be well-presented, clean, and tidy.

DENTISTRY: JAF

ENTRY REQUIREMENTS

Applicants need a minimum of two years' experience as a dental nurse plus a recognized Certificate in Dental Nursing. Five GSCEs/S grades (A–C/1–3) are normally required, including English language and either biology or human biology; some schools also ask for two A levels. A suitable personality for dental hygiene work is also necessary. Applicants should normally be at least 20 years old. Student dental hygienists are not paid a salary, but can apply for bursaries from the Department of Health.

TRAINING

Full-time courses in dental hygiene, leading to the examination for the Diploma in Dental Hygiene, last two years and are offered at most dental schools throughout the UK.

During the first part of the training, students supplement their theoretical training with practical experience on 'phantom heads'. The syllabus is very broad, and includes the following subjects: general histology, which is the study of the cells and tissues of the body; dental histology; general anatomy and physiology – the study of the body and its functions; first aid; diet and nutrition; microbiology and sterilization; oral pathology – the study of diseases of the mouth, especially tooth and gum disease; dental radiography; the study of tooth form; preventive dentistry; dental health education; and operative techniques such as scaling, polishing, and applying fissure sealants.

Tests are normally given weekly during the course, and the final examinations comprise written papers, a practical test, and an oral examination. Once the Diploma in Dental Hygiene has been obtained, dental hygienists may become enrolled dental hygienists by having their name entered in the roll of dental hygienists kept by the General Dental Council. Dental hygienists may not practise in the United Kingdom unless they are enrolled.

Some hygienists take the Certificate in Oral Health Education awarded by the University of Nottingham. Other refresher courses are available as well. It is also possible to take a joint course in dental hygiene and dental therapy, at the Dental Auxiliary School of the London Hospital Medical College, which lasts for two years.

LATE ENTRY

The majority of applicants for dental hygiene training are about 21 years old, although there is no upper age limit. Dental hygiene is a relatively new profession, with most staff having qualified since 1970. Most dental hygienists are currently under 40 years of age. Dental schools do not normally relax entry requirements for mature candidates.

OPPORTUNITIES

Preventive dentistry is increasingly important in the UK, with dental hygienists playing a vital role. Demand for dental hygienists varies in different parts of the UK, particularly in Scotland and Wales; it can therefore be difficult to find work readily. At present there are about 3,000 dental hygienists in the UK.

Dental hygienists may find work in the following areas:

General dental practice: about 85% of hygienists spend at least part of their working week in general practice.

Community dental services include working with pregnant women, and disabled and elderly people, as well as children.

Hospital services: hygienists may work in a specialized department of a dental hospital, or in the dental department of a general hospital.

Teaching and research employs a few hygienists.

Armed Forces: dental hygienists are normally trained by the branch they have joined. Occasionally the Army has spare places on its courses; civilians may take up the places, although they have to pay their own course fees.

Occupational dental practice: hygienists occasionally work in the dental surgery of a company. Toothpaste manufacturers sometimes employ dental hygienists to take part in exhibitions, displays etc.

Outside general practice the majority of dental hygienists are employed in hospital or community service. There are some opportunities overseas, eg in continental Europe and the Middle East.

PAY AND CONDITIONS

Salaries vary according to whether hygienists work in general practice, in hospitals or in the community service.

In general practice, they are paid by the dentist; salaries are not agreed by the NHS. It is up to individual hygienists to negotiate their salaries with their employers. The British Dental Hygienists' Association (BDHA) recommended rate starts at £12,756 and rises to £18,025. Salaries are reviewed annually.

Dental services have become increasingly flexible. It may be possible to work an adjusted working day, or there may be the opportunity to work part-time.

Most hygienists in general practice work surgery hours, which may start between 8.30am and 9am, and finish between 5.30pm and 6pm. They may be required to work late on one or more evenings, and sometimes on Saturday mornings. Dental hygienists who work in hospitals may have to be on call at night. Those in the community dental service work more-regular 9-to-5 hours.

PROSPECTS

There is no clear career path for dental hygienists within general dental practice. Within a dental school or hospital there is the possibility of becoming a tutor once a Further and Adult Education Adult Teacher's Certificate has been obtained. Prospects are improved if dental hygienists take further qualifications, such as the Certificate in Oral Health Education of the University of Nottingham. This could possibly lead to posts in dental health education within the community dental service. Candidates with joint qualifications in dental hygiene and dental therapy will find they are sought after by employers.

RELATED OCCUPATIONS

Dental nurse, dental therapist, nurse, health visitor, teacher.

FURTHER INFORMATION

The British Dental Hygienists' Association*, 13 The Ridge, Yatton, Avon BS49 4DQ, 01934 876389 (please include sae)

DENTISTRY: JAF

Assistant Director, Army Dental Service*, AMD 6, Keogh Barracks, Ash Vale, Aldershot, Hampshire GU12 5RR, 01252 340321

FURTHER READING

Leaflets/booklets are available from the addresses marked*.

In the careers library classified under JAF.

4. DENTAL TECHNICIAN (JAF)

THE WORK

Dental technicians make dental appliances from prescriptions given to them by dental surgeons. Using a variety of traditional and more modern materials, technicians use several techniques in their work that demand a high level of skill. These include plaster casting, wax carving, metal casting, moulding plastic, bending wire, sand-blasting, grinding and polishing, involving the use of specially designed equipment. Dental technicians work in the following areas:

Prosthodontics. Dental technicians make dentures, which can be removed from the mouth, in plastic and cast metal alloys. Either complete or partial dentures may be made, according to the needs of the patient. Technicians have to understand exactly what the dentist requires in order to make a comfortable and visually pleasing denture. They must also ensure that a partial denture does not harm the health of any remaining natural teeth.

Various materials are used for making dentures, including plaster, wax, acrylic, cobalt chrome, stainless steel and precious metals.

Crowns and bridges. Dental technicians help dentists in their restorative work by making crowns and bridges, which are permanently fitted into the mouth. Crowns or caps are made in acrylic, porcelain or metal, and are cemented to the prepared roots of remaining natural teeth. Bridges are made in a similar way, but fit into gaps in the dentition. Plaster, wax, acrylic, porcelain, metal alloys and precious metals are used to make crowns and bridges.

Orthodontic appliances. Orthodontists and dental surgeons in general practice rely upon dental technicians to make orthodontic appliances (braces – special clasps and springs) that help to straighten a patient's teeth. Plaster of Paris, stainless steel wire and tape, and acrylic resins are all used to make orthodontic appliances.

Maxillo-facial surgery. Dental technicians working mainly in hospitals help dental and oral surgeons in their work with patients who have suffered facial or jaw injury or illness, or who have been born with an abnormal or deformed face. They make artificial parts of the face, known as prostheses. These are skilfully modelled in plastic, and fitted to the patient's face. The prostheses help to improve patients' appearance, as well as enabling them to eat and speak. Dental technicians play a crucial part in the recovery of these patients, and have a vital role in the dental team. Technicians also make splints for patients with broken jaw bones so that the oral surgeon can perform urgent operations.

In addition to practical work, dental technicians are sometimes involved in administrative and clerical tasks, particularly if they are self-employed.

WORK ENVIRONMENT

Whatever branch of dental technology they are employed in, dental technicians work in laboratories. They may work alone (particularly if they are self-employed), with one or two other people, or as part of a larger team. In hospitals, there is the greatest opportunity for contact with other people, since the technician will have direct contact with dental and oral surgeons. Dental technicians do not usually have contact with patients. The work is mainly performed whilst sitting down.

SKILLS AND INTERESTS

Dental technicians are involved in highly skilled craftwork, and therefore need to be practical and good with their hands, preferably with an interest and ability in art. A good eye for detail, along with well developed colour perception, is also required. Dental technicians need good concentration to cope with the often painstaking work. An interest and ability in science is also important, as they will be expected to follow and interpret detailed scientific instructions.

ENTRY REQUIREMENTS

Good eyesight (aided or unaided) is essential, along with good colour vision for some aspects of the work. The initial qualification the dental technician should aim for is the BTEC/SQA National Diploma/Certificate in Science (Dental Technology).

Candidates should possess either a BTEC/SQA First Certificate/Diploma in Science or Engineering; or four GCSEs/S grades (A–C/1–3), to include maths and a science, or Intermediate GNVQ/GSVQ Level II in Science.

For dental technician trainees in hospitals entrance requirements may vary. Some ask for four GCSEs/S grades (A–C/1–3), in English, maths, physics and biology, or Intermediate GNVQ/GSVQ Level II in Science.

Occasionally, other qualifications or experience may be acceptable as alternatives, particularly for mature entrants over the age of 21 years or by Accreditation of Prior Experience and Learning.

Entry requirements for commercial laboratories vary, with many laboratories requesting four GCSEs/S grades (A–C/1–3) to enable candidates to study for the BTEC/SQA National Diploma/Certificate in Science (Dental Technology). It is now possible to take a BTEC First Certificate in Science with an option in dental technology, which leads on to the BTEC National Diploma. Entry requirements for the BTEC First Certificate are GCSEs grade E in a science, English and maths, although specific requirements may vary between colleges. Candidates may be accepted for apprenticeships with fewer qualifications if employers consider they have the ability to succeed as a dental technician with education and training.

TRAINING

There are three main ways of training to become a dental technician, all of which combine practical experience with theory work:

Paid training in a commercial dental laboratory or in a dental laboratory associated with a dental practice. Students train for five years, and normally attend college for one day and one evening a week to study for the BTEC/SQA National Diploma in Science (Dental Technology). The first two years of the training may be organized as part of a training opportunity for young people. Most dental technicians in Scotland (outside hospitals) train via this method, which includes day release. The SQA National Diploma in Science (Dental Technology) is normally studied on a day release or block release basis for four years.

The following subjects form part of the courses for the BTEC/SQA National Diploma/Certificate in Science (Dental Technology): dental anatomy, dental materials; basic laboratory techniques; complete denture prosthetics; dental materials technology; orthodontics; partial prosthetics and conservation, porcelain and metal bridges.

Students normally spend four days a week in the laboratory, and start by learning the more straightforward tasks, such as making 'trays' for impressions, and wax 'bite blocks'. They may then make repairs to dentures, before moving on to making dentures, crowns and bridges, and eventually more advanced work.

Full-time college course. The full-time courses for the BTEC National Diploma in Science (Dental Technology) last for three years, and include practical experience in a commercial or hospital dental laboratory as part of the training. Grants for full-time courses at this level are discretionary. The subjects covered are as above.

Higher training. After taking the BTEC/SQA National Diploma/Certificate in Science (Dental Technology), it is possible to take a BTEC/SQA higher national diploma or certificate, on a two-year day release basis, covering more advanced aspects of dental technology. Degree courses are also becoming available, following successful completion of the BTEC/SQA National Diploma/Certificate in Science (Dental Technology).

It is also possible to take advanced City and Guilds 7390 courses in dental ceramics, crown and bridge work, orthodontics, and maxillo-facial work. These are usually taken on a part-time evening basis.

Paid training within a hospital. Eight hospitals in the United Kingdom recruit student dental technicians for a training programme, which lasts up to four years, and includes block release for the BTEC National Diploma in Science (Dental Technology). Hospital trainees receive a salary whilst training.

LATE ENTRY

Some hospitals are reluctant to accept trainee dental technicians over the age of 30 years. Employers are often unwilling to train adults for a five-year apprenticeship, mainly because the wages of trainees are fairly low.

There may be specific training opportunities directed at adults available in some areas for this type of work. Candidates may have to satisfy certain conditions to be eligible. Contact your local Jobcentre, careers office or TEC/LEC for details.

Colleges may be prepared to relax entry requirements for mature students; contact individual colleges for more information. The Accreditation of Prior Experience and Learning may provide exemption of units/modules of the programme of study.

OPPORTUNITIES

Dental technicians work in the following four main areas, where they may perform specialist or general work:

Commercial dental laboratories – dental technicians provide a variety of services to dentists, mainly to those working in general practice. The dentist may be based at some distance from the laboratory, and the technician must interpret the dentist's prescription accurately. Commercial laboratories often undertake highly specialized work. Qualified and experienced dental technicians may be able to set up their own laboratory and become self-employed.

General practice – dental technicians may be employed on a dentist's premises to provide work for the dentists, usually of a fairly general nature.

Community dental service – dental technicians provide the necessary appliances for the work of community dentists – those working for the school dental service and in clinics. Much of the work involves supplying orthodontic braces.

Hospital work – involves maxillo-facial work as well as the more general work of a dental technician.

In total there are about 8,000 dental technicians working in the UK.

There are prospects for dental technicians to work abroad.

PAY AND CONDITIONS

NHS salaries are payable in hospitals. Student dental technicians earn from about £6,371 to £8,627. Trained dental technicians are paid on a salary scale of £10,821 to £13,693. Senior grade technicians earn from £14,242 and chief technicians from £17,326. Senior chief technicians earn from £21,079 to £24,660.

The National Joint Council negotiates minimum pay and conditions for qualified dental technicians following an agreed consolidating period working in commercial dental laboratories. The minimum rate is about £202 for a 39-hour week, or £202.09 if certain qualifications are held, such as the BTEC National Diploma in Science (Dental Technology). An extra £9.50 a week is payable to people registered with the Dental Technician Education and Training Advisory Board (DTETAB). Trainee dental technicians earn a percentage of the full rate, which ranges from 45% in the first year, to 75% in the fifth and final year of training. Dental technicians, particularly if self-employed, can earn higher salaries.

Within the NHS, dental technicians normally work approximately 37 hours, from 8.30am to 5pm, Monday to Friday. In commercial laboratories a 39-hour week is worked, although there may be the opportunity to work paid overtime. Technicians employed in maxillo-facial work may work irregular hours with occasional on-call duties. There is the opportunity to work part-time.

PROSPECTS

Within the NHS there is a clear promotional ladder. After three years' training and a consolidation year a student becomes a qualified dental technician. Promotion to senior grade technician may be possible after two years in a basic grade post. Further prospects are to become a chief dental technician in charge of either a laboratory or a section of a larger laboratory. The senior chief dental technician may be in charge of a large laboratory or group of laboratories, and it is unlikely that anyone would reach this level until the latter part of their career. There are often many more

DENTISTRY: JAF

applicants than vacant posts at the higher levels, and candidates are expected to have gained higher qualifications during their career.

Prospects within commercial dental laboratories are good, and experienced dental technicians may move on to become quality controllers, or section or laboratory managers. It may also be possible to move into dental research, or dental supply company employment.

RELATED OCCUPATIONS

Laboratory technician, orthotist/prosthetist, medical physics technician, medical technical officer, dental nurse.

FURTHER INFORMATION

Dental Technician Education and Training Advisory Board (DTETAB)*, Partners In Practice, 5 Oxford Court, St James Road, Brackley, Northants NN13 7XY, 01280 702600

Dental Laboratories Association Ltd, 92-94 North Sherwood Street, Nottingham, NG1 4EE, 0115 948 2400, www.derweb.ac.uk/dla

FURTHER READING

Leaflets/booklets are available from the address marked*.
In the careers library classified under JAF.

PHARMACY WORK: JAG

1. PHARMACIST CLCI:JAG
2. PHARMACY TECHNICIAN CLCI:JAG

BACKGROUND INFORMATION

Pharmacy is a scientific profession concerned with the development of medicines, their preparation, dispensing and eventual use. There are three main areas of work available to qualified pharmacists: community (or retail) pharmacy, hospital pharmacy, and industrial pharmacy.

Pharmacists wishing to practise must be registered with the Royal Pharmaceutical Society of Great Britain, which has approximately 41,000 members.

1. PHARMACIST (JAG)

THE WORK

Community pharmacist

Community or retail pharmacy is the largest branch of the profession and involves a qualified pharmacist working in a retail environment.

The main duties of a community pharmacist are to prepare and dispense medicines on prescription to the general public, although there is now a general trend towards prepackaged and prepared products. Prescriptions, dosages and labels must be checked for legality and accuracy. The pharmacist must also check for interactions among prescribed medicines.

A pharmacist gives advice to customers on how to use prescribed medicines and ensures that customers realize when prescriptions should not be taken in conjunction with alcohol or with other medication. They also provide information on the sale of over-the-counter medicines and general health care issues. If a patient's condition is serious, then a pharmacist may need to refer them to a doctor or dentist.

The community pharmacist is in frequent contact with the public. However, they also oversee stock control, stock rotation and ordering. Records must be maintained, such as the Poisons Register, and use is increasingly made of computer technology. Pharmacists normally undertake the supervision and training of assistants and technicians. It is unlawful for a pharmacy to operate without the presence of a qualified pharmacist.

A community pharmacist is also likely to be a business manager and must run a pharmacy efficiently and profitably. Most sell a wide range of products, including toiletries, cosmetics and photographic materials. The work therefore includes financial management, merchandising and responsibility for staff and premises.

Hospital pharmacist

Hospital pharmacists prepare and dispense medicines, special feeding solutions and diagnostic agents. They are involved in stock control, ordering, labelling and financial management. Computer technology assists the pharmacist with administration.

In many hospitals, the pharmacist meets patients during ward rounds to discuss the supply and form of appropriate medicines, in addition to consulting with doctors, nurses and other hospital staff.

Newly qualified staff join the NHS at basic grade A under the supervision of more experienced staff. After this transitional period, pharmacists may choose to specialize, for example, in radiopharmacy (preparing radioactive substances for administration to patients, in collaboration with radiologists).

Senior pharmacists may also supervise the training of pre-registration trainees and junior pharmacists.

Industrial pharmacist

Industrial pharmacists are concerned with researching and developing pharmaceutical products. There are many different areas in which an industrial pharmacist can specialize. One field is clinical trials, where drugs are tested for safety and effectiveness with the co-operation of volunteers and patients. Another branch is production, where medicines and drugs are manufactured, packed, stored and delivered. Other areas are research and development, information, marketing and quality assurance.

WORK ENVIRONMENT

Community pharmacists employed in large pharmacies work in a team of pharmacists, technicians and sales staff. In smaller community outlets, the pharmacist works with only one or two other staff. They may travel locally, eg to visit patients in their homes.

Hospital pharmacists work in health centres or hospital laboratories or dispensaries. They work as part of a team that includes doctors, nurses, technicians and many others. In addition to providing inpatients and outpatients with medicines, they may visit patients on the wards and, in some cases, residents in nursing homes and patients at health centre clinics.

Industrial pharmacists are normally based in a laboratory, although some are more office-based and others travel frequently to meet customers.

Pharmacists operate in clean and sometimes sterile conditions. Protective clothing may be necessary.

SKILLS AND INTERESTS

All pharmacists must have an interest in science and medicine, and the ability to study a scientific subject to degree level. The ability to work carefully and accurately is essential. Pharmacists should be able to work methodically and think logically when carrying out laboratory tasks and ordering supplies. It is important that a pharmacist is able to co-operate with others as part of a team. Pharmacists dealing with the public or patients must have a caring and sympathetic manner, a friendly personality and excellent communication skills.

Pharmacists with staff responsibility must have effective management skills and the ability to supervise and delegate work to junior staff. Pharmacists may also have to provide training for other staff.

Those working in the retail sector require merchandising, selling and financial management skills in order to run a successful business.

ENTRY REQUIREMENTS

Pharmacists must have a degree in pharmacy from an approved school of pharmacy.

Minimum requirements for entry to pharmacy degree courses are three A levels/four H grades plus five GCSEs/S grades (A–C/1–3), including English language and maths. A level/H grade chemistry is essential and most

PHARMACY WORK: JAG

universities usually require two A levels/H grades from maths, a biological science and physics. Some universities accept relevant BTEC/SQA national awards and Advanced GNVQ/GSVQ Level III, eg in science, but usually require an additional qualification, such as A level/H grade chemistry.

Postgraduate courses

Many of those working in hospital or industrial posts as pharmacists have studied for postgraduate qualifications. Candidates normally require a first- or second-class degree in pharmacy, or a related discipline, to be considered for entry to a higher degree programme.

TRAINING

Pharmacists must be registered with the Royal Pharmaceutical Society of Great Britain to practise in retail and hospital. Registration is available only to those who have obtained a degree in pharmacy from an approved school of pharmacy, satisfactorily completed a one-year period of pre-registration training in a pharmacy, and passed the Society's registration examination. Both the pharmacy and the tutor appointed to supervise the graduate must be approved by the Royal Pharmaceutical Society for training purposes.

Degree courses

Four-year degree courses are available at the following universities: Robert Gordon (Aberdeen), Aston, Bath, The Queen's University of Belfast, Bradford, Brighton, De Montfort (Leicester), Liverpool John Moores, King's College London, School of Pharmacy (London), Manchester, Nottingham, Portsmouth, Strathclyde, Sunderland and University of Wales, Cardiff.

The University of Bradford also offers a five-year sandwich course which incorporates two six-month blocks of professional training. This enables the student simultaneously to graduate and register as a pharmacist.

Courses include pharmaceutical chemistry (study of the origins and chemistry of drugs); pharmaceutics (the formulation and preparation of medicines); pharmacology (the study of the actions and uses of drugs); and pharmacy practice, which covers dispensing, communication and counselling skills, and the legal aspects of pharmacy practice. Courses also include clinical experience, sometimes in the form of accompanying hospital consultants on ward rounds and observing general medical practitioners at work.

Postgraduate courses are offered at many universities including: Robert Gordon (Aberdeen), Aston, Bath, The Queen's University of Belfast, Bradford, Brighton, Derby, Keele, Leeds, De Montfort (Leicester), Liverpool John Moores, King's College London, School of Pharmacy (London), Manchester, Nottingham, Portsmouth, Strathclyde, Sunderland and University of Wales, Cardiff. Courses are either full-time, usually for one year, or part-time for one to five years, or through distance learning.

LATE ENTRY

There are no upper age limits for training or entry to work. All applicants follow the training route described in TRAINING. Mature applicants may be accepted on to a degree course without the normal academic requirements, although candidates must be able to demonstrate that they are capable of academic study at this level. Applicants may achieve this by successful completion of a science Access course. Details are available from individual institutions.

OPPORTUNITIES

There are numerous opportunities for qualified pharmacists. However, the great majority enter community or hospital pharmacy.

Pharmacies vary in size, and a community pharmacist may be the owner of a small pharmacy or may work for one of the high street chains. There are excellent opportunities for promotion within the larger companies.

Hospital pharmacists can work within the National Health Service, in private hospitals and in health centres. In hospitals, qualified pharmacists enter at a basic grade and diversify or specialize after they have gained some experience. For those who want temporary work, locums are employed in both hospital and community pharmacies.

In the pharmaceutical industry there are a number of varied posts available to qualified pharmacists. Pharmacists are usually employed in clinical trials, production and quality assurance, or research and development. There are also opportunities available in chemical plants producing such items as fertilisers. Pharmacists may also find work in establishments that specialize in agricultural and veterinary products, animal medicines and crop protection products.

Opportunities for advancement in the pharmaceutical industry are considerable. Higher management positions are available to pharmacists from all branches of industry.

Information about vacancies is available from *The Pharmaceutical Journal, New Scientist* and the local and national press.

PAY AND CONDITIONS

A pre-registration pharmacist working in the NHS can expect a starting salary of £8,948. On qualifying, Grade A pharmacists can expect to earn £14,072. A senior pharmacist working at a regional level could earn over £40,000. Terms and conditions of service may differ for pharmacists working in NHS trust hospitals.

There is a wide range of salaries for community pharmacists. A pre-registration pharmacist working in a high street pharmacy could expect a salary of approximately £9,000. Employed pharmacists usually receive salaries between £19,000 and £30,000, although those with senior positions in the large chains may receive far higher salaries. Many of the large high street chains also offer staff discounts, pensions schemes and private health insurance. The income of those who are self-employed varies considerably.

Industrial pharmacists start at around £18,000 often exceeding £60,000 in a senior management position.

Community pharmacists usually work shop hours – 9am to 5.30pm or 6pm for five or six days a week. The use of a rota system is common in pharmacies. Some stores are open for late evening dispensing until 10pm and, in major cities, a few are open all night. A few hospital pharmacists work on a shift system but most usually work from 9am to 5pm. Industrial pharmacists normally work regular hours from Monday to Friday.

PROSPECTS

Newly qualified pharmacists enter employment at a basic level, but some high street pharmacy companies have in-house training schemes, which enable employees to move to a managerial level quickly. Promotion prospects are excellent in larger pharmacies and may lead to regional management. Some pharmacists may wish to run their own establishments, although this requires capital.

Pharmacists working in a hospital pharmacy may be able to specialize in a particular clinical area or in database management or other technical services. Career progression can also lead to district or regional management within a health authority or the NHS Executive.

Industrial pharmacists may move into general or commercial managerial positions, in personnel, or marketing and sales, within or outside the pharmaceutical industry.

RELATED OCCUPATIONS

Dentist, doctor, pharmacologist, biochemist, chemist.

FURTHER INFORMATION AND READING

Please see article 2. PHARMACY TECHNICIAN.

2. PHARMACY TECHNICIAN (JAG)

THE WORK

Community (retail) pharmacy technicians assist qualified pharmacists with their work in retail outlets. They help pharmacists with labelling and dispensing drugs and issuing prepackaged prescriptions. Prescriptions received must be checked for legality, accuracy, and the absence of errors or forgery. Technicians may need to make simple dilutions or count the prescribed number of tablets. It is important that technicians are familiar with the range of different drugs and brand names for similar products and arrangements for emergency supply of drugs.

An important task of the technician is record keeping. Individual records of patient's prescriptions are usually stored on a computer. A community pharmacy technician also helps the pharmacist in a range of other duties such as stock checking and ordering.

Technicians may have to sell over-the-counter medicines and other items stocked by the chemist, such as cosmetics, toiletries, baby food and photographic supplies. Customers may seek advice and information on the use of medicines or general health issues, and the pharmacy technician must know when to refer the customer to the pharmacist or other health care professional.

Hospital pharmacy technicians assist the hospital pharmacist. The majority of work involves dispensing drugs and medicines under close supervision by hospital staff. Hospital technicians also manufacture individual medicines. They ensure that each hospital department and ward has sufficient supplies and the correct dosages for patients. Technicians also check stock levels and ensure that the correct orders are made to the pharmaceutical companies. These orders are often made with the use of a computer.

Senior technicians can specialize, eg in analytical control for checking the quality of hospital medicines, or in the preparation of radioactive materials, under the supervision of a pharmacist.

Industrial pharmacy technicians work as chemical or laboratory technicians and assist the pharmacists who have specialized in a certain field, such as research and development, clinical trials or production. The work may involve setting up scientific tests of medicines to ensure their safety and effectiveness before they go to the production and manufacturing stage. They maintain accurate records of results.

WORK ENVIRONMENT

Please see article 1. PHARMACIST.

SKILLS AND INTERESTS

Technicians should have an interest in medicine, science and technical subjects. They need a basic understanding of the contents and use of common medicines. They should be accurate and meticulous when carrying out practical work. An understanding is required of the basic physiology of the body, together with the action and uses of drugs. As much of the work is routine, a high level of concentration is required, and they must be methodical and logical. It is important that a pharmacy technician is able to operate with other colleagues and work as part of a team.

Technicians employed in the retail sector should be friendly, patient and sympathetic when they deal with patients who may be worried about their condition, or seeking advice about their medication. They may also require sales ability, as a wide variety of products are sold in community pharmacies.

ENTRY REQUIREMENTS

There is no minimum requirement for entry. Many employers, however, follow the recommendation of The National Pharmaceutical Association (NPA) that entrants have some GCSEs/S grades, including a science subject at grade A–C/1–3. There are also minimum entry requirements for some courses. Employers seeking to send trainees on such courses are likely to require applicants to have these qualifications.

BTEC National Certificate in Science (Pharmaceutical). The usual entry requirement is four GCSEs/S grades (A–C/1–3) but applicants in relevant work may be accepted without these qualifications.

SQA National Certificate in Pharmaceutical Sciences. Minimum entry requirements range from a good standard of general education to four S grades (1–3), including English and a science, with maths preferred.

BTEC Higher National Certificate in Science (Pharmaceutical) and SQA Higher National Certificate in Pharmaceutical Sciences. Courses usually require either a pass in the BTEC/SQA National Certificate or one A level/two H grades plus four GCSEs/S grades (A–C/1–3).

NVQs/SVQs. There is no minimum entry requirement for NVQ/SVQs. The NPA recommends that a student working towards NVQ/SVQ in Pharmacy Services at Level 3 should be employed for at least 20 hours a week in the dispensary of a pharmacy.

TRAINING

Few pharmacy technicians train full-time before entry to work but SQA National Certificate modules for pharmacy technicians are offered full-time for one year by Edinburgh's Telford College, James Watt College of Further and Higher Education and Stow College, Glasgow.

PHARMACY WORK: JAG

All trainee technicians receive on-the-job training from their employer. Many hospitals run training sessions for technicians on a regular basis. All pharmacy technicians may attend college part-time or study through distance learning to work towards a qualification.

BTEC National Certificate in Science (Pharmaceutical). Courses include human physiology, pharmaceutical microbiology, pharmaceutics and pharmacy law, actions and uses of drugs, pharmacology and therapeutics. Courses are currently offered at over 30 colleges for two or three years on a day release basis.

SQA National Certificate in Pharmaceutical Sciences. This covers similar subjects to the BTEC award. The two-year part-time day release course is offered at Aberdeen College, Edinburgh's Telford College, James Watt College of Further and Higher Education and Stow College, Glasgow.

NVQ/SVQ Level 3 Pharmacy Services. The introduction of this NVQ/SVQ may lead to some colleges offering NVQ/SVQ courses rather than the BTEC or SQA national certificate. Others may continue with their national certificate courses and enable students to use the underpinning knowledge and understanding required to help them to achieve the NVQ/SVQ in Pharmacy Services at Level 3.

The National Pharmaceutical Association has a distance learning course that enables students to gain the essential knowledge required for the NVQ in Pharmacy Services at Level 3.

BTEC Higher National Certificate in Science (Pharmaceutical) and SQA Higher National Certificate in Pharmaceutical Sciences. Courses last for two years on a day release basis. They are designed mainly for students who have completed BTEC/SQA national award courses. They aim to train candidates for senior and chief pharmacy technician positions.

LATE ENTRY

There is no upper age limit for entry to this work and mature entrants tend to be successful pharmacy technicians. Opportunities for late entry and training, though, depend on the attitude of individual employers.

OPPORTUNITIES

There is a steady demand for pharmacy technicians. Many work for the high street chains. Self-employed community pharmacists may employ one or two pharmacy technicians in their dispensary.

Hospital pharmacy technicians can work within the National Health Service, in private hospitals and in health centres. There is a continuous demand for all levels of hospital technicians.

PAY AND CONDITIONS

The salaries of community pharmacy technicians can vary depending on the size of the pharmacy they are working in. Technicians in the retail sector follow usual shop hours – 9.30am to 5.30pm or 6pm, five or six days a week on a rota system. Part-time work and Saturday jobs are offered by some pharmacies.

The average salary of a pharmacy technician working in a hospital is approximately £8,600 rising to £13,500. With two or three years' experience, this salary could rise to £15,500. Most hospital pharmacies operate shift and rota systems. In some hospitals part-time work may be available.

The salaries of industrial pharmacy technicians vary, depending on which field they are working in, but the hours worked would be similar to office hours.

PROSPECTS

Pharmacy technicians are unable to pursue a career as a pharmacist without successfully completing the relevant degree course and the compulsory pre-registration training period (see article 1. PHARMACIST).

Technicians in a large community pharmacy may be able to work in management or specialize in marketing or sales. Technicians employed in hospitals must complete a training programme and have appropriate experience to be considered for promotion to a higher grade of senior technician. (In NHS hospitals there are five grades of technicians.) In some hospitals there are chances for technicians to specialize in areas such as quality control – analysing the medicines that are dispensed – and radiopharmacy – acquiring expertise in the handling of radioactive materials.

There are numerous fields of specialization available in the pharmaceutical industry, such as research and production.

RELATED OCCUPATIONS

Laboratory technician, medical laboratory technician, medical technical officer, pharmacist.

FURTHER INFORMATION

The Association of Pharmacy Technicians, 15 Southerngate Way, New Cross, London SE14 6DN

The Association of The British Pharmaceutical Industry, 12 Whitehall, London SW1A 2DY, 0171 930 3477

Health Service Careers*, PO Box 204, London SE99 7UW, 0171 972 2000

The National Pharmaceutical Association*, Mallinson House, 38-42 St Peter's Street, St Albans, Hertfordshire AL1 3NP, (please enclose sae), 01727 832161

The Royal Pharmaceutical Society of Great Britain*, Education Division, 1 Lambeth High Street, London SE1 7JN, 0171 735 9141 (please include sae)

FURTHER READING

Leaflets/booklets are available from the addresses marked*.

Working in Hospitals – COIC

Careers in Medicine, Dentistry and Mental Health – Kogan Page

In the careers library classified under JAG.

OPHTHALMICS: JAL

1. **OPTOMETRIST/OPHTHALMIC OPTICIAN CLCI:JAL**
2. **DISPENSING OPTICIAN CLCI:JAL**
3. **ORTHOPTIST CLCI:JAL**

BACKGROUND INFORMATION

Optometrists (also known as ophthalmic opticians) examine eyes and prescribe and dispense optical aids. Dispensing opticians supply optical aids but are not qualified to examine eyes and prescribe. Orthoptists investigate and treat vision defects and abnormal eye movements such as squints. Optometrists must register with the General Optical Council, as do dispensing opticians in certain circumstances. Regulations on spectacle sales have been relaxed, but it is still illegal for unregistered vendors to examine eyes, supply contact lenses, or supply spectacles to children and those who are registered blind or partially sighted.

1. OPTOMETRIST/OPHTHALMIC OPTICIAN (JAL)

THE WORK

Optometrists, when examining a patient, determine the reason for the visit, the symptoms, history and visual needs of the patient, their present state of health and any current or past medication. They also establish whether the patient is a driver, their sports, hobbies etc.

Optometrists have a series of tests available for examining the eyes: objective – that do not need the patient's input, such as retinoscopy (which determines the optical status of the eyes); and subjective – where the patient answers questions about how they see test objects. By combining the results of the various tests, the optometrist prescribes lenses to correct any optical errors.

They may also carry out other tests, such as colour vision tests, tonometry (to measure the pressure in the eyes), or visual field plots (to ensure the eyes are not suffering from glaucoma, neurological or other pathology affecting the visual field).

Optometrists examine the inside of the eye with an ophthalmoscope to see if there are indications of disease or injury. A slit-lamp biomicroscope is used to reveal scratches and scars on the surface of the eye, to help with the prescription of contact lenses, and for internal examination, using supplementary lenses.

When optometrists detect early signs of eye abnormalities, such as glaucoma or detached retina, or of general conditions, such as hypertension or diabetes, they refer the patient to their GP for further investigation, and possible referral to a hospital eye department.

Prescriptions for spectacles consist of mathematical instructions on the lens powers, such as the cylindrical (astigmatic) power and axis, needed. Optometrists are qualified to fit and supply spectacles, but this may also be done by dispensing opticians (please see article 2. DISPENSING OPTICIAN). The lenses they supply must give clear and comfortable binocular vision at the distance needed for the patient's work or recreation. Frames must hold the lenses securely in the right position, be comfortable, and suit the patient, and must take account of any protective requirements of sport and some occupations.

When contact lenses are appropriate, optometrists choose from a range of hard, soft and gas-permeable lenses, tell the patient how to insert, remove, and care for the lenses, and ensure the patient returns for regular check-ups.

Optometrists provide magnifiers, electronic devices and other aids for people whose vision is so poor that conventional spectacles or contact lenses are of little use.

Optometrists also give advice on eye care; some give orthoptic treatment (see article 3. ORTHOPTIST) and advise people such as pilots, VDU operators and others who have particular vision needs connected with their occupations.

Hospital optometrists work as part of a team with other medical professionals. They do the tests described above and help eye surgeons in the diagnosis and post-operative treatment of complex eye conditions. They can specialize in certain types of vision disorder.

Most optometrists also have administrative and management responsibilities.

WORK ENVIRONMENT

Optometrists in private practice work in owned or rented premises, often with a shop front, or in rooms. They work in clean and comfortably furnished examination rooms. They sometimes leave their premises for home visits.

Optometrists also work in eye hospitals and hospital eye departments, where they may have research facilities, as well as examination rooms, and in university departments, where they teach and conduct research.

SKILLS AND INTERESTS

Optometrists require scientific and mathematical aptitude. Patience and precision are essential, as well as the manual dexterity to use delicate instruments and fit contact lenses.

Optometrists must have the enthusiasm and flexibility to respond to the rapid advances in their field, but also be willing to do repetitive, sometimes mundane tasks.

They must like people and deal with them confidently and sympathetically. An interest in style and fashion is an asset.

All optometrists need to be self-motivated and well organized, but in private practice they also require organizational and administrative skills.

ENTRY REQUIREMENTS

Practising optometrists must be registered with the General Optical Council. They need a degree in Optometry (Ophthalmic Optics), a year's clinical experience under supervision and to have passed the Professional Qualifying Examination Part II of the College of Optometrists. Requirements for entry to a degree course vary and may depend on the candidate's performance at an interview.

Usual entry requirements in England and Wales are three A levels, two of which must include biology, physics, maths or chemistry, plus five GCSEs (A–C) including English, maths and either physics or dual science. Average entry grades vary, usually between 20 and 24 A level points.

Entry requirements in Scotland are four or five H grades or three H grades and two S grades (1–3). Preferred H grades are maths, physics, chemistry and biology. Maths and English are required at H grade or S grade (1–3).

Relevant BTEC/SQA national awards and Advanced

OPHTHALMICS: JAL

GNVQ/GSVQ Level III, eg in science, are considered for entry to some courses. Applicants should check with individual universities.

Before applying for a degree course, prospective applicants are advised to seek work experience or work shadowing with an optometrist to see what the work entails.

TRAINING

Candidates must undertake a three-year BSc Degree in Optometry (Ophthalmic Optics) at one of six universities in England, Wales, or Northern Ireland (Aston, Bradford, City (London), Wales at Cardiff, Ulster and UMIST) or equivalent four-year BSc course at Glasgow Caledonian University.

Subjects studied include anatomy and physiology, optics, optometry, pharmacology and the use of drugs, recognition of ocular abnormalities, dispensing practice and management and professional studies, including law. Satisfactory completion of the degree usually exempts trainees from Part I of the professional qualifying exam run by the College of Optometrists.

The degree is followed by a pre-registration year of training and experience supervised by a registered optometrist. This can be with either a high street or hospital practice or occasionally in a university department. Trainees are paid a small salary. They then take Part 2 of the Professional Qualifying Exam towards the end of the year. This combines practical and oral assessment of the ability to manage patients and to practise safely as an independent optometrist. Successful candidates are eligible for registration with the General Optical Council and election to membership of the College of Optometrists (MCOptom).

Optometrists' basic training qualifies them to fit and supply contact lenses, but advanced training is available in this growing field, as well as in orthoptics, children's sight problems, vision in industry, low vision and other areas.

LATE ENTRY

Optometry attracts a number of late entrants. There is no upper age limit and requirements may be relaxed for mature students entering university or college, providing they have equivalent qualifications or experience. Adults may prepare for application to a degree course by taking a science Access course.

Some dispensing opticians retrain to be optometrists. Although university entry requirements may be relaxed, they must still obtain an optometry degree and work the pre-registration year.

OPPORTUNITIES

There are 7,500 registered optometrists in the UK, of whom the great majority work in general practice. About 55% work for small independent firms or run their own business, alone or in partnership.

Opportunities exist in the high street multiples, in independent firms run by optometrists and dispensing opticians, and in hospitals.

PAY AND CONDITIONS

Trainee optometrists in their pre-registration year are paid £7,600. Newly registered optometrists in private practice earn £15,000 to £25,000, their earnings rising, as they become more experienced, to £30,000 or more.

Hospital Eye Service salaries are graded and extra responsibility payments are made within the grades. Salaries range from £11,823 for newly registered optometrists to £39,877 (or exceptionally, £48,517). London allowances are paid. Terms and conditions of service may differ for optometrists working in NHS trust hospitals.

Most optometrists work a 35-hour week, though in private practice hours vary according to local demand. Optometrists working on Saturday take time off in lieu during the week. Some large practices work rotas in which days-off vary. In the Hospital Eye Service optometrists work a 35-hour week, Monday to Friday.

Part-time opportunities are readily available.

PROSPECTS

Career structures vary from firm to firm. Small companies may only employ an assistant optometrist, while the multiples have assistants and branch managers, regional directors, and head office personnel. Advanced qualifications increase prospects of promotion (see TRAINING).

Optometrists hoping to start their own business or enter a partnership usually work as an assistant for two or three years first, to gain experience of patient and practice management. The chances of becoming self-employed are better than in many professions. The Association of Optometrists gives advice on the financial assistance available to optometrists setting up their own practice. The newly self-employed often take part-time or locum work elsewhere for two or three days a week until their own practice is established.

Opportunities are available in teaching and research in universities or colleges, or consultancy or research work in the optical industry.

RELATED OCCUPATIONS

Dispensing optician, ophthalmologist, orthoptist, speech and language therapist, hospital doctor, optical technician.

FURTHER INFORMATION AND READING

Please see article 3. ORTHOPTIST.

2. DISPENSING OPTICIAN (JAL)

THE WORK

Dispensing opticians work mainly in private practice. They dispense, fit and supply spectacles and other optical aids.

Dispensing opticians interpret prescriptions from optometrists and ophthalmic medical practitioners; these give details of the power and angle of lenses needed. They advise patients on lens type – spherical or aspherical, clear or tinted, single vision or bifocal etc – and on spectacle frame, weight, colour and style. They fit sample frames – several sizes are available in each style – and specify lens measurements accordingly. Frames must be chosen that position the lenses correctly in front of the eyes, and opticians may need to take exact measurements to establish, for example, the distance between the pupils, the height of the segment in bifocals etc.

Helping patients choose frames is time-consuming, as they must suit the face and general appearance, as well as holding the lenses securely in the right position.

Dispensing opticians order the spectacles from prescription houses. When the finished spectacles are returned, opticians make sure that they meet specifications and fit the patient correctly and comfortably.

Dispensing opticians may see the same patient a number of times if their spectacles need to be adjusted or repaired, if their vision requirements change, or if their sight deteriorates.

Demand for contact lenses is growing, and many dispensing opticians take the additional training that qualifies them to fit and supply contact lenses. Others specialize in areas such as aids for the partially sighted.

Selling is an important part of a dispensing optician's work. Management skills are essential for those wishing to run a branch or start their own business.

WORK ENVIRONMENT

Dispensing opticians usually work in high street shop premises. Reception and sales areas are clean and comfortable, designed to welcome the public. Many practices have separate fitting rooms.

SKILLS AND INTERESTS

The work of dispensing opticians is intricate and requires exceptional accuracy and precision. As well as interpreting scientific and mathematical information, dispensing opticians must be able to handle ophthalmic instruments and fit spectacles, and probably contact lenses. They come into contact with a variety of people, and their communication skills are as important as their technical ability. They should like people and deal with them confidently and sympathetically. A pleasant manner, tidy appearance, patience and a sense of humour are essential. An understanding of fashion and design is a great asset.

Dispensing opticians in private practice need good sales ability. Management skills and drive are vital when they are holding a responsible post or running their own business.

ENTRY REQUIREMENTS

Dispensing opticians have to be registered with the General Optical Council. They must complete three years' training and pass the Association of British Dispensing Opticians (ABDO) examinations before being eligible for registration and fellowship of the Association (FBDO).

The minimum entry requirement for training is specified by the ABDO as five GCSE/S grades (A–C/1–3) including English and either maths or physics, and a science-based subject. Relevant BTEC/SQA national awards and Intermediate GNVQ/GSVQ Level II, eg in science, are also acceptable.

Students may also meet the minimum entry requirements by successful completion of the ABDO's distance learning Access courses in maths, human biology, physics and general science. These are open to students who have GCSE/S grade (A–C/1–3) in English.

Minimum requirements for entry to the ophthalmic dispensing diploma courses at City and Islington College and Anglia Polytechnic University are those specified by the ABDO. The minimum requirements for entry to Bradford and Ilkley Community College's diploma course are five GCSE/S grades (A–C/1–3), plus one A level, including English, maths and a science, or success in the ABDO's distance learning Access course. Relevant BTEC/SQA national awards and Intermediate GNVQ/GSVQ Level II, eg in science, are also acceptable for all three courses.

Entry to Glasgow Caledonian University's Diploma of Higher Education (DipHE) is with either two or three H grades (BC or CCC), preferably in English, maths and physics, and S grade (1–3) in English and maths if not offered at H grade; or two A levels (minimum grades DE) from English, maths or physics, plus GCSEs (A–C) in English and maths if not held at A level; or a BTEC/SQA national award or Advanced GNVQ/GSVQ Level III in such as science.

Entry to Anglia Polytechnic University's Optical Management degree and combined degree including ophthalmic dispensing is with either a minimum of two A levels, with a science subject preferred but not essential, plus five GCSEs including a science subject; or Part 1 of the ABDO's Ophthalmic Dispensing award; or with equivalent qualifications, eg a relevant BTEC/SQA national award or Advanced GNVQ/GSVQ Level III. It is preferred that applicants have relevant work experience.

TRAINING

There are five methods of training to be a dispensing optician.

1. A two-year full-time course leading to a Diploma in Ophthalmic Dispensing at Bradford and Ilkley Community College (one A level is required for this course) and City and Islington College, or to a Diploma in Higher Education at Glasgow Caledonian University. This is followed by a pre-registration year of salaried work, supervised by a registered optometrist or dispensing optician.

Bradford and Ilkley Community College offer a BSc (Hons) in Opthalmic Dispensing with Management Course, (two A levels are required) in addition to the existing Diploma in Ophthalmic Dispensing.

2. A three-year day release course in ophthalmic dispensing at Bradford and Ilkley Community College, City and Islington College, or Anglia Polytechnic University. Students have to be employed throughout as trainee dispensers, supervised by a registered optometrist or dispensing optician.

3. A three-year distance learning course in opthalmic dispensing run by the Association of British Dispensing Opticians. A GCSE or equivalent pass in mathematics at Grade A or B is required. Students must be employed throughout as trainee dispensers. The course includes block attendance for two two-week periods at one of the above mentioned colleges. Students' pre-registration year is counted as part of the course.

4. A BSc (Hons) Optical Management course offered by Anglia Polytechnic University. This three-year full-time degree qualifies students for ophthalmic dispensing, covers the theory of contact lens fitting and provides training in retail management. The University also offers an honours degree, in which ophthalmic dispensing is combined with another subject such as biology, chemistry or psychology.

5. A national day release course in opthalmic dispensing lasting three years, available only at Anglia Polytechnic

OPHTHALMICS: JAL

University. It is designed for students who wish to study through day release but who do not live near enough colleges offering the day release courses. Students attend college for three and a half days at the beginning of each month.

LATE ENTRY

There is no upper age limit. Some people train late to be dispensing opticians, particularly those with previous optical experience, eg optical technicians or opticians' receptionists.

The minimum entry requirements may be relaxed for applicants with at least ten years' optical experience. They are, though, recommended to have GCSE/S grade (A–C/1–3) standard in maths if they are to benefit from training.

Applicants to Glasgow Caledonian University's DipHE course or to one of Anglia Polytechnic University's degree courses may be accepted on successful completion of an Access course. Access courses are offered by many local colleges.

OPPORTUNITIES

There are more than 4,000 registered dispensing opticians in the United Kingdom. Of these, 65% are employed in private practice, 30% are self-employed or in partnership, and the rest work in hospitals, in prescription houses, as college lecturers etc.

Opportunities arise for dispensing opticians to work for independent optometrists and dispensing opticians, and in the multiple practices – the largest of which has 700 branches. The job market has become more competitive in recent years but prospects remain good, particularly for dispensing opticians willing to relocate and undertake managerial responsibility. Increasing numbers are starting their own businesses.

Registration with the General Optical Council is recognized in many countries abroad. Positions are advertised in the *Optician*.

PAY AND CONDITIONS

Trainees in full-time employment can earn about £9,000. Incremental payments are made as trainees complete key stages of their training. On registration, dispensing opticians employed in private practice earn £14,000 to £17,000, rising to £25,000 or more as experience and responsibility increase. The earnings of self-employed dispensing opticians may be substantially higher.

Dispensing opticians work a five-day, 35-hour week. Many work a half or full day on Saturday, which is often the busiest time of the week, and take time off in lieu. It is possible for dispensing opticians to work part-time and as locums.

PROSPECTS

Each company has its own career structure, but many trainees reach the position of assistant manager by the time they are qualified. In multiple stores, dispensing opticians' promotion may be to managerial positions in larger branches or a move into regional or head office management. Promotion depends on ability to deal courteously and efficiently with customers and on willingness to take responsibility.

Advanced training increases promotional prospects, and geographical mobility is essential at all career stages.

Outside private practice, dispensing opticians work in hospital eye departments, in prescription houses, where they provide technical support for other opticians, in lens and frame manufacture, as college teachers, or as sales consultants for ophthalmic instrument manufacturers, lens suppliers, and frame-makers and importers.

RELATED OCCUPATIONS

Optical technician, ophthalmic instrument technician, optometrist/ophthalmic optician, orthoptist, retail manager.

FURTHER INFORMATION AND READING

Please see article 3. ORTHOPTIST.

3. ORTHOPTIST (JAL)

THE WORK

Orthoptists diagnose and treat disorders of vision and eye movement, including squint, reduced vision and double vision.

Most orthoptists work in hospitals, assessing patients referred by general practitioners and local consultants. Many of their patients are children under eight, although increasing numbers of adults are being referred, including elderly patients with impaired binocular vision.

Orthoptists carry out a range of tests, then decide on appropriate treatment and monitor its progress at subsequent appointments. They aim to re-educate the eyes by exercises to improve eye co-ordination, and this may include giving patients eye patches to wear. Sometimes they refer patients back to a consultant to discuss and recommend the next stage of treatment, which may be optical, pharmacological, or surgical. They may also find that brain scans or other special x-rays are needed.

Orthoptists work with equipment ranging from prisms (to measure a squint) to computerized visual field analysers. They also use charts and cards and – in assessing the vision of very young children – toys and games.

When surgery is needed for squint, orthoptists do the pre- and post-operative assessments and monitoring. They are also involved in the diagnosis and monitoring of glaucoma and the treatment of double vision caused by strokes, accidents and systemic illnesses, such as thyroid disorders. They often help neurologists, neurosurgeons and doctors diagnose complex disorders of eye movement. Orthoptists also assess the visual abilities of physically and mentally impaired children. Their diagnosis, observations and treatment have to be noted in the patient's records and written up in reports for consultants and GPs.

Some orthoptists are involved in screening pre-school and school children for vision defects.

WORK ENVIRONMENT

Orthoptists work in eye hospitals and in eye departments and clinics in general hospitals and children's hospitals. They spend time on the wards as well as in clinics, and may work at several different locations. Many orthoptists now also work in the community.

Most orthoptists work as a member of a team including

dispensing opticians, nurses, optometrists and doctors, headed by an ophthalmic surgeon. They may have their own examination room or share one with another orthoptist.

Orthoptists in the community work in health centres and schools, and sometimes from specially equipped mobile units.

SKILLS AND INTERESTS

Orthoptists have to be enquiring and observant, able to work to high standards of accuracy and interpret the information supplied by their tests and examinations. They need the manual dexterity and technical competence to use ophthalmic instruments and computerized equipment.

They must also be able to communicate well with children and adults from widely differing backgrounds. Orthoptists see some patients over a long period of time and have to gain their confidence and put them and anxious relatives at ease. As well as patience, a pleasant manner and a sense of humour, they need the imagination to attract a young child's attention or to improvise when a patient is unable to respond to conventional methods of testing. They must retain their enthusiasm and persevere when a patient's progress is slower than expected. Their work with physically and mentally impaired children may be particularly demanding, but also very rewarding.

Orthoptists need to be self-motivated and well-organized, working confidently and professionally in a team or on their own. Management skills are necessary for career advancement.

ENTRY REQUIREMENTS

Orthoptists working in the National Health Service have to be registered with the Council for Professions Supplementary to Medicine. Entrants to the profession are required to obtain a degree in Orthoptics. Three-year degree courses are offered at Liverpool and Sheffield universities.

Entry requirements for Liverpool University are three A levels (grades BBC), including at least one science subject, preferably biology; plus five GCSEs (A–C), including English, maths and physics or dual science.

Entry requirements for Sheffield University are three A levels (grades BCC), four H grades (BBBB) including at least one science subject, preferably biology (but excluding general studies); plus five GCSEs (A–C), S grades (1–3) including English language, maths and two science subjects if not offered at A level/H grade.

For both courses alternative qualifications, such as BTEC/SQA national awards or Advanced GNVQ/GSVQ Level III in science, are acceptable in place of A levels/H grades.

Potential applicants are advised to check current course entry requirements.

Prospective candidates are advised to seek work experience or work shadowing in an orthoptic clinic before applying.

TRAINING

The three-year degree courses combine theory and practice and lead to a degree in Orthoptics. Course content includes general study of anatomy and physiology, cell biology, child development, behavioural sciences, and genetics; detailed study of the eyeball, ocular muscles, brain and central nervous system; ophthalmology and diseases affecting the eye.

Students gain practical experience on day and block placements in hospitals, child development centres and assessment centres for the physically and mentally impaired. Training also covers refraction techniques and methods of diagnosing and monitoring glaucoma.

LATE ENTRY

There is no upper age limit for entry to orthoptics training. Mature applicants may be accepted without the usual entry requirements, particularly if they have relevant qualifications and/or experience.

Adults may prepare for application for a degree course by studying a science Access course.

OPPORTUNITIES

There are about 1,000 orthoptists working in the United Kingdom, most of them employed by the National Health Service.

Opportunities arise for orthoptists to work in hospitals (NHS, NHS trust and private practice), in the community and in universities. Many jobs are part-time. It may be necessary to move location in order to find a suitable position.

A list of vacancies – including a few overseas – is circulated with the British Orthoptic Society monthly newsletter.

PAY AND CONDITIONS

National Health Service salaries range from £12,990 for a basic grade orthoptist to £27,950 for the highest grade head orthoptist. A senior orthoptist in charge of a unit or department earns a minimum of £17,840. Annual increments are paid within each of the eight grades. Allowances are paid to orthoptists working in inner and outer London.

Orthoptists work a 36½-hour week, usually Monday to Friday.

NHS trust hospitals may set their own scales of pay and terms of employment.

Part-time jobs are available in the NHS and in private practice, and some orthoptists work in both sectors. Locum work is also available.

PROSPECTS

The National Health Service has a well defined career structure which recognizes special skills and responsibilities. It is possible for a basic-grade orthoptist working in a team to progress to head orthoptist in charge of a department.

Promotion depends on willingness to take increased responsibility, and to move from one region to another.

Some orthoptists work in private practice and a few are employed as researchers, teachers or lecturers. Opportunities may be available in management positions in other areas of health care.

RELATED OCCUPATIONS

Physiotherapist, speech and language therapist, optometrist/ophthalmic optician, medical technical officer.

OPHTHALMICS: JAL

FURTHER INFORMATION

Association of Optometrists*, 90 London Road, London, SE1 8NW, 0171 261 9661, www.assocotom.co.uk

The Association of British Dispensing Opticians*, 6 Hurlingham Business Park, Sulivan Road, London SW6 3DU, 0171 736 0088

College of Optometrists*, 10 Knaresborough Place, London SW5 0TG, 0171 373 7765

British Orthoptic Society*, Tavistock House North, Tavistock Square, London WC1H 9HX, 0171 387 7992

The Federation of Ophthalmic and Dispensing Opticians*, 113 Eastbourne Mews, Paddington, London W2 6LQ, 0171 258 0240

General Optical Council*, 41 Harley Street, London W1N 2DJ, 0171 580 3898

FURTHER READING

Leaflets/booklets are available from the addresses marked*.

Working in Hospitals – COIC

In the careers library classified under JAL.

THERAPY AND TREATMENT: JAN-JAV

1. PHYSIOTHERAPIST CLCI:JAN
2. RADIOGRAPHER CLCI:JAP
3. OCCUPATIONAL THERAPIST CLCI:JAR
4. SPEECH AND LANGUAGE THERAPIST CLCI:JAS
5. CHIROPODIST/PODIATRIST CLCI:JAT
6. DIETITIAN CLCI:JAV

1. PHYSIOTHERAPIST

BACKGROUND INFORMATION

Most physiotherapists work for the National Health Service. They are important members of the health care team, working in close co-operation with doctors, nurses, social workers, other therapists and specialists.

Physiotherapy is concerned with the rehabilitation of people who are suffering from injury, disability or other conditions. Increasingly, physiotherapists undertake preventive work, health education and research.

THE WORK

Physiotherapists aim to return or develop patients to as near normal function of body and limbs as possible, so that they can resume active lives with maximum independence. When treating patients with progressive diseases, physiotherapists aim to make the best of the functions that remain at each stage.

Techniques of physiotherapeutic treatment are mainly based on movement and manipulation. Other treatments may include electrotherapy, ultrasound and heat treatments.

Some patients are treated in groups, but most of the work is with individuals. Those who are too ill to be moved are treated in bed. The emphasis is on encouraging patients to exercise, rather than on prescribing passive treatments. However, some patients may not be able to move at all, for example paraplegics, and it is necessary to move their limbs for them.

Physiotherapists encounter a wide range of disabilities. These include the result of certain diseases (such as arthritis, multiple sclerosis and cystic fibrosis), post-operative conditions, and disabilities resulting from injury or that have been present since birth.

At some stage in their careers physiotherapists usually deal with patients who have suffered strokes. They must encourage them to reach their full potential and cope with permanent disabilities.

The work can be very strenuous – moving limbs, helping patients to move and providing support. It is important that physiotherapists are able to lift without strain.

Physiotherapists must monitor and evaluate the progress of each patient at each session. This involves making records and carefully documenting progress. Where treatments are not as successful as they could be, the physiotherapist may refer back to the doctor to discuss alternatives.

Physiotherapists work with people of all ages, from babies to the elderly.

After gaining experience of general physiotherapy, usually in a hospital, it is possible to specialize in developing a major skill, such as manipulation; treating specific conditions, such as intensive care or respiratory disorders; or treating a particular group, such as children or the elderly. An increasingly important area of work is with mentally disabled and mentally ill people – physiotherapy can help to improve quality of life and assist rehabilitation.

Patients in all types of hospital department require physiotherapy. In maternity wards physiotherapists may advise expectant mothers on relaxation and exercise and help them regain muscle strength after childbirth.

Most physiotherapists begin work in hospitals but the trend is towards community-based health care – patients are treated in their own homes, at local health centres, at schools and in nursing homes.

WORK ENVIRONMENT

The majority of physiotherapists work in the National Health Service; physiotherapists work on hospital wards with patients, or in specially equipped gymnasia and treatment units.

Some physiotherapists work in different kinds of sports clubs, including gymnasium work in health clubs, work for GPs, professional football clubs etc. Others work on-site in industrial concerns, where therapists treat employees and give health education information.

SKILLS AND INTERESTS

Skills in teaching and counselling are needed; physiotherapists must teach the patient exercises, explain the treatment plan and gain the patient's co-operation. It may be necessary to persuade patients to persevere and reassure those who lack self-confidence or are in pain. Progress can be slow and disappointing, but the physiotherapist must be prepared to provide encouragement and build up determination. A tactful and sympathetic personality, patience and tolerance are essential qualities.

Physiotherapists should be able to work well with their hands and have the ability to give manipulative treatments. Lifting and supporting patients can be physically strenuous and individuals should have the stamina and physique required to carry out these duties. Physical fitness and good health are essential. An interest in physical education is helpful.

ENTRY REQUIREMENTS

The minimum entry requirements are the same as for all degree courses, ie five GCSEs/S grades (A–C/1–3) with two A levels/three H grades. However, in practice the usual requirements are as follows:

England and Wales: School-leavers are normally required to have three A levels at grade C or above, including a biological science, and a minimum of five GCSEs (A–C) taken at one sitting, including maths, English language and a spread of science subjects.

Scotland: Typically, Scottish students will have five H grades at grades AAA, BB, taken at one sitting, with a minimum of two science subjects.

Alternative qualifications A range of other qualifications may be accepted, for example:

– BTEC National Diploma in Health Studies (Science) with distinctions/merits in all units;

– Advanced GNVQ/GSVQ Level III in Health and Social Care or Science (usually a biological science A level/H

THERAPY AND TREATMENT: JAN-JAV

grade is also required);

– Higher national diploma in a relevant subject.

Each course has its own individual entry requirements, and applicants should write to the institution of their choice for a prospectus, which will include details of specific course entry requirements.

Applicants have to pass a medical before being admitted into training. The minimum age for entry into training is normally 18 years, but those achieving satisfactory qualifications early may be accepted at 17 years. It is also useful to be able to swim.

It is essential that those considering training in physiotherapy should arrange to visit a physiotherapy department to observe the work, either before applying or before interview.

TRAINING

Candidates training in physiotherapy take an approved degree course that is acceptable for membership of the Chartered Society of Physiotherapy and for UK state registration, essential for work in the NHS.

First degree courses are for three or four years of full-time study and are available at Aberdeen, Birmingham, Bradford, Bristol, Cardiff, Colchester, Coventry, Eastbourne, Edinburgh, Glasgow, Hatfield, Huddersfield, Keele, Leeds, Liverpool, London, Manchester, Middlesborough, Newcastle-upon-Tyne, Norwich, Nottingham, Oxford Brookes, Salford, Sheffield, Southampton, Ulster. (Contact the Chartered Society of Physiotherapy for details.)

Courses combine theoretical and practical training and cover a wide range of subjects including anatomy, physiology, physics, behavioural science, pathology, and the theory and practice of therapeutic movement and manipulation and electrotherapy.

A two-year accelerated postgraduate degree is available at Glasgow Caledonian University for good-honours graduates from a biological or sports science background.

LATE ENTRY

Applications from mature students are welcome. Schools may waive some of the academic entry requirements for applicants aged 21 years and over who can show some evidence of recent successful academic study, for example A levels/H grades, Open University or Access courses.

Separate guidelines for mature applicants are available from the Chartered Society of Physiotherapy.

OPPORTUNITIES

There are over 32,000 practising members of the Chartered Society of Physiotherapy (including students and assistants). About 15,000 are employed by the National Health Service – they may be either hospital or community-based. About 2,000–3,000 physiotherapists are self-employed, running private practices. Employment has been rising for a number of years, but entry to training is very competitive, with three to four applicants for each place.

Vacancies for qualified physiotherapists appear in *Physiotherapy Frontline* (a publication of the Chartered Society of Physiotherapy), which is published and circulated twice monthly to members of the Society.

PAY AND CONDITIONS

National Health Service pay scales range from approximately £13,420 for the newly qualified, to a maximum of £31,960 for a physiotherapy services manager. In addition, there is a range of allowances and benefits, including London weighting. NHS employees have the option to join the NHS pension scheme. Certain conditions of employment may vary for physiotherapists working in NHS trust hospitals; pay rates are currently set nationally, but these may be 'topped up' by some trusts.

Salaries in employment outside the NHS are negotiated individually, but are generally related to NHS scales. The Chartered Society of Physiotherapy has a recommended scale for physiotherapists working in industry and private practice.

Working hours in the sport and leisure sector can involve weekend working (mainly Saturday) and evening work (eg to cover evening football matches). Otherwise, daytime working is usual and there are opportunities for part-time work.

Full-time posts usually follow the five-day week pattern, although there may be demands to work early mornings and evenings, and for on-call duties.

PROSPECTS

There are opportunities for physiotherapists working in the NHS to progress to senior and superintendent physiotherapist grades. Promotion routes extend into senior management positions. Training continues throughout physiotherapists' careers and they may attend postgraduate courses. Some choose to become clinical specialists, rather than moving into management, and career paths are available for those taking this route. Research is a small but growing area and provides opportunities for experienced physiotherapists.

There are also opportunities to teach physiotherapy, once experience has been gained clinically in the profession. Prospective teachers are normally expected to have gained a higher degree.

RELATED OCCUPATIONS

Osteopath, chiropractor, radiographer, occupational therapist, speech and language therapist, teacher, nurse, prosthetist/orthotist.

FURTHER INFORMATION

The Chartered Society of Physiotherapy*, 14 Bedford Row, London WC1R 4ED, 0171 306 6666

FURTHER READING

Leaflets/booklets are available from the address marked*.

Working in Hospitals – COIC

In the careers library classified under JAN.

2. RADIOGRAPHER (JAP)

BACKGROUND INFORMATION

Radiography is a health care profession with two distinct branches: diagnostic and therapeutic. Both types of radiographer need considerable technological, anatomical, physiological and pathological knowledge to carry out their work..

THE WORK

Diagnostic radiographers are specialists who use ionizing radiation and other imaging modalities such as ultrasound and magnetic resonance imaging. This assists in the diagnosis of a wide range of diseases or injuries, or to monitor processes within the body. This could mean, for example, taking an x-ray of a suspected broken limb or an ultrasound scan to ensure all is well in pregnancy.

While most diagnostic radiographers carry out a range of procedures in their daily work, there are also opportunities to specialize in areas such as computerized tomography (CT) scanning, ultrasound, radionuclide imaging, and magnetic resonance imaging. Special post-qualifying courses are available in these areas.

Therapeutic radiographers administer radiation to patients, to treat diseases such as cancer. Therapeutic radiographers often work with the same patients over a period of time and build relationships with them; diagnostic radiographers more often only see patients once. The therapeutic radiographer administers the radiation treatment, keeps detailed records, and ensures that the patient's needs are looked after through liaison with other professionals in the team. Patient care is a vital part of therapeutic radiography.

WORK ENVIRONMENT

Most radiographers work in a hospital. The imaging or radiotherapy department is usually in a central position convenient to all referring departments and wards.

Diagnostic radiographers carry out most of their work in the hospital imaging department, but where necessary they work in wards and operating theatres using mobile units. Large modern hospitals have a series of x-ray rooms, each specially equipped for different procedures. Diagnostic radiographers often work alone on a specific procedure although they are part of a departmental team.

Therapeutic radiographers work almost exclusively in a radiotherapy department, which is usually part of a large general hospital. Their work involves working closely in a team with other colleagues, such as clinicians, physicists, nurses, physiotherapists, dietitians etc.

SKILLS AND INTERESTS

Both diagnostic and therapeutic radiographers need the skill to deal with patients of all types and ages, most of whom will need reassuring about the radiographic procedures. They also need to be able to work with complex high-technology equipment. The work of all radiographers involves knowledge of anatomy. Safe use of radiation and knowledge of the equipment and techniques are vital. A radiographer needs the ability to communicate and give great care and attention to detail, combined with the flexibility to treat each patient as an individual case.

The many new developments in radiographic techniques and treatments mean that radiographers are constantly learning new skills and the work is normally very varied.

ENTRY REQUIREMENTS

The minimum academic entry requirements for degree courses in radiography are the same as for all degree courses, ie five GCSEs/S grades (A–C/1–3) with two A levels/three H grades, or equivalent.

Radiography education centres may require additional or more specific qualifications, for instance science subjects at A level. For candidates offering Advanced GNVQ, there may be requirements for merit/distinction in specific subjects. More detailed information is given in *Radiography Education and Training* – Directory of Courses, available from the College of Radiographers.

The minimum age on entry to training is 17 years.

Before applying for a course, it is advisable to visit a radiography and/or radiotherapy department at a local hospital to gain a clear impression of what the work involves.

TRAINING

Radiographers must be state registered for employment in the NHS. State registration is achieved by gaining a degree in radiography from an approved education centre.

All radiography qualifying courses are at degree level and most are three-year courses, except for Northern Ireland where the course at the University of Ulster is four years. Students are normally based in a university and in hospital departments for an equal amount of time.

Diagnostic radiography and therapeutic radiography are separate disciplines, and candidates must decide which discipline they wish to study before making their applications.

LATE ENTRY

There is no upper age limit for training.

Many radiography education centres especially welcome applications from mature candidates. Alternative qualifications, such as validated Access courses, may be accepted.

OPPORTUNITIES

The NHS employs 90% of all radiographers, with other opportunities in private clinics and industry. There are about 18,000 state registered radiographers in the UK. The ratio of diagnostic to therapeutic radiographers is ten to one.

Radiographers who can speak an appropriate foreign language can often obtain jobs overseas. There are a small number of diagnostic radiographers in the Armed Forces.

PAY AND CONDITIONS

Salaries for newly qualified staff in the NHS start at about £13,300 and rise to about £15,500. Staff working in the London area receive an additional London allowance. Senior Radiographers Grade II earn from £15,500 to £18,400 and Senior I from £18,400 to £21,100. Superintendent scales range from £18,400 at Grade IV to £27,900 at Grade I.

Posts in private clinics do not normally offer higher salaries. Posts in industry might offer a higher salary but are normally only available to experienced radiographers. The Armed Forces pay radiographers a higher basic salary, linked to service grades, but do not provide for emergency payments.

Radiographers employed in the NHS normally work a five-day, 35-hour week. Diagnostic radiographers are normally required to participate in an on-call scheme, to provide cover for emergencies at night, weekends and during public holidays.

THERAPY AND TREATMENT: JAN-JAV

There are growing opportunities for both part-time work and for job sharing up to the most senior levels.

Annual leave starts at five weeks a year and increases by three days after ten years.

PROSPECTS

The NHS has a formal career structure for radiographers. Promotion is by interview and based on merit. Once qualified, a radiographer can progress to senior radiographer. Radiographers in charge of departments are graded as superintendents. There are two grades of senior radiographer and four grades of superintendent radiographer. The grades are related to the level of skill or expertise, as well as the number of staff for whom a superintendent is responsible. The most senior posts are managerial, and there are now a considerable number of radiographers in senior general management posts.

There are courses designed to enhance promotion prospects. A large number of postgraduate courses are available in specialist areas.

There are also opportunities in university education and research.

RELATED OCCUPATIONS

Medical photographer, radiologist, medical physicist, medical technical officer, physiological measurements technician, nurse, medical laboratory scientific officer.

FURTHER INFORMATION

The College of Radiographers*, 2 Carriage Row, 183 Eversholt Street, London NW1 1BU, 0171 391 4500

FURTHER READING

Leaflets/booklets are available from the address marked*.

Working in Hospitals – COIC

In the careers library classified under JAP.

3. OCCUPATIONAL THERAPIST (JAR)

BACKGROUND INFORMATION

Occupational therapists (OTs) work with people with temporary or permanent physical or mental disability or mental illness. The use of carefully selected and graded activity is a key part of the assessment and intervention process, which is designed to maximize independent functioning. OTs consider physical, psychological and social needs, helping people to become as self-reliant and independent as possible. Much of the work is hospital-based but, increasingly, many OTs work for local authority social services departments and general practices, in the community and in people's homes.

THE WORK

Occupational therapists (OTs) assist people to build up confidence and independence after injury, illness or disability, and adjust to everyday living. They assess and treat people of all ages. After an assessment they will design programmes to increase clients' self-reliance, teach skills in self-care and offer activities suited to the person's lifestyle and interests. They enable clients to cope with work, leisure and everyday tasks. Occupational therapists help people with mental health problems gain confidence and a sense of purpose through a range of approaches. These include group work, improving memory and social skills, work-related activities, which can assist in employment, and the constructive use of leisure time. They help elderly people live as independently as possible or maintain full, meaningful lives in residential accommodation.

OTs work with people on an individual and group basis. Those who make home visits work with clients and their families/carers, assisting them to deal with and adjust to disability and to maximize independence. Counselling both the client and carers can be a key part of this. Prevention of illness and promoting a healthy lifestyle are also inherent in the process, as are planning and preparation for coping with increasing stages of illness (if the client has a chronic and/or deteriorating condition).

WORK ENVIRONMENT

Occupational therapists work as part of the health and social care teams in hospitals and the community, in clinics, schools, day centres and clients' homes, and increasingly in facilities provided by the voluntary and independent sectors. A growing number work in private practice.

Some posts, involving local travel, require a driving licence.

SKILLS AND INTERESTS

In addition to their medical knowledge and practical skills, OTs must have good judgement – to make accurate assessments and plan courses of treatment – and have keen powers of observation. Their work brings them into contact with a wide range of people – health and social care workers and clients – so they need a sympathetic and understanding personality, good communication skills and the ability to encourage and teach both individuals and groups. Integrity is essential. They also need energy and stamina.

ENTRY REQUIREMENTS

The minimum age to start training is 18 years.

The minimum academic entry qualifications for degree courses in occupational therapy are five GCSEs/S grades (A–C/1–3) with two A levels/three H grades; however, individual schools may require additional passes and specific grades. Passes should include a science subject. Biology at A level/H grade is particularly useful, and sometimes required.

Alternative qualifications including Advanced GNVQ/GSVQ Level III, NVQs/SVQS, BTEC national diplomas and approved Access courses are also considered.

The requirements of individual schools vary and applicants are advised to consult prospectuses.

A candidate's personal qualities are very important and are usually assessed at interview.

TRAINING

Occupational therapists must be state registered for employment in the NHS and in local authorities in England and Wales. State registration is achieved by gaining a degree in occupational therapy.

Most degree courses last for three years full-time (four

years in Scotland) and are run by schools of occupational therapy, usually based in universities. Two-thirds of the course focuses on the theory of occupational therapy, including subjects such as biological and behavioural sciences, while the other third, the equivalent of a year, is spent in fieldwork practice, some of which may take place during the summer vacation period.

Graduates in relevant disciplines – preferably scientific – may be able to take an accelerated two-year course.

There are also in-service courses for people employed in occupational therapy services as assistants or technical instructors, and who want to become professionally qualified.

These courses last for four years on a part-time, day release basis.

LATE ENTRY

Mature candidates are welcomed and their applications are considered even if they do not have the normal academic entry requirements. It is usually necessary to show evidence of recent study, for example A levels/H grades, Open University or Access courses. Consult individual institutions for further advice.

OPPORTUNITIES

The NHS is the largest employer of OTs. OTs can also find work in local authority social services departments, in prisons and with voluntary organizations. There are increasing opportunities in private hospitals, the independent sector (eg hospices) and in private practice. Job opportunities are good; the demand for qualified OTs exceeds supply.

PAY AND CONDITIONS

NHS salaries start at £13,655, rising to £15,785 in the basic grades (Whitley scale). The next grade is Senior Grade II with a salary of £15,785 to £18,755, followed by Senior Grade I at £18,755 to £21,485. The most senior posts have salaries around £29,000, depending on opportunities and range of responsibilities.

NHS occupational therapists normally work a five-day, 36-hour week. Occasionally they have on-call, weekend and holiday duties. Conditions similar to these are usual with other employers of OTs. Part-time work and job share opportunities are available.

Pay and conditions of service may vary, according to local conditions.

PROSPECTS

In the NHS, OTs can move into the management of occupational therapy services or general management. OTs with additional qualifications can move into teaching or research.

RELATED OCCUPATIONS

Music therapist, drama therapist, art therapist, speech and language therapist, physiotherapist, nurse, counsellor.

FURTHER INFORMATION

The College of Occupational Therapists*, Education Department, 104–106 Borough High Street, Southwark, London SE1 1HL, 0171 357 6480 (please include A4 envelope with 55p stamp), www.cot.co.uk

FURTHER READING

Leaflets/booklets are available from the address marked*.
Working in Social Work – COIC
In the careers library classified under JAR.

4. SPEECH AND LANGUAGE THERAPIST (JAS)

BACKGROUND INFORMATION

Speech and language therapists treat speech, language, fluency and voice disorders. The profession is closely linked to medicine, education and psychology. Speech and language therapists are responsible for the assessment, diagnosis and treatment of clients. Speech and language therapy should not be confused with elocution, which improves poor speech that is otherwise normal.

THE WORK

Clients may be referred to speech and language therapists by GPs, hospital consultants, parents or teachers. Therapists deal with all types of communication problems, but mainly treat disorders of fluency, speech, voice and language, which may be caused by congenital disabilities (eg a cleft palate, deafness, mental or physical disability) or may be acquired (eg through illness and disease, psychological or neurological problems).

To assess clients' problems and devise remedial programmes, speech and language therapists spend a lot of time observing and getting to know the patients and gaining their confidence. When the cause of a problem is not obvious, the speech and language therapist has to use a combination of skills and personal qualities and relies upon medical and scientific knowledge (eg phonetics, psychology, anatomy, physiology, neurology and acoustics), acquired during their education.

Much of the work is concerned with children, for instance those who are slow to talk, have stammers, or have hearing difficulties. Many of the children have learning difficulties or are physically disabled. A lot of work with adults involves the rehabilitation of people after accidents or illnesses. Someone who has had cancer of the larynx, for example, must be taught to speak using the oesophagus or a speaking valve. A patient whose brain has been damaged by an accident or a stroke may have to relearn how to speak or use a communication aid.

Speech and language therapists spend much of their time with individuals on a one-to-one basis, but they also organize group sessions for either adults or children.

They attend case conferences and liaise with other specialists, such as doctors, teachers, social workers and psychologists. They write reports and keep records, some of which are for the use of other professionals. Speech and language therapists counsel relatives to help them cope with the problems created by a patient's disability, so that they are involved in the therapy.

WORK ENVIRONMENT

Most speech and language therapists work for the NHS. Some work in one location, but many divide their time

THERAPY AND TREATMENT: JAN-JAV

between clinics, hospitals, schools and clients' homes; their jobs therefore involve a lot of travelling. Those in rural areas may have to travel long distances.

SKILLS AND INTERESTS

An interest in and an aptitude for both linguistics and science are essential. Speech and language therapists must be effective communicators with clear, accurate speech, a sensitive ear and a good command of written English. Speech and language therapy is demanding and responsible and calls for understanding, patience and the ability to get on well with people and win their confidence.

The work can be very rewarding in terms of results; however, clients progress very slowly and some make little progress. Speech and language therapists need a positive, encouraging approach, particularly where therapy is long and difficult. They work on their own, arranging their schedules and deciding treatments, so they need initiative and good organizing skills.

ENTRY REQUIREMENTS

Entry to the profession is all graduate. The minimum educational requirements for a relevant degree course are two A levels plus five GCSEs (A–C), or three H grades plus five S grades (1–3), including English, or equivalent. Some universities require an A level/H grade in a science. Different courses may require different essential subjects; contact the Royal College of Speech and Language Therapists for details. Competition for student places is strong, and successful applicants normally have more than the minimum qualifications. Students with qualifications in English, a second language, maths and a science subject are often at an advantage.

TRAINING

A speech and language therapist must be issued with a certificate to practise from the Royal College of Speech and Language Therapists, in order to practise in the NHS. There are two routes:

1. By completing a recognized three- or four-year degree course usually including an honours project; *or*

2. Candidates holding a degree (usually in a related subject, such as linguistics or psychology) can qualify by successfully completing a two-year postgraduate course. These are available at City University and University College London, Reading, Sheffield and Newcastle universities and all lead to a Master's degree.

The courses combine theory and clinical practice. The theoretical work has a strong scientific bias. Subjects include: psychology; phonetics and linguistics; anatomy and physiology; language pathology and therapeutics; acoustics; audiology; disorders of ear, nose and throat; education; neurology; orthodontics; plastic surgery; psychiatry; research methodology; and aspects of statistics and sociology. Practical work includes visits to clinics, schools and hospitals and observing, assisting and working under the supervision of a qualified speech and language therapist. Students also have to prepare case studies.

Successful completion of a course makes students eligible for a certificate to practise and membership and registration by the Royal College of Speech and Language Therapists. They may then seek employment as qualified speech and language therapists. After qualifying there is a period of, normally, one year of supervised practice before members of the Royal College of Speech and Language Therapists enter the professional body's full practice register.

LATE ENTRY

There are no age restrictions on entry to the profession, and mature students with evidence of recent study are accepted onto degree and postgraduate courses. Some universities relax entry requirements and take relevant experience into account.

It is possible to take a career break and return to the profession. Refresher courses are available. It is essential to keep up with current knowledge and practices.

OPPORTUNITIES

Most speech and language therapists are employed by the NHS, usually based in clinics and responsible for a geographical area. There are some static posts in specialist hospital departments, or in special schools for children. Some voluntary and charitable organizations offer employment, for example with disabled children or hearing impaired clients. Some therapists work in independent practice.

PAY AND CONDITIONS

Salary scales for speech and language therapists range from £13,316 to £34,129.

Speech and language therapists in the NHS usually work 9am to 5pm, Monday to Friday. There are part-time posts available and occasional job share opportunities.

PROSPECTS

There is a promotion ladder that depends on ability and experience. Further qualifications are an advantage. There are good prospects for advancement in clinical and management fields. Experienced speech and language therapists can move into teaching or research.

RELATED OCCUPATIONS

Social worker, drama therapist, clinical psychologist, teacher, music therapist.

FURTHER INFORMATION

The Royal College of Speech and Language Therapists*, 7 Bath Place, Rivington Street, London EC2A 3DR, 0171 613 3855 (sae required)

FURTHER READING

Leaflets/booklets are available from the address marked*.
Working in Hospitals – COIC
In the careers library classified under JAS.

5. CHIROPODIST/PODIATRIST (JAT)

BACKGROUND INFORMATION

Chiropodists, also known as podiatrists, diagnose and treat ailments, diseases and deformities of the foot, and advise patients how to avoid a recurrence of some foot problems.

Patients can see a chiropodist without having to be referred by their GP, so chiropodists must be able to distinguish between conditions local to the foot and the symptoms of a general disease, eg a circulatory disease or metabolic disorder, which requires medical or surgical attention.

State registration is required of all chiropodists working in the NHS. To become state registered, candidates need to have successfully completed a degree course approved by the Council for Professions Supplementary to Medicine. It is possible to train at private schools of chiropody; however, these schools do not offer state registration.

THE WORK

Much of a chiropodist's time is spent dealing with superficial conditions such as corns, callosities, warts, bursae, blisters, abrasions, disorders of the toenails, bacterial and fungal infections of the skin, and other conditions brought about by systemic disease, eg chilblains, ulcers, cysts and ganglia. They also treat structural and functional disorders, which may be congenital, or abnormalities caused during the period while the foot is growing. The chiropodist can cure many conditions if treatment starts early, but for many elderly patients treatment is palliative.

Chiropodists use heat and cold treatments, hydrotherapy (exercising the foot in warm water), ultrasound and wax baths. Treatment may include the use of active and passive exercises, drugs, analgesics, and fungicides or antiseptics. They make dressings and appliances to ease pressure or redistribute weight. Occasionally they perform skin or nail operations under local anaesthetic. Some also undertake minor surgery, eg involving bones of the toe. Chiropodists have an educative and advisory role; they give foot-care talks in schools and health centres, and counsel on footwear and hosiery.

WORK ENVIRONMENT

NHS chiropodists work in a variety of environments. They see patients in clinics, hospitals, health centres, mobile surgeries, schools, residential homes and they make house calls. They spend part of their day travelling and often work in rooms not ideally suited to their requirements. They keep in contact with doctors, nurses, other chiropodists and specialized professions. Private practitioners see patients by appointment in a rented surgery, or in their own homes, and they make house calls. Chiropodists employed in industrial and commercial organizations usually work in the organization's clinic or sick bay.

SKILLS AND INTERESTS

Chiropodists need patience and understanding, as many of the patients they treat are in pain or discomfort. The work calls for dexterity and good eyesight. Sharp observation and attention to detail are needed.

Chiropodists should be well organized, able to work to an appointments system and deal with administrative work in an orderly way. They need the initiative to work on their own and to take responsibility for their own judgements. They should also be able to work as members of a health care team.

ENTRY REQUIREMENTS

The minimum age of entry is 18 years.

State registration is required of all chiropodists working in the NHS.

To apply for state registration, candidates need to have successfully undertaken a degree course in chiropody, podiatry or podiatric medicine, approved by the Council for Professions Supplementary to Medicine.

Minimum entry requirements are five GCSEs/S grades with two A levels/three H grades. Subjects should include English and preferably two sciences. Some schools require higher qualifications and may prefer A level/H grade science. Alternative qualifications, including BTEC, GNVQ Health and Social Care/Science supported by a science to A/S level, are also considered. Check with individual institutions for detailed entry requirements.

TRAINING

The degree course lasts for three years, full-time. Some centres plan to offer the course on a part-time basis. Courses combine theoretical and practical training.

Universities adopt their own course structure but, typically, in the first year, students follow an introductory life sciences course; they study theoretical chiropody under supervision, and begin practical work, which occupies at least half the total training time. There is a written examination and a practical examination, during which students are assessed in diagnosis, operating skills, therapeutic procedures and chiropodial appliances.

In the second year, they study medicine, surgery and biomechanics, particularly in relation to the foot.

In the third year, students develop research skills, study the principles of medicine and surgery, with emphasis on their application to foot disorders, and pedology (the detailed study of the foot in health and disease), aetiology (the science of the cause of disease), pathology, diagnosis of foot abnormalities, and theory and practice of therapeutics. There are written and oral examinations and two sessions of practical chiropody. Students have to present appliances they have made, with supporting case notes.

On successful completion of the degree course, candidates are eligible for state registration.

LATE ENTRY

Most chiropody training schools accept mature students and an appropriate Access course would be acceptable for entry.

OPPORTUNITIES

The Society of Chiropodists and Podiatrists has about 6,500 members. Most work for the NHS.

Most chiropodists take a first post within the NHS but move on to private practice, supplementing their income with NHS session work. There are a few full-time and part-time posts with industrial or commercial firms. The Armed Forces employ civilian chiropodists. Vacancy information can be obtained from the newsletters of the Society of Chiropodists and Podiatrists.

PAY AND CONDITIONS

Salaries for full-time NHS chiropodists range from £12,990 to £17,840 for Senior Grade II chiropodists, and £17,840 to £20,440 for those at Senior Grade I. A small number of senior posts have salaries up to about £29,870. There are

THERAPY AND TREATMENT: JAN-JAV

London weighting allowances. NHS sessional rates vary according to the chiropodist's grade and the number of sessions worked. Terms and conditions of service may differ for chiropodists working in NHS trust hospitals. Private practitioners can earn considerably more than those in the NHS.

Most NHS chiropodists work a five-day, 37_-hour week, as the main groups of patients (children, elderly people, expectant mothers, hospital in-patients) are available during normal working hours. Chiropodists in private practice must expect to work long and irregular hours, since most of their patients are not available during the day. Many private practitioners supplement their income by doing a number of sessions for the NHS; they receive a fixed sum for a three-hour clinic. There are many opportunities for part-time work.

PROSPECTS

There is a formal promotion structure in the NHS, and in the higher grades work is both clinical and administrative; however, there are very few senior posts. There are very limited prospects for advancement in private practice. There is a formal promotion structure for chiropody teachers, but very few posts.

RELATED OCCUPATIONS

Nurse, orthotist/prosthetist, occupational therapist, physiotherapist, health visitor.

FURTHER INFORMATION

Society of Chiropodists and Podiatrists*, 53 Welbeck Street, London W1M 7HE, 0171 486 3381

Private (non-state registered) courses:

British Chiropody and Podiatry Association, New Hall, 149 Bath Road, Maidenhead, Berkshire SL6 4LA, 01628 32440

Institute of Chiropodists*, 27 Wright Street, Southport, Merseyside PR9 0TL, 01704 546141 (please include sae)

FURTHER READING

Leaflets/booklets are available from the addresses marked*.

Working in Hospitals – COIC

In the careers library classified under JAT.

6. DIETITIAN (JAV)

THE WORK

Dietitians work in a wide range of settings, practically applying the science of nutrition to the diets of all groups of the population, from those who are sick through to preventing illness in the healthy person. Poor diet and ill health are closely linked to many present-day medical conditions, and dietitians play an important role in nutrition education, offering independent, consistent advice to health professionals, the public and many other agencies. In many ways, by encouraging people to look at the food they eat, one can help prevent disease and the dietitian has an important role to play in this aspect of health promotion. Dietitians also work with people who have illnesses or conditions that require major modification of their food intake. These 'special diets' can often be prescribed for life and it is important that people understand the implications of their diet from a person qualified to undertake this task.

The work is very diverse and varies according to which area of the profession the dietitian is employed in. The work of a dietitian must not be confused with that of a nutritionist. The latter name may be used by a dietitian practicing outside the Health Service. However, a nutritionist is unlikely to call themselves a dietitian, as they must be state registered to operate in this capacity.

The main areas for employment for dietitians are as follows:

Within the National Health Service

Hospitals. In consultation with doctors, dietitians advise on therapeutic diets for patients, liaise with the catering department about their preparation, and ensure that all members of the care team – people such as the nurses and speech and language therapist – are aware of the implications of the diet. Dietitians are responsible for ensuring that the patient receives the appropriate therapeutic diet whilst in hospital, as well as advising them on the correct procedures to follow the diet at home. The dietitian's expertise is required in many areas of patient feeding. In some instances, this may be by tube feeding directly into the patient's stomach, looking at food consistency for those unable to chew, or by especially calculated diets for those on a kidney machine.

Within hospitals, the dietitian is closely involved with general aspects of nutrition, eg ensuring hospital menus provide healthy choices for patients and staff, education of medical staff about nutrition, as well promoting the important role food plays within a healthy lifestyle.

Many hospitals have outpatient clinics. Patients may be referred to a dietitian by their GP or a consultant for a variety of reasons. They may be suffering from diabetes, intestinal disorders, allergies, weight problems (underweight or overweight) or heart disease. The dietitian helps and advises the patient in planning a suitable diet, bearing in mind their financial situation and any religious or cultural factors influencing diet. They may see up to 30 patients a day in this setting, although it is more usual for this to be a session of half that number of referrals.

Research. Within hospitals, dietitians may undertake varying areas of research that are diet- or food-related. Such research involves working closely with other professionals, such as biochemists and statisticians. Dietitians may carefully analyse all the nutrients in a patient's diet, and measure its effect on the patient's health. They are involved with ensuring accurate diet histories are obtained, and with interpreting the results.

Community dietetics. Increasingly, the demand for dietetic expertise is required outside the hospital environment, within community settings. The service may be provided from a hospital nutrition and dietetic department, but more often today it is based within a community service. Dietitians working within the community are working with all groups of the population. However, they diversify into several different areas: the majority are either employed to undertake clinical outpatient work within general practice, being based in a health centre and providing training and support to all the members of the primary health care team, or they work solely in the area of nutrition education. As the demand for dietitians is high, they have to work as members of a multidisciplinary team, educating other health professionals, such as teachers, health visitors, social workers, home care workers. They are also involved in the preparation of information packs and leaflets, covering many aspects of food, but especially healthy eating. These may be used by schools, residential homes for the elderly, community hospitals etc.

Outside the National Health Service

The expertise of the dietitian outside the Health Service is highly valued and much sought after, such that the opportunities for employment are various and diverse. Dietitians may be employed in industry, by food manufacturers, public relations companies, trade associations. Many also work in a freelance capacity, working in and with the media, as consultants to outside bodies, in specialist areas such as sports nutrition and in private practice. Job opportunities also exist within higher education, teaching nutrition across a variety of courses, as well as training future dietitians.

WORK ENVIRONMENT

Dietitians may work in a variety of environments, depending on their specialism. The work may be performed within a hospital or health centre, and may involve travelling from place to place in the course of a day. Dietitians involved in research or working for a food manufacturer may be based in a laboratory. This usually involves less contact with people than work in a hospital or the community, where dietitians meet many people from a wide variety of backgrounds. The working conditions are generally good. Dietitians work as part of a team, and may work alongside other professionals such as nutritionists, biochemists, doctors, nursing and other staff allied to medicine, as well as care staff in the community.

SKILLS AND INTERESTS

Dietitians need an interest and ability in science, particularly chemistry, along with a practical approach to the work. An interest in diet and food is also important. Good verbal communication skills are very important in order to talk to people, both individually and in groups. Written communication skills are also important, as dietitians are often involved in writing leaflets and other material used in health education. Dietitians should enjoy working with people, and may need persuasive skills for those patients reluctant to change life-long patterns of eating. An understanding, non-judgemental approach is essential. Dietitians hoping to become managers need determination, resilience and leadership qualities.

ENTRY REQUIREMENTS

Entry to the profession is all graduate. The entry requirements for a degree in Dietetics are five GCSEs/S grades (A–C/1–3), including maths and English, with two/three A levels (which may have to include chemistry and one other science subject, often specified as biology) or three/four H grades (including chemistry and one other science). Two AS levels may be offered as an alternative to one A level (not chemistry). Various institutions have other GCSE/S grade requirements, some specifying maths as essential. It is important to consult individual prospectuses, since the requirements vary between institutions, with some asking for Bs and Cs at A level/H grade. Alternative qualifications may also be considered. Write to institutions for further information.

TRAINING

A dietitian must be registered by the Dietitians' Board of the Council for Professions Supplementary to Medicine (CPSM) in order to become state registered and practise in the NHS. Those who hold an approved degree or postgraduate diploma are eligible for registration. Two-year postgraduate diplomas are available to graduates holding science degrees in other relevant subjects such as biochemistry or physiology.

Degree courses in dietetics, that include state registration, last four years in total. Sometimes the courses are integrated four-year BSc degrees; in other cases there is a three-year BSc degree followed by a postgraduate diploma lasting one to two years. Some institutions may offer part-time study for the first and second year of degree courses. Optional subjects vary between institutions; full details are given in prospectuses.

Subjects normally include human nutrition and dietetics, food and catering studies, sociology and psychology, biochemistry, physiology (the study of the structure and function of the human body), microbiology and medicine. Practical work forms an important part of all courses, with a period of practical training in a hospital and a community setting undertaken by all students aiming for state registration. Management studies, quantitative methods, and interviewing and communication skills feature in most courses.

LATE ENTRY

Many institutions are prepared to consider mature applicants (over the age of 21 to 23 years) who do not have the traditional entry requirements. An approved Access course in science may provide an appropriate bridge for the mature student, and colleges may consider mature students holding BTEC/SQA qualifications. Recent study of some sort is normally required, so that the college can assess whether the student has the necessary academic potential to complete a science degree. Relevant work experience – in a scientific, social, or health-related context – is useful in a profession where maturity is an asset.

OPPORTUNITIES

A significant number of dietitians work within the NHS, and a few are employed in private hospitals. There is also a widening area of opportunities for dietitians in many other fields, although these jobs often go to dietitians with experience, probably gained within the NHS.

Openings exist within food and pharmaceutical manufacturers and large caterers, as well as with promotional bodies such as the Meat and Livestock Commission. The Ministry of Agriculture, Fisheries and Food employs dietitians, who look at the nutritional quality of the food supply. Research is carried out by various bodies employing dietitians, including the Medical Research Council.

An increasing number of dietitians work on a freelance basis, in an advisory or research capacity, and in this case are usually self-employed. If dietitians wish to work abroad, their skills and experience are valued in Third World countries, where they may work for an international relief agency or the Food and Agriculture Organization of the United Nations. British dietetic qualifications are not automatically recognized in the USA. In Australia or Canada, dietitians wishing to practise there may have to

THERAPY AND TREATMENT: JAN-JAV

take examinations set in those countries. Opportunities are available in Europe for those who can offer the necessary language skills.

Dietetics is a small but rapidly expanding profession, expected to be the second of all professions to show significant growth within the NHS. Recently qualified staff should not experience difficulty in finding a first job, provided that they are prepared to be geographically mobile.

Due to reorganization within the National Health Service there is significant demand for dietitians to work in the field of nutrition education within the community environment. Monthly lists of vacancies are published by the British Dietetic Association and circulated to members, but non-members can buy copies from the Association.

PAY AND CONDITIONS

Basic grade dietitians in the NHS start on an annual salary of around £14,000 and progress through four incremental points to about £15,500. Senior dietitians grade 2 earn from about £15,500 to £18,400, and seniors at grade 1 earn from around £18,400 to £21,000. At the top of the NHS ladder, dietitians can currently earn a maximum of about £31,000. Dietitians also receive additional payments for on-call duties and student training allowances.

NHS dietitians normally work a five-day $36\frac{1}{2}$-hour week. Talks and lectures may involve occasional evening work, and dietitians working in the hospital environment may sometimes work on Saturdays. Dietitians whose work includes on-call duties sometimes work evenings and weekends. More flexible patterns of working are increasingly becoming established, with many opportunities for part-time and job share working.

NHS trust hospitals are increasingly setting their own scales on pay although at present they vary little from the above.

PROSPECTS

There is a formal career path for NHS dietitians, and a basic grade dietitian can expect a first promotion after about two years. Experienced dietitians (Senior II, Senior I, and Chief grades) either have clinical expertise, for example, in renal work, paediatrics, or community work, or they manage teams of dietitians. The dietetic manager or head of service is the top-grade post, and can hold responsibility for the whole dietetic service across a wide area. This is, however, now becoming less common, with the advent of trusts. A dietetic manager is normally responsible for staff only working within his/her unit or trust rather than across several trusts (provider units). A dietitian can also enter full-time teaching or lecturing (usually with a research degree), or move into health service management.

Whilst working within the profession, dietitians may take various post-registration training courses, for example in paediatrics or care of elderly people. Dietitians wishing to teach may take the City and Guilds Teaching Certificate or a Health Education Diploma.

RELATED OCCUPATIONS

Health visitor, home economist, food scientist/technologist, health education officer, nurse, pharmacist.

FURTHER INFORMATION

The British Dietetic Association, 7th Floor Elizabeth House, 22 Suffolk Street, Queensway, Birmingham B1 1LS, 0121 643 5483, www.bda.co.uk

FURTHER READING

Working in Hospitals –COIC

In the careers library classified under JAV.

MEDICAL TECHNICAL OFFICER
CLCI:JOB

BACKGROUND INFORMATION

As medical technology is growing, so hospitals are using an increasingly wide range of complex equipment to diagnose and treat illness and then monitor the results of the treatment. The medical technical officers (MTOs), who are responsible for operating and/or maintaining this equipment, usually specialize in a particular area of work, with responsibility for a particular type of equipment. MTOs specialize in either medical physics or physiological measurement.

Medical technical officers (medical physics) – previously known as medical physics technicians – specialize in radiation protection, lasers, clinical instrumentation or engineering, and may have little or no patient contact. Those specializing in radiotherapy, ultrasound, renal dialysis, rehabilitation engineering or nuclear medicine have a high rate of patient contact, dealing with them in clinical situations and, in some cases, at the patient's home. They are involved in the research and development of new techniques and apparatus, the monitoring of its performance, the maintenance and repair of the specialized medical equipment, together with some aspects of its operation. They work closely with scientists within the medical physics department and with medical staff, nurses and other healthcare professionals.

Medical technical officers (physiological measurement) – sometimes known as physiological measurement technologists – usually specialize in audiology, cardiology, gastroenterology or respiratory physiology. Working closely with patients, they measure the capacity of various parts of the body to function – to help medical staff diagnose and treat diseases.

THE WORK
Medical technical officer (medical physics)

Radiotherapy is one of the main treatments of cancer. A beam of radiation is directed at the tumour while the other areas of the body are protected. MTOs construct devices to hold the patient in the correct position during treatment and make masks and shields to ensure that areas of the patient are protected from radiation – vitally important in directing radiation beams at the affected area and away from the rest of the body, so the tumour is treated in the safest and most effective way. Some MTOs are involved in treatment planning, computing doses to be given to patients and ensuring that the treatment is accurately prescribed. The equipment used in planning and administering treatment to the patient in the radiotherapy department is maintained by MTOs who work within the clinical engineering specialities.

Radiation protection is a separate speciality, in which MTOs are responsible for ensuring the safety of staff and patients. They carry out frequent tests and measurements to monitor the exposure levels of staff, patients and the general public in nuclear medicine, diagnostic radiology and radiotherapy, helping to ensure that radiation doses are kept to a minimum and that staff follow safe working practices.

Ultrasound uses sound waves to monitor functions and identify abnormalities with the body. It is best known for its use with pregnant women, showing an image of the unborn baby on the screen to check the progress of development, but is also used to study tissue structure, blood flow and other physiological functions. MTOs working in this speciality offer technical support and back-up to medical and scientific staff, sometimes becoming involved in research and development projects.

Nuclear medicine involves amounts of radioactive material being introduced into the patient. The MTO may be responsible for preparing and purifying radioactive materials safely and for administering them to the patient. The patient is then positioned by the MTO in front of a gamma scanner or radioactivity camera to measure the concentration and distribution of the radioactive material inside the patient's body, testing the uptake of a specific organ. The distribution and uptake of the radioactive material gives a good indication of organ function. It is also the MTOs job to safely and accurately dispose of this radioactive material after use.

Clinical engineering may involve electronic or mechanical specialization. MTOs are involved in the development, construction and maintenance of the specialized medical and scientific equipment that is used by clinicians throughout the hospital. The work ranges from regular calibration, fault diagnosis, servicing and safety checks to designing and building particular pieces of apparatus. Bioengineering involves the development of artificial replacements for parts of the body that no longer work – such as hip or knee joints – or adaptations to help people with disabilities.

Rehabilitation engineering involves providing technical advice and support to clinical colleagues on all aspects of wheelchairs and other mobility equipment – adapting, repairing and conditioning powered and non-powered wheelchairs.

Clinical instrumentation demands considerable knowledge of electronics and/or instrument technology using appropriate skills to construct, maintain, or adapt simple or complex equipment or instruments. Some MTOs may specialize and work mainly in particular clinical departments.

Renal dialysis involves an artificial kidney machine pumping a patient's blood, containing waste products, through ultra-thin tubing so that only the waste products diffuse to the dialysing fluid. MTOs must ensure that the equipment functions correctly and make sure that the dialysis proceeds correctly. When repair is necessary, the MTO removes the apparatus to the workshop to correct faults. If equipment fails at a patient's home, the MTO visits, diagnoses the fault, replaces or repairs the part, and instructs the patient or family on how to operate the equipment and avoid the fault in future.

Lasers are increasingly used in ophthalmology, surgery and gynaecology to burn away diseased, or to repair torn tissue in otherwise inaccessible organs. The accuracy of the laser must be very high and it may be the responsibility of the MTO to check and maintain the equipment.

Medical technical officer (physiological measurement)

Audiology involves the measurement and evaluation of people's hearing capacity. If a child or adult is suspected of having a hearing problem, the audiology MTO's measurements enable the medical staff to diagnose and prescribe the appropriate treatment. Audiology MTOs also test balance and auditory-evoked potentials (electrical responses in the brain to test sounds). Another aspect of the work is to test and fit hearing aids and teach people

MEDICAL TECHNOLOGY: JOB

how to benefit most from them; rehabilitation and counselling are an important part of the job. MTOs make minor adjustments to hearing aids and take impressions of the ear so that they can prepare specially moulded ear inserts.

Cardiology MTOs work with patients who either have, or are suspected of having, heart disease. They measure the electrical activity of the heart, recording its electrical changes by fitting electrodes onto the patient's body and linking them with wires to the ECG (electrocardiograph) machine to pick up the heartbeat. The machine reads the impulses and prints out a chart. Any irregularities are shown up and the doctor can decide on the correct course of action. If a problem does not show up immediately, 24-hour 'ambulatory' readings may be taken using a portable monitor. People with intermittent heart problems may be given a cardio-memo machine, which records the problem when it occurs. Cardiology MTOs may also give a stress test where the patient walks on a treadmill whilst linked up to monitors. Ultrasound may also be used to aid diagnosis. Medical staff assess the results, identify the problem and its severity and decide on a course of action. Cardiology MTOs monitor patients who have electronic pacemakers to regulate their heartbeat, making sure that they are working efficiently. They also may be called upon to monitor the condition of a patient's heart during surgery, or in the intensive therapy unit.

Gastroenterology involves the measurement of pressure and pressure changes and acidity along the alimentary canal. MTOs insert sensitive instruments contained in thin tubes into the patients stomach and beyond and interpret the readings obtained under different circumstances such as different kinds of meals or drugs.

Neurophysiology involves the measurement and recording of the electrical activity of the brain and central nervous system. The MTO monitors the measurements by using electrodes placed on the patient's head to transmit information to an EEG (electroencephalograph) machine. The results are recorded and printed out onto paper. An abnormal pattern may indicate disease. The EEG MTO may also record 'evoked potentials' that are produced by the brain in response to specific stimuli.

Respiratory physiology refers to the functioning of a patient's breathing system. The respiratory physiology MTO takes measurements that reflect the function and efficiency of the patient's breathing system. Patients are normally referred to the department with breathing problems, chest pain or abnormality on a chest x-ray. The tests vary in complexity. Usually, patients breathe into a mouthpiece attached to the equipment used by the MTO to measure and record the volume of the lungs and how well they transfer gas; alternative tests could combine exercise studies and circulatory measurements in more complicated procedures. Respiratory MTOs also analyse respiratory gas and do blood gas analysis. Computer technology is being used increasingly for test calculations.

WORK ENVIRONMENT

MTOs work within different hospital departments, according to their speciality. They may work closely with medical physicists and other MTOs in laboratories, or with doctors and nurses. Those specializing in clinical instrumentation and clinical engineering may work in departments around the hospital, or based in workshops that contain the necessary sophisticated tools and instruments. Cardiology and respiratory MTOs work in clinical departments, outpatient clinics or on wards; neurophysiology MTOs in some hospitals may work on clinical departments, wards, intensive therapy units or operating theatres; audiology MTOs spend much of their time with patients in outpatient clinics.

SKILLS AND INTERESTS

MTOs working in medical physics and physiological measurement need to be responsible and meticulous since medical, nursing, and other medical physics staff rely on them to ensure that the equipment gives the most accurate results.

Manual dexterity and appropriate academic knowledge is required to set up, operate and maintain complex equipment. Accuracy is needed in using equipment.

MTOs need to communicate effectively with patients and staff. They carry out tests on patients who may be anxious and unwell; it is important to be sympathetic and reassuring whilst ensuring that the tests are carried out fully and accurately. They need to be calm and competent, so that patients can have complete confidence in them.

ENTRY REQUIREMENTS

There are no formal entry requirements but employers usually require a minimum of four GCSEs/S grades (A–C/1–3) in English, maths and two science subjects or a double science award; or a relevant BTEC first award, eg science; or appropriate SQA national certificate modules; or a relevant Intermediate GNVQ/GSVQ Level II, eg science. These are the minimum requirements for entry to the BTEC National Certificate in Medical Physics and Physiological Measurement. Employers may require two A levels including physics.

Some entrants in engineering or clinical instrumentation have BTEC National Certificate/Diploma or SQA National Certificate in Electronics or Electrical/Electronic Engineering; or Intermediate GNVQ/GSVQ Level II in Engineering; or A levels/H grades. Some enter on completing a higher national award or degree in science or engineering. MTOs are usually age 18 or over on entry, because of the amount of direct contact with patients.

Modern Apprenticeships (part of the Skillseekers Initiative in Scotland) may be available for young people leading to at least an NVQ/SVQ Level 3. Contact your local careers office, Jobcentre, TEC/LEC for details.

TRAINING

Trainee MTOs undertake a programme of in-service training related to their particular specialism. They also gain an insight into other specialisms. Training is mainly in the practical skills of the specialism but also includes lectures from senior MTOs, clinical scientists and medical staff.

Trainees working in radiotherapy, radiation protection, ultrasound, nuclear medicine or physiological measurement usually attend a college of further education part-time, on day release or block release, to work towards the BTEC National Certificate in Medical Physics and Physiological Measurement or the SQA Certificate in Medical Science, followed by a higher national certificate. Areas studied include physics, maths, medical physics and physiological measurement techniques, medical instrumentation, human physiology, core sciences, computers, and common skills.

MEDICAL TECHNOLOGY: JOB

Trainees working in medical electronics or mechanical engineering will often undertake BTEC or NVQ courses in an appropriate subject and/or may be enrolled within the Modern Apprenticeship Scheme.

Most trainee neurophysiology MTOs also sit Part 1 of the professional examination organized by the Electroencephalography and Clinical Neurophysiology Educational Board. There is also a two-year full-time course available to trainee neurophysiology MTOs.

Trainee audiology MTOs sit examinations set by the British Association of Audiology Technicians. A few hospitals run full-time courses for audiology MTOs rather than sending them to a college of further education.

Respiratory MTOs can take the in-service training examination set by the Association of Respiratory Technicians and Physiologists.

Entrants with relevant BTEC/SQA higher national awards, or degrees, complete a period of in-service training, rather than study for the BTEC national diploma or SQA certificate.

There are some opportunities each year in England for supernumerary trainees, who are employed in a particular hospital trust with funding from a regional office. They spend time in different departments over two or more years while attending a BTEC or NVQ course. NVQs/SVQs in Health Care are available at Level 3 in audiology, neurology and respiratory physiology.

Modern Apprenticeships (part of the Skillseekers Initiative in Scotland) are designed for some young people entering work in either medical physics or physiological measurement. Apprentices work towards the appropriate NVQ at Level 3 and the BTEC National Certificate in Medical Physics and Physiological Measurement. Apprenticeships are not for a set length of time but may last for between two and four years. Contact your local careers office, Jobcentre or TEC/LEC for details.

LATE ENTRY

Some MTOs are recruited straight from school or college, and some may enter as graduates. Most MTOs are not usually recruited under age 18. There is no upper age limit for entry to the profession.

OPPORTUNITIES

The majority of MTOs and physiological measurement technicians work for the NHS. A few MTOs are employed by the Armed Forces, particularly the RAF. Vacancies are advertised in local newspapers, trade journals and scientific publications such as *New Scientist*.

PAY AND CONDITIONS

There are fixed pay scales for NHS employees negotiated annually. All MTO posts are allocated to specific points within a pay spine, normally with annual increments. Trainees pay starts at £6,968. The salaries for qualified MTOs range from £9,437 for MTO1 to £30,341 for MTO5.

MTOs work a five-day, 37-hour week. This may include some weekend or on-call duties. There may be some overtime work. There may be opportunities for part-time work.

PROSPECTS

To apply for promotion through the grades, applicants must have had significant experience, which merits the promotion. Through the grades the skills and responsibilities expected will increase significantly. The MTO5 grade is a post with very substantial responsibilities attached. Top of the scale is the Senior Chief or Principal managing a department, or major sub-division.

RELATED OCCUPATIONS

Radiographer, medical laboratory assistant, laboratory technician, prosthetist/orthotist, pharmacy technician.

FURTHER INFORMATION

Institute of Physics and Engineering in Medicine (IPEM), 4 Campelshon Road, York YO2 1PE, 01904 610821

British Society of Audiology*, 80 Brighton Road, Reading, Berkshire RG6 1PS (please include 31p SAE), 01189 660622

Association of Respiratory Technicians and Physiologists, Dept. of Respiratory Medicine, Queen Elizabeth Building, Royal Infirmary, Alexandra Parade, Glasgow G31 2ES 0141 652 3535

Cardiothoracic Measurement Department, Derbyshire Royal Infirmary, London Road, Derby DE1 2QY 01332 47141 ext 2252

Health Service Careers, PO Box 204, London SE99 7UW

Scottish Office Home and Health Dept, Police Division, Room E1-7, Saughton House, Broomhouse Drive, Edinburgh EH11 3XD, 0131 2442156

FURTHER READING

Leaflets/booklets are available from the address marked*.

Working in Hospitals – COIC

Working in Physical Sciences – COIC

In the careers library classified under JOB.

AMBULANCE WORK: JOC

AMBULANCE PERSON CLCI:JOC

BACKGROUND INFORMATION

Ambulance services are often associated with emergency 999 calls to road accidents and major disasters, or to people suffering sudden illness or injury. However, this forms only a small, though very important, part of ambulance service work. The majority of calls are to non-urgent cases, such as elderly patients, who need ambulance transport to and from hospital and daycare centres.

There are 67 ambulance services in the UK; there is no national ambulance service, so there are some differences between individual services, particularly in recruitment and training patterns. The following sections describe common features; further information on local requirements can be obtained from local chief executives/ambulance officers.

THE WORK

All ambulance personnel spend most of their time working with people – patients, hospital staff, members of other services or agencies. Features common to the work of all personnel are lifting and carrying patients; answering queries from patients, medical staff etc; checking/replenishing stocks of first aid equipment and other supplies; basic vehicle checks (oil, water, tyre pressure); filling up with petrol; ambulance cleaning; completing log sheets.

Ambulance personnel sometimes work in pairs, one driving the ambulance, the other attending to patients' needs.

In most services, operational ambulance personnel are divided into three main grades: care assistants, technicians and paramedics. There are considerable differences in the levels of skill and range of tasks carried out by each grade.

Ambulance care assistants, sometimes known as dedicated day transport personnel, are mainly concerned with transporting infirm, disabled, mentally ill, elderly patients, or patients unable to get to and from hospital outpatient clinics, day centres etc. They help patients into the ambulance and make sure they are secure and comfortable – fastening safety straps and seat belts, wrapping blankets around patients where necessary. Care assistants often enter the patient's home – particularly when the patient is elderly – to help the patient to the ambulance. While in the patient's home, care assistants may carry out simple safety checks, such as making sure the gas is turned off, or that the doors are locked. Assistants sometimes help with patient care in hospital units – carrying out nursing auxiliary duties – as well as undertaking ambulance work.

Ambulance technicians are involved in the full range of accident and emergency duties. They respond to 999 calls for assistance at road traffic accidents and other emergencies and incidents. They are also called on by GPs who require ambulance transport for urgent cases, and their services are needed for the admission, transfer and discharge of patients requiring skilled treatment – such as the administration of oxygen – whilst travelling by ambulance.

Technicians need to be able to make decisions about the treatment and movement of patients; this involves making provisional diagnoses. They give emergency treatment, such as splinting broken bones or using various types of life-saving equipment; these include ventilators, which introduce air into the lungs, or semi-automatic defibrillators, used to restore a co-ordinated rhythm to the heart.

Ambulance paramedics are technicians who have taken significant additional training, and are qualified to use the more advanced forms of life support equipment. They may, for example, administer intravenous infusion (setting up a drip to introduce substances into the patient's bloodstream) and endotrachial intubation (introducing a tube into the throat to create an airway). They are also qualified in coronary care, and may administer drugs in certain situations.

Both technicians and paramedics complete patient report forms, for the use of medical staff; these describe signs, symptoms and any actions that have been taken.

Control room assistants work in ambulance stations or central control units, answering emergency and urgent calls from GPs and the public, and maintaining radio contact with ambulance crews. They operate switchboards, receive and pass on messages, and use other communications equipment, such as computer terminals, fax machines and telex. Assistants may also be involved in planning ambulance crew journeys.

WORK ENVIRONMENT

Ambulance crew spend the majority of their time in vehicles, on the move. They start the working day at the ambulance station, and may return there in mid-shift for a meal break. Throughout the shift they are in radio contact with their control room. Technicians and paramedics work nights, and this may involve being outside in the dark, in all weather conditions – for example, at the scene of an accident. Physically, ambulance work is strenuous, involving heavy lifting, carrying and bending.

Ambulance personnel wear uniforms, and protective clothing for emergency work and where appropriate.

SKILLS AND INTERESTS

Ambulance personnel should enjoy working with people from a variety of backgrounds. A friendly personality is important, together with the ability to deal tactfully and compassionately with sick and injured people. Understanding and patience are essential.

A clear voice and good spoken communication skills are necessary for communicating with patients, hospital staff, representatives of other emergency services and organizations such as social services. Written communication skills are also required, particularly at technician and paramedic level, for completing patient report forms and for formal study on training courses.

A responsible attitude, reliability and punctuality are essential. A smart appearance is required, to inspire the public's trust and confidence.

It is important to be able to remain calm in crises and to be able to cope with distressing sights and situations. It is also necessary to take decisions about the treatment and movement of patients and to be responsible for the results of those decisions.

Ambulance personnel need to be physically fit, and capable of lifting and moving patients. Their weight and body size should be proportionate to their height.

AMBULANCE WORK: JOC

Control room assistants need to be able to communicate clearly, both orally and in writing. Good eyesight and hearing are important. Keyboard skills are an advantage and may be required in some services.

ENTRY REQUIREMENTS

Ambulance services throughout England and Wales set their own entry requirements. The whole of Scotland, though, is served by The Scottish Ambulance Service, so entry requirements in Scotland are standard. The minimum age on entry for ambulance crew varies between services but is usually between 18 and 21 years, although two services have cadet schemes for 17- and 18-year-olds. In Scotland there is no minimum age specified but the need for driving experience means that entrants are at least 19 years old.

Ambulance care assistants need to have had a full, clean, current driving licence for a period specified by each individual service, usually one or two years (two years in Scotland). They may require experience of working with elderly or disabled people, or have other caring experience. In Scotland, it is desirable for applicants to have a minimum of three S grades (1–3) or equivalent, including English and a numerate or scientific subject.

The selection process involves an interview and series of tests. Before the interview, applicants outside Scotland are sent a booklet on medical care, which they are expected to study. The assessment process includes questions on this material. All candidates are tested on basic maths, English, manual dexterity, driving and knowledge of the Highway Code. They must pass a medical examination, including a vision test, although not every service insists on good colour vision.

Ambulance technicians usually have experience as ambulance care assistants but, in some ambulance services, direct entry as a technician is possible. The selection process is the same as for care assistants, but some employers require three to five GCSEs/S grades (A–C/1–3), preferably including English, maths and a science subject, or the equivalent, eg Intermediate GNVQ. In Scotland candidates must show that they are able to progress to paramedical status, so evidence of qualifications equivalent to two H grades is desirable but not essential.

Cadet schemes. It is preferred if applicants to the cadet scheme run by South Yorkshire Metropolitan Ambulance Service have GCSEs (A–C) in English, maths and human biology or dual science. They should be between 17 and 18 on appointment, with a full driving licence. Applicants to the West Midlands Ambulance Service cadet scheme are at an advantage if they have GCSEs (A–C) in English, maths and science subjects. They should be between 1.63 metres (5 feet 4 inches) and 1.88 metres (6 feet 2 inches) in height and at least 17 by the end of September of the year of entry and under 19 before Christmas of the intake year. Both services accept alternative qualifications to GCSEs, eg Intermediate GNVQ in Health and Social Care. Applicants to both services must pass aptitude tests, a medical and physical fitness tests.

Control room assistants may enter at a minimum age of 16 to 18 years. Applicants should have good communication skills and VDU experience – they may have to pass a test of keyboard skills. They may apply to be considered for ambulance duties after reaching the minimum age of entry for ambulance crew.

TRAINING

Ambulance care assistants start by taking an in-house course, usually lasting between two and four weeks. The course includes basic health and safety at work, first aid, the role of the ambulance service in the community, ambulance driving, working with patients (including techniques for lifting and carrying) and, sometimes, experience in a hospital.

Ambulance technicians have normally completed the care assistant training course and gained experience in that position. Technician training starts with an eight-week residential course at a regional ambulance training school (nine weeks in Scotland). Six weeks of the course (seven in Scotland) are spent on the study of patient care, anatomy, physiology, diagnosis, treatment, casualty management, basic midwifery and related subjects. For the remaining two weeks, trainees receive instruction in advanced driving techniques.

The residential course is followed by twelve to eighteen months' experience in the full range of accident and emergency work, with continuous assessment and exams at the end of the twelve-month period. Those who successfully complete the course and assessments, gain the National Ambulance Proficiency Certificate awarded by the Institute of Health and Care Development.

Paramedics. Those who have completed a minimum of twelve to eighteen months' (eighteen in Scotland) post-qualifying experience in the full range of ambulance duties, as ambulance technicians, are eligible to be selected for paramedic training. The selection process involves an interview with clinical staff and ambulance officers, and a written and practical examination in ambulance aid.

Those who are selected for paramedic training take a four-week intensive course at a nationally accredited training centre. The course covers advanced anatomy and physiology, with particular reference to the nervous, cardiovascular and respiratory systems, and training in the use of advanced life-saving equipment. The course is divided into modules of one week and three weeks, each followed by examinations of theory and practical procedure.

After the course, there are four weeks of hospital training, supervised by clinical and medical consultants, which includes experience in different hospital departments. Successful completion of the course modules and hospital training, plus assessment by the Chairman of the local Ambulance Paramedic Advisory Council, leads to the Certificate for Ambulance Paramedic Skills, awarded by the National Health Service Training Directorate.

Cadet schemes are run by South Yorkshire and West Midlands Ambulance Services. South Yorkshire's scheme lasts for two years, West Midlands' for eighteen months. Schemes involve on- and off-the-job training. They include driving instruction, Outward Bound courses, community projects, experience in hospitals and different departments within the ambulance service, and, possibly, a trip abroad to observe how another country's ambulance service operates.

On successful completion of training, South Yorkshire cadets become trainee ambulancemen/women, while West Midlands cadets become qualified ambulance technicians.

Control room assistants receive on-the-job training in the use of switchboards, radio communications and other control room equipment. In Scotland they must also successfully complete a two-week course on computerized

AMBULANCE WORK: JOC

command and control systems.

Ambulance Service Institute qualifications are not essential for ambulance personnel, but they are advantageous, particularly for staff who intend to train as paramedics, and for promotion to supervisory and management grades. Serving personnel (other than cadets) usually study for the examinations via distance learning courses. The Institute awards qualifications at four levels: licentiate, associate, graduate and fellow.

Updating courses. Ambulance personnel take further courses at regular intervals throughout their careers. This enables them to learn new skills and keep up with technical developments.

LATE ENTRY

Ambulance work is often a second career and employers recruit applicants who are over the minimum entry age of 18 to 21 years. Previous experience in nursing or with elderly people is an advantage, although recruits to ambulance services come from a wide range of backgrounds. The age range on entry is about 18 to 55 years. It can be more difficult, however, for people over the age of around 35 to 40 years to be selected for training as technicians and paramedics, because of the length of training involved.

OPPORTUNITIES

The National Health Service employs about 15,000 operational ambulance personnel; the total number of people employed by ambulance services, including officers, is about 18,000.

The UK's ambulance services are usually run by district health authorities or NHS trusts.

Apart from the NHS, there are opportunities to train in ambulance work in the Armed Forces. Other employers include private ambulance services, catering for private hospitals, and large industrial firms that sometimes run small on-site ambulance services. Private sector employers usually engage staff with NHS training and experience.

Overall, employment in ambulance services is stable. The availability of vacancies varies in different parts of the country, with greater demand for staff in London and South East England. In rural districts and areas of high unemployment, there is likely to be considerable competition for vacancies. If an application to the local ambulance service is unsuccessful, it may be worth applying to an ambulance service in another area.

There are occasional opportunities to work overseas, for instance with Voluntary Service Overseas (VSO).

PAY AND CONDITIONS

Salaries vary between different services. Most entrants of 18 years or over start as ambulance persons, earning a salary of £11,362 (pro-rata for part-timers). Ambulance technicians and paramedics earn around £16,000. London staff receive an additional London allowance (£1809).

Additional hours over and above the normal working week are paid, but at the basic rate.

Ambulance personnel work 39 hours a week. Ambulance persons usually work days, Monday to Friday; starting and finishing times vary. Many work part-time. Ambulance technicians and paramedics work a rotating shift pattern, including nights and weekends. In remote areas, additional stand-by and on-call duties may be required.

Control room assistants also work 39 hours a week. Some work days; others work rotating shifts.

Rates of pay and conditions of service may vary in NHS trusts.

Please contact your local ambulance service for more details.

PROSPECTS

All ambulance staff are eligible for promotion if they have the potential and meet the required criteria. Supervisory work involves responsibility for a group of staff. There are further opportunities to progress to management grades – specializing in operations, control room communications, training or administration.

The majority of senior management have risen through the ranks.

In some services, control room assistants can be promoted through various grades and reach management level without gaining operational ambulance experience. Other services require control room assistants to gain experience as care assistants/technicians before they can be considered for more-senior posts.

RELATED OCCUPATIONS

Nurse, health care assistant/nursing auxiliary, care assistant, fire-fighter/officer, coastguard officer, police constable, hospital porter.

FURTHER INFORMATION

Contact the local chief executive/ambulance officer for further information; the address can be found in the telephone directory.

London Ambulance Service*, Personnel Department, 220 Waterloo Road, London SE1 8SD, 0171 928 0333

The Scottish Ambulance Service NHS Trust, National Headquarters, 4 Maitland Street, Glasgow G4 0HX, 0131 447 7711

FURTHER READING

Leaflets/booklets are available from the addresses marked*.

Working in Police and Emergency Services –COIC

In the careers library classified under JOC.

ALTERNATIVE/COMPLEMENTARY MEDICINE: JOD

1. ACUPUNCTURIST CLCI:JOD
2. AROMATHERAPIST CLCI:JOD
3. CHIROPRACTOR CLCI:JOD
4. HERBALIST CLCI:JOD
5. HOMOEOPATH CLCI:JOD
6. NATUROPATH CLCI:JOD
7. OSTEOPATH CLCI:JOD
8. REFLEXOLOGIST CLCI:JOD

BACKGROUND INFORMATION

Many of the therapies profiled in this article see themselves as complementary to conventional medicine, rather than as an alternative to it. They are complementary to each other as well, since different therapies may be seen as more appropriate for different patients, as well as conditions. They are sometimes called natural therapies, as their aim is to work with natural processes.

Complementary medicine can be described as holistic, which means it takes the whole person into account, examining their physical, mental, emotional and spiritual state. The patient's physical, social and personal environment is also taken into consideration. Holistic practitioners may encourage patients to take responsibility for changing elements in their life that may be contributing to their affliction – such as their posture or the amount of exercise they take. Often patients present chronic conditions.

On completion of training, practitioners become eligible for membership of a professional association with its own register, code of ethics and disciplinary procedures. Current changes mean both osteopaths and chiropractors are soon likely to have national registers regulated by law, the others remain voluntary.

GPs, especially from fund-holding practices, may refer patients for complementary treatment, as long as they remain in charge of the patient. Most therapies are available privately, although homoeopathy has been available on the NHS since 1948. Interest in complementary medicine has increased in recent years.

THE WORK

1. Acupuncturist

Acupuncturists aim to regulate their patients' body functions and promote the restoration of health using methods from a system of medicine that originated in China thousands of years ago. As well as therapeutic acupuncture, some acupuncturists offer acupuncture anaesthesia and ear acupuncture, a system to help people overcome addictions.

The main method used is insertion of very fine stainless steel needles into particular points beneath the skin. Sometimes the acupuncturist may treat these points by moxibustion – warming them with a burning aromatic herb (moxa or dried mugwort) – or by massaging them. The underlying theory is that the body has a network of channels (or meridians) along which vital energy (chi) flows. The acupuncturist aims to reduce or increase the flow as required by the stimulation that the inserted needles, or other methods, provide.

Acupuncturists take full case histories from their patients, including their food preferences and emotional reactions to various situations, to get a whole picture before they start a diagnosis. Then they take a series of pulse measurements on the patient's wrist and may examine their tongue. A recent technological introduction to the art is electro-acupuncture, where a machine examines the points on the patient's body, although many acupuncturists prefer to do their examinations by hand.

2. Aromatherapist

Aromatherapists treat a variety of conditions using essential oils extracted or distilled from flowers, trees, herbs, spices and fruit. Practitioners often massage their clients with these oils (blended with carrier vegetable oils), which can also be used in baths or inhaled.

The aromatherapist takes a detailed personal and medical history of the client, often covering areas such as diet, exercise, environmental factors, allergy and emotional problems. From this, the essential oils to be used in treatment are selected and administered in the way the aromatherapist thinks is most appropriate. Different oils are used for their therapeutic properties, depending on the condition being treated. Aromatherapy is used especially for stress-related problems and for a variety of chronic conditions.

3. Chiropractor

Chiropractors specialize in mechanical disorders of joints, especially of the spine, and their effects on the nervous system. They use a wide range of manipulative techniques to improve spinal function and relieve pain. In addition, they may offer advice on exercise, lifestyle, nutrition and work. Chiropractic was established as a health science in 1895 in the USA.

Chiropractors take a detailed medical history of their patients, followed by a physical examination, which may include x-rays, blood samples and neurological examinations. They examine the patient's spine and joints with their hands, observing mobility and any changes in tissue. Treatment comprises a wide range of adjusting and supporting techniques, taking the form of twists and pulls, with the practitioner and patient in different positions.

4. Herbalist

Herbalists use plant remedies to treat disease. Western pharmaceutical drugs use only the 'active' part of a plant, either concentrated or synthesized, while herbal drugs use extracts of the whole plant to achieve a more balanced effect. Herbal remedies include infusions (made like tea), powders, tablets, liquids, lotions, creams and ointments.

Herbalists take detailed medical histories, offer advice about diet and lifestyle, and prescribe herbal remedies for the specific complaint. While qualified herbalists treat a wide range of complaints, they also refer patients to a doctor or another therapist, where appropriate.

Herbal medicine is known as phytotherapy in Europe. Practitioners may specialize in the western tradition, using plants mainly from Europe and North America. Other herbal traditions practised widely in the UK include the Chinese (often known as Traditional Chinese Medicine – a mixture of Chinese herbs and acupuncture) and Ayurreda from India.

5. Homoeopath

Homoeopaths use a system of medicine, based on a Law of Similars, to treat disease with substances that produce similar symptoms in healthy people. The idea is to use very minute quantities of substances to stimulate the body's own natural healing powers. Homoeopathy aims to treat the underlying cause of a disease, rather than just its symptoms.

ALTERNATIVE/COMPLEMENTARY MEDICINE: JOD

Homoeopaths take a wide range of detailed personal and medical information from their patients. They then prescribe remedies, normally in the form of a pill, suited to the individual patient and their illness. Remedies are derived from vegetable, animal or mineral substances. They are prepared through increasing dilution of these substances and vigorously shaking with water and alcohol between dilutions.

6. Naturopath

Naturopaths work on the basis that the body naturally knows how to heal itself, but that most people are out of touch with the knowledge, pointing to animals' instinctive tendency to fast or eat foods with healing properties when they are sick. In the naturopath's view, disease may be caused by congenital or developmental factors, or the patient's environment or diet, as well as by infection or trauma. Naturopaths use standard medical examination procedures to diagnose conditions and assess the patient's potential for health and vital reserves.

The naturopath's main work is to promote the body's own self-healing systems. This work often involves giving advice about nutrition, exercise and rest. Hydrotherapy may also be used, where patients are given special baths or hot and cold shower sprays. Herbs, or hot or cold packs, to be applied to problem areas may be prescribed. In some cases, the naturopath may provide psychological counselling. Where appropriate, if disease is outside the scope of naturopathy, patients are referred to conventional medicine. Naturopaths sometimes practise osteopathy as well.

7. Osteopath

Osteopathy is a system of medicine concerned with the well-being of the musculo-skeletal system (the bones, joints, muscles, ligaments and connective tissue) making up the body's framework. Osteopaths use their hands both to discover the underlying causes of pain and to treat disorders. They use a variety of soft tissue and manipulative techniques in order to restore function and improve mobility. The work is physically quite demanding, although manipulative skills are required rather than particular strength.

Osteopaths take detailed medical histories before examining how the patient walks, stands and sits. They use their hands to examine muscles, ligaments and vertebrae and, in some cases, may use x-rays or other orthodox tests. After treatment, osteopaths often advise on remedial exercises to adjust posture and help in maintaining a realistic level of health. If the problem cannot be helped by osteopathic treatment, the osteopath may refer the patient to a doctor or another type of therapist.

8. Reflexologist

Reflexologists work on the basis of the theory that every part of the body is connected by energy pathways, which end in reflex areas on the feet, the hands and the head. They work systematically on these reflex areas and, by applying controlled pressure, stimulate the body's own healing mechanisms.

Reflexologists treat patients' bare feet (and sometimes hands), feeling for any tiny deposits under the surface of the skin, or imbalances in the feet (or hands). By working on these points, they aim to release blockages and ease tension, thus restoring the body's energy flow and improving circulation and elimination.

WORK ENVIRONMENT

Practitioners work mostly indoors, and often have a couch (or similar) for patients to lie on. Some practitioners work from a room in their home, others in very large buildings (such as the Royal London Homoeopathic Hospital or the British School of Osteopathy), or smaller rented rooms and in clinics or health centres. Some practitioners visit patients in their own homes, using a transportable table/couch. Practitioners may work outdoors, eg at sports events. Some chiropractors treat animals, especially horses.

SKILLS AND INTERESTS

It is essential for practitioners in complementary medicine to be ethical, and to be able to establish a good rapport with a wide range of patients. Good communication skills are vital, as are sympathy and understanding when treating patients who may be in some pain. Clear, logical problem-solving skills, and detached observation, help with case assessments.

A willingness to pursue their own personal development is required, since some self-knowledge and stability is necessary to help other people. A genuine desire to help people is essential, along with a certain amount of sensitivity, especially in therapies that involve touching the patient. For most complementary medicines, a lot of stamina is needed to cope with the physical and emotional demands of healing. For some, such as chiropractic and osteopathy, manipulative skills are needed as well.

ENTRY REQUIREMENTS

Entry to training for most areas of complementary medicine is expressed in terms of A levels/H grades. Where A levels/H grades are specified, relevant BTEC/SQA national awards and Advanced GNVQ/GSVQ Level III, in subjects such as science, are usually acceptable as alternatives. Entry to some courses in acupuncture, homoeopathy, osteopathy and naturopathy is restricted to those with previous medical or health care training.

1. Acupuncturist

Automatic membership of the British Acupuncture Council (BAcC) is open to those who have trained at specified colleges. Other applicants are interviewed for membership. Entry to most colleges is normally with a minimum of five GCSEs/S grades (A–C/1–3) and two A levels/three H grades. Some schools demand an A level/H grade in a science subject. The minimum age on entry to training varies between 18 and 21.

The British College of Acupuncture accepts only those who are already qualified in some branch of medicine or natural therapeutics, eg doctors, osteopaths, radiographers, pharmacists and nurses.

2. Aromatherapist

There are no set entry requirements. Some GCSEs/S grades, including biology or science, are desirable but not essential.

3. Chiropractor

Practising chiropractors must by law be registered with the General Chiropractic Council (GCC). Registration follows successful completion of training at a recognized college. People considering training should check with the GCC which courses will lead to registration.

Entry to training is usually with either a minimum of two A levels, preferably in biology, human biology, physics or

ALTERNATIVE/COMPLEMENTARY MEDICINE: JOD

chemistry; or three A levels including one of those subjects. GCSEs (A–C) in English and maths may be required, as may physics, chemistry and biology/human biology (or dual science) if not held at A level.

Also acceptable are three or four H grades, minimum B pass, preferably including two natural science subjects, one of which should be either human biology, physics or chemistry, plus S grades (1–3) in these sciences (if not held at H grade) and English and maths. Entrants must be at least 18.

4. Herbalist

The College of Practitioners of Phytotherapy and The National Institute of Medical Herbalists (NIMH) only accept onto their registers graduates of The School of Phytotherapy (Herbal Medicine) in Hailsham, East Sussex, and of the four-year full-time herbal medicine degree course at Middlesex University. The NIMH has recently developed an Accreditation Board and expects other training institutions to become accredited soon.

The usual minimum requirements for entry to both courses are two A levels/three H grades, preferably in science subjects, plus three GCSEs/S grades (A–C/1–3). The minimum age on entry to The School of Phytotherapy is 19.

5. Homoeopath

Entry to homoeopathy training can be as a qualified medical practitioner or health care professional with state registration, such as a dentist, pharmacist, chiropodist, nurse or midwife. Alternatively, it can be with a minimum of either two A levels/three H grades and three GCSEs (A–C)/two S grades (1–3); or four H grades. Science subjects, particularly biology, are most useful.

6. Naturopath

Entry to the only full-time training course is with two A levels/three H grades including chemistry and biology and three GCSEs/S grades (A–C/1–3) including English.

Entry to training organized by The Incorporated Society of Registered Naturopaths is restricted to health professionals with at least three years previous full-time training, such as osteopaths, chiropractors, physiotherapists and nurses.

7. Osteopath

Practising osteopaths must be registered with the General Osteopathic Council. In order to register, osteopaths have to train at an approved osteopathic school. Entry is with a minimum of two A levels/two H grades in science subjects, plus three GCSEs/S grades (A–C/1–3) in other subjects. The minimum age on entry to training is 18.

The British School of Osteopathy (BSO) recognizes that some mature individuals who wish to enter training may lack the normal entry qualifications; experience suggests that highly motivated mature individuals can make an invaluable contribution to patient care and they may therefore be accepted on the course with alternative qualifications or relevant experience, provided they can demonstrate an ability to benefit from the course and make a positive contribution to the profession.

There are also training courses designed only for qualified medical doctors, state registered health care professionals and trained complementary therapists from recognized schools.

8. Reflexologist

The Association of Reflexologists (AoR) accepts into membership those who have either trained on AoR accredited courses or undertaken additional training to reach accredited standards. Other organizations accept into membership practitioners who have trained with specific schools. There are no set entry requirements. Some GCSEs/S grades are desirable but not essential. The minimum age of entry to many training courses is 18.

TRAINING

1. Acupuncturist

Six colleges in England and Scotland offer training that leads to automatic membership of the British Acupuncture Council – The London College of Traditional Acupuncture, The London School of Acupuncture and Traditional Chinese Medicine (three years full-time), The International College of Oriental Medicine UK (East Grinstead) (four years full-time), The Northern College of Acupuncture (York) (four years part-time), The College of Integrated Chinese Medicine (Reading) and The College of Traditional Acupuncture (Royal Leamington Spa and Glasgow) (both three years part-time).

2. Aromatherapist

Training courses approved by the Aromatherapy Organizations Council (AOC) are offered at almost 100 establishments throughout the UK. Most are fee-paying, private training schools. Courses normally last at least nine months and are offered full-time and part-time. They include a minimum of 80 hours of aromatherapy, 60 hours of massage and 40 hours of anatomy and physiology, plus ten to fifteen case studies over 50 treatment hours. Shorter courses tend to be an introduction to aromatherapy or for interest only.

3. Chiropractor

The Anglo-European College of Chiropractic in Bournemouth offers a four-year full-time BSc degree in Human Sciences (Chiropractic), with a fifth year leading to the Postgraduate Diploma in Chiropractic.

The McTimoney Chiropractic College in Oxford and the Oxford College of Chiropractic offer four-year part-time courses leading to a Diploma in Chiropractic. Both colleges are currently planning to offer degree courses.

4. Herbalist

The School of Phytotherapy offers a four-year full-time course and a five-year distance learning course, both of which lead to a BSc (Honours) degree in phytotherapy. It also offers a two-year part-time course for trained medical people only, which leads to The Diploma in Herbal Medicine. All three courses lead to membership of the College of Practitioners of Phytotherapy (CPP) or the National Institute of Medical Herbalists (NIMH).

Middlesex University offers three-year and four-year full-time courses and a five-year part-time course. Only the four-year course includes clinical training and leads to professional practice of herbal medicine and registration with the National Institute of Medical Herbalists.

5. Homoeopath

The Faculty of Homoeopathy only promotes training to health care professionals. It accredits courses in Bristol, Glasgow, London and Oxford. Courses vary in length. They lead to the Primary Health Care Certificate. Doctors and veterinary surgeons are also admitted to medical or veterinary membership of the Faculty.

Homoeopaths and some health care professionals train at

ALTERNATIVE/COMPLEMENTARY MEDICINE: JOD

schools or colleges of homoeopathy. On completing a course a student may apply for Licensed Membership of The Society of Homoeopaths, followed by registration on gaining clinical experience. The Society lists 14 establishments in England and Wales that offer recognized training. Most courses last four years part-time. There are four three-year full-time courses, including that run jointly by The London College of Classical Homoeopathy and the University of Westminster that leads to a degree in Health Sciences: Homoeopathy.

6. Naturopath

The British College of Naturopathy and Osteopathy in London offers a four-year full-time course that leads to a degree in osteopathic medicine and a Diploma in Naturopathy.

The Incorporated Society of Registered Naturopaths' course for health professionals lasts four years part-time. It includes attendance at Malvern for at least 15 weekends.

7. Osteopath

There are courses in eight osteopathy schools in England that lead to registration with the General Osteopathic Council. The British College of Naturopathy and Osteopathy (London), The British School of Osteopathy (BSO)(London) and The European School of Osteopathy (Maidstone, Kent) offer four-year full-time degree courses. The BSO also offers its degree through an 'Extended Pathway', where three years' part-time study is followed by two years' full-time study. The London School of Osteopathy offers a five-year part-time degree course. Courses run by Maidstone College of Osteopathy (four-year full-time) and The College of Osteopaths Educational Trust (Borehamwood, Herts) (five-year part-time) lead to a Diploma in Osteopathy.

The London College of Osteopathic Medicine runs a 13-month course for qualified medical doctors only. The Oxford School of Osteopathy has a three-year part-time degree course only for state registered health care professionals and trained complementary therapists from recognized schools.

8. Reflexologist

Reflexology professional bodies accredit over 90 courses at private schools and colleges, colleges of further education and colleges of higher education throughout the UK and Eire. Courses are part-time and last at least nine months, including a minimum of 60 hours contact time. They are held at weekends, in evening or daytime classes and include much home study and practice.

LATE ENTRY

Many entrants to complementary medicine are mature, often with previous experience or qualifications in medically related work. Mature applicants from a wide range of backgrounds, with varying experience and qualifications, may be accepted onto training courses without the usual entry requirements. Interested people should contact training establishments for advice.

OPPORTUNITIES

Interest in complementary medicine has increased in the last few years, with demand exceeding supply in most areas, so that opportunities are generally good. Many areas lack complementary medicine practitioners, so there is often room for new practices to start. These opportunities are most apparent in cities and large towns, where there is a large population to provide potential patients.

Many practitioners are self-employed in private practice, although some work in multidisciplinary complementary health centres. It is sometimes possible for newly qualified practitioners to start work as assistants to other practitioners before setting up their own private practice. This is often the case with osteopaths. Newly qualified chiropractors must work as an assistant to another practitioner for at least one year before setting up their own private practice. Some practitioners work within or alongside the National Health Service, in either hospitals or GP practices.

PAY AND CONDITIONS

Many practitioners are self-employed, so income varies considerably. Most charge a session or hourly rate, which is usually in the range of £25 to £40 an hour. However, as the number and flow of patients can fluctuate, some practitioners supplement their income by practising more than one therapy, or by teaching and related work. The income of self-employed practitioners must also cover costs, such as rent of the therapy room and any administrative staff, such as receptionists. A number of practitioners work part-time.

PROSPECTS

Apart from private practice, where future prospects depend on building up the business alone or with partners, there is a variety of related careers to which practitioners can progress. Some practitioners opt to include teaching in their workload, or move into research. A few move into journalism or publishing in the health care field.

Opportunities may sometimes exist in related manufacturing. This is particularly the case for medical herbalists.

Practitioners in one discipline may add others to their skill base and so build their career. For instance, a reflexologist may practise aromatherapy as well, or vice versa. Opportunities also exist to move into or add related disciplines, such as counselling.

RELATED OCCUPATIONS

Doctor, nurse, counsellor, midwife, occupational therapist, psychotherapist, physiotherapist, paramedic.

FURTHER INFORMATION

British Complementary Medicine Association (BCMA)*, 249 Fosse Road South, Leicester LE3 1AE

Council for Complementary and Alternative Medicine (CCAM)*, 206–208 Latimer Road London W10 6RE, 0181 968 3862 (10am–5pm, Monday–Thursday)

Institute for Complementary Medicine (ICM)*, PO Box 194, London SE16 1QZ, 0171 237 5165

British Acupuncture Council*, Park House, 206–208 Latimer Road, London W10 6RE, 0181 964 0222

Aromatherapy Organizations Council*, PO Box 355, Croydon, CR9 2QP, 0181 251 7912

Anglo-European Chiropractic College*, Parkwood Road, Bournemouth, Dorset BH5 2DF, 01202 436200, www.aecclib.demon.co.uk

ALTERNATIVE/COMPLEMENTARY MEDICINE: JOD

National Institute of Medical Herbalists*, 56 Longbrook Street, Exeter, Devon EX4 6AH, 01392 426022

British Homoeopathic Association*, 27a Devonshire Street, London W1N 1RJ, 0171 935 2163, www.nhsconfed.net/bha

The Faculty of Homoeopathy*, Hahnemann House, 2 Powis Place, Great Ormond Street, London WC1N 3HT, 0171 837 9469

Society of Homoeopaths*, 2 Artizan Road, Northampton NN1 4HU, 01604 621400 (please include sae)

General Council and Register of Naturopaths*, Goswell House, 2 Goswell Road, Street, Somerset BA16 0JG, 01458 840072 (please include sae), www.naturopathy.org.uk

British School of Osteopathy,* 275 Borough High Street, London SE1 1JE, 0171 407 0222

Osteopathic Information Service*, Premier House, Room 432, 10 Greycoat Place, Victoria, London SW1P 1SB, 01734 512051 (please include sae)

Association of Reflexologists*, 27 Old Gloucester Street, London WC1N 3XX, 0990 673320, www.reflexology.org/aor

FURTHER READING

Leaflets/booklets are available from addresses marked*.

Working in Medicine and Dentistry – COIC

Working in Complementary and Alternative Medicine – A Career Guide – Kogan Page

A–Z of Alternative Medicine – Abercorn Hill Associates

Osteopathy by Stephen Sandler – Optima

In the careers library classified under JOD.

PROSTHETICS/ORTHOTICS: JOL

PROSTHETIST/ORTHOTIST CLCI:JOL

BACKGROUND INFORMATION

Prosthetists/orthotists are professionals who work with doctors and therapists as members of rehabilitation teams to provide care for disabled people. Prosthetists design and fit artificial limbs (prostheses) as replacements for limbs lost through amputation. These have to be functional, with working joints, and yet look natural. They are made from lightweight materials and have electronic and pneumatic mechanisms incorporated into the design so that, when fitted, they look and move like the limb they replace. Orthotists design and fit orthoses such as callipers, braces, neck collars and spine supports, which provide support to the patient's limbs or spine to relieve pain or prevent physical deformities from becoming worse. These may be worn permanently by the patient, or temporarily until natural healing restores the normal function of their body.

THE WORK

Prosthetists/orthotists work in a clinic team and help surgeons in deciding on suitable prostheses or orthoses for individual patients. They measure, make tracings and take plaster casts of the part to which the prosthesis/orthosis is to be fitted. They design the prosthesis/orthosis and give instructions to the technician who will make the device. (Prosthetists and orthotists working at small centres may also be involved in making the prostheses.) Prostheses and most orthoses are made to measure and, in designing them, the prosthetist needs to take the patient's life style into consideration.

Once the prosthesis or orthosis is made, the prosthetist/orthotist fits it onto the patient, making sure that it fits well and is comfortable. In the case of prostheses and orthoses for lower limbs, these may need further adjustments to give the patient a walking pattern that looks as natural as possible. They show the patient and their family how the prosthesis or orthosis works, how to put it on and take it off and, in some cases, they may have to help the patient to come to terms with wearing it. They liaise with the physiotherapist responsible for the patient's exercise regime, and also liaise with the occupational therapist who trains the patient in the use of the device in the activities of daily living. They later monitor the effectiveness of the appliance and carry out checks, adjustments and repairs as necessary.

WORK ENVIRONMENT

Prosthetists can work for the NHS, or manufacturing and service companies, and usually work in disablement service centres or artificial limb and appliance centres, which are normally in the grounds of a hospital. Orthotists may work for the NHS and be based in hospitals, or work for manufacturing and service companies, in which case they spend some of their time driving to clinics to see their patients.

Prosthetists/orthotists spend much of their time seeing patients in clinic rooms – large spacious rooms where they measure patients and see how well they move with their prosthesis/orthosis. They also spend time in the centre's office and workshop.

SKILLS AND INTERESTS

Prosthetists/orthotists need both technical and practical skills to measure, design, fit and adapt prostheses and orthoses. They also need to be innovative, as all prostheses and many orthoses are designed for each individual patient. An awareness of computer technology is necessary, as it is becoming increasingly important in this work.

Prosthetists/orthotists need an interest in people, in how the body works, in mechanics, and a desire to help people with disabilities.

Good communication skills are vital in working with patients and other members of the team. They should be sensitive to the needs of the patients, tactful and understanding. The work may involve giving some patients physical assistance and so prosthetists/orthotists should be fit and healthy.

ENTRY REQUIREMENTS

Entry into this career requires an BSc (Hons) degree in Prosthetics and Orthotics. At present there are two such courses:

Department of Rehabilitation – University of Salford. The entry requirements for this course are a combination of A and AS level passes, or equivalent qualifications, that gives a total of around 14 points (grades B and C). A levels in biology and either maths or physics are preferred. GCSEs (A–C) should include English, maths and physics or combined/integrated science.

Alternative qualifications are acceptable, such as BTEC/SQA national awards with distinctions in at least four relevant subjects, normally including maths or physics and human biology; or an Advanced GNVQ/GSVQ Level III in science, plus compulsory and optional additional units (for details of specific units required – contact the university).

The National Centre for Training and Education in Prosthetics and Orthotics – University of Strathclyde. The entry requirements for this course are four H grades including maths and a science subject at minimum grade B, and preferably physics, biology or chemistry; or three A levels including maths and a science subject, both at minimum grade C, and preferably physics, biology or chemistry.

Applicants with alternative qualifications, such as BTEC/SQA national awards or Advanced GNVQ/GSVQ Level III, are considered on an individual basis.

TRAINING

Training for this career takes four years. The courses at University of Salford and University of Strathclyde qualify students in both prosthetics and orthotics. At the end of the course, students can decide in which discipline they wish to specialize, although a small number of prosthetists/orthotists practice in both disciplines.

University of Salford. This course comprises three interlinked elements: academic studies, practical training in the fabrication and forming of prosthetic and orthotic devices, and clinical experience in the assessment and fitting of patients. These three aspects of the course are developed together in the first three years. The fourth year is spent working in clinical practice in the Health Service or with an orthotic or prosthetic manufacturing company under contract to the NHS.

The core subjects for this course are: life sciences and maths refresher (studied during weeks two to four of the

PROSTHETICS/ORTHOTICS: JOL

course), electronic and engineering design and materials sciences, maths, computing, mechanics and biomechanics, clinical studies, prosthetic and orthotic science, health professional studies and research methods.

Students learn about the human body and the conditions that affect it, the biomechanics of normal and abnormal function, and the application of force to the body. They must also understand the properties of the materials from which devices can be made.

During the course students learn to design, fabricate and fit all types of prosthetic and orthotic devices. They work with volunteer patients to gain experience in prescription, measurement and fitting techniques. During these three years they spend short periods in NHS clinics. The final year is devoted to two blocks of six months' clinical experience in each discipline, where students gain practical experience in a clinical working environment.

There is also an optional language training programme which runs throughout the first three years and includes a period of residence abroad in the summer period following the second year of the course.

University of Strathclyde. This is a four-year honours degree course that combines academic studies, practical and clinical training, and clinical experience. Core subjects include life sciences, mechanics and biomechanics, prosthetics and orthotics science, maths and statistics, total design and graphical communication, electrotechnology, computer science, and materials technology.

During the first three years students learn to construct and fit all types of prosthetic and orthotic devices using volunteer patients. The fourth year is spent in approved clinical centres applying the theory and skills they have learnt to real patients in the clinical situation. They work as part of the clinic team, spending six months in prosthetics and six months in orthotics.

LATE ENTRY

Applications from mature entrants are welcome for both courses. Each applicant is considered on their individual merit, and normal entry qualifications may not be needed. Candidates may prepare for application to courses by undertaking a science Access course.

OPPORTUNITIES

In England and Wales most prosthetists work for private manufacturing and servicing companies or private clinics. There are only limited job opportunities for prosthetists within the NHS. Orthotists can work for the NHS or for manufacturing and servicing companies.

In Scotland prosthetists/orthotists work for NHS, private clinics or private manufacturing and servicing companies.

At present there are about 200 prosthetists and 500 orthotists in Britain and it is possible that demand for them will increase.

The two courses only take about 28 students each year and so there is considerable competition for places. Opportunities for prosthetists/orthotists to work abroad are excellent. At present, prosthetists/orthotists are working in Canada and the USA, Australia, China and South East Asia, India, Africa and the Middle East, and in the European Union. They can work for overseas health organizations and manufacturing and servicing companies, British companies with branches abroad, and voluntary organizations such as the Red Cross.

PAY AND CONDITIONS

Starting salaries for newly qualified prosthetists/orthotists range from approximately £17,000 to £22,000, rising to a maximum of around £28,000. Managers may earn in excess of £30,000.

Orthotists working for private companies usually have a company car provided. Most prosthetists/orthotists work a five-day, 40-hour week. Hours are normally from 8.30am to 5pm, Monday to Friday.

PROSPECTS

Although students, on graduating, choose to specialize in either orthotics or prosthetics, they are not restricted by their choice and can later change specialization if they wish. Promotion prospects are very limited in this career. There is no formal career ladder in either the NHS or with private companies. Some may become managers of teams of prosthetists/orthotists and technicians. There are also a few who move into education to train student prosthetist/orthotists or who move into sales posts with manufacturing companies.

RELATED OCCUPATIONS

Medical physics technician, dental technician, occupational therapist, physiotherapist, biomedical engineer.

FURTHER INFORMATION

Department of Rehabilitation*, University of Salford, Blatchford Building, Frederick Road, Salford M6 6PU, 0161 745 5000

National Centre for Training and Education in Prosthetics and Orthotics*, University of Strathclyde, Curran Building, 131 St James Road, Glasgow G4 0LS

FURTHER READING

Leaflets/booklets are available from the addresses marked*.

In the careers library classified under JOL.

OTHER HEALTH WORK: JOZ

1. **HOSPITAL PORTER CLCI:JOZ**
2. **OPERATING DEPARTMENT PRACTITIONER CLCI:JOZ**

1. HOSPITAL PORTER (JOZ)

BACKGROUND INFORMATION

Porters move patients, equipment and other items around the hospital. During a typical day they have short social contacts with many people, including patients, nurses, technicians and other ancillary workers. Portering suits people who enjoy contact with the public and are physically active, as the work can be strenuous.

THE WORK

The organization of porters varies in different hospitals, but generally there is a 'pool' of porters who serve all wards and departments, responding to requests from the nursing staff. There are also other porters attached to particular departments or rostered to carry out specific duties, such as refuse disposal.

Porters in the 'pool' receive instructions from their supervisor – often by radio. A typical task would be to go to a ward, help a nurse to lift a patient from bed to a wheelchair and wheel the patient down to the x-ray department.

Sometimes porters move patients in their beds, when they are too ill to be transferred to wheelchairs. They also use trolleys or stretchers.

Other tasks may include moving furniture and heavy medical equipment, taking blood samples and specimens from wards to laboratories, delivering meal trolleys to wards, cleaning, and reception/telephonist duties.

One aspect of porter's work that may be distressing is the removal of dead bodies from wards and other departments. The body is prepared for movement by the nursing staff, then a porter takes it by trolley to the mortuary and helps to transfer the body to a storage container.

Porters who are not part of the 'pool' are attached to a particular department, such as accident and emergency, the operating department or pharmacy, or specialize in one specific type of duty.

Those who work in the operating department wear sterile clothing, and take patients who are under sedation from the wards to the theatre, and from the recovery room back to the wards. They are accompanied by a nurse.

Some porters are responsible for removing dirty laundry and refuse (including clinical waste, such as used hypodermics and bloodstained dressings) from the wards, and for refuse disposal. Others work in the mail room, sorting and delivering post around the hospital.

Porters may be responsible for checking gas cylinders used on wards (usually oxygen cylinders, used by patients with breathing difficulties) and replacing them with new cylinders as necessary.

In some hospitals, porters are responsible for security – investigating suspicious circumstances and dealing with disturbances or intruders – but in other hospitals, this work is undertaken by separate security staff.

Porters may also be responsible for enforcing parking regulations in the hospital grounds.

Porter/drivers are employed in some hospitals, particularly those with split or spread-out sites. They drive minibuses to take patients from wards to clinics, and delivery vehicles to transport specimens, post and other items.

WORK ENVIRONMENT

Most of the time is spent indoors, walking from one part of the hospital to another. There may be some outdoor work, such as car parking duties. In hospitals with split sites, it is necessary to go out of doors when moving from one part of the building to another.

Portering is very active and physically demanding, involving a lot of walking, lifting, carrying and bending.

Porters wear uniforms – a heavy-duty jumper, dark trousers and shirt. They wear protective clothing for specific duties, such as refuse disposal.

SKILLS AND INTERESTS

Porters need stamina and a good standard of physical fitness.

An outgoing disposition and friendly, cheerful personality are important – they meet a wide variety of people during the course of a working day.

They must be reliable, mature, and not easily upset by sickness and distress. As with all hospital work, it is essential to respect patient confidentiality.

At times, porters deal with people who are under severe stress, and the work may be pressured, for instance when there is a major road accident or other emergency.

They should be flexible, and prepared to carry out a variety of tasks.

ENTRY REQUIREMENTS

There are no specific educational entry requirements, although literacy is essential.

Most entrants are adults, rather than school-leavers, although there is no set minimum entry age.

Selection is by interview and medical examination, which includes a test of physical fitness.

A driving licence is required for porter/driver posts.

It is sometimes possible to work as a volunteer in a hospital, assisting porters; this experience is a useful background for those applying for paid jobs.

TRAINING

Porters start by taking a short induction course covering general information about the hospital, health and safety, and lifting techniques.

Further training is carried out on the job, with guidance from experienced staff. New porters work under supervision for the first few weeks. They often rotate through the various duties until they have gained experience of all the different types of work.

LATE ENTRY

Most entrants are adults. Maturity may be an advantage, and employers may prefer applicants who are over 30 years of age.

Experience in any kind of work that involves contact with the public is useful.

OTHER HEALTH WORK: JOZ

OPPORTUNITIES

Porters work in hospitals of all kinds, both in the public and private sectors. They may be directly employed by the hospital, or they may be employed by private contractors that provide ancillary services for hospitals.

A typical provincial hospital, with around 600 beds, would employ about 30 porters, plus supervisors and a head porter.

Many hospitals are cutting back on the numbers of porters they employ. There is keen competition for any vacancies that arise.

The majority of porters are men, but there is no barrier to the employment of women, provided they meet physical fitness requirements.

PAY AND CONDITIONS

Pay rates may be set locally, but generally porters are paid on the Whitley Council scale; this sets basic pay at between £140.48 and £146.19 a week, with additional payments for shift and weekend work and London allowances. Hospital porters work a 39-hour week. They have to be prepared to work shifts, including nights and weekends. Some day jobs (8am to 5pm) are available. It is possible to work additional hours on the ancillary bank when these are available.

Part-time work may be available.

PROSPECTS

Experienced porters may be promoted to supervisory posts and from there to head porter or porter-manager. However, opportunities for promotion are limited by the relatively small number of porters employed by each hospital.

It is possible to move into related areas such as health care assistant/nursing auxiliary.

RELATED OCCUPATIONS

Ambulance person, health care assistant/nursing auxiliary, sterile services assistant, hotel porter, security guard/officer, operating department practitioner, caretaker.

FURTHER INFORMATION

Further information about training and vacancies may be available from local careers offices and/or Jobcentres. Vacancies may be advertised in local newspapers. Local telephone directories may provide a suitable list of local employers.

FURTHER READING

Working in Hospitals – COIC
In the careers library classified under JOZ.

2. OPERATING DEPARTMENT PRACTITIONER (JOZ)

BACKGROUND INFORMATION

Operating department practitioners (ODPs) are part of a team that cares for patients during anaesthetic procedures and surgical operations. They provide skilled assistance to surgeons and anaesthetists, as part of the theatre team.

THE WORK

ODPs are trained to perform various duties.

'Scrubbed' ODPs are members of the operating team, working alongside surgeons and nurses. Like the rest of the team, they 'scrub up' – scrubbing their hands and arms up to the elbows, and putting on surgical masks, caps, sterile gowns and gloves.

Their duties involve handing instruments and dressings to the surgeon during the operation, anticipating the needs of the surgeon and providing the right instruments quickly, without being prompted. They also have to check instrument trays before the operation and keep account of all swabs and dressings used during the operation. Afterwards, they make a final check, the purpose of which is to make sure no stray swabs, dressings or instruments have been accidentally left inside the patient's body. They sign a register to confirm they have carried out the necessary checks.

Other terms used instead of 'scrubbed ODP' are 'instrument person' and 'scrubbed assistant'.

Circulating duties involve supplying the surgical team with items such as dressings, drugs, swabs and equipment, and providing general assistance as required. ODPs on circulating duties do not wear sterile gowns, and can therefore supply any additional items required during surgery.

Their duties also include overall care for patients, moving them from beds or trolleys onto the operating table and positioning them correctly before and after surgery. They also check patients' identity before treatment, and make sure all necessary records are available for medical staff.

Assistance to anaesthetists involves preparing the area to be used for administering anaesthetic, checking machinery and equipment for faults, and making sure appropriate drugs are available. ODPs assisting anaesthetists have some responsibility for the preparation and storage of drugs and ensuring their use is recorded according to hospital policy.

ODPs help anaesthetists during the administration of general or local anaesthetic, handling equipment and instruments. In the operating theatre they help to monitor the patient's vital signs (such as blood pressure, heart rate and temperature) throughout the proceedings, acting as the anaesthetist's 'second pair of eyes'. They also assist the anaesthetist by preparing and supplying additional items such as drugs, intravenous fluids or blood. After operations, ODPs help monitor patients as they recover from the anaesthetic/surgical procedure.

ODPs are trained to carry out all the roles described above, and they rotate between the different duties. They work as part of a team and, during a typical working day with numerous operations, they swap roles – particularly between circulating and scrubbed duties. Those who are rostered to assist anaesthetists usually spend the whole day in that specialism.

WORK ENVIRONMENT

Most ODPs work in operating departments, which consist of operating theatres, anaesthetic areas and recovery rooms.

An increasing number of ODPs work in accident and emergency departments, intensive care units or as part of cardiac arrest teams. They are employed in these departments mainly for their skills in working with anaesthetists.

OTHER HEALTH WORK: JOZ

ODPs spend most of the time standing.

SKILLS AND INTERESTS

Communication skills and the ability to work with others, as a team member, are essential. A caring, sympathetic attitude is needed for dealing with patients – who may be conscious, and worried about their operations – when they are arriving at or leaving the operating department. Strict confidentiality about patients' treatment is essential.

ODPs need manual dexterity for handling equipment. They should be able to anticipate the needs of surgeons and anaesthetists. A careful, methodical and conscientious attitude is required.

Good health and fitness are important as the job involves a considerable amount of physical work – moving patients and equipment. It is not suitable for people with back problems.

Working in an operating department can be distressing – for instance, some patients may die on the operating table. ODPs need to be mature enough to cope with such situations.

ENTRY REQUIREMENTS

There are no set academic entry requirements, but a good general education is needed and numeracy and literacy are essential. Centres running ODP training usually set selection tests covering basic English, maths and reasoning. Candidates are selected by interview. They have to pass a medical examination. Normal colour vision is required, as it is necessary to be able to recognize colour-coded items.

Entry may be possible for young people through Modern Apprenticeships (part of the Skillseekers Initiative in Scotland) leading to at least an NVQ/SVQ Level 3. Contact your local careers office, Jobcentre, TEC/LEC for details.

The minimum age for entry is usually 18 years. Younger people may gain experience in other types of hospital work – for instance, as health care assistants – and undertake training in ODP work later on.

Courses leading to the GNVQ in Health and Social Care at Intermediate level or the GSVQ in Care at Level II are an appropriate background for those seeking to enter this type of work.

TRAINING

Student ODPs are hospital-based, attending ODP training centres for the theoretical part of their training. There are 27 ODP training centres, based at large hospitals or colleges/institutes of health studies around the country. A list of centres is available from the British Association of Operating Department Assistants or Theatre Personnel Nationwide.

Students are normally trained over two years. Their education and training programme begins with a short induction course at the ODP centre and hospital. They then spend about eight weeks working in operating departments before returning to the ODP centre for a further one- or two-week theory course. A similar pattern of training continues throughout the two years, although the intervals between theory courses gradually become longer. Altogether, about 18–20 weeks are spent on theoretical training, and just over 80 weeks on practical training in hospitals.

The practical training includes experience in a variety of hospital departments – including surgical wards, intensive care units and accident and emergency departments – as well as in operating departments. The theoretical training covers subjects such as anatomy and physiology, basic chemistry and physics, pharmacology, microbiology, sterilization and disinfection, infection control, patient care, and surgical and anaesthetic techniques.

At the end of the two years students are expected to achieve an NVQ/SVQ in Health Care at Level 3: Operating Department Practice, awarded by City and Guilds and the Institute of Health and Care Development in England and Wales and SQA in Scotland. The qualification is made up of seven units: health and safety in the workplace; controlling cross-infection; preparing the environment/workplace; preparing patients for clinical/operative procedures; providing assistance in clinical/operative procedures; providing immediate post-operative care; and providing initial emergency care. Continuous assessment of students is carried out in the workplace; theoretical knowledge is assessed via tests, exams and written case studies.

LATE ENTRY

Entrants are normally over 18 years, and the most usual age to enter this type of work is in mid-twenties.

There is keen competition for training places and it is an advantage to have hospital experience, particularly in a job with a reasonable amount of patient contact, such as health care assistant or nursing auxiliary. Experience in residential care is also useful.

Relevant qualifications may give exemption from part of the ODP training course, via Accreditation of Prior Learning (APL).

There is no fixed upper age limit, but entry after the age of about 45 is likely to be difficult.

OPPORTUNITIES

ODPs are employed by most hospitals with a sizeable operating department, both in the public and private sectors.

About 2,500 to 3,000, nationally, hold a qualification to work as an ODP.

There are some opportunities to work abroad. Employment agencies recruit holders of the ODP qualification to work in hospitals in the Middle East. There are also opportunities in the Netherlands for qualified staff with at least two years' experience.

Temporary work is available in the UK through employment agencies.

PAY AND CONDITIONS

Pay varies according to local policy, but is usually on the Medical Technical Officers' scale. Students are normally paid £6880. Salaries for qualified ODPs range from about £11,000 to £30,000 (Senior ODP).

Operating departments are open 24 hours a day, 365 days a year, and the staff work shifts, including nights and bank holidays. They may have on-call and stand-by duties.

During training, students normally start by working on days, 8am to 5pm. They transfer to shift work once they have gained some experience.

After qualifying, it may be possible to work part-time, depending on the employer's policy. Job share may be available.

PROSPECTS

Promotion is initially to Senior ODP – this involves responsibility for theatre suites, ordering, service contracts, staff management and supervision of students in training.

From Senior ODP it is possible to move into higher managerial positions. Some practitioners move into full-time education posts in health care – they may be able to take courses leading to NVQs/SVQs in Training and Development at Levels 3 and 4.

RELATED OCCUPATIONS

Health care assistant, paramedic, trained hospital nurse, medical technical officer.

FURTHER INFORMATION

British Association of Operating Department Assistants*, 70a Crayford High Street, Dartford, Kent DA1 4EF, 01322 550544

Theatre Personnel Nationwide* (formerly known as The National Association of Professional and Technical Theatre Personnel), PO Box 51, Pontyclun CF72 944, 01443 238880 (please include sae)

Health Service Careers*, PO Box 204, London SE99 7UW

FURTHER READING

Leaflets/booklets are available from the addresses marked*.

Working in Hospitals – COIC

In the careers library classified under JOZ.

GROUP K – SOCIAL AND RELATED SERVICES

1. **FIELD SOCIAL WORKER CLCI:KEB**
2. **RESIDENTIAL SOCIAL WORKER CLCI:KEB**
3. **CARE ASSISTANT CLCI:KEB**

BACKGROUND INFORMATION

Social workers provide support for many kinds of people who need help and protection. They are employed by local authority social services departments in England and Wales, by social work departments in Scotland, and by independent agencies such as the National Society for the Prevention of Cruelty to Children (NSPCC). They act as the administrators, supervisors, programme planners and evaluators of the welfare systems. Their main areas of work are: child welfare and protection; fostering and adoption; and caring for the elderly, people with disabilities, people with physical and mental illness, people with learning disabilities, and people recovering from alcohol and drug misuse.

1. FIELD SOCIAL WORKER (KEB)

THE WORK

Field social workers work within the community as part of locality or specialist teams, helping both groups and individuals. They develop relationships with their clients, gaining their confidence so that they can provide the most effective help, and plan the best strategies for improving their situation in both the long and short term.

Working with children and families: social work with children can be very challenging and requires high levels of skill and judgement. A social worker's intervention can often make a critical difference at a key moment in a child's life.

The law requires that local authority social services departments identify, support and protect children in need and at risk who live in their area. The main focus of their work is always the best interests of the child, and social workers can play an important role in keeping families together by giving advice on issues such as parenting, and drug and alcohol abuse. Social workers who work for specialist agencies are commissioned by local authorities to help with this work.

Sometimes a child's behaviour may be difficult while in other cases a child may have severe disabilities which the parents cannot cope with alone. It is sometimes necessary to take a child away from their parents but this is only done after consultation with other professionals, which may involve a court case or children's hearing. When a local authority looks after or accommodates a child, it is the job of the social worker to ensure adequate arrangements are made for the child's care and that a plan is made, in partnership with the child and the parents, for their future. This may involve arranging foster, residential or adoptive homes for children who cannot be cared for by their own families. Social workers are responsible for interviewing potential foster and adoptive parents to ensure they are suitable and then advising, training and preparing them for some of the difficulties involved in taking on a child who has experienced problems or abuse.

Field social workers also work with schools, helping children with physical, emotional or learning disabilities, and discussing issues such as sexuality, suicide, violence and career planning with teenagers.

Some social workers are employed in hospitals to support parents whose children are seriously ill or dying. They also help parents who have other children at home, or who need assistance travelling to hospital, or who may need help coping when their child is discharged. Hospital social workers may be involved in child protection work when an injury to a child is thought to be non-accidental.

Working with adults: some social workers work within health care settings such as hospitals, GPs' surgeries, psychiatric hospitals or hospices. They assess the social and emotional needs of adult patients, and help them adjust to their illnesses. They also assist older people and their families to make decisions about their future and care, and provide support to patients who do not have relatives to care for them. People with developmental disabilities and their families may also require social work services to help plan for the future.

In a GP's surgery they may deal with people who are depressed, becoming involved in helping people recuperate in their own homes, and offering bereavement counselling to relatives of patients who have died. Some social workers specialize with particular groups, such as people with mental health problems, or in issues such as AIDS and HIV.

Other work: the roles of purchaser and provider within social services are now split, meaning that many social workers spend time assessing needs and arranging for others to provide the specific help that is required. Social workers also carry out routine office work such as report writing, and part of every week is spent dealing with enquiries at the office. They also attend meetings and conferences. In Scotland, social work also covers the work of probation officers.

WORK ENVIRONMENT

Time is split between many different locations, such as the office, a client's home, day centres, hospitals and health centres. Some time may also be spent in court and travel will be involved. Social workers in rural areas require a car.

They need to be prepared for many difficult and unpleasant situations such as visiting squalid housing and dealing with violent clients.

SKILLS AND INTERESTS

Social workers need to have an interest in people and the ability to help them face up to painful and distressing problems. They should also be good at listening, understanding and empathising, and be able to put themselves in their client's place. They must be open-minded and be prepared to examine and change their own attitudes and prejudices. Patience and persistence are other core skills.

Social work can be both physically and emotionally stressful and a sense of humour is very important.

Social work requires the ability to manage a complex and demanding workload, and to work as part of a team, combining specialist areas of knowledge. This may also involve co-ordinating others and guiding their efforts.

Being able to process information is extremely important, as is being able to identify and uncover necessary and relevant information. This information will often be used to produce a report, which must be logically structured and clearly expressed.

SOCIAL WORK: KEB

ENTRY REQUIREMENTS

The Diploma of Social Work (DipSW) is the professional qualification in social work in the UK, and is awarded by the Central Council for Education and Training in Social Work (CCETSW). The minimum age on qualification is 22.

Candidates following a programme that provides a postgraduate route will need a degree in any subject or an equivalent professional qualification.

Programmes offered as a degree course, known as undergraduate routes, are designed for students who, if they are under 21, must meet CCETSW's academic requirements. Admission requirements for applicants under 21 years are: two A levels/ three H grades and three GCSEs (A–C)/two S grades (1–3) in other subjects; or NVQ/SVQ Level 3 in Care, Criminal Justice Services, Community Work, Special Needs Housing or Child Care and Education; or a BTEC/ SQA national award; or the Council for Awards in Children's Care and Education (CACHE) Diploma in Nursery Nursing (NNEB); or Advanced GNVQ/ GSVQ Level III; or equivalent qualifications.

The non-graduate route is for entrants who may not have any formal academic qualification but who must be able to demonstrate their ability to study at a higher education level.

Programmes known as employment routes provide training for people who continue in employment on a part-time basis during their training.

Most programmes also require applicants to have had one year's relevant experience to demonstrate they understand the demands of social work.

Applicants who already have a qualification such as an NVQ or SVQ Level 4 in Care or a related subject; or have considerable relevant experience, may be exempt from certain elements of the DipSW programme.

Certain types of convictions may prevent employment as a social worker. The provisions of the Rehabilitation of Offenders Act do not apply to social service employers, who may require applicants to declare any convictions and may seek information from police records.

TRAINING

DipSW programmes are offered at many centres throughout the UK and social work training is provided jointly by universities and social services. Most programmes offer overall training and the opportunity to practise in a particular area such as working with children. Training normally lasts two years full-time at college, although longer part-time courses are available, with candidates training on-the-job. Distance learning, and accreditation of prior learning (APL) programmes which allow candidates to claim credit for previous learning experiences, are also available.

Full-time students spend up to 160 days on placement under supervision and most programmes operate a system of continuous assessment. Areas of study include: knowledge and understanding of human growth and behaviour; the process of observation and assessment; various aspects of practice such as aims, methods and theories; and client's rights and ethical issues. Some courses have exams and all will test the students' knowledge of relevant laws.

It is possible to follow a particular pathway through the DipSW, as the qualification allows you to move between different settings and user groups as your career progresses. Contact CCETSW for Handbook 9.3, How to Qualify for Social Work.

LATE ENTRY

Adult entry is usual, with experience of life and work greatly valued. There is no upper age limit for entry to a DipSW programme. Entrants must show they can cope with the study involved and this can be done by successfully completing an approved higher education Access course, which is offered by local colleges on a full or part-time basis.

The Open University also offers a route into social work training and there are also extended DipSW Programmes for candidates with family commitments.

OPPORTUNITIES

There are some 26,000 field social workers in the UK and those with a DipSW are very much in demand. They are employed by local authorities in schools, hospitals, homes and GP surgeries, and by specialist agencies such as the NSPCC.

Some social workers are employed as Forensic Social Workers in hospitals that offer psychiatric services, in prisons, or in special hospitals such as Rampton or Broadmoor. They work closely with other professions to assess, treat and support people with mental health problems who have committed serious offences. Approved Social Workers/ Mental Health Officers (in Scotland) work with people who are a danger to themselves or others, ensuring they are adequately supported and treated in the community, or go to hospital if necessary. This work can involve a rota system in evenings and at weekends.

The Ministry of Defence also employs social workers in military hospitals and opportunities exist with the Navy Personal and Family Service, and with the Soldiers', Sailors' and Airmen's Families Association (SSAFA).

Some opportunities exist to specialize with independent social work agencies and there are also openings to teach on training courses in universities and colleges, and as training officers in agencies.

Vacancies for qualified field workers are advertised in *Community Care, Public Service, Local Government Appointments, The Voice, The Scotsman, The Herald, The Independent* and *The Guardian*.

PAY AND CONDITIONS

Although pay scales do exist, salaries are usually based on qualifications, experience and the responsibilities of the post. They also differ from area to area. A newly qualified field social worker could expect to earn between £14,000 to £20,000; a care manager or senior social worker between £17,500 and £21,000. Directors of social service departments are paid considerably more. Social workers employed by agencies are paid according to the resources available.

Hours are long and irregular – social workers do not work nine to five, five days a week. Most local authorities and agencies provide a 24-hour, seven-day-a-week service which requires staff to work a rota, and provide night-time and weekend cover, for which they will receive extra pay or time off in lieu. Some part-time work may be available.

SOCIAL WORK: KEB

Social workers in a medical environment often work normal office hours but may be required to go on a rota for stand by duty.

PROSPECTS

Social work has a well-defined career structure, with opportunities to move from the basic grade of social worker to senior worker in an area team, to team leader and eventually to a managerial and advisory post, although this will involve less direct work with service users. Social workers who have reached this level and have specialized skills can continue working with clients in agencies.

CCETSW has its own post-qualifying framework allowing continual professional development and covering all areas such as family therapy, management, team leader and principal social worker. The framework leads to the Post Qualifying Award and the Advanced Award in Social Work. Further details are available from CCETSW.

RELATED OCCUPATIONS

Probation officer, residential social worker, counsellor, prison governor, teacher, youth and community worker.

FURTHER INFORMATION AND READING

Please see article 3. CARE ASSISTANT.

2. RESIDENTIAL SOCIAL WORKER (KEB)

THE WORK

Residential social workers look after the welfare of residents in long-stay or short-stay residential centres, and in day-care units. The residents will be normally all from the same 'group', that is either children, adults or older people, although all will have individual physical and emotional needs. The work involves physical care, individual counselling, teaching and group therapy. Skilled care is needed with some clients who have behavioural and other problems, and social workers will need to identify the psychological, emotional or social causes of problems.

The homes are run by a local authority social services department or by a voluntary or private agency. Social workers are not necessarily residents in the centres.

Every case a residential social worker deals with will be different, as will the course of action for each individual. Building relationships with clients is very important and will enable the social worker to help residents deal with problems, and perhaps make the transition to independence.

In addition to direct work, residential social workers spend time writing reports and attending meetings and conferences.

Children and young people: children cared for in children's homes are often teenagers who have not been placed with foster parents or who have complex difficulties. Some children will have suffered neglect or abuse from their families; some will have experienced repeated rejection and numerous changes of carer; some may have broken the law, and some are subjects of various court orders; or, in Scotland, a supervision requirement made by a children's hearing.

There are also children's homes that cater specifically for children with learning disabilities, physical disabilities or behavioural and emotional difficulties.

The work involves assessing the particular needs of children; providing support over a range of issues; helping to find, and settle children into, family placements; and preparing young people for when they leave care to live independently. Residential social workers also supervise their day-to-day routine and organize recreational activities.

Some residential units cater for parents and their children together, providing help to parents who have difficulties looking after their children. In this instance social workers also supervise parents who, under a court order or supervision requirement must be supervised when they see their children because of previous abuse or neglect.

Working with adults: many institutions for adults with mental or physical disabilities have now been closed down and replaced by smaller residential establishments. These group homes, or hostels, are more informal places, where groups of 'service users' live together with staff, within the community. Residential social workers help residents to claim benefits, to budget their money, and with the development of personal and social skills. They also liaise with other professionals such as GPs and psychiatric nurses, and encourage residents to participate in recreational and leisure activities, helping people who were previously institutionalized to live independently again. Sometimes staff will help residents move into their own home.

Some units (nursing homes) are managed and supervised by trained nurses as most residents will need some form of nursing care. Greater responsibility for the day-to-day management of staff and finance, comes with experience

There are also hostels for adults needing rehabilitation or an adjustment period before returning home; for ex-psychiatric patients; single parents and parents who need support raising their children; young homeless adults; and people with temporary disabilities.

WORK ENVIRONMENT

Many residential homes are converted houses, while others are modern, purpose-built facilities, with the latest specialist equipment. Most residential social workers spend some nights sleeping in, usually in self-contained apartments, and they work shifts, including weekends.

SKILLS AND INTERESTS

Residential social work is a very demanding career, both emotionally and physically. It can be highly stressful and frustrating, so the ability to detach from work is important, as is a sense of humour.

Social workers need to be patient, sympathetic and good listeners. They must be able to develop positive relationships with clients, gaining their trust and helping them with their problems. They must be mature and capable of assessing their clients' needs in order to provide the necessary care. Tolerance and persistence are other key skills, but social workers also need to be able to establish effective control, be able to establish and maintain firm boundaries, and show firmness when necessary.

Residential social workers must be able to work as part of a team – which may include care assistants, kitchen staff,

SOCIAL WORK: KEB

domestics and ancillary staff – managing people and carrying out some administrative duties.

ENTRY REQUIREMENTS

The professional qualification for social work in the UK is the Diploma of Social Work (DipSW), which is awarded by the Central Council for Education and Training in Social Work (CCETSW) – please see article 1. FIELD SOCIAL WORKER. However, most residential social workers do not have to be professionally qualified, although many use their experience in homes and hostels as a stepping stone to gaining a place on a DipSW course.

Entry may be possible for young people through a Modern Apprenticeship leading to at least an NVQ/SVQ Level 3. Contact your local careers office, TEC/LEC for details.

TRAINING

Please see article 1. FIELD SOCIAL WORKER for details of social work training.

All Diploma in Social Work (DipSW) programmes provide training on residential care.

CCETSW offer a number of NVQs/SVQs in Care and Community Work at Levels 2, 3 and 4 which are designed for people in a wide range of settings including residential and nursing homes and day centre.

LATE ENTRY

Adult entry is usual, with experience of life and work greatly valued. There is no upper age limit for entry to a DipSW programme (please see article 1. FIELD SOCIAL WORKER) by successfully completing an approved higher education Access course, which is offered by local colleges on a full- or part-time basis.

It can be possible for adults to discover whether they would be suitable for residential care work by gaining temporary employment in a residential home or day centre. See FURTHER INFORMATION for contact details.

OPPORTUNITIES

Competition for jobs is generally keen but varies by location and depends on social service funding. Local authorities and voluntary agencies such as Barnardos are the biggest employers of residential social workers, although many homes for young and older people are now run by the private sector. With the closure of many of the larger institutions, there are now many smaller units, developed as part of the Care in the Community policy. Some voluntary organizations also employ residential social workers. The groups may have strong religious or social convictions.

Vacancies are advertised in *Community Care, Public Service, Local Government Appointments, The Voice, The Scotsman, The Herald, The Independent* and *The Guardian*.

PAY AND CONDITIONS

Salaries for staff in local authority residential homes begin at around £11,000, rising to £20,000, depending on the type of the home and the level of responsibility. Salaries may be lower in the private sector. For senior care workers, team leaders and unit manager the scale starts at £22,000.

Allowances are paid for working unsociable hours. Social workers will be expected to sleep-in on a rota basis. There is some scope for self-employment and some local authorities and private homes keep an 'on-call' list. Job sharing and part-time work may also be available

PROSPECTS

Experience is the most vital factor governing promotion in residential social work, although qualifications also count, as will the type of home or hostel and levels of responsibility.

Within private homes, an experienced social worker may become an assistant or deputy to the home's manager, while local authorities have a more formal promotional structure, with opportunities to move into management.

There is also the option to move into other fields of social work, although again this will depend on experience and qualifications. Transfer from the public to the private sector is common, although the reverse is less likely, and there are opportunities for specialization.

RELATED OCCUPATIONS

Nursery nurse, nurse, youth and community worker, play leader, field social worker, care assistant.

FURTHER INFORMATION AND READING

Please see article 3. CARE ASSISTANT

3. CARE ASSISTANT (KEB)

THE WORK

Care assistants (sometimes known as support workers) work in residential homes or hostels, and day-care centres, looking after groups or individuals who may be children and young people, people with disabilities, adults, families or elderly people. Sometimes they will help look after people in their own homes.

The level of care needed depends on the individual or group. Work with the elderly and people with disabilities involves providing physical care such as dressing, bathing, toileting and feeding. Work with children involves a greater degree of emotional support.

Care assistants do not require any qualifications but they must be mature, patient and caring and they will be expected to liaise with other professionals such as doctors, district nurses, occupational therapists and social workers.

Children and young people: care assistants help to look after children whose parents need assistance because the children have special needs, such as physical or mental disabilities. They also work with children who have behavioural problems or have been ordered by a court to live in the home.

Care assistants carry out many of the day-to-day tasks involved in looking after children such as helping them to dress and wash, as well as helping other staff with domestic tasks around the home. They also play an important role in the child's development, by befriending and entertaining them, and encouraging them to learn. They may also accompany children on outings and there are sometimes opportunities to work with children within the community, in schools or nursery groups.

People with disabilities: care assistants help individuals to live as normal a life as possible. They work at centres that

SOCIAL WORK: KEB

provide support for people who are unable to live in their own homes, and also at day centres where people with disabilities are cared for to provide respite for their family and other carers.

They are again responsible for many of the practical tasks such as washing and dressing the clients, and also help people with disabilities to walk and get in and out of wheelchairs. They are also encouraged to develop good relationships with the clients, and under the direction of an instructor, may help with training classes that teach social skills such as reading and writing.

Older people: care assistants give practical help to older people in residential centres and day centres Sometimes they will work in the client's own home, carrying shopping, doing housework and, just as importantly, befriending them.

Day centres provide a caring, supportive environment, where people who are otherwise isolated or house bound are able to socialize and make friends. Care assistants help with meals, organize activities and generally make the centre as friendly as possible. Some residential homes cater for elderly people with particular problems such as blindness, and duties will vary according to individuals' needs.

Work with other groups: care assistants also work in halfway houses with single parents, homeless people or ex-drug addicts who need support until they are able to re-adjust to life in the community.

WORK ENVIRONMENT

Many residential homes are converted houses, with only minor alterations. Others are large, modern, purpose-built facilities, with the latest specialist equipment and facilities to help care for residents.

The work involves a lot of bending and carrying and care assistants need to be able to cope with jobs that are messy and unpleasant. Care assistants may be required to live-in, usually in a self-contained apartment. Those who work in the community will travel a lot, and may need a car to make their regular visits.

SKILLS AND INTERESTS

Patience, tolerance and compassion are three qualities a care assistant needs, as well as an interest in supporting and assisting other people to lead a more fulfilling and valued lifestyle. They must be good listeners, and able to get on with a wide variety of people, yet be strong enough to remain sufficiently detached from the situation so that it doesn't have an adverse effect on their own life.

Reliability is also important and care assistants must be mature enough to deal with distressing situations. They need to be fit as the work involves lifting, carrying and helping people to walk, and be able to work as part of a team.

ENTRY REQUIREMENTS

There are no set entry requirements for work as a care assistant although many relevant courses do exist, which are outlined in the Training Section below. Most employers prefer applicants to be over 18 years. Previous experience of working in a care environment is beneficial.

Certain types of convictions may prevent employment as a social worker. The provisions of the Rehabilitation of Offenders Act do not apply to social service employers, who may require applicants to declare any convictions and may seek information from police records.

TRAINING

Pre-entry

These courses give candidates a general insight into caring, supportive and enabling work, along with practical experience. Because care work is such a growing area, specialist courses are being added to all the time. For full, up-to-date details contact your careers office.

SQA national diploma – one- or two-year course; entry is with a good general education, although some colleges do have specific entry requirements.

BTEC First Diploma in Care – requires a good general education and is offered by a few colleges as a one-year course.

BTEC National Diploma in Caring Services (Social Care) – many colleges offer this two year course and entry is with either: four GCSEs/S grades (A–C/1–3): or a BTEC first award; or an Intermediate GNVQ/ GSVQ Level II.

NVQs/SVQs – CCETSW offer a number of NVQs/SVQs in Care, Community Work and Special Needs Housing at Levels 2, 3 and 4; and Child Care and Education at Levels 2 and 3. There are also SVQs in numerous areas including Direct Care, Developmental Care and Special Care Needs, up to Level 3. No particular exam passes are required and the courses are available at various centres. Contact CCETSW for full details.

Intermediate GNVQ in Health and Social Care – one year course that does not require particular entry requirements but some educational institutions may specify their own requirements.

GNVQ in Health and Social Care/GSVQ in Care – usually requires either: Intermediate GNVQ; or four GCSEs/S grades (A–C/1–3); or BTEC/SQA national award. Some colleges may have their own requirements. The course is offered at some schools and many colleges. The advanced level course takes two years. There are no formal entry requirements for GSVQ in Care Level II (one year) and Level III (two years).

On entry

There are a number of training options for young people that introduce them to work with elderly people, disabled people and/or children. Trainees work towards NVQs/SVQs at Level 2 and 3. Contact your local career's office, TEC/LEC for details.

Modern Apprenticeships (part of the Skillseekers Initiative in Scotland) in Care are designed for care assistants working with disabled people, elderly people or children. Apprentices will work towards an NVQ/SVQ in Care at Level 2 and 3, as well as taking training in areas such as communications and information technology. Apprenticeships do not last for a set period of time but usually take at least three years. Contact your local careers office, TEC/LEC for details.

On-the-job-training is an important aspect of work as a care assistant and there may also be opportunities to attend college on a day release or evening-basis. Courses are detailed above and many care assistants choose to follow general courses, such as an NVQ/SVQ in Care, which gives them a better idea about caring for people in a wide range of settings.

SOCIAL WORK: KEB

LATE ENTRY

Care work calls for maturity and experience so adult entry into the profession is encouraged. There is no upper age limit. The City and Guilds Community Care Practice award (3250) is designed for adults in social care and no qualifications are required for entry.

OPPORTUNITIES

Support services for adults have changed significantly since the 1980s with the closure of large institutions and the transfer of services into the community to support people in smaller residential hostels, or their own homes. However, there are still in the region of 550,000 care workers employed by local government and 466,000 independently employed throughout the UK. The demand for residential or respite services continues to increase as the proportion of old people in the population grows.

Local authorities are the largest employers of care workers, and voluntary organizations employ care assistants in residential homes and day centres. These groups may have strong religious or social convictions. Many homes for young and older people are now run privately.

Vacancies may be advertised in *Community Care, Public Service, Local Government Appointments* and *Care Weekly* and local newspapers.

PAY AND CONDITIONS

Pay scales differ within different local authority areas, and also vary if the work is within the private sector. Location, type of work and experience also have an effect on salary.

Care assistants working a five-day week in day centres, with regular hours and only occasional weekend work, will be on a scale of between £9,500 and £10,500.

Those working in a residential home, when shift work and sleep-overs are involved, will start at around £10,500 rising to £11,500, while senior care workers can be on scales that reach in excess of £18,000. Salaries may be lower in the private sector and with voluntary agencies, who pay according to the resources they have available.

Free accommodation may be provided, and allowances for working unsociable hours. Few care assistants will be required to live in permanently, but will be expected to sleep-over on a rota basis.

There is some scope for self-employment and some local authorities and private homes keep an 'on-call' list. Job sharing and part-time work may also be available.

PROSPECTS

Promotion within care work depends on experience and qualifications. Most care assistants will start working towards relevant qualifications as soon as they begin work. It is unlikely that care assistants will move up to supervisory and senior positions without qualifications.

To progress into other areas of social work as, for example, a Field Social Worker or Residential Social Worker, candidates require the Diploma of Social Work (DipSW); please see article 1. FIELD SOCIAL WORKER. Competition for places on DipSW courses is fierce but experience as a care assistant is an excellent way of gaining a place. Further details are available from the Social Work Admissions System (SWAS).

RELATED OCCUPATIONS

Nursery nurse, nurse, residential social worker, youth and community worker, play leader, nanny/home help, health care assistant, nursing auxiliary.

FURTHER INFORMATION

British Association of Social Workers, 16 Kent Street, Birmingham B5 6RD, 0121 622 3911

Central Council for Education and Training in Social Work:

England: CCETSW Information Service, Derbyshire House, St Chad's Street, London WC1H 8AD, 0171 278 2455;

Scotland: 5th Floor, 78–80 George Street, Edinburgh EH2 3BU, 0131 220 0093; *Wales:* 2nd Floor, West Wing, Southgate House, Wood Street, Cardiff CF1 1EW, 01222 226257

London Voluntary Service Council, 356 Holloway Road, London N7 6TA, 0171 700 8107

National Association for Voluntary Hostels, Fulham Place, Bishops Avenue, London SW6 6EA, 0171 731 4205

National Council for Voluntary Organisations, Regents Wharf, 8 All Saints Street, London N1 9RL, 0171 713 6161

Scottish Council for Voluntary Organisations, 18–19 Claremont Crescent, Edinburgh EH7 4QD, 0131 556 3882

Social Care Association (SCA), 23a Victoria Road, Surbiton, Surrey KT6 4JZ

Social Work Admissions System (SWAS), Fulton House, Jessop Avenue, Cheltenham, Gloucestershire GL50 3SH, 01242 544600 *or* 01242 223707 for an application pack

Wales Council for Voluntary Action, Llys Ifor, Crescent Road, Caerphilly, Mid-Glamorgan CF8 1XL, 01222 869224

FURTHER READING

Leaflets and booklets are available from all the organizations listed above.

Working in Social Work – COIC

Working in Work with Children – COIC

Careers in Social Work – Kogan Page

Careers Working with Children – Kogan Page

In the careers library classified under KEB.

PROBATION AND AFTERCARE: KEB

PROBATION OFFICER CLCI: KEB

BACKGROUND INFORMATION

Probation officers work as part of the criminal justice system, dealing with offenders before their trial, during any prison sentence, and on their release. The Probation Service in England and Wales is made up of 54 local service areas, each one funded mainly by the Home Office, with 20 per cent coming from local government. The Home Secretary has overall responsibility for the service, which is subject to regular inspections by HM Inspectorate of Probation.

In Scotland, probation work is carried out by local authority social work departments.

THE WORK

The role of a probation officer (or criminal justice social worker in Scotland) is to supervise offenders within the community, ensuring that they comply with court orders. Their profile has increased over recent years and they now work in a large range of areas, although their main role remains preventing offenders from re-offending by trying to change the way in which they think and act. This involves advising, assisting and befriending offenders even though some may be difficult and uncooperative.

Court work

Court work takes up much of a probation officer's time. They offer independent advice and information to the courts about a person's offence, their personal circumstances, the most suitable sentence, their likelihood of re-offending, and the risk to the public from further crime. They do this by interviewing the offender and other relevant people, and then producing pre-sentence reports which they must write in a clear, concise, relevant and objective way.

As well as working with the courts, probation officers enforce court orders and serve the public by providing a wide range of supervision programmes for those who receive a community sentence.

In Scotland, social workers also work with young offenders through the children's hearing system, within which they have a key role in requesting further investigations. The hearings have the power to make supervision requirements but matters of proof are dealt with by the courts.

Community sentence work

Community Service is a punishment that involves offenders giving up their time to do unpaid work on community projects such as conservation work, or work with the elderly. The offenders are supervised by a Community Service Officer who is part of the local probation service. Offenders perform five million hours of unpaid work each year for local authorities. Community Service can lead to full employment and all probation services work closely with employment and training agencies to improve the prospects of unemployed offenders.

Probation orders

Probation Orders require offenders to report regularly to a probation officer for close supervision, for between six months and three years. The officer will draw up a probation plan with the offender and then help them to follow it, advise them on any work, help them with any social or family problems they may have, and generally help them to stay out of prison. Each case is different and calls for patience, integrity and understanding on the officer's part.

Combination Orders involve both Community Service and Probation Orders and are intended to deal with offenders who have committed more serious types of crime.

Work with prisoners

Some crimes are so serious that prison is the only solution and some probation staff are seconded to prisons to help the prison service plan and manage sentences. They work with offenders, giving advice on problems such as drug and alcohol abuse, as well as addressing areas such as training needs. They also provide an after-care service once they are released, and help with such things as getting a place in a hostel and finding work or training.

Probation officers also run hostels, or halfway houses, where courts can require offenders to live as part of their probation order, or where offenders go once they are released from prison.

Family court welfare work

Except in Scotland, Family Court Welfare Officers work with families, usually parents, who are separated and in dispute about the arrangements for children. They also mediate in family disputes, although they always represent the best interests of the child.

Probation officers/criminal justice social workers regularly liaise with other bodies such as the police, and draw on the resources of other specialists. Increasingly, probation officers are involved in managing the contributions other agencies make, especially in areas such as training needs or drug dependency. They also work with victims of crime. Probation officers will spend part of every week in the office and there may be some supervision of junior staff.

WORK ENVIRONMENT

Work is split between the office, visiting clients at home or in prison, and attending court. Therefore a lot of travelling is necessary. Probation officers operate as part of a team managed by a Senior Probation Officer and have regular meetings with colleagues to discuss cases.

SKILLS AND INTERESTS

The ability to work with difficult and sometimes violent people is an essential skill. Probation officers need to be patient and enjoy building one-to-one relationships with people in order to help them solve their problems. Probation officers require a high degree of personal commitment and must be able to cope with the pressures of a very stressful job, yet remain objective at all times.

They need to be strong, persuasive communicators, and be able to write clear, concise reports and also speak in court. They must be able to deal with case-loads that involve people of many ages and from many different backgrounds.

ENTRY REQUIREMENTS

England and Wales

From the end of 1998, a new entry system will be in place whereby probation services will be able to select and recruit trainees directly. Trainees will study for a new

Diploma in Probation Studies which will be linked to a National Vocational Qualification in Community Justice (Level 4) and an academic award at degree level. This offers a mixture of academic teaching and work-based supervised practice. Training for probation officers will no longer be linked to social work education.

Selection procedures will be aimed at determining a candidate's suitability, together with a flexible approach to training, making it easier for people with wider experience and talents to join the probation service.

Undertaking voluntary probation work, such as becoming a prison visitor or a volunteer to befriend offenders, is very beneficial. The Community Service Volunteers offer a wide range of pre-course placements and those interested in voluntary work should contact their local probation office and speak to a senior probation officer.

Scotland

Entry to criminal justice work in Scotland is through a course of professional training leading to the Diploma in Social Work (DipSW), which is awarded by the Central Council for Education and Training in Social Work (CCETSW). The minimum entry requirements for a DipSW depend on age, and the minimum age for receiving a DipSW is 22.

Candidates following a programme that provides a postgraduate route will need a degree in any subject or an equivalent professional qualification.

Programmes offered as a degree course, known as undergraduate routes, are designed for students who, if they are under 21, meet CCETSW's academic requirements. Admission requirements for applicants under 21 years are: three H grades and two S grades (1–3) in other subjects; or SVQ Level 3 in Care, Criminal Justice Services, Community Work, Special Needs Housing or Child Care and Education; or an SQA national award; or the Council for Awards in Children's Care and Education (CACHE) Diploma in Nursery Nursing (NNEB); or Advanced GNVQ/GSVQ Level III; or equivalent qualifications.

The non-graduate route is for entrants who may not have any formal academic qualification but who must be able to demonstrate their ability to study at a higher education level.

Programmes known as employment routes provide training for people who continue in employment on a part-time basis during their training.

Most routes also require applicants to have had one year's relevant experience, to demonstrate they understand the demands of social work. Applicants who already have a qualification, or who have considerable relevant experience, may be exempt from certain elements of the DipSW programme.

Certain types of convictions may prevent employment as a social worker. The provisions of the Rehabilitation of Offenders Act do not apply to social service employers, who may require applicants to declare any convictions and may seek information from police records

TRAINING

The skills a probation officer needs are refined by continuous training, using a framework of core competencies and the NVQ system. Working in a hostel is a good introduction to probation work, and most local authorities run on-the-job training schemes.

England and Wales

Due to the proposed changes in the way in which probation officers are selected, applicants should contact the Home Office Probation Unit for the most up-to-date information.

Scotland

DipSW programmes are offered at many centres throughout the UK. Social work training is provided jointly by universities and social work agencies. Most programmes offer an overall training or the opportunity to specialize in a particular area such as working with children. Training normally lasts two years full-time at college, although longer part-time courses are available, with candidates training on-the-job. Distance learning and accreditation of prior learning programmes (APL), which allows candidates to claim credit for previous learning experiences, are also available.

Full-time students spend up to 160 days on placement under supervision and most programmes operate a system of continuous assessment. Areas of study include: knowledge and understanding of human growth and behaviour; the process of observation and assessment; various aspects of practice such as aims, methods and theories of social work; and client's rights and ethical issues. Some courses have exams and all will test the student's knowledge of relevant laws.

It is possible to follow a particular pathway through the DipSW, as the qualification allows you to move between different settings and user groups as your career progresses. Contact CCETSW for Handbook 9.3, How to Qualify for Social Work.

LATE ENTRY

Experience is considered a vital element of probation work, and in England and Wales the new method of recruitment is likely to put even more emphasis on maturity and experience of life.

In Scotland, there is no upper age limit for entry to a DipSW programme. Entrants must show they can cope with the study involved and this can be done by successfully completing an approved higher education Access course, which are offered by local colleges on a full or part-time basis.

The Open University also offers a route into social work training, and there are also extended DipSW Programmes for candidates with family commitments.

OPPORTUNITIES

There are approximately 8,000 trained probation officers in the UK, concentrated largely in urban areas. Some probation officers are seconded to the courts as court liaison officers because of their strong interviewing skills and expertise at report writing, while others may work in prisons or with agencies and charities working in related fields.

All services employ a number of non-qualified staff at the grade of Probation Service Officers (PSO). Further information is available from your local probation office.

There are no opportunities for freelance work although it is possible to become self-employed as a trainer or counsellor.

Vacancies are advertised in *Community Care*, the national

PROBATION AND AFTERCARE: KEB

press and via a weekly national bulletin that is available to all those in training.

PAY AND CONDITIONS

In England and Wales, salaries begin at around £15,000 and rise to £30,000 plus for senior probation officers and management grades. In Scotland, social workers in criminal justice work are paid on a scale of £17,000 to £21,000.

A working week can be between 37 to 40 hours, with irregular hours depending on when clients are available for you to visit them at their home. Officers are often given the opportunity to organize their own working hours but some rota work, when staff provide night-time and weekend cover, is necessary. A car user allowance, child care facilities, and time off in lieu for working unsociable hours, may be offered.

PROSPECTS

Promotion in probation work often means moving up to management level rather than working with people, hence many probation officers prefer not to seek promotion and therefore keep their case work. Subsequently the prospects are good for those seeking promotion to senior, advisory and managerial posts.

RELATED OCCUPATIONS

Field social worker, residential social worker, counsellor, prison governor, teacher, youth and community worker.

FURTHER INFORMATION

Central Council for Education and Training in Social Work (CCETSW):

England: CCETSW Information Service, Derbyshire House, St Chad's Street, London WC1H 8AD, 0171 278 2455

Scotland: 5th Floor, 78–80 George Street, Edinburgh EH2 3BU, 0131 220 0093

Wales: 2nd Floor, West Wing, Southgate House, Wood Street, Cardiff CF1 1EW, 01222 226257

The Home Office, Probation Training Unit, Room 414, Queen Anne's Gate, London SW1H 9AT, 0171 273 3718

National Association of Probation Officers, 3–4 Chivalry Street, London, SW 1HT, 0171 223 4887

FURTHER READING

Leaflets and booklets are available from all the organizations listed above.

Working in Social Work – COIC

Careers in Social Work – Kogan Page

The Probation Service – Working to Reduce Crime and Protect the Public – Home Office, Probation Unit

In the careers library classified under KEB.

NURSERY WORK: KEB

NURSERY NURSE CLCI:KEB

BACKGROUND INFORMATION

Nursery nurses work with children, from new-born babies to seven-year-olds (eight in Scotland), in a variety of settings including nursery, infant or primary schools, day nurseries and hospitals, in both the private and voluntary sectors. They are also often employed in private households to care for children in their own home environment.

There have been enormous changes in the role of the nursery nurse over the last ten years, with an increasing emphasis on the pre-school education of young children, which requires teaching as well as the more traditional caring skills. The growing number of working mothers has meant that more children of pre-school age are being cared for in nursery provision and the demand for qualified nursery nurses remains high.

Nursery nurses work with a wide range of children, including those with disabilities and special needs, and often liaise with other professionals such as social workers, teachers and medical staff.

THE WORK

Nursery nurses are involved in planning, initiating, and supervising work and play activities for individuals or groups of children, including story sessions, reading, cooking, computer activities and music sessions.

Promoting the physical, social, emotional and educational development of a child is an essential part of the work. This is done by encouraging children to make meaningful choices, have consideration for others, engage in exploration and develop self-esteem and confidence, through a programme of learning and play activities. A nursery nurse often has to take sole responsibility for children in outdoor areas where a variety of activities are available. Observing, monitoring and assessing individual children at play is also an important aspect of the job, as is reporting on areas of concern to parents, guardians, teachers or hospital staff. The work also involves carrying out domestic duties such as tidying up, preparing meals and washing soiled clothes. Caring for sick children and administering first aid when necessary as well as washing, feeding and dressing the very young, and taking them to the toilet, are all part of the nursery nurse's work.

With the increasing emphasis on pre-school education, the maintenance of accurate records has become an important aspect of the job, as has the encouragement of, and assistance with, early reading and number work.

Nursery nurses often work as part of a multidisciplinary team providing care and education.

WORK ENVIRONMENT

Nursery nurses work in a variety of settings from private homes to large day nurseries. Working conditions can often be noisy, untidy and messy. Supervision of children can be indoors or outdoors and sometimes involves taking children on outings to local parks or places of interest. The workplace itself may be modern, light and airy or can be an older property with more-outdated facilities.

SKILLS AND INTERESTS

It is essential that nursery nurses have a genuine interest in children and a desire to be involved in their social and educational development. Physical fitness and stamina are essential, as bending and being active are a major aspect of the job. Nursery nurses must be alert, in order to look out for any potential dangers. A responsible attitude is needed at all times. Children are not always predictable and their demands can be stressful, so patience and the ability to remain calm in crisis situations is crucial. Creative ability and imagination are important, in order to produce stimulating activities for children. A nursery nurse must be able to work as part of a team as well as being able to work alone. Planning, organization and presentation skills are necessary in order to provide an interesting programme of work and play. A cheerful disposition along with a sense of humour, are also invaluable. An awareness of the social, emotional and educational needs of a child and sensitivity to children are essential. Good communication skills are important when liaising with other professionals, as well as parents and guardians.

ENTRY REQUIREMENTS

In England, Wales and Northern Ireland the recognized qualifications are the Certificate in Child Care and Education (CCE), the CACHE Diploma in Nursery Nursing (NNEB), and the Advanced Diploma in Child Care and Education (ADCE) – all awarded by the Council for Awards in Children's Care and Education (CACHE). The BTEC National Diploma in Caring Services (Nursery Nursing) is also a nationally recognized qualification. For those already involved in the care of children, NVQs/SVQs in Child Care and Education are available at Levels 2 and 3.

In Scotland, the Scottish Child Care and Education Board (SCCEB) issues certificates of Registration and Preliminary Registration. The normal requirement for work as a Nursery Nurse is a Certificate of Registration, awarded to individuals who successfully complete approved programmes of education and training usually via either an SVQ Level 3 or a one-year programme of Scottish Qualification Authority (SQA) National Certificate modules plus a one-year HNC in Child Care and Education. For those who enter the profession at the lower level of Nursery Nurse Assistant (or similar description), a Certificate of Preliminary Registration is the appropriate qualification and this is awarded to those who successfully complete either an SVQ Level 2 or the one-year programme of SQA National Certificate modules. The Board will consider other qualifications or combinations of qualifications for Registration at both Preliminary Registration and Registration grades.

There are no specific academic requirements but most institutions prefer two or three GCSEs/S grades (A–C/1–3) in English and other subjects such as sociology, music, human biology, psychology and art. The ability to play a musical instrument is useful, as is previous experience of care work either on a paid or voluntary basis. Most colleges of further education accept students at 16 years, although the private colleges have a minimum entry age of 18 years.

Modern Apprenticeships (part of the Skillseekers Initiative in Scotland) may be available for young people leading to at least an NVQ/SVQ Level 3. Contact your local careers office, Jobcentre, TEC/LEC for details.

NURSERY WORK: KEB

TRAINING

The CACHE Diploma and the SQA National Certificate programme consist of both theoretical and practical training on a continuous assessment basis.

The CACHE Diploma is a two-year full-time course, but is also available part-time, which may take up to five years maximum. Forty per cent of course time is spent working in practical placements with children and families. The age groups covered are: birth to one, one to four, and four to seven years – in a variety of settings. Amongst the areas of study are: work with young children, equality of opportunity, physical care and development hygiene, first aid, emotional and social development, and nutrition. Students are expected to demonstrate their competence in a variety of situations and show their ability to work in a professional and responsible manner.

The CACHE Certificate in Child Care and Education is a one-year full-time award. It is a module-based course, the two main areas being knowledge and understanding, and practical skills and competency. There are no academic entry requirements for the Certificate other than a minimum age of 16 years. Students who successfully complete the Certificate can progress on to the CACHE Diploma.

The CACHE Advanced Diploma in Child Care and Education (ADCE) consists of six modules which can be completed within a two- to five-year period and is aimed at experienced professional child care and education workers. The ADCE offers professional development and includes management modules. It may also be run as a one-year full-time course. Under the Credit Accumulation Transfer Scheme (CATS), the Open University awards credit points on completion of the ADCE to candidates who wish to progress to higher education.

The BTEC National Diploma in Caring Services (Nursery Nursing) is also available at many further education establishments; courses usually last two years full-time. A 'First Certificate in Caring' – a one-year full-time course is also offered enabling candidates who lack academic achievement at GCSE to progress to the NNEB Diploma or the BTEC National Diploma (Nursery Nursing).

In Scotland, the SQA one-year National Certificate modular programme and the one-year Higher National Certificate Course in Child Care and Education both include theoretical and practical work and placement time in child care establishments.

NVQs/SVQs in Child Care and Education at Levels 2 and 3 are available nationally. At Level 2 the units covered are: work with babies, work in support of others, work in a pre-school group and work in a community-run pre-school group. Level 3 covers group care and education, family day-care, pre-school provision, family support and special needs.

Training opportunities for young people, including National Traineeships and Modern Apprenticeships (part of the Skillseekers Initiative in Scotland), may be available – contact your local careers office, Jobcentre, TEC/LEC for details.

LATE ENTRY

There is no upper age limit for entry to nursery nurse training and adult students are welcome. Those with previous experience and skills may be able to go through the APEL route in order to gain recognized qualifications.

OPPORTUNITIES

Demand for qualified nursery nurses in both the private and public sector is high, and vacancies are available not only in the UK but often abroad. The majority of nursery nurses work in local authority nursery schools or classes, day nurseries and companies offering workplace crèche or nursery provision.

Vacancies are normally advertised in the local press or in national publications such as *The Lady, The Times Educational Supplement* and *Nursery World*. Local authorities also provide details on all vacancies within various departments. There are several agencies who specialize in finding work for nannies both in the UK and overseas.

PAY AND CONDITIONS

Pay and conditions for nursery nurses vary depending on the type of employer and can range from £8,000 to £13,000. Those in senior positions can earn from £13,500 to £22,500. Nursery nurses employed in private homes as nannies can receive an average wage of £80 to £90 a week, although this can vary depending on the location of the job and the number of children needing care. Private nannies who are required to live in have accommodation provided and this is usually reflected in the salary.

Most nursery nurses work between 32 and 40 hours a week involving early starts and late finishes. Some workplace and day nurseries can be open from 7am until 8pm, and staff normally work on a shift basis. Staff employed in schools usually work school hours and have school holidays.

In residential nurseries it is essential that adequate supervision and cover is available all year round, 24 hours a day (including weekends and public holidays), so staff need to work to a strict shift system.

For nannies working in the private sector, the hours tend to be longer and time off is not always available on the same day or at weekends. Due to the fact that they live in, nannies are sometimes required to attend to, and care for, children during the night.

It is possible to obtain part-time work as a nursery nurse. Job share opportunities are available and encouraged.

PROSPECTS

Promotion prospects for nursery nurses are limited, particularly in the public sector. Eventually, it is possible to become an officer-in-charge, which involves managing budgets, administration duties and arranging and organizing supervision of children.

A qualified nursery nurse may open their own nursery, crèche or child-minding provision but this would also require some business expertise.

RELATED OCCUPATIONS

Nurse, care assistant, child-minder, teacher, social worker, youth and community worker, playgroup leader.

FURTHER INFORMATION

Council for Awards in Children's Care and Education (CACHE), 8 Chequer Street, St Albans, Hertfordshire AL1 3XZ, 01727 847636 (A4 sae please), ourworld.compuserve.com/homepages/cache

NURSERY WORK: KEB

Professional Association of Nursery Nurses (PANN), 2 St James' Court, Friar Gate, Derby DE1 1BT, 01332 343029

Scottish Child Care and Education Board, Office S3, The APL Centre, Stevenston Industrial Estate, Stevenston, Ayrshire KA20 3LR, 01294 470380 (sae please)

FURTHER READING

Working in – Work with Children – COIC

Careers Working With Children and Young People – Kogan Page

In the careers library classified under KEB.

CAREERS WORK: KED

CAREERS ADVISER CLCI:KED

BACKGROUND INFORMATION

The Careers Service is provided by around 80 independent companies working under contract to the Department for Education and Employment or, in Scotland and Wales, with the Scottish and Welsh Offices.

The local careers services provide information, guidance and practical help to school and FE college students (and those who have recently left) to enable them to take up suitable education, training and employment. Most careers services also provide some information and advice to adults who wish to change career.

Careers services are not responsible for work with students in universities and colleges of higher education which employ their own careers staff.

THE WORK

Careers advisers help their clients make informed, realistic decisions about their future education, training and employment, use of the Learning Card, and to put these decisions into practice. Most careers advisers' work is varied, although some careers services have advisers specializing in work with particular client groups, such as members of disadvantaged groups or those with special needs.

Careers advisers spend much of their time in schools, often working in a team with other careers advisers and careers service support staff. They inform and advise young people at times when they make decisions that have career implications. Activities include interviewing young people, sometimes with their parents, and talking to, and initiating discussions with, groups. Careers advisers work closely with school staff to advise on schools' careers education and to arrange interviews and group work. They may conduct training for teachers to advise them of developments in employment and training.

Careers advisers are responsible for providing support and advice to young people when trying to enter and once in work based training. This applies to young people in Modern Apprenticeships (part of the Skillseekers Initiative in Scotland), National Traineeships or other forms of supported training. They also liaise with training providers.

Some careers advisers work in local sixth-form colleges, tertiary colleges and colleges of further education, with similar activities to those in schools.

Careers advisers keep in touch with unemployed young people. They advise them of job and training vacancies, arrange interviews for vacancies notified to the careers service, help them with applications and interview techniques and advise them of any financial help that may be available.

Careers advisers make frequent contact with employers for several reasons – learning about jobs and training; keeping up-to-date with the local labour market; seeking vacancies for clients; arranging work experience placements; setting up education-business projects; advising employers of developments in education and training and on recruitment of young employees; establishing what an employer needs from the careers service and marketing its services.

Careers advisers produce information for their clients on a range of subjects, such as local opportunities, career ideas and higher education. It may be in the form of booklets, leaflets or information from computer databases.

In addition, many careers services have some advisers who spend time working with adult clients. Careers services sometimes charge adults for careers guidance.

All careers advisers are responsible for administrative tasks, including making notes after each interview; writing reports; liaising with staff in schools and colleges, social services, youth service etc; attending meetings and making frequent telephone calls. Some supervise clerical support staff. Careers advisers increasingly use IT systems in their work and must be confident and competent in doing so.

WORK ENVIRONMENT

Careers advisers are based in offices that are open to the public, but spend much of their time in schools, colleges and on employers' and training providers' premises. Most of their work is in clean, light surroundings.

The work usually involves travelling in the local area and many jobs require that careers advisers hold a driving licence and own a car.

SKILLS AND INTERESTS

Careers advisers must be able to get on well with a wide range of people and be capable of establishing good working relations with them.

They have contact with all kinds of young people and their parents, school and college staff, employers, training providers, social workers etc.

Careers advisers should be interested in young people and understand and care about them without being judgemental. They need the ability to gain young people's confidence and to motivate them. An interest in educational matters is important. Careers advisers must keep abreast of developments in education and the labour market and interpret them to young people, parents, employers and training providers.

Careers advisers should understand and be interested in industry and commerce, if they are to advise clients realistically. This should include a thorough understanding of training matters, including new developments and qualifications.

An interest in information gathering is essential, as information plays a central part in careers work. Careers advisers have to research information and communicate it clearly to clients.

Good communication skills are essential. Careers advisers need to be able to express themselves clearly and simply, both in speech and in writing. They also need the ability to speak effectively to groups of people, such as young people, parents or teachers.

Careers advisers are responsible for arranging much of their own work, which needs good organizing and time-management skills. They are usually also part of a team and must operate well as team members.

It is increasingly important that careers advisers can work with computers and other new information technology. Many of them use portable computers to produce clients' career action plans and summaries of advice given to clients. Careers information is increasingly provided on occupational databases and CD ROMs; computer-assisted guidance systems programs are also increasingly used in careers offices, schools and colleges.

Senior staff need to be capable of managing staff and careers service resources.

ENTRY REQUIREMENTS

The nationally recognized professional qualification for careers advisers is the Diploma in Careers Guidance (DCG). A National Vocational Qualification (NVQ) in Guidance is also available and can provide an equivalent qualification to the DCG.

Applicants to DCG courses normally need one of the following:

– a degree, for which the minimum entry requirement is normally two A levels/three H grades and five GCSEs/S grades (A–C/1–3), or equivalent;

– an approved diploma or certificate in social science or social studies;

– an approved diploma in municipal or public administration, political science or management studies;

– qualified teacher status;

– a certificate in municipal administration, higher national diploma, or certificate or other approved qualification of comparable standard; *or*

– a diploma in higher education.

In practice, most younger entrants have a degree.

Two specialised university courses can lead to a degree and Part 1 of the DCG:

1. A degree in Human Organizations at the University of Northumbria, Newcastle – requires three A levels/four H grades plus five GCSEs/S grades (A–C/1–3) or equivalent.

2. A degree in Occupational Psychology – requires three A levels/four H grades and five GCSEs/S grades (A–C/1–3) including mathematics or equivalent.

TRAINING

Most careers advisers achieve their DCG qualification through a one-year full-time course (Part 1) followed by one year's on-the-job training as a probationary careers adviser while employed by a careers service (Part 2). An increasing number, though, are being employed by a careers service and attending college part-time, in which case Part 1 and Part 2 run concurrently.

One-year full-time courses only are offered at: University of Northumbria at Newcastle, and Paisley, Strathclyde, Reading, Glamorgan, Nottingham Trent and South Bank Universities.

The following institutions offer both one-year full-time courses and two-year part-time courses: University of Central England (Birmingham), University of the West of England (Bristol), University of East London, University of Huddersfield, The College of Guidance Studies (Swanley), Manchester Metropolitan University and Napier University (Edinburgh).

Part 1 training is intensive and includes both theoretical study and practical training. Areas covered include careers guidance and careers education, the careers service, the education system, employment and unemployment, training, equal opportunities. Skills training is given in interviewing and working with groups. Courses include visits to employers, educational establishments and training organizations, with practical placements at careers offices.

Part 2 of the DCG takes place in post as a probationary careers adviser. The year is closely supervised and activities assessed.

An open learning course is also offered at The College of Guidance Studies. This involves working through open learning packages, attending several five-day residential blocks at the college, monthly regional tutorial meetings and two weeks' placement at a careers office. Most students take two years to complete Part 1 of the DCG on this basis and, if employed in a careers service, may also complete Part 2 at the same time.

The University of Northumbria at Newcastle offers a three-year full-time Human Organizations degree that can lead to completion of Part 1 of the DCG during the third year.

A recently introduced alternative method of qualifying is via an NVQ in Guidance (at Level 4) awarded by the Local Government Management Training Board/Institute of Careers Guidance, City and Guilds, the Open University Validation Service and the Scottish Qualifications Authority (SQA). As with part-time DCG, this method of training is intended mainly for those currently working in a careers service.

LATE ENTRY

There is no upper age limit for entry. Mature applicants are particularly welcome for the experience they can bring to the work, particularly if that experience is relevant, eg work in industry or commerce, teaching, social work or youth work. The normal entry requirement for entry to DCG courses may be waived for applicants of 25 years and over who have five years' good employment experience. Course tutors need to be satisfied that such applicants can cope with the academic demands of the course and they may have to demonstrate this by passing an entry test.

Adult entrants to DCG training with relevant qualifications or experience may be able to gain exemptions from some aspects of Part 1 through Accreditation of Prior Learning (APL).

Some careers service support staff, often known as **employment assistants** or **careers assistants**, become careers officers by attending a full-time DCG course or by being supported by their employer to study part-time for the DCG. The new NVQs in Advice and Guidance for employment assistants (Level 3) and careers advisers (Level 4) should make it easier for mature entrants to progress in the careers service.

OPPORTUNITIES

Careers advisers work in careers offices in towns and cities throughout the UK. There are approximately 470 main careers offices and a slightly greater number of branch and sub-offices.

Careers advisers work for the private companies that are contracted to provide local careers services. Some colleges of further education and sixth-form colleges employ their own advisers.

The number of careers advisers increased considerably during the late 1980s and there are currently over 4,500.

On completing DCG Part 1 courses, probationer careers advisers may need to move to another location to find a post. Vacancies have tended to be more plentiful in South East England than elsewhere. Vacancies are advertised in *PORTICO* (the Institute of Careers Guidance's fortnightly vacancy bulletin), in the *Times Educational Supplement*

CAREERS WORK: KED

and in the *Guardian* education edition on Tuesdays.

PAY AND CONDITIONS

Most careers advisers currently begin on a salary scale of approximately £14,000 rising to £19,000. Senior careers advisers can earn £19,000 upwards. Chief executives may earn £40,000 plus.

Most careers advisers work a 37-hour week, Monday to Friday. Most work is in normal office hours, but some evening work is usual to attend parents' evenings and careers conventions and to allow late evening opening of careers offices.

The new careers services are encouraging flexibility over working hours. Part-time work, job sharing and working on a supply basis (on call to fill temporary vacancies) are becoming more common for qualified careers advisers.

PROSPECTS

Most careers advisers begin in a general post working in a number of schools. After gaining experience they may move on to a specialist post working with special needs clients, the unemployed, further education students, adults, careers information, industrial liaison, ethnic minority clients etc.

Promotion to senior careers adviser may involve either advising generalist colleagues about these specialist areas, supervising a team of careers advisers, or running a small branch office. Further promotion involves additional management responsibilities and, for instance, it is possible to progress to operations manager and chief executive.

Some graduate careers advisers seek employment as careers advisers in higher education institutions.

It is possible for careers advisers to study part-time for a Master's degree in Guidance. In many cases the DCG has a credit value which can be 'topped up' to Master's level by taking some additional modules.

RELATED OCCUPATIONS

Personnel officer, counsellor, teacher, social worker, youth and community worker, training manager, university careers adviser, employment agency consultant/interviewer.

FURTHER INFORMATION

The Institute of Careers Guidance*, 27a Lower High Street, Stourbridge, West Midlands DY8 1TA, 01384 376464, www.icg-uk.org.uk

FURTHER READING

Leaflets/booklets are available from the address marked*.

Guidance, Counselling and Advisory Work – AGCAS

In the careers library classified under KED.

EMPLOYMENT AGENCY WORK: KED

EMPLOYMENT AGENCY CONSULTANT/INTERVIEWER CLCI:KED

BACKGROUND INFORMATION

Employment agencies act as intermediaries between employers and job-seekers. They earn fees from employers by matching suitable applicants with permanent and temporary vacancies.

There are several types of employment agency:

General staff agencies deal mainly with office workers, but may place other categories of staff, such as drivers or factory workers, in employment. The large national chains – Brook Street, Reed and 'Adecco', for instance – are general staff agencies. There are also smaller local chains and independent agencies, with just one office.

Specialist agencies specialize in particular categories of staff, such as accountants or computer personnel.

Medical and nursing agencies supply nurses and other medical staff to National Health Service and private hospitals.

Executive selection agencies concentrate on permanent recruitment of managers and executives.

Executive search agencies (also known as 'head hunters') are concerned with filling senior posts, and usually make the first approach to potential candidates.

The employment agency business tends to expand rapidly in times of general economic prosperity, and to contract when the economy slows down.

THE WORK

The terms 'interviewer' and 'consultant' generally have the same meaning, although the terms 'consultant' or 'recruitment consultant' are more widely used within the industry.

The work includes the following aspects:

Contacting employers – by telephone, correspondence and in person. A lot of time is spent 'selling' job-seekers to employers. For example, if a skilled candidate is available, a consultant may telephone a number of potential employers to see if they have a suitable vacancy. Employers also telephone the agency when they are in need of extra staff, and it is the consultant's job to take details of their requirements and draw up job specifications. Consultants may circulate lists of candidates to potential employers. 'Prospecting' – finding new clients for the agency – is also important. It involves telephoning and/or making personal visits to local employers, with the aim of selling the agency's services.

Interviewing job-seekers and trying to match their experience, qualifications and personality with suitable vacancies. It may be necessary to advise or counsel job-hunters – eg to persuade them to take further training or to make realistic decisions about the types of work for which they are qualified. Consultants also test candidates' skills.

Organization and administration. Consultants advise on interview preparation, arrange interviews and ensure that candidates know the time, date and venue. Afterwards consultants make follow-up telephone calls, to find out whether the interviews were successful. They also keep records of applicants, introductions and placements – either on record cards or computers. Administration also includes drafting press advertisements and placing them in newspapers and magazines.

Many employment agencies deal with both temporary and permanent placements, but, within an agency, consultants tend to specialize in working with either permanent or temporary staff.

The pattern of work varies with different employers, but a typical consultant would probably spend about half the time dealing with client firms (essentially sales work) and the other half selecting and interviewing candidates and carrying out back-up administration.

WORK ENVIRONMENT

The majority of employment agencies are to be found in town or city centres. Some occupy shop premises, using the shop window to display job vacancy cards; others are situated in offices, usually above street level.

Most agency branches are small – typically employing no more than four or five staff.

The work is largely desk-based, but there may be some travel, to visit clients. A driving licence is useful for this aspect of the work.

SKILLS AND INTERESTS

The work involves a great deal of contact with people, and it is important to be able to gain the confidence of others and to put people at ease. Communication skills – especially a good telephone manner – are essential. Selling is an important part of the work, demanding persuasiveness and persistence. A smart, well-groomed appearance is required to inspire the confidence of clients and job-seekers.

Interviewers/consultants need to be able to cope with pressure, remaining calm and polite at all times. They deal with varying demands and conditions, requiring adaptability and a flexible approach. Good organizational skills are needed to schedule telephone calls, interviews and appointments, keep track of job-seekers and vacancies, and maintain accurate records.

ENTRY REQUIREMENTS

There are no specific entry requirements – a suitable personality is more important than academic qualifications. It is possible to enter this type of work with no exam passes, although it may be an advantage to offer some qualifications, such as GCSEs/S grades.

Most employers – and particularly executive recruitment and executive search agencies – welcome applications from graduates. Any subject is acceptable.

Employment agency consultant/interviewer is typically a second job, entered at the age of around 21 to 25 years (although there are no fixed minimum or maximum age limits). Previous experience in sales, personnel or office work is useful; other backgrounds may be acceptable. Initial appointment will generally be as a trainee consultant. Another entry route involves starting work as an administrator or secretary in an employment agency; promotion may then lead to consultant status.

TRAINING

The large staff agencies run induction training programmes, lasting up to twelve weeks, which include on-the-job training and courses in the companies' own training centres or run by the Institute of Employment

EMPLOYMENT AGENCY WORK: KED

Consultants (IEC). Smaller agencies often send staff on external courses run by IEC.

The IEC offers courses at two levels:

The Foundation Vocational Award in Employment Agency Practice is a distance learning course and examination for recent entrants to employment agency work. The course lasts six months and covers: background to employment agencies; essential legislation and procedures; the agency and the client; and the agency and the applicant. The IEC organizes study and revision seminars, at which students have the opportunity to meet and discuss difficulties. (It is possible to take the Foundation Vocational Award before starting work with an agency.)

The Certificate in Recruitment Practice is a national qualification, offered in conjunction with the Associated Examining Board. Part-time evening courses lasting one year are offered by a number of colleges of further education; a list of colleges is available from the IEC. Distance learning courses are also available. The courses cover recruitment practice, interviewing (including a practical test of interviewing skills) and relevant legislation. (Please note that the syllabus will change with effect from exams in the year 2000.) The standard required is similar to A level. Consultants usually take the Certificate in Recruitment Practice after gaining some experience in an employment agency or other personnel-related fields.

IEC qualifications are not always required for employment, but they are an advantage. The IEC encourages employers to recruit qualified consultants, and recommends that people looking for employment as consultants check that potential employers recognize the value of qualifications and training.

Some consultants take the Institute of Personnel and Development examinations, although this is less common than the IEC qualification route.

LATE ENTRY

Late entry is usual – the majority of entrants are in their twenties. There are no maximum age limits.

OPPORTUNITIES

There are over 16,000 employment agencies in Great Britain. About 70% of these are general staff agencies. There is a greater concentration of agencies in London and South East England than in other parts of the country, although opportunities are available nation-wide.

Vacancies are advertised in local and national newspapers, and in the specialist magazines, *The Interviewer, Selection,* and *Recruitment International.* It is also possible to find work by making direct approaches to agencies. Sometimes applicants who have registered with an agency, seeking other types of work, are offered trainee consultant posts.

PAY AND CONDITIONS

Salaries are a combination of a basic payment and commission. Consultants in London are generally the highest paid, with a typical starting salary of £13,000 to £17,000. Outside of London, starting salaries are likely to be between £8,000 and £12,000. With two to three years' experience, consultants – in London and elsewhere – can earn £30,000 plus. However, earnings depend on results.

Working hours are usually 8.30am to 6pm, Monday to Friday. Some evening work may be necessary. Specialist agencies – such as those dealing with nurses or industrial workers – may open early in the morning, or 24 hours a day (on shifts).

A company car is sometimes provided, usually only to senior staff. Private medical insurance may be offered to senior staff.

PROSPECTS

Entrants usually start as trainee consultants, and can expect to become consultants/interviewers within a few months of joining an agency. Thereafter, prospects depend on the size of the agency – there may not be much scope for promotion in smaller local firms, although it is possible in most agencies to reach branch management level. Large firms have a more clearly defined promotion structure, with opportunities for promotion to divisional management and beyond.

There may be occasional opportunities for experienced consultants to work abroad, with the European divisions of major agencies.

Self-employment – running one's own employment agency – is common, but it is important to gain experience of the industry first.

Experienced consultants also move into related work, such as sales or personnel.

RELATED OCCUPATIONS

Sales representative/manager, sales negotiator (estate agency), telephone salesperson, careers adviser, personnel officer.

FURTHER INFORMATION

Federation of Recruitment and Employment Services Ltd*, 36–38 Mortimer Street, London W1N 7RB, 0171 323 4300, www.fres.co.uk

Institute of Employment Consultants*, 3rd Floor, Steward House, 16a Commercial Way, Woking, Surrey GU21 1ET, 01483 766442, www.iec.org.uk

FURTHER READING

Leaflets/booklets are available from the address marked*.
In the careers library classified under KED.

YOUTH AND COMMUNITY WORK: KEG

YOUTH AND COMMUNITY WORKER (ENGLAND AND WALES)
COMMUNITY EDUCATION WORKER (SCOTLAND) CLCI:KEG

BACKGROUND INFORMATION

Youth and community work involves a broad spectrum of activities, concerned with education in its widest sense, with encouraging active participation in community affairs, and with the promotion of equal opportunities, irrespective of age, gender, class, race or disability. A key theme in current practice is 'empowerment' – the idea that it is possible for individuals or groups of individuals to make significant changes to their lives and the life of their community, with appropriate support from professionals.

THE WORK

There is a wide range of jobs under the general heading of 'youth and community work'.

Youth work is the most easily defined area, and is concerned with the education and development, both social and emotional, of young people aged between 11 and 26 years, particularly those aged 13 to 19 years

Over 50% of youth workers are based in a club or centre. Youth workers in clubs or centres organize activities such as sports, art projects, drama, discos. Centres may provide an informal setting for young people to meet (a coffee bar, for instance), where youth workers provide guidance in an unstructured way. They may also be involved in more formal group discussions and individual counselling, and may focus on particular groups such as the young unemployed, or young people with special needs.

A great deal of face-to-face youth work is carried out by part-time and voluntary workers (who outnumber full-time staff). Full-timers are often responsible for centre management, and divide their time between administrative duties, supervising part-time and voluntary youth workers, and direct work with young people. They may also liaise with and support part-time and voluntary workers running youth clubs in village halls, churches, mosques and other places of worship.

Some youth workers are 'detached' – not based in a centre, but concerned with meeting young people on their own ground: in the street, arcades, pubs and cafes, and working with them on the central issues of their lives.

There are also some youth workers based at schools, who may divide their time between youth work, teaching or pastoral duties, and others who are based in a neighbourhood or district working, for example, on housing estates. Some youth services employ outreach workers, whose aim is to encourage young people to make use of youth service provision.

Community workers work with a variety of people who share common concerns or problems, helping them to identify their problems and move towards a solution. They are concerned with giving people from all walks of life the opportunity and confidence to take part in social, community and political activities. They may, for instance, work with tenants' groups, working to improve facilities on housing estates; encourage parents to establish playgroups and toddler groups; help to set up credit unions; or work with homeless people.

In Scotland, community education services are concerned with adult education, as well as youth and community development. Training covers generic skills, but once employed, some staff specialize in working with young people, community work or adult education. Community education workers in local authorities often continue to have a mixture of responsibilities, whilst those in voluntary organizations tend to specialize.

WORK ENVIRONMENT

Youth workers may be based in clubs, centres, schools, or premises owned and managed by voluntary organizations. Some youth workers, along with community workers, are based at community education centres, community schools, neighbourhood or district offices. In Scotland community education workers may be based in community centres, or have responsibility for a specific geographic area. Most jobs involve some travel; in rural areas, this can be quite substantial. A driving licence is often essential.

SKILLS AND INTERESTS

Youth and community work and community education demands the ability to relate to, and communicate with, a wide variety of people. Empathy and good communication skills (especially the ability to listen) are essential. It is important to be sensitive and emotionally mature, with the capacity to earn the trust of others, and to be able to offer information, advice and guidance in a way that is acceptable and useful. Resilience and toughness may be needed to cope with conflict and deprivation. To get projects off the ground, initiative and enthusiasm are required. Planning and administrative skills are also necessary.

Many posts require a commitment to work unsocial hours.

Wide interests are useful, and for some posts it is an advantage to have specialist skills or interests such as sports or arts.

ENTRY REQUIREMENTS

Although A levels/H grades, or in some circumstances GCSEs/S grades, might be required as minimum entry qualifications for training and degree courses, maturity and experience are often more important.

In Scotland, entry into qualified community education posts is via a first degree or postgraduate certificate in Community Education. Entry requirements are usually three H grades (including English) plus one GCSE (A–C)/S grade (1–3).

The majority of qualifying courses in youth and community work are for mature students (21 years and over); school-leavers are generally advised to gain experience before studying for a full professional qualification. Applicants for degree and training courses have a better chance of acceptance if they have carried out youth or community education work on a paid or voluntary basis. Further information about part-time and voluntary opportunities is available from youth officers in local authorities and voluntary and independent bodies.

Local authorities and voluntary youth organizations run training courses for their part-time staff and volunteers. Basic training courses are sometimes compulsory but further training is up to the individual. In England, Regional Accreditation and Moderation Panels give national recognition to local and regional training for part-

YOUTH AND COMMUNITY WORK: KEG

time volunteer workers.

Degree courses are available but employers are now organizing their own work-based training courses. The courses are designed for entrants who may not be attracted to full-time study.

Entry to degree courses is with a minimum of two A levels/three H grades and five GCSEs/S grades (A–C/1–3) or equivalent. Entry requirements may be waived for mature and experienced entrants but they may need to show that they have the ability to meet the academic standards required. Applicants who have completed Access courses or other non-traditional ways of study are also accepted, with appropriate experience.

Students with HND in a related subject can gain entry to the second year of some degree courses provided they have the relevant experience.

Graduates in subjects unrelated to youth work or community education can qualify by taking postgraduate courses in youth and community work (although some colleges or universities may prefer a 'relevant' discipline, such as social sciences).

Apprenticeship routes to training are available in certain regions of Scotland as an alternative for those with significant experience of working in their communities but who do not have a recognized qualification.

All prospective youth workers must be prepared to disclose any criminal record they may have, even if it would normally be considered 'spent'. However, a criminal record does not necessarily disqualify an individual from working with young people; factors such as the nature of the offence, and how long ago it took place, are taken into account.

TRAINING

There are a number of different routes to becoming a qualified youth and community worker, and there are different levels of qualification, local and national, part-time and full-time.

England and Wales

1. The majority of full-time youth and community staff in England and Wales hold qualifications endorsed by the National Youth Agency (NYA) or Wales Youth Agency (WYA) on behalf of the Joint Negotiating Committee (JNC). In most cases this is a diploma in higher education or postgraduate diploma in youth and community work.

2. Two-year full-time or three-year part-time training courses are available. An initial certificate of youth and community work is awarded but this leads to a full professional qualification, usually a diploma in higher education, which may be followed by an optional third year of study for a degree. Courses are available at a number of colleges.

3. Degree courses, lasting three to four years (with a diploma in higher education awarded after successfully completing the first two years), are available at a number of colleges of higher education and universities.

4. In England a two-year full-time course and a four-year part-time (by distance learning) course – leading to a BA Informal and Community Education degree – are run by the Young Men's Christian Association (YMCA) George Williams National College. The BA is also endorsed in Scotland by CeVe.

5. The College also runs a Diploma in Higher Education over two years full-time.

6. The YMCA George Williams National College has a BA (Hons) Informal and Community Education degree which can be obtained by three years' full-time study or a combination of full-time and part-time study spread over four years.

7. In Wales, the North East Wales Institute (NEWI) runs a two-year Diploma in Higher Education followed by a one-year BA (Hons) in Higher Education (Youth and Community Work). Both are validated by the University of Wales.

8. A teaching qualification gained before 31 December 1988 is, in theory, an acceptable alternative to a youth and community qualification. However, employers may not regard teaching qualifications and experience (particularly with infants or juniors) as relevant for work with adolescents, and in these cases it may be necessary to take a one-year postgraduate course. Those who qualified as teachers after 1988 have to take a further qualification in youth and community work.

Scotland

1. In Scotland, community education workers must have qualifications that are endorsed by the Community Education Validation and Endorsement (CeVe) committee of the Scottish Community Education Council. This covers training at various levels from part-time courses though degree level to postgraduate certificates and diplomas

2. Degree courses are available in Community Education at Moray House Institute of Education, Northern College of Education and the University of Strathclyde.

3. Postgraduate certificate courses are available for those over 22 years of age with a UK degree (or equivalent) who also have substantial experience of work in community education.

4. There is also a postgraduate diploma course at Northern College.

5. Graduates with the BA in Community Education from Scottish Universities or those with a Diploma in Community Education can obtain BA (Hons) in Community Education.

LATE ENTRY

Late entry is positively encouraged, as maturity and experience are important.

OPPORTUNITIES

The number of full-time posts for youth and community workers is relatively limited. The total for full-time youth workers employed by local authorities in England and Wales has been estimated at around 5,000, plus around 700 officers and advisers. There is also a large number of qualified community workers employed by other local authority departments, such as leisure and recreation, social services and housing.

Additionally, youth and community workers are employed by voluntary organizations such as the YMCA, the National Association of Boys' Clubs, and small neighbourhood-based community groups.

In Scotland, it has been estimated that there are about 1,300 to 1,400 full-time posts in community education with many other community education workers holding posts in voluntary sector organizations and other local authority services such as social work and economic development.

YOUTH AND COMMUNITY WORK: KEG

PAY AND CONDITIONS

Qualified full-time youth and community workers in local authority employment are paid on a scale that ranges from £12,447 (starting point of level 1) to £23,967 (top of level 3).

Hours vary, but most staff are contracted to work a set number of hours (35 to 37 a week) that may include specified evening and weekend sessions. In practice, the actual time worked may considerably exceed the contracted hours.

In Scotland pay scales are linked to local authority A.P.T+C spinal points.

PROSPECTS

In local authority youth work and community education services in Scotland, a promotion structure exists. Usually a youth worker will start as an assistant, then move on to running a youth centre, then into a senior role, with responsibility for youth work in a particular neighbourhood. Thereafter, there are opportunities for promotion to management grades – area youth officer, county youth officer. It is also possible to become a lecturer or trainer.

There is less of a formal promotion structure in voluntary sector youth work and in community work.

RELATED OCCUPATIONS

Field social worker, residential social worker, careers adviser, probation officer, volunteer organizer, school teacher, play worker, leisure centre manager.

FURTHER INFORMATION

National Youth Agency*, 17–23 Albion Street, Leicester LE1 6GD, 0116 247 1305, www.nya.org.uk.minicom

Scottish Community Education Council, Roseberry House, 9 Haymarket Terrace, Edinburgh EH12 5EZ, 0131 313 2488

Wales Youth Agency, Leslie Court, Lon-y-Llyn, Caerphilly CF8 1BQ, 01222 880088

Community Youth Work Association & The Youth Development Association, Youth Development Office, 122 Rochdale Road, Oldham OL1 1NT, 01457 834943

National Council for Voluntary Youth Services, The Peel Centre, Percy Circus, London, WC1X 9ES, 0171 833 3003

FURTHER READING

Leaflets/booklets are available from the address marked*.

Working in – Work with Children – COIC

Service to the Community – AGCAS Careers Information Booklet

NYA Guide to Becoming a Youth Worker – National Youth Agency

In the careers library classified under KEG.

PSYCHOLOGY: KEL

PSYCHOLOGIST CLCI:KEL

BACKGROUND INFORMATION

While psychology is a relatively young science, it has made an impact on most people's lives. Psychologists observe and interpret normal and abnormal human behaviour. The knowledge and understanding gained is applied in a wide range of situations.

This article covers the six main professional specialisms: **clinical psychology, educational psychology, occupational psychology, forensic psychology, health psychology** and **counselling psychology**.

The British Psychological Society (BPS) has set up a register of chartered psychologists. It is open to appropriately trained psychologists who are members of BPS. The BPS also approves first-degree courses and professional training courses in psychology.

THE WORK

Clinical psychologists are concerned with their patients' mental health. They work in teams with psychiatrists, nurses and other professionals in hospital and community clinics, or even in the patient's own home. Although there are no absolute boundaries between the work of psychologists and psychiatrists – one major difference is that psychologists do not prescribe medication.

Their clients are all kinds of people, such as the elderly, children and mentally or physically disabled people. They interview and assess their patients, using psychometric testing where necessary. Once a problem has been identified it is discussed with others in the team, and a treatment programme is drawn up and carried out.

Therapy is designed to suit each individual's needs. It helps to improve the quality of patients' lives by teaching them to avoid or control their problems.

Psychologists train nursing and other staff in strategies for coping with problems like disruptive and violent patients, or bereavement. They write reports, attend meetings and case conferences, and carry out research.

Educational psychologists deal with the needs and problems of children from birth to age 19 years. They liaise with teachers, social workers and other professionals in schools, hospitals, child guidance clinics and social service departments.

They deal with all types of children, from the unhappy or disruptive to those who have special needs or who are gifted children. They choose the most suitable course of action from a range including counselling, learning programmes or family therapy. They help parents and teachers when necessary, training them in skills like behaviour management.

Educational psychologists also look at wider issues – for example, the organization and management of a school or home – identifying strengths and weaknesses and solving problems. They provide in-service training for staff dealing with young people. The work includes meetings, case conferences, report writing and research.

Occupational psychologists specialize in the world of work. They advise companies on improving training, job satisfaction and productivity. They study and assess the functions of organizations or groups, preparing and presenting reports, as well as advising on performance, ergonomics (the interaction of people with their workplace, equipment and efficiency), health and safety and other factors. Their skills are used to help individuals' needs as well, handling such behavioural problems as low self-esteem or workplace bullying.

They may specialize in one topic, such as industrial relations, vocational guidance and counselling, or selection and recruitment.

Forensic psychologists (or criminological and legal psychologists) work in prisons, youth custody centres, special hospitals and secure units. They work with staff and inmates, and provide a range of rehabilitative programmes including social skills training, stress management and anger control. An important part of the work is assessing prisoners; some psychologists prepare reports for mental health review tribunals. They provide individual and group therapy. They are involved in the day-to-day running of these institutions and provide support and training for prison staff.

All are involved in research to some extent. They examine criminal behaviour and evaluate their therapies. Senior staff help with policy making and planning. They advise other professionals in this field including prison staff, the police and probation officers. Some specialize in court work, assessing clients, preparing reports and giving 'expert' evidence.

Health psychologists advise other professionals, for example, in patient communication. They may work with others in hospitals, health authorities, universities etc.

Counselling psychologists are concerned with helping people cope with stress, resolve their problems and make decisions for themselves. They may work with individuals, couples, families and groups.

Many of the techniques that psychologists use are common to all the specialisms. Computers, video recording and other specialized equipment are widely used in experimental work.

Psychological investigation uses a variety of methods. These range from laboratory-controlled scientific testing to informal situations where people are assessed in a relaxed environment.

WORK ENVIRONMENT

This varies depending on the specialism. Psychologists may work in laboratories, offices, clinics, schools and colleges, prisons, and in commercial or industrial settings. Some visit clients or patients in their own homes.

SKILLS AND INTERESTS

Psychologists need to be interested in people, their abilities, interests and temperaments. They should be keen to help others without getting too personally involved – working with clients and patients can be emotionally draining. As problem solving can be such a major aspect of the work, they should be able to think logically and creatively and to examine issues from every aspect.

The work needs above-average written and spoken communication skills, as psychologists spend much of their time listening and talking to clients, colleagues and patients, and writing reports and other material. Patients' and clients' confidentiality should be respected. There is an obvious ethical aspect to the work and psychologists need a mature attitude and sound judgement in deciding on the best interests of their clients. It is important to be tolerant and to refrain from judging others.

Team work is an important aspect of the work and psychologists must be able to get on with other people.

Psychology, like other sciences, uses statistics to evaluate the outcomes. This requires psychologists to be numerate, able to analyse and interpret figures, and use computers.

They should be accurate and methodical workers who are able to organize their own workload and meet their objectives.

ENTRY REQUIREMENTS

A psychology degree from a course recognized by the BPS is necessary for anyone wishing to work in most psychology posts. The minimum entry requirements for a degree course are five GCSEs/S grades (A–C/1–3) with two A levels/three H grades; Advanced GNVQ/GSVQ Level III, or BTEC/SQA national qualifications may be accepted for entry. Most valuable subjects are biology or human biology, English, maths, history or economics, also psychology where it is available.

When choosing a degree it is helpful if applicants consider their future career choices, because some first-degree courses are more relevant than others. The BPS awards the 'Graduate Basis for Registration as a Chartered Psychologist' (GBR) to those applicants who have completed approved courses. Normally only graduates with appropriate degrees and 'GBR' can progress to further training and professional work.

Competition for specialized training places and first appointments is very intense. It is essential that applicants obtain good honours degrees (minimum 2:2, more usually a first or 2:1) if they are to find a training place.

TRAINING

Clinical psychology training is mostly hospital-based, although some academic teaching may take place in a higher education institution. A British Psychological Society (BPS) accredited first degree is needed, followed by an additional three-year BPS-accredited training course, where participants are supervised by senior staff and gain experience in working with all client groups.

Educational psychology training requires a BPS-accredited first degree, a teaching qualification and usually two years' postgraduate teaching experience with children and young adults up to the age of 19. (The two years' teaching experience, however, is not required in Scotland.) This is followed by a year's professional training and a further year's supervised practice.

Occupational psychology training require a BPS-accredited first degree. Graduates can go straight on to an accredited training course which should be followed by at least two years' appropriate practice under the supervision of a chartered psychologist. Graduates who do not take an accredited training course are required to sit the BPS Postgraduate Certificate in Occupational Psychology.

Many graduates who are interested in criminological and legal work join the Prison Psychological Service on graduation with a BPS-accredited first degree. An MSc in Forensic/Criminological Psychology, followed by at least two years' supervised practice is required to become a forensic psychologist. Those working in prisons and other institutions that are not secure/special units often need no extra professional qualifications, though many study further for a Master's degree in criminology, criminological psychology or similar.

Those working in special hospitals or regional secure units often have to be qualified in clinical psychology.

To become a chartered counselling psychologist requires a BPS-accredited first degree followed by three years postgraduate training leading to the BPS Diploma in Counselling Psychology; alternatively an accredited postgraduate training course can be taken.

For research psychology, registration is via a research route and is usually only open to those holding a BPS-accredited first degree in addition to a doctoral level degree in psychology.

LATE ENTRY

There is no upper age limit. Those without a degree need to complete a BPS-approved degree course to be eligible for further training. If applicants lack the usual educational requirements they should contact the institution of their choice to enquire if a mature entry scheme is available. Graduates with a non-relevant degree should contact the BPS and enquire about conversion courses.

OPPORTUNITIES

Psychologists work in the public services and the private sector. Part-time and job share vacancies are sometimes available.

Clinical psychologists form the largest professional group. The NHS has about 2,200 posts in the United Kingdom and this number is increasing annually. There are generally regular vacancies at the basic grade. Local authorities employ psychologists mainly in education or social services departments, working in child guidance, assessment centres and community homes. The Civil Service employs psychologists in many departments, including the Home Office Prison Service, Department for Education and Employment and Ministry of Defence.

Those involved in research and teaching are often attached to institutes of higher, further and tertiary education.

Psychologists in the private sector are often found in human resources management, private practice, market research or freelance consultancy. Opportunities are increasing because psychology has such a wide range of applications, relating, as it does, so closely to people in their daily lives.

PAY AND CONDITIONS

Salaries vary depending on specialism, seniority and levels of responsibility. Psychologists working for the National Health Service, local education authorities and the Prison Service have national pay scales. The earnings of freelance psychologists and those in industry and commerce can reach the highest of the salaries mentioned below.

Trainee clinical psychologists start at £14,386. Senior clinical psychologists rise to £50,468. The starting salary for a qualified educational psychologist is £21,642 which rises to £39,270 for a principal educational psychologist. These salaries are slightly lower in Scotland. Occupational psychologists' earnings are more variable. In the public sector, they start at £12,369 rising to £37,539, but in the private sector they can rise as high as £50,000.

Those working in prisons have a pay scale linked to Civil Service pay and conditions, unless they are employed in a clinical capacity, when their pay is similar to NHS scales.

PSYCHOLOGY: KEL

Working hours depend on their duties. Many work normal office hours, 8.30am to 5pm, Monday to Friday. Some research projects and clinical appointments may require attendance out of office hours.

PROSPECTS

Promotion prospects are good for chartered psychologists. Membership of the Register is essential for most vacancies as it denotes a recognized standard of professional attainment and training.

The NHS, Prison Service, Civil Service and local education authorities all have clearly defined career paths for suitably qualified psychologists. The prospects in the private sector are as attractive. People seeking promotion may have to move to another area to take up a suitable vacancy.

RELATED OCCUPATIONS

Psychiatrist, ergonomist, psychotherapist, counsellor, field social worker, teacher.

FURTHER INFORMATION

The British Psychological Society (BPS)*, St Andrews House, 48 Princess Road East, Leicester LE1 7DR, 0116 254 9568 (please include sae)

The BPS has sections for all areas of specific interest, divisions for major professional groups and national branches in Scotland, Wales and Northern Ireland.

FURTHER READING

Leaflets/booklets are available from the address marked*.

Working in Mathematics –COIC

Compendium of Postgraduate Studies in Psychology in the UK and Ireland – BPS

CRAC Degree Course Guide to Psychology – Hobsons Publishing

In the careers library classified under KEL

VOLUNTARY HELP MANAGEMENT WORK: KEM

VOLUNTEER MANAGER CLCI:KEM

BACKGROUND INFORMATION

Voluntary work is unpaid activity which benefits the community. It is carried out in a wide range of settings, and includes activities such as working in charity or hospital shops, befriending the lonely, driving, decorating an elderly person's flat, counselling, fund-raising, delivering meals on wheels, countryside conservation and office administration.

As the scope and complexity of voluntary work has grown, it has become increasingly common for organizations in the voluntary sector to employ paid managers to recruit, train and manage volunteers.

Many different job titles are used in this area, for example, voluntary help organizer, volunteer development officer, voluntary services manager, volunteer co-ordinator and volunteer bureau manager.

THE WORK

The work is concerned with relating to a very wide range of people; some volunteer managers come into contact with a much broader cross-section of the community than is usual in most other jobs, even in related areas such as the social services and health care.

Prospective volunteers may come from any section of the community – from unemployed teenagers to retired executives. They are interviewed by the volunteer manager, who needs to be skilled at drawing people out and discovering their interests, skills and experience, as well as the degree of commitment they are able to make to voluntary work. Managers then try to match volunteers with work that they will find interesting and satisfying from the point of view of their own personal development – and where they will be able to make a useful contribution to whatever project is chosen.

Volunteer managers try to encourage the public to come forward and offer their services, by publicizing the need for volunteers in their organization. This may involve arranging advertising and public speaking.

Liaison with others is an important part of the job – it is necessary to obtain advice, consent, support and sometimes finance for projects. In the NHS, volunteer managers liaise with medical staff and management. In social services departments, they liaise with social workers and other staff, such as home helps. In voluntary organizations, liaison can be with a wide range of other organizations, both statutory and voluntary.

The work may involve organizing training sessions for volunteers and providing ongoing support for them in their voluntary work (eg checking that they are satisfied with the type of work they are doing and dealing with any difficulties that may arise). Managers also promote good practice in the recruitment and use of volunteers by local organizations within the voluntary sector.

Managers may manage/supervise volunteers, or advise and liaise with other organizations/individuals concerned with the day-to-day management of volunteers. Some recruit volunteers for a range of different tasks, whereas others are concerned with organizing volunteers in one specific field.

The work usually involves administration: keeping records/accounts, writing letters, reports, guidelines for volunteers and other documents, applying for grants, organizing fund-raising, attending committee meetings.

Managers may be responsible for budgets and keeping accounts, and for supervising paid staff, such as secretaries, as well as volunteers.

WORK ENVIRONMENT

The work is office-based but is likely to involve travel to meetings with representatives of other organizations, to meet volunteers at their placements etc.

SKILLS AND INTERESTS

The ability to relate to individuals from a very wide range of backgrounds is essential; this involves adaptability, tolerance, patience, open-mindedness and a sense of humour.

Excellent spoken communication skills are required for interviewing, managing and training volunteers, giving talks etc. Volunteer managers also need to be able to express themselves clearly in writing. Self-confidence and a positive, outgoing attitude are required for liaising with people from other organizations.

The post of volunteer manager, even when the work takes place in a large institution, such as a hospital, can be somewhat lonely: manager's concerns are different from those of other professional staff, and at the same time they do not share the perspective of the volunteers with whom they work.

As many posts require the ability to lead and motivate others, enthusiasm is important. Managers need initiative to start up and develop new projects.

The work requires adaptability and commitment – it is not a 9-to-5 job – and it is important to be flexible about attending meetings and other events in the evening or at weekends.

Volunteer managers who keep accounts should be numerate.

ENTRY REQUIREMENTS

There are no specific entry requirements in terms of academic qualifications or previous experience, although a degree and/or professional qualification may be an asset.

Entrants are usually, but not always, older individuals with experience and training in other fields. Experience in any or all of the following is useful – volunteering, organizing people (perhaps in the NHS or in teaching), committee work. It is particularly helpful to have had experience in a field that includes voluntary workers. A full, clean, current driving licence and use of a car are an advantage and may be essential for some jobs.

TRAINING

Training varies according to the organization and area but usually involves learning on the job, possibly under supervision. There may be opportunities to take short courses, typically lasting between one and five days.

Some organizations, eg those in health care and social services, provide short training courses for all their staff. Volunteer managers may attend such courses on areas including counselling and health and safety.

Most training specific to the role of volunteer manager, however, is external. There are a number of organizations running training events of various kinds. They include the following:

VOLUNTARY HELP MANAGEMENT WORK: KEM

The National Centre for Volunteering arranges a large number of training courses. These normally last one or two days and cover topics such as training volunteers, recruitment and selection, and interviewing skills. Details of other training courses can be provided.

The National Association of Volunteer Bureaux (NAVB) provides one-day training courses throughout the UK for managers who have been in post for at least twelve weeks. NAVB also holds training seminars at its annual three-day conference for volunteer bureau managers.

The National Association of Voluntary Service Managers offers a number of short training events (usually lasting one day) for volunteer managers working in the field of health care.

National Association of Councils for Voluntary Service runs a wide range of short training courses throughout England, some of which are designed for volunteer managers.

Directory of Social Change offers a number of short training courses specifically for volunteer managers. Most take place in London but some are in other English cities.

Volunteer Development Scotland has a core training programme for volunteer managers, covering the recruitment, training, selection and support of volunteers. It also offers courses for newly appointed managers and for those with experience.

Wales Council for Voluntary Action runs short courses for volunteer managers at different centres throughout Wales. They include managing for the first time, training skills and managing staff development.

Northern Ireland Volunteer Development Agency (NIVDA) organizes a number of training courses, lasting between a half-day and three days, on such topics as recruitment and selection of volunteers, effective management of volunteers and training volunteers.

Regional networks of voluntary organizations may run their own training events. An NVQ for volunteer managers is being developed.

LATE ENTRY

All entrants are adults and there are no maximum age limits. Most have experience and training in other fields.

OPPORTUNITIES

The main employers are:

– voluntary organizations such as MIND, Age Concern, or local Victim Support Schemes. Some staff in voluntary organizations combine the role of volunteer manager with other responsibilities;

– hospitals, hospices, community health and social services departments, which employ about 400 volunteer managers;

– Local Volunteer Bureaux, which function like employment agencies, matching prospective volunteers with voluntary sector organizations needing their services. There are about 350 such bureaux in England, Wales and Northern Ireland, and about 34 in Scotland. Most are charities or part of charitable organizations. Bureaux respond to local needs, and the range of tasks they carry out varies from one part of the country to another.

Entry is competitive and, because many voluntary sector organizations are affected by constraints on local authority spending, there is little or no expansion of this work at present.

PAY AND CONDITIONS

Rates of pay vary widely. Some organizations recommend rates of pay, eg a minimum of £12,000 to £18,000 for basic manager duties, with more for increased and managerial responsibilities (and higher rates for working in London). However, not all volunteer managers are paid these rates. Many jobs are part-time (salaries may be pro rata). Some are paid more – up to about £23,000 in London.

Full-time volunteer managers work a basic 35 to 37 hours a week, Monday to Friday, though extra evening/weekend work may be required. Organizations in the voluntary sector rarely pay for any overtime work, but instead allow time off in lieu.

PROSPECTS

Promotion prospects are limited, but this type of work can be a good background for related careers, such as social work, and for other posts within the voluntary sector, at managerial level, for instance.

RELATED OCCUPATIONS

Field social worker, youth and community worker, employment agency consultant/interviewer, charity fund-raiser, personnel manager, health service manager, volunteer.

FURTHER INFORMATION

Directory of Social Change, 24 Stephenson Way, London NW1 2DP, 0171 209 5151, www.d-s-c.demon.co.uk

National Association of Councils for Voluntary Service, 3rd Floor Arundel Court, 177 Arundel Gate, Sheffield S1 2NU, 0114 278 6636

National Association of Voluntary Service Managers, Teresa Cullen (Hon. Secretary), University Hospital, Nottingham NG7 2UH, 0115 924 9924 ext 42836

National Association of Volunteer Bureaux*, New Oxford House, 16 Waterloo Street, Birmingham B2 5UG, 0121 633 4555

Northern Ireland Development Agency*, Annsgate House, 70–74 Ann Street, Belfast BT1 4EH, 01232 236100

The National Centre for Volunteering, Regent's Wharf, 8 All Saints Street, London N1 9RL, 0171 388 9888. E mail: Centrevol www.volunteering.org.uk

Volunteer Development Scotland, 72 Murray Place, Stirling FK8 2BX, 01786 479593

Wales Council for Voluntary Action, Crescent Road, Caerphilly, Mid Glamorgan CF83 1XL, 01222 855101

FURTHER READING

Leaflets/booklets are available from the addresses marked*.

Directory of Volunteering and Employment Opportunities – Directory of Social Change

How to Work for a Charity – Directory of Social Change

Voluntary Agencies Directory – Bedford Square Press

Graduate Guide: Working for Charities and Pressure Groups – University of Sussex Career Development Unit

In the careers library classified under KEM.

GROUP L – LAW AND RELATED WORK

1. BARRISTER/ADVOCATE CLCI:LAB
2. SOLICITOR CLCI:LAC
3. BARRISTERS' CLERK CLCI:LAZ
4. LEGAL EXECUTIVE CLCI:LAD
5. SHORTHAND WRITER CLCI:LAG
6. COURT USHER/COURT OFFICER/ MACER CLCI:LAG

BACKGROUND INFORMATION

In the United Kingdom there is one legal system for England and Wales and a different one in Scotland. Each is based on its own set of legal principles.

Both systems consist of two separate, complementary branches – barristers and solicitors (England and Wales); advocates and solicitors (Scotland). They are trained in different ways to qualify for the specialist service they provide.

Solicitors are normally the first point of contact for any person wanting legal advice. They may be general legal experts or may specialize in a particular area of law. In many cases they deal with the matter personally; in others a barrister/advocate is briefed.

Barristers/advocates are consultants offering specialist legal advice or representing clients in court or before tribunals. They are not approached directly by clients but through solicitors or, in some cases, through other professionals who have the right to brief them, such as accountants, architects and surveyors. They have almost exclusive rights to appear in the higher courts. Some barristers practise general common law, although the majority specialize in certain areas. The majority of advocates do not specialize, although a larger number build up expertise in particular areas through doing a considerable amount of work in them.

Other legal careers featured in this chapter are peculiar to one or other of the two legal systems. Court officer/macer, for example, is a Scottish profession; legal executive, an English and Welsh one.

1. BARRISTER/ADVOCATE (LAB)

THE WORK

Practising barristers/advocates are always consulted by a member of another profession – in most cases by a solicitor. They may not work directly for a member of the public. They do not at first meet the client, but are briefed by the solicitor or other professional intermediary who wishes them to give specialist advice to their clients or to represent them in court.

Barristers/advocates are often consulted on points of law on which they give their opinion – after conducting research into similar cases and analysing them.

Solicitors often ask for an opinion on the likelihood of a case succeeding should it come to court. Based on their knowledge of past decisions and of the courts, barristers/advocates advise. If, in their opinion, the claim or defence is not likely to succeed, matters may be taken no further.

If a case comes to court, barristers/advocates concentrate on the conducting of the case, while the preparatory work of collecting evidence is carried out by the solicitor. One of the barrister's/advocate's skills lies in presentation in the courtroom, but in order to do this they have to spend a lot of time in preparation. Their preparatory work consists of becoming thoroughly acquainted with the facts of the case, reading statements and law reports, understanding any relevant technical or scientific terminology, and consulting clients, as and when necessary, in the presence of a solicitor.

In court they present the facts of the case to the judge and jury, cross-examine witnesses who are giving evidence, and finally sum up the reasons why the court should decide in their client's favour.

Court appearances are not always easy to plan, since it is difficult to predict how long a particular case will last. When delayed by one case, a barrister/advocate may not be able to appear as planned in another. This may mean finding someone else – where possible, a colleague – to take on the work.

The division of time between court appearances, advising and drafting written opinions, depends on clients, solicitors and the chosen area of specialism. Chancery work (trusts, property, estates, taxation and company law) involves much more advisory work, preparing detailed and complex opinions and drafting agreements. Common law (criminal, family, contract law, torts) may involve a lot of time spent on court cases, but, even here, civil cases are less likely to lead to proceedings and demand less time in court than on advisory work. (90% of civil cases are, in fact, abandoned, or a compromise is reached.) Barristers specializing in criminal work spend a high proportion of their time in court.

Although the majority of barristers/advocates are in private practice and work for clients, about 25% of barristers and a smaller proportion of advocates work at the **Employed Bar** – in industry, commerce and central and local government, where they work in specialist legal departments, advising only their own employers.

Barristers in commerce and industry may be general legal advisers, or may specialize in areas such as company law or taxation. The greater part of their work is likely to be concerned with drafting, advising on and negotiating contracts, but they may also advise on aspects of employment law, patents, health and safety law, and acquisitions and mergers.

Those working in central government departments provide an advisory service to civil servants and ministers. Others work for the Crown Prosecution Service, which conducts prosecutions on behalf of the police. Barristers review charges and evidence to decide whether a case should proceed to court. They may conduct the prosecution in magistrates' courts, but they brief practising barristers in cases going to the Crown Court.

More and more barristers are using computers in their work, for research, report writing and record-keeping.

WORK ENVIRONMENT

Most of the barristers in private practice work in chambers – their base. Some sets of chambers are specialist, home to groups of barristers who have chosen the same branch of legal work.

In London, chambers were once all in the same area, near the Inns of Court and the High and Central Criminal Courts. Many still are, but some barristers are seeking a wider variety of accommodation just outside the Inns. Outside London, chambers tend to be near the court buildings.

LAW AND RELATED WORK: LAB-LAZ

Some barristers work from home or from rented offices. This accommodation is still technically chambers, but they are known as sole practitioners.

Barristers in practice may base themselves in London and travel anywhere in the country to attend court, or may practise almost exclusively on one of six circuits, or administrative areas, in England and Wales: Northern, North Eastern, Midland and Oxford, West, South East, Wales and Chester. Even within one circuit, they spend a lot of time travelling.

Most advocates work from the Advocates' Library in Parliament House, Edinburgh, which provides the facilities they need to practise and which is open 24 hours a day, 365 days a year. If they are based elsewhere, they must still arrange to collect papers delivered to them by solicitors at the Library.

Employed barristers/advocates work in their company's or employing authority's premises.

SKILLS AND INTERESTS

Barristers/advocates need intellectual ability. The work calls for the ability to assimilate facts quickly, analyse, distinguish the relevant from the irrelevant, weigh the evidence and apply the law to the current situation.

They need fluency, clear speech and excellent presentation skills. In court they must be able to persuade, convince, argue, explain obscure points of law for the jury, and interrogate or cross-examine defendants and witnesses to establish the facts for both judge and jury.

They must be self-confident and able to inspire confidence in others. They must not allow their own or others' prejudices to affect the work they do for a client, but consider every problem dispassionately. Barristers/advocates working in criminal law accept that everyone is entitled to representation, whatever their financial means and whatever crime they are alleged to have committed. Even if their clients are unpopular with the media and general public, they are obliged to defend them to the best of their ability.

They must have complete integrity of character and need mental and physical stamina in order to cope with the long hours, travelling and stress.

ENTRY REQUIREMENTS

England and Wales

Entrants must have:

– a law degree of at least 2:2 honours standard that has included study of the seven foundations of legal knowledge: obligations I, obligations II, criminal law, equity and the law of trusts, the law of the European Union, property law and public law. Entry requirements for law degrees vary but are usually a minimum of five GCSEs/S grades (A–C/1–3) with three A levels/five H grades at high grades, or equivalent; *or*

– a non-law degree at the same standard, plus completion of the one-year full-time or two-year part-time Common Professional Examination (CPE) course or an approved postgraduate diploma in law (PgDL) course. Please see article 2. SOLICITOR. It is important to note, however, that not all CPE/PgDL courses satisfy the Bar's requirements. Suitability must be checked with the General Council of the Bar.

Scotland

Candidates, known as *Intrants,* must:

– have a degree with honours, second class (division 2) or above, in Scottish Law from a Scottish university; *or*

– have an ordinary degree in Scottish Law from a Scottish university, together with a degree with honours, second class (division 2) or above, in another subject from a university in the United Kingdom; *or*

– have an ordinary degree with distinction in Scottish Law from a Scottish university; *or*

– be a member of the Bar of England and Wales, or of Northern Ireland, and have completed a pupillage there; *or*

– provide evidence entitling him/her to practise in another Member State of the EU.

TRAINING

England and Wales

Currently, to become a barrister a person must:

– complete the academic stage of training by one of the routes above; *and*

– join one of the four Inns of Court and complete twelve qualifying units which can be achieved through a number of different ways, including weekends either at the Inn, or, at residential centres, Education Days, Education Dinners, Domus Dinners or Social Dinners. Further information can be obtained from the Inns of Court; *and*

– complete a one-year full-time or two-year part-time Bar Vocational Course (BVC) at one of the validated institutions throughout the country. Applications for a BVC will be made on a computerized form held on floppy disk through a centralized clearing system known as CACH (Centralised Applications and Clearing House). Students are called to the Bar after the successful completion of the BVC.

Two-thirds of the vocational course is devoted to skills training. Students practise the techniques of interviewing clients, take part in mock trials, learn how to draft documents, develop writing, numeracy, communication and presentation skills. They also study legal research, problem solving and opinion writing.

Following completion of the BVC, barristers intending to practise must complete a period of pupillage. Pupillage consists of two six-month periods spent under the guidance of an experienced barrister. During the first six months – the non-practising pupillage – pupil barristers must work in chambers (that may be outside London), gaining experience in drafting, opinion writing, preparing cases, attending court and attending external short courses and conferences. Their activities must be recorded against an approved check-list. They are then given a Provisional Practising Certificate, may appear in court and accept work in their own right. The Final Certificate is issued after the second six-month period.

The second pupillage may be spent outside chambers, in the Government's Legal Service, in industry, the Crown Prosecution Service or even in another EU country or at the European Commission.

Pupillage must also incorporate a certain amount of continuing professional development. Compulsory elements involve attendance at a course entitled 'Advice to Counsel' and further advocacy training that each Inn administers for its own members. Optional courses are available in Accounts, and European and Human Rights Law.

On qualifying, a practising barrister must obtain a tenancy in a set of chambers and work from there for at least three years, or with someone who has had five years' experience.

Barristers choosing to work in commerce and industry usually complete a pupillage even though it is not a requirement. Otherwise, they are unable to represent their employers in court.

Scotland

Intrants first follow a one-year full-time postgraduate course at a Scottish university leading to the Diploma in Legal Practice.

They then serve a period of salaried training of 21 months subject to possible partial exemption in a solicitor's office, during which time they may experience all work undertaken by solicitors, not merely that concerned with litigation. Up to one-third of this time may be in another of the Member States of the EU.

The final stage consists of a nine-month period of pupillage, known as *devilling*, spent with a member of the Scottish Bar approved by the Dean of the Faculty. This is a full-time pupillage, with devils forbidden to undertake any form of paid work which would interfere with their training.

During this time they must pass the Faculty of Advocates' examinations. There are no formal lecture courses or tuition for these. Since the majority are graduates in Scots Law, they are exempted from almost all of the examinations except those in Evidence, Procedure and Practice. After successfully completing the devilling period and passing the examinations, they are called to the Bar. Only then do they decide whether or not to practise.

There are transitional arrangements for five years from 31st July 1996 for those who in the preceding academic year were Solicitors, in training in a Solicitors' Office, or studying a degree in Scottish Law or a Diploma in Legal Practice at a Scottish university.

LATE ENTRY

England and Wales

There is no upper age limit. Adults may follow the normal entry routes described above, and may take an Access to Law course instead of A levels.

Individuals over 25 years of age who do not intend to take a degree should first contact The General Council of the Bar to establish whether any qualifications they do hold would entitle them to enter training. The Council has discretion to rule on previous qualifications and experience.

The decision by a mature entrant to become a practising barrister demands careful thought, given the financial implications of funding CPE and BVC (see below) and the uncertain income during the early years of practice.

Solicitors wishing to become barristers should apply to the Joint Regulations Committee.

Scotland

Adults may follow the normal entry route. Certain exemptions are, however, granted to:

– Scottish solicitors who have practised for a minimum of three years (they are automatically exempted from taking the Diploma in Legal Practice);

– legal practitioners from another Member State of the EU;

– students who do not wish to become practising advocates; they may receive partial exemption from training in solicitors' offices and/or devilling.

Subject to the academic requirements, and pupillage, solicitors may apply to become advocates at any time.

OPPORTUNITIES

There are about 8,500 independent barristers practising at the Bar, of whom 22% are women. Two-thirds are based in London; the remainder in large towns and cities on the circuits. Those with a strong concentration of barristers include Birmingham, Bristol, Cardiff, Chester, Leeds, Liverpool, Manchester and Newcastle. A Northern Chancery Bar has been formed, reflecting the increasing amount of this work done outside London.

Barristers/advocates in independent practice are self-employed. They have to build a reputation for themselves so that solicitors will return to them with cases. There is, however, no longer any prohibition on barristers advertising. They can now market their services.

It is thought that over 2,000 barristers work at the **Employed Bar** and approximately 500 work in central government departments. There are other opportunities in the Crown Prosecution Service. A fairly small number work for local authorities.

There are opportunities to specialize in European or international law, and some to work or travel overseas. Some barristers, for example, have chambers in both Brussels and London. Others work at international and EC institutions. Some barristers have links in Commonwealth countries, or North America, and may travel to represent clients in courts there.

There are increasing opportunities to work on behalf of overseas clients with interests in the UK. These clients may brief barristers direct, without using a solicitor or intermediary, where the work does not involve court proceedings. Barristers wishing to be approached for such work usually make this known to the International Practice Committee of the Bar, which provides guidance to clients on the selection of barristers.

There are about 530 advocates, 300 of whom are in practice. Most are based in Edinburgh. Those who choose not to enter practice work in industry, commerce, government service etc.

PAY AND CONDITIONS

Training

Non-law graduates find the same situation as regards funding full-time courses as do solicitors. Please see article 2. SOLICITOR.

During pupillage, most pupil barristers receive a minimum award of £3,000 for six months and £6,000 for twelve months. However, many chambers choose to provide substantially larger awards. Pupillage served in commerce, industry and public service are salaried. Both the Crown Prosecution and Government Legal Services offer a limited number of sponsorships, under which pupil barristers serving the first six months of non-practising pupillage receive a salary before serving the second six months with them. They, in addition, occasionally sponsor students through the CPE and Vocational course.

Intrants serving their period in a solicitor's office receive a salary on a scale laid down by the Law Society of Scotland.

LAW AND RELATED WORK: LAB-LAZ

They receive no fees or salary during the nine months' pupillage. Some scholarships are available but the majority of intrants must finance themselves.

On qualification

Practising barristers/advocates are all self-employed individuals. (They are not allowed to form partnerships or associations in independent practice.) Earnings therefore vary considerably, depending on success and workload.

It can take three to five years to build up a practice.

Fees may not come in until sometime after a case, and in the meantime overheads have to be met. Barristers share the expenses of running chambers, paying a share of the cost of premises and the salaries of barristers' clerks and other staff. Advocates pay a sum, graduated according to earnings and seniority, to the Faculty, for use of the premises, and a percentage of fees received to a service company, which provides administrative and secretarial services. The latter are not payable until fees are received.

Employed barristers/advocates receive a salary. Salaries in industry and commerce vary. In the Crown Prosecution Service they range from £20,579 to £55,836.

Hours of work vary considerably, but are usually long and often involve unsocial hours and time spent in travelling.

PROSPECTS

Prospects for barristers/advocates employed in government service depend on their gaining promotion to higher grades. The same applies to those working in local government. They sometimes move out of legal work into administration and take up senior management posts with local authorities.

At the independent Bar there are obviously no guarantees of earnings, security or prospects. Newly qualified barristers/advocates spend the early years in building up a practice, getting themselves known while working in the lower courts and in industrial or rent tribunals. Work is allocated to them by the barristers'/advocates' clerks. (The group of advocates assigned to the same clerk at the Library is known as a *stable,* while barristers share a clerk in chambers.)

Barristers/advocates usually know by the end of three years whether or not they are going to succeed.

After 10 to 15 years' experience they may apply to 'take silk' (become a Queen's Counsel), which is necessary if they wish eventually to become a High Court or Court of Sessions judge. Barristers may also become Circuit judges, Crown and County Court recorders (part-time judges) and stipendiary magistrates, while advocates may become sheriffs. Both may be appointed to tribunals.

Some become (salaried) justice's clerks in magistrates courts. Others move to salaried posts outside the profession.

RELATED OCCUPATIONS

Solicitor, justice's clerk.

FURTHER INFORMATION

The Faculty of Advocates*, The Clerk of Faculty, Advocates Library, Parliament House, Edinburgh EH1 1RF, 0131 226 5071

The General Council of the Bar of England and Wales*, Education and Training Departments, 2/3 Cursitor Street, London EC4A 1NE, 0171 440 4000

The Students' Officers at: Gray's Inn Treasury Office, 8 South Square, Gray's Inn, London WC1R 5EU, 0171 405 8649

Students Department, Treasury Office, Lincoln's Inn, London WC2A 3TL, 0171 405 0138

The Honourable Society of the Middle Temple, The Treasury, Middle Temple, London EC4Y 9AT, 0171 427 4800

The Bar Association for Local Government and The Public Service*, Bolton MBC Legal Services, Town Hall, Bolton, BL1 1RU, 01204 522311 ext 1111

The Bar Association for Commerce, Finance and Industry*, PO Box 3663, Bracknell, Berkshire RG12 2FH, 01344 868752

GLS Recruitment Team, Queen Anne's Chambers, 28 Broadway, London SW1H 9JS, 0171 210 3304

The Crown Prosecution Service*, Personnel Branch 2, 50 Ludgate Hill, London EC4M 3EX, 0171 273 8000

FURTHER READING

Leaflets/booklets are available from the addresses marked*.

Legal Profession – AGCAS

In the careers library classified under LAB.

2. SOLICITOR (LAC)

THE WORK

Solicitors give legal advice to clients and act for them, when necessary, in legal matters. Clients may be individuals, organizations, businesses or government departments. The cases undertaken by solicitors depend on the area of work they have chosen, and on their employer. A small firm, or a solicitor working as a sole practitioner, may deal with business affairs, commercial property matters, residential conveyancing, family law, crime, injuries and probate. Medium-sized and large firms tend to specialize, or have specialized departments dealing with international law, litigation, insurance, probate, or company and commercial law etc.

The main areas of work are as follows:

Business and commercial law: contract law, tax and VAT legislation, employment law, patents, export law, acquisition and sale of companies. Small firms usually consult solicitors as the need arises; large ones have their own legal departments staffed by solicitors and possibly barristers.

Probate: wills, estates and property. Solicitors advise clients on how to draw up wills and ensure that their wishes are carried out when they die. They may act as trustees of estates left in wills and deal with the affairs of people who die without making a will.

Conveyancing: involves the buying and selling of both business and domestic property. Solicitors ensure the vendor has the right to sell the property and they obtain all necessary information which may affect the new owners – known as conducting searches (eg in a domestic purchase, on the existence of rights of way or the likelihood of future planning development) – and draw up the contract. In commercial property transactions, they may work closely with the client's source of finance, such as a merchant bank; in domestic ones, they help the client carry out transactions with banks or building societies.

Litigation: clients involved in any kind of dispute with another person might consult a solicitor, who advises on whether the matter could be settled by correspondence or the threat of action, or whether legal action will be necessary. In the latter case, solicitors may represent clients in magistrates' and county courts. In more serious cases heard in the higher courts, they brief barristers. Litigation covers civil law cases like unfair dismissal, debt, landlord and tenant disputes, breach of contract, divorce and custody of children. Examples of criminal cases include theft, motoring offences and personal injury.

Some solicitors choose to specialize in criminal law, defending clients against prosecution.

Others are employed in industry and commerce, where they deal solely with their employer's legal affairs. This work is likely to include drafting, advising on and negotiating contracts, and advising on aspects of employment law, patents, and health and safety law, and on the legislative implications of decisions made, often at board level.

Some work for local authorities, where their clients are the council's staff and the elected members or councillors. They advise on current legislation as it affects local authorities, on matters ranging from child care to planning enquiries, education provision, libraries and social services. They also represent the authority in court when necessary.

Those working for central government advise civil servants and ministers about the legislation relevant to their own department and also oversee the implementation of appropriate legislation. The work varies according to that of their employing departments (eg Environment, Transport and the Regions; Education and Employment; Health).

Solicitors employed by the Crown Prosecution Service (CPS) advise the police about prosecutions. If a case goes to prosecution following their recommendation, a CPS solicitor conducts the case in the magistrate's court.

Wherever they work, solicitors spend a lot of time interviewing clients. They ascertain the facts, form an opinion, and give advice, using their own legal knowledge and consulting books and legal references when necessary. There is a lot of paperwork in the form of letters and contracts.

WORK ENVIRONMENT

Solicitors are based in offices, but some travel may be involved to visit clients at their premises or homes. Solicitors working for big commercial firms may travel overseas. Those involved in litigation may spend a large proportion of their time in court. Some may have to visit clients held at police stations or in prison.

Offices vary in size from large city centre practices with hundreds of employees to smaller ones with less than ten. A small number practise alone, working with just one secretary or clerk. Solicitors employed in government services or by local authorities may work in a legal department housed in a large central government building or county hall.

SKILLS AND INTERESTS

Solicitors need a high level of academic ability. They must be able to assimilate and analyse large amounts of information and must pay great attention to detail. They must also be prepared to read widely and undertake post-qualification training by attending courses, in order to keep abreast with the Law, which is constantly changing.

Communication skills, both written and verbal, are important. Solicitors must be able to write clearly and succinctly. If appearing in court, they need excellent presentation skills and the ability to argue a case successfully. When dealing with clients they need the ability to explain the legal position clearly and simply to people who may find the concepts difficult to understand. Some clients are distressed and solicitors have to be tactful and sympathetic when interviewing them. They must also be discreet.

Numeracy is important in some branches of the work, when dealing with property purchase or divorce settlements, for example.

Solicitors working in large departments are sometimes expected to work as members of a team. Others, particularly on the private client side, work mainly alone. Solicitors running practices need business skills and the ability to manage staff. Those working on their own need self-discipline and motivation.

All solicitors must be able to work under pressure, to deadlines, and cope with large amounts of work.

ENTRY REQUIREMENTS

England and Wales

All students aiming to qualify as a solicitor must complete both the academic and vocational stages of training. The academic stage is obtained through one of three routes:

– by the award of a qualifying law degree, which may be law combined with other subjects, but must include the seven Foundations of Legal Knowledge: Obligations I (Contract); Obligations II (Torts); Foundations of Criminal Law; Foundations of Equity and the Law of Trusts; Foundations of the Law of the European Union; Foundations of Property Law; and Foundations of Public Law. (A list of approved degree courses may be obtained from the Law Society.) A level/H grade subjects are not stipulated, other than that they must be academic ones. Most universities require high grades – usually A and B passes – for admission to a law degree course; *or*

– by the award of a non-law degree plus completion of the Common Professional Examination (CPE), which is a one-year full-time or two-years part-time/ distance learning course, resulting in the award of a Post-Graduate Diploma in Law (PgDL) or a two-year Senior Status Law Degree. These courses cover the seven Foundations of Legal Knowledge and one other area of substantive law. The CPE/PgDL is offered at the four branches of the College of Law and at a number of universities. The Senior Status Degree is awarded at universities only. Exceptionally, mature persons with a professional qualification that is deemed equivalent to a degree may be granted a certificate of academic standing to take a CPE; *or*

– as a Fellow of the Institute of Legal Executives (please see article 4. LEGAL EXECUTIVE), being over the age of 25 years and having five years' qualifying legal experience, of which two years must have been completed after obtaining Membership status. To claim exemption from the academic stage a legal executive must pass, in the Institute's part II examinations, those seven papers that

LAW AND RELATED WORK: LAB-LAZ

correspond to the seven Foundations of Legal Knowledge and one other substantive law paper.

These are the only accepted qualifications for completing the academic stage. Entry with a qualifying law degree is the most usual method; because of the intense competition for posts, it is likely that at least a 2.1 Honours degree will be required.

Scotland

Entrants must:

– hold an LLB law degree from one of the five Scottish universities offering an LLB degree in Scots Law.

Admission requirements to the LLB Degree are high, typically five H grade passes with AAAAB grades, The only preferred subject is English; *or*

– have completed three years' pre-Diploma training and have passed the examinations of the Law Society of Scotland (for which no formal tuition is provided).

Applicants intending to qualify by this (much less common and extremely difficult) route must have five H grade passes including English at B or above and either maths or a science subject or a foreign language. The total H grade passes must be at least eight points on a scale where A=3, B=2 and C=1. Applicants possessing a degree in any discipline, a Higher National Diploma in Legal Studies from an approved college, plus H grade English at B or above, automatically qualify to attempt this route to qualification.

Those holding these qualifications, must, after these courses of study, undertake the one-year postgraduate Diploma in Legal Practice at one of the five Scottish universities offering the course and then undertake a two year period of post-diploma training with a firm of solicitors in Scotland to qualify as a solicitor.

The entry qualifications may be relaxed for applicants over the age of 23 years with experience of legal work.

TRAINING

England and Wales

Vocational training is in three stages in the following order:

– gaining a thorough grounding in the main principles of law, through any of the methods outlined above in ENTRY REQUIREMENTS; *and*

– successful completion of the Law Society's one-year full-time or two-year part-time Legal Practice Course (LPC).

The Legal Practice Course is intended to teach both the legal knowledge necessary to practise as a solicitor and some of the essential skills – such as legal research and problem solving, interviewing skills, legal drafting, negotiation and advocacy (pleading).

– completion of a two-year period of training with solicitors approved to offer training by the Law Society (the solicitors' professional body), known as a Training Contract. (The Training Contract will normally be waived for legal executives if they are a Fellow within six weeks of commencing the Legal Practice Course) *and*

The Training Contract combines on-the-job training with attendance at some external courses. With their employers – firms, local authorities or the Crown Prosecution Service – trainee solicitors gain practical experience in a minimum of three different areas of law from a list laid down by the Law Society (although many employers offer the chance to work in more than the minimum). Trainees are attached to qualified solicitors, at first observing, soon assisting and undertaking some of the work under supervision. Possible areas of experience vary according to the type of work done by the employer. Some might offer only commercial work, others might not offer crime or matrimonial law.

All LPC students have to undertake a Professional Skills course, covering Advocacy, Ethics & Client Responsibility, and Finance & Business Skills, and taking 72 hours in total.

Scotland

All entrants must complete the following:

– a one-year full-time course at one of five universities, leading to a Diploma in Legal Practice. The course teaches the practical skills and knowledge required by solicitors; *and*

– two years under a training contract with a practising solicitor in Scotland. After the first year they may apply for a qualified Practising Certificate from the Law Society of Scotland that permits them to appear in court for their employer's clients. At the end of two years they are entitled to hold the full Practising Certificate, once they have discharged their training contract.

The training contract may be served with solicitors in private practice, industry and commerce or with some public sector departments, eg local authorities or the Department of the Solicitor to the Secretary of State for Scotland.

Six months of the training contract may be spent in England or another EU country, with the employer's consent.

LATE ENTRY

There are no upper age limits. Mature entrants follow any of the training routes available to school-leavers. Some institutions may relax their degree course entry requirements, but all expect evidence of recent academic study – through Access, part-time or evening classes for example.

In England and Wales the legal executive route is the most usual method of entry for mature entrants.

OPPORTUNITIES

There are about 60,000 qualified solicitors in practice in England and Wales; 7,600 in Scotland. The majority work in private practice, where they may choose from a range of employers and specialisms or be self-employed.

In England and Wales approximately 3,000 are employed in industry and commerce. A further 3,000 work for local authorities.

In Scotland approximately 6,000 work in private practice.

Others work in the Civil Service (central government departments), in the Magistrates' Court Service or in the Crown Prosecution Service/Procurator Fiscal Service, both of which have increasing numbers of openings.

Smaller numbers work for law centres, charities, Citizens' Advice Bureaux and in the Armed Forces and industry and commerce.

There are opportunities to travel or to work overseas by: working for an international practice that has branch offices in several countries; working for international and EU institutions like the United Nations or the European Commission; working for a firm engaging in public international law, which may require solicitors to attend

LAW AND RELATED WORK: LAB-LAZ

the World Court, European Court of Human Rights or European Courts of Justice on behalf of clients.

It is possible to work in some Commonwealth countries that have legal systems based on English Common Law, but it is often necessary to attend a familiarization course in order to obtain a licence to practise.

The EU is committed to mutual recognition of professional qualifications. Solicitors wishing to be admitted in any of the EU member states may do so after passing a *transfer test*. It is therefore becoming easier for solicitors qualified in one member state to practise in another.

PAY AND CONDITIONS

Training

Non-law graduates usually have to fund themselves through the CPE course as local education authorities rarely give grants for this – and some do not give grants for the compulsory course in Legal Practice. Many trainees obtain bank loans. Some graduates opt for the longer training route of first becoming a legal executive, as most trainee legal executives study part-time whilst working full-time in a legal environment.

Some large commercial law firms offer sponsorships, under which they pay students' tuition fees and give them a further sum to cover living expenses. Students are then expected to complete the training contract with the firm.

During the training contract, trainee solicitors are paid a salary. The figure varies, but for trainees in England and Wales the Law Society stipulates a minimum of £12,150 in Central London and £10,850 elsewhere.

The Law Society of Scotland recommends trainee salaries of £8,840 and £11,960 for first- and second-year trainees, respectively. These levels are, however, not mandatory.

On qualification

Once fully qualified, solicitors may earn around £18,000 in a small town practice, and from £28,000 in the City of London. Within a few years of qualifying, salaries can vary enormously.

Solicitors normally work standard office hours, plus as much (unpaid) overtime as is necessary to complete the work. Many spend most of the day with clients and have to complete their research and paperwork at home, or in the office, during the evening and at weekends.

Some have to visit clients after working hours or may be called to police stations at any time.

Solicitors working in law centres see a lot of clients in the evenings.

PROSPECTS

Solicitors in private practice begin as salaried assistant solicitors. Later, they may become salaried partners (salaried associates in Scotland) or equity partners, investing a sum in the practice and taking a share of the profits. Many become partners in their early thirties.

They may become self-employed, or principals/sole practitioners, but, they are not allowed to establish their own practices until they have practised for three years.

Solicitors in commerce and industry may become heads of legal departments, or often become company secretaries. In local government they may progress in the legal department or may move into general local government administration. Many chief executives of councils are former solicitors.

In the Civil Service, solicitors may move to bigger or different departments to gain promotion. Some become parliamentary counsels, responsible for drafting legislation.

RELATED OCCUPATIONS

Barrister, justice's clerk, procurator fiscal, legal executive.

FURTHER INFORMATION

The Law Society, Legal Education Information Services, Ipsley Court, Berrington Close, Redditch, Worcs B98 0TD, 01527 504433, www.lawsociety.org.uk

The Crown Prosecution Service, Personnel Branch 2*, 50 Ludgate Hill, London EC4M 3EX, 0171 273 8000

GLS Recruitment Team, Queen Anne's Chambers, 28 Broadway, London SW1H 9JS, 0171 210 3304

The Deputy Secretary (Legal Education)*, The Law Society of Scotland, 26 Drumsheugh Gardens, Edinburgh EH3 7YR, 0131 226 7411, www.lawscot.org.uk

FURTHER READING

Leaflets/booklets are available from the addresses marked*.

In the careers library classified under LAC.

3. BARRISTERS' CLERK (LAZ)

THE WORK

Barristers' clerks work for groups of barristers, who all practise independently in a set of chambers.

The word 'clerk', although a historic term, can be misleading and some chambers now call their senior clerks 'practice managers' or 'chambers' directors'.

Barristers' clerks are responsible for the running of chambers as a business, developing its practice, managing the flow of work, liaising with solicitors, and for day-to-day administration. Most chambers have a team of clerks who, between them, normally carry out the following duties:

Junior clerks

Court work – accompany a barrister to court, carry documents, papers and robes. In cases being heard some distance from chambers they make travel and accommodation arrangements.

Messenger work – deliver documents by hand.

Administrative work in chambers – prepare the accounts, send out bills (sometimes done by clerical staff), keep the chambers reference library tidy and file reports.

Experienced clerks

Arrange the barristers' schedules – keep a master diary with the names of each barrister, the cases they are working on, the names of clients and instructing solicitors, information relevant to cases and barristers' daily engagements.

Run the chambers' petty cash system.

Senior clerks

The senior clerk (also known as clerk of chambers) is the office manager, responsible for the work, recruitment and training of junior barristers' clerks, and other clerical staff where employed – typists, receptionists and, sometimes, VDU operators.

337

LAW AND RELATED WORK: LAB-LAZ

Their most important role, however, is liaison with solicitors. It is through this that work comes into chambers, and clerks must work to establish good relationships with solicitors. A solicitor wishing to brief a barrister first approaches the senior clerk who, through familiarity with previous similar cases and knowledge of the specialisms of the barristers in the set, can recommend particular barristers for the case. They can be extremely influential on the career development of young barristers.

Although it is in their interests to keep work for their own chambers, in some instances they will recommend the solicitor to consult another set, where barristers specialize in the matter in question.

They are also responsible for negotiating their barristers' fees, based on length and difficulty of the case, and the seniority of the barrister.

In Scotland, advocates' clerks fulfil the same duties.

WORK ENVIRONMENT

Barristers' clerks work in small teams in chambers, usually three or four clerks working for 15 to 20 barristers. Some of the London chambers can be very small and cramped. Others, and the majority of provincial chambers, are in more modern premises.

Junior clerks spend much of their time on messenger duties, or accompanying barristers to court. As they become more senior the work is more office-based. Even contact with solicitors is done largely by telephone.

Seventy per cent of barristers' clerks are based in London, with the remainder working in chambers near the courts in other cities in England and Wales.

Advocates' clerks all work at Parliament House in Edinburgh.

SKILLS AND INTERESTS

Barristers' clerks must be completely reliable and able to work under pressure to meet deadlines. They should be able to move from one job to another as the situation demands, putting one task to one side in order to deal with something more urgent. They must pay great attention to detail and make sure that all arrangements work smoothly. If they make mistakes in diary details or bookings for court appearances, the chambers could lose future business from solicitors.

They need a good command of written and spoken English and a good telephone manner.

Loyalty to chambers and discretion are expected. Clerks must be careful to respect client confidentiality, especially if barristers in their set are appearing for opposing sides in the same case.

Senior clerks need to be skilled financial negotiators, especially over the telephone; they must be tactful and at times persuasive. They are essentially the chambers' public relations officers and have to build good working relationships with solicitors. In order to do this they sometimes offer advice on the level of fees or market rate for a particular case without necessarily expecting to get the brief for one of their own barristers.

Although their job is to get business for their chambers, it is within their discretion to refuse a case; if they feel none of their barristers is an expert on a particular problem, they will do so, rather than risk an unsatisfactory outcome.

They need to know their barristers well, since they essentially act as agents. Clerks are particularly careful when selecting cases for young barristers, ensuring that they are not given work as yet outside their experience.

ENTRY REQUIREMENTS

The majority of new entrants start after completing GCSEs/S grades or A levels/H grades. Minimum entry requirements are four GCSEs/S grades (A–C/1–3) or equivalent, including English and maths.

Some junior clerks are expected to be able to type.

TRAINING

All training is carried out in chambers. Junior clerks are assigned to routine jobs of filing, delivering messages, carrying books and papers for barristers going to court and possibly typing out the accounts. They learn the more advanced duties by observing the work of senior clerks and assisting them.

Junior clerks may be given day release to attend the BTEC National Certificate course in Business, Finance and Chambers Administration at Kingsway College, London, which contains specialist modules devised in association with the Institute of Barristers' Clerks.

On obtaining employment in chambers, students may become members of the Institute of Barristers' Clerks.

There is no formal training or qualification for advocates' clerks. They begin as deputy clerks and are trained on the job by senior clerks.

LATE ENTRY

Most barristers' clerks start as school-leavers or graduates. Some chambers recruit adults with previous managerial or administrative experience.

OPPORTUNITIES

This is a particularly small profession. There are approximately 1,300 barristers' clerks in England and Wales. In Scotland, there are ten advocates' clerks and ten deputy advocates' clerks. Over half the jobs for barristers' clerks are in London, in chambers near the Inns of Court. The remainder are found in chambers in towns on the circuits. Please see article 1. BARRISTER.

The number of clerks' posts depends on the number of barristers in a set. Some barristers work in groups as small as six, and employ one clerk. The recent tendency is towards sets of approximately 20 barristers. A set of this size is likely to employ a senior clerk, three clerks and reception and typing staff.

Finding a first position is difficult. Although the more senior positions are sometimes advertised in the national press, the majority of vacancies are filled through a scheme run by the Institute of Barristers' Clerks. Details of vacancies are given to members and people who join the Institute's mailing list. Details are available from the Institute. There is a fee for this service.

Vacancies for trainee advocates' clerks are advertised in the press. There is very little turnover, and so entry opportunities are severely limited.

LAW AND RELATED WORK: LAB-LAZ

PAY AND CONDITIONS

Junior clerks are paid a fixed salary. Figures vary, but £7,000 to £10,000 would be an average starting salary in London.

Senior clerks are paid in one of several ways. A small number receive a salary. The majority receive a percentage of the gross fee paid to each barrister. Traditionally, these were set at either five, seven-and-a-half or ten per cent, but no new ten per cent contracts are now negotiated. Three to six per cent is the average range. A third practice is for the clerk to receive a fixed salary plus one or two per cent of fees.

Earnings potential therefore varies and depends on the size and income of the set of Chambers. There is therefore no typical level of remuneration for senior clerks or experienced junior clerks. For the majority of senior clerks earnings can range from £30,000 to £100,000 and above. For the majority of experienced junior clerks in mid to large size sets earnings can range from £30,000 to £60,000 and above. It is comparatively rare for any clerk to receive employment benefits such as pension contributions in addition to their salary and/or percentage.

Advocates' clerks are all employed by the organization Faculty Services Ltd, which provides support services to *stables* of advocates. They are employed on a salary scale from £15,000 to £28,000.

The work involves long hours, including evenings and weekends.

PROSPECTS

Barristers' clerks begin as junior clerks, may obtain promotion to first junior clerk, then to a senior clerk. It is sometimes necessary to move to different chambers to achieve this.

Once in a senior clerk's position, it is usual to remain with that chambers. Most barristers' clerks do not move again.

In recent years Chambers have been opening in towns other than the traditional main court centres such as London, Birmingham, Bristol, Liverpool and Manchester. Many Chambers have established links with local schools and offer work experience placements.

There is no possibility of transferring to legal work as a barrister, other than by following the full training route.

RELATED OCCUPATIONS

Legal executive, office manager, administrator.

FURTHER INFORMATION

The Administrator of the Institute of Barristers' Clerks*, 4a Essex Court, Temple, London EC4Y 9AJ 0171 353 2699

FURTHER READING

Leaflets/booklets are available from the address marked*.
Careers in the Law – Kogan Page
In the careers library classified under LAZ.

4. LEGAL EXECUTIVE (LAD)

THE WORK

Legal executives work (in England and Wales) with solicitors in private practices, local authority and commercial companies' legal departments and in the Civil Service.

The work falls under three main headings:

Work with clients

Legal executives interview clients, advise them and do much of the preparatory work before cases come to court. Wills are administered and transactions like sale and purchase of property are carried out. They may attend court to assist solicitors or barristers with the presentation of a case.

They are also able to exercise a right of audience before a judge sitting in Chambers in most matters, as well as appearance in some county court arbitrations and tribunals.

Administration

They do much of the practical and technical work in a solicitor's office or legal department. They may, for example, draw up wills, check titles to deeds, issue writs, take out summonses, collect information needed for affidavits and draft documents.

Management

In some law firms, legal executives are practice managers. They assign work to junior staff, supervise the work of clerks and secretaries, and do all the accounts.

Most legal executives specialize in one area of the law:

Probate

If specializing in this, they help to ensure that the property of people who have died is disposed of in the way they had wished. They calculate inheritance tax, work out the sum each beneficiary will receive and explain the terms of the will to relatives. They may work closely with appointed executors who are not relatives, including accountants or bank managers.

Conveyancing

Conveyancing involves helping the client through all the stages of house purchase, reading and checking documents, telephoning the seller's or purchaser's solicitors, estate agents and building societies and conducting searches. Please see article 2. SOLICITOR.

Litigation

Working in litigation involves working for clients who are in a dispute, interviewing them to find out the details and noting the information down. They may write letters on the client's behalf or prepare material for a court case.

There is no direct equivalent to a legal executive in Scotland. Some solicitors employ staff known as legal, or unqualified, assistants who may carry out some of the duties described above.

WORK ENVIRONMENT

Please see article 2. SOLICITOR.

Legal executives work mainly at a desk. Those specializing in litigation may go to court regularly.

SKILLS AND INTERESTS

Much of the routine work – of form filling, document drafting and doing calculations – requires concentration and precise attention to detail.

Legal executives must be able to write clear English, often

LAW AND RELATED WORK: LAB-LAZ

first consulting documents that are written in complicated legal language. They must understand the legal terms and concepts.

They need to be able to relate well to clients of all backgrounds – some of whom may be very distressed – be sympathetic when interviewing them, and be capable of explaining matters clearly. When dealing with court officials or representatives of banks, accountancy firms or other legal firms, they may have to be persistent, but at the same time polite and persuasive.

In probate and conveyancing work, numeracy is essential.

Legal executives are expected to meet deadlines and work under pressure. They work on many different cases at the same time and may be responsible for the work of junior staff. They need to be good organizers, able to plan their time and priorities.

ENTRY REQUIREMENTS

The normal minimum entry requirements are four GCSEs/S grades (A–C/1–3) or equivalent. These must include English, and at least three subjects must be on the Institute of Legal Executives (ILEX) Approved Subjects list of academic subjects. Technical and craft subjects are not normally accepted.

In practice, many entrants have A/AS levels, GNVQ Advanced *or* a EDEXCEL/BTEC national level qualification or equivalent, and 15% are graduates.

An alternative entry qualification is the Vocational Legal Studies qualification.

TRAINING

In order to become a Fellow of The Institute of Legal Executives (ILEX) – that is, fully qualified – it is necessary to be aged at least 25, have passed ILEX membership examinations and worked for five years in **qualifying employment,** ie under the supervision of a solicitor in a practice, public authority, industry or commerce. Two of these years must be served after passing the examinations.

Most legal executives study for the exams on a part-time basis while in approved employment. Although most students work in a legal environment whilst studying part-time, this is not a requirement. Colleges throughout England and Wales run courses leading to the exams. The Institute has set up a home study programme for students who cannot or do not wish to attend a college.

Membership exams are in two stages. Part I, set at A level standard, consists of papers in law, legal practice and procedures. Part II, equivalent to a degree standard, contains one paper on legal procedure and three from specialist areas of law – land law, criminal law, conveyancing, contract law etc. Students may choose papers appropriate to their specialism in their own offices.

It is possible to take a one-year full-time course at certain colleges leading to the Part I exams, then gain suitable employment to train for the necessary five years.

The Graduate Entry Diploma (GED) has been introduced to allow students studying for a qualifying law degree to obtain ILEX membership (MInstLEx) on graduation. The number of universities offering this scheme is expanding.

The average time taken to pass all the exams is four years, although some trainees complete them in three. At this stage they may become Members of the Institute.

Practical training, carried out at employers' premises, consists of assisting legal executives and solicitors with their work, observing, learning and then progressing to doing some casework under supervision, gradually assuming more responsibility.

It is common for trainee legal executives to work as 'outdoor clerks' for a period. This involves delivering documents, such as taking briefs to barristers, taking documents to court for entry by court officials and paying any fees required and attending court cases to take notes for senior colleagues. Some trainees start as secretaries in solicitors' offices and are given the opportunity to progress to legal work.

Scotland

There is no single route to qualify for similar work in Scotland. Some employers prefer to train their own staff: entry requirements are at the discretion of employers, some expect four S grades (1–3). Others employ those who have completed the University Diploma in Legal Studies at Glasgow Caledonian University, or an HND or HNC in Legal Services course available at a number of further education colleges.

The Diploma in Legal Studies has been accredited by the Scottish Conveyancing and Executry Board as appropriate to a qualified conveyancer or executry practitioner. Students may also take an HND in Legal Studies course.

Diplomates can discharge the duties of a conveyancing clerk, an executry clerk and an assistant cashier in a law office. After completing the Diploma, diplomates enter into a one-year period of practical training to qualify as a conveyancer or executry practitioner.

LATE ENTRY

About 60% of legal executives are over 20 years of age on entry and many have worked as legal secretaries.

The Institute of Legal Executives is prepared to waive the entry requirements for mature students over 21 years with suitable references. Each application is considered individually.

OPPORTUNITIES

There are 22,500 members of The Institute of Legal Executives in England and Wales (5,750 of them Fellows). The majority work for solicitors, but they may also work for any of the organizations that employ solicitors. Most opportunities are with medium and large-sized law practices, in industry, commerce and with local authorities.

Registration with the Institute is not compulsory for employment, but only Fellows of the Institute may be described as legal executives.

Opportunities to work overseas are limited. There may be openings in countries that have a legal system based on English Common Law and in the EU with English firms that have offices in member countries.

PAY AND CONDITIONS

Salaries vary throughout the country and according to employer. There is no recommended minimum salary for trainees as there is for trainee solicitors, but most newly appointed trainee legal executives can expect to earn between £8,000 and £12,000. Fully qualified Fellows can earn between £20,000 and £24,000, and experienced Fellows of ILEX £25,000 plus; some receive salaries of £40,000 upwards.

Not all employers give help with course or examination fees, although over 70% do make some contribution. (The total training costs, including fees and books, is approximately £2,100 over the four years.)

Most legal executives work normal office hours over a five-day week but, when necessary, may be expected to work overtime.

PROSPECTS

In large organizations, legal executives have prospects of promotion to head a department of legal executives. In a small number of law firms they may become the practice manager. Promotion prospects are limited in small firms.

Legal executives may also qualify as solicitors and this is now the principal route for a non-graduate wishing to become a solicitor. Fellows of The Institute of Legal Executives may choose whether to attend a one-year Legal Practice course or to take a two-year part-time course whilst remaining in employment. They do not have to undertake the two-year training contract under articles. Please see article 2. SOLICITOR. They do, however, have to complete their training by undertaking a Professional Skills course.

RELATED OCCUPATIONS

Barrister, justice's clerk, procurator fiscal, barristers' clerk, solicitor.

FURTHER INFORMATION

The Institute of Legal Executives*, Kempston Manor, Kempston, Bedford MK42 7AB, 01234 841000, www.ilex.org.uk

The Institute of Legal Executives, Ilex Tutorial Services Ltd, Kempston Manor, Kempston, Bedford MK42 7AB, 01234 841000 (for details of home study courses)

FURTHER READING

Leaflets/booklets are available from the address marked*.
In the careers library classified under LAD.

5. SHORTHAND WRITER (LAG)

THE WORK

Shorthand writers, who are also known as court reporters, shorthand reporters and verbatim reporters, attend court hearings and take records of the hearings in shorthand, either by hand or by the use of stenotype machines. Their work varies, depending on whether they work in England and Wales or in Scotland.

England and Wales

Shorthand writers attend most criminal cases, which are held in Crown Courts throughout the country. Today, most civil cases held in the High Court and all County Courts are recorded officially on audio tape, and shorthand writers are not used, although some are engaged privately in the High Court. Shorthand writers also attend private cases such as arbitration, public inquiries, industrial tribunals, trade union and political conferences, annual general meetings and disciplinary hearings. They are also employed in the House of Commons and House of Lords.

In most Crown Court cases, only one shorthand writer is present. They have to be in court before proceedings start and are present throughout the day's proceedings. They use computer-aided transcription (CAT) systems – which are rather like a small typewriter, but with a different keyboard, which enables whole words and phrases to be typed at one stroke. CAT writers can achieve very high shorthand speeds – over 200 wpm (words per minute).

The machines produce a paper tape, which looks rather like a till roll and enables the shorthand writer to read back what has been said when required. The machine also produces the shorthand on a computer disk and, if a transcript is needed of the day's hearing, the shorthand writer can transfer the text to a computer, which transcribes it. The shorthand writer can then add any words not transcribed by the computer, correct any mistakes and edit the text.

Sometimes lawyers ask for a transcript of the proceedings to be completed before the next day – this means that the shorthand writer has to transcribe the day's work during the evening.

Some parts of the case, such as the witnesses' statements, are transcribed verbatim, whereas other parts may be edited to make them grammatically correct – for instance, many judges do not like the use of colloquialisms, and shorthand writers therefore make the necessary changes. The court reporter has to use common sense and experience to decide what should be changed or included – for instance, some judges like their jokes included in the transcript. In private cases and very complex court cases, lawyers may want a daily copy of the proceedings and this requires the shorthand writers to use a real-time system. To do this, they sometimes work in teams of three. The CAT system is linked to a computer, which immediately transcribes the notes into longhand, which can be seen by those participating in the proceedings. In the team, one shorthand writer records the proceedings on the stenotype machine and one 'scopes', which means that he/she reads what comes up on the screen and corrects any unusual words that have not been translated by the writer's dictionary. A third member of the team proofreads, checking for punctuation and grammar.

Shorthand writers also record and transcribe witness statements prior to the court hearing.

Scotland

At present, shorthand writers work in the Sheriff Courts (on civil cases), the High Court, Senior Criminal Court and the Court of Session. There is little private work in Scotland. In all other courts, tapes are used. In Scotland, although a few shorthand writers use CAT systems, most still use pen and paper. Writers again make a record of the proceedings, with the exception of the lawyer's summing up. If daily transcripts are needed, writers work in teams. After each period of reporting they then leave the court and dictate what they have written onto audio tape – this is then typed up by an audio typist.

WORK ENVIRONMENT

Shorthand writers spend much of their time working in courts. In private hearings such as arbitration, public inquiries etc, they travel to wherever the hearing is held – this could be in a conference room or a court. The work involves sitting for long periods of time. They usually have to do considerable travelling, carrying their CAT machine and computer, so the ability to drive is helpful. Some of their transcription work may be carried out in their homes.

LAW AND RELATED WORK: LAB-LAZ

SKILLS AND INTERESTS

Shorthand writers must be very responsible and work accurately. They need to be able to concentrate for long periods of time. Sharp hearing is important. It is vital that they have an excellent command of English – both written and spoken – and have a very good knowledge of grammar, to transform what might be ungrammatical speech into a grammatical record.

Punctuality is vital, as court cases cannot start until they are present. They have to be flexible in their approach to working hours, being prepared to work in the evenings with virtually no notice. They should be able to work on their own in what can be quite a lonely job. They also have to be able to work in teams when providing a real-time service. In operating stenotype machines, manual dexterity is needed.

Shorthand writers need to present a smart appearance. They need to be confident – if at any point in the proceedings they cannot hear what is being said, or if a witness is talking too quickly, they may have to ask for the proceedings to be stopped and for the witness or lawyer to repeat what they said. They also need a clear speaking voice to read back parts of the script when required.

ENTRY REQUIREMENTS

England and Wales

Employers usually require new applicants to have had training and gained qualifications in the use of stenotyping machines and to have reached a minimum speed of 140 wpm. Training for this is offered in a number of colleges – for addresses contact the British Institute of Verbatim Reporters, or the Association of Professional Shorthand Writers. Entry onto these courses usually requires three or four GCSEs (grades A–C) including English. Many students have A levels or degrees.

Scotland

There are no formal entry requirements, although most firms ask for some S grades (1–3) including English. Applicants must also have shorthand speeds of at least 120 wpm.

All would-be shorthand writers need excellent skills in both spelling and grammar. A familiarity with medical and technical terminology is also a distinct advantage.

TRAINING

England and Wales

Most shorthand writers start by undergoing a course in machine shorthand, either full-time at a college or by distance learning. Addresses of colleges running these courses are available from the British Institute of Verbatim Reporters and the Association of Professional Shorthand Writers.

When trainees are taken on by a firm they usually start by working in one of the courts that is taped, to gain experience of court proceedings, giving them practice at reporting and increasing their speeds. The trainee acts as a logger, keeping a detailed record of the times when each person starts and stops speaking. They also take records of the proceedings in shorthand. In addition, some firms also run evening training sessions, where trainees can practise transcribing.

This period of training usually lasts between three and twelve months. During this time, trainees also start to produce their own dictionary. All shorthand writers have their own way of writing things, so each writer has their own dictionary of how the computer should transcribe their shorthand. They start this dictionary when they first start training, and add to it as they progress in the work.

Once trainees achieve speeds of 160 wpm they can apply to become associates of one of the professional bodies. This involves taking a practical test in court, which consists of taking an hour's proceedings in shorthand and then transcribing it without the aid of tapes. They then become provisionally accredited shorthand writers and can work on their own in court.

After a further three years experience, they can apply for membership of their professional body. This entails producing a transcript of another hour's court proceedings. Members can apply to become fellows two years later, at which time they have to undergo two tests in different types of court – for instance, one test in a civil court and one in a crown court.

Scotland

New shorthand writers in Scotland are trained by the firms they work for – there are no courses. Usually they start learning on straightforward cases, such as custody or divorce. They work with an experienced shorthand writer and both take notes of proceedings. This enables the trainee to practise and increase their speed, as well as become familiar with court procedures. During this time they are given regular tests to see if they are making progress. After about three months they are usually able to undertake a straightforward civil case on their own.

LATE ENTRY

There is no maximum age for entry into this career, and many firms prefer more mature entrants. See ENTRY REQUIREMENTS and TRAINING.

OPPORTUNITIES

Most are employed by firms of shorthand writers, who are contracted to provide reports of court proceedings. The British Institute of Verbatim Reporters (previously the Institute of Shorthand Writers) and the Association of Professional Shorthand Writers provide lists of the member firms who may employee trainees.

In England and Wales, firms hold appointments to the High Court, the Central Criminal Court and other courts, and outside London to the Crown Court centres which are in all the larger towns. They do not hold appointments to the County and Magistrates' Courts and the district courts. Firms also undertake work for public inquiries, trade union and political conferences, industrial tribunals, board meetings and disciplinary hearings. Firms use their own employees and freelances.

In Scotland, they work for one of the three firms of shorthand writers, or are freelance. There is a move in Scotland towards taping cases, rather than using shorthand writers. This means that, over the next couple of years, opportunities for shorthand writers may decrease considerably. There is a shortage of suitably qualified shorthand writers in England and Wales. In addition to full-time work there are opportunities for part-time work and self-employment.

PAY AND CONDITIONS
England and Wales
Shorthand writers are often employed on a freelance basis.
Scotland
Those shorthand writers in employment are paid for the hours that they actually work.

Rates vary accordingly.

Shorthand writers may work irregular hours. Courts usually sit from 10am until 4pm, but if a court case continues into the evening, the shorthand writer is required to stay until the end. In situations where a transcript is needed for the next day the shorthand writer has to complete the work in the evening.

PROSPECTS
There is no promotional ladder for this career. However, there are opportunities for experienced shorthand writers to work freelance. They can also work for Hansard, producing reports of the day's proceedings in the House of Commons and House of Lords. There are also opportunities for caption writing for the deaf, and in television.

RELATED OCCUPATIONS
Shorthand typist, secretary, journalist, copy editor, legal executive, barrister's clerk.

FURTHER INFORMATION
British Institute of Verbatim Reporters, 61 Carey Street, London WC2A 2JG (please include sae)

Association of Professional Shorthand Writers, Edial Farm, Burnt Wood, Near Walsall, West Midlands ST17 9FS

Verbatim Reporters, 1 Atholl Place, Edinburgh EH3 8HP

FURTHER READING
Working in Law – COIC.

In the careers library classified under LAG.

6. COURT USHER/COURT OFFICER/MACER (LAG)

BACKGROUND INFORMATION
In England and Wales, court ushers work in Crown Courts, the Court of Appeal and Magistrates' Courts, all of which deal with both civil and criminal cases. They also work in County Courts and High Courts, which deal with civil cases only.

In Scotland, those working in Sheriff courts are known as court officers, those in the Court of Session (the Supreme Civil Court) and in the High Court of Justiciary (the Supreme Criminal Court) are known as macers.

THE WORK
England and Wales
The work of a court usher varies depending on the type of court they work in. For most ushers, the main part of their work is in ensuring that everything required for a hearing is in the right place at the right time. Before the start of a hearing, they gather all the necessary papers, ready for the court clerk or clerk of the court. They prepare the courtroom for the day's hearings, putting out glasses and drinking water etc. They also have a responsibility for safety, eg by making sure that fire exits are clear.

They check that witnesses, lawyers and defendants have arrived for the case and inform the court clerk of the situation.

In Crown Courts they also receive the judge on arrival and have their wig and gown ready.

At the start of the hearing, when the magistrate or judge enters the court, it is the usher who tells everyone to stand. During the case, they call the defendants and witnesses into the court and administer the oath – giving them the Bible (or other scripture, depending on the defendant's or the witness's religion) and hold up a card printed with the oath for the witness or defendant to read. They fetch anything required by the clerk and pass any evidence to the judge or jury. If the clerk wishes to communicate with one of the lawyers, then the usher passes the message. They also make sure that people waiting outside the court do not make too much noise.

In Crown Courts, which deal with more serious criminal cases, there may be a small team of ushers. As these cases have a jury, one of the ushers acts as jury bailiff. This involves making sure that the jury are sent reminders before the case, so that they know which court they are in and what time to arrive. They welcome the jurors on their arrival at court and escort them to the jury waiting room. When the jury are assembled, they explain the procedures to them, such as how they will be sworn in. For most jurors this will be their first time in court and they may be nervous, so the usher needs to calm their fears and put them at ease. The usher escorts the jury into and out of the court and, during the hearing, passes the jury any evidence such as photographs or documents that they have to look at.

At the end of the hearing, while the jury deliberates its verdict, the usher remains outside the jury room and acts as the communications link between the jury and the court clerk. If the jury does not reach a verdict at the time and has to stay overnight, the usher organizes hotel accommodation for them, takes them to the hotel and stays there with them.

In County Courts with a number of district judges, the majority of hearings are held in chambers, not in public courts. In these situations, the usher acts as a receptionist, taking a note of people as they arrive and escorting them to the correct room for their hearing.

At the end of a session in any court, the usher clears the court or chambers and secures the rooms. They collect any papers and return them to the clerk; they also gather any lost property, record it and store it in a safe place.

Scotland
In Scotland, court ushers, known as either court officers or macers, are civil servants. In the Sheriff Courts they are known as court officers and their main job is to attend the sheriffs. In the Supreme Courts, they are macers and, here, they attend the judges. They also carry out similar jobs to the court ushers in England and Wales and may also deal with a range of other tasks, such as collecting and delivering the mail, and even operating a switchboard.

LAW AND RELATED WORK: LAB-LAZ

WORK ENVIRONMENT

Court ushers spend part of their time in the courtroom itself. They also usually have an office, often in the court buildings, from which they carry out their administrative work. Ushers in Magistrates' Courts may have to travel between a number of different courts. In County Court chambers they work on the reception desk. If they are acting as jury bailiff they may occasionally have to spend a night away from home.

SKILLS AND INTERESTS

Ushers need a considerable amount of confidence and an authoritative manner. They need to be well organized and methodical, as they are responsible for making sure everything needed for a case, from the appropriate people to the relevant papers, is there. They need excellent communication skills as they deal with a wide range of people, from offenders to judges. Defendants are often frightened and witnesses may be nervous, so ushers need to be understanding and have the skills to calm them down and put them at their ease. They have a wide range of problems to cope with, from abusive defendants and people complaining about having to wait for their case to be heard, to lawyers who are not ready when their case starts. Dealing with these takes a considerable amount of patience and good interpersonal skills. Ushers work in a team with the clerk of the court/court clerk and sometimes with other ushers.

ENTRY REQUIREMENTS

There are no entry requirements for this work. The minimum age is 21 (16 years in Scotland) but most courts prefer to recruit more-mature people. Courts often prefer ushers who have a background in the police or Armed Forces. In the more rural areas of Scotland, there can be considerable travelling and ushers may need to be able to drive. This is also the case with ushers whose work covers a number of Magistrates' Courts in a rural area.

TRAINING

Training takes about a year. Some courts in England and Wales run short courses for ushers covering such areas as: security issues, dealing with difficult people, working with jurors and ethnic awareness. However, most training is given on the job, with ushers learning the operations of their particular court from experienced ushers.

LATE ENTRY

Many courts tend to employ more-mature entrants. There is no upper age limit. Entry requirements are as described above.

OPPORTUNITIES

England and Wales – in the Crown Courts, County Courts, the Court of Appeal and the High Court, ushers work for the Court Service (part of the civil service). In Magistrates' Courts they work for the Magistrates' Court Committee. There are some 700 magistrates' courts, 400 county courts and 100 high courts in England and Wales, which employ about 1,000 ushers between them. Courts are found in all cities and most major towns.

In Scotland, all court officers and macers are civil servants. Court officers work in Sheriff Courts, of which there are 49 – divided between the six Sheriffdoms of Grampian, Highlands and Islands; Tayside, Central and Fife; Lothian and Borders; Glasgow and Strathkelvin; North Strathclyde; and South Strathclyde, Dumfies and Galloway. There are 110 court officers at present. Twenty-two macers work in one of the two Courts of Session in Glasgow or Edinburgh and they also work in the High Court of Justiciary. Court ushers, court officers and macers can be employed full-time, part-time or work on a casual basis. Entry into the work is fairly competitive.

PAY AND CONDITIONS

In magistrates' courts, some ushers are paid by the hour at about £4.60 an hour, plus their travelling expenses; others may be salaried. Ushers in England and Wales and macers in Scotland are usually paid between £9,577 and £11,309. Ushers usually work Monday to Friday, starting about 8.30am in the morning and finishing about 5pm. However, occasionally they may have late sittings and be required to stay on in the evening.

PROSPECTS

Within large magistrates' courts, it is possible for an usher to be promoted to a supervisory role with responsibility for a number of other ushers; prospects, however, are limited. In other courts, ushers gain promotion to supervising usher or administrative officer (civil service) and could be promoted to more senior grades, such as court clerk.

In Scotland, court officers/macers can be promoted to supervisory levels, running a team of officers or macers. They can also be promoted to the grade of support manager, where they would be in charge of officers, macers, messengers and other support staff. At present, however, there are only two such posts within the Scottish Court Service.

RELATED OCCUPATIONS

Court clerk, TV floor manager, receptionist.

FURTHER INFORMATION

England and Wales

Contact local Crown Courts or Magistrates' Courts.

Scotland

The Scottish Court Service, Hayweight House, 23 Lauriston Street, Edinburgh EH3 9DQ, 0131 2216837

FURTHER READING

Working in Law – COIC

In the careers library classified under LAG.

GROUP M – SECURITY AND PROTECTIVE SERVICES

1. **POLICE CONSTABLE CLCI:MAB**
2. **TRAFFIC WARDEN CLCI:MAB**

1. POLICE CONSTABLE (MAB)

BACKGROUND INFORMATION

The Police Service in England and Wales is made up of 43 police forces, with eight in Scotland – each run under the command of a chief officer. The chief officer is responsible for the direction and control of the force and its day-to-day management. A police authority has a duty to secure the maintenance of an efficient police force for its area.

The work of the police is to enforce the law, keep the peace and protect the community.

THE WORK

The work of a constable involves maintaining law and order, protecting people and property, preventing and detecting crime, providing reassurance and help, and coping with society's emergencies.

After training, all entrants begin work as uniformed constables. The largest proportion of constables are involved in work 'on the beat'. They are the first point of contact between police and public and act as a visible deterrent to the criminal.

Their work is extremely varied and includes dealing with accidents, disturbances and traffic problems, handling complaints, apprehending and interviewing suspects, investigating crimes, obtaining statements from witnesses, checking the security of premises, and answering questions from the public. They deal with large public events like sports meetings, shows and demonstrations.

Some constables work in car patrols, while others work in the police station, either on the front desk dealing with the public, or in the communications room in two-way contact with their colleagues out of the station. Some time is spent in court giving evidence.

A number of constables specialize some time after completing their two-year probationary period. The specialisms include:

The traffic department, which deals with traffic accidents and offences, promotes road safety and the smooth running of traffic.

Criminal Investigation Department (CID), which is concerned mainly with the investigation of more serious crimes and with crime prevention. It also includes specialist areas like the Fraud Squad and the Special Branch.

Dog handling, where dogs are used to catch and arrest criminals or to find hidden drugs or explosives. Dog handlers are responsible for their own dogs, which live and train with them.

Mounted police, who are concerned with the use of horses for crowd control and countryside searches etc.

River police, who patrol rivers and coastal waters. Their responsibilities include preventing theft and smuggling, life-saving and the recovery of bodies.

Underwater search units, which have teams of divers who have to search rivers, lakes, canals and deep ponds for missing people, stolen property and dumped weapons etc.

WORK ENVIRONMENT

Police constables may spend much of their time outdoors in all weathers. They may be on foot or in a car. When indoors, they may be in a police station, a court of law, or in private or business premises.

Many constables drive regularly in their work.

SKILLS AND INTERESTS

Police constables should be tolerant and show courtesy to the public. They need physical courage and fitness to deal with incidents and disturbances. Mental resilience is needed to cope with difficult tasks such as informing people of the death of a relative.

Initiative is important, as constables often find themselves in charge of situations like road accidents.

Communication is a central part of a constable's work. Good written skills are necessary to record details of incidents and arrests – records that may later be used in court. Good spoken skills are needed to deal with the public in appropriate ways, such as when giving advice, sympathy or a reprimand. Clear speech and confidence are required when giving evidence in court.

Police work is based on a team approach, so the ability to work as part of a team, as well as being able to work alone, is vital. A police force is a disciplined unit where a willingness and ability to accept discipline is necessary.

ENTRY REQUIREMENTS

1. The minimum age for entry to most forces is $18^{1}/_{2}$ years at the time of application. In England and Wales there is no specified upper age limit but some forces do set upper limits around age 49. In Scotland the upper age limit is 40 years and in Northern Ireland it is 52.

2. Entrants must be: British citizens; Commonwealth citizens whose stay in the UK is not subject to restrictions; *or* citizens of the Irish Republic.

3. No particular educational qualifications are specified but all applicants must sit a standard entry test. The tests used in both England and Wales and those in Scotland include use of English language, numeracy, information checking, logical reasoning and observation.

4. There is no minimum or maximum height requirement.

5. Applicants must be in good health and of good physique. They have to pass a full medical examination and a test of fitness, strength and agility.

6. Eyesight standards vary between forces, but all require good eyesight, including colour vision. Most forces accept officers with spectacles or contact lenses (although unaided vision must be of a reasonable standard).

7. Many forces require a driving licence.

8. A criminal record is not always a bar to joining the police, but applicants must declare any convictions, even for juvenile offences, and the Chief Constable of their chosen force will make a decision on their case.

9. People with a degree in any subject (or in the final year of a degree course) may apply for the Accelerated Promotion Scheme for Graduates (APSG). They must first pass selection as a police constable by the police force of their choice and then undergo the APSG selection procedure. This consists of aptitude tests, interviews and an 'assessment centre' (individual and group exercises, personality questionnaires and interviews) lasting about three days (two or three days in Scotland). Only a minority of graduates are selected for this scheme; most enter forces

POLICE AND RELATED WORK: MAB

in the standard way.

10. For those under 18 years, some colleges of further education offer courses like the BTEC National Diploma in Public Services which combine educational qualifications with a preparation for the public services. Some police forces operate voluntary cadet schemes, with very few (Durham, Staffordshire, Central Scotland, Fife, Grampian, Tayside) employing full-time cadets, who must live locally.

TRAINING

All police officers serve a probationary period of two years.

During this time they spend one or more blocks (amounting to between 15 and 25 weeks in all, depending on the force) at one of the national residential police training centres (one of six in England and Wales, Tulliallan Castle, Kincardine in Scotland or Garnerville in Northern Ireland). Training includes law, police procedure, physical education, self defence and community relations.

The remaining time in this probationary period is spent based at a local police station, under the supervision of a tutor constable. Training continues with various post-foundation courses, and attachments to specialized departments, like CID, traffic and the dog section.

Those accepted on the APSG in England, Wales and Northern Ireland follow the same two-year probationary training as all recruits, before taking their Sergeants' exam which they must pass first time. They then begin the Accelerated Promotion course which includes periods at the Police Staff College, Bramshill. When not at police college, they work as a sergeant at a local police station. After two or three years they take the Inspectors' exam and if successful take further courses at Police College. They are expected to continue progressing to the most senior positions and attend further management courses throughout their careers.

In Scotland, those accepted on APSG must also pass their promotion examinations first time. There is no separate examination for promotion to sergeant and inspector. On passing the exams, they are generally promoted to temporary sergeant for around 18 months after which the promotion may be made substantive. After 30 months on the programme they would be eligible for promotion to inspector. The programme is managed by the Scottish Police College, Tulliallan Castle.

LATE ENTRY

There is no specified upper age limit for entry to the police forces in England and Wales although a few individual forces set limits. Some forces may consider applicants in their forties. In Scotland the upper age limit is 40, in Northern Ireland it is 52. All police constables and sergeants must retire at age 55. Officers in higher ranks must retire at a later age.

In Scotland, chief constables may consider applicants from the Armed Forces or the Merchant Navy a year or two above the normal upper age limit of 40 years.

OPPORTUNITIES

Approximately 6,000 police officers are recruited annually throughout England and Wales, and about 600 in Scotland, with fierce competition for places.

There is no annual quota of places open through the accelerated promotion scheme for graduates. The selection procedure is particularly rigorous, but there are places for all who meet the standards. Many other graduates join the police as standard entrants.

In addition to the regular police forces, there are other separate police organizations: for example, the British Transport Police – responsible for railways, docks and harbours, stations etc; and the UK Atomic Energy Authority Constabulary – responsible for security of nuclear establishments.

PAY AND CONDITIONS

Constables begin on £15,478 during initial training and then move to £17,274. They are on a pay scale that reaches £24,432 after 14 years' service. London officers receive additional allowances. Salaries on promotion depend on rank and length of service: eg sergeants earn between £23,583 and £27,504, superintendents between £41,484 and £51,495.

Constables and sergeants work an eight-hour day on a shift system with two days' rest a week. Overtime, or work on a rest day, is paid at an increased rate, or compensatory time off is taken for officers in the ranks of constable or sergeant.

PROSPECTS

After their initial two years, constables may specialize in branches such as the CID, traffic, dog section, mounted branch, community relations, crime prevention.

Promotion is on merit and is initially to sergeant, which may be achieved within about five years by passing a promotion examination in police subjects and being recommended by senior officers.

RELATED OCCUPATIONS

Security officer, prison officer, firefighter, private detective, Armed Forces serviceman/woman, traffic warden.

FURTHER INFORMATION

British Transport Police*, Force Headquarters, PO Box 260, 15 Tavistock Place, London WC1H 9SJ

Police Graduate Liaison Office*, Room 466, Home Office, Queen Anne's Gate, London SW1H 9AT, 0171 273 3353

Police, Personnel and Training Unit*, Room 514, Home Office, 50 Queen Anne's Gate, London SW1H 9AT, 0171 273 3797

Scottish Office Home and Health Department*, Police Division, Room E1-7, Saughton House, Broomhouse Drive, Edinburgh EH11 3XD, 0131 244 2156

UK Atomic Energy Authority Constabulary*, Building E6, AEA Technology, Abingdon, Oxfordshire OX14 3DB, 01235 463757

POLICE AND RELATED WORK: MAB

FURTHER READING

Leaflets/booklets are available from the addresses marked*.

Working in Police and Emergency Services – COIC

Careers in the Police Force – Kogan Page

In the careers library classified under MAB.

2. TRAFFIC WARDEN (MAB)

BACKGROUND INFORMATION

The 1991 Road Traffic Act decriminalized parking offences and led to the introduction of a new, related job known as Parking Attendant, which has been introduced in some areas. The role of parking attendants is to enforce on-street parking restrictions, together with supervising car parks and ensuring that vehicle owners have paid to use them. Some of their duties are broadly similar to those of a traffic warden, described as follows, although they do not share their responsibility for keeping traffic moving freely.

Parking attendants are employed by local authorities or by private companies contracted to them, whereas traffic wardens are employed by police forces.

THE WORK

The traffic warden's main duty is to keep vehicles moving freely through cities and towns which are increasingly under heavy pressure from the volume of traffic. They monitor schemes which have been introduced to prevent traffic problems, including: waiting restrictions, parking meters and one-way street systems, plus controlled parking zones and restrictions on loading and unloading of goods (identified by yellow lines). They also report parking offences and issue fixed penalty notices, commonly known as tickets, to offenders. In addition, they are frequently asked for information and directions by members of the public.

At the beginning of a shift, traffic wardens report to their office and receive instructions from a traffic warden supervisor, who allocates them to specific areas. Wardens are not necessarily always assigned to the same part of a town every day. They are given notice of any special events which may be occurring, such as weddings, funerals, parades or festivals that are likely to cause delays to traffic flow or increase parking problems.

When out on duty, they patrol the streets, acting as a visual deterrent to illegal parking and looking out for vehicles that are wrongly parked and may cause an obstruction, or that may be parked at meters whose time has overrun. When necessary, they issue fixed penalty notices and may have to arrange for a vehicle to be clamped or to be removed by the police to a parking 'pound'. They make checks to ensure that parking meters and some car park ticket machines are in working order.

While on patrol, they also watch for vehicles displaying out-of-date motor vehicle licences (tax discs) or no disc at all. They also assist the police by keeping a look out for vehicles that have been reported stolen.

Their other duties include advising drivers on where they may park, and answering questions from pedestrians who may be unfamiliar with the town and need directions.

Sometimes they do point duty – directing traffic by means of hand signals. This may happen when traffic lights have failed or when traffic has to be re-routed through a town centre due to an event being held. They may also patrol school crossings.

A further duty may be at police car pounds, where they receive vehicles being brought in and register the details.

At the end of a shift, traffic wardens return to the office to hand in duplicate copies of any tickets they have issued and to report incidents, like road accidents, that are causing delays – necessary information for wardens on the next shift.

Occasionally they have to appear in court to give evidence against offenders.

Parking attendants do the above duties with the exceptions of point duty, school crossing patrol and attendance at police pounds.

Traffic wardens wear a distinctive uniform. They have protective clothing for wet weather. Parking attendants wear the uniform of their own employers. These vary in design, the only requirement being that parking attendants' uniforms must be clearly distinguishable from those worn by traffic wardens or police officers and must state clearly the name of the employing local authority.

WORK ENVIRONMENT

Traffic wardens and parking attendants work outdoors in all weather conditions. They are on their feet for most of the day and may walk as far as five miles during one shift. They are based at offices in police stations and may share canteen and social facilities there with police officers.

SKILLS AND INTERESTS

Both traffic wardens and parking attendants must be fit and active.

They work alone for much of the time and must be capable of working without close supervision. They should be observant and honest.

They must be assertive, yet polite and tactful, when dealing with people. Motorists are often aggressive and hostile. They must be able to cope with this and not be easily upset. Self-confidence is important. They need good communication skills, as they are constantly in contact with the public. Traffic wardens also work in close co-operation with the police.

ENTRY REQUIREMENTS

Exact requirements vary from area to area.

No formal educational qualifications are required in most areas, although some may ask for GCSE (A–C) /S grade (1–3) in subjects including English. Applicants should, however, have a good standard of education and are usually expected to pass a written entrance test in English, to show that they can write out tickets, keep notes of incidents and produce written reports which may be used in court. In some areas there may also be a maths test.

The minimum age varies according to the area. In some areas it is 18 years, in others 20 or older.

Some areas require applicants to have experience in dealing with the public and evidence of the maturity to handle difficult or angry people.

Applicants should be in good health and are usually required to take a medical examination. Good eyesight is

POLICE AND RELATED WORK: MAB

necessary. Glasses are permitted. Some employers stipulate a minimum height, others require a certain height–weight ratio and do not allow visible tattoos. Some employers insist that applicants are British subjects and/or reside in the area.

TRAINING

Traffic wardens and parking attendants receive much of their training on the job, from experienced colleagues and, in the case of wardens, sometimes from a police officer with responsibility for supervising traffic wardens. They usually spend several weeks working with an experienced colleague before going out alone.

Since they are often recruited as specific vacancies arise, there is not usually a sufficiently large number of entrants joining at the same time to warrant the provision of a full-time instruction course.

However, in many areas a special introductory course may be arranged for a large intake and in London and other major cities, all traffic wardens attend a training course at their police training centre.

Trainees learn traffic regulations and how to complete and issue tickets for parking offences. They may also learn methods of note-taking and of writing short reports. The training of traffic wardens also covers the techniques of giving evidence in court. In some areas they also take a short first aid course so that they can deal with emergencies that may occur on the street.

LATE ENTRY

This type of work is very suitable for older entrants, as it requires maturity and evidence of ability to deal with people. Some areas set a maximum age limit of 55, while others will consider people up to retirement age.

OPPORTUNITIES

Approximately 4,000 traffic wardens and parking attendants are employed in the UK. Opportunities vary from area to area and the largest number of openings is in cities and large towns.

Traffic wardens are civilians who work in local police districts under the general control of the police force.

Parking attendants are employed by local government district authorities, that is by town or city councils. The London boroughs have contracted out the work to private companies, who directly employ the staff.

The number of opportunities for parking attendants is increasing, as more local authorities take over the responsibility for enforcing parking regulations from the police force. The number of openings for traffic wardens is consequently decreasing.

Vacancies may be held by local Jobcentres or be advertised in the local press. Alternatively, contact local police headquarters (traffic wardens) or council headquarters (parking attendants) directly to enquire about current opportunities. In London, enquiries about traffic warden vacancies should be made to the Metropolitan Police Selection Centre.

PAY AND CONDITIONS

Pay scales vary in different areas. A trainee might begin on a minimum salary of £11,445 rising to a maximum of £12,225. In London, the starting salary is about £11,000 with a London weighting allowance.

Full uniform is provided. Some employers also provide a shoe allowance.

Duties are carried out during the times when traffic regulations are in force. Hours of work could be between 6.30am and 8pm. It is normal to work a 36_-hour week (slightly shorter in some areas) on a shift system spread over seven days.

PROSPECTS

Traffic wardens and parking attendants may gain promotion to senior grades. Career prospects vary in different areas and may be extremely limited in areas where few are employed.

Progression is based on ability. Staff employed in the more senior grades become increasingly involved in the administrative, supervisory and training aspects of the work.

RELATED OCCUPATIONS

Police constable, security officer, Armed Forces personnel, store detective.

FURTHER INFORMATION

From local police constabularies/district councils – addresses in the telephone directory.

Metropolitan Police Service, Selection Centre, 26/27 Aybrook Street, London W1M 3JL, 0171 230 0511 (traffic warden recruitment information: 0345 676876)

FURTHER READING

Working In Police and Emergency Services – COIC
In the careers library classified under MAB.

PRISON SERVICE: MAD

1. PRISON GOVERNOR CLCI:MAD
2. PRISON OFFICER CLCI:MAD

BACKGROUND INFORMATION

Her Majesty's Prison Service serves the public by keeping in custody those committed by the courts. It also has a responsibility to treat prisoners with humanity and to help them lead law-abiding lives in custody and after release.

The Prison Service in England and Wales is a Home Office Agency, whilst the Scottish Prison Service is an Executive Agency of the Scottish Office. Staff are public employees. Both prison services are going through a period of considerable change, with many of the functions previously undertaken centrally by the Home Office or Scottish Office now devolving to individual prisons. In England and Wales, this includes recruitment of prison officers. Some prisons in England have been 'contracted out' to the private sector and are run by private companies, who employ their own staff.

Some prisoners in the care of the prison service are on remand, still awaiting trial or sentencing by the courts, following their conviction. Others have been sentenced for varying lengths of time and are dealt with according to their category. Category A prisoners are the highest security risk and are dispersed between top security prisons, whilst Category D can be trusted not to attempt escape and may be housed in open prisons. Categories B and C fall between these extremes. Other types of prison establishment include remand centres and young offender institutions, which provide training for young people under 21 years of age. Local prisons keep a cross-section of prisoners, and security varies from one part of the prison to another.

The situation in Scotland is slightly different, with local closed prisons, specialized closed prisons, open prisons and young offender institutions.

1. PRISON GOVERNOR (MAD)

THE WORK

Governors are the managers in the prison service. They are responsible for the control and security of prison establishments, managing both staff and resources. The work varies considerably with the size and type of establishment and the grade and level of experience of the governor.

A senior governor is in overall charge and is assisted by a team of governor-grade staff who have responsibility for particular functions or areas of the prison.

Governors organize the work of prison officers and carry out staff training. They supervise security, oversee the maintenance of prisoners' records, deal with parole requests, and have responsibility for discipline procedures. They may also chair admission, release and review boards, and undertake risk assessments of all types of prisoners.

Governors have frequent contact with prisoners, either in a one-to-one situation, or as part of regular 'walkabouts' to check what is happening in the prison. They are responsible for organizing and supervising prisoners' development and progress. They counsel and advise prisoners and liaise with other professionals including doctors, chaplains, probation officers and psychiatrists. They also arrange prisoners' educational, leisure and work activities. Much of the inmates' work is carried out on a commercial basis for organizations outside the prison, and governors oversee contracts.

As governors progress through the grades, they take on more responsibility and may eventually be in charge of a prison. Before this, however, there may be times when they are the most senior member of staff on duty and are responsible for the prison for short periods. Governors also have the opportunity of working at headquarters, perhaps as part of a team looking after several prisons in an area, or offering strategic support to individual prisons when a major disturbance occurs. They may also work at a prison service college, training other staff.

'Contracted out' prisons have a different structure and may not use the term 'governor'. However, similar functions are undertaken by their management teams.

WORK ENVIRONMENT

Governors usually work in prisons, although some are based at headquarters, or in a prison service college or field training unit.

Prisons vary from very modern buildings to old and overcrowded centres, although a great deal of refurbishment is going on in some of the older establishments. The environment will also vary, depending on the amount of security in the prison.

Governors often work in offices within the prison, but their jobs take them to all parts of the establishment. They also spend time in meetings, conferences and courses outside the prison.

SKILLS AND INTERESTS

Governors need management skills to organize the prison and its resources. They must be able to lead and motivate both staff and prisoners. Good communication skills (both written and verbal) are essential. The ability to make decisions, sometimes in response to an urgent situation, is needed. Decisions must be well thought out and clear.

Governors need maturity and patience to help the prisoners, and must be interested in their welfare. They should be able to understand and sympathize with inmates, without condoning their behaviour.

The ability to enforce discipline without being authoritarian is essential. Difficult situations may arise and must be dealt with. The work can be stressful and demanding and requires a flexible approach.

ENTRY REQUIREMENTS

England and Wales

Entry to governor grade is by promotion to governor 5 (the first governor grade) from principal officer (the highest prison officer grade), or by open competition – the Accelerated Promotion Scheme (APS) or the new Direct Entry Scheme. The APS is open to serving prison officers and to graduates or those with equivalent qualifications from outside the prison service. All applicants must pass an examination to progress to a three-day extended interview.

The APS recruits annually, starting each September. It is primarily aimed at new or recent graduates and most entrants are in their early 20s. Applicants are selected on the basis of psychometric tests, experience ('biodata') and performance at a Job Simulation Assessment Centre. They then undergo a three-day extended interview, and only those who meet the required standard are selected.

PRISON SERVICE: MAD

The Direct Entry Scheme has been designed to recruit people with at least five years' experience of managing people. They are likely to be aged between about 26 and about 45 years and will undergo a similar selection procedure to APS applicants.

Scotland

In the new prison staffing structure, the first management post is that of Unit Manager, of which there will be approximately five to ten in any one prison, depending on its size. Entry to this level is either by promotion from prison officer grade or via a direct entry scheme. Direct entry recruitment is held from time to time, depending on need, and is normally aimed at people with a degree or equivalent qualification plus at least three years' experience of managing people and budgets. Recent schemes have set age limits at 24–56 years.

In both England and Wales and in Scotland, health, physical fitness and eyesight standards are as for prison officers, as are nationality, residency and conviction criteria – please see article 2. PRISON OFFICER.

Contracted out prisons operate their own systems.

TRAINING

England and Wales

Entrants to the APS spend a week at the Prison Service College, followed by two weeks' observation in a prison near their home. A nine-week residential course at either Wakefield or Newbold Revel Prison Service College (near Rugby) follows. This deals with the practical skills of prison work, including cell searching and controlling violent inmates. It also covers assertiveness skills and issues such as race relations and suicide prevention. This is the course undertaken by newly appointed prison officers, as all APS entrants begin by spending nine months as a basic grade prison officer.

During this time they sit the senior officer examination and, if successful, take the principal officer board. (APS entrants who were serving prison officers continue from the grade they had reached.) Before taking up a twelve-month posting at principal officer rank they undergo two months' training, and have a further two months' training before their next placement as governor 5. The APS ends when candidates have spent two years at governor 5 level and have passed their governor 4 Board. This will take a minimum of four years.

Scotland

Direct Entry Unit Managers undergo a twelve-month training programme. This is competency-based, and a probationary year runs at the same time. Trainees are based in prisons and work as Unit Managers whilst training.

LATE ENTRY

Older and experienced managers are welcomed on direct entry schemes. In England and Wales there is no upper age limit but in practice those under 45 will be preferred. In Scotland, the upper limit on recent recruitment drives has been 56 years.

Most entrants to the APS in England and Wales are young graduates.

'Contracted out' prisons may have different age limits.

OPPORTUNITIES

Over 40,000 people are employed in prisons in Britain, including over 1,000 governors in England and Wales and about 150 in Scotland. The number of staff in the prison service has increased by around a third in recent years.

Governors are employed by the Prison Service (England and Wales), the Scottish Office or by private companies operating 'contracted out' prisons. There are over 130 prison establishments, including headquarters, colleges and training units in England and Wales, with more planned. Scotland has 22 prisons, plus a headquarters and a prison service college. Prisons are located all over the country in both urban and rural locations. Male and female prisoners are usually housed separately, but a long-established tradition of 'opposite sex posting' means male governors can work with female prisoners and female governors with male prisoners. Governors must be prepared to move, as they can be posted to any prison establishment within the Prison Service (England and Wales) or within the Scottish Prison Service. Those working for private companies are employed at a particular prison.

Entry is very competitive, whether through APS, by direct promotion from principal officer grade, or by direct entry. The APS does not run every year, but is advertised in the national press in October of the year it is to run. Opportunities for Direct Entry Unit Managers in Scotland are advertised in the national and Scottish press and on television (STV).

PAY AND CONDITIONS

Except for direct entrants in Scotland, governors start their careers on prison officer grades. Please see article 2. PRISON OFFICER.

Governor salary scales range from basic pay for governor 5 of £28,568 to £52,224 for governor 1. A London supplement is also payable. Governors wear civilian clothes.

Governors work the hours needed to complete the job, and busy working days may extend beyond eight hours. There are no additional payments for extra hours. The nature of the job involves some evening duties and working weekends, but night hours are less common. There are opportunities to work part-time.

'Contracted out' prisons have their own salary and working patterns, and managers may be required to wear a uniform.

PROSPECTS

The first governor grade is governor 5 and the most senior (which might mean running a large prison) is governor 1. Someone at governor 3 grade (governor 4 in Scotland) may be in charge of a smaller prison.

Promotion to higher grades is on merit through promotion board or assessment centre and the length of time taken varies between candidates. For example, someone entering the service on the APS could reach governor 4 in five years, whereas the non-accelerated route would take considerably longer.

Experienced governors can work at headquarters on the administrative side, for example, as area managers or operational directors with responsibility for several prisons. They may also work at prison service colleges or training units running courses for other staff.

PRISON SERVICE: MAD

Grades and promotion routes are under review in both England/Wales and Scotland. 'Contracted out' prisons have their own structures.

RELATED OCCUPATIONS

Police constable, probation officer, Armed Forces – commissioned officer, social worker, Civil Service executive officer, Civil Service administration trainee, prison officer.

FURTHER INFORMATION AND READING

Please see article 2. PRISON OFFICER.

2. PRISON OFFICER (MAD)

THE WORK

Prison officers' work varies with the type of prison and its level of security as well as with the category and age of the prisoners.

They have security duties that ensure prisoners remain in custody. These involve supervising prisoners in all areas, including work areas and cells, and in all activities such as eating, recreation and exercise. They also patrol buildings and grounds and carry out cell searches. They have to deal with disruptive behaviour and ensure the safety of inmates and staff.

Officers are involved in tasks such as receiving new prisoners, issuing clothing, completing reports and other paperwork, and passing on prisoners' requests to senior staff.

An important part of the work is rehabilitating prisoners. This involves helping them with their problems and preparing them for life outside the prison. Prison officers advise and counsel prisoners and ensure they have access to professional help when needed. They are also responsible for prisoners' training.

Entrants with specific skills can carry out specialist work after prison officer training. They remain prison officers with discipline duties, but may become catering officers, health care officers, PE instructors, works officers (building trades) etc. They practise their skills and teach them to prisoners who work with them in workshops, on farms, in prison hospitals or kitchens, on building sites or in maintenance programmes and in trade training schemes. Inmates can take appropriate vocational qualifications.

Higher grade prison officers have additional responsibilities, such as supervising other officers or looking after an area or wing of the prison.

'Contracted out' prisons have a different structure and may not use the term 'prison officer', but staff carry out similar work.

WORK ENVIRONMENT

Prison officers usually work in prison establishments as part of a team. Some are based at headquarters or in a prison service college or field training unit.

Prisons vary from very modern buildings to old and overcrowded centres, although a great deal of refurbishment is going on in some of the older establishments. The environment will also vary depending on the amount of security in the prison.

Except for certain trades, the majority of a prison officer's work will take place indoors, although patrolling and supervisory duties may mean spending time outside. Escort duty and some trades mean spending time away from the prison.

SKILLS AND INTERESTS

Prison officers must like working with people, gaining their trust and helping with their problems. They need patience, understanding and tact, but must also be firm and be able to exercise authority. They must be able to deal with a variety of people, from those who are abusive and potentially violent, to those lacking in self-confidence and personal skills. Difficult situations may arise and prison officers must be able to use their leadership skills to cope. Prison officers should be able to understand and sympathize with inmates without condoning their behaviour.

They must be able to work as part of a team and liaise with others concerned with the welfare of the prisoners. Good communication skills are very important. The work can be stressful and requires a flexible approach. Self-control, resilience and a sense of humour are all essential.

ENTRY REQUIREMENTS

A minimum of five GCSEs/S grades (A–C/1–3) including English and Maths (or a qualification of equivalent level) is required. However, in Scotland, those with at least three years' experience supervising or managing people may be considered without these qualifications. In addition applicants have to pass an aptitude test and a fitness test before being interviewed.

In England and Wales, those without the required qualifications may enter the prison service on the operational support grade, where they do not deal directly with prisoners. They need the same fitness standards.

There is also a full medical examination.

In England and Wales, applicants have to undergo a half-day 'Job Simulated Assessment Centre' to show they have the interpersonal skills to cope with the demands of the job.

Applicants must also:

– be aged 20 (and under 49_ years in England and Wales, under 57 in Scotland);

– be a British citizen, a British protected person, a Commonwealth citizen with indefinite leave to remain in the UK, or an EU national;

– to work in England and Wales, have been resident in the UK for at least three years at the time of application;

– be physically fit and in good health; weight will be taken into consideration;

– have a minimum standard of vision (glasses and contact lenses are not necessarily a bar);

– be fully mobile (although basic grade officers are recruited locally by prisons in England and Wales, postings for senior and principal officers are controlled centrally. In Scotland, officers themselves apply for postings or promotions in other establishments but, under some circumstances, postings may still be controlled centrally);

– declare any convictions (including those considered 'spent' under the Rehabilitation of Offenders Act) on the application form. An offence is not an automatic bar, as each case is considered on its own merits.

PRISON SERVICE: MAD

'Contracted out' prisons have their own entry requirements.

TRAINING

England and Wales

New prison officers spend one week on pre-training experience at the prison that appointed them before undertaking a nine-week residential course at one of the two Prison Service Colleges (Wakefield or Newbold Revel, near Rugby). After the fourth week, a week is spent at the home establishment. This course covers a wide range of skills necessary for the care and control of prisoners, including cell and body searching, radio procedures, court and escort duties, supervision, physical restraint and self-defence. It also includes a strong element of physical training. After the course there is a one-week induction at the prison before prison officer duties start. New prison officers have a twelve-month probationary period.

Those on operational support grades may progress to prison officer posts by working towards the NVQ Level 2 in Custodial Care.

Scotland

Newly appointed officers undergo a two-year probationary period during which time they work towards the SVQ Level 2 in Custodial Care. They are trained mostly at their establishment but spend several periods (amounting to about nine weeks in total) at the Scottish Prison Service College in Falkirk

'Contracted out' prisons provide their own training for staff.

LATE ENTRY

The upper age limit for entry to the prison service is 49 years in England and Wales and 57 in Scotland. All entrants must meet the requirements listed above and follow the same pattern of training.

Relevant experience such as Armed Forces or police work is useful.

'Contracted out' prisons may have different age limits.

OPPORTUNITIES

Over 40,000 people are employed in the prison service in Britain and, of these, more than 27,000 are prison officers. The number of staff in the prison service has increased by approximately one third in recent years.

Prison officers are employed by the Prison Service (England and Wales), the Scottish Prison Service, or by private companies operating 'contracted out' prisons. There are over 130 prison establishments, plus headquarters, colleges and field training units, in England and Wales, with more planned. Scotland has 22 establishments, a headquarters and a college. Prisons are located all over the country and, in England and Wales, each is responsible for recruiting prison officers locally. Vacancies are advertised in Jobcentres and the local press. In Scotland, recruitment is still carried out centrally. A new recruitment campaign began in March 1998.

Prison officers must be prepared to move, as they can be posted to any prison establishment within the Prison Service (England and Wales) or within the Scottish Prison Service. Those working for private companies are employed at a particular prison. Male and female prisoners are usually housed separately but 'opposite sex postings' mean that female officers can work in male prisons, and male officers in female prisons.

PAY AND CONDITIONS

The starting salary for a basic grade prison officer (England and Wales) is £14,863, rising to £21,257. The basic pay for a senior officer is £22,570 and that for a principal officer is from £23,400 to £24,643. Shift allowances and London supplements are also payable. Specialist officers, such as trade instructors and hospital officers receive an additional £1,041 a year. Officers are provided with a free uniform.

New recruits in Scotland have a starting salary of £9,600 rising to £16,850. Residential officers start at £11,800 which rises to £22,100.

Officers work a 39-hour week in shift patterns that vary between establishments. Night, evening and weekend working are likely to form part of the shift pattern.

'Contracted out' prisons have their own salary and working patterns.

PROSPECTS

Prison officers can progress to senior officer grade (after a minimum of four years in England and Wales) by examination and promotion board. After this, promotion to principal officer grade is by merit, and officers go before a promotion board. Principal officers are eligible for promotion to governor grades (please see article 1. PRISON GOVERNOR).

Prison officers in England and Wales can also apply to join the accelerated promotion scheme (APS) (please see article 1. PRISON GOVERNOR), although this does not run every year.

Experienced officers who wish to specialize can take additional training courses. For example, those without nursing qualifications, who wish to work as hospital officers, can take an intensive course that includes NHS hospital placements as well as classroom and practical instruction.

Grades and promotion routes are under review in England and Wales.

In Scotland, prison officers who successfully complete their two-year probationary period are eligible to apply for advertised vacancies for jobs in higher pay bands. Natural progression would be to a residential officer position. However, after successfully completing one year's probation, officers would be eligible to apply for specialist officer posts, for example instructor positions in industries, physical training and prison catering.

'Contracted out' prisons have their own structures.

RELATED OCCUPATIONS

Police constable, prison instructor, Armed Forces serviceman/woman, probation officer, social worker, youth and community worker, prison governor, security officer.

FURTHER INFORMATION

England and Wales – individual establishments: see Yellow Pages for addresses/telephone numbers.

England and Wales – Accelerated Promotion Scheme: The APS Section, Directorate of Personnel, Prison Service

PRISON SERVICE: MAD

HQ*, Room 418, Cleland House, Page Street, London SW1P 4LN, 0171 217 6437/6055 (please include sae)

Scottish Prison Service*, Recruitment Unit, Room 131, Calton House, 5 Redheughs Rigg, Edinburgh EH12 9HW, 0131 244 8591/2

FURTHER READING

Leaflets/booklets are available from the addresses marked*.

In the careers library classified under MAD.

FIRE SERVICE: MAF

FIREFIGHTER/FIRE OFFICER CLCI:MAF

BACKGROUND INFORMATION

The Fire Service exists to save and rescue people and property from all types of accident and disaster. In fact only one in five calls, on average, is for help at a fire.

Firefighters respond to fire calls, road traffic accidents, floods, bomb incidents, spillages of dangerous substances, rail and air crashes, and also rescue people and animals who are trapped inside buildings, lifts and other confined spaces. They often work closely at the site of a disaster with members of the other emergency services, including the ambulance and police services.

The Fire Service also has a role in promoting fire safety (including safety when using fireworks) and is responsible for enforcing standards of fire safety in public and commercial premises.

There is no national fire service. Instead, there are 58 local fire authorities, each under the command of a chief fire officer (firemaster in Scotland). There are 50 separate fire brigades in England and Wales, provided by county councils, metropolitan authorities and in London by the London Fire and Civil Defence Authority. The majority of fire brigades divide their geographical area of responsibility into Divisions. In addition to an overall Brigade Headquarters each has Divisional Headquarters in the charge of a Divisional Commander, responsible for several fire stations.

There are three types of firefighter: whole-time, 'retained' and volunteer. The latter two types are sometimes called 'part-time'. The Home Office (for England and Wales) and The Scottish Office Home Department lay down guidelines based on the risk of fire occurring in each area and how severe the damage might be to the people. These help determine whether a fire station is staffed by whole-time, retained or volunteer firefighters. Retained firefighters are usually found in rural areas and small towns. They are paid an annual fee or retainer plus fees for attending drill nights and training sessions in addition to a fee for each call they attend. They must live or work within four minutes of the fire station.

In the remoter parts of Scotland there are units of volunteer firefighters who serve their local communities.

THE WORK

Firefighters work in teams and respond to an emergency call or 'shout' as it happens. They may be required to attend an incident in which they have to use cutting and lifting gear to free people who are trapped under masonry or in vehicles and may have to give first aid before the ambulance crew arrive. They may be called to a fire that produces toxic fumes and heavy smoke, which necessitates the use of special breathing apparatus. Whatever the situation, their responsibility is to save life and property with minimum damage and to clear and check the safety of the site.

Firefighters work in crews of five or six allocated to one appliance (fire engine). When a shout comes a controller assesses how many appliances will be required and, from information on high risk buildings and hazardous materials that is kept on the control room computer, decides whether specialist equipment will be required. A sub-officer or station officer is briefed before leaving the station, then takes charge of the operation and leads the crew(s). With a major incident, a more senior officer attends and co-ordinates the work.

Firefighters' appliances are fully equipped with ladders, water hoses, foam equipment, bolt cutters, air cutting saws, sledge-hammers, slate rippers, breathing apparatus and sometimes thermal imaging cameras to help them to locate people in smoke-filled rooms. They wear helmets and protective equipment and, for attendance at chemical spills, they have additional protective suits. They may carry personal radio sets with them to enable them to stay in contact with each other and with the fire station.

When the crews arrive at an incident the officer in charge must assess the situation as quickly as possible, noting, for instance, whether a fire involves any hazardous substances or modern materials such as foam-filled furniture, which generates heavy smoke. The fire officer decides on the method of containing the fire or dealing with other incidents and directs the crew who work in close co-operation with each other. Team work is vitally important. Every member of a crew is responsible for the lives of colleagues and of people involved in the situation. They have to deal with unforeseen circumstances as they arise and think quickly.

After dealing with an incident, firefighters clean up the site then return to the station, where the officer in charge has to write a full report of the incident.

Between shouts, whole-time firefighters are based at their station, where they have a variety of duties. They inspect, clean and maintain their appliance and its equipment, do drills and physical training, and study and learn new techniques. If they have the time, they may study for promotion exams. The night shift, or watch, are able to rest if they are not called out. Each station has sleeping quarters.

Other duties carried out by firefighters and particularly by fire officers, include providing specialist advice to institutions, such as hospitals and residential establishments, and to local authorities, which are responsible for licensing places of entertainment; inspecting premises and issuing fire certificates; talking about fire safety in schools and to local organizations.

Fire officers have a dual role. In addition to leading teams of firefighters at incidents they have managerial duties. The most senior officers spend a large part of their time on administrative and training duties and in giving talks on fire prevention and safety.

WORK ENVIRONMENT

Generally, most full-time firefighters work in urban areas, whereas retained firefighters cover rural ones.

Firefighters work in dangerous and often very unpleasant conditions: heat, cold, at heights, in enclosed spaces, in smoke-filled buildings, and in all kinds of weather conditions. They are exposed to danger from collapsing buildings or vehicles, explosion and fumes.

The work is hard physically and can be very uncomfortable, since firefighters have to wear heavy protective clothing and breathing apparatus and carry heavy and awkward equipment.

Crews normally stay in the same watches, which is important for building up team spirit.

Firefighters spend much of their time at the station, where they carry out routine duties, study or do physical training. Sometimes they leave the station to carry out practice

FIRE SERVICE: MAF

drills and to give fire safety talks and lectures or carry out inspections of premises.

SKILLS AND INTERESTS

Firefighters require stamina and a high level of physical fitness. They need quick reactions and the ability to stay calm in hazardous situations. Their work requires courage and determination. They must be able to accept discipline and enjoy working as a member of a close-knit team. At the same time they are expected to use their initiative and respond to changing circumstances when at an incident.

They must be prepared to accept restrictions on their personal appearance. Most brigades insist that hair should not show below the helmet. Male firefighters are not permitted to have beards or sideburns which could impinge on the breathing apparatus face mask.

They need to be practical and able to work with a range of tools and equipment.

Communication skills are important. Verbal skills and a reassuring manner are required when dealing with members of the public who are injured or in a state of shock. They must be able to deal firmly but politely with bystanders who may be hampering rescue work at an incident.

Written communication skill is essential when writing incident reports. These will often be used by accident investigators and insurance companies as a basis for their work.

ENTRY REQUIREMENTS

There is no minimum educational entry standard. A good general education is required and applicants may have to pass written entrance tests. Some fire brigades may require specific GCSE examination passes.

All recruits begin as firefighters. There is no separate officer or fast-stream entry, although entrants with A levels or degrees are expected to pass promotion exams more quickly.

The minimum age for entry is 18 years. There is no national maximum age, although individual brigades may set their own minimum and maximum ages.

There are no height restrictions.

There are national fitness entry tests that include lung function and aerobic capacity, strength of hand grip and combined lifting strength of back and legs. Applicants must be in good health and must pass a medical examination. They should have good vision in each eye without the aid of glasses or contact lenses and must not be colour blind.

Brigades also set a series of initiative and physical tests – often over a two-day period. They may also test for mental agility and stamina and the ability to work as a team.

Modern Apprenticeships (part of the Skillseekers Initiative in Scotland) may be available for young people leading to at least an NVQ/SVQ Level 3. Contact your local careers office, Jobcentre, TEC/LEC for details.

For those under 18 years, some colleges of further education offer courses like the BTEC National Diploma in Public Services which combine educational qualifications with a preparation for a range of public protective services.

TRAINING

New recruits in England and Wales follow a full-time training course lasting approximately three to four months. This is held at their own or a nearby fire authority's training centre and will include some residential periods. In Scotland, 16-week recruit-training courses are provided at the Scottish Fire Service Training School, which is maintained by the Scottish Office.

Induction training is rigorous, with military-style discipline. It is divided between theory and practical work covering basic rescue techniques – use of firefighting and breathing apparatus; entering smoke-filled rooms; foam and fire extinguishers; ladders, hoses, knots, hydraulic and other equipment; fire safety; and first aid.

Recruits then move to their fire station, where they spend up to two years as probationary firefighters learning from experienced firefighters. There is continuous assessment during this period.

Some fire brigades encourage firefighters to work towards NVQ/SVQ at Levels 2 and 3 in Emergency Fire Fighting.

Firefighters can progress to becoming fire officers by undergoing training at the Fire Service College and passing a series of examinations.

Training continues throughout a firefighter's career. Refresher courses are held in fire safety, use of breathing apparatus and appliance driving. Lectures and courses are held on new techniques. Fire Service training centres often have buildings which can be filled with smoke and whose layout – floors, walls, staircases – can be changed so that both recruits and experienced firefighters can practise rescues continually in realistic conditions.

Firefighters are encouraged to gain specialist qualifications, such as an LGV licence, necessary for driving a fire appliance, or in fire safety, and to study for statutory promotion exams. Most brigades encourage firefighters who wish to do so to take additional professional qualifications, such as membership of the Institution of Fire Engineers, or a degree in Fire Engineering or qualifications in public administration or management studies.

Officers attend short courses on technical firefighting and management skills at the Fire Service College in Gloucestershire.

Retained firefighters do basic training over a series of weekends and attend weekly drill nights throughout their service. They may occasionally have to attend some short courses held during the day.

LATE ENTRY

There is no maximum age for entry as a firefighter although applicants of all ages must pass the demanding physical selection tests.

OPPORTUNITIES

There are about 40,000 whole-time firefighters in England and Wales and approximately 17,000 retained firefighters. In Scotland there are approximately 4,500 whole-time, 2,800 retained and 1,200 volunteer firefighters.

The majority of firefighters work for local fire brigades. Competition for entry is fierce and there are always far more applicants to the full-time Fire Service than there are vacancies. Many brigades have periods when they do no recruitment at all. There is almost always a shortage of retained firefighters.

FIRE SERVICE: MAF

There are opportunities to work for a small number of other employers, like the British Airports Authority, which maintains fire brigades at airports, and for the Defence Fire Service of the Ministry of Defence.

PAY AND CONDITIONS

A firefighter earns £14,700 on entry, rising to £18,678 over five years. Leading firefighters earn from £20,004 to £20,826. Sub-officers and officers earn higher salaries. A station officer, for example, earns £23,793 to £26,659 and a senior divisional officer £33,912 to £36,579. Assistant chief officers and chief officers/firemasters are not paid on fixed scales. Their salaries vary with different fire authorities.

Retained firefighters are paid £1,632 to £1,782 a year plus attendance and turn-out fees.

Firefighters work a 42-hour week, which is divided into day and night shifts. They have an average of at least two days off each week. Many stations operate a system under which firefighters work two day shifts from 8am to 6pm followed by two night shifts from 6pm to 8am. The four shifts are then followed by four days' leave. When necessary, paid overtime is worked.

PROSPECTS

All recruits start in the same grade and promotion is on merit. Progression through the ranks is as follows: leading firefighter, sub-officer, station officer, assistant divisional officer, divisional officer grades 1–3, senior divisional officer, assistant chief fire officer/firemaster, chief fire officer/firemaster.

A firefighter who has passed the promotion exams could rise to the rank of station officer after five years' experience. This, however, would be exceptional. It normally takes longer than the minimum possible period to gain each promotion.

Up to the rank of station officer, promotions are largely made internally. Vacancies that arise are generally advertised throughout the Service, so that anyone with appropriate experience and qualifications may apply.

It is usually necessary to move to different areas for promotion and most senior officers have worked in several brigades.

RELATED OCCUPATIONS

Police constable, security officer, Armed Forces serviceman/woman, ambulanceman/woman.

FURTHER INFORMATION

Contact the personnel or recruitment departments of local fire services; addresses are in the local telephone directory.

FURTHER READING

Working in Police and Emergency Services – COIC
In the careers library classified under MAF.

SECURITY WORK: MAG

SECURITY OFFICER CLCI:MAG

BACKGROUND INFORMATION

Security is often required by both private and public organizations whose premises and property may be at risk of theft, malicious damage, or accidents such as fire and flood. Many organizations have their own security staff, while others make use of services provided by specialist security companies.

Services offered by contract security companies include: transporting cash and valuables in secured vehicles; guarding premises; planning and installing security systems; protection against industrial espionage; protecting retail premises; and protecting people.

THE WORK

The prime function of security officers (sometimes known as security guards) is loss prevention (one of the major causes of this is fire). They protect property, goods, money and people for commercial, industrial and public organizations. Their work can range from patrolling industrial premises to guarding ships and their cargoes, providing security for important meetings or conferences, being guards at sporting events or providing protection for important people.

There are three main types of security officers: static security officers; mobile security officers; and security drivers/cash-in-transit security officers.

Static security officers: are based in one place, which could be an office block, a factory, warehouse, building site etc. Part of their work may involve working in the reception area, where they receive visitors to the company, get them to sign the visitors' book, issue them with a pass and direct them to where they are going. Security officers are usually responsible for personnel and visitors in case of an emergency such as fire, so they need to know where a visitor will be. Their work may include checking delivery vehicles in and out of premises; in factories and other large premises, guards may be on the gate checking all who enter and leave.

If an emergency does arise, security officers are usually responsible for ensuring that everyone can leave the building easily – so they control all doors and gates and ensure that fire exits are kept clear. They also ensure all personnel are out of the building and accounted for, and that no one re-enters until the emergency is over.

At night, security officers use closed circuit television to watch the premises. They also patrol the premises regularly, checking doors and windows, making sure that no one has broken in, and looking for fire and flood hazards.

Security officers may be issued with two-way radios, so that, if they come across intruders, they can radio for assistance.

Mobile security officers: do similar work to the static guards but are not based in one place. Mobile security officers patrol and visit a number of sites. Part of their job may be visiting premises as the staff are leaving at the end of the day.

Throughout the night and at weekends they carry out patrols of the outside of buildings, checking windows, gates and doors. They also patrol the inside of the building, checking to see that there are no water leaks or fire hazards. They also need to be on the alert to deal with intruders, if found.

A security company may act as a key-holder for a number of premises, so that if an alarm goes off, mobile guards are sent to premises to find out what has happened. They open the premises for police or fire brigade, assist them while they are there and then make sure the building is secure when they have left. It is important that mobile security officers vary their routine for visiting premises. Some mobile security officers also use dogs.

Cash-in-transit operatives: collect valuables such as cash, precious metals or jewellery and transport them in safety to their destination. The operatives wear protective clothing and they are in constant radio contact with their base station. Drivers may also be used as couriers delivering packages, documents, computer data and almost any other important item.

WORK ENVIRONMENT

This varies depending on the job. Static security officers could be based in offices, building sites, industrial premises, retail premises etc. They may work alone, although some companies may have a number of static security officers on duty at one time. Mobile security officers often work alone and spend a considerable amount of their time driving from one set of premises to another. Both static and mobile security officers' work involves patrolling the inside and outside of buildings and this can mean being outside in the dark in all weathers. Cash-in-transit operatives spend much of their time in security vehicles.

SKILLS AND INTERESTS

All security officers need the qualities of honesty, common sense and reliability. It is vital for this work to be able to think quickly and clearly in an emergency, and confidence is essential, as security officers are expected to approach and challenge suspicious persons in the course of their duty. They must have a firm, polite and helpful manner, and be fit and in good health. Mobile and static security officers need to be able to work alone and on their own initiative, while cash-in-transit operatives must be able to work in a team.

ENTRY REQUIREMENTS

There are no specific entry requirements to work as a security officer. Personal qualities and good health are considered more important than educational qualifications. Security officers must be able to produce written reports. Applicants will have to provide a checkable record of all periods of employment, self-employment or unemployment, and give details of any criminal convictions, which will be checked along with their credit rating. Employers carry out a ten-year vetting procedure on all applicants. They may have to pass a medical examination – perfect health and fitness are not always required, provided applicants are able to carry out their duties safely. For some jobs, a current clean driving licence is required.

TRAINING

Training varies depending on the organization for which the security officer works. Organizations may run their own training or may send employees on training courses run by other security firms. All firms that comply with British Standard 7499 must give new entrants at least two days' induction training with an examination at the end.

SECURITY WORK: MAG

The Security Industry National Training Organization has established a range of NVQ/SVQ courses linked with City & Guilds qualifications which it encourages employers to offer their security staff. These include: City & Guilds in Professional Guard, Retail Guarding, and Cash in Transit; NVQ Level 2 in Security Guarding, Retail, Security and Door Supervision, and Transporting Property under Guard; SVQ Level 2 in Security, Safety and Loss Prevention, Retail and Leisure Security and Transporting Property under Guard. NVQs/SVQs can be achieved by being assessed in the workplace although it may be necessary to attend short courses or study by distance learning for the background knowledge required for the City & Guilds examinations. There are also NVQs/SVQs Levels 2 and 3 in Security and Emergency Systems for those who move into this more technical work.

Security officers may also attend short courses on specialized aspects of the work, for example dog handling, closed circuit television (CCTV) control room operation, fire training and security surveying. Most security officers will receive training in first aid.

Those wanting to move into investigation, supervision or management can take NVQ/SVQ qualifications at Levels 3 and 4 as well as the International Institute of Security's Certificate in Security Management which can lead to Graduateship, Membership and Fellowship of the Institute.

For young people wanting to enter the industry, Modern Apprenticeships and National Traineeships are available in some areas. Opportunities may also be available under training schemes for adults. Information can be obtained from SITO, local careers offices, Jobcentres and TECs/LECs.

LATE ENTRY

Most security organizations want more mature applicants and the usual age for recruitment into this work is between 21 and 45 years although some companies recruit people from age 18 to over 60. There are good opportunities for ex-servicemen and women, police, prison officers and firefighters. There are no formal academic requirements for this work – see ENTRY REQUIREMENTS for details.

OPPORTUNITIES

This area of work is expanding by about 15% each year and employs about 200,000 people. Employers include industrial and commercial organizations, retail stores, property companies, central government, local government and contract security firms. Amongst the specialist security companies, there are a few large companies and many smaller ones. With large international security companies, there may be chances to work abroad.

PAY AND CONDITIONS

In contract security companies, security officers tend to earn between £200 and £300 a week. Shift allowances may be paid and overtime is common. Security officers working for in-house security teams may earn slightly more – often between about £250 and £350 a week (or possibly even more). Hours vary – most security officers work shifts. Some officers work permanently at night. Cash-in-transit operatives and some static security officers may work mainly during the day. Security officers in the contract side of the industry normally work between 50 and 60 hours a week. The in-house security officers tend to work a maximum of 40 hours.

PROSPECTS

Opportunities for promotion are usually better in large companies. Security officers can be promoted to supervisory posts, eg supervising a number of static security officers, visiting them to make sure that all is going smoothly and being on hand in case they have any problems they cannot deal with. There are also opportunities for promotion from supervisory posts to management.

RELATED OCCUPATIONS

Police constable, prison officer, store detective, safety officer.

FURTHER INFORMATION

British Security Industry Association, Security House, Barbourne Road, Worcester, WR1 1RS, 01905 21464

The Security Industry National Training Organization, Security House, Barbourne Road, Worcester WR1 1RS, 01905 20004

The International Professional Security Association, IPSA House, 3 Dendy Road, Paignton, Devon TQ4 5DB , 01803 554849

The International Institute of Security, Suite 8, The Business Centre, 57 Torquay Road, Paignton, Devon TQ3 3DT, 01803 663275

FURTHER READING

Working in Police and Emergency Services – COIC

In the careers library classified under MAG.

COASTGUARD: MAZ

COASTGUARD OFFICER CLCI:MAZ/YAL

BACKGROUND INFORMATION

Her Majesty's Coastguard is responsible for the co-ordination of all civil maritime rescue operations around the coastline of the UK and for 1,000 miles into the North Atlantic. The Coastguard Agency is a civilian, uniformed service and an executive agency of the Department of the Environment, Transport and the Regions.

HM Coastguard is organized in six Maritime Search and Rescue Regions (SRRs), each of which contains a number of districts. SRRs are the responsibility of regional controllers operating from Maritime Rescue Co-ordination Centres (MRCCs), and each district is controlled by a district controller working from a Maritime Rescue Sub-centre (MRSC).

Within each district, there are companies of auxiliary coastguards, who are volunteers but are under the management of coastguard sector officers.

Regular coastguards are civil servants and this article is concerned with their role and duties.

THE WORK

Coastguards in rescue centres keep a 24-hour radio watch on the international UVF distress frequencies and also deal with telephone, telex and facsimile messages through specially designed consoles.

Search and rescue

Coastguards co-ordinate all civil marine search-and-rescue operations and are responsible for radio monitoring, calling and co-ordinating emergency services, and leading and training rescue teams.

Radio monitoring: coastguards keep a close watch over the radio frequencies used by ships in distress.

Rescue co-ordination: on receipt of a distress message at the MRSC/MRCC, the coastguard decides on the action to be taken, requests assistance from the appropriate authorities and co-ordinates operations.

Coastguards may call on RNLI offshore and inshore lifeboats, fixed-wing aircraft and helicopters allocated by the Ministry of Defence, civil helicopters under contract, and coastguard equipment and teams. They may also request assistance from vessels in the vicinity of a ship in distress. They keep in constant radio contact with rescue services and pass on accurate information, ensuring messages, signals etc are dealt with promptly and that information is disseminated correctly.

Coastguards also alert and liaise with other interested bodies such as the police, fire brigades and harbour authorities.

Rescue team work: coastguards train and supervise auxiliary coastguards, and lead rescue teams of auxiliaries in cases of cliff rescue.

Channel Navigation Information Service (CNIS)

The HM Coastguard MRCC at Dover operates CNIS on behalf of the Department of the Environment, Transport and the Regions (DETR). They broadcast information for navigators regularly on VHF, and monitor vessels not complying with collision regulations. Unusually large ships and those carrying bulk liquid and gas cargoes must report to the coastguard and receive instruction on passing through the strait. CNIS is in constant contact with its French equivalent.

Reporting pollution

The coastguard is often first to hear about pollution incidents at sea because of its communication coverage. It is responsible for reporting incidents to the Marine Pollution Control Unit (MPCU), which is part of the Department of the Environment, Transport and the Regions (DETR).

Miscellaneous duties

Coastguards provide shipping and casualty information to the Marine Accidents Investigation Branch and Lloyd's of London. They also give safety-at-sea education and assistance to other government departments – such as Customs and Excise, and the Ministry of Defence – and report infringement of Merchant Shipping Acts.

Certain coastguard stations maintain a daily log of weather conditions, and may provide local meteorological offices with weather reports. Readings are collected of wind direction and speed, rainfall, pressure, humidity and hours of sunshine. This may involve taking straightforward readings from meteorological instruments, and some computation.

Coastguards also deal with press enquiries, may be asked to give talks or lectures to local clubs/other bodies on coastguard matters, give navigational information, answer general enquiries, and recommend safety equipment for use in small vessels.

WORK ENVIRONMENT

Most coastguards work solely in rescue centres, but a number work at sector offices where some patrol work at sea can be involved, using small boats in surf and moderate sea conditions. Coastguards work as part of a team in rescue centres.

For the majority of coastguards, most of the work is light and indoors, but for sector officers it may involve going out in all weathers. Rescue work can entail climbing, heavy lifting, pulling and carrying, and can demand a great deal of physical effort at times.

SKILLS AND INTERESTS

Coastguards must be self-reliant, and able to work well alone or in a team. They should be calm and reliable and able to maintain concentration throughout the shift. It is important that they can assess situations quickly, have good judgement and are able to make decisions. Coastguards must be prepared to take the lead and instruct auxiliary coastguards in the event of an emergency.

Coastguards spend much of their time communicating by telephone and radio; they should therefore be competent at handling communications equipment, and have good hearing and a good clear speaking voice. Physical fitness is important in order to carry out the strenuous activities that can be involved in rescue work.

ENTRY REQUIREMENTS

Applicants should:

– have at least six years' practical maritime experience *or* three years' practical search-and-rescue experience;

– hold at least three GCSEs/S grades (A–C/1–3), or equivalent, including English and maths;

– hold a full current UK driving licence;

– have good sight and hearing and pass a medical examination;

COASTGUARD: MAZ

– be prepared to work anywhere in the UK; and
– be a British subject or member of the Commonwealth.

TRAINING

Coastguards are employed as probationers for the first year of service. Most of the training is given on the job, with a seven-week training course at Coastguard Training Centre, Highcliffe, Dorset, after first appointment, and a further short course after nine months' service. After satisfactory completion of the probationary period and passing the proficiency examinations, a probationer becomes a watch officer. A second attempt to pass the test is permitted, but failure at this stage is usually followed by service being terminated.

Candidates must achieve satisfactory theoretical and practical knowledge of a variety of subjects. These include the organization of HM Coastguard, search-and-rescue principles and procedure, navigation and chart work.

LATE ENTRY

All applicants must have six years' previous maritime experience or three years' practical search-and-rescue experience. See ENTRY REQUIREMENTS for further details.

OPPORTUNITIES

HM Coastguard is organized by the Maritime and Coastguard Agency (MCA), an executive agency of the Department of the Environment, Transport and the Regions (DETR). There are around 500 regular coastguard officers, located around the British coastline. Coastguards must be prepared to work anywhere in the UK; it is possible to apply for transfer but applicants must usually have served at least three years at one station before a transfer will be considered. Some stations are in remote areas.

PAY AND CONDITIONS

Coastguard officers (probationer) are paid a scale of £9,774 plus £2,443 allowance. Coastguard officers (watch officer) start on a salary of £10,794 rising to £15,259 depending on performance, plus additional coastguard allowance of 25% of salary. Additional allowances may be payable to officers stationed in the Scottish Islands. Uniforms are provided.

Coastguard watch officers work on average a 42-hour week in 12-hour shifts.

PROSPECTS

A formal promotion structure exists, leading to the higher posts of watch and section manager, station officer and district officer.

Promotion is dependent on success in qualifying examinations. District officers may go on to achieve inspector grade through promotion via a selection board. Opportunities to progress are limited by the small number of higher-grade posts.

RELATED OCCUPATIONS

Air traffic controller, Merchant Navy officer, Royal Navy officer/rating, RAF officer/airman/airwoman, police constable, firefighter/fire officer, lifeboatman/woman.

FURTHER INFORMATION

The Maritime and Coastguard Agency*, Bay 1/18, Spring Place, 105 Commercial Road, Southampton SO15 1EG, 01703 329462

FURTHER READING

Leaflets/booklets are available from the address marked*.
Working in Police and Emergency Services - COIC
In the careers library classified under MAZ; YAL.

GROUP N – FINANCE AND RELATED WORK

1. **PRIVATE PRACTICE ACCOUNTANT CLCI:NAB**
2. **INDUSTRY AND COMMERCE ACCOUNTANT CLCI:NAB**
3. **PUBLIC SECTOR ACCOUNTANT CLCI:NAB**
4. **ACCOUNTING TECHNICIAN CLCI:NAB**

BACKGROUND INFORMATION

Accountants work in private practice, for local and central government, public organizations and in industry and commerce. They manage the financial affairs of individuals and organizations, giving advice on broad areas such as record-keeping, taxation, investments and other aspects of finance. Within industry and commerce, an increasing number are also becoming business advisers.

Although they work in a numerate environment, accountants must also be good communicators and be able to explain complex, financial information to qualified colleagues, as well as clients without financial training.

All accountants share common accountancy skills and broadly work in either of two overlapping areas: financial accounting or management accounting.

Financial accounting deals largely with recording and analysing financial information through the maintenance of accounting records. This information is used to provide reports for other areas of the business, and to meet legal requirements. The reports take the form of profit and loss accounts, budgets, and cashflow forecasts. Financial accountants also oversee the payroll, internal audits and stock control.

Management accounting is a more strategic role, and deals with the production and analysis of one-off reports which help with the running of the business and assist managers in making significant decisions on expenditure.

All accountants routinely use computers and calculators in their work.

Accounting is seen as a good stepping-stone to other careers in business and many of the top positions in companies are held by people with a background in finance. There are more than 100,000 accountants in the UK working in three areas: private (public) practice, industry and commerce, and public service.

1. PRIVATE PRACTICE ACCOUNTANT (NAB)

THE WORK

Private practice (sometimes known as public practice) accountancy firms range in size from two or three partners, to those with more than 100 employees. The bigger the practice the more diverse the workload, with the larger practices dealing with major companies, while smaller practices deal with individuals and small firms. When working with any size of business, however, accountants must solve real financial problems, as well as anticipating future ones.

All accountancy firms have a basic workload which includes the auditing of accounts and the preparation of statutory reports such as balance sheets and tax returns. They will also specialize in certain areas such as mergers and take-overs, and corporate finance. The main areas of work are:

Financial services: general tax advice, keeping daily records of the company's financial performance and advising on financial management. It also involves explaining complex financial and legal matters in a clear, straightforward way.

Audit: these can take a few hours or a few months, depending on the size and complexity of the business. Accountants check company accounts and present an analysis of the state of the organization's finances. They then give advice on the basis of their findings. Within larger commercial and industrial organizations, accountants investigate and review the operations and internal controls of the entire business. Audits allow shareholders, investors, suppliers and customers to gain an independent view of the performance and strength of a company.

Insolvency/Corporate recovery: involves evaluating the financial difficulties faced by troubled businesses and putting together suitable rescue packages. Sometimes a business cannot be saved and accountants may have to sell off the assets of the business, limiting the financial impact of the company's collapse.

Management consultancy: accountants can become actively involved as part of the management team, working on strategy, planning, budgeting and financial management.

Taxation: an expert knowledge can help to minimize a client's tax bill. Accountants will also negotiate with the tax office and advise clients on the tax implications of certain business deals.

Corporate finance: dealing at the highest level, accountants help to identify suitable companies for acquisition, evaluating their worth and negotiating the purchase on behalf of their client.

Information technology: advising clients on new accountancy software and appropriate systems for the company's use.

WORK ENVIRONMENT

Private practice accountants spend most of their time either in their own offices or in those of their clients. They will also attend meetings at banks and other financial institutions; the amount of time spent travelling will depend upon where their clients are based. This may mean some time spent away from home.

SKILLS AND INTERESTS

Private practice accountants need strong numerical skills, the ability to organize and analyse information, and a broad knowledge of all areas of accountancy. They manage their own workload and so must be reliable and responsible, and be able to produce accurate results under pressure and when working to tight deadlines. They need to be imaginative, with an enquiring mind which can produce alternatives, while tact, diplomacy and independence are also important, ensuring they are able to act with integrity and offer detached advice when dealing with confidential information.

In order to offer the best possible service, accountants need a working knowledge of the areas of business in which their clients operate and need to be up-to-date with current legislation and understand the implications of changes for their clients.

They need to be sociable and will meet a wide range of people with differing needs, from staff of large multinational companies to the self-employed. They must

ACCOUNTANCY: NAB

be effective communicators, both orally and in writing, and be able to explain difficult financial subjects in laymen's terms.

ENTRY REQUIREMENTS

Private practice accountants qualify by taking professional exams with the Institute(s) of Chartered Accountants (England and Wales, Ireland, Scotland), the Association of Chartered Certified Accountants (ACCA) and the Association of International Accountants (AIA). About 95% of the intake of the Institute(s) of Chartered Accountants, and 40% for ACCA, are graduates. There is a heavy demand for places on degree courses, with high passes in A levels/ H grades often required. Most universities offer courses in accountancy. GCSE English and maths are required, and some courses will specify A level maths too.

Minimum entry requirements to the Institutes are: five GCSEs/S grades (A–C/1–3), with English language and maths, and two A levels/three H grades, or equivalent; the Association of Accounting Technicians qualification; or a BTEC Higher National Diploma; or relevant NVQ/SVQ Level 4 qualification.

TRAINING

To qualify as a chartered accountant through the Institute of Chartered Accountants in **England and Wales** (ICAEW), entrants must secure a training contract with an organization authorized by the Institute. This is the most common route and takes a minimum of three years. In addition to practical work experience, the employer will also normally provide paid study leave. The length of the block release will depend on the type of pre-entry qualification held. Students take three sets of professional exams: Technical Core 1 (TC1) with six papers and Technical Core (TC2) with four papers plus a final admitting exam. Students are not usually allowed more than two attempts at the exams and must pass the final admitting exam within four years of the start of the last year of their training contract.

A Prospective Student route also exists that allows students to take the Institute's TC1 and TC2 exams without a training contract but the candidate must obtain a training contract before they take the final admitting exam. They will need to complete the training contact before they become members of the Institute.

An increasing number of training places are available with approved organizations in industry, commerce, and the public sector via The Training Outside Public Practice (TOPP) scheme.

For the Institute of Chartered Accountants of **Scotland** (ICAS), there are 13 exam subjects covered in three study levels: the Test of Professional Competence, the Test of Professional Skills and the Test of Professional Expertise. All candidates attend block release courses at ICAS training centres in Aberdeen, Birmingham, Edinburgh, Glasgow or London, and candidates can train in other European countries while still attending classes at a UK centre. Graduates with accountancy degrees may be exempt from some exams and should contact ICAS for full details.

The course at the Institute of Chartered Accountants in Ireland is split into four sections: Professional One, Two and Three, and the Final Admitting Exam. Graduates and members of the Institute of Accounting Technicians in Ireland (IATI), who have passed their technician exams with a credit, are exempt from Professional One. Study involves block release, home study, lectures and study weekends. Candidates also have to successfully complete a course in Information Technology.

For details of training with the AIA and ACCA please see article 2. INDUSTRY AND COMMERCE ACCOUNTANT.

All accountancy training is very demanding, and candidates need to be committed and self-disciplined.

LATE ENTRY

Although most candidates enter through one of the routes described above, opportunities do exist for mature candidates, and entry requirements may be relaxed for those with relevant financial or accounting experience. The AIA and ACCA have mature student entry routes. Please see article 2. INDUSTRY AND COMMERCE ACCOUNTANT.

OPPORTUNITIES

Typical employers range in size from small one-partner practices, to medium-sized firms with two or three partners which employ accountants and other staff, to huge international and national firms employing hundreds of staff. Jobs are available in most parts of the UK but mostly in cities and larger towns.

There are an estimated 113,000 chartered accountants in the UK and overseas but job availability is good with more and more people becoming self-employed and therefore needing the services of an accountant. Additionally, changes to the way tax is calculated and the introduction of Self Assessment has also led to an increase in the demand for accountants. Some of the bigger practices operate offices abroad.

Vacancies are advertised in the local and national press, and journals such as: *Accountancy Age, Accountancy, Accountant, Local Government Chronicle, Management Accounting,* and *Vacancies* and *PASS* magazines. The ICAEW and ICAS publish a comprehensive guide to training vacancies every year.

PAY AND CONDITIONS

Salaries start at around £8,500 for trainees in public practices, rising to up to £23,000 for graduates and newly qualified accountants. Salary will depend on the size and location of the practice, with higher salaries in London compared to the rest of the UK. Salaries will then rise with seniority and experience.

Accountants will typically work 9am to 5pm, Monday to Friday, and rarely at weekends but extra hours will be needed during busy periods such as year end.

Part-time work, flexible hours and job share may be possible after qualification and some practices may offer part-time training contracts.

PROSPECTS

Promotion depends upon experience and aptitude, and it can take up to ten years before a private practice accountant becomes a partner in a firm. Those who intend to set up in practice require a Practising Certificate which

ACCOUNTANCY: NAB

is awarded by the qualifying body to those with a minimum of two years' recent, relevant and practical experience.

As well as moving between practices, accountants also work directly for commercial companies and those who become experts in a particular field can command high salaries.

RELATED OCCUPATIONS

Actuary, insurance loss adjuster, economist, stockbroker, building society manager, local government service manager, health service manager, investment analyst, statistician, bank manager, operational researcher.

FURTHER INFORMATION AND READING

Please see article 4. ACCOUNTING TECHNICIAN

2. INDUSTRY AND COMMERCE ACCOUNTANT (NAB)

THE WORK

Accountants working in industry and commerce do so for one business rather than dealing with separate clients. Their work is divided into three broad areas, although often these overlap, and they will deal with most areas of accounting, except external audits.

Financial accountants deal with the day-to-day running of the business, ensuring that accurate financial records are kept and that efficient, computerized accounting systems are in place. They are directly involved in areas such as book-keeping, taxation, VAT payments, invoicing, wages, and generally managing the company's income and expenditure, including stocks and fixed assets.

They also liaise with other managers on financial aspects of the business, and using financial data and their knowledge of the company accounts, they produce reports, profit and loss accounts and financial forecasts which are used in the overall business planning process; and are responsible for negotiating loans and grants to finance major projects.

Management accountants are involved with statistical and financial management information and providing 'snapshots' of the company's trading position for other members of the management team. They have a major impact on company policy, putting the financial aspect of the business into a wider commercial context. They assess the value and contribution to profit of all aspects of the business and make recommendations to improve the company's financial returns. They monitor financial trends and evaluate future performance based on previous activity. They also establish, develop and maintain financial policies and management information systems.

Internal auditors mainly work within larger commercial and industrial organizations. They undertake internal audits, investigating and reviewing the efficiency and effectiveness of the operations and internal controls of the entire business. This may involve everything from financial procedures to stock control systems and staff working hours. Because of their reliance on computers, they will often require an expertise in information technology.

Accountants in these environments must be able to handle a complex workload and produce accurate information to meet tight deadlines.

WORK ENVIRONMENT

Work is largely office-based, whether within the company or attending meetings with other businesses. The amount of travel required will depend on the size of the business. Some will have offices in other areas of the country and some may have international offices, too.

SKILLS AND INTERESTS

Accountants need excellent numerical skills matched with a strong commercial awareness and knowledge of the company for whom they work. They need to be able to organize and analyse information and must be able to communicate effectively, conveying the necessary information clearly and succinctly, both orally and in writing. They need to be imaginative, with an enquiring mind that can produce alternatives, yet still be able to work under pressure and to deadlines.

Tact, diplomacy and independence are also important, ensuring they are able to act with integrity and offer detached advice when dealing with confidential information. Accountants need good interpersonal skills and must be able to deal with different sorts of people.

During training candidates must study whilst working, and can fulfil exam and training requirements separately for both the Association of Chartered Certified Accountants (ACCA), the Association of International Accountants or the Chartered Institute of Management Accountants (CIMA). This requires commitment, long hours, high levels of determination and application. IT and language skills may be useful.

ENTRY REQUIREMENTS

Industry and commerce accountants qualify by taking professional exams via ACCA, AIA or CIMA.

Entry to CIMA and ACCA professional qualification programmes is fiercely competitive and the usual minimum entry is with three GCSEs/S grades (A–C/1–3), with English language and maths, and two A levels/three H grades or equivalent such as Advanced GNVQ/GSVQ Level III in Business. Candidates with higher level qualifications will be exempt from some of the professional examinations.

TRAINING

There are a variety of ways to work towards the ACCA, AIA and CIMA qualifications, including full-time or part-time while in employment, by day release, evening classes, distance learning, correspondence, home study, or a combination.

ACCA – all students must complete three stages of exams comprising 14 papers: Foundation stage (four papers), Certificate stage (four papers) and Professional stage (six papers). ACCA training is competence based and students are required to demonstrate their competency in ten out of forty technical areas (which can be obtained in any employment sector), and their proficiency in five mandatory management competencies.

Entrants with the Association of Accounting Technicians (AAT) final examination, BTEC Higher National Certificate/Diploma in Business and Finance, or NVQ/SVQ in Accounting at Level 4 are exempt from the Foundation stage. Graduates with degrees in non-relevant subjects may obtain exemptions from papers 2 and 4;

ACCOUNTANCY: NAB

graduates with a more relevant qualification such as a degree in Accounting or Business and Management, may gain further exemption at the certificate stage. However, irrespective of exemptions, all entrants must complete three years' approved practical experience before, during or after the exams. Students are allowed ten years to complete the course, but in reality most achieve the qualification in three to four years.

AIA – examinations are at three levels, Foundation, Professional I and Professional II, testing theoretical knowledge and progressively its application to practical situations. As well as passing examinations, students complete three years approved practical training, acquired before during or after study, to achieve membership. Students are encouraged to gain experience in as many accountancy sectors as possible.

CIMA – the qualification takes about three years and has four separate stages, each with four exams. Candidates must also gain three years' practical experience, which is usually completed in a training post with an employer while studying for exams. Experience from any of the three fields of accounting is relevant and should cover the following areas: basic accounting, management accounting and financial management.

Candidates with the AAT exam, BTEC Higher National Certificate/Diploma in Business and Finance, SQA Higher National Certificate/Diploma in Accountancy, or graduates with a relevant degree (and non-relevant degree holders who have passed a graduate conversion course) may claim exemptions from certain papers in stages 1 to 3.

Contact the relevant body for full exemption details.

LATE ENTRY

There are no age restrictions for entry to either ACCA, AIA or CIMA.

ACCA – mature students (21 years and over) who lack the minimum qualifications can apply via the Mature Students Entry Route (MSER). Entrants are allowed four attempts at passing papers 1 and 3 of the Foundation Stage. If successful, they transfer to the ACCA main scheme register and continue with the remaining twelve exams. Work experience of accountancy is useful for mature entrants and can count towards ACCA's three-year experience requirement, provided it can be verified by an employer.

CIMA – mature students (25 years and over) who lack the minimum qualifications, but whose employers can confirm their experience of accountancy, may be accepted.

OPPORTUNITIES

Typical employers include all types and size of industrial, commercial and public sector organizations. Jobs are available in most areas but are most common in cities and larger towns. Demand for accountants is increasing across all sizes of organizations, particularly in financial services.

There is the possibility of some freelance work and some agencies do have project work. Some accountants become financial/management consultants, while some firms may offer openings for a business advisory role. Once qualified, ACCA and AIA members have the opportunity to obtain registered audit status and a practising certificate, and may then set up their own practice.

Vacancies are advertised in the local and national press, and journals such as: *Accountancy Age, Accountancy, Accounting & Business, PASS Magazine, Accountant, Local Government Chronicle* and *Management Accounting. Vacancies*, produced by ACCA three times a year, and CIMA's *Directory of Opportunities* are available free.

PAY AND CONDITIONS

Starting salaries range from between £12,000 to £18,000 for graduates (lower for A level candidates), although experience and seniority can bring salaries in excess of £50,000. Size and location of the business can also affect salary, with those in London receiving the highest pay. Accountants will typically work 9am to 5pm, Mondays to Fridays and rarely at weekends but extra hours will be needed during busy periods such as year end. Part-time work may be available with larger employers.

PROSPECTS

Promotion, particularly in larger organizations, will occur as candidates complete examinations. Project work may be used to gain expertise or a more strategic role in general management, and professional qualifications are essential to progression. Mobility can aid advancement as some larger employers encourage transfers within the company as part of an accountant's professional development.

The breadth of experience gained as a trainee ensures that senior management positions within industry are attainable. Many accountants move into other roles within business that are not purely financial such as general management, marketing or computer services.

RELATED OCCUPATIONS

Actuary, insurance loss adjuster, economist, stockbroker, bank/building society manager, local government service manager, health service manager, investment analyst, statistician, managemnt consultant, sole practitioner (for ACCA and AIA), operational researcher.

FURTHER INFORMATION AND READING

Please see article 4. ACCOUNTING TECHNICIAN

3. PUBLIC SECTOR ACCOUNTANT (NAB)

THE WORK

Public sector accountants are generally employed as financial managers for local authorities, state-owned industries, the National Health Service, in central government departments and other non-private bodies such as charities and housing associations.

Public services are constantly evolving as organizations that must cope with many different pressures both from the public and from central government. Subsequently, some public sector accountants have highly influential jobs, dealing with large budgets and with the responsibility for ensuring the public gets the best value for money.

Their work involves both financial and management accounting. They prepare budgets and final accounts, and expenditure and cash flow forecasts which help managers keep their departments within budget. They contribute to the planning and implementation of policy objectives and form an integral part of the management team, influencing decisions through their sound financial judgement. Public sector accountants also advise management boards and

ACCOUNTANCY: NAB

elected bodies.

The work also involves assessing the financial viability of a whole range of proposals that influence public services. The resources used to provide services are finite and accountants must find the correct balance between supply and demand. They must also understand and implement changes in legislation, while remaining accountable for their actions.

Working within the NHS requires many tough decisions about the allocation of resources that will directly affect people's lives. Accountants also work with organizations, such as health authorities and boards, that are responsible for purchasing supplies and services.

Working within local authorities means making funding decisions about schools, housing, and social services, and ensuring that departments allocate their budgets wisely. As a financial manager, accountants must ensure that the authority's elected politicians understand the importance of acting with financial integrity and of keeping accurate financial records which can be audited or scrutinized.

Public sector accountants also work for the four national audit bodies: the Audit Commission; The Accounts Commission; The National Audit Office; and The Northern Ireland Audit Office. They assess whether the public are getting the best quality, value for money and efficient public services, and investigate whether public sector organizations are spending money wisely. Accountants work as either technical advisers who specialize in an area of the public sector or in a field service role, making on-site visits across the breadth of public services and evaluating their effectiveness.

Opportunities exist to work within the private sector for major accountancy firms providing consultancy and training on aspects of public sector finance; or working for a private company delivering a 'contracted out' sector.

Other areas include working with one of the UK's 2,500 housing associations, which involves responsibility for the internal finance of the organization, budgeting and providing advice for the best use of funds for current and future projects.

In charities, an accountant's main concern is to minimize administration costs and so maximize the amount of help the charity can give.

Working in the regulated industries – such as water, gas and electricity – often means balancing profit generation and shareholder requirements with the need to provide a public utility that gives value for money.

Public sector accountants also work across the range of central government agencies and departmental bodies such as the Employment Service and Home Office. Like all other areas of the public sectors, resources are finite and so the role of the financial manager is critical in determining the implications of policies.

WORK ENVIRONMENT

Most work is carried out in an office but accountants will need to attend meetings. Travel can be frequent but it is uncommon to spend long periods away from home. There are few opportunities to travel abroad.

SKILLS AND INTERESTS

Public sector accountants need excellent numerical skills matched with a thorough knowledge of the role of the public sector and current legislation. They need to be able to organize and analyse information and must be able to communicate effectively, conveying the necessary information clearly and succinctly, both orally and in writing. They need to be imaginative, with an enquiring mind that can produce alternatives, yet still be able to work under pressure and to deadlines.

Tact, diplomacy and independence are also important, ensuring they are able to act with integrity and offer detached advice when dealing with confidential information. Accountants need good interpersonal skills and must be able to deal with different sorts of people.

ENTRY REQUIREMENTS

Public sector accountants may qualify by taking professional exams with the Chartered Institute of Public Finance and Accountancy (CIPFA), the Association of Chartered Certified Accountants (ACCA), the Association of International Accountants (AIA) or the Chartered Institute of Management Accountants (CIMA). Minimum entry is with three GCSEs/S grades (A–C/1–3), with English language and maths, and two A levels/three H grades; or Advanced GNVQ/GSVQ Level III; or NVQ/SVQ Level 3; or BTEC/SQA national certificate. Alternatively: the AAT Technician exam, ACCA Accounting Technician qualification; BTEC/SQA higher national certificate/diploma; or a degree. Otherwise candidates may need to undertake pre-entry study for the CIPFA foundation course.

Many accountants in the public sector hold other accountancy qualifications, particularly accountants of ACCA and CIMA. Please see articles 1. PRIVATE PRACTICE ACCOUNTANT and 2. INDUSTRY AND COMMERCE ACCOUNTANT for relevant training and entry details.

TRAINING

The CIPFA qualification combines both academic study and relevant hands-on experience and is usually undertaken in-sector. Study is part-time and combines open learning with opportunities for block/day release, evening classes and residential weekends. The course is split into four stages and covers all the main areas of public sector accounting including: financial accounting; management accounting; treasury management; auditing; information management and control; and management. The Foundation and first two Professional stages (P1 and P2) involve course work and exams. The third Professional stage (P3) involves a practical case study exam and a written project based on a work situation.

The course involves a minimum of 400 days' workplace experience and candidates must complete the course within six years, although most do so within three and a half.

Degree holders (relevant and non-relevant), those with the AAT exam and holders of the SQA Higher National Certificate/Diploma in Accounting are exempt from certain stages or papers. For full details of exemptions and other training, contact CIPFA

LATE ENTRY

CIPFA has two categories of entry for students with no formal qualifications, senior and mature entrants. Candidates over 21 years, who have at least three years' work experience and have the support of their employer, can undertake CIPFA studies as Mature Entrants starting

ACCOUNTANCY: NAB

at the Foundation stage.

Candidates over 25 years, with at least five years' relevant experience, can apply for Senior Entrant status and begin studying at the first Professional (P1) stage. This is a fast-track route that allows candidates to fit in work around their studies. Senior entrants are also exempt from the workplace training requirement.

OPPORTUNITIES

Jobs exist across the whole of the UK, and typical employers include local government, educational institutions, housing associations, charities, public utilities, national audit bodies and some large private sector organizations. More and more decisions about resource allocation are being taken at a local level, where the decision making process can be speeded up. These pressures mean that the demand for qualified accountants who understand the public sectors has never been greater.

CIPFA members who become partners in chartered firms are self-employed but normally there are very few opportunities for self employment.

Although not essential, experience of working in the public sector is beneficial. About 40% of accountants' jobs that are advertised do not specify the need for a degree but do require a professional accounting qualification.

Opportunities exist to work abroad with government departments, in British dependency states and with the Voluntary Service Overseas.

Vacancies are advertised in the local and national press, and journals such as: *Accountancy Age, Accountancy, Accounting & Business, PASS Magazine, Accountant, Local Government Chronicle, Management Accounting* and *Health Sector Journal*. CIPFA also produces a regular, free vacancy list.

PAY AND CONDITIONS

Starting salaries range from between £9,000 to £15,000, rising to £26,000 after three years. Experience and seniority, as well as the size and location of the organization also affects salary. Accountants typically work 9am to 5pm, Monday to Friday, and rarely at weekends but extra hours are needed during busy periods. After qualification part-time careers and job sharing opportunities are possible.

PROSPECTS

Career development is based on ability, and opportunities exist with a wide range of employers. Movement between the public and private sector is possible but competition is keen and the ability to show interests outside work, as well as other employment experience, is important.

Promotion structures vary with organizations but those who rise to senior positions, such as chief executive, usually have a financial background. The national audit bodies follow a set structure for career progression.

RELATED OCCUPATIONS

Actuary, insurance loss adjuster, economist, stockbroker, building society manager, local government sector manager, health service manager, investment analyst, statistician, bank manager, operational researcher.

FURTHER INFORMATION AND READING

Please see article 4. ACCOUNTING TECHNICIAN

4. ACCOUNTING TECHNICIAN (NAB)

THE WORK

Accounting technicians are the skilled staff who work alongside accountants in managing an organization's financial affairs. As well as working with accountants, some technicians carry out similar duties. They produce and analyse figures, keep day-to-day records of the company and deal with invoices, payments, tax returns and wages. As a result of this, experienced technicians can rise to positions of seniority and responsibility such as finance managers, assistant financial accountants or finance officers. Some are also in overall charge of the accounts, while others specialize, becoming payroll supervisors, credit controllers and audit seniors.

Their work is demanding and requires a solid grounding in the techniques of accountancy, as well as in wider business applications. Technicians have many accountancy skills that are common to financial and management accountancy, but the emphasis of their work differs according to the sector or organization in which they are employed.

Financial accounting involves recording sales and purchase transactions, carrying out internal audits of the accounting system and managing credit controls. Technicians also liaise with clients, ensuring they make their payments on time and do not exceed agreed credit limits, as well as ensuring invoices and payments are correct and sent out on time. They may deal with the payroll, calculating wages and salaries, and may oversee stock control.

As part of an audit team, accounting technicians monitor a company's accounting systems to ensure the accounts are being effectively and efficiently maintained.

They also play an important role in advising clients, often representing the company during one-to-one meetings when they may explain accounting techniques such as book-keeping methods, or gather information that will help the chartered accountant to give relevant financial advice.

Their role within management accounting involves collating and analysing financial and statistical information, and producing written reports for other managers in the company.

Computers and calculators are vital tools of the technician's work.

WORK ENVIRONMENT

Accounting technicians spend most of their time in the office, sitting at their desk. There will be some local travel, with the occasional visit to clients. If in auditing, they will often be required to visit clients' premises; if working with large industrial or commercial organizations, they may be seconded to subsidiaries.

SKILLS AND INTERESTS

Accounting technicians work with numbers all the time and so need strong numerical skills. They need to pay great attention to detail at all times and be able to produce accurate work, often to tight deadlines. They must also be able to organize and analyse information, and have a broad

ACCOUNTANCY: NAB

knowledge of all areas of accountancy.

A good commercial awareness and a working knowledge of the areas of business in which their clients operate is also important, as is an up-to-date knowledge of current legislation.

Technicians work as part of a team but must also be responsible enough to work without supervision. They need good written and spoken skills and must be able to communicate complicated information to professional colleagues as well as lay-people.

Technicians also need to be professional when meeting clients, hard working and have a good understanding of computerized accounting systems.

ENTRY REQUIREMENTS

There are two ways to qualify as an accounting technician: through the Association of Chartered Certified Accountants (ACCA) which offers the opportunity to qualify as a Certified Accounting Technician (CAT); or the Association of Accounting Technicians (AAT). Neither qualification requires formal entry requirements to register but entrants must be over 16 years old.

Entry may be possible for young people through Modern Apprenticeships leading to at least an NVQ/SVQ Level 3. Contact your local careers office, TEC/LEC for details.

TRAINING

To qualify as an accounting technician with AAT, candidates enrol in the AAT Education and Training Scheme, either on a two-year full-time or three-/four-year part-time course. These are provided by the AAT-approved colleges and private training organizations, while some AAT-approved employers offer in-house training schemes. The approved assessment centres will advise candidates on the best methods of study, be it by correspondence, day release or evening classes; full- or part-time. All routes lead to the award of NVQs/SVQs in Accounting at Levels 2, 3 and 4: the Foundation, Intermediate and Technician stages respectively.

The scheme is designed to be flexible and allow candidates to work at their own pace. There is no time limit to complete the course and those in full-time employment take, on average, a year to pass each stage. Students may also study for individual modules of each stage, as appropriate.

A number of exemptions apply: candidates with one A level (A-E)/H grade in Accounting, plus one other H grade (A-C); or two A levels (A-E) in academic subjects; or three H grades (A-C) in academic subjects; or an Advanced GNVQ in Business Studies; or a BTEC National Diploma in Business Studies (with accounting options); or an SQA Certificate in Business and Finance, are exempt from the Foundation stage. Candidates with a degree in Accounting can move directly to the Technician stage.

To achieve full membership of the AAT, allowing the use of the letters MATT, students must complete all stages of the scheme and have at least one year's approved work experience in accounting, gained during or after qualification.

The AAT Accelerated Learning Programme is for entrants wishing to follow a career in one of the many sectors of accounting. It is designed to give the student accounting knowledge and skills, enhanced career prospects and a basis for the AAT Technician Stage after one year's study. Completion of the AAT Education and Training Scheme means students can gain subject exemptions from a range of other professional qualifications.

To qualify through ACCA, there are nine examinations split into three levels, all designed to test the knowledge and understanding candidates will need to work in accounting support roles. Applicants can also link their exams to an NVQ in Accounting, and achieve both qualifications at the same time, or students can satisfy ACCA's experience requirements by working in an accounting support role and completing the Technician Training Record (TTR), which is based around NVQ competence at technician level.

There is no time limit to completing the qualification and entrants can qualify at their own pace. Candidates with qualifications above GCSE/S grade level may receive exemptions from some technician exams.

Many non-graduates use technician qualifications as a stepping stone to professional accountancy. Contact the AAT and ACCA for full details.

LATE ENTRY

There are no age restrictions and adult entrants can join either qualification route at any stage of their career.

The AAT also offers a mature entrant route for those 21 years and over, which recognizes relevant work experience gained prior to registration. Some students may also be eligible for Accreditation of Prior Learning (APL), when candidates gain credit towards the qualification for skills they have already demonstrated. For full details on both these programmes, contact the AAT.

OPPORTUNITIES

There is a steady demand for qualified accounting support staff in central and local government, health and public service industries, manufacturing, commerce (banks, building societies and insurance companies), as well as private practices. As with all accountancy jobs, they are available throughout the UK, although are concentrated in urban areas. There may be opportunities to work abroad. Further information about types of employer is available in the **OPPORTUNITIES** sections of articles 1, 2 and 3.

Additionally, changes to the way tax is calculated and the introduction of Self Assessment has also led to an increase in the demand for financial services. Some technicians are self-employed.

The AAT works with 30,000 employers world-wide, and has more than 90,000 members and students.

Vacancies are advertised in the local and national press, and journals such as: *Accountancy Age, Accountancy, Accountant, Accounting & Business, Local Government Chronicle, Management Accounting* and *Accountant Technician*.

PAY AND CONDITIONS

Salaries start at around £6,000–7,000 for trainee technicians, rising to up to £19,000 and above for fully qualified technicians. Salary will depend on the size and location of the practice, with higher salaries in London compared to the rest of the UK. Salaries rise with seniority and experience, and self-employed technicians can earn higher than average salaries.

ACCOUNTANCY: NAB

Accountants will typically work 9am–5pm Monday to Friday and rarely at weekends but extra hours may be needed during busy periods such as year end. Flexible hours may be possible with some employers and there are good opportunities for part-time and home-based work.

PROSPECTS

Career development is based on ability, and opportunities do exist with a wide range of employers because accounting technicians are skilled in a number of accounting areas. Promotion depends upon experience and aptitude. Movement between companies is common in order to gain specialization and/or promotion. Qualified and experienced accounting technicians can move up to senior management positions within organizations.

RELATED OCCUPATIONS

Taxation technician, accounts clerk, finance clerk, bank/building society officer/customer services assistant, insurance clerk, insurance broker, accountant.

FURTHER INFORMATION

The Association of Accounting Technicians*, 154 Clerkenwell Road, London EC1R 5AD, 0171 837 8600

The Association of International Accountants*, South Bank Building, Kingsway, Team Valley, Newcastle Upon Tyne, NE11 0JS, 0191 482 4409

The Association of Taxation Technicians*, 12 Upper Belgrave Street, London SW1X 8BB, 0171 235 2544

The Association of Chartered Certified Accountants*, Student Promotions, 29 Lincoln's Inn Fields. London WC2A 3EE, 0171 296 5800; Irish Branch*, 9 Leeson Park, Dublin 6, Eire, 00353 1 496 3144.

The Chartered Institute of Management Accountants*, 63 Portland Place, London W1N 4AB, 0171 637 2311.

The Chartered Institute of Public Finance Accountancy*, Recruitment Liaison Officer, 3 Robert Street, London WC2N 6BH, 0171 543 5678

The Institute of Chartered Accountants in England and Wales*, Student Recruitment and Promotion, Gloucester House, 399 Silbury Boulevard, Central Milton Keynes, MK9 2HL, 01908 248108

The Institute of Chartered Accountants in Ireland*, Student Recruitment, Chartered Accountants' House, 87-89 Pemroke Road, Dublin 4, Eire 00353 1 668 0400; and 11 Donegal Square South, Belfast, BT1 5JE Northern Ireland, 01232 321600

The Institute of Chartered Accountants in Scotland*, Student Recruitment, 27 Queen Street, Edinburgh EH2 1LA, 0131 225 5673

The Institute of Financial Accountants*, and The International Association of Bookkeepers, Burford House, 44 London Road, Sevenoaks, Kent TN13 1AS, 01732 458080

FURTHER READING

Leaflets/booklets available from the addresses marked*

Working in the Money Business – COIC

Careers in Accountancy – Kogan Page

Accountancy, Taxation and Financial Management – AGCAS Careers Information Booklet.

Classified under NAB in the careers library.

BANKING AND BUILDING SOCIETY WORK: NAD/NAF

1. **MANAGER CLCI: NAD/NAF**
2. **BANK OFFICER/CUSTOMER SERVICE ASSISTANT CLCI: NAD/NAF**

BACKGROUND INFORMATION

When banks were first invented, their main functions were to keep customers' money safe, pay interest to them on the amount deposited in their accounts and lend them sums of money, charging interest for this service.

Nowadays their role has broadened, particularly over the last 15 years. They also provide foreign exchange facilities and financial services, which include investment and insurance advice, mortgages, personal and business financial advice. They also act as executors and trustees. For each of these services they charge a fee or commission.

Many services are also offered by other financial services institutions such as insurance companies, building societies and even supermarkets. This means that banks are in a very competitive environment and their employees must be prepared to market services and meet targets.

There are four main types of bank:

Retail or high street banks look after the accounts of personal and business customers. The best-known names are the 'big four': Barclays, Lloyds TSB, Midland and National Westminster, together with the Clydesdale, the Co-operative Bank, the Bank of Scotland, the Royal Bank of Scotland and a number of former building societies such as Abbey National, Alliance and Leicester, Bristol and West, Halifax, Northern Rock and Woolwich. They have been joined by ones newly formed by supermarket chains and insurance companies. This sector is still growing since more building societies are intending to become retail banks.

The Bank of England is banker to the Government, providing advice to the Treasury, raising finance for the Government and issuing bank notes. It also acts as banker to all the other banks. All clearing banks have accounts there. It does not operate personal or business accounts.

Investment or merchant banks provide banking services to companies (corporate clients), to governments and to a small number of very wealthy individuals. In addition to the investment banks themselves there are investment banking divisions in many retail banks.

International banks have overseas branches or own banks in other countries. Most of the overseas banks in Britain are based in London, with some in other major cities. British banks have branches in different countries. In general, branches of international banks offer the services provided by the investment banks while some also offer the ones provided by the retail banks. They tend to recruit mainly local staff except at management level.

At management level staff are often seconded to work abroad for periods of varying lengths.

Building societies used to have two functions only. They took deposits from savers, paying them interest on their accounts and lent money in the form of mortgages to prospective property purchasers. They are now allowed by law to offer a much wider range of services and may now offer many of the same facilities as the retail banks: run cheque accounts, issue foreign currency, make personal loans, devise and sell financial products, provide financial planning etc. Some have also branched out into estate agency and insurance broking. A large amount of their work, however, is still concerned with their two original functions of providing mortgages and running savings schemes. Building societies do not usually have many business customers.

Building societies choose which services they will offer. Some provide almost the same range as the retail banks while others still do not offer current accounts. Some have chosen to concentrate on mortgage and savings work plus a small number of financial products like insurance provision or pension planning. On the whole, the societies that wish to provide most of the possible services have already become or are planning to convert to banks.

It is therefore not easy to define precisely the roles of building society managers and other staff. Much of the information in this chapter is common to careers in both retail banking and building societies, but some of the duties described under THE WORK are different.

1. MANAGER (NAD/NAF)

THE WORK

Retail banks and some building societies have management teams that may run one large branch or have additional responsibility for a number of smaller ones in the same area or for sub-branches that open for limited hours. The team is responsible for providing quality customer service, running the branches, managing and motivating staff and for marketing services and products. Branches are given targets by their regional head offices and are expected to achieve these by selling the range of services. There are many different grades of *manager* and the number of staff known by this title varies according to the size of the branch or to their job duties. In a small branch there may be only one manager while in larger ones there are more: for example, an administration manager who deals with the day-to-day running of the branch and staff training and assessment; a lending account manager, who supervises the work of the lending team and makes sure that all loans are repaid; and, in overall charge, the branch manager.

The branch manager has overall responsibility for staff training and for encouraging all staff to reach sales targets. They also deal with any complaints.

All managers need to know their area well, the type of customers they have and what their requirements are. They must be familiar with all the services and *products* – the word used to describe savings schemes, insurance policies etc. A good deal of their time is taken up in interviewing customers to offer advice or to decide whether to agree their requests for loans or overdrafts. Individual managers who deal with requests for loans usually have a maximum sum they are allowed to lend. Above this limit they must refer to a senior manager or, where large sums are concerned, to the bank's regional office.

Managers spend a proportion of their time visiting existing and potential customers, to promote the bank's products and generate new business. They also establish links with professionals such as accountants, estate agents and solicitors who may encourage clients to come their way.

Some employees known as managers do not work in branches or deal with day-to-day banking work. In regional and head offices the term may describe a level of seniority in specialist functions that are also conducted in other businesses like marketing, personnel and training. Other managers specialize in investment, taxation, corporate finance (particularly in investment banks) or

BANKING AND BUILDING SOCIETY WORK: NAD/NAF

trust work, which involves administering the estate of a person who has died and left money and property to be invested on behalf of another person named in their will. They may advise branch managers required to take important decisions, or have clients referred to them for detailed advice. Some managerial-level staff work as inspectors (now often known as auditors), visiting and assessing the work of branches.

In the Bank of England, employees who would be described as managers in other banks are Officials who hold managerial responsibility or who work in high-level economic research.

WORK ENVIRONMENT

Some senior branch managers or those who work in large branches have their own offices. Other managers often work in an open-plan office, but may take customers to interview rooms to discuss confidential matters. Some banks prefer to have open-plan offices for all their staff and even the manager in charge works in one.

Some managers spend up to half their time out of the branch visiting business customers at their premises, where they can assess how the business is being run. All branch managers of both retail banks and building societies are usually expected to be active members of local business and community organizations and to attend evening meetings.

Specialist managers are usually based in regional or head offices.

SKILLS AND INTERESTS

All managers need general management skills. They must to be able to lead and motivate their staff, to arrange for them to attend appropriate training courses and to recommend suitable staff for promotion. They conduct annual appraisals of the staff who work directly for them.

They need good communication skills, both verbal and written, for dealing with their own staff and with customers. They need to be able to form accurate judgements, negotiate and take decisions.

Numeracy is important.

They must be willing to work in what is increasingly a sales-orientated environment.

Managers must also be honest and demonstrate integrity in their dealings with customers and staff.

They also need technical knowledge, ie they must have a thorough understanding of banking procedures, services and products.

ENTRY REQUIREMENTS

There are generally speaking, three levels of entry to management work. It is possible to enter in a junior grade with GCSEs and gain promotion to management level, although most such entrants might more realistically hope to reach supervisory level. For entry qualifications to this level please see article 2. BANK OFFICER/CUSTOMER SERVICE ASSISTANT.

Others enter with A levels (or equivalent) and could expect to reach junior management level posts or above.

The majority of senior managers now join initially as graduate trainees on fast-track programmes that are designed to give them experience of most of the jobs done in branches and some at head or regional offices (please see article 2. BANK OFFICER/CUSTOMER SERVICE ASSISTANT) and help them to reach managerial level in a shortened period of time, provided that their work is suitable.

Investment banks normally recruit entrants with degrees for their management training programmes, as does the Bank of England.

Most banks and building societies accept any degree subject, although banking, business studies, law and economics are particularly relevant. Degrees particularly relevant to banking are offered at some universities: Bangor (Banking, Insurance and Finance), Birmingham, Middlesex (Money, Banking and Finance), University of Wales Cardiff, Loughborough, Ulster (Banking and Finance), City (Banking and International Finance), Greenwich (Economics with Banking), Reading (International Securities, Investment and Banking). London Guildhall's Business Studies degree offers specialization in Banking or Corporate Finance.

Great stress is laid on the personal qualities and skills outlined above.

Some graduates with relevant degrees enter as specialist managers.

The Bank of England's specialist economists must all have at least a postgraduate degree in economics.

TRAINING

Most retail banks and some building societies run two kinds of accelerated management training programmes: one for applicants with A levels/H grades or Advanced GNVQs/GSVQs Level III; the other for graduates. Training is a combination of on-the-job training, attending courses at residential training centres and study for Chartered Institute of Bankers' (CIB) qualifications. Practical experience is normally gained by working briefly in most of the jobs in the bank or building society. This is normally done in several different branches. Trainees must be willing to be mobile. The length of scheme varies with different employers. Graduates, however, are normally expected to pass the Institute's examinations within three years. Some banking programmes include all aspects of a bank's work – domestic, corporate and foreign, while some have separate programmes for those who wish to work in UK banking alone.

To become a manager in either retail banks or building societies, it is usually necessary to have passed the examinations leading to Associateship of the Chartered Institute of Bankers (CIB) or the Chartered Institute of Bankers in Scotland. The Associateship of the Chartered Institute of Bankers (England and Wales) is linked to a BSc (Hons) Financial Services degree. The examinations consist of compulsory papers in: law and practice; the monetary and financial system; management and organization; and financial reporting, analysis and planning; plus a further four papers chosen from a range of options such as: administration of trusts; investment; international trade finance; branch banking, law and practice; corporate banking, practice and law; law and practice for mortgage lenders; retailing of financial services; taxation; and insurance.

In England and Wales, candidates must follow an approved course of study based on tuition material provided by the Institute in partnership with the University of Manchester Institute of Science and Technology. Courses are offered

BANKING AND BUILDING SOCIETY WORK: NAD/NAF

through a network of academic centres in England and Wales. Courses may include lectures, group-work, tutorials, distance learning and revision seminars. Candidates have a maximum of six years in which to complete the associateship. On successful completion they are also awarded the BSc degree in Financial Services.

The Chartered Institute of Bankers in Scotland offers training for associateship via distance learning. This may be followed by its higher level membership course which is taken on block release at a university over 16 weeks.

Staff who join as bank officers/customer service assistants may also study for CIB qualifications via the Banking Certificate as they progress through a bank. Please see article 2. BANK OFFICER/CUSTOMER SERVICE ASSISTANT.

The Bank of England has a training scheme for graduate entrants known as the Trainee Officials Programme. Any academic degree subject is acceptable. In addition the Bank sponsors a small number of economics graduates through MSc courses in Economics before they join.

Investment banks run their own training programmes which are much shorter than those in other banks. They have their own training departments and also make use of external training centres. Some encourage their staff to take CIB examinations and give them financial support – and sometimes limited time off – to study for these and other relevant professional qualifications.

LATE ENTRY

There is no maximum age limit for entry to banking. Applicants over 30 years old, however, are unlikely to be recruited direct to management training programmes – with the exception of people who may have had previous banking experience – for instance women who took a break from bank officer work to have a family.

OPPORTUNITIES

The retail banks' total intake of graduate management trainees is about 700 each year. This has declined from over 1,000 a few years ago. Most are recruited for national schemes, on which they are expected to work anywhere in the UK, but some banks have separate regional programmes for graduates who wish to restrict their careers to working in one geographical area. Figures for A level/equivalent entry vary and are difficult to calculate since recruitment is done at regional or branch level.

There are between 13,500 and 14,000 branches. Despite the closure of some branches with the increase of telephone banking, the overall number is still rising due to the numbers of converting building societies which have a strong branch structure.

The head offices of many retail banks are in London. They also have a network of regional offices. Few building societies' head offices are in London. The majority are in the North and Midlands.

Investment banks recruit in much smaller numbers – about 100 to 150 graduate trainees in total annually.

PAY AND CONDITIONS

Managers' salaries depend on the size of the branch and/or their level of responsibility. Newly appointed managers could expect to earn approximately £24,000, while a very senior manager could earn over £70,000. They may also receive performance-related bonuses, which now form an important part of the overall salary package, if branch targets are met. Additional allowances are paid to managers working in the London area.

Managers also receive benefits in the form of reduced rate mortgages and other loans, pension and insurance schemes. They may also receive company cars, particularly if their work involves travel outside the branch to visit customers.

Working hours are officially 9am to 5pm Monday to Friday plus some Saturdays, worked on a rota basis. Most managers work much longer hours and may have to arrange early morning or evening meetings to suit customers' convenience. They receive around 30 days annual holiday.

PROSPECTS

Promotion is strictly on merit and managers have regular appraisals. The first appointment as a manager is either to branch manager of a small branch with no more than ten staff, or to manager of a department within a larger branch, or to a specialist head or regional office position. They may eventually be responsible for over 200 staff, or head a specialist department.

Career development depends on ability and on the degree of mobility of a manager – ie the amount of relocation they are willing to undertake. The best prospects are for those who are willing to move frequently when promotion is offered.

A career in investment banking or in the Bank of England is spent mainly in London with openings in some other cities.

RELATED OCCUPATIONS

Accountant, retail manager, insurance underwriter, insurance broker, financial services consultant, bank officer.

FURTHER INFORMATION AND READING

Please see article 2. BANK OFFICER/CUSTOMER SERVICE ASSISTANT.

2. BANK OFFICER/CUSTOMER SERVICE ASSISTANT (NAD/NAF)

THE WORK

The term bank officer is used to describe bank employees below management grade (formerly known as bank clerks). In retail banks, bank officers do a variety of different jobs which are graded according to difficulty and responsibility. Some banks still use the terms grade 1 officer to grade 5 officer; others use specialized job titles.

Some bank officers work in a branch office on the administration of customers' accounts, while others work in the banking hall, where they have direct contact with customers. In a small branch, one person may combine several duties; in larger ones jobs are specialized.

Some now work in regional processing centres or telephone centres as opposed to branches, and do not see customers face to face.

Bank officers have different roles with different levels of seniority. As they gain experience, they may be promoted to higher grades. They may spend considerable time in each one before moving on.

BANKING AND BUILDING SOCIETY WORK: NAD/NAF

Grade 1 or processing officers feed information on customers' accounts into computer terminals, answer telephone enquiries and process the cheques paid into the branch each day. They may deal with accounts held at several branches. This is the level of work most likely to be done from an area or regional centre – or to be done in the processing room of one large branch which also handles processing work for several of the bank's smaller branches in the same locality.

Processing the cheques and credits paid into customers' accounts is done by passing the cheque through an encoding machine which enters the amount written on it. The computer sorts the cheque and credits customers with the correct withdrawals and deposits. Processing officers have to check, at the end of each day, that the total amount shown on the computer balances with the cheques paid in.

Grade 2 officers usually meet customers and, in some banks, these officers are known as customer service officers. They may work on the counter as cashiers, paying money into and out of accounts; or as personal banking advisers, opening and closing accounts and dealing with enquiries. They are expected to suggest use of the bank's financial services and products to customers. Another job is that of standing order officer, arranging for regular payments to be made from customers' accounts for items such as mortgages or bills. This job corresponds to the job of cashier or customer service assistant in most building societies.

Grade 3, 4 and 5 officers do more complicated work. This varies in different banks. Some work in a branch's foreign section, where they issue foreign currency and travellers' cheques and help customers with business overseas to settle their invoices and arrange insurance. Others arrange for customers to purchase or sell stocks and shares or advise on insurance policies. At this stage, officers are often supervisors, responsible for the work and training of junior staff in the processing office, or in one section of the branch.

They also do more technical banking duties. They may work as loans officers with authority to lend customers sums up to a certain amount. They undertake more complicated investment and advisory work and, at grade 4 or 5 level, often work as assistants to one of the managers. Managers' assistants write letters to customers, analyse balance sheets, prepare reports for managers, frequently interview customers and agree loans and overdrafts. They work closely with the management team and, at this level, are gaining management experience.

WORK ENVIRONMENT

Most retail bank officers are based in branches, which may have from ten to over 200 members of staff. In some banks, processing officers work together in the branch processing area. Other banks have removed all processing functions to regional processing centres, which are staffed by processing and customer service staff.

Most bank officers at grade 2 and above work in the part of the branch that is open to customers as do building society customer service assistants. In larger bank branches this is known as the banking hall. Cashiers and some officers who handle enquiries work behind counters. In some branches, cashiers sit behind security glass. Some banks and building societies, however, have introduced counter areas with no protective glass. Staff are given certain protective devices and procedures that they can follow in an emergency – eg panic buttons or rising screens.

Bank officers who advise customers often have their own desks in the open-plan banking hall. They are normally able to move to private interviewing rooms if they sense that a customer does not wish to discuss business in an open area.

Some banks offer a total telephone banking service to customers. Bank officers working in such banks respond to requests from, and advise, customers by phone rather than face to face.

SKILLS AND INTERESTS

Bank officers/customer service assistants must enjoy providing a service to customers. They must be accurate and pay great attention to detail, even when they are under pressure because several customers are waiting for attention or if a particular customer is in a hurry.

They must be honest. Tact is often required when dealing with customers and they must always respect confidentiality.

Bank officers/customer service assistants should enjoy working in what is increasingly a sales-orientated environment and must also have sufficient knowledge of the bank's products to be able to advise customers on them. Those working in the higher grades also need further technical knowledge and understanding of banking procedures and services.

ENTRY REQUIREMENTS

Although there are no minimum entry requirements, some banks and building societies require a minimum of two to four GCSEs/S grades (A–C/1–3), normally including English and maths. Some training programmes for young people are also run. However, many banks recruit at well above the minimum, often preferring holders of A levels/H grades or Advanced GNVQs/GSVQs Level III.

The Bank of England recruits junior clerical staff with GCSE/S grades (A–C/1–3) or equivalent, including maths and English, and senior clerical staff with at least two academic A levels/H grades, or equivalent qualifications in addition.

Modern Apprenticeships may be available for young people leading to at least an NVQ/SVQ Level 3. Contact your local careers office, Jobcentre, TEC/LEC for details.

TRAINING

Bank officers/customer service assistants learn their work on the job from more experienced staff and supervisors. They may also attend short courses at banks/building societies' residential training centres.

If they wish, they may study for the examinations of the Chartered Institute of Bankers (CIB) or Chartered Institute of Bankers in Scotland (CIBS). These are not compulsory but are almost essential for promotion. The first stage is the Certificate in Financial Services Practice which is aimed at anyone whose job involves customer contact. This is followed by the Banking Certificate for employees aiming at supervisory or junior management work. Six compulsory subjects are studied: economics and the bank's role in the economy; introduction to accounting; banking: the legal environment; business operations – UK lending and international business; customer services – marketing and the competitive environment; and supervisory skills.

BANKING AND BUILDING SOCIETY WORK: NAD/NAF

Specialist CIB/CIBS qualifications are also available in areas such as financial advice, mortgage advice and practice, and professional investment advice for staff wishing to improve their knowledge in these areas.

NVQ/SVQs are available at Levels 2, 3 and 4 in banking and building society work.

Please see article 1. MANAGER for further training details.

All new entrants to the **Bank of England** receive extensive on-the-job training delivered in the workplace and at the Bank's own training centre. Staff may also be nominated to join the Trainee Official Programme (TOP) at any stage of their career, but will normally have worked in the Bank for at least four years and competition is tough.

LATE ENTRY

It is possible to enter banking/building society work as an adult, particularly for work in a bank's regional processing centre. Retail banks now recruit many more older applicants, although promotion prospects are likely to be limited, due to the length of time required to work through the grades and take examinations. The majority of entrants are still aged 18 to 25 years.

OPPORTUNITIES

There are between 13,500 and 14,000 branches of retail banks where bank officers may work. The number of branches is increasing, but this does not mean that there are more job opportunities since the increase includes branches of former building societies. The number of bank officer jobs at grade 1 level has declined sharply with the introduction of new technology and in particular, of the introduction of automatic cash machines. Most banks have closed branches. However, there are some new opportunities to work at cashier level in telephone banking centres. (All banks now offer a telephone banking service of some kind, and this area may well expand.) There are opportunities for career breaks, job sharing and part-time employment. Some retail banks now offer short-term contracts of two to three years.

The number of jobs open in investment banks to entrants below degree level has also declined.

Building societies employ about 44,000 staff, of whom around 20,000 work in branches. The number has reduced over the last few years because, following conversion by several former societies, they are now employed by banks.

The head offices of many retail banks are in London. They also have a network of regional offices. Few building societies' head offices are in London. The majority are in the North and Midlands.

PAY AND CONDITIONS

Salaries vary with different employers but bank officers/customer service assistants are paid on salary scales from approximately £6,000 (£7,000–8,000 for an A level entrant) to approximately £15,000 depending on their seniority. They receive benefits such as cheap loans and mortgages and may receive profit-related pay if the bank meets sales targets.

Hours are usually 9am to 5pm, Monday to Friday, but may vary. If the computer records and till balances do not match at the end of the day some employees have to stay on to find the mistake. At busy times some overtime working may be required.

Many branches now open on Saturdays. Staff are expected to work on these days and are paid extra for doing so. Sufficient volunteers may be found; otherwise weekend work is done on a rota basis.

Some telephone banking services operate on a 24-hour basis. Shift work is therefore required.

Flexible hours are very common.

PROSPECTS

Bank officers/customer service assistants may progress through the grades to reach higher positions. Promotion prospects vary, however, according to the movement of staff in the higher grades and the number of staff who may leave. Bank officers/customer service assistants may be qualified and ready for promotion only to find that they have to wait a considerable time for a vacancy in the next grade to arise. It can help to be willing to move to other branches.

All promotion comes on merit and on consideration of officers' annual appraisals. Bank officers/customer service assistants can increase their prospects by taking professional examinations.

Those hoping to reach senior supervisory grades normally take the CIB certificate examinations, while those who hope to become managers study for the associateship. Please see article 1. MANAGER.

RELATED OCCUPATIONS

Accounting technician, post office counter clerk, bank/building society manager.

FURTHER INFORMATION

Local branches and regional offices of retail banks.

The Building Societies Association, 3 Savile Row, London W1X 1AF, 0171 437 0655

The Chartered Institute of Bankers*, Emmanuel House, Canterbury Kent CT1 2XJ, 01227 762600 (for information on banking examinations only)

The Chartered Institute of Bankers in Scotland*, 19 Rutland Square, Edinburgh EH1 2DE, 0131 229 9869

London Investment Banking Association*, 6 Frederick's Place, London EC2R 8BT, 0171 796 3606

The Bank of England*, Schools Liaison Officer, Threadneedle Street, London EC2R 8AH

FURTHER READING

Leaflets/booklets are available from the addresses marked*

Working in the Money Business - COIC

Careers in Banking and Finance - Kogan Page

In the careers library under NAD/NAF.

INSURANCE WORK: NAG

1. **INSURANCE UNDERWRITER CLCI:NAG**
2. **INSURANCE BROKER CLCI:NAG**
3. **FINANCIAL ADVISER CLCI: NAG/NAK**
4. **INSURANCE CLAIMS OFFICIAL CLC:NAG**
5. **INSURANCE CLERK CLC:NAG**
6. **INSURANCE SURVEYOR CLC:NAG**
7. **INSURANCE LOSS ADJUSTER CLC:NAG**
8. **RISK MANAGER CLCN:NAG**

BACKGROUND INFORMATION

Insurance provides financial protection against loss and misfortune for individuals, their families, the business community and other organizations. Insurance policies are taken out by people to protect their homes, their possessions and their life styles, they need to know that if their possessions suffer damage or are stolen then they will be compensated. Individuals and businesses also take out insurance against incidents occurring to people and property. They may wish to insure against premature death, ill health, permanent injury or unemployment. Sometimes this is required in law as is the case with motor insurance or employer's liability for accidents to employees.

Insurance works on the principle that large numbers of people pay sums of money into a common fund but a smaller number will need to draw money out when the risk occurs that has been insured against.

Insurance brokers and financial advisers advise clients. Underwriters will negotiate the premium the client will have to pay and the detailed terms of the policy. Insurance surveyors provide reports on factors that may influence the degree of risk. Claims officials supported by clerks will process any claim and determine whether the claim is covered by the policy and if so, how much should be paid. When large claims are made loss adjusters may perform this task.

Insurance companies also employ actuaries to assess and minimize risk and uncertainties. Many commercial companies employ risk managers to identify areas of risk in the company's business and to work out ways of reducing those risks in order to reduce the cost of insurance cover.

There are seven main classes of insurance: aviation, marine, motor, liability, property, life and pensions. There are three areas of specialism: life, general insurance and reinsurance. Life is about insuring people against premature death or permanent injury and providing for the financial needs of individuals through changing circumstances. General insurance divides into two sections. Personal insurance deals mainly in motor, household insurance and cover against accidents. This represents about half of all insurance in Britain. Commercial insurance provides companies and employees with a whole range of insurance from damage to premises to protection if the company is proved to have caused loss or suffering. Reinsurance occurs when insurers spread the risk by taking out insurance against claims.

Insurance is a major industry employing over 350,000 people (source CII) in Britain. Employees work for insurance companies that may deal with one aspect of insurance like motor insurance or a whole range like motor, life and property. They vary in size from small privately owned companies to multi-branch, stock exchange listed companies operating in Britain and internationally. Employees also work for brokers who act as intermediaries between clients and the insurers. Brokerage companies may also specialize and vary considerably in size.

Lloyd's is an insurance market where 200 firms of brokers arrange insurance for their clients. They bring business from all over the world representing insurance and reinsurance of every kind. Underwriters at Lloyd's accept risks on behalf of syndicates (groups of individuals called names and corporate members). Lloyd's syndicates often specialize in covering large-scale risk like spacecraft, oil rigs and natural disasters.

1. INSURANCE UNDERWRITER (NAG)

THE WORK

Underwriters issue policies to meet customers' insurance needs. They understand and measure the risks associated with business and social activities and negotiate the premiums and terms of policies.

Underwriters receive a proposal or proposition from a broker or a client. They cannot take the information on the form at face value and they study it carefully and assess all the facts. They may have to ring a doctor to check medical history or check statistics on burglary rates or car thefts in a certain town or neighbourhood.

If the risk is considered straightforward then the premium will be a standard rate that underwriters calculate using computer software, a calculator or books of tables. They provide a quotation and, if that is acceptable, issue a standard policy immediately in line with company guidelines. If there are unusual circumstances that represent a higher risk than usual the underwriter may adjust the premiums or add special terms and conditions. If the request is for house content insurance in an area with a high burglary rate the client may be asked to install an industry standard burglar alarm.

Policies written by underwriters must clearly define the liabilities that have been accepted and any exceptions or exclusions must be fully explained to the broker or client.

Some risks are not standard and underwriters will tailor a unique policy to meet a client's special needs. A film company may wish to insure a famous actor's life when embarking on a multi-million pound film production or a pharmaceutical company may wish to insure for claims against them when they launch a new drug.

Underwriters sometimes need more detailed information than is contained in a proposal form and may ask an insurance surveyor to prepare a detailed report to help them assess the degree of risk. They will also use other information like statistical information on life expectancy and market analysis of a company's products produced by other professionals like actuaries and risk managers.

Underwriters sometimes decide that a risk is too great and they will not accept it or they may spread the risk among different insurers by reinsuring it. They choose appropriate insurers or specialist reinsurance companies and negotiate the terms of a reinsurance contract.

In cases of very large risk sometimes underwriters decide to share it with other insurers and and may only accept a percentage of the full risk. This is particularly true at Lloyd's where underwriters usually only accept a tiny percent of one risk and brokers have to approach a large number of underwriters to put together a contract for their client.

Most underwriters specialize in one type of insurance.

WORK ENVIRONMENT

Insurance underwriters are based in offices where they work with teams of other underwriters and supporting clerks and other professionals like actuaries. They may travel to attend meetings with clients and brokers at their own premises. They may also occasionally be required to travel abroad for short periods.

SKILLS AND INTERESTS

Underwriters need thorough expert knowledge of factors that are likely to be involved in the class of insurance they are dealing with. They must keep abreast of industrial, technological and business developments as well as changes in the law and taxation in the UK and throughout the world.

They need to be clear thinkers with analytical minds and able to absorb complicated information. They should be numerate with good written and communication skills; everything they say and write must be clear and understandable and capable of withstanding scrutiny from others. They have to collect information from clients and negotiate with them.

They should be confident, decisive and prudent. Any mistake could cost their company millions of pounds. They must pay attention to detail and learn when they can act alone and when they need the support of experts.

Underwriters working in Lloyd's work face to face with brokers and need to cope with a cut and thrust environment. They must be assertive and quick-witted.

Underwriters deal with confidential information and must be discrete and mindful of ethical issues like freedom of information

Computers are used extensively by underwriters.

Since the introduction of the 'European Market' many underwriters are required to speak one or more European languages. For those wishing to work for international companies an Asian language may be useful

ENTRY REQUIREMENTS

Most insurance companies expect entrants to have the background necessary for entry to the professional examinations of the Chartered Insurance Institute (CII). These are :

– two A levels/four H grades, plus two GCSEs (A–C)or S grades (1–3) including English;

– Advanced GNVQ/GSVQ level III;

– a BTEC/SQA national qualification;

– a pass in Certificate of Insurance Practice (CIP) (a CII qualification at technician level);

– a pass in the Financial Planning Certificate (FPC) (held by qualified financial advisers).

Although it is not essential to register as a student member and take CII examinations most companies will only promote those who do. It is essential for those who wish to work as Lloyd's underwriters to have associate membership of the CII.

Many new entrants are graduates and whilst any degree is acceptable some degrees in risk management, insurance or with financial or insurance options are preferred. A list of insurance related degrees is available from CII.

Entrants who do not have appropriate qualifications may start as clerks and be promoted to trainee underwriters. Please see article 5. INSURANCE CLERK.

TRAINING

Training varies from company to company and depends on a trainee's background and previous experience. Most companies have a systematic programme that includes study for appropriate CII examinations.

Most start with an induction course introducing entrants to the insurance business and their company methods. They then receive on the job training in a department. This is usually under the supervision of an experienced underwriter and will involve doing routine clerical work to familiarize the trainees with systems before moving on to issuing standard policies and dealing with enquiries.

As trainee underwriters become competent they will be assigned their own case-load and allowed to issue policies up to a given sum. They will then specialize and undertake more complex work.

Larger companies run training schemes for graduates and A level/H grade students wishing to enter the insurance industry; these cover all aspects of the industry including underwriting and allow the trainee to spend time in a number of different sections before specializing.

Insurance companies emphasize continued professional development (CPD) and encourage trainees to attend appropriate courses which are often linked to NVQ/SVQ qualifications in such topics as customer care and the Diploma in Life and Disability.

Underwriters are usually expected to study for the associateship examinations of the CII (ACII) which takes three years or more. They may be given time off work to attend college or may study at evening classes or by distance learning. Correspondence and computer-based learning packages are available. Many employers allow study leave before examinations take place.

Examination consists of three core subjects in:

– risk and insurance;

– company and contract law and their application to insurance;

– the business environment.

A further six units are chosen from a wide range which allows trainees to concentrate on their chosen specialism. A final paper must be taken on a management subject chosen from:

– principles and practice of management in insurance;

– accounting principles and practice for managers in insurance;

– either of the above with specific reference to working at Lloyd's.

LATE ENTRY

There is no official maximum age for entry to the career of underwriter. Some people aged over 30 years may gain entry if they are promoted from a related technical field within an insurance company. Sometimes people with relevant financial or business experience may be accepted. Mostly trainees are recruited directly on to training schemes when they leave school or university.

INSURANCE WORK: NAG

OPPORTUNITIES

There are over 500 insurance companies in Britain. Insurance underwriters work for specialist insurance companies and those providing a wide range of insurance cover. They may also work for syndicates at Lloyd's.

Underwriters who can speak languages, particularly European languages, are increasingly in demand to work for British companies at home and abroad.

PAY AND CONDITIONS

Trainees with A levels/H grades could expect a starting salary of around £7,250 to £10,500. Graduates could expect between £12,000 and £15,000. Many companies link graduates' pay rises to progress in CII exams with additional increments as each stage is passed.

Salaries for experienced underwriters depend on performance and responsibility but an underwriter with five years' experience could expect a salary of between £16,000 and £27,000.

Many companies and most Lloyd's syndicates pay salaries linked directly to performance, measuring success by the value of business successfully attracted by underwriters.

Most insurance companies provide benefits such as pension schemes, mortgage subsidies, medical insurance and life cover.

Underwriters usually work between 35 and 37 hours a week, Monday to Friday, but work outside these hours may be necessary.

PROSPECTS

Underwriters usually gain promotion to more-responsible posts dealing with more complex cases which represent greater risk and greater sums of money. As their knowledge increases, underwriters may supervise other members of their departments including support staff before moving on to management positions taking charge of a team of underwriters or a Lloyd's syndicate.

Some gain promotion by specializing in a particular field of underwriting like marine or aviation. Others move into marketing departments where their skills are used to devise new policies. There are also opportunities to move into other areas of insurance like loss adjusting, claims, brokering or training.

RELATED OCCUPATIONS, FURTHER INFORMATION AND READING

Please see article 8. RISK MANAGER.

2. INSURANCE BROKER (NAG)

THE WORK

Brokers help their clients select and buy the best insurance policies to meet their needs. They act as independent intermediaries between the clients and the insurers. Clients may range from individuals wishing to insure sole items like a car, or holiday, to large companies wishing to insure very large risks like business premises and stock.

Brokers ask clients questions to identify and assess the need the client wishes to insure. Brokers condense their client's need into an insurable proposition and present it to underwriters in a professionally acceptable form.

Using their knowledge of their client's business and their knowledge of the insurance industry they advise their client what price they will have to pay for an insurance policy. In many cases they can provide immediate quotations for cover from companies that operate standard book rated schemes. Sometimes they will need to negotiate special terms and conditions to cover a client's particular circumstances.

In some cases a tailor-made policy will be necessary. Brokers may have to write a detailed report or commission an expert report from an insurance surveyor. They may also have to collect supporting evidence like photographs or medical records. They may approach a number of underwriters for separate quotations or to ask them to accept only a part of the total risk. They then advise their client which quotation is the most suitable explaining the detailed terms and conditions and outlining the level of cover accepted and any exceptions or exclusions. They may also point to the merits of the claims procedure as well as assessing the long-term benefits of renewal rates if the policy is for a set period and will need to be renewed.

Brokers at Lloyd's deal with the most complicated risks which sometimes involve millions of pounds and may be international in nature. They take instruction from high-ranking professionals, senior company managers and government officials. Brokers approach underwriters working for Lloyd's syndicates with full details of the risk to be insured and ask them to accept it all, or in most cases, a small proportion of it. Brokers then advise their client and produce a document for all the parties to the agreement to sign.

Brokers working for large companies are likely to specialize in a certain type of insurance like aviation or marine. In smaller broking businesses brokers may advise on many types of insurance.

Brokers also assist their clients to make claims. They may advise them on how to proceed by making a telephone call or writing a letter. In some cases they may assist a client in defending a claim by using their experience and knowledge to argue over technicalities. Some specialize in this field as claims brokers.

Although brokers earnings come from commission from insurers with whom they successfully place business they are legally obliged to put the interests of their clients first . They build up a relationship with their clients and give them ongoing advice on their need as the clients' circumstances change.

WORK ENVIRONMENT

Brokers are based in offices which are often open plan. They will work with other brokers and a support team of clerks and other professionals. They may spend a great deal of time outside their office visiting clients and underwriters. Brokers working at Lloyd's are likely to be out of their office for two days a week.

Much of the time in the office will be spent at a desk using a computer terminal or microfiche screen.

If the broker works for a firm that negotiates policies for clients with overseas interest they may travel abroad and be away from home for short periods.

SKILLS AND INTERESTS

Insurance brokers need good oral communication skills. They have to establish relationships with clients and

INSURANCE WORK: NAG

underwriters and negotiate with them. They must be able to explain complicated issues to their clients and win their trust and confidence. They may deal with a very wide range of people with differing levels of understanding and must be able to explain complicated policies and propositions in a simple way. They may work for high- ranking officials of international companies or even governments and they have to be confident in their approach. On occasions they are required to be persuasive.

They need to communicate well in writing. They must condense their client's insurance needs into a proposal that will be acceptable to underwriters. They may put together contracts for a number of parties to agree. They will also spend a lot of time writing letters and reports.

Insurance brokers need to be technically competent. They need a wide knowledge of their chosen class of insurance and the insurance market generally as well as their client's business. They must keep abreast of changes and need to have inquiring minds and the ability to absorb information quickly.

They need to be numerate and analytical to make effective comparisons between different insurance policies for their clients. They must also pay attention to detail and be scrupulously honest and discreet.

Brokers need to have strong personalities. Those working in Lloyd's face to face with underwriters must be confident and quick-witted.

Most brokers use computers.

Brokers working in the international market need to speak one or more languages.

ENTRY REQUIREMENTS

Brokers do not always need formal qualifications. Many broking firms do however recruit students straight from school, college or university. Many companies require trainees to sit CII examinations. See article 1. INSURANCE UNDERWRITER for qualifications. Companies may also want evidence of competence in maths and English at GCSE/S level grade(A–C/1–3) or equivalent.

If candidates wish to become registered insurance brokers and conduct business at Lloyd's they will be required to achieve associateship status of the CII and demonstrate practical experience of insurance broking.

Some brokering companies recruit claims clerks and other support staff with the intention that they will become brokers when they have sufficient knowledge, experience and maturity. Please see article 4. INSURANCE CLAIMS OFFICIAL.

Smaller companies prefer to recruit people who already work in insurance as underwriters or financial advisers.

TRAINING

Most of the training is on the job and may begin with an introduction to the company and its departments before working in a specific department. Trainees usually start by setting up claims or proposals on computer and inputting data which helps them get familiar with the company's systems. They will then move on to taking routine enquiries and giving general advice about straightforward insurance cover. They will work under the supervision of a senior broker or team leader. When they have covered the basics they will be allocated clients and the degree of complexity and the degree of risk involved in their work will be gradually increased.

Many employers require trainees to pass CII exams. Please see article 1. INSURANCE UNDERWRITER.

Most broking companies require staff to undertake continuous professional development (CPD) and staff will be encouraged to attend courses that the company will often arrange. The British Insurance and Investment Brokers' Association (BIIBA) and CII run a variety of courses on brokering and other subjects like information technology and marketing. These may be linked to National Vocational Qualifications (Levels 2, 3 and 4) and CII studies. Details from BIIBA and CII.

LATE ENTRY

There is no upper age limit for this work although many companies recruit school-, college- or university-leavers. Older applicants with associated qualifications in finance or banking and work experience in those fields may be accepted. Those who have worked in an associated insurance area like claims or underwriting are also sought, especially by smaller companies. Entry and training requirements are the same for all entrants irrespective of age.

OPPORTUNITIES

Brokers are employed by insurance broking companies throughout the country. Some are small high street operations dealing in personal or general insurance, others are international companies dealing with insurance generally or specific areas like marine or aviation. Some employ only a few people while others employ thousands.

Larger insurance broker operations are usually organized into departments and brokers may specialize in a class of insurance and advising clients on appropriate policies or claims work. In a smaller company they may advise on many types of insurance and may specialize in dealing with corporate accounts or individual members of the public.

There are increasing opportunities to work overseas especially for those who speak European languages or Japanese.

There are opportunities to become self-employed and some part-time work may be available.

PAY AND CONDITIONS

Trainees with A levels/H grades could expect to earn between £7,500 and £9,000. Graduates would start on £11,000 to £15,000. The pay for experienced brokers is often performance related and may vary considerably depending on the area of specialism and degree of responsibility. A broker with five years' experience could expect to earn between £16,000 to £28,000. Brokers working in London, for Lloyd's and for companies dealing internationally may earn considerably more than this.

Most insurance companies also provide other incentives like private health care and subsidized loans and low rate mortgages.

Brokers normally work office hours – 35 to 37 hours a week Monday to Friday. They may be required to work outside these hours if clients are not available and deadlines need to be met. Those required to travel abroad could work considerably longer because of differences in time zones.

INSURANCE WORK: NAG

PROSPECTS

Brokers usually specialize in certain types of insurance and become team leaders or department managers. There may be opportunities to become directors or partners in their firm. Many brokers establish their own businesses or become self-employed.

Brokers require the same knowledge and qualifications as other professions within the insurance industry and there may be the chance to move into other areas like risk management or loss adjustment. Some may also move into training or marketing.

Senior positions are usually only available to those who achieve associate level or higher within CII.

RELATED OCCUPATIONS, FURTHER INFORMATION AND READING

Please see article 8. RISK MANAGER.

3. FINANCIAL ADVISER (NAG/NAK)

THE WORK

Financial advisers or sales consultants are important to any insurance company. They are responsible for bringing in new business and maintaining existing business by encouraging clients to renew or extend their policies in line with their changing need. They sell all types of insurance to the general public, companies and other institutions.

They must give clients clear and comprehensive information about the products they are buying and must understand the rules specified by the industry's regulatory bodies. People involved in insurance sales have many different titles depending on the company they work for, or the product they sell, but broadly speaking the work can be divided into three categories:

Inspectors/broker consultants are the link between an insurance intermediary and their own company. Intermediaries include accountants, solicitors, estate agents, car sales staff, holiday company sales persons and brokers. They have technical knowledge about their company's products and they advise intermediaries or agents who are not always insurance professionals. They will visit the agents they deal with on a regular basis to explain new products. They will visit potential agents to encourage them to sell their company's products, and may appoint new agents, which involves drawing up contracts. They will also encourage agents to promote their company's business. In some cases they will train new agents in the company's products and procedures and demonstrate any marketing materials.

Direct sales consultants fall into two kinds. The company representative sells only their company's products directly to the public. They deal mainly with life products like savings plans, investment products and life assurance. They advise clients as their needs change and identify and attract new clients by visiting them and explaining the benefits of their products. They have to gain the confidence of clients and analyse their need often taking into account their financial outgoings, dependants and commitments. Sometimes they need to adjust an existing scheme to suit a client and sometimes they need to offer alternative choices if the circumstances of a client change. They may visit a client in their own home to explain their product and may call to collect premiums on a regular basis.

The appointed or 'tied' agent works for a third party like an estate agents or solicitors or other intermediary and sells the products of the company that has appointed them in the same way as the direct company representative. Although some may specialize entirely in insurance others may well perform other duties within their own organization.

The third category is **independent financial adviser** who may recommend the insurance and investment schemes of many different companies to their clients. The work of independent advisers is governed by strict regulation. Their advice must be genuinely independent and they must keep constantly up to date with every aspect of the insurance market to be sure of giving the best advice to their clients.

WORK ENVIRONMENT

Insurance advisers are usually based in offices where they are supported by clerical staff and other professionals. Some work from home. They spend a lot of their time visiting clients in their business premises or in their own homes. They usually cover specific geographical areas and usually work in sales teams under the direction of a sales manger or sales director. Extensive travelling may be necessary in rural areas and a driving licence is usually required.

SKILLS AND INTERESTS

Financial advisers need good communication skills. They must be able to win the confidence and trust of their clients. They must establish relationships with all types of people. They need an analytical mind and a sharp intellect to recognize, assess and satisfy each individual client's need. They must also be able to explain the terms and benefits of different schemes clearly to clients who will have varying degrees of financial understanding.

They need to be numerate and capable of making calculations with computer systems and calculators. Those working in life products need knowledge of law and taxation. They need to be trustworthy and able to treat personal information confidentially.

They may need managerial skills to supervise support staff.

Increasingly they need up-to-date knowledge of financial services and the wide range of products available within their own companies and available from their competitors. They may also need knowledge of the benefits system and changing government legislation.

Like all sales people they also need to be persuasive .

Most companies expect all sales staff to use computers and those who visits clients may be provided with a desktop computer which enables them to give immediate advice to clients.

ENTRY REQUIREMENTS

Qualifications are not always necessary but many companies do prefer their entrants to have four GCSEs/S grades (A–C/1–3). Some require a pass in English.

Some companies recruit school- or college-leavers to work in clerical support posts until they have sufficient maturity and experience to move on to sales work . This is unusual, and most companies prefer older entrants. Please see LATE ENTRY.

Financial advisers working on life products are required to meet the minimum standards of the Personal Investment

INSURANCE WORK: NAG

Authority (PIA) which is the official regulator for financial service advice. (The Financial Services Act is likely to be amended during 1998 and regulation of life insurance and pension business will be conducted by the Financial Services Authority.)

The Financial Planning certificate (FPC) awarded by the Chartered Insurance Institute (CII) is recognized by the PIA as a minimum standard. There are no age or educational requirements for those wishing to take the FPC. The CII does not set any limit on the number of times FPC exams can be taken. Employers will expect entrants to be able to achieve this.

Some employers also encourage their sales staff to complete CII associateship exams. Please see article 1. UNDERWRITER.

TRAINING

Training is usually given on the job and involves learning from experienced sales people and attending courses on product knowledge, selling skills and market trends. Anyone who sells insurance or advises on investment must be qualified.

The FPC consists of three papers. Papers I and II are multiple choice and cover financial services and their regulation and protection, savings and investment products. Paper III consists of three case study applications which test a student's ability to identify and satisfy clients needs. For candidates who are 55 years or over with ten years' relevant experience, paper III can be taken as an oral exam.

Some exemptions are available to students holding other financial, investment or accounting qualifications.

Candidates can use a variety of study methods. Correspondence courses, audio tapes and computer-based training are available.

One-week residential courses, two-day courses and study days are organized by the CII in Sevenoaks.

Exams can be taken at centres throughout the UK. Some employers arrange for examinations to be taken in-house.

An Advanced Financial Planning Certificate is available for students wishing to demonstrate their ability to advise clients on more complicated investments. Subjects studied include taxation and trust, financial planning, with a choice of technical papers. Holders of the Advanced FPC can apply to become members of the Society of Financial Advisors (SOFA) and take further professional exams.

The PIA recognizes certain other qualifications for example those offered by the Chartered Institute of Bankers, the Securities Institute or the Institute of Investment Management and Research.

It is mandatory for independent financial advisers to spend at least 50 hours a year on continuous professional development.

LATE ENTRY

There is no upper age limit on entry. Previous experience in a related area, eg insurance, accounting or banking is an advantage. Most selling representatives are rarely recruited under the age of 20 and many are much older than this.

OPPORTUNITIES

There are over 500 insurance companies in Britain and many new organizations are providing insurance cover like banks and building societies. There are also new entrants like retail outlets and other big corporations who are capitalizing on powerful brand names and existing sophisticated marketing techniques. They cover all types of insurance and some specialize in certain areas like life or motor. There are opportunities for advisers to become self-employed or to work with a group of other independent advisers or consultants. Companies are distributed throughout Britain.

Changes in government legislation and the increasing pressure on government to control spending on pensions and benefits means many more people are seeking insurance advice.

PAY AND CONDITIONS

Salaries vary considerably and are mainly based on commission. Those working as tied agents may work on a commission only basis.

For those selling life products that are paid by results, usually related to the financial volume of business, earnings can be very high.

Basic salary is usually quite low, in the region of £8,000 to £15,000. Sometimes arrangements are made for a new entrant to receive a higher basic salary which is reduced as they become more experienced and earn more commission.

Many companies also offer performance bonuses and sales incentives like consumer goods and exotic holidays.

PROSPECTS

Promotion is to senior adviser or area manager. There may be opportunities to move into general management or training. Some sales people move into marketing or other areas of insurance business like new product development.

RELATED OCCUPATIONS, FURTHER INFORMATION AND READING

Please see article 8. RISK MANAGER.

4. INSURANCE CLAIMS OFFICIAL (NAG)

THE WORK

Claims officials check claims that have been made by policyholders who have suffered loss or damage and decide whether the claim should be settled. They may decide to pay the full sum insured or only part of it.

There are two types of claims officials: **claims settlers** and **claims inspectors.**

Claims settlers deal directly with clients, their brokers and their solicitors by letter, telephone and in person. They issue appropriate claims forms when loss or damage occurs. When the forms are returned to them they check details and check that the policy covers the claim and the necessary premiums have been paid. If the claim is small and falls within the terms of a standard policy, the claims clerk may settle it immediately. They write letters to clients outlining their decision and issue cheques up to a set limit. Sometimes their recommendation will be checked and authorized by a senior claims settler. Claims settlers ask

INSURANCE WORK: NAG

clients to return receipts and they update records. They may advise clients if the claim has any effect on the terms of their policy or premiums in the long term.

In some cases the claims settlers ask for more information from the client before settling the claim. They may want estimates of the work to be done on property and motor vehicles or receipts or photographs of property that has been lost or stolen. If a crime has been committed, or a motor accident has occurred, they may wish to see police reports.

If additional information is required the claim may be passed to **claims inspectors.** Claims inspectors visit the client to inspect the damage or loss. They may talk to third parties like police officers and witnesses as well builders and motor mechanics who have submitted estimates for the work.

Inspectors write reports and make recommendations to claims settlers stating whether the claims should be met. They give reasons for their recommendation which may be to meet all or part of a claim. When claims are authorized inspectors often visit clients and negotiate the settlement with them .

If the claim is very large or complex, or fraud is suspected, a loss adjuster may be asked to write a more detailed report.

WORK ENVIRONMENT

Claims settlers are based in offices which are often open plan. They may sit at a desk for long periods using computer terminals or microfiche. The office may have an area open to the public. They use the phone extensively.

Claims inspectors may visit clients and their representatives in their own homes or at their offices. They spend a great deal of time out of the office. They may visit the scenes of accidents or inspect damaged vehicles at garages which may be dirty and oily.

Claims officials usually work in teams. They work standard office hours of 35 to 37 a week. Claims inspectors may have to make appointments outside these hours but usually have time off in lieu to compensate.

SKILLS AND INTERESTS

Claims officials must be good communicators. They must relate to all types of people and be able to explain procedures and decisions in a way clients understand. They will need to do this face to face, in writing and in telephone conversations.

They must be diplomatic and sensitive. Often clients will be distressed and worried if they have had an accident or lost something valuable. They need good negotiating skills and will need to be tactful if a claim is to be reduced or not met. Sometimes clients will be angry and claims officials will need to be firm.

They must pay attention to detail as a great deal of their time will be spent checking information and verifying facts.

They need a thorough knowledge of their company's policies and procedures.

They must work well under pressure.

They must be practical and able to use office equipment like photocopiers and microfiches. Good keyboard skills are usually essential.

Claims inspectors will require a full current driving licence.

ENTRY REQUIREMENTS

The usual qualification is four GCSEs/S grades (A–C/1–3) including maths and English or equivalent. Some employers prefer entrants who have the qualifications necessary to study for CII examinations. Please see article 1. INSURANCE UNDERWRITER. Larger companies recruit graduates for general insurance work and allow entrants to specialize in claims work after a general introduction to all aspects of insurance.

Although not essential, many companies value an NVQ/SVQ in customer care.

Many companies promote insurance clerks who have shown aptitude and a willingness to study. Please see article 5. INSURANCE CLERK.

TRAINING

Training varies from company to company and is mostly on the job with the supervision of an experienced claims official or a team leader. Usually claims officials have an induction course which introduces the various aspects of the company's work with particular focus on their own department. They usually start with routine tasks like checking details on claims forms are correct, before moving on to taking telephone enquiries and assessing standard claims. In the initial training period their decisions will be checked and authorized by senior staff members.

Many insurance companies are committed to continuous professional development and will make arrangements for entrants to have ongoing training in insurance and other related issues like IT and communications. Many will also expect entrants to take CII examinations. These are particular necessary for those who wish to be promoted.

Some companies run training courses for school-, college- or university-leavers that take in all aspects of insurance and allows trainees to specialize in claims after working in a variety of departments. In these cases a formal programme will be organized and trainees may progress in small groups.

LATE ENTRY

There are no official maximum age limits for this career although many companies recruit school leavers. People over 30 years may be successful if they have appropriate work experience in related businesses like accountancy, banking or pensions administration or any type of assessment work.

OPPORTUNITIES

Claims officials work for specialist and generalist insurance companies as well as brokers and Lloyd's.

There may be opportunities to work overseas for experienced claims officials.

PAY AND CONDITIONS

Salaries vary from company to company and may vary according to experience, age and qualifications. Starting salaries vary from £8,000 to £9,500. Graduates are likely to receive a slightly higher amount. Experienced claims officials with five years' experience could expect to earn in excess of £15,000.

INSURANCE WORK: NAG

Insurance companies usually offer other benefits like medical insurance and low rate mortgages. Hours are normally 35 to 37 a week, Monday to Friday. Claims inspectors sometimes work evenings and at weekends.

PROSPECTS

Claims officials are usually promoted to supervisory or management positions specializing in certain types of insurance. They may also become underwriters, brokers or financial advisers if they are prepared to sit the appropriate examinations. Claims inspectors may become loss adjusters.

RELATED OCCUPATIONS, FURTHER INFORMATION AND READING

Please see article 8. RISK MANAGER.

5. INSURANCE CLERK (NAG)

THE WORK

Insurance clerks assist their senior colleagues by providing support and clerical assistance. They work in all aspects of insurance but particularly in claims, brokers offices and underwriting sections.

They perform a whole range of clerical duties like opening post, updating records, dealing with routine correspondence and answering enquiries from clients.

In some areas, especially general insurance where much of the work is based on standard policies, they may deal with clients directly and give advice, draw up routine proposals and policies and adjudicate claims.

They may provide specialist support to a team of brokers and underwriters which may involve making appointments and maintaining diaries as well as preparing papers and obtaining information. They may also prepare and maintain statistical records relating to office performance.

They will have a lot of personal contact with clients and other insurance staff in person and over the phone.

Brokers' clerks check proposal forms filled in by clients. They may contact the client to check details or to obtain additional information or clarify details. They forward information on to insurance companies and write letters to clients advising them of progress. Brokers' clerks sometimes advise clients on appropriate policies for uncomplicated risks. They may give general advice to clients who call in the office and help them complete appropriate forms. They may sometimes liaise with underwriters and ask for information on behalf of the brokers they work with.

Claims clerks work in claims departments of insurance and broking companies. They send out the appropriate claims forms to clients and brokers who may write, telephone or call into their office. When the forms are returned they check the details. If the claim is simple and routine they may check whether the claim is covered by the policy and whether the insurance premiums are fully paid up. They do this by looking at files or at information stored on computer. They will advise the client either by telephone or letter whether or not they are covered. In more complicated cases they put together all the necessary information and pass it on to a claims official. They may write to clients on behalf of claims officials and underwriters asking for additional information to support or verify their claim.

Processing/underwriting clerks work in underwriting departments providing support for underwriters and other professional staff. They transfer information from proposal forms onto computer. They update information and check clients details and policies for underwriters. They may answer enquiries from clients and brokers and give quotes on standard insurance premiums within a set level. They use reference tables and computer systems to access information. They also undertake routine clerical duties like sending out policy documents to clients and issuing reminders and other fairly standard letters. Underwriting clerks may also have to ensure that cheques and cash coming into the office are accounted for and banked.

WORK ENVIRONMENT

Insurance clerks usually work in offices with other clerks and insurance professionals. They may be required to sit and use computers, VDUs or microfiches for long periods. Offices are light and airy and usually based in the centre of towns. They may have areas open to the public. They vary considerably in size.

SKILLS AND INTERESTS

Insurance clerks must pay attention to detail as much of their work involves checking and transferring information from documents. They need good keyboard skills.

They need to be good communicators. A great deal of time will be spent writing letters, talking to people on the phone or when they call into the office. They must be able to explain things and read and write clearly. They need to deal with people in a friendly but professional way. They have to listen, be polite and understanding but know when to be firm and when to seek advice from senior colleagues.

They must be numerate and able to handle numbers accurately using a calculator or computer.

Insurance clerks must be able to organize their time and recognize the unexpected or the non routine.

They must also be practical and able to use equipment like computers, calculators, microfiche readers, photocopiers and fax machines.

ENTRY REQUIREMENTS

No formal qualifications are necessary for this work but in practice many employers expect clerks to have four GCSE/S grades or equivalent including passes in maths and English. NVQs in customer care, although not required, are valued by employers.

TRAINING

Training varies from company to company and is mostly on the job with supervision by an experienced clerk or a team leader. Usually clerks will have an induction course which may last a week and introduces the various aspects of the company's work with particular focus on their own department. If a number of clerks have been employed they may undertake this training together. Clerks will be instructed in health and safety policies and told about leave procedures, flexitime, performance related pay and other personnel issues. They will then be allocated to their departments and will perform routine tasks and observe more experienced clerks undertaking more complicated work.

INSURANCE WORK: NAG

There may be an internal training officer who may organize short training sessions on telephone techniques or company policies. Clerks may be required to attend training courses at another venue or the information may be given to them more informally by an office manager.

Many insurance companies are committed to continuous professional development and will make arrangements for entrants to have ongoing training in insurance and other related issues like IT and communications. Many will also expect entrants to take CII examinations. These are particularly necessary for those who wish to be promoted.

Clerks with no formal qualification can enroll for the Insurance Foundation Certificate (IFC) which is a CII qualification at technician level equivalent to NVQ/SVQ Level 2. To achieve IFC clerks must pass two papers. Paper 1 consists of 100 multiple-choice questions on insurance, the market and the legal and regulatory background. Paper 2 is a general paper covering non-life issues which consists of 60 multiple-choice questions and 40 true-or-false statements, and has two options: general insurance or life insurance. IFC exams are held twice a year and involve 75 to 100 hours of study. Both exams can be taken at the same time. Distance learning packages are available from CII. This qualification allows clerks to apply for membership of the Society of Technicians in Insurance (STI).

Clerks without qualifications may also take the Lloyd's Introductory Test or BIIBA Certificate of Competence which test knowledge gained at work and can count as exemptions to Paper 1 of IFC.

Clerks with 4 GCSEs/S grade (A–C/1–3), the IFC (or Certificate of Proficiency (COP) which pre-dated IFC), the Financial Planning Certificate, or who are aged 21 years or over, may take the Certificate in Insurance Practice (CIP). This is a higher technical qualification and counts as three credits for those wishing to take Associateship of CII examinations. Five examinations must be passed: three at Foundation, two at Branch and one at Specialist level. There are a variety of subjects to chose from which enables clerks to pick those most closely related to their work. Distance learning packages are available from CII and some local colleges run tuition classes.

LATE ENTRY

There are no official maximum age limits for this career although many companies recruit school-leavers. People over 30 years may be successful if they have appropriate work experience in related businesses like accountancy, banking or pensions administration.

OPPORTUNITIES

Clerks work for specialist and generalist insurance companies as well as brokers and Lloyd's.

PAY AND CONDITIONS

Salaries vary from company to company and may vary according to experience, age and qualifications. Staring salaries vary from £6,500 to £7,500. An experienced clerk with five years' experience could expect to earn between £9,000 and £13,000.

Insurance companies usually offer other benefits like medical insurance and low rate mortgages. Hours are normally 35 to 37 a week, Monday to Friday.

PROSPECTS

Clerks are usually promoted to team leader or office manager. They may also become claims officers. Insurance clerks who take CII examinations may become underwriters, brokers or financial advisers.

RELATED OCCUPATIONS, FURTHER INFORMATION AND READING

Please see article 8. RISK MANAGER.

6. INSURANCE SURVEYOR (NAG)

THE WORK

Insurance surveyors prepare reports for underwriters and brokers outlining the details of the risk to be insured and any factors that might affect it. They help brokers and underwriters understand the degree of risk and help them formulate appropriate policies.

Insurance surveyors usually specialize in one of the following areas: fire and perils; accidents and liability; engineering; or theft.

Fire and perils: surveyors often ask to see plans of the building before making a visit. They establish what materials have been used in construction. They collect detailed information on fire protection arrangements like the positioning of fire extinguishers. They talk to the local fire officer. They examine and assess the condition of the heating and ventilating system. They write a report noting any factors that affect the insurance and may draw their own diagrams to illustrate a point. If they have found anything hazardous like faulty wiring, or unsafe storage conditions, they may draw this to the attention of the insurance company and the owner. The company may add terms and conditions asking the owner to put this right before insurance cover is given or may adjust the premium. If the premises are near a river or stream the surveyor will check with the local authority and the river authorities to try and gauge the risk of flooding. Other perils that may require assessment are aircraft accidents, explosions, storm damage and burst pipes.

Liability and accident: surveyors check the potential liability to employees or the public arising from the use of premises and the operation of machinery or the processing of hazardous substances. They will examine the manufacturing process and assess the safety measures in place to protect employees. They will check the condition of machinery and examine safety systems to ensure safety regulations are being followed. They will wish to see any reports made by the local health and safety officer. They will write a report as for fire and perils.

Engineering: surveyors check plant and equipment and the wide variety of risk from simple machinery to huge industrial plant and offshore oil rigs.

Burglary and theft: surveyors examine how goods are stored and may examine financial procedures and other clerical procedures to track stock. They will also assess security arrangements and access to the building.

WORK ENVIRONMENT

Surveyors work partly in their office where they may spend time using computer terminals and attending meetings and partly on sites where surveys are to take place.

INSURANCE WORK: NAG

About half the time is spent on site work which may be dirty and noisy. When looking at installations and buildings they may be required to work at heights.

They usually work alone but have lots of contact with other insurance employees, clients and other professionals like health and safety officers at local councils.

SKILLS AND INTERESTS

Insurance surveyors must pay attention to detail and be observant and inquisitive.

They must be able to understand and absorb technical details. They often need to make sense of plans or draw simple plans illustrating a point they are making in a report.

Insurance surveyors must keep up to date with the laws relating to health and safety at work and fire regulations.

They must write clear reports that will be understood by those who do not have the same levels of technical knowledge.

They must be able to work with a wide range of people and explain technical issues to them. They must also seek technical information from other professionals.

A clean current driving licence is usually necessary.

ENTRY REQUIREMENTS

Most insurance surveyors enter the profession after a period in the insurance industry where they may have worked as an underwriter or a broker. Some companies recruit entrants directly from school, college or university with the necessary qualifications to sit CII exams. Please see article 1. INSURANCE UNDERWRITER.

Graduate entrants are becoming more common, with degrees in insurance, risk management, engineering or any scientific or technical subject being preferred.

People working in insurance who have passed, or are working towards, CII exams are also accepted as trainees. Sometimes specialists with engineering or accounting qualifications may be accepted.

TRAINING

Trainees usually undergo an induction programme which introduces them to company practices and procedures. They may work in an underwriting department where they see a variety of proposal and policy forms – this helps them understand the type of information companies need if they are to insure risks. They will then accompany an experienced insurance surveyor before being allocated work of their own. The cases they deal with will increase in size and complexity as they gain experience.

Some companies run training schemes for graduates and school-leavers which may involve some work in a variety of departments before the trainees are asked to decide which work they would wish to specialize in.

For information on professional exams please see article 1. INSURANCE UNDERWRITER.

Most insurance companies expect employees to undertake a programme of continued professional development and training in a wide variety of subjects which may be offered internally or by CII.

LATE ENTRY

Mature candidates are preferred for this work. Most trainees work in other branches of insurance and enter this profession in their mid-twenties. Those with engineering backgrounds recruited for specialist posts may be older.

OPPORTUNITIES

Insurance surveyors are employed by large insurance companies and increasingly by brokers which may be situated throughout the country.

There are some opportunities to work abroad.

PAY AND CONDITIONS

Trainee insurance surveyors can expect to earn £10,500 to £13,000. A fully trained insurance surveyor can expect a salary of between £16,500 and £26,000. Specialists may earn in excess of this.

PROSPECTS

Promotion is usually to senior surveyor or department head. Insurance surveyors may also move into other types of insurance work like underwriting and risk management. Sometimes they may become consultants.

RELATED OCCUPATIONS, FURTHER INFORMATION AND READING

Please see article 8. RISK MANAGER.

7. INSURANCE LOSS ADJUSTER (NAG)

THE WORK

Loss adjusters are independent professionals who investigate claims for insurance companies. They determine whether claims are valid and recommend levels of payments. The work varies considerably and may involve fire or theft from an office, damage to a domestic property or an oil tanker running into rocks at sea.

Loss adjusters investigate the causes of loss and damage and confirm that the terms of the insurance policy have been observed. In the case of a burglary they may check that the police have been informed and the premises were properly locked according to company procedures.

They will consider whether another party may have caused the loss or been a factor in it. A security company with a contract to patrol a warehouse may be liable for any theft or damage to the warehouse if the security personnel were not on site when they were contracted to be.

Loss adjusters must first survey the physical damage. This could mean climbing on the roof of a building to look at a hole or visiting a company in the aftermath of a fire. If they are unsure what has caused the loss or damage they may ask for forensic evidence to be taken or for a detailed report from a specialist like an accountant or building surveyor. They may ask for stock valuation certificates and reports from any attending services like the police or fire brigade.

They also help arrange to have the damage put right by contacting reputable builders and arranging for repairs to be carried out or, in the case of theft, by employing private investigators or offering a reward for the return of the goods or property.

INSURANCE WORK: NAG

Loss adjusters advise claimants on measures that will help mitigate the loss like selling off any stock not destroyed in a fire.

They present their final report and recommendation to the insurers employing them but also explain the recommendations to claimants, and may suggest that the claimant takes additional precautions before the existing insurance policy can be renewed.

In some cases they explain to the policyholder that their property is not insured or that they must make a claim against another person.

WORK ENVIRONMENT

Loss adjusters are based in offices but spend two-thirds of their time visiting claimants at their homes or business.

They may have to visit a site or property immediately after a disaster which may mean conditions are dirty or dangerous.

There may be opportunities to travel overseas.

Loss adjusters need a clean current driving licence.

Loss adjusters work also brings them into contact with a wide range of other professionals like the police, the fire brigade, accountants, engineers, and forensic scientists.

SKILLS AND INTERESTS

Loss adjusters must have complete integrity and inspire trust and confidence. They must be completely impartial and independent. Although they are appointed by insurance companies, they are acting for both the company and the insured person, and so must be fair to both parties.

They should possess good powers of observation and the ability to assimilate knowledge quickly in situations that are not always very comfortable. They may make an assessment on the causes of an industrial accident where loss of life has occurred. They need wide-ranging knowledge of the area of insurance they deal with, which will include a degree of technical knowledge in order to commission expert reports from other professionals like forensic experts and accountants. They must also be physically fit as they may have to climb on roofs or work their way around debris after a natural disaster.

Loss adjusters must communicate well with people of widely differing backgrounds and must be able to present the results of their work concisely in a well-written report. They must be able to negotiate and be diplomatic. In some cases they will need to be firm.

They will be required to manage a changing workload which may involve dealing with difficult situations at all hours of the day and night.

ENTRY REQUIREMENTS

Most loss adjusters move into the profession after developing skills in another area of work experience. Qualified surveyors, engineers, accountants and insurance claims officials often have the necessary expertise to become loss adjusters.

It is unusual but not unknown for school, college or higher education students to enter a career in loss adjusting.

Loss adjusters may be expected to study for the examinations of the Chartered Institute of Loss Adjusters (CILA). To enter the exams candidates need a professional qualification (list available from CILA) or must have passed the CII examinations. Please see article 1. INSURANCE UNDERWRITER. They must also have at least two years' experience as a loss adjuster.

TRAINING

Loss adjusters are usually trained on the job. They normally enter the profession with an area of expertise like finance or property surveying. They will spend some time with an experienced loss adjuster with similar skills who they will observe. They will then be given small projects of their own before moving on to projects that demand a greater amount of skill and expertise.

They will undertake study for associateship examinations of CILA. Study may be part-time or by distance learning over a period of three to four years.. The examinations offer a choice according to the loss adjuster's areas of specialism like buildings, accounts and theft. In addition all trainees study principles and practice of insurance in relation to loss adjusting, accident and liability claims, and commercial claims.

Many loss adjusting companies also expect trainees to undergo continuous professional development and many courses run by CILA and CII are available in loss adjusting and related fields like technology and business practices.

LATE ENTRY

Most people entering this field are late entrants with other professional qualifications.

OPPORTUNITIES

Loss adjusters work for specialist firms which range considerably in size from two or three loss adjusters to those with more than 100. Firms are situated throughout the country. Some loss adjusters become consultants or set up their own companies.

Work overseas is possible as many foreign companies take out insurance in Britain.

PAY AND CONDITIONS

Salaries vary considerably in this profession and are dictated by previous qualifications, level of expertise and type of specialism. Loss adjusters with five years' experience could expect to earn £20,000. Many earn in excess of this.

Although loss adjusters officially work 35 to 37 hours a week, in practice hours of work are long. They may be called out at weekends and in the evenings to emergencies. They might also visit clients at their own homes during these periods. They have to work to strict deadlines and often take work home or work late in the office to complete reports.

PROSPECTS

In a small firm loss adjusters may become partners or directors. In a larger company they may become the head of a department or a branch manager. Eventually they become area mangers or move to a specialist head office position.

They may also move into other areas of insurance work like surveying or risk management.

INSURANCE WORK: NAG

RELATED OCCUPATIONS, FURTHER INFORMATION AND READING

Please see article 8. RISK MANAGER.

8. RISK MANAGER (NAG)

THE WORK

Risk managers identify, measure, control and finance risks that may threaten property, life and the continuing success of a company

They often use mathematical modelling and statistical analysis to work out the probable impact upon the company of all types of risk. They visit the company's factories, plant and construction sites to inspect equipment and working practices in order to identify areas that may result in loss or damage to the company.

They assess the potential financial impact of risks upon a company. For example, they have to assess whether products are safe and what effect a recall of a product would have on the company's financial position.

When risks have been identified risk managers negotiate with insurance brokers and insurance companies to obtain the best premiums and terms and conditions for their company. They also examine financial reports, lease agreements and contracts the company may produce, or enter into with a third party, and identify weaknesses that may result in loss or damage or a claim against the company.

Risk managers write reports outlining what they have discovered and make recommendations for improvements. These could involve changes to company health and safety procedure, taking out additional insurance cover, or adding terms to a lease. They may suggest additional training on health and safety issues or additional management checks that should be undertaken to ensure a process is being operated according to company policy. Sometimes they recommend that some risks are predictable and will only result in a small loss which the company can absorb.

Risk managers study government regulations and legislation that may affect their company and its business and advise any action necessary in order to comply. A change in the hours a lorry driver can legally drive without break could have considerable impact on a transport company.

Risk managers also develop contingency plans to deal with emergencies and business calamities. Companies based in central London may have plans to move to an alternative address should their property be damaged by a terrorist bomb. The provision of a remote computer site might also be considered to save important information. Risk managers publish and update company documents giving guidance to employees about what action to take when an emergency occurs so that loss is minimized and the company's work is not interrupted. Risk managers also produce a plan for protecting the company's image in the media if a disaster occurs.

WORK ENVIRONMENT

Risk managers are office based. They may work in teams within risk management departments or may be key members of the management team working with other professionals like accountants and solicitors.

They may spend some time at their desks using computer terminals but will also inspect company installations that may be wet, dirty or oily. They are likely to spend between a third and a half of their time out of the office and if the companies' operations are widespread then they may travel extensively.

Most risk managers are contracted to work a normal working week of between 35 to 37 hours. Many work longer than this and they may be called out at evenings and weekends if an emergency arises.

They usually require a clean current driving licence.

SKILLS AND INTERESTS

Risk managers need good planning and problem solving ability. They must be numerate and able to make complicated calculations.

They need to be technically competent in order to understand their company's processes. They must also have a working knowledge of the laws and regulations governing occupational health and safety, employers' liability, and the law of tort and contract. In addition they will need to understand accounting and actuarial systems and have a wide knowledge of the insurance market. They must keep abreast of changes and need to absorb information quickly.

Risk managers need good negotiating skills and need to be persuasive and firm. They must be confident in their own judgement. They must be diplomatic and sensitive to the problems of other professionals when devising company strategies.

They must be good communicators, orally and in writing. They must deal with a whole range of people from the shop floor to the boardroom. They must present their work concisely in well-written reports. They may be required to give presentations and produce slides including diagrams so they need the practical skills to operate office equipment

ENTRY REQUIREMENTS

A number of risk managers enter after working as insurance managers and increasingly after gaining experience as financial managers. A number enter the profession after developing skills in another area of work experience. Sometimes quantity surveyors, solicitors and engineers may have the necessary experience to become risk managers.

Those working in the insurance industry who have passed CII examinations would also be considered.

Some larger companies with risk departments do take trainees straight from school or higher education as junior technicians who may move on to become risk mangers. In many companies risk manager is a senior management position.

Risk managers would be expected to study for the examinations of the Institute of Risk Management (IRM). To register as a student entrants need either a professional qualification, degree or diploma that is considered relevant in the opinion of the governors; examples include a risk management degree, a degree with an insurance or risk management module or an associate membership of the Chartered Institue of Insurance or an accounting body (a full list is available from IRM).

If entrants are over 21 years they may be accepted on the recommendation of a referee such as a fellow of the IRM or a similar professional body.

INSURANCE WORK: NAG

TRAINING

Training is likely to be on the job with an experienced risk manager. Entrants will be required to sit the examination of the IRM. Examinations comprise five core subjects in business organization and finance, risk analysis, risk control, risk financing and corporate risk management. One optional subject must be taken from: occupational safety and health, insurance, liability exposure, local authority risk management and health service risk management.

Candidates are advised to sit not more than four subjects at one sitting. Continuous assessment counts for 25% of the total marks in each subject. Continuous assessment papers are sent out on 1st December to be returned by 1st March and a minimum mark of 40% is required to enable a candidate to proceed to the final examination.

Some exemptions may be available for holders of certain degrees and certain professional qualifications. Contact IRM for details.

Distance learning packages are available and the IRM organizes student forums to support students during their studies.

Most employers expect entrants to undertake continuous professional development and will encourage entrants to undertake additional training courses run by IRM and CII as well as other professional bodies.

LATE ENTRY

Most people enter this career after obtaining another professional qualification. Most enter in their late twenties, early thirties. Some companies may recruit specialist risk managers with accountancy or legal training who are older than this. Larger companies with risk departments may recruit school-leavers.

OPPORTUNITIES

Risk managers are employed by insurance companies and business operations of every kind as well as the public sector. There are also companies that offer consultancy support to companies who do not have their own in-house risk management team.

PAY AND CONDITIONS

Salaries vary considerably in this profession and are dictated by previous qualifications, level of expertise and type of specialism. Risk managers with five years' experience could expect to earn £25,000. Many earn in excess of this.

Although risk managers officially work 35 to 37 hours a week, in practice hours of work are long. They may be called out at weekends and in the evenings to emergencies.

PROSPECTS

In a larger company risk managers may become managers of a specialist department; in a small company they may become directors with a seat on the board. They may become self-employed consultants and specialize in a particular kind of risk like fire or liability.

They may also move into other areas of insurance work like surveying or loss adjusting management.

RELATED OCCUPATIONS

Accountant, accountancy technician, actuary, chartered surveyor, company secretary, solicitor, investment analyst, stockbroker, Stock Exchange market maker/trader, pensions adviser, solicitor, claims engineer.

FURTHER INFORMATION

The Chartered Insurance Institute (CII)*, 20 Aldermanbury, London EC2V 7HY, 0181 989 8464

Insurance and Related Financial Services NTO, The Chartered Institute of Insurance, 20 Aldermanbury, London EC2V 7HY 0171 417 4403

British Insurance and Investment Brokers' Association (BIIBA)*, BIIBA House, 14, Bevis Marks, London EC3A 7NT, 0171 623 9043

The Personal Investment Authority (PIA)*, 1 Canada Square, London E14 5AZ, 0171 538 8860

The Pensions Management Institute (PMI)*, PMI House, 4–10 Artillery Lane, London E1 7LS, 0171 247 1452

The Society of Insurance Technicians*, The Chartered Insurance Institute, 31 Hillcrest Road, South Woodford, London E18 2JP

The Chartered Institute of Loss Adjusters (CILA)*, Manfield House, 1 Southampton Street, London WC2R 0LR, 0171 240 1496

The Institute of Risk Management (IRM)*, Lloyd's Avenue House, 6 Lloyds Avenue, London EC3N 3AX, 0171 709 9809

FURTHER READING

Working In The Money Business – COIC

Periodicals: Pensions World Financial Advisor, Money Management, The Journal (CII publication), The Broker (BIIBA publication).

Leaflets are available from the addresses marked*.

In the careers library classified under NAG.

ACTUARIAL WORK: NAJ

ACTUARY CLCI:NAJ

BACKGROUND INFORMATION

Actuaries form a small but influential professional group. Most of them are concerned with life assurance, pension schemes and other forms of insurance, but all are concerned with long-term financial planning. They design the policy, fix the premiums and repayment values, and decide how to invest the policyholders' money in order to keep the company viable.

THE WORK

Actuaries apply the mathematical theories of probability, compound interest, and statistical techniques to matters with long-term implications, such as life assurance or pension schemes. Actuaries make financial sense of the future by assessing the financial impact of tomorrow's uncertain events. They are experts in analysing the past, modelling the future, assessing the risks involved and communicating what the results mean in financial terms.

Increasing use is made of computers, but an understanding of mathematical theories and statistical techniques is essential.

Insurance: almost 50% of actuaries in Britain work in insurance companies. They carry out an annual valuation – the financial stock-taking required by law. They are concerned with developing new financial products, calculating premium costs and surrender values and investing the vast sums that are received in premiums. The larger insurance companies invest over two million pounds every working day.

Life assurance: the 'appointed actuary' of the company has a statutory responsibility for certifying that millions of pounds of policyholders' money is safe. The actuary to a pension fund similarly has a responsibility to make sure that the finances are sound and that there is money available to pay the benefits that have been promised to present and future pensioners.

Consultants deal with a variety of clients, but most of their work is concerned with advising commercial companies and businesses on pension arrangements for their staff. They advise smaller insurance companies who do not have their own in-house staff, give specialist advice on such matters as take-overs or mergers and, where necessary, the level of damages to be awarded.

Government service: the Government Actuary Department is responsible for devising public service pension schemes, inspecting life assurance companies for the Department of Trade and Industry, and advising the Department of Social Security on benefit rates.

Stock Exchange actuaries give investment advice based on analyses of the market. Their clients are usually insurance companies or pension funds seeking to invest money from premiums. They need specialist advice because they are subject to particular legal liabilities.

A few actuaries work in education, industry and commerce. The jobs range from university teaching to administering the pension funds of multinational companies.

WORK ENVIRONMENT

Actuaries are usually office-based, but those in consulting practice spend a lot of time visiting clients.

SKILLS AND INTERESTS

Actuaries need a flair for maths and an aptitude for analysing facts and figures. The ability to express facts and ideas clearly and simply in speech and writing is essential. They need to be able to explain details to non-specialists and make reports. They also need an intellectual interest in problem solving and in the practical analysis of business problems.

Concentration and attention to detail are essential. Actuaries must be able to amass large quantities of facts, to organize this knowledge, and apply it methodically and accurately.

ENTRY REQUIREMENTS

To qualify as an actuary, candidates must register as a student member of the Institute of Actuaries (England and Wales) or the Faculty of Actuaries (Scotland).

For the Institute of Actuaries, minimum entry requirements for student membership are five GCSEs (A–C), including English; plus two A levels, one of which should be maths at grade B or further maths at grade C, and the other must be at grade C.

For the Faculty of Actuaries, minimum requirements are three H grades, including maths at grade A, and English.

Over 90% of entrants are graduates.

There are several degree courses in actuarial science in the UK. Graduates are accepted from a wide variety of disciplines, providing that they can either meet the A level/H grade requirements, or their degree covers the required mathematical studies.

TRAINING

Training time varies, but an average estimate is from three to five years, combining part-time study and supervised work experience. Tuition for the examinations is mainly through correspondence courses run by the Actuarial Education Company, on behalf of the Faculty and the Institute. Most employers allow time off for study, but much of it has to be fitted in at evenings and weekends. Tutorials and revision courses are arranged in London and other major centres.

There are a series of examinations that must be completed in order to qualify as an actuary. The earlier examinations cover mathematical, statistical and financial techniques. The later examinations test the application of these principles and techniques to institutional investment, life assurance, general insurance and pension funds. In addition, there is a fellowship examination which aims to test the candidate's understanding in greater depth. It is also necessary to have at least three years' relevant experience of actuarial work to qualify as a fellow of the Institute.

In Scotland, the Faculty examinations are the same, but there is no prescribed period of practical experience.

Actuarial science degrees, and some maths degrees, give exemption from parts of the Faculty or Institute examinations.

LATE ENTRY

The Institute of Actuaries prefers training to begin within four years of achieving A levels or a degree. Exceptions can be considered, depending on previous experience and proven aptitude.

ACTUARIAL WORK: NAJ

OPPORTUNITIES

The Institute of Actuaries has approximately 4,500 Fellows and over 4,000 Student Members. The Faculty of Actuaries has over 900 members. Approximately 50% work in insurance or life assurance companies, 40% in firms of consultants, two per cent on the Stock Exchange and a few in industry, commerce, government service and education.

Members of the Institute and the Faculty are employed all over the world, especially in Australia, Canada, the USA, New Zealand, South Africa and the West Indies.

PAY AND CONDITIONS

Salaries start at around £17,000 to about £20,000 for a trainee in London, rising to over £35,000 on qualification. A chief executive can earn £100,000, or more, a year, depending on location.

Actuaries work normal office hours. Trainees have to set aside several hours of their own time every week for studying.

PROSPECTS

Actuarial training can prove an effective foundation for any type of management. It involves analysing facts and figures, perceiving trends and planning ahead. Actuaries are widely respected in business and financial circles, since they play a significant role in many matters. Many actuaries achieve senior management positions.

RELATED OCCUPATIONS

Insurance broker, insurance underwriter, accountant, economist, investment analyst/fund manager, stockbroker, market maker, statistician.

FURTHER INFORMATION

The Faculty of Actuaries (FOA)*, Macleaurin House, 18 Dublin Street, Edinburgh EH1 3PP, 0131 240 1300, www.actuaries.org.uk

The Institute of Actuaries*, Napier House, 4 Worcester Street, Oxford OX1 2AW, 01865 268200, www.actuaries.org.uk

FURTHER READING

Leaflets/booklets are available from the addresses marked*.

Working in Mathematics – COIC

The Ivanhoe Guide to Actuaries – available from careers offices

In the careers library classified under NAJ.

STOCK EXCHANGE WORK AND INVESTMENT ANALYSIS: NAL

1. MARKET MAKER/TRADER CLCI:NAL
2. STOCKBROKER/EQUITY SALESPERSON CLCI:NAL
3. INVESTMENT ANALYST/FUND MANAGER CLCI:NAL

BACKGROUND INFORMATION

Stockbrokers, market makers/traders and investment analysts are all concerned with the trading of bonds, stocks and shares (also known as securities). Bonds are mostly issued by the government when it is in need of additional money and carry a fixed and guaranteed rate of interest. Shares are issued by companies that wish to raise capital to help them carry out their business. When owners or directors of a company decide to 'float' it on the Stock Exchange they have decided to sell part of it. The company gets the money it needs while all new shareholders own a proportion of it and share in its profit or loss. Shares rise or fall in value according to the company's progress and pay out annual dividends or payments to shareholders which are related to the company's profit.

Both individuals and institutions such as pension funds buy and sell shares as a form of investment, hoping that the shares will have increased in value by the time they decide to sell them, thus increasing their investment. Individuals save through shares for a variety of purposes. Pension funds and insurance companies use the profit on share investments to pay pensions or to pay the claims they receive.

Nobody may trade in shares other than through the London Stock Exchange and by using a stockbroker as their agent. Stockbrokers therefore act both as advisers and as the people who actually carry out the transaction. Market makers/traders buy and sell securities, quoting buying and selling prices. Both market makers and stockbrokers are member firms of the London Stock Exchange. There are approximately 400 of these. Some firms are both market makers and stockbrokers.

Investment analysts are employed by either stockbrokers or institutional investors to undertake research into companies, industries or individual securities.

1. MARKET MAKER/TRADER (NAL)

THE WORK

Market makers, sometimes known today as traders, deal in securities as 'principals'. They buy and sell shares on their own account, hoping to make a profit between the buying and selling prices. The system is based on competition between market makers, who are obliged to quote firm bid (buying) and offer (selling) prices for the shares in which they are registered to deal.

They may choose to register to trade in one or more of: UK equities, international equities, the gilt-edged market (loans issued on behalf of the government to fund its spending), AIM securities (the Stock Exchange's Alternative Investment Market for new, small and growing companies) or fixed-interest securities. Some securities are traded so infrequently that there is no competition between market makers and a sole market maker may quote a price.

Market makers decide what prices to quote by studying the supply and demand for investment in various companies. If a company is doing particularly well or if it is the subject of rival take-over bids (a situation which usually increases investor interest) and has shares that are in high demand, any shareholder wanting to sell can expect a high price. If, on the other hand, a company has had recent disappointing results then many shareholders might want to sell. Demand for those shares will be lower however, so they can be bought for a low price.

Market makers gather their information by reading the financial press, consulting investment analysts and making judgements on the basis of the information they are given. Information changes constantly and since it is important that they are always up to date they make great use of computerized information systems which are updated continuously to take account of events that affect the markets.

It is not essential to be a registered market maker to deal in the top 100 securities - i.e. the 100 companies known as the FTSE 100, although some market makers do trade them. These securities are also traded by stockbroking firms directly through the Stock Exchange Electronic Trading System, or SETS, which firms satisfying the Stock Exchange's membership criteria are eligible to use. Orders from clients wishing to buy shares are placed by stockbrokers on this electronic system which is known as the 'order book'. The price at which the client wishes to buy is also displayed. Numbers of shares, with their offer price, are also displayed on the screen by brokers acting for clients wishing to sell. Both buyer and seller have to make a judgement on price, but usually do so following advice from their stockbroker who knows the current state of the book. At the moment a buying order and a selling order match, the sale order is executed automatically. There is therefore no need to employ a middleman.

Other UK securities are still traded through market-making firms.

WORK ENVIRONMENT

Market makers/traders work in their firms' dealing rooms where they have their own workstations containing VDUs and telephones. Dealing rooms are usually very large and so the atmosphere can be very noisy.

SKILLS AND INTERESTS

Market makers/traders need to be able to concentrate for long periods of time and to work under great pressure. They must be constantly alert and quick thinking, able to make split-second decisions. They need to have confidence in their own judgements.

They must be able to absorb information quickly and pick out the relevant parts. They need to be good with figures and quick and accurate in mental arithmetic for calculating prices and profits.

As their income depends entirely on their skill and judgement, they must be able to cope with high levels of risk.

ENTRY REQUIREMENTS

Although there are no formal entry requirements many firms recruiting market makers/traders will only consider graduates. Any degree subject is acceptable but one in economics or a financial subject could be advantageous. Equally important is a strong interest in how the City works and a good knowledge of the financial press.

STOCK EXCHANGE WORK AND INVESTMENT ANALYSIS: NAL

TRAINING

New recruits are trained in-house by working in a firm's different departments and watching established colleagues at work. A trainee market maker/trader might spend the first two to three months at a desk with a qualified dealer, familiarizing himself/herself with day-to-day business and terminology. Some large financial institutions that offer a variety of broking and investment services, including market-making, train new recruits by introducing them to all branches of the firm before they decide to which section they would be best suited. This type of training programme can last for 18 months.

Before market makers/traders are permitted to conduct any business they must qualify to have their names placed on the Stock Exchange's list of persons eligible to trade. In order to qualify they must pass the Domestic Equity Markets Oral Examination, run jointly by the Stock Exchange and the Securities Institute, a professional body which sets examinations on behalf of different regulatory authorities. This examination is held once a month. Candidates who decide that they are ready to take the examination apply to the Securities Institute. They are then sent a study pack. They may study the material at their own pace but are recommended to allow two to three weeks. The examination consists of ten questions based on the study pack and is held by two examiners, one from the Markets Regulation Department of the Stock Exchange and the other an experienced trader.

Successful candidates are awarded a certificate by the Securities Institute showing their status as a registered trader. Unsuccessful candidates are informed of their weaknesses and advised in which areas they must improve. They may have three attempts at the examination. Should they fail all three they may not attempt it again for a two-year period.

LATE ENTRY

This is possible but in most cases, late entrants are expected to have had some other relevant experience. It is essential, nonetheless, to be well-informed about and committed to the financial world.

OPPORTUNITIES

This is a very small field which has seen a reduction in opportunities with the advent of automated share trading. Market-making firms are now often part of larger financial organizations made up of banks, stockbrokers and investment advisers. Although these all recruit from time to time, openings for market-makers/traders as such are limited and highly competitive.

There are opportunities to work overseas, especially in the Far East.

PAY AND CONDITIONS

Earnings can be very high – well in excess of £100,000, but can vary greatly from year to year depending on a firm's trading results.

The working day is from about 7am to 7pm Monday to Friday, but longer hours are often necessary.

This is largely a young person's profession. Many market makers/traders suffer from 'burn out' by their early forties and look for alternative employment.

PROSPECTS

Most firms do not have a well-defined promotion structure. It may be possible to move into other types of work within the employing organization.

RELATED OCCUPATIONS

Actuary, commodities broker, futures trader, insurance underwriter, investment analyst, fund manager, stockbroker.

FURTHER INFORMATION AND READING

Please see article 2. STOCKBROKER/EQUITY SALESPERSON.

2. STOCKBROKER/EQUITY SALESPERSON (NAL)

THE WORK

A stockbroker is an individual or a firm that gives investment advice to a client in return for a commission. The investments are usually stocks and shares – ie equities traded on the London Stock Exchange. Individual stockbrokers, often now known as equity salespeople, act as advisers and agents on behalf of individual clients and as dealing agents for institutional investors. They research and absorb information about the markets in both foreign and domestic equities and interpret analysts' reports in order to recommend to their clients whether they should buy, hold or sell stocks; to advise and persuade clients what action they should take and to buy and sell securities for them. They also advise on other investment products such as unit trusts and options (the right to buy or sell securities at a fixed price within a specified period).

Stockbrokers may not carry out all of the above functions as some stockbroking firms offer different levels of service to their clients who choose the ones they wish to use. Clients may opt for an **'execution only'** service. In this case they make their own decisions and simply instruct the stockbroker to carry out their instructions in making a deal. If they choose an **'advisory, non-managed'** service, they expect the stockbroker to advise them on the decisions to take. The third alternative is a **'managed portfolio'** – this arrangement sub-divides into two groups. **'Discretionary managed clients'** have given the stockbroker authority to trade for them using their professional judgement while **'non-discretionary managed clients'** must be consulted before a deal is made. The ultimate responsibility for all decisions taken however, remains the client's.

Stockbrokers conducting private client work are obliged to follow strict rules. They must conduct a thorough financial analysis including all the client's assets in order to know the full extent of their assets and obligations before they begin to advise them. They are also required to review all portfolios every six months but in practice, most do this more frequently.

Stockbrokers trade through the Stock Exchange's automatic system or through a market maker. (Please see article 1. MARKET MAKER/TRADER). They have a

STOCK EXCHANGE WORK AND INVESTMENT ANALYSIS: NAL

legal obligation to buy at 'best price' for their clients or the lowest price available at the time of the deal. Once a deal has been finalized the Stock Exchange's computerized settlement system transfers the shares between buyer and seller.

WORK ENVIRONMENT

Stockbrokers work from their firms' dealing rooms or from their own offices, using telephones, VDUs and computers. The atmosphere in dealing rooms can be busy and noisy. Shares are no longer traded on the floor of the Stock Exchange.

SKILLS AND INTERESTS

Stockbrokers must be able to master detail and to present information lucidly and clearly to clients. They need an interest in and understanding of how different businesses work and of the factors that can affect share prices. They must be able to cope with stress and pressure. This is a high risk business. Honesty and integrity are vital since they are dealing with (often large sums of) other people's money.

They need to be confident with figures and to have confidence in their own judgement.

They should be prepared to wear conventional business dress.

ENTRY REQUIREMENTS

There are no formal minimum entry requirements, but, in practice, firms recruit graduates with good degrees (minimum 2:1). Although any degree discipline is acceptable particularly useful subjects are business studies, economics, law, mathematics and statistics. Recruits without a relevant degree should be able to demonstrate interest in their chosen field: for example, they may have done vacation work with a stockbroking firm.

TRAINING

Stockbrokers must be registered by their employer as a 'registered person' with the regulatory organization, the Financial Services Authority, and the employing firm must be a member firm of the Stock Exchange. In order to register and so be allowed to conduct investment business on behalf of clients, they must at present pass the Registered Persons examination administered by the Securities Institute. Some changes to the structure of the examination are currently under consideration.

Training also takes place in-house. Many new recruits follow formal training programmes for a year or 18 months, during which time they work in all sections of the firm and are assigned projects to complete. Employers offering a variety of financial services, including stockbroking, may take on graduate recruits and train them in all branches of the firm before they decide what type of work they are best suited to.

LATE ENTRY

This is possible but unlikely after the late twenties, unless moving from a related financial area and perhaps able to introduce new business to the firm.

OPPORTUNITIES

There are about 400 member firms of the London Stock Exchange. Many of these are now large banking and finance houses offering other financial services such as banking, market-making and investment advice. People who hope to become stockbrokers often enter as graduate trainees and express a preference for this area of work.

Most opportunities for institutional work are in London, with some openings also in other cities that have become major financial centres like Birmingham, Bristol, Edinburgh, Glasgow and Manchester. There are opportunities for private client work in other cities for locally based investors.

PAY AND CONDITIONS

Starting salaries range from around £17,000 to £25,000. A successful broker can earn in excess of £100,000 and also has the opportunity to build a personal portfolio of equities.

The working day is from about 7am to 7pm Monday to Friday, but longer hours are often necessary and stockbrokers often take clients' portfolios home to review over the weekend.

PROSPECTS

There are opportunities to become heads of broking teams or partners in firms and to move to other related areas such as fund or investment management.

Very few stockbrokers are entirely self-employed, but some work on a self-employed basis within a firm.

RELATED OCCUPATIONS

Actuary, commodities broker, financial services adviser, insurance underwriter, investment analyst, fund manager, market-maker.

FURTHER INFORMATION

The Securities Institute, Centurion House, 2-4 Monument Street, London EC3R 8AJ

FURTHER READING

Working In The Money Business – COIC

In the careers library classified under NAL.

3. INVESTMENT ANALYST/FUND MANAGER (NAL)

THE WORK

The work and training of an investment analyst and a fund manager is so similar in content that, often, fund managers carry out their own analysis, so the following information is relevant to both titles. Investment analysis and fund management also includes the work of portfolio managers and investment managers.

Investment analysts attempt to predict the long- and short-term future performance of securities and decide what will be a good buy for investors, who may be their clients (for stockbroker analysts) or their employers (for institutional analysts). Investment analysts do not analyse only UK securities. They study foreign securities and other investment media, such as commodities, futures and options. They also look at economies and markets in general, to help them get the full picture of the prospects

STOCK EXCHANGE WORK AND INVESTMENT ANALYSIS: NAL

for a particular company or sector. Investment analysts working for stockbrokers tend to specialize in a particular field, such as utilities (gas, water and electricity) or building materials, building up long-term relationships in their specialist sectors.

Investment analysts study financial and other data, such as past performance of particular securities, published government statistics, company annual reports, government regulations, and legislation that could affect companies in their sector. They also gather information by speaking to contacts via the telephone and by meeting representatives of, and visiting, the companies they analyse. They use this information to produce models and forecasts for internal use, written reports for clients (often accompanied by a presentation) or reports on proposed changes within an investment portfolio. These reports often have to be produced at short notice.

Stockbrokers' investment analysts have regular meetings with clients. Their expertise is important in attracting potential clients. They can become involved in assisting their firm to advise companies in their sector on raising money through issuing shares. In large firms they work as part of a team, all contributing to produce one report, but in small firms, one investment analyst may do all the research necessary to produce a report.

Institutional investment analysts work closely with fund managers (the people who manage an institution's portfolio of investments) and help them decide what to buy and sell; in fact, the distinction between the two is often blurred. They also make presentations to representatives of the funds they manage. These representatives may be fellow employees, in the case of life assurance companies or self-managed pension funds, or they may be clients, for instance, trustees of pension funds or charities who have appointed an external fund manager to look after their investments.

WORK ENVIRONMENT

Investment analysts are based in offices; however, they spend a lot of time out of the office, conducting research and meeting people. They may have to travel long distances to meetings or spend time away from home or even abroad.

SKILLS AND INTERESTS

Investment analysts need to have outgoing personalities and to be able to sell their skills and knowledge to clients and relate to people at all levels. They need the maturity and responsibility to organize their own or their employer's time and work without supervision. At the same time, a capacity for team work is essential. As they often receive unexpected last-minute requests for detailed information, flexibility, emotional resilience and the ability to work under pressure are vital. Tact and resourcefulness are also useful when gathering information, perhaps from companies that are being studied as investment prospects. A high level of commitment to the job is required.

Investment analysts need to be able to extract relevant information from a mass of detail, in order to prepare useful reports on a company as an investment prospect. Numerical fluency, or the readiness to improve it, is important for understanding statistical and financial information. Accountancy skills are useful too. Fluency in written and spoken communication is needed for writing readable reports and making presentations to clients. They need to have, or be prepared to acquire, computer skills.

ENTRY REQUIREMENTS

It is difficult to become a trainee investment analyst without a degree or professional qualification. Many applicants will have both. (There is a *minimum* entry requirement of five GCSEs /S grades (A–C/1–3) or equivalent for registration to take the examinations of the Institute of Investment Management and Research). The most useful degrees or qualifications for prospective entrants are in economics, statistics or accounting, but this does not rule out candidates from other disciplines. For instance, languages may be useful when applying to a firm specializing in overseas work. Relevant industrial experience may also be useful.

TRAINING

Training varies according to the size of the employing organization, but most training takes place on the job. Trainees usually start off as part of a team, with a senior analyst assigned to supervise them. They are given regular tasks, such as updating internal forecasts, and larger projects – designed to teach them how to approach analysis, such as collecting published data on a company or sector and writing a report on it. They are expected to read widely and to take some responsibility for keeping abreast with new information. They can expect to contribute to the decision-making process within six to twelve months of joining.

At the same time, they may study for examinations of the Institute of Investment Management and Research. The Institute's Investment Management Certificate (IMC) is the UK mandatory test of competence and is also recognized in 19 other European countries and in the USA. Exam subjects include: regulatory environment; financial instruments and other investments; accounting; economics; and statistics. Candidates must have six months' experience in the financial services industry before attempting the examination.

After obtaining the certificate, analysts may take a further two-part examination in order to become eligible for election to Associate Membership. Depending on the size of the employing organization, trainees are usually given financial support and time off work to study for these exams. Study for the exams can be by block or day release, evening classes or distance learning courses. In addition to passing the six papers of the Associateship examination, candidates must demonstrate two years' relevant experience before being elected.

It is possible to become an Associate in two years.

Holders of certain other professional qualifications in accountancy or corporate finance and graduates from MSc courses based on the Institute's syllabus at Dublin City and Stirling Universities may claim exemption from some or all of the papers in the Associateship examinations.

LATE ENTRY

There is no upper age limit. Maturity and experience are useful attributes. The majority of new entrants are over 25 years.

OPPORTUNITIES

Investment analysts usually work for stockbrokers of

STOCK EXCHANGE WORK AND INVESTMENT ANALYSIS: NAL

financial institutions, ie pension funds, life assurance companies, unit and investment trusts and banks, including merchant banks and the Bank of England, and large companies who manage their own investments. There are opportunities for work abroad, particularly in the Far East. The employer's size can vary from a small firm with a handful of professionals, to an integrated financial conglomerate with hundreds of investment professionals.

Overall numbers within the profession (around 5,000) are stable and competition for vacancies is fierce. Vacancies occur fairly often, as investment analysts tend to move around within the profession. Jobs are concentrated in the South East of England, Birmingham, Liverpool, Manchester and Edinburgh, and it is necessary to be mobile to secure work.

PAY AND CONDITIONS

Annual salaries are within a range of £18,000 to £20,000 for new entrants to over £50,000 for experienced analysts. Analysts work long and irregular hours to get the job done, as stock markets around the world operate on different time zones. They often come into work very early, before the London Stock Market opens.

PROSPECTS

Career analysts tend to work for stockbrokers, while institutional analysts who do well can expect to progress to assistant fund manager and then to fund manager. It is also possible to become self-employed as a partner in a consultancy or stockbroking firm, though partners in a firm of stockbrokers must pass the Securities and Futures Authority exams.

RELATED OCCUPATIONS

Accountant, actuary, economist, statistician, stockbroker, fund manager.

FURTHER INFORMATION

Institute of Investment Management and Research, 21, Ironmonger Lane, London EC2V 8EY, 0171 796 3000

Publicity and Promotions Department * , The London Stock Exchange, London EC1 1HP, 0171 797 3628

The Securities and Futures Authority Ltd*, Cottons Centre, Cottons Lane, London SE1 2QB, 0171 378 9000

FURTHER READING

Leaflets/booklets are available from the addresses marked*.

Working in the Money Business – COIC

In the careers library classified under NAL.

GROUP O – BUYING, SELLING AND RELATED SERVICES

1. MARKETING MANAGER CLCI:OB
2. MARKET RESEARCH EXECUTIVE CLCI:OB
3. MARKET RESEARCH INTERVIEWER CLCI:OB

BACKGROUND INFORMATION

The purpose of marketing is to provide customers with the goods and services they want, when and where they want them, at a price that suits both the customers and the company.

Marketing involves making sure the company offers what the customer wants to buy, and that the customer buys it. This entails a marketing campaign in which all departments, from design to distribution, work together with the client's wishes in mind.

The main sectors in marketing are:

– fast-moving consumer goods, such as food, drink, toiletries;

– consumer durables, such as furniture, cookers, washing machines;

– industrial products, sold within industry, such as machine tools, engine components, laboratory equipment, raw materials;

– services, including financial, computing, travel, leisure;

– public sector, for example, charities, theatres, schools and colleges.

This division applies to both the home and export market.

1. MARKETING MANAGER (OB)

THE WORK

The main stages in marketing – the 'marketing mix' – are market research, product development, pricing, sales, distribution and promotion. Marketing managers are responsible for planning and co-ordinating each of these stages.

Market research provides managers with information about customer preferences and competitors' activity. They attend meetings with their research executives or a market research agency, deciding what information they need and how to gather it. They use the findings of the research in planning the marketing strategy.

Product development involves the marketing manager advising the design and production departments of the customers' requirements, agreeing what changes need to be made to existing products and discussing the introduction of new ones. They attend meetings, give presentations and write reports based on market research findings.

Pricing means working out prices that are realistic in terms of both production, costs, sales targets, and an acceptable profit level. Managers co-ordinate production and promotion with sales and distribution.

Sales and distribution – the marketing manager makes sure the demand can be met. They analyse the sales figures to find out how effective the promotion campaign has been and to help in planning future production. In some companies, sales and marketing management are combined, and the marketing manager takes personal accountability for sales.

Promotion campaigns involve working and liaising with design consultancies, advertising, direct marketing and self promotion agencies and PR consultancies if not done in-house, also liaising with advertising agencies to discuss the advertising campaign and choice of media.

Export marketing is usually separate from the home marketing department. It often combines responsibility for marketing and sales. Managers have to adapt the marketing mix to local demand and can face problems of communication, cultural differences or consumer legislation. Some managers appoint local agents to handle market research, sales, distribution and promotion. Others become personally involved in assessing the market, setting up promotion campaigns and negotiating with customers. While overseas they often work by themselves, arranging transport and storage, dealing with documentation, customs, local taxes and legal problems. Some spend most of their time overseas; others handle much of the administration from the UK. In multinational companies, the marketing manager works in liaison with overseas branches.

WORK ENVIRONMENT

Marketing managers are office-based but spend much of their time in discussion with other departmental managers and in travelling to visit customers and agencies. Travel overseas may be required.

SKILLS AND INTERESTS

Marketing managers should be good communicators, able to talk and write clearly and persuasively to people at all levels both inside and outside the company. It is important to be a good listener, able to understand other people's points of view without losing sight of the original objective.

Qualities of leadership are very important: the ability to organize and motivate others, set targets, encourage co-operation and accept responsibility. They should also be willing to adapt plans to the needs of the market-place and to work within the management team.

Numeracy is a basic requirement; marketing managers use figures much of the time, in analysing sales and research data, in planning and in pricing. They must be aware of the need for profit.

In initiating and carrying through a project, imagination should be combined with enthusiasm, attention to detail and sound judgement.

ENTRY REQUIREMENTS

The minimum qualifications for a trainee post in marketing are normally four GCSEs/S grades (A–C/1–3) including English and maths. Entrants are usually over 18 years.

Holders of any of the following qualifications who are also over 18 years are able to study for the Certificate in Marketing of the Chartered Institute of Marketing:

– GCSE/S grade passes as above plus one year's full-time experience in sales or marketing;

– GCSE/S grade passes as above and two A levels or equivalents;

– BTEC/SQA National Certificate/Diploma in Business Studies;

– Advanced GNVQ/GSVQ Level III in Business;

MARKETING: OB

- NVQ/SVQ Level 2 in a sales- or marketing-related subject; *or*
- or aged over 20 with at least one year's full-time experience in sales or marketing.

Minimum qualifications for the professional examinations of the Institute of Export are four GCSEs/S grades (A–C/1–3) including English, and one A level/two H grades or equivalent or NVQ/SVQ Level 2 in International Trade and Services.

Many employers require a degree or higher national diploma. The degree may be in any subject, but a business-related course that includes marketing would be most directly relevant. Some employers prefer a language qualification or, for industrial marketing, a scientific or technical subject.

BTEC/SQA Higher National Diploma in Business Studies with marketing specialisms is widely available. Subject entry requirements should be checked with each institution but nearly always include English and maths at GCSE/S grade.

An increasing number of graduates (any discipline) take a full-time postgraduate course in marketing, a Diploma in Management Studies, or a Diploma in Export Marketing.

For export marketing, it is often important to acquire a knowledge of the language used by the company's customers.

A driving licence is often required.

TRAINING

A number of full-time courses are available that include marketing studies. Marketing may be combined with languages, computing, economics or other subjects and it forms part of most business and management science courses.

Whether or not the new entrant has an academic qualification in marketing, some measure of training at work is provided. Much of the training is informal, through working alongside experienced marketing assistants and managers. Employers arrange short in-company or external courses on topics such as public speaking or computer techniques, and may encourage part-time study for a professional qualification, usually the Advanced and/or Postgraduate Diplomas in Marketing of The Chartered Institute of Marketing.

An increasing number of marketing trainees study for the CIM qualifications, usually via part-time courses or distance learning. The syllabuses cover the economic and legal aspects of marketing, management, marketing strategy, business communications, business organization, financial analysis and marketing operations. Alternatively, many short courses/seminars are also available on all aspects of marketing.

The Institute of Export conducts professional examinations in two parts. Courses may be studied by part-time or distance learning. Professional Part 1 ('Work in the Office') includes principles of marketing, principles of law relating to overseas trade, international trade and payments, and international physical distribution. Professional Part 2 ('Work in the Field') covers international marketing, international marketing research and principles of management in export.

NVQs/SVQs are available in Marketing Communications at Level 2 and in Marketing Products and Services at Levels 3 and 4.

LATE ENTRY

Most recruits to marketing begin in their early twenties and expect to become marketing managers at age 25 to 35 years. Older candidates usually have experience in a related field such as sales, market research or advertising.

Most institutions of higher education welcome applications from adult students. Candidates who lack the normal entry qualifications are considered according to individual circumstances.

OPPORTUNITIES

Most industrial and commercial organizations have their own in-house marketing departments, responsible for the marketing process as a whole. Marketing services agencies also offer opportunities for marketing managers. Some agencies specialize, for example, in communications, or other areas such as advertising or market research. Others offer a broad range of marketing support services.

Opportunities exist in the consumer sector, particularly fast-moving consumer goods, for marketing trainees with both manufacturers and retail chains. In industrial marketing, where the products are often complex, expensive and adapted to the requirements of individual customers, the sales and marketing functions may be combined, so that the marketing manager deals directly with the customers. Opportunities also exist in the relatively new and growing service and public sectors.

Opportunities in marketing vary with the state of the economy. Competition for jobs at any level is intense. Vacancies are advertised in the national press, *Marketing, Marketing Weekly* and *Campaign*.

PAY AND CONDITIONS

Salaries for trainees in marketing start at around £10,400 and rise with success in the job. A salary of £35,000 or more is not uncommon for an experienced manager.

Most marketing managers work normal office hours of 37 to 40 hours a week but these are often extended to meet deadlines and attend meetings.

PROSPECTS

It is usual for a new entrant to marketing to make several changes, between jobs and between employers, in order to gain experience. Promotion depends on success in the job. It generally implies taking responsibility for the marketing of an increasing number or range of products. Marketing managers may become marketing directors or go into general management. Some set up their own consultancy.

RELATED OCCUPATIONS

Advertising agency account/media executive, market research executive, sales manager, public relations officer, store manager, sales representative.

FURTHER INFORMATION

The Chartered Institute of Marketing*, Moor Hall, Cookham, Maidenhead, Berkshire SL6 9QH, 01628 427500

The Institute of Export*, Export House, 64 Clifton Street, London EC2A 4HB, 0171 247 9812

MARKETING: OB

FURTHER READING

Leaflets/booklets are available from the addresses marked*.

Working in Marketing and Sales – COIC

Marketing and Sales – AGCAS

How to Get on in Marketing – A Career Development Guide (Second Edition) – Kogan Page

In the careers library classified under OB.

2. MARKET RESEARCH EXECUTIVE (OB)

BACKGROUND INFORMATION

The purpose of market research is to find out what customers want and why, so that the suppliers of goods and services may meet that need. There are three main types of market research: consumer, industrial, and social.

Consumer research is concerned with goods and services sold to the public. Companies that provide these ask questions such as: how do customers react to new prices or packaging? How satisfied are they with the after-sales service? Could this town accommodate another hypermarket? A market research agency usually conducts the research on behalf of the company.

Industrial or 'business to business' research is concerned with goods and services bought for use within industry, such as machine tools or raw materials. It often calls for technical knowledge and is carried out either by a specialist research agency or by the firm's own market research executives. They deal with matters such as the market for electronic components, trends in textile manufacture, potential coal exports.

Social and political research is used by central and local government to investigate people's views on political or economic issues. They use the findings to help plan their policy on, for example, health or housing provision.

THE WORK

Consumer research executives, working for an agency, identify exactly what the client wants to find out, then prepare a proposal outlining the research programme and detailing the costs. They 'sell' this to the client in a written and oral presentation. Once the deal has been negotiated and secured, agency executives control progress. They decide what sample of the population to target and what quantitative or qualitative research methods to use. These could include face-to-face or telephone interviews, postal questionnaires and group discussions. Executives usually train a team of field interviewers to help with face-to-face surveys – interviewing passers-by – while they themselves conduct in-depth discussions and write the questionnaires. They monitor sales and stock records from stores. They also use published information from sources such as government statistics and company reports. Using computers to analyse the data, executives collate and interpret the findings of the research. Finally they deliver a written or verbal presentation to the client.

Many firms supplying the consumer market employ their own market research executives. Their job is seldom to carry out the research themselves but to commission an agency to do it. This means agreeing objectives, terms and methods of enquiry with the agency, and interpreting the results to management.

Industrial research executives gain much of their information from personal or telephone interviews with users of the product in question. Interviews tend to be more detailed than in the consumer sector, and to be based less on a questionnaire than on a discussion about how the product is bought or used in that particular firm. Desk research can also be particularly helpful.

Social researchers work in many different settings on a wide range of subjects. These include unemployment, racial harassment, women's health care, drug dependency. Methods vary with subject and sample, but include questionnaires, interviews, and door-to-door enquiry, followed by statistical analysis using computers.

In large agencies and research institutes, the work may be divided into quantitative and qualitative research. Quantitative researchers spend more time on computing and statistical analysis. Qualitative work calls upon interests in psychology and behaviour, and involves writing questionnaires, conducting in-depth interviews and interpreting the results.

WORK ENVIRONMENT

Market research is mainly office-based, either in agencies or within the firms that supply goods or services. However, executives may travel extensively to meet their clients, at home and, increasingly, abroad. Most agencies are found in large cities.

SKILLS AND INTERESTS

For quantitative research a numerate and analytical mind is essential. Market research executives dealing with numbers and statistics have to analyse the data clearly and objectively. A grounding in statistics and computing is often required. Industrial research executives may need particular scientific or technical knowledge. Qualitative researchers require an interest in psychology and behavioural science.

Executives need the ability to appreciate the client's requirements and to frame a questionnaire that elicits the appropriate information. They should be able to express themselves clearly in speech and writing, for compiling and presenting reports.

Market research executives should like working with a wide variety of people. The work can involve discussions with consumers, managers, technical staff and others; executives should feel at ease in meeting and talking to everybody. Agency executives also require sales ability to some extent, as part of their job is to win commissions.

Market research executives should be good administrators. A thorough, logical approach, and willingness to take responsibility, are important. Pressure can be considerable – working to deadlines, sometimes handling several projects at once.

ENTRY REQUIREMENTS

No formal academic requirements are specified but almost all market research executives hold a degree or higher national diploma. Any degree subject is acceptable, though the most relevant include business studies, social sciences, maths, statistics and economics. A science or engineering degree may be appropriate for industrial market research. Languages can be an advantage for international work.

Students in further and higher education may take the Market Research Society's Foundation and Certificate examination as part of their degree, higher national diploma or A level/H grade studies. These professional examinations can also be taken independently. Details of these schemes are available from The Market Research Society. Candidates must have completed the certificate in order to pass the diploma.

The foundation and certificate qualifications are equivalent to NVQ Levels 2 and 3 respectively.

TRAINING

Postgraduate courses in marketing, market research or social research are available at several institutes of higher education. A degree course lasts three or four years, a higher national diploma course lasts two to three years. Many degree and higher national diploma courses in business subjects offer options in marketing or market research.

Much training is carried out within companies and may be supplemented by short courses and seminars run by the Market Research Society (MRS). Practising researchers who hold the Market Research Society's Certificate may progress to the Diploma.

NVQs/SVQs in Marketing Research are available at Levels 3 and 4.

LATE ENTRY

Most research assistants or trainee market research executives begin in their early twenties. It may be possible to go into market research after experience in other marketing fields – such as advertising or sales – or with a background in statistics, economics or maths. Some find an opening as research assistants after experience in field or telephone interviewing.

Many universities and colleges welcome applications from older candidates who lack the usual formal academic entry requirements. Each application is considered on its merit.

Candidates over 21 years who lack the usual academic qualifications may register for the MRS Certificate and Diploma examinations provided they are working full-time in market research or marketing at an appropriate level.

OPPORTUNITIES

The Market Research Society has about 6,500 members, of whom half work in agencies. There are about 300 market research agencies, mostly in London. They range from one- or two-person businesses to firms of several hundred. Most agencies handle consumer research, a few specialize in industrial topics or social and political research.

Opportunities in social research arise with local and central government, in higher education, with independent agencies and with institutes such as Social and Community Planning Research. There are occasional openings in employer or trade associations. The Social Survey Division of the Office of Population Censuses and Surveys handles much of the research for central government.

Other executives work in industry. Most large industrial and commercial organizations have their own research departments. Advertising agencies employ market researchers, mainly to study the effectiveness of the advertising.

There are about 250 vacancies a year in market research for new graduates. Many start as research assistants, helping with desk research and administration and briefing field workers. Some graduates start as general marketing trainees, with research as one of the options. Vacancies appear in the national press, industrial trade press, *Marketing* and *Marketing Week*.

The MRS publish directories of market research organizations.

PAY AND CONDITIONS

Starting salaries range from £10,000 to £15,000. These rise to £26,000 plus, for senior executives; well over that for managers.

Most executives work normal office hours but may be required to work extra as deadlines approach.

PROSPECTS

Early responsibility and rapid promotion are possible within market research for those with ability and ambition. In consumer research, it is usual to change jobs fairly frequently, and to move between industry and agencies to gain experience.

Market research trainees can expect to take early responsibility for their own clients and their own projects, then to manage a research department or team. Specialization is possible, for example in attitude research or overseas work. Agency executives may become directors, or set up in business themselves. Some market research executives move into advertising or other marketing functions.

Industrial market researchers may gain promotion within their department, or move into other marketing or managerial posts.

In social research institutes, central and local government and higher education, a career structure, dependent on experience, leads to senior grades. However, many posts are on a short-term contract basis.

RELATED OCCUPATIONS

Advertising executive, public relations officer, marketing manager, statistician, psychologist, sales representative, purchasing officer.

FURTHER INFORMATION

Please see article 3. MARKET RESEARCH INTERVIEWER.

3. MARKET RESEARCH INTERVIEWER (OB)

THE WORK

Market research interviewers collect facts and opinions by interviewing the public and members of organizations in person or by telephone. The main areas of work are consumer, executive or specialist research. Interviews may be with individuals or groups and range from brief objective questions-and-answers to lengthy in-depth discussions. Most interviews are one-to-one, but some interviewers hold group or panel sessions. These involve, for example, asking members of the public to keep a diary of the brands they are using.

To make sure that they obtain the information they want, interviewers normally follow a guide and in many cases a

MARKETING: OB

very detailed questionnaire, specifying not only what is to be asked but how. They note down answers as they proceed – by ticking boxes and/or writing, word for word, what each person says. They may use tape or video recorders in group situations. Telephone interviewers may key the responses directly into a computer.

Consumer research can take place on the pavement, inside shops, in local halls or in people's homes. A vast range of topics is covered, from shopping habits and food preferences to political opinions and local transport policy. On the high street, interviewers approach members of the public who, in their opinion, belong in certain selected categories. In most cases, interviewer and respondent together complete a brief questionnaire, which may cover any social, political or consumer subject. In hall tests, respondents are invited into a local meeting place to sample a new product or comment on a display. For home visits, interviewers may be supplied with addresses or may choose their own. They may conduct the interview there and then, or they may leave a questionnaire for the householder to fill in, returning at a later date to collect it or assist with it. They may leave samples on home placement, for example, new brands of washing powder or disposable nappy, and call back to discuss them later. Some interviews may be conducted by telephone from home or office, often during the evening.

Executive interviews are usually long detailed discussions, by telephone or in person. They are arranged by appointment with people in positions of responsibility, such as senior executives, purchasing officers or company secretaries. They may investigate industrial or commercial subjects such as the import of raw materials, choice of machine tools or use of desktop computers in the office.

Specialist interviews are similarly detailed. The interviewer might, for example, question doctors, pharmacists and physiotherapists on the supply of certain medicines or orthopaedic equipment, or visit farmers to compare fertilizers or feedstuff. In-depth interviews demand careful preparation as the interviewer should be sufficiently well-informed to discuss the subject with experts.

WORK ENVIRONMENT

Many market research interviews take place in town or city streets amid noise, bustle and any sort of weather. Others are held in shopping malls, stores, places of work or in private homes. Interviewers usually work in or near their home area. Telephone interviewers usually work from their own homes but sometimes from an office.

SKILLS AND INTERESTS

Market research interviewers should enjoy meeting people and should not be shy to approach them. They should find it easy to talk confidently to anyone, explain what they are doing and ask direct unambiguous questions. They should also be good listeners, careful and observant in noting responses. Legible handwriting and the ability to write clear, concise reports are required.

Gaining people's confidence and winning their co-operation demands tact and patience. Most people are pleased to respond to a courteous, friendly approach, but some object. It can be especially difficult to gain interviews with busy executives. Completing a full quota of interviews can take a great deal of perseverance and self-discipline. A thorough, methodical manner of working is required. Interviewers need to be reliable and work without direct supervision.

Good health and stamina are essential for most field work, as it often takes place outdoors in all weathers and can involve a great deal of walking and standing.

ENTRY REQUIREMENTS

No particular academic qualifications are required. Personal qualities and enthusiasm are more important. These are tested during training and the first experiences of field work, which commonly deter a number of new entrants.

Applicants should have their own telephone, so that they can be contacted when work is available. They should be able to work at short notice and to devote sufficient time each day to complete the job within the allocated period. Except in inner cities, a driving licence and a car are nearly always essential.

TRAINING

Market research agencies organize their own training. Typically this consists of a two- or three-day intensive course covering the principles and practice of market research interviewing. Trainees are taught to recognize socio-economic categories. They learn how to select and approach respondents, what to ask and how, how to complete the returns and write reports. Where appropriate they also learn the skills of telephone interviewing. A supervisor accompanies them on field-work training, and again at twice-yearly intervals. A percentage of their field work is back-checked by telephone.

The Market Research Society's Foundation and Certificate examinations provide a qualification for those new to the industry. Contact the Market Research Society for details.

NVQ/SVQ in Marketing Research (Interviewing) is available at Level 2.

LATE ENTRY

Market research interviewers are recruited at any age over 18 years. There is no maximum age limit. Some agencies may express a preference for older applicants with some experience of dealing with the public.

The availability of part-time work also makes it particularly suitable for adults with domestic commitments.

OPPORTUNITIES

Most interviewers are employed by market research agencies. A smaller number work for research institutes, government departments or opinion pollsters. There are about 300 agencies, mostly based in the London area but using field interviewers throughout the country. The larger agencies undertake all types of market and social research. Consumer research is the main area of employment for interviewers, but a few agencies specialize in industrial or business-to-business research. Social research is carried out either by independent research institutes, the Social Survey Division of the Office of Population Censuses and Surveys, other government departments, or by the social research units of large market research agencies. Some interviewers are self-employed and may work for more than one agency.

MARKETING: OB

Demand for market research interviewers varies with the state of the economy. In recent years many small independent agencies have closed, or amalgamated with larger firms. Vacancies are advertised in the local press. Jobcentres and careers offices may be able to help with the addresses of potential employers.

PAY AND CONDITIONS

The work is part-time and irregular. Agencies contact interviewers already on their pay-roll, or advertise for trainees, as required. Interviewers are allocated work to be completed within a set period. To some extent they can arrange their hours to suit themselves and their family commitments. However, some jobs, such as those involving home visits, have to be done in the evening and at weekends. Field interviewers are normally expected to work about six hours a day. Interviewers may be paid on an hourly or daily rate, but most are paid by the job. The average basic rate for a six-hour day is about £26 to £30 a day plus mileage allowance. Bonuses may be added.

PROSPECTS

Experienced field interviewers may develop preferences and build up skill in certain types of work, such as social surveys, home placement or group interviewing. Some branch into industrial research, which involves learning to interview executives or specialists in depth.

In large agencies there are prospects of promotion to senior interviewer, supervisor and area field-work manager. Occasionally an opportunity to become a research assistant may arise.

RELATED OCCUPATIONS

Telephone salesperson, sales representative, employment agency consultant/interviewer, store demonstrator, market research executive.

FURTHER INFORMATION

The Market Research Centre*, Leicester Business School, The Gateway, Leicester LE1 9BH, 0116 257 7222

The Market Research Society*, 15 Northburgh Street, London EC14 0AH, 0171 490 4911

FURTHER READING

Leaflets/booklets are available from the addresses marked*.

Market Research and Social Research – AGCAS

In the careers library classified under OB.

ADVERTISING: OD

1. **ACCOUNT EXECUTIVE CLCI:OD**
2. **ACCOUNT PLANNER CLCI:OD**
3. **MEDIA EXECUTIVE CLCI:OD**
4. **COPYWRITER CLCI:OD**

BACKGROUND INFORMATION

Advertising is concerned with promoting goods, services and ideas. Advertisements appear in newspapers and magazines, on posters, commercial radio and television, in cinemas and in the form of direct mail and circulars.

Advertising is big business, with thousands of millions of pounds spent on advertising in Britain each year. It is an industry that has to keep aware of changes in the business environment, such as the development of advertising on satellite and cable television and on Teletext.

The advertising industry can be seen as having three parts:
– the organizations that buy advertising;
– the owners of the media who sell advertising, such as newspapers, magazines, commercial radio and television;
– the link between the two, which is usually an advertising agency.

This article deals with four of the main specialist jobs in advertising agencies – account executive, account planner, media executive and copywriter.

THE WORK

1. Account executive

Account executives, also known as account handlers, act as the link between the advertising agencies that employ them and the clients that wish to advertise. In effect, they represent the client to the agency and the agency to the client.

Account executives receive a brief (instructions) from the client. They find out from the client information about the company, its business methods, products or services and whom it wishes to attract with its advertising (the target group).

They work with account planners to devise a marketing strategy and advertising campaign (an advertising programme usually consisting of a series of advertisements) within a given budget. When the client approves the campaign, account executives brief the creative team of copywriter and art director, whose job is to develop ideas for the campaign. They also brief the media planner and buyer, who are responsible for recommending the most effective form of advertising and buying the advertising space or time.

Account executives monitor the progress of the creative and media teams, leading to them giving a presentation of the creative work to the client and advising the client of the media plan (which media are to be used, when and the costs involved). The client may ask for modifications and the account executives negotiate these changes with the agency's creative and media teams.

When the client finally accepts the agency's proposals, account executives arrange for the advertisements to be produced and make sure that deadlines are kept.

Once an advertising campaign has begun, account executives monitor its progress in consultation with the client's marketing staff. If results are not up to expectations they may negotiate with the client to modify the campaign, eg switching from one form of advertising to another.

Account executives work under the supervision of account directors. Typically they handle three or four accounts at the same time. Approximately 80 per cent of their time is spent in discussion with clients, agency colleagues and suppliers. The other 20 per cent is taken up with writing reports, briefs and business correspondence.

2. Account planner

Account planners use their knowledge of consumer attitudes and reactions to make sure that advertising campaigns are targeted effectively. They do this by acting as the consumer's representative at each stage in the development of an advertisement.

At the presentation, agencies try to secure a client's business (the account); account planners contribute their specialist knowledge of consumers.

If the agency is awarded the account they study the brief (instructions) given by the client and decide what research they must do. They need to know who buys the product or service to be advertised, why they buy it and what distinguishes it from competitors' products or services. They also need to understand consumers' attitudes towards their clients and their competitors, their products or services and their advertising.

There may be existing research information available in the form of published market reports, surveys on usage and attitudes, and advertising research. It may, however, be necessary to arrange for fresh market research. Account planners may commission another organization to carry out this research or they may conduct it themselves. This may involve discussions with consumers likely to buy the particular product or service.

Account planners analyse and interpret the research information and decide on a strategy for the advertising campaign based on a thorough understanding of the target audience – the consumers at whom the advertising is aimed. They seek the client's approval for the strategy, then brief the creative team of copywriter and art director. In particular, they seek to describe very clearly the nature of the target audience.

Account planners liaise with the creative team while they are coming up with ideas and join them in presenting ideas to the client for approval, interpreting the appeal of the proposals to the target group.

When a campaign has been approved account planners may arrange for it to be pre-tested to check that the intended message is getting across and the brand name remembered.

While a campaign is in progress account planners research its effectiveness by getting consumer reaction to the campaign. They try to gauge consumer awareness of the campaign and the image of the product or service, and they monitor sales figures. If account planners do not think that a campaign is going as well as expected they may suggest alterations.

Account planners work on several different campaigns at the same time. Much of their time is spent in discussion with account executives and creative staff in the advertising agency, the agency's clients and with consumers.

3. Media executive

Media executives recommend the media that should be used for a client's advertising, and they buy the advertising space and time. Their aim is to place the advertisements where they will be seen or heard by the maximum possible number of the target audience at the lowest possible price.

In small agencies the planning and buying work may be combined and dealt with by a media executive. Large agencies usually have separate planners and buyers, each of whom may further specialize in 'time' (radio, television and cinema advertisements) and 'space' (newspapers, magazines and posters).

Media planners may work alongside the account executive in preliminary discussions with a client. Alternatively they may be briefed by the account executive or account planner on the product or service to be advertised, the advertising strategy, the target audience and the available budget.

When considering the advertising media to use, planners have to take into account information about the different media. They consider circulation and readership figures for newspapers and magazines, viewing figures for different commercial television stations, listening figures for commercial radio stations and figures for cinema audiences. They also consider the costs for each form of advertising. Some information is readily available, such as readership figures from NRS (National Readership Survey) and viewing figures from BARB (Broadcasters' Audience Research Board). Sometimes planners ask their agency's research department to conduct some necessary survey or research.

Planners finally decide on a detailed media plan showing which media are to be used, when, and the costs involved in each. When the client has agreed the plan, planners brief the media buyer.

Media planners spend much of their time in discussion with clients and agency colleagues. They use computers to help in analysing the information they must consider before arriving at the media plan.

Media buyers are instructed by media planners on which media are to be used for an advertising campaign, the budget available and the approximate number of the target audience the agency and the client hopes to reach.

Buyers negotiate with media owners for the advertising space in newspapers, magazines, posters or time on television, radio or in cinemas. They aim to get the best possible deal for the client, which can include being aware of any available discounts.

Much of media buyers' time is spent on the telephone. They keep detailed records of all their transactions and check that they are staying within their budget.

In large agencies media buyers may specialize in one particular medium, such as television.

4. Copywriter

Copywriters work in agency creative departments, providing the words (copy) that are read or heard in advertisements. This can range from slogans, jingles and headlines to more detailed text for catalogues, brochures, leaflets, trade papers and journals. They may also be involved in writing scripts for film, radio and television advertisements. Some copywriters specialize in a particular form of advertising.

Copywriters usually work in partnership with one particular art director who is responsible for the visual part of the campaign.

Copywriters and art directors receive their brief (instructions) from the account executive and/or account planner, with detailed information about the advertiser, the product or service to be advertised and who it wishes to attract with its advertising (the target group). They may want further information, including research material, and may visit the client to learn more about the product or service.

The essential skill of copywriters lies in understanding the product and the target group and in linking them persuasively. Copywriters and art directors together look for an idea that will catch the attention of the target group and put across the selling point of the product. They may produce many ideas, both pictures and headlines, most of which they will discard. In this ideas stage copywriters and art directors discuss visual and textual ideas with each other.

Copywriters and art directors show their more successful ideas to the creative director who may suggest modifications. Neater drawings are then produced and presented to the client, who may also ask for changes. Once the client accepts the concept the layout is modified and the copywriters write the 'body copy' (smaller print containing more detailed information).

Copywriters must always keep in mind the need for their writing to meet legal requirements and be within the Codes of Advertising Practice. They are involved in constant revision and rewriting of their work, either to seek improvement or following a request for modification.

After the client has approved the design and copy, the work is handed on to the production team for typesetting and the production of photographs and drawings (in the case of printed advertisements), or recording or filming (for radio or television commercials). Copywriters and art directors may attend recording and filming (shoots) to make sure that the creative aspects meet their requirements.

Copywriters work under the supervision of a creative director and usually work on several briefs at any one time. Although coming up with ideas and writing copy is central to their work, copywriters spend much of their time in talking to people – agency colleagues, clients and others.

WORK ENVIRONMENT

Account executives, account planners, media executives and copywriters work indoors in office surroundings that are usually comfortable and well furnished.

All spend some time travelling to meetings with clients. Account executives, in particular, may spend up to a day a week travelling to and attending meetings with clients and suppliers outside the agency. Copywriters may travel to studios or locations when advertisements are being recorded or filmed.

All spend much of their time sitting.

SKILLS AND INTERESTS

Advertising is, above all else, a commercial activity. However attracted staff feel towards the creative aspects of advertising they need both an interest in and a commitment to advertising as a business.

Communication skills and the ability to get on well with people are essential in all these jobs, as much of the working day for account executives, account planners, media executives and copywriters is spent in discussion with clients, agency colleagues and others.

Writing skills are important for producing briefs and reports.

ADVERTISING: OD

Advertising is based on team work, so the ability to work well in a team is essential.

Having to meet deadlines is a feature of advertising work, as is the need to cope with several different jobs at the same time. Ability to work under pressure is therefore important, as is willingness to work long, irregular hours.

Account executive

As the link between clients and the agency, account executives have to balance clients' wishes with the agency's recommendations. This needs self-confidence, diplomacy, persuasiveness and good negotiating skills.

Account executives should be able to present ideas and strategies clearly and accurately, both in speech and in writing.

They must be systematic and well organized, as they have to co-ordinate different activities in several accounts at the same time.

Good staff management skills and the ability to lead a team and work within it are important. They must be able to motivate staff to give of their best, although they are under pressure themselves.

Account planner

An interest in human nature is essential. If account planners are to represent consumers to their colleagues and clients they must be able to understand people, what motivates them, how their attitudes are formed and why they behave as they do.

Account planners must keep constantly aware of changes in society that affect consumer attitudes, such as the state of the economy, the role of women in society, changing leisure patterns and changing eating habits. They need to be alive to trends and fashions and take them into account.

Account planners should be numerate and imaginative in order to translate research data into advertising action.

Media executive

Media planners must be able to express themselves well in speech and in writing in order to negotiate with clients and to brief agency colleagues. A persuasive manner is necessary to gain acceptance of recommendations.

Planners need computer aptitude and numerical and statistical ability for analysing data.

Media buyers should have a confident telephone manner, as much of their time is spent on telephone work. They should have good negotiating skills if they are to get the best possible deals for their clients.

Numerical ability and computer aptitude are important, as buyers have to analyse statistics, calculate expenditure and keep within their budget. They have to be well organized, attentive to detail and capable of careful record-keeping.

Copywriter

Copywriters need the ability to write well. They must be able to express themselves in writing in a clear, concise and persuasive way. They need to have imagination and a good command of different writing styles. It is important that they are capable of the painstaking rewriting and polishing necessary to produce quality work.

It is not enough for copywriters to be interested only in the creative side of their work. They must also have a strong interest in the commercial aspects of advertising if they are to understand the products and services they are advertising and the readers, viewers or listeners they are targeting.

Visual understanding is important. Although they are responsible for the written and spoken parts of advertisements, copywriters should be able to contribute ideas about the visual aspects.

Copywriters must be able to accept criticism and be prepared to modify their work if requested by their creative director or the client.

ENTRY REQUIREMENTS

There are no minimum educational requirements but entry to advertising is fiercely competitive and most entrants have at least A levels/H grades. Many agencies recruit only graduates.

Degree courses in communication studies, media studies and business are useful and there are some higher national certificate/diploma and degree courses that specialize in advertising. While these courses are good preparation for a career in advertising they do not guarantee acceptance into the industry. Most employers do not ask for degrees in any particular subject and select the applicants they think are most suitable.

BTEC higher national diplomas require either four or five GCSEs/S grades (A–C/1–3) and one A level/two H grades, or a BTEC/SQA national award, or Advanced GNVQ/GSVQ Level III. Some colleges offer a BTEC HND in Design with an advertising option. They usually require a Foundation art course or Advanced GNVQ/GSVQ Level III in Art and Design.

Aberdeen College's SQA Higher National Certificate in Advertising, Marketing and Public Relations requires either two H grades, including English, or an SQA national certificate with appropriate modules (including communication at Level 4).

Central College of Commerce, Glasgow offers an SQA Higher National Diploma in Advertising and Public Relations that requires either two H grades at C or above, including English, or an SQA national certificate with appropriate modules, including communication at Level 4.

Degree courses require a minimum of two A levels/three H grades plus five GCSEs/S grades, or Advanced GNVQ/GSVQ Level III, or BTEC/SQA national award. Specific grade and subject requirements vary from course to course.

West Herts College has three relevant courses: the HND in Advertising and Marketing Communications requires five GCSEs/S grades (A–C/1–3) and one A level/two H grades or a BTEC/SQA national award, or Advanced GNVQ/GSVQ Level III. This may be followed by a one-year top-up degree course. The Postgraduate Diploma in Advertising requires a higher national diploma or degree in any subject. Applicants for the Postgraduate Diploma in Copywriting/Art Direction wishing to specialize in copywriting should have two A levels/three H grades.

West Thames College's Higher National Diploma in Graphic Design and Advertising prefers a good grade in A level English or equivalent for entry to its copywriting option. Ability in art and design is not essential but basic visual understanding is.

The Communication Advertising and Marketing (CAM) Education Foundation's Certificate in Communication Studies requires a degree, or BTEC/SQA national award in business studies, or two A levels/H grades and three GCSEs/S grades (A–C/1–3), or five GCSEs/S grades (A–C/1–3) and at least one year's relevant UK

ADVERTISING: OD

employment, or at least five years' relevant work experience, or the London Chamber of Commerce and Industry Third Level Group Diploma in Advertising, Marketing and Public Relations. Some qualifications give full exemption from the Certificate examinations.

For the CAM Diploma in Advertising, entrants must have the CAM Certificate or have exemption from it.

TRAINING

Pre-entry

There are several courses that specialize in advertising:

- BTEC Higher National Diploma in Marketing and Advertising is offered by the London Institute (two years full time). It is concerned with the business aspects of advertising.

- SQA Higher National Certificate in Advertising, Marketing and Public Relations is offered by Aberdeen College (one year full time), while SQA Higher National Diploma in Advertising and Public Relations is offered by Central College of Commerce, Glasgow (two years full time). These courses introduce students to advertising techniques and practices.

- Degree courses are offered by Bournemouth University (Advertising Management), Lancaster University (Advertising and Marketing) and London College of Printing and Distributive Trades (Marketing and Advertising). These courses are all full time for three years. Ulster University offers a four-year full-time course in Communications, Advertising and Marketing. All courses are good preparation for work as an account executive, account planner or media executive.

- A number of universities and colleges offer higher national diploma and degree courses in graphic design that offer an advertising option that includes either copywriting or the business aspects of advertising. These courses are designed primarily for those with art and design ability.

- West Herts College's Diploma in Advertising and Postgraduate Diploma in Advertising (both one year full time) include advertising and sales promotion, media, advertising administration, marketing, market research, psychology, print processes and production, copywriting, design and typography.

- West Herts College's Postgraduate Diploma in Copywriting/Art Direction (one year full time) trains students in the working practices of advertising agencies. They learn the copywriting skills relevant to a broad range of media. During the course copywriters have the opportunity to form creative partnerships with those training for art direction.

- West Thames College's Higher National Diploma in Graphic Design and Advertising (two years full time) has a copywriting specialism that includes studying advertising, scriptwriting, copywriting, television and radio. Copywriters team up with art directors during the course to form creative partnerships.

On entry

Training received by new staff varies between agencies. In some agencies entrants begin work straight away and learn from experienced staff. Other agencies have a more formal programme of training that includes lectures, periods of time spent in different departments within the agency and visits to media owners.

In addition the Institute of Practitioners in Advertising (IPA) runs a number of courses for staff employed by an IPA member agency.

Account planners may attend short courses on specific skills run by the Market Research Society and the Account Planning Group.

Media executives may attend a series of introductory lectures by the Media Circle followed by an intermediate level course. They may also attend a four-day Media Business Course organized by The Advertising Association.

Copywriters may attend Advertising Creative Circle seminars and workshops.

Account executives who deal with overseas clients and have at least three years' experience may study for The International Advertising Association's diploma by attending a six-month evening course at Martran College, London.

Some agencies encourage their staff to study for the qualifications of The Communication Advertising and Marketing (CAM) Education Foundation:

- CAM Certificate in Communication Studies: students must pass examinations in: marketing, advertising, public relations, media, sales promotion and direct marketing, and research and behavioural studies.

- CAM Diploma in Advertising: students must pass an examination in management and strategy and two advertising papers – consumer and business-to-business.

Both the Certificate and the Diploma can be studied full-time but are usually studied part-time on a day release, evening, weekend or distance learning basis. Thirty-four colleges throughout the UK offer tuition for the Certificate and 13 for the Diploma. The length of time needed to complete the courses varies, but is typically around two years for the Certificate and one year for the Diploma.

NVQs/SVQs in Advertising are available at Levels 3 and 4.

LATE ENTRY

There are no upper age limits for entry but advertising is largely a young person's profession. Fifty per cent of agency staff are under 30 years, 80% under 40. Mature applicants find entry very difficult unless they have previous relevant experience, such as in marketing or communications work.

Some agency staff such as secretaries, media assistants, production assistants and administrative assistants may manage to progress to become account executives.

Account planners have often had previous experience in advertising, research being a common background.

Late entry to media planning and buying is more likely with experience of selling advertising for a media firm or in marketing.

Mature applicants may be considered for the courses described in TRAINING without the usual minimum entry requirements.

OPPORTUNITIES

There are approximately 800 recognized advertising agencies in the UK. Most agencies are small and employ fewer than 50 staff, although two agencies employ over 500. Most of the larger agencies are subsidiaries of American companies and are situated in London.

The Institute of Practitioners in Advertising has 220

ADVERTISING: OD

member agencies, which employ a total of 11,800 staff. They include most of the larger agencies and account for over 80% of those employed in advertising in the UK. Approximately three-quarters of those 11,800 work in London.

Large agencies are often 'full service agencies' that offer a complete range of advertising services to clients. Many small and medium-sized firms specialize in one area of work and buy in expertise in other areas when required.

The number employed in advertising decreased considerably during the late 1980s and early 1990s but has begun to stabilize. There is always intense competition for all posts. Those seeking to enter advertising should approach agencies direct, rather than seek job advertisements. It can help if applicants have had some voluntary or vacation work experience in an agency.

It is not usual for those in advertising to work abroad, although there may be some opportunities for those who work for multinational agencies.

PAY AND CONDITIONS

Rates of pay vary according to the size of agency and the geographical area, with salaries usually higher in London. The starting salary for a graduate entrant may be between £13,000 and £15,000.

Account executives and account planners earn between £17,500 and £19,000, while media executives earn between £22,000 and £24,000. Senior posts for account executives, account planners and media executives can command over £30,000. Copywriters usually earn between £20,000 and £40,000, while successful copywriters working for a top agency may earn over £50,000.

Advertising staff tend to work long, irregular hours, Monday to Friday, although pressure of work can often lead to weekend work.

PROSPECTS

Large agencies have a promotion structure that may allow account executives and account planners to become account supervisors or account directors, media executives to become media directors, while copywriters may become senior copywriters or creative directors. Moving to another agency is common, either for a salary increase or for promotion, although most agencies regularly promote staff internally.

Experienced account executives may set up small advertising agencies of their own, possibly offering a specialist service and buying in expertise as required.

Media executives may transfer to media specialists – organizations that specialize in buying and, sometimes, media planning and research.

Copywriters may become freelance.

RELATED OCCUPATIONS

Market research executive, buyer, public relations officer, graphic designer, illustrator, marketing manager.

FURTHER INFORMATION

Account Planning Group*, 16 Creighton Avenue, London N10 1NU

The Advertising Association*, Abford House, 15 Wilton Road, London SW1V 1NJ, 0171 828 4831 (2pm–4pm, Tuesday to Friday)

The CAM Foundation*, Abford House, 15 Wilton Road, London SW1V 1NJ, 071 828 7506

Institute of Practitioners in Advertising*, 44 Belgrave Square, London SW1X 8QS

FURTHER READING

Leaflets/booklets are available from the addresses marked*.

Working in Marketing and Sales – COIC

Careers in Marketing, Advertising and Public Relations – Kogan Page

Advertising, Public Relations and Market Research – AGCAS

Getting Into Advertising – The Advertising Association

In the careers library classified under OD.

RETAIL DISTRIBUTION: OE–OFZ

1. STORE MANAGER CLCI:OE
2. STORE ASSISTANT CLCI:OE
3. STORE DEMONSTRATOR CLCI:OE/OFZ
4. SUPERMARKET WORKER CLCI:OE
5. TYRE/EXHAUST FITTER CLCI:OFM/RAE
6. FORECOURT ATTENDANT CLCI:OFM
7. RETAIL BUTCHER CLCI:OFM
8. FLORIST CLCI:OFM
9. DISPLAY PERSON CLCI:OFM/ET
10. SHOE REPAIRER CLCI:OFZ

BACKGROUND INFORMATION

Retailing is the final stage in getting goods and products to the final user, the consumer. Although it includes mail order operations, its main aspect is the wide variety of shops and stores from which we do our shopping. The retail industry has a workforce of over two million. Some 45% of these work part-time.

Its range covers anything from a market stall to a big chain of supermarkets. The main categories are: small individual or independent shops, often specialising – such as a fashion boutique, a greengrocer or a newsagent; department or variety stores which sell a range of different products, though often with a separate department specialising in each product type (a carpet department, a hardware department etc); and multiple retailers which operate chains of stores, though these stores may be small or large, specialist or variety, self-service or traditional.

They may be run by an owner/manager whose staff may be mainly members of the family, by a co-operative of friends, or by a limited company whose head office is in the same building, in a town miles away, or, in the case of a multinational, in another country.

The range of specialisms includes chemists, DIY and hardware, books, antiques, builders merchants, cars, clothing and footwear, florists, furniture, jewellery, toys, sports equipment, stationery and office equipment, as well consumer durables like cookers and refrigerators.

The industry is still undergoing change. Supermarkets, hypermarkets and out-of-town shopping centres have already had a major impact on the types, style and location of stores. Electronic tills connected direct to central computers keep a running record of goods sold and initiate re-ordering processes, as well as simplifying analysis of changing consumer demand and staff performance. Giant warehouse-style operations and shopping from home by phone and computer may affect stores in the future. Also, experiments with eliminating cash and having customers in self-service stores tally up their own bills with portable bar-code readers could affect staffing levels.

1. STORE MANAGER (OE)

THE WORK

Store managers are sometimes called retail sales managers or, increasingly, customer services managers, and there are other titles denoting level on a promotion ladder. The manager of an independent store or of a branch of a specialist multiple may, in a department store, be the department manager, sometimes called controller. In fact they may manage more staff and have a bigger sales turnover.

The work of a store manager is similar to that of the store assistant – please see article 2. STORE ASSISTANT – except in self-service stores. Store managers may work as a senior salesperson, selling to customers, dealing with complaints, and leading by example. They deal with problems that junior staff cannot handle, give special attention to regular customers, and listen to their suggestions. They supervise and direct the assistants to ensure that shelves and counters are fully stocked and neat, and that everything is clean, tidy and safe. As managers, they also have to encourage and motivate the assistants in order to meet sales targets devised by themselves or imposed by head office. They draw up rotas for staff, deal with holiday arrangements, interview and recruit new staff, arrange and conduct training, discipline and sometimes dismiss staff who cannot achieve the required standard.

The manager may have responsibility for stockroom staff or for receiving deliveries themselves. They may initiate special offers, promotions of specific items or ranges, and decide or recommend price changes. They may see sales representatives from suppliers, place orders, complain about quality or late delivery, and handle or oversee the accounts. They also deal with paperwork – instructions from head office and forms to complete. They have a responsibility for the security and safety of premises and stock as well as for staff and customers.

Generally, the manager of an independent store is likely to have much more freedom to use their own initiative than a manager within a multiple, who has to work within standardized procedures.

In many stores, there are supervisors and assistant or deputy managers who may handle some of these responsibilities. In some large stores, duties are divided so that a trading or commercial manager looks after stock levels, display areas and their staffing and running; a customer service manager looks after the checkout area and the cash received; and a systems manager oversees the operation of the computerized aspects of the work. In a large department store, there may also be a personnel manager who handles hiring and training, an accounts manager, a marketing manager, a purchasing manager etc. In a major multiple, these would be roles occupied by senior managers at a regional or head office.

WORK ENVIRONMENT

The offices of managers are often small and cramped and may be windowless, because space devoted to selling goods is more profitable. Except when managing specialist departments such as personnel, store managers are expected to spend as much time as possible supervising in the sales areas and as little as possible on paperwork, telephoning etc.

The work involves a lot of standing and walking. Sales areas of stores are usually open, light and attractive. All areas of large stores are likely to be lit mainly by artificial light and be air-conditioned.

SKILLS AND INTERESTS

This is a labour-intensive industry, so skills in leading and managing people are essential. This includes the ability to communicate clearly, and to lead and encourage, often by

RETAIL DISTRIBUTION: OE–OFZ

example. Good communication skills, tact and politeness are also important in dealing with customers, when handling their suggestions and criticism. Store managers have to be able to think quickly and take decisions to cope with emergencies and solve often complex problems. They must be able to work within the procedures laid down by the company to ensure efficiency, safety and accuracy. Self-confidence and self-motivation are essential. Attention to detail, ability to plan and set priorities, and analytical skills are all important, as is a constant commercial awareness of the possible impact on takings and profits of any course of action. Managers should know the role of their staff and be able to take over in the event of absence or sickness. Managers are expected to be smartly dressed in the style required by the company. It is often necessary to move to different parts of the country during training and during employment with multiples.

ENTRY REQUIREMENTS

Direct entry to management training schemes operated by medium-sized and large companies is usually between 18 and 23 years. Some of these schemes are open to graduates (degrees in any subject), others accept people with BTEC/SCOTVEC National Certificate/Diploma or Higher National Certificate/Diploma in Business Studies, Distribution or Retailing, and some ask for GNVQs/GSVQs or two A levels/three H grades in any subject. In addition, many companies expect GCSEs/S grades (A–C/1–3) in English and maths. Specialist qualifications may be useful for work in specific sectors such as food marketing or food science for the grocery sector, or a functional department such as accounts.

Entry may be possible for young people through Modern Apprenticeships (part of the Skillseekers initiative in Scotland) leading to at least an NVQ/SVQ Level 3. Contact your local careers office, TEC/LEC for details.

Sound health and physical fitness is a requirement and some employers give applicants a medical examination. Employers look for a pleasant personality, neat appearance and evidence of an interest in retailing.

However, many people reach store management after entering as a store assistant and subsequently being placed on a management training course or by working their way up via supervisory positions, sometimes gaining relevant qualifications whilst in employment (see LATE ENTRY). Entry to junior clerical and accounts posts may also offer the possibility of promotion within function departments.

TRAINING

Most management training schemes involve a period as a sales assistant in a selling department followed by attachments in a junior capacity to departments such as buying, marketing, personnel. Training involves gaining experience in positions of greater responsibility in various sales departments or at stores in different parts of the country. Between these assignments are periods that are spent in the company's training department or, for higher level entrants, at a management training college following a specialist course or, for lower level entrants, at an FE college studying for a BTEC/SCOTVEC qualification. Some graduate entry schemes involve study for a postgraduate qualification.

The structure of schemes varies from company to company as does duration. Graduate entry schemes are from three months to 18 months, lower level entry schemes two years.

Training is to NVQ/SVQ Level 3 or 4 in Retail Operations. Modern Apprenticeships also lead to NVQs/SVQs in Retail Operations plus units of Advanced GNVQs/GSVQs in Distribution at Level III and other broad-based skills. For these some training may be off the job in a training centre or FE college. Modern Apprenticeships are expected to average three years.

Retail Traineeships, for people aged 16 to 19 prepared to work towards NVQ Level 2 in Retail Operations, will be available shortly.

LATE ENTRY

Though graduate trainee schemes normally recruit people in their early twenties, some of them are officially open to individuals up to 35 years. Other companies accept applicants of any age to management and trainee vacancies if they have supervisory or management experience elsewhere.

Sales and supervisory staff in stores who show ability and potential may be encouraged and assisted to take management courses with a view to promotion. Most companies have a policy of promoting from within. Individuals working as store assistants may increase their chances of promotion to management by taking distance learning courses and exams with bodies such as the Institute of Sales and Marketing Management (ISMM) or the British Shops and Stores Association (BSSA). Other organizations cater for specialist and functional areas.

Anyone may become a manager at any age by raising the necessary finance to buy or rent premises, purchase stock to sell and open their own store.

OPPORTUNITIES

Despite a decline in the total numbers employed in retailing in recent years, the number of managers has declined much less than lower levels of staff. The need for effective management has led to a growing tendency for large concerns to seek management recruits with higher qualifications at higher national certificate/diploma or degree level. Openings still exist for those with lower qualifications. However, competition for places on management training schemes is intense, especially with the major publicly recognized companies.

Stores of all kinds exist in towns and cities throughout Britain but, for major multiple chains, management recruitment is often at national level through company headquarters.

PAY AND CONDITIONS

Salaries differ widely at different points on the promotion ladder. A graduate trainee may start at around £12,000. Managers may earn from £8,000 in a small store or branch to £50,000 plus for a managing director, general manager or chief executive in a large concern. Team and individual bonuses may increase these figures significantly. The range of other benefits also tends to increase with promotion and may include concessions on purchases, subsidized meals, assistance with loans and mortgages, free health insurance, and company cars.

Managers generally tend to start work before other staff and finish afterwards. This leads to long hours, although generally over five days, alternating with other managers to cover Saturdays (and Sundays in some cases). Above junior levels, overtime is not paid for the extra hours.

PROSPECTS

Compared to many industries, retailing offers the possibility of reaching a responsible managerial position very early, often in one's twenties. Department stores and retail chains have established promotion ladders and often have a policy of promoting from within. This may lead from assistant or deputy departmental manager, to departmental manager, to deputy store manager, and store manager, or possibly sideways into a functional department within a big store in a managerial role in one of the functions of personnel, marketing, buying, systems etc. In a multiple, the ladder may go on to area or district manager, regional manager and national manager, or sideways to management of one of the functions at any of these levels.

In independent stores, the promotion ladder is limited but may give a greater degree of responsibility over a wider range of activities. Experience even at relatively junior management levels is valuable in applying to other retail concerns or if one decides to set up one's own store or take over an existing business. Taking a retail franchise is a step some managers take.

There are chances to work abroad either in the overseas outlets of British chains or by applying directly, once experienced, to overseas companies in Europe, the USA and other countries.

RELATED OCCUPATIONS

Sales manager, buyer, marketing manager, personnel manager, store supervisor, store assistant, warehouse manager, distribution manager, restaurant manager.

FURTHER INFORMATION AND READING

Please see article 4. SUPERMARKET WORKER.

2. STORE ASSISTANT (OE)

THE WORK

Store assistants are also called general assistants, customer care assistants, or sales assistants. The move to self-service in many stores has narrowed the job in these shops to the tasks of making sure shelves and counters are fully stocked and attractively displayed, taking the customer's payment and wrapping or bagging the purchases. (Please see article 4. SUPERMARKET WORKER.) However in many stores, especially department stores and smaller specialist shops and boutiques, the complex and varied task of selling is still important. In larger stores, the trend towards multiskilling means various duties are rotated among staff, giving greater work variety.

Every customer is different and has different needs and reasons for coming into the store. Some know exactly what they want, ask for it and buy it, but many are not sure and, if not dealt with correctly, may go somewhere else to buy. The store assistant must assess when and how to ask if the customer wants help, win their confidence with the appropriate amount of questioning about their requirements, and give information and advice about suitable products that might best suit their needs. To do this, assistants draw on their interpersonal skills and also on their product knowledge. Outlining possible payment methods, especially easy-payment ones, may also be important in gaining a sale.

Finally they have to edge the customer into making the decision to buy and 'close the deal'. If the customer is merely assessing possibilities to buy, the store assistant offers efficient and friendly service so that they may return next time they need that type of product or goods. Many stores depend on their regular and repeat customers for survival. Assistants also handle returns and complaints.

Actual tasks vary with the type of product sold. In a men's outfitter, these could include measuring a customer for a suit. In an electronics store, it may be vital to be able to demonstrate how a computer or hi-fi unit works, and to ensure the customer has any accessories they need. In food areas, cutting and weighing the quantities requested may be part of the service.

In smaller independent stores, the work may include tasks such as arranging window and in-store displays, lettering sales and special offer cards, and helping to receive deliveries from suppliers into the stockroom.

WORK ENVIRONMENT

Please see article 1. STORE MANAGER.

Store assistants are normally expected to wear a uniform provided by the employer or to be smartly dressed. They are on their feet most of the time, except for assistants regularly on till duty at checkouts who sit most of the time in a confined area. Most big stores are located in city centres or on the outskirts of urban areas.

SKILLS AND INTERESTS

It takes physical and mental stamina to stand and walk around a store or department for long hours each day. Considerable self-reliance, patience and resilience are needed during quiet periods with few customers and the hectic rush of busy times. They should enjoy working with people and must be able to remain polite even when they are tired, under pressure or dealing with a complaining customer. A lively mind and good memory are valuable in learning about a product range and answering queries or offering advice. They must be able to work in a team yet accept responsibility for their own tasks.

ENTRY REQUIREMENTS

No minimum qualifications are required, though there may be basic tests of reading, writing and ability with numbers. Many employers look for some GCSEs/S grades (A–C/1–3). They also expect physical fitness, normal eyesight (with or without glasses) and hearing. Many companies offer training schemes for young people as an entry route at 16 to 17 years, but entry is possible at later ages.

Modern Apprenticeships (part of the Skillseekers Initiative in Scotland) may be available for young people leading to at least an NVQ/SVQ Level 3. Contact your local careers office, Jobcentre, TEC/LEC for details.

National Traineeships (England and Wales) are also available leading to NVQ Level 2, Key Skills and broad based skills. Contact your local TEC for details.

Candidates have to be able to speak clearly and present themselves well. An interest in the store and its product range is useful. This means an interest in sports may help in obtaining work in a sportswear and equipment shop, or hi-fi and photography in an electronics or camera store.

RETAIL DISTRIBUTION: OE–OFZ

TRAINING

In independent stores, a new recruit is likely to be trained on the job by working alongside experienced staff in a succession of duties and departments. At a later point, they may be sent on short courses in sales techniques at training centres or in product knowledge with manufacturers.

In large department stores and multiples, where several assistants may be recruited at the same time, initial training is more likely to be away from the shop floor in a training room or department. It includes company structure and policy, the product range, operation of tills and the various methods of taking payment (cheque, credit card, debit card etc). Short videos and role-play sessions may be used to teach techniques for handling customers wanting to buy or to complain. Further training may follow after a probationary period.

Specific training opportunities for young people, including Modern Apprenticeships (part of the Skillseekers Initiative in Scotland), may be available – contact your local careers office, Jobcentre, TEC/LEC for details.

Training programmes may include part-time study at college for a relevant qualification or NVQs/SVQs in Retail Operations at Levels 1 and 2.

LATE ENTRY

Though there are no age limits, in practice many store assistants are recruited after leaving school or college. However, increasingly employers are recruiting older staff. Some supermarkets and chains now deliberately seek staff over 50 years for some positions, though those with some experience of jobs involving contact with the public are likely to be preferred. People returning to work after family commitments are generally welcomed.

OPPORTUNITIES

Numbers employed in retailing have fallen significantly in recent years and many stores have closed, especially in rural areas and smaller communities, with supermarkets taking over from small local shops. However, there are still opportunities in most urban areas. Part-time and temporary work is available in many stores.

Vacancies may be advertised in stores themselves, in local newspapers and in Jobcentres. Even where vacancies are not advertised, direct application to the personnel manager at large stores or at the head office of retail chains should obtain information on recruitment policy and availability of jobs.

PAY AND CONDITIONS

Different sizes and types of employer pay at different rates. Pay is dependent on the size of the business and special terms, such as commission rates or bonuses. Rates may increase with experience, skills and seniority. Seasonal work may be paid at a lower rate.

The basic working week is usually 35 to 39 hours spread over five days. However, most stores open Saturdays (though some close on Mondays), many open late on at least one or two evenings, and an increasing number open on Sundays for a few hours. This may mean working rotas or shifts and overtime, with overtime pay or time off in lieu as compensation. In small local and family shops hours may be very long.

PROSPECTS

Although, with independent stores, promotion possibilities are limited, retail chains, department stores and supermarkets offer opportunities for their own staff who show ability and keenness, for promotion to senior store assistant and supervisor. They may also consider such people for further training, for transfer to a specialist department or for a place on a management training scheme. Many managers in retailing have started as store assistants. Some assistants study in their spare time for appropriate qualifications to improve their chances of promotion. The NVQ/SVQ system of validating growing experience may form a way of proving readiness for promotion. For those with fluency in another language, there may be the possibility of work for a branch of a British multiple store in a European country.

RELATED OCCUPATIONS

Counter service assistant, supermarket worker, receptionist, store demonstrator, forecourt attendant, store supervisor, store manager, ticket agency clerk, travel agency clerk.

FURTHER INFORMATION AND READING

Please see article 4. SUPERMARKET WORKER.

3. STORE DEMONSTRATOR (OE/OFZ)

THE WORK

Demonstrators show potential customers in a store or at an exhibition or roadshow how to use an appliance or gadget, explain the advantages of a product, offer free samples or tastings of food or drink, and hand out leaflets or recipe cards, stickers, badges or cut-price coupons. Their purpose is to promote interest in a new product or increase sales of an established product.

Freelance demonstrators are normally hired by a manufacturer or supplier or, sometimes, by a large store, to promote a product. This could be a washing machine or a washing powder, an item or range of food, drink or confectionery such as French cheeses, household goods, a DIY tool, or a kitchen gadget such as a new fruit and potato peeler.

The demonstrator receives a training session or written brief about the item, so that they can talk knowledgeably about it and answer questions. They may use wording provided or have to prepare their own speech. They set up a table or specially made unit in the relevant department of the store or at the manufacturer's or supplier's exhibition stand. They unpack and put out examples of the product and any accessories needed such as glasses for a wine-tasting, portions of cheese, a small grill for cooking sausage samples, lengths of carpet for demonstrating a carpet cleaner, etc. For some items, a small room, area or theatre with seating may be provided and demonstrations advertised for set times. They may offer samples or a demonstration to individuals passing, by or draw a small audience around them before starting their routine.

The demonstrator may be responsible for ensuring point-of-sale material about the product is displayed on the shelves where it is sold, and for taking some record of sales before and during the promotion period. Promotions often coincide with a TV or poster advertising campaign. In some instances, a competition may be involved, or an element of consumer research requiring forms to be completed and returned to their employer.

At the end of the promotion they pack up and leave the area clean and tidy. They may be engaged for one or a few days, a week or for the duration of an exhibition. They may travel with a roadshow, or visit stores or pubs in different towns or areas on successive days.

WORK ENVIRONMENT

Demonstrators work in all kinds of stores, shopping centres (indoors and outside), pubs and hotels, exhibitions, motorway service stations etc. They may need their own transport and spend time travelling between locations. In some cases, overnight stays may be involved.

Work situations are usually pleasant but may be crowded. Demonstrators stand for long periods. They may have to wear a uniform or costume and an apron or tabard and hat are supplied when handling foodstuffs. Otherwise they wear their own clothes but are expected to maintain a smart appearance.

SKILLS AND INTERESTS

Demonstrators should be sociable, self-confident and able to converse easily with strangers of a variety of ages and backgrounds. They need to remain cheerful and friendly, however unsympathetic the response of their audience may be. A clear voice that projects well is important.

Manual dexterity may be needed and the ability to learn quickly both how to use a new product and the information about it. Demonstrators have to appear to believe fully in the value of the items, whatever their personal preferences.

Although demonstrators may work with a wide variety of goods, individual promotions may be repetitive. Resilience and a sense of humour are essential, as well as the energy and physical stamina to stand in one place for long periods.

Owning a car and a clean driving licence may be important.

ENTRY REQUIREMENTS

A clear speaking voice and attractive appearance are essential requirements. No exam qualifications are needed but knowledge of the retail industry, and experience or qualifications in home economics, technology, cookery, bar work and DIY activities can help obtain certain types of demonstrating engagements.

Demonstrators are normally hired through marketing services companies, employment agencies, model agencies or performers' agencies. To register with such companies and agencies, individuals may need to show good photographs of themselves, both portrait and full length in smart clothes, together with a cv giving relevant experience such as performance/modelling, public speaking, teaching, work as a store assistant, party plan or catalogue selling. Most demonstrators are aged 20 years and over but some individuals are younger.

A Food Hygiene Certificate may be needed for demonstration involving food.

TRAINING

There are no training courses for this occupation. Some marketing or merchandising agencies that keep a register of approved demonstrators run short training programmes for new candidates which cover persuasion techniques, how to handle questions and complaints, safety, hygiene and food handling, and aspects of appearance and body language.

Those engaged to demonstrate more technical products may attend briefing sessions given by the manufacturer or supplier to learn their features. Some types of presentation may require briefings/rehearsals in ways of moving and speaking in a special costume, slogans and catchphrases.

Courses that provide certificates in elocution, public speaking, acting, modelling, selling, cookery and homecrafts may be useful.

One-day courses leading to a certificate in food hygiene are available at many FE colleges and training centres.

LATE ENTRY

Many agencies only accept applications from people over 20 years. Some product demonstrations may call for a specific age-range of demonstrator.

OPPORTUNITIES

Most store demonstrators work on a freelance basis. To obtain a reasonable amount of work, it is sensible to register with several agencies. Once registered with a few agencies, work should be possible but this may average no more than a day or two a week even for the most popular demonstrators. Few people make a full living as demonstrators and there is always considerable competition for the available work. A few stores employ their own demonstrators, usually at specific times of the year such as Christmas. Obtaining the first engagement is the most difficult, but, after a few successful engagements, obtaining work usually becomes easier.

Generally, there is more demonstration work in London and the big cities, though even here it varies considerably by region.

PAY AND CONDITIONS

Freelance demonstrating is paid at a daily rate of £30 to £60 a day. Rates are higher in London and major cities. Travel, subsistence and incidental expenses may be paid. Engagements are normally only for one or a few days but may last for several weeks. They are usually on days when stores are busiest, ie Thursday, Friday, Saturday, and may extend into evening opening hours. Most work often takes place over periods such as Christmas, Easter, bank holidays or local anniversaries or festivals. A day's hiring is normally eight hours, excluding travel time, but may be longer. Tea and meal breaks may be allowed.

PROSPECTS

As this is a freelance occupation, promotion prospects are limited. Some demonstrators are engaged regularly or full-time by marketing, merchandising or advertising companies as field supervisors or booking agents to supervise and/or book demonstrators. This may open up channels into other aspects of marketing, merchandising or promotions.

It may also be possible to move into party plan selling where similar skills are required.

RETAIL DISTRIBUTION: OE–OFZ

RELATED OCCUPATIONS
Store assistant, market research interviewer, telephone salesperson, merchandiser, receptionist, beauty consultant, catalogue sales agent, party plan sales agent.

FURTHER INFORMATION AND READING
Please see article 4. SUPERMARKET WORKER.

4. SUPERMARKET WORKER (OE)

BACKGROUND INFORMATION
Supermarkets differ from most other types of store since they are self-service. As the customer selects products from shelves themselves, the sales function performed by store assistants in other stores is eliminated. Most supermarkets are based on grocery products, but the same principles are applied in some cases, to clothing, DIY products, and other areas. This field includes medium and large supermarkets, superstores, hypermarkets, and cash and carry operations.

THE WORK
The main operations are: receiving products from delivery trucks into the warehouse or stockroom attached to the shop floor; placing the products onto the shelves as needed and possibly attaching prices to them; and taking payment from the customer. These may be seen as separate jobs or stages in a training and promotion process. These duties may be rotated among staff providing a variety of work known as multiskilling. In smaller neighbourhood supermarkets, the same workers may perform all these tasks at different times during the day or week.

Checkout operator
The checkout operator sits at an electronic till and feeds into the till the prices of goods chosen by the customer. This is increasingly done by 'scanning', passing each item over a device that reads the bar code on it and automatically registers this in the till. In other cases, the operator presses numerical keys to enter the price or may use a light-pen to read a code. They may weigh some products such as fruit on a weighing scale by the till. When all the goods have been scanned the till provides a total, the operator takes payment in cash, by cheque or by credit or debit card, and gives a till receipt and any change required. They provide plastic bags and may help the customer to pack. They change paper till rolls when necessary, and make sure there is enough change, credit card forms, and plastic bags. The operator rings a bell or buzzer to summon a supervisor to help with problems, and bags up notes and cheques for periodic collection. They enter their personal details and start and finish time in the till, so that their performance can be analysed later. General cleanliness and tidiness of the till area is their responsibility.

They may also have to deal with customers changing their mind or not having enough money to pay for the full load, broken or split packaging, unreadable or missing price labels and other problems.

Shelf filler
Working under instruction from a supervisor, shelf fillers take quantities of products from the warehouse or stockroom on a wheeled trolley into the store. They stack these on the appropriate shelves, display stands or refrigerator cabinets, making sure that the older items remain at the front. If the packages are not already priced by bar code or otherwise, they use a gun to attach small sticky labels showing the price to each item. They keep shelf and display areas clean and tidy, clear any breakages or spillages, and answer questions from customers or call a supervisor for any they cannot answer. They may also have the duty of moving empty baskets and trolleys from the checkout area back to a point near the entrance. Major shelf refilling work may be done by part-time staff after closing time.

Warehouse/stockroom staff
They receive and check in deliveries from suppliers or the company's main warehouse and move them by lift truck or hand truck onto the correct racks and shelves in the warehouse/stockroom. They may unpack some products from larger containers. They may take quantities off the racks and load them onto hand trolleys for the shelf fillers.

Supervisor
Most large supermarkets have a number of supervisors on duty at any time. They direct the shelf fillers and are available to answer queries from customers and staff and to deal with problems as they arise. They may also collect money from tills, bring extra change and other supplies to operators, move staff to different duties to deal with customer demand, and tell staff when to go for meal breaks. Some supervisors act as managers of specialist areas.

Specialist worker
Some supermarkets contain within them specialist areas that operate like small shops with products requiring individual attention to make, prepare or serve. Principal among these are: butcher areas, where meat is cut or minced, weighed and packed into suitable portions; bakery areas, where bread and pastries may be baked and packed; and delicatessen counters, where cooked meats, cheeses and salads are sliced, weighed and portioned often to individual order. These workers need appropriate skills and knowledge of hygiene rules.

WORK ENVIRONMENT
The store area of supermarkets is usually a big open space with rows of shelving and cabinets divided by wide gangways. Despite this functional layout, they are usually decorated in light colours, have good even lighting and are warm. Specialist areas may be like their small shop equivalents: meat and fish areas may be cooler and have refrigerated areas, bakeries may be hot because of ovens, sometimes in view of the customers. Warehouses/stockrooms are big open spaces with tall racks. They also have refrigerated cold stores for meat, fish and frozen foods, and chilled areas for other perishables. Checkout operators work in a very restricted space. Some aspects of warehouse and shelf-filling work may be dirty and messy.

Supermarket workers are usually required to wear distinctive uniforms supplied by the employer. This often includes a hat, especially in areas of high hygiene requirements. Plastic gloves are worn for handling unwrapped foods.

SKILLS AND INTERESTS
A pleasant, polite personality and patience are important in dealing with customers and coping with their problems and complaints. Supermarket workers must be willing to work under close supervision. The ability to work fast and

accurately is called for, especially on checkouts, where performance is measured from till records via the computer. The lifting, bending and stretching involved in shelf filling and warehouse work demands physical fitness. Workers must be honest and trustworthy.

ENTRY REQUIREMENTS

There are no minimum academic requirements, though there may be basic tests of reading, writing and ability with numbers. Some employers look for GCSEs/S grades (A–C/1–3) in English and maths. They also expect physical fitness, normal eyesight (with or without glasses) and hearing. Many companies offer training schemes as an entry route at 16 to 17 years, but entry is possible at later ages.

Previous experience in retailing in a part-time capacity or in work involving contact with the public helps in obtaining full-time employment. Specialist staff may be recruited from those with experience and training in independent butchers, bakers etc.

TRAINING

Supermarkets in large chains give short induction courses in a training room. This covers company policy on employment, welfare, holidays, health and safety, handling of food and hygiene. Some tuition is given in store and warehouse/stockroom layout, product ranges and stock control systems, use of tools such as trolleys and sticker guns, and safe lifting techniques. Unless recruited specifically for checkout duties, instruction in using the till may follow. Training for checkout duties may be complex and could be carried out away from the shop floor but using a training simulation programme linked to the store's computer. Tuition is also given in handling cheque and debit, charge and credit card transactions. A period of working under supervision of experienced workers follows. Trainees may also help with bagging up customers' purchases during busy periods, checking missing prices for till operators or replacing damaged packets for customers. Warehouse/stockroom workers may be sent on a short course in lift truck operation after an initial period of work. Workers in specialist areas may receive training in the specific craft involved.

In independent supermarkets, training on the job is the common practice, with the new recruits receiving instruction from an experienced worker in the simpler activities and performing these before moving to instruction and practice in the more complex and responsible areas.

Specific training opportunities for young people, including Modern Apprenticeships (part of the Skillseekers Initiative in Scotland), may be available – contact your local careers office, Jobcentre, TEC/LEC for details.

Entrants may be sponsored for courses working towards NVQ/SVQ in Retail Operations at Levels 2 and 3 depending on the company's training policy and budget.

LATE ENTRY

Though there are no age limits, in practice many store assistants are recruited after leaving school or college (or before that for part-time work). However, employers welcome applications from mature entrants and some supermarkets now deliberately seek staff over 50 years for some positions especially those with some experience of jobs involving contact with the public. Those with experience in specialist shops such as butchers may be recruited directly as supervisors of specialist areas.

OPPORTUNITIES

There are supermarkets in most towns and cities, though superstores and hypermarkets are much fewer and generally on large sites away from towns. Despite the decline in the retail industry in recent years and the impact of electronic till systems on staffing levels, the number of self-service stores continues to grow. Recruitment is more or less continuous, due to promotion and people leaving for study or other types of work, and is usually handled at local store level.

PAY AND CONDITIONS

Different employers pay at different rates. Hourly rates average between £3.50 and £4.00 an hour, increasing with experience and for skills in a specialist area. Some employers pay group bonuses to staff for meeting sales targets for the store.

The majority of jobs are part-time ranging from eight hours per week to over 30 hours worked over one to five or more days per week. The basic full-time working week is usually 39 hours. Saturday working may be obligatory. Many supermarkets open late on at least two evenings, and an increasing number open on Sundays for a few hours. This may mean working rotas or shifts and overtime, with overtime pay or time off in lieu as compensation. In neighbourhood supermarkets, hours may be very long.

Supermarkets in large chains usually offer a subsidized canteen and staff concessions on purchases in the store.

PROSPECTS

Many supermarket chains have a policy of promoting from within, at least to supervisor level. Workers who show ability and enthusiasm may be offered supervisory training. Some go on from this to management training to become supermarket managers or even move into senior management. Such promotion may involve having to move to other parts of the country.

The possibility of promotion in independent supermarkets is more limited, but experience in them could form a good basis for applying for posts with larger concerns. Some workers study in their own time for relevant qualifications, which make them eligible for supervisory or managerial posts or for management training schemes.

RELATED OCCUPATIONS

Store assistant, counter service assistant, store demonstrator, forecourt attendant, supermarket manager, ticket office clerk, box office clerk, warehouse worker.

FURTHER INFORMATION

National Retail Training Council (NRTC)*, 5 Grafton Street, London W1X 3LB, 0171 647 1500

Scottish Distributive Industries Training Council, Federation House, 222 Queensferry Road, Edinburgh, EH4 2BN, 0131 343 3300

Institute of Grocery Distribution*, Careers Information Service, Grange Lane, Letchmore Heath, Watford, Hertfordshire WD2 8DQ, 01923 857141

RETAIL DISTRIBUTION: OE–OFZ

Consortium of Retail Training Companies (CORTCO), c/o J Sainsbury PLC, Stamford House, Stamford Street, London SE1 9LL, 0171 695 6742

FURTHER READING

Leaflets/booklets are available from addresses marked*.
Working in Retailing – COIC
Retailing and Buying – AGCAS
Careers in Retailing – Kogan Page
Running Your Own Shop – Kogan Page
Marketing, Retailing and Sales Casebook – Hobsons
A Guide to Careers: Retailing and Wholesaling – DITT
In the careers library classified under OE.

5. TYRE/EXHAUST FITTER (OFM/RAE)

BACKGROUND INFORMATION

Tyre and exhaust fitters work alongside mechanics in garages and commercial and public service vehicle workshops, or in specialist tyre and exhaust centres.

In garages, it is usually up to the tyre/exhaust fitters to decide on whether tyres are so damaged or worn as to require repair or replacement, although customers may initially have been informed by a mechanic carrying out a repair or MOT test. In the larger tyre and exhaust fitting centres, instructions and work assignments usually come from supervisors.

THE WORK

Tyre/exhaust fitters check and fit tyres and exhausts to vehicles. Some may only carry out tyre fitting, although many fit both tyres and exhausts. They may work on cars or light vehicles or large goods/public service vehicles.

Tyre fitting

Cars and light vehicles. It is usual to replace a damaged tyre as modern car tyres are mostly tubeless although a repair service may be offered. The first step is to remove the wheel from the vehicle – in most tyre and exhaust centres, large garages and workshops this is done very quickly, by raising the vehicle on a hydraulic jack to remove the wheels from the axles. The hub-cap/wheel trim is removed, the wheel nuts are loosened with a box spanner or power tool, the axle is raised with a jack until the wheel clears the ground, the wheel nuts are removed and the wheel is taken off. The valve is then removed, and the tyre is deflated and separated from the wheel by an automatic machine that breaks the seal between tyre and wheel. The above steps are reversed when fitting the replacement tyre.

The wheel must then be 'balanced' on a balancing machine to ensure even wear in road use and avoid steering vibration. A machine is run to rotate the wheel, and an indicator is read to determine the size and position of lead weights that are attached to the wheel rim. The machine is then re-run to check that the wheel is in balance.

Fitters may also occasionally advise customers on whether tyres need switching round to even out wear patterns, on which treads are best to use according to their driving needs, and on legal requirements for tread depth and tyre type.

Large goods/public service/passenger vehicles. In large-vehicle garages and workshops, fitters undertake regular inspections of the tyres looking for stones, nails and so on, embedded in the tyre, and any serious cuts or cracks. The stones/nails are removed, the tyre pressure is checked and the fitter decides if the tyres need repositioning because of wear, or need repair or replacement. To remove tyres from commercial vehicles up to seven tons, procedures are as for light vehicles, but the removal of tyres for vehicles over this weight is more complicated. The size of the wheels makes them awkward to handle, and special equipment is needed to remove and replace them. Once the tyre is removed it is inspected on the inside for any defects and it is then repaired or replaced. Special care is again taken when assembling and re-inflating the tyres; large vehicle tyres must be inflated within a protective steel cage. In some workshops and depots, the wheels are removed and replaced by mechanics, though any check and repair work is carried out by the tyre fitters.

Field duties. Some fitters work on agricultural and construction plant vehicles on-site. This mainly involves using a water pump to pump water into tyres to act as ballast for large vehicles. The work involves working alone in awkward places and observing strict health and safety regulations.

Exhaust fitting

This requires a wider range of tools than tyre fitting, and is carried out on both cars and light vehicles and large goods and public service vehicles. The vehicle is lifted up on a ramp so that the straps holding the exhaust onto the vehicle can be undone. The faulty parts are then replaced and the exhaust refitted to the vehicle.

WORK ENVIRONMENT

Fitters work in awkward places, sometimes in cramped conditions, eg lying down under a car. Some workshops can accommodate several large lorries at a time, whilst others are much smaller. All are equipped with work benches, power tools, ramps and pits. Strong artificial lights may be used, and the work is oily and greasy.

SKILLS AND INTERESTS

This is heavy and dirty work, especially if done by hand, so candidates should be physically fit, able to stand all day and do heavy lifting and carrying. Fitters may also work in cramped conditions when working under a car.

As team work is involved it requires a person that can get on well with workmates. Fitters dealing with the public need to be polite and be able to explain things clearly and give customers advice. They may have to handle cash and credit card transactions, so require numerical ability.

ENTRY REQUIREMENTS

No educational qualifications are required but employers might ask for GCSEs/S grades (A–E/1–5). Evidence of practical ability (eg qualifications in school subjects such as technology) and/or an interest in motor vehicles may be an advantage. Some employers require their fitters to be able to drive or be willing to learn.

TRAINING

Training is on the job, working alongside an experienced fitter. Some companies also have their own internal training programmes. Trainees learn the exact procedure to adopt depending on the type of tyre involved, which tools and equipment to use, which tyre types are best for various makes and size of motor vehicles, and which combinations of tyres are best for certain types of motoring. They must also know the standard rate of pressures for tyres of various makes of vehicles. It can take as little as six weeks to train a fitter to a reasonable standard in one of the specialist fitting centres, but to become a fully trained fitter, able to work on all sorts of vehicles and use all types of equipment, can take up to two years.

NVQs/SVQs in Vehicle Maintenance: Service Replacement are available at Levels 1 and 2. National Traineeships are available for Level 2. Relevant areas covered include identifying, inspecting and testing parts for replacement; removing, selecting and refitting replacements and final testing and adjustment. This covers tyres for light and heavy vehicles and for specialist vehicles such as earthmoving, industrial and agricultural machinery or silencers, exhaust pipes and joints.

Fitters can also study for City and Guilds qualifications such as C&G 3911 Tyre Fitting (Car and Van Types), 3912 (Truck Tyres), 3986 (Motor Cycle Tyres) and 3984 (Solid Tyres) or C&G 3981 Exhaust Fitting. Other C&G qualifications that can be obtained include 3913 (Advanced Tyre Fitting), 3916 (Agricultural Tyre Fitting), 3983 (Earthmover Tyre Fitting) and 3906 (Roadside Breakdown). Study is via day or block release courses at a local college or on internal training programmes.

LATE ENTRY

No upper age limit is set, but the heavy physical nature of the job demands a very high standard of physical fitness, which limits opportunities for those over 40 years.

OPPORTUNITIES

The major employers of fitters are the specialist tyre and exhaust centres. Their purpose is to provide a quick tyre/exhaust replacement service for car owners. Garages vary from one- or two-person businesses to big main dealers specializing in a certain make of vehicle. The smaller businesses do not generally employ tyre/exhaust fitters. Transport firms employ tyre fitters in their workshops to carry out regular inspections, repairs and maintenance work on commercial/passenger vehicles.

PAY AND CONDITIONS

Trainee wages start at £50 per week rising to £70 per week in the second year. The average rate of pay for a tyre or exhaust mechanic or fitter is about £166 for a 39-hour week. Many establishments open seven days per week with staff working five to six days per week. Some fitters do overtime in the evenings and at weekends especially if called out to breakdowns. Incomes can rise to over £200.

Fitters employed by transport companies do most of the work at night when most of the firm's vehicles are off the road; such fitters will usually work shifts. Many tyre and exhaust fitting centres offer a Monday to Sunday service, with late evening opening. Staff work a duty rota with days off in lieu.

PROSPECTS

Experienced fitters working for specialist tyre and exhaust fitting centres or large garages or workshops can progress to supervisory positions.

RELATED OCCUPATIONS

AA/RAC patrolman/woman, motor mechanic/vehicle technician, motor partsman/woman.

FURTHER INFORMATION

The Motor Industry Training Standards Council, 201 Great Portland Street, London, W1N 6AB, 0171 436 6373

National Tyre Distributors Association,* Elsinore House, Buckingham Street, Aylesbury, Bucks, HP20 2NQ, 01296 395933.

Retail Motor Industry Federation Ltd*, 201 Great Portland Street, London W1N 6AB, 0171 307 3411

The Scottish Motor Trade Association*, 3 Palmerston Place, Edinburgh EH12 5AF, 0131 225 3643

FURTHER READING

Leaflets/booklets are available from the addresses marked*.

Working in the Motor Industry–COIC

In the careers library classified under OFM.

6. FORECOURT ATTENDANT (OFM)

BACKGROUND INFORMATION

Forecourt attendants work for petrol filling stations. Some filling stations offer an attended service where the forecourt attendant (also known as a petrol pump attendant) puts petrol or diesel into the customer's car. Most, however, are self-service; the forecourt attendant acts primarily as a cashier, performing similar duties to those of a cash till operator at any other retail outlet.

THE WORK

Attended service

The attendant asks how much petrol/diesel the customer wants. Various types of petrol are available, such as unleaded and four star, which can be measured in litres or money value, eg £5 worth. The attendant establishes what type of petrol the customer wants, and removes the car's petrol filler cap. The nozzle of the petrol pump is then put into the tank, checking that all the pump dials have returned to zero, before putting in the required amount of petrol. The attendant then replaces the filler cap and returns the petrol pump nozzle to its housing, before taking the customer's money and issuing change and, if required, a receipt.

Some customers may require additional services such as filling up with oil or water, checking and adjusting tyre pressures, or washing windows and lights.

Self-service stations

Forecourt attendants spend virtually all of their time in an office as a cashier controlling sales from the forecourt and the shop.

Customers come to the forecourt and serve themselves with air, petrol and water before coming into the shop to pay for their purchases. The attendant operates a 'console' machine which has a series of lights and buttons relating to each petrol pump on the forecourt. When a pump is in use a button lights up. When the nozzle is replaced the 'pay' sign lights up and the console displays the amount of petrol

RETAIL DISTRIBUTION: OE–OFZ

sold and the price. The attendant can then re-set the pump dials to zero in preparation for the next customer. If a customer leaves the forecourt without paying for their petrol, the attendant must note the date and time together with the vehicle registration number and telephone the police immediately.

Most other functions are common to both self-service and attended petrol stations. Many customers pay cash for their petrol; the amount must be entered on a cash register and change given. Modern cash registers display how much change should be given but in other stations the attendant will need to calculate this. The attendant must also know how to deal with cheques and debit/credit card sales. Regular customers at the garage may hold an account whereby they just sign a receipt for their petrol and a bill is sent to them – usually on a monthly basis.

Many stations have a shop where they sell a range of foods, sweets, drinks and cigarettes, and car accessories such as dusters, polishes and sponges. Some also stock a small supply of replacement parts, such as thermostats, windscreen wiper blades, bulbs and fuses. The attendant may need to advise the customer on what type they need for their car by referring to literature and displays available within the petrol station.

At the end of each working day, or in 24-hour stations at the end of each shift, the attendant balances the cash in the till with the purchases recorded by the till. They also read a meter on each petrol pump and compare the readings with those taken at the start of a shift. The pump readings should correlate with the recorded sales on the cash register. Cashiers must be very security conscious and most companies enforce a maximum amount which should be held in the cash register at any one time. Anything over this amount should be transferred to the safe and a record kept of all such transfers.

In addition to sales work, attendants perform a number of other tasks concerned with the day-to-day running of the station such as dealing with petrol deliveries; re-ordering supplies for the shop; keeping the forecourt area safe, clean and tidy (including cleaning toilets); and giving directions to motorists.

WORK ENVIRONMENT

At self-service stations, attendants, by law, spend most of the shift indoors in the shop, only going outside occasionally to take readings from pumps and deal with petrol deliveries when the forecourt is temporarily closed.

At petrol filling stations with attended service, attendants work outdoors for most of the time in all types of weather conditions. The smell of petrol fumes can be quite strong. Forecourt attendants work largely alone with minimum supervision.

SKILLS AND INTERESTS

Attendants must be able to get on well with people and should have a pleasant, polite and helpful manner. For large parts of the day they will have control over the station and must therefore be able to work alone or with minimal supervision. It is important to work well under pressure without becoming flustered and making mistakes. Forecourt staff handle large sums of money, so must be trustworthy and security conscious.

An interest in cars and some mechanical ability is an advantage but not essential. Sales skills are also an advantage due to the range of products now sold from petrol stations.

ENTRY REQUIREMENTS

The level of entry qualification varies from area to area but usually there are no minimum educational qualifications required. Employers might ask for GCSEs/S grades (A–C/1–3) especially in maths. Some employers set an aptitude or arithmetic test at the interview. Local by-laws set minimum ages for people able to sell petrol; this is usually 18 years.

TRAINING

Training takes place on the job under the supervision of an experienced attendant or other qualified individual. Trainees learn how to use the petrol pumps in an attended station or how to use the console in a self-service station. They will also learn to operate the cash register including cancelling a sale that has been entered incorrectly and dealing with customer accounts, cheques and charge, credit and debit cards. They are also shown the various routine maintenance tasks, such as changing till rolls and balancing cash at the end of the shift. Where relevant they will also be trained on how to handle deliveries of fuel to the site. All training emphasizes the importance of health and safety awareness.

NVQs/SVQs are now available in Petrol Retailing.

LATE ENTRY

This work is ideally suited to adults. Many employers favour older applicants due to the responsibility of working alone in the station and handling large sums of cash.

OPPORTUNITIES

Forecourt attendants are employed by all types of filling station. Many stations operate under franchise or other agreements with the oil companies. Some stations are attached to garages offering car sales and/or servicing and repairs. Others are linked to supermarkets. Filling stations are found throughout the country with higher concentrations in urban areas. Staff turnover is quite high, so jobs occur quite regularly in most areas.

PAY AND CONDITIONS

The average rate for forecourt staff is £151 for a 39-hour week but can be higher in some parts of the UK. Earnings can be improved by additional payments for overtime and unsocial hours including nights, weekends and bank holidays, and from bonus payments earned from shop sales.

Filling stations open for long hours, and some are open 24 hours a day, so shift work is normal. Many stations are open from about 7am to 11pm; they usually operate a two-shift system whereas 24-hour stations usually have a three-shift system. Saturday, Sunday and bank holiday working is to be expected, with compensatory time off in the week.

There are many opportunities for part-time work, often covering just the evening period or weekends and bank holidays.

PROSPECTS

Prospects of progression into managerial positions is severely limited for those without qualifications. Attendants who are particularly good at selling shop produce, have a pleasant manner and accept responsibility for handling cash may find that jobs in other areas of retailing are open to them. Those whose particular interest is in cars may find it possible to progress into car sales work or tyre/exhaust fitting on sites with these facilities.

RELATED OCCUPATIONS

Store assistant, supermarket worker, tyre/exhaust fitter, counter service assistant, filling station manager, cashier.

FURTHER INFORMATION

The Motor Industry Training Standards Council, 201 Great Portland Street, London, W1N 6AB, 0171 436 6373

Petrol Retailers Association, 201 Great Portland Street, London, W1N 6AB, 0171 436 6373

Retail Motor Industry Federation Ltd*, 201 Great Portland Street, London W1N 6AB, 0171 307 3411

The Scottish Motor Trade Association*, 3 Palmerston Place, Edinburgh EH12 5AF, 0131 225 3643

FURTHER READING

Leaflets/booklets are available from the addresses marked*.

In the careers library classified under OFM.

7. RETAIL BUTCHER (OFM)

BACKGROUND INFORMATION

The meat retailing sector is the major employer in the meat industry. Some 60,000 people work in independent retailers and 8,000 in the meat operations of supermarkets and multiple stores. This article is concerned particularly with the independent retailers.

Retail butchers' shops increasingly offer a range of foods – including cheeses and delicatessen – as well as meat. Customers are demanding higher quality and a wider choice of goods, particularly products such as stir-fry or kebabs.

THE WORK

The main activity is selling meat and related products. Retail butchers need a thorough knowledge of the products they are selling, so that they can advise customers and answer enquiries about preparation, cooking, nutrition etc.

In some shops, one or more staff work in a back room, cutting, boning and trimming meat to prepare it for sale, whilst staff at the front of the shop concentrate on serving customers. Both in the back room and in the store itself, staff must maintain a high standard of safety and hygiene.

Meat arrives at butchers' shops as carcasses, bone-in primal cuts and boneless pre-packed primal cuts, from which butchers prepare joints, chops, mince and meat products.

Buying and ordering supplies is an important part of the work; butchers need to take into account the quantities they have in stock and the anticipated demand – for instance, customers usually buy more joints in colder months, whereas in the summer, when barbecues are popular, there is a greater demand for chops, chicken joints, burgers and steaks.

Some retail butchers visit meat markets to purchase supplies; some buy their meat from local farms; and others receive deliveries from wholesalers. When a delivery arrives, it is important to check the contents against the order form. Stock is transferred from the supplier's van either manually, or with trolleys, hoists, lifts etc. The meat is examined, any unsuitable products are rejected, and supplies are then transferred to the cold store. Operating the cold store involves following the correct procedures governing temperature indicators and controls. (There are legal requirements governing temperature and hygiene in meat retailing.)

Another important aspect of the work is setting up attractive, eye-catching displays in the store, using both the shop window and internal display cabinets. Sometimes there are practical promotions to arrange (eg encouraging customers to buy more lamb), with posters and leaflets advising customers on preparation and cooking.

Accurate handling and processing of payments is essential, as in all retail operations. Butchers need to operate the till and understand payment procedures. They weigh many purchases, using either electronic or manual scales, and wrap products hygienically. They may use an automatic ticketing system.

Some retail butchers run their own delivery services.

Butchers working in supermarkets are mainly backroom staff, engaged in cutting, boning and packaging, but much of this work is being transferred to supermarket suppliers. There is less contact with customers than in independent retailers' shops. However, there is a trend to develop in-store serve-over butchery counters within supermarkets.

WORK ENVIRONMENT

Butchers' shops are generally well ventilated and well lit. The selling area is maintained at a controlled, cool temperature. Staff also enter chill rooms and cold stores, mostly for brief periods.

Much of the working day is spent standing. Unloading and storing stock involves lifting and carrying, although mechanical aids may be used.

Some jobs involve driving vans to markets, wholesalers and customers' premises – for these posts, a full driving licence is required.

SKILLS AND INTERESTS

It is important to enjoy meeting customers and advising them on choice of products, cooking and preparation. An outgoing personality is essential for success as a retail butcher. Good spoken communication skills, with the ability to listen as well as to give information, are required. Butchers work as a team and need to be able to get on well with colleagues.

An interest in cooking and a taste for good food is a distinct advantage. Some visual flair is useful for producing attractive window/counter displays.

Butchers need manual dexterity and good hand-to-eye co-ordination for cutting and preparing meat.

Personal cleanliness and strict attention to hygiene are essential.

Numeracy is required for cash handling.

RETAIL DISTRIBUTION: OE–OFZ

ENTRY REQUIREMENTS

No specific educational qualifications are required, although The Meat Training Council recommends entrants have GCSEs/S grades (A–D/1–4) in English, maths and a science subject. Some larger firms may set aptitude tests. A Saturday job or work experience placement in a butcher's shop is a useful background for applicants.

Completion of a training scheme for young people (as an unemployed trainee) and attainment of an NVQ in Meat Processing at Level 2 is an advantage for those seeking employment with retail butchers.

TRAINING

For school-leavers, the most common route is via National Traineeships. Training both on and off the job normally lasts two years and can lead to an NVQ in Meat Processing at Level 2. Contact your local careers office, TEC/LEC for details.

To attain the NVQ in Meat Processing at Level 2, trainees have to reach set standards in a specified number of units. These include hygiene and cleaning procedures, use of tools and equipment for cutting and boning, displaying and selling meat and meat products, and health, safety and security procedures. There is a core of units that must be taken and a choice of options. Additional units may be taken by those wishing to gain a wider level of competence. Units are awarded on the basis of continuous assessment, usually in the workplace. Holders of NVQ Level 2 are eligible to become affiliates of the Worshipful Company of Butchers Guild.

In Scotland, SVQs are available at Levels 1, 2 and 3 and the Scottish Federation of Meat Traders' Associations runs its own training scheme and prepares young people for certification as Modern Apprentices within the overall Meat Training Council scheme.

Opportunities may be available to train via Modern Apprenticeships leading to at least an NVQ Level 3. In Scotland Skillseekers may be available.

The Meat Training Council offers further qualifications leading to associateship and graduate membership. These are aimed at those seeking advancement in the industry. They include modules in: abattoir; catering butchery; manufacturing plant; poultry industry; retailing; supermarket butchery; and wholesale distribution. Each module is accompanied by practical training and experience, and there is a written and practical examination.

Over 60 colleges and training centres offer courses leading to NVQs/SVQs and some also offer the Meat Training Council's examination courses. Courses are generally part-time, over two years, and some also offer the Meat Training Council's examination courses, but one-year full-time courses are available at some centres.

Opportunities for specialist study and work experience abroad are available through the Worshipful Company of Butchers Guild. Participants can gain experience in the continental meat trade and study specialist subjects such as *charcuterie*.

LATE ENTRY

Traditionally, employers have preferred to recruit school-leavers. However, as the number of 16-year-olds is declining, there may be better opportunities for adults, particularly those with experience in other retail sectors, to enter this type of work.

Related NVQs or SVQs are useful; it may be possible for adults with experience, who lack formal qualifications, to gain NVQs/SVQs via Accreditation of Prior Learning (APL). Further information is available from the Meat Training Council.

OPPORTUNITIES

In the independent retail sector there are opportunities for employment with firms that run a single shop, or a chain of shops. Traditionally, many independent retailers have been family businesses, handed down from generation to generation, but this is now becoming less common. However, there are opportunities for others – without family connections but with training and experience as retail butchers – to start their own businesses.

In some areas (mainly in large cities) there are halal and kosher butchers catering for the specialist needs of local communities.

PAY AND CONDITIONS

Wage rates and hours of work are a matter of negotiation between employer and employee. Rates of pay vary considerably in different areas of the country. In general terms, for a 40-hour week, 18-year-olds may earn between £90 and £130 a week; general assistants, aged 20 or over, £140 to £190 a week; skilled butchers £190 to £220+ a week; shop managers £230 to £280+ a week. Paid overtime may be available.

Most butchers work Saturdays, with a day off during the week. Part-time work may be available.

PROSPECTS

There are opportunities, particularly in supermarkets and major chains, for rapid progress. Many people reach managerial positions in their twenties.

It is possible, after further training, to become a meat inspector. The Royal Society of Health (RSH) qualification for meat inspectors may be taken after the associateship of the Meat Training Council, via a one-year part-time course, or as part of a one-year full-time course leading to the graduate membership and the RSH. Inspectors, who are employed by the Meat Hygiene Service, check quality and standards in abattoirs and meat plants.

RELATED OCCUPATIONS

Meat process worker, meat inspector, store assistant, store manager, self-employed franchisee, food scientist/technologist.

FURTHER INFORMATION

Meat Training Council*, PO Box 141, Winterhill House, Snowdon Drive, Milton Keynes MK6 1YY, 01908 231062

The Worshipful Company of Butchers Guild, Butchers' Hall, Bartholomew Close, London EC1A 7EB, 0171 606 4106

The Scottish Federation of Meat Traders' Associations, 8/10 Needless Road, Perth PH2 0JW, 01738 637785

FURTHER READING

Leaflets/booklets are available from the address marked*.

Working In Retailing – COIC

In the careers library classified under OFM.

8. FLORIST (OFM)

BACKGROUND INFORMATION

Although most floristry shops are small, the floristry industry is a significant part of the retail trade, with sales each year in the UK exceeding one billion pounds.

Florists use their creative skills to make up floral designs and sell flowers and plants.

THE WORK

Florists create and make bouquets, wreaths and floral tributes to order and sell them to the public. They also sell cut flowers, pot plants and sometimes dried and artificial flowers and gift arrangements.

Florists buy fresh flowers, taking into account customers' orders and likely sales to passing trade. They may visit a wholesale market or buy from a wholesaler who delivers to florists. Some florists also buy direct from local nurseries, while some telex or telephone orders to overseas growers, particularly in Holland.

They also buy other items they need for floristry make-up work and for sale in the shop, such as special wire, ribbon, cellophane, oasis (water absorbent foam), silk, dried and other artificial flowers, cards, tools and fertilizers. This can involve visiting a wholesale market or warehouse or having the goods delivered.

Florists use flowers to design and make up floral arrangements, often for special occasions, such as weddings, anniversaries, birthdays, funerals and gift presentations. Many designs are traditional but florists will work to a customer's own ideas or may create their own designs. They use a knife or scissors to make the design with fresh flowers and materials such as wire, tape, oasis, sprays of leaves and evergreen, baskets and gift wrap.

Care of the flowers is important. This involves removing damaged branches, cutting the stems and putting them into deep water containing flower nutrient, watering pot plants and checking them for pests and treating them where necessary.

Florists display flowers, plants and accessories and price goods for sale. They serve customers, both in person and by telephone, advise them on their choice and on how to care for their flowers or plants. They may arrange for orders to be delivered and process orders by the flower relay services such as Interflora, Teleflorist and Flowergram. They handle cash, give change and process credit card orders. They keep the premises clean and tidy.

Florists who are managers or who run their own shops must keep accounts and other business records, such as VAT returns.

Some florists provide contract services on customers' premises such as hotels, offices, public buildings, private homes and at exhibitions. They may also supply and care for the house plants in these premises, which is known as 'interior landscaping'.

Florists should wear protective overalls and comfortable shoes.

WORK ENVIRONMENT

Florists work indoors, mainly in shops open to the public. While the selling areas are bright and cheerful, many shops have workrooms where design and make-up work is undertaken. They also have cold rooms designed to provide the right environment for flower care, and these are therefore cool and shaded.

Florists spend much of their time standing, either when working at a bench or in dealing with customers. Work can be dirty, wet, heavy and strenuous.

Work can involve travelling to wholesalers, nurseries or customers' premises.

SKILLS AND INTERESTS

Florists must be creative and have artistic ability. A sense of colour, shape and design is important, both when discussing customers' requirements and when making up floral designs.

Good hand skills are required, together with nimble fingers for wiring flowers. They need to work carefully and gently when making up designs, as flowers are easily damaged.

Florists should be able to work well as part of a team and get on well with other staff, as well as with customers. They need good communication skills to advise customers, understand their instructions and sell to them. Clear speech is necessary, particularly in dealing with telephone orders. They need to be particularly sympathetic and tactful when dealing with customers who may be upset, eg when ordering flowers for a funeral.

Figurework ability is necessary for estimating the cost of orders, handling cash and giving change. Those who manage or run a business also need this ability for keeping financial records, such as wages and VAT returns.

Florists must be able to work under pressure when completing orders by an agreed time and at busy times of the year, such as Mothers' Day, Easter, Valentine's Day and Christmas.

ENTRY REQUIREMENTS

There are no minimum requirements for entry to floristry, although some employers prefer some GCSEs/S grades (A–C/1–3). English, mathematics, art and craft subjects are particularly useful. It is important that entrants can write clearly and spell well. Good health and stamina are required.

Direct entry

It is possible to enter floristry direct, or following a full-time course. Direct-entry school-leavers begin on training schemes for young people through Modern Apprenticeships. National Traineeships in floristry will be available from summer 1998 – contact local careers offices for details.

NVQs/SVQs in Floristry: no set entry qualifications.

Full-time vocational studies

BTEC First Diploma in Floristry: no particular entry qualifications are required, although some GCSEs/S grades are useful.

BTEC National Diploma in Floristry: usually requires four GCSEs/S grades (A–C/1–3), or a relevant BTEC first award, or Intermediate GNVQ/GSVQ Level II.

BTEC Higher National Diploma in Floristry: usually

requires one A level/two H grades and some GCSEs/S grades (A–C/1–3), or a relevant BTEC/SQA national award, or Advanced GNVQ/GSVQ Level III.

National Certificate in Professional Floristry: usually requires NVQ/SVQ Level 2 in Floristry.

Professional development

The Intermediate Certificate of the Society of Floristry (ICSF) requires evidence of at least three years' practical experience in floristry plus attendance at a one-day seminar run by the Society. Seminars are held at various locations throughout the UK.

The National Diploma of the Society of Floristry (NDSF): requires entrants to hold the ICSF.

TRAINING

Pre-entry

Full-time further education vocational qualifications

There are a number of full-time courses that can be taken to prepare for entry into floristry.

BTEC First Diploma in Floristry: courses are offered at a few English colleges and last for one year. They are designed as an introduction to floristry.

BTEC National Diploma in Floristry: courses are offered at several colleges in England and Wales and last for two years full-time or three years on a sandwich basis. They aim to provide thorough training in the principles and practice of floristry.

BTEC Higher National Diploma (HND) in Floristry: two- and three-year courses are offered at some colleges. Higher National Diploma courses prepare students for managerial work or self-employment.

Direct entry qualifications

NVQ/SVQ Floristry Levels 2 and 3: many colleges offer courses preparing students for NVQ/SVQ Levels 2 and 3.

Continuous professional development qualifications

National Certificate in Professional Floristry: a number of colleges offer one-year courses that allow students to develop existing floristry skills to a higher level. Successful completion of the course helps students to prepare for ICSF and NDSF qualifications, but is not essential for this purpose.

On entry

Entrants are trained by an experienced florist. On starting work they learn shop procedures, the care of flowers and plants, flower and plant names, the principles of colour and design, techniques of making bouquets, wreaths and other displays, selling skills, cash handling, estimating costs and customer relations.

Those on training schemes and others wanting to gain qualifications work for NVQ/SVQ qualifications in floristry, often through part-time attendance at a local college.

NVQ/SVQ in Floristry is designed for a wide range of floristry activities including producing designs, conditioning and caring for fresh materials, product presentation, providing a service to customers, selling, handling stock, display. Topics covered include customer care, health and safety, plant care, flower arrangements, merchandising, wedding floristry, gift wrapping, communications, funeral designs, tied assemblies.

NVQ/SVQ in Floristry at Level 3 includes assessing and evaluating designs and displays, work planning, floristry designs, receipt, storage and condition of stock, receipt of payments, security, health and safety, customer care, complaints and returns, information, staff training, working relationships. It also has an optional unit on assessing performance.

Florists can also attend short courses on specific topics that are run by colleges and flower relay services.

Experienced florists can gain the Intermediate Certificate of the Society of Floristry (ICSF) by passing examinations on the theory and practice of floristry. Holders of the ICSF can take further theory and practice examinations to gain the National Diploma of the Society of Floristry (NDSF). The ICSF and NDSF are intended for professional florists with full practical experience and a thorough knowledge of the flower industry. It is the highest award in the UK and has international recognition. Some colleges offer courses to prepare for the ICSF and NDSF.

LATE ENTRY

There is no upper age limit for entry to floristry.

Mature applicants may be considered for the courses described in TRAINING without the usual minimum entry requirements.

There may be specific training opportunities directed at adults available in some areas for this type of work. Candidates may have to satisfy certain conditions to be eligible. Contact your local Jobcentre, careers office or TEC/LEC for details.

OPPORTUNITIES

Most florists work in small specialist shops that are in every town and city throughout the UK. Some work in floristry shops based in large hotels or shops that are departments within larger stores or garden centres. Shops tend to be small and usually employ fewer than ten staff.

The number of florists decreased during the recession in the early 1990s but has since stabilized.

Vacancies may be advertised in Jobcentres, local newspapers and trade magazines such as *The Florist Trade Magazine*.

There is an increasing trend for those leaving higher-level full-time courses to seek financial backing to open their own shop, possibly having first gained experience as an employee.

There are opportunities for experienced florists to work abroad.

PAY AND CONDITIONS

There are no set pay scales for florists. Their earnings tend to be similar to those in retail work generally and can range from approximately £65 to £200 a week, depending on the size and location of the shop.

Florists usually work normal shop hours for 40 hours a week including Saturdays. Early starts are often necessary to complete large orders for weddings or funerals or if visiting a wholesaler to buy stock. Sunday work may be necessary on occasions.

There are opportunities for part-time work.

RETAIL DISTRIBUTION: OE–OFZ

PROSPECTS

Career development involves broadening the range of skllls, as well as specializing in aspects of the business.

It may be possible to become a buyer in a large floristry shop, or be promoted to supervisor or manager. Experienced florists with business skills may choose to set up their own business.

There are openings for some florists to teach floristry full-time or part-time and opportunities for part-time work demonstrating floristry and judging competitions.

Florists may use their experience to transfer to supervisory or management work in the retail trade outside floristry.

RELATED OCCUPATIONS

Window dresser, horticultural worker, garden centre worker, interior landscaper, gardener, store assistant, store manager.

FURTHER INFORMATION

Floristry Training Council*, Roebuck House, Hampstead Norreys Road, Hermitage, Thatcham, Berkshire RG18 9RZ, 01635 200465 (please enclose an sae)

The Secretary, Society of Floristry, 59 Treetops, Portskewett, Gwent NP6 4RT, 01291 424039 (please include sae)

FURTHER READING

Leaflets/booklets are available from the address marked*.
In the careers library classified under OFM.

9. DISPLAY PERSON (OFM/ET)

BACKGROUND INFORMATION

The primary purpose of display design is to sell goods. It is usually intended to interest customers in merchandise, to encourage them into the shop and to focus the customers' attention on goods that the company's marketing plans are currently concentrating on selling. In-store and exhibition displays should make it easy for sales people to demonstrate and sell the products and make it easy for customers to find and examine the goods they want.

A good display can inform and advise, introduce new merchandise and products, help to establish new fashions, educate public tastes in furnishing fashion, promote the company's corporate image and keep customers in contact with price changes.

THE WORK

This varies considerably depending on where they work. In some cases, display personnel can use all their creativity; with other employers, such as cosmetic manufacturers or high street chains, the style of display may be dictated by the employer.

The work of a display person often starts months before the display is needed. In department stores for example, plans are made in January for the displays for the following Christmas. Designers, together with store directors, shop managers or manufacturers, plan future displays bearing in mind the image they want to create and the message they want to communicate, and what their competitors might be doing.

Many displays are based upon a theme or event, eg Christmas, Easter, spring, summer holidays, back to school, or autumn. In some cases they may be based on a show or film in the area, a national celebration or a topical occasion. The choice of merchandise for display depends on a number of factors – time of year, fashion, the location of the shop, the corporate identity of the manufacturer or shop and whether there is a national or local promotion for the goods at the time.

Once plans have been decided, design personnel draw designs for windows, shop interiors, show cases, exhibition stands etc. In doing this they consider the areas to have displays, the size and shape of the areas and where they are positioned. For instance, in a store some windows facing a main street may be more important than those down a side street which may not be seen by so many people.

Display personnel design the displays to be pleasing to look at and to show the merchandise off to its best advantage. They consider such things as the shapes and colour of the merchandise and the balance and grouping of props. They decide what they want the customer to focus on in the display, how they will draw their eye to that area and the impression they want the display to create.

Lighting is a vital part of displays as, depending on the atmosphere required, the display may be softly lit, dim, bright or have coloured lighting. Lighting is also used to focus the customers' attention on particular parts of the display.

The next stage is planning what they need to create the impression they want, and how the props used in the display are to be made. In some cases the display team make their own display props, in other cases they contract the work out or may hire items. They plan the time needed, the materials, and the resources for the display.

In making props for the display they require a range of skills including painting, carpentry and plastering and may have to use a variety of tools from sewing needles and pins to hand drills and saws. A window displaying ski clothing, for instance, may require them to paint panels with snow scenes on them to go at the back of the window. They would also have to create artificial snow for the floor of the window. For a display based on an Egyptian theme they might make models of pyramids and the Sphinx.

Before the display is ready to assemble, display personnel dismantle the previous display and return the merchandise to the relevant departments and clean the window areas. Assembling the new display may involve placing panels at the back of the window, laying the flooring, arranging the merchandise, dressing mannequins etc.

Although the description above details the work of display personnel in a store the principles are similar in all types of display and exhibition design.

WORK ENVIRONMENT

Display personnel usually work indoors – in studios where they make the props being used to create the displays, in shop windows, on shop floors, and on exhibition stands. Some work in theme parks, advertising, TV or film studios, in museums or art galleries, airports, seaports or on board ship.

The work can involve climbing ladders, lifting carrying and bending. Display people working for manufacturers, high street chains or for a group of shops may have to travel and a driving licence could be an advantage. Occasionally they may be required to stay away from home overnight.

RETAIL DISTRIBUTION: OE–OFZ

SKILLS AND INTERESTS

Display people need a considerable amount of creativity and artistic flair, with a good eye for colour, balance and composition. They also need imagination, ingenuity and the ability to improvise and adapt available materials. They need good hand skills and the ability to work with a wide range of materials – wood, paper, polystyrene, fabric etc.

They work in teams and so need good interpersonal skills. They also meet customers and should be able to communicate well with them. Display staff also need to be reasonably fit as this can be physically hard work.

ENTRY REQUIREMENTS

It is possible to start straight from school with no academic qualifications and train on the job, together with day release to college. However, the majority of display people start with a full-time college course.

Entry requirements vary depending on the course applied for.

British Display Society (BDS): the Technician's Certificate and BDS General Certificate Grade I do not require any academic qualifications. In order to apply for the BDS General Certificate Grade II it is necessary to have passed Grade I.

The BDS National Diploma Advanced Level course in Retail Display requires three GCSEs/S grades (A–C/1–3), including art and English.

The BDS National Diploma Advanced Level course in Exhibition Design requires three GCSEs/S grades (A–C/1–3), including art, English and a technical subject, plus a one-year foundation course such as the BDS General Certificate Grade I.

BTEC: the BTEC National Diploma in Design (Display) requires four GCSEs/S grades (A–C/1–3), including art or a related subject, or Intermediate GNVQ in Art and Design/GSVQ in Design Level II. Applicants should take a portfolio of their work along to the interview.

SQA: the GSVQ Level III in Design requires GSVQ Level II in Design, or five S grades (1–3).

Higher national diplomas/certificates require two H grades, or GSVQ Level III in Design. Applicants should take a portfolio of their work along to the interview.

TRAINING

Training may be full-time at colleges or part-time working as a display assistant and attending college on a day release basis. There are three major bodies offering qualifications in display – the British Display Society, BTEC and SQA. Courses may be full- or part-time.

British Display Society (BDS): BDS General Certificate grade I – a one-year full-time course. Entry at 16 years.

BDS General Certificate grade II – one-year full-time course entry. Entry at 17 years.

BDS National Diploma Advanced Level in Retail Display – a two-year full-time course. Entry at 16 years.

BDS National Diploma Advanced level in Exhibition Design – a full-time two-year course.

BDS Technician's Certificate – a three-year, day release course with three levels – Preliminary, Intermediate and Final stages. Students who successfully complete the BDS National Diploma Advanced Level courses, the BDS General Certificate course grade II or the final part of the Technician's Certificate can use the letters Cert BDS after their name on becoming members of the Society.

Students at colleges recognized by the BDS offering BTEC national diplomas or SQA GSVQ Level III in Design, are eligible on qualification to apply for Cert BDS membership.

BTEC: the National Diploma in Design (Display) is a two-year full-time course and is offered at a number of colleges throughout the country. However, at present there is only one college offering the BTEC National Certificate in Design (Display) and one college offering a National Diploma in Design (Exhibition).

SQA: in Scotland the equivalent college course is the GSVQ Level III in Design which has options in display design and exhibition design. This is a two-year full-time or three-year part-time course. SQA Higher National Diplomas and Certificates are also available in Design. Titles of these courses vary but include Retail Display, Exhibition Design, Visual Merchandising and Marketing Design. SQA courses may be full- or part-time and some parts may be available through distance learning.

There is also a considerable amount of on-the-job training in this work which can lead to NVQs/SVQs in Interior or Exhibition Design at Levels 2, 3 and 4.

New display personnel usually start as juniors and learn from more experienced staff.

LATE ENTRY

There is no upper age limit for the work. Entry and training for mature entrants is as described above. However, applicants for college courses with relevant experience and a very good portfolio may be accepted without the usual academic entry qualifications.

OPPORTUNITIES

Display personnel are employed by many different types of employers. They work for shops – this includes large department stores, high street chains and small groups of shops. They can also work for manufacturers doing displays for them in shops, exhibitions or pubs.

There are opportunities for work in advertising, in films and TV and in airports or seaports designing and dressing showcases. They can also work on board cruise liners.

It is also possible to work on a freelance basis and display personnel can work anywhere in the world. There are also opportunities to move into other types of design work such as interior design or theatre set design.

The chances of finding employment for those leaving college with recognized display qualifications is good.

PAY AND CONDITIONS

This depends on the type of work but on the whole most staff work flexitime, usually about 40 hours a week. Display staff work on Saturdays and Sundays and sometimes may have to work during evenings. Occasionally they may have to work on bank holidays.

Salaries vary tremendously depending on where the display person works and for whom. An assistant may be paid in the region of £10,000 to £12,000.

PROSPECTS

Promotion prospects vary depending on where display people work but usually the prospects are good. For instance, in a large department store they start as a junior, progressing to display assistant and then to senior in charge of windows. They could then progress to assistant manager and then to display manager. Although it is not absolutely necessary to do the more advanced courses in order to gain promotion they can be a considerable advantage.

There are also opportunities for those with the necessary experience and qualifications to become lecturers in colleges offering display design courses.

RELATED OCCUPATIONS

Store manager, merchandiser, model maker, TV and theatre set designer, graphic designer, interior designer, store assistant.

FURTHER INFORMATION

British Display Society Ltd*, 146 Welling Way, Welling, Kent, DA16 2RS, 0181 856 2030

FURTHER READING

Leaflets/booklets are available from the address marked*.

Working in Retailing – COIC

In the careers library classified under OFM/ET.

10. SHOE REPAIRER CLCI:OFZ

BACKGROUND INFORMATION

There are different kinds of shoe repairer. Most are skilled craftspeople based in shops who accept repairs to be collected a few hours or days later. An increasing number of shoe repairers work in outlets that not only offer a shoe repair service but also key cutting, engraving, making house signs and replacing watch straps as well as acting as agents for dry cleaning in some cases. They also sell a range of shoe-care products, such as polishes, dyes, laces, insoles and ranges of small gifts (such as trophies), leather goods and key rings etc. Many of these services are done while customers wait. A small number of shoe repairers work in factories that make shoes. They deal with shoes returned to the factory for repair, usually shoes that have cost at least £90 a pair.

THE WORK

Shoe repairers mend all types of shoes and boots. This can involve replacing soles or heels, re-stitching, patching, replacing faulty fasteners (eg zips), dyeing, staining and polishing.

Advising Customers

Shoe repairers begin by examining the damaged or worn footwear to decide whether repair is possible. They use their knowledge of how the shoes were manufactured and how different materials respond to wear and tear to decide on the most appropriate materials for the repair. They advise the customer of the recommended repair, the cost involved and when the footwear will be ready for collection.

Benchwork and Repair

Shoe repairers use pincers to remove the worn sole or heel. They then attach the replacement sole or heel. This may be done by using adhesive and a compressed-air staple gun, brad (nail) gun or hammer and nails. Leather soles are fixed to the shoe by a stitching machine or by other forms of attachment. When they have fitted the replacement sole or heel, repairers use a knife to trim away the excess material. They may then use an electrically operated trimmer to produce an exact fit to the shape of the shoe.

Finishing

Shoe repairers use a brush to stain the edges of leather soles and heels to match the colour of the shoe. They use an electrically operated machine to polish footwear when repairs have been completed. The shoes are then wrapped, labelled with the customer's name, address, code number and price, and stored ready for collection.

Most shoe repairers are responsible for keeping their own machines and equipment in good working order. They sharpen cutting tools frequently and regularly service the electrically operated machinery.

Shoe repairers working in shops and heel bars usually offer a repair service for leather goods, such as stitching leather belts, jackets, handbags and suitcases, which often involves using sewing machines.

Key Cutting

Another important part of retail shoe repairers' work is key cutting. They use a range of small electrically powered machines to cut a variety of commercial, domestic and vehicle keys. Some also use machinery to engrave items such as key-rings, nameplates and trophies.

Retail shoe repairers collect money from customers and deal with cash, cheques and credit cards.

Shoe repairers need to work quickly when trying to meet a promised deadline for repair. All shoe repairers wear protective clothing.

WORK ENVIRONMENT

Shoe repairers work indoors. Most work in small shops, either alone or with one or two others. A small number of shoe repairers work in workshops in shoe manufacturing companies.

The work can be dirty, with fumes from strong adhesives and smells from leather and rubber. It can be noisy when operating machinery.

Most work is done standing at a workbench or machines.

SKILLS AND INTERESTS

Repairing shoes is practical work, so shoe repairers should have good hand skills, be nimble-fingered, and enjoy working with machines and people. They must be able to work neatly and accurately for repairs to be of acceptable quality to customers.

Shoe repairers should be safety conscious as some hand tools and machinery they use are potentially dangerous.

Product knowledge is important to decide on the most suitable method of repair. Initiative is required to complete each job alone.

Those working in shops must be able to get on well with customers. They need good communication skills to listen to customers' requirements and to explain the repairs they recommend. They should also be capable of working in a

RETAIL DISTRIBUTION: OE–OFZ

team with others in the shop.

Shoe repairers should be able to cope with pressure when working to meet promised deadlines and when their work is interrupted to serve customers. Lunch-times and Saturdays can be particularly busy. They must have the ability to estimate the cost of work and cope with handling money and giving change.

Good eyesight is needed to cope with small, neat stitching. Normal colour vision is required for matching dyes and threads.

ENTRY REQUIREMENTS

There are no minimum entry qualifications required for shoe repairers but some employers may ask for GCSEs/S grades (A–E/1–5). In addition, entrants might be asked to show evidence of practical ability such as GCSEs/S grades in CDT or technology.

Some national organizations require applicants to pass an aptitude test that includes English, arithmetic and practical skills.

TRAINING

Most 16- and 17-year-olds entering shoe repairing do so via training to standards developed by the Shoe Repair Industry Training Organisation Ltd (SRITO). Contact your local careers offices, jobcentresTECs/LECs for details.

Training in shoe repairs is usually on the job, with the trainee learning from an experienced repairer such as the owner or manager of the business. Some companies have their own training schemes which can include trainees attending their national or regional training centres.

Trainees work towards an NVQ/SVQ in Footwear Repair at Level 2. This includes dealing with customers to advise on repairs that may be needed and preparing the work including selection of materials and methods. It also covers repair techniques, finishing and quality control as well as the skills required to manage the workplace and the business.

Modern Apprenticeships (or similar schemes under the Skillseekers Initiative in Scotland) may be available working towards NVQ/SVQ Level 3 and encompassing key cutting and engraving – contact your local careers office, Jobcentre, TEC/LEC for details.

LATE ENTRY

There is no upper age limit for entry to shoe repair and the majority of entrants are adults rather than school- or college-leavers.

Independent training providers offer courses to learn shoe repairing and the ancillary skills now carried out in shoe repair businesses.

There are specific training opportunities directed at adults available in some areas for this type of work. Candidates may have to satisfy certain conditions to be eligible. Contact your local Jobcentre, careers office or TEC/LEC for details.

OPPORTUNITIES

There are between 7,000 to 8,000 shoe repairers in the UK. Nearly all of them work in the estimated 6,000 shoe repair outlets. An increasing percentage of shoe repair outlets are part of national companies or part of larger shops, such as department stores or shoe retailers. About 70% of outlets, though, are small, independent businesses, each typically having one to three workers.

The number of shoe repairers employed by factories is less than 50.

Vacancies may be advertised in *Footnotes, Shoe and Leather News, Shoe Repairer* and *Shoe Service*.

The shoe repair industry is influenced by footwear fashion. Fashions can either produce a lot of work for shoe repairers (eg court shoes with high heels which need frequent repair) or little work (eg trainers, which can be repaired but frequently are not).

The influx of cheap imported shoes has not helped shoe repairers, as people are reluctant to spend money on repairing very cheap shoes, preferring to buy a new replacement pair.

On the positive side, key cutting has become an increasingly important part of most shoe repairers' work. The recent increase in interest in security has led to a strong demand for additional and replacement keys, and key cutting now accounts for up to 40% of business for some shoe repairers.

PAY AND CONDITIONS

There are no standard rates of pay for shoe repairers. The earnings of shoe repairers with their own business depend on the shop's takings. Employed shoe repairers may earn between £4 to £7 an hour, with national companies commonly offering a bonus scheme.

Shoe repairers usually work a 40-hour week. This includes Saturdays, except for those in factories. Part-time work is possible.

PROSPECTS

Shoe repairers working for small, independent businesses have little or no chance of promotion. Instead, many choose to set up in business on their own.

National organizations have a structure that allows promotion to assistant manager and shop manager through to area and regional manager.

RELATED OCCUPATIONS

Saddler, leather craftworker, footwear manufacturing worker, sewing machinist, upholsterer, store assistant, textile operative, store manager.

FURTHER INFORMATION

Shoe Repair Industry Training Organisation Ltd (SRITO)*, Claverton Road, Wythenshawe, Manchester M23 9NE, 0161 946 6200

Society of Master Shoe Repairers*, 21 Station Road, Desborough, Northamptonshire NN14 2SA, 01536 760374

FURTHER READING

Leaflets/booklets are available from the addresses marked*.

In the careers library classified under OFZ.

PUBLIC RELATIONS OFFICER CLCI:OG

BACKGROUND INFORMATION

Public relations (PR) is concerned with presenting a favourable understanding of an organization to various audiences or publics, such as consumers, businesses, the financial community and employees.

The Institute of Public Relations (IPR) describes PR as having "the responsibility of managing an organization's reputation, credibility and corporate image: shaping, protecting and promoting it".

Many kinds of organization use PR – commercial and industrial, central and local government, hospitals, charities, religious bodies, educational institutions, trade unions, trade and professional associations, lobbyists and arts organizations. They use PR to present their organization in the best possible light, so that their policies, products or services are regarded favourably.

PR is a two-way activity. PR staff seek to influence others on behalf of an organization but also to gather and feed back outside opinions of the organization.

PR operates in two distinct settings. **In-house PR** departments are concerned solely with their employing organization, while **PR consultancies** provide a service to a number of clients. Some organizations have an in-house PR department but also use an external consultancy.

THE WORK

Public relations officers plan, organize and conduct activities that bring favourable attention to an organization's image, policies, products or services. This involves a number of functions, including:

Programme planning. Public relations officers analyse PR problems in consultation with clients or management. They agree on aims and objectives and plan activities to meet them within an agreed budget.

Writing and editing. A major function of PR work is writing and editing press releases, reports, articles, newsletters, annual reports, leaflets, brochures, speeches and film and video scripts.

Production. Public relations officers co-ordinate the production of radio tapes, company newsletters, leaflets, brochures, videos and films.

Liaison with the media. Public relations officers make sure the message they want to put across is published or broadcast. They make and maintain good relationships with newspaper, magazine, radio and television staff to help make it more likely.

Public speaking. The work involves talking to individuals and groups through interviews, meetings, presentations and conferences.

Special events. Public relations officers plan events and participate in them. Press launches, news conferences, exhibitions, open days, trade fairs and corporate hospitality at sports events, for example, are an important part of PR activity.

Research and evaluation. Surveys, interviews and opinion polls are used to gauge how a PR activity may be received. After an activity, public relations officers may use similar methods to judge its effectiveness.

In-house PR is often more specialist than work in consultancies. This is reflected in some job titles used, such as press officer, publicity officer, information officer.

PR consultancy w... an account director, ... secretary. Teams may ... account – corporate, fin... business, public affairs or emp...

WORK ENVIRONMENT

Public relations officers are based in offi... involves travelling for a variety of purpo... clients, to attend press conferences, exhibitions... radio and television studios and design studios.

SKILLS AND INTERESTS

Public relations officers must be able to get on well with many different people, including journalists, managers and employees of an organization, and members of the public.

They should be able to express themselves clearly in speech and in writing. Oral skills are needed for press briefings, meetings, conferences and presentations. Written ability is required for preparing news releases, leaflets, reports, articles etc.

PR work demands good organizational skills to cope with a number of different activities and to arrange events, such as news conferences, open days and exhibitions.

Numeracy is important as PR work must be costed and kept within budget.

Public relations officers must be able to analyse problems before deciding on action. Initiative and enterprise are needed to devise activities that provide solutions.

It is important to be able to work well in a team. Self-motivation and the ability to work under pressure are necessary.

ENTRY REQUIREMENTS

Although no specific qualifications are required, in practice most entrants have a degree. Any degree subject is acceptable. The minimum requirements for entry to degree courses are five GCSEs/S grades (A–C/1–3), plus two A levels/three H grades.

There are some BTEC Higher National Certificate/Diploma courses in Business Studies with a PR specialism. They require either one A level/two H grades with four GCSEs/S grades (A–C/1–3), or a BTEC/SQA national award.

Postgraduate courses in PR require a degree for entry.

Some entrants to PR have taken the Communication Advertising and Marketing (CAM) Foundation's Certificate in Communication Studies. Candidates applying for Certificate registration must be age 18 or over with a minimum of two A levels/three H grades and three GCSEs/S grades (A–C/1–3), or a BTEC/SQA national award in business studies, or five GCSEs/S grades (A–C/1–3) and one year's relevant work experience, or at least three years' relevant experience.

Most entrants to PR have had previous experience of other work, such as journalism, marketing, advertising, engineering, science or law.

TRAINING

Pre-entry

There are a number of relevant full-time courses, although none guarantees entry to PR.

On entry

The Institute of Public Relations (IPR) lists three PR consultancies with in-house graduate training programmes. They involve experience in various departments of the consultancy, internal training sessions, attending talks and visiting media organizations.

Training for most entrants to PR is given in-house. They may also attend workshops, seminars, courses and conferences organized by IPR and by the Public Relations Consultants Association (PRCA).

Public relations officers are encouraged to study for the CAM Certificate in Communication Studies and the CAM Diploma in Public Relations. The diploma is concerned specifically with management and PR. Courses are available at 28 centres, full-time, part-time or by distance learning. Course length varies from centre to centre.

NVQs/SVQs in Public Relations are available at Levels 3 and 4.

LATE ENTRY

Most entrants to PR have had experience of other work. Journalism, marketing and advertising are particularly useful. Other experience, such as engineering, financial management or law, can be useful in relevant areas of PR work.

Entry beyond the age of 35 becomes increasingly difficult.

Adults may be able to enter higher education courses described in TRAINING without the usual entry qualifications.

OPPORTUNITIES

There are approximately 11,000 professional PR practitioners in the UK, although it is estimated that there are over 28,000 with substantial PR experience. Approximately 70% work outside London.

In-house PR staff are employed by a wide range of organizations. The largest single employer is the Government Information Service with over 1,300 employees. Other employers include local authorities, commercial companies, professional bodies, trade associations, charities and television companies.

There are approximately 2,000 consultancies, which employ about one-third of all PR staff. Consultancies vary from those run by one or two individuals to large national firms employing over 100 staff.

Entry to PR work is extremely competitive. Vacancies are advertised in *Campaign*, *PR Week* and *Public Relations Consultancy* and in the national press, but those seeking entry are advised to contact potential employers direct. It may be necessary to begin in PR as an information assistant or publicity assistant with an in-house department, with the aim of later becoming a public relations officer.

PAY AND CONDITIONS

There are no set salary scales in PR. Starting salaries can be around £10,000. Experienced public relations officers earn between £15,000 and £22,000. Senior managers in PR earn over £30,000.

Public relations officers usually work a five-day week, with pressure of work sometimes leading to evening and weekend work. An average working week may be approximately 45 hours.

PROSPECTS

Both in-house departments and consultancies have promotion possibilities but both are very competitive.

In-house public relations officers may seek promotion to management posts, such as communications manager or media relations manager.

Consultancy staff may progress from junior account executive to account executive, senior account executive or account manager, associate or account director.

Movement from company to company for advancement is a common feature of PR careers. Some public relations officers move to the related fields of advertising or marketing, while others set up consultancies on their own or in partnership.

There are some opportunities for experienced public relations officers to work abroad for international companies and consultancies.

RELATED OCCUPATIONS

Market research executive, advertising account executive, advertising copywriter, marketing manager.

FURTHER INFORMATION

CAM Foundation*, Abford House, 15 Wilton Road, London SW1V 1NJ, 0171 828 7506

The Institute of Public Relations*, The Old Trading House, 15 Northburgh Street, London EC1V 0PR (please include sae) 0171 253 5151

Public Relations Consultants Association*, Willow House, Willow Place, Victoria, London SW1P 1JH, 0171 233 6026

Scottish Public Relations Consultants Association, Scottish Council for Development and Industry, 23 Chester Street, Edinburgh EH3 7ET, 0131 225 7911

FURTHER READING

Leaflets/booklets are available from the addresses marked*.

Working in Journalism – COIC

Working in Marketing and Sales – COIC

Careers in Marketing, Public Relations and Advertising – Kogan Page

In the careers library classified under OG.

SALES REPRESENTATIVE/MANAGER
CLCI:OM

BACKGROUND INFORMATION

Every product and service needs to reach prospective customers – whether that product or service is food, clothes, hi-fi equipment, roads, aircraft, stationery, insurance or cleaning services.

The jobs of all the people who design and manufacture goods or provide services depend on the work of the sales people. For instance, however good a new novel is, it will not sell unless the sales team do their job well and get the book into the bookshops.

Sales representatives may be involved in selling their products to shops or retail outlets or may sell direct to the customer who may be an individual buying home improvement products or a developing country buying major engineering works or road-building programmes.

THE WORK

Sales representative

The work of sales representatives – who may also be known as sales executives, sales consultants, agents or technical representatives – varies considerably from company to company. Most sales representatives are responsible for a particular area (usually called territory) of this country or abroad. In some companies, especially new companies or ones that have a new product and no existing customers, representatives may have to decide on the potential market for the product and then build up their list of customers. Other representatives have already established customers on whom to make regular calls.

Some sales people working in consumer sales sell their company's products to retailers, whereas others in technical or specialized sales sell products such as parts and components or items such as road systems or aircraft to other industries.

Selling to retail outlets – the products sold by representatives working in this field depends on the company they work for. They could be selling shoes, sports equipment, jewellery, cleaning materials, food, stationery, electrical goods, farm foods etc.

Representatives work in partnership with shop owners, managers and buyers. They find out what their customer wants then advise on appropriate products. They supply information about the product and any other information the customer needs to know. They visit their retail outlets on a regular basis to show the buyers or managers new products and promotions, or invite buyers to a showroom to show them the products.

When buyers have decided what they need to buy, representatives help them build an order, which may be done on computer. As stock is sold, the shop or company notifies the representative who arranges to replace it.

Sales representatives also help shop owners and managers to sell the products. This may include advising about display and providing the shop's sales staff with product information and sales techniques.

Services may be sold in a similar way. For instance, insurance sales people work closely with brokers, accountants and travel agents to keep them up to date on their company's products and services.

Technical sales representatives usually sell to senior staff of technical departments, such as aeronautical or civil engineers or architects, and need technical knowledge about their products. One sale may take months of negotiating and when the sale is completed the sales representative may oversee the installation of the product – the building of a road system, for example – so projects may take years to complete. Other technical sales, such as medical or pharmaceutical products, are sold to doctors, vets and hospitals in the same way as consumer product sales people sell to retail outlets.

All representatives have considerable paperwork to complete, they keep records and accounts of all their sales, which may be on paper or computer. They handle the initial stages of complaints from their customers.

Sales manager

A large part of sales managers' work is to organize and control their teams of representatives. They recruit representatives, which involves arranging for job vacancy advertisements, interviewing and appointing staff. They are usually responsible for organizing training courses for their staff in such areas as product knowledge, company procedures, communication skills and sales techniques. In some cases they may carry out some of the training themselves. Sales managers have regular meetings with their teams to motivate and manage them, carrying out assessments, appraisals and counselling.

They organize their sales force, allocating the territories to be covered by each representative, and they set sales targets. They compile accounts and analyse sales results (often using computers), monitor the progress of all their team, and use sales figures to plan and budget for future sales campaigns. Sales managers also organize regular sales conferences where the company's new products are explained to the representatives. In some companies, sales managers may deal with a number of customers themselves.

Another large area of their work is in dealing with problems or complaints that customers have. Some problems are dealt with by representatives but major problems require the sales manager to resolve the situation.

Sales managers can also be involved with market research carried out on a product before it is ever manufactured. They attend meetings with other managers and advise on whether a product is likely to meet a market need (however good a product is, it is not worth making unless it is going to sell). Sales managers may also be able to advise other managers on what products the buyers want.

WORK ENVIRONMENT

Representatives usually spend a considerable amount of their time driving to visit customers who may be within a relatively small geographical area like Avon or a much larger area such as the North of England. They may use their homes as a work base, only visiting their companies very occasionally. Others may spend a day or two a week in their offices.

Some representatives spend much time abroad selling goods. Representatives may have to spend days or even weeks staying in hotels away from their home.

Sales managers spend considerable time in the field advising sales representatives and visiting major customers. They also spend time in their office. They travel to attend trade fairs and exhibitions.

SALES: OM

SKILLS AND INTERESTS

Representatives should be friendly, outgoing, self-assured and able to get on with all types of people. They need excellent interpersonal skills to build good relationships with customers and to negotiate sales with them. They need good telephone skills to arrange appointments. They must be able to work on their own, and be very self-motivated. Determination and perseverance is also needed. Representatives should have good numeracy skills to deal with orders and costings, and the ability to absorb large amounts of information about products and customers' needs.

Sales managers need many of the same skills as representatives with the addition of administrative abilities, and management skills to motivate and assess their teams.

ENTRY REQUIREMENTS

There are no set entry requirements for this work other than a clean driving licence. However, more and more companies are recruiting graduates and people with professional skills. Technical and scientific products usually need representatives with relevant qualifications and experience. For instance, engineering sales representatives are invariably engineering graduates.

Some companies recruit trainees, usually graduates, with no experience; others recruit people with relevant experience. Experience can usually be gained in the following way: working in a sales office carrying out clerical jobs such as maintaining sales records and dealing with customers by phone and letter, starting in a particular profession or speciality such as engineering and moving into technical sales, working in the retail industry and gaining experience of sales work.

The Managing amd Marketing Sales Association (MAMSA) offers training and qualifications for sales staff. To study for the Diploma in Salesmanship requires five GCSEs/S grades (A–C/1–3), including English and a mathematical subject; or to have reached a minimum age of 20 years with two years' approved and certified employment; or by assessment of the college/institute lecturer. Sales representatives can also study for City and Guilds/Institute of Sales and Marketing Management (ISMM) examinations in Professional Salesmanship – candidates are usually required to have GCSEs/S grades (A–C/1–3) in English and maths.

Most sales managers have previous experience as sales representatives. Some companies recruit graduates as direct-entry trainees.

TRAINING

Sales representative

Most training is given on the job with representatives learning from experienced members of the team. Companies often run courses in the practical skills of selling such as how to take an order, negotiating, presentation skills, and finance. Representatives can study for the Diploma in Salesmanship from MAMSA which covers communication, salesmanship, organization and business, and market distribution, or City and Guilds/ISMM 6701 Professional Salesmanship which covers salesmanship, organization for selling, communication, advanced salesmanship, and marketing practice.

Sales manager

Training is also usually given on the job. MAMSA offer an Advanced Diploma in Sales Management which covers communication control, advertising and marketing research, personnel control, time control, cost control, legal control, and statistical control. ISMM/City and Guilds offer an examination in Sales Management.

A number of NVQs/SVQs are available, including Selling at Levels 2 and 3, Sales Supervision at Level 3, and Field Sales Management at Level 4.

LATE ENTRY

There is no maximum age limit for entry into this career and adult candidates are often preferred. However, applicants should be healthy, with considerable stamina because of the travelling and long hours required. Many people move into sales work from other careers.

OPPORTUNITIES

Most sizeable manufacturing companies and companies offering commercial services such as insurance companies provide opportunities throughout the country and have their own sales representatives and sales managers. Employment is also possible overseas. There are opportunities for self-employment as freelance sales agents, who may sell products for a number of different companies.

PAY AND CONDITIONS

Pay varies enormously from one company to another. Some representatives work on a salary; some have a salary plus commission; others may just work on a commission-only basis. Many companies have bonus schemes as well. Starting salaries for representatives commence at £6,500 rising up to £50,000 on target earnings. Most companies provide a company car and expense allowance to cover meals and hotel expenses. Working hours are not regular and there may be some evening work.

Sales managers – again pay varies a great deal. Managers can earn between £18,000 and £47,000; some firms pay a bonus if the company does well. Managers usually have a company car and an expense account.

PROSPECTS

The promotion route for representatives is usually to become field sales managers, running a team of representatives. Many move on to become sales managers and from there into general management, and then possibly become directors of a company.

RELATED OCCUPATIONS

Insurance salesperson, marketing executive, buyer/purchasing officer, sales assistant.

FURTHER INFORMATION

The Institute of Sales and Marketing Management (ISMM), Romeland House, Romeland Hill, St Albans, Herts AL3 4ET, 01727 812500

Managing and Marketing Sales Association (MAMSA), PO Box 11, Sandbach, Cheshire CW11 3GE, 01270 526339

SALES: OM

FURTHER READING
Working in Marketing and Sales – COIC
In the careers library classified under OM.

BUYING: OP

BUYER/PURCHASING OFFICER CLCI:OP

BACKGROUND INFORMATION

Every organization needs to purchase supplies, whether for its own internal use (office stationery), for the manufacturing process (raw materials, components) or for re-sale (goods purchased by retail, wholesale and mail order businesses). As well as goods, many organizations purchase services such as cleaning, transport and consultancy.

Purchasing can make a direct contribution to the effectiveness and profitability of an organization, by cutting costs, by ensuring that sources of supply are reliable, and by reducing the amount of capital tied up in stock. Greater management awareness of the importance of these factors has improved the status of purchasing departments in recent years.

Various different terms are used to describe the purchasing function and the people who carry it out. Retailers generally refer to 'buyers'. Buyers are also found in industry, as are 'purchasing' or 'supplies' officers. In the public sector, the terms most commonly used are 'procurement' and 'supplies'.

THE WORK

Buyers/purchasing officers aim to obtain goods and services 'of the right quality, in the right quantity, from the right source, delivered to the right place at the right time, at the right price'. These aims may be difficult to reconcile – for instance, a company that can supply goods of the 'right' quality may not have the capacity to deliver them at the 'right' time. Buyers and purchasing officers have to achieve a balance between often-conflicting objectives, with the aim of making the best possible arrangement that circumstances allow.

There are a number of stages in the purchasing process:

– define requirements, in consultation with other departments such as design and production;

– obtain quotations from potential suppliers;

– negotiate with suppliers, in response to their queries, both technical and commercial;

– choose supplier(s) and commit to purchase, in the form of a contract. The buyer needs to be confident that the product will meet specifications and that the supplier can deliver by the due date. Price is an important, but not overriding factor; buyers aim to achieve a fair price, rather than the lowest possible figure;

– monitor the progress of the contract;

– accept delivery and check that the product or service is of an acceptable standard; and

– pay processing suppliers' invoices, taking advantage of any discounts for prompt payment, and checking that suppliers are paid on time.

Purchasing is often seen in the wider context of the management of materials, storage and stock control. Buyers may have additional responsibilities in these areas, such as making sure that supplies arrive 'just in time' for use, but not too soon (because it is wasteful for an organization to hold unnecessary stock).

In retailing, the fundamental aspects of purchasing are similar to those in other organizations; however, retail buyers need a keen awareness of consumer tastes and preferences, with the ability to pick out merchandise that will sell successfully in the shops. This can be particularly difficult in areas such as fashion buying, where it is important to predict future trends and consumer buying patterns.

Retail buyers, and purchasing officers in other sectors, often specialize in buying a particular category of merchandise.

The work usually involves a great deal of contact with people, including members of other departments within the organization and suppliers' representatives. Buyers and purchasing officers are likely to spend a lot of time on the telephone and in meetings.

Handling, sifting and evaluating information is another important aspect of the work. This involves tasks such as reading catalogues, consulting trade directories, and using computers for recording and analysing supplier performance, or monitoring stock levels.

WORK ENVIRONMENT

The work is office-based, but there may be trips out of the office to visit suppliers. These journeys may involve staying away from home for short periods.

It is usual to work as a member of a team, except in the case of small firms, where there may only be one buyer or purchasing officer.

SKILLS AND INTERESTS

Purchasing is very responsible work, demanding sound judgement, decisiveness, maturity and the ability to cope with pressure and crises. Buyers and purchasing officers need a firm, tough, business-like approach. Absolute integrity is essential; there are greater temptations (for instance, to accept gifts from suppliers) than in many other jobs.

Excellent communications skills – oral and written – are required for liaising with other departments and negotiating with suppliers.

Buyers/purchasing officers need to be well organized and methodical, with an eye for detail (to read the small print in contracts, for instance). The ability to assimilate information is also important. Numeracy is required to interpret market data, to make commercial decisions and negotiate effectively.

Buyers need initiative to seek out new sources of supply.

A driving licence is useful; it is usually required for posts involving travel.

ENTRY REQUIREMENTS

Entry qualifications vary with different employers. No specific academic entry requirements are laid down but, increasingly, employers are looking to recruit candidates with A levels, H grades, BTEC/SQA national or higher national awards, or degrees.

A degree in any subject is acceptable. Business studies or closely related subjects are usually regarded as the most relevant disciplines, and graduates in these may be granted exemption from all or part of the foundation stage of the Chartered Institute of Purchasing and Supply (CIPS) examinations. Technical and scientific disciplines are useful, where relevant to the employers' business. Foreign languages are an asset in international companies, or for jobs involving contact with overseas suppliers.

Holders of BTEC/SQA Higher National Certificates or Diplomas in Business Studies may also be granted full or part-exemption from the CIPS foundation stage. Entry to BTEC/SQA higher national certificate/diploma courses is with one/two A levels or three H grades, or a BTEC/SQA national certificate diploma.

The minimum entry qualifications for student registration with CIPS are two A levels or three H grades and three additional GCSEs/S grades (A–C/1–3), or an Advanced GNVQ/GSVQ Level III, or a BTEC/SQA national certificate/diploma, or a relevant NVQ/SVQ at Level 3, or an equivalent qualification. Exact details are available from the CIPS.

About 60% of CIPS students have degrees or BTEC/SQA higher national awards.

Applicants without the necessary qualifications listed above may register for the CIPS Supervisory Qualifications (First and Second Certificates in Purchasing and Stores). These provide the opportunity to start working towards a professional qualification.

In retailing, it is possible for people with sales experience, but no formal qualifications, to become buyers. Increasingly, however, employers are recruiting A level or H grade school-leavers and graduates – either providing general management training or direct entry to buying departments.

TRAINING

Many employers run their own training schemes. Graduates or A level entrants may start on a general management training scheme and then specialize in purchasing, or they may enter a purchasing or buying department directly, typically as trainee buyers or purchasing clerks. They may take part-time courses for CIPS qualifications; these are becoming increasingly necessary for career progression.

The majority of CIPS students qualify via part-time day/evening courses, with employers paying tuition and examination fees. However, block release, full-time and correspondence or distance learning courses are also available. Over 120 educational establishments offer courses for the CIPS examinations.

The examinations leading to the Graduate Diploma are in two stages:

1. The Foundation Stage covers introduction to purchasing and supply chain management, management principles and practice economics, quantitative studies, and business accounting.

2. The Professional Stage includes four compulsory papers in purchasing and supply chain management: strategy, tactics and operations, legal aspects, and a case study. This stage also includes specialist option papers and electives.

Courses for BTEC/SQA Higher National Certificate or Diploma in Business Studies, with purchasing options, are available at a number of colleges. Both full- and part-time courses may be taken, usually over a period of two to three years.

The CIPS Supervisory Qualifications (First and Second Certificates in Purchasing and Stores) are aimed at young people with fewer academic qualifications, who are typically employed in purchasing at a clerical level, or in stores and warehouses. They may, after obtaining the qualifications, proceed to courses for the CIPS qualifications, as described above, although this is a lengthy training route. First and Second Certificates in Purchasing and Stores are offered by many of the colleges running CIPS courses. The majority of courses are part-time; it takes one year to complete each certificate.

NVQs/SVQs in Procurement at Levels 2, 3 and 4, and completion of Levels 3 and 4 offer a route to membership of the CIPS, subject to the completion of a project and a case study examination.

LATE ENTRY

There are good opportunities for adult entry. Most CIPS students are aged 23 years or over. Academic entry requirements for CIPS examinations are waived for candidates aged 23 or over, providing they are working in a business or commercial environment. Study for the CIPS Supervisory Qualifications is open access.

OPPORTUNITIES

Purchasing/buying departments vary enormously in size and scope. In a small organization, one person may be responsible for all purchasing. In a large organization there may be a centralized purchasing department with a number of purchasing officers or buyers, each specializing in buying a particular category of goods or services. Alternatively, purchasing may be decentralized, so that it serves the needs of the individual branches of the organization more closely. Sometimes purchasing is partly centralized, with certain supplies being purchased centrally, others at local level.

Buyers and purchasing officers are employed by organizations of all kinds – including manufacturing and service industries, retailing and mail order firms, wholesalers, the Civil Service, the National Health Service, local authorities, public service industries, and the Armed Forces.

The Chartered Institute of Purchasing and Supply (CIPS) has around 21,000 members, but this figure does not represent the total number of people employed in purchasing.

Recruitment is competitive; employers are looking for well-qualified candidates. Those who are prepared to be mobile are at an advantage.

There are some opportunities to work abroad, particularly with multinational firms. There is also the possibility, in organizations of many kinds, of making short overseas buying trips.

PAY AND CONDITIONS

Starting salaries for trainee buyers are dependent upon industry and location and range from £10,000 to £15,000. Three to four years after qualifying via the Chartered Institute of Purchasing and Supply, a typical salary would be in the range £13,000 to £23,000 with an average of £17,000. Managerial posts offer salaries from around £20,000 to £45,000 plus a company car and health insurance.

Holiday entitlement varies with different employers, but is likely to be around 20 to 35 days a year.

Purchasing staff normally work office hours, sometimes with extra hours in the evenings or at weekends.

BUYING: OP

PROSPECTS

There are good promotion prospects in larger organizations with sizeable purchasing departments. People who enter as trainee buyers or purchasing clerks can become assistant buyers within two to three years; thereafter, progress is very much dependent on ability, as well as formal qualifications. It is quite possible to become a purchasing manager by the age of 28 to 30 years.

Some buyers/purchasing officers move into other, related areas of work, usually within their own organizations. Computing, distribution, logistics, stores and materials control, marketing or sales are the most likely areas for a career move. Small firms offer more limited prospects, and people employed by small companies should be prepared to move in order to progress.

RELATED OCCUPATIONS

Distribution manager, warehouse manager, marketing manager, market research executive, store manager, sales representative.

FURTHER INFORMATION

Chartered Institute of Purchasing and Supply*, Easton House, Easton on the Hill, Stamford, Lincs PE9 3NZ, 01780 756777

FURTHER READING

Leaflets/booklets are available from the address marked*.
Working in Retailing – COIC
Retailing, Retail Buying and Purchasing – AGCAS
In the careers library classified under OP.

FASHION MODELLING: OT

FASHION MODEL CLCI:OT

BACKGROUND INFORMATION

Fashion modelling has a very glamorous image. Top models are constantly in the news, shown in exotic locations or on the catwalks in designer shows. For a select few, fashion modelling can be glamorous and well paid. For the majority, however, it is a tough, competitive, insecure and short-lived career.

The main areas of modelling are catwalk and press advertising and editorial photographic work. There is much overlap between the two and many models do both.

THE WORK

Fashion models display clothes and/or accessories to potential customers to the best effect, either live at a fashion show or in photographs.

Live modelling

'House' models work for wholesale or retail fashion houses displaying garments to private buyers, professional fashion buyers and fashion journalists from newspapers, magazines and television.

They work closely with designers who create clothes on a live model. The model must stand still for long periods of time while the designer drapes and pins the fabric and makes adjustments to the garment.

House models display the finished garments. This involves walking and turning with natural, flowing movements and bringing details of the garments to the attention of spectators. They must allow spectators to have a close view of the garments and may answer their questions about available fabrics, colours and sizes.

House models may undertake other duties when not modelling, such as greeting clients, answering telephones and helping visitors.

Freelance show models work in fashion shows at a variety of venues, displaying clothes produced by fashion houses. High fashion models demonstrate *couture* (exclusive fashion) and *prêt-à-porter* (ready-to-wear) collections, while general show models display all types of clothes as required. These models are often also photographic models.

The major international fashion shows take place in the spring and autumn. They are generally more flamboyant than showroom work, designed to give an overall impression of the clothes. Shows are often fast-paced and choreographed. Models rehearse the schedule of clothes and display the garments by performing movements to music, sometimes to simple dance routines.

During the show there is very little time allowed for models to change outfits and the atmosphere can be hectic.

Designers also take stands at fashion exhibitions held in major cities. Models stand and walk about for much of the day, although exhibitions usually include at least one large show each day.

Models may also do some promotional non-fashion work, for example, at motor shows, product launches and exhibitions.

Photographic modelling

Photographic models work in a studio or on location. A small number of top models obtain work with high fashion and women's magazines but most opportunities are with mail order catalogues and advertisements that appear in magazines, newspapers, advertising brochures and on posters.

Mail order catalogues are produced twice a year and models are used to display clothes in a simple and straightforward way. They are also used to display other catalogue products, such as furniture.

Models with exceptionally good features, such as teeth, hands, eyes or hair, can specialise in modelling particular products that emphasise these features but they may not be able to make a living relying on this alone. Some experienced models appear on television and cinema advertisements.

In photographic work models have to follow the photographer's directions on pose, movement and facial expression. They may have to hold a particular pose for a long time. The work involves sitting, standing, moving and posing, while looking natural and relaxed. Photographic sessions can be lengthy, with periods of inactivity while the photographer adjusts the set and lighting.

All models spend time caring for their complexion, hair and figure. When not modelling, freelance models spend much of their time seeking work by attending auditions, and visiting fashion editors and designers.

WORK ENVIRONMENT

Fashion models work mainly indoors in showrooms, studios, stores, hotels or exhibition centres. Dressing rooms and studios can be hot, cramped and overcrowded. Working conditions can be uncomfortably hot or cold. When on location, models may work outside in all weathers.

Models are likely to spend all day on their feet, either standing or walking to display clothes.

Modelling involves travelling to auditions and jobs. Some jobs result in long and short stays away from home.

SKILLS AND INTERESTS

Fashion models should have an interest in fashion and an awareness of new trends in clothing, make-up and hairstyling.

Models must be well groomed at all times. They must look after themselves if they are to keep a good complexion and not put on weight.

Good physical co-ordination is required for the natural, flowing movements of live modelling and for interpreting directions during photographic work. An interest in dance and drama is helpful for this.

Personality is very important in modelling – models work closely with others, including designers, photographers and agents. This requires a pleasant manner and the ability to get on well with people.

Models need to develop a professional approach and be punctual and well prepared for each job. Patience is vital – models may spend long periods waiting around. They must keep smiling and look interested even when they are tired or bored. Self-confidence is important, and models must be able to accept criticism and rejection.

ENTRY REQUIREMENTS

There are no minimum educational qualifications required for fashion modelling. Appearance and personality are more important than qualifications.

FASHION MODELLING: OT

Models should have a slim figure, be well proportioned with good even physical features. A clear and healthy complexion is required, as are good hands, skin, teeth and hair. Photographic models, in particular, should have a good facial bone structure and be photogenic.

Modelling is physically demanding and tiring, so models need to be fit, healthy and energetic to cope with live shows or lengthy photographic sessions.

Females. The Association of Model Agents recommends that females should be approximately 86–61–86 cm (34–24–34 inches) and at least 1.72 metres (5 feet 8 inches) tall, although most top models are taller. Some females begin modelling part-time before they are 16 years of age.

Males should be at least 1.83 metres (6 feet) tall. Many male models are taller. The Association of Model Agents recommends that males should also have at least a 97–102 cm (38–40 inch) chest, 76–81cm (30–32 inch) waist and 84 cm (33 inch) inside leg measurement. Males usually begin modelling between 17 to 35 years.

Entry to modelling is usually by acceptance onto the books of a reputable modelling agency. Less often, entry is by gaining employment in a showroom.

TRAINING

It is possible to take a training course at one of the commercial modelling schools before trying to enter modelling but care should be taken. Reputable schools only accept applicants they feel have a chance of succeeding as a model. Such training is not essential and certainly cannot guarantee success in finding work as a model.

The training varies from courses that last for a few evenings to those that are full-time for several weeks. Courses provide the basic techniques of fashion and photographic modelling and may also cover grooming, hygiene, diet, exercise, skin care and make-up, deportment and fashion clothing and accessories. Commercial modelling courses tend to be very expensive. There are no educational entry requirements for their courses.

When models are accepted onto an agent's books they are advised about dress, appearance and hair styles. Agents may recommend hairdressers and cosmetic experts. Experienced models teach new recruits basic walks, turns, stands and poses.

LATE ENTRY

There is no strict upper age limit for entry to modelling. Most female models, though, begin in their teens, while most males start between the ages of 17 and 25 years. Entry beyond those ages is unusual and extremely difficult.

OPPORTUNITIES

Most fashion models work freelance and find work through model agencies, some of which specialize in either show or photographic work. Model agencies are regulated by the Employment Agencies Act, 1973, which does not allow them to charge a model for joining an agency.

It is important that models seek representation with reputable agencies, such as those belonging to the Association of Model Agents (AMA). Reputable agencies only accept models they feel may be successful in finding modelling work.

Entry to modelling is highly competitive. Even after acceptance onto an agency's books it may be very difficult to obtain work.

There are few openings for permanent positions as a house model with wholesale and retail fashion businesses.

Most modelling work is for females, although there has been an increasing demand for male models over the past few years. Male models are employed more in photographic work than in live modelling.

Most work for fashion models is in London and it can be very difficult to make a reasonable living from modelling outside London. The AMA, for example, has 19 member agencies in London and just one elsewhere, in Glasgow.

Modelling careers tend to be short. Some live models may continue modelling into their thirties but photographic models usually finish before they are 30. There are some opportunities for experienced, older models to promote products aimed at a more mature market.

PAY AND CONDITIONS

Most models are self-employed and earn only when they work. Earnings can therefore vary tremendously. They obtain work through modelling agencies which negotiate fees for each job. The agencies deduct a percentage of the modelling fees as commission, typically 20% to 25%.

It is unusual for most new models to find regular work, and earnings can be low – often below £4,000 a year – unless and until they establish a reputation for their work. Few people ever make a living from modelling. Successful models, however, can earn £200 to £400 a day for photographic work. Catalogue work earnings vary according to a model's popularity, but may be up to £500 a day, although the work is seasonal. Advertising can pay up to £150 an hour. Editorial work pays less than these rates – from £50 a day – but it is very useful for getting models seen and in building up their careers.

Freelance models do not obtain as many bookings as those that are represented by agents as virtually all jobs and work comes via agencies. Shows and showroom work and a limited amount of photographic work is undertaken by freelance models; they often have to pay their own expenses, such as travel to auditions and jobs and maintaining a wardrobe.

There are no set working hours for freelance models, although a working day can be as long as ten hours.

Models employed full-time by fashion houses work more regular hours, with overtime usual at show times. These models receive a set wage.

There is little opportunity for part-time work.

PROSPECTS

Modelling has no career structure. Successful employed models may seek to increase their income by becoming freelance. Freelance models progress by being offered more prestigious and highly paid jobs.

When their modelling career is finished, models may seek to use their experience in a number of ways. They may teach in a modelling school. Some run or manage a modelling agency. It may be possible to enter fashion journalism, fashion consultancy, public relations in a fashion house or store, retailing or sales work.

FASHION MODELLING: OT

RELATED OCCUPATIONS

Beauty therapist/beautician, beauty consultant, make-up artist, actor, dancer, fashion designer.

FURTHER INFORMATION

The Association of Model Agents*, 122 Brompton Road, London SW3 1JE (please enclose sae), Model Information Line 0891 517644 (premium rate line)

FURTHER READING

Leaflets/booklets are available from address marked*.

Working in Fashion – COIC

Careers in Fashion – Kogan Page

In the careers library classified under OT.

GROUP Q – SCIENCES, MATHEMATICS AND RELATED WORK

1. **SCIENTIST/TECHNICIAN CLCI:QOB-QOM**
2. **BIOMEDICAL SCIENTIST CLCI: QOB**
3. **FOOD SCIENTIST/TECHNOLOGIST/ TECHNICIAN CLCI:QON**
4. **MATERIALS SCIENTIST/ TECHNOLOGIST/METALLURGIST CLCI:QOS**

1. SCIENTIST/TECHNICIAN (QOB–QOM)

BACKGROUND INFORMATION

Scientists are involved in the systematic study of the nature and behaviour of the material and physical world, based on observation, experiment and measurement. The scientific subjects taught at school – biology, chemistry, maths and physics – form the basis for an enormous range of scientific careers. It is possible to qualify and work in these familiar subject areas or to choose a more specialized field, such as biochemistry, metallurgy, food science, forensic science, environmental monitoring or a related subject like computer science or engineering.

Employment opportunities range from laboratory-based posts in areas such as research and development or quality control to work in technical marketing, production management or science teaching. Professional scientists and technicians work for both public and private sector organizations, in this country and overseas.

Most professional scientists and technicians qualify in one of the following disciplines, although much scientific study and many fields of scientific work combine two or more of these.

Biological science is concerned with the study of living organisms and includes many different specialisms. Zoology is concerned with animals, botany with plants. Microbiology involves the study of micro-organisms, while biochemistry and pharmacology are concerned with chemical compounds and reactions in living organisms. All of these areas of biology are important in the pharmaceutical and food industries and in medicine. Biotechnology, where the scientific theory of biological processes is applied to technological development, is an expanding area. It involves the production of man-made molecules, such as hormones and enzymes, and is closely linked to genetic engineering.

Chemistry is concerned with the composition, reactions and properties of substances. Laboratory-based chemical research leads to the development of new products, such as drugs for combating disease, foodstuffs, dyes and paints, fertilizers, detergents, synthetic fibres for textiles, plastics and cosmetics. Analytical chemistry is vital in areas such as environmental protection and medicine and is important in ensuring the quality of production in the chemical, pharmaceutical and food and drink industries. It also plays an essential part in public health protection and in such work as forensic science.

Physics is based on the properties of matter and energy, and the relationship between them. Through physics we can understand how and why things behave as they do. It includes topics such as heat, light, magnetism, electricity, electronics, sound, atomic physics, laser optics, cosmology, astrophysics, quantum physics, plasma physics, opto-electronics and low temperature physics. The work of physicists often involves both experimental investigations and theoretical analysis, and forms the basis for solving a wide range of scientific and engineering problems.

Mathematics forms the basis for increasingly important fields such as computing, systems analysis, statistics and operational research. Mathematical operations and processes are therefore involved in the solution of many scientific problems in industry and commerce. Mathematics is also very important in physics and engineering fields.

Professional scientists and technicians are also active in more specialized areas:

Food science concentrates on developing processes of cooking, preserving and storing food, and on quality control procedures. Food scientists and technologists are employed by industrial and manufacturing companies as well as government bodies such as the Ministry of Agriculture, Fisheries and Food. Please see article 3. FOOD SCIENTIST/TECHNOLOGIST.

Medical laboratory sciences cover a wide range of related fields including pharmacology, biochemistry, microbiology, cytology, immunology, cellular pathology and haematology. Medical laboratory scientists and technicians work in the National Health Service and private hospitals, government departments, higher education institutions, manufacturing industry and the Armed Forces.

Materials science involves the study of a wide range of natural and man-made materials including glass, ceramics and polymers, while **metallurgy** is concerned with metals and alloys. Metallurgists and materials scientists/technicians are therefore involved in the development of new materials and in the selection of appropriate materials for new products. Metallurgists are also employed in the mining industry. Please see article 4. MATERIALS SCIENTIST / TECHNOLOGIST /METALLURGIST.

Environmental science has become increasingly popular as awareness of 'green' issues increases. Environmental scientists work in such diverse areas as geology, hydrogeology, geophysics, meteorology, ecology and astrophysics, to improve and maintain our environment.

Other areas in which professional scientists and technicians are active include: agriculture, horticulture, natural resources, biomedicine, health care and education.

THE WORK

Scientists often work as part of a multidisciplinary team in a laboratory experimenting, monitoring and analysing the results. They are required to write up the results of tests and experiments, perhaps using a computer for analysis of data. Information technology skills are increasingly important.

There is also a growing emphasis on being able to communicate scientific information in an understandable way to non-specialist audiences, such as marketing staff and customers.

Many scientists have a management role, including responsibility for staff, premises and work scheduling. They may also have financial responsibilities in areas such as purchasing, planning and managing a department budget. Scientists must pay close attention to health and safety requirements.

It is essential for scientists to devote time to keeping up to date with new developments in their area of specialization, for example, through reading scientific journals,

SCIENCES: QOB–QOS

membership of a professional body, or attending conferences.

Technicians play an important role as part of the scientific team. The work varies enormously from one environment to another – from analysing blood samples in a hospital to operating physical testing equipment in a research centre, from assisting with the development of a new polymer to preparing equipment for use by students at a college. The work frequently involves taking measurements, so accuracy is vital. A working knowledge of computers is often necessary as complex calculations are common. Technicians also have to keep equipment – such as measuring devices – clean and in good working order. Senior technicians require good financial and management skills.

The main areas of work are:

Research, design and development (R&D) covers a wide spectrum of activity from basic, original research through applied research to the development of new products to meet a particular market need. Research requires innovative ideas, together with the ability to develop creative and practical solutions. Universities often undertake pure research, and some projects may have no immediate practical application. Others, such as those undertaken by commercial organizations, are designed to develop saleable new products or to improve existing ones. Scientists and engineers often work together on exciting and challenging projects to design and develop new products.

Analysis involves a wide variety of tests using highly sophisticated equipment, as well as complex manual procedures. The work of analysts ranges from quality assurance to aid manufacturing production, to testing samples of water, food, drugs or chemicals. In medical laboratories, the majority of the routine tests are carried out by technical staff (medical laboratory scientific officers), while scientists are involved in specialized analyses and the development of new techniques.

Production is usually a commercial enterprise and involves the manufacturing of products. Scientists and technicians work as part of a production team to ensure the manufacturing process is carried out efficiently, safely and practically. The end product must also be tested for quality and effectiveness.

Management services covers a broad range of activities which include: marketing and sales, technical support, operational research and data processing. Marketing and sales is a vital area for many businesses, such as chemical and pharmaceutical companies, as international competition is fierce. An excellent understanding of the customer, the product and its competitors is vital.

Technical support staff provide a back-up for the marketing and sales team, offering technical advice and information. If there is a problem with a product, they have to resolve it.

Education. There is a great demand for science teachers in schools and colleges, particularly teachers of the physical sciences. Please see TEACHING articles (FAB). Many science graduates find work within institutions of higher education as lecturers or choose to carry out research and gain further qualifications. Others train to teach young people at schools, tertiary colleges and colleges of further education. Teachers and lecturers need to be able to communicate effectively, and to demonstrate their enthusiasm for science.

WORK ENVIRONMENT

Many scientists/technicians are laboratory-based, but scientists/technicians also work in offices, on production lines or building sites, at mines or weather centres.

Scientists work with team members of every discipline, supervising technicians and other support staff, as well as working alone. Many scientists travel to other laboratories or libraries, attend meetings, seminars and conferences, both in this country and overseas. Some scientists take part in video conferences and may communicate via the Internet.

SKILLS AND INTERESTS

Scientists and technicians both need to have a keen interest in science. It is important to have a clear logical mind and a practical approach to problem solving. Accuracy and attention to detail are vital. Technicians should be methodical, as they often carry out routine tests and applications. Research activities require persistence.

Imaginative and creative abilities are required to find solutions to problems. Good communication skills, both spoken and written, are important. Scientists/technicians need to be able to explain clearly scientific and technical concepts to the non-specialist. It is also important to work well with others as a team member.

ENTRY REQUIREMENTS

Graduate entry

A recognized science degree is necessary. Minimum entry requirements for degree courses are two A levels/three H grades and GCSEs/S grades (A–C/1–3) in three other subjects – specific subjects may be required, eg maths, English and relevant sciences, or a relevant BTEC/SQA national award, or a relevant Advanced GNVQ/GSVQ Level III.

Applicants with non-science A levels may be accepted onto a foundation year preceding the first year of a degree course in some institutions. Many professional bodies offer recognized qualifications equivalent to a first degree, which also allow membership at different grades.

Technician level entry

The minimum requirements for technician entry are four GCSEs/S grades (A–C/1–3), or a relevant BTEC first award, or appropriate SQA national certificate modules, or Intermediate GNVQ/GSVQ Level II.

BTEC/SQA higher national diploma/certificate courses require a minimum of one A level/H grade and three GCSEs/S grades (A–C/1–3), or a relevant BTEC/SQA national award, or a relevant Advanced GNVQ/GSVQ Level III.

BTEC national diploma and certificate courses usually require four GCSEs/S grades (A–C/1–3), or a BTEC first award, or Intermediate GNVQ/GSVQ Level II.

SQA national certificate courses have no set entry requirements. Applicants should check with individual colleges, who may set their own requirements as they wish, to be satisfied that students are able to benefit from the courses.

Advanced GNVQs/GSVQs Level III usually require either four GCSEs/S grades (A–C/1–3), or Intermediate GNVQ/GSVQ Level II.

SCIENCES: QOB–QOS

The Institute of Science Technology's (IST) Ordinary Diploma and Certificate have a preferred minimum entry requirement of four GCSEs/S grades (A–C/1–3), preferably including a science subject, or equivalent. Candidates for the IST's Higher Diploma should have A levels/H grades or equivalent. There are no formal entry requirements for the IST/City and Guilds Core Vocational Qualification (CVQ).

Modern Apprenticeships (part of the Skillseekers Initiative in Scotland) have been introduced for young people in some areas of chemical work, including process operations and laboratory operations. There are no set entry requirements and selection is based on entry tests and evidence of relevant academic success. Contact your local careers office, TEC/LEC for details.

An NVQ in Laboratory Services for schools and colleges will soon be available for technicians working in these institutions. A Modern Apprenticeship framework relating to the Level 3 award is under development.

TRAINING

A number of professional and industrial organizations offer sponsorship to science students. Bursaries are available from a number of organizations and salaries are normally paid while students are on industrial placement at the company/organization.

Graduate training

A wide range of degree courses in scientific subjects is offered by many universities and colleges of higher education. Courses are either three or four years in duration. Four-year sandwich courses allow a period of time for placement with an employer, where students can get hands-on experience. Courses include agriculture/horticulture, biomedical/healthcare, natural resources/environment, food and drink, as well as the more familiar basic sciences.

Many graduates with a science degree follow this with a postgraduate course. A good degree (first or upper second class) is normally needed to progress to a research degree. There are specialized options from which to choose for both taught courses and research degrees.

Technician training

Technicians may take a full-time course before joining an employer. They may study for a higher national diploma with a view to entry as a higher level technician (two years full-time or three years sandwich), or a BTEC national diploma (two years), or a SQA national certificate (one year), or an Advanced GNVQ/GSVQ Level III.

Those seeking to work in animal science can take the Institute of Science Technology's (IST) Ordinary Diploma (one year full-time) in Animal Science at Blackpool and The Fylde College, West Cheshire College or Swindon College.

Alternatively technicians may enter work and study part-time on a day release or evening class basis for BTEC higher national certificate (two years), or SQA higher national certificate (one year), or BTEC national certificate (two years), or SQA national certificate (one year). Those working in animal science can study for the IST's Ordinary Certificate in Animal Science by attending one of the colleges listed above, part-time for two years.

The IST's Higher Diploma is intended for employed technicians. It is not a taught course but is designed to recognize technicians' understanding and competence. It is offered in the following subjects: analytical chemical laboratory techniques, biochemical laboratory techniques, electron microscopy laboratory techniques, physiology and pharmacology laboratory techniques and microbiological laboratory techniques. It consists of two written papers and a practical project overseen by the candidate's employer.

The IST, in conjunction with City and Guilds, has introduced the Core Vocational Qualification (CVQ), a work-based qualification for laboratory technicians. Preliminary, Intermediate and Advanced levels are being planned.

Those on Modern Apprenticeships (part of the Skillseekers Initiative in Scotland) work towards a relevant NVQ/SVQ at Level 3, eg Process Operations or Laboratory Operations. They also undertake training in team work, communication, application of number, problem solving, information technology and self-development. There is no set length of time for Modern Apprenticeships, but training is likely to take at least three years.

In-service training is provided by most public and private sector organizations for both scientists and technicians, through external short courses, in-house programmes or distance learning. This training may cover advanced technical skills or business management areas. Many employers also encourage staff to participate in the career development opportunities offered by professional bodies.

There are a number of NVQs/SVQs available in science areas up to Level 4.

LATE ENTRY

There are no upper age limits for entry to scientific work, but adult entrants must have science qualifications. However, as scientific knowledge develops so rapidly, opportunities may be limited. Refresher courses are run by some colleges for scientists wishing to return to work after a career break.

Access courses for adults, who wish to study for a degree but do not have the necessary qualifications, are offered at many local colleges. Courses are usually one year full-time or one/two years part-time with daytime and/or evening attendance.

Mature applicants may be accepted onto a foundation year preceding the first year of a science degree or higher national diploma course in some institutions.

OPPORTUNITIES

Within specialized scientific fields, there is a massive range of jobs available to qualified scientists and technicians. For example scientists can choose a laboratory-based career or work in sales and marketing. Starting a career in one sector of industry does not mean staying there, and scientists are able to move around as their career develops.

The main areas of employment are within industry. Scientists and technicians are employed in a wide range of private sector organizations, such as pharmaceutical companies, food manufacturers and research consultancies.

Public sector organizations are also major employers of scientists, including education establishments, government departments and the National Health Service.

SCIENCES: QOB–QOS

Jobs are advertised in magazines and newspapers such as: *The New Scientist, The Institute of Biomedical Science Gazette, Laboratory News, Chemistry in Britain, Chemistry and Industry, Process Engineering, Energy World, Physics World, Food Manufacture, Food Processing, Farmers' Weekly, The Guardian, The Daily Telegraph, The Independent, The Sunday Times, Times Educational Supplement* and *Times Higher Educational Supplement*.

PAY AND CONDITIONS

Laboratory technicians may earn between £9,000 and £14,000, assistant scientists £13,000 to £19,000 and senior scientists £18,000 to £28,000.

Figures for scientists/technicians employed in industry depend on qualifications, experience, ability and employer location. Large manufacturing and industrial companies offer highly competitive salaries.

Many scientists/technicians work normal office hours, 9am to 5pm, Monday to Friday. Laboratories in hospitals, however, operate 24 hours a day, and staff work to a rota. Weekend and evening work may also be necessary for scientists and technicians employed in industry, who are often required to meet tight deadlines.

Temporary and part-time work and job sharing are sometimes available.

PROSPECTS

Promotion and prospects vary within private and public sectors. Medical laboratory science officers follow a grading scale within the National Health Service as do scientists/technicians who are part of the Scientific Civil Service. Within private organizations promotion can be fast and scientists are likely to be given managerial responsibilities, including the possibility of director-level posts.

Some scientists may have to move around the UK to obtain promotion. Employment opportunities exist not only in the UK but elsewhere in the world, particularly Europe and North America.

Scientists can use their knowledge to enter careers in other areas such as production, scientific publishing and information technology.

RELATED OCCUPATIONS

Engineer, telecoms engineer, pharmacist, pharmacy technician, technical brewer, geologist, oceanographer, meteorologist.

FURTHER INFORMATION

The Association of Clinical Biochemists*, 2 Carlton House Terrace, London SW1Y 5AF, 0171 930 3333, www.leeds.oc.UK/acb/

The Biochemical Society*, 59 Portland Place, London W1N 3AJ, 0171 580 5530

Bio-Industry Association, 14–15 Belgrave Square, London SW1X 8PS, 0171 565 7190

British Pharmacological Society*, 16 Angel Gate, City Road, London EC1V 2PT, 0171 417 0113

Food and Drink Industry Training Organization*, Training and Careers Executive, 6 Catherine Street, London WC2B 5JJ, 0171 836 2460

The Institute of Biology*, 20–22 Queensberry Place, London SW7 2DZ, 0171 581 8333 (sae required), www.iob.org.uk

Institute of Biomedical Science*, 12 Coldbath Square, London EC1R 5HL, 0171 636 8192, www.ibms.org.uk

The Institute of Food Science and Technology*, 5 Cambridge Court, 210 Shepherd's Bush Road, London W6 7NJ, 0171 603 6316, www.easynet.co.uk/ifst/

The Institute of Materials*, 1 Carlton House Terrace, London SW1Y 5DB, 0171 839 4071

The Institute of Physics*, 76 Portland Place, London W1N 4AA, 0171 470 4800, www.iop.org.uk

Institute of Science Technology, Stowe House, Netherstowe, Lichfield, Staffs WS13 6TJ, 01543 251346

Institution of Mining and Metallurgy, 44 Portland Place, London W1N 4BR, 0171 580 3802, www.imm.org.uk

The Royal Society of Chemistry*, Burlington House, Piccadilly, London W1V 0BN, 0171 437 8656, www.chemistry.rsc.org/rsc

The Science, Technology and Mathematics Council, 20-22 Queensbury Place, London SW7 2DZ, 0171 225 1155

FURTHER READING

Leaflets/booklets are available from the addresses marked*.

Working in Physical Sciences – COIC

Student Helpbook Series – Careers With a Science Degree – CRAC/Hobsons

In the careers library classified under QOB/QOD/QOF/QOM.

2. BIOMEDICAL SCIENTIST (QOB)

BACKGROUND INFORMATION

Biomedical scientist is a broad term encompassing scientists who work in the NHS as medical laboratory scientific officers (MLSOs) and those who work in other fields such as the pharmaceutical industry, universities and government departments. NHS medical laboratory scientific officers make up the majority of the biomedical science profession.

THE WORK

In hospitals, biomedical scientists carry out laboratory tests on samples of patients' body fluids and tissues. The results of these tests are used by doctors to diagnose illness, evaluate treatment and carry out research into the causes and cures of disease.

In modern laboratories much of the routine analysis of clinical samples is carried out using automated processing equipment. There is also more specialist, intellectually challenging work, involving a range of advanced techniques and sophisticated computer-controlled equipment.

Biomedical scientists usually specialize in one of the following areas:

Medical microbiology – involves the identification and study of micro-organisms (bacteria, mould fungi, parasites etc) that cause disease, and the correct choice of antibiotics.

SCIENCES: QOB–QOS

Haematology – the study of the physiology, morphology and microscopic appearance of blood. It is used both for the diagnosis of disease and monitoring of treatment.

Transfusion science – involves identifying individual blood groups, screening donated blood and preparing blood components and plasma. It also involves testing donors' blood and that of patients for compatibility, for transfusion.

Histopathology – the light and electron microscopic study of human tissues removed during surgery, used to identify disease. Also the examination of tissues removed post mortem, to determine the cause of death.

Clinical chemistry – analysis of blood and biological materials for purposes such as diagnosis of disease, studies of poisonous agents, and monitoring drug therapy.

Virology (often included within medical microbiology) – detection of viruses such as HIV, influenza and herpes simplex. The work may also relate to population screening programmes and monitoring the effectiveness of vaccines.

Immunology – the study of the body's immunity and immune systems. Tests in this specialization form the basis of investigations into allergies, immune deficiency, infectious disease and tumour growth.

Cytology – the microscopic examination of cell samples, as distinct from bulk samples and whole organs, to detect possible disease. Cytology is an important aid in the early detection of cancer, particularly of the uterus and lung.

Biomedical scientists in the early years of their careers spend most of their working day at the laboratory bench. As they progress, they may have other duties related to quality control, supervision and management of staff and services.

There may be hazards in working with potentially infected material, but biomedical scientists are trained in procedures which minimize the risks. They wear protective clothing.

In the NHS, medical laboratory scientific officers are supported by medical laboratory assistants (MLAs) who perform routine tasks such as making up solutions of chemicals, preparing test materials or clerical work, using computers. Other support staff include *phlebotomists*, specialized MLAs who collect blood from patients for examination to help diagnose disease. *Cervical cytology screeners*, are supervised by MLSOs, and trained to recognize normal cells and pass on any smears that seem abnormal to biomedical scientists who will then call in a highly specialized doctor. Their role is highly responsible.

In other sectors, biomedical scientists carry out closely related work, but they may test different types of sample. For instance, in Public Health Laboratories – which are responsible for the diagnosis, prevention and control of infectious and communicable diseases – biomedical scientists test samples of sewage, drinking water, milk and foodstuffs.

WORK ENVIRONMENT

All the work is laboratory-based. In the NHS biomedical scientists generally work in clinical pathology laboratories. These are usually divided into separate specialist departments or sections.

Laboratory work involves being active much of the time, and may involve moving around between different sections or hospitals.

SKILLS AND INTERESTS

Scientific interests and an aptitude for meticulous, accurate work are essential – mistakes can have far-reaching consequences. A responsible, mature attitude is required.

An organized mind, with the ability to set priorities, is important. Good powers of concentration are essential.

As with all scientific laboratory work, manual dexterity is required for handling samples, use of the microscope and other equipment.

ENTRY REQUIREMENTS

An honours degree is now essential for entry to the profession. Minimum entry requirements for degree courses are five GCSEs/S grades (A–C/1–3) with two A levels/three H grades, or equivalent. Requirements of individual institutions vary, but for relevant courses it is usual to offer biology and chemistry at A level/H grade and mathematics at GCSE/S grade (A–C/1–3).

The most appropriate degree courses are those designed specifically for the profession – ie biomedical science(s) – and accredited by the Institute of Biomedical Science and approved by the Council for Professions Supplementary to Medicine. A list of accredited courses is available from the Institute. Some courses are organized on a sandwich basis, enabling students to gain practical laboratory experience before graduating.

Other degree courses in related subjects may be acceptable for entry to the profession. These include courses offering as principal subjects one or more of the following: animal physiology, biochemistry, biology, chemistry, microbiology, physics and zoology.

There are also several part-time degree courses, allowing candidates with appropriate A levels/H grades to enter employment as trainee MLSOs, and to study part-time whilst working. This option is only available in certain parts of the country.

Those intending to work in the NHS need to make sure, before starting a degree course, that it is acceptable for state registration with the Council for Professions Supplementary to Medicine. Written advice should be obtained from the Council.

Job applicants may need to fill in a medical questionnaire.

For medical laboratory assistants, there are no formal entry requirements but a mature approach is essential.

TRAINING

To become state registered with the Council for Professions Supplementary to Medicine (essential for NHS employment in the qualified MLSO grades) graduates must take in-service training in an approved laboratory and pass the National Examination of the Council for Professions Supplementary to Medicine. The length of in-service training varies, but is generally one to two years, depending on the relevance of the candidate's first degree. Those in training are employed in the MLSO trainee grade.

Medical laboratory assistants receive on-the-job training. Certificates of competence are issued for safe working in MLA duties, and for *phlebotomists* to work without close supervision in the hospital. *Cervical cytology screeners* take a qualifying examination for the NHSCSP certificate although their work will still be supervised.

Working as a medical laboratory assistant does not provide

SCIENCES: QOB–QOS

entry to a career as a medical laboratory scientific officer, although some graduates may find temporary work at this grade, while waiting for a vacancy to arise in the MLSO trainee grade.

LATE ENTRY

Adults may qualify for entry to relevant degrees by taking Access courses.

Those who qualified in the past via the higher national certificate/diploma route (not now available) may take a 'top-up' course in order to gain a degree.

OPPORTUNITIES

Biomedical scientists are employed by hospitals in the NHS and the private sector, and by the Public Health Laboratory Service, whose facilities are normally situated in, or closely attached to, NHS hospitals. They also work for the blood transfusion service (National Blood Authority), manufacturing industry (particularly pharmaceuticals), government departments, universities and veterinary services.

The Institute of Biomedical Science has about 14,000 members, the majority of whom work in the healthcare sector. However, not all biomedical scientists are Institute members.

There are opportunities for employment throughout the country, but greater chances of finding a job in major centres of population.

Vacancies are advertised in *Biomedical Scientist*, the Institute's monthly magazine, and in *New Scientist, Nature* and the local press. There is likely to be considerable competition for trainee vacancies, but it is not difficult for qualified, experienced biomedical scientists to find suitable posts. Agency work may be available.

There are opportunities to work abroad – the most popular destinations are Australia, Canada and Saudi Arabia.

Occasionally, biomedical scientists become self-employed, as proprietors of private laboratories.

PAY AND CONDITIONS

In the NHS, salaries for grade 1 medical laboratory scientific officers (the basic grade) range from £11,608 to £17,183 (£11,812 to £17,486 w.e.f. 1 December 1998). Salaries for grades 2–4 range from £15,889 to £32,185 (£16,169 to £32,753 w.e.f. 1 December 1998). Trainees are paid on a scale ranging from £7,346 to £9,626 (£7,476 to £9,796 w.e.f. 1 December 1998). Salaries offered by other employers are likely to be higher.

Hours of work are normally 37 a week. Most work is carried out between 9am and 5.30pm, Monday to Friday, but NHS clinical pathology labs usually have an emergency 24-hour service, requiring on call duties. The larger laboratories may work on shifts, with hours varying from site to site.

There are many opportunities for part-time work.

PROSPECTS

Those who want to progress in their careers usually study for higher degrees, often on a part-time basis whilst working in a laboratory. Fellowship of the Institute of Biomedical Science, which may be achieved by gaining a relevant higher degree (or by examination or thesis) is normally required for promotion to senior MLSO posts in the health service, and is extremely useful in other sectors.

Well-qualified MLSOs can progress to become business or laboratory managers or to other administrative posts.

It is possible to move from MLSO work into related careers such as technical sales (of laboratory equipment and reagents, for example) or teaching in higher education.

RELATED OCCUPATIONS

Clinical scientist, medical technical officer, forensic scientist.

FURTHER INFORMATION

Institute of Biomedical Science*, 12 Coldbath Square, London EC1R 5HL, 0171 636 8192, www.ibms.org.uk

Health Service Careers*, PO Box 204, London SE99 7UW, 0171 972 2000

Council for Professions Supplementary to Medicine, 184 Kennington Park Road, London SE11 4BU, 0171 582 0866 (mornings only)

FURTHER READING

Leaflets/booklets available from the addresses marked*.

Working in Hospitals – COIC

Working in Natural Sciences – COIC

Scientific Analysis, Investigation and Technical Support – AGCAS

In the careers library classified under QOB.

3. FOOD SCIENTIST/TECHNOLOGIST/TECHNICIAN (QON)

THE WORK

Food scientists examine the chemical, biological and nutritional aspects of food from raw materials through to the finished product while food technologists use their expertise to turn raw materials into finished products, but the two overlap and most food scientists/technologists use a combination of both subjects in their work.

They work in four main fields.

Applied research. Food scientists/technologists work on projects to solve problems that occur in the development or processing of new food products as well as on the safety of food and its processing.

They work as part of a small team on their own, on both long- and short-term projects, normally on several at the same time. They design experiments, use the latest equipment, and prepare reports on their findings. Examples of projects include: testing a starch in a range of mayonnaise, ice creams and low-fat spreads to establish whether it could be an effective substitute for fat; evaluating the effect of microwave cooking on raw ingredients; or investigating the safety of irradiation as a method of preserving food.

Technicians assist the scientists and technologists by operating equipment under guidance. They help to collate results and statistics and may be in charge of one section of the laboratory, and responsible for ordering supplies and controlling stock.

SCIENCES: QOB–QOS

Research of this nature is carried out in institutions of higher education, government-funded and independent research establishments and large food companies. Trouble shooting and problem solving are also carried out in small to medium-sized companies, or consultancies to the food industry.

Product/process development. This can mean development of new products, making changes to existing ones or improving the manufacturing process.

In most food manufacturing companies this type of work goes on all the time. Food scientists/technologists make up small batch samples and test them on panels of tasters, sometimes drawn from the general public. They note suggestions and comments and prepare full-scale trial runs on processing equipment. Problems often occur at this stage, in transferring small samples to factory processes. If the product is not of the required quality or safety standard they analyse the ingredients at each stage of manufacture. Problems can occur at any stage, including packaging.

Product development involves food scientists/technologists in liaison with other departments in the company, such as sales and marketing. They often have to work within a strict budget and to tight deadlines.

Quality control. This involves analysing raw materials, monitoring stages of production and checking storage and distribution conditions. Food scientists/technologists conduct tests on taste, texture, nutritional value, microbiological content, and ensure that products conform to legislation and safety standards. They are also responsible for the overall appearance of a finished product, ensuring, for instance, all the biscuits in a batch look the same after baking.

They use varying techniques, for example sophisticated gas chromatography for compositional analysis of oils and fats and near-infra-red reflectance spectroscopy to determine the moisture, fat and protein content of foods.

Much routine testing is done by machines, some of which may be operated by technicians. Quality control technicians carry out the bulk of the testing and monitoring work, take samples from the conveyor belt, analyse them and keep records at each production stage. Statistical evaluation is important.

Production management. Food scientists/technologists have to make sure production is as efficient as possible. When there is a drop in quality or a time delay, they try to find out which stage of production is causing the problem. Many of the problems are technical, eg to do with faulty equipment, but this specialism also requires them to manage people and resources. They are often involved in recruitment and training, and may take part in negotiating industrial relations.

Retailing. Food scientists/technologists are involved in quality assurance for new and existing products. This may involve developing new ideas, testing ingredients, arranging trials, helping to control quality and hygiene and working with other specialists such as marketing and sales personnel. The work is very customer focused.

Other work. Some food scientists/technologists work for government organizations, investigating food safety, collecting and interpreting information and acting as advisers, possibly also dealing with problems of pesticides and food contamination. Others specialize in packing technology or process equipment engineering.

Other opportunities exist in consultancy, technical sales, technical journalism, trading standards, education and, increasingly, in environmental health.

WORK ENVIRONMENT

Food scientists/technologists involved in research and development work mainly in laboratories or pilot plants. Those specializing in food manufacturing spend much of their time on the factory floor; those with management responsibilities may be based in an office.

Food scientists/technologists who work for food manufacturers may spend time away from their own research laboratories visiting other factories in the group where different products are made, and visiting firms that supply ingredients. Those working for retailers spend a lot of time visiting the companies that manufacture their products.

SKILLS AND INTERESTS

Food scientists/technologists need a strong interest and ability in science combined with an enquiring mind. They should be accurate and methodical and enjoy applying an analytical approach to problem solving. It helps to be innovative and creative, particularly in the area of product development.

Self-motivation is important as much work has to be completed to deadlines. Since the job often requires them to work on several different projects simultaneously they should also be flexible and able to allocate time to different priorities. Personal hygiene is also a priority for anyone involved with food handling, due to the responsibility for people's safety.

Many jobs also require management skills and the ability to communicate with all different types of people and to write clear reports.

ENTRY REQUIREMENTS

Food scientists/technologists. Most qualify by taking a full-time or sandwich degree or higher national diploma in food science and/or technology.

Degrees in food science/technology usually require a minimum of two A levels, preferably including chemistry, with the other being either biology, physics or maths, plus three GCSEs (A–C) in other subjects; or three H grades, preferably including maths, chemistry and physics, plus two S grades (1–3) in other subjects; or a relevant BTEC/SQA national award (eg science or food technology); or a relevant Advanced GNVQ/GSVQ Level III (eg science).

BTEC higher national diploma and certificate courses usually require one science A level, preferably chemistry, plus GCSEs (A–C) in maths and English; or a relevant BTEC/SQA national award (eg science or food technology); or a relevant Advanced GNVQ/GSVQ Level III (eg science).

SQA higher national diploma and certificate courses usually require two H grades, including a science, plus three S grades (1–3); or a relevant BTEC/SQA national award (eg science or food technology); or a relevant Advanced GNVQ/GSVQ Level III (eg science). Those with a higher national diploma may be eligible for third-year entry to a degree course.

Different institutions prefer different combinations of subjects and it is advisable to check entry requirements.

Applicants with non-science A levels may be accepted onto a foundation year preceding the first year of a food science/technology degree or higher national diploma in some institutions.

It is also possible to enter most areas of employment with a qualification in a closely related subject, such as chemical engineering, microbiology, biology or analytical and applied chemistry. Some graduates in these areas take a postgraduate course in food science or food technology, entry to which is with a first degree.

Technician entry. The usual entry qualifications are a minimum of four GCSEs/S grades (A–C/1–3), often including English, maths and a science subject; or a relevant BTEC first award (eg science); or appropriate SQA national certificate modules; or a relevant Intermediate GNVQ/GSVQ Level II (eg science).

BTEC national diploma and certificate courses usually require four GCSEs/S grades (A–C/1–3), or a BTEC first award, or Intermediate GNVQ/GSVQ Level II.

SQA national certificate courses usually require a minimum of four S grades (1–3), including chemistry, or equivalent.

Advanced GNVQ courses usually requires four GCSEs/S grades (A–C/1–3) preferably including science, or a BTEC first award, or Intermediate GNVQ/GSVQ Level II.

Defective colour vision or skin allergies may be a problem in this career.

TRAINING

Food scientist/technologist. A number of universities and colleges offer degree courses in food science/studies/technology. Titles vary as does course content. Most cover the basic disciplines of food processing, biochemistry, microbiology, physics, mathematics and statistics, nutrition, quality control, management studies and basic engineering. Each course also offers additional options and specialisms. Courses usually last three or four years full-time or four years on a sandwich basis, where some time is spent on placement with an employer. All honours degree courses in Scotland last four years.

Graduates in other science subjects may either take a postgraduate course in food science or food technology or find employment with an employer who arranges any necessary training for them.

A number of colleges offer higher national diploma courses relevant to food science and technology. Courses usually last two years full-time or three years on a sandwich basis. For some students these courses can lead to eventual transfer to a degree course.

The Institute of Food Science and Technology (UK) – the food scientists' and technologists' professional body – awards its own Postgraduate Diploma in Food Control. Graduates working full-time in the food and allied industries may join the programme. The Diploma combines academic study with work-based experience and requires the successful completion of three of six modules. Final assessment is by case study and oral examination.

Technicians may take a full-time course before joining an employer. They may study for a higher national diploma with a view to entry as a higher level technician; or a BTEC national diploma (two years); or an SQA national certificate (one year); or an Advanced GNVQ in Science with food technology specialism which is offered at Grimsby College (two years).

Alternatively they may enter work and study part-time on a day release or evening class basis for a BTEC higher national certificate (two years), or an SQA higher national certificate (one year), or a BTEC national certificate (two years); or an SQA national certificate (one year).

Many BTEC/SQA courses, particularly those that are part-time, have specialisms geared to the needs of the local industry, for example, baking or meat, while others have options in business or management studies.

NVQs/SVQs relating to food science and technology – Food and Drink Manufacturing Operations Levels 1 and 2 are available.

Modern Apprenticeships (Skillseekers programme in Scotland) in Food and Drink Manufacturing Operations are available. Ask your careers service or local TEC/LEC for further details.

LATE ENTRY

Late entry is not difficult for mature graduates in food science and related subjects due to the national shortage of food scientists/technologists.

Access courses for adults who wish to study for a degree or higher national diploma course but do not have the necessary qualifications are offered at many local colleges. They are usually one year full-time or one or two years part-time with daytime and/or evening attendance.

Late entry technicians may have difficulty in finding posts if not able to move to another location.

OPPORTUNITIES

There are about 4,000 food scientists/technologists working in the UK. About one-third work in research and development and another third in production and quality control.

The majority of opportunities are with the food processing and manufacturing industry – with manufacturers of products or ingredients, packaging and equipment manufacturers – in research laboratories and in government departments (especially the Ministry of Agriculture, Fisheries and Food); and with retailers. Supermarket chains are now major employers. They have teams of food technologists who are concerned with new product development, food control and product distribution. The latter requires knowledge of refrigeration and packaging techniques, and shelf-life of individual products.

Food scientists/technologists may work as public analysts in laboratories, move into the catering industry or become specialist environmental health officers with local authorities. It is possible to work for consultancy organizations.

There are also opportunities in education. Food scientists/technologists may work in universities and colleges that teach food science and technology as specific subjects but also may teach courses concerned with agriculture, catering, dietetics, nutrition and food management and marketing.

There are some opportunities to work for international organizations like the United Nations and to work overseas on short-term projects in developing countries.

Jobs are available throughout the UK, although most of the research establishments are in the South East of England (with the exception of the MAFF research station in Norwich and the Campden Food and Drink Research

SCIENCES: QOB–QOS

Association in Gloucestershire).

Recruitment is fairly regular and, as there is a shortage of well-qualified food scientists and especially technologists, there is a good choice of openings. There is competition, however, for entry to the food research associations which may only need a small number of new entrants each year.

PAY AND CONDITIONS

Earnings vary according to employer, specialism, qualifications and location. A new graduate may expect from £11,000 to £16,000.

Hours of work depend on the type of work being done. Food scientists/technologists working in research and development may work a standard five-day 37-hour week, Monday to Friday. Those involved with food manufacturing processes may have to work the usual hours of the factory which can include some shift, evening or weekend working. Most positions of responsibility will demand more than the contractual hours.

PROSPECTS

Promotion prospects for food scientists/technologists depend on where they work. In central or local government there is a structured career path with prospects of promotion to a higher grade, ultimately running a research laboratory, selecting research topics and managing staff.

Some similar positions exist in the private sector, but senior positions in industry generally depend on business and management skills or may mean a move away from bench laboratory work into more general management.

Those who want promotion in a particular field may have to move between companies or between employment sectors.

Self-employment in consultancy work is possible. A small number become journalists, technical writers and information scientists.

RELATED OCCUPATIONS

Analytical chemist, dietitian, nutritionist.

FURTHER INFORMATION

The Institute of Food Science and Technology (UK)*, 5 Cambridge Court, 210 Shepherd's Bush Road, London W6 7NL, 0171 603 6316 (please send 9 inch by 6 inch sae), www.easynet.co.uk\ifst\

Food and Drink National Training Organization*, 6 Catherine Street, London WC2B 5JJ, 0171 836 0580

FURTHER READING

Leaflets/booklets are available from the addresses marked*.

Where to Study for a Career in Food Science and Technology – Institute of Food Science and Technology

An A–Z of Careers in Food Science and Technology – Institute of Food Science and Technology

Working in Manufacturing – COIC

In the careers library classified under QON/SAC.

4. MATERIALS SCIENTIST/TECHNOLOGIST/ METALLURGIST (QOS)

BACKGROUND INFORMATION

All products are made from materials. Quality products depend on the most effective use of materials. Some materials, like wood and stone, are used in their natural state. Most materials, though, are made by applying physical and chemical processes to natural raw materials and their compounds to make **polymers** like plastics (which are derived from oil, coal, natural gas and salt) and rubbers; **metals** (eg steel, aluminium); and **ceramics** including glass. There are currently no fewer than 110,000 different materials.

Materials scientists/technologists and metallurgists are concerned with the behaviour of metals and materials and improving our knowledge of what they can be made to do or how they can be exploited. The results of research are applied to the manufacture and production of the alloys, compounds etc.

Materials science/metallurgy has been responsible for the development of products as different as jet engines, ships, lasers, aircraft, bathroom fittings, microchips, computer disks, house guttering, contact lenses, double glazing, cling film, car bodies and replacement hip joints. The materials industry is large and rapidly developing. By the year 2000 it will be worth an estimated £266 billion.

There is much overlap between the disciplines of materials science and metallurgy, such that they are often studied together, although there are specialist courses.

There is no standard materials scientist. Some people use the name of the material in which they specialize in their job titles, calling themselves ceramics, glass, plastics technologists or paper scientists instead of using the more general term.

Strictly speaking however, metallurgists study metals alone; polymer scientists, polymers; ceramicists, ceramics; while people who study *all* materials, ie, metals, polymers and ceramics, are called materials scientists. Similarly, the job titles scientist, engineer and technologist are used interchangeably.

THE WORK

As the range of materials is so vast it is usual for materials scientists/technologists and metallurgists to specialize. Their work, though, is increasingly multidisciplinary, as they often work with people from other branches of science and with engineers, designers and marketing specialists.

Materials scientists apply the principles of chemistry and physics to structures, uses and production of all kinds of materials, but may specialize in working on one or two only, depending on the research and manufacture undertaken by their employers.

Materials technologists and **engineers** are concerned with selecting the best and most cost-effective material for a particular product, whether it is a cutting tool, a component for electronic devices or an artificial limb design, and the associated fabrication of materials into products. They also work to discover why failures occasionally occur.

Metallurgists normally specialize in one of three areas:

Chemical metallurgists are concerned with the extraction and purification of metals from their ores, the reclamation of metals from scrap, corrosion prevention and the development of new, lighter alloys.

Physical metallurgists specialize in the structure and physical properties of metals and alloys and, in particular, how they behave when subjected to stress, temperature or other physical effects.

Process metallurgists are concerned with the manufacturing process. They are the experts on the best way to produce the required product, deciding whether to use forging, welding, bonding or other techniques, and how to alter a metal's properties by controlled heat treatment.

Materials scientists/technologists and **metallurgists** work in three main areas:

Research and development. This is carried out in laboratories in educational establishments, government research institutes or on manufacturers' premises.

Government and university-funded projects are usually concerned with finding solutions to problems over a long period. Industry tends to support research over a short time-scale that is designed to improve, invent or modify its own products.

Scientists frequently work at a laboratory bench – the term used is actually 'bench research'. They usually work in a small team with colleagues, some of them specialists in other scientific disciplines. They supervise junior staff and may be responsible for managing the project's budget and staying within the agreed sum made available for research.

Research may be directed at the development of new materials ranging, for example, from those for hip replacements to those for building bridges. Research is also undertaken into new and better ways of using existing materials. Much research effort is currently being put into improving methods used to form, treat and shape materials. Development involves developing new ideas from existing products.

Research and development staff make use of laboratory tools – microscopes, testing equipment, sophisticated analytical machinery, much of it controlled by computer. They use computer modelling to test and evaluate the properties of materials. They also use computers when analysing data and results of experiments. All staff, but particularly the project director, have to keep accurate written records of the project's progress. The senior scientists and director have to write the final report.

Technicians assist the scientists and technologists by setting up experiments and operating equipment and they may become the experts in using particular equipment. They also help to collate results and statistics and may be in charge of one section of the laboratory, and responsible for ordering supplies and controlling stock.

Quality control. All products have to be tested at stages during manufacture to ensure they meet the purpose for which they were designed, are safe, with all components reaching the same standard. In addition to standards imposed by individual manufacturers, British Safety Standards (laid down by government) must be met. Quality control is also responsible for ensuring that goods are being produced as economically as possible.

Materials scientists/technologists take samples for analysis; this is done either in the laboratory or on the factory floor, depending on the size of the parts being tested. Samples may be destructively tested by chemical, physical or mechanical methods. Some testing methods, using x-rays for example, leave the component in its original state. These are known as non-destructive testing.

Routine testing is done by machine. Samples that need to be tested by hand or bench equipment are usually the responsibility of technicians who carry out the bulk of the testing and monitoring work, taking samples from a conveyor belt, analysing them and keeping records at each production stage.

Production. Some materials scientists/technologists and metallurgists become production managers or manufacturing engineers.

Production managers and manufacturing engineers use managerial rather than scientific skills, although in this area of work a technical background and understanding of the processes involved is important.

They are responsible for the manufacture of products or components on time and in line with the agreed budget. Their work includes planning every stage of production to ensure that equipment is being used to full capacity and that parts and supplies arrive on schedule in order to keep the production process in operation.

Anyone working in research, quality control or production, but particularly the latter, may have to wear protective clothing. This depends on the materials being worked with. Some substances are dangerous and there are strict government health and safety regulations regarding the control of substances hazardous to health (COSHH regulations). In other cases, protective clothing is used to protect the product. Processing of silicon, for example, is done in clean rooms with all the staff wearing full head-to-toe anti-contamination suits, gloves and face masks to protect the silicon from dust.

Other opportunities exist in technical sales and marketing, technical journalism, information work, consultancy, teaching and lecturing.

WORK ENVIRONMENT

The workplace of materials scientists/technologists and metallurgists depends on their specialism. They might work in laboratories, in scrupulously clean production plants wearing special suits or in noisy and possibly uncomfortable conditions. A metallurgist or metallurgical technician may use portable testing equipment outdoors. Others have to spend time on noisy factory floors or visit industrial plants operating furnaces at very high temperatures to ensure that production achieves appropriate results.

Most materials scientists/technologists and metallurgists also spend time in offices, writing reports or attending meetings.

SKILLS AND INTERESTS

Materials scientists/technologists and metallurgists must be interested and have ability in maths, physics and chemistry. Scientific ability, curiosity and an interest in the practical application of science is essential. They should enjoy working accurately, patiently and methodically, even when conducting the same test or experiment repeatedly. They must be capable of clear, logical thought and have a practical approach to problem solving.

As research and development work is normally carried out in teams, they must be able to work well as a team member.

SCIENCES: QOB–QOS

Tact and diplomacy are required, as is the ability to relate to all levels of staff.

Good communication skills, both written and spoken, are important. Many jobs also require the ability to write clear, concise reports. Computer skills are necessary.

ENTRY REQUIREMENTS

The usual qualification to become a materials scientist, materials technologist or metallurgist is a degree in either metallurgy, materials science, polymer chemistry or ceramics. Some entrants, though, have a degree in such as physics, chemistry or engineering.

Minimum entry requirements for relevant degree courses are either: two A levels from physics, chemistry and maths plus GCSEs (A–C) in three other subjects; or three H grades (in maths, physics and chemistry) plus five S grades (1–3); or a BTEC/SQA national award in science or an applied science such as polymer technology, ceramics science and technology, materials science or materials technology; or a relevant Advanced GNVQ/GSVQ Level III, eg science, engineering, manufacturing or technology.

Applicants with non-science A levels may be accepted onto a foundation year preceding the first year of a relevant degree course in some institutions.

Entry to materials higher degree courses is with a good class first degree, either in a materials related discipline or in science or engineering.

The minimum qualifications for technician entry are usually four GCSEs/S grades (A–C/1–3) or a BTEC first award in science, or appropriate SQA national certificate modules, or Intermediate GNVQ/GSVQ Level II.

BTEC Higher National Diploma/Certificate in Materials Science/Metallurgy requires study of two A levels from physics, chemistry or maths, with at least one being passed; or a relevant BTEC/SQA national award; or a relevant Advanced GNVQ/GSVQ Level III. In Scotland those with H grades normally complete the last year of an SQA certificate before starting the higher certificate/diploma, but direct entry is possible with the Certificate of Sixth-Form Studies.

BTEC national diploma and certificate courses usually require four GCSEs/S grades (A–C/1–3), or a BTEC first award, or Intermediate GNVQ/GSVQ Level II.

SQA national certificate courses have no set entry requirements. Applicants should check with individual colleges, who may set their own requirements, as they wish to be satisfied that students are able to benefit from the courses.

Advanced GNVQ/GSVQ Level III courses usually require either four GCSEs/S grades (A–C/1–3), or Intermediate GNVQ/GSVQ Level II.

Modern Apprenticeships (part of the Skillseekers Initiative in Scotland) are available in various industries relevant to materials, including ceramics and building products, chemicals, engineering construction, engineering manufacture, glass, polymers, steel, telecommunications, paper and board, and surface coatings. Entry requirements vary between industries. Some require three to five GCSEs/S grades (A–C/1–3), often including English, maths and science. Others do not specify entry qualifications but look for ability in English, maths and science and may set entry tests. Contact your local careers office, TEC/LEC for details.

Defective colour vision or any skin or respiratory problems could present difficulties in this career.

TRAINING

A number of universities and colleges of higher education offer degree courses in materials science/technology/engineering or metallurgy. Course titles vary, as does the emphasis of each course. It is important, therefore, to check carefully before choosing a course. Some courses concentrate on a single material, others on all materials. Some courses combine study of materials with study of a language, management or another science or engineering discipline. The Institute of Materials has a list of degree courses they accredit. Students on such courses may receive a £1,000 bursary from the Institute if they meet certain academic requirements.

Degree courses last three years full-time or four years on a sandwich basis, where students spend a period of time on placement with an employer.

There are many postgraduate materials courses offered at universities. Some courses are designed for those with a materials related first degree and some for those with a first degree in science or engineering. Courses usually last one or two years full-time or three or four years part-time.

Technicians usually enter work and study part-time on a day release or evening class basis for a BTEC higher national certificate (two years), or SQA higher national certificate (two years), or a BTEC national certificate (two years), or an SQA national certificate (two years). They may work towards relevant NVQs/SVQs.

Alternatively technicians may take a full-time course before joining an employer. They may study for a higher national diploma (two years full-time or three years sandwich) with a view to entry as a higher level technician, or a BTEC national diploma (two years), or an SQA national certificate (one year), or an Advanced GNVQ/GSVQ Level III science, manufacturing, engineering or technology (two years).

Those on Modern Apprenticeships (part of the Skillseekers Initiative in Scotland) work towards one of the Level 3 NVQs/SVQs relevant to their particular industry. There is no set length of time for Modern Apprenticeship training but it is likely to be at least three years.

Training is provided by employers for both materials scientists and technicians. They may work towards membership of The Institute of Materials and the status of Chartered Engineer, Incorporated Engineer or Engineering Technician.

LATE ENTRY

There is no set upper age limit for entry to this work but attitudes of individual employers to mature entrants vary.

Mature applicants may be accepted onto university and college courses without the usual entry requirements, particularly if they have relevant experience and/or qualifications.

Access courses for adults who wish to study for a degree but who do not have the necessary qualifications are offered at many local colleges. They are usually one year full-time or one to two years part-time with day and/or evening attendance.

SCIENCES: QOB–QOS

OPPORTUNITIES

Materials scientists/technologists and metallurgists work throughout the UK for employers of widely differing size. Most work in private industry, in research and development, quality control and production. There are opportunities in the industries that produce materials, including metals, plastics, polymers, synthetic rubbers, natural and manmade fibres, ceramics and glass.

There are also openings in the wide range of industries that use materials, including aeronautical, civil, mechanical, electrical, electronic and telecommunications engineering, gas, electricity and nuclear power companies, chemical, oil, building, packaging, vehicle manufacturing and biomedical industries.

Major employers include such companies as British Steel, ICI, Imperial Metal Industries (IMI), Shell Chemicals, BP Chemicals, Pilkington, GEC, British Gas and Rolls Royce.

In addition to the research opportunities in private industry there are openings in university laboratories, industrial research associations, contract research laboratories and government laboratories, such as the Defence Research Agency, the National Physical Laboratory and the Building Research Establishment.

Self-employment is possible, as a consultant working on projects for companies on a contract basis.

Britain is the base for several foreign companies that employ materials scientists/technologists and metallurgists. In addition, some companies based in mainland Europe recruit British graduates.

There is currently strong demand for materials scientists/technologists and metallurgists. Vacancies may be advertised in *Materials World* and *New Scientist*.

PAY AND CONDITIONS

Hours of work are usually 9am to 5pm or 8.30am to 4.30pm (often the case in industry) Monday to Friday, with some employers offering flexitime. Staff working to deadlines or travelling to visit clients at different sites may work extra hours when necessary.

Work in quality control and production management usually involves shift work. Patterns vary with different employers.

Salaries vary widely between companies but tend to follow those for engineering in general. A newly qualified graduate might expect to earn at least £14,000 a year. A 1997 survey by the Engineering Council found that the average salary for a Chartered Engineer was £40,131 a year. The average for an Incorporated Engineer was £29,918, while that for an Engineering Technician was £26,311.

PROSPECTS

It is possible for materials scientists/technologists and metallurgists to progress to senior positions within their area of work, such as senior scientist, project director or production manager. Some progress into general management.

There are openings for materials scientists/technologists and metallurgists to specialize in purchasing of raw materials, as well as in sales or marketing management, and information work. Some go into technical writing, lecturing or specialist journalism

RELATED OCCUPATIONS

Medical laboratory scientist, engineer, textile technologist, scientist, medical technical officer, laboratory technician.

FURTHER INFORMATION

The British Polymer Training Association, Coppice House, Halesfield 7, Telford, Shropshire TF7 4NA, 01952 587020

Institute of Materials*, 1 Carlton House Terrace, London SW1Y 5DB, 0171 839 4071, http://www.instmat.co.uk

Plastics and Rubber Advisory Service, 6 Bath Place, Rivington Street, London EC2A 3JE, 0171 457 5000

FURTHER READING

Leaflets/booklets are available from the address marked*.

Working in Physical Sciences – COIC

Scientific Research and Development – AGCAS

Process Technology – AGCAS

In the careers library classified under QOS.

STATISTICS: QOG

STATISTICIAN CLCI:QOG

BACKGROUND INFORMATION

Statistics is the science of collecting, classifying, presenting, analysing and interpreting numerical information to assist in problem-solving and decision-making.

This is a relatively new career area, which has expanded greatly since the 1950s, when industry and commerce recognized the value of employing specialist statisticians rather than relying solely on scientists or managers to analyse their own numerical data. Computers also have had a major impact – extending the range and scope of the work.

Statisticians are employed in many different fields: government service; industry; finance; teaching; research and development; market research; medicine; agriculture and forestry; environmental health; commerce. In addition they are involved in a wide variety of different tasks. Examples of a few of these are: economics and resource forecasting; management services; quality control and production problems; health and safety research (such as the risks of work-related diseases); medical research (the relationship between disease and smoking, the spread of epidemics, effects of new drugs etc); road safety (eg optimum speed limits); ecology (extinction rates of plants and animals); planning (future needs of housing, schools, roads etc); and insurance (probabilities of death or accident).

THE WORK

Statistical analysis

Figures can be used to indicate current situations, currency reserves and census figures, for instance. Taken alone such figures are of little interest, but after analysis the information can form the basis of models for use by decision makers. Statisticians compare the latest figures with previous ones; they can then produce information about changes, such as percentage increases in users of a product or rises/falls in population. Decision makers may use the information when determining policies, such as where to market products.

Efficiency evaluation

Statistics can be used to assess the efficiency of policies, new products, equipment etc. In industry this could mean using figures to assess whether production plant is being used efficiently and economically. Another example is where a policy of increasing salaries may have been intended to boost the number of recruits entering a particular profession; statisticians could review the effectiveness of the policy through analysing the recruitment figures, taking into account other variable factors.

Forecasting

Statistical techniques are used to forecast the results of policies, future requirements, marketing campaigns, performance of products or industrial processes etc. Information may be obtained by interviewing random samples of the population and analysing replies to a range of carefully worded questions, or by observing a range of measurements which predict trends or changes in processes etc.

Quality assurance

Statistical techniques are used to ensure that all types of products/services are of an acceptable and consistent standard. Statisticians may help to define the precise specifications and standards that must be achieved, as well as advising on methods of collecting data, evaluating quality control tests and reports, and devising new tests.

Activities involved in statistical work

Statisticians work in a variety of fields and may specialize in particular applications. However, the work involves a number of common tasks:

1. Working with client to establish goals for the project

It is first important to consider whether statistical methods can be applied to the problem and, if so, how this should be done. Clear and accurate definitions are essential to ensure that those collecting the information gather exactly what is required so that findings may have a wide application. Statisticians also need to establish valid, reliable and efficient research designs, in both experimental and survey studies.

2. Statisticians' ability to deliver a solution

Statisticians analyse the information and must indicate the reliability with which any conclusions can be drawn.

Computers are widely used and they can be programmed to act as working models and determine the effects of changing variables. When analysing a mass of information, statisticians take account of the variables that might affect the results.

3. Communicating the result to the client

Interpreting figures is a major element of a statistician's work so that results need to be presented as models for decision makers who need to know the reasons behind the results, the likely effects and implications. Analysis and information must be presented in a meaningful way by the statistician and this can involve making written and oral reports, explaining details in a way that is understandable to non-specialists. They may use diagrams, graphs and tables to show results and the relationships between factors.

WORK ENVIRONMENT

Many statisticians are office-based and can expect to work in fairly comfortable surroundings. They often work in teams with other professionals such as scientists, market researchers, management services personnel, engineers and managers.

Work on some investigations may involve travelling to different locations, and sometimes may include trips abroad. Scientific work may include surveys and experiments away from the office.

SKILLS AND INTERESTS

Statisticians need a high level of numeracy and a thorough understanding of the modelling tools of statistics.

Statisticians should be methodical, logical and show a high level of reasoning, as well as having problem-solving skills. Statisticians must be able to handle large amounts of information easily and must work accurately with attention to detail. Interests and skills in computers are essential.

The work offers opportunities for initiative and creativity in problem solving; however, it is also necessary for statisticians to carry out work that is routine.

Consultancy skills are also important for all statisticians if their efforts are to be used and valued. They need to develop effective working relationships and be able to communicate with clients or specialists in other disciplines with whom they work. They should be able to weigh up the evidence and communicate their results. It will often be necessary to explain complicated aspects of the work to non-experts in a clear and straightforward manner.

ENTRY REQUIREMENTS

Entrants need to show competent levels of numeracy with GCSEs/S grades, A levels/H grades or BTEC/SQA national certificates in a mathematical subject or similar. However, most entrants to statistician jobs have to obtain qualifications such as BTEC/SQA higher national certificates or diploma, degrees or The Royal Statistical Society examinations on either a full-time or sandwich training course.

Entrants to BTEC/SQA higher national certificate or diploma courses generally require an appropriate BTEC/SQA national award or one A level plus three to four GCSEs (A–C), or two H grades plus two or three S grades (1–3) (including study of a mathematical subject to A level/H grade), or equivalent.

Candidates for degree courses need a minimum of two A levels plus five GCSEs

(A–C), or three H grades plus five S grades (1–3), or equivalents. In addition to maths, other useful subjects include computing, sciences and economics. Contact universities for details of specific requirements.

The three Royal Statistical Society qualifications are the Ordinary and Higher Certificates and the Graduate Diploma. Entry to the Ordinary Certificate is with GCSEs/S grades or equivalent in maths and English, or with relevant work experience. Exemption to the Ordinary Certificate is given to candidates with A levels/H grades in maths and statistics or pure maths and one other subject. The Higher Certificate follows on from the Ordinary Certificate and is recognized as an advanced qualification in its own right as well as being accepted for degree course entry or entry to the Graduate Diploma, which is recognized as equivalent to an honours degree in applied statistics.

The Government Statistical Service (GSS), which is one of the largest employers of statisticians, operates a fast-track development programme. There is an annual competition for permanent posts in January but GSS also employs temporary statistical officers throughout the year for graduates with degrees that include 25% statistical theory. Candidates must have a first- or second-class honours degree in a numerate subject, Graduate Diploma of the Royal Statistical Society, or equivalent. Contact the Government Statistical Service personnel section for further details.

TRAINING

Several institutions of higher education offer full-time courses leading to BTEC/SQA higher national awards. Appropriate subjects include, for example, maths, statistics and computing, statistics and physics, and applied maths. A number of sandwich courses are available; these include placements to give work experience.

Full-time or sandwich degree courses are available at higher education institutions throughout the UK. Statistics can be taken as a single subject or combined with other subjects such as maths, operational research, or computer science.

It is important that candidates check the syllabuses of courses, as there may not be a strong enough statistical content to qualify the graduate as a specialist statistician. Most specialist courses include study of maths, statistics and computing.

Postgraduate courses may be available for those with good mathematical, statistics or scientific degrees to undertake research leading to doctorates or masters degrees. Students may specialize in particular applications or fields, such as medical or agricultural statistics. Those with degrees in related subjects but with less emphasis on statistics - such as engineering sciences, psychology and social sciences - may attend postgraduate diploma or MSc courses in statistics. Maths graduates might also attend these courses to study advance statistics.

The Royal Statistical Society examinations:

Courses are available at some institutions of higher education in the UK, mainly on part-time day release or evening class basis, for those in work. A small number of full-time courses are available and it is possible to study through correspondence courses. Contact The Royal Statistical Society for further details.

Ordinary Certificate in Statistics. The aim of this qualification is to provide a grounding in the principles and practice of statistics. The emphasis is on practical data collection, presentation, and interpretation as a basis for the more advanced exams. It is intended as a qualification for clerical assistants in statistics.

Higher Certificate in Statistics. In addition to the knowledge required at Ordinary Certificate level, entrants study statistical theory and methods and applied practice. It is intended for those in relevant work, for example, at assistant level, and for those wishing to progress to graduate level work in statistics.

Graduate Diploma in Statistics. The diploma involves further and intense study on statistical theory and methods and applied practice and options such as economics and statistics for medical applications or for industry and quality improvement. Other options are biometry, econometrics or operational research. Statistical computing features in all parts of this examination.

In the Civil Service, training takes place mainly on the job, with recruits working alongside experienced staff. It may also include formal courses, including classroom training, to cover specialist elements of the work, such as computing and consultancy skills.

The training period will vary according to the type of job, organization and experience of the individual. New statisticians often work on a number of projects with experienced statisticians, until they have sufficient experience to work alone.

Membership of professional organizations

The Royal Statistical Society is the professional body representing statisticians.

Candidates can become a Chartered Statistician (CStat) with either the RSS Graduate Diploma or an honours or higher degree in statistics and a number of years' practical and management experience in statistics. They can also qualify with ten years' varied experience at a responsible level. Graduate Statistician (GradStat) status is awarded to those with the graduate diploma or academic qualifications but who have not yet the necessary practical experience. Anyone with an interest in statistics may also join as a (non-professional) fellow.

STATISTICS: QOG

LATE ENTRY

Entry to this type of work is normally via the routes described.

Adult candidates may achieve promotion from clerical posts in statistical work. They often take The Royal Statistical Society qualifications on a part-time basis. Adults may also gain entry to relevant degree and/or postgraduate diploma courses. Many higher education institutions are flexible in their entry requirements for adult students. However, applicants should normally show they have the required ability in numeracy and have relevant experience of statistics in business, industry or commerce.

Appropriate Open University degrees can be acceptable.

OPPORTUNITIES

Computers have had an enormous impact on the profession. They have taken over many of the complicated and time-consuming calculations. The statistician's expertise is still necessary and it is unlikely that they will be replaced by new technology. The practice of statistics requires skills of judgement which cannot be automated. This is a fairly small profession, however, with around 2,000 professionally qualified members of The Royal Statistical Society and a further 4,000 fellows who have applied for CStat status or have a non-professional interest in statistics.

Statisticians work in many sectors of the economy. In industry and commerce, employers include those involved in manufacturing, market research and finance.

Opportunities also exist within local government, for example, in planning. The Civil Service is a large employer.

The main employing departments include the Inland Revenue, Department of Social Security, Department for Education and Employment, Department of Health, Department of Trade and Industry, Department of the Environment, Transport and the Regions, Home Office, Farming and Rural Conservation Agency, The Office for National Statistics, Scottish Office, Treasury and Welsh Office.

In addition, statisticians may also be employed by higher education and by research institutions. There are opportunities for statisticians to work abroad, either with overseas employers or representing British companies on overseas projects.

Statisticians may also work on a self-employed basis, often as members of management consultancy teams.

Advertisements may be carried in the national press, and also in the monthly newsletter of The Royal Statistical Society, *RSS News*, which goes to all members of the Society.

PAY AND CONDITIONS

Salaries vary according to employer, location and experience. Assistant statisticians are expected to progress rapidly, on merit, to statistician (grade 7) with a salary of £27,000 to £44,000. Assistant statisticians normally start at around £15,000 and rise to £27,000. Salary for a statistical officer normally starts at £11,500 (£14,000 in London) rising to a maximum of £17,000 (£20,000 in London). Starting salaries outside the Civil Service are likely to be comparable. Average salaries for people with experience are £16,000 to £25,000, with those in senior posts able to earn in the region of £35,000.

Most statisticians work flexible hours – where starting and finishing times can vary to suit an individual's preference or needs.

When working on particular projects, it may be necessary to work extra hours so that deadlines can be met.

PROSPECTS

Many statistician groups are small and there may, therefore, be limited opportunities for internal promotion except in Government departments. However, statisticians are not restricted to one area of application and there may be promotion opportunities by moving between companies into areas making increasing use of statistics, such as the pharmaceutical industry, environmental sciences and market research. Prospects may exist for progression to senior statistician, then to project leader and department head.

There are opportunities for statisticians, usually with experience, to work for consultancies – either specialist or general management consultancies. There may also be opportunities for statisticians to progress into general management; statistics can provide a useful background for senior management positions.

RELATED OCCUPATIONS

Operational researcher, actuary, computer systems programmer, computer hardware designer (electronics), economist, professional scientist.

FURTHER INFORMATION

The Royal Statistical Society*, 12 Errol Street, London EC1Y 8LX, 0171 638 8998

Government Statistical Service, The Office for National Statistics, D4/22, 1 Drummond Gate, London SW1V 2QQ, 0171 533 5040/5043

Office of Public Service and Science (OPSS)*, Cabinet Office, Fast-stream and European Staffing Division, Room 127/2, Horse Guards Road, London SW1P 3AL, 0171 270 5697

FURTHER READING

Leaflets/booklets are available from the addresses marked*.

Working in Mathematics – COIC

In the careers library classified under QOG.

ECONOMICS: QOK

ECONOMIST CLCI:QOK

BACKGROUND INFORMATION

Economics is a small profession – comparable in size with actuarial or archive work. Competition for entry is fierce, and only the most able economics graduates become professional economists.

However, there are many other careers for which an economics degree is a useful background, including other financial professions such as accountancy, banking or insurance, general business careers such as marketing, market research or management services, economic journalism and lecturing/teaching.

THE WORK

Economists perform an advisory role in government and business, providing information on which policy decisions can be based. They analyse and research economic problems, and produce forecasts of future developments.

The work of professional economists varies considerably according to the sector in which they are employed, but there are certain tasks that are common to all jobs.

1. All economists are experts in finding information from sources such as databases, libraries, newspapers and government departments. They manipulate data drawn from these sources, using mathematical and logic tools to find answers to questions such as:

– what have the recent economic trends been?

– what are the driving forces behind these trends?

– what forecasts can be made for the future?

2. The problems economists deal with may be macro-economic – concerned with large economic units such as nation-states; or micro-economic – concerned with the financial characteristics of firms, industries, individual households, and so on, and the way individual elements in an economy (such as consumers or commodities) behave. A typical macro-economic task might be to forecast the GDP (gross domestic product) of the USA in the coming year, or to assemble the arguments for and against a change in interest rates, whilst the kind of question dealt with at micro-economic level could be concerned with predicting the demand for furniture in South East England over the next quarter, or analysing the costs and benefits of regulating or taxing some form of pollution.

3. Personal computers are essential tools for professional economists, who use them to access information, make calculations, run economic models and word process reports and other documents.

4. There is a public relations aspect to the work of most professional economists. They may be required to speak at seminars, conferences and other public gatherings, or to present their views via the media. They go out and meet representatives of other organizations, and may deal with their employers' clients.

In specific sectors, the emphasis of economists' work is as follows:

Government Economic Service (GES)

Economists in the Government Economic Service advise ministers and senior officials on a broad range of economic issues. Work on macro-economic problems, especially in the Treasury, involves forecasting, policy development and analysis of trends in incomes, output, prices, balance of payments etc.

They advise on micro-economic issues in the Treasury and in all the major departments – including Health, Social Security, Agriculture, Environment, Transport and the Regions, Education and Employment, Industry and Overseas Development – and in 20 or so other government departments and agencies.

Some economists specialize in particular policy areas, but it is usual for them to change jobs every few years, either within or between departments.

Bank of England

Economists employed by the Bank of England specialize in areas such as monetary economics, financial economics, international economics or econometrics.

Other banks and financial institutions

Economists investigate and analyse national and international trends affecting financial markets. They may specialize, for instance in particular sectors of the economy such as housing, or in producing reports on foreign countries.

Commerce and industry

Economists are concerned with the effect of economic trends and changes in the economy on their own industry or organization. They produce forecasts which managers can use as a basis for forward planning.

Only the largest 'blue chip' companies employ their own economists – and then only in very small numbers.

Consultancies

Many management and specialist consultancies employ economists to help produce reports for governments, local authorities, commercial enterprises and other customers, on a wide range of issues from macro-economic forecasting to capital project appraisal.

WORK ENVIRONMENT

Economists are mainly desk-based. They spend much of the time working alone, but are usually part of a small team.

Some jobs involve travel, for instance to meet clients. Travel is likely to be mainly within the UK, except when the economist is working for an overseas client, or attending the occasional international conference.

SKILLS AND INTERESTS

Economists need to be good at working with figures. They should enjoy looking at a page of numbers and working out what they mean. Mathematical and information technology skills are essential.

Economists need to be able to explain their ideas simply, in plain English, to non-specialists. They should be able to express themselves clearly, both in writing and in speech.

Once they have drawn conclusions from a set of figures, economists should be prepared to stand by their judgements and argue a case. They should not be swayed easily by the views of others.

Economists need to be decisive, logical, quick-thinking and able to cope with pressure – they may, for example, be given only a few minutes to come up with a reasoned reaction to a set of statistics.

It is important to be able to get on well with a variety of people, both inside and outside the employing organization.

ECONOMICS: QOK

ENTRY REQUIREMENTS

The minimum entry requirement is normally a good first degree in Economics (preferably first- or second-class).

Entry to first degree courses is with a minimum of five GCSE/S grades (A–C/1–3) with two A levels/three H grades, or equivalent. Maths at A level or H grade is often required for entry to courses, and is increasingly regarded as essential for those who intend to become professional economists.

Many entrants have postgraduate qualifications – masters or doctorates.

TRAINING

Government Economic Service

Economics graduates join the GES as Assistant Economists. Their training is largely given on the job but is supplemented by a structured programme of courses. In addition to academic ability in economics, they are expected to develop administrative, managerial and communication skills.

There are also opportunities for economists to join the GES via the European Fast-stream, which helps candidates to prepare for the recruitment competitions of the European Union institutions. If successful, they leave the GES for employment with one of the European institutions; if not, they have the option of staying in the GES.

Bank of England

The Bank runs a graduate training programme (Trainee Officials Programme), covering all the Bank's operational and policy areas. In addition, a number of postgraduate sponsorships are offered either to students on leaving university or to staff who have begun their Bank career; the Bank will pay tuition fees and living expenses on one-year masters courses.

Other organizations

In other organizations training is largely given on the job. Some employers encourage staff to study for higher degrees via part-time or evening study.

Professional bodies

Many economists join the professional bodies – the Royal Economic Society and the Society of Business Economists – but these bodies do not confer specific qualifications.

LATE ENTRY

Adults may qualify by taking first degrees and postgraduate qualifications in economics. Entry is so competitive, however, that in most cases they are not likely to find employment as professional economists unless they have closely related experience.

There is no upper age limit on entry to the GES, apart from the European Fast-stream, but most successful applicants have graduated in the past ten years.

OPPORTUNITIES

With 530 staff in the Government Economic Service, government departments are the main employers of economists in the UK. Each year there are up to 60 vacancies for assistant economists, plus up to ten in the European Fast-stream. Most posts are in London, but there are some opportunities in Birmingham, Sheffield, Leeds, Edinburgh, Glasgow and Cardiff.

The Bank of England is another major employer of economists. Most begin their careers in the Monetary Analysis Division, which employs around 90 economists, but there are some opportunities in other divisions. As their careers develop, economists are able to choose between remaining as specialists or becoming all-round central bankers.

Other banks and financial institutions such as building societies, insurance companies and securities houses also have some openings for economists.

There are some opportunities in local government, particularly in larger urban authorities which may employ economists as economic development officers.

Some large industrial and commercial firms employ economists, but in very small numbers. There are also a few opportunities with other large organizations such as health authorities and utilities. In some cases a specialist qualification such as health or transport economics may be required.

Opportunities for teaching and research are available in universities and colleges. Independent economic intelligence units also offer a few posts.

An increasing number of organizations prefer to use the services of economic consultants, rather than to employ their own economic teams. There is therefore a growing number of opportunities with firms of consultants.

Overseas work with international organizations such as the European Union institutions, the World Bank or the Organization for Economic Co-operation and Development (OECD) is possible, although the number of posts is small and competition intense.

PAY AND CONDITIONS

Starting salaries for assistant economists in the Government Economic Service are in the region of £15,000 to £18,500. In other sectors starting salaries may be higher – up to about £20,000 in financial institutions. In the Bank of England, the minimum graduate entry salary is about £18,000; those with relevant further degrees and/or experience may be offered a higher starting figure.

For experienced economists, the salary range is very wide, with the most successful commanding six-figure salaries. In general, however, salaries are likely to be in the £30,000 to £50,000 bracket. There may also be fringe benefits such as a company car, assisted loan for house purchase, medical insurance, non-contributory pension, profit shares and an annual bonus.

Economists work a five-day week, but are likely to work long hours – in the financial sector, for example, twelve-hour days are common.

PROSPECTS

Promotion prospects are generally rather limited, because economists are employed in such small numbers by most organizations.

In the GES, however, there is a promotion structure and staff can expect to be promoted through the grade of assistant economist to economic adviser. Economists at that level, if they stay in the Civil Service, can transfer into administration. There are, however, some prospects of promotion, as an economist, to Senior Economic Adviser, and to a very few more senior posts.

ECONOMICS: QOK

Experienced economists may become self-employed, setting up their own consultancies. Alternatively, they may move into more specialist areas of economics – for example, experience in the GES or Bank of England can be a useful background for work in one of the international organizations. It is also possible to move into related careers such as financial or investment management.

RELATED OCCUPATIONS

Statistician, mathematician, accountant, investment analyst, bank manager, actuary, financial consultant/adviser.

FURTHER INFORMATION

Society of Business Economists*, 11 Bay Tree Walk, Watford, Herts WD1 3RX, 01923 237287, www.sbe.co.uk/index.html

Royal Economic Society, Dept of Economics, London Business School, Sussex Place. Regents Park, London NW1 4SA, 0171 262 5050

Government Economic Service*, Economist Group Management Unit, HM Treasury, Room 122/2, Parliament Street, London SW1P 3AG, 0171 270 5073/4581, www.hm-treasury.gov.uk

Bank of England (Personnel Division)*, 1–2 Bank Buildings, Princes Street, London EC2R 8EU

FURTHER READING

Leaflets/booklets are available from the addresses marked*.

Management Services and Economic and Statistical Work – AGCAS Careers Information Booklet

In the careers library classified under QOK.

EARTH SCIENCES: QOL

1. GEOLOGIST CLCI:QOL
2. METEOROLOGIST CLCI:QOL
3. OCEANOGRAPHER CLCI:QOL

1. GEOLOGIST (QOL)

BACKGROUND INFORMATION

Geology is the science of the Earth's history, composition and structure. It has applications in mining, civil engineering and the exploitation of natural resources such as oil, gas, minerals and underground water.

Geology covers a range of specialisms including: petrology – the composition, character and origin of rocks; mineralogy – the composition, occurrence and origin of minerals; palaeontology – the study of fossils and the evolution of life; stratigraphy – the study of history; structural geology – the study of work deformation; and geomorphology – the origin and development of land forms.

Two closely related subjects are geophysics and geochemistry. Geophysics is the scientific study of the physical properties, structure, composition and dynamic changes that affect the Earth and its atmosphere. Geophysics uses the principles of physics to measure and analyse the Earth's seismic activity (earthquakes and related phenomena), electromagnetism, gravity and radiant energy. Geochemistry is the study of the chemical composition of the Earth – it provides information about, for example, the evolution of the oceans and the atmosphere, the ages of rocks and fossils, the occurrence of elements and the effects of pollutants in the earth, oceans and atmosphere.

The term 'geoscience' is sometimes used to cover all the geological disciplines, particularly since geologists, geophysicists and geochemists are increasingly required to engage in multidisciplinary studies.

THE WORK

Geologists identify and survey areas where valuable natural resources may be present. They take samples in the field, test and evaluate them, and use the results as a basis for maps, reports and computer models.

The main areas of work are:

Exploration for natural resources such as oil, gas, coal, ground water and raw materials for industry

Geologists identify areas where resources are likely to be found, both onshore and offshore. In the oil industry, for example, geologists carry out seismic surveys, generating seismic waves and recording reflections from sub-surface layers. They evaluate the data collected, and, if the results are favourable, drilling and further geophysical and geochemical testing are carried out to confirm the presence of oil. Geologists then assess whether oil is present in sufficient quantities to justify commercial development. Comparable activities, with a heavy emphasis on geochemistry, sustain the minerals industry.

Hydrogeologists are responsible for identifying, measuring and analysing sources of water. They evaluate the quality and quantity and assess the possible threats posed by pollution. In the case of reservoirs, geologists advise on siting, accessibility and suitability of construction materials.

Engineering and environmental geology

Geologists are involved in carrying out investigations before the foundations and earthworks for large civil engineering projects – such as roads, dams or tunnels – are constructed. They assess the condition of bedrock and sub-soil, and evaluate risks such as landslides or earthquake. Once projects are under way, they monitor progress. They may also advise on the suitability of materials used in construction, such as sand, gravel and limestone.

Environmental geology can involve dealing with questions such as disposal of waste of all types – from household rubbish to nuclear waste – or evaluating the environmental impact of construction projects.

Geological surveying

Geologists collect geological information, both on land and at sea, which is used as a basis for maps and databases.

The subject is so important to national economies that most countries have geological surveys or equivalent bodies. The British Geological Survey, founded in 1835, surveys and maps the British land-mass and offshore areas. It provides a national geoscience information service, and has extensive international experience.

Education and research

Many geologists are concerned with teaching and academic research in universities, or with teaching earth sciences and related subjects in schools and colleges.

There are also geologists working as museum curators.

WORK ENVIRONMENT

The work often involves travel, sometimes to areas with extreme climates and arduous conditions. However, an increasing proportion of the work is laboratory- and office-based, mainly as a result of the greater emphasis now placed on the use of computer modelling and information technology.

SKILLS AND INTERESTS

A scientific approach is essential. Geologists need to be observant, objective and analytical, and capable of thorough, methodical work. They need investigative and enquiring minds, with the ability to think logically and clearly, to deal with numerical data, statistics, maps, and so on, and to interpret them with clarity and precision. Most jobs involve the use of information technology.

Geologists should be flexible, prepared to adapt to new theories, techniques and practices. It is important to keep abreast of new developments and current research.

Good communication skills – spoken and written – are required. It may be necessary to explain complex information clearly to non-specialists.

Geologists should be able to work alone (when carrying out field work, for example) and as members of a team. They need to be practical and resourceful and willing to act on their own initiative. A sense of responsibility is important. Some jobs require the ability to supervise the work of technicians.

Manual dexterity is needed for using surveying instruments. Many jobs require good health and normal colour vision.

ENTRY REQUIREMENTS

Entry is usually with a first degree in one of the geological sciences. Some support staff enter the profession after taking a first degree in a subject such as maths, physics or

EARTH SCIENCES: QOL

chemistry, followed by a postgraduate degree in one of the geosciences. First degree courses are currently being accredited by the Geological Society of London; intending professional geologists are well advised to ensure they attend such a course.

Minimum entry requirements for degree courses are five GCSEs/S grades (A–C/1–3) and two A levels/three H grades in scientific subjects – but for some geoscience courses, more than the minimum requirements may be needed. Relevant GNVQs/GSVQs or BTEC/SQA national awards may be acceptable for entry to some courses. Preferred subjects include physics, chemistry, biology, geology, mathematical subjects. A level/H grade geography is also accepted for entry to some courses.

Minimum entry requirements for the British Geological Survey, at scientific officer level, are a good degree or higher national certificate/diploma in a scientific, engineering or mathematical subject.

TRAINING

Many universities and other institutions of higher education offer first degree courses, lasting three or four years, in the geological sciences. Subject choices include geology, geophysics, geochemistry and applied courses – for instance, engineering geology, petroleum geology or exploration geology. Almost all courses include practical experience of field work and basic training in the use of computers within the sciences.

Geologists often go on to take higher degrees in specialist or applied geoscientific subjects. One-year taught masters courses provide the specialist vocational training, required by some employers. For research posts or teaching in universities, a PhD is usually required.

For those wishing to teach, postgraduate teacher training courses are available at nearly 100 educational institutions. Specialist courses in teaching earth sciences are offered at Bath and Keele Universities.

Employers usually provide induction training and an initial period of supervised work. Some sponsor staff on postgraduate courses. Further in-service training may be provided as necessary. Large organizations such as the British Geological Survey run extensive training and development programmes for staff at all stages of their careers. Such training is linked to gaining Professional Accreditation as a Chartered Geologist and to continuing professional development.

LATE ENTRY

Most geology departments welcome applications from mature students, and may accept older applicants with non-standard qualifications, depending on their background and experience. Science Access courses are a useful background. Check detailed requirements with individual institutions.

For mature applicants intending to teach, experience in industry, and of working with young people (eg in a voluntary setting), are useful.

OPPORTUNITIES

There are about 6,000 geologists and other geoscientists employed in the UK. The largest single employer is the British Geological Survey, which is part of the Natural Environment Research Council (NERC). The NERC, which is the leading UK agency for research and surveying of the natural environment, also offers some opportunities for geologists in its other research institutes and units.

Other major employers of geologists are oil and gas companies, mining and quarrying firms, and companies that provide these industries with technical services.

Some geologists are employed by the water industry, civil engineering companies and environmental agencies. Others work as teachers in schools, colleges and universities.

In the long term, there is likely to be a steady increase in demand for geologists. Growth areas include hydrogeology, pollution control and other work related to environmental problems.

It is possible to enter employment directly after taking a first degree. Initial employment, for instance in junior posts in seismic exploration, provides entry to the profession and can lead on to more responsible technical or managerial work.

Evidence of commitment to the subject – for instance, through junior membership of the Geological Society, or relevant vacation work – is helpful for those seeking employment.

Mobility is necessary for those who want to take full advantage of job opportunities. Many geologists – particularly those working in the oil, mining or civil engineering industries – spend part of their careers working abroad.

PAY AND CONDITIONS

Short-term contracts are common, both in industry and academic research.

Many jobs involve office hours, Monday to Friday, but in areas such as oil exploration, civil engineering or mining, shift work may be necessary.

In the British Geological Survey, salaries are similar to those of the scale for the science group in the Civil Service. This starts at £13,700 for a scientific officer, rising to a top rate of £25,000 for a senior scientific officer, and supplemented by a range of allowances.

Rates of pay are likely to be higher in industry, particularly for those with postgraduate qualifications. There may be special allowances for those working overseas.

PROSPECTS

Promotion prospects vary in different organizations. There may be opportunities to progress to senior scientific or managerial posts. Experienced geologists may become self-employed consultants.

RELATED OCCUPATIONS

Meteorologist, oceanographer, engineer: chartered civil/structural, surveyor: land/hydrographic, surveyor: mineral/mining, scientist, laboratory technician.

FURTHER INFORMATION

The Geological Society*, Burlington House, Piccadilly, London W1V 0JU, 0171 434 9944, www.geolsoc.org.uk

British Geological Survey*, Kingsley Dunham Centre, Keyworth, Nottingham NG12 5GG, 0115 936 3100

British Geological Survey, West Mains Road, Edinburgh EH9 3LA, 0131 667 1000

EARTH SCIENCES: QOL

FURTHER READING

Leaflets/booklets are available from the addresses marked*.

Exploration, Extraction and Protection of Natural Resources – AGCAS Careers Information Booklet

Degree Course Guide – Geological and Environmental Sciences – Hobsons

Working in Natural Sciences – COIC

Periodicals: Geology Today, New Scientist

In the careers library classified under QOL.

2. METEOROLOGIST (QOL)

BACKGROUND INFORMATION

Meteorologists monitor and interpret changes in the Earth's atmosphere and analyse and predict their effects. All aspects of the atmosphere are relevant, from the Earth's surface to the beginning of 'outer space'.

The science of meteorology is developing rapidly, leading to a greater understanding of the natural environment and climate. It is now possible, thanks to the development of Earth satellites and extremely powerful computers, to study the weather over the entire globe in a way that could not be done in the past.

The work of meteorologists varies from regular collection and forecasting of weather information for airlines, the media, farmers, shipping, industry, government departments and other organizations, to research into the long-term effects of climate change such as global warming.

THE WORK

Operational: meteorologists collect and interpret information continuously from sources such as weather stations, satellites, observation vessels, and civil and military aircraft. The information has to be co-ordinated and processed via computer systems and the resulting charts and computer models analysed. General and specific forecasts and maps are prepared.

Research: the research conducted by meteorologists is very varied. Many researchers try to improve the scope and range of forecasting. Their studies can extend to the oceans and polar regions and a long-term view of climatic change.

Applied: meteorologists also give specific advice on many practical matters, such as crop spraying, the effects of atmospheric pollution (eg acid rain, car exhausts), or the siting of bridges, oil rigs and power stations.

A large proportion of meteorologists work for the Meteorological (Met) Office. Met Office staff are best known for presenting weather forecasts on TV and radio, but this is only a small part of their work. Other major activities include providing meteorological services to government departments, civil and military aviation, local government and industry. For example, electricity, water and gas companies rely on information from the Met Office to predict demand; and local authorities use frost warnings to save money, by salting the roads only when necessary.

Met Office headquarters in Bracknell houses one of the most powerful computer complexes in the UK, used for forecasting and research. Over 100,000 messages from weather observation stations are received every day at the Met Office's telecommunications centre; they are fed into computers which generate global forecasts. The Met Office also operates a national network of local weather centres, many of which provide specialist services – such as shipping forecasts.

The Met Office undertakes an extensive research programme in meteorology and geophysics. Its Hadley Centre for Climatic Prediction and Research makes it possible for meteorologists to study large-scale changes in the world's climate, caused by the greenhouse effect.

WORK ENVIRONMENT

Work environments vary from comfortable offices to remote weather stations at airfields, defence bases, and so on. Some posts involve spending time out of doors, collecting weather information and possibly non-standard working hours, for example in shift work.

SKILLS AND INTERESTS

Meteorologists need a methodical and practical approach to collecting information, analysing data and solving problems. Meticulous accuracy, patience, attention to detail and good powers of observation are essential.

Good communication skills – written and spoken – are needed for answering enquiries, interacting with colleagues and advising clients. Meteorologists should be able to work with others as members of a team. Some posts require supervisory and management skills though numeracy and computational skills are more fundamental.

Meteorologists should be responsive to new ideas and technological developments. They need to be adaptable, enthusiastic and innovative. A flexible approach, together with a willingness to acquire new skills, are important.

ENTRY REQUIREMENTS

Entry at meteorologist level is with a degree or higher national certificate/diploma. Minimum entry requirements for degree courses are two A levels/three H grades and five GCSEs/S grades (A–C/1–3) or equivalent, for example, Intermediate GNVQs/GSVQs Level II in appropriate subjects. Many institutions' requirements are above the minimum – for example, some require three A levels, with good grades. For higher national certificate/diploma courses, entry is normally with one A level/two H grades and four GCSEs/S grades (A–C/1–3), or equivalent. The most useful A level/H grade subjects are maths and physics.

Relevant first-degree subjects include meteorology (as a single subject or as part of a combined degree), mathematics, physics or computing science. Other subjects that may be acceptable include astrophysics, electronics and physical chemistry. Environmental science or geography may be accepted if applicants have a good grounding in maths and physics. All applicants must have English language up to GCSE/S level (or equivalent).

Meteorological Office

To enter the Met Office at scientific officer grade, applicants need a degree in Mathematics, Physics or Meteorology (or a combination of these), Computing Sciences or Electronics; or a BTEC/SQA Higher National Certificate/Diploma in Mathematics, Computing or Applied Physics; or an equivalent qualification. The Met Office also gives consideration to applicants who have a

EARTH SCIENCES: QOL

degree in a relevant subject such as Physical Chemistry, Oceanography, Environmental Science or Geography, together with proven ability (usually A level or equivalent) in maths and physics, or if they have a relevant higher degree, for example in computing, together with a less relevant first degree. Degree courses usually last between three and four years.

Applicants must meet Civil Service residency requirements.

TRAINING

The main centre for the study of meteorology at first degree level is the University of Reading. Reading offers a single subject degree in Meteorology, combined first-degree courses in Meteorology with Mathematics or Physics, and an interdisciplinary course in Environmental Science of Earth and Atmosphere, containing substantial meteorological components.

Other universities offering a substantial amount of meteorology as an option within more general degree courses include East Anglia – Environmental Sciences; Edinburgh – Physics; Lancaster – Environmental Science or Geophysical Science; Plymouth – Ocean Science; Southampton – Geophysical Sciences.

The following postgraduate courses are appropriate: Birmingham – MSc Climatology and Applied Meteorology; Dundee – MSc Remote Sensing, Image Processing and Applications; East Anglia – MSc Atmospheric Sciences; Edinburgh – MSc Remote Sensing and Image Processing Technology; London, Imperial College – MSc Remote Sensing; Reading – MSc or Diploma in Applied and Agricultural Meteorology, also in Weather, Climate and Modelling.

The Meteorological Office College provides practical training at graduate and non-graduate level, both for Met Office staff and for sponsored students from other organizations.

The Royal Meteorological Society organizes meetings in London and at its local centres. It also has a professional qualification, Chartered Meteorologist.

LATE ENTRY

Adults may be accepted on relevant degree or higher national certificate/diploma courses – many educational institutions encourage adult applicants, and may relax entry requirements to courses. Enquiries should be made to the university or institution concerned.

The Met Office does not set age limits for entry (apart from normal retirement age). Adult applicants are welcome, provided they have appropriate scientific background. Previous experience in any kind of scientific work, and IT skills, are useful.

OPPORTUNITIES

The main employer is the Meteorological Office, which is an agency within the Ministry of Defence and employs over 2,000 staff. About half of them work at Met Office headquarters in Bracknell, Berks. Others work at around 100 smaller offices at locations throughout the UK, or overseas – mainly in Germany, Cyprus, Gibraltar and the South Atlantic. Met Office staff must be willing to move to another location.

Other employers include research councils such as the National Environment Research Council or the Agricultural and Food Research Council, universities and other educational institutions, government departments and industry – particularly oil, gas, electricity and water. Small numbers of meteorologists are employed by instrument manufacturers and geophysical contractors. An increasing number of consultancies offer forecasting services, and consultancy work offers opportunities for self-employment for experienced meteorologists.

The Overseas Development Agency and United Nations technical aid programmes, as well as the Met Office, offer opportunities for overseas employment.

PAY AND CONDITIONS

Current Met Office salary scales for graduates start on a salary band starting at £13,500 rising to £16,429.

These scales are supplemented by additional allowances, for shift work, for example. Many posts in meteorology involve shifts, because information about the weather is collected on a round-the-clock basis.

In the Met Office the basic working week is 42 hours, including meal breaks.

It may be possible to work part-time.

PROSPECTS

There are opportunities within the Met Office to transfer from one type of work into other areas – for instance, from forecasting to research or computing. Staff are encouraged to study for further qualifications which may be useful when they are considered for promotion.

Other organizations employ only small numbers of meteorologists, so promotion prospects are likely to be limited.

RELATED OCCUPATIONS

Scientist, geologist, oceanographer, hydrographic surveyor, ecologist, physicist, laboratory technician.

FURTHER INFORMATION

Association of British Climatologists, Roehampton Institute London, Whitelands College, West Hill, London SW15 3SN, 0181 392 3000

Royal Meteorological Society*, 104 Oxford Road, Reading, Berkshire RG1 7LJ, 0118 956 8500

Meteorological Office*, Personnel Department, London Road, Bracknell, Berks RG12 2SZ, 01344 856032/3

FURTHER READING

Leaflets/booklets are available from the addresses marked*.

Working in Natural Sciences – COIC

Exploration, Extraction and Protection of Natural Resources – AGCAS Careers Information Booklet

Periodicals: New Scientist; Weather (monthly): RMS

In the careers library classified under QOL.

EARTH SCIENCES: QOL

3. OCEANOGRAPHER (QOL)

BACKGROUND INFORMATION

Oceanography, the study of the seas, is a multidisciplinary field, drawing on biology, chemistry, physics, geology and geophysics, supported by mathematics, computer sciences and engineering. It encompasses the study of the shoreline, estuaries, coastal waters, shelf seas and deep oceans – including their history, present state and likely future development.

THE WORK

Two major issues that currently preoccupy oceanographers are:

– pollution of the seas, through their use as a dumping ground for waste;

– climate change, and how this is affected by, and affects, the oceans.

Both these questions need to be approached from a multidisciplinary point of view. For instance, to study the effects of pollution on organisms requires, in addition to a knowledge of biology, an understanding of the chemistry of the ocean environment, together with a knowledge of physics and geology, to understand how the pollutant is carried from its source by currents and turbulence and how pollutant particles find their way to the seabed and become part of its geological structure. Similarly, the study of climate change involves not only physics, which is closely connected with meteorological forecasting, but also marine biology, chemistry and geology.

Nevertheless, within oceanography there is some degree of specialization.

Oceanographers whose interests are primarily biological are concerned with organisms living under the sea or on the shoreline. There are practical applications to biological research in fisheries research and in other branches of oceanography – eg the development of medicines based on aquatic plant life.

Chemists are concerned with the ocean as a chemical system, and with understanding how chemicals are distributed within the ocean and are eventually transferred into the rocks and seabed. Chemical oceanography has applications in the study of pollution – and it is linked closely to physics, because the distribution of material in the water is largely determined by the laws of physics.

Geologists working in oceanography are concerned with the formation of sediments – this has practical applications, varying from the study of the effects of offshore dredging on beaches to the effects on the environment of offshore extraction of natural gas. On a much larger scale, they are concerned with plate tectonics – large-scale movements of the Earth's crust – much of which is occurring beneath the oceans.

Many geophysicists work in the oceanographic field, interpreting geological structures using sound waves and drill cores. They work particularly in the offshore hydrocarbon industry helping to discover new oil and gas fields.

Physicists study the movements of waves, tides, ocean currents, turbulence and the temperature and salinity of the ocean.

Much of the work of an oceanographer involves gathering data, for instance, from moored or drifting instruments deep below the sea surface, and recording the results. Techniques such as acoustics or satellite remote sensing are also used to collect information.

At some stage in their careers, almost all oceanographers carry out field work, going to sea on research vessels for periods lasting from around two weeks up to about two or three months. They may go down to the seabed, using diving equipment or submersible vehicles.

Onshore, oceanographers may be engaged in delicate laboratory work, using sophisticated analytical equipment. Much of the mathematical and physical calculations are done in the laboratory. A major task is in the use of computers, for example, to produce forecasting models. They also write and present reports, attend meetings and conferences.

Many oceanographers are purely concerned with research, but others work in a more commercial environment. In this context, they may, for example, carry out surveys and advise on the siting of sewer outlets, or the environmental consequences of extracting gravel from the seabed.

WORK ENVIRONMENT

Much of the work is laboratory- or office-based. In some cases, depending on the area of specialization, oceanographers may spend up to about three months a year at sea, on research vessels.

There is an international dimension to oceanography, which will involve attendance at conferences in Europe and elsewhere, as well as seagoing research on foreign vessels.

SKILLS AND INTERESTS

Oceanography, like other scientific disciplines, demands an enquiring mind, good powers of observation, numeracy, meticulous accuracy and close attention to detail.

Research work in oceanography is often carried out on an individual basis, but there are many situations in which it is important to interact well with others and work as a member of a team.

Good communications skills – oral and written – are essential. Mathematical ability and information technology skills are also very important.

For carrying out research at sea, a reasonable standard of physical fitness is helpful though not essential– but disability is not necessarily a barrier to employment in this field.

ENTRY REQUIREMENTS

Entry is usually with a first degree in physics, maths, chemistry, geology, biological sciences or a related subject, such as meteorology. Alternatively, graduates with a first degree in oceanography or combining oceanography with other subjects such as marine biology, maritime studies, geology, physics or maths.

Entry to first degree courses is with a minimum of five GCSEs/S grades (A–C/1–3) with two A levels/three H grades, or equivalent. For most courses, maths at GCSE/S grade (A–C/1–3) is essential; technological subjects and one or more foreign languages are useful. At A level/H grade, intending oceanographers need at least two sciences; maths or statistics are the most useful third subjects. Advanced GNVQs/GSVQs Level III or BTEC/SQA national qualifications in relevant subjects are acceptable for entry to some courses.

EARTH SCIENCES: QOL

TRAINING

There are universities offering broad-based first degrees in oceanography, covering the four main disciplines: physics, chemistry, biology and geology.

Bangor (The University of Wales) offers single honours courses in ocean science, geological oceanography, marine biology and marine chemistry. Joint honours courses in marine biology with oceanography, biochemistry or zoology, and in physical oceanography with mathematics, are available.

The University of Southampton offers a degree in oceanography, marine sciences and combined degrees in oceanography with geology, marine biology, marine environmental chemistry, French, mathematics, physics or physical geography.

The University of Plymouth offers a single honours degree in ocean science. It is also possible to combine ocean science with a range of other subjects.

In addition, a number of other universities offer more specialized first-degree courses in relevant areas – for example, marine biology, applied marine biology.

At postgraduate level, it is usual to specialize in the study of marine aspects of one of the four main disciplines. Postgraduate facilities are therefore available at a wider range of universities.

Specialist on-the-job training may be provided by employers.

LATE ENTRY

Adults may apply for first-degree or postgraduate courses on the same basis as school-leavers or graduates. Universities may be prepared to waive or lower standard entry requirements in the case of mature applicants – check with individual institutions.

OPPORTUNITIES

The Natural Environment Research Council (NERC) is the main employer of oceanographers. The council, which was established in 1965, is responsible for planning, encouraging and carrying out scientific research to explain the natural processes of the environment. It runs two institutions concerned with oceanography:

– the Southampton Oceanography Centre (which brings together the former Institute of Oceanographic Sciences' Deacon Laboratory and the James Rennell Centre, the NERC's Research Vessel Services and the University of Southampton's departments of geology and oceanography); and

– the Centre for Coastal and Marine Science, which comprises the Plymouth Marine Laboratory, the Proudman Oceanographic Laboratory in Birkenhead, and the Dunstaffnage Marine Laboratory in Oban.

The British Antartic Survey (part of NERC) also employs oceanographers.

Other employers include the National Rivers Authority, water companies, university departments, pharmaceutical companies and the Royal Navy. Some government departments – mainly the Department of the Environment, Transport and the Regions (DETR), the Ministry of Agriculture, Fisheries and Food, and the Ministry of Defence – employ oceanographers. There are opportunities abroad, particularly in Europe.

Consultancies providing advice on environmental matters offer a growing number of opportunities for employment. These bodies may, for instance, advise on matters relating to construction of offshore structures. Advisory and consultancy work is likely to increase in the next few years as more legislation concerned with environmental matters is introduced. It is expected that there will be opportunities in fields such as marine environmental law – for those with legal training coupled with relevant scientific knowledge.

It is also expected that, in future, interest in predicting changes in climate will lead to greater emphasis on the observation and study of the oceans. The creation of a 'Wet' Office – similar to the Met Office – has been proposed, and another possible development is the setting up of a Global Ocean Observing System (GOOS) to aid in climate prediction. These are likely to be international projects, not necessarily in the UK. Good numerate skills will be required.

There is also likely to be a large rise in the number of employment opportunities at universities over the next decade.

PAY AND CONDITIONS

The pay scale for scientists employed by the NERC is similar to the scale for the science group in the Civil Service. This starts at £12,700 for a scientific officer, rising to a top rate of £31,920 for a senior scientific officer and supplemented by a range of allowances.

In universities, lecturers are paid between £16,655 and £29,048; senior lecturers £30,496 to £34,464.

Short-term contracts lasting between one and four years are common.

Oceanographers are likely to work normal office hours when engaged in onshore work, but they may work round-the-clock when engaged in research at sea.

PROSPECTS

Recruitment in the UK is quite low at the moment. The growing prevalence of short-term contracts means that it can be difficult to predict long-term career paths. A series of sideways moves – from university into the NERC and back, or between contracts and fellowships, for example – are possible.

RELATED OCCUPATIONS

Geologist, chemist, biologist, physicist, meteorologist, hydrographic surveyor, laboratory technician.

FURTHER INFORMATION

Southampton Oceanography Centre, Empress Dock, Southampton SO14 3ZH, 01703 596435

Natural Environment Research Council*, Polaris House, North Star Avenue, Swindon, Wilts SN2 1EU, 01793 411500 (refers enquiries to nearest marine laboratory)

Society for Underwater Technology*, 76 Mark Lane, London EC3R 7JN, 0171 481 0750

EARTH SCIENCES: QOL

FURTHER READING

Leaflets/booklets are available from the addresses marked*.

Working in Natural Sciences – COIC

Exploration, Extraction and Protection of Natural Resources – AGCAS Careers Information Booklet

Oceanography, an illustrated guide – Summerhayes & Thorpe, Mansion Publishing, 1996

Periodicals: New Scientist, Nature

In the careers library classified under QOL.

FORENSIC SCIENCE: QOT

FORENSIC SCIENTIST CLCI:QOT

BACKGROUND INFORMATION

Forensic scientists examine materials associated with crimes to provide information or evidence that may be used in the legal process.

Forensic scientists are independent of police authorities although most of their work is undertaken for the police.

Forensic evidence has become increasingly important in crime investigation as techniques have advanced. Research is constantly being undertaken to make forensic techniques faster, more specific and more precise and the information and evidence provided more useful.

The importance of forensic science cannot be overstated. In many crime investigations it can provide the only hard evidence to indicate the guilt or innocence of an individual.

THE WORK

The work carried out in forensic science laboratories is usually dealt with in three main sections:

Chemistry

The main concern is with crimes against property such as burglary and arson. The work includes examination of glass, paint, chemicals, shoe-prints and tool marks. Forensic scientists also deal with fire investigation and vehicle accident reconstruction.

Biology

This involves offences against people, such as murder, assault and rape. The work includes blood grouping, blood pattern analysis, DNA profiling, and the examination of damage to clothing and of weapons, hairs, fibres, paper and other such materials.

Drugs and toxicology

Forensic scientists examine materials for restricted drugs and other toxic substances and look into cases of suspicious death, such as overdose or poison.

Laboratories have wide-ranging facilities, including, in some cases, for examining vehicle engines, defective parts and tyres, and for the analysis of blood and urine samples in drink-driving cases. Some work is undertaken in specialist departments, for example, at Huntingdon for the examination of firearms, and at Birmingham for the examination of forged documents.

The work of forensic scientists depends on their grade and specialism. Scientists examine exhibits arising from a wide variety of crimes, make comprehensive notes, handle small samples, analyse a range of materials and work with appropriate instruments. Techniques used include gas and high-pressure liquid chromatography, infra-red spectroscopy, specialized microscopy, microspectrophotometry, electrophoresis and DNA analysis techniques.

On completion of tests, scientists present the results of their examinations in the form of written statements for production in court. The more experienced scientists may be required to produce reports for court and give verbal evidence in court.

Senior scientists also allocate work to other staff and support their work. Assistant forensic scientists in England and Wales, and technicians and trainees in Scotland, are involved in examining and analysing a range of materials under the supervision of qualified scientists.

WORK ENVIRONMENT

Most forensic science work is laboratory-based. Some time is spent travelling to and attending scenes of crime, which can be indoors or outdoors in any conditions or weather. Good personal mobility may be required at scenes of crime, with bending and crouching necessary. The more experienced scientists attend court to give evidence.

SKILLS AND INTERESTS

Forensic scientists need an interest and ability in science. Mathematical ability is required as test results may be in numerical form. Their work demands a logical, methodical, problem-solving approach. Painstaking attention to detail, accuracy and sound judgement are essential.

Good written ability is necessary. Forensic scientists compile detailed reports on all examinations, with conclusions they have drawn from the scientific evidence. The reports must be clearly written and capable of being understood by whomever hears them in court.

Forensic scientists should be articulate and self-confident, as they may have to give evidence in court and be cross-examined.

It is important that forensic scientists are not squeamish, as scenes of crime can be unpleasant and distressing.

Forensic scientists must be able to work in a team. Although scientists tend to specialize in one area of forensics, they often need to work closely with scientists from different sections during a major police inquiry, as well as with police officers and lawyers.

ENTRY REQUIREMENTS

England and Wales

The minimum entry requirements are those for entry as an assistant forensic scientist.

Assistant forensic scientist: entry is with a minimum of either four GCSEs/S grades (A–C/1–3) including English and either maths or a relevant science, or Intermediate GNVQ/GSVQ Level II. In practice, most entrants have A level/H grade in chemistry and two from physics, maths and biology. BTEC/SQA higher national diploma in a science is accepted, entry to which requires a minimum of one relevant A level/H grade and three GCSEs/S grades (A–C/1–3), or Advanced GNVQ/GSVQ Level III science, or a relevant BTEC/SQA national award.

Forensic scientist: entry requires a good honours degree in science, usually chemistry- or biology-based, or degree-standard membership of a professional institution, or a BTEC/SQA higher national diploma/certificate in science.

In practice, most entrants have a degree in science, such as chemistry, physics or biology, or in an appropriate technology, such as metallurgy. Entry to degree courses is with two or three A levels/three or four H grades, usually including sciences and sometimes maths, and three GCSEs/two S grades (A–C/1–3) including maths and usually English; or a relevant Advanced GNVQ/GSVQ Level III; or a relevant BTEC/SQA national award.

Applicants with non-science A levels may be accepted onto a foundation year preceding the first year of a degree course in some institutions.

The University of Strathclyde's degree in Forensic and Analytical Chemistry requires three A levels including chemistry and maths and preferably either physics, biology or a modern European language; or four H grades

FORENSIC SCIENCE: QOT

including chemistry, maths and physics and preferably either English or a modern European language; or Advanced GNVQ/GSVQ Level III science with evidence of sufficient chemistry and maths and some physics; or BTEC/SQA national award, again with evidence of sufficient chemistry and maths and some physics.

The University of Bradford's degree in Chemistry with Pharmaceutical and Forensic Science requires three A levels including chemistry and at least one other science and a minimum of grade B in GCSE maths; or four H grades including chemistry and at least two other science or maths subjects; or Advanced GNVQ/GSVQ Level III in science plus A level/H grade chemistry; or a BTEC/SQA national award with sufficient chemistry content.

NB: The Universities of Strathclyde and Bradford require above average grades for entry to these degree courses. Consult the university prospectuses for detailed entry requirements. Postgraduate courses in forensic science require a relevant degree for entry.

Senior forensic scientist: entry is with a first- or second-class honours degree in a relevant subject, such as science or technology, and a number of years' relevant postgraduate experience.

Scotland

The minimum entry requirements are those for entry as a technician. Few are recruited at this level, however, the majority entering as basic grade forensic scientists.

Technician: entry is with a relevant SQA national award.

Basic grade forensic scientist: entry is with at least a first- or second-class honours degree in chemistry, biology or another relevant subject.

Good colour vision is essential. There are nationality rules that restrict entry to British, Commonwealth, EU and Irish Republic citizens and British protectorate persons.

TRAINING

Pre-entry

The University of Strathclyde offers a degree in Forensic and Analytical Chemistry (three or four years for A level entrants, four or five years for H grade entrants), which includes an industrial placement of five or twelve months' duration.

The University of Bradford offers BSc and MChem courses in Chemistry with Pharmaceutical and Forensic Science. The BSc course lasts three years full-time or four years on a sandwich programme with one year spent in industry. The MChem course is full-time over four years. The courses combine chemistry with forensic science and crime scene investigation, pharmaceutical and analytical chemistry and elements of forensic archaeology and anthropology.

Neither of these courses is exclusively concerned with forensic science, and graduates can seek openings in other fields open to chemistry graduates.

Strathclyde also offers postgraduate courses in forensic science – a diploma (nine months full-time) and an MSc (one or two years full-time). Kings College, London, offers an MSc course (one year full-time).

Although extremely useful, none of the above courses guarantees employment in forensic science.

On entry

Most forensic science training is in-house. It is laboratory-based and provided by experienced staff at the establishment concerned. Forensic Science Service staff may attend induction training at the training unit at Chepstow. All forensic science staff may attend specialist courses at Chepstow, dealing with subjects such as examining techniques, blood grouping and note taking.

Where appropriate, assistant forensic scientists and technicians are encouraged to continue their education up to degree level by day release.

NVQ/SVQ in Investigating Scenes of Incident at Level 3 and NVQ/SVQ in Recovery of Evidential Value (Laboratory Based) at Level 3 are available. NVQs/SVQs at Levels 4 and 5 are being developed.

LATE ENTRY

Mature entrants must have the qualifications described in ENTRY REQUIREMENTS and recent relevant experience, such as scientific research.

Adults may be considered for relevant higher education courses without the usual entry requirements. They may also prepare for application to higher education by taking an Access course. Access courses are offered at many colleges throughout the UK. They are usually one year full-time or one/two years part-time, with daytime and/or evening attendance.

OPPORTUNITIES

Most forensic scientists in England and Wales are employed by government or police laboratories. The largest single employer is the Forensic Science Service, an agency of the Home Office that employs approximately 500 scientists; the number has increased slightly in recent years, particularly at assistant forensic scientist level. The Service has six operational laboratories at Aldermaston, Birmingham, Chepstow, Chorley, Huntingdon and Wetherby, and a Central Research and Support Establishment at Birmingham, where forensic techniques and equipment are developed.

The Metropolitan Police Service Forensic Science Laboratory employs over 200 scientists.

Forensic scientists in Scotland are employed by the police in four laboratories – Strathclyde (Glasgow), Lothian and Borders (Edinburgh), Grampian (Aberdeen) and Tayside/Fife/Central (Dundee). The Scottish laboratories employ approximately 100 forensic scientists – an increase on past years.

There are also a number of private forensic science consultants in the UK and many official forensic laboratories abroad that may recruit British staff.

Vacancies are scarce. Any vacancies for assistant forensic scientists and technicians are advertised in the local press and at Jobcentres. Vacancies for other grades are advertised in the national press and in scientific journals such as *New Scientist*.

PAY AND CONDITIONS

The Forensic Science Service and Metropolitan Police forensic staff are on similar annual salary scales, with starting points depending on qualifications and experience.

The ranges are from £10,496 to £17,150 for assistant forensic scientists. Senior forensic scientists can earn up to £39,869. Those working in London receive an additional allowance.

FORENSIC SCIENCE: QOT

Forensic scientists in England and Wales usually work 41 or 42 hours a week (inclusive of lunch breaks) over five days. They work an on-call rota outside those hours to deal with serious crimes.

In Scotland annual salaries range from £16,281 to £20,337 for technicians. Basic grade forensic scientists start at £11,658 rising to £23,298. Senior scientists earn between £23,298 and £25,158. Principal scientists' pay rises to around £33,000. These rates and grades may vary between each Police Forensic Science Laboratory.

Forensic scientists in Scotland work a 36-hour five-day week (excluding lunch breaks), with an on-call rota outwith standard hours.

PROSPECTS

In England and Wales promotion is from assistant forensic scientist to forensic scientist, higher forensic scientist and senior forensic scientist. Further promotion in the Forensic Science Service is to grade 7 and beyond. With the Metropolitan Police further promotion is to principal scientific officer, senior principal scientific officer, assistant director and director. Promotion boards interview candidates recommended by their line managers as suitable for promotion. Transfer from one regional laboratory to another for promotion is common.

In Scotland, technicians who obtain a relevant degree may apply for a vacancy as a basic grade forensic scientist. Thereafter, promotion is to senior chemist or biologist, head of chemistry or biology (in Strathclyde only), deputy principal scientist and principal scientist. Transfer between laboratories for advancement is possible when vacancies arise.

RELATED OCCUPATIONS

Chemist, biologist, medical laboratory technician, biochemist, microbiologist, pharmacologist, laboratory technician.

FURTHER INFORMATION

The Forensic Science Service*, Priory House, Gooch Street North, Birmingham B5 6QQ, 0121 607 6800

The Forensic Science Society (FSS)*, Clarke House, 18A Mount Parade, Harrogate, North Yorkshire HG1 1BX, 01423 506068

Forensic Science Laboratory, Grampian Police Office, Nelson Street, Aberdeen AB2 3EQ, 01224 639111

Lothian and Borders Police Forensic Science Laboratory, 11 Howden Hall Road, Edinburgh EH16 6TF, 0131 666 1212

Metropolitan Police*, Forensic Science Laboratory, 109 Lambeth Road, London SE1 7LP, 0171 230 6181

The Police Forensic Science Laboratory, PO Box 59, West Bell Street, Dundee DD1 9JU, 01382 312291

Strathclyde Police Forensic Science Laboratory, Police Headquarters, Pitt Street, Glasgow G2 4JS, 0141 532 2318

Individual laboratories listed usually send requests for careers information to The Forensic Science Service.

FURTHER READING

Leaflets/booklets are available from the addresses marked*.

In the careers library classified under QOT.

GROUP R – ENGINEERING

ENGINEER CLCI: RAB

BACKGROUND INFORMATION

The results of engineering skills and knowledge surround us: from household goods, gadgets, clothing and medicines to transport, energy and telecommunications. Engineering is one of the widest occupational groups in the UK.

It is a multidisciplinary field which can be broadly divided into the following areas:

Civil and structural: working on different structures such as roads, tunnels, bridges, dams and housing;

Mechanical: working on all parts of machinery that move and keeping things running smoothly;

Electrical and electronic and manufacturing: involving power generation, telecommunications, electronics, controlling systems and computing;

Chemical: how raw materials change chemically and the processes involved;

Materials: working to maximize the performance of existing materials and develop new ones;

Aeronautical: design, manufacture and maintenance of aircraft, equipment and systems;

Information systems: designing and building computer systems to solve practical problems;

Systems: planning and implementing large-scale projects that require the integration of contributions from several groups of engineers in a wide variety of disciplines.

Other types of engineering include: agricultural, marine, mining and nuclear engineering. Within each area, there are different specializations. In electrical and electronic engineering, these specializations are areas in their own right. For example, electronics include: telecommunications, radar, satellites, microelectronics and information displays.

Engineers from different disciplines and specializations are involved at different stages in a particular process: from research and design to development and production through to running and maintaining and testing.

There are also different levels of engineering occupations. These levels relate to qualifications, the type of work done and the level of responsibility held. There are broadly five levels of engineering occupation: operator, craftsman/woman, engineering technician, incorporated engineer; chartered engineer.

At the levels of Engineering Technician, Incorporated Engineer and Chartered Engineer, each area of engineering has its standards set by its own professional institution. The Engineering Council is the institution for the profession as a whole.

THE WORK

Engineers are employed in all types of industries and with experience, they can choose from a variety of jobs in different types of organizations. As such, there is no typical engineering job. What engineers do depends on which stage of a process or project they are involved in and their level of responsibility.

There are different kinds of engineers in each specialization:

Research engineers find new or improved ways of doing things;

Design engineers turn ideas into plans for a real product;

Development engineers turn the design into a model for testing;

Production engineers decide how it is made and the skills, equipment and costs involved;

Control engineers regulate the systems and processes that produce the product.

System engineers have a broad knowledge of all areas and are able to perform trade-offs and decision making in complex projects.

One thing that is common to all engineering roles is working as part of a multidisciplinary team, whatever the level they start at. Engineers do not work in isolation. Liaison with others to find out the causes of a problem and the right solution is essential. They often work on a particular project and on a specific stage in that project. They also work with other engineering disciplines as well as with other specialists from areas such as research science, law and especially finance. Another thing they have in common is that they are likely to be using the latest technology, such as computer-aided design (CAD) and computer-aided engineering. The wide range of work involved is described below:

Operators might operate machinery or be involved in assembly work as part of the manufacturing process.

Craftsmen/women may install electrical circuits as electrical fitters, or produce and fit machinery parts together as mechanical fitters. Craftsmen/women will learn other skills, eg how to interpret engineering drawings and turn the design into a product.

The traditional boundaries dividing skills between a craftsperson and a technician are blurring as people learn a variety of skills at different levels.

Engineering Technicians are involved in designing, planning, testing, lab work or product development. As individuals in a team they are responsible for solving problems using standard procedures. They have some technical responsibility and usually work under the general supervision of incorporated or chartered engineers who head up the team. With experience, engineering technicians and craftsmen/women may work at supervisory level.

Incorporated Engineers have more individual responsibility for large amounts of complex equipment, for example. They may also have managerial responsibility as team leaders, responsible for the efficiency of the team. They may be responsible for managing quality, supervising inspection and test procedures or involved in developing diagnostic procedures and techniques.

There is an inevitable overlap in duties between Incorporated and Chartered Engineers.

Chartered Engineers would normally have more overall responsibility and be concerned with a broader range of activities. With experience, a chartered engineer may be responsible for an entire project, involved in strategic planning of engineering activities and functions or managing the development and implementation of new technologies.

In the manufacturing and construction industries, Chartered Engineers are managers of high-risk, capital-intensive projects. They liaise not only with other specialists and suppliers, but with clients to ensure a project meets their requirements and comes within the agreed budget.

ENGINEERING: RAB

WORK ENVIRONMENT

Engineers work in a variety of environments: on the factory floor, in a laboratory, outside on a building site or inside in an office. Working on a particular project, engineers can find themselves in different locations at different times. At the higher engineering levels, many projects are multi-site and that may involve working abroad.

Using highly sensitive, computer-operated equipment in laboratories and on the factory floor means that both the workplace and their hands are kept clean. On a building site or down a tunnel, the situation would be different. Safety procedures, however, are strictly adhered to throughout the industry.

Clothing is appropriate to the task engineers do at a particular time: overalls in a factory, safety wear outside on a construction site or a suit for a meeting with other specialists and clients.

SKILLS AND INTERESTS

Engineers should be interested in technology, mathematics and science. An interest in craft and design is also useful. Manual dexterity is important especially at the levels of operator and craftsman/woman.

A liking for problem solving is essential. Engineers need to have enquiring minds and be able to think logically. Creativity and imagination are also useful for example, in design. The ability to analyse complex information is important as is attention to detail. As a lot of work involves computers, IT skills are becoming more and more important. Engineers must be committed to improving their own learning and performance throughout their careers as they work in a fast changing environment.

Good communication and presentation skills both spoken and written are important. Engineers often have to explain complex scientific information to non-technical people.

Engineers must be able to work as part of a team and, if they are working in research for example, on their own as well. Being able to listen, compromise and negotiate with others is an important part of team working. Flexibility is essential and engineers sometimes need to take decisions based on incomplete data.

As engineers take on more responsibility, as project leaders for example, effective management skills are becoming more and more important. Good organizational skills, such as time management, are useful at all levels and increasingly, interpersonal skills and the ability to understand the needs of customers are highly valued. Engineers are increasingly being asked to combine their technical skills and training with good business skills and knowledge.

Team and cell working is increasingly becoming the way that work is organized in engineering production and requires increased levels of multiskilling and multifunction working.

ENTRY REQUIREMENTS

Operator

There are no formal entry requirements for entry into engineering as an operator. Those without qualifications, or with qualifications such as GCSEs/S grades (A–G/1–7) with no specific grades may become trainees. Employers will normally take people at any age. Sometimes employers require medical tests to be taken if the work requires a level of physical skills or fitness. Good colour vision is required particularly in electrical areas.

Craftsman/woman

Educational qualifications required are GCSEs/S grades (A–G/1–7) including maths, science or technology and English. Modern Apprenticeships (Skillseekers in Scotland) is the normal training route for craftsmen and women and many employers require grades A–C/1–3 in these key subjects. Age at entry is usually 16 to 17 years although 18- to 19-year-olds are also accepted. Some employers also use aptitude tests.

Engineering Technician (EngTech)

Entry requirements are five GCSEs/S grades (A–C/1–3) or equivalent including maths, science and English to study for a BTEC national diploma full time at college or start training with an employer and study for a BTEC national certificate on day release.

Incorporated Engineer (IEng)

To study for a BTEC/SQA certificate or higher national certificate/diploma course at university or college requires at least one A level/two H grades in maths, science or technology, or a BTEC/SQA national certificate/diploma in a practical or science based subject; or at least four GCSEs/S grades (A–C/1–3) including maths, English and science to start work and study for a qualification on day release.

Chartered Engineer (CEng)

The requirements for acceptance onto degree courses are two/three A levels, three/five H grades, including maths, English and science/technology or exceptional performance in a Higher National Certificate (HNC) or Higher National Diploma (HND) in Engineering or BTEC/ SQA or appropriate Advanced GNVQ/GSVQ Level III qualification,

TRAINING

There is increasing coherence between academic and vocational training for an engineering career. National Traineeships in Engineering became available in December 1997. Whilst they are aimed at 16- to 18-year-olds, other young people may also be eligible if they can complete the training before the age of 25 years.

Criteria for National Traineeships will include initial engineering training lasting eight weeks and covering a basic introduction to engineering. Following this, there are two routes: firstly a broad-based route designed for those without the full requirement of a Modern Apprenticeship but which includes the Foundation stage of a Modern Apprenticeship. The other route is an occupationally specific route (ie operator training) for those in skilled and semi-skilled employment, leading to at least NVQ/SVQ Level 2.

Operator

An operator receives on-the-job training under the charge of a supervisor. This training will include an overview of the company, its structure and policies, health and safety, as well as skills training on specialist machinery. As one of the training routes under National Traineeships it can lead to achieving an NVQ/SVQ Level 2.

Craftsman/woman

Training for young people is through Modern Apprenticeships, which provide a basis in engineering and

ENGINEERING: RAB

a route to higher level qualifications. They have two components: a foundation stage and a higher level post-foundation stage. Contact your local careers office, Jobcentre or TEC/LEC for details.

The foundation stages consist of mandatory components plus six technical units selected from a wider list. Formal Vocational Education (VE) is mandatory at this stage. Typically, attainment is a continuous pattern of off-the-job training in a centre and education at college. No fixed time for attainment is specified at this stage, although 24–26 weeks is usual.

The post-foundation stage takes place mostly on-the-job to develop skills leading to NVQ/SVQ Levels 3 and 4. Formal VE continues to be mandatory at this stage and normally leads to a BTEC/SQA national or higher national qualification, City and Guilds Part 2 or higher, or Advanced GNVQ/GSVQ Level III. Most Modern Apprentices attend college on day release.

Engineering Technician (EngTech)

Training can be full-time at a further education college leading to a BTEC/SQA national or higher national certificate, followed by at least two years' appropriate on-the-job training. The other route is a Modern Apprenticeship leading to an NVQ/SVQ Level 3 or 4, with day release for vocational education leading to BTEC/SQA national or higher national certificate.

Incorporated Engineer (IEng)

Training is by enrolment on a university degree course accredited for IEng. Alternatively, two years' full-time study for a BTEC/SQA Higher National Diploma or a three-year sandwich course can be undertaken. Another route is on a Modern Apprenticeship leading to an NVQ/SVQ Level 4 with study on day release leading to a BTEC/SQA higher national certificate. All routes must be followed by appropriate training and responsible experience, both of which take a minimum of two years.

Chartered Engineer (CEng)

A CEng-accredited university degree course usually lasts three years full-time and can include industrial placements. There are various sandwich courses lasting four or five years. After qualifying, periods of appropriate training and responsible experience are required. A minimum of two years each is required for corporate membership of a nominated chartered engineering institution.

Degree courses vary, some specializing in a particular branch of engineering, some combining various branches and others combining with subjects like languages or business studies. There are many new developments, such as semester terms and modular courses. Some university courses also offer a four-year Master of Engineering degree as a first degree.

Those with a non-accredited degree or who have taken different routes, may take Engineering Council Examinations (Parts 1 and 2). There are university preparatory courses for these examinations.

Professional qualifications

Enrolment on the professional register held by The Engineering Council has to fulfil criteria at three stages: Stage 1 – registration with the Engineering Council (after achieving the required academic standard); Stage 2 – approved and appropriate level of training; Stage 3 – responsible engineering experience.

Stage 1: Registration with the Engineering Council

This is fulfilled by passing a course accredited by a particular engineering institution. Accreditation means that courses meet the requirements of that institution as well as the Engineering Council for course content, technical grounding and quality of facilities. Enrolment on a non-accredited course requires qualifications being assessed by the relevant institution, and Engineering Council examinations may be necessary as well.

All candidates for registration are assessed at a standards-based professional review. This includes an interview which covers current competence to practise and also the candidate's commitment to continuing professional development (CPD).

Stage 2: Appropriate training

Approved levels of training may be gained through an accredited training scheme, which many engineering institutions administer and which usually lasts at least two years.

Stage 3: Responsible engineering experience

To qualify, a candidate must demonstrate having gained responsible engineering experience, which charts at least two years of career development. This means having a degree of autonomy in decision making, problem solving and the exercise of independent judgement. To become a Chartered Chemical Engineer with IChemE, for example, candidates undergo a professional appraisal. This is an assessment of a report showing the nature and extent of training and experience across a number of chemical engineering aspects and practices.

NB: After a review, the Engineering Council is in the process of reshaping its qualification requirements for CEng and IEng qualifications. The proposals are that the educational standard for an incorporated engineer will be a three-year BEng degree, replacing previous/current higher national certificate/diploma criteria.

For Chartered Engineers, the proposed path will be a four-year accredited MEng degree or a three-year honours degree plus appropriate complementary postgraduate study. This will replace the current three-year honours degree.

Engineering Technician will remain unaltered at national certificate level, but with the NVQ/SVQ, GNVQ/GSVQ and Modern Apprenticeship routes being emphasized for 16- to 19-year-olds.

For further information, contact the Engineering Council or the specific institutional body.

LATE ENTRY

Although there are minimum age limits for attaining engineering titles, there are no upper age limits for those wanting to progress through the profession. In practical terms, the limiting factors are the time taken to achieve the training and the levels of experience and qualifications obtained. Usually the decision to become an engineer is made relatively early.

As there are so many paths to reach the different levels, training can, in theory, begin at any age. Because of the time it takes to reach the higher levels, however, it is unusual for very late entry. It is uncommon for people to choose engineering as a second career. Those working in related occupations may decide to specialize at a later stage and they can choose one of the many work-based training options available. In this instance, they may be able to obtain funding from their company.

ENGINEERING: RAB

OPPORTUNITIES

Demand for engineers is high, particularly those with the highest qualifications. This demand is across many industries, not just in engineering, especially in management roles. This is because engineers are numerate, are used to making decisions and are able to adopt inter-disciplinary approaches to problem-solving and project work. More and more, flexibility of skills and adaptability is what industry is asking for.

Seventy-eight per cent of graduates take up jobs in industry, twelve per cent go into finance or commerce and the remaining ten per cent into other fields like teaching, training or the armed forces. Many job opportunities exist, from self-employed to working for small specialized companies through to multinationals. There are many areas of work: research, design and development of new products and processes; manufacture and construction, from component parts at one extreme to large scale projects at the other; jobs involved in maintenance of machines or structures; specialist back-up and support functions, such as accountants and salesmen.

Greater levels of experience make an engineer more valuable across a range of industries, and a range of areas across a company. Technical knowledge gained in an engineering speciality is valued in non-technical areas like marketing or accountancy.

Engineering is becoming more attractive to women and the numbers enrolling on degree courses rose from seven per cent to fifteen per cent of total enrolment between 1984 and 1995. Many women are attracted by some areas of engineering that are newer and faster developing such as information systems sector.

Sponsorship is one method firms are using to help them attract the best recruits. Candidates usually receive a bursary while studying at university and are expected to spend vacation periods on paid work for the company.

Engineering work, particularly for multinationals, offers the opportunity for overseas postings. This may sometimes be for several years, but more often for a short duration of a week to several months on specific projects.

Engineers are valuable as generalists. Knowledge of the latest tools, materials and technologies is a key attribute. Technology is increasingly cross-disciplinary which is now being reflected in engineering training courses.

Use of technology, computers and telecommunications is growing in all industries and there has thus been a growth in support industries to serve this. The manufacture of electronic, telecommunications and IT equipment, plus software engineering has shown large growth rates over the last 15 years. This means there are opportunities for highly qualified engineers, regardless of age, to earn high salaries and receive rapid promotion.

PAY AND CONDITIONS

Engineering, especially at professional level is a highly trained occupation. This is reflected in salary levels. Chartered engineers' salaries are comparable to those of solicitors and financial specialists and higher than marketing managers and accountants.

Salaries vary according to the branch of engineering you are in, the level of qualifications obtained and whether you are a member of an association. Chemical engineering is traditionally the highest paid of the professional groups. The higher your qualification, the more you will be paid.

Average starting salaries for graduates aged under 25 range from £15,000 to £17,000. With experience, qualifications and membership of a professional association these can rise to £20,000 to 28,000 by the age of 29 and then up to £29,000 to 38,000 by the age of 39. Engineering Council research shows that the average salary for chartered engineers is £40,000, incorporated engineers £30,000 and engineering technicians £26,000. The Institution of Chemical Engineers report that one in twenty chartered chemical engineers earn over £50,000.

Working days vary according to the industry. Starting times vary according to the type of work and industry. Some may involve working unsocial hours, such as in factories that operate 24-hour shifts. As in many jobs, working to a tight deadline may involve putting in a lot of hours, especially if it means that a delay in one part of a project will cause delays in other areas.

PROSPECTS

Engineering includes highly versatile training and is a highly respected profession. The prospects for promotion are directly linked to increased qualifications as well as having the necessary experience. Engineers usually change jobs and departments as their careers develop. As they go up each level, they have more seniority and responsibility. From starting having a small role in a project, they can become a project leader – responsible for all aspects of running a project – up to running a whole department or section.

At the higher professional levels, there are many opportunities to cross into other less obviously technical fields, such as marketing, sales and general management. Given the diverse nature of the career, there are also many opportunities to move across different industries. As engineering standards and qualifications are respected internationally, there are a large number of opportunities overseas. Like any other job, it is experience and ability that counts.

There are also many high-level engineers who are self-employed and work on a freelance basis and run or are part of specialist consultancy firms.

RELATED OCCUPATIONS

Principal planner, project leader, development technologist, laboratory technician, estimator, draughtsperson, toolmaker, building operative, machinist, fitter.

FURTHER INFORMATION

Engineering and Marine Training Authority (EMTA)*, Vector House, 41 Clarendon Rd, Watford, Herts WD1 1HS, 01923 238 441 or 0800 282167 (careers information), ww.emta.org.uk

The Association of Cost Engineers, Lea House, 5 Middlewich Road, Sandbach, Cheshire CW11 1XL, 01270 764798

The British Computer Society*, 1 Sanford St, Swindon SN1 1HJ, 01793 417417

The British Institute of Non-Destructive Testing*, 1 Spencer Parade, Northampton NN1 5AA, 01604 30124, www.powertech.co.uk/bindt

ENGINEERING: RAB

The Civil Engineering Careers Service*(CECS), 1 Great George Street, London SW1P 3AA, 0171 222 7722, www.ice.org.uk

The Chartered Institution of Building Service Engineers*, Delta House, 222 Balham High Rd, London SW12 9BS, 0181 675 5211, www.cibse.org.uk

The Chartered Institution of Water and Environmental Management, 15 John St, London WC1N 2EB, 0171 831 3110, www.ciwem.org.uk

The Engineering Council*, 10 Maltravers St, London WC2R 3ER, 0171 240 7891, www.engc.org.uk

The Institute of Acoustics, Agriculture House, 5 Holywell Hill, St Albans, Herts AL1 1EU, 01727 848195, ioa.essex.ac.uk.ioa

The Institute of British Foundrymen *, Bordesley Hall, The Holloway, Alvechurch, Birmingham B48 7QA, 01527 596100, ourwall.compuserve.com

The Institute of Energy, 18 Devonshire St, London W1N 2AU, 0171 580 7124

The Institute of Engineers and Technicians*, 100 Grove Vale, London SE22 8DR, 0181 693 1255. www.instenergy.org.uk

The Institute of Healthcare Engineering and Estate Management*, 2 Abingdon House, Cumberland Business Centre, Northumberland Rd, Portsmouth PO5 1DS, 01705 823 186

The Institute of Highway Incorporated Engineers, 20 Queensberry Place, London SW7 2DR, 0171 823 9093, www.hemming-group.co.uk/logon

The Institute of Marine Engineers, The Memorial Building, 76 Mark Lane, London EC3R 7JN, 0171 488 8493, www.imare.org.uk

The Institute of Materials*, 1 Carlton House Terrace, London SW1Y 5DB, 0171 839 4071

The Institute of Measurement and Control, 87 Gower St, London WC1E 6AA, 0171 387 4949

The Institute of Physics, 76–78 Portland Place, London W1N 4AA, 0171 470 4800, www.iop.org.uk

The Institute of Plumbing, 64 Station Lane, Hornchurch, Essex RM12 6NB. 01708 472 791, www.plumbers.org.uk

The Institute of Quality Assurance, PO Box 712, 2 Southwark St, London SE1 1SB, 0171 401 7227

The Institute of Road Transport Engineers, 22 Greencoat Place, London SW1P 1PR, 0171 630 1111

The Institution of Agricultural Engineers, West End Rd, Silsoe, Bedford MK45 4DU, 01525 861 096. www.silsoe.cranfield.ac.uk

The Institution of Chemical Engineers*, 165–189 Railway Terrace, Rugby CV21 3HQ, 01788 578 214, www.icheme.org.uk

The Institution of Civil Engineers*, 1 Great George St, London SW1P 3AA, 0171 222 7722, www.ice.org.uk

The Institution of Electrical Engineers*, Educational Activities, Michael Faraday House, Six Hills Way, Stevenage, Hertfordshire SG1 2AY 1438 313311, www.iee.org.uk

The Institution of Electronics and Electrical Incorporated Engineers*, Savoy Hill House, Savoy Hill, London WC2R OBS, 0171 836 3357

The Institution of Engineering Designers*, Courtleigh, Westbury Leigh, Westbury, Wilts BA13 3TA, 01373 822801, www.ied.org.uk

The Institution of Gas Engineers, 21 Portland Place, London W1N 3AF, 0171 636 6603

The Institution of Incorporated Executive Engineers*, Wix Hill House, West Horsley, Surrey KT24 6DZ, 01483 222383

The Institution of Lighting Engineers, Lennox House, 9 Lawford Rd, Rugby CV21 2DZ, 01788 576492

The Institution of Mechanical Engineers*, Schools Liaison Service, Northgate Avenue, Bury St Edmunds, Suffolk IP32 6BN. 01284 763 277. www.imeche.org.uk

The Institution of Mechanical Incorporated Engineers*, 3 Birdcage Walk, London SW1H 9JN, 0171 799 1808.

The Institution of Mining and Metallurgy, 44 Portland Place, London W1N 4BR, 0171 580 3802, www.imm.org.uk

The Institution of Mining Engineers*, Danum House, South Parade, Doncaster DN1 2DY, 01302 320 486

The Institution of Nuclear Engineers, Allan House, 1 Penerley Rd, London SE6 2LQ, 0181 698 1500

The Institution of Plant Engineers, 77 Great Peter Street, London SW1P 2EZ, 0171 233 2855

The Institution of Structural Engineers*, 11 Upper Belgrave St, London SW1X 8BH, 0171 235 4535

The Institution of Water Officers, 12 Summerhill Terrace, Newcastle-upon-Tyne NE4 6EB, 0191 230 5150

The Royal Aeronautical Society, 4 Hamilton Place, London W1V 0BQ, 0171 499 3515, www.raes.org.uk

The Royal Institution of Naval Architects, 10 Upper Belgrave Street, London SW1X 8BQ, 0171 235 4622

The Welding Institute, Abington Hall, Abington, Cambridge CB1 6AL, 01223 891162

FURTHER READING

Leaflets and booklets are available from the addresses in the previous section marked*.

Working in Engineering – COIC

The Engineering Profession – Ivanhoe Career Guides – in association with The Engineering Council.

In the careers library classified under RAB.

VEHICLE MAINTENANCE: RAE/RON

1. **MOTOR MECHANIC/VEHICLE TECHNICIAN CLCI:RAE**
2. **VEHICLE BODY REPAIRER CLCI:RON**

1. MOTOR MECHANIC/VEHICLE TECHNICIAN (RAE)

BACKGROUND INFORMATION

There are about 24 million motor vehicles in Britain. These range from the family car to heavy lorries, passenger transport buses to racing cars and motorcycles. All of these vehicles require regular maintenance and repairs in order to keep them functioning efficiently and safely. This work is carried out by mechanics, technicians, and vehicle body repairers.

Broadly speaking, motor mechanics carry out the routine work, while vehicle technicians tend to occupy senior positions such as workshop foreman or supervisor and carry out the more complicated diagnostic tasks.

Mechanics and technicians may choose to specialize in light vehicles; cars, vans, or motorcycles, whilst others tackle the big lorries or public service vehicles; buses and coaches. They apply their skills in a range of environments; fast-fit centres, local garages, car or motorcycle dealerships, haulage companies, bus and coach companies or even providing emergency roadside assistance to stranded motorists.

In some garages they may undertake all types of work including working on petrol and diesel engine vehicles. There are also opportunities for fitters who specialize in vehicle systems replacement such as exhausts or tyres. Please see article TYRE/EXHAUST FITTER (OFM/RAE).

THE WORK

The day-to-day work involves routine servicing and tuning, replacing worn components and units, fitting accessories, overhauling and reconditioning components, carrying out road tests, using specialized equipment to measure performance, make adjustments and diagnose, locate and repair faults including electrical and electronic faults.

A good deal of the work involves servicing and changing parts rather than actually repairing them. This is because modern cars are more reliable than they used to be, and it is often quicker and therefore cheaper, to replace a part rather than make a time-consuming (and costly) repair.

Light vehicle maintenance

Mechanics and technicians working in garages that service and repair cars for private and business customers carry out a wide range of tasks:

Routine servicing is performed at regular intervals based on time or mileage according to instructions laid down by the vehicle manufacturer. Some services are basic and involve checking components, changing the oil and filter and checking lubricants, while a major service can involve checking all the systems on the car.

Mechanics/technicians work through a checklist of items. They record faults on a job card, noting the part number of any replacement parts. Usually the customer is contacted for authorization before the new part is fitted. Each type of service has to be carried out in a specified time, so the mechanic/technician must work quickly and accurately.

Mechanical faults reported by the customer are investigated and appropriate steps are taken to remedy the problem. This may involve stripping down the relevant unit (engine, gearbox etc.), identifying and replacing faulty components, and re-assembling the unit, ensuring parts are secure and correctly adjusted.

Electrical and electronic systems in modern vehicles are becoming increasingly sophisticated. These may include computer-controlled engine management systems, electronic ignition, digital display dashboards and electrically operated seats and windows.

On modern vehicles, mechanics/technicians can connect a laptop computer to the vehicle's Electronic Control Unit (ECU) and use a keyboard to enter details about the vehicle. From an on-screen menu they can select the system they want to access (eg brakes, suspension, transmission etc). The computer reports the fault, for example, loose connections or a break in the circuit wiring. Appropriate action is then taken to remedy the problem. This makes the whole business of diagnosing electrical faults very much quicker than it used to be.

Many older vehicles do not have an ECU. Components therefore, are checked using electrical testing equipment such as voltmeters and ammeters. Most testing is done in the car, using portable equipment, or on a test bench. Mechanics and technicians must be able to read and understand wiring diagrams to guide them in their work.

Pre-delivery inspections are carried out to ensure new vehicles are in good order before the customer takes possession: engine tuning – using specialized equipment to measure and adjust engine performance; road testing – to confirm that faults have been corrected.

Heavy vehicle maintenance

Much of the work of heavy-vehicle mechanics/technicians is similar to that of light-vehicle mechanics/technicians and is carried out in large workshop/garage premises.

Heavy-vehicle mechanics and technicians also carry out routine servicing. The aim is to ensure vehicles are maintained in a road-worthy condition to minimize off-road time caused by breakdowns. As well as routine servicing of steering, brakes, carburettors etc, major overhauls are undertaken at regular intervals. Vehicles are stripped of their working parts. These are dismantled, cleaned, checked and re-assembled in the shortest possible time.

Because the cost of new parts for heavy vehicles is so much higher, worn-out parts often have to be repaired rather than replaced. Heavy-vehicle mechanics/ technicians may have to make replacement parts such as body panels.

Motorcycle maintenance

The sale and repair of motorcycles is usually carried out by garages that specialize in this kind of work. Mechanics/technicians undertake all aspects of motorcycle maintenance. They also assemble new motorcycles for sale, as these are delivered by manufacturers in parts. They work on a wide variety of machines, and in small dealerships also do some reception and sales work.

Mechanics/technicians use a variety of hand and power tools including spanners, wrenches, screwdrivers and drills. They may also use soldering and welding equipment in the course of their work.

VEHICLE MAINTENANCE: RAE/RON

WORK ENVIRONMENT

Most modern workshops/garages are large, airy and well lit, and many are heated. However, these can still be cold environments in the winter months when doors may be left open to provide access or to help clear exhaust fumes. Workshops/garages normally have concrete or tiled floors with inspection pits and ramps. The presence of lubricants can mean conditions are oily/greasy at times. Mechanics and technicians also work outside when attending vehicle breakdowns at the roadside. This can mean working in all weathers.

SKILLS AND INTERESTS

Much of the work involves bending, stretching and lying in or under vehicles, often in cramped or uncomfortable positions. Lifting gear is used, for example, when removing engines. Mechanics and technicians need sufficient manual dexterity to work with small, delicate components such as washers, nuts and bolts. They need good practical skills such as soldering and welding. They must work safely and wear correct safety clothing (eg overalls and safety boots) as appropriate.

They must be able to work accurately and methodically, paying close attention to detail. They need the ability to follow spoken and written instructions, work as part of a team, and independently without supervision, using their own initiative especially when diagnosing faults.

Good interpersonal skills are required in order to communicate with colleagues and to explain faults and corrective procedures to non-technical persons, particularly the general public. For most mechanics a driving licence is essential.

ENTRY REQUIREMENTS

No minimum entry qualifications are specified, however, employers look for a reasonable standard of education and many require four GCSEs/S grades (A–C/1–3) including maths, English and a science subject or equivalent, for example Intermediate GNVQ/GSVQ Level II in Engineering.

All applicants to ReMIT are required to take an aptitude test, the results of which are taken into consideration when deciding an applicant's level of entry.

Entry to BTEC national diploma/certificate courses in motor vehicle engineering is with four GCSEs/S grades (A–C/1–3) or equivalent, including maths, English and a science subject. Entry requirements to SQA national certificate module courses vary between colleges.

TRAINING

Craft level

Training for school-leavers leads to craft level qualifications at NVQ/SVQ Levels 2 and 3. Most train in the workplace with day or block release at college. However, assessment may take place solely in the workplace. Most normally complete training to NVQ/SVQ Level 3 within three and a half years.

NVQs/SVQs are available at Level 2 in Vehicle Mechanical & Electronic Systems – Unit Replacement; at Level 3, Vehicle Mechanical & Electronic Systems – Maintenance and Repair (Light Vehicles; Heavy Vehicles; Motorcycles).

Technician level

Training for school-leavers leading to technician level qualifications may be via a Modern Apprenticeship. These last between three and four years and are progressed through NVQ/SVQ awards at Levels 2 and 3 as well as BTEC HNC/HND awards.

Alternatively, BTEC national certificate/diploma courses are offered at further education colleges throughout the country. These may be studied full-time, or part-time with day or block release whilst in employment. Success at this level can lead directly to HND/HNC studies.

Beyond this level, manufacturers run their own specialist training schemes successful completion of which can lead to technician status.

National Traineeships (leading to NVQ/SVQ Level 1 and 2) are available.

Modern Apprenticeships (part of the Skillseekers Initiative in Scotland), leading to at least an NVQ/SVQ Level 3, may be available for young people. Contact your local careers office, TEC, LEC or ReMIT for details.

The Retail Motor Industry Federation (RMIF) has established ReMIT as the training arm of the Federation. ReMIT runs a wide programme of training courses at every level – from unskilled beginner to top management. Although ReMIT covers every type and level of training, a large proportion of courses concentrate on training for young people funded by the Government through Training Enterprise Councils (TECs) and Local Enterprise Companies (LECs). These courses are based on the framework of NVQs/SVQs. Subject to the ability of each trainee, ReMIT aims to bring trainees to Level 3 standard. At least half of ReMIT's 8,000 trainees are in Modern Apprenticeship schemes.

LATE ENTRY

Though most join as school-leavers, training opportunities for adults – including NVQs/SVQs and BTEC certificates and diplomas – are available as above.

OPPORTUNITIES

More than 800,000 people work in the motor industry and there is a steady demand for trained mechanics and technicians. Opportunities exist throughout the country. Most light-vehicle mechanics work in garages that range from one-person operations to large main dealers specializing in one particular make of vehicle. A mechanic in a small garage is likely to carry out a range of tasks, while in larger garages they may specialize in a particular area (eg engines). As vehicles have become more technologically advanced, there are opportunities for mechanics and technicians to specialize in electrical and electronic systems. Opportunities also exist for semi-skilled workers in 'fast-fit' outlets which specialize in a particular repair or service (eg tyre and exhaust fitting).

Heavy-vehicle mechanics are usually employed by organizations with a fleet of vehicles that must be regularly serviced and maintained. These include haulage and distribution companies, bus companies and public utilities.

Other possible employers include the Armed Forces (who run their own training schemes). The AA and RAC employ those with a proven auto mechanical background and excellent communication skills to operate as patrol persons. Both these organizations offer induction and ongoing training. The AA employ women as well as men as patrol persons; the RAC employ only male patrol persons.

PAY AND CONDITIONS

Mechanics, technicians, apprentices and trainees receive hourly rates of pay on a scale guided by the National Joint Council (NJC) of the Retail Motor Industry Federation. Rates for qualified mechanics and technicians depend on qualifications and experience and therefore vary from employer to employer. In addition, company supplements, bonuses and allowances can increase pay by 100 per cent or more. Some employers offer discounts and free overalls. Trainees normally have to buy their own tools, but most employers will help with loans or credit.

Mechanics and technicians normally work a 39-hour week, from 8am to 5pm, Monday to Friday. Some firms work evening or Saturday morning overtime. Garages operating a 24-hour breakdown service have a shift rota system, though heavy vehicle firms may operate a 24-hour on-call system instead. Some heavy-vehicle companies only service vehicles at night.

As a guide, pay-scales are:

Motor mechanics and technicians: between £3.25 and £4.48 per hour;

Modern Apprentices: between £1.99 and £3.76 per hour according to phase of training;

Unindentured Trainees: between £1.97 and £2.79 per hour according to their stage of training.

PROSPECTS

Promotion to supervisory and management positions is common and most progress through jobs as motor mechanics/vehicle technicians or related occupations. Qualified and experienced motor mechanics and technicians may set up in business on their own, although the cost of equipment and premises can be considerable.

Opportunities may also exist to work overseas in Europe and elsewhere. For those with supervisory qualifications and experience, opportunities may also exist in developing countries.

RELATED OCCUPATIONS

Agricultural/horticultural machinery mechanic, tyre/exhaust fitter, AA/RAC patrolperson, plant fitter/mechanic, sheet metal worker, welder.

FURTHER INFORMATION AND READING

Please see article 2. VEHICLE BODY REPAIRER.

2. VEHICLE BODY REPAIRER (RON)

BACKGROUND INFORMATION

Vehicles require repair as a result of accident damage or metal corrosion. Vehicle body repairers carry out this work. They build or alter vehicle bodies according to the customer's or employer's specifications. Duties may include fabrication and welding, jig assembly manufacturing, glazing, finishing and fitting special equipment.

Vehicle body repair tends to divide into panel work and spray-painting. In some workshops body repairers will do both types of work, while in others specialist spray painters are employed who may not do any panel work.

THE WORK

A vehicle with a badly damaged chassis needs first to be straightened on a 'jig'. The vehicle is bolted to brackets on a large ramp and then a machine is used to pull it into square.

Before painting, the vehicle must be cleaned with solvents and new panels rubbed down by sanding. In some cases panels are sandblasted down to bare metal to expose any defects. Areas not to be painted have to be masked off. The new body panels are then primed and rubbed down to give a smooth and shiny surface to which paint will adhere smoothly and evenly.

A difficult part of the work can be matching the colour of the re-spray paint to the rest of the vehicle. Most cars have a colour code number which allows the repairer to check on the exact mix of colours required, but this is not available for all vehicles. The exact colour and shade may then have to be mixed by hand.

Paint spraying is carried out in spray booths. Several coats of paint are normally required, with each one allowed to dry before the next is applied. The final coat is polished to a high gloss finish. Finally, masking materials are removed and fittings and accessories re-fitted.

Panel work involves repairing or renewing body panels that have been damaged as a result of corrosion or accidents. Minor damage such as dents can be hammered out using a 'dolly'. Small depressions or corroded areas have to be filled with resin, body solder or other filler compounds. Where damage is too great for repair, a new panel has to be fitted. This may be obtained from stock, ordered from the manufacturer, or cut and shaped from sheet metal. It must then be carefully aligned, and riveted or welded into position.

WORK ENVIRONMENT

Most body repair work is carried out indoors in workshops or paint-spraying booths which are fitted with extractor fans. However, these can still be cold environments in the winter months when doors may be left open to provide access or to help clear dust and paint fumes. Workshops/garages normally have concrete floors with inspection pits and ramps fitted with jig assemblies. The presence of lubricants can mean conditions are oily/greasy at times.

SKILLS AND INTERESTS

Much of the work involves bending, stretching and lying in or under vehicles, often in cramped or uncomfortable positions. Lifting gear is used, for example, when dismantling vehicles in preparation for body work. Vehicle body repairers need normal colour vision, and good practical hand skills eg for dismantling and welding vehicle parts. They must work safely and wear correct safety clothing (eg protective masks, glasses, gloves) as appropriate.

Repairers need patience to carry out sometimes laborious tasks (such as sanding down filler) and must be able to work accurately and methodically, paying close attention to detail. They need the ability to follow spoken and

VEHICLE MAINTENANCE: RAE/RON

written instructions, work as part of a team and independently without supervision, using their own initiative to decide on repair methods.

Good interpersonal skills are required in order to communicate with colleagues and to explain faults and corrective procedures to non-technical persons, particularly the general public. For most repairers a driving licence is essential.

ENTRY REQUIREMENTS

No minimum entry qualifications are specified, however, employers look for a reasonable standard of education and many require four GCSEs/S grades (A–C/1–3) including maths, English and a science subject or equivalent, for example Intermediate GNVQ/GSVQ Level II in Engineering.

All applicants to ReMIT are required to take an aptitude test, the results of which are taken into consideration when deciding an applicant's level of entry.

TRAINING

Craft level

Training for school-leavers leads to craft level qualifications at NVQ/SVQ Levels 2 and 3. Most train in the workplace with day or block release at college. However, up to NVQ/SVQ Level 2, assessment may take place solely in the workplace. Thereafter trainees also attend college on day or block release. Most normally complete training to NVQ/SVQ Level 3 within three and a half years.

NVQs/SVQs are available at Level 2 in Vehicle Body Fitting, and at Level 3: Vehicle Body Repair, and Vehicle Re-finishing.

Technician level

Training for school-leavers leading to technician level qualifications may be via a Modern Apprenticeship. These last between three and four years and are progressed through NVQ/SVQ awards at Levels 2 and 3.

Beyond this level, manufacturers run their own specialist training schemes successful completion of which can lead to technician status.

National Traineeships (leading to NVQ/SVQ Level 1 and 2) are available.

Modern Apprenticeships (part of the Skillseekers Initiative in Scotland) leading to at least an NVQ/SVQ Level 3, may be available for young people. Contact your local careers office, TEC, LEC or ReMIT for details.

The Retail Motor Industry Federation (RMIF) has established ReMIT as the training arm of the Federation. ReMIT runs a wide programme of training courses at every level – from unskilled beginner to top management. Although ReMIT covers every type and level of training, a large proportion of courses concentrate on training for young people funded by the Government through Training Enterprise Councils (TECs) and Local Enterprise Companies (LECs). These courses are based on the framework of NVQs/SVQs. Subject to the ability of each trainee, ReMIT aims to bring trainees to Level 3 standard. At least half of ReMIT's 8,000 trainees are in Modern Apprenticeship schemes.

LATE ENTRY

Though most join as school-leavers, training opportunities for adults – including NVQs/SVQs – are available as above. Related experience (eg in vehicle maintenance) can be useful.

OPPORTUNITIES

There is a steady demand for trained vehicle body repairers. Opportunities exist throughout the country. Most work in garages that range from one-person operations to large main dealers specializing in one particular make of vehicle. In small garages, they carry out both vehicle body repair and vehicle paint-spraying, while in larger garages they may specialize in either vehicle body repair or vehicle paint-spraying. Other opportunities are with specialist vehicle repair firms, and with firms of vehicle restorers. Large fleet operators employ vehicle body repairers in their maintenance workshops. These include haulage and distribution firms, bus and coach companies and public utilities.

PAY AND CONDITIONS

Vehicle body repairers, apprentices and trainees receive minimum hourly rates of pay on a scale set by the Retail Motor Industry Federation. These rates are similar to those for motor mechanics (please see article 1. MOTOR MECHANIC/VEHICLE TECHNICIAN).

Pay rates for qualified vehicle body repairers depend on qualifications and experience and therefore vary from employer to employer. In addition, company supplements, bonuses and allowances can increase pay by 100 per cent or more. Some employers offer discounts and free overalls. Trainees normally have to buy their own tools, but most employers will help with loans or credit.

Vehicle body repairers normally work a 39-our week, from 8am to 5pm, Monday to Friday. Some firms work evening or Saturday morning overtime. Large companies that run fleets of vehicles may have a shift rota system. Some operators may only conduct vehicle body repairs at night.

PROSPECTS

Promotion to supervisory and management positions in larger organizations is common and most progress through jobs as vehicle body repairers. Those who are qualified and experienced may set up in business on their own, although the cost of equipment and premises can be considerable.

RELATED OCCUPATIONS

Sheet metal worker, welder, vehicle restorer, motor mechanic/vehicle technician, agricultural/horticultural machinery mechanic, tyre/exhaust fitter.

FURTHER INFORMATION

AA, Fanum House, Basing View, Basingstoke, Hampshire RG21 4EA, 0990 448866

Bus and Coach Training Limited, Regency House, 43 High Street, Rickmansworth, Herts WD3 1ET, 01923 896607

Engineering and Marine Training Authority (EMTA), 41 Clarendon Road, Watford, Hertfordshire WD1 1HS, 0800 282167

VEHICLE MAINTENANCE: RAE/RON

RAC, M1 Cross, Brent Terrace, NW2 1LT, 0181 4528000

ReMIT:

England: 201 Great Portland Street, London, W1N 6AB, 0171 580 9122;

Scotland: 5B, The Knowes, Kelso TD5 7BH, 01573 224377

Retail Motor Industry Federation (RMIF), 201 Great Portland Street, London W1N 6AB, 0171 580 9122

Road Haulage & Distribution Training Council (RHDTC), 14 Warren Yard, Warren Farm Office Village, Stratford Road, Milton Keynes MK12 5NW, 01908 313360

The Scottish Motor Trade Association, 3 Palmerston Place, Edinburgh EH12 5AF, 0131 225 3643

Society of Motor Manufacturers and Traders Ltd (SMMT), Forbes House, Halkin Street, London SW1X 7DS, 0171 235 7000

FURTHER READING

Leaflets/booklets from the above addresses.

Working in the Motor Industry – COIC

Working in Engineering – COIC

Careers in the Motor Industry – SMMT

In the careers library classified under RAE/RON

ELECTRICAL WORK: RAK

ELECTRICIAN CLCI:RAK

BACKGROUND INFORMATION

Although the skills and knowledge of the craft electrician apply to all electricians, their actual jobs vary considerably depending on the industry in which they are trained and employed.

Installation electricians install the wiring in new buildings and conversions of old buildings. The wiring includes that needed for equipment and machinery as well as for light, heat and power points.

Maintenance electricians maintain the basic circuitry, and service the machines used in manufacturing processes.

Production electricians install the wiring and electrical components in more complex electrical and electronic appliances and products.

Electricians in the electricity supply industry install and maintain transformer stations, and **in electricity power stations** maintain the electrical aspects.

Service electricians repair faults in domestic appliances and office and factory machines. Please see articles DOMESTIC APPLIANCE/GAS SERVICE ENGINEER (ROK) and BUSINESS EQUIPMENT SERVICE ENGINEER (ROK).

Auto-electricians service the electrical wiring and components in cars, trucks and buses. Please see article MOTOR MECHANIC/VEHICLE TECHNICIAN (RAE).

Safety

Electricity is dangerous; electricians rarely work where the system is live. Installation electricians' work is often done before the electricity supply is connected. The work of production electricians only receives current when the test technicians take over. A first rule for electricians, whether in homes or in factories, is to isolate the circuit before starting work.

However, some faults can only be located with the current flowing, eg in electronic circuits. Specially insulated tools and test instruments are used for these.

Where high voltages are involved, as in electricity generation and distribution, a strict 'permit to work' system is enforced. Electrical engineers certify that equipment being serviced is isolated from power.

THE WORK

Installation electricians install the wiring in houses. They decide from the architect's or contractor's drawing where to run the wiring (carcassing). The 'first fix' is to put in the boxes that will hold power points and to put protective strips over the cables. The 'second fix' is to strip the insulation off the ends of the wires and connect the fitments – light fittings, wall sockets, fuse box, immersion heater, central heating controller etc. The system is earthed and tested to make sure all circuits are correctly installed, before calling in the regional electricity company for a connection to the supply.

Working on an office block or factory will involve a similar pattern. Cables may be laid in metal trunking in the floor and in metal pipes, called conduit. Cables for lifts or machinery may be bigger to carry higher currents.

On a conversion of an old building, the work starts with stripping out the old wiring and installation system.

Much of the work can be non-electrical – lifting floorboards, bending and cutting conduit or trunking, fixing cables, boxes or other equipment to walls, drilling holes for cables or screws etc.

Production electricians' work may involve interpreting drawings provided by the drawing office or production engineers. The electrician decides the best way to make the connections, probably working at a bench or in a workshop.

Maintenance and service electricians' work involves travelling to where the faulty equipment or wiring is located. They use visual indications, past experience and instruments to check the faults.

WORK ENVIRONMENT

Installation electricians normally work in private houses, shops, offices or on building and construction sites. They can be exposed to cold, damp, dirt and dust. Electricians may also wire the lights on airfields, signals on railways and instruments in oil refineries and chemical plants. Some of the work can be in very exposed locations. Long journeys to and from work or staying away from home may be necessary.

Maintenance electricians in factories work indoors, but servicing machine tools, for example, may be oily and greasy.

Production electricians may work in the same workshop all the time, connecting up the wiring inside a complex product with a range of variations, or they could, for example, be in a shipyard, wiring out a cross-channel ferry.

SKILLS AND INTERESTS

Good hand skills are needed to deal with often quite intricate connections and to handle a range of tools skilfully and quickly. The work is active and can involve standing for long periods, bending, stretching, pulling, kneeling and lifting heavy equipment. Electricians should be able to work at heights and in confined spaces and in the heat or cold, damp and dust of building sites.

Electricians often work on customers' premises so they need to be tidy and clean and respectful of other people's property.

An ability in maths and physics is needed to follow technical drawings and calculate formulae. Electricians have to be able to work without supervision and to make decisions either on their own or in a small team. They must be meticulous and careful when working on installations/equipment that carry high voltages. Patience is needed to locate and diagnose faults.

ENTRY REQUIREMENTS

Entry is mainly at 16 years or 17 years by applying for an apprenticeship with an electrical contractor, an engineering company or an electricity supply company. Vacancies may also be advertised in local newspapers.

Training opportunities for young people are mainly through Modern Apprenticeships (part of the Skillseekers Initiative in Scotland), leading to at least NVQ/SVQ Level 3. Contact your local careers office, Jobcentre, TEC/LEC for details.

ELECTRICAL WORK: RAK

Though not essential, GCSEs/S grades in English, maths, science or a practical subject are desirable. Craft and technology subjects can be useful. GNVQs/GSVQs Level 2 may also be useful. Applicants take aptitude and selection tests followed by an interview.

They also need to be physically fit with normal colour vision.

TRAINING

Training of installation electricians in England and Wales is usually managed by JT Limited which is owned jointly by the Electrical Contractors Association (ECA) and the Amalgamated Engineering and Electrical Union (AEEU). In Scotland, training is supervised by SECTT (Scottish Electrical Charitable Training Trust) on behalf of the Scottish Joint Industry Board (SJIB).

The Modern Apprenticeship training programme in England offers paid status with an employer and usually leads initially to NVQ Level 2 in Installing Electrical Systems and Equipment. This requires apprentices to attend college on a day/block release course and take City and Guilds (Part 1) and the Achievement Measurement (AM1) practical test. Following success in C&G Part 1 and AM1, apprentices continue to attend college to undertake City and Guilds (Part 2).

Apprentices also gain on-site experience which is recorded by them in a Field Evidence Record Book. When it is considered that apprentices are nearing full competence they undertake the industry's final practical test, Achievement Measurement (AM2), which leads to the awarding of NVQ Level 3 in Installing and Commissioning Electrical Systems and Equipment, and which signifies the end of the apprenticeship and subsequent qualified electrician status. Modern Apprenticeships in Scotland are part of the Skillseekers Initiative and lead to at least SVQ Level 3.

NVQs/SVQs in Servicing Electronic Systems are now available at Levels 1 to 3.

Full Modern Apprenticeship training usually lasts approximately four years.

LATE ENTRY

It may be possible for adults to do a Joint Industry Board-approved (JIB) course through government-sponsored training for adults. The JIB gives recognition, through employers. No formal route exists for engineering but some employers will take on adults and train them, increasingly so in view of the shortage of school-leavers. The electricity supply industry does recruit adult entrants for craft training.

OPPORTUNITIES

There are approximately 35,000 electricians in the electrical contracting industry, 112,000 in engineering, and 42,000 in electricity generation and supply.

The wide range of employers includes specialist electrical contractors, building contractors, manufacturers of electrical appliances and products with a significant electrical and electronic content, local authorities, hospitals, colleges, retailers and rental companies of domestic appliances, and power generating and supply concerns.

PAY AND CONDITIONS

Wages vary according to employer and experience. In many large firms, the basic wages are around £260 (£265 in London) a week. Pay rates determined by the Joint Industry Board for the Electrical Contracting Industry are around £242 a week for an electrician, and £267 (£284 in London) a week for an approved electrician, for a 37½-hour week. From 4th January 1999 the rates will be around £254, and £278 (£295) respectively. Hours depend on the company; shift work may be involved.

Overtime and holiday arrangements vary between industries and firms. Overtime is common; maintenance electricians, for instance, often do their work when everyone else has gone home, which means work at night, at weekends and during holidays.

PROSPECTS

After at least two years' experience, installation electricians may become eligible for re-grading to approved electrician. In all areas, promotion to senior hand, chargehand or forehand is available with the possibility of moving on to managerial positions.

Further training can lead to transfer into non-craft and supervisory grades, working on estimating, designing or planning electrical installations, or specializing in electronics. Some people go on to take degrees in electrical engineering, sometimes with the financial support of their employer.

It is possible to work freelance or start a small business.

RELATED OCCUPATIONS

Motor mechanic/vehicle technician, domestic appliance service engineer, business machine service engineer, telephone technician, electrical/electronic assembler, telecoms technician.

FURTHER INFORMATION

Amalgamated Engineering and Electrical Union (AEEU), EETPU Section*, Hayes Court, West Common Road, Bromley, Kent BR2 7AU, 0181 462 7755

Electricity Training Association (ETA), 30 Millbank, London SW1P 4RD, 0171 963 5770 (electricity supply industry in England, Wales, Scotland and Northern Ireland)

Engineering and Marine Training Authority (EMTA)*, Careers Department, 41 Clarendon Road, Watford, Herts WD1 1HS, 01923 238441, 0800 282167 (freephone)

JT Limited*, South Block, Central Court, Knoll Rise, Orpington, Kent BR6 0JA, 01689 891676

Scottish Electrical Charitable Training Trust (SECTT)*, Bush House, Bush Estate, Penicuik, Midlothian EH26 0SB, 0131 445 5659 (electrical contracting industry in Scotland)

NET (National Electrotechnical Training), 34 Palace Court, London W2 4HY, 0171 229 1266

ELECTRICAL WORK: RAK

FURTHER READING

Leaflets/booklets are available from the addresses marked*.

Working in Construction – COIC

Working in Engineering – COIC

Would you like to be an electrician – JT Limited

Plug into Electrical Apprentice Training – JT Limited

Women in the Electricity Industry – JT Limited

In the careers library classified under RAK.

TELECOMMUNICATIONS WORK: RAL

TELECOMS TECHNICIAN CLCI:RAL

BACKGROUND INFORMATION

At one time, telecommunications essentially meant telephones and it was a British Telecom monopoly, with private systems within large organizations. Since privatization and deregulation, the industry has changed, extending the range of possible employers to some 5,000 organizations and increasing the technical knowledge demanded of technicians. The technology is now a complex mix of telephone cable (metal or fibre-optic), radio and computers, with some technicians being specialists, others multiskilled.

Major manufacturing and commercial companies have internal telecommunication systems spanning office and manufacturing complexes, regions and countries. These have been expanded to computer networking as well as voice and fax communication. Some use telecoms systems to transmit signals automatically from unstaffed plant and to adjust switches and valves remotely from a control room a considerable distance away. All of these use microwave radio links as well as cable (whether metal or fibre-optic), and, in some cases, satellite uplinks.

Major concerns that have their own telecommunications systems include: Railtrack, London Transport, British Gas, Powergen and other electricity companies, big oil and chemicals companies, water utilities etc.

In addition, there are now cellular phone networks (which work on a basis of interlinking radio areas or cells) and a number of private mobile radio network operators. Cable TV companies offer local telephone connections as well as TV programmes, and satellite companies have a role to play in international communications.

Other technical developments include digital telephone exchanges and digitized signals, fibre-optic cable, car phones and pagers. The interface with computers often calls for some knowledge of computer hardware and software. The incorporation of live and recorded moving pictures into computer and phone systems will change things further.

The titles telecoms technician and telecoms engineer are used to cover a wide range of jobs and include craft, technician and incorporated engineer qualifications.

THE WORK

There are a whole range of jobs and the work varies accordingly. Many telecoms technicians work on the installation and maintenance of communication systems at customers' premises. These could be switchboards (PBXs), telephones, telex and fax machines, and the internal cabling for phones and for computer networks. Installation of a whole system in a new office block, or in an old office being modernized, could take weeks or even months, laying cables in ducts below flooring, then connecting up equipment and testing it, using complex test equipment.

A maintenance technician might travel in a van from customer to customer, responding to calls following faults, discovering the cause of the fault and then correcting it. If based at the exchange (sometimes called a switch or switching centre or distribution node), they might install extra capacity, test lines where a fault has been reported, connect new or additional circuits for subscribers, and locate and repair faults within the exchange responding to flashing codes on a screen indicating the area of a fault.

Based at a satellite earth station, they could work either on operations and maintenance, ensuring the satellite dish is lined up correctly with the satellite and correcting faults, or on connecting circuits through the satellite to a telecoms system in another country.

With a cellular network, they could be based at the switching centre, as described above, or work as a radio base station (RBS) engineer, travelling by van to each base station in their area, either on routine testing of circuits or responding to faults reported by the engineers at the exchange.

With a user company, the work may be designing a system or preparing a detailed brief of what is required as well as installation and fault-finding. This may involve detailed talks with other departments in the company, and then liaising with suppliers and contractors who provide the appropriate equipment and software, cabling or radio links.

With an equipment manufacturer, technicians may be involved in the design, construction, inspection, testing, installation or technical sales of switchboard or exchange equipment, fax, telex and answering machines, mobile phones and radios etc.

WORK ENVIRONMENT

Workplaces vary. A technician could be based permanently at a telephone exchange. Here they would divide their time between the control room/area and the switchroom, or they might travel in a van between sites (homes, offices etc.) of customers, or to radio base stations. This may involve carrying heavy test equipment from van to site.

Some technicians work outdoors laying and connecting cables in the street or in uncompleted buildings on construction sites. Other telecoms technicians work in factories or design offices or development laboratories.

Many technicians work on their own. They communicate with base by radio or mobile telephone, apart from occasional visits to pick up spare parts etc. Whether they wear overalls, a uniform or smart clothes depends on the type of work and the degree of contact with customers.

SKILLS AND INTERESTS

Dexterity is a prime requirement for using a wide range of hand tools and meters and making connections of tiny wires and electronic components. Engineering calculations and the use of meters require some mathematical skills. Deductive ability and a methodical approach are needed in analysing a fault and tracing its cause. Technicians often have to work alone and take responsibility for their own work, but also have to perform quickly under pressure when customers, or their employer, want facilities back in operation as quickly as possible.

They need good communication skills to discuss requirements and the symptoms of faults with customers or users. An interest in technology and a willingness to read magazines to keep abreast of new developments is valuable. Wires and electronic components are colour-coded so normal colour vision is required. Physical fitness may be important for lifting, carrying, bending and stretching. A clean driving licence is a requirement for some posts. A requirement to work at heights on radio towers or underground in tunnels and ducts; therefore claustrophobia or fear of heights may affect employment.

TELECOMMUNICATIONS WORK: RAL

ENTRY REQUIREMENTS

Minimum academic qualifications are GCSEs/S grades (A–C/1–3) in maths, English, science and technology. Other qualifications include BTEC/SQA National Certificate in Electronics, Telecommunications Technology, Higher National Certificate in Computing or Computing Sciences or City and Guilds Certificates or Diplomas in Telecommunications and Electronics.

Modern Apprenticeship: the minimum requirements are to be between 16 to 18 years of age (some slightly older applicants considered) and have a good general education, but many successful applicants have three or four GCSEs/S grades (A–C/1–3), including maths, English and a science subject preferably with a higher physics content. Technology and engineering subjects may be useful. Intermediate GNVQs/GSVQs Level II may be an alternative. Application is direct to employers. Entrants who perform well may be moved on to a higher level of training/study/qualification.

National Traineeship: there are no mandatory entry requirements but employers expect applicants to show ability and ambition to complete training. A NVQ/SVQ award, including nationally-accredited Key Skills Units (Communication, Application of Number, Information Technology, Working with Others or Improving own Learning and Performance), could be useful. Employers may set other specifications according to their needs. Candidates must complete by age 25.

Incorporated engineer level: entry to a traineeship is with a relevant BTEC/SQA higher national diploma/certificate in electronic engineering or telecommunications, for example. For higher national certificate/diploma level study, one A level/two H grades or BTEC/SQA national certificate/diploma or Advanced GNVQ/GSVQ Level III in Manufacturing or Telecommunications is required.

TRAINING

Telecommunications Modern Apprenticeship Scheme: an extended period of off-the-job workshop training, as well as tuition in theory at college, followed by work alongside experienced technicians under supervision. Most employers expect applicants to complete the scheme within three years. Funding is available up to 25 years of age. Assessment is to at least NVQ/SVQ Level 3, including all Key Skills at Level 3 (Core Skills in Scotland).

Telecommunications National Training Scheme (TeNTS): a flexible programme where applicants are employed and given technical and generic training, most of which is competence based, and opportunities to progress to higher technical awards. Assessment is to NVQ/SVQ Level 2; Key Skills at Level 2 except Communication Skills at Level 3 (Core Skills in Scotland).

Incorporated engineering: training is likely to be similar to Modern Apprenticeship above. Assessment to NVQ/SVQ Level 4.

Professional engineering: for engineering technicians, this gives the letters EngTech after their name. Those with national certificate/diploma qualifications and three years' engineering experience, including two years' training, may obtain this by registering with The Engineering Council direct or through the Institution of Electronics and Electrical Incorporated Engineers (IEEIE). Incorporated engineers gain the letters IEng, by the same process, after achieving BTEC/SQA higher national certificate/diploma standard qualifications or a degree including maths and science (normally physics), plus five years' practical experience including two years' training.

LATE ENTRY

Adult entry is fairly common. Newer, rapidly growing companies, needing capable technicians quickly, have recruited to a large extent from experienced or qualified people. Individuals from comparable posts in the Armed Forces, on radio/radar, for example, have been welcomed, as have those from electronic engineering with craft and technician skills/qualifications.

The NVQ/SVQ system makes possible the assessment of competencies, however gained, which is valuable when applying to new employers. Training periods are usually shortened for recruits with relevant experience. Full-time and part-time college courses are open to mature applicants for whom formal educational requirements may be lowered or waived.

OPPORTUNITIES

Downsizing of major companies, especially privatized ones, has led to a reduction in staff numbers and severe restrictions on recruitment of apprentices and trainees.

However, some cellular companies are still expanding, and cable TV is a growth area. The demands of computer networking, checkout tills linked directly to computers for stock re-ordering and sales analysis, travel agencies making bookings directly with tour operators' computers, bank accounts debited electronically, and so on, means that large companies increasingly find they need telecoms technicians as well as computer experts on their staff.

The major employers, especially public and cellular telephone systems, function throughout the UK, though their offices are likely to be in major towns and cities. The big industrial and commercial companies, such as gas, electricity and water utilities, and transport such as Railtrack, which maintain their own internal communications systems, are also usually found in towns and cities.

Telecommunications equipment manufacturers employ technicians in the more complex assembly roles, in test and inspection, in design and development, and in installation and service areas. Suppliers of imported equipment and specialist service companies have technicians for installation and service work.

An increasing number of technicians now work freelance, subcontracting their skills to large companies and developing business skills to obtain customers. Others set up small businesses supplying telephone or communications equipment to domestic or commercial customers or offering a maintenance service.

Some move into inspection or regulatory work in manufacturing or with supervisory bodies or government departments.

Installation work can take technicians to other countries. Opportunities arise for employment in Europe, USA, the Middle East etc.

PAY AND CONDITIONS

Salaries are generally supplemented with payments for overtime and shift working and some companies also pay bonuses. However, salaries and conditions such as holiday entitlement can vary significantly.

TELECOMMUNICATIONS WORK: RAL

In most areas, the basic working week is 37 to 38 hours, and many technicians work evenings/weekends as part of their normal working hours.

PROSPECTS

Job titles and promotion routes vary depending upon the employer.

In some cases it may be necessary to take further courses, in order to gain promotion, or to gain BTEC/SQA higher national certificate/diploma qualifications or a relevant degree.

RELATED OCCUPATIONS

Maintenance fitter (instrument/electronics), broadcasting engineer, computer service engineer, aircraft maintenance engineer (avionics), contract electrician, production fitter (electronics), railway signal/telecoms technician, incorporated engineer/technician (electronics).

FURTHER INFORMATION

Telecommunications Industry Association (TIA)*, Douglas House, 32–34 Simpson Road, Fenny Stratford, Milton Keynes MK1 1BA, 01908 645000

Telecommunications Vocational Standards Council (TVSC) - (NTO), Blackfriars House, 399 South Row, Central Milton Keynes MK9 2PG, 01908 240120

Institution of Electronics and Electrical Incorporated Engineers (IEEIE)*, Savoy Hill House, Savoy Hill, London WC2R 0BS, 0171 836 3357

Scottish Engineering*, 105 West George Street, Glasgow G2 1QL, 0141 221 3181

Cable Communications Association, 5th Floor, Artillery House, Artillery Row, London SW1P 1RT, 0171 222 2900

Federation of Communication Services (FCS)*, Keswick House, 207 Anerley Road, London SE20 8ER, 0181 778 5656

Fibreoptic Industry Association (FIA), 10–15 The Arcade Chambers, High Street, Eltham, London SE9 1BG, 0181 850 0040

Mobile Radio Training Trust, PO Box 10, Twyford, Reading RG10 8AZ, 01189 223 828

Confederation of Aerial Industries, Fulton House Business Centre, Fulton Road, Wembley Park, Middlesex HA9 0TF, 0181 902 8998

FURTHER READING

Leaflets/booklets available from the addresses marked*.

Working in Armed Services – COIC

Working in Electronics – COIC

Your Choice for Life – A Career in Electronic, Electrical and Mechanical Engineering – IEEIE Periodicals

Periodicals: Communications Monthly, Electronics Weekly

In the careers library classified under RAL.

OIL AND GAS PRODUCTION AND DRILLING: ROB

1. ROUSTABOUT CLCI:ROB
2. ROUGHNECK CLCI:ROB
3. DERRICKMAN CLCI:ROB
4. DRILLER/ASSISTANT DRILLER CLCI:ROB
5. TOOLPUSHER CLCI:ROB
6. PRODUCTION STAFF CLCI:ROB

BACKGROUND INFORMATION

Oil is one of our most valuable commodities. We need it to run cars, ships, aircraft and railways; to provide power, heat and light, and to lubricate machinery. From oil we also get chemicals and other products used in industry, agriculture and our homes. The UK offshore oil and gas industry only started 30 years ago and is still a relatively new employment field.

From offshore oil platforms two key operations take place – drilling and production. In addition to drilling from established oil platforms, drilling is also done from a number of other offshore drilling units. There are mobile offshore drilling units, which can be moved from place to place. Different types of drilling rigs can be either mounted on barges or supported on the seabed by legs. In deeper water semi-submersible drilling units are used.

After forecasting by geologists that oil is present in viable quantities, the first activity is exploratory drilling to establish whether there is an oil reservoir suitable for commercial production. When this is confirmed the temporary rigs are replaced by a permanent fixed platform, which is attracted to the sea bed. This platform houses facilities for both drilling and production as well as living quarters, storage areas for all the equipment and supplies, a helicopter pad and power generation for the platform.

Drilling – is normally done using a rotary drill which revolves at the end of a string of drill-pipe rather like a giant power drill. The drill string is suspended from the derrick – steel framework which may be up to 140 feet high. At the top of the derrick is a crown block to enable the drill string to be raised and lowered. During drilling, mud is circulated down the drill pipe to make the process easier.

Drilling is done from both offshore and onshore. Onshore rigs are mobile and can be dismantled and moved from one site to another.

Production – once the well is drilled and completed, production starts. Lighter-weight tubing is inserted into the well through which hydrocarbons – a mixture of oil and gas together with water – can flow to the well-head. These then have to be separated so the oil is free of dissolved water and gas and is ready for pipeline or tanker transport. The gas must be purified and free of any liquids. If the hydrocarbons cannot reach the surface unaided then other methods such as pumping or injecting gas or water may be required to stimulate flow.

This article concentrates on the work of drilling and production teams; however, there are many other jobs on an oil platform – engineers, geologists, safety officers, divers, caterers and medical orderlies.

THE WORK

Drilling

Offshore drilling crews consist of a toolpusher, drillers, assistant drillers, derrickmen, roughnecks and roustabouts. Onshore drilling crews are often smaller and usually have a toolpusher, driller, derrickman and roughnecks; they rarely employ roustabouts.

1. Roustabout

This is the basic manual labouring job on a drilling platform or rig. Roustabouts work in both oil drilling and production (deck crew). They keep work areas clean, remove rust from structures and paint them. They offload supplies from boats and store them in storage areas and move supplies from storage areas to where they are going to be used. Some more experienced roustabouts lead a small team (as lead roustabout).

2. Roughneck

Working under the direction of the driller, they do the manual work associated with the drilling operation. They run the drill pipe into the hole and pull it back out. They make up the appropriate length of drill string by joining lengths of drill pipe together. As drill bits become worn the roughnecks assisting pull the drill string out of the hole, disconnect the lengths of pipe and put a new drilling bit in, they then reconnect the drill string. This operation is repeated depending on the drilling programme. In doing their work roughnecks use hoisting gear, ropes and air winches.

In addition to working on the drill string they clean the de-sanding and de-silting equipment through which the mud passes. They also maintain drilling equipment. Roughnecks also carry out some of the duties of the roustabout.

3. Derrickman

The term 'derrickmen' stems from their work up the derrick. Under the direction of the driller, they handle and stack the sections of drill pipe, latching and unlatching the lifting equipment used to support the pipe when it is being pulled out of or run into the hole. Derrickmen also have responsibility for the proper working of the mud pumps, the condition of the drilling mud system and mixing additives into the mud. They supervise the mud pumping operators.

4. Driller/assistant driller

Drillers control the hoisting and drilling equipment and are in charge of the drilling crews. They control operations on the drill floor and operate the machinery that raises and lowers the drill string and bit. Under the advice of the drilling supervisor they maintain the speed of rotation of the drill string, the weight on the bit and the appropriate mud circulation rate. In addition they keep records of the drilling and its progress. Assistant drillers do the same job as drillers but under the supervision of the driller.

The driller is responsible for controlling a well if an influx of hydrocarbons is experienced.

5. Toolpusher

The toolpusher is the rig superintendent in overall control. They oversee the entire drilling operation. They ensure everything runs smoothly and all the necessary equipment and materials are available. They are also responsible for the crews, shifts, rotas and safety. The toolpusher is the link with the oil company's representative who makes regular visits and inspections.

OIL AND GAS PRODUCTION AND DRILLING: ROB

Production

6. Production Staff

The production team is involved in the management of the hydrocarbons (oil and gas) from the reservoir to the initial customer. They deal with production from the wells and the processes through which the hydrocarbons go. The team comprises a production supervisor, control room operators, foremen/women operators, lead operators and operators. Roustabouts may also work in production. Operators work in one of three areas: utilities, oil production and gas compression.

New operators start working in utilities – controlling the systems that provide such things as sanitation and electricity. With experience they move to oil production and then gas compression – the most complex of the operations.

Operators in oil production keep a constant watch on the instrumentation, making sure all the valves and instruments work properly. If there are problems they correct them – often by operating valves manually. In gas compression they look for abnormalities in flow rates and pressure and condition of gas.

Their work varies depending on their level of experience. Less experienced operators carry out manual tasks such as opening and shutting valves, offloading tankers, and warehouse work. Skilled operators work in the control room, taking and analysing samples for quality, operating computers, and managing equipment used to measure and control the substances being refined. They are responsible for making sure that equipment is working properly and safely. If the flow rate of a substance slows down they are responsible for finding out the reason and having the fault repaired.

From operator (gas compression) they can be promoted to lead operator (utilities), then lead operator (oil production) and on to lead operator (gas compression). In this job they are chargehands supervising a team of operators. Their next promotion is to foreman/woman operator, running the plant and instructing the operators. The next level is control room operator – these people control the whole operation. They monitor everything that is happening in all three areas. If, for instance, the gas is not up to the correct standard they recycle it. They also manage the crews.

The most senior job in production is that of production supervisor. They have a more strategic role involved in forward planning, as well as having overall responsibility for the production operation and safety. They also handle any major problems that arise. A major part of their work is controlling the production of oil. There are limits to the amount of oil that can be produced at any one time. These limits are determined by OPEC and by the oil buying market. So, under the direction of the oil company, the production supervisor controls the production rate. This is done by shutting down a well or reducing the rate of flow. The production supervisor decides on the most appropriate method and then instructs the crew.

WORK ENVIRONMENT

Crews working offshore may be on oil platforms or rigs and are away from home for two weeks at a time. Those involved in offshore drilling are often exposed to dirty, wet and noisy conditions. Production operators, however, work mainly in control rooms. Derrickmen work at heights. Drilling jobs involve a great deal of bending and lifting.

On the platform there are leisure facilities such as games rooms, films, videos and libraries. Smoking on the platforms is restricted to certain areas and no alcohol is allowed.

Roustabouts and production operators sleep in two-berth cabins, but only one sleeps there at a time, as the other one will be working. Food and accommodation are provided free.

SKILLS AND INTERESTS

It is very important that crew members are able to cope with periods spent away from home. They should be able to live with and get on with other people and to work as a team. They are transported to the platform by helicopter, so punctuality is necessary. Work on oil platforms can be hazardous so employees must be responsible, reliable and safety conscious. Those involved in drilling must be willing to work outside in all weathers.

ENTRY REQUIREMENTS

There are no minimum academic entry requirements to start as a roustabout, although applicants must be physically fit. They also have to be able to work at heights and have no speech defects. There is a tendency nowadays for companies to prefer operators to be multiskilled, for instance, as operator/mechanics or operator/electricians, and employers look for relevant training and experience. Those who wish to become operators but have no transferable skills can start as roustabouts. For some jobs defective colour vision is a bar. All applicants undergo a medical which may include tests for substance abuse. The minimum age for this work is 18 years although many companies prefer applicants who are between 25 and 35 years.

Graduate entry – there are schemes for graduates with relevant degrees in science to enter and progress quickly in production or drilling to production supervisor or toolpusher.

TRAINING

All offshore employees must first undertake an offshore survival course which covers safety, survival and firefighting. Some companies sponsor new employees for this course. The cost of this course is around £570. For a list of centres running this course contact OPITO.

Other training is given on the job under the supervision of chargehands, combined with relevant short courses which crew members may do during their shore leave. This can lead to NVQs/SVQs in Process Operations: Hydrocarbons at Levels 1, 2 and 3 and Offshore Drilling Operations at Levels 1, 2 and 3.

LATE ENTRY

It is unusual for applicants to be accepted after 35 years, unless they have transferable skills such as engineering or mechanic work or they have a background in the Armed Forces.

OPPORTUNITIES

The UK offshore industry is mainly based off the east coast of England and Scotland, in Morecambe Bay and

OIL AND GAS PRODUCTION AND DRILLING: ROB

Liverpool Bay and west of the Shetlands. There are three types of offshore companies: operating companies (usually major oil companies) hold the exploration and production licences and operate the production platforms; drilling companies are contracted to undertake the drilling work. There are also service companies providing assistance to both operating and drilling companies, such as caterers, well services etc. Operators usually work for the operating companies and drilling teams for drilling contractors.

There is considerable competition for jobs, so the more skills and relevant work experience applicants have the better. Experience in offshore installation construction yards or an onshore drilling company is useful. For experienced personnel there are opportunities to work anywhere in the world.

PAY AND CONDITIONS

Roustabouts and production operators earn up to about £18,000 with increases on promotion. Offshore crews typically work on the rig for two weeks followed by two weeks' shore leave. The crews work in shifts of twelve hours on and twelve hours off. Onshore crews also work night shifts but they usually work a week of days followed by a week of nights.

PROSPECTS

Drilling

Most people start as a roustabout. Promotion is gained on experience and ability. Promotion to roughneck usually takes from one to three years. From there to derrickman another two to three years and a further four to six years to reach assistant driller. To reach driller takes about five to eight years and then eight to ten years to become a toolpusher.

Production

Production operator (utilities) is the first rung on the ladder for those who have relevant experience. Those without relevant experience start as roustabouts. From utilities the next steps are to production operator (oil) and then production operator (gas). This is followed by promotion to chargehand (utilities), chargehand (oil) and chargehand (gas). Then it is possible to move to control room operator and then to production supervisor.

There are accelerated training schemes in both drilling and oil/gas production for graduates who can reach senior jobs more quickly. There are a range of courses in both these areas, which can enhance promotion prospects – information on these is available from individual training schools (for addresses contact the Institute of Petroleum).

RELATED OCCUPATIONS

Chemical plant process operator, construction operative, crane driver, motor mechanic, dock labourer.

FURTHER INFORMATION

The Institute of Petroleum*, 61 New Cavendish Street, London W1M 8AR, 0171 467 7100, www.petroleum.co.uk/petroleum/

OPITO The NTO for Oil and Gas Extraction Industry*, Inchbraoch House, South Quay, Ferryden, Montrose, Angus DD10 9SL, 01674 662500

UK Offshore Operators Association (UKOOA):

England: First Floor, 30 Buckingham Gate, London, SW1 6NN, 0171 802 2400;

Scotland: 9 Albyn Terrace, Aberdeen, AB1 1YP, 01224 626652

For information about firefighting and survival courses only, contact OPITO.

FURTHER READING

Leaflets/booklets are available from the addresses marked*.

In the careers library classified under ROB.

ELECTRICAL AND MECHANICAL SERVICING: RAB/ROK

1. **MAINTENANCE FITTER CLCI:RAB**
2. **BUSINESS EQUIPMENT SERVICE ENGINEER CLCI:ROK**
3. **DOMESTIC APPLIANCE/GAS SERVICE ENGINEER CLCI:ROK**

BACKGROUND INFORMATION

Our society depends upon the continued and efficient running of its machines and appliances, whether these are machines used in manufacturing processes in industry, business machines in offices or domestic appliances in our homes. Yet, due to overwork, misuse or the simple wear and tear of normal operation, these machines are liable to break down.

The answer to this is called maintenance or servicing. This may be routine inspection and maintenance where, at set intervals, the equipment is checked, cleaned, lubricated, the parts most liable to wear replaced, and the machine adjusted to work as well as possible. This gives longer life and trouble-free performance. Or it may follow a breakdown, after which the cause of the failure has to be found and corrected, possibly including repair or replacement of a faulty part.

In many cases, the people responsible for maintenance also deal with the installation and commissioning of machinery, though for more complex equipment this may be a separate occupation, often at technician or incorporated engineer level.

Some trends have lessened the amount of servicing required such as greater built-in reliability and modular construction which allows major components to be replaced and either discarded or taken to a workshop for repair. With computer/microchip control, some machines now have in-built diagnostic ability and signal the cause of common faults which may then be corrected by the user, or which simplifies the task of the engineer, indicating where the fault lies and what is required to repair it.

Engineers who go into customers' premises are often called field engineers as opposed to workshop engineers who remain in the repair workshop.

In industry

In manufacturing and process industries, maintenance has traditionally been split between different engineering disciplines, with fitters skilled in mechanical, electrical or electronic/instrument aspects, partly because each field is so complex. Although there has been a measure of multiskilling, which avoids having to call out someone with one of the other skills when the fault is predominantly in one area, this split still broadly applies. It has broken down most in areas of strong automation and robotization, though these tend to require technician level knowledge and skills.

In offices

Increasingly, business machines of all kinds are leased or rented from an agent or dealer rather than bought from a manufacturer. Part of the deal may be a service contract under which the agent or dealer takes responsibility for maintenance. If the equipment is purchased, there is a period under guarantee during which the manufacturer or dealer is responsible for maintenance. After that, they may offer a service contract or the user company may contract with a service company.

Some of these providers have regional and local workshops with their own maintenance staff. Others use a network of small independent service companies subcontracted to them. Some organizations such as large educational establishments employ a small number of maintenance staff to deal with most problems.

In homes

The increased reliability of appliances, which has reduced the number of breakdowns, has led to a reduction in the need for domestic appliance servicing in recent years. This is especially true of electronic devices where the microchip has greatly reduced the number of components that can go wrong. In addition the much lower cost of small appliances, such as electric irons and hair dryers, means that it is often cheaper for the user to buy a new one than to pay for repair.

In gas appliance servicing, the major change is the downsizing of British Gas following privatization and the increase of competition. This has drastically curtailed the main entry and training route for gas service jobs.

1. MAINTENANCE FITTER (RAB)

THE WORK

Maintenance fitters ensure that machinery and equipment used in making or processing products keeps working and that, when it breaks down, it is put back into order as quickly as possible. Another group of maintenance fitters may perform similar tasks for the plant services, ensuring that supplies of electricity, water steam, compressed air, and so on, continue and that lighting, heating, lifts, conveyor belts, security and sprinkler systems and communications networks function as required.

Following instructions from a work docket or call-out sheet, or working to a routine maintenance schedule, fitters leave the workshop to repair/service machines. A mechanical fitter involved in servicing isolates the machine from power, replaces parts that have worn, or can be expected to wear out shortly, and lubricate and adjust machines as necessary. Their field includes pneumatic and hydraulic aspects.

An electrical fitter checks the electrical components, they may replace items such as brushes, check that contacts are free from dirt and oil, replace and repair the electric motor or overhaul the old motor in the workshop.

The electronics or instrument fitter examines the instrument and control aspects, which have increased with computerization and the microchip. This may involve mechanical aspects such as the delicate moving of arms that draw pens across revolving graph sheets to record changes in temperature or pressure. Increasingly machines have a built in electronic monitoring system so that a printout indicates the fault or the area of a fault. For these, it may be necessary to keep the power flowing to be able to check faults; this may call for additional safety precautions such as insulation mats and insulated tools.

Periodically, equipment needs a major service or complete overhaul, involving dismantling, and repair or replacement of any damaged parts, re-assembly and testing. A large factory may do this during the annual summer holiday shutdown.

Maintenance fitters are also involved in the installation of new machines, instrumentation and facilities, possibly working alongside suppliers or contractors from whom the new machines or services have been bought.

ELECTRICAL AND MECHANICAL SERVICING: RAB/ROK

Maintenance fitters may repair parts in the workshop – machining, welding etc. In some firms they may be employed solely in the workshop as specialist maintenance fitters.

Fitters work on their own or with a semi-skilled mate to assist with heavy lifting, handing them tools etc. They use a wide range of hand and power tools, measuring and testing devices, and may refer to technical manuals and drawings.

WORK ENVIRONMENT

Fitters are based in a workshop which may be within the manufacturing area or away from it. This is equipped with workbenches, specialist machine and power tools, and test equipment for checking and repair. These workshops are usually well lit and warm.

From this base, fitters go out into manufacturing areas where environments vary. Engineering machinery may be dirty and greasy. Shipyards and coal-fired power stations may be dirty and dusty. Some chemicals plant is in the open air. So work areas may be cold in winter, and involve long walks. In contrast the surroundings of a highly automated food processing plant are clean, warm and comfortable.

SKILLS AND INTERESTS

Good powers of observation are necessary to be able to deduce the reason for a failure from the symptoms reported by the machine operator. This may involve good hearing, good eyesight for anything out of the ordinary, and even smell and touch. The work involves checking meticulously all the possible faults.

Fitters need good communication skills to question the operator and to understand their instructions and the manual. They also have to complete forms reporting on their tasks. With production held up until they can restore the machine or conveyor belt, they have to be able to work quickly and accurately under pressure.

Nimble fingers, dexterity with hand and machine tools, understanding of engineering principles, and ability to follow technical descriptions and diagrams are all involved.

ENTRY REQUIREMENTS

Normal entry in future will be through a Modern Apprenticeship at craft level. GCSEs/S grades in maths, physics and English are required, although many successful applicants have three/four GCSEs/S grades (A–C/1–3). Engineering and technology subjects help, as does an interest in mechanics/electrics/electronics illustrated by hobbies such as model making. GNVQ/GSVQs in engineering may be accepted.

An alternative route may be to take a course at an FE college leading to a City and Guilds (C&G) or BTEC/SQA national certificate/diploma qualification such as mechanical and manufacturing engineering or electrical and electronic craft studies, and then apply to an employer. For BTEC/SQA national certificate/diploma, entry is usually with four GCSEs/S grades (A–C/1–3).

TRAINING

Modern Apprenticeships (part of the Skillseekers Initiative in Scotland) are structured on an established pattern. They initially involve one-year off-the-job training in a company training centre or a group or industry training centre, primarily in general engineering craft skills with day or block release at a college. This is followed by on-the-job training, working alongside experienced fitters, in relevant modules (at least two) accompanied by assessments towards NVQ/SVQ in Engineering Maintenance at Level 3 and college study towards a C&G craft or BTEC/SQA qualification. In engineering, this leads to the EMTA Modern Apprenticeship Certificate as well as an NVQ/SVQ in Engineering Maintenance at Level 3.

Modern Apprenticeships (part of the Skillseekers Initiative in Scotland) are skill-based not time-based, but usually take three to four years.

LATE ENTRY

The NVQ/SVQ system may make it possible for engineering operators, assemblers or craftsperson's mates to acquire and be accredited with the relevant skills and knowledge and so be accepted as qualified fitters.

Some employers may train people with an appropriate C&G or national certificate/diploma qualification gained in further education; or re-train someone with similar experience, eg a production fitter, in maintenance skills.

OPPORTUNITIES

There is a continuing demand for maintenance fitters. However, the decline in manufacturing industry generally has reduced the number of openings and the recruitment of apprentices. Also the application of computer control and the introduction of integrated manufacturing systems has tended to mean more reliable machinery with less need for servicing/repair. When servicing/repair is needed, technician level skills are required.

Employers include:

– large concerns in engineering, manufacturing, process and extraction industries;

– manufacturers of industrial machinery and equipment who employ fitters as field engineers to install, test, service and repair on customers' premises;

– service industries and commercial concerns including hospitals, local authorities, universities, chains of stores and restaurants, insurance companies etc, who may retain or call in maintenance staff to service heating and ventilation systems, communication systems, lifts, lighting, computers/tills, conveyor belts, catering equipment etc;

– the Armed Forces.

However, not all of these recruit and train apprentices.

Opportunities to work abroad may come through working on overseas contracts for UK or multinational companies or by employment by foreign companies in other EU countries, the USA, Eastern Europe, Middle East etc.

PAY AND CONDITIONS

Average earnings for a qualified fitter are about £370 per week, including overtime and bonuses. The basic week is 37 to 39 hours. Shift work may be involved, especially in process industries such as chemicals and power generation. In others, overtime in evenings or weekends allows servicing or repairs to be done when machines are not in use. In some cases, fitters may have to be prepared to be called out by phone in off-duty hours to deal with a breakdown. In large companies that close down for annual holidays, fitters may work through on major overhauls or

ELECTRICAL AND MECHANICAL SERVICING: RAB/ROK

installations, taking their own holidays at another time.

Protective clothing, such as overalls, boots, helmets and earmuffs, are normally provided by employers. Apprentices are expected to build up their own toolkit of hand tools and basic measuring devices during training while the employer makes available power and machine tools, electrical or electronic test equipment etc.

PROSPECTS

The promotion route is to senior fitter, chargehand, foreman/woman and possibly to workshop manager or maintenance department manager, though these higher level posts are more likely to be held by incorporated or chartered engineers in large companies. Some fitters go on to train further to engineering technician or incorporated engineer level by studying for BTEC/SQA national certificate/diploma or higher national certificate/diploma qualifications or through the NVQ/SVQ system. It is also possible to qualify for Engineering Council examinations leading to professional engineer status by open learning through a National Extension College course.

The detailed knowledge of machines gained during maintenance work makes possible specialization in installation work or transfer to inspection and testing or to sales and marketing posts for those with the appropriate abilities.

RELATED OCCUPATIONS

Production fitter, motor vehicle mechanic, business machine service engineer, domestic appliance service engineer, gas service engineer, incorporated engineer/technician (mechanical), aircraft maintenance engineer, auto-electrician, computer service technician, construction plant mechanic, plumber, telecoms technician.

FURTHER INFORMATION

Engineering and Marine Training Authority, Engineering Careers Department*, Vector House, 41 Clarendon Road, Watford, Herts WD1 1HS, 01923 238441, freephone 0800 282167, www.emta.org.uk

Scottish Engineering*, 105 West George Street, Glasgow G2 1QL, 0141 221 3181

FURTHER READING

Leaflets/booklets are available from the addresses marked*.

Working in Engineering – COIC

Engineering Explained – ECIS

Training and Working in Engineering – ECIS

In the careers library classified under ROK.

2. BUSINESS EQUIPMENT SERVICE ENGINEER (ROK)

THE WORK

Business equipment service engineers install, service and repair a wide range of office equipment including computers, printers, photocopiers and fax machines.

Engineers usually spend their day visiting clients, who have contacted them because there is a fault with their machinery, or because their equipment is under contract and due to be serviced. Field engineers, who are 'on-the-road', receive details of their next jobs through regular contact with their office.

Using a variety of tools, manuals, meters and electronic testing equipment and laptop computers, engineers are expected to locate and fix a problem, or alternatively take the machinery to be repaired by workshop engineers. The work is often technically rewarding.

Engineers must work efficiently because the equipment is often vital to the running of an office. They must also be able to keep records detailing the problem and the amount of time they have spent fixing it, and any spare parts used.

Some specialist engineers are based in workshops where they use specialist equipment and tools to repair equipment too intricate to be mended on site. Other engineers may work in an office, as many business machines are now linked directly to the manufacturer by computer and telephone lines. Engineers can now anticipate problems before they happen, by monitoring the performance of equipment and then informing customers when, for instance, a computer's hard disk needs 'attention', or a printer's toner cartridge needs replacing.

Increasingly, companies expect their engineers to offer extra services to retain customer loyalty, such as consultancy and training.

WORK ENVIRONMENT

Engineers who visit customers premises in their machine rooms may find some of the work physical, such as bending and stretching when changing a part. The work may also be high-tech, making decisions from computer generated information. Engineers also spend a lot of time driving from one client to another. Workshop engineers are based at a site and do not meet clients. Engineers who monitor machines using computers use high-tech equipment and spend long periods sitting down.

SKILLS AND INTERESTS

Business equipment service engineers require a good knowledge of electronics and how many different kinds of office machines work. They need to be able to make decisions quickly, diagnose and solve problems, and work efficiently and accurately when under pressure.

Engineers must be mature and responsible enough to work without supervision, because they often have to manage their own workload. They must be confident when dealing with people and have good communication skills so that they can find out exactly what the problem is with the equipment, and then be able to explain the solution to the customer. Good customer skills are important, because clients may be annoyed that the machine has broken down and interrupted their work. Engineers are representatives of their company and must be courteous when visiting clients.

Numerical and literacy skills are important for completing the paperwork that accompanies most jobs. Physically, engineers need to be fit and agile, with nimble fingers for reaching into awkward places. However, more disabled people are being employed in engineering workshops.

ENTRY REQUIREMENTS

There are no standard qualifications required for entry

ELECTRICAL AND MECHANICAL SERVICING: RAB/ROK

into the profession, although few people join straight from school. Most entrants have a qualification in electronics or electrical engineering, such as City and Guilds, BTEC/SQA or a degree depending on the job.

The following are standard entry guidelines, although they may vary from college to college: City and Guilds – no set minimum requirements but colleges may require three GCSE/S grades; BTEC national awards – entry with four GCSEs (A–C) or equivalent; SQA National Certificate modules – entry requirements vary from college to college.

Entry to BTEC/SQA higher national certificate/diploma courses is with four GCSE/S grades (A–C/1–3) and one A level/two H grades, or equivalent, eg Advanced GNVQ/GSVQ Level III.

A National Traineeship, leading to an NVQ Level 2 or a Modern Apprenticeship (Skillseekers in Scotland), leading to an NVQ/SVQ Level 3 in Electronic & Software Services is another possible entry route. There are no formal entry requirements for the National Traineeship but for the Modern Apprenticeship it is recommended that candidates have a minimum of three GCSEs/S grades (A–C/1–3), including English language and maths, or an equivalent GNVQ/GSVQ or BTEC national award.

The Traineeship and Apprenticeship mix practical on-the-job training with college courses, and includes customer care modules, as well as theoretical lessons in electrical engineering. Further information may be available from local careers offices and TECs/LECS.

Engineers are also recruited from other service/maintenance industries where many of the foundation skills are transferable, and much of the training is relevant.

Engineers need to have normal colour vision so they can differentiate between electrical wires, and a clean driving licence is also important.

TRAINING

A number of courses are available at many colleges throughout England, Wales and Northern Ireland. These include:

C&G 7261 Information Technology, 2348 Servicing Electronic Systems – these offer an introduction to the practical skills needed to work in the sector. 2230 Microcomputer Technology covers areas such as programming and data manipulation, as well as maintenance and repair.

NVQs/SVQs in Servicing Electronics Systems at Levels 2 and 3. Service involves maintaining equipment with an emphasis on developing and maintaining relationships with other people.

BTEC First course in Engineering includes an option involving electronics and microelectronics systems, and lasts one year part-time.

BTEC National in Engineering offers a more advanced course, developing skills in a broader area including communicating and working with others and problem solving. The course lasts two or three years on a part-time basis.

The BTEC National in Electrical and Electronic Engineering is aimed at people who wish to become technicians and covers practical areas such as maintenance and fault diagnosis, as well as subjects electrical and electronic principles. The course lasts two or three years on a part-time basis.

BTEC/SQA Higher National Diploma/Certificate in Electrical and Electronic Engineering (two years full-time, three years part-time) is for senior technicians and provides a detailed knowledge of advanced electrical components, devices and systems and how to apply this knowledge to solve engineering problems.

The Electronics Examination Board runs a four-year part-time course on day release, leading to the Electronic Servicing Certificate.

However, an increasing number of employers offer recruits the opportunity to study for qualifications on a part-time or day release basis. Training takes place on the job or in the employer's own workshops under the supervision of an experienced engineer. Some manufacturers run special courses that relate directly to their own machinery.

LATE ENTRY

Employing mature people with relevant experience in other related fields is a recognized path into business machine service engineering.

Adults can gain recognition of their skills and experience by working towards NVQs/SVQs. There is open access to NVQs/SVQs – no academic qualifications are required and there are no age limits.

Past experience can be put forward as evidence of competence, via Accreditation of Prior Learning (APL).

OPPORTUNITIES

Although engineers now make fewer visits to customers, as equipment is now more reliable and can be maintained by the client, maintenance companies are diversifying into new areas such as data recovery and training, offering engineers the opportunity to diversify into new areas.

Employment is often with leading manufacturers of office machinery, or smaller independent contractors who work on their behalf.

There are also opportunities to enter the profession with one of the increasing number of courier companies who now stock spare parts for popular makes of office machines, and employ staff trained to make basic repairs.

Opportunities in the industry have also been increased by state-of-the-art computer links that now exist between some equipment and the engineer's office. This means engineers can now service equipment all over the world.

Many employers now expect far greater productivity from their engineers, requiring them to become multiskilled, and offer value-added services to clients such as consultancy and training.

Some opportunities exist for in-house service engineers, working in office blocks, local authority buildings or other places with a high number of office machines.

Experienced engineers may consider becoming self-employed and setting up their own business.

PAY AND CONDITIONS

Pay is very much determined by experience and qualifications. Overtime is common. The average wage for engineers, including overtime and bonuses, is £330 a week.

Engineers normally work office hours (9am–5pm) but sometimes may have to work outside these hours in order to be able to service a machine when it is not in use. Some contracts offer 24-hour servicing, and engineers may work

ELECTRICAL AND MECHANICAL SERVICING: RAB/ROK

a rota when they are called on outside normal hours.

PROSPECTS

There is a natural progression within the industry, from engineer to senior engineer, to supervisor and then manager. Engineers with the necessary experience and skills may move into technical sales, marketing or management. Larger companies may offer the opportunity to work abroad, but this is very limited.

RELATED OCCUPATIONS

Computer systems support person, audio-visual aids technician, electrician, chartered electrical engineer, telephone technician, domestic appliance service engineer.

FURTHER INFORMATION

Electronics and Software Services NTO,*, Old Chambers, 93–94 West Street, Farnham, Surrey, GU9 7EB, 01252 720843

FURTHER READING

Leaflets/booklets available from the address marked*.

Working in Electronics – COIC

In the careers library classified under ROK.

3. DOMESTIC APPLIANCE/GAS SERVICE ENGINEER (ROK)

THE WORK

Appliances on which we depend in our homes include cookers, washing machines, tumble dryers, TV sets and video recorders, microwave ovens, vacuum cleaners, heaters and central heating installations.

When a new or second-hand appliance is brought or rented, a domestic appliance or gas service engineer installs it in the home. They connect to electricity, water or gas supply as necessary, installing new cables or pipes if needed. Testing and adjustment follows and instructing the owner in correct use, safety etc.

Engineers also visit homes under routine service agreements to service equipment such as a central heating system or a cooker once a year. This involves inspection, cleaning, replacing worn parts, adjusting and testing.

However, most visits are call-outs when an appliance has broken down or is performing badly. The engineer has to detect the cause of the fault, tracing it with meters or other test devices or relying on past experience, to correct the fault. This may mean replacing a basic component, or involve dismantling a part of the appliance. Increasingly, serious faults are dealt with by removing the whole appliance or a faulty sub-unit to the workshop for repair, replacing it with a working appliance or sub-unit.

Engineers question the owner to find out the symptoms of the fault and how it came about, suggest ways to prevent it happening again, provide estimates of cost for work to be done, make out invoices or receipts, and take payment by cash or cheque if the work is not covered by a guarantee or service agreement. Gas engineers, especially, may have to inform the owner if an appliance is unsafe, fixing a tag prohibiting its continued use.

Engineers handle electrical, electronic and mechanical/plumbing aspects SNS - most gas appliances now have electrical and electronic aspects. They make use of a wide range of hand and power tools and test devices, bending/cutting equipment etc. Some tasks call for use of technical devices, equipment for bending and cutting pipes etc. Other tasks call for reference to technical manuals. Links with base are maintained by mobile phone or radio. Spare parts are kept in the van and replenished on occasional visits to the workshop. Domestic appliance service engineers may be trained in one manufacturer's range or be capable with several types of appliance. Gas service engineers are normally trained in the range of gas domestic appliances, unless working for one manufacturer.

Field service engineers may also be involved in installing appliances in new houses and in installing and servicing appliances in non-domestic premises, such as cookers in company or school canteens or in restaurants, tumble dryers in launderettes, heating in offices etc.

Workshop engineers have the facilities, tools and test equipment for complete analysis, dismantling and re-assembly of appliances, including the complete renovation or updating of older appliances for resale or rehire as second-hand models. With smaller local shops, members of the public may bring portable appliances to them for service, with larger appliances only arriving when brought in by field engineers. In some companies, field engineers spend some time, perhaps one day a week, in the workshop on workshop repairs, and only a small number of specialists stay in the workshop.

WORK ENVIRONMENT

Field service and gas engineers travel between cutomers in a car or van, and communicate with base by radio or phone. Actual work is done mainly in people's homes, so conditions vary. Usually, they are warm and clean, but they may be cluttered. Engineers must work carefully and neatly.

Bending, kneeling and physical effort may be involved. With electrical and gas appliances safety is of prime importance, including explaining safety factors to customers.

Workshop engineers normally remain in the workshop, where they have use of more sophisticated tools and test equipment.

SKILLS AND INTERESTS

Tact, friendliness and the ability to converse easily are essential in getting customers to explain symptoms, to deal with complaints about the breakdown or delays and to explain what has gone wrong and advise on future use of the appliance. Engineers need analytical skills to diagnose and trace faults and a methodical approach. They need to build up, from training and experience, a thorough knowledge of the appliances and what can go wrong with them.

They must have a concern for safety, be fit and agile with manual dexterity. Those dealing with electrical and electronic devices need normal colour vision. They should be self-motivated, working alone without supervision at speed to achieve the number of calls required in a day. They represent their employer, so they must be neat in their appearance, usually in a uniform or overall. Technical calculations, estimating what to charge the customer, and record-keeping all call for mathematical ability. Field

ELECTRICAL AND MECHANICAL SERVICING: RAB/ROK

engineers also require a clean driving licence, though some large employers may assist with training for this during an apprenticeship.

ENTRY REQUIREMENTS

Domestic appliance service engineer

For craft level and a NVQ/SVQ qualification, a general education including maths, physics (or other science) and English may be acceptable. Those employers who train to QCA/SQA national level may ask for three to four GCSEs/S grades (A–C/1–3). Most entrants have some GCSEs/S grades (A–E/1–5) or equivalent such as Intermediate GNVQ/GSVQ Level II in Engineering.

Another route is to acquire training through the further education system by taking a full-time college course leading to GNVQ/GSVQ engineering qualification before applying to an employer.

Gas service engineer

Recruitment within British Gas Services is now handled centrally. Entry requirements are Advanced GNVQ/GSVQ Level III in Engineering or equivalent. Candidates should be over 18 years.

Most other gas installation and service companies do offer apprenticeships. Entry requirements will vary however three GCSEs/S grades (A–C/1–3) in English, mathematics and a science/technology subject would satisfy most employer's criteria.

All gas installation/service companies must be registered with the Council of Registered Gas Installers (CORGI).

TRAINING

Domestic appliance service engineer

Apprenticeships may include a period of off-the-job training in a training centre and on-the-job training in a workshop followed by working alongside an experienced field engineer, observing, assisting and performing increasingly complex tasks under supervision. Day or block release may be included to study at college in theoretical and practical aspects of NVQ/SVQ qualifications. Short courses on specific appliances and models provided by appliance manufacturers may form part of or supplement this training. NVQs/SVQs in Domestic Appliance Engineering at Level 3 are available.

Gas service engineer

STS Apprentice training is similar to that described above. Both apprenticeship training and college courses incorporate assessment for NVQs/SVQs in Mechanical Engineering Services, Gas Services Installation and Maintenance Domestic at Level 2, and Gas Service Installation and Maintenance at Level 3.

In addition to NVQ/SVQ qualifications, gas service engineers need to prove their competence by undertaking assessments from the Nationally Accredited Certification Scheme for Individual Gas Fitting Operatives (ACS). This is a legal requirement and applies to any occupation associated with work on gas systems or appliances.

LATE ENTRY

Many individuals enter these occupations after training and experience in other fields, including gaining craft or technician qualifications. This might be in electrical and electronic maintenance, or work as an assembler or production fitter in light engineering. For gas work it might be as a plumber or heating and ventilating fitter/welder.

Mature entry is possible to college courses mentioned above. Formal entry requirements may be reduced or waived for applicants over 21 years.

OPPORTUNITIES

Domestic appliance service engineers are employed by electricity supply companies, stores and chains selling or renting appliances, local electrical shops, manufacturers of appliances, and specialist service companies. However, the electricity companies and the large chains are the most likely to recruit apprentices. Others prefer to recruit people with training in and/or experience of maintenance and give additional training in specific appliances.

Gas service engineers are employed by British Gas Services and by independent gas installers, gas appliance stores, department stores retailing gas appliances, and central heating companies. They all have to be members of CORGI (Council of Registered Gas Installers), which maintains the necessary safety standards. However, some employers tend to recruit people who have already acquired basic maintenance training and possibly experience; they then provide the training in gas service work.

Employers or their workshops are situated throughout the UK, mainly in urban areas. The growth in the range of appliances and the steady consumer demand mean there is a continuing need for service engineering. However, the increased reliability of appliances and the practice of removing and replacing faulty units such as printed circuit boards has cut down on the number of calls and the amount of work per call, allowing fewer engineers to handle the total work. Disposability of small appliances has reduced the amount of repair work, though renovation of large second-hand appliances continues.

PAY AND CONDITIONS

Salaries vary around the country and with different employers. Average earnings in some fields are about £280 a week. Overtime, call-out, shift and bonus payments may operate. A nominal working week is 38 hours, but an actual average of 40 to 45 hours is more common, including early starts to collect instructions and spares from base and reach the first call at an early hour, as well as continuing into the evening to complete calls at the only time when the customer is at home. Most companies operate a five-day week, but some offer Saturday service. British Gas Services offer a 365 days a year service to all its customers.

Overalls or uniform are often provided, as is a car or van.

PROSPECTS

Some maintenance teams are small, offering little chance of promotion. In larger companies, the promotion route is from engineer to senior engineer, then supervisor and then service manager. With the increasing computerization of products, some engineers go on to train for technician-level qualifications. The detailed knowledge of appliances they gain allows some to transfer to sales and marketing posts or, if employed by a manufacturer, to inspection and test jobs in the factory.

Some gas engineers receive additional training to install and service large-scale industrial heating equipment and gas-fired manufacturing plant for industrial and

ELECTRICAL AND MECHANICAL SERVICING: RAB/ROK

commercial customers. Gas-fired power stations may present other opportunities. Some experienced engineers opt to start their own small service business or open electrical shops, or they may become freelances, contracting to large concerns or to specialist service companies.

RELATED OCCUPATIONS

TV/Video repairer, business machine service engineer, plumber, incorporated engineer/technician.

FURTHER INFORMATION

Electronics & Software Services NTO, Old Chambers, 93–94 West Street, Farnham, Surrey GU9 7EB, 01252 720843

Amalgamated Engineering and Electrical Union (AEEU), Hayes Court, West Common Road, Bromley, Kent BR2 7AU, 0181 462 7755, www.aeeu.org.uk/

Human Resource Department, British Gas Services, Lakeside East, 30 The Causeway, Staines TW18 3BY

FURTHER READING

Working in Engineering – COIC

Working in Electronics – COIC

In the careers library classified under ROM/RAN.

FABRICATION ENGINEERING: RON

1. **SHEET METAL WORKER/PLATER/ FABRICATOR CLCI: RON**
2. **WELDER CLCI: RON**

BACKGROUND INFORMATION

These are major occupations involved in making or constructing engineering products or processing plant by shaping and joining metal parts, which is often called fabrication. In the main, these parts are tubes, pipes, cylinders, boxes, flat or shaped plates or sheets of metal. Usually this concerns fixed metal constructions; mechanical fitters are responsible for assembling and adjusting aspects of metal machines with moving parts. Machine operators or foundry workers may have been involved in the creation of some of the metal parts.

The products made cover a massive range from laboratory sinks to oil rigs and refineries, ships, and aeroplanes. Industries involved include domestic appliance and industrial machinery manufacture, aerospace, engineering construction, shipbuilding and civil engineering. However, there is a major difference between the manufacture of light engineering products and heavy engineering ones.

In light engineering areas, the metal involved is in sheets up to 3 mm thick and often thinner (and, therefore, light and easily shaped). This is what sheet metal workers work with.

Heavy engineering and construction use metal plate which is thicker, and often much thicker, than 3 mm. This is handled by platers or fabricators (a job title increasingly used in shipbuilding). Welders work in both sectors using the same basic skills, but the quality demanded of the weld and the level of weld inspection and testing are often much higher in heavy engineering.

1. SHEET METAL WORKER/PLATER/ FABRICATOR (RON)

THE WORK

Sheet metal workers

They use thin metal sheets which can be bent and formed into different shapes by beating it with hammers. Skill is needed to create a smooth, regular curve or bowl shape without dents, and without the metal becoming significantly thinner and weaker at any point. Sheet metal workers use small presses, roller machines and hammers for the simpler bends and curves and they cut it with snips, with hand or machine saws, and with guillotines.

Sheet metal workers use a technique called pattern-development, which involves mathematical calculations, when marking out (drawing) the shapes on flat metal, so that stretching and contraction of the metal is allowed for. The joining of shaped pieces is done by riveting or welding. Often the welding work is done by a specialist welder, though the sheet metal worker may set up the workpiece for the welder.

Platers/fabricators

The techniques for handling heavy metal plate are quite different. Cranes and hoists are needed to move the metal plate around, with platers possibly doing the guidance and slinging (fixing the chains securely). Straight cuts may be done by powerful guillotine machines. More complex shapes are cut out by computer-controlled burning machines which are programmed by technicians and operated by platers or by caulker-burners using hand-operated flame burners.

The marking on the plate of lines for cutting and of codes for assembly is done by marker-offs, who are senior platers, working to drawings prepared by technicians. Shaping is done by massive machines called rollers and presses capable of creating curves and bends. A complex shape like a bowplate may take a series of partial bends at slightly different angles. Some platers (usually in a team of two) specialize in the operation of these machines.

Other platers specialize in assembly – setting up the cut pieces of metal in the positions specified by the drawings. They use metal wedges and blocks and clamps to hold it in place until it can be tack-welded (small temporary pieces of weld). They use power grinders or hand files to prepare cut edges for a craft welder to do the finished weld and, after the weld is done, they may grind down surplus weld metal to leave a smooth surface. They may build sub-assemblies in a big workshop, or work outside putting sub-assemblies and units together to create the finished ship, chemical plant etc.

They may work closely with others, not only welders and crane drivers, but, in shipbuilding, for example, caulker-burners, who prepare edges and who cut with hand burners, and shipwrights who are especially concerned with the shape of the hull. On repair work, damaged plates may have to be cut away and replaced or patched.

WORK ENVIRONMENT

Sheet metal workers work alone or in small teams. Their workshops are usually relatively small. Work items normally fit onto a bench with devices for holding them.

Platers work in huge workshops or on construction sites outdoors in all weather conditions. They may work in a team with other craftspeople.

They both use earmuffs to protect against noise and wear boiler suits, gloves, helmets and safety boots. Goggles or visors are needed when close to welding activity.

SKILLS AND INTERESTS

Both need physical fitness for lifting, bending and using a range of hand and machine tools. Good hand-to-eye co-ordination is called for, especially from sheet metal workers. They should be meticulous and logical in planning how to tackle each task.

Sheet metal workers – need good eyesight to spot a blemish or dent, however small, and a subtle sense of touch to feel any too small to see. An ability with numbers is vital in handling the formulae and calculations involved in working out the size of the flat shape from which the three-dimensional one can be made. They have to be able to imagine the three-dimensional shape they will be making from looking at two-dimensional technical drawings. Powers of concentration are important to see a job through accurately.

Platers/fabricators – should be able to visualize the finished assembly and have an eye for the right line or curve. Good colour vision may be important in differentiating colours used in codes marked on the plate to show which edge butts against which, various kinds of metal etc. As well as hand and power tools, they use spirit levels, water levels, laser devices, and so on, to ensure accuracy of positioning. In much plating work, a head for heights is important, as is willingness to live away from

FABRICATION ENGINEERING: RON

home and to work in all weather conditions.

ENTRY REQUIREMENTS

Engineering – the minimum requirement for entry to a Modern Apprenticeship at 16 to 17 years is a good general education, but most successful applicants have three/four GCSEs/S grades (A–C/1–3), including maths, English and a science subject (physics is preferred). Technology and engineering subjects may help. GNVQs/GSVQs may be an alternative.

Shipbuilding/repair – for Modern Apprenticeship entry, there are no minimum requirements but preference is given to those with GCSEs/S grades (A–C/1–3) in maths or a science or a related GNVQ/GSVQ.

Engineering construction – the National Apprenticeship Scheme for Engineering Construction (NASEC) caters for craft-level occupations. For NASEC apprenticeships, entrants are expected to gain GCSEs/S grades (A–C/1–3) in maths, English and a science. Those with engineering drawing, metalwork or other practical subjects in addition have an advantage.

Hobbies that show a keen interest in technology always help. The selection process may include aptitude tests (to show manual dexterity, co-ordination etc) and interviews.

An alternative route may be to do A levels/H grades, or undertake a course at an FE college leading to a City and Guilds (C&G), BTEC/SQA, or Advanced GNVQ/GSVQ Level III qualification, covering subjects such as sheet metal working and fabrication skills or mechanical and manufacturing engineering, and then apply to an employer.

TRAINING

Engineering – training often starts with one year off-the-job training in engineering workshop skills. This is followed by up to three years' on-the-job training, working alongside experienced sheet metal workers or platers. There may be day or block release throughout for study at college for a C&G or BTEC/SQA qualification, such as sheet metal working and fabrication skills or fabrication and welding competencies. They also take assessments for an NVQ/SVQ in Engineering Materials Processing at Level 3 and receive an EMTA Modern Apprenticeship Certificate.

Shipbuilding/repair – skill training may be to NVQs/SVQs Levels 1, 2 or 3. It can include off-the-job and on-the-job training for an NVQ/SVQ in Engineering Foundation at Level 2. It may include day or block release as above. A Modern Apprenticeship Certificate is awarded to trainees achieving NVQ/SVQ in Engineering Assembly (Fabrication) at Level 3 and other required standards.

Engineering construction – NASEC apprentices do two years' off-the-job training at a training centre in Stockton-on-Tees in north-east England. Apprentice platers start with general workshop skills, then do basic training in fabrication and welding skills and go on to specialized plating training. The college element is a C&G course. On-the-job training on actual engineering construction sites follows for 12 to 18 months. They are assessed for an NVQ/SVQ in Engineering Construction at Level 3, and receive a Modern Apprenticeship Certificate.

LATE ENTRY

College courses are open to mature applicants but adult entry to these occupations is rare except for individuals from related skill areas, for instance, a vehicle body repairer. People in other heavy engineering trades may be able to re-train as platers or extend their training into this field. Semi-skilled platers' assistants or mates may be able to add to their basic plating skills and confirm their competence using the NVQ/SVQ system.

OPPORTUNITIES

The decline in manufacturing industry in the UK, and especially of shipbuilding, aerospace and defence work, has reduced the number of jobs and the amount of apprentice recruitment. Computer-controlled manufacturing systems and robotization have also had an impact in some areas, as has machine pressing of sheet metal and the use of plastics for housing some appliances.

Heavy engineering companies and the bases of engineering construction companies, which employ platers, tend to be in Scotland and the north of England. Shipbuilding/repair is now found in cities on a very few major rivers only. The Midlands, south Wales and London and the south east of England probably offer most sheet metal work opportunities. Large engineering companies may have a sheet metal work department, but there are also smaller companies that specialize in sheet metal work for other manufacturers or direct to end-users.

Employers are usually companies making or constructing one-off or small batches of products where machine-pressing would be uneconomic. For sheet metal workers, these products could be aircraft, railway carriages, lorry cabs or coaches, laboratory sinks and other equipment, housings for packaging or other manufacturing or agricultural machinery, ventilation ducting etc. For platers, they would be ships, tanks, oil refineries, chemicals plant, power stations, large storage vessels, oil rigs etc.

PAY AND CONDITIONS

Average earnings, including overtime and bonuses, are in the region of £300 a week for sheet metal workers, and for platers. However, this depends on the industry, the scale of the company, experience and responsibilities, as, to some extent, do conditions such as holiday entitlement. The basic week is 37 to 38 hours, but there may be overtime or shift working in some areas. Protective clothing, steel-capped boots, or helmets are usually provided by the employer.

PROSPECTS

Promotion is to marker-off (marking out the lines for cutting or shaping on metal plate or sheet from engineering drawings), foreman/woman, and manager. Some platers and sheet metal workers become inspectors, checking the work done by others, usually after specialist training. Others move into training. Some study for technician or incorporated engineer qualifications on part-time or full-time BTEC/SQA courses, and move into design, planning, production control, estimating or similar fields.

In engineering construction and civil engineering, there may be possibilities of freelance work, contracting as an individual or as a small team to a construction company for the duration of specific projects. Some individuals start their own metal-working business, either alone or with

FABRICATION ENGINEERING: RON

colleagues.

There is the possibility of work on construction projects in other countries, either for UK companies or for foreign ones.

Multiskilling may ultimately create a new trade that merges plating, welding and other metal-handling/construction skills into a new occupation.

RELATED OCCUPATIONS
Motor vehicle body repairer, pipefitter, heating and ventilating fitter/welder, steel erector, mechanical fitter, shipbuilding caulker/burner, plumber, welder.

FURTHER INFORMATION
Engineering and Marine Training Authority*, Engineering Careers Department, Vector House, 41 Clarendon Road, Watford, Herts WD1 1HS, freephone 0800 282167, www.emta.org.uk

NASEC Administration*, Engineering Construction Industry Training Board (ECITB), Blue Court, Church Lane, Kings Langley, Herts WD4 8JP, 01923 260000, www.ecitb.org.uk

(For further information about pipefitters/mechanical fitters/erectors please contact NASEC Administration.)

Institute of Sheet Metal Engineering, Exeter House, 48 Holloway Head, Birmingham B1 1NQ, 0121 622 2860

Scottish Engineering*, 105 West George Street, Glasgow G2 1QL, 0141 221 3181

FURTHER READING
Leaflets/booklets are available from the addresses marked*.

Working in Engineering – COIC

Engineering Explained – ECIS

Training and Working in Engineering – ECIS

Modern Apprenticeships in the Engineering Construction Industry – ECITB NASEC – ECITB

Leaving School at 16+ – ECITB

Fact Sheet 11, Welding as a Career – TWI

Providing a Wealth of Opportunity – M&ETA

National Standards and Qualifications for Engineering – M&ETA

In the careers library classified under RON.

2. WELDER (RON)

THE WORK
Welding uses intense heat to join together pieces of metal with a joint. The heat may melt the edges of two pieces of thin metal butted up together so that they merge, or, for thicker metal, it may melt 'weld metal' from a rod or electrode to fill a V-shape gap between the pieces of metal or to join pieces at right angles. The pieces to be welded are often set up by other craftspeople, such as a plater or sheet metal worker.

The five principal fusion welding methods are: oxy-acetylene (OA), manual metal arc (MMA), metal inert gas, metal active gas (MIG/MAG), submerged arc (SA) and tungsten inert gas (TIG). Not all welders are expert in all of these, as different processes suit the work of different industries or companies, and relate to which metals and thicknesses are involved.

Their work instructions or welding procedure specification gives the welder technical information to support the engineering drawings showing what is required. Depending on size, the items are welded at the welder's workplace or where the weld is needed. They connect equipment to power and to gas cylinders with cables and pipes. They plan the weld, deciding how to do it most effectively. In some cases, they make sure the metal surfaces are clean, though often this preparation is done by another craftsperson.

With the equipment correctly adjusted to suit the job to be done, the welder switches on and strikes an arc, which is the hot bright zone between the metal and the electrode tip. In OA and TIG welding, a filler rod has to be held in the other hand to supply the extra metal to fill the gap. In MMA, MIG/MAG, and SA the electrode becomes molten and is used to fill the gap, so the welder has to maintain a constant distance between the electrode tip and the work to ensure the arc does not go out.

Welds can be downhand or overhead – looking down or up at them. They may be on a curve, an angle, in any direction.

Welds in critical products are subject to strict inspection to check their quality, using measuring instruments and non-destructive testing methods such as x-ray, ultrasonic and dye testing, so welds are expected to be of a standard that will not fail these tests.

Automatic and robotic welding equipment is more usually set up and operated by welding technicians than by craft welders. Spot-welding may be of sheet metal panels, a robot operation as in car manufacture or is carried out by semi-skilled operators.

WORK ENVIRONMENT
Factory workshops may be large or small, with the noise of machine and hand tools. The welder may work in a small booth created by heavy curtains to protect other workers from glare. Other work situations might be in the hollow sections in the bottom of a ship's hull or, exposed to the weather, welding sections of a pipeline or chemical plant.

A head shield with protective filter glass, or tinted goggles, gives essential protection for the welder's eyes from the glare. Overalls, apron and gloves give protection against sparks and molten metal. Where fumes could be a problem there is an extractor above their work and, in some situations, breathing apparatus is used. In noisy work situations, they wear earmuffs. On construction sites, hard helmets have to be worn.

Except for welders based permanently in a factory workshop, they are likely to travel to different locations for long or short periods, which could be a long way from home, living in site accommodation or lodgings.

Though they may work closely with a sheet metal worker or plater, they essentially work on their own.

SKILLS AND INTERESTS
Obtaining a good weld calls for the ability to concentrate intensely, with accurate co-ordination of hand and eye. Strength and steady hands are needed to be able to work holding a welding torch.

FABRICATION ENGINEERING: RON

Other attributes are good eyesight to see into the welding glare through tinted goggles or mask, and good hearing to spot changing sounds of the welding arc. Welders need fitness and strength to carry heavy equipment, climb ladders and crawl into cramped spaces.

They need mental and physical stamina to keep up the level of concentration all day and withstand the loneliness of much of the work. They must take full responsibility for their work, adhere to safety regulations and technical instructions, and may liaise closely with platers, sheet metal workers and other craftspeople.

ENTRY REQUIREMENTS

Engineering – the minimum requirement for entry to a Modern Apprenticeship at 16 to 17 years is a good general education but most successful applicants have three/four GCSEs/S grades (A–C/1–3), including maths, English and a science subject (physics is preferred). Technology and engineering subjects may help. GNVQs/GSVQs may be an alternative. Welders must be physically fit. In some cases defective colour vision may restrict entry.

Shipbuilding/repair – for Modern Apprenticeship entry, there are no minimum requirements but preference is given to those with GCSEs/S grades (A–C/1–3) in maths or a science or a related GNVQ/GSVQ.

Engineering construction – the National Apprenticeship Scheme for Engineering Construction (NASEC) caters for craft-level occupations. For NASEC apprenticeships, entrants are expected to gain GCSEs/S grades (A–C/1–3) in maths, English and a science. Those with, in addition, engineering drawing, metalwork or other practical subjects have an advantage.

Hobbies that show a keen interest in technology always help. The selection process may include aptitude tests (to show manual dexterity, co-ordination, and so on) and interviews.

An alternative route may be to do A levels or to undertake a City and Guilds (C&G) 229 or CENTRA/EMFEC 165 course, or equivalent, at an FE college, and then apply to an employer. However, it is not yet clear how this system will operate for this particular occupation.

TRAINING

Engineering – training often starts with one year's off-the-job training in engineering workshop skills. This is followed by up to three years' on-the-job training working alongside experienced welders. There may be day or block release throughout for study at college for a C&G or BTEC/SQA qualification. The resulting qualification is an NVQ/SVQ in Joining Materials by Welding at Level 3 plus an EMTA or M&ETA Modern Apprenticeship Certificate.

Shipbuilding/repair – skill training may be to NVQ/SVQ Levels 1, 2 or 3. It can include on- and off-the-job training for an NVQ/SVQ in Engineering Foundation at Level 2. It may include day or block release as above. A Modern Apprenticeship Certificate in Welding is awarded by M&ETA to trainees achieving NVQ/SVQ in Joining Materials by Welding at Level 3 and other standards.

Engineering construction – NASEC apprentices do two years' off-the-job training in one of three training centres (Grangemouth in Scotland, Stockton-on-Tees in north-east England and Tipton in the west Midlands of England). They start with general workshop skills, then would-be welders do basic training in fabrication and welding skills and go on to specialized welding skills. The college element is a C&G course. On-the-job training follows for 12 to 18 months, on actual engineering construction sites. The resulting award is NVQ/SVQ in Engineering Construction at Level 3 and a Modern Apprenticeship Certificate.

To find employment, a skilled welder must be able to pass a Welder Approval Test which demonstrates their skill on that type of welding work. These tests may be in accordance with, for example, BS:4872, BS EN:287, ASME IX or other similar standards. This may mean frequent re-testing, as with Ministry of Defence work, which is re-tested every six months.

LATE ENTRY

Adult entry is not common without previous experience in a related area. With multiskilling, basic welding has become a small part of other jobs, such as plater, which may offer the possibility of additional training to become a welder. TWI and other organizations run training courses of two to ten weeks leading to a recognized Welder Approval Certificate. Contact your local Jobcentre, TEC/LEC for details.

OPPORTUNITIES

Skilled welders are important in heavy engineering, where products like vessels and pipework for chemical plants or boilers and turbines for power stations are made, or in similar industries, such as shipbuilding/repair and engineering construction, which handles the building of chemical plants and power stations. In this area the decline in manufacturing, construction and shipbuilding generally and cuts in arms manufacture mean fewer welders are needed. In light engineering, they work with thinner metal sheet alongside sheet metal workers who prepare the metal for welding. There is reduced demand in this area due to the increase in plastics and the shaping of metal sheet by giant presses with panels joined by robotic welding processes. Welders also work in building engineering services (heating and ventilating) and civil engineering.

In all areas, multiskilling has passed some basic welding tasks, such as tack-welding to hold a piece of metal plate in position, to other trades such as platers or shipwrights. In time, there may be some merging of these crafts, as has already happened in heating and ventilating where the title fitter/welder applies. However, at its most skilled levels, welding is a distinct and important skill.

PAY AND CONDITIONS

Different skill classifications, ie certification for different types and qualities of welding, demand different levels of pay. An average would be around £296 a week, including overtime and bonuses. In some areas, piecework rates may apply. The basic working week is 38 hours. There may be shifts or overtime.

PROSPECTS

In companies with a team of welders, promotion may be possible to foreman/woman and supervisor and possibly to fabrication shop manager over welders and other craftspeople. With additional training and qualifications, some welders move on to technician or higher level work and into inspection and non-destructive testing. Further training is also needed to obtain European qualifications

FABRICATION ENGINEERING: RON

such as European Welding Practitioner, Specialist and Technologist.

In construction and engineering construction industries, some welders operate on a freelance basis, contracting their skills for the duration of a job such as the laying of a gas or oil pipeline. In some instances, welders work abroad on overseas construction projects.

RELATED OCCUPATIONS

Heating and ventilation fitter/welder, vehicle body repairer, sheet metal worker/plater, shipbuilding caulker/burner, gas distribution worker, plumber, blacksmith.

FURTHER INFORMATION

Engineering and Marine Training Authority*, Engineering Careers Department, Vector House, 41 Clarendon Road, Watford, Herts WD1 1HS, freephone 0800 282167, www.etma.org.uk

TWI (The Welding Institute)*, Abington Hall, Abington, Cambridge CB1 6AL, 01223 891162, www.twi.co.uk

NASEC Administration*, Engineering Construction Industry Training Board (ECITB), Blue Court, Church Lane, Kings Langley, Herts WD4 8JP, 01923 260000, www.ecitb.org.uk

Scottish Engineering, 105 West George Street, Glasgow G2 1QL, 0141 221 3181

FURTHER READING

Leaflets/booklets are available from the addresses marked*

Working in Engineering – COIC

Engineering Explained – ECIS

Training and Working in Engineering – ECIS

Modern Apprenticeships in the Engineering Construction Industry – ECITB NASEC – ECITB

Leaving School at 16+ – ECITB

Fact Sheet 11, Welding as a Career – TWI

Providing a Wealth of Opportunity – M&ETA

National Standards and Qualifications for Engineering – M&ETA

In the careers library classified under RON.

GROUP S – MANUFACTURING INDUSTRIES

1. **PRODUCTION MANAGER CLCI:SAB**
2. **QUALITY CONTROLLER/TESTER CLCI:SAB**
3. **PRODUCTION WORKER CLCI:SAB**
4. **ASSEMBLER (LIGHT INDUSTRY) CLCI:SAB**
5. **PACKER CLCI:SAB**

BACKGROUND INFORMATION

Almost all products in everyday use – domestic items, food and drink, electrical goods and furniture – are provided by manufacturing industry, which also supplies different industries with components such as bricks, tubing, integrated circuits and optical fibres. Manufacturing is divided into sectors: biotechnology; ceramics, glass and minerals; chemical industry; defence industries; electrical, electronic and information technology; energy; food and drink manufacturing; mechanical engineering; metal manufacturing; packaging; paper making; plastics processing; printing; shipbuilding; textile, clothing and related industries; timber and furniture; and the vehicle industry.

Production is central to manufacturing; methods of production vary from industry to industry and according to type of product. The major aspects of production are described below.

Production/processing takes a number of forms. In some industries, though, traditional techniques are still used, increasingly the emphasis is on introducing new technology to automate production. Production workers are required mainly to monitor the working of the machinery/equipment, operate controls, maintain a supply of raw materials etc.

Assembling – components are brought together to produce partly assembled or finished products. Workers may assemble on a line, bench or floor and may be involved with assembling light or heavy goods.

Packaging may be the final stage on a production line or a separate procedure. It may be automated, or carried out by skilled or unskilled workers.

Quality control – all the way through production, the quality must be monitored, and tests carried out to ensure specifications are being met. The types of checks made by quality controllers and/or checkers/testers vary in sophistication although there is an increasing trend to give production workers greater responsibility for checking the quality of their own work.

Production management is an essential element of efficient manufacturing, necessary to ensure forward planning, scheduling, co-ordination and organization.

Manufacturing engineering is concerned with planning, managing and maintaining manufacturing production/processing. Manufacturing engineers plan and set up the production line, so that goods are manufactured making the most efficient use of resources.

Research and development engineering is concerned with practical problem solving on current and new products, taking into account the often continuous and rapid product changes that are necessary to keep up with and beat competitors in world markets. Research and development departments work closely with design and production teams.

Design engineering involves consulting other experts and drawing up the specifications of the plans and processes to be used in manufacturing a product. Normally the work is done within tight financial and time restraints.

These articles are concerned with the work of production managers, quality control inspectors, production workers, assembly workers and packers who are employed in almost all manufacturing industries. For information about engineering, see ENGINEER (RAB).

1. PRODUCTION MANAGER (SAB)

THE WORK

A production manager's role is to oversee the activities associated with production. Functions include: ensuring production targets are met; planning and controlling resources, product quality, labour relations and discipline; avoiding disruptions to the continuous operation of the production line; and future planning. Their main concern is to make the best use of available resources to achieve given objectives. Customers are given a delivery date and estimate of costs when ordering manufacturing products. It is the responsibility of the production department to ensure orders are completed by the agreed date and conform to requirements.

The production manager has overall responsibility; tasks may be carried out, however, by members of the production team.

The numbers and titles of jobs vary within different production management departments. The production supervisor may be called the shift supervisor and may be responsible to a production controller and/or planner at middle management level. Controllers and planners may have a number of staff under their control, eg progress chasers/clerks or production clerks or planning technicians, and can be responsible to senior planners and/or the production manager.

In general, as managers become more senior, they spend less time on the factory floor and become increasingly involved in future planning, co-ordinating, attending management meetings etc.

The major production functions include:

Planning and control

On receiving an order, the planner must devise a production programme to be agreed by the manager and/or production director. The type of programme required depends on the method of production:

continuous/flow production – the programme may remain unchanged for long periods of time;

batch production involves limited numbers (batches) of each of a range of different products, or of the same product with variations of style, colour, aroma etc, being produced in succession. The production programme may be based on sales estimates and previous experience, or on orders from customers, and is likely to be adjusted quite regularly;

non-standard item/job production – every order is of a different specification, involving frequent machine changes and for which it is very difficult to draw up a regular programme. Where the item being produced is big and complex, eg a turbine for a power station or an aircraft, the production schedule may stretch over many months and involve input from a large number of departments or factories and even countries.

MANUFACTURING: SAB

The production programme states the output figures for each quantity and type of product for each period – day, week, month etc. It is necessary to calculate the number of machines and time required to produce the operations, taking into account constraints such as time required for servicing equipment.

The allocation of resources – people, equipment and time – to production operations is known as loading. The aim is to achieve optimum loading – parity between supply and demand – which may be difficult since there are often conflicting requirements.

Production control involves making sure that production is maintained and refining the master programme – scheduling and re-scheduling work to ensure the targets are met, taking day-to-day problems into account.

Data is received from all production departments giving details of the current position. Many problems arise, such as machine failure, staff shortages or increasing rates of machine rejections or scrap. Adjustments must be made to daily schedules according to the established priorities.

Planning and control involves liaison with many other people including senior managers and production workers, managers of design, estimating, sales and purchasing departments, and outside suppliers. The collection and analysis of data entails a great deal of figure work, which in larger companies is computerized. Various techniques may be employed for planning, analysing, scheduling and controlling, including critical path analysis.

Production supervision

This is mainly concerned with supervising the production workers involved.

Much of the work takes place on the shop floor, and involves touring production areas. Supervisors observe work and ensure the production schedule and targets are adhered to. They anticipate problems, take action to forestall them, or deal with them if they do arise. They are required to take frequent decisions. Decisions are mostly of a short-term and immediate nature, but must be made independently as higher management is often unavailable, for example during night shifts.

Day-to-day duties vary considerably. Supervisors receive production reports and check that production is proceeding to schedule. They take a co-ordinating role – liaising with planners, controllers and departmental managers, co-operating with colleagues (for example, in quality control and dispatch), and organizing and motivating production workers. It is essential that they establish good working relationships.

Supervisors take responsibility for handling problems of absenteeism, maintaining good labour relations and attending to health and safety. They need to consider the workloads on individual operatives and sort out group problems, directing the workforce towards achieving the overall production goals.

Other activities may include taking corrective action to reduce sudden increases in rejects, ensuring operatives adhere to specified procedures, making sure machine fault analysis is correct, anticipating future problems etc.

Production management and supervision may include: preparing and submitting budgets; cost control; responsibility for productivity and efficiency, for planned maintenance and equipment replacement, and for employee training programmes; negotiating with employees and trade union representatives on industrial relations matters; health and safety; as well as problem-solving on a day-to-day basis.

WORK ENVIRONMENT

This depends on the type of manufacturing unit and, to some extent, on the type of production. Modern factories are often light, airy and clean, but there are exceptions in some industries and workshops, eg foundries.

The more senior members of the production management team tend to be office-based. Offices may be clean and fairly comfortable, large and open-plan, or small and cramped. Middle and junior managers may have offices close to the shop floor and spend a proportion of their time in the manufacturing facility. Supervisors may have office space within the manufacturing area but spend most of their time on the shop floor, touring the production areas, dealing with problems etc.

SKILLS AND INTERESTS

Personal qualities are very important in production management. Managers in junior grades are primarily concerned with dealing with people. They should have good skills in persuading and influencing and must develop good working relationships with production workers, colleagues and senior managers. It is necessary to be approachable as well as being a good leader.

Good communication skills, both spoken and written, are essential at all levels. Production managers are required to present arguments, write reports and keep records. For planning and controlling work, individuals need to be numerate, and should be able to master basic analytical and planning techniques. Production managers also need to understand the processes involved. The emphasis on technical knowledge varies according to the industry and products being manufactured. A knowledge of marketing and finance is also helpful.

Problem-solving skills are required to find the cause of the problem, initiate corrective action and carry out follow-up procedures. Managers need good investigative skills and should be able to set priorities.

Individuals must be self-reliant and capable of making decisions quickly. Many problems can arise and it is important to be able to work under pressure while remaining calm and in control.

Supervisors may spend much of their time on their feet on the shop floor, and require energy and stamina to endure work that can be physically as well as mentally demanding.

ENTRY REQUIREMENTS

There are no minimum qualifications for production management. However, for direct entry to a management trainee scheme, which may result in a post in production management, candidates are normally educated to degree level or equivalent. Direct entry to a post as assistant or trainee production manager may be possible with a degree in a relevant subject and/or a management qualification. Other production managers are recruited after experience in other posts in manufacturing industry such as production supervision, quality control, production planning and control, sometimes by internal promotion.

Entry to degree courses is with a minimum of five GCSEs/S grades (A–C/1–3) with two A levels/three H grades or equivalent, such as Advanced GNVQs/GSVQs

Level III in Manufacturing. Exact requirements vary and applicants should check prospectuses.

Any degree may be acceptable although the subject may affect the type of industry the graduate enters. The high-technology sectors often require entrants with degrees predominantly in technical subjects, such as technology, science, or maths. Degrees in specific engineering disciplines may be needed for some jobs. Other industries prefer a qualification specifically in management.

In some industries there may be openings for some candidates with BTEC/SQA higher national awards.

Industrial experience, such as that gained on a sandwich course or in an industrial placement, can be an advantage.

TRAINING

It is possible for an individual to work up to production supervisor level through the ranks – eg from production worker to chargehand to production supervisor. Some entrants move into production from other functions such as work study, quality control, purchasing or works engineering.

Direct entrants to production departments may start their training by following an induction course, lasting anything from a few weeks to several months. Specific job-related training follows; this normally entails working alongside experienced staff. Trainees may start on the factory floor in a manufacturing/production supervisor role, or in a related department, such as production planning or control, to get an overview.

Classroom training in specialist functions may be provided, particularly if there are specialist elements in the work, such as complex production processes or computer applications. Trainees may take courses in management or technical subjects at further/higher education establishments on a part-time or full-time basis or as part of in-company training.

Some companies recruit management trainees into broad-based schemes that do not involve a commitment to production – trainees spend time in different functions, such as sales, personnel and finance departments as well as production. Trainees gain wide experience and may then specialize in one function as a route to senior management.

There are a number of qualifications relevant to production management. They include:

– National Examining Board for Supervision and Management (NEBS Management) courses which relate to supervisors and first-line managers. These may be formal courses, open learning, or through NVQs/SVQs at Levels 3, 4 and 5;

– The Institute of Management's Certificate in Supervisory Management, Certificate in Management, and Diploma in Management. These relate to NVQs/SVQs at Levels 3, 4 and 5 respectively and also provide a pathway to masters-level degrees (MBA/MSC). A postgraduate diploma is also offered for senior managers;

– Certificate in Management Studies (CMS) awarded by BTEC/SQA for people in junior management posts;

– Certificate in Management (CM) and Diploma in Management Studies (DMS) which are postgraduate or post-experience courses offered by colleges and universities. In some cases, the CM is the first year of a two-year linked course; in others the DMS is a two-year stand-alone course;

– Master of Business Administration (MBA) courses at colleges, universities and private sector business schools, usually for individuals already in, or aiming for, senior manager posts;

– NVQ/SVQ in Supervisory Management (Level 3), First-line Management (Level 4) and Middle Management (Level 5) to standards set by the Management Charter Initiative (MCI) and awarded by organizations such as BTEC, SQA, IM, NEBS Management, Henley Management College and the Institute of Supervisory Management. This can be by workplace assessment or courses at colleges, universities and private sector organizations;

– NVQ/SVQ at Level 4 relevant to specific manufacturing industries, eg engineering manufacture and production planning in engineering.

Though some qualifications can be gained on a full-time course before a first management job, many are intended for those with management experience and already in post, so they can be taken on a part-time, open or distance learning basis.

These qualifications do not specialize in production management, but choice of topics, modules or units allows a degree of specialization.

Several years' experience in relevant functions such as production planning and control or production supervision are often required for production manager posts.

LATE ENTRY

Production management is a career highly suitable for adult entrants, though increasingly it is necessary to acquire one of the qualifications listed in TRAINING to be considered eligible.

Experience of production work at any level can be an advantage. There are no upper age limits specified although individual companies may set their own. It may be more difficult to be accepted for posts at production level if aged over 40 years and considering production work for the first time.

There may be specific training opportunities directed at adults available in some areas for this type of work. Candidates may have to satisfy certain conditions to be eligible. Contact your local Jobcentre, careers office or TEC/LEC for details.

OPPORTUNITIES

Production managers are employed by manufacturing companies. Prospects vary according to sector, individual factory location, and a variety of local and economic factors. The nature of manufacturing industry is changing with the decline of the traditional heavy industries and the increasing introduction of automation. This may have implications for production managers. In future, recruits with technical knowledge who are able to understand the more complex production technology may be favoured by employers. In addition, as production lines are increasingly automated, fewer workers (including production supervisors) may be required on the shop floor. The need to maintain competitiveness, however, and the pressure to meet production targets will ensure a continuing demand.

Experienced individuals employed by large companies with overseas subsidiaries or connections may have opportunities to work overseas. This will depend on company policy where it may be necessary to speak a foreign language.

MANUFACTURING: SAB

PAY AND CONDITIONS

Salaries vary according to the company, its location, the responsibility of the job and experience of the manager.

Production supervisors receive in the region of £11,500 to £17,800. Extra payments are made for overtime and shift work. Production controllers and planners receive between £12,900 and £20,700, and production managers from around £17,000 to £30,000. Senior production managers working for large companies can earn in excess of £40,000.

Official working hours are usually from Monday to Friday, 37 to 40 hours a week. The demands of production, however, often mean that flexibility and overtime are required making the actual hours very irregular. In senior positions, this overtime may be without additional pay.

Supervisors and junior managers are required to work the same hours as production and process workers. This can often involve shift work, including nights and weekends. In addition, they deal with immediate problems, and some supervisors in continuous production industries are effectively on call day and night for seven days a week. Overtime is often required.

PROSPECTS

Career development depends on the organization and the manager's individual performance. Production managers may advance into general management. Some people move into different functions at a senior level to gain wide experience before moving into general management. There is a formal promotion hierarchy in most organizations. Individuals may also move to different employers to improve their position.

RELATED OCCUPATIONS

Work study/organization and methods officer, transport manager, general manager, engineer, marketing manager, quality controller, warehouse manager, distribution manager.

FURTHER INFORMATION

Institute of Operations Management, University of Warwick Science Park, Sir William Lyons Road, Coventry CV4 7EZ, 01203 692266, www.comnet.demon.co.uk

The Institute of Management*, Management House, Cottingham Road, Corby, Northants NN17 1TT, 01536 204222, www.inst-mgt.org.uk

The Institute of Manufacturing, 58 Clarendon Avenue, Royal Leamington Spa, Warwickshire CV32 4SA, 01926 855498

National Examining Board for Supervision and Management, 1 Giltspur Street, London EC1A 9DD, 0171 294 2468, www.nebsmgt.co.uk

FURTHER READING

Leaflets/booklets are available from the address marked*.

Production and Plant Management – AGCAS

In the careers library classified under SAB.

2. QUALITY CONTROLLER/TESTER (SAB)

THE WORK

Quality controllers or testers, ensure everything, from raw materials entering a factory to finished goods leaving the factory, is tested and meets the specified requirements.

Inspection and testing involves a wide range of duties, determined to some extent by the product. In the food and drink industry, for example, inspectors may test for consistency, flavour, colour and nutritional value. Pharmaceutical products may be tested for composition, purity and safety. In textiles, yarns may be tested for strength, colour/dye, grease and water content. Packages must also contain correct quantities and be in perfect condition.

Methods of inspection include visual inspection, which involves checking the product by viewing with or without aids, such as microscopes or magnifying glasses. Products are also checked for physical characteristics, such as weight or size. Functional tests may be required to ensure products perform adequately. Electronic measuring instruments are often used and are being introduced to take over some of the more routine tasks. Complicated scientific testing can involve using a wide range of instruments and scientific equipment. Accuracy and precision is vital to ensure meaningful results.

Analysing and interpreting the results of tests is a major part of the work. Quality controllers/testers, may use a variety of distribution charts and statistical and arithmetical techniques to translate their results and determine whether specifications, eg British Standards etc, have been met. The analyses are also used to determine whether the production processes are drifting even if the product is within specification. This can involve calculating percentages, averages, means and modes, determining whether results fall within normal distribution ranges, and identifying deviations.

Some tests may be very straightforward and take only a few minutes to complete; others are complicated, and it can take hours or days to obtain the results. Quality controllers/testers make notes of the tests for each product as they work, and write up detailed reports on completion.

Quality controllers/testers advise shop floor staff who are increasingly responsible for the quality of their output.

WORK ENVIRONMENT

The work environment depends on the type of factory and product being manufactured. In most cases the quality control department is located in a room similar to a laboratory or workshop away from the shop floor.

For some tests, a dust-free and scrupulously clean environment is essential for accurate results. Materials and products may also be dangerous and must be handled safely and carefully. It may be necessary to wear protective clothing and head coverings.

For sample-collecting and liaising with workers, quality controllers/testers spend time on the shop floor. The temperature in factories is often controlled but in some places it may be very hot or cold. In addition, the shop floor may be noisy, dusty, dirty etc – depending on the type of manufacture.

MANUFACTURING: SAB

SKILLS AND INTERESTS

Carrying out test and inspection work requires practical skills and manual dexterity. The work is often precise and requires careful attention to detail and a thorough approach. Inspectors should have an interest in science subjects. They must be prepared to carry out routine tasks time and time again whilst maintaining concentration and accurately following specified procedures.

Some quality control is based on statistical sampling and arithmetical methods; controllers or testers, therefore, should be numerate and comfortable working with figures.

Quality controllers or testers must be able to deal with people and therefore need a mature outlook. They need to gain the co-operation of shop floor workers and encourage operators to produce work of a satisfactory quality.

ENTRY REQUIREMENTS

There are no minimum academic qualifications required to become a quality control inspector.

Many individuals gain shop floor experience as production workers and then move into quality control. School-leavers without qualifications may enter quality control departments as assistants and progress to inspector posts; however, it is more likely that employers will ask for qualifications – typically a minimum of four GCSEs/S grades (A–C/1–3), including maths, English and science subjects.

Some employers may train controllers/inspectors/testers via a Modern Apprenticeship or Technician training scheme and may ask for some GCSEs/S grades or A-levels/H-grades. Employers in high technological industries may require BTEC/SQA NC/D or HNC/D or, in some cases, relevant degrees, eg in electronic engineering, materials science, or chemistry.

The City and Guilds does not ask for formal qualifications for entry to the C&G 7430 Certificate in Quality Assurance.

TRAINING

Training varies according to the type of industry and methods of production. Mainly it takes place on-the-job with instruction from experienced staff and/or senior instructors. The length of training varies but it may take up to four years. Classroom training may be arranged to give instruction in specific techniques, complicated production methods or computer applications etc.

Many trainees are required to study for qualifications on a part-time basis through day release and/or evening classes. The main qualification for inspectors is the C&G 7430 Quality Assurance. Courses are normally run at educational establishments and C&G examinations are usually taken after one or two years' study.

The certificate is in two parts which may be taken separately. Candidates who pass both parts are then exempt from the first of the Institute of Quality Assurance's (IQA) series of associate membership examinations – contact the IQA for further details.

Training may include further specialist courses in aspects of quality control/quality assurance, and courses specifically geared towards quality control inspectors working in particular industries, such as engineering or food processing.

Other relevant qualifications include BTEC/SQA higher national certificate/diploma courses with quality control/quality assurance elements. Such courses tend to have a manufacturing bias.

A small number of first degree courses in technology include quality control/assurance elements. Several MSc courses are also available.

NVQs/SVQs for quality controllers at Levels 2 and 3 are being introduced by different manufacturing industries under titles relevant to those industries. In engineering, for instance, Control of Quality is one possibility within the Providing Technical Services NVQ/SVQ. Other NVQ/SVQs up to Level 4 for different manufacturing industries have quality assurance units and/or testing elements. In engineering, Engineering Manufacture (Testing) Level 4 would be appropriate for some posts.

LATE ENTRY

There are opportunities for mature entrants in quality control. This is particularly true for those already working in production with a company; those who show the necessary aptitude may be offered opportunities to move into quality control. Background experience will be taken into account.

Dealing with people in ways which may be critical of their work demands individuals with maturity, who can rely on experience and personal qualities. Mature applicants may, therefore, be preferred by employers for inspector posts.

Training opportunities specifically for adults may be available in some areas for this type of work. Candidates may have to satisfy certain conditions to be eligible. Contact your local Jobcentre, careers office or TEC/LEC for details.

OPPORTUNITIES

Quality controllers/testers are employed by manufacturing companies of all types. Firms employing quality controllers/testers vary in size and type from the highly automated to basic factories with large or small workforces. High-technology sectors with complicated production and processing techniques, may tend to employ those with higher-level scientific or technological qualifications.

The Institute of Quality Assurance issues a monthly magazine *Quality News* which usually contains advertisements for quality control assurance vacancies.

PAY AND CONDITIONS

Salaries vary according to employer, location, responsibility and experience. Quality Control Inspectors have starting salaries of around £9,000 to £12,000, depending on age, experience and qualifications. This can rise to over £14,000 for experienced and senior staff. Overtime rates are usually payable and there may be shift allowances.

Regular working hours – of 37 to 40 hours a week – are available in manufacturing industry. Some companies run shift systems and may require quality control departments to be staffed 24 hours a day. Shift systems can involve day and night shifts and include work at weekends. Working to production schedules may mean that overtime is available or required.

There are some opportunities for part-time working.

MANUFACTURING: SAB

PROSPECTS

Quality controllers/testers may progress to senior technician/team-leader posts and to quality control management positions. Several years' experience is necessary and inspectors often study for advanced qualifications.

Other avenues for quality controllers, with sufficient experience and expertise, may be into supervisory or management posts in production or research and development.

RELATED OCCUPATIONS

Engineer/technician, work study/O&M officer, production manager, laboratory technician, safety officer, production worker.

FURTHER INFORMATION

Institute of Quality Assurance*, PO Box 712, 61 Southwark Street, London SE1 1SB, 0171 401 7227

Engineering and Marine Training Authority*, Careers Department, 41 Clarendon Road, Watford, Herts WD1 1HS, 01923 238441, freephone 0800 282167, www.emta.org.uk

FURTHER READING

Leaflets/booklets are available from the addresses marked*.

In the careers library classified under SAB.

3. PRODUCTION WORKER (SAB)

THE WORK

Operatives carry out key, though often routine, jobs in order to produce the variety of items manufactured in industry. As many as 60 people may work on a production line requiring workers to co-operate as members of a team. Others work as individuals either sitting or standing at a bench or table. There are wide individual variations between jobs at this level. They may be grouped, however, into the following areas of work.

Machine minding and operating is concerned with the monitoring and/or operating of the automatic and semi-automatic machinery involved in producing manufactured products. The level of skill required and the types of tasks performed, vary.

With automated processes, certain levels – temperature, pressure, rates of flow or speed of lines – need to be maintained. Deviations from specified conditions must be recognized immediately. The appropriate action by operatives may involve calli+g in the maintenance or engineering staff, or operatives may be required to make adjustments – opening and closing valves or altering levers, switches etc. Operatives, such as those working in the food or chemical industries, may follow menu-type directions that require the weighing and measuring of different materials or ingredients for adding to the main mixture at specified times.

Those working with machines are required to be aware of, and adhere to, safety regulations. This may involve, for example, wearing protective clothing or ensuring machine guards are properly fitted.

Finishing work is concerned with adding the finishing touches to the manufactured product – often metals, plastics or textiles – usually involving special treatments, such as adding protective coatings, smoothing down rough edges, and heat or special cleaning processes.

As dangerous substances may be used, such as acids or other corrosive/explosive chemicals, a careful and systematic approach is necessary in this sort of work. Skill is required in setting up the work and ensuring the part has been adequately treated, cleaned, protected etc.

In addition, workers may label finished items with their name or number and batch identification tag or label. Items must go for inspection on completion, and those that are not passed will be returned to be done again.

Other duties: operatives may have other duties combined with production. Much of the work is now on automated production lines, for example, those where machines fill, cap, label and pack items including pharmaceuticals, food products, paint or chemicals. On semi-automated lines, operatives may undertake a variety of duties, along with other workers, possibly on a rota, and may be concerned with assembling and packing (please see articles 4. ASSEMBLER (LIGHT INDUSTRY) and 5. PACKER).

Some workers may be responsible for checking products for faults or testing products as they come off the production line, checking aerosol cans for leaks or weighing samples to ensure they are of the correct weight, for example (please see article 2. QUALITY CONTROLLER/TESTER).

WORK ENVIRONMENT

The work may be light or heavy. For some types of work, a dust-free and scrupulously clean environment is essential – pharmaceuticals or food in particular – and workers may wear special clothing, such as head coverings, gloves and slippers.

Those working in a dusty environment may wear face masks, for example, when dealing with flour or refractories. Other types of protective clothing, including goggles, aprons and boots, may be required when dealing with dangerous substances or heavy materials. In some factories workers may be subject to hot or cold conditions and unpleasant smells or fumes.

The work can be tiring and entail remaining in one position, either sitting or standing, throughout the day.

It is important that production workers are able to work well as members of a team, particularly when working on production lines with others.

SKILLS AND INTERESTS

Workers require stamina to cope with long periods of sitting or standing, and those handling heavy materials or products require a degree of physical strength. The work can be repetitive and operatives have to work consistently and often quickly.

Workers should be able to get on with people of all ages and co-operate, if required, as members of a team.

The operating and monitoring of machines requires attention to detail, concentration and a sense of responsibility. Good timekeeping and reliability are important personal qualities.

MANUFACTURING: SAB

ENTRY REQUIREMENTS

No educational qualifications are required to enter work as a production operative. Proof of proficiency in practical subjects can be advantageous.

Some employers set an aptitude test for applicants, particularly where the work requires good manual dexterity and/or following detailed instructions. Tests are used to determine the individual's practical ability and suitability for the type of work. Good eyesight and accurate colour vision may be essential in some areas, eg electronics. For some posts, physical fitness and stamina may be important, though mechanical aids are usually available for heavy lifting and moving.

TRAINING

This varies according to the employer and type of product manufactured. The training may be in two parts.

Induction training is an introduction to the company – its structure and policy, company practices and products. Subjects usually include conditions of employment; layout of the factory – medical facilities, restaurant/canteen, recreation areas, and so on; staff welfare; and health and safety matters. Induction training may be held in the firm's training centre, or may be a brief introductory talk and tour round the factory.

Skills training is largely given on the job, and normally involves supervision from an experienced worker, chargehand or supervisor. For routine work, new recruits may receive instruction for a few hours or from two to twelve weeks, depending on the job. It may take some time for individuals to learn all the aspects of the work and to develop speed, if required.

For semi-skilled and or more specialist jobs, there may be short classroom training courses held on the premises and supervision for longer periods.

In some industries, employers send operatives to study on a part-time basis at technical colleges. Training may be through day or block release and can lead to relevant qualifications, including NVQs/SVQs, awarded by City and Guilds or other bodies. Subjects may include operating equipment and machinery, instrumentation and production and process techniques, and safety or emergency procedures.

NVQs/SVQs are available at Levels 1 and 2 in a number of manufacturing industries, with each industry setting its own standards and requirements. For instance, in the engineering industry, relevant titles might be Engineering Machining, Engineering Material Processing, Engineering Assembly or Engineering Finishing. Level 3 may be available for those who move into supervisory or more technically skilled positions.

Specific training opportunities for young people may be available, including Skillseekers in Scotland. Contact your local careers office, TEC/LEC for details.

LATE ENTRY

Manufacturing is an area of work providing many opportunities for adult entrants. Acceptability will vary according to the policy of the individual employer. Most companies consider adult applicants on an equal basis to school-leavers. Personal qualities are most important, especially reliability. There are also opportunities for part-time working at times that fit in with personal and family commitments – these vacancies are often more attractive to the adult entrant or returner.

There may be specific training opportunities directed at adults available in some areas for this type of work. Candidates may have to satisfy certain conditions to be eligible. Contact your local Jobcentre, careers office or TEC/LEC for details.

OPPORTUNITIES

Production workers are employed throughout the country by manufacturing companies of all types. The Engineering Training Authority covers almost half of those employed in manufacturing. Production or process workers are required in all sectors including ceramics, glass and mineral products, chemical industry, electrical, electronic and information technology, energy production, food and drink manufacturing, mechanical engineering, metal manufacturing industry, packaging, paper making, plastics processing, textile, clothing and related industries, timber and furniture, and the vehicle sector.

Employment in manufacturing is changing with the introduction of new technology, and the number of semi-skilled and unskilled jobs is falling. Future opportunities are likely to be for production workers who monitor machines that carry out a variety of tasks.

PAY AND CONDITIONS

Rates of pay vary according to employer, location, the type of job, experience and age. Wages may also vary if a piecework rate is paid, that is, a rate of pay set by the rate of production.

Production workers, after training and with sufficient experience to have built up speed, earn around £180 to £250 a week.

Additional payments may be made for shift work and as productivity bonuses. Extra pay for overtime may also significantly increase wages.

Regular working hours, of 37 to 40 hours a week, are available in manufacturing industry. Some companies have shift systems that include work in the evenings, and at nights and weekends. Meeting the requirements of production schedules may mean that overtime is available or required. There are good opportunities for part-time working. Some firms operate production machinery during the night, and may require permanent night shift workers.

PROSPECTS

Promotion prospects are fairly limited for most production workers.

There may be opportunities, for those with speed and aptitude, to move on to more specialist and complex work; some may become skilled craft workers and undertake formal training programmes.

Some individuals may progress to supervisory grades such as inspector, chargehand or supervisor. Another alternative may be to move into quality control work.

There may be opportunities for some production workers to move into related areas such as transport, distribution, storage, warehouse or clerical work.

MANUFACTURING: SAB

RELATED OCCUPATIONS

Packer, bottler, brewery worker, chemical plant process operator, quality control inspector, assembler, sewing machinist, engineering machine operator, textile operative, ceramic/pottery maker, lift truck operator.

FURTHER INFORMATION

Engineering and Marine Training Authority*, Careers Department, Vector House, 41 Clarendon Road, Watford, Herts WD1 1HS, freephone 0800 282167, www.emta.org.uk

FURTHER READING

Leaflets/booklets are available from the address marked*. In the careers library classified under SAB.

4. ASSEMBLER (LIGHT INDUSTRY) (SAB)

THE WORK

Assemblers are involved in fitting together components, made by others, to produce finished products or sub-assemblies – used as components of other products. Assemblers are responsible for carrying out one or more stages of the making-up procedure. Some assemblers construct complete products; most assemble part of an article, such as integrated circuits or mechanical components for hearing aids, washing machines or vacuum cleaners. Goods may be completed within the factory, or sub-assemblies may go to other factories, companies or industries for fitting into finished products.

On an assembly line, each assembler may carry out a different task – adding bits to an item as it moves on a conveyor – to result in a finished product or complex component.

The parts required to carry out the assembly – such as clips, screws, pins, washers, wires and transistors – are usually to hand in trays or bins.

Partly assembled items may be taken from a conveyor belt, or a batch brought to the assembler. Each assembler fits components to the items and then replaces them on the conveyor belt or trolley ready for the next person.

The assembler normally remains in one place, and is brought new supplies by warehouse/ stores staff as required. Items are often kept in order on the assembler's bench and there is usually a specified routine for fixing parts together. This is so that the operation may be carried out quickly and efficiently.

The work can involve a series of simple but repetitive tasks. It may be necessary to follow sets of detailed instructions and diagrams.

The work may be held in a jig or frame, which allows the assembler to fix pieces more easily and rotate the part. Simple tools may be used, such as screwdrivers, pliers or tweezers, and some assemblers use soldering irons to link wires between pins on circuit boards etc. Where components are very small, regular breaks are given to allow rest and avoid eye strain. Some assemblers use simple machinery, eg crimping machines for soldering tags on to wires, drills or grinding equipment – operated by foot pedals, switches or hand levers.

WORK ENVIRONMENT

This varies according to the type of manufacturing unit and to some extent to the type of product being assembled. Modern factories are often light, airy and clean. For some types of work, a dust-free, scrupulously clean environment is essential; in electronics, for example, conditions resemble those of a science laboratory. Workers may have to wear overalls and head-coverings.

The work can be tiring and may require assemblers to remain in one position, either sitting or standing, all day. Using a soldering iron for lengthy periods may mean that the worker is subject to hot conditions with unpleasant fumes.

SKILLS AND INTERESTS

For light assembling, individuals should have patience and good manual dexterity.

It is important to have good eyesight and for some operations, such as wiring, good colour vision is essential. The work demands accuracy, neatness and well-developed powers of concentration. Assemblers should be quick and methodical, and capable of following instructions or diagrams.

Particularly on production lines, it is important that assemblers are able to work as members of a team.

ENTRY REQUIREMENTS

No educational qualifications are required to enter assembly work. GCSEs/S grades or equivalent qualifications in English and maths are useful. Proof of proficiency in a practical subject can be advantageous.

Some employers set an aptitude test for candidates, particularly when the work is the assembly of very small components, demanding a high level of accuracy. Tests are used to determine an individual's manual dexterity and suitability for the type of work. Good eyesight may be essential, and accurate colour vision is vital for jobs in electrical and electronic assembly, because of the colour coding of components.

TRAINING

Training is given on-the-job or there may be a short training course lasting up to a month, for the more complex assembly work. This can entail classroom instruction where trainees learn to identify different components and follow instructions and diagrams accurately. Special techniques – such as wiring, soldering and inspection – will be taught.

NVQs/SVQs are available at Levels 1 and 2 in a number of manufacturing industries, with each industry setting its own standards and requirements. For instance, within engineering, Cable and Wiring Loom Manufacture, or Electronic Product Assembly, or Engineering Assembly, or another similar title, might be appropriate to a specific job. Level 3 may be available for those who move into supervisory or more technically skilled positions.

Specific training opportunities for young people may be available, including Skillseekers in Scotland. Contact your local careers office, TEC/LEC for details.

LATE ENTRY

Manufacturing is an area of work providing many opportunities for adult entrants. Personal qualities are

MANUFACTURING: SAB

most important to employers, especially reliability. There are also opportunities for part-time working at times, that can fit in with personal and family commitments. These vacancies are often more attractive to the adult entrant or returner.

Specific training opportunities directed at adults may be available in some areas for this type of work. Candidates may have to satisfy certain conditions to be eligible. Contact your local Jobcentre, careers office or TEC/LEC for details.

OPPORTUNITIES

Assembly is traditionally very labour-intensive work. However, with increasing automation, the divisions between different stages of work and types of jobs – production, assembly and packing, for example – are breaking down. It seems probable that future jobs will be mainly concerned with machine monitoring and maintenance, or at technician and professional level.

Much of the work for assemblers is in the electrical, electronic and information technology sectors. Assemblers may be concerned with assembling components for domestic appliances such as refrigerators, washing machines, vacuum cleaners and dishwashers; TV, video and audio equipment; air conditioners; office equipment; aerial, aeronautical, scientific and medical equipment and instruments etc. Many components are assembled for use by different companies and for industries in different sectors such as electronics for the defence industry.

Assembly work of components and/or complete items is also required in the metal manufacturing, paper-making, plastics processing and timber and furniture sectors. Individuals should also refer to ENGINEER (Operator) (RAB) for details of heavy assembly work and SEWING MACHINIST (SAH) for textile and clothing assembly.

PAY AND CONDITIONS

Assemblers, after training and with sufficient experience to have built up speed, earn around £180 to £227 a week. Additional payments may be made for shift work and as productivity bonuses. Extra pay for overtime may also significantly increase wages.

Regular working hours of 37 to 40 hours a week are available, although some companies operate shift systems. There are good opportunities for part-time working.

PROSPECTS

Promotion prospects are fairly limited for most light assemblers. Some individuals may progress to supervisory grades such as inspector, chargehand or supervisor. Another alternative may be to move into quality control work (please see article 2. QUALITY CONTROLLER/TESTER).

RELATED OCCUPATIONS

Engineering operative, production worker, quality control inspector, packer, electronic bench tester, sewing machinist, domestic appliance repairer, electrician, telephone technician.

FURTHER INFORMATION AND READING

Please see article 3. PRODUCTION WORKER.

5. PACKER (SAB)

THE WORK

Modern packaging has a variety of functions: as well as containing the product, the package may help to preserve perishable goods, make transportation easier, prevent damage, advertise, and provide directions/instructions. A package can form a constituent part of a product – as with aerosol cans, matchboxes etc.

Goods of all types are packed in the factory ready for sale. A variety of materials are used for packaging including paper, board, cellulose film, thermoplastics, glass, tin plate, aluminium foil, textiles, laminates and wood.

Products may be in liquid (eg beverages, chemicals and pharmaceuticals), powder or solid form, and are packed into packages including bottles, jars, cartons, tubes, boxes, bags, cans, crates, drums and sacks.

Packing may be divided into two main types:

Routine packing

The tasks involved in packing vary according to type of product. Bottles/jars, for example, may be packed into cartons of a dozen or more. The packer makes up cartons from flat sheets and inserts dividers to protect the bottles. Using both hands, the packer picks up a number of bottles at once, for slotting into the boxes. Other items may be packed into bags, sacks or drums, or put into trays for shrink-wrapping – this involves loading batches into a machine that shrinks plastic-film wrapping by heat. Different methods of sealing packages – tape, staples, glue etc – are used and can entail operating various types of equipment, tools and machinery, such as staple guns or banding machines.

Packing may be a full-time job or combined with other work. Much of the packaging in factories is now automated and many of those working on production lines are concerned with machine operating (see article 3. PRODUCTION WORKER). Operators monitor equipment carrying out filling, capping, labelling, and so on, and make adjustments to the speed of operations and the quantities being packed into individual containers. They ensure the machines are supplied with raw materials, component parts, boxes, labels etc.

In routine packing, a continuous flow or batches of a product are all packed in the same way. It may take anything from a few hours to several weeks to complete a batch.

Specialist packing

Different-sized, awkwardly shaped and particularly heavy or fragile articles need special attention. A great deal of skill is required to pack delicate items, such as scientific instruments, ceramics and glassware.

Packers normally work alone or in small teams of three or four people.

Additional duties

All types of packing work often entail carrying out other relevant duties, including labelling. Products may be labelled automatically on production lines, although it may still be necessary to mark packs with information such as the batch number, date and destination. In addition, some packers are responsible for checking items for faults and testing products as they come off the production line, by weighing samples, for example.

MANUFACTURING: SAB

WORK ENVIRONMENT

Working conditions vary. Certain products need to be packed in sterile conditions. The workplace may in some cases be dusty or hot. Packing may involve long periods of sitting or standing.

Protective clothing – such as overalls or head coverings – may be worn.

SKILLS AND INTERESTS

Packers should enjoy practical tasks and take pride in producing neat and tidy work. They should be able to work quickly and carefully. Specialist packers should be patient and able to decide how to pack items securely. Those who label packages need clear handwriting.

Good timekeeping and reliability are important.

ENTRY REQUIREMENTS

No educational qualifications are required. Proof of proficiency in practical subjects can be an advantage.

Ability to read and write is important for reading labels and filling in forms. Some employers set aptitude tests for manual dexterity etc. Physical fitness and stamina may be important in some industries.

TRAINING

Training is largely given on the job. Large companies may run short induction courses for new staff covering conditions of employment, company policies, health and safety etc.

Skills are gained through experience, with entrants learning from experienced workers or supervisors.

NVQs/SVQs are available at Levels 1 and 2 in a number of manufacturing industries, with each industry setting its own standards and requirements. The pharmaceuticals industry has a specific title, Packaging Operations (Pharmaceuticals), while, in other industries, packing units of a more general NVQ/SVQ might be relevant. Level 3 may be available for those who move into supervisory positions.

Packer in the removals industry is a specialist occupation due to the skills required for packing delicate and valuable items. Short courses for removals staff, which include packing for export, are run by CENTREX.

Specific training opportunities for young people may be available, including Skillseekers in Scotland. Contact your local careers office, TEC/LEC for details.

LATE ENTRY

Packing is an area of work providing many opportunities for adult entrants. Personal qualities are most important to employers, especially reliability. There are also opportunities for part-time working at times that can fit in with personal and family commitments. These vacancies are often more attractive to the adult entrant or returner.

There may be specific training opportunities directed at adults available in some areas for this type of work. Candidates may have to satisfy certain conditions to be eligible. Contact your local Jobcentre, careers office or TEC/LEC for details.

OPPORTUNITIES

Packers are employed throughout the UK by manufacturing companies of all types. They are also employed to pack manufactured goods by export firms, shipping and forwarding agents, mail order companies and warehouse/storage services. Similar work is available with large stores and other retail outlets, removal firms and specialist exporters dealing with antiques, fine arts etc.

In manufacturing, the introduction of new technology is reducing the demand for routine packing, and opportunities are decreasing. Demand for specialist packers is more stable.

PAY AND CONDITIONS

Packers usually work 37 to 40 hours a week. Some work shifts. Overtime may be available. There are also opportunities for part-time work.

Rates of pay vary according to employer, location, the type of job, experience and age. Wages may also vary if a piecework rate is paid, that is, a rate of pay set by the rate of production.

Packers, after training and with sufficient experience to have built up speed, earn around £150 to £250 a week.

Additional payments may be made for shift work and as productivity bonuses. Extra pay for overtime may also significantly increase wages.

PROSPECTS

Promotion prospects are limited. It may be possible to progress from routine to specialist packing but this may involve moving to another company. Some packers progress to supervisory grades such as chargehand or supervisor.

RELATED OCCUPATIONS

Production worker, checker, quality control inspector, assembler, engineering machine operator, warehouseman/woman, removal man/woman, fork lift truck operator, post-room worker, laundry/dry cleaning worker.

FURTHER INFORMATION

CENTREX Training and Conference Centre*, High Ercall, Telford, Shropshire TF6 6RB, 01952 777777

FURTHER READING

Leaflets/booklets are available from the address marked*.

In the careers library classified under SAB.

BAKING AND CONFECTIONERY: SAC

BAKER CLCI:SAC

BACKGROUND INFORMATION

The large white sliced loaf is still the most popular type of bread in Britain, but other types of bread such as wholemeal, French sticks, pitta bread, malt loaves, and organic bread have grown in popularity. Bread sales declined for a number of years but are now static; however, 'morning goods' – products such as rolls, croissants, crumpets, muffins and pastries – are being bought in increasing quantities. Public interest in a more varied range of bakery products means there is scope for the small, specialist concern, as well as for the large-scale bread producer.

Bread and morning goods are made by three main types of bakery:

Plant bakeries are mainly large firms, with a factory-like environment. They use modern technology to bake on an automated production line. Their main product is bread of all types and morning goods.

Traditional craft bakeries bake bread for sale in their own shops and also supply local outlets such as hotels, pubs and sandwich bars. Craft bakeries vary in size – some may consist of a single shop and bakery, others own a network of shops in a local area. As well as bread and morning goods, many craft bakeries produce cakes, pies and pastries, and offer sandwiches and snack meals.

In-store bakeries are found in supermarkets and other large stores. The growth of these outlets has been helped by technical developments that enable retailers to purchase pre-mixes, part-baked or unbaked frozen dough. These can be stored until needed, then processed and baked on site – enabling stores to sell freshly baked bread throughout the day.

About 70% of Britain's bread is produced by plant bakeries, about ten per cent is made by craft bakeries, and the rest by in-store bakeries.

THE WORK

The main difference between the work in craft, plant and in-store bakeries is the degree of mechanization involved. In plant and in-store bakeries, most operations are mechanized and routine, whereas in craft bakeries, some proportion of the work may be carried out by hand, or with hand-operated machinery, and is usually non-routine.

The main operations in all types of bakery are: weighing and measuring ingredients; mixing doughs and other mixtures; portioning and shaping mixtures (for loaves, rolls etc); conditioning and baking mixtures; cooling, slicing, wrapping and labelling where required; and delivery to customers.

In plant bakeries, baking is a continuous operation, with dough and loaves moving automatically through the various stages of production on a conveyor belt. The baker's work involves operating machinery and ensuring each stage of the process progresses smoothly. Bakers may move between different tasks during the course of each working week, so there may be some variety in the work, though the number of production lines is usually limited.

In-store bakeries operate on the same lines as plant bakeries, but not usually with a continuous production line, as batches are smaller. There is more manual work – such as lifting and carrying trays of bread from one stage of production to the next.

Craft bakers use fewer machines and may carry out some processes – such as moulding dough and check-weighing finished loaves – by hand. They need to develop the skills necessary to adjust recipes, taking into account the variability of ingredients (such as the quality of flour used). There is more variety of tasks and products in craft baking, as batches are smaller and it may be necessary for a small team to produce a wide range of different products. Craft bakers may also make and decorate cakes, as well as other jobs such as driving delivery vans, ordering supplies, or cleaning the bakery.

WORK ENVIRONMENT

Plant bakeries are a factory environment. In-store bakeries are large rooms, attached to a supermarket or store. Craft bakeries are usually attached to a baker's shop.

Conditions are often noisy – with tins clattering against racks, and the sound of machinery. There may also be dust from flour, although this problem has been virtually eliminated in the larger automated bakeries and is controlled in others. Conditions for people working near ovens are warm, but not all jobs involve working in a warm environment; putting cream on cakes, for instance, is a task that must be done in a cool room.

There are legal requirements covering health, safety and hygiene, which all bakeries must meet.

Bakers work as members of a team: the number of people working together varies considerably, from two or three in a small craft bakery to 200–300 in a large plant bakery.

Protective clothing and equipment, consisting of hats and overalls and, for some tasks, safety shoes, gloves and ear defenders, is normally provided by employers.

SKILLS AND INTERESTS

As the work involves food handling, a high standard of personal hygiene is essential. It is important to be conscious of safety procedures when operating machinery and using hot ovens.

Bakers need to be able to work quickly. Good timing is crucial in baking, and it is important, particularly in craft bakeries where there may be several different types of bread being baked at once, to be well organized – remembering to take each batch out at the right time.

Good health and physical fitness are important; bakers are on their feet all day, and the work can be tiring. In smaller bakeries (craft and in-store), staff may need to lift sacks of flour, tins of loaves etc; some strength is required.

Manual dexterity and some artistic ability are required for hand moulding of dough (to make bread plaits, for example) and decorative work. Some jobs require numeracy, for measuring ingredients, ordering supplies, working out costings and calculating cooking times.

Bakery work may be unsuitable for people who suffer from dust allergies, asthma and certain skin complaints.

ENTRY REQUIREMENTS

In the majority of cases, there are no formal educational entry requirements; however, GCSEs/S grades in English, maths, science or food technology are useful.

BAKING AND CONFECTIONERY: SAC

Entry requirements for the BTEC national diploma or SQA national certificate modules are four GCSEs/S grades (A–C/1–3) including English, maths and a science subject, or equivalent qualifications.

TRAINING

There are a number of different training routes:

On-the-job training – many entrants begin as trainees and receive on-the-job training from employers. In some cases this may be supported by flexible and video learning material produced by the National and Scottish Associations of Master Bakers. Training may also include day release study at a local college.

Skillseekers – in Scotland only, Skillseekers opportunities are available for young people in all LEC areas, with entry usually at 16–18 years but also possible, in some areas, up to 25 years. This is a structured form of youth training, mainly on the job, which may lead to an SVQ in Craft Baking at Level 2. It can also lead to a Modern Apprenticeship and SVQ Level 3. For placements, contact the Scottish Association of Master Bakers (see FURTHER INFORMATION).

National Traineeships – in England and Wales only, are available to young people in all TEC areas, with usual entry at 16–18 years with some possibility up to 25 years. Training is mostly on the job leading to an NVQ Craft Bakery Level 2. It can lead on to a Modern Apprenticeship and NVQ Level 3.

Modern Apprenticeships – part of the Skillseekers Initiative in Scotland – are available for young people mainly in craft bakeries. Training is on the job, plus college studies, and normally takes about three years. The Apprenticeship leads to NVQ/SVQ in Craft Baking at Level 2 and NVQ/SVQ in Craft Baking (Technical Operations) at Level 3. Additional qualifications may be acquired such as GNVQ/GSVQ units or BTEC Baking Technology modules/SQA Craft Baking units.

NVQs/SVQs – available in Craft Baking at Level 2 and at Level 3 in Craft Baking (Technical Operations). Employees of any age can be assessed for these, as they are based on competencies acquired.

For plant bakers, the relevant NVQs/SVQs are in Food and Drink Manufacturing Operations at Levels 1 and 2. Level 3 in Supervisory Management and Technical Operations is also available. Modern Apprenticeships and National Traineeships in food manufacturing have been developed by the Food and Drink National Training Organisation.

BTEC National Diploma in Science (Baking Technology) – is a two-year full-time course, which may be taken before applying to employers, available at a number of colleges, including Thomas Danby College, Leeds, and the University of the South Bank, London. BTEC qualifications are particularly useful for intending supervisors and managers. In addition to the national diploma, first diploma/certificate, national certificate and higher national diploma/certificate courses are available.

SQA Scottish National Certificate in Craft Baking – is a one-year full-time course, which needs no formal entry qualifications. An SQA Higher National Certificate in Bakery and Confectionery Production is also available, for which entry requirements may be the SNC, SVQ Level 2, or appropriate work experience within a bakery. The HNC is particularly useful for people aiming to work at technician or supervisory levels.

Basic hygiene training is compulsory for all food handlers, and health and safety qualifications are recommended for all bakers.

LATE ENTRY

There are no age restrictions on entry, but employers have, traditionally, tended to favour school-leavers. However, shift working in the plant baking industry means that employees usually have to be at least 18 years.

There may be specific training opportunities directed at adults available in some areas for this type of work. Candidates may have to satisfy certain conditions to be eligible. Contact your local Jobcentre, careers office or TEC/LEC for details.

OPPORTUNITIES

There are estimated to be about 125,000 people employed in the British baking industry of which about 50,000 to 60,000 work as bakers. There are opportunities throughout the country. Overall, employment in the industry has been decreasing for a number of years, as baking processes have become increasingly automated. The decrease in employment has been mainly in the plant baking sector, which currently employs about 25,000 people in about 70 bakeries. The majority of employees in the plant baking industry are adults.

In-store bakeries are increasing their share of the bread market, and most large supermarkets now have their own in-store bakery. There is a growing number of jobs in this sector.

The National Association of Master Bakers, which represents craft bakeries in England and Wales, has some 1,600 member firms. Some of these are very small, with just one shop and a bakery attached; others are chains, supplying five or six shops or, in a few cases, a much larger number of outlets. In Scotland, some 350 craft bakeries – also varying considerably in size – are represented by the Scottish Association of Master Bakers.

PAY AND CONDITIONS

In plant bakeries a skilled (Group 2) operative receives approximately £174 for a basic 39-hour week; around £380 when overtime plus shift premiums are taken into account. A Group 4 worker earns approximately £163 as a basic and approximately £350 with shift and overtime payments.

Standard working hours are 39 a week, over five days. Very early starts (4am or earlier) are less often required than in the past, and starting times of 6am to 7am are now more common. Plant bakeries operate 24 hours a day; staff work shifts, on a rota system. Shift and overtime working for full-time workers is usually compulsory.

In craft and in-store bakeries, Saturday work (to produce bread for sale the same day) is fairly common. This may attract overtime rates of pay, or may be part of a standard Tuesday to Saturday week.

In plant bakeries, employees covered by negotiated agreements receive 25 days' paid holiday. In craft bakeries, the agreements allow for 20 days' paid holiday a year, plus one extra day holiday over the Christmas and New Year period. After five years' service, staff are entitled to an extra two days' holiday. Holiday entitlement for in-store bakery staff depends on the policy of individual employers.

There are limited opportunities for part-time employment.

BAKING AND CONFECTIONERY: SAC

Some specialist types of work – such as cake decoration – are quite often done on a part-time basis. Part-time work is also available in retail bakers shops, for which separate Bakery Service NVQs/SVQs are available.

PROSPECTS

Plant bakeries offer a full range of career opportunities. It is possible for young people entering plant baking at any level to reach production management, provided they gain an understanding of production techniques and have managerial capabilities.

In-store and craft bakeries, which are generally fairly small, offer prospects for promotion – to supervisor level, for example. Prospects are better for those who are prepared to be mobile, moving to different areas to take up more responsible posts.

Self-employment – setting up and running a small bakery – is possible for those with several years' experience of the work. The National Association of Master Bakers offers guidance on self-employment and runs a finance company that provides loans to people wishing to purchase a bakery business.

Some bakers transfer into related areas of work, for instance, with flour-milling companies and baking equipment manufacturers. These firms employ test bakers, who experiment with different baking methods and ingredients, and they also employ bakers as technical advisers, trainers or sales representatives.

There are also opportunities to teach bakery skills at colleges of further and higher education.

RELATED OCCUPATIONS

Chef, cook, kitchen assistant, production operative (food manufacturing), retail assistant (bakery).

FURTHER INFORMATION

The Federation of Bakers*, 6 Catherine Street, London, WC2B 5JW, 0171 420 7190

The National Association of Master Bakers (NAMB)*, 21 Baldock Street, Ware, Herts SG12 9DH, 01920 468061 (please include A4 sae)

The Scottish Association of Master Bakers (SAMB)*, Atholl House, 4 Torphichen Street, Edinburgh EH3 8JQ, 0131 229 1401

The Craft Bakery Training Organisation (Scotland)* – as for SAMB

Bakery Training Council (NTO)*, Dovecote Barn, South Wraxall, Bradford-on-Avon, Wiltshire BA15 2SE 01225 864500

FURTHER READING

Leaflets/booklets are available from the addresses marked*.

In the careers library classified under SAC.

MEAT INDUSTRY: SAC

MEAT PROCESS WORKER CLCI:SAC

BACKGROUND INFORMATION

The most visible part of the meat and poultry industry is the high street butcher, but independent retailers (who are covered in a separate article: RETAIL BUTCHER: OFM) only form one part of the meat chain. There are also those who work in abattoirs, process plants, wholesalers, manufacturers and supermarkets, and those who work as meat inspectors and catering butchers. Increasingly, these activities overlap – for instance, slaughtering, processing and manufacturing may be combined on one site. Factories combining these operations are known as meat plants.

THE WORK

Meat process workers usually specialize in one of the following:

Abattoirs

Animals are humanely slaughtered in abattoirs, which may be part of meat plants or may be separate. Livestock arrive at the meat plant or abattoir in lorries. Some workers are responsible for unloading the animals and receiving them into pre-slaughter pens (known as 'lairage'), where they are kept for a short time. The animals are then moved from the lairage to the stunning pen. Slaughtermen/women stun the animals – to render them insensitive to pain – then kill them quickly. The carcasses are hoisted onto an overhead line where they are bled. Further on, the hides are removed. After skinning, carcasses are 'dressed', which involves trimming, cleaning and the removal of the edible offals.

The carcasses are now ready for cutting into sides and quarters (known as 'primary cutting'). In some abattoirs they are then prepared for dispatch as whole carcasses, to be further cut up (or processed) at wholesalers or retail butchers. In the larger meat plants, further cutting and boning continues, both mechanically and by hand, to prepare joints and cuts. In poultry plants, slaughter and processing is largely an automated process.

All work in an abattoir is subject to strict public health controls, monitored by the Meat Hygiene Service.

Meat wholesalers

Some staff of meat wholesalers buy livestock from markets; others cut and prepare carcasses that have been supplied by the abattoir; others sell to retailers and other customers, including meat manufacturers, from depots and meat markets, including overseas customers.

Catering butchers

Companies vary in the type of work they do. Some workers take deliveries from abattoirs and meat plants, process and distribute them to restaurants, caterers or public institutions. Some carry out primary cutting, leaving the final preparation to the caterer. Others are involved in producing cuts, joints, oven-ready dishes and other products to the caterer's strict specifications. There is particular emphasis in catering butchery on portion size, weight, cost and packing.

Meat manufacturing

In larger meat and poultry plants, some of the meat passes through to the manufacturing stage, but meat manufacturing is also carried out in specific factories, large and small, which may not be related to abattoirs. Workers produce sausages, pies, pâtés, ready-made dishes, frozen foods and other meat products, and cure bacon and ham. Much of the work is broken down into simple, repetitive tasks, carried out on a continuous production line, in factory conditions. In smaller companies, more traditional craft skills are required, with staff carrying out a wide range of processing operations.

In all sectors of the meat processing industry, there is an emphasis on cleanliness, hygiene and food safety. In smaller factories the cleaning and maintenance may be carried out by the process workers, but in larger factories this will be a specialist function.

WORK ENVIRONMENT

Abattoirs and meat plants are cool and airy. The environment is designed to protect the health and safety of workers and to ensure the food safety of products, with hygienic practices observed at all stages. All workers wear protective and hygienic clothing, including head coverings.

Many workers (though not all) experience very cold conditions during brief periods spent in chill rooms and refrigerated areas, used for storage. Special clothing is provided for this.

In abattoirs and meat and poultry processing plants conditions can be noisy, and it may be necessary to wear ear defenders in fully automated plants. Smells can be unpleasant, particularly in abattoirs.

Much of the work involves standing.

SKILLS AND INTERESTS

All staff working with meat must pay strict attention to food safety and hygiene. Personal cleanliness is essential.

Most jobs demand the ability to work with others as a member of a team.

Workers who are directly involved in slaughtering need a straightforward, unsentimental approach to killing animals for food. In the abattoir and in other stages of the meat processing chain, it may be necessary for some workers to handle carcasses, and for these manual lifting and carrying jobs some strength is required.

Manual dexterity is required for jobs that involve cutting and boning meat.

On the production line, it is important to be able to carry out repetitive tasks consistently and quickly whilst maintaining high standards of hygiene.

ENTRY REQUIREMENTS

There are no formal educational entry requirements. However, for those aiming to reach supervisory or technical level, it is an advantage to have some GCSEs/S grades or GNVQs/GSVQs.

The job of slaughterman/woman is restricted by law to people aged 18 or over.

Every slaughterman/woman involved in killing must, under European Union legislation, be licensed by the local authority. Licences must be renewed annually.

TRAINING

National Traineeships are available in England and Wales leading to NVQs in Meat Processing at Levels 1 and 2. All NVQs at this level include compulsory units in health and safety, hygiene, teamwork and quality procedures. Units

MEAT INDUSTRY: SAC

are awarded on the basis of continuous assessment at colleges, training centres and in the workplace.

Some companies offer opportunities for young people via a Modern Apprenticeship leading to NVQ/SVQ Level 3 in Meat Processing (Technical Operations). In Scotland, Skillseekers may be available.

The Meat Training Council offers further qualifications leading to Associateship and Graduate Membership. These are aimed at those seeking advancement in the industry. They include modules in abattoir, catering butchery, manufacturing plant, poultry industry, and wholesale distribution. These qualifications are examination-based.

Nearly 70 colleges and training centres offer courses leading to NVQs/SVQs and the Meat Training Council's other qualifications. Courses are generally part-time, over two years, but one-year full-time courses are available at some colleges.

The Royal Society of Health (RSH) qualification for meat inspectors may be taken after the Associateship of the Meat Training Council, via a one-year part-time course, or as part of a one-year full-time course leading to the Associateship and RSH.

LATE ENTRY

Adult entry is very common, particularly in the manufacturing sector of meat plants. Most employers welcome applications from mature people. There are good opportunities in manufacturing for women returners, and part-time jobs are plentiful. Experience on a production line is useful, but not essential.

Related NVQs/SVQs are useful; it may be possible for adults with experience, who lack formal qualifications, to gain an NVQ/SVQ via Accreditation of Prior Learning (APL).

There may be specific training opportunities directed at adults available in some areas for this type of work. Candidates may have to satisfy certain conditions to be eligible. Contact your local Jobcentre, careers office or TEC/LEC for details.

OPPORTUNITIES

It is estimated that about 60,000 people are employed in meat manufacturing. A further 11,000 work in abattoirs, and about 4,000 in catering butchers and wholesalers.

The overall trend is towards consolidation into larger units, combining all or most of the stages in the meat chain from slaughter to shrink-wrapping for supermarkets. At the same time, however, there has been an increase in the number of small firms that concentrate on specialist products, such as pâtés.

The number of abattoirs not linked to meat plants has been decreasing for some time, and further closures are expected, as more stringent domestic and European Union hygiene legislation comes into force.

PAY AND CONDITIONS

Minimum wage rates for adults is approximately £150 gross a week, depending on the individual's level of skill and the area of the country. However, bonus and other incentives boost take-home pay significantly for most people.

Full-time staff work a 40-hour week, usually Monday to Friday. Some employers may operate a shift system. There are many part-time jobs in meat manufacturing.

PROSPECTS

There are good prospects of promotion to supervisory and management posts, and into quality control, product development and other related specialisms, for committed and able people.

After further training it is possible to become a meat inspector; inspectors are employed by the Meat Hygiene Service to check quality and standards in abattoirs and meat plants.

NVQs/SVQs in Meat Processing at Levels 3 and 4 and other Meat Training Council qualifications may be advisable for the more responsible posts.

RELATED OCCUPATIONS

Retail butcher, meat inspector, production worker, quality control inspector, packer, warehouse worker.

FURTHER INFORMATION

Meat Training Council*, PO Box 141, Winterhill House, Snowdon Drive, Milton Keynes MK6 1YY, 01908 231062

Worshipful Company of Butchers, Butchers' Hall, Bartholomew Close, London EC1A 7EB, 0171 606 4106

Scottish Federation of Meat Traders' Associations, 8–10 Needless Road, Perth PH2 0JW, 01738 637785

FURTHER READING

Leaflets/booklets are available from the address marked*.
In the careers library classified under SAC.

BREWING: SAC

TECHNICAL BREWER CLCI:SAC

BACKGROUND INFORMATION

British brewing companies produce about 30 million pints of beer every day. There are over 1,200 brands of beer on the market, each with its own special flavour and characteristics. Almost half of all beer produced is now lager; the more traditional bitters, mild, pale ale and stout make up the remainder.

There are about 60 substantial brewing companies in the UK, operating around 100 breweries. There are also regional brewing companies and small companies. The small breweries offer few opportunities for employment. The majority of openings for technical brewers are with the large firms.

THE WORK

Brewing is a biochemical process in which malt, barley and other cereals or cereal products, water, hops and yeast are combined to produce beer. Variations occur in the properties of these ingredients; it is the brewer's responsibility to ensure beer of a consistent quality, which suits public taste, is produced.

Technical brewers (also called technical or process managers) manage the complex process of beer production, which in most breweries is highly automated. They are responsible for resources – raw materials, plant and equipment – and for managing the work of operators and technicians. They monitor the production process, testing samples (for instance, to check specific gravity, which determines the strength of a beer). Where necessary, technical brewers make adjustments to processes in order to maintain product consistency.

Technical brewers' responsibilities vary according to the size of the company. In a large firm, they are likely to specialize in managing one stage of the brewing process, such as production of wort (malt liquor), fermentation, packaging or quality control. In a small company, a technical brewer may be responsible for several or all aspects of beer production.

In both large and small organizations, technical brewers need a knowledge of the chemistry, biochemistry and biology of the raw materials and their conversion into the finished product. To understand the plant and equipment used in brewing, they also need some knowledge of mechanical, chemical and electrical engineering. The work is likely to involve the use of computers for large-scale operations such as process control; technical brewers may also use personal computers for tasks such as technical calculations.

WORK ENVIRONMENT

Technical brewers spend much of their time in production areas, where conditions can be noisy, hot, wet and sometimes dusty. The work involves a lot of walking and standing; it may involve climbing up and down ladders (fitted to fermentation vessels, for instance). Only a small part of the working day is likely to be spent in the office.

Managing people is an important aspect of the work and there is continual contact with staff at all levels in the organization.

Technical brewers wear protective clothing – laboratory coats, rubber gloves, rubber boots or stout shoes. In noisy parts of the production area they may wear ear defenders; in dusty areas, face masks.

SKILLS AND INTERESTS

Technical brewers need leadership qualities, including initiative, the ability to manage people, and the capacity to develop general business management skills. They have to be able to interact well with other people and to communicate easily.

An interest in science and its practical application is important. Some aptitude for mechanical engineering is required, to understand the operation of plant and machinery.

Numeracy and computer literacy are essential.

Brewers need to be fit and active. Normal colour vision is required to read colour-coded control panels. Good hearing is important, for safety reasons.

ENTRY REQUIREMENTS

Most entrants are now graduates. They enter through one of two routes:

– a degree in a pure or applied scientifically based discipline such as chemistry, biochemistry, food science/technology, microbiology or chemical engineering; or

– a BSc (Honours) in Brewing and Distilling at Heriot-Watt University. Entry to the course is usually with three A levels/four H grades including chemistry, biology and maths or physics. Maths must be offered at GCSE/S grade (A–C/1–3) if not at A level/H grade.

Entrants are usually expected to sit and pass the Institute of Brewing (IOB) Associate Membership Examination (AME), which covers the underlying scientific and engineering knowledge required. The BSc (Hons) in Brewing and Distilling at Heriot-Watt University gives associate membership and exemption from the exam.

TRAINING

The large companies run graduate technical management training programmes, consisting of intensive on- and off-the-job training, together with practical experience, over a period of between one and four years.

Trainee technical managers study for the AME of the IOB. The examination syllabus covers scientific and engineering topics. Candidates may attend intensive modular courses, run by the IOB, covering engineering, malting, wort production, fermentation, and post-fermentation treatments. They are also expected to carry out a substantial amount of private study in their own time.

The practical aspects of technical brewing training are covered by the International Brewers' Guild Certificate of Brewing Competence (CBC). This scheme has been introduced to replace the former pupillage system, and to ensure entrants to the industry obtain practical experience in all aspects of brewing production, in addition to their academic training. The minimum time to complete the syllabus is twelve months, but a considerably longer period may be required. Assessment, in the form of an oral examination in a brewery, is carried out by an experienced senior brewer.

Alternative entry and training routes include the following:

BREWING: SAC

– entry to laboratory-based research and development or quality control in a brewing company, with a relevant degree. After several years it may be possible to transfer to technical management; or

– candidates with relevant degrees and experience in other industries are sometimes recruited as 'direct replacements', taking up operational appointments without going through the normal management training scheme route; or

– A level/H grade entry, with day release or evening study for higher national certificate qualifications. This route is now rare. People who enter via these routes will be expected to study for the AME of the IOB, as above.

Advanced qualifications

Brewers may take the Diploma Master Brewer Examination (DMB) of the IOB. A pass in or exemption from the AME is a prerequisite for those taking the DMB.

An MSc and a postgraduate diploma in brewing are available at Heriot-Watt University. Employers may sponsor recruits with non-brewing degrees on these.

LATE ENTRY

The majority of entrants are recruited directly from institutions of higher education. There are no special provisions for mature entrants, although they may be accepted on relevant degree courses. It is now rare for people to enter technical brewing by promotion from operative and supervisory jobs in the industry.

OPPORTUNITIES

The majority of opportunities are with the large brewing companies, which recruit via the university 'milk round'; smaller companies tend to advertise when they need to fill a specific technical vacancy.

As a result of automation, employment in the production side of brewing has been declining over the years. The number of vacancies for technical brewers is very limited.

Related areas of work in brewing companies, where entry may be easier, include laboratory-based research, development and quality control, brewing engineering, sales, marketing, personnel and distribution.

With large brewing companies, which often have overseas divisions, there may be opportunities to work abroad. Foreign languages may be required.

A list of brewing companies and their addresses is included in the Brewers' and Licensed Retailers' Association (BLRA) information pack, *Technical Management in the Brewing Industry*.

PAY AND CONDITIONS

The large brewing companies have graduate recruitment schemes, and generally offer starting salaries of between £14,000 and £17,000.

Technical brewers who have completed company training schemes are likely, in their first operational appointments, to earn from £20,000 to £30,000. Earnings vary according to the size of the brewery, and geographical area. Salaries for experienced brewers can be substantially higher.

Large breweries operate a two- or three-shift system, and technical brewers are expected to work shifts and weekends. Small breweries may only brew one batch a day, and so do not operate shifts. However, hours of work in a small brewery are likely to be variable and irregular, and on-call duties may be required.

Working away from home for short or long periods of time may be necessary. This is particularly likely during training, when it is important to gain experience in a wide range of operations, but it may happen at any time in a brewer's career – for instance, if the company is setting up a new plant in another area of the country.

PROSPECTS

The IOB Diploma is recognized as the standard of technical excellence by employers. In major companies, it is unlikely that individuals will advance in their careers without this qualification.

The IOB Diploma, along with appropriate personal qualities and management skills, gives a proven competitive advantage, which has seen many IOB members progressing rapidly to the higher echelons of their particular business.

RELATED OCCUPATIONS

Scientist/technician, food scientist/technologist, microbiologist.

FURTHER INFORMATION

Brewers and Licensed Retailers Association*, 42 Portman Square, London W1H 0BB, 0171 486 4831, www.blra.co.uk

International Brewers' Guild*, 8 Ely Place, Holborn, London EC1 6SD, 0171 405 4565

The Institute of Brewing*, 33 Clarges Street, London W1Y 8EE, 0171 499 8144, e-mail: enquiries@iob.org.uk

FURTHER READING

Leaflets/booklets are available from the addresses marked*.

Working in Manufacturing – COIC

In the careers library classified under SAC.

GLASS: SAD

GLASSMAKER CRAFTSMAN/WOMAN
CLCI:SAD

BACKGROUND INFORMATION

Glass is a transparent, hard, brittle substance used for a wide range of purposes in modern industrial societies. It is formed from certain liquids that have the property of cooling below their freezing point without crystallizing. They become liquids of increasingly high viscosity (stiffness) until they are, to all intents and purposes, solid.

The main ingredient of most glasses is silica (sand). This is combined with lime and soda in varying proportions to make the soda lime glass used for many purposes, including windows, light bulbs, bottles and inexpensive tableware. Glass can also be given special qualities by adding other ingredients. Crystal glassware, is made from silica, potassium carbonate, potassium nitrate and red lead. Coloured glasses are produced by adding metallic oxides.

Glass is made by heating the ingredients, together with cullet (scrap glass) of the same type being made, to a very high temperature in a furnace. At these temperatures glass behaves like a normal liquid, but as it cools it becomes malleable. It can then be fabricated into the shape required by one of three main methods: mouth blowing; pressing; and pouring, rolling or drawing. Although all these operations were originally performed by hand, automatic processes have been developed for large-scale production and by far the majority of glass products today are made in this way.

Automated production lines employ relatively small numbers of staff. Many are professionally trained engineers and technologists, but there are also jobs for production workers who tend the machinery and intervene when problems arise. These occupations are discussed in articles elsewhere in this book. The most common items still hand-made by traditional methods are lead crystal glassware, other decorative glassware and tableware, and special scientific glass articles.

The glass industry today can be divided into four main sectors. These are: the **container sector,** which produces bottles, jars, light bulbs, vacuum flask interiors, and so on; the **flat glass sector,** which manufactures flat glass for window and vehicle glazing and mirrors; the **fibre sector,** which produces glass fibre products such as glass wool and optical fibres for use in communications systems; and the **tableware and scientific products sector.**

The article below deals with the work of craftsmen/women who produce hand-made tableware and scientific products, as well as art and sculptural glass.

THE WORK

Traditional glassblowers form glass roughly into the shape of the finished article by blowing down a tube, spinning the tube and swinging it backwards and forwards. They then either pass the pipe on to the chairman/servitor to complete the article, or blow it into a mould to shape it further.

Chairmen/servitors (sometimes called **finishers**) receive the partly shaped object still attached to the blow pipe or rod and form it into shape using shaping tongs, a palette knife, wooden blocks and other implements. They usually sit in a chair with long, horizontal, metal-plated arms and roll the blow pipe backwards and forwards to help them shape the glass.

Glass benders bend glass by placing sheet glass or smaller pieces of glass over moulds and putting them in a furnace or kiln. When heated the glass becomes pliable and falls into or over the shape of the mould. Products made this way include curved shop windows, roof-lights and glass domes. Glass benders place the glass and moulds in the kiln and remove them when the glass has bent. They also check the kiln temperature and adjust this if necessary.

Scientific glassblowers (sometimes called **bench glassblowers**) make scientific and industrial glassware by heating glass tubes in a bench burner until they are pliable. They can then make bends and bulbs in them by bending by hand and by blowing into the tubes. Blowing is also used to even out constrictions or sagging in the glass caused by bending.

Glass lathe workers use lathes for large pieces of glassware that cannot be handled on a bench. They join separate pieces of glass together, such as the neck and bulb of a scientific flask, and, like benchworkers, make straight joints and 'T' joints. They also shape glass on the lathe as it rotates heated by burners. Lathe workers use thermally protective gloves where necessary.

Designers develop new designs and products in glassware, taking into account the production methods and costs involved. Some, particularly in the craft sector, combine this with working as glass decorators.

Glass decorators apply decorative designs and finishes to glassware. They use a variety of techniques, including mitre wheel cutting, engraving, sand blasting and stencilling, acid etching and polishing. Decorators work to traditional designs or to new ones created by designers or, in some cases, themselves. Some decorative work involves freehand drawing. This is highly skilled.

Designer craftsmen/women combine the work of designer, glass-blower, chairman/servitor and decorator to produce glass articles from start to finish. They make mainly decorative glassware in small craft workshops or studios. Some craftsmen/women specialize in stained glass work, restoring old stained glass windows and screens, or creating new products. Recent advances in technology mean that it is now possible for craftsmen/women to build and operate their own small glass-making furnaces.

WORK ENVIRONMENT

Conditions in a glass factory can be hot, particularly in the summer months and when workers have to go near the furnaces and kilns. For the most part, however, working conditions are warm though not uncomfortable. Glass factories can also be noisy.

Glassblowers and glass benders have to be on their feet for much of the day, whereas chairmen/servitors, scientific glassblowers and lathe workers tend to do most of their work sitting down. Designers, decorators and designer craftsmen/women also do much of their work seated.

Chairmen/servitors and glassblowers usually work in teams, with workers passing articles from one to another for further shaping. Glass benders, scientific glass blowers and lathe workers work largely alone, though they may occasionally join with others on large jobs.

GLASS: SAD

SKILLS AND INTERESTS

Chairmen/servitors and glassblowers need to be good with their hands and in the use of tools and equipment to control the distribution and shaping of the hot glass. Some physical strength and stamina are needed to manipulate the weight of the rod and metal. Scientific glassblowers need to have nimble fingers and a steady hand. The main requirements of a glass bender are patience and care.

All glass workers need a good eye for shape and size, and to be able to work quickly and accurately. They need to be able to work with others as part of a team.

Self-employed craftsmen/women need to have or develop a range of business skills, including marketing, bookkeeping, pricing and estimating, negotiating and time management.

Glass decorators and designer craftsmen/women may, depending on the nature of their work, require good colour vision.

ENTRY REQUIREMENTS

For jobs as glassblowers, scientific glassblowers, lathe workers, benders and chairmen/servitors, most employers do not require any specific educational qualifications, although exam passes in science and craft subjects are an advantage.

The main way to become a designer or a craftsman/woman is to take a course in design with an option in glass. These are mostly degree level courses, for which the minimum requirement is five GCSEs/S grades (A–C/1–3) and two A-levels/three H-grades, or an equivalent qualification, such as the BTEC National Diploma in Design or Advanced GNVQ/GSVQ Level III in Art and Design. Applicants are also usually expected to show practical evidence of their ability and commitment to art and design by submitting a portfolio of their work.

A non-degree full-time course is available at Dudley College of Technology. No specific academic qualifications are required for this course, but enthusiasm and commitment, as well as satisfactory references, are needed.

In Scotland the requirements for degree-level design courses are five GCSEs/S grades (A–C/1–3) including English, and three H-grades or two A levels. Art and English at A-level or H-grade are normally expected but not mandatory. A degree course in Glass Technology is available at Edinburgh College of Art.

TRAINING

Glassblowers and chairmen/servitors learn mainly by working alongside experienced workers, by being shown and by carrying out the operations themselves. The same applies to glass benders, though in a few cases a trainee bender may attend college on day release to study for the City and Guilds award in Glass Technology.

For scientific glassblowers and lathe workers, some companies have training schools where trainees learn how to manipulate glass, how to form bends and constrictions, and how to join pieces of tubing together. Similarly, lathe workers learn by starting on simple jobs and gradually develop skills and expertise. In many firms trainees learn both scientific glassblowing and lathe work.

Some London-based firms send trainees to college on day release to study for the qualifications of the British Society of Scientific Glassblowers (BSSG) or City and Guilds.

Designers are usually graduates from courses where they learn all aspects of glass making and decorating. Glass decorators are often trained on the job, and may also be sent on part-time college courses.

Youth training in the glass industry is supported by Glass Training Limited (GTL). Programmes are run by a number of firms, each of which adapts the programme according to the type of glassware it produces. Trainees are first given an all-round introduction to the glass industry followed by specialist training suited to their abilities and needs.

Trainees can study an open learning course called Glass Manufacture which was set up by Glass Training Limited in conjunction with Dudley College of Technology. This course is also available to other employees. Students who successfully complete the course receive a Dudley College/Glass Training Limited certificate. They may also sit for the City and Guilds 0690 examinations (Sections 1 and 2) in Glass Manufacture.

Another open learning course is the BTEC National Certificate in Engineering Process Technology (Glass), run via Wakefield College and St Helens College. The section of the course relating to glass is mainly provided by the Glass Manufacture open learning course materials.

Entry through Modern Apprenticeships (part of the Skillseekers Initiative in Scotland), leading to NVQ/SVQ at Level 3 may also be available. Contact your local careers office or TEC/LEC for details.

Designer craftsmen/women usually take a full-time training course such as the BA (Honours) degree in Three-dimensional Design. The University of Sunderland and Edinburgh College of Art offers BA Honours in Design and Applied Arts with specialisms in Glass or Architectural Glass. Surrey Institute of Art and Design offers a three year course in Three-dimensional Design–Glass and Stourbridge College of Technology and Art offers various glass courses. Many other design courses include glass as an option, though not always to the same extent as those mentioned.

A non-degree course in glass techniques and technology is run by Dudley College of Technology at its International Glass Centre in Brierley Hill. This is a full-time 36-week course starting in September and lasting till June. It is primarily aimed at students who wish to work in a glass studio, or set up their own businesses. The course is, however, accredited by the West Midlands Access Federation, which means that students can gain credits towards higher education entrance requirements. Students spend about a third of their time on glass making, a third on the technology of glass (including furnace building and design) and a third on glass decoration. Dudley College also organizes short courses on demand.

NVQs/SVQs in Glass Processing and Scientific Glass Product Fabrication are available at Levels 1, 2 and 3. NVQs/SVQs in Glass Batch Processing Operations, Glass Melting Operations, Glass Forming Operations and Production Support Operations – Glass (Cold End Operations) are also available at Level 2.

LATE ENTRY

Many of the colleges running the courses mentioned in TRAINING are prepared to waive their normal entry requirements for mature candidates.

GLASS: SAD

The course at Dudley College is particularly popular among adults changing career.

OPPORTUNITIES

Opportunities for craft glass workers are limited. Only a very small number are being recruited at present. Manufacturers of glass articles of this kind are situated in all parts of the country, but with a particularly strong concentration in London, the West Midlands and the North East of England, and Perthshire in Scotland.

Some companies may be NVQ/SVQ assessment centres and can offer access to qualifications within the national framework.

Self-employment as a designer craftsman/woman is possible by setting up a workshop or studio. As well as excellent craft skills, a range of business skills are needed for success.

PAY AND CONDITIONS

The average earnings of the glass craft workers covered in this article are around £260 a week. Chairmen/servitors and scientific glassblowers usually earn more than other craft workers as their work is the most skilled. Some workers such as glass decorators are paid at piece-rates, so their earnings can vary.

Most craft glassmakers work a 39-hour week, Monday to Friday, usually starting at 8am. Overtime may sometimes be required. Some companies operate a shift system. Craft crystal workers often work 6am to 2pm.

PROSPECTS

Glassblowers can go on to become chairmen/servitors, but for the most part, craft glass workers are limited to reaching positions as supervisors or foremen/women. There is no promotion ladder for self-employed designer craftsmen/women. For them a rising income depends on hard work, business acumen, skill, and – to some extent – luck.

RELATED OCCUPATIONS

Glazier, three-dimensional designer, carpenter/joiner, ceramics/pottery glazer/painter/decorator, materials scientist/technologist, glass technologist, production worker.

FURTHER INFORMATION

Glass Training Limited*, BGMC Building, Northumberland Road, Sheffield S10 2UA, 0114 266 1494, www.glasstrg.demon.co.uk

British Society of Scientific Glassblowers, 24 St Michael's Avenue, Houghton Regis, Dunstable, Beds LU5 5DN

Dudley College of Technology*, International Glass Centre, Moor Street, Brierley Hill, West Midlands DY5 3EP, 01384 455433 (ext 4267), www.dudleycol.ac.uk

Glass and Glazing Federation*, 44–48 Borough High Street, London SE1 1XB

Guild of Glass Engravers*, 19 Wildwood Road, London NW11 6UL. 0181 731 9352

Rural Development Commission*, 141 Castle Street, Salisbury, Wilts SP1 3TP, 01722 336255

Made in Scotland Ltd, Station Road, Beauly, Inverness-shire IV4 7EH, 01463 782578, www.made-in-scotland.co.uk

Scottish Glass Society*, 11 Inverleith Place Lane, Edinburgh EH3 5QJ, 0131 552 3392

North Lands Creative Glass, Quatre Bras, Lybster, Caithness, KW3 6BN, 01593 721325

University and Colleges Admissions Service (UCAS)*, Fulton House, Jessop Avenue, Cheltenham, Glos GL50 3SH, 01242 544867

FURTHER READING

Leaflets/booklets are available from the addresses marked*.

In the careers library classified under SAD.

LEATHER GOODS: SAF

LEATHER TECHNOLOGIST CLCI:SAF

BACKGROUND INFORMATION

Leather is made in a tannery from animal skins and hides. In Britain the main animals used are cows, pigs, sheep and goats. The raw hides and skins are cured or preserved immediately to prevent decay.

After pre-treatment to remove unwanted components such as flesh, hair and salt, the hides and skins are ready for tanning. Tanning agents bond the protein fibres in the skin giving leather its unique, flexible, hard-wearing qualities.

A variety of tanning substances may be used. The most common are chromium salts, though for environmental reasons traditional tanning methods using vegetable extracts are enjoying a revival. Other tanning substances include aluminium and zirconium salts, oil (used mainly for chamois leather) and synthetics.

Tannages are often used in combination, consecutively or simultaneously, to produce leather with just the right qualities for the application intended. Vegetable-tanned leather, for example, is retanned with chrome to produce semi-chrome shoe uppers and suede and glove leather.

After tanning, and retanning if required, the leather is then dressed and finished, through processes such as shaving, dyeing, rolling, fat-liquoring, softening, lubricating and surface coating. It is then ready to be crafted into any of the wide range of domestic and industrial leather products.

Domestic leather products include: boot and shoe soles, heels, inner soles and uppers; saddles, bridles, harnesses and horse collars; travelling bags, suitcases and briefcases; straps; book bindings; handbags, purses and wallets; gloves; upholstery; belts, jackets and other garments; razor strops; and footballs, cricket balls and other sporting goods. Industrial products include: aprons; buffing wheels; textile carders and combers; washers; hydraulic packings; lithographic equipment; and machinery belting.

The leathercraft industry in the UK is made up mainly of small firms with an average of 25 to 30 employees, though there are a few larger firms. The major geographical centres are Walsall – where saddles, harnesses and small items such as purses and wallets are produced – and London – where handbags are made. Leathercraft businesses do, however, exist in all parts of the UK.

THE WORK

Leather technologists apply scientific and technical principles in the process of leather manufacture. They aim to ensure the leather's aesthetic appeal is maintained without compromising physical attributes such as durability. Technologists must be familiar with: all the processes and operations that are needed to prepare skins for tanning; the tanning process itself; and the many subsequent operations that determine the thickness, softness, texture, colour and water resistance of the leather.

Leather technologists must continually balance the practical requirements of day-to-day production (including the need for the tannery to make a profit) with the strict disciplines of the pure sciences.

Technologists have to understand the nature of the materials used in leather production and the ways in which they react. They control these reactions by methods such as varying the time a reaction is allowed to proceed and altering the mix and concentration of chemicals used. They test and analyse the finished products in laboratories, using chemicals, dyestuffs and small-scale apparatus, to ensure the leather produced has all the required qualities.

Technologists do some office work, writing reports on research projects and on management topics such as plant production and performance. This may involve statistical analysis, which is likely to require the use of computers.

Depending on the size and the nature of the company, technologists may supervise operatives and technicians, and may in turn be responsible to senior managers or to a board of directors. The UK leather industry is becoming increasingly automated, and technologists are responsible for designing production layouts and for engineering aspects of processing. They have to ensure plant performs efficiently, by minimizing costs incurred on items such as energy, labour, time and raw materials.

Finally, leather technologists are responsible for the monitoring and control of effluent, as well as ensuring the health and safety of the workforce.

WORK ENVIRONMENT

Most leather technologists work indoors in tanneries. Much of the work is practical, dealing with hides and chemicals and controlling and monitoring large-scale machinery. Some office work is also involved.

Although modern tanneries are usually clean, light and airy, some noxious substances are used, and protective clothing has to be worn at least some of the time.

The leather industry obtains its supplies and sells its products all over the world. Hence the job of the technologist may well involve travel, both within the UK and overseas.

SKILLS AND INTERESTS

Technologists must be flexible and adaptable, always seeking to solve problems in new and different ways. An aptitude for science, particularly chemistry, is essential, and practical ability is required for working with large-scale machinery.

An aptitude for staff management is important for supervising operatives and technicians. Good communication skills are needed when giving verbal and written reports to senior staff. The work is occasionally physical so technologists should be reasonably fit, but they are not required to do any heavy lifting.

Colour-blindness may be a disadvantage, and an allergy to chemicals or hides would cause major difficulties.

ENTRY REQUIREMENTS

Entry is possible at several levels. For courses leading to the City and Guilds (C&G) Operatives Certificate (4560) and the C&G Craft Certificate (4570), no formal qualifications are required, but candidates would normally already be employed in the leather industry.

For the BTEC Certificate of Achievement in Leather Technology, GCSEs/S grades (A–C/1–3) in maths, chemistry, a second science and a subject showing use of English are the minimum requirements. City and Guilds qualifications provide an alternative entry route.

LEATHER GOODS: SAF

Students with some science qualifications (GCSE or equivalent) and relevant industrial experience (normally of at least two years' duration) can be admitted to the Nene Certificate course (please see TRAINING for details).

Applicants for the BSc Honours Degree in Leather Technology at Nene University College, Northampton, normally require a minimum of five GCSEs/S grades (A–C/1–3) including maths, physics and chemistry, with two A levels/three H grades including at least one from maths, physics and chemistry. The BTEC Certificate of Achievement in Leather Technology also gives entry to the BSc course. Alternative qualifications with a similar physical science content are also considered.

TRAINING

The following courses are available at the British School of Leather Technology (BSLT) at Nene University College, Northampton, which is the only establishment in the UK offering formal training for leather technologists. The school's purpose built Leathersellers Centre has a well equipped modern tannery as well as testing and research laboratories.

For those joining the industry direct from school, on-the-job training is supplemented by courses leading to City and Guilds Operatives and Craft Certificates. The Operatives Certificate (4560) gives an introductory overview of leather manufacture, while the Craft Certificate (4570) is a more advanced and comprehensive course which covers the operations of leather processing in more detail, with reference to the underlying science, mathematics and management principles. These courses are normally studied via open learning. Students on open learning courses work at their own pace, assisted by a mentor at their workplace and a tutor based at BSLT.

The one-year full-time BTEC Certificate of Achievement in Leather Technology is designed as a preliminary course to the BSc honours degree, and successful students would normally progress to the degree course in the next session. The subjects covered are: maths, physics and chemistry; the principles and practice of leather production; laboratory techniques; chemical engineering; tannery engineering; quality assurance; the use of computers; health and safety; and environmental issues (clean technology).

The major course offered by the British School of Leather Technology is the BSc Honours Degree in Leather Technology. The major themes of the course developed through the three years are: leather science and technology; evaluation and testing; chemistry and engineering; and the management of production. A final-year project brings together these themes in a practical investigatory study.

A one-year taught MSc in Leather Technology is available for graduates working in the leather producing and allied industries. Higher degrees (MPhil and PhD) are also available by research. It is possible for a student with no initial qualifications to progress from the C&G Operative's Certificate via BTEC qualifications and a BSc degree to a PhD.

All courses at Nene University College are flexible, and it is possible for students to have different entry and exit points according to their needs and experience. It is also possible for students to take a break from their studies and return later to complete their education.

LATE ENTRY

Adult entry at technologist level is normally restricted to applicants who have followed one of the formal training courses described above.

Graduates in related subjects such as chemistry may be recruited into the industry. They are often sponsored to take a course such as the one-year MSc in Leather Technology. Students who already have at least one year's previous tannery experience (and, normally, have reached the age of 20) can take the one-year full-time Nene Certificate in Leather Studies. This course combines the study of practical leather-making with leather science, management and other relevant subjects.

OPPORTUNITIES

Most technologists work in tanneries. Centres of production have been traditionally sited near rivers. The main production areas today are in the East Midlands, the west of England, Lancashire, Yorkshire and the Scottish lowlands.

Leather manufacturing in the UK has contracted in recent years due to factors such as increased foreign competition and the replacement of leather in some applications by synthetic products such as plastics. However, a number of companies with high quality products and modern manufacturing methods are trading successfully, and appear to have good prospects for the future.

A number of companies in the UK employ leather technologists, though the job may not always be given that title. Job descriptions vary between companies, particularly with regard to areas of responsibility and the amount of supervisory work involved. Generally, smaller companies offer greater variety of work, a shorter management hierarchy and, therefore, more responsibility. In larger companies, the technologist can expect a more clearly demarcated job and a more clearly defined position on the management ladder.

Most leather technologists are directly involved in leather tanning and processing. Technologists also work in the footwear industry, in companies specializing in the import or export of leather, and in companies supplying chemicals and equipment to tanneries. There are many opportunities to work overseas. Teaching posts are occasionally available, as are research and commercial posts with BLC Leather Technology Centre, the technical and consulting centre for leather world-wide.

PAY AND CONDITIONS

Newly qualified leather technologists earn between £8,000 and £12,000, with about 20+ days' paid holiday, plus public holidays. Many firms have private pension schemes.

Leather technologists usually work the same hours as the factory. As leather production is a continuous process they may be required to work outside these hours, especially if problems arise.

PROSPECTS

A technologist may progress to production manager or technical manager. It is also possible to become a works chemist, or to work on the commercial side of the business in buying, sales or marketing. Formal qualifications in leather science and technology are increasingly a necessity for promotion to senior positions.

LEATHER GOODS: SAF

RELATED OCCUPATIONS

Scientist, technician, materials scientist, engineer, textile technician, production manager, leather craft worker.

FURTHER INFORMATION

BLC Leather Technology Centre*, Leather Trade House, Kings Park Road, Moulton Park, Northampton NN3 6JD, 01604 679999, www.blcleathertech.com

The British School of Leather Technology*, Nene University College, Park Campus, Boughton Green Road, Northampton NN2 7AL, 01604 735500, www.nene.ac.uk

Leather Producers' Association, contact J Purvis (Secretary), 8 Queensbury Road, Kettering, Northants, 01536 483668

National Union of the Knitwear, Footwear and Apparel Trades, 55 New Walk, Leicester LE1 7EB, 0116 255 6703

The Society of Dyers and Colourists*, Perkin House, PO Box 244, 82 Grattan Road, Bradford BD1 2JB, 01274 725138

Society of Leather Technologists and Chemists Ltd, 38 Roseholme Road, Abington, Northampton NN1 4TQ, 01604 639306

Society of Master Saddlers*, Kettles Farm, Mickfield, Stowmarket, Suffolk IP14 6BY, 01449 711642

FURTHER READING

Leaflets/booklets are available from the addresses marked*.

Relevant books are available from the Nene University College bookshop.

In the careers library classified under SAF.

TEXTILES: SAG/SAV

1. **TEXTILE TECHNICIAN CLCI:SAG**
2. **TEXTILE DYEING TECHNICIAN CLCI:SAV/SAG**
3. **TEXTILE OPERATIVE CLCI:SAG**

BACKGROUND INFORMATION

Technology has transformed the textile industry in recent years. Intricate and time-consuming jobs, such as splicing yarn or threading the loom, have been largely automated. In many modern textile mills, computers govern the pattern of warp and weft in weaving, the degree of twist and tension in spinning, and can translate a design on the drawing board into an electronic pattern-card controlling the looms or knitting machines.

The result of such changes is ever-increasing productivity from a decreasing workforce. Even so, textile manufacture remains one of the largest industries in Britain. It employs 160,000 people in firms that range from small businesses specializing in a single process, such as spinning or weaving, to big conglomerates dealing with every stage from raw fibre to finished garment.

The raw materials of the textile industry are natural fibres (such as cotton, wool, angora, silk or jute), man-made ones (and include nylon or viscose) and combinations (such as cotton/polyester). Textile mills turn these materials first into yarn, then into fabric. The products include lace, rope and carpets as well as woven and knitted cloth for fashions, furnishing or industrial uses.

The four main stages of textile production are: yarn preparation; yarn production; weaving or knitting; and dyeing and finishing. New bales of wool or cotton are first sorted and cleaned. Carding machines spread out and straighten the fibres to form a sliver, or soft rope. Man-made fibres may be added at this stage. The sliver is further drawn out, combed and twisted until it is fine and strong enough to be spun into yarn.

Weaving and knitting are the basic processes of cloth production. Cloth comes off the looms or knitting machines in continuous lengths. Some circular knitting machines produce garment shapes such as stockings in linked chains.

Bleaching, dyeing, printing and finishing impart colour, pattern and qualities such as water-resistance, fire-resistance or lustre to the cloth.

1. TEXTILE TECHNICIAN (SAG)

THE WORK

Textile technicians work in most sections of a mill – in production, in design and in dyeing, printing and finishing.

Technicians are responsible for the machinery. They make sure all the mechanical and electrical parts work efficiently, installing the equipment, stripping it down and servicing it regularly. Before each production run they set up the machines for the operatives. When something goes wrong, the technician finds and repairs the fault. Technicians learn to operate the computers that control the machines and will learn basic electronic engineering skills as well, to help them diagnose problems in the electronic components.

Each technician usually looks after the machinery for one particular process, such as spinning or weaving. Weaving technicians, or supervisory technicians, are in charge of the looms, which are large, complex and expensive. Warp (lengthwise) threads are raised and lowered in step as the weft (crosswise) yarn flashes to and fro between them. In the most modern looms, tension, pattern and speed are automatically controlled. With older machines the supervisory technician adjusts and checks the settings. Jacquard looms, which weave the design into the cloth (as opposed to having it printed) are governed by pattern cards. These control a 'harness' of wires, which raise and lower individual warp threads. In some firms a computer translates the design on the drawing board into an electronic pattern card. In others, technicians code the design onto paper pattern and fix up the intricate mesh of wires which forms the harness.

In addition to machine maintenance and adjustment, technicians are responsible for making sure the work of their section goes on safely and efficiently. This involves showing the machine operators what to do, explaining safety procedures and making sure the area is kept tidy. They fill in time sheets and write reports.

WORK ENVIRONMENT

Conditions in textile mills vary widely, but modern factories can be spacious and bright. In some sections the noise level may be high, and ear protectors are required. Some of the processes make the atmosphere warm and humid. Dust is less of a problem as most of the larger particles are eliminated by dust extractors.

Much of the work involves standing, stretching and walking about, ie patrolling.

SKILLS AND INTERESTS

Technicians should enjoy solving mechanical problems. Practical ability is essential. Setting up and adjusting machinery calls for accuracy in measurement and calculations. They should be interested in the rapidly changing technology of the textile industry.

Technicians should be able to work alone, but also to fit in well with others, for example, discussing problems with designers, managers or operatives. They need to express themselves clearly in speech and writing, to give instructions, keep records or write reports.

Technicians need good eyesight, with or without glasses, and, for most jobs, good colour vision.

ENTRY REQUIREMENTS

Candidates for technician training at 16 or 17 years usually require GCSEs/S grades (A–C/1–3) in maths, English and science, with an additional subject at grade D/4 or above, or a qualification of similar standard such as Intermediate GNVQ/GSVQ Level III in relevant subjects such as manufacturing or science. They are also required to show some practical/mechanical ability and for most jobs they need good colour vision. Other qualifications may be considered at the employers' discretion. People over 18 years may also apply for technician training. Entry standards are similar, but most employers are willing to consider a fairly wide range of qualifications and experience provided the candidate is keen and able. Employers may set their own selection tests.

It is also possible to enter technician training after full-time study on the following courses:

– BTEC National Diploma in Textiles: entry requirements are four GCSEs/S grades (A–C/1–3) including maths,

TEXTILES: SAG/SAV

English and science, or a BTEC First Qualification in science;

- SQA national certificate modules: suitable GCSE/S grades are usually required;
- BTEC National Certificate in Science (Textile Coloration): entry requirements are three or four GCSEs/S grades (A–C/1–3).
- BTEC/SQA Higher Diploma in Textiles: entry requirements are BTEC/SQA national certificate/diploma, or Advanced GNVQ/GSVQ Level III, or four GCSEs/S grades (A–C/1–3) including maths, English and science, plus one A level/two H grades.

TRAINING

Opportunities are available via a Modern Apprenticeship, part of the Skillseekers Initiative in Scotland, for young people, leading to at least an NVQ/SVQ Level 3. Contact your local careers office or TEC/LEC for details.

All apprentices work towards NVQ/SVQ Level 3 or above. During their training they may also take appropriate City and Guilds and/or BTEC/SQA national certificates in textiles. Apprentices who are already part-qualified on entry – for example, they may have begun a college course – are expected to cover the same training and achieve NVQ/SVQ Level 3 in a shorter time. The training programme for each entrant is modified to take into account existing qualifications and experience. There are similar arrangements for older entrants.

In the wool industry, apprenticeships are integrated into the Career Structure Scheme of the Confederation of British Wool Textiles. This is a training programme for technicians and supervisory technicians of any age. Trainees under 21 years follow the terms and conditions of a Modern Apprenticeship. The scheme combines structured experience on the job, under continuous monitoring, with part-time study for appropriate qualifications. These include NVQs/SVQs up to at least Level 3. In year two, trainees also take C&G exams or BTEC/SQA national certificates. In the third year, they may begin studying for BTEC/SQA Higher National Certificate in Textiles and/or supervisory studies leading to NVQ/SVQ Level 4 or NEBS Management (National Examining Board for Supervision and Management) qualifications.

NVQs/SVQS are available in: Manufacturing Textiles or Products from Textiles at Levels 1 and 2; Product Development: Apparel at Level 3; and Textile Technician at Level 3.

A new NVQ/SVQ Manufacturing Textiles at Level 3 is proposed and should be available by the end of 1998. There are no set entry requirements. Contact your local TEC/LEC for details.

LATE ENTRY

Most candidates for technician training are aged 16–24 years. However, adults over this age are welcome to apply. They are selected by test and interview. Training takes account of previous qualifications and experience. People of any age can take NVQs/SVQs. Existing qualifications may afford exemption from part or all of the units at any level (Accreditation of Prior Learning).

OPPORTUNITIES

West Yorkshire, Lancashire, the Midlands and the borders of Scotland are the main areas of textile manufacture, with smaller centres all over the country. Many craft and operative jobs have disappeared. However, there is great demand for people with technical interests and abilities who want to learn about the new and developing technology of textile production.

The journal *Textile Month* carries job vacancies.

PAY AND CONDITIONS

Rates of pay differ from place to place, and are usually enhanced by shift allowances, overtime etc. A 16- or 17-year-old trainee starts at about £82.40 to £92.70 a week. Salaries for fully trained and experienced technicians range from about £10,300 to £16,995 (£198 to £327 a week).

PROSPECTS

Promotion to senior technical positions can lead on to more specialized scientific and technical work in quality control or research and development.

Technicians who are following the Career Structure Scheme of the Confederation of British Wool Textiles, and experienced technicians who like to teach or take responsibility for others, may go on to supervisory grades. From there they may go into professional management, technical sales or business management. Study to at least BTEC/SQA higher national certificate level is required. It is possible to continue studying part-time for a BSc honours degree in textile technology.

These professional qualifications open up a wide range of opportunities in textile research, marketing and management both in the UK and abroad.

RELATED OCCUPATIONS

Textile operative, textile technologist, textile designer, textile dyeing technician, engineering technician, scientist/technician.

FURTHER INFORMATION

The Confederation of British Wool Textiles Ltd*, Merrydale House, Roydsdale Way, Bradford BD4 6SB, 01274 652207

The Cotton and Allied Textiles Industry Training Organisation*, Suffolk Street Works, Pendleton, Salford, M6 6DX, 0161 745 8333

FURTHER READING

Leaflets/booklets are available from the addresses marked*.

In the careers library classified under SAG.

2. TEXTILE DYEING TECHNICIAN (SAV/SAG)

THE WORK

Dyeing technicians are responsible for dyeing materials to the shade the customer wants. Dyeing involves a series of chemical processes, and each type of material requires different treatment. Technicians in collaboration with

TEXTILES: SAG/SAV

other colleagues can decide which dyes and which machine processes to use. They work out the dye recipes for each shade of dye and calculate the machine settings that govern temperature, heating rate and timing. In some dye houses this information is specified on a computer database.

Recipes are tested in laboratories before being applied in quantity. On the factory floor, dyeing technicians supervise operatives, who mix the dyes and feed the materials through the machines. They make sure the machinery is running smoothly, check the dyeing process at each stage, and take samples for testing.

Quality control is an important part of the job. Dyeing technicians are responsible for testing the treated materials for colour fastness, colour match, finishes, and so on, using a variety of physical and chemical tests. Computers are often used in colour matching.

Technicians keep records of orders, materials, recipes and processes. They may be involved in choosing and buying the dyestuffs. Assistants or trainees may work under their direction in the laboratory.

Most dyeing technicians specialize in dyeing, but their training includes printing, finishing and the preparation processes of bleaching and cleaning. They may be involved in these, for example by choosing pigments for printing or by making sure that the chemicals used are compatible with the dyestuffs.

WORK ENVIRONMENT

Bleaching, dyeing, printing and finishing may take place either in a general textile mill or in specialist bleach and dye works. In a textile mill, the dye house is usually set apart from the main shop floor. Conditions vary from place to place. Modern dye houses are warm but spacious and airy, so the fumes and steam from the dyeing processes are well dispersed. Dyeing technicians spend a good deal of their time in laboratories or in the dyer's office partitioned off from the shop floor.

SKILLS AND INTERESTS

Dyeing technicians should be interested in science, particularly chemistry and physics, and should enjoy practical laboratory work. Mathematical ability and an interest in working with computers are desirable. Good colour vision is essential. A thorough, methodical approach is called for, checking and testing at every stage in the dyeing process.

Dyeing technicians should be prepared to take responsibility for planning and organizing their own and other people's work, for making decisions and supervising staff.

ENTRY REQUIREMENTS

Please see article 1: TEXTILE TECHNICIAN. Good colour vision is essential for work in dyeing.

TRAINING

Coloration and Finishing is one of the programmes available under a Modern Apprenticeship, part of the Skillseekers Initiative in Scotland in the textile industry. Apprentices gain practical experience of all processes in dyeing and finishing. This is combined with off-the-job study and leads to NVQ/SVQ Level 3. They may also take a BTEC/SQA national certificate in textile coloration in the second year. Students are encouraged to begin studying for Higher National Certificate in Science (Textile Coloration) during the third year of the Apprenticeship, and to continue with this during subsequent training. Contact your local careers office, TEC or LEC for details.

NVQs/SVQS are available in: Manufacturing Textiles or Manufacturing Products from Textiles at Levels 1 and 2; and Product Development: Apparel and Textile Technician at Level 3.

A new NVQ/SVQ Manufacturing Textiles at Level 3 is proposed and should be available by the end of 1998. There are no set entry requirements. Contact your local TEC/LEC for details.

Technicians aged 23 years or over, with an HNC/HND and at least two years' experience, may study for the SDC Certificate in Colouration and later for Licentiateship of the Society of Dyers and Colourists (LSDC). A suitable degree may lead to Licentiateship. Candidates must provide evidence of having appropriate experience in one or more branches of colour science or colour technology or in an associated discipline. They may then continue their studies to apply for Associateship of the Society (ASDC), the professional qualification granting the title Chartered Colourist. Applicants who fall outside the age limits for apprenticeships follow a similar training plan. The programme can be modified to take account of existing qualifications and experience.

LATE ENTRY

There is no upper age limit. Adults for whom a full NVQ/SVQ or BTEC/SQA course would be inappropriate may take single units from the programme, or short college courses complementing intensive training at work. Mature applicants with alternative qualifications or experience may be considered for full-time courses at the discretion of the college.

OPPORTUNITIES

West Yorkshire, Lancashire, the Midlands and the Scottish Borders are the main areas of textile production, with smaller centres elsewhere. Dyeing technicians work either in textile mills or in specialist dye works.

PAY AND CONDITIONS

Technicians are usually salaried, paid monthly on rates agreed by local negotiation. Salaries vary widely, from about £10,300 to about £17,510.

Hours vary from factory to factory. Some run a 24-hour three-shift system; others work 35 to 40 hours a week, daytime only.

PROSPECTS

Promotion to senior posts can lead to work in research and development, technical or general management, or technical sales. Associates of the Society of Dyers and Colourists find a wide range of career prospects in management, marketing, research and development, both in Britain and abroad. Some transfer from the textile industry to other areas of colour science and technology, such as the manufacture of dyes and pigments or the coloration of paper, plastics, leather etc. Demand for dyeing technicians from the trainee level upwards is high and increasing.

TEXTILES: SAG/SAV

RELATED OCCUPATIONS

Textile technician, printing technician, scientist/technician, leather technologist, paint technologist, materials scientist/technologist.

FURTHER INFORMATION

Confederation of British Wool Textiles Limited*, Merrydale House, Roydsdale Way, Bradford BD4 6SB, 01274 652207

Cotton and Allied Textile Industry Training Organisation*, Suffolk Street Works, Pendleton, Salford, M6 6DX, 0161 745 8333

Society of Dyers and Colourists*, Perkin House, PO Box 244, 82 Grattan Road, Bradford, West Yorkshire BD1 2JB, 01274 725138

FURTHER READING

Leaflets/booklets are available from the addresses marked*.

In the careers library classified under SAG/SAV.

3. TEXTILE OPERATIVE (SAG)

THE WORK

Textile operatives work in every section of a textile mill. Some work in the warehouse on loading, unloading, packing and dispatch. Others run the machines that turn raw fibre into yarn or yarn into fabric. Their jobs include scouring, carding, combing, spinning, weaving, knitting, bleaching and dyehouse work.

Operatives engaged in any of these processes start the machine and watch the passage of the material through it. They look out for faults that could indicate breakages or mechanical failure and report these to a technician. On some spinning or weaving machines, broken threads have to be repaired by the operative, who finds the broken ends and joins them together. On modern machines the yarn is automatically mended. Weavers check cloth as it comes off the loom and mark any flaws for the attention of the mender. Badly damaged sections are removed. Operatives are always moving along the rows of machinery watching for problems. They may also replace empty bobbins and take off the cones of spun yarn or the completed lengths of cloth. A knitting operative may control a bank of high-precision machines; a weaver attends to several looms.

Operatives in the dye house load the grey (untreated) cloth onto rollers and start the machine that feeds it through vats of dye and fixative, through the drying chambers or over the stenter to stretch it to shape. They make sure it runs smoothly and evenly, and watch for any problems that need the attention of a technician. In between batches they clean the dye off the rollers.

Operatives are responsible for keeping their work area as tidy as possible. As with any machine work, they need to pay attention to safety procedures in handling the machines or moving between them.

WORK ENVIRONMENT

Conditions in textile mills vary widely, but modern factories are spacious and bright. In some sections, the noise level may be high and ear protectors are required. Some processes, such as scouring, make the atmosphere warm and humid. Dust is less of a problem as most large particles are eliminated by dust extractors.

Operatives spend much of the day on their feet. Lifting, bending and stretching are unavoidable.

SKILLS AND INTERESTS

Textile operatives should enjoy practical work using machines. Many operative jobs require nimble fingers and good eyesight (with or without glasses) and, in some cases, good colour vision. They need to remain alert and observant, and be able to concentrate while carrying out routine tasks. They should be reliable and conscientious workers.

ENTRY REQUIREMENTS

There are no particular academic requirements. Some employers test eyesight and colour vision before entry.

TRAINING

Training is mainly on the job but may include part-time attendance at a training centre or college. Trainees take NVQs/SVQs at Levels 1 and 2. They follow one of 13 routes, depending on which job they do. Each route consists of several units covering skills used at each stage of the production process. Some companies train operatives in more than one job. Some jobs, such as operating a bank of knitting machines, are multiskilled in themselves.

LATE ENTRY

There are no upper age limits. Older people, job-changers and returners may enter the work. Special training and re-training courses may be arranged for them by the company.

OPPORTUNITIES

West Yorkshire, Lancashire, the Midlands and the Scottish Borders are the main areas of textile manufacture, but there are smaller centres elsewhere.

Many older mills have been closed and many workers have been made redundant in recent years. There is now a shortage of people skilled in using modern equipment, however, and new entrants at all levels are in demand.

PAY AND CONDITIONS

Wage rates are fixed by negotiation with local unions and differ from place to place. A 16-year-old trainee might expect to start at about £93 to £98 a week. Basic wages for those aged 18 years or over range from £131 to £168. This would be the basic minimum, invariably boosted by overtime, shift allowance, bonus schemes etc.

Hours vary. Some factories work round the clock in three eight-hour shifts. Others work a 37- to 40-hour week. Overtime and part-time work are often available.

PROSPECTS

Promotion is initially to supervisor or instructor, then section management, sales or administration. It is usually an advantage for people seeking promotion to gain BTEC/SQA qualifications. These can lead eventually to positions in management.

TEXTILES: SAG/SAV

RELATED OCCUPATIONS

Production worker, textile technician, textile dyeing technician, machine printer, warehouse worker, sewing machinist.

FURTHER INFORMATION

Confederation of British Wool Textiles Ltd*, Merrydale House, Roydsdale Way, Bradford BD4 6SB, 01274 652207

Cotton and Allied Textile Industry Training Organisation*, Suffolk Street Works, Pendleton, Salford, M6 6DX, 0161 745 8333

FURTHER READING

Leaflets/booklets are available from the addresses marked*.

In the careers library classified under SAG.

CLOTHING: SAH

1. **TAILOR/DRESSMAKER CLCI:SAH**
2. **PATTERN CUTTER/GRADER CLCI:SAH**
3. **SPREADER/CUTTER CLCI:SAH**
4. **SEWING MACHINIST CLCI:SAH**
5. **CLOTHING PRESSER CLCI:SAH**

BACKGROUND INFORMATION

Clothing is one of the United Kingdom's largest manufacturing industries, with over 175,000 employees. Companies usually specialize in making certain types of garments, for example rainwear or sportswear, in a range of styles and fabrics.

Wholesale manufacturing is the largest sector, producing ready-made clothes for high street stores and mail order, and special clothing for specific companies. Most modern factories are highly automated and often use computers to help control the work and systems. Some people, however, still prefer to buy individually made clothes. Their needs are catered for by haute couture houses, tailors and dressmakers. Haute couture houses make designer garments, available from high-class fashion houses at very high prices. Only one or two copies of each garment are made almost entirely by hand. Individual clothes are made to order for customers by bespoke tailors and dressmakers.

In every case, the production cycle begins with design followed by the creation of a pattern, fabric cutting, sewing, pressing and checking for quality before despatch. With the increase of working in teams, checking for quality is now more often done by workers at each stage in the production process rather than by specialist garment examiners or quality controllers.

Intense competition from abroad and new technology are affecting the whole industry, demanding increased professionalism from management and a more highly skilled and adaptable workforce.

1. TAILOR/DRESSMAKER (SAH)

THE WORK

Bespoke tailors make made-to-measure suits and heavy outer clothes; dressmakers make dresses and other light clothing. Tailoring and dressmaking involve very similar techniques.

In a small firm the tailor/dressmaker is responsible for the garment from commissioning to collection; in a larger firm some of the tasks may be shared with others.

Tailors/dressmakers firstly take the customer's measurements and advise on fabric and style. When the fabric is selected they quote a price for the work, taking into account the time involved and the cost and quantity of the material. If the quote is accepted, the measurements are converted into a cardboard or paper pattern, which the tailor/dressmaker cuts round on the cloth, also cutting linings, canvas interlinings and tapes as required. The cardboard pattern can be stored and used again for the same customer. Occasionally, the pattern may be drawn straight on the cloth. Cutting is delicate work, demanding a high level of accuracy; allowances have to be made for fitting ease and possible alterations in the future. Wastage must be kept to a minimum.

After cutting, the tailor/dressmaker carefully sews the garment together. Various stitches are used, to hold the garment firm or to produce special effects such as making a collar lie neatly. A sewing machine may be used on long seams, but hand sewing is used wherever it produces a better finish.

The tailor/dressmaker presses each part of the garment as it is completed. The customer may be fitted with the garment on two or three occasions and it is altered where necessary. Bodies are not symmetrical; left and right sides can differ markedly. A skilful tailor or dressmaker can disguise shoulders that are different heights or a slightly curved spine.

Tailors/dressmakers must keep up with changing fashions and must be aware of new techniques and materials. Each customer has different needs and the garments have differing wear and tear: eg a sports jacket may be worn daily whilst an evening dress or kilt may be used only once a year.

It is possible to specialize in particular garments. Dressmakers may concentrate on children's clothes or wedding dresses, while tailors may specialize, for instance in military uniforms.

WORK ENVIRONMENT

Many firms are based in town-centre premises comprising a small shop with workroom attached. Some clothing factories have small tailoring and dressmaking sections, while many people work in workrooms in their homes. Accommodation is generally well lit and clean.

SKILLS AND INTERESTS

Tailors and dressmakers need an aptitude for, and interest in, sewing, and the ability to concentrate on fine work for long periods. They should enjoy seeing a task through from the beginning to end, and have an interest in fashion and design. Good eyesight and good colour vision are essential. Numerical ability is useful for doing calculations and measurements, and good communication skills are required to deal effectively with clients and colleagues.

Self-employed tailors and dressmakers require good business skills. They need to monitor buying and spending, pricing their work realistically.

ENTRY REQUIREMENTS

Modern Apprenticeships (part of the Skillseekers Initiative in Scotland) are available, though some employers may still offer a traditional apprenticeship. No formal educational qualifications are stipulated, but some firms prefer candidates with GCSEs/S grades (A–C/1–3) in maths and English.

Personal aptitudes are more important than academic achievement.

TRAINING

A Modern Apprenticeship is not time-based, relating instead to the time it takes the individual trainee to acquire competencies, but it is expected to take three years as against the four to five years of a traditional apprenticeship. Modern Apprenticeships lead to an NVQ/SVQ in Handcraft Tailoring at Level 3. On-the-job instruction by experienced tailors/dressmakers and work experience is combined with day/block release or evening study at local colleges for underpinning knowledge. With traditional apprenticeships, this study would be for City and Guilds 4600 craft certificates.

CLOTHING: SAH

The C&G 4600 certificates are available through full-time and part-time study at a few centres around the country. Some people take these courses as a pre-entry qualification before applying to an employer.

LATE ENTRY

Some colleges are making increasing provision for mature students. It is also possible to apply direct to employers who may either train or re-train applicants, as required. The NVQ/SVQ system may allow individuals with experience in the industry to be trained and assessed for Level 3 qualifications.

OPPORTUNITIES

There will always be a demand for made-to-measure garments from people who do not conform to standard sizes or who value hand-crafted, well-fitting clothes. Most large bespoke tailoring houses are in London, but openings also occur with shops and factories throughout the country. Dressmakers work for fashion retailers or clothing manufacturers nationwide. Opportunities for self-employment are particularly good, both for dressmakers and for tailors. Many firms employ outworkers, who visit the firm to collect bundles of work and are paid as pieceworkers.

Several employment agencies in the West End of London specialize in tailoring and dressmaking vacancies. Vacancies may also be found in *Drapers Record* – a weekly publication.

PAY AND CONDITIONS

Workers over 18 years earn about £150 a week or over. Experienced tailors and dressmakers are paid according to their skill, experience and responsibility. Many are self-employed, with earnings linked directly to business prosperity.

Waged tailors and dressmakers work a standard 39-hour, five-day week. Those employed in retail outlets may work Saturdays. Extra hours are common, bringing in overtime payments or enhancing piecework productivity. Self-employed tailors and dressmakers can arrange hours to suit themselves and their customers and can put in a lot of hours if demand warrants it.

PROSPECTS

Tailors and dressmakers may progress to become supervisors in charge of a workroom, or may enter self-employment with their own small shop. Some tailors/dressmakers specialize in cutting and move into larger-scale production, while others develop the selling side and spend more time dealing with customers. There is a wide range of courses to prepare staff for management positions; details can be obtained from the CAPITB. There are a few opportunities for teaching in colleges of further education.

RELATED OCCUPATIONS, FURTHER INFORMATION AND READING

Please see article 5. CLOTHING PRESSER.

2. PATTERN CUTTER/GRADER (SAH)

THE WORK

Pattern cutters make the patterns that enable a designer's sketch to be made into a garment. Pattern graders work from a basic size pattern and create the patterns needed for a range of garment sizes. Jobs vary from company to company. In small companies the designer may also be responsible for pattern cutting and grading. In larger companies there are specialist pattern cutters and/or graders.

There are two ways of making patterns; the method used depends on the style of garment concerned.

Flat pattern cutting – the pattern cutter works from the designer's sketches or working drawings and makes a pattern for each part of a garment by creating a block (a cardboard pattern piece). Some pattern cutters create their own blocks, while some companies have their own basic blocks and the pattern cutter adapts the shape of these for the new garment. Increasingly, computers are used to help in designing garments and creating patterns.

Modelling onto a stand – working from the designer's drawings the pattern cutter drapes and pins fabric onto a dummy and fits it in accordance with the drawings. The fabric is then cut and the resultant pattern shape or toile is pinned to paper which is cut out to form the pattern shape. This method is mainly used for designer/couture garments.

With both processes, the pattern cutter produces patterns as near as possible to the designer's sketches, while taking into account the type of fabric to be used and the demands of the manufacturing process. When the pattern has been completed, it goes to a sample machinist who produces a sample garment. When the designer and pattern cutter inspect the sample garment they may decide on slight alterations before the final patterns are made.

Pattern grading has become increasingly computerized. The pattern grader pastes a standard size 12 pattern onto a computerized digitising table and assigns rule numbers. There are different rules for different garments. The grader feeds the rule numbers into the computer with a cursor pen and the computer automatically grades the pattern into different sizes and plots the patterns full-size onto paper. Some companies do not use computers for pattern grading, working instead from size charts and using conventional drafting skills to draw up the graded patterns.

WORK ENVIRONMENT

Pattern cutters' and pattern graders' work environment can vary considerably from employer to employer. Some work in a factory sharing their work space with those involved in garment manufacture, others work with clothing designers in studios. Work can involve long periods sitting or standing with some bending.

SKILLS AND INTERESTS

Pattern cutters/graders should be interested in fashion if they are to appreciate what their designers are aiming for.

Numerical ability is essential for measurement and calculation. It is useful if pattern cutters and graders have some technical drawing skill, both for understanding drawings and for adapting existing blocks. Aptitude for working with computers is very helpful. Accuracy and a meticulous approach are important as patterns must be

CLOTHING: SAH

exact. An eye for proportion and shape are necessary, as is good manual dexterity.

Their work demands patience but pattern cutters and graders often work to deadlines. They must be able to work under this pressure while maintaining accuracy and quality of work.

Pattern cutters and graders should be able to work as part of a team. Good communication skills are needed, as they must liaise with designers and sample machinists.

ENTRY REQUIREMENTS

Most entrants come into these jobs after pre-entry training, usually full-time, on a course leading to one of the qualifications listed below. These include pattern cutting and grading within general clothing manufacture skills and knowledge. However, by selection of units, the SQA courses mentioned below can be tailored specifically towards pattern cutting and grading. Increasingly, employers look for design expertise as well.

City and Guilds (C&G) 4600 Clothing Craft Certificate: no specific qualifications are required for entry but applicants should have practical ability and numerical skills. This course is offered at a number of centres across the country.

London College of Fashion Foundation Course in Clothing: no specific qualifications are required.

London College of Fashion Certificate in Clothing Production: applicants must be at least 21 years old and have a minimum of four GCSEs/S grades (A–C/1–3), including English.

BTEC National Diploma in Clothing: requires either four GCSEs/S grades (A–C/1–3), or a relevant BTEC first award offered at a number of centres across the country.

SQA National Certificates in Fashion Technology, in Clothing Technology, and in Clothing Studies: no particular qualifications are required, but an interest in this type of work is essential.

BTEC Higher National Diploma in Clothing: requires one A level/two H grades and four GCSEs/S grades (A–C/1–3), or, more usually, a BTEC National Diploma in Clothing offered at a number of centres across the country.

SQA Higher National Diplomas in Fashion Technology and in Clothing Technology: applicants should have evidence of having achieved national certificate modules in garment making.

Degree in Clothing Studies: entry is with either two A levels/three H grades and three GCSEs/S grades (A–C/1–3) including English, maths and a science subject, or a relevant BTEC National Diploma.

Some fashion design courses include pattern making and grading skills. Entry requirements range from having a good portfolio of drawings and designs, to those required for entry to degree courses.

A Modern Apprenticeship in Product Development leading to at least an NVQ/SVQ Level 3 may be an alternative route into this work. Most employers would look for GCSEs/S grades (A–C/1–3) in maths, English and art as entry qualifications.

TRAINING

Pre-entry

C&G 4600 Clothing Craft Certificate (two years full-time or three years part-time) is offered at a number of centres in England.

London College of Fashion Foundation Course in Clothing (one year full-time) prepares students for entry to a national diploma course in, for example, clothing or fashion. It includes the possibility of taking C&G 4600 Clothing Craft Certificate.

London College of Fashion Certificate in Clothing Production (one year full-time) concentrates on the design, cutting and making of sample garments.

BTEC National Diploma in Clothing (two years full-time) is offered at eight centres in England.

SQA National Certificates in Fashion Technology and in Clothing Technology (one year full-time) are offered at Cardonald College, while the SQA National Certificate in Clothing Studies (one year full-time) is run by Motherwell College.

BTEC Higher National Diploma in Clothing (two years full-time) is run at Handsworth College, Birmingham, Leeds College of Art and Design, Kent Institute of Art and Design, City of Liverpool Community College, and Manchester Metropolitan University and other centres.

SQA Higher National Diplomas in Fashion Technology and in Clothing Technology (two years full-time) are run at Cardonald College.

Degrees in Clothing Studies are offered at London College of Fashion and Heriot-Watt University (four years sandwich), Manchester Metropolitan University, and Nottingham Trent University (both three years full-time).

On entry

Pattern cutters and graders receive further training from experienced staff. There are a number of courses they may attend on a day release or evening basis to develop their skills. Courses are of varying length and include C&G 4600 Pattern Cutting stages 1, 2 and 3, as well as courses leading to individual colleges' certificates or diplomas. In Scotland, SQA national certificate modules in clothing are offered by Cardonald College, Motherwell College, and North Glasgow College.

After entry, pattern cutter/graders may be assessed on relevant units of NVQ/SVQ in Product Development at Level 3 to gain the full qualification.

LATE ENTRY

There is no upper age limit for entry to pattern cutting and grading. Adults may find that they can be accepted for courses described in ENTRY REQUIREMENTS without the usual academic entry requirements. Some people move into these jobs from work in the industry as machinists or spreaders/cutters and are given additional training. They may be assessed on units of NVQ/SVQ in Product Development at Level 3.

Access courses may be available in some areas to prepare adults for entry to higher national diploma and degree courses in clothing studies.

CLOTHING: SAH

OPPORTUNITIES

Pattern cutters and pattern graders may work for individual designers, for large manufacturers, for specialist pattern cutting and/or pattern grading firms, or they may work on a freelance basis. Pattern graders have first had experience of pattern cutting. Most employers require both pattern making and grading skills.

The clothing manufacturing industry is large, with garment manufacturers in many towns and cities. The industry has, however, decreased in size over the past few years and computerization has speeded up much pattern cutting and grading. In spite of this, there is a shortage of skilled pattern cutters and graders. Vacancies are advertised in periodicals, including *Drapers' Record*, *Fashion Weekly* and *Manufacturing Clothier*.

PAY AND CONDITIONS

There are no set salary scales for pattern cutters and pattern graders, with individual employers paying their own rate. Some pay annual salaries, while others pay on a piecework basis. Earnings vary tremendously and range from £6,000 to £20,000.

Working hours are usually between 37 and 39 a week, Monday to Friday. Many firms in the clothing industry finish early on Friday afternoons. Part-time work is possible. Overtime may be worked.

PROSPECTS

Pattern cutters and pattern graders may seek to improve their situation by moving from one employer to another. They may become head pattern cutters and head pattern graders, either within their employing organization or by moving to another employer. Some link pattern cutting with clothing designer, particularly if their original training specialized in design.

The clothing industry is important world-wide and there are openings for trained pattern cutters and pattern graders overseas.

There are opportunities for pattern cutters and graders to become self-employed and work on a freelance basis.

RELATED OCCUPATIONS, FURTHER INFORMATION AND READING

Please see article 5. CLOTHING PRESSER.

3. SPREADER/CUTTER (SAH)

THE WORK

The spreader or cutter checks the cloth for flaws – it must be smooth and free of wrinkles and any patterns or other features must match up when it is sewn together. This laying-up process can be done manually by two people, or by machine. The next step is to put a lay-plan on the cloth which may be pre-painted. The lay-plan is worked out by a technician, sometimes using a computer. The fabric is then ready for cutting either by hand or machine.

Hand cutting is done using shears, an electric knife, or a vertical band knife. Cutters must ensure that the bottom pieces of the lay remain in unison with the top ones to avoid distortions in shape and must try to minimize fabric wastage.

Die-cutting is done by machine. A press, whose blades have been set according to the lay-plan, is lowered on to the fabric, cutting the pattern shape right through the lay. This process is very accurate but uses more fabric than does cutting by hand. It is often used when large numbers of identical garments are being made or for cutting linings and trimmings where the fabric is less expensive.

Computer-controlled cutting machines are gradually being introduced which are capable of cutting up to 250 inches per minute, depending on the depth of the lay. These machines are capable of great accuracy.

Laser cutting – with this, computer images are used to operate the laser cutter with great accuracy.

After cutting, the cloth is made into bundles containing everything necessary to make up a given number of a particular garment.

WORK ENVIRONMENT

Cutting rooms are generally clean and well lit. There may be some dust in the air, and it can be noisy at times. Cutters must be safety-conscious, as the cutting edges are very sharp; chain mail gloves are worn as protection for band knife cutting.

Cutters spend much of the day standing.

SKILLS AND INTERESTS

Cutters need to be physically fit, able to bend over tables and lift heavy bales of cloth. Good eyesight and perfect colour vision are important, and it is useful to be able to visualize the finished garment so as to minimize marking-up errors. Some numerical ability is required.

The work demands a methodical and meticulous approach; mistakes can rarely be rectified, so accuracy is very important. Cutters should be able to cope with pressure, be decisive and able to rely on their own judgement – cutting an expensive pile of cloth is a big responsibility. Cutters work directly with the designers and sometimes technicians, trainees and other assistants so ability to work well in a team is important. An interest in fashion is useful as cutters must keep up with new styles, ideas and techniques.

ENTRY REQUIREMENTS

No educational qualifications are necessary, but a good standard of secondary education is expected. Some GCSE/S grade qualifications are an advantage; maths is particularly useful.

TRAINING

Training is largely given on the job. Some employers offer the HEADstart training programme with the Kingscourt training organization (details from local careers offices or from Kingscourt). This leads to an NVQ/SVQ in Manufacturing Sewn Products at Level 2.

Trainees learn about different types of fabric and all the flaws that may be found; how to interpret written and spoken instructions; correlation of pattern parts with the garment sample; using the laying-in instructions on a pattern; cutting procedures and routine maintenance of cutting tools; spreading fabrics by hand and machine; lay planning; marker making; and advanced computerized cutting-room methods.

CLOTHING: SAH

LATE ENTRY

As the industry comes out of recession and with the challenge of new technology, employers are increasingly willing to take on adults with experience in other industries or returners. Training is mainly on-the-job and usually shorter than for youth entrants. Adults can also be assessed for NVQ/SVQ and previous experience may be taken into account.

OPPORTUNITIES

Garment manufacturers are found in towns throughout the country producing a great variety of clothes from sober suits to high fashion. Firms vary greatly in size and in the techniques and manufacturing equipment used. Some employment is part-time.

PAY AND CONDITIONS

Experienced cutters are paid according to their skill and the level of responsibility in their job.

PROSPECTS

There is no fixed promotion pattern. Cutters can move into a supervisory/management level.

RELATED OCCUPATIONS, FURTHER INFORMATION AND READING

Please see article 5. CLOTHING PRESSER.

4. SEWING MACHINIST (SAH)

THE WORK

Machinists guide fabric through a sewing machine. Different machines do different jobs: lockstitch for plain seams; overlocking for neatening seams; button-holing machines; lace attaching machines.

Traditionally, machinists were trained to use one particular machine. By sewing one type of seam over and over again, they could build up their speed and skill. Now, however, it is increasingly common for machinists to work together in teams to produce a whole garment – individuals carry out several operations, and this makes the work more interesting. This is known as team working.

Sample machinists make up a few examples of every new style to show to potential buyers. They work closely with the designers and pattern cutters.

WORK ENVIRONMENT

Clothing firms range in size from small businesses with half a dozen people in a workshop to large factories where there may be up to 500 machinists. Factories, however, tend to be split into small units working with individual unit supervisors.

Most, though not all machinists, work sitting down. The work is often done under artificial light.

SKILLS AND INTERESTS

Machinists need good eyesight, manual dexterity, a liking for fine, close work and the ability to concentrate.

It is important to be able to work quickly, neatly and accurately. Nimble fingers are required for tasks like changing needles and cleaning machines as well as for guiding fabric through the machine.

An interest in fashion and design is useful for visualizing the appearance of the completed garment. An eye for colour is useful for matching pieces together.

Machinists need to be able to get on with colleagues and work as part of a team.

ENTRY REQUIREMENTS

No formal entry qualifications are required. Most companies give applicants a practical aptitude test, plus a medical which includes an eyesight test.

A qualification awarded by Qualifications for Industry, 'Introductory Industrial Stitching', can be taken by pupils at school or students in further education. It accredits the basic skills needed for entry to the industry.

TRAINING

Training is largely given on the job. Some employers offer the HEADstart training programme with the Kingscourt training organization (details from local careers offices or from Kingscourt). This leads to an NVQ/SVQ in Manufacturing Sewn Products at Levels 1 and 2.

Trainees experience a variety of work before specializing in machining. During the scheme, trainees have approximately 20 weeks' off-the-job training, usually on the employer's premises.

Most companies have a training section, where new machinists spend the first few weeks learning to operate a machine. While training, they receive a basic weekly wage. It takes about three weeks to become skilled enough to go out onto the factory floor. Re-training is constant as new products are introduced. Keen workers with aptitude can train to operate several different machines, so increasing their choice of jobs.

LATE ENTRY

As the industry comes out of recession and with the challenge of new technology, employers are increasingly willing to take on adults with experience in other industries or returners.

Adult entrants follow the training described above. Employers normally offer a few weeks' training or re-training to those who have experience working with other companies or machines or who have taken the City and Guilds Certificate so that machinists become familiar with the firm's machines and procedures.

Adults can also be assessed for NVQ/SVQ and previous experience may be taken into account.

There may be specific training opportunities directed at adults available in some areas for this type of work. Candidates may have to satisfy certain conditions to be eligible. Contact your local Jobcentre, careers office or TEC/LEC for details.

OPPORTUNITIES

There are plenty of vacancies for skilled or trainee machinists in all areas. The biggest employer is the clothing industry but machinists also work in other parts of the textile industry, for example making household goods such

CLOTHING: SAH

as bedlinen or curtains or speciality items like sails and tents. They work in the furniture industry on upholstery, and even in the motor car industry making seat covers.

Some machinists work as outworkers.

PAY AND CONDITIONS

Many machinists receive bonuses or sew for piece-rates. The more practised and skilled they become, the more they can earn.

A 39-hour week is normal. Some factories work shifts and there are often opportunities for part-time work.

PROSPECTS

Experienced machinists can become supervisors in charge of a unit of up to 30 workers. Supervisors are responsible for keeping the unit supplied with work, for monitoring output and doing an initial check on the work as it comes in. Alternatively, machinists could turn to garment examining, packing or sample-room machining. Experienced machinists could also become instructors or go into quality control. Instructors are responsible for training new machinists and for re-training existing workers in new methods or when a style is changed.

RELATED OCCUPATIONS, FURTHER INFORMATION AND READING

Please see article 5. CLOTHING PRESSER.

5. CLOTHING PRESSER (SAH)

THE WORK

Pressers use steam, pressure and temperature to press clothes. Pressing of separate pieces of garments may be done during production before they are made up, known as underpressing. Pressing also takes place at the end of production, when the garments are given a final pressing before they are put on sale.

Different machines and methods of pressing are used depending on the type of garment and the fabric concerned. Pressers have to follow set procedures for all pressing work, whatever the machinery used.

A common type of pressing involves a hand iron and ironing table/board. The hand iron is fed with steam from a central boiler, and the board has a vacuum on it. The presser places the iron onto the garment and steam is drawn through the cloth by the vacuum, which dries the garment, while preventing the board from becoming wet. The irons have to be set for temperature and steam control according to the fabric concerned and may be fitted with a Teflon shoe to protect the garment and reduce friction.

Some pressers use a steam form which looks like a tailor's dummy. The presser puts a garment such as a skirt or shirt on the press and steam is blown from inside the shape to get rid of creases.

Garments such as trousers are pressed on a flat press where the presser lowers a large press onto the whole garment, which has been laid on a flat surface.

Some pressing is automatic with sophisticated machinery, often computer controlled. With tunnel presses and carousel presses, pressers carefully hang garments onto shaped supports, which are then fed into the machine where they are steam-pressed automatically.

Pressers working manually have to work quickly, while those on automatic machines have to work to the speed of the machine.

In small factories, pressing may be just part of a job, with some time spent on machine sewing. In larger factories it is usual for people to specialize in pressing – some use one machine; others use different pressing processes.

WORK ENVIRONMENT

Clothing pressers work in factories. Conditions in clothing factories vary. Some are light and spacious with extractor systems to keep a reasonable working temperature and also prevents an uncomfortable build-up of steam; others can be cramped and hot.

Pressing involves standing all day, with some bending.

SKILLS AND INTERESTS

Clothing pressers should be interested in practical work. Some pressing operations, such as hand ironing, require manual dexterity.

There are set procedures to follow in pressing different types of garment to produce the best finish in the quickest time. Pressers need to be methodical and able to follow those set procedures. Pressing is done to shape a garment or to remove creases. Speed of work is important. Pressers should be able to work quickly while maintaining good quality work.

Pressers should be able to concentrate and work consistently at what tends to be repetitive work. An eye for detail is required.

Pressers should be flexible and prepared to operate different types of machinery depending on the type of garment that is being produced and the fabric concerned. They need also to be willing to learn the operation of new pressing machines that may be introduced.

Some pressing work is energetic. It is important for pressers to like active work and to have the stamina to cope with it.

ENTRY REQUIREMENTS

No formal academic qualifications are required for entry to pressing although an aptitude for practical subjects is helpful. Employers are concerned with personal qualities, seeking reliable, conscientious workers who can follow instructions.

Some employers give applicants a practical test. Some arrange for a medical examination to make sure that applicants are fit for the work.

TRAINING

Training is largely on the job. This may lead to an NVQ/SVQ in Manufacturing Sewn Products at Levels 1 and 2. Trainees experience a variety of work before specializing in pressing.

On starting work all pressers are trained by an instructor. They may begin by practising on training garments, then on reject garments, before progressing to full-quality garments. It can take several weeks to become efficient on one type of pressing operation but years to gain full proficiency and experience on a range of pressing operations.

CLOTHING: SAH

As new pressing machines are introduced into the factory, pressers are trained in their use by an instructor.

LATE ENTRY

There is no upper age limit for entry to pressing. As the industry comes out of recession and with the challenge of new technology, employers are increasingly willing to take on adults with experience in other industries. Training is mainly on-the-job and usually shorter than for youth entrants. Adults can also be assessed for NVQ/SVQ and previous experience may be taken into account.

There may be specific training opportunities directed at adults available in some areas for this type of work. Candidates may have to satisfy certain conditions to be eligible. Contact your local Jobcentre, careers office or TEC/LEC for details.

OPPORTUNITIES

There are more than 4,000 clothing factories throughout the UK making all kinds of clothing – skirts, dresses, sweaters, jeans, sports wear, men's and boys' clothes, overalls, uniforms etc. Most of them employ pressers. The clothing industry has been decreasing in size over the past few years, however, with a consequent reduction in the number of pressers employed.

Opportunities may be available via training schemes for young people. Contact your local careers office, TEC/LEC for details.

Vacancies for pressers may be advertised in *Drapers' Record, Manufacturing Clothier,* or local newspapers. Those seeking work as a presser should contact local clothing manufacturers to ask about vacancies.

PAY AND CONDITIONS

There are no national pay scales for pressers. Most pressers are paid on a piecework basis. Trained pressers may receive between £120 and £240 a week. Working hours vary between 37_ and 39 a week, Monday to Friday. Many firms finish early on a Friday afternoon. Some part-time work is available. Overtime is common.

PROSPECTS

Pressers may be promoted to supervisor and be responsible for a number of pressers – allocating their work, monitoring output, and checking the quality of work.

It may be possible to become an instructor, responsible for training new staff and re-training existing staff on new presses that are introduced into the factory.

Promotion to supervisor or instructor is usually internal. Most companies prefer to promote internally rather than bring in supervisors from outside the firm.

The clothing industry is world-wide. Pressers who move abroad may find pressing work in any one of a number of countries.

RELATED OCCUPATIONS

Clothing alteration hand, textile operative, packer, theatre costume maker.

FURTHER INFORMATION

CAPITB Trust*, 80 Richardshaw Lane, Pudsey, Leeds LS28 6BN, 0113 227 3345

Qualifications for Industry (address as for CAPITB)

FURTHER READING

Leaflets/booklets are available from the address marked*.

Working in Fashion – COIC

In the careers library classified under SAH.

FURNITURE CRAFTS: SAJ

1. **CABINET MAKER CLCI:SAJ**
2. **UPHOLSTERER CLCI:SAJ**
3. **FRENCH POLISHER CLCI:SAJ**

BACKGROUND INFORMATION

Making fine furniture by hand and restoring furniture requires three main skills: cabinet making, upholstery and French polishing. Many of these craftspeople work on their own or with one or two other craftspeople, but their skills are also needed by furniture manufacturers.

1. CABINET MAKER (SAJ)

THE WORK

Cabinet makers are craftsmen/women who make fine furniture mainly by hand. In addition to making cabinets – which are pieces of furniture containing shelves, drawers or cupboards used for storage or display – they may also make other items such as chairs and tables. Cabinet makers usually specialize in traditional designs; others produce furniture, sometimes one-off pieces, to their own designs and are often called designer/makers. Cabinet makers may also restore damaged furniture.

The first stage in their work is to make a drawing of the piece to be made, the joints to be used, and so on. They calculate the timber required to make it, then select and buy the wood. Usually they work with hardwoods such as oak, tropical hardwoods, walnut or American cherry. They rarely work with softwoods such as pine.

When they have selected the appropriate timber, they cut it using circular, hand and band saws, and plane to get a smooth finish. This is a very important process as the timber has to be cut and planed in such a way as to get exactly the grain effect the cabinet maker wants. The pattern of grain on the fronts of drawers, for instance, may be cut so that the grain pattern on each one is identical. Decorative veneers, if used, are normally applied to panels before they are cut to size. They are bought in sheets and cut to give the right grain effect in the right place.

The cabinet maker then assembles the piece of furniture. Any decorative effects such as mouldings or inlays are added and the whole piece is then carefully sanded. The latter is a lengthy operation, some of which, is done by machine or by hand. Sometimes the cabinet maker will then pass the piece on to a French polisher to provide the final finish; others may do this themselves.

WORK ENVIRONMENT

Most cabinet makers work in workshops that are light and airy, though conditions in some smaller workshops can be cramped. There may be dust from sanding but most workshops have dust extractors and masks are also worn. The workshop may be noisy when using machinery so ear defenders are worn. Some cabinet makers may have to travel to timber yards to buy wood and deliver their goods. Occasionally they may have to work at customers' premises, for example, in the case of making and fitting kitchen units. The work involves considerable standing and walking as well as bending and carrying.

SKILLS AND INTERESTS

This work requires excellent hand skills and hand-to-eye co-ordination. Cabinet makers need a great deal of patience and perseverance – to carry out very detailed accurate work. They also need a certain amount of artistic ability – an eye for what looks good and a sense of proportion. Numeracy is important in calculations, measuring and estimating costs.

Self-employed cabinet makers need good business skills, self-discipline and self-motivation. They also require good interpersonal skills to deal with customers.

ENTRY REQUIREMENTS

No minimum educational qualifications are required. The courses leading to relevant qualifications, however, may have specific entry requirements. There are a number of appropriate courses for cabinet making.

City and Guilds 5550 in Furniture Craft subjects and 5640 in Furniture Crafts (Special): there are no formal entry requirements for C&G courses but some colleges may look for about three GCSEs in maths, English and a science subject.

BTEC/SQA National Diploma/Certificate in Design (Crafts): entry requirements are four GCSEs/S grades (A–C/1–3), or an Intermediate GNVQ/GSVQ Level II.

BTEC/SQA Higher National Diploma/Certificate in Design (Furniture), Design (Restoration) or Furniture: entry requirements are usually five GCSEs/S grades (A–C/1–3), with two or three subjects studied to A level/H grade and one or two passed; or an Advanced GNVQ/GSVQ Level III; or a BTEC/SQA national diploma/certificate.

Degree courses, national diplomas/certificates in subjects such as restoration and conservation, furniture design and craftsmanship, and furniture restoration and craftsmanship. Entry requirements for degree courses vary. Normal qualifications for some courses are five GCSEs/S grades (A–C/1–3) including English, plus an art foundation course; Advanced GNVQ/GSVQ Level III; or BTEC/SQA diploma in art and/or design. Other courses may require two A levels/three H grades or equivalent.

TRAINING

Training may be either full-time at college or by becoming a trainee with a cabinet maker learning on the job and attending college on day release. There are a number of colleges offering full-time courses.

Courses include City and Guilds 5550 in Furniture Crafts, a one-year full-time or three-year part-time course which covers timber preparation and construction, metal and plastics preparation and construction, upholstery and bedding preparation and construction, finishing preparation and modern finishing, soft furnishing, carcass and wooden frame construction, and hand-made furniture construction. This can lead to C&G 5640 Furniture Crafts: Cabinet Making (Special), a one-year full-time or three-year part-time course.

BTEC/SQA national diploma and higher national diploma courses vary. A typical BTEC national diploma is a two-year full-time course and is likely to cover the skills needed to design and make furniture, working with wood, metal and plastics. Courses also include material and workshop technology, information technology, business studies and design history.

BTEC Higher National Diploma in Furniture Design is a two-year full-time course and is likely to cover both traditional and modern methods of making furniture, restoration of furniture and replica-making, as well as design and business management.

There is also a range of relevant BSc and BA courses for cabinet makers, eg the BA (Hons) Furniture Design and Craftsmanship course at Buckinghamshire College (a college of Brunel University). This covers designing and producing furniture with instruction in creative design and practical skills together with business training.

There are also private fee-paying courses in cabinet making lasting from a couple of days to two years.

NVQs/SVQs in Furniture Production and Producing Handcrafted Furniture are available at Levels 1, 2 and 3, and in Assembled Furniture Production and Upholstered Furniture Production at Level 2. NVQs/SVQs are also available at Levels 2 and 3 in Woodmachining, and at Levels 1, 2 and 3 in Producing Hand-crafted Furniture.

A Modern Apprenticeship Programme is available in cabinet making leading to at least NVQ/SVQ Level 3. Further information is available from BFM Training Ltd, the furniture industry training organization.

LATE ENTRY

There are no maximum age limits for this work and some colleges run full and part-time courses especially for mature students.

The BA (Hons) Furniture Design and Craftsmanship course at Buckinghamshire College accepts many mature students (over 22 years) who do not have the normal minimum academic qualifications for a degree course but can demonstrate ability and commitment.

OPPORTUNITIES

Cabinet makers are found in many cities, towns and rural areas throughout Britain. They may be self-employed or work for companies of cabinet makers. A few may specialize in one type of furniture but most design and make a range of different items.

PAY AND CONDITIONS

As some cabinet makers are self-employed, pay may vary considerably. Hours are also variable to suit the needs of the job. Self-employed cabinet makers may work more than 39 hours a week.

PROSPECTS

Cabinet makers can progress by moving from being employed by a company to owning and running their own company. Some move into teaching.

Cabinet makers starting their own business need capital. This may be borrowed from a bank. There may also be some grants available, for instance from the Rural Development Commission.

RELATED OCCUPATIONS

Furniture designer, boat builder, musical instrument manufacturer, patternmaker, upholsterer, French polisher, carpenter/joiner.

FURTHER INFORMATION

BFM Training Limited*, 30 Harcourt Street, London W1H 2AA, 0171 724 0851, www.bfm.org.uk

Buckinghamshire College*, Queen Alexandra Road, High Wycombe, Bucks HP11 2JZ, 01494 522141

The Crafts Council*, 44A Pentonville Road, Islington, London N1 9BY, 0171 278 7700, www.craftscouncil.org.uk

Guild of Master Craftsmen*, 166 High Street, Lewes, East Sussex BN7 1XU, 01273 478449

Rural Development Commission, 141 Castle Street, Salisbury, Wilts SP1 3TP, 01722 336255

FURTHER READING

Leaflets/booklets are available from the addresses marked*.

Woodworkers' Career and Educational Source Book – Guild of Master Craftsmen

In the careers library, classified under SAJ.

2. UPHOLSTERER (SAJ)

THE WORK

Upholsterers build up a piece of furniture from a frame into a finished covered item; they cover chairs and sofas with fabric or leather. Some of their work is re-upholstering and covering furniture. Their first job is to discuss with the customer what they want. Once the customer has chosen the fabric to be used, upholsterers measure the furniture to work out how much material is needed, so they can quote a price.

In re-upholstering, they first remove all the previous upholstery using a staple remover and a ripping chisel. If it is an old piece of furniture they may have to strengthen the frame by removing the old dried-out glue and re-glueing it. They then upholster the furniture following the way it was made originally. If it had springs, they start by attaching webbing to the frame. Springs are then placed on the webbing and lashed with cord to the frame. Hessian is stretched over and attached to the frame, and padding of curled hair, soft cotton wadding or felt is added. This is often followed by calico before covering with fabric.

To cover the chair or sofa the upholsterer carefully cuts out the fabric making sure patterns match and little material wasted. The pieces of material are stretched over the part to be covered and then tacked down. When it is covered, braid, piping, fringing or other trimmings are added. They also make cushions if required.

The backs of chairs and sofas are upholstered in a similar way but twine is woven into the base layer of hessian and stuffing such as curled animal hair is tucked under the twines. This is followed by adding a layer of felt or wool flock to stop the hair coming through. Finally the item is covered in the chosen upholstery fabric.

Most modern furniture uses latex or polyurethane foam rather than the traditional stuffing materials. In the mass production of furniture, some of the work is done by machine. Upholsterers working in factories are generally responsible for handling one particular operation rather than the entire job working as a team.

Many factories employ a few upholsterers to upholster and cover sample pieces of furniture (eg for trade shows and exhibitions). They may also make patterns for cutting the material, and work out templates for the production line. They are known as prototype upholsterers.

FURNITURE CRAFTS: SAJ

WORK ENVIRONMENT

Most upholsterers work in workshops that are light and airy; there may be some dust when removing old upholstery. Some work in factories. Self-employed upholsterers may have to visit a customers' houses to measure, collect and deliver furniture. They may occasionally do some upholstery work on a customers' premises. Considerable standing, bending and walking is involved. There is also a lot of carrying of material, chairs and sofas.

SKILLS AND INTERESTS

This work requires a good range of hand skills from sewing to hammering. Considerable patience and perseverance is needed to carry out detailed work with accuracy. Upholsterers need to work carefully and neatly. A certain amount of artistic ability is helpful and an eye for colour, proportion and co-ordination is needed for building upholstery and matching fabrics, patterns and colours. Numeracy is important in calculations, measuring and estimating costs.

Self-employed upholsterers need good business skills, self-discipline and self-motivation. They also require good interpersonal skills to deal with customers.

ENTRY REQUIREMENTS

There are no formal educational requirements for this career although some employers may look for GCSEs in subjects such as technology, maths, English, and science, and courses leading to relevant qualifications may have specific entry requirements.

The main courses for upholstery are City and Guilds (C&G) 5550 in Furniture Craft Subjects and 2955 in Upholstery. There are no formal entry qualifications for C&G courses but some colleges may ask for three GCSEs in maths, English and a science subject.

TRAINING

Training may be full-time at college or part-time working as a trainee with skilled upholsterers, learning on the job and attending college on day release. Study is usually via a two-year part-time course for C&G 5550 in Furniture Crafts or via a one-year full-time/three-year part-time course for C&G 2955 in Upholstery. The Furniture Crafts course covers timber preparation and construction, upholstery and bedding preparation and construction, metal and plastics preparation and construction, finishing preparation and modern finishing, soft furnishing, carcass and wooden frame construction, and hand-made furniture construction. There are also modules in upholstery that can be taken with this course which include related subjects such as drawing, history and safety.

C&G 5640 Furniture Crafts: Upholstery (Special) includes basic traditional techniques in upholstery, use of tools and equipment, upholstery construction materials, and upholstery and soft furnishing fabrics and trimmings. It also covers soft furnishing, furniture history, frame making and repair, wood finishing and polishing, small business studies, and applications of information technology.

Further study can lead to C&G 5550 Advanced Studies (Upholstery) which takes the studies to a deeper level and introduces workshop management and structure of the industry.

For a list of colleges offering the courses contact the Guild of Master Craftsmen. All courses are listed in *The Woodworkers' Career and Educational Source Book*.

NVQs/SVQs in Upholstered Furniture Production and Traditional Upholstery are included in a comprehensive range of NVQs/SVQs available in the furniture industry at Levels 1, 2 and 3. For full details, please see article 1. CABINET MAKER.

A Modern Apprenticeship Programme is available leading to at least NVQ/SVQ Level 3. Further information is available from BFM Training Ltd, the furniture industry training organization.

For apprentices employed by firms located in a rural area of England (where the population is less than 10,000) there is an assisted programme of upholstery training run by the Rural Development Commission.

LATE ENTRY

There are no maximum age limits for this work. Some colleges run full- and part-time BTEC continuing education courses, designed for mature students, in relevant subjects such as furniture restoration, which includes upholstery.

OPPORTUNITIES

Upholsterers are found in many cities, towns and rural areas throughout Britain. Many work for, or in association with, furniture restorers, antique dealers or interior decorators. Others are self-employed, work for other upholsterers or furniture manufacturers.

PAY AND CONDITIONS

As some upholsterers are self-employed, pay may vary considerably. Hours are also variable to suit the needs of the job. Those employed by furniture manufacturers are likely to work a 39-hour week, Monday to Friday. Self-employed upholsterers frequently work far more than 39 hours a week.

PROSPECTS

Upholsterers can gain more advanced qualifications by studying for C&G 5553 Advanced Studies (Upholstery) and the BA (Hons) Furniture Restoration and Craftsmanship course with specialism in Traditional Upholstery offered by the Buckinghamshire College, High Wycombe. They may progress by moving from working for another upholsterer to owning and running their own company. In factories there may be possibilities of moving into supervisory or management posts. Some upholsterers move into teaching.

Upholsterers starting their own business need capital (though the cost of tools and equipment is much less than for cabinet making). This may be borrowed from the bank. There may also be grants available, for instance from the Rural Development Commission.

RELATED OCCUPATIONS

Tailor, dressmaker, French polisher, cabinet maker.

FURNITURE CRAFTS: SAJ

FURTHER INFORMATION

The Association of Master Upholsterers, Francis Vaughan House, 102 Commercial Street, Newport, Gwent NP9 1LU, 01633 215454, www.upholsterers.co.uk

BFM Training Limited*, 30 Harcourt Street, London W1H 2AA, 0171 724 0851

The Guild of Master Craftsmen Ltd*, 166 High Street, Lewes, East Sussex BN7 1XU, 01273 478449

Rural Development Commission, 141 Castle Street, Salisbury, Wilts SP1 3TP, 01722 336255

The Guild of Traditional Upholsterers, 5 Station Road, West Runton, near Cromer, Norfolk, NR27 9QD

FURTHER READING

Leaflets/booklets are available from the addresses marked*.

Woodworkers' Career and Educational Source Book – Guild of Master Craftsmen

Upholstery: a Complete Course – Guild of Master Craftsmen

In the careers library classified under SAJ.

3. FRENCH POLISHER (SAJ)

THE WORK

French polishers work on the sheen and colour of a piece of wood to fill in the grain, give it a smooth finish and bring out the beauty of the timber. They work on pieces of furniture and occasionally other wooden items such as staircases, doors and panelling in old houses. They may work on new items or on the restoration of old ones.

Before polishing, French polishers have to prepare the piece of furniture. For restoration work simple repairs may need to be carried out; more complex ones are usually sent to a cabinet maker or restorer. If the furniture has previously been painted, varnished or lacquered, they remove this with paint stripper, steel wool and possibly sandpaper. They fill in any holes in the wood and ensure that it has a smooth surface.

Once the wood is prepared they decide on the type of stain needed to produce the necessary colour. This is mixed and then applied using a rubber (which is a piece of cloth with wadding inside it) or mop. French polish consists of shellac dissolved in methylated spirit – and this is applied to the wood using the rubber. The shellac is applied by rubbing it onto the wood, using an overlapping circular motion. This process is repeated many times until the correct finish is achieved.

Furniture may also be lacquered, varnished, painted, oiled or waxed, and many French polishers apply these finishes. They also reproduce and create other different types of finishes. These processes may be quicker than French polishing. For instance, in the case of a lacquer, the furniture may first be sprayed with a tinted lacquer, or stained and then sprayed with a clear lacquer.

French polishers are sometimes employed in factories that mass-produce furniture. As very little mass-produced furniture is French polished, their job is usually to work out how to achieve the finish the designer requires in the manufacturing process. If the factory does produce furniture French polished then machines may do some of the work, but French polishers polish parts, such as chair legs, that can not be done by machine.

WORK ENVIRONMENT

Most French polishers work in workshops that are usually light and airy. There may be dust from sanding and masks are worn. There may also be some fumes from the lacquers and polishes although most workshops are well ventilated. Some types of finish require the use of protective clothing, masks and (when using polyurethane, for example) a respirator hood with air supply. French polishers may have to visit a customer and may occasionally work in customers' homes. Some work in factories which may be noisy. The work involves considerable standing, bending and lifting.

SKILLS AND INTERESTS

French polishers should enjoy working with natural materials and have an appreciation of (and a good eye for) colour. They require good hand skills to apply stains and polishes. The work needs a great deal of patience and perseverance as it can be slow and repetitive. The work can be physically demanding and French polishers should be agile and fit. An interest in antique furniture and the history of furniture production is useful. French polishers should have an appreciation of the pattern, texture, feel and design of wood.

Self-employed polishers need good business skills, self-discipline and self-motivation. They need good interpersonal skills to deal with customers. Numeracy is important for calculating quantities and estimating costs. A knowledge of science is useful in working with chemicals.

ENTRY REQUIREMENTS

There are no specific entry requirements for this career although some employers may look for GCSEs in subjects such as technology, maths, English and science. Courses leading to relevant qualifications may have specific entry requirements.

The main course for French polishing is City and Guilds (C&G) 5550 in Furniture Craft Subjects. There are no formal entry qualifications for C&G courses but some colleges ask for three GCSEs/S grades in maths, English and a science subject.

TRAINING

Training may be full-time at college or part-time working as a trainee with skilled French polishers, learning on the job and attending college on day release. Study is usually for C&G 5550 in Furniture Craft Subjects, with specialist modules in finishing.

C&G 5550 in Furniture Craft Subjects covers timber preparation and construction, metal and plastics preparation and construction, upholstery and bedding preparation and construction, finishing preparation and modern finishing, soft furnishing, carcass and wooden frame construction and hand-made furniture construction.

FURNITURE CRAFTS: SAJ

All students follow a common course during part 1 (normally one year block or day release), and select from a range of specialist modules for part 2 (which normally takes two years). All courses are listed in the *Woodworkers' Career and Educational Source Book*.

There are also private fee-paying courses in French polishing such as those run by the Midland School of French Polishing, in Nottingham.

A number of NVQs/SVQs in Furniture Production and Producing Handcrafted Furniture are available at Levels 1, 2 and 3. For full details, please see article 1. CABINET MAKER.

A Modern Apprenticeship Programme is available in polishing and finishing leading to at least NVQ/SVQ Level 3. Further information is available from BFM Training Ltd, the furniture industry training organization.

A BA(Hons) in Furniture Restoration Craftsmanship (with specialism in Surface Finishing in years 2 and 3) is available at Buckingham College, High Wycombe.

LATE ENTRY

There are no maximum age limits for this work. Some colleges run BTEC continuing education courses, both full and part-time, in relevant subjects such as furniture restoration, which includes French polishing.

OPPORTUNITIES

French polishers are found in many cities, towns and rural areas throughout Britain. Many work for or in association with furniture restorers or antique dealers. Others are self-employed, working for other French polishers or for furniture manufacturers.

PAY AND CONDITIONS

As many French polishers are self-employed, pay may vary considerably although there is a minimum wage rate of around £181 a week. Hours are also variable to suit the needs of the job. They may work in excess of 39 hours a week.

PROSPECTS

French polishers can progress from working for another French polisher to owning and running their own company. Those working for furniture manufacturers may have promotion routes into supervisory and management posts. Some move into teaching.

French polishers starting their own businesses need capital. This may be borrowed from a bank. There may also be some grants available, for instance from the Rural Development Commission.

RELATED OCCUPATIONS

Boatbuilder, musical instrument manufacturer, museum conservation officer, cabinet maker, upholsterer, painter/decorator.

FURTHER INFORMATION

BFM Training Limited*, 30 Harcourt Street, London W1H 2AA, 0171 724 0851, www.bfm.org.uk

The Guild of Master Craftsmen Ltd.*, 166 High Street, Lewes, East Sussex BN7 1XU, 01273 478449

Rural Development Commission, 141 Castle Street, Salisbury, Wilts SP1 3TP, 01722 336255

FURTHER READING

Leaflets/booklets are available from the addresses marked*.

Woodworkers' Career and Educational Source Book – The Guild of Master Craftsmen

In the careers library, classified under SAJ.

THE FOUNDRY INDUSTRY: SAM

1. **FOUNDRY WORKER CLCI:SAM**
2. **PATTERNMAKER CLCI:SAM**
3. **MOULDER/COREMAKER CLCI:SAM**

BACKGROUND INFORMATION

The foundry industry produces metal castings, such as engine blocks, turbine blades for jet engines, surgical instruments, crankshafts and other car parts. They also make products such as church bells, taps, ornate metal garden furniture and gates. Castings are produced in a wide variety of metals including iron, aluminium, brass, bronze, steel, and even silver, gold and platinum. They range in size from large ships' propellers to delicate pieces of jewellery. Foundries usually specialize in one type of metal although some deal with a range of materials.

In foundries, metal ingots, other raw materials and in some cases, scrap metal, are put into a furnace and melted down. The molten metal is then poured into moulds made of sand or metal, where it solidifies into the correct shape.

1. FOUNDRY WORKER (SAM)

THE WORK

Foundry workers carry out a wide range of tasks within a foundry ranging from jobs such as cleaning or lift truck driving, to more complex work such as that of furnace operators. Many of the foundry workers assist specialist craftspeople in the foundry. For instance, some assist moulders/coremakers by mixing the moulding sand to the correct specification adding water and binders. The main types of workers are:

Furnace operators load the furnaces with the correct specification of metal which can include new and scrap metal. After melting the metal, a sample is taken to the laboratory for testing or, in more modern foundries, the furnace operators may carry out their own analysis with special equipment. Temperatures are also taken to ensure they are correct for casting. Operatives check that furnace linings are not worn out. They may have to be replaced if they are worn down.

Casters use ladles to pour molten metal into the prepared moulds. They are also involved in lining the ladles with a heat-resistant material and checking that the temperature in the ladles is correct. In more modern foundries this process is automated.

Knock out operators remove castings from moulds when they are cool and break the sand after it has been used, in foundries where this process is not automated.

Fettlers and grinders remove any unwanted pieces of metal from castings and grind off any rough edges, in foundries where this process is not automated.

Machine moulding operators operate machinery. In fully automated foundries, their main task is controlling the moulding machine which may make as many as 300 moulds per hour. In other foundries, they may work hand-operated moulding machines set up for the production of small batches of castings. If this is not automated, they place cores into the moulds and close the mould prior to casting. When the castings have been produced in the moulds they knock the castings out and put them into a shot blaster to knock the sand off.

WORK ENVIRONMENT

Foundry workers work mainly indoors in the foundry itself where the furnace area can be hot, although some work outside in all weathers sorting out scrap metal. The work may be physical with some lifting and carrying but European legislation and the introduction of mechanical aids have removed most strenuous tasks. Foundries can be dirty and dusty and there may be fumes from moulds and cores although most modern foundries have fume and dust extractors. In some iron foundries, coal dust is used in the sand which makes the environment very dirty, though many have introduced an alternative that is dust-free. The industry has established many modern practices that are designed to improve the working environment within a foundry.

SKILLS AND INTERESTS

Traditionally, foundry workers have needed to be fit and strong for the physical work, which used to involve a lot of lifting but, increasingly, automation and mechanical aids and the use of sophisticated equipment mean there is more mental activity involved. Hand skills are very important for some jobs – such as fettling and controlling the moulding machine. Basic communication skills are needed to be able to understand instructions and communicate with other workers.

Foundry workers should be careful, thorough in their work and able to understand and follow safety regulations. Foundries can be potentially dangerous with hot metal and metal splinters being some of the hazards. Adaptability is also needed so that workers can do more than one job in the foundry. They need to be able to work on their own but under supervision, and to work as part of a team.

ENTRY REQUIREMENTS

There are no academic entry requirements for this work. Physical fitness, however, may be vital and workers usually have to pass a medical examination. Although it is possible to come into this work at 16 years, this is unusual; most workers are over 18 years.

TRAINING

Training varies according to the needs of the person and the complexity of the job. Usually all new foundry workers will go through induction training and a course in safety, and safe working practices. The rest of their training is given on the job and can take from a couple of hours to a couple of months, depending on the work they are to do. Lift truck drivers, for instance, require about two weeks' training. Furnace operators may take five to six months to train. In some cases a worker will start with a job such as general labouring work at the furnace, gradually learning more complex work. Many workers are now being trained to carry out a wide range of different tasks. Those may lead to the awarding of an NVQ.

NVQs/SVQs in Engineering Material Processing or High Pressure Aluminium Diecasting at Levels 1 and 2 are available. Modern Apprenticeships (Skillseekers Initiative in Scotland) are now available which lead to the Apprentice obtaining an NVQ/SVQ up to Level 2 or 3, with a City and Guilds certificate. A whole range of NVQs/SVQs have now been introduced.

THE FOUNDRY INDUSTRY: SAM

LATE ENTRY

There is no upper age limit for this work and many employers accept or prefer adults, especially those with experience of production work. Some jobs require physical strength and fitness; workers may have to pass a medical examination.

There may be specific training opportunities directed at adults available in some areas for this type of work. Candidates may have to satisfy certain conditions to be eligible. Contact your local Jobcentre, careers office or TEC/LEC for details.

OPPORTUNITIES

Foundry workers are employed in large engineering companies that have their own foundries but most opportunities are in independent foundries. Foundries fall into two types – automated and jobbing foundries, with some foundries being both. Automated foundries make large quantities of identical castings and the work is done by machines, whereas jobbing foundries make small quantities of castings and much of the work is done by hand.

There are over 700 foundries throughout England, Wales and Scotland, ranging from very large foundries to small ones with fewer than 25 staff. They are found in most industrial areas, particularly in the Midlands, but many foundries are also found in Lancashire, Yorkshire, the North East coast, the Clyde, South Wales and the South East of England.

PAY AND CONDITIONS

Basic pay for foundry workers is likely to be around £220 a week, or £180 in a small foundry dependent upon the size and type of work carried out, specialists and team leaders can expect to earn up to £270 per week. The working week is usually 37 hours, Monday to Friday. The industry is currently very busy and most foundries are working overtime and earnings can be in excess of £300 per week. It is possible, although not common, for foundry workers to work abroad for overseas companies.

PROSPECTS

Promotion is usually to supervisor or foreman/woman where NVQ/SVQ in Supervisory Management at Level 3 is available. Foundry workers often progress further into management and even senior management, as local knowledge and experience are highly valued.

RELATED OCCUPATIONS

Patternmaker, moulder/coremaker, blacksmith, forklift truck driver, engineering operator, production worker.

FURTHER INFORMATION AND READING

Please see article 3. MOULDER/COREMAKER.

2. PATTERNMAKER (SAM)

THE WORK

Patternmakers make the models or patterns of the required casting shape from which the moulds are produced. Patterns can be of wood, metal, plastic, resin or polystyrene.

Patternmakers work from a technical drawing of the part required, they plan how to make the pattern and then produce a full-scale working drawing by hand or computer. They decide from which material the pattern should be made, and then decide on the type of wood or metal. For instance, some woods such as mahogany are very long lasting, while others are particularly good for cutting with a chisel. For complicated shapes they may first make a metal template to assist them. Next they make the pattern parts using machines and hand tools including saws, planes, and milling and grinding machines working to extremely fine tolerances. During this process they use precision instruments to measure the dimensions of the pattern to make sure they are accurate. They then assemble the patterns and finish them by hand. Finally the pattern may be painted or varnished.

Some patterns are made on computer numerically controlled machines (CNCs), which are operated by a machine operator, the job of the patternmaker being to program the machine.

WORK ENVIRONMENT

Patternmakers usually work in a workshop. Modern dust and fume extraction systems mean that these are not particularly dusty. Working with wood, however, can produce dust that may cause problems for people with chest complaints. The workplace can be noisy on occasion.

SKILLS AND INTERESTS

Patternmakers need good hand skills and the ability to work with both machines and hand tools with a variety of different materials including wood and metal. They should be able to visualize in three dimensions to work out how to construct patterns. Mathematical ability is needed for calculations and a good understanding of engineering drawings is vital.

Communication skills are important as liaison with others is involved in the design and use of patterns. They should be able to work as part of a team but also on their own if necessary. They should be safety conscious, thorough and methodical. They also need the self-motivation to see a job through from start to finish.

ENTRY REQUIREMENTS

Entry for young people is possible in England via a Modern Apprenticeship in Patternmaking and Foundry Work or, in Scotland, through the Skillseekers Initiative. Application may be made to an employer or through a TEC/LEC or, for Modern Apprenticeships, through one of the four colleges that are approved training providers: Coventry Technical College, Sandwell College, Chesterfield College and Openshaw College.

Qualifications may vary but many companies look for GCSEs/S grades (D/4 or above) in maths and an engineering subject. GNVQ/GSVQ in Engineering could also be helpful.

TRAINING

Both Modern Apprenticeships and Skillseekers lead to an NVQ/SVQ in Engineering Material Processing: Foundry or Patternmaking at Level 2 or Level 3 in Patternmaking. They are based on acquiring competencies rather than

THE FOUNDRY INDUSTRY: SAM

being time-based, and usually take about three years. Apprentices may also study for C&G 2110 Part 3 in Patternmaking.

Training varies but usually consists of one year's broad-based off-the-job training in a college or company training school followed by modular training within the company and day or block release to college. Modules/units will be chosen to suit the requirements of the particular employer.

Practical training includes pattern construction and how to make patterns in different materials, such as wood, metal and plastic.

LATE ENTRY

Traditionally most new entrants into this career are school-leavers aged 16 to 17 years. However, nowadays some companies employ adults, especially those with relevant experience in related areas of work, such as mechanical engineering crafts, or construction crafts, such as woodmachining and joinery, and give them additional training.

Training for adults varies from employer to employer and usually depends on the qualifications and experience of the trainee. Training is likely to be shorter and more condensed than that of a school-leaver. Adults may also be assessed for NVQs/SVQs, and skills acquired in other industries can be taken into account.

There may be specific training opportunities directed at adults available in some areas for this type of work. Candidates may have to satisfy certain conditions to be eligible. Contact your local Jobcentre, careers office or TEC/LEC for details.

OPPORTUNITIES

Please see article 1. FOUNDRY WORKER.

In addition to patternshops attached to foundries, patternmakers also work for specialist pattern-making companies.

PAY AND CONDITIONS

Basic pay for trained patternmakers is about £300 to £350 a week, dependent upon the size and type of work carried out by the patternshop. Hours are usually 37 a week, Monday to Friday. The industry is currently very busy and most shops are working overtime. Rates of pay on average including overtime and shift allowance vary between £380 to £420.

PROSPECTS

Promotion for patternmakers is usually to supervisor or foreman/woman and from there they may move into management. It is also possible for patternmakers with good results in their City and Guilds (C&G) examinations to move on to technician training in a range of areas, such as: quality control, estimating, work study, production planning, or mechanical testing.

Employers may give some patternmaking apprentices the opportunity to attend university for degree courses in materials sciences.

Work abroad is possible, as British C&G qualifications are recognized world-wide. Patternmakers can become self-employed.

RELATED OCCUPATIONS

Carpenter/joiner, engineering craft machinist, foundry moulder/coremaker, wood machinist, engineering toolmaker.

FURTHER INFORMATION AND READING

Please see article 3. MOULDER/COREMAKER.

3. MOULDER/COREMAKER (SAM)

THE WORK

Moulders/coremakers make the moulds in which metal castings are made, by packing sand into a box, round a pattern usually made of wood or metal that is the same shape as the required casting. They start by deciding how the mould should be made, choosing the correct size of box for the job as it has to hold enough sand to make the mould strong, yet not use too much sand as that would be too expensive. They then carefully position the pattern into the box. Before putting the sand into the box and packing it firmly round the pattern they check that the sand mix is right.

When the sand is hard they carefully remove the pattern. If the mould shape is damaged they repair it using hand tools. Often they apply a mould coating, which means mixing the coating to get the right consistency then applying it with a brush or hose pipe to give a better surface finish on the castings.

If the casting has hollow sections, they make a core – a mass of sand in the shape of the hollow – and place it carefully into the mould ensuring the correct space for the molten metal to pass between the core and the mould walls. Some very intricate castings may have a large number of cores. Finally the mould halves are closed ready for the molten metal to be poured in.

WORK ENVIRONMENT

Moulders/coremakers' work environment varies depending on the type of mould they are working on. They could be working with a moulding box at a workbench or, in the case of very large moulds, they work in specially designed moulding pits. The work is physically strenuous with some lifting and carrying. Their environment may be dirty, hot if near the furnaces, and there may be fumes, although most foundries have fume and dust extraction systems. In iron foundries, coal dust is used in the sand, which makes the environment very dirty.

SKILLS AND INTERESTS

Moulders/coremakers need good hand skills. Care and patience are needed as some of the work such as smoothing the sand in the mould can be very delicate. It is important that they work accurately; measurements for moulds and cores may need to be accurate to 1 mm. Care is also needed to follow safety procedures. They need the

THE FOUNDRY INDUSTRY: SAM

ability to visualize in three dimensions to work out how to make moulds. Physical fitness is important as the work involves some lifting and bending. Moulders/coremakers need good communication skills to follow instructions and communicate with other moulders/coremakers and foundry workers.

They also need an understanding of the casting process and how sands and metals react. They should be adaptable as they have to work on both simple moulds and complex moulds which have a number of cores. They need to be organized, able to think for themselves and be methodical to plan and make moulds.

ENTRY REQUIREMENTS

In England, it is possible to enter via a Modern Apprenticeship or, in Scotland, Skillseekers training for young people. Application may be made to an employer or through a TEC/LEC or, for Modern Apprenticeships, to one of the three colleges involved: Coventry Technical College, Sandwell College and Chesterfield College.

For these, companies may look for GCSEs/S grades (D/4 or above) in maths and an engineering subject. GNVQ/GSVQ in Engineering could also be helpful.

However, moulders/coremakers may also be recruited directly as trainee moulders/coremakers within an in-company training scheme, or start as foundry workers and progress to become moulders/coremakers. For this, no formal educational qualifications may be required, as many employers consider practical ability to be more important than academic ability.

TRAINING

Both Modern Apprenticeships and Skillseekers lead to an NVQ/SVQ in Engineering Material Processing at Level 3. This is based on acquiring competencies and usually takes about three years. Modules/units selected are relevant to the requirements and processes of specific employers. Apprentices may also study for C&G 2100 Part 3 in Foundry Craft Studies.

Training varies. In many foundries, trainees spend their first year in a training centre learning the basic skills of moulding and coremaking. During this time they may also spend one day a week at a college learning the theory. At the end of that year they start work in the foundry, beginning with straightforward jobs such as making a smaller mould from a plated pattern, gradually progressing to more and more complex work, such as moulds with many cores and complex joints. On more complicated jobs they often assist an experienced moulder/coremaker, to learn their skills.

LATE ENTRY

There is no maximum age limit for this work although some foundries may not recruit people over the age of 30 years. Previous experience, especially in relevant work such as other foundry or engineering work, may be an advantage in getting a job. Length of training may vary depending on the experience of the trainee. Adults may be assessed for NVQs/SVQs and previously acquired knowledge and skills can be taken into account.

There may be specific training opportunities directed at adults available in some areas for this type of work. Candidates may have to satisfy certain conditions to be eligible. Contact your local Jobcentre, careers office or TEC/LEC for details.

OPPORTUNITIES

Please see article 1. FOUNDRY WORKER.

Moulder/coremaker is a traditional craft. While opportunities for training in it still exist, computerization and automation, together with pressure for higher production rates, mean that there is a tendency for these positions to be replaced by multiskilled machine operators in some foundries. In some instances, this is within a team-working system that includes maintenance skills. This craft may be redefined or a new one evolved to replace it.

PAY AND CONDITIONS

Pay for trained moulders/coremakers is likely to be around £250 a week. Hours are usually 37 a week, Monday to Friday. They may have to work shifts, weekends and overtime, depending on the foundry.

PROSPECTS

Promotion for moulders/coremakers is usually to supervisor or foreman/woman and from there they may move into management. It is also possible for moulders/coremakers with good results in their C&G examinations to move on to technician training, in a range of areas, such as quality control, estimating, work study, production planning or mechanical testing.

RELATED OCCUPATIONS

Patternmaker, foundry worker, engineering craft machinist, engineering operative, engineer.

FURTHER INFORMATION

British Metal Castings Council*, The McLaren Building, 35 Dale End, Birmingham B4 7LN, 0121 200 2100

Institute of British Foundrymen*, Bordesley Hall, The Holloway, Alvechurch, Birmingham B48 7QA, 01527 596100, ourworld.compuserve.com/homepages/instituteoffoundrymen

Metcom*, Savoy Tower, 77 Renfrew Street, Glasgow G2 3BZ, 0141 332 0826, www.metcom.org.uk

Engineering and Marine Training Authority*, Engineering Careers Department, Vector House, 41 Clarendon Road, Watford, Herts WD1 1HS, 0800 282167, www.emta.org.uk

Training Publications Ltd*, PO Box 75, Stockport, 0161 480 5285

FURTHER READING

Leaflets/booklets are available from the addresses marked*.

In the careers library classified under SAM.

PLASTICS PROCESSING: SAN

PLASTICS PROCESS OPERATIVE
CLCI:SAN

BACKGROUND INFORMATION

Plastics are used throughout the world – everything from household goods to the most advanced science and technology. The range of uses is endless because plastics are so versatile. There are roughly 24 main types, including polythene, polypropylene, melamine and glass reinforced plastic (GRP), which is very hard. Plastics have many properties – they are strong and light, soft and flexible; can be moulded; are heat-resistant; and are free from corrosion. They can be welded, pre-coloured, printed upon or be used to coat or laminate goods. Another type of plastic – known as thermosetting plastic – is malleable when it is first heated and formed but, when further heat is applied, it is 'cured', setting like pottery in a kiln and remaining permanently shaped and heat-resistant.

THE WORK

Process operatives – also called machine operators – are responsible for product quality, feeding raw materials into machines and removing the finished product. They weigh and measure, then remove and trim the finished product checking its quality. Some process operatives also label and pack the finished goods.

Process operatives check that semi-automatic and non-automatic machinery involved in producing plastic products runs correctly. They check the machines' pressures and temperatures, and ensure the goods are being produced at the right speed. Machines are set by machine setters but operatives may need to make minor adjustments to machines, altering valves and switches to check the machines run smoothly. When there is a fault, operators may need to tell the chargehand or supervisor, or call in the maintenance team.

Process operatives need to work at a steady, quick pace. Some machines produce goods at a set rate, others can be altered to produce goods to different speeds so the operator can work at their own rate. Some operators may be responsible for more than one machine.

The operative may work on a range of different goods; one machine may make a variety of products. The operative may also move from machine to machine and learn how several different machines work.

WORK ENVIRONMENT

Process operatives work on the shop floor, in factories and workshops.

There may be fumes from the raw material but most shop floors are well ventilated. In most factories, operators work in clean, well lit surroundings.

SKILLS AND INTERESTS

Process operatives need to work quickly and steadily to handle the regular flow of goods being produced by the machine.

Operating machinery can be repetitive and requires concentration and careful attention. All operators need to be responsible and check that safety regulations are followed.

Technical knowledge is necessary for monitoring and correcting machines. A scientific understanding is useful, as plastics processing involves the effect of chemical reactions and heat treatments.

Operatives may need to make some straightforward calculations when measuring and mixing quantities of raw materials.

Working on the shop floor involves team work – the ability to co-operate with other workers and follow instructions is needed.

Workers should be physically active – long periods are spent standing or sitting, and some work may involve lifting heavy materials.

ENTRY REQUIREMENTS

For many operative jobs, no educational qualifications are required, but exam passes can be useful.

Applicants should be able to follow instructions and understand straightforward calculations as the work may involve weighing materials.

Increasing complexity of machinery and processes, however, means that qualifications are becoming more important. To meet this, a new entry route is a Modern Apprenticeship, leading to an NVQ/SVQ in Polymer Processing at Level 3. Entry requirements are GCSEs/S-grades (A–C/1–3), or being able to demonstrate the ability to cope with an NVQ/SVQ Level 3 content.

In Scotland, entry to Modern Apprenticeships is via Skillseekers.

National Traineeships are also available leading to NVQ Level 2. Please contact your local careers office or TEC/LEC.

TRAINING

Training for Modern Apprentices includes on- the-job skills training to acquire competencies, which are assessed, and study for underpinning knowledge. Apprentices also study to obtain a BTEC Certificate in Polymer Technology and some Foundation units in Engineering.

Other entrants learn specific tasks mainly on-the-job but a wide range of other courses are offered to meet the needs of the industry; these combine both study and practical work. Apprentices may be sent on BPTA short courses, lasting three or four days, related to new technology and specific job duties. These include courses about plastic materials, the physical testing of plastics, the use of additives such as stabilizers and colorants during processing and their effect on production.

Other courses teach operators to recognize faults in finished goods and carry out tests for quality to national standards.

LATE ENTRY

Opportunities are available for older entrants to work as a process operative. Most companies consider adults who meet their requirements; see ENTRY REQUIREMENTS and TRAINING. Adults can also be assessed towards NVQ/SVQ qualifications, and previous relevant experience in other industries may be taken into account.

PLASTICS PROCESSING: SAN

OPPORTUNITIES

There are over 4,000 plastics processing companies employing 200,000 people, a large number being process operatives.

After falling for a number of years, there has been some increase lately in the number of people employed in plastics processing. Indeed, the plastics processing industry has been identified by the government as a growth sector both for output and for employment, so opportunities will increase for individuals willing to obtain the appropriate qualifications.

PAY AND CONDITIONS

Rates of pay vary and depend on the company and its location. An experienced operative can earn an average basic wage of around £260 a week. Extra may be paid for shift work and productivity bonuses. Opportunities may also exist for overtime work.

Most companies have shift working which includes evening, night and weekend work. Some firms may require permanent night-shift workers.

PROSPECTS

For those interested in, and with an aptitude for, working with machines, machine moulding or setting is a possible prospect.

The BPTA runs various courses to enable process operatives to increase their skills. Courses include practical knowledge about how to set up and close down machines and correct faults. Some operatives may progress to supervisory grades, such as chargehand, inspector or supervisor.

Other prospects may include moving into quality control work.

RELATED OCCUPATIONS

Production worker, chemical plant process operative, engineering operative, brewery worker, foundry worker.

FURTHER INFORMATION

Polymer and Associated Industries NTO*, Coppice House, Halesfield, Telford, Shropshire TF7 4NA, 01952 587020
www.bpta.co.uk

Institute of Materials*, 1 Carlton House Terrace, London SW1Y 5DB, 0171 839 4071

FURTHER READING

Leaflets/booklets are available from the address marked*.
In the careers library classified under SAN.

PAPER MANUFACTURE: SAP

PAPER MANUFACTURING WORKER
CLCI:SAP

BACKGROUND INFORMATION

The paper manufacturing industry makes paper and board which are converted into a wide range of products from packing boxes and writing paper to kitchen work surfaces. In Britain we produce half of our paper; the other half is imported. Over half the paper made in Britain is made from recycled wastepaper with the rest made from wood pulp, either imported or home-grown. A little is made from other vegetable fibres, such as cotton or grasses – bank notes are made of cotton, for example. Most paper is made by machines, but there are a few remaining paper mills where paper is hand made.

THE WORK

Pulpmen/women operate the machinery that converts the raw material into fibres called pulp which is suitable for further processing. To do this, they use conveyors to load the raw materials into the pulpers, control the process time, add chemicals and adjust the temperature and pressure of machines. They then test the pulp to make sure it is suitable for papermaking. The mixture of treated raw materials eventually becomes the paper or board known as stock.

Beatermen/women operate the mechanical and chemical processes that refine the stock so that it is of the correct colour, fibre length and wetness to provide the characteristics of the paper or board required. For instance, they operate the control systems from a computer keyboard or by opening and closing valves that add the correct colourings at the right temperature and in the right amount to produce paper of the required colour. In addition to operating the machinery, they monitor the processes, making sure that the machines are working correctly.

The stock then passes to the papermaking machine where the fibres are intermeshed to form a continuous sheet. **Machinemen/women** control the papermaking machine, usually by computer. They use a variety of data such as laboratory tests and readings from the computer to keep a constant check on the quality of the paper being produced. They also maintain the condition of the machines by ensuring that all moving parts are working correctly, sensors are operating and worn parts are replaced. Often this means liaising with engineers. They also supervise and train other members of the machine crew.

The water is then removed to leave a dry continuous sheet of paper, which is then sprayed with size to seal its surface. **Dryermen/women** or **backtenders** control the dryers to make sure that the paper dries uniformly, and monitor and control the size press. They use VDUs to monitor the processes and the condition of the paper, making sure the processes are working correctly.

Reelermen/women operate the reeler that converts the reels of paper at the end of the production into finished reels of the right size for the customer. They set and change the knives used to do this. They check any sub-standard reels for re-winding.

Coating machinemen/women control the coating machines, usually by computer, making sure the machines run at the right speed and apply a coating of the right quality. They make sure that the coating is mixed to the right consistency and add appropriate chemicals. They supervise the rest of the coating crew.

Sometimes paper gets damaged in the manufacturing process and the job of the **inspection windermen/women** is to cut out any marked or damaged paper from the reels and remake any bad joints. If the paper is to be coated it then goes through another process.

Cuttermen/women operate a sheet-cutting machine that cuts the paper into sheets. They set up the machine to cut the paper to the correct size and inspect the paper for faults. They also direct their crew.

Finally, the paper passes to a finishing area, called the *salle*, where packers and sorters take out any faulty sheets of paper.

At various stages during the manufacturing process **paper testers**, using a variety of types of measuring equipment, carry out tests to determine the paper's thickness, weight, smoothness, strength and moisture content.

Paper making uses a lot of water, but at the end of the production process most of the water is recycled. Mills use millions of gallons each day. The **effluent operative/fibre recovery attendants** operate and maintain the water systems and operate the plant that recovers fibres for re-use. They make sure the correct volume of effluent is directed to the appropriate stage in the process. They do this by checking flow rates and by opening and closing gates or valves. Many modern effluent treatment plants have systems containing live microscopic organisms that devour the effluent, and the attendants have to ensure the organism's environment is correctly maintained.

WORK ENVIRONMENT

Paper mills can be noisy and workers may have to wear ear defenders when working near machinery. Nowadays, however, most of the processes are controlled by computers and workers work within soundproof rooms. Paper testers work in laboratories. The work can involve standing and a lot of walking as mills are usually very large. There is some lifting, although most of which is done by machine.

SKILLS AND INTERESTS

Paper manufacturing workers need an interest in mechanical and computer-controlled equipment. Some ability in science, technology and maths is useful, to make calculations and to understand the manufacturing process.

They need to be very observant as much of the work is observing the various processes to check that the paper is being produced to the right quality.

Communication skills are required in order to give and understand instructions.

Paper manufacturing workers need to be able to work as part of a team.

ENTRY REQUIREMENTS

There are no minimum entry requirements for this work. Most employers look for a good general education and some may give candidates a maths test.

For Modern Apprenticeships or Skillseekers, employers may require GCSEs/S grades (A–C/1–3) in maths, English and science, plus passes in two other subjects (D/4) or equivalent awards such as GNVQs/GSVQs.

PAPER MANUFACTURE: SAP

Physical fitness is important and candidates usually have to pass a medical.

TRAINING

Training varies from employer to employer. Most training is given on-the-job, with trainees starting with more straightforward jobs, such as testing, reeler's assistant, machine assistant, dryerman/woman's assistant.

Some employers encourage trainees to study for the City and Guilds 5120 in Paper and Board Making either at college or in the mill's own training department. This covers the technology of paper and board manufacture plus related industrial studies and students can study at a pace to suit themselves. In Scotland, Skillseekers may be available.

Some mills offer a Modern Apprenticeship. In Scotland, this is via Skillseekers. Apprentices spend their first weeks moving round the different sections of the paper mill and then start their on-the-job training, at the same time going to college on day release, or studying in the mill's training department. The training leads to NVQs/SVQs in Paper and Board Making at Level 2, and in Controlling the Process of Making Paper and Board at Level 3.

In Scotland, SQA National Certificate in Paper Production can be taken by workers with appropriate qualifications and/or experience. S grade (1–3) is preferred.

LATE ENTRY

There are no age limits for entry into this work. However, it is important for all workers to be physically fit. Adult applicants with previous experience in relevant work, such as other manufacturing work, may be preferred.

OPPORTUNITIES

Paper mills are mainly found in South East and South West of England, Lancashire and Scotland although there are a few mills in other areas. As a great deal of water is used in the papermaking process, mills are normally found close to rivers, well away from towns.

The size of mills varies from quite small recycling firms to enormous sites covering acres of land.

There are currently 110 mills operating in the UK, employing over 33,000 people.

Opportunities for paper manufacturing workers are decreasing because of new technologies enabling greater output per employee.

PAY AND CONDITIONS

Paper manufacturing workers work a range of day and shift systems with the majority employed on seven-day shift-working systems. Weekly hours vary between 37 and 40 dependent upon the shift system.

Minimum pay ranges from £150 to £290 a week for adult employees. Actual rates paid by paper mills are higher than the minimum and are further supplemented through bonuses and overtime payments.

PROSPECTS

Promotion for paper manufacturing workers is usually, firstly, to shift supervisor – possibly in charge of a couple of machines – and then to superintendent, where they might be in charge of the preparation area or the papermaking machines or dealing with waste products from manufacturing and the warehouse.

RELATED OCCUPATIONS

Textile operative, chemical process worker, production worker.

FURTHER INFORMATION

Paper Education and Training Council (PETC)*, Papermakers House, Rivenhall Road, Westlea, Swindon, Wilts SN5 7BD, 01793 886086, www.paper.org.uk

FURTHER READING

Leaflets/booklets are available from the address marked*.

In the careers library classified under SAP.

PRINTING: SAR

1. ORIGINATOR CLCI:SAR
2. MACHINE PRINTER CLCI:SAR
3. PRINT FINISHER/BOOKBINDER CLCI:SAR

BACKGROUND INFORMATION

This article refers to the general commercial sector of the printing industry but excludes printing for national newspapers.

Printing is a growing industry. It is the UK's fifth largest, with over 10,000 companies employing approximately 165,000 people. The majority of companies employ fewer than 25 people and many employ fewer than ten. There are printing companies throughout the UK but with a concentration in London, and, to a lesser extent, in Leeds and Bradford.

Printing firms tend to specialize in the type of work they do as it is more efficient and profitable to do so. This is mainly because each end product requires slightly different printing presses, and folding, binding and glueing processes – all of which use expensive machinery.

The main specializations are: magazines; cartons (for food and other packaging); stationery; labels; print on metal (for such as beer cans and metal badges); books; high-quality colour printing (for brochures, cards and fine art reproductions); newspapers (short-run local papers and free sheets); security printing; and general printing (anything from mail order coupons to catalogues).

A number of different processes are used in printing, depending on the end product – lithography, flexography, gravure, screen printing and letter press. Developments in technology have led to the use of letter press being uncommon now, except in the production of self-adhesive labels.

The printing industry has been through great change, particularly with the introduction of computer technology. This has particularly affected origination work.

Jobs and training in printing can be grouped under the three main stages of the printing process – origination (also known as pre-press), printing and finishing.

1. ORIGINATOR (SAR)

THE WORK

Originators are responsible for the first stage in the printing process. They prepare text and illustrations for printing. There are several stages in origination. Staff in large firms may specialize in one stage, but increasingly, one person is responsible for some or all of the stages. Job titles differ but the following are all 'originators'.

Customers may send in the required text and illustrations and discuss requirements such as typeface and layout with **desktop publishing (DTP) operators** (who may be known as **keyboard operators** or **typesetters**). DTP operators use a keyboard to input the original copy into a computer then use desktop publishing software to manipulate the words on a VDU (visual display unit) into headlines, columns and text to produce the image. This may include making decisions on the typeface, size of type and spacing of text. More often, though, customers send in a computer disk with the text, in which case DTP operators follow instructions to produce what the customers require. Throughout the work, DTP operators check it as it appears on the VDU and make any necessary amendments.

DTP operators produce a proof (sample print). The proof is checked for any errors. This is often done by DTP operators but may be done by a specialist **proofreader**. DTP operators then combine all the elements of text and graphics into complete make-up pages. They may output these pages to film to go to planning and platemaking. Increasingly, though, they output the pages to machinery that produces a plate ready to go to a machine printer.

Scan operators, planners and **platemakers** are employed where DTP operators output to film rather than direct to plate.

Scan operators operate the machinery that photographs illustrations to be used in printed material. They are given the colour transparencies, photographs or artists' originals that are to be reproduced and printed. They set the controls of electronically controlled scanners to ensure that the colours are reproduced accurately.

Planners assemble the photographed pages in sets of four, eight, 16 or 32 pages, according to the design system. This makes sure that, eventually, the printed pages, after folding and cutting, will be in the correct order.

Platemakers use a special camera or scanner to produce the final plates that go to the machine printer. They do this by exposing the prepared plate to ultraviolet light – this transfers the image from film onto the printing plates. They use special fluids to remove any blemishes, then treat the plates to protect them.

WORK ENVIRONMENT

All origination work takes place indoors. DTP operators work in an office environment and spend most of their time sitting at a computer.

Scan operators, planners and platemakers work in workshop conditions. They stand for much of the time. Platemakers use chemicals and water in some processes.

SKILLS AND INTERESTS

The different tasks in the origination process require differing skills and interests but there are some that are common to them all. All involved in origination should be interested in computers and have computer skills. Computer use is now so central to origination. It is important that originators work accurately and that they are conscientious and careful. All origination processes require some ability with figures to make calculations. Tasks that involve the assessment of colours require normal colour vision. Origination work combines working individually and in a team, so it is important to be able to do both successfully.

DTP operators must be thoroughly familiar with DTP software and be able to type quickly and accurately. They need a good standard of English, particularly spelling, grammar and punctuation. This is especially the case if they are also responsible for proofreading. They need the skill to visualize layout of work and should have a flair for design. They spend long periods of time at a computer, which demands good powers of concentration.

Scan operators, planners and platemakers should be interested in photography. They need good eyesight and an appreciation of detail.

PRINTING: SAR

ENTRY REQUIREMENTS

There are no specified entry requirements. Recruitment policy varies between employers but most employers prefer applicants to have three or four GCSEs/S grades (A–C/1–3), including English, maths and a science subject. Computer studies is useful. Intermediate GNVQ/GSVQ Level II in, for example, Media Communication and Production, Art and Design or Design, may be accepted.

BTEC First Diploma in Printing – usually has no formal entry requirements, although individual colleges may have their own, such as The London Institute, which requires a minimum of three GCSEs/S grades (A–C/1–3).

City and Guilds (C&G) 5260 Printing and Graphic Communications – no particular entry requirements.

SQA National Certificate in Printing – no particular entry requirements.

Modern Apprenticeships – for young people who enter full-time employment. Entry is with at least three GCSEs/S grades (A–C/1–3) including English and maths. Technology subjects are useful. Some employers may seek more than the minimum entry requirements.

National Traineeships – for young people. Entry is with a good general education.

NVQs/SVQs in Origination – no particular entry requirements.

TRAINING

Pre-entry

It is possible (but not essential) outside Scotland to enter printing by studying for the BTEC First Diploma in Printing. There are six main study areas: origination processes; machine printing; print finishing and design; printing material studies; business organization, communication skills and administration; printing technology and related computer studies. The course lasts one year full-time and is offered at eleven colleges in England and one in Belfast.

On entry

Some entrants outside Scotland attend college to study for C&G Printing and Graphic Communications 5260-21 Origination Level 2 and 5260-22 Level 3. These reflect the knowledge requirements of the NVQs in Origination Levels 2 and 3. Courses are offered at several colleges on a day release basis and usually last two years.

In Scotland, some entrants attend college to study the SQA National Certificate in Printing, specializing in origination. The course is offered by Glasgow College of Building and Printing and lasts three years. In the first year students attend four periods of four weeks' block release, while in years 2 and 3 they attend four periods of two weeks' block release.

Entrants into printing may train through pre-press Modern Apprenticeships. Apprentices are trained by their employers but they may also attend a printing school or training provider on a part-time basis. They work towards NVQs/SVQs in Origination at Levels 2 and 3. They also work for additional NVQ/SVQ units in communication, information technology, application of number, problem solving and personal skills. Modern Apprenticeship training is not for a set length of time but usually takes at least three years. Modern Apprenticeships are also to be introduced for desktop publishing.

Entrants into printing may train through a National Traineeship that leads to NVQ/SVQ in Origination at Level 2. Trainees are trained by their employer and may attend a printing school or training provider part-time. Although not for a set length of time, National Traineeships are likely to last around two years. Contact your local careers office for information on Modern Apprenticeships and National Traineeships.

All those working in origination can work towards NVQs/SVQs in Origination at Levels 2 and 3.

LATE ENTRY

There are no upper age limits for entry to printing, although most entrants are school-/college-leavers.

There may be specific training opportunities directed at adults in some areas for this type of work. Candidates may have to satisfy certain conditions to be eligible. Contact your local Jobcentre, careers office or TEC/LEC for details.

OPPORTUNITIES

Originators work throughout the UK for printing companies and for firms that specialize in providing an origination service for the printing trade. As a consequence of technological change, there are now many fewer scan operators, planners and platemakers but many more DTP operators. A lot of staff in the industry have undergone re-training to equip them with the computer skills now needed for origination.

Vacancies for originators are advertised in *Print Week*, *Printing World* and in local newspapers. Those seeking entry into printing, though, ought to write speculatively to local employers.

There are a few opportunities for originators to work abroad.

PAY AND CONDITIONS

The British Printing Industries Federation (BPIF) recommends a minimum grade rate for skilled occupations of £212.02p a week but many companies pay considerably more than this. The minimum recommended weekly rate is £106.01p for a Modern Apprentice under 20 and £169.62p a Modern Apprentice over 20. This rises in both cases to £180.22p on achievement of NVQ/SVQ Level 2 and to the full rate on achieving NVQ/SVQ Level 3. In Scotland, apprentices are paid £84.80p a week during the first year, £137.80p in the second, £159.00p in the third and £178.25p in the fourth year.

The standard working week is 37½ hours but, in practice, hours vary between employers and can be between 35 and 40 a week. Day work is most common, although some work double day shifts (6am to 2pm and 2pm to 10pm). Where companies operate 24 hours a day, some work treble shifts or three shifts of twelve hours. A few work night shifts. With printing machinery becoming increasingly expensive, an increasing number of companies are getting a return on their investment by moving away from day work. More are now operating 24 hours a day for six or seven days a week.

Part-time work is possible, while overtime is very common.

PRINTING: SAR

PROSPECTS

Promotion is possible to supervisory and then to management positions, such as production controller/manager, estimator and account executive.

RELATED OCCUPATIONS, FURTHER INFORMATION AND READING

Please see article 3. PRINT FINISHER/BOOKBINDER.

2. MACHINE PRINTER (SAR)

THE WORK

Machine printers set up and run printing presses (machines) that print ink onto paper and other materials. The work involved differs according to the printing process – lithography, flexography, gravure, screen printing or letterpress.

Printers position one or more plates onto the press to make sure that the image is transferred exactly onto the surface. This can involve using hand tools and, in some cases, climbing on to the press. They select the correct inks and load them into reservoirs. They then load the machine with paper or other material before setting the machine to work at the correct speed, pressure and ink flow. This is done on modern machines by operating a push-button computer control console.

Printers have a trial run, if necessary adjusting the machine until it produces a print of acceptable quality, which is then used as a master sheet. They then start the print run. Printers are responsible for monitoring the quality of the printing. They do this by making regular checks of printing against the master sheet to make sure that print quality remains constant. If any problems occur during printing, printers diagnose the fault and make necessary adjustments before continuing the print run.

When a print run has finished, printers unload the printed material and stack it in readiness for print finishing. They then clean the machine before preparing it for the next job. Machine printers are responsible for routine maintenance of their machines.

WORK ENVIRONMENT

Machine printers work indoors in a factory environment.

Work can be dirty, dusty and noisy, particularly with older machines.

Machine printers spend much of their time standing. Work can involve heavy lifting. Some printers have to climb ladders and work at heights.

SKILLS AND INTERESTS

Machine printers should enjoy practical work and have good hand skills. They need mechanical ability, as they are responsible for setting, operating and maintaining machines. This is also important for dealing with machine problems during a print run. It is helpful if they have an interest in technology. With modern machinery, it is useful if printers understand electronics.

Some ability with figures is required for printers to set and adjust machines. They need normal colour vision and an eye for colour, shape and design to judge the quality of their work. An interest in art and design is useful.

Careful attention to detail and the ability to work accurately is necessary, not least for setting up machines. Concentration and vigilance is important to detect any faults during a print run. Printers have to re-train as more advanced machinery is introduced. Willingness to re-train when necessary is, therefore, essential.

As machine work is just part of the whole printing process, machinists must be able to work as part of a team. They should have stamina and reasonable health, as they spend a lot of their time standing.

ENTRY REQUIREMENTS

There are no specified entry requirements. Recruitment policy varies between employers but most employers prefer applicants to have three or four GCSEs/S grades (A–C/1–3), including English, maths and a science subject. Computer studies is useful. Normal colour vision is essential.

BTEC First Diploma in Printing – usually has no formal entry requirements, although individual colleges may have their own, such as The London Institute, which requires a minimum of three GCSEs/S grades (A–C/1–3).

City and Guilds (C&G) 5260 Printing and Graphic Communications – no particular entry requirements.

SQA National Certificate in Printing – no particular entry requirements.

Modern Apprenticeships – for young people who enter full-time employment. Entry is with at least three GCSEs/S grades (A–C/1–3) including English and maths. Technology subjects are useful. Some employers may seek more than the minimum entry requirements.

National Traineeships – for young people. Entry is with a good general education.

NVQs/SVQs in Machine Printing – no particular entry requirements.

TRAINING

Pre-entry

It is possible (but not essential) outside Scotland to enter printing by studying for the BTEC First Diploma in Printing. There are six main study areas: origination processes; machine printing; print finishing and design; printing material studies; business organization, communication skills and administration; printing technology and related computer studies. The course lasts one year full-time and is offered at eleven colleges in England and one in Belfast.

On entry

Some entrants outside Scotland attend college to study for C&G Printing and Graphic Communications 5260-23 Machine Printing Level 2 and 5260-24 Level 3. These reflect the knowledge requirements of the NVQs in Machine Printing Levels 2 and 3. Courses are offered at several colleges on a day release basis and usually last two years.

In Scotland, some entrants attend college to study the SQA National Certificate in Printing, specializing in machine printing. The course is offered by Glasgow College of Building and Printing and lasts three years. In the first year students attend four periods of four weeks' block release, while in years 2 and 3 they attend four periods of two weeks' block release.

PRINTING: SAR

Entrants into printing may train through machine printing Modern Apprenticeships. Apprentices are trained by their employers but they may also attend a printing school or training provider on a part-time basis. They work towards NVQs/SVQs in Machine Printing at Levels 2 and 3. They also work for additional NVQ/SVQ units in communication, information technology, application of number, problem solving and personal skills. Modern Apprenticeship training is not for a set length of time but usually takes at least three years. Modern Apprenticeships are also to be introduced for non-impact printing, possibly in late-1998.

Entrants into printing may train through a National Traineeship that leads to NVQ/SVQ in Machine Printing at Level 2. Trainees are trained by their employer and may attend a printing school or training provider part-time. Although not for a set length of time, National Traineeships are likely to last around two years. Contact local careers offices for information on Modern Apprenticeships and National Traineeships.

All machine printers can work towards NVQs/SVQs in Machine Printing at Levels 2 and 3.

LATE ENTRY

There are no upper age limits for entry to printing, although most entrants are school-/college-leavers.

There may be specific training opportunities directed at adults in some areas for this type of work. Candidates may have to satisfy certain conditions to be eligible. Contact your local Jobcentre, careers office or TEC/LEC for details.

OPPORTUNITIES

Machine printers are employed throughout the UK by printing companies and companies that specialize in machine printing alone. Some organizations such as local authorities also employ machine printers. There is currently a shortage of skilled machine printers – this has not been improved by many employers tending to prefer to attract skilled machinists from other firms rather than train new entrants.

There are good opportunities to become self-employed and also to work abroad.

PAY AND CONDITIONS

Please see article 1. ORIGINATOR.

PROSPECTS

Promotion is possible to supervisory and then to management positions, such as production controller/manager, estimator and account executive. Some experienced machine printers set up their own businesses.

RELATED OCCUPATIONS, FURTHER INFORMATION AND READING

Please see article 3. PRINT FINISHER/BOOKBINDER.

3. PRINT FINISHER/BOOKBINDER

THE WORK

Most printed items need finishing in some form or another to turn them into a product such as a book, brochure, label or carton. Print finishers are responsible for converting printed materials into that finished form.

Print finishers work mainly on machines, such as cutting machines that trim paper, card or books, and folding machines that fold single printed sheets into sections. They use other machines for creasing, stitching, stapling, binding, glueing, sewing, indexing, round-cornering, padding, numbering, perforating and wrapping. Some machines carry out just one operation, while others carry out several. An increasing number of machines are automated.

Print finishers set up machines, making sure that they do so accurately. They load the machines with the printed material, then operate them. While the machines are operating, finishers are responsible for checking that they are working accurately. They unload the printed material when the process is complete and stack it, either ready for the next process or for final packaging. Some print finishers specialize in just one finishing operation, such as cutting, but most work on a whole range of different machines.

Skilled print finishers may be helped by other workers in the finishing department.

Most bookbinding is done on specialist machines, which make hard covers for books, cover them with cloth fabric and secure the contents. There are, however, some bookbinders who design and make bindings for books and journals by hand. They use specialist hand tools to make outer cases for books, sew pages and glue them to the covers. Bookbinders may decorate books with gilding or gold lettering.

Some bookbinders specialize in restoring or conserving old or damaged books in need of repair or restoration.

WORK ENVIRONMENT

Print finishers and bookbinders work indoors in factories or workshops. Premises may sometimes resemble warehouses with completed and partly completed work stacked over wide areas.

Work with machines can be noisy and dusty. Print finishers spend much of their time standing. Their work involves lifting and carrying printed materials.

SKILLS AND INTERESTS

Print finishers and bookbinders need mechanical ability for setting and operating machines. They should enjoy practical work and working with machinery. Print finishing and bookbinding are the final stages in the whole printing process. If print finishers or bookbinders make a mistake, it can waste the materials and the time of the originators and print machinists involved. Accuracy and attention to detail is therefore very important.

Figure work ability is necessary to calculate and measure. Finishers and bookbinders must be keen to produce quality work. They should have good eyesight and normal colour vision.

Print finishers and bookbinders must be safety conscious and aware of the potential hazards of using machinery. They need to be willing to re-train and update their skills from time to time when changes in technology make it necessary.

Print finishers and bookbinders must be capable of working both in a team and on their own. They require stamina and reasonable health as they spend much of their time standing.

Bookbinders working by hand need good hand skills and be capable of working neatly and accurately.

ENTRY REQUIREMENTS

There are no specified entry requirements. Recruitment policy varies between employers but most employers prefer applicants to have three or four GCSEs/S grades (A–C/1–3), including English, maths and a science subject. Computer studies is useful. Normal colour vision is essential.

BTEC First Diploma in Printing – usually has no formal entry requirements, although individual colleges may have their own, such as The London Institute, which requires a minimum of three GCSEs/S grades (A–C/1–3).

Degree in Print Media (Book Arts and Crafts) – requires either: three A levels/four H grades and a portfolio of creative work; or two A levels/three H grades plus three GCSEs/S grades (A–C/1–3); or one A level/two H grades and completion of a foundation art and design course; or five GCSEs/S grades plus completion of a foundation art and design course; or a relevant BTEC National Diploma; or Advanced GNVQ/GSVQ Level III.

SQA Higher National Certificate (HNC) in Print Media Fine Bookbinding and Book Repair – requires one A-level/two H-grades and two GCSEs/S grades (A–C/1–3) or an appropriate group of SQA national certificate modules.

City and Guilds (C&G) 5260 Printing and Graphic Communications – no particular entry requirements.

SQA National Certificate in Printing – no particular entry requirements.

Modern Apprenticeships – for young people who enter full-time employment. Entry is with at least three GCSEs/S grades (A–C/1–3) including English and maths. Technology subjects are useful. Some employers may seek more than the minimum entry requirements.

National Traineeships – for young people. Entry is with a good general education.

NVQs/SVQs in Print Finishing, Mechanised Binding and Carton Manufacture – no particular entry requirements.

TRAINING

Pre-entry

It is possible (but not essential) outside Scotland to prepare to enter printing by studying for the BTEC First Diploma in Printing. There are six main study areas: origination processes; machine printing; print finishing and design; printing material studies; business organization, communication skills and administration; printing technology and related computer studies. The course lasts one year full-time and is offered at eleven colleges in England and one in Belfast.

The London Institute offers a degree in Print Media (Book Arts and Crafts). The course covers the art and craft of making books and is designed to prepare for a career in fine binding, designer binding, private press, fine print, restoration, library binderies, museum archives or restoration workshops. The course lasts three years full-time.

Glasgow College of Building and Printing offers an HNC in Print Media Fine Bookbinding and Book Repair. The course includes fine bookbinding, book restoration, stationery and library binding, finishing and blocking, bookbinding design, marbling and edge decoration and managing a small business. It is designed to prepare for a career in fine bookbinding and book restoration within commercial companies, art galleries, museums and archives, and in antiquarian book selling and private collections. The course lasts one year.

On entry

Some entrants outside Scotland attend college to study for either C&G Printing and Graphic Communications 5260-25 Print Finishing Level 2 and 5260-26 Level 3, 5260-27 Mechanised Binding Level 2 and 5260-28 Level 3, or 5260-29 Carton Manufacture Level 2 and 5260-30 Level 3. These reflect the knowledge requirements of the NVQs in those areas of work. Courses are offered at several colleges on a day release basis and usually last two years.

In Scotland, some entrants attend college to study the SQA National Certificate in Printing, specialising in print finishing. The course is offered by Glasgow College of Building and Printing and lasts three years. In the first year students attend four periods of four weeks block release, while in years 2 and 3 they attend four periods of two weeks' block release.

Entrants into printing may train through Modern Apprenticeships in print finishing, mechanized book binding or carton manufacture. Apprentices are trained by their employers but they may also attend a printing school or training provider on a part-time basis. They work towards NVQs/SVQs in either Print Finishing, Mechanised Binding or Carton Manufacture at Levels 2 and 3. They also work for additional NVQ/SVQ units in communication, information technology, application of number, problem solving and personal skills. Modern Apprenticeship training is not for a set length of time but usually takes at least three years.

Entrants into printing may train through a National Traineeship that leads to NVQ/SVQ in either Print Finishing, Mechanised Binding or Carton Manufacture at Level 2. Trainees are trained by their employer and may attend a printing school or training provider part-time. Although not for a set length of time they are likely to last around two years. Contact local careers offices for information on Modern Apprenticeships and National Traineeships.

Glasgow College of Building and Printing offers the HNC in Print Media Fine Bookbinding and Book Repair on a day release basis over two years – see above for information.

All print finishers can work towards relevant NVQs/SVQs in Print Finishing, Mechanised Binding or Carton Manufacture at Levels 2 and 3.

PRINTING: SAR

LATE ENTRY

There are no upper age limits for entry to printing, although most entrants are school/college leavers.

There may be specific training opportunities directed at adults in some areas for this type of work. Candidates may have to satisfy certain conditions to be eligible. Contact your local Jobcentre, careers office or TEC/LEC for details.

Adult applicants for the degree course at The London Institute and for the HNC at Glasgow College of Building and Printing may be accepted without the normal entry requirements, particularly if they have relevant experience.

OPPORTUNITIES

Print finishers and mechanized bookbinders work throughout the UK in the finishing departments of printing companies or for specialist companies that provide a finishing service to the printing industry. There is currently a shortage of skilled print finishers and mechanized bookbinders. Opportunities for new entrants, though, can be limited by some employers tending to prefer to attract skilled workers from other firms rather than train new entrants. There are few opportunities for print finishers or mechanized bookbinders to work abroad or to become self-employed.

Many hand bookbinders are self-employed. Others are employed by printing firms, while a few work for libraries, records offices, restoration workshops, museums and private collectors. There are few opportunities for work abroad.

PAY AND CONDITIONS

Please see article 1. ORIGINATOR

PROSPECTS

Promotion is possible for print finishers and employed bookbinders to supervisory and then to management positions, such as production controller/manager, estimator and account executive.

RELATED OCCUPATIONS

Wordprocessor operator, computer operator, sub-/copy editor, reprographic assistant, photographic technician, cameraman/woman, graphic designer, production worker/process operator.

FURTHER INFORMATION

British Printing Industries Federation (BPIF)* , 11 Bedford Row, London WC1R 4DX, 0171 242 6904, www/bpip.org.uk

Institute of Printing, 8a Lonsdale Gardens, Tunbridge Wells, Kent TN1 1NU, 01892 538118, globalprint.com/uk/iop

Scottish Print Employers Federation*, 48 Palmerston Place, Edinburgh EH12 5DE, 0131 220 4353

FURTHER READING

Leaflets/booklets are available from the addresses marked*.

Working In Publishing – COIC

In the careers library classified under SAR.

CHEMICAL PLANT PROCESSING: SAV

CHEMICAL PLANT PROCESS OPERATOR
CLCI:SAV

BACKGROUND INFORMATION

The chemicals industry is one of Britain's largest manufacturing industries and its highest-value exporter. It spends heavily on research and development – to keep at the forefront of science and technology – and on high-cost manufacturing plant. Its products include plastics, paints, medicines, fertilizers, adhesives, pesticides, herbicides, inks, dyes, polishes and cosmetics.

The industry includes firms that refine feedstocks such as oil and natural gas to make base chemicals, firms that use these to create more sophisticated chemicals for industrial use, and firms that mix together chemicals to make finished products such as paints. Process plant is found mainly in the first two types of firm.

Chemicals manufacture is carried out either on a continuous process or by batch production. Continuous process plant runs 24 hours a day, seven days a week. A batch process may last for 24 hours or longer, and the same equipment may be used to make different chemicals. Usually one or more chemical reactions occur during these processes. Production in both cases can take place in massive vessels connected by large amounts of pipework.

THE WORK

Chemical plant process workers operate and look after the process plant that makes the chemicals. On continuous process plant, operators walk around the plant. They check what is happening by taking meter and instrument readings.

To start another stage of the process, or to speed up or slow down the process, they open or close valves by hand or automatically. They draw off small samples of the product to test that its quality meets the specification. They may do a simple chemical reaction test themselves by adding another substance or pass the sample to technicians in a laboratory.

In the main, however, they are looking to prevent a fault occurring in the process – eg a leaking pipe-joint – that may need attention or maintenance. Usually they report faults to the relevant expert, to a maintenance fitter, for example, but increasingly process operators carry out the less complex and time-consuming maintenance tasks themselves.

They may also spend time in the control room, operating a computer-controlled process by taking readings from an electronic instrument panel. This is to check that everything is proceeding normally and to identify any sign that a process is going wrong and take corrective action. This is usually carried out by the plant controller who is an experienced process operator.

Normally a team – of three to four workers a shift – looks after a large section of plant. The team might consist of a senior controller, a plant controller and one or two process operators, for example.

On batch production, the process operator cleans out and prepares the equipment and pipework, measures out the ingredients and adds them into the reaction tanks in the correct sequence. They then switch on any heating, cooling or other operations, take readings as the process continues, make adjustments manually or by pressing control buttons, and take samples for testing. On completion of the process, they close down the plant and may run off the finished product into barrels, container lorries, railway trucks etc. The work involves learning the different processes under supervision first and then working carefully to written instructions.

WORK ENVIRONMENT

The control room, which serves as a base, is dry, clean and usually air-conditioned because of the electronic equipment. Chemical plants are very health and safety conscious and are constantly being updated to protect the environment. They are often modern and clean, though some older, dirtier plants remain.

Workers wear protective overalls, helmets and boots. Some of the chemicals in some plants may be hazardous and involve additional safety precautions to protect employees, the public and the environment.

The work may involve climbing stairs to considerable heights and walking long distances along catwalks around the tanks and pipework. It may also include long periods of sitting or standing. The plant may be covered or outdoors.

At night, lit by floodlights, parts of the plant may be dark and in shadow so that a torch is needed, for example to examine pipework. Communication with the control room is by phones at key points, a mobile phone or a two-way radio.

SKILLS AND INTERESTS

Process operators need to have the patience to cope with regular routines, during which times little may happen, yet be able, if a problem or emergency arises, to react quickly, make the right decisions and take corrective action.

An interest in science and technology is important.

They should be able to work in a team, yet be self-sufficient to cope with the responsibility of patrolling the plant on their own. Physical fitness is needed for climbing, walking, being out in all weathers and lifting or loading chemicals into containers.

Good eyesight and colour vision are required for reading meters, dials and instrument charts. An eye for detail and a good memory for what should be happening at each part of the plant and at each stage of the process is valuable.

ENTRY REQUIREMENTS

Employers seek people who are mature and responsible so they tend to recruit people over 18 years (and in some cases over 23 years) who have held at least one other job since leaving school.

This is beginning to change, however, with the introduction of Modern Apprenticeships (part of the Skillseekers Initiative in Scotland). Specific training opportunities for young people, including Modern Apprenticeships, may be available. Contact your local careers office, TEC/LEC for details.

In many companies, there are no formal educational requirements, though basic numeracy and literacy and a good general education is an asset. Applicants may be asked to take numeracy and general intelligence tests. Some companies ask for GCSEs/S grades (A–D/1–4) in maths and science subjects.

CHEMICAL PLANT PROCESSING: SAV

The increasing complexity of process control systems has resulted in some companies looking for technical qualifications for control staff roles. Relevant qualifications include City and Guilds and NVQs/SVQs (see TRAINING).

TRAINING

On-the-job training is provided. Some new process operators accompany an experienced worker, watching what they do and learning from them, then doing the tasks under their supervision. Normally this follows classroom induction training which includes health and safety information and precautions, and a basic understanding of the main chemical processes involved.

For more complex processes, there may be additional in-company courses. In some plants, there may be day release to study for a City and Guilds qualification in, for example, Instrumentation and Control, Materials Processing, Industrial Studies, and Scientific Calculation.

Increasingly, process operators are assessed in the workplace, carrying out their duties. These assessments of competence lead to NVQs/SVQs in Process Operations at Levels 1, 2 and 3.

It is sometimes possible for process operators with NVQs/SVQs at Level 3 to study for HNCs or degree qualifications.

LATE ENTRY

There is no maximum age limit, though company policies vary. Many firms prefer mature applicants, who have worked in other jobs or have experience in other process industries.

OPPORTUNITIES

There have always been relatively few openings for plant operators. In common with many other industries the number of posts has reduced in recent years even more due to factors such as recession, improvements in remote sensing, and computerization and electronic control of operations.

Employers range from big multinational chemical and oil companies to small firms producing specialist chemicals. The larger chemical process plants tend to be located near ports where feedstocks arrive by sea and where facilities for export are convenient. They may also be sited near natural sources of mineral feedstocks or in major industrial centres close to potential customers.

With the multinationals, there may be opportunities to work overseas, for example, in Europe, the Middle East, Far East and the Americas.

PAY AND CONDITIONS

Pay varies from company to company. However, process operators usually earn £18,000 to £22,000, plus overtime and productivity/bonus payments.

Basic hours are 38 a week. Plants operate 24 hours a day, seven days a week, so shift-working is common, involving night and weekend work. The shift pattern may change every week or two, so as to rotate everyone through the different duties. There are opportunities for overtime.

PROSPECTS

Promotion is from trainee plant operator (who works under instruction) to plant operator (who carries out normal routine operations) and then to plant controller (who runs the team from the control room). Beyond that are senior controller (who is responsible for that area of the plant) and shift supervisor (who is responsible for all areas of plant).

In smaller companies and on batch processes, there are fewer levels. Plant manager positions are normally held by graduate chemists or engineers.

There may be opportunities to take courses in craft maintenance and laboratory work to increase the range of practical skills or to take appropriate NVQ or SVQ qualifications to transfer to craft or technician posts.

RELATED OCCUPATIONS

Plastics process operative, brewery worker, water/sewage treatment plant operator, electricity generation worker, engineer, meat process worker.

FURTHER INFORMATION

Chemical Industries Association (CIA), Kings Buildings, Smith Square, London SW1P 3JJ, 0171 834 3399

FURTHER READING

In the careers library classified under SAV.

BLACKSMITHING: SAW/RAB

BLACKSMITH CLCI:SAW/RAB

BACKGROUND INFORMATION

Blacksmiths are concerned with shaping and constructing metalwork using both traditional and contemporary forge-work techniques. People often confuse the two trades of blacksmith and farrier: farriers shoe horses using blacksmithing skills to make the horseshoes. Only farriers are permitted by law to shoe horses. Some blacksmiths are farriers as well.

THE WORK

Blacksmiths work with a variety of metals. Mild steel is the main material but wrought iron is increasingly being reintroduced. Some also work with stainless steel, copper, brass and bronze. Other metals used are carbon tool steels, cast iron and alloys. Forge work is a series of different techniques involving heating, shaping, cooling, re-heating and re-shaping using a wide variety of tools. First the metal is cut to the sizes laid down in drawings. The blacksmith holds a piece of metal in an open coke, coal or gas fire – the forge or hearth or closed oil- or gas-fired furnace – with a pair of tongs until it is hot and pliable. This is then transferred on to an anvil, where it is gradually shaped with blows from a variety of hammers and other tools.

A variety of tools can be used for decoration and other techniques such as twisting, punching and texturing. The design of traditional blacksmiths' hand tools has changed little over the centuries. Blacksmiths often make their own tools. Power tools such as power hammers, drills, air chisels and hydraulic presses are also now used. Engineering machinery such as centre lathes, millers and grinders may be used. Modern fabrication equipment, including plasma cutters, is used too. Sheet metal is usually worked cold but can also be manipulated while hot.

Once the pieces of metal have been shaped, they are fixed together by, for example, riveting, fire and arc welding, or soldering. A range of equipment such as MIG, TIG and oxy-acetylene torches is used in welding. Surface finishing ranges through coating with gilt or zinc, galvanizing, painting, waxing, anodizing and metal spraying. Grit or shot blasting is a method of cleaning the surface prior to the application of finishes. A wide selection of paints and dangerous chemicals is also employed. Decorative techniques similar to those used by jewellers, such as *repoussage* and *relevage*, are used for intricate work. Protective clothing – leather aprons, overalls, face masks, ear defenders, safety glasses, and shoes – are worn when required.

Blacksmiths make anything from gates for stately homes and canal locks, metal housing for industrial machinery and road barriers, to candlestick holders and decorative brackets. Most blacksmiths specialize in an area of work.

Some work in agriculture, making farm trailers and sheep feeders, and mending agricultural machinery etc. Some steel farm buildings are made and erected by them.

The building trade uses blacksmiths to make and fix fire escapes, security grills and steel doors. Engineering companies may subcontract with, or employ, blacksmiths who have a knowledge of mechanical engineering for fabrication and welding of manufacturing equipment. Industry also uses blacksmiths for heavy forging, fabrication and tool production.

Some blacksmiths have conservation and restoration skills. They use their detailed knowledge of architectural history, maintenance, materials and finishes in the heritage industry, restoring and replacing ironwork in and around old buildings.

Other blacksmiths design, produce and market decorative work for indoor domestic and garden use, and for the tourist trade. Some make limited editions of art objects, both decorative and functional items for sale in museums and galleries.

Architects employ blacksmiths to work on modern office buildings and shopping centres, producing and installing railings, staircases and decorative ironwork. Local councils employ them to design and make street furniture such as seats, lamps and litter bins.

WORK ENVIRONMENT

Forges vary in size from a large engineering workshop to a small brick shed. Most of the work is carried out under cover but installation can involve working outdoors. They work in extremes of temperature from the heat of the area around the forge to freezing site conditions. Some jobs involve visiting customers and fetching supplies.

Blacksmiths' forges are sometimes uncomfortable, noisy, dirty and smelly due to the nature of the work. Safety practices are strictly enforced due to fire hazard and use and storage of dangerous chemicals. Most of the work is done standing up and involves a lot of bending and lifting.

SKILLS AND INTERESTS

Fitness and stamina rather than strength are essential as the craft is physically demanding. Power tools are now used for much of the heavier work. Good hand-to-eye co-ordination is important for working accurately. As the craft uses technical skills a logical approach is required. Artistic ability and design skills are needed by artistic blacksmiths. Much of the work is repetitive and progress can be slow. Persistence and strong powers of concentration are therefore important.

Blacksmiths tend to work alone so they must be well-motivated and self-disciplined.

Many blacksmiths are self-employed. Running a business requires sound business and administration skills. An important element of the job is sales and marketing which means being confident and sociable and able to get on with people at all levels.

ENTRY REQUIREMENTS

There are no formal entry requirements for those seeking employment with a blacksmith or entry on to specialist smithing courses. Attendance on short courses, related qualifications and/or examples of metalwork are helpful.

Related areas include:

Engineering, including welding and sheetmetal work. Useful subjects include maths, engineering, workshop theory and practice, craft (metal), design technology, and integrated science. These are also basic entry requirements for BTEC/SQA, NVQ/SVQ or City and Guilds qualifications.

Art and design: three-dimensional (3-D) design in metalwork. The usual entry requirements for higher national diploma courses are BTEC National Diploma/Certificate in General Art and Design, or three GCSEs/S grades (A–C/1–3) with one A level in a relevant

BLACKSMITHING: SAW/RAB

subject, or five GCSEs/S grades (A–C/1–3) and successful completion of a foundation course in art and design. For degree courses, five GCSEs/S grades (A–C/1–3) are required, with two A levels/three H grades or equivalent.

TRAINING

On the job

Occasionally, job opportunities occur where specific skills such as welding, sheetmetal work, fabrication or 3-D metalwork design are sought. Other blacksmithing and forging techniques are taught on the job.

For those already working in blacksmithing in rural areas, the Rural Development Commission has a programme of courses designed to extend and develop skills and techniques. Contact the Rural Development Commission for further details.

The Worshipful Company of Blacksmiths is active in developing training. It promotes standards of excellence and professional practice through a system of awards made at all levels from apprentices upwards. Diploma holders are associates of the company and are entitled to use AWCB after their name. Medal holders are fellows (FWCB) and licentiates (LWCB).

Apprenticeships

Few blacksmiths are able to offer apprenticeships. Prospective apprentices have to find their own Masters. The Worshipful Company of Blacksmiths administers apprenticeships. Other apprenticeships are administered by the National Joint Apprenticeship Council (NJAC) through the National Association of Farriers, Blacksmiths and Agricultural Engineers (NAFBAE). Attendance at Herefordshire College on a block release basis is a NJAC requirement (see below).

Courses

Herefordshire College of Technology

1. College Diploma in Blacksmithing and Metalworking – one year, full-time. The course covers the full range of blacksmithing including the use of hand and machine tools, cutting and welding, farm machinery maintenance, metal fabrication, wrought iron design, materials, costing, art and design, and business skills.

2. College Diploma in Blacksmithing and Restoration Crafts – one year, full-time. A specialized course for those wishing to pursue a career in restoration work. It covers: blacksmithing and related areas including heat treatment and corrosion control of metals; preservation, conservation and restoration techniques; drawing and design; and business skills. Students visit museums and heritage sites. A project portfolio is produced and the course includes two weeks' practical experience.

3. College Certificate in Rural Smithing – four years, block release. This course is designed for those employed in small firms catering for the rural market. It covers smithing, gas and arc welding, bench fitting, machine shop practice and agricultural implements repair. Subsidiary subjects include electrical safety requirements, engineering science, reading drawings, workshop calculations and business skills. Apprentices indentured with NJAC sit trade tests in smithing, welding and bench fitting, with implements repair option.

4. College Certificate in Industrial Smithing – four years, block release. This course is suitable for those working in small urban workshops handling work for industry, builders, local government etc. Blacksmithing and fabrication craft work is combined with welding, sheetmetal work, bench fitting and lathework. Ornamental ironwork option. See College Certificate in Rural Smithing (above) for subsidiary subjects and details of NJAC tests.

5. BTEC National Diploma in Three Dimensional Design: Blacksmithing – two years, full-time. This course is offered jointly with Herefordshire College of Art and Design. It provides a basic understanding of drawing and design principles, coupled with practical workshop introductions into the structure and use of materials.

6. BTEC Higher National Diploma in Design Crafts: Blacksmithing – two years, full-time. This course is also offered jointly with Herefordshire College of Art and Design. It has been devised to prepare students to enter or establish a workshop in order to produce originally designed works directed towards high quality outlets. There is also provision for students to concentrate on restoration work, should that be where their strengths lie.

West Dean College runs a programme of residential courses lasting from two to five days in basic blacksmithing, wrought ironwork and decorative techniques.

Camberwell College of Arts – BA (Hons) Three-dimensional Design, Ceramics or Silversmithing/Metalwork. The course develops the creative use of materials and processes. Students produce individual pieces as well as learning about batch production. The metalwork option covers blacksmithing and architectural metalwork.

Art and design courses at higher national diploma and degree level, in three-dimensional design specialising in jewellery or metalwork, is another route into blacksmithing. Contact the British Artist Blacksmiths' Association.

Craft engineering/craft training schemes with engineering companies are run through a local network of group training associations (GTAs). Trainees work towards BTEC/SQA, NVQ/SVQ or City and Guilds qualifications in welding and fabrication. Usual age of entry is 16 or 17 years. Contact Engineering Careers Information Service.

Training schemes for young people

Wye Valley Training, based at Herefordshire College of Technology, is the main training provider for blacksmithing. Placements are organized through the agency. The NJAC recognizes the first two years of training as the equivalent of the first two years of its four-year apprenticeship, subject to passing trade tests. For further information, contact Wye Valley Training or your local careers office or TEC/LEC.

The *New Entrants' Training Scheme (NETS) in Forgework,* run by the Rural Development Commission, provides training for young people aged 16–25 years (though older applicants may be considered). Applicants must be employed in a rural area in England. Trainees receive twelve weeks' training over a two-year period. Successful trainees gain a range of qualifications, including two Worshipful Company of Blacksmiths' awards and City and Guilds awards or NVQs.

LATE ENTRY

There is no upper age limit and many take up blacksmithing as a second career. Entry requirements to art and design courses may be waived for adults.

BLACKSMITHING: SAW/RAB

There may be specific training opportunities directed at adults available in some areas for this type of work. Candidates may have to satisfy certain conditions to be eligible. Contact your local Jobcentre, careers office or TEC/LEC for details.

OPPORTUNITIES

Around 900 UK companies employ blacksmiths in mining, docks and engineering for maintenance, repair and production. Job opportunities are limited. There are around 600 artist blacksmiths, and opportunities are increasing. Most are self-employed, working to commission for architects, interior designers and the public.

PAY AND CONDITIONS

Minimum rates of pay, hours of work and holidays laid down by the National Joint Wages Board (NJWB) of the Blacksmithing and Agricultural Engineering Trades are as follows. For apprentices: first year, £69.23p a week; second year, £78.84p a week; third year, £107.69p a week; fourth year, £136.54p a week. Qualified craftsmen/women earn a minimum £208.37p a week.

NJWB recommended hours of work are 40 hours a week, Monday to Saturday. Holidays are four working weeks a year plus eight days statutory bank holidays.

NB: NJWB rates are not mandatory. Pay and hours are subject to individual negotiation between employer and employee.

PROSPECTS

In larger firms there are opportunities for promotion to supervisory posts.

RELATED OCCUPATIONS

Bladesmith, goldsmith/silversmith, farrier, agricultural mechanic, welder, sheetmetal worker, mechanical engineer, machine operator.

FURTHER INFORMATION

British Artist Blacksmiths' Association (BABA)*, Honorary Secretary, The Old Manse, Kilberry, Tarbert, Argyll, Scotland, PA29 6YD, www.baba.org.uk

Engineering and Marine Training Authority, Engineering Careers Department, Vector House, 41 Clarendon Road, Watford, Herts WD1 1HS, 0800 282167 (freephone), www.emta.org.uk

Herefordshire College of Technology, The Library, Folly Lane, Hereford HR1 1LS, 01432 352235

National Organizer, National Association of Farriers, Blacksmiths and Agricultural Engineers (NAFBAE)*, The Forge, Avenue B, 10th Street, National Agricultural Centre, Stoneleigh, Kenilworth, Warwickshire CV8 2LG, 01203 696595

Rural Development Commission, 141 Castle Street, Salisbury, Wilts SP1 3TP, 01722 336255

Training Co-ordinator, Wye Valley Training, Herefordshire College of Technology, Folly Lane, Hereford HR1 1LS, 01432 352235

West Dean College, West Dean, Chichester, West Sussex PO18 0QZ, 0171 379 6344

Worshipful Company of Blacksmiths, 27 Cheyne Walk, Grange Road, London N21 1DB, 0181 364 1522

FURTHER READING

Leaflets/booklets are available from the addresses marked*.

In the careers library classified under SAW/RAB.

GROUP U – CONSTRUCTION AND LAND SERVICES

1. **ARCHITECT CLCI:UB**
2. **ARCHITECTURAL TECHNOLOGIST CLCI:UB**

BACKGROUND INFORMATION

Architects are concerned with the design of new buildings and the alteration of existing buildings. New buildings may be single structures, such as houses, shops, schools, factories, warehouses, offices and hospitals, or may be complete housing estates, shopping precincts, industrial estates and office blocks.

Alterations to existing buildings may mean extending them, converting them to a different use or modernizing them.

Architects are not only concerned with design. They are often responsible for every stage of a building project, through to completion of the building work.

Traditionally, architectural technologists worked entirely under the supervision of architects. Many still do so, but the responsibilities of other technologists have expanded considerably and some technologists now work independently of architects.

1. ARCHITECT (UB)

THE WORK

Architects design new buildings and design alterations to existing buildings. They may also be responsible for complete projects from design to the completed structures.

Architects receive instructions from a client, which detail the work the client requires and the budget available. They discuss and develop the brief for the proposed building work and advise the client, taking into account the type of building required, the proposed site, legal and planning matters and costs involved.

Architects may undertake preliminary research by arranging for the site and its surroundings to be surveyed and by discussing the proposals to decide how they will affect people who will use the building.

The next stage involves architects in preparing a design at a drawing board or, increasingly, on a computer. The design must take into account how the building will be used, its appearance, the materials to be used, how all the services will work and the costs involved. Architects must make sure in their design that the building can be built and maintained safely. In preparing the design, architects combine their creativity with a high level of technical knowledge and social awareness.

Architects present the client with visual ideas of the proposed design, which may include a model of the project, and an estimate of the cost.

When a client has approved the design, architects produce 'working drawings', which are detailed drawings specifying exact dimensions, materials, fittings, services and costings. In some cases the working drawings are produced by an architectural technologist rather than an architect. During this stage architects may work closely with other professionals, including civil and structural engineers, mechanical and electrical engineers, surveyors, landscape architects and quantity surveyors. They may negotiate and agree contracts with those needed for the project.

In many projects architects are in overall charge until completion. In these cases architects make constant visits to sites to check progress, see the work is of the necessary quality, issue instructions to contractors' agents, authorize payments to contractors, and generally take responsibility for solving any problems that may arise.

Some architects specialize in areas such as project management, building investigation, safety planning and energy advisory work.

WORK ENVIRONMENT

Most of architects' work is office-based, in clean, light surroundings. They may be out of their own offices for a good deal of time when visiting clients, planners, builders and others.

Architects responsible for a project until completion spend some time on site, which involves being outdoors in all weathers.

Much of the time indoors is spent sitting, while site work includes walking.

Travelling to meetings and sites can take up a considerable amount of architects' time. The work may involve being away from home for extended periods.

SKILLS AND INTERESTS

Architects need drawing ability as they design by drawing. They must be creative to be able to work through problems to achieve a finished structure that will satisfy both their clients and public opinion. Creativity must be matched by a practical approach to enable them to design buildings that are safe and suited to their purpose.

Ability in science is essential for solving design problems and understanding the properties of building materials. Mathematical ability is necessary for preparing costings and for dealing with financial matters. As computer-aided design (CAD) techniques are increasingly being used for design, architects need to be confident in using CAD instead of a traditional drawing board when appropriate.

Architects must have an awareness of social and environmental factors, as the people who use their buildings can be greatly affected by the design.

Good communication skills are important. Architects are constantly involved in meetings and discussions with clients and others involved in a project.

Architects should have good management skills to organize and lead several projects at the same time. Ability to negotiate and persuade is desirable.

Architects should be physically fit to cope with site inspections. There is, however, scope for people with disabilities to qualify and succeed as architects.

ENTRY REQUIREMENTS

The minimum entry qualifications are those required to enter a degree course accredited jointly by the Royal Institute of British Architects (RIBA) and the Architects Registration Board. Minimum requirements are:

– two A levels/three H grades with five GCSEs/two S grades (A–C/1–3) in other subjects. Both the A levels/H grades must be in academic subjects. The GCSE subjects should include English, maths and either physics, chemistry or dual award science.

Some schools of architecture will accept either:

– Advanced GNVQ Construction and Built Environment/GSVQ Level III Construction, *or*

ARCHITECTURE: UB

– BTEC National Certificate/Diploma in Building Studies, or SQA National Certificate in Building/Building Construction plus GCSE/S grade (A–C/1–3) in English.

Many schools of architecture require more than the minimum requirements. They may also specify certain subjects. Details of each school's requirements are listed in a booklet published by the RIBA – *Schools of Architecture with Courses Recognized by the RIBA*.

It is not essential to have an art qualification but applicants should be able to sketch and draw freehand. Most schools of architecture ask to see an applicant's portfolio of drawings and sketches.

TRAINING

To use the title of architect it is necessary to register with The Architects Registration Board. Registration is permitted when applicants have gained exemption from Parts 1, 2 and 3 of the RIBA Examination in Architecture and spent at least two years working in an architect's office. Most achieve this by following a full-time course that is offered at 35 schools of architecture in the UK.

Training takes at least seven years. There are variations between schools but there are usually four stages in training:

1. Three or four years at a school of architecture to work for a degree in architecture and exemption from RIBA Part 1. (Those who do not wish to continue beyond this stage may seek to become architectural technologists or can use their degree to enter any one of a range of careers open to all graduates.)

2. One year, usually spent working in an architect's office.

3. Two years' further study at a school of architecture to obtain a diploma or higher degree and exemption from RIBA Part 2. This does not necessarily have to take place at the same school at which Part 1 was taken.

4. One year (at least) working in an architect's office before taking the RIBA Part 3 Professional Practice Examination. Successful completion of Part 3 allows registration with ARCUK and membership of the RIBA.

Some schools of architecture offer part-time training on a day release basis for students already working in an architect's office. The degree takes four or five years and the diploma course three years. A further year must be spent in an architect's office before taking the Professional Practice Examination.

A large part of the time at a school of architecture is spent on project work, where, individually or in groups, students design buildings. Subjects studied include design, building science and technology, construction and structure, history and theory of architecture, environmental science, urban studies, town planning, social studies, economics, communication, computer-aided design, and professional practice.

LATE ENTRY

There is no upper age limit for entry to architecture. Adult entrants normally follow the route described in TRAINING, which takes a minimum of seven years.

The RIBA Examination in Architecture for office-based candidates has been suspended pending reorganization.

Alternatively, adults with at least six years' continuous practical architecture experience who have the minimum qualifications needed for entry to an architecture degree may become external candidates. They may work towards the RIBA Examination in Architecture and Examination in Professional Practice and become qualified architects. Those who have already gained RIBA Part 2 from attending a school of architecture need only three years' practical architecture experience to become an external candidate.

OPPORTUNITIES

There are approximately 20,700 architects in full-time employment in the UK. Seventy-seven per cent of them work in private practice, with practices varying in size from those with one or two staff to those with over 50. About half have five or fewer staff. The majority of those in private practice are self-employed. Seven per cent of architects work for private companies such as retail organizations, building and civil engineering firms, industrial firms, and commercial organizations such as banks and breweries.

Nine per cent of architects work for local authorities and seven per cent for central government.

Architects are employed throughout the UK, although almost half are located in London and south-east England.

Architecture is closely linked with the building industry, which is subject to the state of the economy more than most industries. The number of unemployed architects in the workforce in 1997 is three per cent and about a tenth of those in work were underemployed. As a result, newly qualified architects have found it difficult to find a first job, although some continue in employment with the organization with which they worked towards Part 3 of the RIBA exams.

Work overseas is a possibility, either for UK-based private practices that win contracts abroad, or with government bodies such as the Overseas Development Administration.

Vacancies for architects are advertised in *Building Design, Architects' Journal, RIBA Journal, Building*.

PAY AND CONDITIONS

The average salary for an architect's assistant with Part 1 of the RIBA examination was £12,000. An architect's assistant with the Part 2 examination earned an average of £14,217, while a newly qualified architect aged about 27+ averaged £17,500 a year. A partner or director over 45 years earned an average salary of £30,000. There were slight regional variations with those in London earning above average in each case.

Architects have a basic working week of 9am to 5pm, Monday to Friday, but pressure of deadlines can mean that they must work some evenings and weekends.

Architects involved in site management have to deal with problems whenever they arise. They can be on call 24 hours a day or have to be on site while building is being carried out.

Part-time work is common.

PROSPECTS

Architects may become partners in private practices. Many architects set up on their own.

In central and local government there is a promotion structure that enables architects to progress to chief architect.

ARCHITECTURE: UB

Some architects achieve further qualifications and become planners, landscape architects or conservation specialists. Others move into teaching in schools of architecture. A few use their architectural experience to become writers, journalists or researchers.

RELATED OCCUPATIONS

Town planner, engineer, surveyor, landscape architect, construction manager, interior designer, architectural technologist.

FURTHER INFORMATION AND READING

Please see article 2. ARCHITECTURAL TECHNOLOGIST.

2. ARCHITECTURAL TECHNOLOGIST (UB)

BACKGROUND INFORMATION

In 1994 the British Institute of Architectural Technicians became the British Institute of Architectural Technologists (BIAT). This change reflected the increased responsibilities of architectural technicians over the past few years. Members of the BIAT are now known as architectural technologists. Others in the field may be known either as architectural technicians or architectural technologists. For the purposes of this article they are all called architectural technologists.

In the past, architectural technologists worked under the supervision of architects. Many still do so but increasingly they operate as professionals in their own right.

THE WORK

Architectural technologists are concerned with the technological aspects of building design and construction, from the initial client briefing to completion of the project.

There is considerable variation in the work of different architectural technologists, depending on the organization worked for and the experience and seniority of the technologist. Some experienced architectural technologists are responsible for managing the whole building process from start to finish; others may specialize in just one part of the process.

Duties may begin with discussions with a client to understand what the client requires and to advise what is possible.

Architectural technologists conduct preliminary investigations based on the client's brief. They gather, analyse and prepare all the technical information that is necessary before a design can be produced. This can involve surveying sites and buildings and collecting specialist advice and opinion from other professionals, such as structural and civil engineers.

The design itself may be the responsibility of an architect but in routine building or conversion work the design may be done by an architectural technologist. The technologist may prepare drawings or a model of the design and be involved in a presentation of the design to the client.

Whether or not the architectural technologist has been responsible for the design, it is usually the technologist who prepares detailed technical drawings specifying, for example, dimensions and materials to be used. These may be drawn at a drawing board but are increasingly produced by computer-aided design (CAD) techniques. In both design and detailed drawings architectural technologists use their technical knowledge and take into account the legislation and regulations that affect the project.

Architectural technologists may be responsible for inviting tenders for the building work, which can involve liaising with quantity surveyors to prepare the necessary information, and for negotiating contracts with building contractors.

When the building work takes place architectural technologists monitor schedules to check that the project is progressing on time, deal with any problems on site, make sure that the correct materials are used, and carry out regular inspections. They are also concerned with routine project administration tasks, such as the issue of instructions and certification of work satisfactorily completed.

Some architectural technologists manage the day-to-day running of an architect's office. Some operate within architects' offices as CAD systems managers.

WORK ENVIRONMENT

Much of architectural technologists' work is office-based in clean, light conditions, although they may be frequently out of their offices to attend meetings, collect data and visit sites.

Some of their time is spent on site, involving being outdoors in all weathers and wearing boots and safety helmets.

Much of the time indoors is spent sitting, while site work includes walking.

Architectural technologists spend some of their time travelling between their office and meetings on-site and elsewhere. For most that involves driving. For some, the work can include spending extended periods away from home.

SKILLS AND INTERESTS

Architectural technologists should have an interest in design and be able to draw. The ability to visualize objects in three-dimensional (3D) form is helpful. An interest in architecture and the environment is desirable.

Aptitude with figures is required, both for technical and financial calculations. Scientific ability is necessary to understand building technology.

A methodical, accurate approach with an eye for detail is demanded to be able to produce detailed drawings. As computer-aided design (CAD) techniques are increasingly used for design, architectural technologists need to be confident in using CAD when appropriate.

The ability to get on well with people and operate effectively within a team is essential, as architectural technologists spend much of their time in discussions and consultations with clients, architects, contractors and others. They need good listening, spoken and written communication skills, together with a diplomatic but persuasive manner. These skills are also important as architectural technologists may have an important role in co-ordinating the professional consultants involved in a project.

Architectural technologists should be physically fit to cope with site inspections.

ARCHITECTURE: UB

ENTRY REQUIREMENTS

There is no specified minimum qualification required for entry to work as an architectural technologist, although in practice most entrants have at least four GCSEs/S grades (A–C/1–3).

BTEC National Certificate/Diploma in Building Studies requires four GCSEs/S grades (A–C/1–3). Useful subjects include English, maths, science, technology and art.

SQA National Certificate in Building/Construction Studies has no formal entry requirements. Colleges admit students they feel can benefit from the course.

Advanced GNVQ Construction and the Built Environment usually requires either four GCSEs/S grades (A–C/1–3) or Intermediate GNVQ Construction and the Built Environment.

GSVQ Level III Construction has no formal entry requirements. Colleges admit students they feel can benefit from the course, including students who have successfully completed GSVQ Level II Construction.

BTEC Higher National Certificate/Diploma in Building Studies or Architectural Technology usually requires two A levels to have been taken and one passed, plus four GCSEs (A–C); or a relevant Advanced GNVQ (for example, Construction and the Built Environment, or Science); or a relevant BTEC national certificate/diploma.

SQA Higher National Certificate/Diploma in Architectural Technology/Building usually requires two H grades and three S grades in separate subjects, with a preference for English, maths and science; or a relevant GSVQ Level III (for example, Construction or Science); or appropriate SQA national certificate modules.

Degree courses require two A levels/three H grades with three GCSEs/two S grades (A–C/1–3) in other subjects, with English, maths and science often being required; or a relevant Advanced GNVQ/GSVQ Level III (for example, Construction and the Built Environment, Construction, or Science); or a relevant BTEC/SQA national award. Candidates with a relevant higher national diploma may be accepted onto the second or third year of a degree course.

TRAINING

British Institute of Architectural Technologists (BIAT)

The BIAT is the professional body that represents architectural technologists and many employers expect entrants into architectural technology to work towards full membership of the BIAT. To become a member requires one of the following qualifications:

– a degree in architectural technology or a built environment subject with a technology base;

– an approved BTEC/SQA Higher National Certificate/Diploma in Building Studies that includes a number of specified units;

– an alternative BIAT-approved higher level qualification, eg Royal Institute of British Architects (RIBA) Part 1 or Chartered Institute of Building (CIOB) Part 2.

Those who have followed a full-time course of study must have a further year's work experience. All applicants must complete a logbook for two years during practice and pass a professional interview.

The BIAT intends moving to degree entry for membership, probably by the late 1990s.

Pre-entry

There are a number of courses that prepare entrants for architectural technology.

BTEC National Diploma in Building Studies (two years, full-time) is offered at many colleges throughout England, Wales and Northern Ireland.

SQA National Certificate in Building or Building Construction (one year, full-time) is offered at almost 20 colleges in Scotland.

Advanced GNVQ Construction and the Built Environment (two years, full-time) is offered at colleges throughout England, Wales and Northern Ireland.

GSVQ Construction Level III (normally two years, full-time) is offered at colleges.

BTEC Higher National Diploma in Building Studies (two years full-time or three years on a sandwich basis) is offered at many colleges in England, Wales and Northern Ireland. Fifty-two of the courses include the units required by the BIAT for membership.

SQA Higher National Diploma in Architectural Technology/Building (two years, full-time) – five colleges and universities in Scotland offer courses that include the units required for BIAT membership.

Degree courses in architectural technology (three or four years full-time, or four years on a sandwich basis) that are currently accepted by the BIAT as qualifying towards membership are offered at Huddersfield University, University of Luton, South Bank University, Glasgow College of Building and Printing in association with Glasgow Caledonian University, Napier University, the University of Ulster, Coventry University, Southampton Institute of HE, University of Lincolnshire and Humberside, Nottingham Trent University, Sheffield Hallam University and Robert Gordon University.

On entry

Many architectural technologists enter work and attend college on a day release basis for a course appropriate to their entry qualifications.

BTEC National Certificate in Building Studies (two or three years) courses are offered at many colleges throughout England, Wales and Northern Ireland.

SQA National Certificate in Building Construction (two years) courses are offered at almost 20 colleges throughout Scotland.

BTEC Higher National Certificate in Building Studies (two years) – 76 colleges in England, Wales and Northern Ireland offer courses that include the units required for BIAT membership.

SQA Higher National Certificate in Building (two years) – twelve Scottish universities and colleges offer courses that include the units required for BIAT membership.

Subjects studied on national award courses may include all or some of the following: construction drawing, construction processes, the built environment, construction science, construction technology, construction materials, measurement, organization and procedures, site surveying and levelling, communication studies, building construction, design procedures, environmental science, structural mechanics and architectural detailing.

Higher national award courses include similar subjects plus advanced building construction, building services and equipment, contractual procedures, computer-aided design (CAD), law and economics, and architecture

ARCHITECTURE: UB

administration and practice.

Degrees include similar subjects but may also include history of building craft techniques, advanced technology, management theory, advanced CAD, interior architecture, and business studies.

GNVQ/GSVQ courses are designed to develop the general skills, knowledge and understanding that underpin a wide range of occupations relating to construction and the built environment. They are modular courses with units relevant to architectural technology.

LATE ENTRY

There is no upper age limit for entry. Mature applicants may be accepted for courses described in TRAINING without the usual minimum entry requirements, particularly if they have relevant experience, in construction, for example.

Those aged 30 years and over with at least ten years' relevant experience may become members of the BIAT through a special entry route called the profiling route.

OPPORTUNITIES

Architectural technologists work throughout the UK, mostly in private practice for firms headed by architects, architectural technologists or other professionals in the building industry. Others work for building contractors, property developers, housing associations, banks, building societies and commercial and manufacturing companies.

A number of architectural technologists work in the public sector for central government organizations such as the Property Services Agency, and for local authorities in the architects or planning departments.

An increasing number of architectural technologists are self-employed.

The number of architectural technologists has decreased in the past few years as a direct result of economic recession and there are now just under 20,000 in the UK, including approximately 6,000 who are members of BIAT. However, the construction industry in the UK is currently experiencing a gradual recovery.

Vacancies for architectural technologists are advertised in *Building Design, New Builder, Building, Architects Journal, Opportunities*, and *RIBA Journal*.

There are opportunities to work overseas, either for UK-based private practices that win contracts abroad or for government bodies.

PAY AND CONDITIONS

Junior architectural technologists at 18 years with BTEC/SQA national qualifications earn £6,500 to £15,500. Those aged 24 with higher national qualifications and at least three years' experience earn £10,000 to £24,000, while 30-year-old architectural technologists with higher national qualifications and ten years' experience earn £15,000 to £28,000. (Figures from *Building*, 9 April 1998)

The earnings of architectural technologists who are partners or directors of a practice depend on the profitability of the practice.

The standard working week is 9am to 5pm Monday to Friday but pressure of deadlines can involve working in the evenings and at weekends. Architectural technologists in site management may have to be on site while work is going on, or possibly be on call 24 hours a day.

Some architectural technologists work part-time.

PROSPECTS

Architectural technologists may be promoted to senior technical positions within their employing organization, which may include responsibility for supervising other staff.

Many architectural technologists with good experience in private practice set up on their own or go into partnership with other architectural technologists, architects or other building professionals.

It is possible to train to become an architect. Qualified architectural technologists interested in this should approach schools of architecture to check the acceptability of their existing qualifications for entry to an architecture degree.

Alternatively, architectural technologists with at least six years' practical experience who have the minimum qualifications needed for entry to an architecture degree may become external candidates. They may work towards the RIBA Examination in Architecture and Examination in Professional Practice and become qualified architects. Those who have already gained RIBA Part 1 from attending a school of architecture need only three years' practical experience to become an external candidate.

Some architectural technologists train for surveying by studying for the examinations of the Royal Institute of Chartered Surveyors.

RELATED OCCUPATIONS

Town planning technician/support staff, quantity surveying technician, design draughtsman/woman, civil engineering technician, construction manager, building surveyor, surveying technician, architect.

FURTHER INFORMATION

Architects Registration Board*, 73 Hallam Street, London W1N 6EE, 0171 580 5861

British Institute of Architectural Technologists*, 397 City Road, London EC1V 1NE, 0171 278 2206, email: info@biat.org.uk

Royal Incorporation of Architects in Scotland*, 15 Rutland Square, Edinburgh EH1 2BE, 0131 229 7545, www.rias.org.uk

Royal Institute of British Architects*, 66 Portland Place, London W1N 4AD, 0171 580 5533, www.riba/org/library

FURTHER READING

Leaflets/booklets are available from the addresses marked*.

Working in Construction – COIC

In the careers library classified under UB.

BUILDING TECHNOLOGY AND MANAGEMENT: UD

PROFESSIONAL BUILDER/TECHNICIAN
CLCI:UD

BACKGROUND INFORMATION

The construction industry is a major UK employer and accounts for around ten per cent of gross national product. Forecasts of future demand for construction work indicate that 80% of new projects over the next decade will be in building (as opposed to civil engineering). For this reason, and because the technical demands of building are becoming ever more complex, there is a growing need for qualified building professionals.

The following article describes four professional roles in building: estimator; buyer; planner; and construction manager. To understand the relationship between these and allied professions such as architects and quantity surveyors, a brief outline of the various stages in the management of a building project is necessary. These stages are as follows:

Design

The client defines a need – for instance, for a housing estate, factory or office block. The architect interprets the client's ideas into a design, and the architectural technologist produces working drawings. At the design stage, other professionals such as the consulting civil engineer, landscape architect and building services engineer may be involved. The drawings and specifications produced by this design team are then translated by the quantity surveyor into the **bill of quantities**; this document sets out in writing every operation that the building contractor will have to carry out in order to complete the contract, with lists of materials and methods of working. A number of firms of building contractors are then invited to submit tenders for the contract.

Tender stage

Once the contractor receives the design and the bill of quantities, the estimator can calculate the cost of labour, plant and materials. At this stage the planner starts work on planning a programme of operations, and the buyer obtains information on prices, availability and delivery dates. The construction manager advises on potential construction problems, and other professionals – such as the plant specialist, who is consulted on the use of machinery – are called in. At the end of this process, an estimate of the amount it will cost the contractor to complete the contract is reached, and a further amount is added for profit. This represents the tender price, which is submitted to the client.

Site preparation

If the tender is accepted by the client, then a considerable amount of preliminary work must be carried out before construction starts. The main role here is that of the planner, who works out the sequence of operations in detail, liaising with the buyer, construction manager, subcontractors, the design team and others.

Construction

Under the supervision of the construction manager, building work starts. Progress is continually monitored by the construction manager and planner, to ensure that work proceeds according to schedule.

THE WORK
Estimator

The estimator calculates the cost of labour, materials, subcontractors, plant and overheads. Estimating is closely linked to the process of tendering. A tender must reflect all the costs to the company, otherwise no profit will be made, but the price must be competitive or the contract will be won by another firm. It is therefore important to forecast costs as accurately as possible, working from architects' and engineers' drawings, the bill of quantities, and information on prices supplied by subcontractors and the company buyer.

The estimator is a member of the pre-tender team, liaising with the planner, buyer and technical staff to ensure that estimates are realistic, and that the tender submitted to the client will enable the contractor to make a profit.

Estimators are also concerned with comparing actual costs against estimates throughout the building process.

Buyer

The buyer sends out enquiries for quotations and – once the most suitable quotation has been selected – purchases materials, equipment and services required for the contract. The work involves negotiating the most competitive price and making sure that materials can be delivered on time.

Buyers usually invite potential suppliers to submit competitive tenders. They may screen suppliers, investigating their past track record to ensure that they have the ability to supply and deliver materials and/or labour to a set programme.

When tenders have been received, the buyer assesses each one from a commercial point of view, and to check its compliance with the required specifications.

The buyer then selects a particular firm from those that have submitted tenders, and proposes acceptance of a suitable contract to the management team.

The buyer's other responsibilities include checking materials are to be delivered on time, and monitoring the quality of supplies. From time to time the buyer may be involved in commercial disputes over problems such as late delivery or poor quality.

In large firms some buyers specialize, for instance in purchasing timber or steel.

Planner

The planner selects the most appropriate method and sequence for building operations. The aim is to schedule building work so that it can be completed within the shortest possible time.

The work involves planning and co-ordinating all the project's requirements for materials, equipment and labour. Planners make sure that everything is available at the right time, and they set target dates for completion of each stage of the construction process, eg excavating, completing the structure, installation of services. They may be responsible for setting completion dates for whole projects.

Working from designs, plans and bills of quantities, planners construct a programme of the sequence of operations. The programme is usually diagrammatic, with some explanatory text, and is produced on computer. It involves complex calculations, such as of quantities of materials required.

BUILDING TECHNOLOGY AND MANAGEMENT: UD

To plan the sequence of building operations, the planner needs to gather detailed information from the design team, buyer, estimator and others. Precise information on designs and specifications, and how they can be practically translated into bricks and mortar, are needed in order to set a target date for completion of each stage of the project. The planner also has to pass on information to the construction manager, subcontractors and other interested parties. The information gathering and disseminating role involves the planner in a lot of telephone liaison work.

Once construction has begun, planners usually need to modify the programme, taking into account any problems that have arisen, for instance delays caused by bad weather or late delivery of materials. If at all possible, they must try to re-schedule work so that the pre-arranged completion date can still be met. Monitoring the programme involves planners in site inspections.

In a small company planning may be combined with buying.

Construction manager

The construction manager usually oversees between four and six contracts and has overall responsibility for a building site, monitoring three main elements: quality, cost and speed. The construction manager co-ordinates operations, making sure they are carried out to the correct standard, and on schedule. A site manager or agent carries out the detailed work of overseeing the production process, in a similar way to the construction manager, but is usually only responsible for one site.

The majority of the work is at the construction stage, but at the tender and site preparation stages the construction manager liaises with the estimator, buyer, planner and other professionals. It is important that the planner and construction manager agree on the scheduling of operations, as it is the construction manager who actually puts the planner's programme into operation.

At the site preparation stage, the manager visits the site to check on matters such as access, environmental factors (trees, for example, may be left standing) and car parking. Services such as electricity and telephones have to be arranged, and site offices erected.

Once construction is under way, the manager leads and controls practical operations on site. On a large building project, this involves leading a team of professionals and co-ordinating the work of heads of section and supervisors. On a small site, there is more contact with the labour force, and the manager may act as a general foreman/woman. Much of the work involves trouble-shooting: sorting out problems such as labour disputes, non-arrival of plant or materials, and safety matters.

Another major aspect of the work is monitoring or taking overall responsibility for standards of materials and workmanship. On a small project, this can involve going out on site to check records of deliveries, completed work and measurements, then comparing these with plans and specifications; on a larger project, the manager supervises staff carrying out these tasks.

In the site office, records are kept, covering matters such as instructions received from the client and issued to subcontractors, hours worked, materials and plant used, health and safety etc. The records are kept by clerical staff, but the construction manager is involved in the paperwork and is responsible for its organization and maintenance. This may involve the use of computers.

Technician

Technicians provide support to professional staff and act as a link between management and the labour force on site.

In large and medium-sized companies, technicians usually specialize in one of the areas described above, carrying out the less complicated types of work. For example, in the buying area they may deal with purchasing for smaller contracts, working under the supervision of the company buyer.

In small companies, if technicians are employed, they may carry out aspects of all the areas described above.

WORK ENVIRONMENT

Estimators and buyers are generally office-based, working either at the company's head office or regional offices. They sometimes travel to visit sites.

Planners are usually site-based, but they sometimes work at regional or head offices.

Construction managers usually work in a site office – often a temporary structure, such as a Portakabin. They also spend a considerable proportion of the time outdoors, in all weathers, inspecting work on site. Inspection may involve climbing ladders and scaffolding. Travel is an important part of the construction manager's job and it may be necessary to work a long way from home, living in lodgings, whilst a contract is in progress. Construction managers also travel to meetings with clients, architects and other professionals.

Depending on the type of work involved, technicians may be site-based or office-based, or may combine both.

SKILLS AND INTERESTS

Professional builders and technicians need to be able to work well with other people as members of a team, and to liaise with other professionals. Good spoken and written communication skills are important.

A thorough knowledge of building techniques and materials is needed, and it is helpful to have site experience.

Numeracy is required for all professional and technician-level building work, and is particularly important for estimators and buyers, much of whose work involves interpreting figures and making calculations.

Self-motivation and the ability to plan and organize one's own workload are important. It is essential to be able to think logically.

Buyers need commercial awareness, with good negotiating skills, as well as an understanding of the technical aspects of building.

Estimators need to be able to work accurately, and assimilate details quickly.

For all jobs, it is important to be able to cope with working under pressure.

A driving licence is useful and may be required.

BUILDING TECHNOLOGY AND MANAGEMENT: UD

ENTRY REQUIREMENTS

The most common entry route at professional level is via a relevant degree course. Minimum entry requirements are three GCSEs (A–C) or two S grades (1–3) and two A levels or three H grades. English and maths may be required at GCSE/S grade and some colleges require A level/H grade maths.

Entry to degree courses is also possible with a relevant BTEC/SQA national certificate or diploma, or with Advanced GNVQ/GSVQ Level III in a relevant subject, such as Construction and the Built Environment.

Technicians qualify via BTEC/SQA national or higher national awards. Normally, the minimum entry requirements for national level courses are four GCSEs/S grades (A–C/1–3), or Intermediate GNVQ/GSVQ Level II. However, less-qualified candidates may be admitted at the discretion of the college. Entry to higher national diploma/certificate courses is with one A level/two H grades and supporting GCSEs/S grades (A–C/1–3), or a BTEC/SQA national award, or Advanced GNVQ/GSVQ Level III.

TRAINING

Degree level: courses in building, building management, building technology, construction, construction management and related subjects last three/four years; some are sandwich courses, including practical experience in the building industry. Employer sponsorship may be available for degree courses – contact the Construction Careers Service for further details. The degree is normally followed by three years' practical experience in construction, with continuing professional development (this may include further training courses, organized by employers).

Professional qualifications: to be eligible for full corporate membership of the Chartered Institute of Building (CIOB) candidates must either:

– complete the CIOB's own examinations and gain three years of construction management experience and then sit the Professional Interview. If successful they become a Chartered Member (MCIOB), or

– complete an accredited honours degree eg BSc(Hons) Construction Management, BSc(Hons) in Building Engineering and Management and the Professional Development Programme (PDP) – the CIOB's own training programme. The PDP incorporates the Professional Interview; when successfully completed the candidate becomes a Chartered Member (MCIOB).

Higher technician level: training is via a BTEC/SQA Higher National Certificate or Diploma in Building Studies (or equivalent). The higher national certificate is a part-time day release course, over two years, whilst the student is in employment. The higher national diploma is studied as a two-year full-time course, or three-year sandwich course.

Technician level: this involves entering employment and studying on day release for the BTEC/SQA national certificate (two to three years), or taking a full-time BTEC/SQA National Diploma course in Building Studies (or equivalent).

NVQs/SVQs in Building Site Supervision are available at Level 3 and Building Site Management at Level 4.

LATE ENTRY

There is no age limit on entry for candidates with previous experience in the construction industry (for instance at craft level), but it is difficult for adults with unrelated experience to enter this field.

The CIOB has a special entry route to corporate membership for mature candidates. The Direct Membership Examination is open to people who have been employed at higher technician level for at least ten years.

There may be specific training opportunities directed at adults available in some areas for this type of work. Candidates may have to satisfy certain conditions to be eligible. Contact your local Jobcentre, careers office or TEC/LEC for details.

OPPORTUNITIES

Professional builders and technicians are employed by national and international firms of building contractors. Building contractors vary in size and scope, and it tends to be the medium-sized and larger firms, some of which combine building and civil engineering, that employ staff at professional and technician level. There are also opportunities with central and local government, and with other organizations that carry out or supervise their own construction projects – for instance, public utilities and major retailers.

Major international contractors offer opportunities to work abroad.

Self-employment is possible; a planner, for instance, can work on a self-employed basis for several small building companies.

There is a shortage of professional builders; in normal circumstances, when the construction industry is not in recession, most building graduates experience little difficulty in finding employment. It may, however, be necessary to move location to take advantage of the opportunities available.

Technicians also need to be prepared to be mobile.

PAY AND CONDITIONS

Salaries vary with individual employers, but typically are in the region of £10,000 to £12,000 for a graduate entrant. This could quickly rise to around £15,000, with additional benefits such as a company car. The most responsible posts command considerably higher salaries.

Technicians, once qualified to national certificate/diploma level, earn from around £9,000.

The standard working week is 37 to 40 hours, but actual hours worked may be irregular and include evenings and weekends.

PROSPECTS

Building graduates tend to start as planner, buyer, estimator or assistant to a construction manager, usually on the more straightforward building contracts. With experience it is possible to move on to larger and more complex projects, or into construction management. Further promotion could lead to the post of contracts manager, responsible for a number of different projects.

Some professional builders work in teaching or building research.

BUILDING TECHNOLOGY AND MANAGEMENT: UD

Higher-level technicians may qualify as chartered builders by gaining practical experience, with part-time study for the membership exams of the Chartered Institute of Building and the Professional Interview.

Technicians may proceed via the higher national certificate/diploma route or study part-time for the associate grade of the Chartered Institute of Building, followed by further part-time study for the membership examinations and the Professional Interview, although the associate route is becoming less common.

RELATED OCCUPATIONS

Architect, building services engineer, building surveyor, civil engineer, clerk of works, quantity surveyor, town planner.

FURTHER INFORMATION

Careers in Construction, Construction Industry Training Board (CITB), Bircham Newton Training Centre, Bircham Newton, Kings Lynn, Norfolk PE31 6RH, 01485 577577, www.citb.org.uk

Chartered Institute of Building, Englemere, King's Ride, Ascot, Berks SL5 7TB, 01344 630700, www.ciob.org.uk

FURTHER READING

The Construction Industry Handbook of Professional and Management Careers – CITB

Professional and Management Careers in Building – CITB

Periodicals: Building Construction News; New Builder

In the careers library classified under UD.

BUILDING AND CONSTRUCTION TRADES: UF

1. BRICKLAYER CLCI:UF
2. CARPENTER/JOINER CLCI:UF
3. FLOOR LAYER CLCI:UF
4. GLAZIER CLCI:UF
5. PAINTER AND DECORATOR CLCI:UF
6. PLASTERER CLCI:UF
7. PLUMBER CLCI:UF
8. ROOFER CLCI:UF
9. SCAFFOLDER CLCI:UF
10. WALL AND FLOOR TILER CLCI:UF

BACKGROUND INFORMATION

The construction industry is a major UK employer and is engaged in an enormous variety of projects ranging from roads and airports through to house extensions. The traditional focus of the industry has been on the building of houses, offices and factories, and on large-scale civil engineering projects such as bridges and motorways. Now, however, a considerable amount of work involves the restoration and refurbishment of existing buildings.

The industry is constantly tackling new and increasingly complicated projects, which require a well trained, skilled workforce. Essential to any project are the traditional trade or craft skills described below, which offer many opportunities for interesting and challenging work. In construction no project is the same, so the work is varied and every day is different.

1. BRICKLAYER (UF)

THE WORK

Bricklayers build the interior and exterior walls of buildings, and other types of walling, for example, the linings of tunnels, archways, ornamental brickwork. The work may be on new buildings or on the extension, maintenance and restoration of old buildings.

Engineers usually set out the positions at which walls are to be constructed, although on smaller sites bricklayers themselves may be responsible for setting out. Working from these positions, bricklayers build the walls, starting with the corners of the building. They use spirit levels and bricklayers' lines to check vertical and horizontal alignment of walls. They use a trowel to spread mortar, a club hammer and bolster to cut bricks to size, and a brick hammer to trim the brick.

Labourers are usually employed to keep the bricklayers supplied with a steady stream of bricks and mortar. Several hundred bricks may need to be laid in one working day.

Depending on the size of the structure involved, it is usual for teams of bricklayers to be engaged in working on different sections of the site.

WORK ENVIRONMENT

Bricklayers must work on scaffolding when working at high levels. They work outside in most weather conditions. The work can be dirty and dusty.

Working as a bricklayer involves a lot of standing, kneeling, climbing ladders and constant physical motion. Sometimes quite heavy loads of tools, bricks and mortar have to be carried.

Building work inevitably involves travelling from site to site, working on a particular property or building project and then moving on when the job is completed. It may be necessary to work away from home for short and long periods.

SKILLS AND INTERESTS

Bricklaying is primarily a practical craft requiring good hand skills. It also requires a careful and methodical approach to the work and an ability to plan the job well in advance and set about the various tasks in the right order. Arithmetical ability is important as is the ability to understand drawings, plans and written or oral instructions easily.

The work can be physically demanding and it is important to have good health, agility and enough strength to lift and carry tools and equipment. A head for heights is also required.

Safety awareness is essential in all work in the construction industry. Basic safety equipment includes a safety helmet and protective footwear. Items such as gloves, goggles and ear defenders are provided as required.

Team work is a vital aspect of working in construction as each person relies on others to carry out their work to a high standard.

ENTRY REQUIREMENTS

No minimum educational qualifications are required for a trainee bricklayer. However, a good standard in maths, English and science at GCSE/S grade can help with the measurements, calculations and instructions in the job, and also with the theoretical part of the training.

Candidates for apprenticeships or training schemes may have to take a selection test. Contact your local careers office or TEC/LEC for details.

A driving licence is useful, especially for the self-employed.

TRAINING

Many young people now enter the building crafts/trades through specific government-assisted training schemes, and then extend the period of training through a nationally approved training agreement, National Traineeships or a Modern Apprenticeship.

A Modern Apprenticeship is an agreement between a young person aged 16–20 years and an employer or training provider, with the signed approval of the parents and the local TEC. Both apprentice and employer undertake to follow a training programme approved by the Construction Industry Training Board, leading to NVQ/SVQ Level 3 (minimum) in approximately three years. The apprentice receives a wage or training allowance.

Whether on a scheme or an apprenticeship, training combines site experience on the job, in-company training and day or block release to a local college. Additional units in key skills (core skills in Scotland) may also be given. Some employers provide training for C&G qualifications as well as NVQs/SVQs Levels 1, 2 and 3.

Several of the building crafts follow this system of entry and training. They are: brick-laying, carpentry and joinery, painting and decorating, plastering, roofing.

BUILDING AND CONSTRUCTION TRADES: UF

LATE ENTRY

NVQs/SVQs can be taken at any age. Awards can take account of previous experience and qualifications (Accreditation of Prior Learning.) However, opportunities for adult entry are limited, except for those with compatible skills and experience. It can be difficult to find an employer willing to provide training. A building craft training scheme for adults is available in Scotland.

OPPORTUNITIES

The demand for construction workers varies according to a variety of local and economic factors. In recent years recruitment has been low in the building/construction industry. However, the CITB has offered opportunities for training and entry into many of the building trades, including bricklaying.

Bricklayers are often self-employed, working on a subcontract basis for building contractors. They may work as 'labour only' subcontractors, with all their materials provided by the building contractor.

Some are directly employed by building contractors, local authorities and other public organizations. Specialist bricklayers work in foundries and in mining.

PAY AND CONDITIONS

Pay rates are agreed nationally, and minimum rates for skilled workers start from £210.60p a week. Some employers pay above minimum rates, and bonus and overtime pay can increase wages considerably.

Allowances may also be paid for travelling time, travel expenses and cost of lodgings, though this will vary from employer to employer.

The standard working week is 39 hours, worked over five days, Monday to Friday. It is usual for starting and finishing times to vary in summer and winter to take advantage of available daylight. Construction and maintenance contracts usually have to meet deadlines and schedules, so evening and weekend overtime is common.

PROSPECTS

Progression may be made through craft supervisor up to the construction management team.

Qualifications like BTEC/SQA national and higher national certificates/diplomas are useful.

There may also be the opportunity, for the self-employed, to run one's own specialist firm.

RELATED OCCUPATIONS

Carpenter/joiner, plasterer, painter and decorator, scaffolder, roofer, stonemason, construction operative, building technician.

FURTHER INFORMATION AND READING

Please see article 9. SCAFFOLDER.

2. CARPENTER/JOINER (UF)

THE WORK

The main types of work or jobs carried out by carpenters and joiners are:

Formwork joiner

Formwork consists of moulds, made of timber (or other materials such as metal or plastic), used to support and shape wet concrete until it has set. This 'shuttering' is used on major structures such as multi-storey car parks, bridges and motorways, and buildings. The formwork carpenter cuts, shapes, drills and fits together timber or plywood to make the formwork according to required measurements, drawings or instructions.

First fixer

All first fixing work is concerned with the wooden parts used in the basic structure of a building and any wooden fittings fitted prior to having the walls plastered. This includes 'carcassing', which is concerned with fitting floor and roof joists and roof timbers, floorboards, staircases, partition walls, and door and window frames. The work involves setting up the wooden posts in the right position (many of them are now prefabricated) and fixing them in place. Modifications may have to be made and the posts must be checked for correct positioning and fit according to drawings and plans.

Second fixer

This includes putting in skirting boards and door surrounds, hanging doors, and fitting any kitchen cupboards, sink units, wardrobes, shelves etc. Door handles and locks must also be fitted. Again, many parts will have been prefabricated and some items (for example, windowsills) are now made from PVC. However, a variety of materials must be handled, modifications must be made where necessary, and a high level of finish is required, particularly where quality materials are used.

Bench joiner

All of the prefabricated parts fitted by carpenters and joiners on site (like roof timbers, staircases, cupboards etc) have been made by bench joiners in a joinery workshop. All carpenters and joiners are trained in bench and site work, though usually bench joiners remain in the workshop while others work on site. Timbers are marked and cut to the required lengths, planed and smoothed down and then put together to form the prefabricated part. Complicated formwork can also be done in workshops by joiners (though usually these workshops are on site).

Most wood fabrication work is done in joinery workshops sometimes miles from any building site.

Shopfitter

This is a specialist craft engaged in producing and fitting shop fronts and interiors. It is also concerned with hotels, restaurants, banks, offices and other prestigious buildings. It can involve both bench joinery work (producing items such as shop counters and special panelling) and fixing and installing these items on site.

Carpenters and joiners may specialize in one of the major skills, although those employed by small non-specialist firms that carry out a lot of maintenance/repair work and wood fabrication will probably need skills in most aspects of the work.

WORK ENVIRONMENT

Carpenters and joiners may spend a good deal of their time standing, kneeling or crouching to carry out the work. On site, agility is important in order to climb up ladders and onto scaffolding or to enter narrow and cramped spaces or to go out onto roofs and work at various heights.

BUILDING AND CONSTRUCTION TRADES: UF

It is necessary to carry heavy equipment such as ladders and tools; some of the prefabricated parts such as roof timbers need more than one person to move them. Team work is an important part of construction industry work; most carpenters and joiners will find themselves working with other skilled workers.

Bench joiners work in workshops; other carpenters/joiners work on site, both indoors and outside. Outdoor work can involve cold and wet conditions.

Working with timber creates wood dust, although in some workshops it may be minimized by extraction systems.

Site work and shopfitting involves travel; it may be necessary to spend short or long periods away from home.

SKILLS AND INTERESTS

Practical hand skills and good hand-to-eye co-ordination are essential. Carpenters and joiners need to work accurately, carefully and methodically. They should be able to plan and organize their work. It is important to be able to follow plans, diagrams and written instructions. Numeracy is required for measuring and calculating quantities of materials.

Physical fitness is important. Some strength is required to lift and carry timber and tools.

Safety awareness is essential in all work in the construction industry. Basic safety equipment includes a safety helmet and protective footwear. Items such as gloves, goggles and ear defenders are provided as required.

ENTRY REQUIREMENTS, TRAINING, LATE ENTRY

Please see article 1. BRICKLAYER.

OPPORTUNITIES

Carpenters and joiners work for construction companies of all sizes, for local authorities and other public organizations, and for demolition companies. Many are self-employed. Some work in specialist areas such as restoration of old buildings or furniture making.

Shopfitters usually work for specialist firms.

PAY AND CONDITIONS, PROSPECTS

Please see article 1. BRICKLAYER.

RELATED OCCUPATIONS

Plasterer, painter and decorator, glazier, tiler, cabinet maker, designer: three-dimensional (craft), wood machinist.

FURTHER INFORMATION AND READING

Please see article 9. SCAFFOLDER.

3. FLOOR LAYER (UF)

THE WORK

Floor layers work with three main types of floor covering:
– carpets, of all qualities, from Axminster and Wilton through to carpet tiles;
– vinyls, linoleum and rubber, including sheet material and tiles;
– hardwoods, which include hardwood strip – often used in sports halls – hardwood blocks, and mosaic panels, which are similar to parquet.

Floor layers usually follow plans, diagrams and written instructions.

In occupied buildings it may be necessary to move furniture and fittings before starting work.

The skills used in laying vinyls, linoleum and carpet are similar. With these materials, the first consideration is the condition of the sub-floor, which must be flat, because any undulations or damage will spoil the appearance of the floor covering.

Often, the floor layer prepares a flat surface by spreading a layer of levelling compound. Sometimes it is first necessary to remove an existing floor covering. This may be done mechanically, especially in large areas. It is also important to remove all traces of old adhesives.

With a level surface prepared, the next task is to measure the floor area, then measure and cut the material. It is usually cut slightly over-size before laying, because the room may not be exactly regular in shape.

Vinyls, linoleum and some types of carpet are stuck down with adhesive, which is evenly spread with a trowel or roller. Adhesives have to be handled carefully, and it may be necessary to wear a mask or even, in enclosed areas, to use breathing apparatus.

The flooring material is laid to protrude up the skirting board and is cut by hand, with a carpet knife, round the perimeter, to give a snug, neat fit.

Carpet, instead of being fixed with adhesive, may be laid on to a 'gripper' – a piece of wood with upwardly protruding nails. The gripper is fitted at the perimeter of the room, around the underlay. The carpet is then placed over the underlay and gripper. The edges, which protrude over the gripper, are neatly turned under.

Some types of flooring material, including carpet, are simply laid side to side and stuck down with adhesive. But with carpet, the edges may be sealed together with heated tape, or hand sewn. Vinyls are welded at all seams, after they have been stuck down. The simplest types of work involve laying carpet, lino or vinyl tiles. The main concern is maintaining the 'bond', ie laying the tiles straight.

Laying the more expensive types of carpet, particularly carpet with a repeating pattern, can be complicated. Large areas of high-quality carpet are often laid in buildings such as hotels or offices, and the work needs to be carefully planned so that offcuts from one room can be used elsewhere, with as little wastage as possible. The appearance of the fitted carpet is extremely important, and it may be necessary to stretch it to give a good fit, using special equipment. Sometimes a plain border is fitted around a patterned carpet, and doing this neatly is a highly skilled job.

Hardwood flooring involves different techniques. Hardwood strip is laid on battens, and secret-nailed (ie the nails are invisible). The battens provide a level surface; sometimes they are laid on rubber pads, to create a semi-sprung floor. Hardwood blocks and mosaic panels are laid on the sub-floor, which must first be prepared and levelled. Blocks are set out in a pattern, such as herringbone. The floor layer usually works from the centre of the room, moving out to the perimeter. The blocks are dipped into

BUILDING AND CONSTRUCTION TRADES: UF

adhesive. Hardwood mosaic panels, on the other hand, are laid on to adhesive, which is spread by trowel on the sub-floor. Electric saws are used to cut hardwoods so that they fit neatly at the perimeter. The finished floor is then sanded with an electric sander.

Floor laying includes all the above types of work, but in practice floor layers tend to specialize in one or two areas: laying expensive carpet; laying lower-cost carpet, vinyl and linoleum; or hardwood flooring.

WORK ENVIRONMENT

The work environment can be a building of any type – including shops, offices, schools, hospitals, sports halls or private houses. It may be a building site or a building that is currently in use. Floor layers call at their employer's office or yard to collect materials, receive instructions, and so on, but most of their time is spent at customers' premises.

The work involves a considerable amount of travel, which may be in the local area or further afield. It may be necessary to spend the working week away from home, although it is usual to return at weekends. There may be opportunities to work abroad, on contract.

Some adhesives used in floor laying give off unpleasant and potentially dangerous fumes. However, there are strict safety procedures to minimize the risks, and modern adhesives are considerably safer than they were in the past.

SKILLS AND INTERESTS

Physical fitness is important – floor layers spend much of the working day on their hands and knees. They need to be able to lift and carry rolls and boxes of flooring material.

Practical hand skills are required for accurate fitting and cutting of materials.

A courteous and pleasant manner is required for dealing with clients, who may include private householders.

Work on building sites takes place at the final stages of the construction programme, and floor layers often face a situation where other trades, such as electricians or carpenters, are trying to finish their work at the same time as the floor is being laid. This situation requires tact and flexibility.

Floor layers also need to co-operate with others in their team – they normally work in pairs, but may work in groups on larger jobs.

Basic numeracy is required for measuring.

An appreciation of design is useful, particularly for laying and matching patterned carpet.

ENTRY REQUIREMENTS

There are no minimum academic entry qualifications, although a reasonable standard of maths, English and science subjects is desirable for career progress.

Applicants may be asked to take an aptitude test, administered by the Construction Industry Training Board (CITB).

Good colour vision is desirable.

Transport to jobs is often provided by the employer. However, a driving licence is almost essential (trainees may be accepted without).

TRAINING

The Contract Flooring Association, together with the CITB, offers a three-year Modern Apprenticeship. After initial experience on the job, apprentices attend courses, on block release, at Erith Training Centre in Kent, Salford College, or Glasgow College of Further Education. In their third year they may attend manufacturers' short courses, covering specialist aspects. They are expected to attain NVQ/SVQ Level 2 in Floor Covering.

Alternatively, employers may train staff on the job, usually over two years. Again, this leads to NVQ/SVQ Level 2. Trainees are assessed at the end of their first and second years.

NVQs/SVQs Level 3 in Floor Covering are also available.

There are no college facilities for training in hardwood floor laying – all training is with employers.

Specific training opportunities for young people may be available – contact your local careers office or TEC/LEC for details.

LATE ENTRY

The majority of entrants are school-leavers, but some employers do recruit adult entrants.

A background in carpentry/joinery is very useful for laying hardwood floors.

There may be specific training opportunities directed at adults available in some areas for this type of work. Candidates may have to satisfy certain conditions to be eligible. Contact your local Jobcentre, careers office or TEC/LEC for details.

OPPORTUNITIES

The main employers are firms of flooring contractors, who provide services to the construction industry.

Flooring contractors are, by and large, small family businesses, typically employing about eight to ten people. There are, however, some larger firms with a hundred staff or more.

There are a few opportunities for employment with the manufacturers of flooring materials.

Retailers of carpets and other flooring materials generally use the services of self-employed flooring contractors, and rarely offer direct employment.

Self-employment is common, both in the domestic and contracting sides of the industry.

The market for flooring is dependent on the state of the construction industry, declining in times when the industry is stagnant, expanding when there is a construction boom.

There are no particular regional trends in employment – firms of flooring contractors are found throughout the country.

PAY AND CONDITIONS

The standard wage rate, laid down by the Building and Allied Trades Joint Industrial Council, is £210.60p a week. Additional payments are made for specialist skills and there are allowances for travel, lodgings and tools.

BUILDING AND CONSTRUCTION TRADES: UF

The standard working week is 39 hours. When laying flooring in premises such as shops, it may be necessary to work nights and/or weekends, so that there is no interruption to business.

Overtime may be available or required.

PROSPECTS

There are opportunities in flooring contracting firms for promotion to leading hand, supervisor and contracts manager. It is also possible to become self-employed.

RELATED OCCUPATIONS

Wall/floor tiler, carpenter/joiner, ceiling fixer, painter and decorator, upholsterer, interior designer.

FURTHER INFORMATION

Careers in Construction, Construction Industry Training Board (CITB)*, Bircham Newton Training Centre, Bircham Newton, King's Lynn, Norfolk PE31 6RH, 01485 577577, www.citb.org.uk

Contract Flooring Association, 4c St Mary's Place, The Lace Market, Nottingham NG1 1PH, 0115 941 1126, www.cfa.org.uk

FURTHER READING

Leaflets/booklets are available from the address marked*.

In the careers library classified under UF.

4. GLAZIER (UF)

THE WORK

Slightly different techniques and installation methods are required depending on the type of glass/glazed unit being fitted.

Window fixing

Most house windows can be installed by a glazier and assistant/trainee or two glaziers working together. When working on new property under construction it may be necessary to refer to drawings/written instructions to ensure that the right type/size of glass is installed in the right location.

If a broken window is being replaced, then any remaining pieces of the glass must be removed. Large pieces may need to be scored through and broken in sections; pliers are used to remove awkward pieces. If the glass is held in position by wooden or metal beading this must also be removed. The old putty/mastic is then chipped away or cleared off. To fit a new pane into position it may be necessary to trim it to the correct size for an exact fit. This is done by holding the glass in position by hand and using a hand glass cutter.

High-wind/security/safety glass

This is used in shops and offices and in multi-storey buildings above the first two to three floors where wind force would break ordinary glass. The methods of fixing are otherwise much the same as described above, but it is usual to put in some sort of spacers, made of wood or plastic, or spring clips (for metal frames) to help absorb the weight of the glass. Sometimes as many as ten or even twenty glaziers are needed to help move and position the glass (with the aid of webbing straps). Fewer glaziers are needed if a wheeled lifting machine is used – this has a big suction pad to hold the glass plate safely while it is moved into position.

Pre-glazed/double glazed units/doors

While double glazed panes of glass are fitted as described above, with the help of wood/metal beading to hold it in position, a very different method is required for pre-glazed units. These usually come complete in a wooden, metal or PVC framework. Instead of only removing any existing glass, the entire frame must be removed before the new unit can be installed. Installation requires the unit to be screwed directly into the surrounding brickwork and sealed in with a waterproof mastic. Any pre-glazed doors have hinges and handles fitted by the glazier. Security glass used in banks/post offices and elsewhere also comes as a pre-glazed unit with its surrounding framework.

Roof glazing

Skylights and dormer windows are re-glazed in the same manner as house windows or doors. Skylight units, eg Velux, are fitted by experienced roofers because of the amount of work required in making the roof good, but there are workshops/offices, and so on, that are built with glass roofing. Here the glass (normally in two-feet widths) is held in position between bar-strips acting as clamps. The glazier must first attach the bar-strips (up to twelve feet long) parallel to each other to the roof beams. This is done by drilling holes into the beams and bolting the strips to them. A pane of glass is then fitted between two bar-strips (into channels in the strips) and fixed in place. A further strip is then attached over the end of the fitted pane, the next pane slipped into position and so on. Finally the glazier fits lead/aluminium flashings to waterproof the glass roof.

Although glaziers may specialize in any of the above different types of glazing, it is also common for glaziers in the smaller glazing firms to be able to employ any of the above techniques and undertake any type of work.

WORK ENVIRONMENT

A feature of glazing work is having to work at heights. This can be done from a ladder, when fitting small, manageable panes of glass; tower scaffolding is also used. When working on multi-storey buildings where it is not possible to glaze from the inside then a suspended cradle is required.

A lot of the work can be carried out by one glazier, though a team of glaziers or a trainee acting as an assistant will be needed when working with large and heavy panes of glass.

The work can take place indoors or outside.

A lot of travel may be required.

SKILLS AND INTERESTS

Glazing requires considerable hand skills and material-handling ability.

It is not easy to cut glass in straight lines, neatly and without breaking it. Safety considerations also call for a careful, methodical approach. It is important to be able to measure accurately and interpret drawings and written instructions. Glaziers must be physically fit, able to carry quite heavy loads and climb easily up and down ladders and along scaffolding. They must not be afraid of working at heights. Neatness and tidiness in their work is also required when carrying out glazing work in people's homes or in offices and factories where people are working.

BUILDING AND CONSTRUCTION TRADES: UF

ENTRY REQUIREMENTS
Please see article 1. BRICKLAYER.

TRAINING
In most cases, young people enter the glazing industry through a Modern Apprenticeship. An apprenticeship lasts at least three years and follows nationally agreed guidelines.

Apprentices work towards NVQ/SVQ in Glazing Installation, or Installing Architectural Glazing Systems, at Level 3. Some employers also provide training for City and Guilds or BTEC/SQA qualifications.

LATE ENTRY
Please see article 1. BRICKLAYER.

OPPORTUNITIES
Although there is less new building work being carried out at present, existing structures are still in need of constant repair and maintenance. Glass, in particular, is fragile and tends to break and need replacement regularly. Windows in houses, shops, offices etc cannot usually be left broken.

Glaziers are employed by any firm that sells, cuts and installs glass. These can be very small one- or two-person businesses, requiring skilled glaziers capable of undertaking a wide variety of tasks. Then there are middle-sized firms employing several teams of three to four glaziers that will also undertake any type of glazing. There are also the larger glazing firms that employ hundreds of people – glass cutters/general glass operatives in the workshops and glaziers/glazing installers out on the road fixing glass. They may have glaziers specializing in different types of glazing, such as domestic, or pre-glazed units, or leaded and decorative glass. Other glazing firms may specialize totally in one aspect of glazing work, such as glass roofing contractors or commercial greenhouse glaziers.

Self-employment is always a possibility, but it is usually advisable to gain full training and qualification, followed by experience, before attempting self-employment.

PAY AND CONDITIONS
Please see article 1. BRICKLAYER.

PROSPECTS
If a firm is large enough to offer promotion prospects then there may be a chance to become a supervisor in charge of a team of glaziers and responsible for overseeing their work on site and elsewhere, or to become a surveyor of glass installations.

An alternative would be to specialize, for example, in double glazing, security glass, or decorative glazing, and obtain a specialist post within the firm or move to a specialist firm offering these sorts of services. Presentation and accuracy is most important.

RELATED OCCUPATIONS
Window fitter, carpenter and joiner, wall/floor tiler, floor layer, painter and decorator, scaffolder, ceiling fixer, construction operative, building technician.

FURTHER INFORMATION AND READING
Please see article 9. SCAFFOLDER.

5. PAINTER AND DECORATOR (UF)

THE WORK
The sort of work carried out depends on the size of the employing firm and the type of work it does. Generally the smaller the firm the wider the range of work and duties performed, although firms tend to specialize in domestic or industrial work. Even within these fields there can be further specialization – shop and office decoration, civil engineering structures or ships, for example. All of this affects the type of skills an individual is expected to use and the types of tools used to carry out the work.

The work involves:

Preparation work

This involves moving furniture, stripping wallpaper, ensuring the surface is smooth and clean, and so on, as necessary. This is not necessary on new buildings.

Painting

Before any paint can be applied to a surface, a primer or sealing coat is needed if the surface is absorbent, an undercoat is then added and then the required paint. Depending on the finish required and the scale of the job, paint may be applied by brush, roller or spraying equipment; each requires a different application technique.

Wall hanging

Wallpaper is still the most popular form of wall and ceiling covering. However there is a wide range of other types of wall hanging available, such as hessian, silk, wool, felt, suede and cane. The method of hanging therefore varies according to the covering used. Generally, each roll has to be measured, cut, pasted and hung using the correct type of paste for that type of covering, and making sure the material does not stretch during hanging. Sometimes a lining paper is required. Usually a plumb-line and spirit level are used to ensure correct vertical lines.

WORK ENVIRONMENT
The work takes place indoors and outdoors. It involves lifting, carrying, bending, climbing ladders and long periods of standing.

Some paint gives off fumes; it may be necessary to wear a mask and to use extraction equipment.

The work involves travelling to different sites, usually in the local area.

SKILLS AND INTERESTS
Painters and decorators need practical hand skills, with the ability to work accurately and neatly. An eye for detail is important; some appreciation of form and colour is an advantage. Good colour vision is desirable for mixing/matching paints.

Painting and decorating can be repetitive, but it is important to be self-motivated and to maintain a high standard of work at all times.

Often painters and decorators work in teams or pairs, but they may work alone. They need to be able to co-operate and work well with others.

BUILDING AND CONSTRUCTION TRADES: UF

A head for heights is required, as it is necessary to work from ladders or scaffolding.

ENTRY REQUIREMENTS, TRAINING, LATE ENTRY

Please see article 1. BRICKLAYER.

OPPORTUNITIES

Painters and decorators are employed by building contractors, specialist painting contractors, local and national bodies. Some painting and decorating firms concentrate on particular techniques, such as Artexing, marbling or graining, or on high-quality work for prestigious clients, such as banks.

Many painters and decorators are self-employed; they may work as subcontractors and/or for private householders.

There is always a demand for painters and decorators, and the level of demand is fairly constant. However, the type of work depends on the state of the housing market and other local and national factors. During a housing boom, there is more contract work available, especially on new buildings; when houses are hard to sell, there is more demand from private householders who have decided to redecorate rather than move.

PAY AND CONDITIONS

Please see article 1. BRICKLAYER.

PROSPECTS

Promotion is usually to a supervisory position, organizing the work of others in the same specialist craft. Beyond this, a small number may progress to become general supervisors in charge of a number of different trades.

RELATED OCCUPATIONS

Carpenter/joiner, bricklayer, plasterer, electrician, scaffolder, glazier, floor/wall/ceiling tiler, interior designer, construction operative.

FURTHER INFORMATION AND READING

Please see article 9. SCAFFOLDER.

6. PLASTERER (UF)

THE WORK

There are two types of plastering – solid and fibrous.

Solid plastering

The plaster used is not mixed with any hair or fibre to help hold it together. This is the usual type of work associated with plasterers and involves working mainly on the inside of buildings, plastering walls and ceilings, putting down solid flooring, and fitting cornices and mouldings. Plasterers may also give a protective covering to the external walls of the building.

Working on interior walls it is usual to fix angle beads (metal strips) to all exterior corners to achieve a straight and vertical edge (checked by spirit level and plumb-line). A screed of rough plaster is then applied to the wall to form a box around the area to be covered. Once these horizontal and vertical bands are done the rest of the wall is covered up to the level of the screed. The plaster is then ruled off level and the surface scratched with a bevel (board with nails) to provide a key for the final fine coat of plaster. Some high-quality jobs require three coats. The final coat is smoothed over with a water brush and trowel.

Floors are built up in the same way as walls, with plaster or cement screeds on top of which various floor coverings can be laid. Various qualities of floor plasters are available; some are tough enough for hard-wearing use, for indoor car parks, for example, and some plasterers specialize in this sort of work.

Exterior walls are also done in the same way as interior walls except that a board is nailed up to provide a level to work to and a sand and cement mix is normally used in the place of plaster. Various finishes may be required and it is possible to give the impression of stone work, by careful marking off, or a pebble dash finish, achieved by coating the wet cement and sand mix with small pebbles. Other coverings (eg Hi-build) may need to be rollered on or applied by spray gun.

Maintenance and repair work requires the same skills and covers the same sort of work as outlined above. It also involves removing old plaster and bad patches before fresh plaster can be applied.

Fibrous plastering

This involves short lengths of fibre being used to hold the plaster mix together to produce a particular form or decorative pattern. It is the fibrous plasterer who is responsible for producing all sorts of decorative plaster work like cornices and ceiling roses found in most types of older houses, bars and restaurants, and the columns and architraves found in stately homes and public buildings. This sort of work was being replaced by the use of plastic mouldings until new fire regulations banned a lot of plastics from use in buildings.

Fibrous plasterers usually work in specialist firms that produce ornamental plaster work from moulds (synthetic rubber or resin). They may follow architect's or artist's drawings.

The fixing of the decorations in buildings can be done by solid plasterers; they are nailed or screwed into place. More complex and delicate work is usually carried out by fibrous plasterers working on site, although in some firms this is split into two jobs: with fibrous makers working all the time in the workshop and fibrous fixers working on site.

WORK ENVIRONMENT

Plasterers are less affected by the weather than other building trades, in that most of their work is done under cover. However, conditions for solid plastering can be cold and draughty.

Fibrous plasterers work in workshops, and may visit sites.

Plastering may involve working at moderate heights from ladders or scaffolding.

Travel may be necessary, including short/long periods away from home.

SKILLS AND INTERESTS

Plasterers need to be physically fit and active. The work involves continuous movement and demands good co-ordination. Plasterers spend a lot of time standing, bending and kneeling; strong wrists and arms are needed. The plaster, which is held on a board, can be quite heavy.

BUILDING AND CONSTRUCTION TRADES: UF

They should be able to work quickly but carefully to produce flat, smooth plasterwork. Good hand skills are needed for handling trowels and floats. Plasterers may work as part of a team; it is important to be able to co-operate with others.

Some artistic skills are needed for fibrous plastering and other decorative work.

ENTRY REQUIREMENTS, TRAINING, LATE ENTRY

Please see article 1. BRICKLAYER.

OPPORTUNITIES

Plasterers are employed by specialist plastering firms, building contractors, and by local authorities and other public organizations.

Many are self-employed.

PAY AND CONDITIONS

Please see article 1. BRICKLAYER.

PROSPECTS

Please see article 5. PAINTER AND DECORATOR.

RELATED OCCUPATIONS

Bricklayer, floor layer, painter and decorator, roofer, wall/floor tiler, ceiling fixer, construction operative, building technician.

FURTHER INFORMATION AND READING

Please see article 9. SCAFFOLDER.

7. PLUMBER (UF)

BACKGROUND INFORMATION

Plumbing – more accurately termed 'plumbing and mechanical engineering services' – is concerned with the installation of most systems that make a building pleasant and hygienic to work in. These include water supplies, systems of soil and waste disposal, heating and ventilation pipes and appliances.

Plumbers are also responsible for a range of external work on buildings including sheet weathering, cladding, and rainwater discharge systems – pipes and gutters – in various materials.

The role and work of the plumber provides an important service for the community as a whole. Unlike some other building trades, the plumber is not dependent on new construction work and a good deal of time may be spent on maintenance and repair work on existing properties. A house owner is more likely to call for a plumber than for any other building trade worker. The same techniques and skills used in general plumbing work are also used in more specialized plumbing work in the chemical, ship and gas-fitting industries.

THE WORK

In plumbing work the provision of water supplies and facilities can be divided into two main areas.

Internal plumbing: hot and cold water supply; sanitation and waste disposal systems; oil, gas, and solid fuel appliances; and space/heating systems. In industrial buildings, offices, shops, hospitals and schools, plumbers will be responsible for a much wider range of piped services.

External plumbing: weatherproofing joints in roofs and walls against rainwater, and conveying it away in gutters and rainwater pipes. External works may also include the covering of roofs or external walls in sheet metals or non-metallic sheet material.

Each area involves the plumber in different operations, tools and materials. The type of skill and technique required also depends on whether the work is on new property, or maintenance and repair work on existing structures.

New work

In construction contracts involving housing and industrial estates, a lot of detailed planning will have been carried out by the professional design team. Plumbers must, therefore, be able to follow drawings and instructions on the various stages of work required, including details on the types, lengths and sizes of pipes, also the kind of joints to be used. A lot of the plumbing can be assembled in the on-site workshop, leaving a minimum of assembly and jointing work to be done in the buildings. Smaller contracts involve the plumber in a lot more individual decision making.

The main tasks for a plumber are as follows:

Roof weathering – plumbers make and fit flashings or weatherings of copper, aluminium, zinc, lead or non-metallic sheet, to joints between roof tiling/slates, chimney stacks, dormer windows etc. A range of techniques, such as bossing, welting and welding, are used to form details in the different materials.

Rainwater, soil and drainage pipes – rainwater pipes and gutters are fitted to a building to take rainwater discharged from roofs. Soil pipes and drains are fitted to take the discharge from sanitary fittings. These pipes may be in plastic material, which is easily fitted and jointed, but which nevertheless must be fitted properly to avoid problems due to the high expansion rate of plastics. They may otherwise be in cast iron, with the fixing and jointing methods being dependent upon the purpose and situation in which the pipe or gutter is fixed.

Hot and cold water supply, heating systems, gas supply, sanitation and waste disposal – these are fitted as other crafts complete the various stages of the building.

A variety of pipe materials are used for the different systems, and different installation techniques – cutting, jointing, bending, fixing – are used for the different materials and systems. Each system will also have various appliances – baths, toilets, washbasins, sinks, boilers, pumps, storage cylinders, storage cisterns, showers etc – which must be correctly fitted to ensure they work properly.

Maintenance and repair work/jobbing

This is an important part of a plumber's work and many small firms specialize in this type of work. It covers all the types of work and skills required in the plumbing industry. In addition it can involve the plumber in a lot more planning and decision making than is usual in large-scale construction work. Plumbers must decide for themselves the types of material to use, the pipework layout, and how best to tackle the job. The plumber may also have to advise the property owners on the type of system required for

BUILDING AND CONSTRUCTION TRADES: UF

their needs. The type of job to be done can range from very simple to complex: from replacing a worn-out washer to replacing out-of-date pipework and installing a new system.

The plumber will also be required to carry out routine servicing on central heating installations, and must be able to diagnose and rectify faults on plumbing systems.

Plumbing in other industries

Shipbuilding: marine plumbing – the same skills and abilities as plumbers in the building industry. As well as sanitation and water supply, however, refrigeration pipework is also fitted.

Chemical: plumbers' skills and abilities are employed in the chemical industry. Due to dangerous corrosive chemicals used in the industry, lead and plastic pipes are used extensively in their plumbing systems.

Gas: this covers the provision of gas supplies to all types of buildings for central heating, cooking and refrigeration purposes.

It is also important that all plumbers ensure that systems and appliances are fitted safely, correctly, and in accordance with regulations.

WORK ENVIRONMENT

Plumbing involves working both indoors and outdoors (depending on the particular job to be done) and involves work in cold, wet and dirty conditions. Particularly severe wet and cold weather can halt external plumbing work, but even if working indoors it may be cold and draughty in properties and structures lacking any means of heating.

All plumbers often have to work in extremely cramped and uncomfortable positions fitting pipework to baths and wash-basins or crawling about under floorboards. It will also be necessary to be able to work at heights on roofs to fix flashings and gutters. This involves climbing and working from ladders and a variety of scaffolding.

It is usual for plumbers in building and jobbing work to work at a site or building until a particular task is complete and then move on to the next site or property. Usually firms will be operating locally, so requiring workers to travel no further than normal daily travelling distances.

Occasionally, and in particular with large contracting firms, it may be necessary to work away from home for a certain period of time (this can also involve working abroad). The only plumber not likely to travel to varying workplaces is the marine plumber based in a single shipyard.

SKILLS AND INTERESTS

Plumbing is a practical craft and it is important to have a mechanical aptitude and the ability to use a wide range of hand tools and equipment.

However, the plumber also requires a wide range of knowledge of plumbing systems and appliances which must be installed correctly, safely and in accordance with building regulations, water by-laws and codes of practice.

The ability to read drawings and plans, follow oral and written instructions, produce working drawings and carry out craft calculations is essential.

Since plumbers often come into contact with a company's customers, a polite and courteous manner is important. The work can be physically demanding and can involve working at heights and in confined spaces.

ENTRY REQUIREMENTS

There are no minimum stated qualifications for entry into the plumbing industry. However, most employers prefer candidates with GCSEs/S grades, particularly in technical subjects – maths, technology etc.

Some companies have formal selection tests.

A driving licence is useful as most companies operate their own vans.

TRAINING

The industry operates a traditional four-year apprenticeship scheme. Under this scheme, apprentices either go straight into employment on leaving school, with payment of a wage by the employer, or go first into government-assisted training for young people. An increasing number of employers offer Modern Apprenticeships instead of the traditional type. Modern Apprenticeships in plumbing have been developed by the National Training Organisation (NTO) for the plumbing industry and the British Plumbing Employers Council [Training] Ltd (BPEC), and is based on the achievement of NVQ/SVQ Level 3.

Modern Apprenticeships (part of the Skillseekers initiative in Scotland) have no fixed term and provide training in waged employment. Training towards the Modern Apprenticeship will be based on a combination of on-the-job training at a college, usually on a day release basis. National Traineeships (Skillseekers in Scotland) are now available in plumbing. The training outcome is the achievement of NVQ Level 2.

In all cases, once employment has commenced, the employer should apply to the appropriate apprentice registration body to take out a Training Service Agreement (or indenture) for the apprentice.

The apprentice registration bodies for the plumbing industry are: England and Wales – the Joint Industry Board (JIB) for Plumbing and Mechanical Engineering Services in England and Wales; Scotland and Northern Ireland – Scottish and Northern Ireland Joint Industry Board for the Plumbing Industry.

The Training Service Agreement is a written agreement between the JIB, the employer and the apprentice (and the parent/guardian if the apprentice is under 18 years) under which the employer agrees to pay the appropriate wages, employ the apprentice under the correct terms and conditions, and support the apprentice's training, usually at a college or training centre, for NVQs/SVQs in Mechanical Engineering Services (Plumbing) at Levels 2 and 3. Full details of the working rules and training regulations may be obtained from the appropriate JIB.

The plumbing industry has established two organizations who operate as National Training Providers for the plumbing industry. National Training Providers can provide assistance to young people in establishing employment in the plumbing industry. Please see **FURTHER INFORMATION** in article 9.
SCAFFOLDER

The Institute of Plumbing is concerned with promoting technical aspects of the plumbing industry and maintaining nationally accepted standards. Membership is available to any plumber holding technical qualifications and/or whose training and experience satisfies the Institute's Articles and Bylaws. The Institute publishes the annual directory listing over 5,000 registered plumbers in business. Details of the

BUILDING AND CONSTRUCTION TRADES: UF

Institute's other activities are obtainable from the Institute itself.

LATE ENTRY

Entrants are usually school-leavers, but mature applicants are welcome. Adults are normally required to complete the same qualifications as apprentices, over a time-span agreed with the employer, but existing qualifications may count towards their NVQ/SVQ awards (accreditation of prior learning).

Previous experience in related skills that can be transferred to plumbing (for example, certain types of engineering work) is particularly useful.

There may be specific training opportunities directed at adults available in some areas for this type of work. Candidates may have to satisfy certain conditions to be eligible. Contact your local Jobcentre, careers office or TEC/LEC for details.

OPPORTUNITIES

Plumbers work mainly with the following types of employer:

Plumbing contractors – the greater proportion of plumbers are employed by plumbing contractors or mechanical engineering services contractors. These companies range from the small one- or two-person companies to national/international companies employing 100+ plumbers. Some of the larger companies employ other skilled trades people, such as gas fitters, electricians, and welders. Where a large building is being erected, the plumbing company will usually be subcontracted to the main building contractor.

Building contractors – many building contractors, especially those involved in house building, employ their own plumbers.

Public sector bodies – local authorities, health authorities and government departments all employ plumbers who are mainly employed on the maintenance of plumbing systems in buildings.

Ship, chemical and gas industries – these represent an important branch of the plumbing industry, employing between them thousands of skilled plumbers. Plumbers in the gas and chemical industries will be employed directly by firms operating in these fields or by contracting firms.

Self-employment is always a possibility for plumbers, as for other building trade skilled workers.

PAY AND CONDITIONS

Pay rates are agreed nationally and are normally reviewed every year.

Within the JIB National Agreement for England and Wales there are three grades of plumber; the rates are: £5.98 an hour for trained plumbers; £6.70 an hour for advanced plumbers; and £7.48 an hour for technical plumbers (for a basic week of 37_ hours). Similar rates apply in Scotland. Some employers operate bonus schemes, and, on jobs where it is necessary to meet a customer's deadline, overtime may be worked.

National rates are also agreed for travelling time, accommodation allowances, tool money etc.

Plumbers with certain additional qualifications, such as the JIB Certificate of Competency in Welding, qualify for an increased hourly rate.

The standard working week is $37\frac{1}{2}$ hours, worked over five days, Monday to Friday.

It is usual for starting and finishing times to vary in summer and winter to make the most of available daylight. Construction and maintenance contracts usually have to meet deadlines and schedules, so evening and weekend overtime is common. It may also be necessary to work unusual hours if business or industrial activities cannot be interrupted for maintenance work during normal working hours.

PROSPECTS

Under the JIB structure, companies operate a grading scheme, by which plumbers are able to progress from trained to advanced to technical plumber, as their qualifications and experience increase, and according to the size of company.

NVQs/SVQs at Levels 4 and 5, when available, will enhance promotion prospects.

RELATED OCCUPATIONS

Electrician, heating and ventilating fitter/welder, domestic appliance/gas service engineer, maintenance fitter (mechanical), building technician, construction operative.

FURTHER INFORMATION AND READING

Please see article 9. SCAFFOLDER.

8. ROOFER (UF)

THE WORK

Roof slater and tiler

Despite the fact that most modern houses now use roof tiles there is still a lot of work for specialist slaters, especially re-slating and repairing the roofs of old buildings. In any event slates and tiles are fixed to a roof in a similar way.

The technique used in fitting a new roof to an old house is much the same as when working on a completely new house. First of all, reinforced roofing felt is laid over the roof timbers and secured; this increases weatherproofing. Wooden battens are then attached horizontally across the roof to which the slates/tiles are to be nailed. As slate is a natural material it varies in size and thickness. A slater must, therefore, sort slates/tiles according to size before use, needing to vary the batten distance according to the length of the slates. Tiles, although of uniform manufacture, come in a variety of shapes and materials each requiring a different approach.

When fixing slates/tiles the slater/tiler begins at the lowest part and lays them in horizontal rows; the larger slates are laid at the bottom of the roof, smaller ones towards the top. If re-using old slates any flaking edges must be trimmed down. Many modern tiles are moulded to hook over the battens and are nailed down on alternate rows.

Where surfaces meet, such as gable ends, the slates/tiles have to be cut to size. Special capping tiles/slates are fitted along the ridge of a roof. These are bedded in place with cement.

BUILDING AND CONSTRUCTION TRADES: UF

Felt-roofer

On timber roofs a layer of felt is first of all nailed down. Further layers of felt and bitumen are laid on top of this by pouring hot bitumen onto the felt surface, and laying more felt over the bitumen. Modern techniques also include using torch-on materials, a blow lamp being used to melt the bitumen on the back of the felt as it is being laid. Some roofs are then finished off with paving tiles of fibre cement, or slabs, or granite chips.

Mastic asphalter

Mastic asphalt is used to seal and waterproof concrete roofs and other flat surfaces such as car parks, bridges and basements.

Normally the work is carried out by a gang including: the potman/woman who melts the asphalt; a labourer who carries buckets of hot asphalt and pours it out for the two spreaders. It is possible for two people to do the work, one as the potman/woman and bucket carrier and one as a spreader.

For hot roof surfaces the area to be covered must have been swept clean and felt laid down first. Wooden battens are used only to mark the area being worked on and two layers of asphalt are spread using a laying float. A layer of sand may be rubbed into the top surface to form a finish.

Roof sheeter/cladder

This work involves fixing profiled/corrugated iron sheets to roofs (sheeting) and to walls (cladding). The sheets can be made of fibre-cement, plastic, steel or aluminium. The sheets are normally one metre wide and vary in length. They can be difficult to handle in high winds and freezing weather.

This work is always carried out by a team. A worker on the ground hoists up the sheets by hand or rope and tackle while the others stay up on top to position and fix the large sheets. At least two people are needed to handle and fix the sheets.

WORK ENVIRONMENT

The roofer works at heights (often several storeys high) and climbs ladders and works from scaffolding. The work is dusty and dirty at times, especially when removing an old roof; it can also be quite cold.

Travelling to sites is necessary. Some roofers work away from home for long or short periods.

SKILLS AND INTERESTS

The roofing trades suit people who like to work with their hands. It is essential to have a head for heights and be able to climb ladders and scaffolding. The work is mainly outdoors and physically demanding; roofers need stamina, agility and strength.

They need to plan out each job in advance and set about various tasks in the right order. They must be able to understand drawings, plans and written or spoken instructions. Ability to work as part of a team and get on well with other members of the gang is essential.

ENTRY REQUIREMENTS, TRAINING, LATE ENTRY

Please see article 1. BRICKLAYER.

OPPORTUNITIES

The main employers are specialist roofing companies. Roofers may be directly employed by these companies or work as self-employed subcontractors.

PAY AND CONDITIONS

Please see article 1. BRICKLAYER.

PROSPECTS

Please see article 5. PAINTER AND DECORATOR.

RELATED OCCUPATIONS

Ceiling fixer, carpenter/joiner, scaffolder, glazier, wall/floor tiler, steeplejack, roadworker.

FURTHER INFORMATION AND READING

Please see article 9. SCAFFOLDER.

9. SCAFFOLDER (UF)

THE WORK

Access scaffolding

Putlog scaffolds or bricklayers' scaffolds are erected using scaffold tubes tapered and flattened at one end (putlogs) inserted into gaps left by the bricklayer at regular intervals between the courses of bricks. Upright tubes (standards) and horizontal tubes (ledgers) are attached with fittings using a special spanner to tighten the bolts.

Existing buildings do not have gaps in the brickwork, and the scaffold is tied to the building with 'positive ties' and 'reveal pins' which clamp the structure to window apertures, arches and other convenient openings. All the tools used by scaffolders are hand operated and simple to use, such as spirit levels, string lines and plumb-lines, pulleys and winches.

In erecting scaffolding, safety regulations will need to be strictly adhered to – for example, relating to the maximum distance between uprights, minimum width of working platforms, and minimum height of toe-boards and guard rails.

Different trades also have different requirements – bricklayers require a more solid platform for themselves and their stacks of bricks so the standards have to be closer together than for a painter or plumber cleaning gutter-work. Hoists and lifts may also need to be erected so that workers and materials can be taken quickly and easily to higher levels. Scaffolders also need to ensure the safety of any passers-by below and erect safety nets, covered walkways and street-level illumination.

Access scaffolding is not only needed around the exterior of buildings. A lot of repair, cleaning and restoration work is also carried out inside buildings, such as churches. For this a tower scaffold may be used. This consists of special horizontal and upright pieces that slot into each other. The whole tower can be mounted on castors for easy movement.

Falsework scaffolding

Falsework scaffolding uses similar techniques to those used in access scaffolding but for very different purposes. In this sort of scaffolding the scaffold provides a framework to

BUILDING AND CONSTRUCTION TRADES: UF

support the wooden framework (formwork or shuttering erected by carpenters and formworkers) and reinforcement bars used in reinforced concrete structures such as large buildings, motorway bridges etc. The scaffolding is removed once the liquid concrete has been poured into the formwork and has set. With some formwork the scaffolding is designed to just slot and bang together without using bolts.

WORK ENVIRONMENT

Erecting scaffolding involves a lot of work at heights (anything from one metre off the ground to several storeys high). It also involves a lot of movement, climbing up and down ladders, and balancing on narrow structures, while building up parts of the scaffold, and carrying heavy metal poles – up to 6.3 metres long – and heavy wooden boards.

Scaffolders work outside in all weather conditions.

The work involves travel to different sites and working away from home for short/long periods.

SKILLS AND INTERESTS

Scaffolders need to be physically fit and active, and a certain amount of strength is needed. The work involves a lot of bending, lifting and carrying. A head for heights is essential.

They need practical skills and the ability to work with hand tools.

Scaffolders must be extremely safety-conscious – those working on the scaffolding depend on this.

They should be able to work as part of a team, usually of three people.

ENTRY REQUIREMENTS

Please see article 1. BRICKLAYER.

TRAINING

Training follows the Scaffolders' Record Scheme. After gaining some work experience, and with their employer's agreement, new entrants apply for a trainee scaffolder's record card. They then attend a basic training course at a CITB-approved training centre. After a year's satisfactory experience, including some formal training, they may qualify for a basic scaffolder's record card. After 18 months' experience as a basic scaffolder they may take a further course leading to an advanced scaffolder's record card. Trainees take NVQs/SVQs up to Level 3 during their training. The type of work given to an individual by an employer and its complexity will depend on whether a basic or advanced card is held.

Alternatively, the employer may send the trainee on a one-year full-time course at the Civil Engineering College (CECOL) at Bircham Newton. Here they gain a trainee scaffolder's record card, then, after six to twelve months' experience, a basic record card.

LATE ENTRY

Adult entrants may gain experience as scaffolder's labourer in order to obtain a trainee scaffolder's record card. With training and support from the employer they may go on to gain a basic scaffolder's record card. A background in relevant practical work is essential.

OPPORTUNITIES

Scaffolders work on new buildings and those that are being repaired. These include houses, factories, office blocks, steel works, nuclear power stations, oil refineries, oil rigs and cathedrals. Scaffolders work for organizations such as oil and power companies, or for scaffolding firms, which can range in size from large multinational firms to small companies with fewer than ten staff. Some scaffolders are self-employed.

There is a steady need for new scaffolders. They work all over the country in both urban and rural areas; there are also opportunities to work abroad.

PAY AND CONDITIONS

Please see article 1. BRICKLAYER.

PROSPECTS

Please see article 5. PAINTER AND DECORATOR.

RELATED OCCUPATIONS

Bricklayer, carpenter/joiner, roofer, steel erector, ceiling fixer, steeplejack, construction operative.

FURTHER INFORMATION

Careers in Construction, Construction Industry Training Board (CITB)*, Bircham Newton Training Centre, Bircham Newton, King's Lynn, Norfolk PE31 6RH, 01485 577577, www.citb.org.uk

Glass and Glazing Federation*, 44–48 Borough High Street, London SE1 1XB, 0171 403 7177

Glass Training Ltd*, BGMC Building, Northumberland Road, Sheffield S10 2UA, 01142 661494, www.glasstrg.demon.co.uk

The Institute of Plumbing, 64 Station Lane, Hornchurch, Essex RM12 6NB, 01708 472791, www.plumbers.org.uk

Joint Industry Board for Plumbing and Mechanical Engineering Services in **England and Wales** Brook House, Brook Street, St Neots, Huntingdon, Cambridgeshire PE19 2HW, 01480 476925; in **Scotland** 4 Walker Street, Edinburgh EH3 3LB, 0345 656565

National Association of Plumbing, Heating and Mechanical Services Contractors, Ensign Business Centre, Westwood Way, Coventry CV4 8JA, 01203 470626

National Training Providers for the plumbing industry:**England and Wales** BSI Training Ltd, 15 Ensign House, Westwood Way, Coventry CV4 8JA, 01203 470626 **Scotland** SP Training Services, 2 Walker Street, Edinburgh EH3 7LB, 0131 2252255

National Association of Scaffolding Contractors, 18 Mansfield Street, London W1M 9FG, 0171 580 5404

FURTHER READING

Leaflets/booklets available from the addresses marked*.

Working in Construction – COIC

In the careers library classified under UF.

BUILDING AND CONSTRUCTION TRADES: UF

10. WALL AND FLOOR TILER (UF)

THE WORK

Tilers fix tiles made of ceramics, and sometimes of other materials such as stone, terracotta or marble. Tiles come in a variety of shapes, sizes, surface textures and colours, and may be laid in intricate decorative patterns.

Ceramic tiles are fixed on exterior and interior floors and walls, and on other surfaces, for instance, in swimming pools or on worktops. Tiling is used in kitchens and bathrooms in domestic premises, in commercial settings such as shopping centres, and in industry, for instance, in food preparation areas.

Tilers work from plans, diagrams and written instructions.

Before tiles are laid, most surfaces need to be prepared. This may involve removing existing floor or wall coverings, levelling floors by putting down a layer of sand and cement (known as screed), occasionally plastering walls or, for tile panels, fixing grounds (made of timber or other materials) to walls. Tiling is also used on partition walls, where special preparations have to be carried out.

Tilers measure the area where tiles are to be laid, using a ruler, square, plumb-line, spirit level, theodolite and/or laser level. They calculate the quantity of tiles needed for the area and work out how to keep cutting to a minimum (for the sake of cost and appearance).

They select a starting point, spread a layer of sand and cement mix or adhesive with a trowel or serrated float, and onto this they lay the tiles, leaving joints in between. They cut tiles to fit at sides, around pipes, columns etc – wherever necessary. Cutting methods depend on the type of tile used; for household tiles a hand-operated tile cutter is used, whereas heavy industrial tiles are cut with a bench-mounted mechanical cutter.

The adhesive or sand/cement is allowed to dry and the joints between the tiles are then filled with grouting cement.

Sometimes the work can involve making and matching of patterns, or creating a mural effect. It may also involve the use of large or small mosaic tiles.

On larger contracts tilers work as a team, but on smaller jobs they work in pairs or alone.

WORK ENVIRONMENT

About 90% of the work takes place indoors. Locations vary tremendously and can include, for instance, shopping centres, underground stations, factories and building sites, as well as private houses. Most of the time is spent at customers' premises.

The work involves kneeling, bending and lifting. It is sometimes necessary to work at moderate heights, and in confined spaces. Adhesives, used for fixing tiles, may give off unpleasant and/or potentially dangerous fumes, but there are strict safety procedures governing their use. Protective clothing is worn as appropriate.

The work involves travel to different sites, both in the local area and further afield, and it may be necessary to work away from home for short or long periods.

SKILLS AND INTERESTS

Practical hand skills, with good hand-to-eye co-ordination, are required. Tilers need an awareness of shape and colour and an eye for the design aspects of their work. Accuracy is essential – tiles, once laid, may be in place for many years, and any faults are easily visible.

Physical fitness is important, as the work is quite strenuous. Safety awareness is essential and safety equipment or personal protective equipment – such as gloves and goggles – must be used as appropriate.

Basic numeracy is required for measuring and calculating areas and quantities. Tilers need to be able to follow quite complex plans, diagrams and instructions – both written or spoken. They need to be able to plan and organize their work carefully, thinking ahead to ensure tasks are carried out in the right order.

A polite, pleasant manner and good spoken communications skills are required, particularly for working in private houses, where the occupant may be present. It is important to be flexible, to enjoy meeting people and working in different settings.

ENTRY REQUIREMENTS

There are no minimum academic entry qualifications, although a reasonable standard of maths, English and science subjects is desirable for career progress. Entry is either direct to an apprenticeship or traineeship, or through a CITB training scheme. The CITB sets an aptitude test.

A driving licence is usually required, but young people can enter training before they have passed their driving test.

TRAINING

Training involves a three-year apprenticeship or traineeship. It follows guidelines set by the industry and is not a Modern Apprenticeship as such. Training on site is combined with block release attendance at a college or training centre. The periods on block release courses total 20 weeks over a period of two years.

Colleges and training centres running courses include: Glasgow College of Building; Salford College; Leeds College of Building; Birmingham College of Building; Lambeth College, London.

Apprentices and trainees take NVQs/SVQs Levels 2 and 3, supplemented by additional specialist courses. Specific training opportunities for young people may be available at several of the above colleges/training centres or through other organizations. Contact your local careers office or TEC/LEC for details.

LATE ENTRY

Adult entry is possible, but unusual. Experience in any practical type of work involving hand skills is useful.

Adults normally follow the training routes described in TRAINING.

There may be specific training opportunities directed at adults available in some areas for this type of work. Candidates may have to satisfy certain conditions to be eligible. Contact your local Jobcentre, careers office or TEC/LEC for details.

OPPORTUNITIES

Employment is with specialist tiling companies, which are either concerned with tiling alone or, in a few cases, with tiling and an allied area, such as plastering. They are

BUILDING AND CONSTRUCTION TRADES: UF

generally small firms: the smallest employ just one or two tilers; the largest firm belonging to the National Master Tile Fixers' Association employs around 80 tilers. Opportunities for employment depend on the state of the construction industry as a whole; in times of recession, it can be very difficult to find work or training places with tiling companies.

Tiling firms are found throughout the country, although most of them are based in towns or cities.

There may be occasional opportunities to work on contracts abroad.

Self-employment is common: many tilers work as self-employed subcontractors.

PAY AND CONDITIONS

The minimum weekly wage for trained craftspeople is £210.60p for a 39-hour week. Companies may pay in excess of this rate.

Certain projects involve night and/or weekend work.

Paid overtime may be available or required.

PROSPECTS

There are prospects for promotion to supervisory posts. It is possible to move from supervisory posts into contracts management.

Many tilers, once they have been trained and gained experience, become self-employed.

RELATED OCCUPATIONS

Floor layer, roof slater and tiler, plasterer, ceiling fixer, painter and decorator, building/civil engineering operative, professional builder.

FURTHER INFORMATION

National Master Tile Fixers' Association, Forum Court, 83 Copers Cope Road, Beckenham, Kent BR3 1NR, 0181 663 0946

Careers in Construction, Construction Industry Training Board (CITB)*, Bircham Newton Training Centre, Bircham Newton, King's Lynn, Norfolk PE31 6RH, 01485 577577, www.citb.org.uk

FURTHER READING

Leaflets/booklets are available from the address marked*.

Working in Construction – COIC

In the careers library classified under UF.

OTHER CONSTRUCTION WORK: UF/UV

1. CONSTRUCTION OPERATIVE CLCI:UF
2. CONSTRUCTION PLANT OPERATOR CLCI:UV

BACKGROUND INFORMATION

Construction operatives are employed throughout the building and civil engineering industries. They are multiskilled and carry out a variety of general tasks that are as important to the overall success of a project as any of the craft trades.

In building, they are involved in the construction of houses, factories, offices etc. In civil engineering, they work on roads, tunnels, bridges, docks, airports and roads.

Some construction operatives develop one particular area of work as a specialist occupation, particularly on the civil engineering side.

Contractors' plant, or machinery, is used in building and civil engineering to prepare the site for construction and to transport soil and materials.

Plant is particularly important in the first stage of construction, for trench digging and preparing foundations, and for roadworks. On a major civil engineering project, huge amounts of earth need to be moved and the machinery used is heavy and powerful. On smaller sites, plant that can be adapted to a variety of purposes is more suitable.

Throughout the construction process, materials need to be moved around the site, and different types of plant, including trucks and cranes, are used for this purpose.

1. CONSTRUCTION OPERATIVE (UF)

THE WORK

Building

Construction operatives play an important role in preparing the ground for building. Before holes and trenches are dug for the foundations and drains, they help to set out the areas to be excavated. This involves positioning wooden or metal stakes (profiles) at set reference points, and laying string lines between the stakes. They check line and level, so that excavation is done in the correct place.

Most excavation work is carried out mechanically, by plant operators using earth-moving equipment. However, operatives may dig shallow holes and trenches manually. They also trim and square trenches previously excavated by machine, and erect and dismantle timbering to shore up trenches. They lay drains – including pipes, manhole covers and inspection chambers – and cover them with earth, stone or rubble (backfilling).

Other tasks include:

– erecting hoardings, safety signs, barriers and temporary site huts;

– setting up and dismantling access equipment, including trestle scaffolding, ladders and small scaffolding towers;

– preparing materials for use on site, which involves mixing concrete, mortar and plaster;

– transporting, stacking and removing materials and components.

Construction operatives use, clean and maintain a variety of tools and equipment, including hand tools, power tools and small plant such as pumps and compressors. They may drive dump trucks.

All types of work may involve interpreting drawings, specifications, schedules, manufacturers' technical information and written or spoken instructions.

Some operatives specialize in assisting craft workers such as plasterers or bricklayers.

Civil engineering

In civil engineering, the work is similar to the tasks carried out in building, but also includes:

Formwork – this term is used to describe temporary moulds that support and shape liquid concrete until it hardens. Formwork is constructed from wood or metal or a combination of both, and can be made in a wide variety of shapes. Operatives assist with its erection and dismantling, taking care not to damage the finished concrete structure.

Steel fixing and bar bending – concrete structures that have to withstand heavy loads are reinforced with steel rods. The steel rods have to be bent to the required shape – a task known as bar bending. This may be carried out by specialist companies, but on smaller sites bar bending is often done by operatives. Operatives are also concerned with steel fixing – fitting the steel reinforcement in position. Some specialize in this type of work.

Concreting – operatives place liquid concrete, to make foundations, columns, beams, floors etc. The concrete is placed in several layers, vibrated by mechanical vibrators to consolidate, and the top surface smoothed off.

Steel piling – involves the insertion of interlocking steel sheets into the ground. The sheets form a temporary retaining wall, allowing earth to be removed on one side. Operatives transport, place and remove the steel sheets.

Drain laying – in civil engineering, operatives lay large-diameter pipes, for main drainage systems, for example. The sections of pipe are lowered into trenches by crane, with teams of operatives guiding them into position. Operatives seal the sections of pipe together. The trench is then filled in by a plant operator, using earth-moving equipment.

Roadworks – civil engineering operatives carry out most road building, including concreting, kerb laying, paving and surfacing. Some operatives specialize in kerb laying or slab paving. Kerb laying involves laying kerb stones in straight lines or curves, to the correct alignment. They are held in place by a concrete backing (haunching), and joined end to end with dry butted joints. Slab paving involves laying a base of stone or hard-core (rubble) and then bedding the slab on a sand/cement mix. Paving slabs are sometimes laid in patterns, and may require cutting.

WORK ENVIRONMENT

Construction operatives work mainly outdoors, on site. Conditions may be cold, dirty, dusty and muddy. They wear protective clothing, including safety helmets, ear defenders, goggles and boots.

The work involves travelling to different sites, and may involve being away from home for short or long periods.

SKILLS AND INTERESTS

A practical approach and common sense are needed. Construction operatives need an understanding of the

OTHER CONSTRUCTION WORK: UF/UV

basic terminology used in building and civil engineering, together with a knowledge of the materials used, the basic structures and the order of events in the construction process.

A good standard of physical fitness, strength, stamina and agility are required to cope with lifting, climbing ladders and scaffolding, working outdoors in all weathers.

An aptitude for team work and the ability to get on well with others are important.

Working on a construction site can be hazardous; a responsible attitude to safety regulations is essential.

ENTRY REQUIREMENTS

No minimum educational qualifications are required. However, to cope with the theoretical side of the training, GCSEs/S grades in maths, English and science are desirable.

Entrants to training schemes for young people may have to take a selection test.

Those entering the Construction Industry Training Board (CITB) Civil Engineering Apprenticeship Training Scheme should be sponsored by an employer who is prepared to give the trainee on-site training experience. The CITB is usually able to assist applicants in finding a sponsor.

A driving licence is useful, especially for the self-employed.

TRAINING

The Construction Industry Training Board's Civil Engineering College at Bircham Newton, Norfolk runs two courses:

The Civil Engineering Apprenticeship Training Scheme (CEATS) includes 21 weeks' instruction in year 1, covering personal effectiveness and general studies; industrial relations; safety, security and site knowledge; hand and power tools; excavation work; concrete; paving; formwork; steel fixing; proprietary system scaffolding; drainage and pipe laying; timbering and support to excavations; kerb laying. The remainder of year 1, and year 2, consist of on-site training, except for those who choose the option of further training as plant operators, gas distribution operatives, scaffolders or formworkers.

At the end of two years (known as stage A), trainees qualify as general construction operatives. An optional third year (stage B), including off-the-job training in more advanced skills, leads to qualification as general construction craftsman/woman.

The course leads to NVQ/SVQ in General Construction Operations at Level 3. The CEATS course is also available at the CITB's training centres in Glasgow and Birmingham.

The Construction Course includes 43 weeks' instruction in year 1, covering the following practical skills: use of hand tools, power tools and site and plant equipment; recognition and handling of construction materials; operating and routine maintenance of small plant; concreting; formwork erection; pipe laying and other drainage work; kerb laying; scaffolding; steel fixing and bar bending; timbering for trenches and shafts; levelling and setting out; road surfacing; sheet piling and oxy-acetylene cutting; project work; and an Outward Bound course. The second year consists of work experience.

The course leads to NVQs/SVQs in General Construction Operations at Level 3. Similar courses are available at other centres.

Either course may be taken through a government-assisted training scheme, or as part of a Modern Apprenticeship or an approved training agreement. A training scheme can be extended into an apprenticeship. National Traineeships may also be available. The total period of training lasts three to four years. The Construction Industry Training Board (CITB) acts as the primary managing agent for government-assisted training in the construction industry.

An alternative pattern of training is a Modern Apprenticeship or approved training agreement with part-time study by day or block release at a local college, leading to NVQs/SVQs in General Construction Operations at Level 3.

In other cases, all or most of the training may be given on the job. The trainee is placed with a skilled worker who demonstrates an operation, then asks the trainee to carry it out under supervision. It is usually necessary to repeat the operation a number of times before becoming proficient. Ideally, on-the-job training covers a wide variety of tasks, so the trainee obtains maximum benefit. Within the NVQ/SVQ framework, each skill represents a unit or element, which counts towards the eventual award. Trainees may collect a range of units at their own pace, depending on the tasks they do within the job. They may be taught and assessed at the workplace or by attending a college or training centre part-time.

LATE ENTRY

Some employers tend to favour older, more mature applicants for this type of work, particularly if they have related experience. On-the-job training may be provided. However, the CITB courses described under TRAINING are not open to adults.

OPPORTUNITIES

Construction operatives work on all types of building and civil engineering projects, from house building to motorways, bridges and tunnels.

The UK construction industry is a major employer. The industry consists of a small number of relatively large companies and a very large number of smaller building and subcontracting firms, usually with fewer than ten employees.

Operatives are very often self-employed, working on a subcontract basis for building or civil engineering contractors. They may work as 'labour only' subcontractors, with all their materials and tools provided by the main contractor.

Over the past decade, most large contractors have made substantial cuts in their permanent workforce, and now rely to a much greater extent than in the past on smaller subcontracting firms and self-employed workers.

There are, however, still some opportunities for permanent employment with building and civil engineering contractors, with local authorities and other public organizations.

Demand for construction workers varies according to a variety of local and national economic factors. In times of recession there are fewer construction projects and reduced opportunities for employment. However, although the amount of work carried out by the industry varies, there is always demand for construction.

OTHER CONSTRUCTION WORK: UF/UV

PAY AND CONDITIONS

In civil engineering, rates of pay for trainees start at around £81 a week. On completion of training the pay is around £178 a week. Employers may pay more.

Very similar rates apply in the building industry.

A 39-hour week is standard. Overtime is common, to meet construction deadlines. It may be necessary to work unusual hours if business or industrial activities cannot be interrupted for maintenance work during normal working hours.

Some jobs are short-term or seasonal.

PROSPECTS

The CEATS scheme is designed for those who have the potential to become foremen/women, after they have gained relevant experience. Others who take the construction course or receive on-the-job training may also progress to foreman/woman level. Beyond that they can move into site management, particularly if they are prepared to study for relevant qualifications such as the Chartered Institute of Building exams.

RELATED OCCUPATIONS

Plant operator, scaffolder, fencer, steeplejack, bricklayer, roofer, demolition specialist.

FURTHER INFORMATION AND READING

Please see article 2. CONSTRUCTION PLANT OPERATOR.

2. CONSTRUCTION PLANT OPERATOR (UV)

THE WORK

Plant operators operate and control machinery, usually specializing in one particular type of machine. The main types of equipment used are:

Excavators – these machines are used to dig and transport soil, clear and level sites, break up hard surfaces, and load lorries. One of the most commonly used types is a rubber-wheeled machine with a front loading shovel and bucket and a rear digging arm (often known as a JCB). Relatively small, versatile and manoeuvrable, JCBs are widely used on both building and civil engineering sites. There are also larger but less versatile steel-tracked machines, which are used for heavy digging and levelling, and machines known as draglines, with a jib like a crane, which are used for deep or hard-to-reach excavations.

Compaction equipment – includes rollers for compacting materials or soil, mainly on roadworks or civil engineering projects, and smaller machines, known as whacker plates, used for compaction in smaller or restricted spaces.

Cranes – these are used to pick up equipment and materials and deposit them at different parts of the site. They include mobile cranes, which can be moved along normal roads and are fast, efficient and versatile. Rough terrain mobile cranes are also available. The other types of crane are the conventional crane, mounted on steel tracks, which is more complicated to transport and assemble, and the static tower crane, which is bolted to a concrete base.

Trucks – dumper trucks, with a capacity of up to five tons, and dump trucks, with a larger carrying capacity, are used to carry earth, sand and other materials. Rough terrain lift trucks are used to move materials such as bricks, scaffolding and timber. Crawler loaders are used for loading heavy materials etc.

There are also various specialist machines used in road and motorway construction.

All plant has to be operated safely, and it is very important for operators to be aware of other workers close to the machine.

Plant operating frequently involves carrying out work to certain heights and depths – for instance, foundation digging. This must be done to the correct level. A banksman/woman on the ground works with the plant operator, checking the position and depth of the dig according to pre-fixed site guide rails and profiles. The banksman/woman also gives directions to the operator when visibility of any part of the operation is restricted, either by hand signals or by radio.

As well as operating plant, operators change buckets and other attachments – which can be heavy. Operators are also responsible for maintaining their machinery in good working order. They grease the machines and check the water, fuel, oil and hydraulic systems, as well as making daily safety checks.

WORK ENVIRONMENT

The work is outdoor, but much of the time is spent in the cab, which is enclosed and heated.

Conditions can be dusty and noisy (although ear defenders are worn if necessary). In winter, sites can be dirty and muddy; in summer, cabs can become very hot (although some are air-conditioned).

Some jobs (such as operating a tower crane) involve working at heights.

Travel to different sites is involved and it may be necessary to spend short/long periods working away from home.

SKILLS AND INTERESTS

Plant has the potential to be dangerous and operators need to be alert and aware of their surroundings, so as not to cause damage to other workers, equipment etc. Adherence to safe working practices is essential.

Operators need to be able to concentrate for long periods.

Good hand-to-eye co-ordination is required for operating controls.

It is important to be physically fit, as the work involves some lifting and carrying, when changing buckets, for example. Agility is needed for climbing in and out of drivers' cabs. Good eyesight (with glasses if worn) and hearing are important for following directions and maintaining awareness of surroundings. Certain medical conditions – such as vertigo or fits – are a bar to this type of work.

Some knowledge of basic motor mechanics is required, and an understanding of construction processes and materials is desirable, although this can be gained through experience.

OTHER CONSTRUCTION WORK: UF/UV

ENTRY REQUIREMENTS

Regulations require operators to be over 18 years, and because of the potentially hazardous nature of the work, some employers prefer older applicants. However, it is possible to start as a trainee at 16 years.

A full current driving licence is required.

No minimum educational qualifications are laid down. However, GCSEs/S grades in maths, English and science are desirable, particularly for those planning to take the CEATS course (please see TRAINING).

TRAINING

Training for plant operators is largely given on the job, supplemented by short courses (one week, for example) covering the operation of different categories of plant. Off-the-job induction courses are also available.

Under the Certificate of Training Achievements (CTA) Scheme, administered by the Construction Industry Training Board, construction plant operators have to demonstrate that they have attained an acceptable level of basic skills and safety awareness before they are awarded a certificate. These tests are specific to a particular category of machinery. After obtaining a CTA Operator Card for one type of machinery, additional types may be added by taking further tests. All operators are required to obtain a CTA Card.

The objective of the CTA Scheme is to ensure that all plant operators have attained an acceptable standard of basic skills and safety awareness.

Over 80 centres offer CTA testing. They include company training centres, CITB training centres and other CITB-accredited organizations.

School-leavers may train via the Construction Industry Training Board's CEATS scheme (please see article 1. CONSTRUCTION OPERATIVE). In their second year they take a 20-week course in plant operating, followed by 25 weeks' work experience.

NVQs/SVQs are available at Level 1 Plant Occupations, and Levels 2 and 3 Plant Maintenance (Construction). Assessment is built into the CTA Scheme.

LATE ENTRY

Operators must be over 18 years and employers often prefer older applicants, especially if they have experience in the construction industry, for instance at operative level.

OPPORTUNITIES

Plant operators are employed by building and civil engineering contractors and other organizations, such as local authorities, that employ their own construction workforce.

There are more opportunities in civil engineering, because this involves a greater need for plant, both for earth moving and for transportation of materials.

There are also opportunities with specialist plant hire companies.

Self-employment is common, either as an owner-operator or labour-only subcontractor. Owner-operators have their own machines (for instance, a JCB); labour-only subcontractors use contractors' plant.

It is possible to work overseas – there are some specialist employment agencies that arrange contracts.

PAY AND CONDITIONS

The basic working week is 39 hours, Monday to Friday. However, it may be necessary to work overtime in the evenings and at weekends in order to meet deadlines. Minimum rates for trainees (under 19 years) start at £69 a week. Trainees over 19 start on pay of around £130 a week for 39 hours.

After training, employed operators earn around £160 for a 39-hour week; the self-employed (labour only) earn around £220 to £240 a week. However, pay depends on the level of skill – those who are able to operate more than one type of machine may earn more.

PROSPECTS

It may be possible for operators to move into general foreman/woman positions. Beyond that they can move into site management, particularly if they are prepared to study for relevant qualifications such as the Chartered Institute of Building exams.

Experienced operators can also become plant co-ordinators, selecting the machinery used for each contract and evaluating new plant.

RELATED OCCUPATIONS

Construction operative, plant mechanic, lift truck operator, LGV driver, scaffolder, roofer, plant co-ordinator.

FURTHER INFORMATION

Careers in Construction, Construction Industry Training Board (CITB)*, Bircham Newton Training Centre, Bircham Newton, King's Lynn, Norfolk PE31 6RH, 01485 577577, www.citb.org.uk

FURTHER READING

Leaflets/booklets are available from the address marked*.

Working in Construction – COIC

In the careers library classified under UF and UV.

HOUSING OFFICER/MANAGER
CLCI:UH/CAG

BACKGROUND INFORMATION

Over the last decade, the number of people in Britain owning their own homes has increased considerably. Many people, however, still need or prefer to rent accommodation, from either local councils, housing associations (collectively known as the social housing movement) or the private rented sector.

Although government legislation has changed the role of local authority housing departments, to one of enabling other organizations to meet housing needs, the situation is variable - some tenants vote to stay with the council and some councils do not wish to transfer their stock. They are still providers, alongside their strategic role for ensuring that an area's housing needs are met – including ensuring the availability of land for building purposes. Increasingly, responsibility for providing new housing is moving to housing associations, which also own and manage properties, although local authorities still provide the majority of properties available for rent.

Council tenants are able to buy their homes. Those who remain as local authority tenants may choose their own landlords. Some groups are doing so, with the result that in some areas council estates are now managed by housing associations or housing action trusts. With the advent of compulsory competitive tendering for the housing management service, the role of the local authority in housing management is set for further change, with the possibility of private companies taking over the management function.

Various types of accommodation are owned and managed by local authority housing departments and housing associations. Apart from general needs accommodation, special needs accommodation is provided, suited to the needs of particular groups such as the elderly and people with physical disabilities.

Local authorities have, in addition, a statutory duty to house or provide temporary accommodation for certain groups of homeless people.

Some private sector landlords own large blocks of flats or other properties, which are run by professional managers. There are also a very large number of small private landlords – sole traders (owner-managers of small businesses) with a range of houses and flats.

Housing officers (sometimes called housing managers) may work for any of the above, but the work they do varies according to the type of employer.

THE WORK

Housing officers oversee the day-to-day running of rented properties on behalf of the owners, arranging for the signing of leases or tenancy agreements, organizing rent collection, arranging for any necessary maintenance work and repairs to be carried out, appointing and managing caretakers and wardens, and possibly interviewing prospective tenants.

They may allocate properties to waiting-list applicants and arrange transfers or mutual exchanges between tenants. They may also advise on welfare benefits and the statutory rights of private sector tenants.

Housing officers consult with tenants on all relevant matters. Some also attend meetings with tenant groups at which tenants can raise any problems and grievances and, sometimes, participate in decisions about the management of their homes.

As the local authority role is increasingly one of enabling other organizations to meet housing demand, housing officers working for local authorities may be called upon to assess the housing needs of particular localities and make recommendations for improvement.

Some housing officers may specialize in areas of special need such as people with disabilities, and assisting homeless people. This includes making decisions concerning whether clients are homeless in the eyes of the law, giving people assistance in finding their own accommodation, arranging for emergency accommodation or rehousing.

The work involves contact with tenants and other people concerned with housing provision such as social workers. They may also liaise with people connected with house building and repair, such as builders and architects.

WORK ENVIRONMENT

Housing officers are based in offices but spend a lot of time visiting tenants, inspecting properties and attending meetings.

SKILLS AND INTERESTS

Housing officers must be committed to providing a service, which often includes improving people's living conditions. They must be sensitive to the needs of all clients. Good interpersonal skills with the ability to communicate clearly in speech and in writing are required.

Housing officers need to be able to work on their own and make decisions and explain the reasons for these. They must learn to deal with disappointed, angry and sometimes abusive clients.

Numeracy skills are important. All housing managers are expected to work within pre-set budgets, to analyse statistics, the findings of reports and surveys and to assess priorities. Some technical understanding is required when examining structures and assessing the need for repair or improvement.

Housing officers need to be organized, with good administrative skills. Many are responsible for junior staff – housing assistants and clerical workers.

ENTRY REQUIREMENTS

Some posts require no qualifications but most employers expect or encourage staff to work towards membership of the Chartered Institute of Housing (CIH).

Full corporate membership of the CIH is open to housing workers who hold the Institute's professional qualification and who have passed the Test of Professional Practice.

Many entrants have degrees or BTEC/SQA higher national awards.

Minimum entry requirements for a degree course are usually two A levels/three H grades plus five GCSEs/S grades (A–C/1–3), or a BTEC/SQA national award, or Advanced GNVQ/GSVQ Level III, or equivalent.

Entry to BTEC/SQA higher national award courses is usually with a minimum of one A level/two H grades plus GCSEs/S grades, or a BTEC/SQA national award, or Advanced GNVQ/GSVQ Level III, or equivalent.

HOUSING: UH

Entry to postgraduate courses is with a first degree.

Housing Modern Apprenticeships (part of the Skillseekers Initiative in Scotland) for young people have been introduced. There are no standard entry requirements but employers need to be sure that entrants can benefit from training and are capable of achieving an NVQ/SVQ in Housing at Level 3.

TRAINING

A great deal of the training is carried out in the workplace. A trainee may work towards the professional qualifications of the Chartered Institute of Housing through a combination of work experience and part-time study or on a full-time course with placements in housing organizations.

There are several methods of obtaining the qualifications.

Graduates and those with a relevant BTEC/SQA higher level award (business studies, building studies, land administration, public administration or surveying) take a one-year Graduate Foundation Course and the Institute's Test of Professional Practice, followed by a two-year Professional Diploma course.

Non-graduates take a two-year BTEC/SQA Higher National Certificate in Housing Studies followed by the two-year Professional Diploma course and the Institute's Test of Professional Practice. Those who have an NVQ/SVQ in Housing at Level 4 are granted exemption from the higher national certificate.

The Graduate Foundation, Professional Diploma and higher national certificate courses are all offered part-time at universities and colleges, and may also be studied through distance learning. UNISON offers the BTEC higher national certificate and Telford College (Edinburgh) the SQA higher national certificate as distance learning courses.

Alternative routes are available through:

- a four-year degree course that includes housing placements, eg degrees in housing management and development, housing policy and management and housing studies; or
- a two-year full-time postgraduate Master's Diploma in housing that includes housing placements; or
- a three-year part-time postgraduate course recognized by the CIH.

All students must complete the Test of Professional Practice which consists of structured practical experience in the workplace. In addition, students are required to keep a logbook and complete case studies.

NVQs/SVQs in Housing are available at Levels 2, 3 and 4. They assess and certificate competent practice in housing.

Those on Modern Apprenticeships work towards an NVQ/SVQ in Housing at Levels 2 and 3. They also undertake training in communication, application of numeracy, information technology and personal effectiveness. There is no set length of time for Modern Apprenticeship training but it is likely to be at least two years. On completion of the Apprenticeship it will be possible to progress to an NVQ/SVQ in Housing at Level 4. This allows entry to the Professional Diploma course to work towards membership of the CIH. Contact your local careers office or TEC/LEC for details of Modern Apprenticeships.

LATE ENTRY

There are no upper age limits. Maturity is considered an advantage, as is previous experience in a relevant job or in voluntary work. Many people enter housing as a second career.

Adults applying for courses may find they are accepted without the normal entry requirements. They can prepare for applications to degree and higher national courses by undertaking an approved higher education Access course. Access courses are offered at local colleges and are usually one year full-time, or one to two years part-time, with daytime and/or evening attendance.

OPPORTUNITIES

The Chartered Institute of Housing has about 15,000 members.

Most housing officers still work for local authorities, which at present own about 23% of the country's housing stock. With the gradual transfer of responsibilities to housing associations, opportunities for employment with these are increasing. There are already over 2,000 associations, between them managing homes for over one million people.

Openings are also found with voluntary organizations, housing trusts, private landlords and property companies.

Employment is available throughout the UK. Most opportunities are found in large population centres.

Trainee positions are advertised in the local government bulletin *Opportunities*, in *Inside Housing* – the Institute of Housing's weekly magazine, in *Housing Associations Weekly* – the magazine of the National Federation of Housing Associations, and in the local and national press.

PAY AND CONDITIONS

Pay varies from employer to employer. Local authorities pay new entrants £11,000 to £15,000. Senior posts carry salaries of £25,000 plus. Salaries in excess of £60,000 are sometimes paid to Directors of Housing in large local authorities. Salaries in private organizations vary, but in the main are comparable with those paid in local government.

Housing managers normally work 37_ hours a week, within normal office hours – 9am to 5pm, Monday to Friday. Some overtime may be necessary as may some evening work, particularly at more senior levels. Meetings may be held out of office hours.

Flexitime systems are operated by many local authorities.

Part-time/job share posts are often available.

PROSPECTS

There is a clear promotion path in local authorities, from housing officer to senior and principal officer level and onwards to Assistant and Assistant Director posts. It may be necessary to move to another local authority in order to reach the higher grades.

Some private sector employers have similar structures but many are individually organized to reflect the services they provide. It is often necessary to change employers in order to gain higher salaries and more responsibility.

In larger organizations and housing departments it is often possible to specialize in one aspect of the work such as research, housing advisory services, homelessness, welfare benefits, housing finance, development, or administering house purchase schemes and grants.

Many housing officers work for a variety of different organizations during their career.

RELATED OCCUPATIONS

Surveyor, community worker, estate manager, local government administrator, social worker, welfare rights officer.

FURTHER INFORMATION

Chartered Institute of Housing*, Octavia House, Westwood Business Park, Westwood Way, Coventry CV4 8JP, 01203 851776

Chartered Institute of Housing in Scotland*, 6 Palmerston Place, Edinburgh EH12 5AA, 0131 225 4544

Chartered Institute of Housing in Wales*, 4 Purbeck House, Lambourne Crescent, Cardiff Business Park, Llanishen, Cardiff CF4 5GJ, 01222 765760

Chartered Institute of Housing in Northern Ireland*, Carnmoney House, Edgewater Office Park, Dargan Road, Belfast BT3 9JQ, 01232 778222

The National Federation of Housing Associations*, 175 Grays Inn Road, London WC1X 8UP, 0171 278 6571

Local Government Opportunities (LGO), Local Government Management Board*, Layden House, 76–86 Turnmill Street, Farringdon, London, EC1M 5QU, 0171 296 6600, www.datalake.com/lgo/jobsearch

FURTHER READING

Leaflets/booklets are available from the addresses marked*.

Working in Buildings and Property – COIC

Local Government Opportunities in Housing –Local Government Management Board

In the careers library classified under UH and CAG.

BUILDING SERVICES: UJ

1. **BUILDING SERVICES ENGINEER/TECHNICIAN CLCI:UJ**
2. **HEATING AND VENTILATING FITTER/WELDER CLCI:UJ**

BACKGROUND INFORMATION

Building services are all those services that help a building to run: plumbing, lighting, heating, ventilating, air conditioning, power supply, lifts and escalators, refrigeration, cabling for computers, internal telephone systems, fire alarm and sprinkler systems etc. These all relate to control of the working or living environment hence the alternative title environmental engineering. Environmental concerns have increasingly led to more efficient systems being fitted to minimize energy loss.

It is increasingly common for these services to be designed together and installed by the same contractor. In large buildings, the pipes, cables, ducting etc. needed for these services, are normally hidden from view above false ceilings or below floors, with boilers, pumps, refrigeration or air-conditioning plant in basement rooms and on the roof. The installation of these services can typically represent 20% to 35% of the cost of a building. The buildings range from houses (central heating) to offices, factories, schools and hospitals.

In practice, the title 'engineer' is used for all three grades working on the design, planning and management of this work, whether trained at chartered engineer, incorporated engineer or engineering technician level. A large design or contracting company may employ staff at all three levels, in which case the title technician may be used for the less-qualified staff. Smaller companies undertaking the less complex installations may have only engineering technicians. In some instances, heating and ventilating fitters/welders are also referred to as engineers.

1. BUILDING SERVICES ENGINEER/TECHNICIAN (UJ)

THE WORK

Building services engineers and technicians perform a range of roles and tasks in the marketing, design, estimating, planning, installation, commissioning, upgrading and maintenance of building engineering services.

A **chartered engineer** is more likely to take the more senior and managerial roles such as direct negotiation with potential and actual clients, preparing the overall designs and specifications, overseeing the whole project as project engineer or the on-site installation work as site engineer etc.

An **incorporated engineer** could carry out duties similar to those undertaken by a chartered engineer or engineering technician, though, in general, they fill more senior roles than the engineering technician.

An **engineering technician** is more likely to work as a design draughtsman/woman, estimator, purchaser (of materials and equipment), inspector (of quality of materials and workmanship), or as an installation technician. Installation technicians install the more complex and sophisticated equipment requiring a high level of engineering knowledge, or supervise craftspeople and sometimes semi-skilled workers in the more routine aspects of the work.

While work must be done with skill and accuracy, building services technicians frequently have to meet tight production schedules and deadlines. This may involve liaison with the client, the architect, civil and mechanical engineers, representatives of other contractors, craftspeople of a range of trades working on site and their supervisors etc. At higher levels this may include site meetings regarding progress, co-ordination, any changes to plans etc.

Design and draughting may be done on traditional drawing boards with a pen or on computer design terminals. Estimating, planning, scheduling and control may also involve computers. Installation, testing, quality control and maintenance may require a range of tools and instruments/meters, depending on the activity. Use of the telephone, including portable ones, will be important for communications. Accurate record-keeping and regular reports may be required.

WORK ENVIRONMENT

For a design engineer, work may be mainly in a drawing office at a drawing board or computer design terminal. For a planner or purchaser, it may be primarily office-based with occasional visits to or from customers or suppliers, or to sites. Installation work is carried out on a construction site and, for a project engineer or site engineer, a major part of the time may be spent in a temporary office on site or outdoors on site.

Work on site at different stages in the construction or refurbishment of a building may mean areas open to the wind and cold, though normally under cover, and with no heating or only temporary industrial heating. On site, a protective helmet is worn and a coat or overalls to protect clothes against dust and dirt.

Some tasks could involve dirt, dust, grease and noise. Climbing ladders and working at heights may also be required. There may be considerable walking from area to area and the work may involve standing, crouching and kneeling.

There may be long distances to travel from home to reach the work site which may change every few months. This could involve spending long or short periods away from home.

SKILLS AND INTERESTS

Mathematical ability and an understanding of physical science and engineering principles are important. An ability in design and technical drawing, as well as an interest in computers and computer graphics, are useful in understanding and creating designs and drawings.

Communications skills are needed for liaising with clients, architects, colleagues, suppliers and staff of other contractors in person and by phone, as well as for writing reports.

The ability to work with technical accuracy under pressure and yet make sound decisions is vital, as is being able to work as a member of a team. Maintenance and commissioning require the application and analytical ability to locate a fault and trace the cause before deciding on a solution.

BUILDING SERVICES: UJ

Good health and physical fitness are needed when working on site in all weathers.

Foreign languages are an asset for those wishing to work overseas.

ENTRY REQUIREMENTS

Chartered engineers follow an accredited honours degree in Building Services Engineering or Environmental Engineering. Degrees in Mechanical or Electrical Engineering are also accepted but may be less highly regarded. Courses may be three-year full-time, or four-year sandwich, with work experience periods in the industry which may count towards training requirements. Sponsorship may be available. Entry to degree courses is with five GCSEs/S grades (A–C/1–3) with two to three A levels or three to four H grades, including maths and physics. GCSE/S grade English is also required. Other acceptable qualifications are BTEC/SQA national certificate/diploma or higher national certificate/diploma.

Incorporated engineer/engineering technician: normal entry is at 16 to 18 years as a student engineering technician apprentice or student incorporated engineer apprentice for a four- to five-year apprenticeship. Entry requirement for this is two A levels/H grades in maths and physics plus four GCSEs/S grades (for incorporated engineer), or four GCSEs/S grades (A–C/1–3) in maths, physics and English (for engineering technicians). An alternative route is to take a BTEC/SQA national diploma (for engineering technician) or higher national diploma (for incorporated engineer) course full-time at a college; a shorter apprentice training may then be available. But few colleges offer such courses.

Incorporated engineers take an ordinary degree course. Engineering technicians follow the BTEC NC/HNC route.

TRAINING

Chartered engineer: a graduate engineer receives two years' training in employment. This includes induction training in the activities and practices of the employing company, and work under supervision in a number of departments including the final department, where the trainee will be given gradually increasing responsibility. After two further years' work experience, candidates can register with the Board for Engineers' Registration of the Engineering Council via the Chartered Institution of Building Services Engineers (CIBSE). On completion of the appropriate degree course and relevant work experience candidates may apply for Chartered Engineer (CEng.) status.

Incorporated engineer and engineering technician: training, in a large company, may involve some training in a training centre in more basic aspects, followed by work under supervision in different departments, involving increasing individual responsibility in later years of the apprenticeship. Performance in these will determine the job role they are finally placed in, if the company offers them a job on completion. Training will include practical skills as well as design, estimating and programming. Training includes day or block release to study both theoretical and practical aspects at college for a BTEC/SQA higher national certificate (incorporated engineers) or national certificate (engineering technicians).

Following completion of the apprenticeship and three years' work experience, incorporated engineer candidates may register with the Board for Engineers' Registration of the Engineering Council via the CIBSE. This brings the title 'Incorporated Engineer' (initials: IEng). Engineering technician candidates need a total of three years' training and experience before they can register. They gain the title engineering technician (EngTech).

LATE ENTRY

The CIBSE offers a mature candidate route for those over 35 with extended and increasing responsibility in the industry to achieve chartered engineer status.

Incorporated engineers with experience can take appropriate honours degrees to upgrade to chartered status, either full-time (possibly sponsored) or part-time on accredited courses or via Open University. Engineering technicians can also take higher national certificate plus a continuing education diploma (or higher national diploma) in their spare time or with help from employers. Experienced employees at craft or operator level may also find their experience helps them achieve higher technical or educational qualifications.

Many universities and colleges may waive the usual entry requirements for degree courses.

OPPORTUNITIES

Concerns that employ building services engineers and technicians include:

– building services departments of major building contractors;

– building services contractors, which may specialize in one area, such as heating and air conditioning or refrigeration or electrical;

– design consultancies or architectural practices that design building services installations;

– equipment manufacturers, such as lift manufacturers;

– users of large buildings, such as industrial and commercial concerns, big stores, hospitals, local authorities, or government departments, which may have building services engineers and technicians to maintain existing services, plan new ones and liaise with contractors/suppliers;

– specialist servicing and maintenance companies.

These are spread throughout the country, though the larger concerns with most employees are in cities and large towns.

For those prepared to travel, there are opportunities for employment in Europe and in other countries.

Membership of the CIBSE is 15,500, of whom 5,000 are chartered engineers.

PAY AND CONDITIONS

Pay at start of training is from £5,612 (first year) for student apprentices (technician levels). On completion of a technician apprenticeship, it is between £10,000 to £12,000. For graduate engineers, it is likely to be in the range of £13,047 to £16,026.

Those working on design, planning, estimating, purchasing and so on, normally work 36_ hours a week, Monday to Friday, with overtime when project deadlines require it.

BUILDING SERVICES: UJ

Those involved in installation or site management may have to work variable hours to suit the project. This can include weekends and evenings as overtime or with weekdays off in lieu. Servicing and maintenance, especially, may be done in evenings and weekends, and engineers may be on call to attend to breakdowns.

PROSPECTS

Promotion is to team leader, project leader, project manager or section manager, and department manager. In the larger concerns, chartered engineers will normally fill these posts, but, in many cases, it is managerial skills that determine promotion rather than qualifications. Some move on to general management positions or to become directors of companies. Others start their own companies or become self-employed as consultants, especially in the design field.

Employers may send suitable candidates on short training courses to increase supervisory and management skills and/or familiarity with new technical developments and equipment. Engineering technicians and incorporated technicians may take additional courses part-time on their own initiative, or with the support of their employer to gain higher-level qualifications.

RELATED OCCUPATIONS

Chartered electrical engineer, chartered structural engineer, quantity surveyor, incorporated electrical engineer, architectural technologist, building technician, heating and ventilating fitter/welder.

FURTHER INFORMATION

Chartered Institution of Building Services Engineers (CIBSE)*, Delta House, 222 Balham High Road, London SW12 9BS, 0181 675 5211, www.cibse.org.uk

Professional and Management Careers Service, Construction Industry Training Board (CITB)*, Bircham Newton, King's Lynn, Norfolk PE31 6RH, 01485 577577, www.citb.org.uk

HVCA Careers Service*, ESCA House, 34 Palace Court, London W2 4HY, 0171 229 1266

Institute of Domestic Heating and Environmental Engineers, 37a High Road, Benfleet, Essex SS7 5LH, 01268 754266.

FURTHER READING

Leaflets/booklets are available from the addresses marked*.

Working in Construction – COIC

In the careers library classified under UJ.

2. HEATING AND VENTILATING FITTER/WELDER (UJ)

THE WORK

Heating and ventilating fitters/welders install the heating and ventilation equipment in all types of buildings. They install pipes, boilers, pumps, radiators, control valves and other equipment associated with heating and air-conditioning systems. The materials they work with include steel, copper, iron, plastic and stainless steel.

Fitting involves the installation of parts in the correct places with the right amount of space around them. Welding involves joining different metal parts by melting them with intense heat so that they flow together and become permanently joined as they cool.

The heating and ventilating fitter/welder works sometimes in existing buildings, but more often on building sites when a great deal of the construction work has been finished. Pipes can be fitted on the surface of walls or concealed above false ceilings or in ducts constructed in brick and concrete.

For large contractors, a chargehand or foreman/woman directs the work of the heating and ventilating fitter/welders. Otherwise, their first task is to check the plans that detail where everything should go, what length and diameter of pipe is required, and where joins and bends are required. At the same time, they must check what tools they are going to need. A variety of tools are used for pipe fitting, including bending machines to bend pipes, stillsons (pipe-wrenches) that are used to tighten pipes into their fittings, pipe cutters to cut pipes to the required length, and an assortment of hand and power tools to fit valves, pumps and boilers. For welding, different types of gas and arc welding equipment are used. Fitting domestic heating systems may involve minor electrical wiring of boilers, control valves or thermostats.

Heating and ventilating fitters/welders perform a wide range of fitting work. They may start by fixing supports, which need to be stable and strong enough to support the weight of pipes and to withstand expansion stresses. They fit the pipes that link the boiler and other plant to the radiators and other heating units. They also install control valves and other parts to vary the system's output as the weather or time of day changes.

To join the pipework for the heating and ventilating systems, they may use one of a number of different welding techniques. These involve applying an electric arc or gas flame to heat and melt the parts to be joined (please see WELDER: RON) to make permanent, load-bearing, leak-tight joints in the pipes. While welding is more commonly used for joints in metal than plastic pipes, the practice of plastics welding is growing.

Protective clothing is essential, such as a hard hat, leather gauntlets and aprons, and masks or goggles for welding.

WORK ENVIRONMENT

Heating and ventilating fitters/welders frequently work on building sites, towards the end of the construction phase. The site may be dirty, dusty and unheated, and work may be required at heights or on ladders. They may also work in completed buildings that require a new or replacement system. In either case, they sometimes have to work in cramped conditions. They may have to travel some distance to particular building sites, and be prepared to work away from home.

SKILLS AND INTERESTS

Heating and ventilating fitters/welders must enjoy working with their hands and using tools. Good eye-to-hand co-ordination is necessary, and good colour vision is vital for any electrical work. Numeracy skills are needed to ensure accurate measurements and fittings.

Fitters/welders need to be able to read plans and diagrams to see exactly where different parts need to be fitted.

BUILDING SERVICES: UJ

Working very accurately is essential, as the safety of many people, as well as the efficient working of the system, can depend on their work.

Heating and ventilating fitters/welders should enjoy solving practical problems. They need to be able to work on their own initiative as well as part of a team. If they are working in someone's home, they need to exercise tact and work cleanly and tidily.

ENTRY REQUIREMENTS

Formal qualifications are not essential, but an aptitude for maths, physics and science subjects as well as English is helpful for studies at college. All potential apprentices are required to sit a numerical paper and in some cases defective colour vision may restrict entry. Heating and ventilating fitters/welders must be physically fit. A GNVQ in Construction and the Built Environment will be acceptable.

Specific training opportunities for young people, including Modern Apprenticeships (Skillseekers in Scotland), and National Traineeships may be available. Please contact your local careers office or TEC/LEC for details.

TRAINING

Training normally lasts four years, comprising on-the-job training and work experience with study leading to NVQs/SVQs. During this time, apprentices usually study at college on day release or block release.

Learning programmes designed to meet the requirements of NVQs/SVQs have been developed.

The appropriate NVQs for heating and ventilation fitting are at Levels 2 and 3 in Mechanical Engineering Services – Heating and Ventilating (MES – H&V) and include:

– MES H&V Installation Level 2 (Q1027508);
– MES H&V Installation Level 3 (Q1027509);
– MES H&V Service and Maintenance (Maintenance of System Components) Level 2 (Q1027506);
– MES H&V Service and Maintenance (Rectification of Systems) Level 3 (Q1027507);
– MES Ammonia Refrigeration Systems Level 3 (Q1027263);
– MES Refrigeration and Air Conditioning Commercial and Industrial Air Conditioning Systems Level 3 (Q1027262);
– MES Refrigeration and Air Conditioning Commercial and Industrial Refrigeration Systems other than Ammonia Level 3 (Q1027261).

The appropriate SVQs for heating and ventilation fitting are at Levels 2 and 3 in Mechanical Engineering Services (MES) and include:

– MES H&V Installation Industrial and Commercial Level 2 (SFO304703);
– MES H&V Installation Domestic Level 2 (SFO304701);
– MES H&V Ductwork Installation Level 2 (SFO304704);
– MES H&V Service and Maintenance of System Components Level 2 (SFO304702);
– MES H&V Installation Industrial and Commercial Level 3 (SG0304703);
– MES H&V Installation Domestic Level 3 (SGO304701);
– MES H&V Rectification of Systems Level 3 (SG0304702);
– MES H&V Ductwork Installation Level 3 (SG0304704).

For further details contact your local careers office, TEC/LEC or local office of Building Engineering Services Training Ltd (BEST)

LATE ENTRY

It is possible for adults to enter some training schemes, especially if they have relevant experience or skills. There may be specific training opportunities directed at adults available in some areas for this type of work. The Accreditation of Prior Learning (APL) system will help candidates to match their skills against the appropriate NVQ/SVQ. Candidates may have to satisfy certain conditions to be eligible. Contact your local Jobcentre, careers office, TEC/LEC or BEST for details.

OPPORTUNITIES

There are about 30,000 heating and ventilating fitter/welders employed at craft level in the UK.

Although the construction industry has suffered from the recession, new building work is still underway. In the south east of England, major new projects include the opening of international terminals in London and Kent linked to the Channel Tunnel and the extension of the Jubilee Line on London Underground. Elsewhere, many companies and government departments are relocating to the north and west, with business parks and shopping centres opening to accommodate the moves.

Contact companies direct for information on apprenticeship opportunities, and look for advertisements in local and national newspapers. Your local careers office and the local office of BEST may also have details.

PAY AND CONDITIONS

Heating and ventilating fitters/welders (trained craftsmen) earn on average about £290 a week. Pay, holidays and other benefits are agreed annually by the employers' association and the trade union.

Employees usually work 38 hours a week, Monday to Friday, and may be required to work shifts or overtime to meet client deadlines.

PROSPECTS

Heating and ventilating fitters/welders with organizational abilities may seek promotion to foreman/woman or supervisor. With appropriate further City and Guilds, BTEC/SQA or NVQ/SVQ qualifications, it is possible to progress to inspector or instructor. It is also possible to specialize in, for example, either service and maintenance of system components or domestic installation by following appropriate NVQs/SVQs.

For those who wish to progress to engineering technician or incorporated engineer, it is possible to become a building services technician (please see article 1. BUILDING SERVICES ENGINEER/TECHNICIAN). The usual route would be through following BTEC/SQA or NVQ/SVQ courses at higher levels.

RELATED OCCUPATIONS

Welder, sheet metal worker, plumber, engineering craftsman/woman, building services technician.

BUILDING SERVICES: UJ

FURTHER INFORMATION

Heating and Ventilating Contractors' Association (HVCA)*, ESCA House, 34 Palace Court, London W2 4JG, 0171 229 2488

Building Engineering Services Training Ltd (BEST)*, 3 Mill Court, 51 Mill Street, Slough, Berks SL2 5DA, 01753 531188

Building Engineering Services Training Ltd*, Bush House, Bush Estate, Penicuik, Midlothian EH26 0SB, 0131 445 5900

City and Guilds (C&G)*, 1 Giltspur Street, London EC1A 9DD, 0171 294 2468

Institute of Domestic Heating and Environmental Engineers, Dorchester House, Wimblestraw Road, Berinsfield, Oxon OX10 7LZ, 01865 343096. E-mail info@idhe.newnet.co.uk

Engineering and Marine Training Authority*, Vector House, 41 Clarendon Road, Watford, Herts WD1 1HS, freephone 0800 282167, www.emta.org.uk

The Welding Institute (TWI)*, Abington Hall, Abington, Cambridge CB1 6AL, 01223 891162

The Construction Industry Training Board (CITB)*, Bircham Newton Training Centre, Bircham Newton, King's Lynn, Norfolk PE31 6RH, 01485 577577, www.citb.org.uk

FURTHER READING

Leaflets/booklets are available from the addresses marked *.

Working in Engineering – COIC

Working in Construction – COIC

In the careers library classified under UJ.

LANDSCAPE ARCHITECTURE: UL

LANDSCAPE ARCHITECT CLCI:UL

BACKGROUND INFORMATION

Landscape architects, also known as landscape designers, are concerned with the planning, design and construction of the whole outdoor environment.

Landscape architecture is often associated with planning fine gardens and parks but in fact most of the work is concerned with: the grounds and surroundings of public buildings and factories; open spaces on urban estates; playgrounds and recreational areas; or urban schemes in derelict inner cities. Some landscape architects work on water catchment areas and reservoirs, coastal regions and marinas, motorways, and mineral and quarry workings.

In any development that sets out to change the existing scenery – for example, the erection of a building, the excavation of a quarry or the creation of a park – landscape architects aim to create harmony between what is new and what already exists. They try to ensure that developments blend in, with minimal environmental damage.

In addition to landscape architects, other landscape professionals include landscape scientists and landscape managers. Information about these careers can be obtained from the Landscape Institute.

THE WORK

Landscape architects ideally become involved in the early stages of a development project, working alongside architects, planners and surveyors, in which case they can suggest alterations to plans that will help the new development to blend into the existing landscape.

They work to a brief (client's instructions). A project usually begins with an initial site visit to survey and record in detail the nature of the land and soil, the condition and life span of existing vegetation, together with any features such as buildings and roads.

Many different factors influence landscape architects in the drawing up of their plans. Their designs must be practical and make users feel at ease. Scientific considerations are also important; landscape architects must know what plants will flourish where – they must, therefore, have an extensive knowledge of horticulture, geology, soil science, and local ground and weather conditions. Technological considerations – for example, what methods and materials can and should be used to get particular effects and withstand various levels of use – must also be taken into account.

Having evaluated the project bearing all the above factors in mind, they produce drawings/diagrams of their proposals plus complementary written reports; together, these documents set out the possibilities of sites within the clients' guidelines. Negotiations then take place between landscape architects and clients to produce design schemes on which both are agreed. They then produce financial specifications and estimates for the work, which must include maintenance costs.

Having produced an acceptable plan, they put the project out to tender and select contractors who will carry out the digging, planting etc. Landscape architects make regular site visits throughout the duration of the project, checking the work is progressing according to contract and the client is getting value for money. They also often negotiate the long-term maintenance contract.

WORK ENVIRONMENT

Landscape architects divide their time between office work and site visits. The office environment is normally warm, clean and comfortable, usually with good natural light for the drawing work. Site visits can, however, be cold and wet, and can also involve considerable amounts of travelling.

Those employed in the public sector may only be responsible for projects in a given area, but those in private practice may have to travel quite long distances.

SKILLS AND INTERESTS

Landscape architects must have a genuine interest in the creation and maintenance of an attractive physical environment. This requires an interest in both architecture and horticulture.

Design skills and technical drawing ability are important, since a lot of material is presented in the form of plans, sketches and detailed drawings.

Landscape architects work as part of a team alongside architects, planners, surveyors and engineers, and must therefore be able to communicate effectively, both verbally and in writing. The ability to negotiate – persuading clients to accept plans, and contractors to work to specifications – is also important, particularly for those working in private practice. Sound business sense is essential for those considering self-employment.

The work can be physically demanding, requiring site visits in all weather conditions.

ENTRY REQUIREMENTS

Entry is with a first degree or with a postgraduate qualification accredited by the Landscape Institute – the chartered institute in the UK for landscape architects.

Entry to first degree courses is with a minimum of five GCSEs/S grades (A–C/1–3), including English and maths, plus two A levels or three H grades or equivalent. Useful A level/H grade subjects include biology, botany, design, environmental studies and geography. Check prospectuses for detailed entry requirements.

Entry to postgraduate courses is with a good first degree, usually in a related subject such as planning, geography, architecture, biology or horticulture. Some relevant practical experience is useful.

TRAINING

The recognized qualification for landscape architects is Member of the Landscape Institute (MLI). To gain this qualification, it is first necessary to obtain associate membership of the Landscape Institute by completing an accredited first degree or postgraduate course.

First degree courses are available at Cheltenham and Gloucester College of Higher Education, Edinburgh College of Art/Heriot-Watt University, Leeds Metropolitan University, The Manchester Metropolitan University, Sheffield University, the University of Central England, Kingston University and the University of Greenwich.

Postgraduate courses (two years full-time or three to five years part-time) are available at the universities of Edinburgh, Newcastle-upon-Tyne, Sheffield and Central England in Birmingham.

LANDSCAPE ARCHITECTURE: UL

A degree or postgraduate qualification is then followed by a period of practical experience, normally lasting two years, and the Landscape Institute's professional practice examination. This completes the requirements for Member of the Landscape Institute (MLI).

NVQs/SVQs are available in Amenity Horticulture: Constructing and Restoring Landscapes and Designing and Specifying Land Designs at Level 3 and Amenity Horticulture: Designing Landscapes and Planning their Management at Level 4.

LATE ENTRY

All professional landscape architects must follow one of the training routes outlined in TRAINING. Adult applicants are encouraged on all courses.

OPPORTUNITIES

Over 50% of landscape architects work in private practices, which are usually small; most have fewer than ten professional staff.

There are also opportunities with local authorities, public bodies like the Forestry Commission, water authorities, and in the construction industry. Some landscape architects are employed as lecturers in higher education.

Landscape architecture is a small profession, with around 1,800 fully qualified practitioners, but it is growing fast. Most students completing courses in landscape architecture find employment in this field. There tend to be more vacancies in visually unattractive areas – such as inner cities – because in these places there is a greater need to improve the appearance of the outdoor environment.

There are opportunities to work abroad, particularly in other European countries and the Middle East.

Vacancies appear in the following journals: *Landscape Design, Landscape Design Extra, Building Design* and *Architects Journal.*

PAY AND CONDITIONS

Salaries are comparable to those earned by other similarly qualified professionals, such as architects. The starting salary for a degree-qualified entrant is around £10,000 to £16,000. Professionally qualified experienced landscape architects in private practice can expect to earn from £19,000 to £25,000 plus, depending on location and experience.

In the public sector, landscape architects normally work a 37-hour five-day week. Some employers operate a flexitime scheme. Site visits can involve unforeseen difficulties and may occasionally lead to overtime. Extensive travelling can also lead to long working days.

Hours in private practice can be long and irregular. Meetings with clients must usually be held at their convenience and may involve occasional evening and weekend working. Overtime may be available or necessary in order to meet project deadlines.

PROSPECTS

Public sector employers, particularly local government, usually have well-defined promotion structures. Senior positions are difficult to achieve, however, because of the small numbers employed.

Experienced practitioners often move into private practice, where they can aim to become partners or set up their own practice. Some may also move into lecturing at higher education institutions.

RELATED OCCUPATIONS

Architect, town planner, design draughtsman/woman, civil engineer, horticultural manager, interior designer, forest officer, landscape manager, landscape scientist.

FURTHER INFORMATION

The Landscape Institute, 6/8 Barnard Mews, London SW11 1QU, 0171 738 9166, www.l-i.org.uk

FURTHER READING

Architecture, Landscape Architecture and Town and Regional Planning – AGCAS

Working in Geography – COIC

In the careers library classified under UL.

SURVEYING AND LAND MANAGEMENT: UM

SURVEYOR CLCI:UM

BACKGROUND INFORMATION

Surveyors are involved in a wide range of roles related to the measurement, management and development of land, natural resources, buildings, other types of property and infrastructure, such as harbours, roads and railway lines. They work closely with other professionals, including architects, geologists and civil engineers, to provide expert services associated with land management and development.

Professional surveyors are supported by technical surveyors, who are less academically qualified but perform a vital role across the whole range of specializations.

THE WORK

There is a variety of different specialisms. The main areas are as follows:

Marine resource management surveying involves planning and development of marine based projects. The work can include mapping and charting, helping to extract minerals from the sea, reclaiming land, establishing and maintaining fisheries, and coastal engineering schemes.

Minerals surveyors work with other professionals, such as geologists, in the exploration of mineral deposits, from coal or gravel to gold and gemstones. The work involves surveying existing mine workings and valuing mines, quarries and mineral deposits. The valuation of mines and minerals require an understanding of the principles of rating valuation and taxation relating to the acquisition and sale of mineral assets.

When new developments or extensions to existing sites are proposed, the work includes preparing planning applications, anticipating any possible objections, negotiating with local authorities and land owners, and suggesting suitable amendments to overcome problems such as noise, dust or subsidence. They prepare contracts covering infrastructure, facilities, access rights, and infill and restoration of sites after extraction is completed.

The minerals surveyor is also likely to be involved in mine planning, including the design, development and surveying of quarries and underground mines, requiring a knowledge of earth sciences. They are responsible for ensuring the safety of mine workings and tips, and for minimizing the risk of subsidence and land movement, which could lead to claims for compensation. Once mineral extraction is completed, the quarry or mine workings must be left safe and may need to be sealed up, with the location of shafts fully recorded. Tips of mineral waste continue to be surveyed to ensure they remain stable, and arrangements may need to be made for tips to be landscaped to enhance the environment.

Rural practice surveyors are involved in a number of aspects of management and development in the countryside. They are often responsible for the management of estates, farms and forests, including financial and staff management. The supervision of agriculture and forestry activities is an important part of the job, including activities such as managing planting, ensuring the well-being of livestock, protecting crops and trees from damage and pests, harvesting and the marketing of estate or farm products. They may be employed to manage one estate or, alternatively, be responsible for a number of smaller properties.

Increasingly, this work involves the operation of leisure and recreation facilities, such as riding or golf, and perhaps the management and marketing of tourism accommodation. They may also be concerned with granting fishing or shooting licences.

Rural practice surveyors are also concerned with developments in the countryside, and advise on sales and purchases of rural holdings. Chartered surveyors in rural practice are employed to value land, property, livestock, agricultural produce and machinery, requiring a good knowledge of trends in the market. They may also organize and conduct auctions.

Planning and development surveyors in the private sector work on behalf of developers, advising them on the planning implications of their proposals. The work could include identification of suitable sites, analysing the viability of a project, preparing valuations, preparing planning applications, and negotiating with local authority planners to obtain planning permission. Developments normally have to conform to statutory requirements, such as county structure plans, and must be in line with complex legal and administrative requirements.

In the public sector, planning and development surveyors are involved in environmental planning at national, regional and local level. Working with other professionals, they help to plan where new developments, such as housing estates or shopping centres, are to be located and how competing demands for land use are to be reconciled, and priorities set. They balance the economic, social, financial and environmental benefits of different development proposals and recommend the most appropriate solution.

Planning and development surveyors are often required to prepare planning briefs, advise on legal aspects and to give evidence at public enquiries. Surveyors working in this area of the profession may also be concerned with financial arrangements and preparing tenders for building contracts.

General practice (or commercial and residential property) surveyors are involved in valuation, marketing and management of commercial and residential property, and investment management. Valuation is a key activity and surveyors are therefore experts in property markets, land and property values, valuation procedures, construction methods, property and planning law. Surveyors may act for vendors, purchasers, landlords or tenants, and visit different properties to value them.

Some surveyors specialize in the identification, valuation and auctioning of furniture, carpets, fine art, plant and machinery. This work can involve making detailed inventories, arranging for goods to be insured and safely transported to salerooms, producing a catalogue or arranging and conducting an auction.

Surveyors can also handle a property portfolio on behalf of pension funds, insurance companies, charities and other major investors, ensuring they obtain the best possible return on their investment. Property management services are provided by surveyors in all sectors of the economy, including public sector organizations, property companies and charitable trusts.

Estate agency work involves the sale and acquisition of all types of property, from a family home to an office block or industrial estate. A prime role is negotiating between the vendor and the purchaser of a property. A survey is undertaken and a valuation agreed with the vendor. It is then necessary to market the property, which is likely to

SURVEYING AND LAND MANAGEMENT: UM

include preparing written information on the property, arranging for the display of 'For Sale' signs and, perhaps, organizing press advertisements. Prospective buyers are shown the property and the surveyors may be involved in negotiations with solicitors or organizations being asked for a mortgage on the property. An excellent knowledge of property law is required, together with an understanding of local market trends and sales skills.

In some instances, estate agents may be responsible for organizing property auctions.

Building surveyors cover a very wide field of work, which frequently overlaps with other specialisms. Their work is mainly concerned with existing buildings of all types, sizes and uses. It includes undertaking detailed surveys of buildings, preparing accurate plans, advising clients on the suitability of the buildings for specific purposes, preparing schemes for conversion or repair, advising on relevant government legislation and the availability of grants.

If a client decides to go ahead with alterations to a building, the surveyor works with an architect to prepare constructional drawings, detailed specifications and obtain estimates for the work. Schemes may need to be submitted for planning approval. They also advise on the selection of contractors, then supervise the work to ensure it is undertaken according to the specification. The work involves liaising with a number of different individuals and keeping them informed of progress.

Some building surveyors are employed by local authorities and specialize in building control, which includes administering building regulations, public health legislation and improvement grants. They check plans and ensure work is undertaken to a satisfactory standard and all health and safety requirements are met.

Quantity surveyors specialize in calculating what projects will cost. In private practice, they often work in conjunction with the architect, the client and others in undertaking feasibility studies to examine the kind of building required in relation to the money available for the project. Throughout the design stage of a building, the quantity surveyor continually appraises the cost of the work being undertaken using his or her knowledge of the quantities and prices of materials being used and the labour charges likely to be involved.

When the design is completed, a *bill of quantities* is prepared for selected contractors to use as a basis for preparing tenders and detailing what they would charge for the work. The quantity surveyor advises on which estimate should be accepted, monitors expenditure as the project progresses, and arranges stage payments and final payments. It is important to keep an accurate check on the value of work in progress and to ensure any variations are agreed by all relevant parties.

Quantity surveyors also work for contractors and civil engineers. This role involves providing cost and other financial advice, preparing estimates and invoices for work undertaken, establishing the quantities of materials that will be required for a project, agreeing the accounts submitted by subcontractors and preparing work schedules.

Central and local government also employ quantity surveyors, where the type of work is likely to be similar to that performed in private practice.

Technical surveyors (TechRICS) are non-chartered surveyors who work professionally in the built environment. They work within very similar disciplines of the profession as, and often in support of, chartered surveyors, using their technical experience and technical knowledge.

WORK ENVIRONMENT

Surveyors are frequently office-based, and most spend some time at a desk dealing with administration, writing reports, or preparing plans. However, the work is likely to include external meetings and site visits in all weather conditions. Travel within the UK is an essential part of many posts and travel overseas is increasingly common. Employers may require surveyors to have a full driving licence.

Quantity surveyors and planning and development surveyors are likely to spend more time working at their desks than other branches of the profession. However, they are also involved in travelling to meetings and some site visits.

Marine resource management surveyors often work from on board a ship and must be prepared for bad weather and rough seas. Hours of work are often determined by the availability of daylight, and are likely to include weekends. They are likely to spend long periods away from home, sometimes in harsh or isolated conditions.

Minerals surveyors often work underground in mines and quarries where conditions are dirty and can be hazardous. Many posts are based overseas.

For more specific information about careers options in surveying please contact the Careers Section of the RICS (see FURTHER INFORMATION).

SKILLS AND INTERESTS

Surveyors should be practical problem-solvers, able to obtain and analyse information, apply scientific and technological principles, and reach logical decisions within agreed deadlines and budgets. A methodical approach is required, together with an ability to pay attention to detail.

It is important for surveyors to understand fully the economic, social, legal, business and environmental background to a project. They therefore need to acquire technical, financial and legal expertise.

Surveyors and technical surveyors need to communicate effectively with a wide range of different people, face-to-face, on the telephone, and in writing. It is important to be able to present complex information, views and recommendations in a coherent and persuasive manner, sometimes to non-specialists. Surveyors are usually part of a team and therefore need to be able to work effectively with others. Chartered surveyors are often project managers, and leadership skills are therefore valued by employers.

Many posts require surveyors to possess a full driving licence.

ENTRY REQUIREMENTS

The entry requirements for professional bodies vary considerably. Those undertaking a relevant course or working in surveying are, however, usually eligible to join as student members.

SURVEYING AND LAND MANAGEMENT: UM

BTEC/SQA National Certificate/Diploma in Surveying requires four GCSEs/S grades (A–C/1–3), with English, maths, science and geography being useful subjects; or a BTEC first certificate in a relevant subject, such as construction; or Intermediate GNVQ/GSVQ Level II in a relevant area such as Construction and the Built Environment/Construction; or an equivalent qualification.

BTEC/SQA Higher National Certificate/Diploma in Surveying requires at least one A level/two H grades and GCSEs/S grades (A–C/1–3), with physical science, maths, geography and economics the preferred subjects; or a relevant BTEC/SQA national award such as surveying or construction; or a relevant Advanced GNVQ/GSVQ III such as Construction and the Built Environment/Construction; or equivalent qualification.

Degree courses relevant to a career as a surveyor require a minimum of two A levels plus three other subjects at GCSE (A–C) or three H grades plus two other subjects at S grade (1–3). The GCSEs/S grades should include English and maths. A relevant BTEC/SQA national award, such as surveying or construction, or Advanced GNVQ/GSVQ III such as Construction and the Built Environment/Construction may be accepted. Consult individual academic institutions about specific surveying-related courses.

TRAINING

A number of organizations are involved in the training and professional development of surveyors:

Royal Institution of Chartered Surveyors

This is the principal body representing surveyors in the United Kingdom. To become a full member or a professional associate, it is necessary to satisfy the Royal Institution of Chartered Surveyors (RICS) in three areas: academic qualifications (a degree or equivalent), approved probationary training and experience, and professional assessment.

Relevant academic qualifications can be obtained via:

– a RICS-accredited full-time degree course in the relevant discipline, for example, quantity surveying, land management, estate management, building or surveying, and normally lasting three years; *or*

– a RICS-accredited sandwich course that includes a year of practical work experience; *or*

– employment in surveying whilst studying for a RICS-accredited degree or diploma on a part-time basis by block release, day release or distance learning.

Graduates with any degree not directly related to surveying, such as in the arts or humanities, can undertake a postgraduate conversion course. These can either be one year full-time, two years part-time or through distance learning.

After successfully completing the RICS-accredited programme, applicants may enrol onto the Assessment of Professional Competence provided they are working in a surveying environment. This professional training element will last for a minimum of 24 months, during which time candidates will be required to submit documentation for an Interim Assessment (after the first twelve months) and a Final Assessment (towards the end of the second year of training). Applicants will be required to submit the following documentation for Final Assessment:

– diary and log book (including professional development records);
– summary of experience;
– record of progress; and
– critical analysis.

Technical surveyors can start their training by working for an employer and following a part-time or full-time course leading to a BTEC/SQA national certificate/diploma in a relevant surveying subject. Those wishing to become technical surveyors may wish to join as a student of the RICS, having enrolled on their national certificate course. On attaining higher national certificate or equivalent and entering employment, they would progress to Technical Probationer status. The next step is to undertake a two-year period of structured training meeting certain competence levels before attending an interview assessment. This scheme is called the Assessment of Technical Competence.

Those over 30 years, with two years' membership as a technical surveyor, may apply for an abridged route to corporate membership of the RICS.

Architects' and Surveyors' Institute

This organization was formed by the amalgamation of the Faculty of Architects and Surveyors and the Construction Surveyors' Institute. Full membership is available to those who successfully complete the Stage 3 of the Institute's examination and have relevant practical experience. Exemption is given to those with a degree related to surveying. Licentiateship is available to those qualified to higher national certificate/diploma level. An alternative entry route is available to mature candidates with industry experience.

ISVA – The Professional Society for Valuers, Auctioneers and Estate Agents

ISVA is the principal society within the property profession involved with valuation services. There are several entry routes to become an associate of ISVA including: entry with a minimum of five GCSEs/S grades (A–C/1–3) including English language and maths; an NVQ/SVQ Level 2; Intermediate GNVQ/GSVQ Level II; or age 21 and over with relevant experience.

The ISVA Syllabus has six units, each consisting of a number of subject areas. Study can be part-time by day release at various universities and colleges throughout the UK or by distance learning. To achieve associate membership, students must pass the six units (or be granted exemption from some or all of the units) and satisfy the Professional Assessment. That is undertaken over a two-year period of approved employment and comprises a journal and an assignment.

The Association of Building Engineers

The Association of Building Engineers (ABE) was formerly known as The Incorporated Association of Architects and Surveyors and is the professional body for those specializing in the technology of building.

Student membership of the ABE is open to those undertaking a full-time course of study leading to the award of an ABE-accredited degree.

Associate membership (ABEng – senior support staff grade) is awarded to those with an appropriate higher national award with two years' relevant experience in a professional office.

SURVEYING AND LAND MANAGEMENT: UM

Entry to professional membership is through an ABE-accredited honours degree in a construction-related subject. Members have an Evaluation of Professional Competence (EPC), success at which leads to becoming corporate members (MBEng). The EPC consists of two years' approved professional experience, a project and a professional interview.

The Institute of Revenues, Rating and Valuation

The Institute of Revenues, Rating and Valuation (IRRV) is a professional body for those involved in valuation, property taxation, and local authority revenues and benefits. Full professional membership is available to those who pass the Institute's professional examinations and to those qualified members of certain other professional bodies, including the RICS and the ISVA.

Training for young people

For those aged 16 or 17 years, it is possible to enter the profession via training that includes a work placement as well as part-time study for a BTEC/SQA National Certificate in Surveying. Trainees specialize in either commercial and residential property surveying, building surveying or quantity surveying. Further information is available from the Chartered Surveyors Training Trust.

Continuing professional development

A growing range of post-qualification courses are available for surveyors who wish to specialize in a particular area, such as project management, property investment or building conversion. Surveyors may also participate in overseas technical study tours. It is also possible to upgrade knowledge and skills through distance learning programmes, such as those offered by the College of Estate Management.

Larger organizations offer in-house training to surveyors and technical surveyors in areas related to technical as well as business and management skills. Even in smaller organizations, surveyors must continue to develop their professional skills, perhaps by attending external courses or seminars, to ensure they keep abreast of new technical or legal requirements relating to their area of specialization.

NVQs/SVQs relating to surveying are currently being developed.

LATE ENTRY

Adults applying for degree or higher national courses may not need the normal entry requirements. They may prepare for application for such courses by successfully completing an approved higher education Access course. Access courses are offered at local colleges and are usually one year full-time or one to two years part-time with daytime and/or evening attendance.

Professional bodies associated with surveying are also willing to accept mature candidates and most have special late-entry criteria for those with appropriate experience. It may be more difficult for those over 30 years to find a first post, though, unless they have relevant experience.

Refresher courses are available for those wishing to return to work as a surveyor after a career break.

OPPORTUNITIES

Demand is generally good for surveyors and surveying technicians, although it does vary with the state of the property market and the level of construction activity being undertaken. There are over 73,000 fully qualified members of the Royal Institution of Chartered Surveyors.

Opportunities occur most frequently in general practice and quantity surveying as these are the largest areas of specialization. There are good opportunities for mineral surveyors and planning and development surveyors, both in the UK and abroad.

In the private sector, surveyors and technical surveyors are employed by organizations of all types, from utility companies such as British Gas or Thames Water to firms of builders and civil engineers, auction houses to rural estates.

Government departments and executive agencies employ some surveyors, including the Valuation Office Agency, the Ministry of Defence and the Ministry of Agriculture, Fisheries and Food, and the Mapping and Charting Group. Local authorities are also large employers.

Vacancies are advertised in *Building*, *Property Week*, *Estates Gazette*, *Estates Times* and *New Builder*.

PAY AND CONDITIONS

Surveying salaries vary considerably depending on age, qualifications and experience. Demand for staff in particular specialisms also has a major impact on salary levels.

A school-leaver starting work and studying part-time might expect a salary anywhere between £5,000 and £10,000. For newly qualified chartered surveyors, salaries average £24,000 dependent on location.

Progression within the private sector is likely to be based on merit with salaries for experienced practitioners rising to £30,000 plus. Income for partners, for example in general practice, depends on the profits achieved by the business.

Local authorities and other public sector organizations have salary scales although, overall, salaries are usually lower than in the private sector.

PROSPECTS

Prospects for surveyors and technical surveyors are generally good. Larger firms in the private sector and public sector organizations usually have a recognized career structure with promotion opportunities leading to managerial posts.

Promotion prospects can be more limited in smaller organizations and it may be necessary to move around to gain experience. However, these organizations can be very flexible and career progression can be rapid for the most able. It is often possible for experienced chartered surveyors to become partners in commercial organizations or even to start their own firm.

RELATED OCCUPATIONS

Estate agent, land agent, civil engineer, construction site manager, town planner, town planning technician/support staff, architect, housing manager, forestry manager, valuer/auctioneer.

SURVEYING AND LAND MANAGEMENT: UM

FURTHER INFORMATION

Architects and Surveyors Institute*, St Mary House, 15 St Mary Street, Chippenham, Wilts SN15 3WD, 01249 444505

The College of Estate Management*, Whiteknights, Reading, Berks RG6 6AW, 01189 861101, www.cem.ac.uk

Construction Industry Standing Conference, The Building Centre, 26 Store Street, London WC1E 7BT, 0171 323 5270, www.cisc.org.uk

The Association of Building Engineers (ABE)*, Jubilee House, Billing Brook Road, Weston Favell, Northampton NN3 8NW, 01604 404121

ISVA – The Professional Society for Valuers and Auctioneers, 3 Cadogan Gate, London SW1X 0AS, 0171 235 2282, www.isva.co.uk

The Institute of Revenues, Rating and Valuation, 41 Doughty Street, London WC1N 2LF, 0171 831 3505, www.irrv.org.uk

The Royal Institution of Chartered Surveyors (RICS)*, Training Department, Surveyor Court, Westwood Way, Coventry CV4 8JE, 01203 694757; e-mail: nhudson@rics.org.uk

FURTHER READING

Leaflets/ booklets are available from the addresses marked *.

Working in Buildings and Property – COIC

Working in Construction – COIC

The Ivanhoe Career Guide to Chartered Surveyors – CMI Ivanhoe in association with the RICS.

In the careers library classified under UM.

CIVIL ENGINEERING: UN

CIVIL ENGINEER CLCI:UN

BACKGROUND INFORMATION

Civil engineers are concerned with major construction projects – roads and railways, tunnels and bridges, docks and airports. Reservoirs, dams, water supply and sewerage systems are designed and built by civil engineers, so are power supply systems such as hydroelectric or nuclear power installations.

Structural engineers design large free-standing structures, such as dams, bridges, oil rigs, multi-storey car parks or office blocks. They are responsible for the foundations and structural framework of the building, making sure it is strong enough to withstand loads such as the weight of traffic or water and the forces such as heat, cold or earth tremors. They also carry out structural surveys of existing buildings and advise on repair.

Municipal engineering is the public service branch of civil engineering. It normally involves working for local government, other public authorities or utilities, on projects such as road building, traffic management, water supply or sewerage. **Municipal engineers** may undertake design, construction and maintenance themselves, or arrange contracts with consulting engineers or contractors.

Highway and **traffic engineers** are concerned with road building and traffic management. Traffic management entails assessing road use and planning one-way systems, cycle lanes, traffic lights, parking facilities etc.

Water engineers specialize in water supply, sewerage systems and pollution control.

This article deals with the opportunities in civil engineering and its specialisms.

THE WORK

Professional chartered engineers initiate, design and manage projects. Other members of the team, normally incorporated engineers or engineering technicians, translate overall plans and designs into drawings and instructions. At the design stage they produce calculations and make detailed drawings, often using computers. They may be involved in estimating costs, buying materials and planning the sequence of work. During construction they help to set out the site, using surveying instruments to check lines and levels. They pass instructions to the supervisors and craft workers and make sure that any alterations in the plan are noted and acted upon.

Professional incorporated engineers are usually team leaders within the design office or on the construction site who take responsibility for sections of the work, solve day-to-day engineering problems and advise on choices of action.

Engineering technicians apply standard techniques in practical situations.

Civil and structural engineers are involved in all stages of a construction project. The two main areas of work are design and construction management.

Design

Design is based on knowledge and structures of materials, their properties and behaviour and the forces that can be applied to them. It demands an understanding of mechanics, statics and aerodynamics, of hydraulics (the movement and storage of water) and of geotechnics (the properties and behaviour of soil and rock). Civil and structural engineers use their knowledge to create the most efficient and economic design.

The design of a project involves collecting data about the site, planning in detail, producing design calculations and drawings, plans and specifications and estimating costs. The overall plan is turned into a series of working drawings by civil engineering draughting technicians. Computers are widely used in drawing.

Structural design for large buildings involves selecting materials, calculating stresses and making drawings. Structural engineers work in liaison with the architect, builder, building services engineer and quantity surveyor. Their aim is to balance strength and safety against economy and appearance.

Construction management

Civil engineers may work as project managers or site engineers. Project management entails detailed planning; working out the sequence of operations at each stage and organizing workers, equipment and materials. Managers make regular inspections on site, checking measurements, materials and workmanship. They are responsible for the work of site engineers, buyers, planners, quantity surveyors, supervisors and craftworkers.

Site engineers make sure that the design is carried out in detail on site. First they set out the site and establish the site infrastructure (making a compound for workshops and offices, laying on water and erecting fences). Next they supervise ground preparation - excavating topsoil, laying foundations. Thirdly the main structure goes up. Site engineers mark out the positions for buildings, check measurement and levels, assess the quality of the materials and the standard of work. They give instructions to technicians and supervisors and sort out day-to-day problems, such as drainage, mechanical breakdown or the non-arrival of supplies, as they arise. They liaise with gas and electricity authorities over realigning pipes and cables, and consult with local people and pressure groups to explain what they are doing.

WORK ENVIRONMENT

Civil and structural engineers work both in offices and on site. Site work can involve working outdoors in all weathers and at heights on scaffolding or ladders.

Jobs at a senior level usually involve working on several projects, visiting sites, attending meetings and working in an office.

Engineers may work on sites away from home for varying periods of time.

SKILLS AND INTERESTS

Civil and structural engineers are both creative and practical; design and problem-solving call for creative thinking combined with a practical outlook and logical method of working.

It is necessary to be able to make neat, accurate plans and drawings and to use advanced maths to calculate stresses etc, although much of the routine work is done by computers.

Both design and management involve team work. On site, the engineer may be in charge of 100 people or more. Organizing and motivating the workforce demands qualities of leadership and the ability to deal with problems in detail without losing sight of the overall plan.

CIVIL ENGINEERING: UN

Good communication with staff at all levels is essential. Civil and structural engineers need to give clear instructions and hold discussions with everyone on the project, from the client and architect to the site supervisor and plant operatives. They also have to write regular progress reports for the management team.

Dealing with all the problems that occur on a large project, from bad weather to land slippage, demands a great deal of perseverance and adaptability.

ENTRY REQUIREMENTS

Chartered engineer

To become a chartered engineer requires from September 1999 an accredited four-year MEng degree in civil engineering or engineering science, accredited by the Joint Board of Moderators on behalf of the Institution of Civil Engineers, the Institution of Structural Engineers and the Chartered Institute of Building Services Engineers. Alternatively, you may upgrade a three-year BEng (Hons) degree by further learning. To attain the status of 'chartered engineer', the academic qualification is followed by structured postgraduate training leading to the Professional Review or examination of the professional institution.

Minimum entry requirements for a degree course are two A levels/three H grades and three other subjects at GCSE/S grade (A–C/1–3). The A levels/H grades should include maths and physics. A BTEC/SQA national award in engineering or construction may be acceptable as an alternative to A levels/H grades, as may a relevant Advanced GNVQ/GSVQ III, eg Engineering, Construction and the Built Environment, or Construction. The intake requirement is usually 24 UCAS points for the MEng and 18 points for the BEng (Hons).

Applicants with A levels that do not include maths and science may be accepted onto a foundation year preceding the first year of a civil engineering course in some institutions.

Incorporated engineer

Incorporated engineers need an accredited three-year degree, possibly a BSc or a BTech. Alternatively an accredited Higher National Diploma or Certificate in Civil Engineering Studies and further learning, followed by training at work, leading to the Professional Review or examination of a professional institution.

Minimum entry requirements for higher national certificate/diploma are BTEC/SQA national award in an appropriate subject, or four GCSEs/S grades (A–C/1–3) and the study of two A levels/H grades with a pass in at least one, or a relevant Advanced GNVQ/GSVQ III, eg Engineering, Construction and the Built Environment, or Construction. The entry requirements for the degree will be 10 UCAS points.

Applicants with A levels/H grades that do not include maths and science may be accepted onto a foundation year preceding the first year of a civil engineering higher national diploma course in some institutions.

Technician

Engineering technicians need a BTEC/SQA National Certificate in Civil Engineering Studies; or a National Diploma in Construction; or Advanced GNVQ in Construction and the Built Environment; or GSVQ Level III in Construction. They undertake further training at work in order to register as an engineering technician.

Minimum entry requirements for a national certificate, national diploma or Advanced GNVQ/GSVQ Level III are normally four GCSEs/S grades (A–C/1–3), preferably including maths, science and English, or Intermediate GNVQ/GSVQ Level II.

TRAINING

Chartered engineer

Degrees in civil and structural engineering include maths, materials applied mechanics, computing, drawing and communication skills, with structural, water or geotechnical engineering in various proportions. To become a chartered engineer, further postgraduate training is required. This is arranged by the employer and approved by the professional institution.

Schemes run by the Institution of Civil Engineers lead to a Professional Review consisting of a presentation, an interview and two essays. Successful candidates can become Members of the Institution. They are registered with the Engineering Council as chartered engineers and may use the initials CEng MICE after their name.

Those applying to the Institution of Structural Engineers complete a Record of Practical Training and sit a Part 3 exam. Success leads to registration as a chartered engineer, membership of the Institution and the title CEng MIStructE.

Incorporated engineer

The technical content of an HNC/HND programme remains at the core of the IEng qualification with each aspect being developed in greater depth and breadth. The technical content will normally include: structures, materials, geotechnics, fluid mechanics, constructional methods and surveying, an individual project and options such as highways, water treatment or structural design.

Further training at work leads to the Professional Review of the ICE or the Institute of Highway Incorporated Engineers (IHIE) or the Associate Membership examination of the IStructE. Successful candidates are registered with the Engineering Council as incorporated engineers. They gain Associate Membership of the ICE or IStructE or Fellowship of the IHIE and are entitled to use the letters IEng and AMICE, AMIStructE or FIHIE after their name.

Technician

BTEC/SQA National Certificate in Civil Engineering Studies and BTEC National Diploma in Construction include construction, drawing, applied sciences, surveying and maths.

To become an engineering technician, further training at work is required, leading to the Technician Professional Review. Successful candidates are registered with the Engineering Council and become technician members of the ICE or the IHIE.

Most technicians go on to study for a higher national certificate or diploma.

LATE ENTRY

The minimum age for registration as a chartered civil engineer is 25 years. In practice most candidates are in their mid/late twenties by the time they are ready for the Professional Review that leads to registration. There is no maximum age for registration.

CIVIL ENGINEERING: UN

Most universities and colleges welcome applications from adults. There may be some flexibility over entry requirements for applicants who lack the normal academic qualifications but have relevant work experience.

Access courses for adults who wish to study for a degree but do not have the necessary qualifications are offered at many colleges throughout the UK. They are usually one year full-time or one/two years part-time with daytime and/or evening attendance.

The Institution of Civil Engineers and the Institution of Structural Engineers have mature candidate schemes for adults who wish to become chartered engineers, incorporated engineers or engineering technicians but who lack the normal academic qualifications. Applicants should be over 35 with at least 15 years' experience in construction, including responsibility for initiating and managing projects. The scheme entails submitting essays and project reports and attending an interview.

OPPORTUNITIES

The three main areas of work for civil and structural engineers are with consulting engineers, contractors, or client organizations such as local authorities.

Consulting engineers

Firms usually specialize in certain types of project, such as roads, power stations or docks and harbours. They may work for many different clients, including overseas governments. Working with a team of technicians and quantity surveyors, consulting engineers undertake design and feasibility studies. They appoint contractors to carry out the project but supervise the work themselves.

Contractors

Contractors may undertake all types of construction, or specialize in either building or civil engineering. Civil engineers work at head office and on site. At head office they are employed as designers, planners or general administrators. On site they work as construction managers, site managers, site engineers or section heads.

Client organizations

In the public sector, local authorities are major employers of civil engineers. They work as county or municipal engineers, in technical administration or in planning departments. For water authorities they build dams and reservoirs and design water supply and sewerage systems. For dock and harbour boards they build quays, jetties etc. Civil engineers work in various departments of the Civil Service, principally the Department of the Environment, Transport and the Regions (DETR), and in research establishments.

Gas and electricity supply companies employ civil engineers to design storage, generating and distribution systems.

For transport authorities they design and construct lines and stations and plan the services.

In manufacturing industry, civil engineers are employed on the construction and maintenance or industrial plant. Oil companies use them as drilling or field engineers. In the quarrying, cement, brick and tiling industries they work as research and production engineers.

There are also some opportunities in the Armed Forces and as teachers in universities and colleges.

Overseas there are good opportunities with British firms of consulting or contracting engineers working for foreign governments, or with international oil and mining companies. Civil engineering graduates are sought after by many different types of companies due to the broad experience their degrees provide.

There are about 100,000 professional civil and structural engineers in Britain. Demand fluctuates to some extent with the state of the economy. The professional institutions provide lists of firms with approved training schemes and those willing to sponsor students. Journals advertising vacancies include: *Construction News*, *Contract Journal*, *New Civil Engineer*, *Offshore Engineer* and *Structural Engineer*.

PAY AND CONDITIONS

Salaries depend on experience and the type of employer. They range from about £12,000 for a newly qualified graduate to well over £30,000. A 16-year-old trainee technician might start at about £9,000, studying part time towards a BTEC national certificate qualification.

A 37-hour week is normal in design offices, local government and public service. On site, hours are often irregular and can include evening and weekend work with up to and in excess of 50 hours. Site engineers and managers may be on 24-hour call in case problems arise.

PROSPECTS

Progression depends very much on ability, experience and ambition. Civil engineers commonly change their jobs many times in order to gain experience and responsibility and switch between the public and private sectors. The promotional ladder can lead to posts as chief engineer, associate or partner.

The ICE, IStructE and IHIE run mid-career education courses for continuing professional development.

Higher degrees in specialized aspects of civil engineering are available and may be of advantage in applying for some senior posts. Chartered engineers with at least four years' work experience can apply for the status of European Engineer (Eur Ing).

RELATED OCCUPATIONS

Professional engineer, architect, building services engineer, building surveyor, planning and development surveyor, town planner.

FURTHER INFORMATION

The Civil Engineering Careers Service, The Institution of Civil Engineers*, 1 Great George Street, London, SW1P 3AA, 0171 222 7722; e-mail: careers//www.ice.org.uk

The Institution of Structural Engineers, 11 Upper Belgrave Street, London, SW1X 8BH, 0171 235 4535

Construction Careers Forum*, PO Box 976, London, EC1V 1PB

Construction Careers Service, Construction Industry Training Board (CITB)*, Bircham Newton, King's Lynn, Norfolk, PE3 1RH, 01485 577577, http://www.citb.org.uk

FURTHER READING

Leaflets/booklets are available from the addresses marked*.

Periodicals: New Civil Engineer (ICE), The Structural Engineer (IStructE), Highway and Transportation (IHIE)

Working in Construction – COIC

In the careers library classified under UN.

TOWN PLANNING: US

1. **TOWN PLANNER CLCI:US**
2. **TOWN PLANNING TECHNICIAN/SUPPORT STAFF CLCI:US**

BACKGROUND INFORMATION

Planning is a major tool for influencing the environment. Land is in limited supply, and the population is increasingly aware of environmental concerns. Planners have the task of balancing conflicting demands and ensuring sustainable development: protecting both countryside and urban areas from badly planned or unsightly development, while providing for increased requirements for housing, industry, recreation and transport.

Consideration must be given to social and economic factors, for example: population drift from the countryside to towns and vice versa; the need to locate new industries in areas of high unemployment; requirement for transport networks in order to get people to work; the need to undertake urban renewal projects; the rise in car ownership; changes in agriculture. All these factors bring demands for roads, housing, schools, shops, factories and leisure facilities. These must be balanced, wherever they occur, with protection of the landscape, preservation of historic buildings, wildlife conservation and minimum increase in pollution. Planners must consider the future, forecasting likely needs and developments, rather than simply aiming to solve today's problems.

Planning cannot be carried out patchily, with each region or area acting solely on its own concerns. A comprehensive town and country planning system has therefore been established, regulated by Acts of Parliament. Strategic planning sets out the broad framework of policies on development over a given period. Local planning translates these broad proposals into much more detailed plans for specific areas.

Planning decisions are taken ultimately by politicians at either national or local level. Professionally qualified planners prepare and co-ordinate plans for the development of particular areas and advise councillors or ministers on the benefits and drawbacks of various possible solutions. They may also work as private consultants for developers and environmental organizations. They are assisted by town planning technicians/support staff, differently qualified, but working in an important support role.

1. TOWN PLANNER (US)

THE WORK

A town planner's prime task is to find and evaluate information in order to make judgements. They conduct research, carry out surveys and analyse information, before presenting reports giving the different options and likely effects of these to the people ultimately responsible for taking planning decisions. Some information may already be available in the form of published reports or from censuses; some is obtained from other departments within their own councils, from health authorities, transport organizations or from the Department of the Environment, Transport and the Regions (DETR); but in many cases town planners have to devise questionnaires, take advice from other professionals such as architects, engineers and surveyors, or go out on site to assess situations themselves. They frequently make use of computers, feeding in data to construct different models.

Typical problems on which they might work include: assessing the number of people likely to move into an area over a ten-year period, their ages, and consequent demand for houses, schools, sheltered accommodation and leisure facilities; the changing nature of employment, with resulting need for different amounts of industrial or office premises; assessing the impact of a proposed new road system or industrial development on the community, examining environmental factors like noise, pollution and increased traffic; deciding whether a new housing development or shopping centre would put strain on existing transport services or adversely affect existing residents.

In all cases, planners must work within the constraints of existing legislation, national and regional plans – and finance – aiming to reach the best compromise solution.

Public consultation is an important part of the planning process. Planners try to involve residents in the early stages of preparing plans, by organizing displays in public places such as town halls and libraries and holding public meetings at which they speak and answer questions. Since people take an active interest in plans affecting their areas, and it is often difficult to accommodate the conflicting views of different interest groups, meetings are often lively affairs and planners must be able to explain the reasons behind certain proposals convincingly and evaluate people's views carefully and objectively.

As one method of ascertaining people's opinions and of explaining planning policies and constraints, planners increasingly talk to interested groups in the community and may take part in school environmental education classes.

Their exact duties vary according to whether they are engaged in strategic or local planning.

Strategic planning is carried out at the county level or by unitary (all purpose) councils.

County and unitary planning departments prepare structure plans or policy statements, setting out: the amount of industrial development envisaged for an area, what type it should be and where it should be located; the number of houses to be built and in which areas; changes necessary to transportation systems, such as the construction of major roads and bypasses; proposals for new hospitals; protection and management of scenic areas; the consequences of major projects like power stations and mines; policies on waste disposal; and control of mineral extraction.

A structure plan with appropriate diagrams is produced, usually for a ten- to fifteen-year period, and, following public consultation and approval by councillors, is presented to the Secretary of State for the Environment, Transport and the Regions. There may be further public discussion of the main issues before the plan is adopted.

Local planning is done by district councils or by unitary ('all purpose') councils. Planners employed by these authorities, working closely with strategic planners and with colleagues in adjoining districts, convert the structure plan into a detailed local plan. This shows in more detail how any proposed changes in land use would be made, which are conservation areas and how individual properties may be affected. They discuss these proposals with potential developers and other environmental organizations and also respond to their proposals. An

TOWN PLANNING: US

important part of their work is development control or assessing applications to change the use of individual buildings or pieces of land, then advising councillors on granting or withholding planning permission. Individuals have the right of appeal against decisions, in this case to the Secretary of State, which often involves a public inquiry by an independent planning inspector (planning reporter in Scotland).

Planners in private sector consultancy work on a variety of projects. They may do projects for planning departments that sometimes contract out part of their work, or may work for groups or individuals wishing to work up proposals or appeal against planning decisions or proposals. In this case they investigate all the likely implications of the local authority's/central government's proposals and write a report. Many planners specialize as their career develops, for example, in economic development, transport planning, development control, recreation or minerals planning.

WORK ENVIRONMENT

Planners spend most of their time in offices, although they make site visits from time to time. When out on site they can be working in all weathers. They may spend considerable amounts of time in travelling to attend meetings or conduct surveys. A driving licence is useful and, in many jobs, essential.

SKILLS AND INTERESTS

Planners need an interest in the environment and its effect on people's lives and in the future.

They must be aware of the needs of all sections of the community, yet be capable of working realistically within environmental, legal and financial constraints.

They must be able to communicate with a wide range of people, from fellow professionals – they often work in teams with architects, landscape architects, civil engineers and surveyors – to elected politicians and members of the public.

It is important to be able to write clear reports in language that is non-technical and is easily understood. As they become more senior they need to develop public speaking skills in order to present reports at council meetings, address public meetings and conduct or defend planning application appeals.

The work involves researching and analysing a wide range of subjects including law, housing and economics. Much of the information is technical or in chart, graph or statistical form, and increasing use is made of computers.

They need administrative and managerial skills in order to be able to organize their own workloads and supervise the work of junior staff.

ENTRY REQUIREMENTS

Minimum entry requirements to degree courses are normally five GCSEs/S grades (A–C/1–3) plus two A levels/three H grades (useful subjects are English, maths and history, or geography or a foreign language), or a relevant BTEC/SQA national certificate or diploma, or equivalent.

Full details of entry requirements can be obtained from individual educational institutions.

TRAINING

There are three possible routes to qualification as a planner:

1. By following one of the four-year full-time or five-year sandwich degree courses that are accredited by the Royal Town Planning Institute (RTPI) as fulfilling the academic requirements for membership. These are available at a number of universities and, at some, may be studied on a part-time basis while in employment.

2. By taking a postgraduate degree or diploma that also fulfils the academic requirements for RTPI membership. Courses last for two years full-time or three years part-time. In order to gain entry to one of these courses it is normally necessary to have a first degree in a relevant subject such as geography, geology, ecology, economics, architecture, statistics, landscape architecture or transportation.

3. `The Joint Distance Learning MA/Diploma in Town Planning course is also available. This comprises eight courses, five provided by the Open University and three jointly by a consortium of four Planning Schools (at the University of the West of England at Bristol, Dundee University, Leeds Metropolitan University, and South Bank University, London). This permits people to qualify at their own pace through home study. No formal entry requirements are stipulated although a graduate entry route is available which comprises two Open University courses plus three planning courses.

In order to become a member of the RTPI, it is necessary, in addition to passing the academic stage, to complete: *either* two years' experience in professional work directly related to town planning (one year post qualification if a sandwich course was taken); *or* the part-time equivalent if work and study are combined. Normally, one year must have been completed after passing all the relevant examinations. Applicants for membership must provide a brief summary of the work undertaken, a statement of experience and be proposed by two chartered town planners (ie members of the RTPI).

LATE ENTRY

Mature entrants over 25 years who can demonstrate they are capable of postgraduate level study and who have relevant qualifications or experience may be admitted to the postgraduate courses through a special entry scheme.

OPPORTUNITIES

Planning is a comparatively small but growing profession. The RTPI has over 17,000 full and student members.

Around 60% of qualified planners work in the public sector – for a total of over 500 separate organizations.

Those working for local authorities are employed by county, unitary or district councils. A small number work for central government departments – for the Department of the Environment, Transport and the Regions (DETR) or for the Scottish or Welsh Offices – where their role is to co-ordinate local planning policies to ensure they are in line with national and regional policies. Some may work for other government-funded organizations.

There are increasing openings in private practice. There are now over 1,250 planning consultancies that may conduct work for people making planning appeals or carry out projects on a fee-paying basis for central and local

TOWN PLANNING: US

government departments. As a result, there are many more opportunities to move between the public and private sectors during the course of a planning career. It is common practice to gain experience in local government before moving to the private sector, although this is not always the case.

Other opportunities exist with tourist boards, water companies, health authorities, construction companies and environmental organizations.

RTPI qualifications are widely recognized internationally. A small number of British planners are employed in over 70 countries. There are increasing opportunities in the EU for qualified planners able to speak another European language.

PAY AND CONDITIONS

Salaries vary with different employers. Local authorities no longer operate standard salary rates nationally. However, many professional staff are initially on a scale from £12,500 to £19,000, with planners who already possess RTPI membership being appointed well above the minimum. Experienced planners might expect a salary between £19,000 and £29,000, and those in senior jobs, considerably more.

Planners employed in central and local government usually work a 37-hour week. Many authorities operate a flexitime system. Staff reporting to committees often have to attend evening meetings. Hours worked in consultancies are more variable, depending on the flow of work. Periods of long hours worked to meet a deadline may be balanced by quieter times.

Job sharing and flexible work patterns are becoming more common.

PROSPECTS

Formal career and promotion structures exist within local government, although the number of very senior posts is limited. Mobility is usually required to gain promotion, and many young planners choose in any case to move several times during the early stages of their careers in order to gain breadth of experience in different areas and different sectors of employment.

In the private sector it is possible to become self-employed or to open one's own consultancy business after suitable experience.

RELATED OCCUPATIONS

Architect, civil engineer, surveyor, housing manager, town planning technician/support staff.

FURTHER INFORMATION AND READING

Please see article 2. TOWN PLANNING TECHNICIAN/SUPPORT STAFF.

2. TOWN PLANNING TECHNICIAN/SUPPORT STAFF (US)

THE WORK

Town planning support staff, sometimes known as technicians, technical assistants or technical officers, are important members of the planning team, providing essential support to professional staff and carrying out many of the tasks connected with planning work.

Although they are less concerned with policy, they have greater technical skills in some areas of planning work, notably analysis of data, collection of information and use of computers.

Planning departments have to store large quantities of records – plans, photographs, maps, reports and notes on listed buildings. Support staff help to organize, index and store these; make limited revisions to maps; and produce extracts, enlargements or reductions from maps and charts when required.

They help to collect and analyse planning information required by the professional planners. Some of the information is already available from published reports – the census and statistics on, for example, population and employment trends – but some has to be acquired. Support staff do this by helping to conduct surveys – first devising questions and identifying the right people to ask and in some cases conducting the survey. Analysing the collected information, usually with the help of the computer, is the next stage. Finally, they write a report and may produce costings.

They assist with much of the administration connected with development control by recording and checking on the progress of planning permission applications. They may be required to deal with written or verbal enquiries in connection with these from members of the public or councillors on the planning committee.

Meeting and dealing with the public is often an important part of their work. They are heavily involved in the process of public consultation, setting up exhibitions, writing leaflets and making available relevant maps, charts and drawings.

Support staff may also work as planning administrators or planning enforcement officers.

WORK ENVIRONMENT

Planning support staff spend most of their time in the office, but they may do some outdoor work, accompanying planners on site visits. They also travel to various venues when arranging exhibitions, and may carry out field surveys, which involves interviewing the public.

It is useful to hold a driving licence.

SKILLS AND INTERESTS

Support staff must be able to work accurately and neatly. They should be numerate, since they spend much of their time working with statistics.

They must enjoy working as part of a team, but also be able to work on their own. Sometimes they have to work under pressure when figures, statistics or a report are required urgently.

They need the ability to write clear reports and need good verbal communication skills as they frequently interview, or answer enquiries from, members of the public.

ENTRY REQUIREMENTS

Minimum requirements in England and Wales are four GCSEs (A–C) including maths and a subject testing the use of written English such as English, history or geography. In Scotland four S grades (1–3) are required in

TOWN PLANNING: US

subjects including maths; one from science, geography or statistics; and one from English, history, geography, economic organization or modern studies.

Advanced GNVQ in Construction and Built Environment or GSVQ at Level III in Land-based Industries may be regarded as alternative qualifications.

Some entrants have BTEC/SQA National or Higher Certificates/Diplomas in Planning or Land Administration. Some enter with specialist degrees, eg in geology.

TRAINING

Planning support staff are trained largely on the job and take BTEC/SQA national certificate qualifications by part-time study over two years. (SQA modules are available in Planning, Landscape and Townscape; BTEC has a national certificate qualification in Land Administration (Planning), devised in consultation with the RTPI.)

The national certificates include the study of: computing, construction, economics, elements of planning, environmental planning, legal and communication studies, map studies, maths, statistics, public administration and property valuation.

After obtaining the national certificate, it is possible to proceed to a higher certificate via a further two-year part-time course. This includes more advanced subjects such as data management, administrative law, development control, planning law, and social surveys.

Some local authorities and private sector employers give support staff day release.

An NVQ/SVQ in Town Planning at Level 3 is now available and is being developed at Level 4. These are relevant for planning enforcement staff and planning administrators.

While training, support staff are eligible to join the Planning Executives Association of the Royal Town Planning Institute as an associate member. With two years' experience, including at least one after qualifying, or four years' experience before qualifying, they may be able to join the Royal Town Planning Institute as a Technical Member.

LATE ENTRY

There are no upper age limits, although some employers may give preference to school-leavers. Those with relevant national certificate, higher national certificate or degree qualifications gained on full-time courses or specialist skills, eg in graphic design, survey work or information systems, are welcomed for some posts.

OPPORTUNITIES

The majority of posts are with county, unitary and district council planning departments. A very small number of planning support staff work for central government, mainly in the Department of the Environment, Transport and the Regions (DETR).

Some opportunities exist with private sector employers, although planning consultancies often only recruit experienced technicians.

Vacancies occur occasionally with environmental and conservation organizations such as the National Park Authorities and the Countryside Commission.

It is usually necessary to contact a wide range of employers and consider travelling some distance, or moving, in order to find a trainee position.

PAY AND CONDITIONS

Salaries for planning support staff employed by local authorities are paid on nationally agreed scales but vary since authorities may fix different entry points according to age and qualifications. Salaries tend to commence in the range from £7,500 to £11,000, depending on age and qualifications. Senior support staff may earn up to £15,000 or more.

Local and central government planning departments usually work a 37-hour week, many of them operating a flexitime system.

Salaries vary widely in the private sector. Hours vary according to need. When a project deadline has to be met, some overtime may be necessary.

PROSPECTS

There is a clearly defined promotion structure in local authority planning departments, with opportunities for promotion to senior support staff, responsible for the work of several staff.

Promotion to supervisory level work is also possible in planning consultancies and other organizations.

In all cases, it may be necessary to move in order to gain promotion.

It is possible for planning support staff who have obtained the BTEC/SQA national-level qualification to become a professional planner by following one of the training routes described in article 1. TOWN PLANNER. It must be emphasized, however, that this is not a recommended route for entering the profession.

RELATED OCCUPATIONS

Architectural technologist, surveying technician, surveyor, town planner.

FURTHER INFORMATION

The Royal Town Planning Institute*, 26 Portland Place, London W1N 4BE, 0171 636 9107, www.rtpi.org.uk

Society of Town Planning Technicians* (address as RTPI)

FURTHER READING

Leaflets/booklets are available from the addresses marked*.

Environmental Planning, Conservation and Management – AGCAS

In the careers library classified under US.

GROUP W – ANIMALS, PLANTS AND NATURE

1. FARM MANAGER CLCI:WAB
2. FARM WORKER CLCI:WAB
3. FISH FARMER CLCI:WAG

BACKGROUND INFORMATION

Agriculture may be defined as the large-scale raising of animals and crops to provide food. Its importance can be seen by the fact that it occupies over three-quarters of the total area of Britain and produces 60% of all the food needed in Britain. Agriculture has undergone great change, brought about by technological developments, increased mechanization and greater EU and government influence.

Farming can be divided into three main types:

– **livestock** – the raising of dairy and beef cattle, sheep, pigs, poultry, goats, deer etc;

– **arable** – the growing of cereals (wheat, barley and oats), root crops (potatoes, sugar beet etc), oil seed rape, and large-scale vegetable production;

– **mixed** – combines livestock and arable farming.

1. FARM MANAGER (WAB)

THE WORK

Farm managers are responsible for the forward planning and day-to-day running of a farm on behalf of a tenant farmer, owner occupier or commercial organization.

Farm managers have to agree policy with the farm owner or tenant. Some owners and tenants set clear guidelines while others delegate some responsibility for deciding farm policy to the manager. This may include planning the farm's budget and production targets for the following twelve months.

Record-keeping – both financial and of livestock and crop development – is an important part of a farm manager's work. Computers are increasingly used for this purpose. Paperwork can take a lot of a manager's time, although some receive help from clerical or secretarial staff.

Only on the largest of farms are managers engaged solely on administrative work. Most managers contribute to the day-to-day practical work of the farm. With livestock, this may include feeding and watering animals, supervising births, nursing sick animals and milking cows. Arable work involves driving a tractor for a variety of purposes. Work is likely to include using other machinery – such as combine harvesters and straw balers – and driving lorries.

Managers are responsible for making decisions affecting the farm, such as planning livestock breeding and crop planting schedules. They are also responsible for decisions relating to buying, for example, of feed, fertilizer and machinery, and for marketing the farm's produce.

Managers recruit and dismiss staff. They organize and supervise the work of staff, although on large farms they may delegate this to supervisory staff. There are some posts with less responsibility, such as assistant farm managers and unit managers – responsible for a pig, poultry or arable unit. Managers arrange for the repair and maintenance of the farm's buildings, machinery and equipment.

On many farms it has been necessary to diversify into other activities, such as recreation and the provision of accommodation. Farm managers oversee these developments.

WORK ENVIRONMENT

All farm managers spend time indoors carrying out administration, which involves sitting for long periods of time. The proportion of time spent on administration depends on the size of the farm. Managers of large farms spend more of their time carrying out administrative duties (though they may be assisted in this by assistant farm managers and farm secretaries). Managers of small farms are likely to spend a greater proportion of their time outdoors in all weathers on practical work, which can be dirty and, with livestock, smelly. The work can also be heavy and involve standing, bending and carrying. Work usually involves driving, both on and off the farm.

SKILLS AND INTERESTS

Farming is a business, and owners employ managers to maximize profits from the farm. Ability with figures is essential. Managers must be able to prepare production targets and budgets and monitor progress towards meeting those targets within budget. Commercial sense is essential in making decisions on buying materials and equipment for the farm and in selling the farm's produce. It is also needed when considering diversifying into non-farming activities, such as providing bed and breakfast accommodation.

Farm managers should have an interest in science, as agriculture is subject to constant scientific and technological developments. They need to keep abreast of developments that can be used to benefit the farm.

They must be able to communicate effectively with staff, the farm owner and specialists such as veterinary surgeons and accountants.

Factors such as weather conditions make precise planning difficult. Farm managers, therefore, need to be good problem solvers and good organizers, and need to have the ability to make decisions.

It is important that farm managers are fit and healthy and capable of the day-to-day physical work on the farm.

ENTRY REQUIREMENTS

Most managers hold a higher national certificate/diploma or degree and have considerable practical agricultural experience. Some also hold a postgraduate qualification in farm business organization and management.

Degrees in agricultural subjects require five GCSEs/S grades (A–C/1–3) with two A levels/three H grades, two of which should be sciences or equivalent. For most degree courses it is essential to have had at least one year's relevant pre-course experience.

BTEC higher national diploma in agricultural subjects requires four GCSEs/five S grades (A–C/1–3), including English and two maths/science subjects, with one A level/two H grades, including a science; or a relevant BTEC/SQA national award; or equivalent. Applicants may be required to have practical agricultural experience before starting the course.

SQA higher national certificate/diploma in agricultural subjects has preferred entry requirements of five S grades (1–3) including maths, chemistry and English and two H grades including a science or maths; or one A level in a science and four other GCSEs (A–C); or SQA national certificate; or equivalent. For higher national certificate courses it is necessary to have had at least twelve months' practical experience and some formal agricultural training,

FARM WORK: WAB/WAG

eg national certificate.

For higher national diploma courses some evidence of practical agricultural experience is required.

Entry to supervisory-level posts may be with BTEC National Diploma in Agriculture, City and Guilds National Certificate in Agriculture, or SQA National Certificate. Please see article 2. FARM WORKER for details.

TRAINING

Degree courses last for three years full-time or four years on a sandwich basis and range from the general to the specialist. They are offered by a number of universities and by Harper Adams Agricultural College, the Royal Agricultural College, and the Scottish Agricultural College. Courses at universities concentrate on scientific, economic and management principles. Courses at the agricultural colleges combine general agriculture with practical experience and are more suited to intending farm managers.

BTEC Higher National Diploma in Agriculture courses are mostly for three years on a sandwich basis and prepare students for practical farming at supervisory level. They can be general or can allow specialization in, for example, arable, livestock or rural environment management. Courses are offered at several agricultural colleges in England and Wales.

SQA Higher National Certificate in Agriculture courses are one-year full-time and can be general or allow for specialization in crop husbandry, livestock husbandry, farm management, or poultry production. Courses are offered by the Scottish Agricultural College at its Aberdeen, Auchincruive and Edinburgh sites.

SQA Higher National Diploma in Agriculture courses are for two years full-time or three years on a sandwich basis, and are offered at the Scottish Agricultural College at the same sites as the Higher National Certificate in Agriculture. They offer a range of specializations including: crop and animal production, farm mechanization, farm management, and poultry production and management. The courses aim to prepare students for management posts in agriculture.

NVQs/SVQs in Agriculture at Level 3 are available in crop production and livestock production. In addition to units specific to crop or livestock production, each award includes personal effectiveness; obtaining resources to maintain supplies; constructing and maintaining boundaries, drains and temporary buildings.

NVQs/SVQs in Agriculture at Level 4 are available in livestock management and in crop management (NVQ only). They include personal effectiveness and organizing work, procuring resources to obtain services and supplies, obtaining and using information for problem solving, planning production and marketing produce.

LATE ENTRY

There is no upper age limit for entry to farm management but entry still requires considerable practical experience and high-level qualifications – see ENTRY REQUIREMENTS. It may be possible for adults without the normal academic entry qualifications to be accepted onto full-time courses.

OPPORTUNITIES

Farm managers are employed by commercial organizations that own farms, by tenants and by owner occupiers. There are regional variations in agricultural activity. Livestock farming takes place mainly in the uplands of Britain, with sheep farming mainly in Scotland, Wales and northern England. Arable farming is concentrated in lowland areas, particularly in the east and south of England. Mixed farming takes place all over England, Scotland and Wales.

There are approximately 8,000 farm managers in the UK, a number that has been stable. Competition for vacancies is intense and most become farm managers only after considerable experience as a unit manager or supervisor. It is often necessary to move to secure a farm manager post. Vacancies may be advertised in *Farmers Weekly*, *The Scottish Farmer* and *Poultry World*. It is not possible for many who enter as unit managers or supervisors to become farm managers. They either continue in their posts or transfer to work supporting agriculture, with agricultural contractors or in technical sales, for example.

The chances of entry into specific sectors of agriculture, such as arable, beef or poultry production, upland sheep farming, and so on, depend on their current prosperity, which is influenced to some extent by EU and government policy.

PAY AND CONDITIONS

Salaries vary widely, depending on size of the farm or unit for which the manager is responsible. Salaries may range from £9,000 to £30,000. Managers are usually provided with a rent-free tied home and use of a vehicle. Bonuses and profit-sharing schemes boost income for some managers.

There are no set working hours in farm management. Workload can vary according to season and on the pressure of paperwork. Early morning, evening and weekend work may be necessary. A 60- to 70-hour week is normal.

PROSPECTS

A promotion structure for farm managers is only possible on the largest farms.

Self-employment is an option for very few. Land to lease is scarce and very expensive; the cost of buying land is prohibitively high.

It may be possible to work abroad, for example, in New Zealand and Australia. Opportunities in Europe are limited but developing – knowledge of the appropriate European language is necessary.

There are opportunities for experienced farm managers to enter: advisory work, for example, with the Agricultural Development and Advisory Service (ADAS) or the Scottish Agricultural College; the agricultural service industries, for example, with manufacturers of fertilizers, feedstuff and agricultural machinery and equipment; or farm management consultancy.

RELATED OCCUPATIONS

Horticultural manager, forest officer/manager, fish farm manager, estate manager, marketing manager, farm worker.

FARM WORK: WAB/WAG

FURTHER INFORMATION AND READING

Please see article 2. FARM WORKER.

2. FARM WORKER (WAB)

THE WORK

Livestock and arable farms tend to employ specialist workers in those areas. Mixed farms may employ specialists in both livestock and arable work and/or farm workers with experience of both areas. In addition to their specialist tasks most farm workers are involved in farm maintenance work, such as fencing, hedging and building maintenance, although on large farms specialist staff may be employed for this work.

Many farm workers work under the supervision of a farm owner or manager. On large farms their work is overseen by forehands or supervisors. Farm workers may themselves supervise casual staff on occasions.

Livestock farming

There are some tasks common to all livestock workers whatever animals they work with – feeding and watering the animals, supervising births, giving vitamins and medication to the animals, checking on growth, maintaining hygienic conditions, nursing sick animals, and keeping records. Other activities vary according to the animals concerned, which are mainly: beef cattle, dairy cattle, sheep, pigs, and poultry.

Arable farming

Much of the work with arable farming involves driving a tractor with a variety of implements and attachments. Tasks include ploughing fields, breaking down furrows, making a tilth, sowing or drilling seeds, fertilizing, planting, spraying crops, digging ditches and trimming hedges. Other machinery is used, including combine harvesters, straw balers, mowers and forage harvesters.

Farm workers also operate fixed plant, such as grain-drying, storage and milking machines. They also maintain machinery, drive lorries, and prepare and pack crops for dispatch.

Mixed farming

On mixed farms, livestock and arable specialists carry out the tasks described above but are also expected on occasion to get involved in work outside their specialism. Mixed farms also employ general farm workers who are involved with both livestock and arable farming.

WORK ENVIRONMENT

Most farm workers spend the majority of their time outdoors in all weathers. Work can be dirty and, with livestock, smelly. It can be heavy and involve standing, bending and carrying. With some intensive livestock farming, such as poultry or pig production, much of the work is indoors. Many farm workers drive lorries on the farm and for collection and delivery purposes. Arable farming involves much tractor driving.

SKILLS AND INTERESTS

Farm workers should have an interest in science in order to understand the process of rearing livestock or growing crops.

Practical ability is important as is adaptability, as most farm workers have to carry out a variety of tasks. It is helpful if farm workers have an interest in mechanics and can cope with maintenance and simple repairs, as much farm work involves the use of machinery. All farm workers must work carefully and safely.

Numeracy is necessary for such tasks as weighing feed and calculating fertilizer use. Farm workers need to be able to keep written records, for example, of livestock development.

Livestock workers should enjoy working with animals but should not be sentimental about them.

Farm workers should be able to follow spoken and written instructions and carry them out accurately. Farm work can be routine but the well-being of livestock and the growth of crops can depend on that routine being followed closely. Workers should not mind working alone for long periods of time.

Farm workers must be fit, healthy and capable of physically demanding work. They should be prepared to work outside in all weathers.

ENTRY REQUIREMENTS

There are no minimum qualifications required for entry to farm work.

School-leavers may enter direct or follow a full-time course. Most direct-entry school-leavers begin on work-based training.

Entry may also be possible through Modern Apprenticeships (part of the Skillseekers Initiative in Scotland) leading to NVQs/SVQs Level 3. Check with your local careers office or TEC/LEC for details.

BTEC First Diploma in Agriculture – no particular qualifications are required for entry but good GCSEs/S grades are useful.

BTEC National Diploma in Agriculture requires four GCSEs/S grades (A–C/1–3) including English and two maths/science subjects, or BTEC First Diploma in Agriculture, or equivalent. Applicants may be required to have practical experience of farm work before starting the course. Completion of work-based training or the BTEC first diploma satisfies this requirement.

City and Guilds National Certificate in Agriculture (NCA) needs a good general education with some GCSEs/S grades preferred. Entrants normally have to be at least 18 years and have a minimum of one year's practical farm-work experience. Work-based training can meet that requirement.

SQA National Certificate – entry is with a good general education.

TRAINING

Young people on work-based training gain experience on a farm and have day or block release to the local agricultural college. They work towards NVQ Level 2 or, in Scotland, SVQ Level 2 and SQA National Certificate modules.

School-leavers directly employed are trained by their employer. They may attend day or block release courses at a local college and work towards NVQ/SVQ qualifications.

BTEC First Diploma in Agriculture courses are offered at colleges of agriculture in England and Wales, for one year full-time. They provide a general introduction to

FARM WORK: WAB/WAG

agriculture and usually lead to entry to the national diploma. By the end of the course students may have gained credits towards NVQs Levels 1 and 2.

BTEC National Diploma in Agriculture courses are offered at colleges of agriculture in England and Wales. They last for two or three years depending on the practical experience of the student. Courses can be general or specialist and can lead to credits towards NVQs Levels 2 and 3.

City and Guilds National Certificate in Agriculture (NCA) courses are offered at colleges of agriculture in England and Wales, for one year full-time. They are general courses that provide basic training for those seeking to work in practical agriculture. Holders of the NCA may, after a further year's practical experience, take the C&G Advanced National Certificate in Agriculture (ANCA), a one year full-time course, either in general agriculture or in a specialist area. By the end of the courses, credits towards NVQs Levels 2 and 3 may have been gained.

SQA National Certificate in Agriculture courses are offered (one year full-time) at the Scottish Agricultural College (Aberdeen and Auchincruive sites) and at Borders College, Oatridge Agricultural College, and Elmwood Agricultural and Technical College. They cover such areas as crop and livestock production, construction/maintenance of farm boundaries, and operation of farm transport. By the end of courses, credits towards SVQs Levels 2 and 3 may have been gained.

A number of NVQs/SVQs in Agriculture are available at Level 1. They include: crop and livestock production, livestock production, mechanized field crop production/intensive crop production. In addition to units specific to crop and/or livestock production, the awards include personal effectiveness, maintaining services and structures, and transporting mechanically. The NVQ/SVQ in Agriculture (Livestock Production) allows for specialization in dairying, beef, sheep, pigs, goats or poultry.

NVQs/SVQs in Agriculture at Level 2 are available in similar areas, plus estate maintenance. For information on NVQ/SVQ awards at Levels 3 and 4, please see article 1. FARM MANAGER.

LATE ENTRY

There is no upper age limit for entry to farm work. Adults interested in agriculture must be capable of coping with the physical demands of the work.

There may be specific training opportunities directed at adults available in some areas for this type of work. Candidates may have to satisfy certain conditions to be eligible. Contact your local Jobcentre, careers office or TEC/LEC for details.

OPPORTUNITIES

There are opportunities for farm workers in livestock, arable and mixed farming. Please see article 1. FARM MANAGER for the distribution of farms in Britain.

The number of farm workers has decreased steadily because of increased mechanization. That trend has accelerated in the 1990s as financial difficulties, particularly faced by large farms, have led to reduced employment.

Chances of finding work are considerably better for more-skilled workers. The demand for casual, part-time and seasonal workers has decreased substantially. The prospect of finding work in different sectors of agriculture – arable, beef or poultry production etc – varies and is influenced partly by current EU and government policy.

Vacancies for farm workers may be advertised in local newspapers.

PAY AND CONDITIONS

General farm workers working a basic 39-hour week earn £99.65 at age 16 and £116.25 at age 17. The standard basic weekly wage is £141.17 at age 18 and £166.08 at 19 years and over. For those with craft status, the minimum wage rates (age 19 or over) are £190.99, and £195.97 for workers with an NVQ/SVQ Level 3. There is a standard 39-hour week. Overtime is frequently necessary and depends on the demands of the work. Overtime is payable at an enhanced rate of 150% of the appropriate minimum hourly rate of pay.

Many farm workers have a rent-free (or low-rent tied cottage). Some workers in lodgings receive a lodging allowance. Where an employer provides board and lodgings for workers, up to £62.28 (for a worker aged 19 and over) may be deducted from the weekly wage.

PROSPECTS

Promotion to supervisor or unit manager is possible only on larger farms. Competition for such vacancies is intense. Experience and qualifications are important when seeking advancement, as is the willingness to move to another area.

It is difficult for farm workers to find work overseas. Self-employment is rarely possible.

RELATED OCCUPATIONS

Forest worker, gamekeeper, groundsman/woman, horticultural worker, farm manager.

FURTHER INFORMATION

CETAC*, 10 Northgate Street, Warwick CV34 4SR (written enquiries only, accompanied by sae)

Principals of local agricultural colleges – addresses and telephone numbers available from telephone directories or from a list held by CETAC.

FURTHER READING

Leaflets/booklets are available from the address marked*.

Agriculture, Horticulture, Forestry and Fisheries – AGCAS

Careers Working with Animals – Kogan Page

Directory of Courses in Land-based Industries – Nicholas Bond – Farming Press (Miller Freeman Professional Ltd)

In the careers library classified under WAB.

3. FISH FARMER (WAG)

BACKGROUND INFORMATION

Fish farming is concerned with producing fish for food, for angling and, to a lesser extent, for ornamental pools. As the traditional sea fishing industry has declined, cultivating fish for food purposes has grown. There is also a continuing demand from anglers for fish to re-stock rivers and ponds. Most fish farming is concerned with producing fin fish, particularly rainbow trout and salmon, although some fish

FARM WORK: WAB/WAG

farmers specialize in shellfish, such as oysters, mussels and scallops. Some ornamental fish, such as golden orfe, are also bred in this way.

THE WORK

Fish farmers breed and rear fish for sale mainly for food and for angling. Some specialize in hatching eggs and raising fry, while others buy in young fish and rear them until they are ready to be sold. Some are involved in both. Tasks include:

Feeding

Fish are kept in ponds, tanks, cages, pens or concrete raceways. They are fed with specially prepared food. Feeding may be automatic or by hand. Daily feed rations are based on the total weight of stock and water temperature.

Grading

Fish are frequently graded by size and moved to larger tanks. Grading may be done by hand, involving catching fish in hand nets, then sorting them by weight, or it may be done automatically. On some farms without catwalks across the tanks workers wear chest waders and work in the water.

Treatment of disease

Fish farmers keep constant watch for any evidence of disease or infection and apply appropriate treatment. They may add chemicals to the water to safeguard against disease.

Maintaining water quality

Fish farmers use automatic equipment to monitor the oxygen content of water and frequently take the water temperature. Workers keep clean the grills or screens that are used to prevent leaves and weeds entering the water and contaminating it and periodically drain the tanks and hose them down.

Maintenance

Workers carry out any routine maintenance work that may be needed, such as simple plumbing, carpentry and brickwork.

Harvesting

Fish produced for food are killed, gutted and placed in ice for transportation.

Management

Managers have additional duties, including keeping records of fish numbers and average weight, ordering feed and chemicals, marketing, staff supervision and keeping financial records.

Farming salmon is slightly different. Salmon breed in fresh water and mature at sea. After salmon have been reared in fresh water for a year or two they are transferred to pens in the sea, where they are matured until marketable. Salmon farm workers move between the pens by boat.

WORK ENVIRONMENT

Fish farmers work outdoors in all weathers, including the cold and the wet. For some, work includes working in water while wearing chest waders. Salmon farming involves some work in boats at sea.

The job involves much standing, bending and carrying and some heavy lifting.

Many fish farms are in remote and isolated areas.

SKILLS AND INTERESTS

Fish farmers need an interest in science in order to understand the conditions that are necessary for fast, healthy growth of fish.

Good practical skills are required, such as building skills, and workers must be prepared and able to tackle whatever needs doing. Workers should be fit and strong as the work is active and involves heavy lifting.

Workers on fish farms often work alone, so the ability to use initiative is important. They must be conscientious when checking, for example, water temperature and oxygen content, as fish are susceptible to disease if conditions are unsuitable. Good powers of observation are required to spot possible evidence of disease or infection before it can spread.

All fish farm workers should be able to swim. Those working on salmon farms should be capable of learning basic seamanship, as they spend some time in boats at sea moving between salmon pens.

Fish farming is a business, so fish farm managers or owners need commercial skills for budgeting, marketing their fish and keeping financial and other records.

ENTRY REQUIREMENTS

No formal academic qualifications are required for entry to fish farming. An aptitude for science – particularly biology and chemistry – and practical subjects is helpful.

SQA National Certificate in Fish Farming – no specific qualifications are required but it is an advantage to have some GCSEs/S grades (A–C/1–3), particularly in English, maths and science.

BTEC First Diploma in Fishery Studies requires a good general education and enthusiasm for the career.

BTEC National Diploma in Fishery Studies requires a merit or distinction pass in the first diploma, four GCSEs/S grades (A–C/1–3), or equivalent. It also requires a minimum of twelve months' full-time experience of fishery work. Candidates must be at least 17 years on entry.

BTEC Higher National Diploma in Fishery Studies requires one A level/3 H grades including a science and four GCSEs/S grades (A–C/1–3), or equivalent. A minimum of twelve months' full-time experience of fishery work is necessary.

Degrees with relevance to fish farming usually require a good pass in a relevant BTEC national diploma; or SQA national certificate with appropriate modules; or at least two A levels/three H grades, usually in science subjects, and a further three GCSEs/two S grades (A–C/1–3) in different subjects.

Postgraduate courses relevant to fish farming require a relevant degree for entry.

Institute of Fisheries Management Certificate in Fish Farming – no particular qualifications are needed but students must be members of the Institute.

Entrants to fish farming should be physically fit. A driving licence is usually essential.

FARM WORK: WAB/WAG

TRAINING

Pre-entry

SQA National Certificate in Fish Farming (one year, full-time) is offered by The Barony College and Inverness College. Both courses include a short placement on a commercial fish farm. BTEC courses are offered at Sparsholt College, Hampshire. All include practical experience of fish farming.

BTEC First Diploma in Fishery Studies (one year, full-time) provides an introduction to fish farming, fishery management and aquatics.

BTEC National Diploma in Fishery Studies (two years, full-time) is a scientifically based practical training course.

BTEC Higher National Diploma in Fishery Studies (three years, sandwich) covers fish farming, fishery management, fish science, business management, engineering and estate maintenance.

A number of universities offer degree courses (three or four years, full-time) with some relevance to fish farming, such as marine and freshwater biology, and aquatic biology. The Scottish Agricultural College offers a BTechnol course in Aquaculture, based at its Aberdeen site.

Postgraduate courses available include aquaculture, applied fish biology, fisheries science and fisheries management.

Institute of Fisheries Management Certificate in Fish Farming can be studied by correspondence course either before or after entry to fish farming.

On entry

Specific training schemes for young people are run by The Barony College, Lews Castle College, and North Atlantic Fisheries College. Training combines practical experience on a fish farm with some time at college working towards SQA modules.

All entrants to fish farming receive on-the-job training from experienced staff. That may be supplemented by short part-time courses in, for example, fish health and smolt production.

There may be some opportunity to work towards NVQs in Fish Husbandry at Level 2, specializing in either cyprinids, salmon, shellfish or trout, or SVQs in Fish Husbandry at Level 2 in fin fish or shellfish. They include: first aid; assisting operations in a hatchery; routine estate work and maintenance; maintaining fish in a holding unit; operating safely in the workplace; and optimizing water conditions in a fish holding unit. Those concerned with shellfish include operating small boats and managing shellfish stock and equipment on shore or sea sites, while the others include operating and maintaining agricultural tractors, maintaining feeding programmes on a fish farm, selecting and preparing fish for sale or transfer.

LATE ENTRY

There is no upper age limit for entry to fish farming. Mature applicants may be accepted onto the full-time courses described in TRAINING without the usual academic entry requirements, particularly if they have relevant experience.

OPPORTUNITIES

Commercial fish farms are the major employers but fish farms are also run by water authorities, government departments, industrial firms, private estates and angling organizations.

There are approximately 870 fish farms throughout England and Wales, with some concentration in Hampshire, Yorkshire, Wiltshire, south-west England and the Lake District. They employ just under 900 full-time and almost 1,000 part-time workers.

There are approximately 1,000 fish farms in Scotland, the majority concerned with salmon and concentrated along the west coast and in the islands. They employ approximately 1,500 full-time and 700 part-time workers.

Although fish farming has expanded, opportunities for employment are scarce, as most farms operate with minimal staffing. It is often necessary to move to get a job. Vacancies may be advertised in local newspapers, the angling press, *Fish Farmer* and *Fish Farming International*.

PAY AND CONDITIONS

There are no standard rates of pay in fish farming. Some employers pay weekly rates similar to those of general farm workers – £99.65 at 16 years, £116.25 at 17 years, £141.17 at 18 years and £166.08 at 20 years and over. Some employers pay less than these rates. Overtime may be payable. Technicians with large organizations may earn between £10,000 and £13,000 at age 18. Hatchery managers may earn from £13,000 to £16,500.

Self-employed fish farmers' earnings are related to profit and vary considerably.

Working hours are long and irregular. Early morning and evening work may be necessary.

Many fish farms are in remote areas, and tied accommodation may be included in the terms of employment.

PROSPECTS

On small fish farms there is little or no opportunity for promotion. On larger farms there can be a structure that allows promotion to supervisory or management posts.

There are some opportunities for working abroad as many countries have a well-developed fish-farming industry. Trout cultivation, for example, is well developed in France, Germany and Italy, salmon in Norway, carp in Northern Europe, and both salmon and trout in North America.

It is possible to become self-employed, although it involves considerable financial investment.

RELATED OCCUPATIONS

Waterkeeper/bailiff, gamekeeper, forest officer, farm manager, farm worker, fisherman/woman.

FURTHER INFORMATION

The Barony College*, Parkgate, Dumfries DG1 3NE, 01387 860251, www.barony.ac.uk

CETAC*, 10 Northgate Street, Warwick CV34 4SR (written enquiries only, accompanied by sae)

Institute of Fisheries Management*, 22 Rushworth Avenue, West Bridgeford, Nottingham NG2 7LF, 0115 982 2317

Inverness College*, 3 Longman Road, Inverness IV1 1SA, 01463 236681

FARM WORK: WAB/WAG

Lews Castle College*, Stornoway, Isle of Lewis HS2 0XR, 01851 703311, www.lews.uhi.ac.uk

North Atlantic Fisheries College*, Port Arthur, Scalloway, Shetland ZE1 0UN, 01595 880328, www.nafc.ac.uk

Sparsholt College Hampshire*, Sparsholt, Winchester, Hants SO21 2NF, 01962 776441. www.sparsholt.ac.uk

FURTHER READING

Leaflets/booklets are available from the addresses marked*.

Working in Agriculture and Horticulture – COIC

In the careers library classified under WAG.

HORTICULTURE: WAD

1. HORTICULTURAL MANAGER CLCI:WAD
2. HORTICULTURAL WORKER CLCI:WAD

BACKGROUND INFORMATION

There are two main areas of horticultural work, with a wide range of opportunities in related areas.

Commercial horticulture

Commercial horticulture involves the cultivation of salad crops, soft fruit (strawberries, raspberries etc) and top fruit (apples, pears etc), vegetables, flowers for cutting, trees, shrubs, bulbs, and plants for sale through shops and garden centres or for use in parks, planting schemes etc.

Many horticultural businesses specialize in just one or two activities, such as large-scale production of field vegetables or ornamental plants, or raising seedlings, in controlled conditions, for sale to commercial growers.

Some activities are concentrated in particular areas of the country. Orchards are found mainly in south-east England, where the climate is more favourable for fruit growing. Lincolnshire is an important region for field cultivation of vegetables, such as celery, onions and cauliflower, whereas Bedfordshire is traditionally known for its Brussels sprouts.

Protected cropping nurseries, where crops such as tomatoes, lettuce, flowers for cutting, bedding plants and pot plants are grown under glass or plastic, are found in many places, although West Sussex, Lancashire and East Yorkshire are important centres. Tree and shrub nurseries are found in most parts of the country, as are garden centres.

Amenity (or environmental) horticulture

This includes the initial design, and subsequent maintenance and management, of parks, open spaces, sports grounds, roadside areas, public gardens, the gardens of private estates and countryside recreation areas. It also includes landscape design, construction and maintenance.

Traditionally, much of amenity horticulture has been the responsibility of local authorities. However, local authorities are now required to invite competitive tenders for the upkeep of their parks, gardens, recreation areas etc.

Amenity horticulture also includes maintenance of the gardens of large estates, many of which are now owned by organizations, such as the National Trust, and of specialist gardens such as the Royal Botanic Gardens at Kew or those of the Royal Horticultural Society at Wisley.

Developing areas of amenity horticulture include 'interior landscaping' – designing and maintaining indoor plant areas in shopping centres and commercial premises; and horticultural therapy – the provision of gardens and horticultural training for people suffering from mental or physical illness or disability.

The maintenance of sports grounds, which is a specialized branch of amenity horticulture, is covered in the separate article GROUNDSMAN/WOMAN.

1. HORTICULTURAL MANAGER (WAD)

THE WORK

Horticultural managers in both commercial and amenity sectors may be responsible for all, or some, of the following:

– **planning**, which includes overall strategic planning deciding on the general direction of the business or organization, and crop planning – deciding on the crops and/or plants to be grown, and when, where and how to grow them;

– **managing staff**, including hiring and firing, directing, organizing and co-ordinating, either personally or via a team of supervisors, depending on the size of the organization;

– **financial management**, which involves monitoring costs and being responsible for maintaining profits. Managers may tender for contracts (in amenity horticulture);

– **ordering supplies** of seed, plants, fertilizer, equipment etc;

– **marketing** produce, and arranging for its transport and distribution;

– **maintenance and repair**, including arranging for maintenance and repair work to be carried out on buildings, machinery and equipment;

– **day-to-day duties**, involving dealing with problems such as staff disputes or the non-arrival of materials, as they arise.

Managers are increasingly likely to use computers for tasks such as planning, scheduling and financial management.

Managers need to be in close touch with work outside and may carry out practical tasks.

WORK ENVIRONMENT

The work is partly office-based, sometimes with travel to several different production sites.

SKILLS AND INTERESTS

Horticultural managers need business and organizational skills, as well as a thorough knowledge of good horticultural practice. Numeracy skills are required to analyse computerized data and deal with accounts, budgets, costings and other financial matters.

Good communication skills, both spoken and written, are required. Horticultural managers need to be capable of dealing confidently with staff, customers and suppliers. Good negotiating and marketing skills are needed when dealing with retail outlets, growers and distributors.

Managers need technical knowledge of plant stock and a scientific understanding of environmental conditions, crop pests, soil chemistry, plant physiology etc.

ENTRY REQUIREMENTS

Degree courses in horticulture – entry qualifications are two or three A levels or three or four H grades, usually including chemistry and a biological science, with supporting GCSEs (A–C/1–3) including maths and chemistry (if this is not obtained at A level/H grade), or equivalent. Check detailed requirements with prospectuses.

BTEC/SQA higher national diploma in horticultural subjects – candidates should have four GCSEs/S grades (A–C/1–3) in appropriate subjects plus at least one A level (preferably in a science subject), having studied a second subject to A level or two H grades; or a BTEC/SQA national certificate or diploma; or equivalent. Twelve months' practical experience in horticulture may be required.

HORTICULTURE: WAD

BTEC national diploma in horticultural subjects – entry requires four GCSEs/S grades (A–C/1–3), including English or a subject testing command of English and two maths or science subjects, or equivalent. Practical experience in horticulture may be needed. Candidates with a credit or distinction in the National Certificate in Horticulture (please see article 2. HORTICULTURAL WORKER) may enter the second year of a BTEC national diploma course.

Higher National Certificates validated by the SQA are available in Scotland. Study is for one year full time.

Kew Diploma in Horticulture – candidates need two A levels/H grades at grade C or above, preferably in science subjects, two years' practical experience, and associated horticultural training (such as NVQ/SVQ Level 2 in Horticulture, BTEC/SQA national or higher national diploma). There is a special entry scheme for sixth-formers, for which previous practical experience is not required.

Royal Botanic Garden, Edinburgh – candidates for the SQA HND Horticulture with Plantsmanship run jointly with the Scottish Agricultural College (SAC) need GCSEs/SCEs in five subjects, two of which should be at H grade, or one at A Level. These requirements may be relaxed at the discretion of the Principal at SAC and the Regius Keeper at the Garden.

Royal Horticultural Society (RHS), Wisley – candidates for the Diploma in Practical Horticulture need the RHS General Examination in Horticulture Certificate or a National Certificate in Horticulture plus previous practical work experience in horticulture.

TRAINING

The following qualifications are suitable for intending managers. In their first appointments, graduates and diplomates may be expected to gain general experience, including working at supervisory level, before they have sufficient expertise to be appointed to managerial-level posts.

Degree courses in horticulture – three-year courses are offered at the Universities of London (Wye College), Nottingham, and Reading; four-year sandwich courses are offered at Hadlow College (in conjunction with the University of Greenwich), Hertfordshire University (in association with Writtle College), Myerscough College (in conjunction with the University of Central Lancashire), Pershore College (validated by Coventry University), Writtle College (in conjunction with Anglia Polytechnic University), and the University of Strathclyde (in conjunction with the Scottish Agricultural College).

BTEC/SQA higher national diploma courses in horticultural subjects are offered on a three-year sandwich basis at a number of horticultural colleges. Some courses concentrate on amenity horticulture options, some on commercial horticulture.

The SQA higher national diploma is a one-year course available at several colleges.

BTEC national diploma in horticultural subjects – courses lasting two years or three years (sandwich) are available at a number of colleges in England and Wales.

For further information about courses, consult the Institute of Horticulture or *Courses in Land-Based Industries* published by the Association of Colleges in the Eastern Region (ACER).

The Kew Diploma in Horticulture is a degree-equivalent course at the Royal Botanic Gardens, Kew. The course lasts for three years, except for sixth-form entrants without previous experience, who take a four-year sandwich course.

A two-year SQA HND course in Horticulture with Plantsmanship is run by a number of Scottish colleges. Students who achieve the necessary credits may proceed to the third year of the BSc Horticulture offered through Strathclyde University.

Higher national certificate one-year courses validated by SOEID are available at Scottish agricultural colleges.

Royal Horticultural Society, Wisley, Diploma in Practical Horticulture is a two-year course offered at the Society's principal garden. The course leads to an examination in practical skills. Successful candidates are eligible to also complete the RHS Diploma in Horticulture examination.

NVQs/SVQs in Commercial Horticulture at Level 3 are available in: mechanized field crop production; fruit crop production; intensive crop production; nursery stock production. NVQ Level 3 awards are also available in mushroom crop production, while SVQ Level 3 awards are also offered in garden centre operation and general practice. An NVQ/SVQ at Level 4 is available in crop management.

NVQs/SVQs in Amenity Horticulture at Level 3 are available in: constructing and restoring landscapes; designing and specifying landscape designs; managing trees and woodlands; sports-turf maintenance. Level 4 awards are available in: designing landscapes and planning their management; managing landscape construction and maintenance.

Horticultural workers with craft qualifications may enter management posts, sometimes after taking further qualifications. Please see article 2. HORTICULTURAL WORKER.

LATE ENTRY

The usual requirement of twelve months' practical experience in horticulture may be waived or reduced to three months for students of 19 years or over.

OPPORTUNITIES

In the commercial sector there are opportunities with plant, tree and shrub nurseries, vegetable growers and fruit growers, growers of salad and glasshouse crops and bedding plants. Managers may specialize in areas such as crop production or marketing, or may have overall responsibility for all aspects of commercial production.

Garden centres and garden departments in other retail organizations recruit horticulturists as management trainees.

Supermarkets that sell large quantities of fruit and vegetables employ horticulturists to purchase and monitor the quality of supplies. There are also similar opportunities with importers and wholesalers.

There are also opportunities with producer organizations and grower group marketing associations, which grow and sell produce on behalf of commercial growers, mainly to supermarkets.

In amenity horticulture, managers are employed by local authorities and contractors; the work may involve liaising with and monitoring the progress of private contractors, or

HORTICULTURE: WAD

managing a direct labour force employed by the council or private contractors. There is also a limited number of openings with private estates, national parks and botanic gardens.

Vacancies are advertised in specialist magazines such as *The Grower* and *Horticulture Week*.

PAY AND CONDITIONS

Starting salaries for managers with the qualifications outlined under TRAINING vary considerably, ranging from around £11,000 up to £14,000. Senior managers – for example, in charge of large nurseries or garden centres – can earn in the region of £15,000 to £30,000. Similarly, there is a very wide range of salaries for experienced managers. A company car may be provided.

Working hours are around 40 a week, sometimes with additional weekend and evening work.

PROSPECTS

Career prospects may be improved by taking the Royal Horticultural Society's Master of Horticulture (MHort(RHS)) Award, an advanced qualification in practical horticulture at degree-equivalent level. Five years' full-time experience (or three years' experience and two years spent in horticultural education) is required as a minimum academic entry requirement including having successfully passed the RHS Diploma in Horticulture examinations. Advanced horticultural qualifications may give exemption from management parts of the examination. Courses are available (mainly on a part-time basis) at a number of colleges throughout the country, or by distance learning.

The MHort(RHS), or postgraduate qualifications (eg MSc, MPhil, PhD), may lead to academic or research posts.

There tends to be a more defined career structure in amenity horticulture (particularly in local authorities). In commercial horticulture, where there are very varied employment opportunities, prospects depend very much on the policy of the individual employer.

Back-up services to the horticultural industry offer many opportunities, including the following:

– **ADAS** – the Government's Agricultural Development and Advisory Service – employs graduates or people with equivalent qualifications in horticulture as advisory officers. They provide a service to growers, and also work at experimental horticultural stations, developing new techniques and practices for the industry;

– **advisory and consultancy work** is available for the self-employed and with private firms;

– **research** – Horticultural Research International runs three research stations covering horticultural crops and two research centres. There are also several research stations run by commercial firms;

– **teaching, training and lecturing** in horticultural subjects;

– **horticultural journalism**, including publishing;

– **horticultural therapy** in settings such as hospitals and residential homes.

Trained horticulturists are recruited for posts abroad by organizations such as the Overseas Development Administration. Short-term overseas posts are offered by VSO. Horticulturists are also employed overseas by the Commonwealth War Graves Commission.

RELATED OCCUPATIONS

Farm manager, forest officer, retail manager, landscape architect, scientific officer (nature conservation).

FURTHER INFORMATION AND READING

Please see article 2. HORTICULTURAL WORKER.

2. HORTICULTURAL WORKER (WAD)

THE WORK

There are two main areas of work common to both commercial and amenity horticulture.

Propagation includes sowing seeds, in trays or outdoors; raising plants from cuttings; pricking out and potting up seedlings, then 'potting on' (transferring growing plants to larger pots); budding and grafting (techniques used for propagating roses and trees).

Crop husbandry is looking after crops whilst they are growing and involves watering, feeding, and trimming plants. Horticultural workers apply fertilizers, pesticides and herbicides, and maintain a controlled environment for protected crops, with the right levels of temperature and humidity. Much of the control is computerized.

In commercial horticulture, harvesting is an important aspect of the work. Workers pick crops and place them in containers. They grade produce by size and quality, and package it, ready for market. Harvest is the busiest time of the horticultural year, and casual workers are often taken on for the picking season, though mechanization has taken over in areas, especially for field vegetables. Permanent horticultural staff may be responsible for supervising the casual workforce.

In amenity horticulture, propagation and plant husbandry involve similar duties to those required in the commercial sector but there is no harvesting. Amenity horticulture also involves tasks such as mowing lawns, pruning shrubs, applying mulches to protect plant roots, staking plants, keeping edges of beds and lawns tidy, and removing autumn leaves.

In both sectors of horticulture, many tasks are mechanized; digging of large areas, for instance, is usually done with a Rotavator, rather than by hand, and ride-on mowers are used for cutting grass. There is, however, a considerable amount of hard manual work, with the use of hand tools such as trowels, spades and forks.

In garden centres and other retail outlets such as farm shops, workers act as sales assistants and give advice to customers, as well as looking after plants.

For working outdoors horticultural workers may wear overalls, boots, or waterproof clothing.

WORK ENVIRONMENT

Horticultural workers spend much of their time outdoors, unless they are working with protected crops or in retailing.

The work is physically demanding, involving a lot of walking, standing and bending, and some lifting/carrying, for instance of sacks of compost, pots, or trays of plants. Disability, however, is no bar to employment in horticulture, although it may restrict the choice of work available. Working conditions can be cold, wet and muddy, or extremely hot (in glasshouses).

HORTICULTURE: WAD

Horticultural workers often work in small groups of three or four; they may work in larger teams, or alone.

SKILLS AND INTERESTS

It is important to be interested in plants and nature and to understand scientific and technical information relating to plant growth, and control of pests and diseases.

In glasshouse crop production, an understanding is needed of bed rotation and technical information, such as humidity levels and temperature settings, day length and water requirements.

To be capable of the full range of horticultural tasks, workers need a reasonable standard of physical fitness. Manual dexterity is required for jobs such as grafting, budding and potting.

It is important to get on well with others and to be able to work as a member of a team. Horticultural workers in garden centres work closely with the public, so they need good communication skills and a wide knowledge of plants and chemicals used for the control of pests and diseases.

An appreciation of environmental factors, hygiene and food safety are also important.

ENTRY REQUIREMENTS

There are no formal entry requirements for direct entry to employment or training schemes for young people, but some GCSEs/S grades, especially in science subjects, are an advantage.

City and Guilds/SQA National Certificate in Horticulture – applicants must be at least 17 years old and have one year's suitable pre-course practical experience. This requirement may be modified for mature applicants. There are no set academic requirements, although these may be specified by individual colleges.

TRAINING

Many young people enter horticulture via training schemes for young people. This provides practical training at the workplace and off-the-job courses, usually at local colleges, on day or block release. College training normally leads to NVQ/SVQ Level 1 and 2 awards, specializing either in amenity or commercial horticulture. Modern Apprenticeships (part of the Skillseekers Initiative in Scotland) may also be available leading to at least an NVQ/SVQ Level 3. National Traineeships in Horticulture are also available. For details of training schemes for young people contact your local careers office, or TEC/LEC.

Trainees may also take National Proficiency Tests.

Alternatively, in England and Wales it is possible to take a one-year full-time course for the National Certificate in Horticulture, awarded by City and Guilds. In Scotland, one-year full-time programmes of SQA modules are available. Young people must preferably have one year's suitable pre-course experience.

C&G/SQA National Certificate in Horticulture – the curriculum for these courses is set by individual colleges, and relates to local horticultural needs. Various options are available at different colleges, including amenity horticulture, commercial horticulture, garden centre practices, horticultural contractors' operations, nursery practices, and nursery stock production. Similarly, in Scotland there is a flexibility over the modules taken on a one-year course.

The Royal Horticultural Society's General Examination in Horticulture is a nationally recognized qualification covering a wide range of horticulture with open access. Courses for the examination are available on a part-time basis, usually over one or two years offered at about 100 centres nationwide. Distance learning is also available. The standard of knowledge required is equivalent to GCSE/S grade level in science. The more advanced RHS Diploma in Horticulture is also available. This qualification is recognized for associate membership of the Institute of Horticulture. Studied usually as a two-year part-time course, it covers theory and practical and is equivalent to two A levels/H grades.

NVQs/SVQs are available in both Amenity Horticulture and Commercial Horticulture at Levels 1, 2 and 3.

Courses for people with disabilities are offered at various specialist centres. Further details are available from disablement resettlement officers or from the Royal Agricultural Society of England's Careers, Education and Training Advice Centre (CETAC).

LATE ENTRY

There are no upper age limits on entry. Adult applicants for one-year National Certificate in Horticulture courses may be accepted with less than one year's pre-course experience.

Adults may be able to gain certification of horticultural skills without taking a formal training course, via Accreditation of Prior Learning.

There may be specific training opportunities directed at adults available in some areas for this type of work. Candidates may have to satisfy certain conditions to be eligible. Contact your local Jobcentre, careers office or TEC/LEC for details.

OPPORTUNITIES

Horticultural workers are employed in the commercial sector by fruit and vegetable growers, protected cropping and tree/shrub nurseries. There are many opportunities in garden centres and garden departments of other retail organizations.

In amenity horticulture, there are opportunities both for direct employment with local authorities and for work with private contracting firms.

There are opportunities for trained staff to work overseas.

Self-employment is possible; the most likely areas are those requiring little capital investment, such as interior landscaping (looking after plants in shops and offices), or professional gardening and landscaping.

PAY AND CONDITIONS

Commercial horticulture

Wages depend on age, experience and type of employment. General workers aged 16 to 19 years receive basic wages of around £67 to £133 a week. Workers aged over 20 years earn basic salaries of between £129 and £174 a week. Overtime payments can increase wages.

Hours of work in England and Wales are 40 a week; in Scotland, they are either 40 a week throughout the year or 41½ in summer and 36½ in winter. Weekend work may be required, particularly in summer. Some jobs are available on a seasonal basis.

HORTICULTURE: WAD

Amenity horticulture

In local authority employment, pay rates for gardeners (aged 18 years or over) range from about £160 to £180 a week for 39 hours. Overtime and bonus payments may be available. Pay rates for staff employed by private contractors vary with different employers.

PROSPECTS

Horticultural workers with the National Certificate in Horticulture or NVQ/SVQ Level 2, and several years' experience in practical horticulture, may be appointed to supervisory posts. Supervisory work involves directing staff engaged in practical operations, ensuring that production targets are achieved and deadlines met. Supervisors may also be responsible for ordering supplies, stock control, administration of staff timesheets, and bonus payments. In retail operations they may be responsible for dealing with customer complaints.

It may be possible for supervisors with further qualifications to gain management posts.

RELATED OCCUPATIONS

Farm worker, groundsman/woman, gardener, forest worker, fish farmer.

FURTHER INFORMATION

CETAC*, 10 Northgate Street, Warwick CV34 4SR (written enquiries only, accompanied by sae)

LANTRA National Training Organisation, National Agricultural Centre, Stoneleigh, Kenilworth, Warwickshire, CV8 2LG, 01203 696996

The Institute of Horticulture*, 14–15 Belgrave Square, London SW1X 8PS, 0171 245 6943, http://www.horticulture.demon.co.uk/

The Royal Botanic Gardens, Personnel Section, Kew, Richmond, Surrey TW9 3AB, 0181 332 5127/5141

The Royal Botanic Garden, 20A Inverleith Row, Edinburgh EH3 5LR, 0131 248 2825

Royal Horticultural Society*, Supervisor of Studies and Training, Wisley, Woking, Surrey GU23 6QB, 01483 224234, www.rhs.org.uk (please enclose large sae)

Please contact local colleges who may be able to provide information and training.

FURTHER READING

Leaflets/booklets are available from the addresses marked*.

Agriculture, Horticulture, Forestry and Fisheries – AGCAS

Working In Agriculture & Horticulture – COIC

In the careers library classified under WAD.

GROUNDSMANSHIP: WAD

GROUNDSMAN/WOMAN CLCI:WAD

BACKGROUND INFORMATION

The Institute of Groundsmanship (IOG) defines the work as 'managing land for sport and recreation and keeping the soil in the right condition for any given activity'. Soil, and the grass that grows on it to form turf, is the groundsman/woman's basic concern. Very different types of ground are required for different kinds of sport; compare, for example, the fine turf of a cricket pitch with the rougher surface of a football pitch.

Groundsmen/women are responsible for making sure that playing facilities are kept in the best possible condition for any given sport. They also maintain other areas, such as lawns, grass verges and flower beds.

In a broader sense groundsmanship, as a specialist branch of amenity horticulture, is part of the sport and recreation industry. Promotion is likely to lead away from the maintenance of sports grounds into the more general area of leisure facility management.

THE WORK

Groundsmen/women usually organize their own day-to-day work in order to prepare and maintain the sports facilities for which they are responsible. The work varies with different types of ground. Some facilities, such as school playing fields, are used on a year-round basis and are constantly maintained to a given standard. Groundsmen/women working at Wimbledon concentrate their efforts on providing a top quality playing surface for special competitions and also for club play throughout the season.

In both cases, groundsmen/women plan a regular maintenance schedule, but for Wimbledon or any facility used for major events there is additional work to prepare the ground for specific fixtures.

The work involves the following aspects:

Groundsmen/women regularly mow the grass during the growing season (generally from March to September, but this varies with the weather – during a warm winter, the grass does not stop growing). Other tasks include: scarification (removal of dead grass); sowing seeds or replacing turf in worn areas; application of fertilizers and pesticides; rolling where necessary, for a smooth surface.

They also mark out lines, to a high degree of accuracy, for playing areas, and generally maintain the surrounding area, including borders and flower beds, to provide an attractive environment.

Groundsmen/women use a variety of mowers for different jobs. For large areas they use ride-on mowers or sets of 'gang mowers' fitted behind tractors. Whereas for smaller areas or fine surfaces they use small pedestrian mowers.

Other tools and equipment include fertilizer distributors, sprayers, rollers, irrigation equipment and a wide range of hand tools, including shears, spades, hoes and other general gardening tools. Groundsmen/women are responsible for maintaining their tools and machinery.

Groundsmen/women may also manage facilities made of synthetic turf, concrete and tarmac. They may be responsible for seating and for setting out and removing protective coverings over pitches. In local authorities, they may take care of verges along highways and in parks, as well as at sports grounds. Some groundsmen/women order their own supplies of seed, fertilizer etc, calculate costings, and manage a team of staff.

WORK ENVIRONMENT

Almost all the time is spent outdoors.

Groundsmen/women are usually based at one site, but some jobs, particularly at supervisory and management level, involve travel to several sites – for instance, to all the football pitches in the local area.

Groundsmen/women employed by private clubs are likely to spend much of their time working alone; in local authority employment, it is more common for them to work in pairs, or small teams.

SKILLS AND INTERESTS

An interest in gardening is useful. Manual dexterity is required for using hand tools and for work on fine turf areas.

It is important to be physically fit, although slight disability is no bar to employment in groundsmanship, provided applicants are capable of a lot of walking, some bending and lifting, and occasional strenuous effort.

Numeracy skills are required for calculating quantities (of fertilizer, for instance). Groundsmen/women in supervisory posts need to be capable of tasks such as processing staff timesheets and calculating bonus payments.

Groundsmen/women need reasonable spoken communication skills, particularly in private sports clubs where they may have to deal with members' complaints and liaise with a committee. Tact and diplomacy may sometimes be required.

It is necessary to be self-motivated and capable of organizing one's own work.

ENTRY REQUIREMENTS

There are no formal entry requirements but individual employers may specify their own.

TRAINING

Practical experience is supplemented by on-the-job training from senior staff.

Qualifications in groundsmanship are not essential, but are advantageous, and may be required for the more responsible posts.

A number of NVQs/SVQs in Amenity Horticulture are available at Levels 1, 2, 3 and 4 in Sports Turf Management.

The Institute of Groundsmanship (IOG) offers the National Practical Certificate, the National Technical Certificate, the National Intermediate Diploma and the National Diploma in Turfculture.

The National Practical Certificate is based on practical groundsmanship skills. Attendance at a formal course of study is not essential (although courses are available). Successful completion of the Certificate gives accreditation towards part of the NVQ/SVQ in Amenity Horticulture at Level 1.

The National Technical Certificate is based on the NVQ/SVQ in Amenity Horticulture (Greenkeeping – Sports Turf – Sports Ground Maintenance) at Level 2. It is now being offered in the majority of horticulture colleges in the UK, either as a full-time or day release programme.

Specific training schemes for young people are available. Contact your local careers office, TEC/LEC or the IOG.

LATE ENTRY

There are no formal age limits, and maturity can be an asset for this type of work. Experience in a related occupation, such as farming, is an advantage. Adults may improve their chances of finding employment by studying for the Institute of Groundsmanship qualifications.

There may be specific training opportunities directed at adults available in some areas for this type of work. Candidates may have to satisfy certain conditions to be eligible. Contact your local Jobcentre, careers office or TEC/LEC for details.

OPPORTUNITIES

The main employers are: private sports clubs – for example, football clubs, tennis clubs, and cricket clubs; local authority parks or leisure and recreation departments; horticultural contractors that provide services for local authorities and other organizations such as sports clubs; universities or hotels with sports facilities.

Groundsmen/women are employed throughout the country, although there are more jobs available in the major centres of population. The number of opportunities is increasing slightly.

Vacancies are advertised in *The Groundsman* and *Horticulture Week*. Self-employment, as a horticultural contractor, is possible. There is considerable demand from employers overseas for trained groundsmen/women.

PAY AND CONDITIONS

Pay varies for groundsmen/women. The Institute of Groundsmanship recommends minimum salary scales of £6,970 to £8,360 for juniors. Groundsmen/women can expect from £10,950 to £13,655 depending on skill level. A head groundsman/woman would earn in the region of £17,000 plus. The IOG recommends additional increments for those with qualifications.

Pay in the private sector varies with individual employers. Some private sports clubs provide accommodation.

Hours of work are usually 37½ to 40 a week, but flexibility over work schedules is needed because the spring and summer growing season is busier than autumn and winter. Some jobs are offered on a seasonal basis. A lot of part-time work is available. Weekend work may be required to prepare the ground for specific events.

PROSPECTS

Promotion prospects are improved by the possession of formal qualifications (see TRAINING). Qualifications can lead to the post of head groundsman/woman or grounds manager responsible for managing a small team of staff.

There are opportunities to progress into general sports and leisure management, particularly with local authorities. Qualifications suitable for intending supervisors and managers include the following:

Institute of Groundsmanship Intermediate Diploma – candidates need at least four years' relevant experience and should hold the IOG National Technical Certificate or an equivalent qualification.

Institute of Groundsmanship National Diploma – for candidates with the Intermediate Diploma and at least six years' experience.

BTEC National Diploma in Horticulture (specializing in Turf Science and Sports Ground Management Amenity Horticulture) – courses are normally available on a three-year sandwich basis, with the second year spent on a work placement.

City and Guilds National Certificate in Horticulture (C&G 0350) – this is a one-year full-time course offered at a number of agricultural colleges. Specialist options (at certain colleges) include groundsmanship, greenkeeping and sportsground management.

NVQs/SVQs in Amenity Horticulture are also available at Levels 3 and 4 in Sports Turf Maintenance.

RELATED OCCUPATIONS

Horticultural worker, horticultural manager, sports/leisure centre assistant, gardener, golf greenkeeper, farm worker, forest worker.

FURTHER INFORMATION

The Institute of Groundsmanship*, 19–23 Church Street, The Agora, Wolverton, Milton Keynes MK12 5LG, 01908 312511

FURTHER READING

Leaflets/booklets are available from the address marked*.

In the careers library classified under WAD.

FORESTRY: WAF

1. FOREST OFFICER CLCI:WAF
2. FOREST WORKER/RANGER CLCI:WAF

BACKGROUND INFORMATION

A major force in modern forestry during the past 60 to 80 years has been the development of industries based on wood (such as wrapping and writing papers, cardboard packaging, insulating boards, and plywood). These require a large and regular supply of wood of uniform quality.

Another factor has been the increasing recognition of the role played by trees in stabilizing soil and regulating the flow of water into streams and rivers. Forests also provide a source of shelter for houses, buildings, crops, wild and domestic animals, and many plants. Not least in terms of importance is the aesthetic appeal of wooded areas, with their peace and tranquillity being enjoyed and appreciated by many.

So, although forestry is primarily to do with the production of timber for sale, it is also closely connected with enhancement of landscape, conservation of wildlife, and public recreation.

Growing commercially useful timber on the land available has meant an emphasis on softwoods (such as conifers), which grow on the more exacting upland soils in Scotland, Wales and northern England. Now, however, the Government is encouraging the planting of broad-leaved trees (such as oak, ash, beech) with the use of grants. These more traditional hardwoods usually require good soil and milder climatic conditions, generally found in the lowlands.

The forestry industry in Great Britain is small, employing approximately 20,000 people. Another 11,000 are employed in related wood-processing industries.

The state-owned Forestry Commission manages about 40% of the forests in Britain. The Commission is divided into two main sub-divisions:

– Forest Enterprise is the operational arm responsible for the Forestry Commission's forests and woodlands. It markets timber, provides recreational opportunities and safeguards forest flora and fauna;

– The Forestry Authority administers grants, provides control functions such as felling licensing, carries out research, advises private woodland owners and liaises with local authorities and countryside groups on land uses.

The remainder of the forestry industry is managed by private estate owners (especially in Scotland), co-operative forestry societies, commercial firms (particularly contractors who provide tree-care services), local authorities and some timber merchants. Private woodlands vary greatly in size and organization, although work tends to be broken down into three groups – managerial staff, foresters and forest workers.

Like forestry companies, the co-operatives provide management and marketing services, including specialist areas. They employ forest officers (also known as woodland managers) and foresters who either engage forest workers directly or put work out to contract.

1. FOREST OFFICER (WAF)

THE WORK
Forestry Commission

Forest officers, working for Forest Enterprise, are technical managers responsible for the annual planning and day-to-day organization of a particular area of forest/woodland. Forest officers plan the annual work programme to ensure cultivation and harvesting take place at the correct times. The work involves decisions concerning seed collection, preparation of land for tree planting, raising and planting trees for afforestation and replanting, tree thinning including organization of marking, sometimes felling, and transportation of timber. General day-to-day care of woodland areas includes the checking of trees for pests and disease, ensuring problems are rectified by administering proper treatment.

Forest officers are also responsible for fire protection arrangements within their area.

Forest Enterprise provides and supervises recreational and leisure facilities for the general public. Forest officers are becoming increasingly involved with recreational aspects of forest and woodland areas. This may include organizing the layout of nature trails and provision of caravan sites and information centres. Conservation aspects also have priority and can involve anything from the management and provision for deer and other wildlife, to landscaping motorways and derelict sites.

Forest officers working for Forest Enterprise are responsible for staff, organizing them according to annual and daily management plans. This includes supervising forest workers, organizing the training of existing staff or new entrants, and becoming directly involved with the training of new forest officers. The forest officer is responsible for safety standards, estimating costs, setting piecework rates, and measuring and controlling work programmes.

Forest officers working for the Forestry Authority act as advisers for private estates in the area, administer grants and liaise with local authorities and countryside groups.

Experienced forest officers may have specialist duties, such as research, education and training, or technical development (work study). These are normally undertaken on a five-year tour of duty.

The private sector

Within the private sector the work is similar, with emphasis on tree crops and timber, management of woodlands, land evaluation, marketing of timber, and provision of contract services.

In both the public and private sectors a further area of responsibility is the control of financial affairs. This may range from simple accounts and book-keeping to controlling capital assets, including sophisticated machinery, amounting to thousands of pounds depending on size and scope of the employing organization.

WORK ENVIRONMENT

Forest officers are office-based, but work outdoors for part of the day dealing with the practicalities of the work. Approximately three-fifths of forest officers' time is spent outdoors whatever the season or weather conditions. Although forest officers are likely to work in the most beautiful parts of the country, locations are generally remote, away from towns and cities. The larger forests are mostly in the upland areas, particularly Scotland, Wales and northern England.

FORESTRY: WAF

SKILLS AND INTERESTS

Forest officers need to be able to plan, organize and supervise the work of others. Ability to plan ahead for the long-term is essential; the forest officer may have the satisfaction of creating a lasting resource for future generations, but must be aware that mistakes are also long-lasting.

The work involves careful collection and analysis of facts and figures, so numeracy is essential.

Written and spoken communication skills are required for negotiating, answering enquiries, liaising with outside organizations, managing and supervising staff, writing reports and correspondence.

Some scientific knowledge and an interest in the environment are also required.

Physical fitness is important; the work involves a lot of walking, often over rough terrain.

ENTRY REQUIREMENTS

Entry to the Forestry Commission is with one of the following:

BSc in Forestry – minimum entry requirements for degree courses are five GCSEs/S grades (A–C/1–3) including maths, with two A levels or three H grades (usually three/four A levels/H grades in science subjects are preferred or required, depending on the course). It is helpful to gain some practical experience in forestry before starting on a course.

BTEC/SQA Higher National Diploma in Forestry – minimum entry requirements are normally one A level or two H grades and supporting GCSEs/S grades (A–C/1–3), or a BTEC/SQA national award, or equivalent.

BTEC National Diploma in Forestry or SQA equivalent – entry is normally with: four GCSEs/S grades (A–C/1–3) including maths, English and a science subject; or a relevant BTEC first diploma, or equivalent.

City and Guilds Phase IV Certificate in Forestry or SQA equivalent – there are no minimum entry requirements, but practical experience is a condition of entry to courses.

Possession of a full driving licence is essential.

Private sector employers' requirements vary.

Candidates should check with universities and colleges for details of specific entry requirements.

TRAINING

Degree courses

First degree courses in forestry or forestry-related subjects are available at the following universities:

Aberdeen University – three-year ordinary and four-year honours degree in Forestry, with two parallel programmes, one in Forest Management and one in Arboriculture and Amenity Forestry.

Edinburgh University – four-year honours course leading to BSc in Ecological Science and Forestry. A four-year joint honours degree in Agriculture, Forestry and Rural Economy is also available.

University College of North Wales, Bangor – three-year honours degrees in Agroforestry, Forestry, Soil and Forest Science, Forestry and Wood Science, or Wood Science. (Wood science courses are primarily for those who wish to work in timber-using industries.)

BTEC/SQA higher national diplomas

Newton Rigg College: a three-year course, including one year's work experience, leading to the BTEC Higher National Diploma in Forestry and NVQ Level 4.

Inverness College – a three-year programme, including a year's practical experience, leading to the SQA Higher National Diploma in Forestry.

BTEC/SQA national certificate/diplomas

NC/ND courses usually last two years full-time, or three years including a year's practical experience. Colleges running courses include: Newton Rigg College, Inverness College, De Montfort University, Askham Bryan College, The Barony College, Herefordshire College of Agriculture, and Sparsholt College.

City and Guilds

C&G courses are for those already employed in the industry, and are taken on a part-time basis. The existing City and Guilds Phases I–IV are being replaced by courses leading to National Vocational Qualifications.

NVQs/SVQs in Forestry at Levels 2 to 4 have been accredited.

A Forestry Modern Apprenticeship Scheme is available in Scotland and will be submitted for endorsement for use in England and Wales.

The Institute of Chartered Foresters' examinations are for those in employment in the industry. Possession of other forestry qualifications may grant exemption from part of the examinations.

Once in a post, forest officers may take short technical courses organized by the Forestry and Arboriculture Safety and Training Council (FASTCO).

LATE ENTRY

Competition for the limited number of available vacancies is keen. It is, therefore, unlikely that adults looking for a change of career, without any previous forestry qualifications or experience, will be successful. Mature student applications are considered by those universities offering forestry degree courses, but, again, relevant forestry experience is likely to be essential.

OPPORTUNITIES

Despite an increase in resources available to forestry, the introduction of mechanization and improved methods has meant a significant reduction in the number of jobs. Competition is intense, with more people training than can be absorbed. Even finding a job or practical experience before college or university can be difficult.

The Forestry Commission is the largest employer overall and covers the whole of Great Britain. The concentration of forestry, however, tends to be in Scotland, Wales and northern England – with corresponding employment opportunities often in remote, outlying areas. Research work is mostly based at Alice Holt Lodge, near Farnham, Surrey, with another main research station at Bush Estate, near Edinburgh.

Other employers include private landowners, local authorities, national companies, co-operative forestry societies and contracting companies.

Vacancies for forest officer posts within the Forestry Commission are filled by competitive interviews, which are

FORESTRY: WAF

normally held annually.

The following journals may carry advertisements for vacancies in the private sector: *Quarterly Journal of Forestry, Forestry, Forestry Machinery Journal, British Timber, Timber Grower,* and *Scottish Forestry.*

PAY AND CONDITIONS

Wages and salaries in the Forestry Commission are as follows: Forest Officer III – £12,380 to £21,600; Forest Officer II – £14,315 to £25,260; Forest Officer I – £17,575 to £31,965.

No average pay scales are available for the private sector. Pay is generally less than for comparable positions in the Forestry Commission, except at the higher end of the scale. A vehicle may be provided.

In the Forestry Commission and local authorities a 42-hour week is standard. Overtime is worked when required. Forestry Commission salaries include an element for 'all hours worked' and no additional overtime payments are made. In the private sector, especially in the larger commercial companies, supervisory staff must be willing to work hours as required by the employer, including evening and weekend work. More often than not, extra time worked is balanced by time off in lieu.

PROSPECTS

Management of private forests is likely to be the growth area for future forestry employment with promotion opportunities being reflected accordingly. There is, however, no formal structure for promotion; prospects vary according to size and structure of individual organizations.

For higher-level posts, many employers require full membership of the Institute of Chartered Foresters.

Promotion within the Forestry Commission depends on merit, ability and the number of vacancies that arise.

There are opportunities for self-employment, for instance as a forestry consultant.

There may be opportunities for forestry graduates to work overseas, as requests from foreign countries arise. These are usually on limited-term appointments and candidates may be required to have specialist experience.

RELATED OCCUPATIONS

Arboriculturist, horticultural manager, farm manager, landscape architect, land agent/agricultural surveyor, forest worker/ranger.

FURTHER INFORMATION AND READING

Please see article 2. FOREST WORKER/RANGER.

2. FOREST WORKER/RANGER (WAF)

THE WORK

The duties of a forest worker are all practical, concerning the general upkeep of forest and woodland areas. This includes clearing scrub to promote the healthy growth of young and established trees, helping to control harmful diseases, pests or wildlife, planting and tending young trees, pruning and felling trees, and the general upkeep of boundary fences, ditches and drainage systems.

The work is increasingly mechanized, with skilled forest workers using tractors and chain saws. Such jobs as ploughing and drain making are all mechanized, but hand tools such as billhooks and handsaws are also used. Although the forest worker is likely to work out in all weathers, maintenance of forest machinery and sharpening of tools is likely to be carried out during poor weather.

Fire prevention and control is also part of the forest worker's duties. A constant look-out is kept for fire hazards. Where an area of forest or woodland is close to industry or houses, fires can be frequent. Duties also include maintaining firefighting equipment.

Forest workers may specialize in harvesting, tractor driving and the extraction of wood to transportation point.

Depending on the type of employer, it may be possible for some forestry workers to specialize in nursery work. Many plants are raised from seeds carefully collected from trees in this country or obtained from North America, Japan and Europe. A variety of native and exotic species are raised for replanting in such places as city streets and open spaces, along motorways etc.

Some forest workers within the Forestry Commission (Forest Enterprise) may work as forest rangers. Forest rangers deal with wildlife control and conservation. They protect animals and birds by creating and maintaining habitats; they control pests and conserve the forest environment. They are also responsible for protecting forests from misuse by the general public. This includes reminding people about fire risks and supervising and generally taking care of public facilities such as car parks, picnic sites, and caravan areas.

WORK ENVIRONMENT

Forest workers work mostly outside in all weathers, whatever the season. Only when the conditions are very bad or wet do they work indoors on machine and tool maintenance, gate making etc.

The work is dirty and can be hazardous. Special protective clothing is supplied although this may be restrictive. Chemical spraying, which has to be carried out in warm weather, can be uncomfortable because it involves wearing plastic protective clothing, which can be hot.

Larger forests and woodland areas are mostly in the upland parts of Britain, particularly Scotland, Wales and northern England. Workers must be prepared to live and work in isolated places. Accommodation may sometimes be provided by the employer.

SKILLS AND INTERESTS

Forest workers need to be fit, as the work is physically demanding. They should be capable of sustained hard work – moving around in undergrowth and branches, carrying and using a chainsaw etc is physically demanding. Felling trees is strenuous work and may involve working at heights.

Forest workers must be good at manual work and able to use machinery and handtools safely with skill and speed. Common sense is required because of the hazardous nature of the work. They should be observant – able to detect changes in drainage and soil features that may affect the performance of machinery and general standard of work.

Forest workers need the ability to work on their own initiative as well as forming part of a team. Even when

FORESTRY: WAF

working in pairs for safety, it can be a solitary job as workers may be isolated by protective clothing, machinery may be noisy, and they may be working at a fast pace.

The forest ranger and warden must be able to deal with visitors tactfully, but firmly if needed. Rangers should be interested in animals and birds.

Respiratory and skin disorders (including asthma, hay fever, chilblains and eczema) may cause difficulties.

ENTRY REQUIREMENTS

No minimum formal educational qualifications are required. Those with GCSEs/S grades (A–C/1–3) may have an advantage because of the intense competition for places.

A driving licence is an advantage, although not essential.

TRAINING

Specific training schemes for young people are available within the forestry industry. They include work experience and college training. Trainees work towards NVQs/SVQs at Levels 1 and 2, and may take City and Guilds qualifications. The schemes are available through a number of colleges of agriculture/forestry and other training organizations.

It is also possible to enter forestry after taking a one-year full-time BTEC first diploma. Colleges running courses for this qualification include Newton Rigg College, Sparsholt College, Llysfasi College of Agriculture, and De Montfort University. In Scotland, one- or two-year SQA national certificate courses are available at Inverness and Barony Colleges.

Courses for the National Certificate in Forestry, awarded by City and Guilds, are available at a number of colleges, either full-time or part-time, over a period of at least one year.

All forest workers, including those who do not follow any formal college training, are expected to do in-service training, to gain considerable skill with forest tools and machinery. Safe handling of equipment is essential.

NVQs/SVQs in Forestry are available at Levels 1, 2, 3 and 4 covering skills such as planting, fencing, draining, pruning, timber harvesting and nursery work. The NVQ/SVQ at Level 3 includes supervisory skills and monitoring contract work to ensure standards are maintained.

The Forestry and Arboriculture Safety and Training Council (FASTCO) runs skill courses in various areas according to local demand. Courses vary from basic forestry techniques, chainsaw basic handling and maintenance, to advanced chainsaw and tree-climbing courses, lasting between one and five days. Details from FASTCO or individual colleges.

LATE ENTRY

There is no upper age limit but applicants should consider the physical demands of the job. Health and fitness determine suitability. Those with a land-based sector background and knowledge of the machinery and tools used, may have an advantage.

There may be specific training opportunities directed at adults available in some areas for this type of work. Candidates may have to satisfy certain conditions to be eligible. Contact your local Jobcentre, careers office or TEC/LEC for details.

OPPORTUNITIES

There are few direct openings, either with the Forestry Commission or private sector employers. However, there are good opportunities for those who are prepared to undertake contract work on a self-employed basis – increasingly, the Forestry Commission and other organizations use the services of contractors rather than directly employed labour.

The following journals may carry advertisements for vacancies in forestry work: *Quarterly Journal of Forestry*, *Forestry*, *British Timber*, *Timber Grower*, and *Scottish Forestry*.

PAY AND CONDITIONS

There are wage agreements for forestry workers. Unskilled workers aged 18 years and over earn minimum wages of £157.17p. Wages for other workers vary according to experience, type of work and seniority. Ranger trainees – £163.41p a week; head rangers – £275.73p a week.

Skilled workers, including foremen/women, receive a higher basic wage of around £180 to £250 a week. Pieceworkers are usually able to earn substantially more than the basic rate. Overtime may be available.

A 42-hour week, inclusive of meal breaks, is standard for forest workers, although some overtime and weekend work may be necessary. Starting and finishing times often depend on the season. Ranger grades work a flexible five-day week.

PROSPECTS

Forest workers with suitable experience and personal qualities may be promoted to foreman/woman.

The duties and responsibilities of a foreman/woman include supervising the work of a group of forest workers or contractors, to maintain standards, output and safety measures. Foremen/women are also responsible for the timing of work and keeping accurate time sheets. They are involved with on-the-job training and generally keeping a watch for hazards such as damage by fire, insects, wild animals, disease and trespass.

Forest workers who show suitability may become wardens or rangers, although vacancies are few and sought after.

Within the private sector, it may be possible to progress to supervisory and even managerial posts by experience only. Absence of a clear hierarchy of responsibility, however, may mean comparatively fewer opportunities occur.

The Forestry Commission and many private sector employers encourage employees in the development of their full potential by providing the opportunity for further training and education.

RELATED OCCUPATIONS

Farm worker, horticultural worker, wood mill worker, gamekeeper, fish farmer, countryside ranger/warden, forest officer.

FORESTRY: WAF

FURTHER INFORMATION

Forestry and Arboriculture Safety and Training Council (FASTCO)*, 231 Corstorphine Road, Edinburgh EH12 7AT, 0131 314 6247, e-mail: fastco\www.btinternetcom\jindex.html

Enquiries about employment with Forest Enterprise as a forest worker can be made to Local Forest District Offices; the address and telephone number can be found in local telephone directories.

FURTHER READING

Leaflets/booklets are available from the addresses marked*.

Working in Outdoor Jobs – COIC

In the careers library classified under WAF.

VETERINARY WORK: WAL

1. VETERINARY SURGEON CLCI:WAL
2. VETERINARY NURSE CLCI:WAL

BACKGROUND INFORMATION

Veterinary surgeons (vets) work mainly in general practice, where they treat a variety of animals. Much of the work, particularly in urban areas, is with domestic pets, but some vets treat farm animals, poultry, horses and ponies. There are also specialist areas, such as public health and research and investigation into animal disease, in which vets are employed. Just as surgeons treating human patients are assisted by hospital nurses, so veterinary surgeons are assisted by veterinary nurses (VNs). VNs help during treatment and operations, and also assist with the general running of veterinary practices.

1. VETERINARY SURGEON (WAL)

THE WORK

Around three-quarters of all vets in the UK work in general practice; others hold appointments in the State Veterinary Service, universities, research establishments, pharmaceutical companies and other organizations. The work varies considerably in these different settings.

General practice

The main emphasis in general practice is on diagnosis and treatment of disease and injury. Vets also inoculate animals against disease, carry out neutering to prevent unwanted breeding, and advise owners on matters such as food intake and breeding.

A substantial proportion of the work is with domestic pets such as dogs, cats, rabbits, hamsters and caged birds. Many vets may also treat horses and ponies.

Some practices in rural areas work mainly with farm animals or horses, others with 'small animals' (mainly pets); mixed practices deal with the whole range of species.

Vets working with farm animals are concerned with matters such as animal health and welfare, improvements in productivity, artificial insemination, and disease control programmes. Modern farming demands a high standard of veterinary service – this may include providing written reports.

A considerable amount of practice time may be spent on 'part-time' appointments. Many vets in farm practice are local veterinary inspectors for the Ministry of Agriculture; their duties include testing cattle for disease, inspecting cattle markets, and working in abattoirs to ensure welfare and hygiene standards are met. Vets may also inspect conditions at greyhound race tracks, riding establishments, zoos, dog breeding and boarding kennels, and pet shops, on behalf of local authorities. They may advise on the welfare of laboratory animals used in scientific experiments.

Other appointments

Vets employed by the animal welfare societies or the Royal Army Veterinary Corps are engaged in similar duties to those in general practice, whereas those working for organizations such as research institutes and pharmaceutical companies may concentrate entirely on research. In university veterinary schools, vets teach and carry out research.

In the State Veterinary Service, investigation and field officers are involved in matters such as the control of disease, special investigations, general advisory work and the improvement of farm animal welfare. There is no clear distinction between investigation and field officers, although the former provide most diagnostic services, the latter statutory work, carried out where there are legal obligations – for instance, after a notifiable disease, such as foot-and-mouth, has been reported.

WORK ENVIRONMENT

Vets in small animal practices spend much of their time in the surgery. In mixed practices and practices dealing with farm animals or horses, a lot of the time is spent travelling – 100 miles a day is not uncommon.

Vets in general practice have a great deal of contact with people from a variety of social backgrounds, and also with practice staff, including other vets, veterinary nurses and other workers, such as receptionists.

Research and investigatory work is carried out in both laboratory and clinical areas. Most research jobs involve some contact with people from within the organization and outside it.

All vets must be prepared to work in smelly and messy conditions; they need to wear appropriate protective clothing for the job they are tackling.

SKILLS AND INTERESTS

Vets need to be dedicated to animals and their welfare. Veterinary practice is not a '9am-to-5pm' job, and the training is lengthy; commitment and a sense of vocation are essential.

Dealing with people is an important part of the work; vets should be tactful, patient and sympathetic, with good communication skills. They often need to help owners to make difficult decisions, such as whether to have an elderly and much loved pet put down.

Good powers of observation are required – animals cannot, of course, describe their symptoms; to make a diagnosis, the vet must be aware of small and important changes in an animal's appearance and behaviour.

Manual dexterity is needed for animal handling and performing surgical procedures. The work can be physically demanding, particularly when it involves horses or farm animals. Vets often work in cold, wet, dirty and smelly conditions.

It is important not to be squeamish about messy tasks, such as making internal examinations.

Veterinary practice is unsuitable for people who are allergic to fur or hair.

Vets in private practice need to develop all the skills associated with running a business. In public appointments, vets carry considerable responsibility and require strong personalities to enforce hygiene regulations that may affect the livelihood of other people.

ENTRY REQUIREMENTS

Entry is via a veterinary degree. This is extremely competitive; it is harder to obtain a university place to study veterinary science than to enter any other course.

The minimum academic requirements for university entry are two A levels/three H grades and three other subjects at GCSE/S grade (A–C/1–3). In practice, however, applicants for places at university veterinary schools need three A levels/five H grades, with high grades. The most usual

VETERINARY WORK: WAL

subjects are chemistry, biology and either physics or maths, but other subject combinations (which must include chemistry) may be accepted, for instance chemistry, physics and zoology. At GCSE/S grade, preferred subjects include English, chemistry, physics, biology and maths or another numerate subject. Intending students should check detailed entry requirements with university veterinary schools. Advanced GNVQ/GSVQ Level III in Science is not yet accepted as equivalent to A levels/H grades.

Before applying for a place, it is important to spend at least two weeks helping out in a veterinary practice. All university veterinary schools also now insist on applicants having had experience in handling healthy animals including livestock – for instance on a farm, in kennels, catteries or riding stables. This experience helps intending students to decide whether they are really suited to the work and enables them to prove their interest and commitment to the university veterinary schools.

TRAINING

The university veterinary schools in Great Britain have been allowed to increase their intake to a 'core' of about 400 students, with the schools free to admit additional numbers on payment of fees, subject to the requirements of their university.

Six university veterinary schools offer degrees in veterinary science, veterinary medicine or veterinary medicine and surgery. They are: Bristol, Cambridge, Edinburgh, Glasgow, Liverpool, and London. The length of the course is five years, except at Cambridge, which runs a six-year course.

Degrees from the six university veterinary schools confer on holders the right to membership of the Royal College of Veterinary Surgeons (RCVS) and the right to practise as a vet in the UK and other European Union countries (provided they are citizens of the UK or another EU country). No one can practise as a vet in the UK without being a member of the RCVS.

The way subjects are spread through the veterinary degree course varies from university to university; there is no uniform pattern. All, however, cover: scientific disciplines dealing with animal structure and functions (for example, anatomy, physiology and biochemistry); pharmacology, pathology, microbiology, parasitology and bacteriology; animal health and husbandry; clinical medicine and surgery; reproduction; and veterinary public health.

Courses cover all the main domestic and agricultural species. Students learn to handle and examine animals from the first year onwards. They also receive instruction in matters such as legal requirements, meat inspection and food hygiene.

In the vacations, all students are required to obtain specific experience in farm and veterinary work. This includes 26 weeks' 'extra-mural tuition' during the later years of the course, spent mainly in veterinary practices, but also at laboratories, investigation centres and abattoirs as well as twelve weeks' animal husbandry experience within the first two years of the course.

After graduation, those who enter general practice start as assistants. They usually remain assistants for several years, until they have the experience to be accepted as partners. To acquire a partnership, it is necessary to make a financial investment in the practice.

LATE ENTRY

The university veterinary schools consider the selection of a few mature students each year; the majority of those who are accepted are graduates with first or upper second class honours degrees in related subjects such as biochemistry or zoology.

Mature applicants are advised to write to the university veterinary schools for advice on their individual cases.

OPPORTUNITIES

There are some 11,600 active vets in the UK – including general practitioners and those employed in other fields. The Royal College of Veterinary Surgeons has over 18,000 members, but this figure includes retired and overseas members.

At present, the demand for veterinary surgeons exceeds supply.

About 9,700 vets work in **private practice.** On average, there are three or four vets in a practice, but there are variations: some practices are single-handed, whereas others are staffed by as many as 15 vets.

Vets in private practice are self-employed. However, newly qualified vets are employed by practices, as assistants, on a salaried basis. Once they have gained experience, they may be able to purchase a share in a practice; alternatively, they may set up a new practice.

The State Veterinary Service is part of the Food Safety Directorate of the Ministry of Agriculture, Fisheries and Food (MAFF). The Veterinary Field Service is responsible for the control and eradication of notifiable diseases of animals, control of the animal health aspects of international trade in animals and animal products, and the monitoring and promotion of farm animal welfare. Animal Health Divisional Officers are located throughout Great Britain.

Several agencies of MAFF also employ vets. The Veterinary Laboratories Agency provides diagnostic services to practising vets, as well as disease surveillance and laboratory support to the Veterinary Field Service via its Veterinary Investigation Centres and the Central Veterinary Laboratory. The Veterinary Medicines Directorate is responsible for the licensing of veterinary medicines for use in the UK. The Meat Hygiene Service (MHS) is responsible for the enforcement of public health regulations in slaughterhouses and other meat premises. Additionally, the proposed Food Standards Agency will give veterinary advice to policy makers on public health matters relating to food, including licensing of slaughterhouses and auditing the MHS.

University veterinary schools– in the six universities offering veterinary courses, the work includes research, undergraduate and postgraduate teaching, and the provision of clinical and pathological services.

Research institutes– include Agricultural and Food Research Council and Medical Research Council establishments and the charity Animal Health Trust.

In **pharmaceutical companies, industry and commerce** the work includes investigations into medical or veterinary problems, biomedical research and technical advice on the development of drugs, vaccines and food additives. There may be opportunities for overseas travel.

In **local government** some veterinary surgeons are employed on a full-time basis to advise on animal-related

VETERINARY WORK: WAL

matters and to supervise the enforcement of public health and animal welfare legislation. Some of these have transferred to the new Meat Hygiene Service. This work is also carried out on a part-time basis by vets in private practice.

Animal welfare societies employ about 230 vets, and include the People's Dispensary for Sick Animals (PDSA), the Royal Society for the Prevention of Cruelty to Animals (RSPCA) and the Blue Cross. The main employer is the PDSA.

In the **Royal Army Veterinary Corps** the work mainly involves looking after the Army's horses and dogs. Vets normally enter on short service commissions, although regular commissions are available. There are opportunities to serve in every country in which the British Army is stationed.

Overseas Development Administration– contract appointments in developing countries are available.

Apart from the opportunities to work abroad described above, it is also possible for vets from the UK to practise in other European countries, as their qualifications are recognized throughout the European Union.

PAY AND CONDITIONS

Veterinary assistants in general practice (the majority of vets start their careers in such posts) usually earn between £15,000 and £25,000. In addition, most veterinary assistants are paid housing and car allowances. Earnings of principals and partners depend very much on the success and location of the practice.

Vets in government service, the universities, research institutes and commercial organizations usually work office hours, but may still be called upon to work extra hours as necessary.

There are some opportunities for part-time work.

Running a veterinary practice is a 24 hours a day, 365 days a year responsibility. Every practitioner has an obligation to deal with emergencies. In a single-handed practice, the vet can only take time off if a member of a neighbouring practice agrees to provide cover or if a locum is employed. Even in practices with several vets, someone has to be on call at all times.

PROSPECTS

The majority of newly qualified vets start their careers as assistants in general practice; they may move into other branches of the profession later on.

In general practice, vets generally become senior assistants after two or three years. After gaining further experience, they may become partners or set up their own practices. Both options require a substantial financial investment.

In the State Veterinary Service, there is a clear promotion structure; the same applies to university work (candidates for promotion are usually expected to hold a postgraduate degree or diploma). In industry, promotion opportunities depend on the size of the company; progression may mean moving out of veterinary work into a more general management role.

The contracting policy of the government agencies means there may be opportunities for freelance work as a vet, either direct or via a specialist employment agency, but, due to the shortage of vets in the UK, there is an inflow of vets from other European countries for these posts.

Prospects for promotion in animal welfare societies are limited.

RELATED OCCUPATIONS

Zoologist, biologist, doctor (GP), doctor (hospital), veterinary nurse, RSPCA/SSPCA inspector.

FURTHER INFORMATION AND READING

Please see article 2. VETERINARY NURSE.

2. VETERINARY NURSE (WAL)

THE WORK

Veterinary nurses (VNs) assist vets with the care and treatment of animal patients. They work mainly with dogs, cats, small mammals such as hamsters and rabbits, and caged birds, although in some practices they may also work with farm animals and horses, or with exotic species such as snakes, which are becoming increasingly popular as pets.

The nursing duties of a VN involve generally assisting the vet in the practice. VNs hold animals whilst vets carry out examinations and treatment. They collect specimens, make simple laboratory tests, and, when specimens require more extensive testing, prepare samples for posting to commercial laboratories.

Assisting vets during operations is an important aspect of the work. VNs prepare animal patients for surgery, for instance by shaving the operation site. They assist with administering and monitoring anaesthesia, and hand instruments and dressings to the vet during the operation. They monitor the animal's condition during surgery and after the operation.

VNs also maintain the equipment used for anaesthesia, radiography and laboratory testing. They keep stocks of drugs, and may dispense drugs, under the direct supervision of the veterinary surgeon.

Other nursing duties include developing x-rays, assisting with the preparation and positioning of animals for x-rays, and preparing and administering drugs (this includes giving injections under the supervision of the veterinary surgeon). VNs deal with emergencies and may give first aid in the vet's absence. Occasionally they accompany vets on their rounds.

Veterinary nurses also carry out other practice duties. They prepare the consulting room and diagnostic equipment. Before operations, they get the theatre ready, and sterilize and lay out surgical instruments. They may have general cleaning duties.

In practices that have hospitalization quarters, VNs are involved in general daily care of the animals. They clean pens or cages, provide fresh bedding, feed the animals and ensure that a supply of fresh drinking water is available. They also exercise and groom animals in their charge.

VNs may also have reception and clerical duties, including answering the telephone, keeping an appointments book, maintaining and filing case records and other documents such as laboratory reports, and dealing with correspondence. They also advise owners on matters such as vaccinations, neutering, house-training and nutrition.

Uniforms (green and white striped for student VNs, bottle green for qualified VNs) are provided by employers.

VETERINARY WORK: WAL

WORK ENVIRONMENT

The work takes place in the practice premises and animal quarters. In mixed practices, veterinary nurses may sometimes work out of doors, helping with the treatment of large animals.

Working conditions, particularly in the animal quarters, are noisy, sometimes cramped, and, on occasion, smelly.

Veterinary nurses spend much of their working day with vets, often on a one-to-one basis. They also have a great deal of contact with animal owners.

SKILLS AND INTERESTS

Veterinary nurses need a strong interest in animals, but without over-sentimentality. An interest in science, particularly biology, is also important.

VNs need to be able to receive and transmit information accurately; during training, they learn the terminology used by vets, and are expected to have a good command of the correct terminology by the time they qualify. It is also important to be able to communicate well with other members of the practice staff and with animal owners. A good telephone manner is required. Tolerance and patience are needed for dealing with owners who are anxious or upset about their pets.

Manual dexterity is required for animal handling and delicate tasks such as giving injections.

A sense of responsibility is important, to ensure that the animals are properly cared for and treatment routines followed precisely.

VNs need neat, legible handwriting for keeping records. Keyboard skills are an advantage.

Willingness to carry out messy jobs such as cleaning up blood and vomit is essential.

ENTRY REQUIREMENTS

For the Royal College of Veterinary Surgeons (RCVS) Veterinary Nursing Scheme, entry requirements are as follows:

1. Five GCSEs/S grades (A–C/1–3), including English language and two passes in maths or science subjects plus two others of the student's choice, or equivalent/higher qualifications, eg Intermediate GNVQ/GSVQ Level II in Science.

2. Applicants must be 17 years or over. (Consent of a parent or guardian must be obtained for applicants under 18 years.)

3. Applicants must have obtained paid employment at an approved training and Assessment Centre (ATAC). An ATAC is a veterinary practice or similar establishment approved by the RCVS for training and assessing veterinary nurses; not all practices are ATACs. A list of ATACs is available from the British Veterinary Nursing Association (BVNA). The BVNA's employment register may help with finding a position.

Application for enrolment application forms to become a student is made to the BVNA with a statement showing you can meet these entry requirements. Fees are charged for enrolment and for each examination.

Applicants who cannot meet the educational requirements can take the BNVA Pre-Veterinary Nursing exam which qualifies for entry. The Pre-VN is a one-year course, and the only entry requirement is being currently employed in a veterinary practice, not necessarily an ATAC. Employment in a nursing auxiliary role in veterinary practices may be obtainable without qualifications.

TRAINING

RCVS Veterinary Nursing scheme

Training lasts for a minimum of two years and includes the study of anatomy, physiology, first aid and nursing, human first aid, husbandry and dietary requirements, theatre practice, kennel and hospital management, quarantine procedures, laboratory techniques, anaesthesia, dispensing, radiography and dark room techniques, health and safety, and exotics.

Students gain practical experience, with tuition from employers and colleagues, by working in an ATAC. Theoretical knowledge may be gained by attending full-time, part-time, day release or evening courses at colleges, by correspondence course or by private study. Although a few colleges offer full-time residential courses (of varying length), it is not possible to attend these without having completed a period of training at an ATAC. Details of all courses are available from the BVNA.

Two examinations must be passed before a student qualifies as a veterinary nurse and becomes eligible for entry to the List of Veterinary Nurses maintained by the RCVS. The Part I examination is usually taken one year after enrolment with BVNA. The Part II examination can be taken nine months after passing Part I. However, a student will not be deemed to be qualified until they have completed 24 months in an approved ATAC.

Entry may be possible via training schemes for young people, for those who fulfil the RCVS VN entry requirements. Contact your local careers office or TEC/LEC for further information.

LATE ENTRY

There are no fixed upper age limits. Adults must have the qualifications described in ENTRY REQUIREMENTS, and their training is the same as for young people. Rates of pay are also likely to be the same as for younger entrants, and this may be a deterrent.

OPPORTUNITIES

There are about 5,500 qualified VNs in the UK. The majority work with vets in general practice. Some work in veterinary hospitals, which are veterinary practices fulfilling certain RCVS requirements. There are also a number of VNs employed by animal welfare societies. Over 180 are employed by the People's Dispensary for Sick Animals (PDSA) at its 57 veterinary centres throughout Britain. All PDSA entrants train for the VN qualification. Other animal welfare societies like the RSPCA and the Blue Cross also train and employ VNs.

Some veterinary nurses work in university veterinary schools and in research establishments. There are a few opportunities in zoos and animal laboratories. Breeding and boarding kennels may employ VNs as managers. Some move into jobs as representatives for companies in the fields of veterinary medicine or insurance.

The BVNA runs an employment register that puts prospective students and qualified VNs in touch with potential employers. Vacancies are also advertised in *Veterinary Nursing Journal* and *Veterinary Record*.

There are opportunities to work abroad; a number of VNs are employed in Australia and New Zealand.

Temporary locum work is available, particularly during peak holiday periods.

PAY AND CONDITIONS

There are no nationally agreed rates of pay for veterinary nurses. Salaries vary according to employer, geographical location and the individual nurse's experience.

The PDSA pays students a starting salary of £6,199 up to £6,758, depending on age and qualifications. On passing the Part II examinations, nurses are paid between £9,761 and £11,811. The scale for head nurses extends from £13,609 to £16,466.

Hours of work depend on the individual employer, but will generally be at least 35 hours a week and often 37 to 40. Hours are likely to be variable, with on-call duties. Weekend work is often required. There are some opportunities for part-time work.

PROSPECTS

Until recently, prospects for promotion have been rather limited, but they are now improving. In general practice, VNs may become head nurses or practice managers; duties include organizing staff rotas, interviewing prospective staff, assisting with training, dealing with banking and carrying out basic book-keeping.

Further qualifications may improve prospects. Qualified veterinary nurses working in approved training centres may study for the two-year Diploma in Advanced Veterinary Nursing (Surgical). Nutritional certificates are also available.

VNs are also moving into related careers such as product management (marketing) with pharmaceutical companies, lecturing and training.

RELATED OCCUPATIONS

Zoo keeper, kennel worker, horse groom, RSPCA/SSPCA inspector, dog groomer, guide dog trainer/mobility instructor.

FURTHER INFORMATION

The Blue Cross*, Shilton Road, Burford, Oxon OX18 4PF, 01993 822651

British Veterinary Nursing Association Ltd*, Level 15, Terminus House, Terminus Street, Harlow, Essex CM20 1XA, 01279 450567 (please enclose a large sae)

The Royal College of Veterinary Surgeons (RCVS)*, Belgravia House, 62–64 Horseferry Road, London SW1P 2AF, 0171 222 2001 (sae required), www.rcvs.org.uk/rcvs/

People's Dispensary for Sick Animals (PDSA)*, Whitechapel Way, Priorslee, Telford, Shropshire TF2 9PQ, 01952 290999

RSPCA*, Causeway, Horsham, West Sussex RH12 1HG, 01403 264181, www.rspca.org.uk

FURTHER READING

Leaflets/booklets are available from the addresses marked*.

Working with Animals – COIC

A Career as a Veterinary Surgeon – Royal College of Veterinary Surgeons

Careers Working with Animals – Kogan Page

In the careers library classified under WAL.

ANIMAL WELFARE: WAL

RSPCA/SSPCA INSPECTOR CLCI:WAL

THE WORK

Inspectors aim to prevent cruelty to animals and to encourage kindness and humanity in their treatment.

Inspectors spend most of their time working independently, dealing directly with animals and with the owners/people concerned. They perform a variety of different tasks each day, travelling around in a specially equipped van containing ropes, rescue equipment, overalls, drugs (for the humane destruction of animals etc) and a radio/mobile telephone allowing speedy contact in cases of emergency.

An inspector's work can be roughly divided into three parts.

Law enforcement and investigatory work

Inspectors carry out the policing function of the Society, attempting to enforce the legislation affecting animals. The principal laws are the Protection of Animals Act 1911 and the Protection of Animals (Scotland) Act 1912; other laws concern such things as the transit of animals, the protection of birds and pets, and animal welfare. There are also a large number of specific regulations concerning different species.

The majority of complaints come from the public. All are investigated, logged and reported, even though around three-quarters are unfounded. Inspectors visit premises and try to gain access to the animal suspected of suffering. They may give advice, take statements and ask the police to assist by obtaining search warrants in suspicious circumstances. They have no powers to force entry or to remove animals (unless the owner agrees), however bad the conditions. The inspector decides on what action to take, for instance educating an owner or attempting to remove the animal.

Court proceedings are taken against people suspected of wilful cruelty or neglect. If investigations lead the inspector to believe that court action may be possible, details are sent to the headquarters so that proceedings can begin. The inspector's evidence to the court must be accurate and detailed, following strictly the requirements of the Police and Criminal Evidence Act 1984, if a case is to be successful.

Other duties include detecting the occurrence of illegal acts: eg dog fighting, cock fighting, badger baiting etc.

Inspection

Inspectors are responsible for the general patrol, observation and routine inspection of a designated area, to try and ensure all establishments selling or dealing with animals (eg pet shops, boarding kennels, riding stables, zoos, circuses, farms and slaughterhouses) maintain proper standards. An important aspect of the work is attending local events such as cattle markets and race meetings.

Inspectors are concerned with the transportation of live animals, by road, sea or air. They may check the conditions in which animals are transported – calling at railway stations when a consignment of animals is expected, or inspecting a wagon transporting animals.

Welfare work

On receiving a victim of cruelty, or an abandoned or unwanted pet, the inspector calls the veterinary surgeon, if necessary, and then attempts to secure accommodation for the animal. The Society runs its own shelters, and maintains lists of volunteers willing to accept animals either temporarily or permanently. A good many animals, although kept as long as possible, are not found homes and must be destroyed. The inspector is required to slaughter farm animals humanely at times and euthanase pet animals.

Some animals become injured as a result of accidents, for example, in road accidents, or birds that are victims of oil spillages. The inspector attempts to alleviate their suffering, in whatever way is possible. The inspector is also involved in rescue work. This can cover anything from rounding up strays, to complex and difficult operations involving animals stranded on cliffs, or sinking in mud. In some cases expert assistance is sought from, for instance, climbers or coastguards.

Inspectors receive large numbers of telephone enquiries, usually from members of the public seeking advice about animal welfare. If they are unable to advise individuals directly, they usually know to whom to refer them. They sometimes have to respond to emergency calls after normal hours.

WORK ENVIRONMENT

Inspectors usually cover an area of between 50 and 2,000 square miles, depending on location. Much of their time is taken up investigating complaints. A major problem in urban areas may be abandoned animals; while, in rural areas, much time may be spent visiting farms and livestock markets. Coastal regions have particular problems relating to the effects of pollution on wildlife.

Inspectors spend about half of their time on the road between visits. Outdoor work can involve cold, wet and dirty conditions; rescue work may be dangerous. They may be called out at any time, day or night, though there is normally a rostering system for out-of-hours work.

Inspectors work largely alone, keeping in regular contact with their chief inspector. They liaise closely with other specialists, such as veterinary surgeons, the police, the fire brigade and rescue workers.

SKILLS AND INTERESTS

Inspectors should be dedicated and caring, with a genuine concern for animals and an ability to cope dispassionately and calmly in emergency situations. They should not be squeamish, and must be prepared to slaughter animals humanely if necessary to prevent suffering.

Inspectors must be tactful, diplomatic, confident and level-headed, since people suspected of cruelty may be resentful, obstructive or even aggressive. The work can be frustrating at times, since inspectors' powers are limited and they may be unable to act in every situation seeming to demand it. They should be able to plan their own work and should have good standards of verbal or written communication. They must be prepared to work long hours, spending a lot of time outdoors, often in adverse weather conditions.

ENTRY REQUIREMENTS

Applicants for the RSPCA and the SSPCA need a good general education and a full, clean, current driving licence. They must pass a medical. The RSPCA requires applicants to be able to swim 50 metres fully clothed, be fit and able to take part in physical training, have animal-handling experience, and be prepared to relocate to any part of England and Wales after training. They must also have good interpersonal skills.

The SSPCA requires applicants to have had previous experience working with animals, preferably from a farm or veterinary background.

The minimum age for entry is 22 years for the RSPCA, or 25 years for the SSPCA.

TRAINING

RSPCA training lasts approximately six months. The course comprises an initial twelve weeks' training at the Society's headquarters in Horsham, followed by eight weeks' field training under the supervision of an experienced officer and a final five weeks' study at headquarters in Horsham.

Theoretical training covers such subjects as: the law relating to animal welfare, animal injury and disease; investigative and interview techniques; court procedure; rescue techniques; humane slaughter; the work of animal clinics, hospitals and homes; report writing; and animal first aid, care and welfare instruction. Trainees must pass written exams. After training there is a one-year probationary period.

Training with the SSPCA usually lasts six months. Part of this is spent at the Society's headquarters in Edinburgh, part gaining field experience. As with the RSPCA, a final examination is necessary.

Successful trainees may be posted anywhere, and become permanent members of staff at the rank of inspector.

LATE ENTRY

All entrants are adults. The maximum age for entry to the RSPCA is normally 40 years, although applicants leaving the Armed Forces may be admitted up to the age of 42 years. The upper age limit for the SSPCA is 45 years. The SSPCA requires practical experience of work with animals, preferably farm animals. The RSPCA gives preference to applicants who have had experience working with the public. Experience of working with animals is not essential for the RSPCA, although it may be an advantage. Experience may be gained in veterinary practices, farming, kennels etc.

OPPORTUNITIES

The RSPCA employs around 300 inspectors; the SSPCA employs around 45 inspectors who cover the whole of Scotland apart from the city of Aberdeen and county of Aberdeenshire (which are the responsibility of a small, local society).

Competition for available posts is severe. The RSPCA receives several hundred applications every year for around 24 vacancies. The SSPCA has about two vacancies a year and receives 20 to 30 applicants a week.

PAY AND CONDITIONS

RSPCA. Trainee inspectors receive a basic salary of £10,085 plus accommodation allowance. Experienced inspectors are paid on a scale from £15,268 to £17,450.

Inspectors also receive overtime payments for evening and weekend work. Those working in or around London receive an additional supplement. RSPCA Inspectors work Monday to Friday, 9am to 6pm.

SSPCA. Probationary inspectors earn £11,987 rising to £14,118 on completion of a six-month training period. After training, the salary scale then increases to a maximum of £15,891. With continuing experience and passing examinations, inspectors can progress to Chief Inspector and earn £17,571. Most inspectors live in tied houses but there is an allowance for those who wish to live in their own property. SSPCA Inspectors work Monday to Friday, 8.30am to 5pm with weekends, evening duties etc by roster.

PROSPECTS

Inspectors may receive promotion to higher grades. Some RSPCA inspectors move into specialist work at the headquarters in Horsham, investigating matters such as the transport and slaughter of livestock in the UK and EU, or illegal blood sports.

RELATED OCCUPATIONS

Veterinary nurse, kennel worker, zoo keeper, countryside ranger/warden, guide dog trainer/mobility instructor.

FURTHER INFORMATION

The Royal Society for the Prevention of Cruelty to Animals*, Causeway, Horsham, West Sussex RH12 1HG, 01403 264181, www.rspca.org.uk

The Scottish Society for the Prevention of Cruelty to Animals*, Braehead Mains, 603 Queensferry Road, Edinburgh EH4 6EA, 0131 339 0222

FURTHER READING

Leaflets/booklets are available from the addresses marked*.

Working with Animals – COIC

Careers Working with Animals – Kogan Page

In the careers library classified under WAL.

OTHER WORK WITH ANIMALS: WAM

1. **GUIDE DOG TRAINER/MOBILITY INSTRUCTOR CLCI:WAM**
2. **KENNEL WORKER CLCI:WAM**
3. **DOG GROOMER CLCI:WAM**
4. **HORSE GROOM CLCI:WAM**
5. **RIDING INSTRUCTOR CLCI:WAM**
6. **ZOO KEEPER CLCI:WAM**

BACKGROUND INFORMATION

Many people are very keen to work with animals. This leads to great competition for jobs. Every employer, from zoos to kennels to riding schools, is inundated with applications from young people.

Looking after animals all day is very different from caring for family pets. The work is hard, often dirty, with long, unsocial hours. Some jobs can be very lonely, with only the companionship of animals for much of the day. However, there will usually be some contact with people – owners, customers and the general public; in several jobs outlined in the articles following, skills in dealing with people are important.

In addition, jobs with animals are rarely well paid. Careers with the national organizations, or in research, offer salaries that compare favourably with those in other jobs. Some of the larger commercial establishments pay reasonable wages, but rates of pay with the small privately owned concerns can be very low indeed. Profits in the animal care business are not large, and employers cannot afford high wages.

The jobs described here are all different, but they all have certain similar requirements. Anyone interested in a career with animals must be fit, healthy, unsentimental and not allergic to fur and hair. There is always some risk of picking up an infection from the animals. The most popular jobs are those with dogs and horses.

1. GUIDE DOG TRAINER/MOBILITY INSTRUCTOR (WAM)

BACKGROUND INFORMATION

The Guide Dogs for the Blind Association was formed in 1931 to train guide dogs and their new owners to work together. Most guide dog owners regard their dogs as an extension of themselves, enabling them to do all the everyday things sighted people take for granted: shopping, walking to work, crossing roads and using public transport. Owners and dogs are matched very carefully, and are helped to form a good working partnership.

About half of the guide dogs currently used are crosses between Labradors and golden retrievers, although other breeds are also used.

Young puppies are placed with families, known as puppy walkers, who take care of them for a year, getting them accustomed to home life, public transport and busy streets. Young adult dogs then go to one of the Association's regional centres where they are placed with guide dog trainers for training. During their training at the centre, the dogs live in kennels. When the dogs are ready, usually after about six months, they are handed over to guide dog mobility instructors who carry out advanced training, and then train dogs and owners together for four weeks.

THE WORK

Guide dog trainers begin to work with the dogs when they leave their puppy walkers and come to the regional centre. At first they help the dogs to settle in, spending the first few weeks taking them for pleasure walks and assessing their suitability for training. After about three weeks, proper training begins.

Dogs are first taught to walk in the centre of the pavement and to obey simple commands – 'Forward', 'Left', 'Back' etc. They then learn to sit at every kerb and not to cross if traffic is approaching. Next they are introduced to wearing a harness and begin more specialized training, learning obstacle avoidance. Dogs learn that when they are in harness they are working; when not in harness they are as free as any other family dog.

All the time the trainer is building up close communication with the dog – praising it and teaching it to respond to voice and hand. Before handing the dog on to the mobility instructor, the trainer spends some time wearing a blindfold whilst working with the dog.

The **guide dog mobility instructor** takes over the training in the last few months before the dog meets its owner. More advanced guiding skills are taught, such as shoulder work – helping the person handling it to get through a crowd without bumping into people. Dogs are then carefully matched with their new owners. An elderly retired person, for example, has different requirements from a younger person still at work with a more active social life. Visually impaired people spend a month at the centre and are taught – in groups of four owners and dogs to an instructor – how to get to know and work with their animal. Instructors encourage the owners to have confidence in their dogs, and to work in gradually more complicated situations. They teach owners how to handle their animals correctly, without damaging the training that has already been given.

After the owners and dogs have gone home they are visited by a guide dog mobility instructor. The instructor makes further visits periodically to provide support and help with any problems.

WORK ENVIRONMENT

Both trainers and instructors spend most of their working hours outdoors, in all weathers.

SKILLS AND INTERESTS

Instructors and trainers need to be physically fit and prepared to work for long hours at a time. They need good physical co-ordination, a great deal of patience and, of course, a love of animals.

Instructors need to be good with people too. They must be able to sympathize with the fears of a visually impaired person about to receive a guide dog, and to sort out any worries and apprehensions. They must be able to establish good relationships with people and, as teachers, know when to be firm. A sense of humour often helps.

ENTRY REQUIREMENTS

Guide dog trainers – entry requirements are three GCSEs/S grades (A–C/1–3) including English language. The minimum age is 18 years.

Guide dog mobility instructors – entry requirements are five GCSEs/S grades (A–C/1–3) including English, maths,

OTHER WORK WITH ANIMALS: WAM

a science subject and preferably a social science subject. Minimum age is 18 years.

A full driving licence is essential for both types of work.

Experience of handling dogs or other animals is also required, as is work or social experience with adults from various backgrounds.

TRAINING

Guide dog trainers join the Association as training entrants, spending two months learning basic dog care skills, in the kennels. They then spend eleven months working towards the guide dog trainer qualification. All training is carried out by qualified Association staff at the regional centres, and all trainees are paid. Guide dog trainers work towards a City and Guilds qualification (guide dog trainer).

Guide dog mobility instructors serve a three-year apprenticeship. This is modular, and culminates in the Guide Dogs for the Blind Association's guide dog mobility qualification.

LATE ENTRY

Applications from older candidates are encouraged, since previous work experience is often valuable, especially if in a caring role or one working with animals. This experience may have been gained in either a paid or voluntary capacity.

OPPORTUNITIES

Between 16 and 20 apprentice guide dog mobility instructors are engaged each year. Guide dog trainers are engaged on an ongoing basis; however, there tend to be waiting lists for such positions. The Association receives around 100 enquiries every week from people interested in a career with guide dogs.

Employment is at The Guide Dogs for the Blind regional training centres at Middlesborough, Bolton, Leamington Spa, Redbridge, Wokingham, Exeter and Forfar in Scotland, and at the breeding centre at Tollgate, Warwickshire. There are also smaller support centres at Maidstone, Nottingham, Southampton, Liverpool, Sheffield, Cardiff, Belfast and Larkhall, Scotland.

PAY AND CONDITIONS

Guide dog trainers commence on £8,992, rising to £11,990 on qualifying (after a minimum of 13 months). The maximum salary is £14,106 reached by annual increments. Hours of work are 35 a week.

Apprentice guide dog mobility instructors commence on £13,576 rising to £19,540 on qualifying (after a minimum of 37 months). Guide dog mobility instructors work an average of 35 hours a week, but this includes weekends and bank holidays whilst training students with dogs. However, time off in lieu is given.

A six-month 'living in' period is compulsory for all new guide dog trainers and instructors, during which time food and accommodation are provided free of charge at the centre. After this period, accommodation is sometimes available, subject to appropriate charges and availability.

PROSPECTS

There are opportunities for dog trainers to be promoted to senior guide dog trainer or puppy walking supervisor. Guide dog mobility instructors may be promoted to supervisory and managerial posts.

RELATED OCCUPATIONS

Veterinary nurse, horse riding instructor, animal technician, dog groomer, kennel worker, farm worker, RSPCA/SSPCA inspector, zoo keeper.

FURTHER INFORMATION

Please see article 2. KENNEL WORKER.

FURTHER READING

Please see article 6. ZOO KEEPER.

2. KENNEL WORKER (WAM)

BACKGROUND INFORMATION

Kennels vary in size, some employing very few staff and others having several hundred dogs to look after. The latter are more likely to have managers, experienced kennel workers and trainees on the staff.

THE WORK

The work is hard and often dirty. Typical daily duties in all kennels include: cleaning out the kennels and changing bedding; exercising the dogs; checking for illness – dealing with minor ailments personally or sending for the vet; preparing meals and mixing special diets; and cleaning and grooming the dogs. From time to time kennel staff may also have to stay up all night with a bitch about to produce a litter. Those with hunt kennels may act as 'whippers-in', learning to train and control hounds.

Dogs may be in kennels for very short periods, in which case there is little chance to get to know them. But in various charities' kennels, staff may have cared for a dog for several months and come to know it well before it is handed over to a new owner. There will also be some contact with people.

Staff in some kennels meet prospective buyers and show them round; in others they may also have to advise customers on animal care. Kennel staff employed at training centres of the Guide Dogs for the Blind Association are expected to talk to and get to know the visually impaired people who have come to train with their dogs.

WORK ENVIRONMENT

This is largely outdoor work, exercising and feeding the animals, often in the cold and wet. Conditions can be dirty and smelly.

SKILLS AND INTERESTS

Kennel workers must love and care for dogs. They need to be hard-working and dedicated to the job.

An unsentimental love of animals is needed, and, because of the nature of some of the duties, staff should not be squeamish.

OTHER WORK WITH ANIMALS: WAM

Kennel workers require a firm but gentle manner and need to be able to handle all sizes and types of dogs. They need patience and the ability to encourage and calm nervous dogs.

The work requires a sense of responsibility and the ability to work without supervision and as part of a team.

Good health and physical fitness are essential; the work is physically demanding and active.

ENTRY REQUIREMENTS

Entry is possible without formal qualifications, although GCSEs/S grades (A–C/1–3) are an advantage.

Some private training schools ask for GCSEs/S grades (A–C/1–3) in English, biology and maths.

The Guide Dogs for the Blind Association requires applicants for kennel work to be over 18 years, with GCSEs/S grades (A–C/1–3) in English and maths, or equivalent.

An NVQ/SVQ Caring for Animals Level 2 would be useful but not essential.

There are no set entry requirements for BTEC first diploma courses in Animal Care, although colleges may require one to two GCSEs/S grades (A–C/1–3). For BTEC national certificate/diploma courses in Animal Care entry requirements are four GCSEs/S grades (A–C/1–3) or equivalent, preferably including maths and a science subject.

TRAINING

Training is generally given on the job, but there are also some full-time and part-time courses at colleges of further education and private training schools.

On-the-job training in private kennels: involves practical experience, supervised by the owner or manager. Young people often enter work in private kennels via training schemes for young people such as National Traineeships (contact your local careers office or TEC/LEC for details). Trainees may be able to take part-time courses at local colleges, leading to NVQs/SVQs in Animal Care at Levels 1 and 2. Alternatively, they may take an open learning course, run by the Animal Care College and Canine Studies Institute.

NVQ/SVQ in Animal Care is available at Level 1.

BTEC First Certificate/Diploma in Animal Care courses (generally one year, full-time, although some part-time courses are available) are offered by a number of colleges including Bishop Burton College of Agriculture, North East Surrey College of Technology, Cambridgeshire College of Agriculture and Horticulture, Carmarthenshire College of Technology and Art, Sparsholt College, Rodbaston College, Lancashire College of Agriculture and Horticulture, Pencoed College, Reaseheath College, Derbyshire College of Agriculture and Horticulture, Bicton College of Agriculture, Dorset College of Agriculture and Horticulture, Gloucestershire College of Agriculture, West Sussex College of Agriculture and Horticulture (Brinsbury College), and the College of Animal Welfare (Godmanchester, Cambridge).

BTEC National Diploma in Animal Care courses (usually two years, full-time) are available at Bicton College of Agriculture, Gloucestershire College of Agriculture, Sparsholt College, Bishop Burton College of Agriculture, Lancashire College of Agriculture and Horticulture, Pencoed College, and Rodbaston College, Staffordshire.

Training is also provided by private training schools attached to boarding kennels. Private training schools, which operate on a fee-paying basis, should be chosen with care.

Charitable and voluntary organizations, such as the Guide Dogs for the Blind Association, usually provide full-time training for their own staff.

The Animal Care College and Canine Studies Institute offers a variety of open learning courses covering various aspects of the care of dogs and other small animals.

LATE ENTRY

Late entry is unusual. The rates of pay for a trainee are not attractive, and unless capital is available to staff one's own kennels, prospects are limited. However, there is no formal upper age limit provided that one is keen and physically fit.

OPPORTUNITIES

There are several different types of kennel.

Breeding kennels are often fairly small family businesses specializing in the breeding of one or two types of dog.

Boarding kennels are where owners leave their pets for any period from a weekend to several weeks whilst they are away on holiday or business.

Quarantine kennels – dogs brought into this country must spend six months in a kennel approved by the Ministry of Agriculture, Fisheries and Food to ensure they are free from disease, particularly rabies.

Hunt kennels – hunting stables keep their own hounds and employ staff who act as kennel workers and 'whippers-in', training and controlling the hounds.

Racing kennels – greyhound kennels may be quite large with a trainer looking after groups of dogs and supervising one or two handlers.

Kennels maintained by animal welfare organizations – such as the RSPCA or the National Canine Defence League (NCDL). The RSPCA and NCDL care for strays and unwanted animals until they can be found a home.

There are also some opportunities in the **Armed Forces**.

Competition for vacancies with any of the above is very intense, with hundreds of people applying for very few posts. Vacancies are sometimes advertised in the specialist dog magazines. Preference is often given to those with experience of kennel work on a voluntary basis.

PAY AND CONDITIONS

Pay is variable, but can be up to £100 a week plus a bonus. In some establishments both pay and conditions can be very poor. Generally speaking, larger private establishments and charitable organizations tend to offer the best conditions, with set pay scales. Anyone applying for a job in kennels, particularly a training post, should try to choose an employer with a good reputation, and insist on a proper contract.

Kennel staff work unsocial hours including weekends and holidays. Boarding kennels are particularly busy in the summer holiday season and at Christmas and Easter.

OTHER WORK WITH ANIMALS: WAM

PROSPECTS

Prospects for advancement are not good except in some of the larger establishments, where kennel staff may progress to kennel supervisor, assistant kennel manager or kennel manager. Many entrants aspire eventually to run their own kennels; this requires a lot of capital, experience and a head for business.

RELATED OCCUPATIONS

Guide dog trainer/mobility instructor, dog groomer, RSPCA/SSPCA inspector, farm worker, veterinary nurse, zoo keeper.

FURTHER INFORMATION

Animal Care College and Canine Studies Institute*, Ascot House, High Street, Ascot, Berkshire SL5 7JG, 01344 28269

College of Animal Welfare*, Woodgreen Animal Shelter, Kingsbush Farm, London Road, Godmanchester, Cambridge PE18 8LJ, 01480 831177

Guide Dogs for the Blind Association*, Hillfields, Burghfield Common, Reading, Berkshire RG7 3YG, 01189 835555

National Canine Defence League, 17–26 Wakley Street, London EC1V 7LT, 0171 837 0006

Royal Society for the Prevention of Cruelty to Animals (RSPCA)*, Causeway, Horsham, West Sussex RH12 1HG, 01403 264181, www.rspca.org.uk

FURTHER READING

Please see article 6. ZOO KEEPER.

3. DOG GROOMER (WAM)

THE WORK

Dog groomers are concerned with dog trimming. They may also be known as dog or canine beauticians.

Many long- and short-haired breeds of dog require the attention of dog groomers; poodles may be the best known but others include spaniels, terriers, Old English sheepdogs and Afghan hounds. Some dogs need trimming every six weeks, to keep their coats manageable.

The dog should first be bathed, dried and brushed through. Clipping then follows, for which the dog is usually placed on a table. Careful attention must be given when clipping delicate areas, particularly around the face, between the pads and over the paws. Clipping involves using electric clippers, though a stripping knife (similar to a razor) may be used for those breeds with an inner protective coat of thick hairs (such as West Highland White Terriers), which could be damaged by clippers.

The animal's coat is brushed or combed and a final trim with scissors completes the grooming.

In addition to trimming and bathing dogs, groomers provide other services, which include nail clipping, teeth cleaning, ear cleaning and treatments for parasites. A dog groomer might expect to deal with around four to six dogs a day, depending on the attention the dogs require.

Some dog groomers prepare dogs for shows and competitions.

WORK ENVIRONMENT

Dog groomers work inside, usually based in a shop of some type. This may be a room adjoining a pet shop, part of a boarding kennel or breeder's premises, or a dog grooming salon. Some groomers work from their own homes and travel to owner's homes to give grooming services.

Working areas usually comprise a working table or bench, baths, sinks and kennels or places for dogs to wait between each stage of the process.

Much of the working day is spent standing. The atmosphere may be warm and humid.

SKILLS AND INTERESTS

In addition to liking animals, dog groomers must be able to handle dogs of all types. Talking to the animals while grooming can help to calm those that are nervous or agitated. Dog groomers should handle dogs with care and in a gentle manner. Manual dexterity is required for handling the equipment used in trimming and clipping. Accuracy when using clipping equipment is essential and great care is necessary to avoid injury to the animal.

Groomers should be able to work alone or as part of a team. The work may be considered creative to some extent; an eye for detail and good eye-to-hand co-ordination are important.

ENTRY REQUIREMENTS

There are no minimum educational requirements. Personal characteristics and practical ability are often considered more important than academic qualifications.

TRAINING

It is useful to have had some sort of experience in handling, bathing and grooming dogs before beginning training, though these skills can be learned during training. There are two main methods for training as a dog groomer: fee-paying course or traineeship. Training varies in quality and length.

Private fee-paying courses are available at a number of private training establishments and last anything from three months to one year, depending on the content of the course. The longer courses tend to include other aspects of dog care and give the student experience of different breeds of dog and types of cut and style. On completion of the course a certificate or diploma is usually awarded. A list of approved schools is available from the British Dog Groomers Association.

Traineeships – many dog groomers learn their craft by joining established parlours or experienced groomers as juniors, or by learning the trade as part of general kennel work. Training is given on the job, although it may include off-the-job training, and lasts for around one to two years.

It is also possible to learn basic grooming as part of a full-time course in animal care – see article 2. KENNEL WORKER.

There may be opportunities for school-leavers to obtain places in salons via specific training schemes for young people such as National Traineeships. Contact your local careers offices or TECs/LECs for details.

Dog groomers may take the Dog Grooming Certificate 775, which is a written paper and a series of skills tests developed by City and Guilds and the British Dog

OTHER WORK WITH ANIMALS: WAM

Groomers Association. It is recommended that entrants to the exam have had 18 months' to two years' experience.

The Advanced Grooming Diploma is open to anyone who has gained the C&G Dog Grooming Certificate 775.

NVQs/SVQS in Dog Grooming at Levels 2 and 3 will be available in late 1998.

LATE ENTRY

Entry onto fee-paying courses is open equally to adults and school-leavers. Mature candidates may find difficulty entering employment as trainees, since employers may tend to favour younger applicants.

There may be specific training opportunities directed at adults available in some areas for this type of work. Candidates may have to satisfy certain conditions to be eligible. Contact your local Jobcentre, careers office or TEC/LEC for details.

OPPORTUNITIES

There has been an increase in demand for the services of dog groomers in recent years. Many of the establishments traditionally providing services for, or with, animals – such as pet shops and boarding kennels – are offering grooming facilities as additional services.

However, the opportunities to work as a full-time dog groomer are limited and vary according to area, local demand and competition.

Demand for services may vary seasonally, as owners often let their dogs' coats grow in cold weather.

It may be difficult to find traineeship places and competition may be high for those that are available.

Vacancies may be advertised in *Our Dogs* and *Dog World*.

PAY AND CONDITIONS

Hours vary. In a salon, groomers usually work Monday to Saturday. Some groomers work weekends. Part-time work is possible.

It is not possible to give the wages of trainees or experienced dog groomers, since there are no national standards and many groomers are self-employed. Work with animals is sometimes poorly paid and both job opportunities and pay vary across the country.

PROSPECTS

Having completed their training most dog groomers become self-employed, although some may continue to work for the employer that trained them. There are few, if any, opportunities for promotion for dog groomers.

RELATED OCCUPATIONS

Kennel worker, riding instructor, horse groom, horse breeding stud assistant/groom, jockey/stablehand, guide dog trainer/mobility instructor, RSPCA/SSPCA inspector, veterinary nurse.

FURTHER INFORMATION

British Dog Groomers Association/Pet Care Trust*, Bedford Business Centre, 170 Mile Road, Bedford MK42 9TW, 01234 273933

FURTHER READING

Please see article 6. ZOO KEEPER.

4. HORSE GROOM (WAM)

THE WORK

The daily routine for grooms varies according to the type and size of yard and level of the groom's skill. The basic tasks, however, are mucking out, quartering, sometimes exercising, grooming, rugging, watering, feeding and bedding down.

First thing in the morning the groom inspects the horses, making sure they have suffered no injury during the night and have finished their late night feed. They are then usually given fresh water and a small feed, are mucked out and given a day bed. When this is done, the horse is brushed over quickly and stable stains removed with a water brush. The mane is laid – brushed out and set on the correct side and dampened with the water brush. A tail bandage is usually applied, the feet oiled and the horse is then ready for either its owner or the stable staff to exercise it.

Grooms are expected to be competent riders, with the ability to ride at walk, trot and canter and on occasions to ride and lead.

After exercise, the horse is fully groomed – sometimes called strapping. This is done while the horse is still warm and the pores are open. It takes 30–45 minutes to groom a horse properly.

Other duties usually include fitting riding tack, which includes a variety of bridles, head collars, halters, saddles etc. Grooms must be able to fit this equipment correctly, avoiding any risk of injury to the horse (or rider). In addition, tack is regularly cleaned to maintain a good condition, preventing mould and perishing, and checked for wear, especially in the stitching.

Grooms may use a variety of tools to clip and trim the horse's coat or hair. Clipping machines are used on the main body, and different types of clip are used according to how the horse is to be worked. Trimming can be with scissors and comb.

Additional duties include attending to sick or injured animals. Grooms may treat minor wounds and keep basic health records. When the veterinary surgeon is called the groom must closely follow directions and provide relevant information about the horse's condition. The nursing that follows may include taking and recording temperature, pulse and respiration, administering medicines etc.

General knowledge about horse shoeing is essential, such as the fact that special shoes are used in particular cases. Grooms must know shoeing procedure and how to remove broken or twisted shoes.

WORK ENVIRONMENT

Duties involve working outdoors in all weather. Horses must be attended to every day, all the year round, and this can mean working in extremely cold and wet conditions. In addition, mucking out, stable and yard duties are dirty, routine and can be tiring. Physical fitness is required and there can be much bending, climbing, lifting and carrying involved in the work.

Due to the nature of the work, and because stables are often in remote areas, grooms often live in and may share

OTHER WORK WITH ANIMALS: WAM

meals, household chores etc. Working with horses, in many respects, is more a way of life than a job.

Grooms may travel, eg to competitions, and spend time away from home.

SKILLS AND INTERESTS

Grooms must genuinely love and care for horses. It is essential that grooms are fit and have the stamina to endure long hours of hard physical work for modest rewards in terms of pay.

Practical hand skills are necessary and great care must be taken when performing some of the more delicate tasks, such as trimming and bandaging. Grooms should be observant and notice any changes in a horse's condition. A responsible attitude is required. Intricately plaiting manes and grooming for competitions, shows etc requires patience and attention to detail. The groom must also be able to work quickly and remain calm when under pressure, particularly on competition days.

Clear spoken communication skills are important for speaking to employers, other staff, owners, vets etc. Legible handwriting is required for record-keeping and writing messages. Grooms need basic arithmetic for tasks such as rationing feeds.

Grooms should ride confidently and competently.

ENTRY REQUIREMENTS

Though formal educational qualifications are not required for entry to work as a groom, candidates should have a good basic education with GCSE/S grades, particularly for entry to colleges offering courses for formal qualifications. NVQs/SVQs are available. The British Horse Society (BHS) and Association of British Riding Schools (ABRS) also offer courses.

Some knowledge of biology is essential, to understand how the horse's body functions and how to keep the animal in a healthy condition. Experience of working with horses is useful, and may be required.

Entrants for British Horse Society (BHS) exams must be BHS members. The minimum age for BHS Horse Knowledge and Riding exams, including the BHS Groom's Certificate, is 16 years; 17 years for Stage 3; and 20 years for Stage 4.

The minimum age for the ABRS Preliminary Horse Care and Riding Certificate Levels 1 and 2 is 16 years. It is open to candidates who are in full-time training or employment with horses. The ABRS Groom's Certificate is open to those with practical experience in the handling and care of a variety of horses. The ABRS Groom's Diploma is open to holders of the ABRS Groom's Certificate and a current first aid certificate, and who are 18 years or over. They must also have a wide knowledge and experience of a great variety of horses, and be capable of organizing and supervising other staff.

Individuals would be expected to have their own clothes for riding and a safety standard riding hat.

A driving licence is useful/required for some jobs.

TRAINING

There are a number of recognized qualifications for grooms; those with awards may have improved chances of employment.

NVQs/SVQs are available in Horse Care at Levels 1 and 2, and in Horse Care and Management at Level 3.

NVQs/SVQs are also available in Racehorse Care at Level 2 and Racehorse Care and Management at Level 3.

British Horse Society (BHS)

BHS offers exams in Horse Knowledge and Care in four stages:

Stage 1 – students are tested on their understanding of the basic principles of horse care. They must show, working under supervision, knowledge and practice of caring for a horse in the stable and at grass.

Stage 2 – entrants must have passed Stage 1 and the BHS Riding Road Safety Test. They must understand the general management and requirements of horses and should be able to work under regular but not constant supervision. Candidates need to show a higher standard of efficiency in knowledge and practical ability.

Stage 3 – applicants must have passed Stages 1 and 2 Horse Knowledge and Care. Candidates must show that they are able to care for up to four horses in stables and at grass, and pass a written test. Success in Stage 3 leads to the award of Groom's Certificate.

Stage 4 – candidates are of a more advanced level and must be capable of taking charge, without supervision, of a group of horses of various types. Success in Stage 4 leads to the award of Intermediate Stable Manager's Certificate.

An advanced qualification – BHS Stable Manager Certificate– is available for experienced candidates aged 22 years and over who possess the Intermediate Stable Manager's Certificate. The senior BHS qualification is the BHS Fellowship Examination, the minimum age for entry to which is 25 years.

Association of British Riding Schools (ABRS)

Examinations that can be taken, include:

Preliminary Horse Care and Riding Certificate Levels 1 and 2 – this exam is designed to show that a young groom is competent in the basic skills but must work under supervision.

ABRS Groom's Certificate – this exam is designed to show the practical ability of grooms working basically on their own, but with some supervision.

ABRS Groom's Diploma – those holding this qualification have wide knowledge and experience with horses, and are able to work without supervision, and, if required, supervise the work of other staff.

No written papers are required for any of the ABRS examinations, and there is no requirement that candidates must be members of the Association. All exams are of one day's duration, and are of a practical nature.

Formal training methods for grooms

Training schemes for young people – school-leavers may gain work experience and training as grooms via specific training schemes. Most training is on employers' premises, with an element of off-the-job training. Some courses are based at agricultural colleges; these include work placements. There is no guarantee of a full-time job on completion of training; however, trainees are generally preferred by employers to those without experience. Candidates may have the opportunity to enter for BHS or ABRS exams.

OTHER WORK WITH ANIMALS: WAM

National Traineeships are available for employees or for those wishing to enter the industry. Please contact your careers office or TEC/LEC for details.

Working pupils – training is offered to young people by employers and in return the trainee works at the school/centre. There may be opportunities for taking recognized BHS/ABRS qualifications. Terms and conditions vary and the BHS and ABRS advise that employers and pupils should agree a contract covering aspects such as duties, hours, rules, holidays, training, approximate date of exams and financial arrangements. Pupils do not usually receive a wage and may have to pay contributions towards accommodation and meals.

Fee-paying students – riding schools run courses to train students for examinations. These can be fairly intensive, of three to twelve months' duration. However, fees can be very high and although pass rates are also fairly good they are not guaranteed.

Private study – individuals may prepare for BHS/ABRS exams in their own time. The difficulty is in gaining the required practical or work experience, and achieving a sufficiently high standard without coaching.

LATE ENTRY

Individuals of any age may become grooms. Traditionally, it has been a career pursued by young people of 16–18 years. However, this is changing, and employers are now looking towards employing more mature people.

OPPORTUNITIES

Grooms are employed at all types of yards/riding schools/centres.

Riding schools – there are many schools situated throughout the country. Most employ grooms, although smaller stables may use instructors to perform the groom's duties.

Polo yards – polo is played in Britain from the end of April to October. Grooms are usually in charge of a string of four ponies and will exercise them daily. At matches the groom will have to bandage (sometimes boot) legs up, put studs in the ponies' shoes, groom and tack up. During the game they ensure a change of mount is ready and attend to ponies coming off the field – untacking, washing down and cooling off, removing studs and preparing them for the journey home. The hours can be long but grooms get opportunities for riding and exercising, sometimes joining in a chukka. Polo being an international sport, grooms accompany players and teams overseas for matches during the winter months.

Hunt stables – hunting generates many jobs within the horse industry. The season runs from October to March. Horses spend the summer out at grass but it is an important part of the groom's work to ride and exercise them to ensure that they are fit for the season. The groom will be expected to plait the horses up and turn them out smartly for the day's hunting.

Grooms may prepare fresh horses to change at a given point during the hunt, and will deal with the tired horses appropriately. At the end of an exhausting day, horses will need to be throughly groomed when the mud has dried, fed and watered, and made comfortable.

Competition stables – individuals keeping horses for showjumping, dressage, showing, eventing etc, employ grooms at their stables to care for and exercise their horses. The work can involve travelling overseas with the top riders and teams. The BHS now offer a Competition Groom's Certificate.

Livery stables – look after horses for those owners who do not have their own stables. Riding schools often accept a number of livery horses.

Trekking centres and riding holiday hotels – seasonal work is available for grooms during summer months to care for horses, lead treks etc; also looking after the horses during the winter months. The BHS offer British Equestrian Tourism Certificates at three levels: Assistant Ride Leader, Ride Leader, Holiday Riding Centre Manager.

Other opportunities – a limited number of grooms may be employed in circuses and zoos (pony departments). The large stud and breeding side of the horse industry also offers opportunities for grooms.

Vacancies may be advertised in local careers offices, Jobcentres and local newspapers. Yellow Pages should provide a list of local employers.

Vacancies for jobs and training courses are advertised in the equestrian magazines – *Horse and Hound*, *Pony*, *Riding* and other leading equine magazines. There are also a number of employment agencies that deal solely with vacancies for stable staff, eg Stable Relief Services.

There are a number of opportunities to work overseas, for which a second language can be an advantage.

PAY AND CONDITIONS

Rates of pay vary enormously, making it difficult to give accurate figures. Accommodation, meals and training received are usually taken into account when calculating wages.

A 40-hour week is usual, but extra hours may be required on competition or event days. Hours may be spread over seven days, sometimes involving early starts, but in general a five-and-a-half-day week is a planned working target for grooms.

Working with horses involves a certain amount of risk of injury. Grooms should ensure in their contract that they are covered by employers' liability insurance. They are also advised to take out personal accident insurance.

PROSPECTS

Grooms may improve their prospects by taking NVQ/SVQ Level 3 in Horse Care and Management, or the ABRS and British Horse Society qualifications up to stable-manager standard. Minimum age for entry to the BHS Stable Manager examination is 22 years. This is an advanced qualification for those experienced in all aspects of horse care. Holders of any of these qualifications will be capable of organizing and running a stable – planning, staffing, construction, stocking, purchasing, book-keeping etc. Additional qualifications may help the groom achieve senior and/or better jobs.

Some employers have a hierarchy that allows progression to head groom for the experienced and capable. Other grooms may improve their position by changing employers.

OTHER WORK WITH ANIMALS: WAM

RELATED OCCUPATIONS
Horse breeding stud assistant/groom, riding instructor, jockey/stablehand, kennel worker, veterinary nurse, zoo keeper, farrier, farm worker.

FURTHER INFORMATION
Please see article 5. RIDING INSTRUCTOR.

FURTHER READING
Please see article 6. ZOO KEEPER.

5. RIDING INSTRUCTOR (WAM)

THE WORK
Instructors will have to teach all kinds of people, from beginners to experts, in all weather conditions, and will be expected to help them to develop their performance techniques and abilities. They may work with highly skilled professional riders or solely with beginners. The qualification level of instructors, such as British Horse Society Assistant, Intermediate or full Instructor standard, affects the type of work they can carry out. Only very experienced and exceptionally skilled instructors train top-level riders.

Instructing professionals
An instructor may be responsible for coaching a team of riders. This involves ensuring individual talents are used to greatest effect and appropriate team tactics are employed; individuals must be moulded and encouraged as team members, co-operating as a unit. It also involves assessing the strengths and weaknesses of opposing competitors and planning strategies with their riders. The instructor works closely with the team manager determining who will ride in particular events or in what order the competitors will compete.

Instructing amateurs
Instruction is given in basic techniques – mounting the horse correctly, riding in the correct position and with the correct aids. Many pursue the sport as a recreation; others want to develop their abilities seriously and get involved in high-level competitions. Much of the work is concerned with children, including children with disabilities, and good teaching skills are essential. One of the most important aspects is to ensure participants are trained safely. Bad techniques can result in injury, and great care must be taken to make certain that riders know their own capabilities.

Instructors must take command, particularly in cases of emergency.

Developing a training programme, aiming for the highest possible level of mental and physical fitness for competition riders, can prove difficult when riding is a part-time activity and there are other demands on instructors' time. Instructors must be prepared to pass their trainees on to other instructors more able to help them fulfil their potential.

Instructing involves giving trainees vocal and practical demonstrations. Instructors should observe performances, identify problems and organize training to overcome weaknesses. They must also provide interesting and varied ways of practising the same activity time after time. It is important that a participant's skills are developed gradually, with progression from one level of competition to the next at their own pace.

In addition to preparing riders for showjumping, dressage, eventing etc, the instructor must also be fully conversant with the rules and regulations of competitions.

Horse schooling and care
As well as instructing people, the riding instructor is responsible for schooling horses. Similar skills are required. A training programme of practice and exercises must be devised to organize the breaking in and obedience of the horse to a rider's command. The instructor prepares a fittening programme according to the condition of the horse. When training or exercising, the instructor may lunge the horse using a rein designed for this purpose, and as with any equipment/tack, safe use is essential to avoid injury to the horse and trainer. Observation, leading to early detection of problems, can benefit both horse and rider; the instructor can then plan future exercises that concentrate on the problem area.

Instructors, at all grades, often have responsibility for a number of horses and/or ponies. This involves making sure that they are watered, fed, groomed and exercised each day, and that the boxes, fields and yard are kept clean. Tack – saddles, bridles, harnesses etc – must also be checked and cleaned to ensure good condition is maintained.

Pupils are taught stable management, horse care and riding.

WORK ENVIRONMENT
Instructors may be involved in work inside at times – large centres may have facilities for indoor training during winter months – but often duties are undertaken outdoors, and in all weathers.

Mucking out, stable and yard duties are dirty, routine and may be tiring. There may be a significant amount of travelling involved, accompanying pupils to gymkhanas, showjumping competitions and other events. Some freelance instructors travel to work at different schools and centres. Travelling can require short and long stays away from home. At top levels, instructors may go abroad with competitors.

SKILLS AND INTERESTS
Instruction has played a major part in the development of horsemanship for work and leisure. Instructors should be enthusiastic, self-confident and patient, with the ability to inspire the same qualities in their pupils.

The work is both physically and mentally demanding and requires the stamina to endure long hours of hard work. Physical fitness and stamina is important if jobs are to be carried out effectively.

Instructors teach people of all ages from a variety of backgrounds. Much of the work is often with children. Patience and good communication skills are required. They should be articulate in order to explain clearly what is required of their pupils.

Instructors should be able to assess and motivate people: some may respond best to encouragement and gentle persuasion; with others, a firm approach may bring results. The difficult task of getting riders to persevere during the bad times is as important as being able to motivate a good performer to continue to work to maintain form or strive to improve.

OTHER WORK WITH ANIMALS: WAM

Instructors are also concerned with schooling horses and must apply similar skills to teaching the animals, as to teaching the riders. Patience, tolerance and self-control are essential. The horse must be kept physically fit and healthy, and trained to a high standard. Some understanding and appreciation of horse psychology is demanded.

It is important that instructors can establish discipline and keep control of situations. They may need to act quickly without panic in a crisis, and should be able to anticipate the actions of both horse and rider.

Instructors need not be exceptional performers but must have enough riding expertise to inspire confidence.

Self-employed instructors need knowledge of business management. A knowledge of book-keeping, accounting and secretarial skills would be advantageous.

ENTRY REQUIREMENTS

Instructors are qualified and hold British Horse Society qualifications at Assistant, Intermediate, Instructor or Fellow standard. Entry, for candidates under 18 years, to the Assistant Instructor's Preliminary Teaching Test examinations is with a minimum of four GCSEs/S grades (A–C/1–3), or equivalent. Subjects must include English. After 18 years, there are no academic requirements.

For the BHS Assistant Instructor award, candidates must be aged at least 17 years 6 months, and for the Intermediate Instructor award 20 years. The minimum age of entry to the BHS Instructor's exam is 22 years. For the Fellowship exam candidates must be at least 25 years.

There is no minimum age for the ABRS Initial Teaching Award. For the ABRS Teaching Certificate, the minimum age at which the exam may be taken is 19 years.

It is good practice, and often yard rules, to wear an approved hat to safety standard, gloves, hard boots and riding clothes.

A driving licence is useful but not essential.

TRAINING

The British Horse Society (BHS) runs examinations leading to internationally recognized qualifications. Professional qualifications for riding instructors are as follows:

BHS Assistant Instructor – there are four examinations leading to this qualification: Stages I to III of the BHS Horse Knowledge and Riding examinations (please see article 4. HORSE GROOM) and the BHS Preliminary Teaching Test. Candidates then hold the BHS preliminary teaching certificate and are required to complete 500 hours' teaching practice in order to gain the BHSAI. Assistant instructors are qualified to work in a stable yard and teach basic riding and stable management.

BHS Intermediate Instructor – this is achieved by passing the BHS Horse Knowledge and Riding examination Stage IV and the BHS Intermediate Teaching Examination. Candidates must also hold a first aid certificate from British Red Cross, St John's Ambulance or a recognized equivalent. The Intermediate Instructor's award requires a high standard of horsemanship and teaching, and the instructor should be able to work without supervision.

BHS Instructor's Certificate – this is awarded to candidates who hold the Intermediate Instructor's Certificate and pass two examinations: the BHS Stable Manager's Examination and the BHS Equitation and Teaching Examination. The Instructor's Certificate is the main BHS professional qualification.

BHS Fellowship Certificate – this is a senior qualification, for which candidates must demonstrate an advanced knowledge of equitation and horse care.

The Association of British Riding Schools (ABRS) offers two teaching qualifications: the ABRS Initial Teaching Award and the ABRS Teaching Certificate. The *ABRS Initial Teaching Award* is a foundation qualification for those who are capable of teaching at a basic level in a riding school. The *ABRS Teaching Certificate* is a more advanced qualification for teachers with greater experience. Both examinations are of a practical nature, and no written papers are required. An ABRS Teacher's Helper Certificate and an Advanced Teaching Diploma are being developed.

NVQs/SVQs Levels 1 and 2 in Horse Care, and Level 3 in Horse Care and Management, are available, although there are no NVQs/SVQs specifically for riding instructors. However, within the next few years it is anticipated that coaching units will be incorporated in the NVQ/SVQ at Level 4.

Training for BHS/ABRS examinations

The main routes for training for BHS/ABRS qualifications include:

Working pupils – training is offered to young people by employers, riding schools and stable proprietors. In return the trainee works at the school or centre. This is a popular and economical way to train. Training for Assistant Instructor exams usually lasts for around one year depending on previous experience.

Fee-paying students – riding schools run courses to train students for exams and these can be fairly intensive, of three to twelve months' duration. However, fees can be very high and, although pass rates are also fairly good, there is no guarantee of passing the examinations.

Training schemes for young people – in many areas school-leavers have the opportunity to start a career with horses through these schemes.

National Traineeships are available for employees or for those wishing to enter the industry. Please contact your careers service or TEC/LEC.

Full-time college courses – a number of colleges offer courses leading to BHS awards, usually in the context of a BTEC first certificate/diploma or national diploma. They include: Cambridgeshire College of Agriculture and Horticulture, Sparsholt College, Bishop Burton College, Lancashire College of Agriculture and Horticulture, Brooksby College, Pencoed College, Askham Bryan College, Writtle College, Duchy College of Agriculture and Horticulture, Bicton College, Gloucestershire College of Agriculture, Coleg Glynllifon, Otley College of Agriculture and Horticulture, Craven College, Moulton College, Myerscough College, West Oxfordshire College, Walford College of Agriculture, Cannington College, Hartpury College, and Warwickshire College.

In Scotland, colleges offering full-time courses leading to BHS awards and SQA national certificate modules in subjects such as equitation and horse care include: Oatridge Agricultural College, Aberdeen College, Thurso and Borders.

Private study – individuals may study and prepare for BHS exams in their own time. The BHS will provide their syllabuses (priced).

OTHER WORK WITH ANIMALS: WAM

LATE ENTRY

People of any age can become riding instructors. Most instructors are qualified and the BHS may waive the academic qualifications required for entry to exams for older applicants. There are no upper age restrictions for entry to BHS or ABRS exams.

Employers tend to favour young applicants/school-leavers for this type of work. Mature candidates should be active and outdoor people, with the physical fitness and stamina required for the work.

OPPORTUNITIES

Horse riding is becoming increasingly popular, and the number of riding schools is growing. Therefore the need for instruction is also increasing.

Some of the work is seasonal and employers often require experienced instructors who can work without supervision. This is particularly the case with those employed by private stables, and so on, and they are also often required to undertake groom duties. In addition, instructors employed by trekking centres are usually qualified or pass a company training course.

Jobs with top-level competitors is competitive, yet highly qualified instructors will be rewarded.

Riding instructors are employed at various types of stables and equestrian centres.

Riding schools – many qualified instructors work at schools situated throughout the country. Some small schools employ an instructor to work as an instructor/groom. Opportunities for qualified instructors are good.

Competition yards – individuals keeping horses for showjumping, dressage, showing, eventing etc, may employ instructors as grooms and to exercise their horses. The work can involve travelling overseas with the top riders and teams. Very few instructors – only those who are highly successful – train horses and riders at the top levels.

Private stables – private individuals who keep horses in their own stables may employ an instructor, often with the combined job of groom and teacher for family and friends.

Pony trekking centres and riding holiday hotels – seasonal work is available during summer months for instructors, as trek leaders. Experienced instructors may be employed, or some work freelance and provide services for a number of riding establishments.

For self-employment, individuals need to be established and should have had a degree of success with riders, as well as having business skills. Some instructors buy and run their own riding schools; however, this requires a large capital investment.

Employment opportunities with commercial stables – using horses to show and/or make deliveries – and with the uniformed forces, are competitive. The police may employ instructors who have been trained outside the force, at the discretion of the Chief Constable; however, this is very uncommon. Most instructors in mounted police sections are trained police officers who have specialized – progressing from work as a mounted police rider to instruction.

Vacancies for jobs and training courses are advertised in leading equine magazines such as *Horse and Hound, Pony,* and *Riding*. There are also a number of employment agencies that deal solely with vacancies for stable staff and instructors, eg. Stable Relief Services.

There are a number of opportunities to work and teach overseas. A second language can be helpful here.

PAY AND CONDITIONS

The British Horse Society issues guidelines to pay rates for people holding BHS qualifications. However, rates of pay vary enormously, making it very difficult to give any meaningful figures. In addition, instructors may receive accommodation, meals and further training at the employer's expense. Such provisions are usually taken into account in the payment of wages. The guidelines suggest the following rates: Fellows of the Society (FBHS) – £25,000; BHS Instructor (BHSI) – £20,000; BHS Intermediate Instructor (BHSII) – £14,000; BHS Assistant Instructor (BHSAI) – £9,000.

Wages for self-employed freelance instructors depend on their experience, skill, success in attracting business and the area they cover.

Working with horses involves a certain amount of risk of injury. Trainees and instructors should ensure they are covered by employers' or their own insurance.

Many people want to take riding lessons outside usual working hours, in the evenings and at weekends. Instructors therefore tend to work unsocial hours. In addition, horses need regular attention – feeding, watering etc. – which may mean early morning and late evening duties.

Some riding schools have rotas for days off and for late night stable duties. In general, many instructors work long hours – up to 60 each week. Part-time work may be possible, especially for freelance instructors who find work with local riding establishments. In some types of work there are seasonal variations – pony trekking holidays offer opportunities for instructors during the summer months.

PROSPECTS

Once fully qualified, an instructor may find opportunities, with employers of large riding centres, to advance within the hierarchy to head or senior instructor.

Many instructors work freelance, dividing their time between a number of riding schools and riding clubs. It is possible – and an ultimate aim of some instructors – to open and run a riding school. As well as requiring a good deal of expertise and business knowledge, this demands a substantial capital investment to buy and equip the stables and horses.

There are other opportunities for good riding instructors; for example, they may become judges for showjumping or dressage competitions run by the British Show Jumping Association or British Horse Society. There may be scope for instructors to design and set up courses for different sorts of horse-riding competition. Some instructors may be selected to become British Horse Society examiners.

Most Pony Clubs organize summer camps and for the week or more of the camp, instructors will be required.

An employer may allow an instructor to ride in shows and other events, and provide training and practice facilities. However, even for those with outstanding ability and use of the facilities of a school or stable, it is very difficult and also expensive to become a successful professional competitive rider.

OTHER WORK WITH ANIMALS: WAM

RELATED OCCUPATIONS

Sports coach/instructor, guide dog trainer/mobility instructor, groom, horse racing jockey/stablehand, kennel worker, veterinary nurse, zoo keeper.

FURTHER INFORMATION

The Association of British Riding Schools*, Queen's Chambers, 38-40 Queen Street, Penzance, Cornwall TR18 4BH, 01736 369440

The British Horse Society, Training Office, The British Equestrian Centre Building, 16–17 Stoneleigh Deer Park, Kenilworth, Warwickshire CV8 2XZ, 01926 707700, www.equiweb.co.uk/bhs/index.html

The National Horse Education and Training Company, 2nd Floor, The Burgess Building, The Green, Stafford, ST17 4BL, 01785 227399, www.horsecareers.co.uk

FURTHER READING

Please see article 6. ZOO KEEPER.

6. ZOO KEEPER (WAM)

BACKGROUND INFORMATION

In Great Britain there are about 250 zoos, safari parks, bird collections and aquariums. The major collections, in terms of numbers of visitors, are at London, Whipsnade, Chester, Bristol, Edinburgh and Paignton.

Smaller zoos tend to specialize.

Many zoos are involved in educational projects and in scientific research. They also help to ensure the survival of rare species by planning breeding programmes; indeed, it is often a matter of pride amongst zoo staff that most of the collection has been bred in captivity.

Zoos are run by zoological societies, charitable trusts, local authorities or private businesses.

THE WORK

An important part of the work is providing routine daily care for the zoo's animals. Keepers muck out and clean pens and cages. They prepare food which may involve, for instance, chopping up vegetables and adding vitamins. Some animals require hand feeding. Keepers also ensure fresh water and clean bedding are available, and animal houses are kept at the right level of temperature and humidity.

Keepers are responsible for checking the general health and condition of the animals in their care. They observe animals for signs of illness and injury, keep records of health, diet and behaviour, and assist vets when animals need treatment. If animals display aggression towards each other, keepers may try to intervene and separate them.

To ensure the safety of both animals and visitors, keepers make regular checks of fences and barriers for signs of wear or damage. They also prevent the public from feeding the animals or climbing the barriers. Other responsibilities include removing harmful or poisonous weeds from animal enclosures and, in smaller zoos, keeping paths and flowerbeds clean and tidy. At the end of each day, keepers check that animal quarters and public gates are securely locked.

Keepers usually come into contact with visitors and answer questions about the zoo and its collection. In some zoos they give talks or lectures, and participate in special events organized for schools and other groups.

In safari parks, the animals roam about in large enclosures and an important part of the keepers' work involves patrolling, in jeeps, to make sure that visitors are safe and do not behave irresponsibly – for instance, getting out of their cars and approaching animals, or even picnicking close to groups of lions or tigers. Keepers also deal with any accidents or vehicle breakdowns that occur.

An area of increasing importance in keepers' work is environmental enrichment – that is to say, making the conditions for the animals as near natural as possible, combating the boredom of captivity, and enhancing their quality of life. This can involve such measures as varying feeding times and places (to prevent the animals becoming inured to a stereotyped routine), and providing toys, shelter from the public's gaze etc.

WORK ENVIRONMENT

Depending on the type of animals they care for, keepers may work indoors or may spend much of their time out of doors, in all weathers. Conditions can be wet, cold, dirty, muddy and smelly. Indoors, the atmosphere may be humid.

Keepers wear uniforms or overalls, provided by employers.

They may work alone, in pairs or in small teams, depending on the job in hand. Food preparation may be carried out as a group activity. Keepers work in pairs when entering enclosures containing dangerous animals.

SKILLS AND INTERESTS

Keepers need to be enthusiastic about animals, and able to convey their enthusiasm to visitors. A pleasant manner and good spoken communication skills are required for answering enquiries about the animals' background, habits etc. An interest in geography is useful, to understand and convey information about animals' natural habitats.

It is important to be prepared to carry out hard physical work, cleaning and mucking out pens and cages – in all weathers.

Keepers need to be patient with both animals and public. Reliability and punctuality are necessary; animals rely on a consistent routine.

Working with wild animals can be hazardous and it is essential for keepers to have a responsible attitude towards safety, and to adhere to codes governing safe working practices.

Physical fitness is required. The work is unsuitable for people with allergies to fur or hair, and for those with certain disabilities. Walking, standing, bending and some lifting (of sacks of animal feed, for instance) are required. Keepers must be prepared to be inoculated against various animal diseases.

ENTRY REQUIREMENTS

There are no set minimum educational entry requirements, but employers often prefer applicants with three to five GCSEs/S grades (A–C/1–3), including maths, English and a science subject. Geography, a foreign language and subjects indicating practical abilities are also useful.

OTHER WORK WITH ANIMALS: WAM

Because entry is highly competitive, it is an advantage to have had experience of voluntary work with animals. Experience in a zoo volunteer scheme is valuable for those who are interested in working in a zoo or in other jobs involving the care of animals. If voluntary zoo work is not available, then experience with animals in other settings – such as farms, kennels or stables – is also helpful.

Entry as a trainee is possible at 16 years, but some employers prefer more mature applicants and set a minimum age of 19 or 21 years (especially for work with large animals such as elephants).

In safari parks, a driving licence is essential.

TRAINING

Training on entry to zoo work involves practical experience in different departments, to enable trainee keepers to gain experience with a range of animals.

They receive on-the-job training from other members of staff and study for the City and Guilds Certificate in Zoo Animal Management (C&G 7630), which is available as a correspondence course run by the National Extension College, Cambridge. The course consists of study units, assignments and a project. It takes about two years to complete, on a part-time basis. Employers may pay tuition fees and allow for some study to take place during working hours.

The course has the following four elements:

1. Introduction: reasons for the existence of zoos; record-keeping, finance and management; housing and zoo design; nutrition and diet; safety, hygiene, restraint and transport; breeding; and animal behaviour.
2. The study of particular animal groups such as amphibians and reptiles, primates, mammals living in water, elephants and other large mammals.
3. The study of children's zoos, endangered species and the supply of animals to zoos.
4. Completing a project.

Students take a written examination, and their practical work is assessed by a representative of the zoo's management.

Please note that this course is currently under review and will include a new unit on Horticulture. The revision is expected to be complete in Spring 1999 ready for examination in 2000.

NVQs/SVQs in Animal Care are available at Levels 1 and 2. They are not specifically for zoos but cover the whole animal-care industry. The Level 3 NVQ/SVQ may be more appropriate to those working in zoos, and work will be undertaken to provide a link between the NVQ/SVQ and the C&G Zoo Animal Management Certificate.

Opportunities may be available through training schemes for young people such as National Traineeships. Contact local careers offices or TECs/LECs for further details.

LATE ENTRY

Zoos tend to prefer applicants under the age of about 30 years, and it may be difficult for older people to become zoo keepers unless they have closely related experience.

OPPORTUNITIES

Only about 1,500 people work in zoos and wildlife collections in Britain.

Entry is highly competitive and there are many more applicants than vacancies. Many employers keep waiting lists of applicants. The best way of finding work is to write to local zoos (always enclose a stamped addressed envelope). Employers usually prefer handwritten letters, addressed to a named individual.

It may be possible to start on a voluntary basis, perhaps at weekends, for example, in order to gain experience and to be known to the zoo when a full-time vacancy arises. Many zoos have special volunteer schemes. Another possibility is to find other work in a zoo – as a car park attendant or gardener, for instance – on the understanding that a keeper's post may later be available.

Jobs are advertised in *Cage and Aviary Birds*, *International Zoo News* and the journal of the Association of British Wild Animal Keepers (ABWAK) – *RATEL*.

PAY AND CONDITIONS

Rates of pay vary with different employers. Wages are often comparatively low but in some establishments, subsidized accommodation – often a single room with shared facilities – may be provided.

Zoo opening hours and hours of work are longer in the spring and summer season – which lasts from April to September or October – than in the autumn and winter. During the season, there may be a staggered shift system, for instance one shift of 7.45am to 5pm and a second of 9.45am to 7pm. Hours of work are shorter in winter.

Smaller zoos sometimes close during the winter, but keepers are employed on a year-round basis to provide animal care.

Keepers work a five-, five-and-a-half-, or six-day week. Weekend and bank holiday work (on a rota) is required, as these are the busiest times.

PROSPECTS

The promotion structure varies in different zoos. Generally, however, keepers are responsible to senior keepers or section leaders, who in turn report to the head keeper. Head keeper is a managerial role, with responsibility for all practical matters related to animal care. Promotion prospects beyond head keeper level are extremely limited, and even becoming head keeper can be very much a case of waiting until the current post-holder reaches retirement age. Frequently, finding more responsible work is likely to involve moving to another zoo.

Some keepers move into related areas of work such as the RSPCA inspectorate, kennels or stables.

RELATED OCCUPATIONS

RSPCA/SSPCA inspector, horse groom, kennel worker, dog groomer, veterinary nurse.

OTHER WORK WITH ANIMALS: WAM

FURTHER INFORMATION

Association of British Wild Animal Keepers (ABWAK)*, 12 Tackley Road, Eastville, Bristol BS5 6UQ (sae required), www.wwwebspace.co.uk/abwak/

National Extension College*, 18 Brooklands Avenue, Cambridge CB2 2HN, 01223 316644, www.nec.ac.uk

Federation of Zoological Gardens of Great Britain and Ireland*, Zoological Gardens, Regent's Park, London NW1 4RY, 0171 586 0230 (please send sae)

FURTHER READING

Leaflets/booklets are available from the addresses marked*.

Working with Animals – COIC

Working in Outdoor Jobs – COIC

Careers Working with Animals – Kogan Page

How to Work with Dogs – How to Books

In the careers library classified under WAM.

NATURE CONSERVATION: WAR

1. **COUNTRYSIDE/CONSERVATION OFFICER CLCI:WAR**
2. **COUNTRYSIDE RANGER/WARDEN CLCI:WAR**

BACKGROUND INFORMATION

In Britain, several statutory organizations have responsibility for conservation of the natural environment.

The Countryside Commission is an advisory body aiming to conserve the beauty and charecter of the English countryside and make it more accessible to the public. Its tasks include designating national parks, providing grant aid for conservation projects and sponsoring training for countryside staff. Each national park authority is responsible for developing and managing its area.

English Nature promotes nature conservation in England. It advises government on conservation issues, conducts research, runs 150 national nature reserves and identifies Sites of Special Scientific Interest (SSSIs).

Scottish Natural Heritage and the Countryside Council for Wales combine the functions of the Countryside Commission and English Nature, nature and natural heritage conservation; they undertake both the administrative and the practical aspects of conservation in Scotland and Wales respectively. They are responsible for protecting the countryside so that people can use and enjoy it in a sustainable manner. They have an advisory and educational role, conduct research and provide grant aid for conservation work. They also develop and manage Natural Heritage Areas, SSSIs and national nature reserves.

Forest Enterprise is concerned with timber production, but also with conserving forest wildlife and providing recreational facilities.

Local authority countryside and recreation departments run country parks, regional parks and other outdoor recreation sites. Planning for urban and rural development also involves conservation issues.

In addition, many voluntary and charitable organizations promote the interests of wildlife and conservation. They include the National Trust and National Trust for Scotland, the Royal Society for the Protection of Birds and national and local wildlife trusts, whose work is co-ordinated by The Wildlife Trusts.

Work in countryside conservation is diverse but not plentiful. Long-term planning, policy-making and research is generally the province of countryside or conservation officers. Day-to-day management of sites and visitors is the responsibility of rangers and wardens.

1. COUNTRYSIDE/CONSERVATION OFFICER (WAR)

THE WORK

Countryside and conservation officers are responsible for the scientific planning and management of areas of land. They aim to protect the countryside and help people to value and enjoy it without harming it or inconveniencing its inhabitants. Many posts carry a strong public relations role – not only encouraging people to learn about their natural heritage but influencing policy at local and national level, so that roads are built or industrial sites planned with conservation in mind.

The range of duties varies from one place to another but in differing proportions. Most include ecological surveys, practical land management and educational or advisory work. In general, the title of conservation officer implies greater concern with protecting wildlife; countryside officer with managing public access.

Surveys involve identifying plant and animal species, mapping their habitat and drawing up plans to conserve it, for example, by checking the spread of bracken or erecting deer fences. Surveys to identify SSSIs and national nature reserves are organized by conservation officers and scientists with English Nature and Scottish Natural Heritage. In liaison with local planning authorities and conservation organizations, they establish the sites and explain to land owners how they are affected. Surveys of visitors – their activities, attitudes etc – are also an important aspect of managing many natural heritage sites. The results of these surveys are applied in site and visitor management practice.

They also carry out environmental assessments on proposed new developments – for example, predicting the effect of a new airport or motorway on wildlife and landscape. They may represent their authority at public inquiries.

Land management involves forward planning and immediate action. For example, a long-term plan to regenerate woodland entails organizing and supervising a series of conservation projects such as scrub clearance, drainage and tree-planting. Officers may be in charge of full-time and part-time wardens and rangers, trainees and volunteers. Explaining the job to staff and showing them how to do it can involve a good deal of practical work.

Developing a project involves working closely with agencies and people such as Forest Enterprise, the Countryside Commission, local wildlife trusts, other conservation organizations, planning officers and local councillors. Officers meet farmers and land owners to explain what is going on, enlist their co-operation, and negotiate access or other problems.

Providing information to the public is an important part of the work. This can include setting up displays at information centres, writing leaflets and talking to local groups and to the press. Some are appointed as education officers to run courses at study centres and to involve schools or other groups in conservation projects of their own.

Being in charge of any group involves administrative work – the management of staff, resources and finance. Officers take part in the recruitment and training of staff, allocate money and equipment between sites, and plan the budget for future developments.

WORK ENVIRONMENT

Many posts combine indoor and outdoor work. Much of the planning and administration is done in an office and in meetings, but site surveys, instruction and maintenance go on outdoors in all weather conditions. Most jobs entail driving to different sites.

SKILLS AND INTERESTS

An enthusiastic commitment to countryside and wildlife conservation is essential, together with the ability to convince others of its importance.

Countryside/conservation officers need to combine

NATURE CONSERVATION: WAR

scientific interest in the natural environment with a practical outlook on its day-to-day management. Keen powers of observation, an enquiring mind and a methodical approach are required for assessing a site.

Officers should be able to talk to a variety of people from experts to amateurs. In the course of a week they could help a primary school plant trees, negotiate access with a land owner, instruct volunteers on fencing and ditching, and put the case for preserving ancient woodland at a public inquiry into road building.

Officers should be efficient, well organized managers, able to set goals, and organize people and resources to achieve them. Team work is important as they work in liaison with land agents, scientists, planners, statutory and voluntary agencies.

For most jobs it is necessary to be fit and active and prepared to join in with the heavy work.

ENTRY REQUIREMENTS

Most countryside/conservation officers hold a degree or BTEC/SQA higher national diploma. Appropriate degree subjects include life sciences, ecology, environmental science, geography or geology. BTEC/SQA higher national diploma courses are available in subjects such as environmental planning and management, conservation management, landscape or amenity horticulture, and leisure studies.

The usual minimum requirements for a degree course are five GCSEs/S grades (A–C/1–3) and two A levels/three H grades, or a relevant BTEC/SQA national award, or equivalent, such as Advanced GNVQ/GSVQ Level III. For higher national diploma courses they are one A level/two H grades with four GCSEs/S grades (A–C/1–3), or a relevant BTEC/SQA national award, or equivalent.

It may be possible to work for voluntary bodies and charitable organizations with A levels/H grades and evidence of both commitment and experience.

Competition for posts is extremely fierce. It can be an advantage to hold a postgraduate diploma or higher degree in conservation, ecology, land management or related subject. In all cases practical experience is essential. There are some opportunities to gain paid experience as a part-time or seasonal ranger or warden, and many more to do voluntary work with agencies such as the British Trust for Conservation Volunteers (BTCV), the National Trust or local wildlife conservation groups.

An alternative entry route is to gain professional qualifications and experience in a related field such as planning, landscape management, ecology, leisure management or teaching.

A driving licence is required.

TRAINING

In-service training is provided by employers in health and safety and management skills, often using distance learning packages. Short courses in a range of management and ecological topics are offered at many colleges and field study centres. Many are sponsored by the Countryside Commission. Environmental employers' training needs are now focused on the work of the national training organization for the sector – Lantra NTO, based at Stoneleigh, Warwicks.

Full-time and part-time courses leading to a higher degree or postgraduate diploma are offered at many institutions. A wide range of subjects is available in the field of ecology, nature conservation and environmental or leisure management.

Open learning and correspondence courses in these subjects are run by the Open University, Open Business School, Institute of Leisure and Amenity Management (ILAM) and other institutions.

NVQs/SVQs in Environmental Conservation are available at Levels 2 and 3 for people working in a range of conservation or countryside management jobs. Standards are set by the environmental sector industry group of Lantra National Training Organisation (NTO). The awards are based on competence at work and may also involve short or part-time courses at a college or training centre. The awarding bodies are BTEC, SQA and C&G/NPTC (National Proficiency Tests Council).

Modern Apprenticeships and National Traineeships frameworks are available (enquiries please to Lantra NTO)

LATE ENTRY

Maximum age limits are not usually stated. Previous experience in related fields such as planning, leisure management or teaching may be helpful, and it is essential to have extensive experience and knowledge of conservation and natural history.

OPPORTUNITIES

Conservation and countryside management is a relatively small but slowly increasing profession, with 2,000 to 3,000 posts at present at officer grade. In many areas, similar or related work goes under different job titles, such as field officer, scientific officer or adviser.

In the public sector, conservation and countryside officers work for English Nature, national parks, the Environment Agency and local authority countryside, recreation or planning departments. Scottish Natural Heritage and the Scottish Environment Protection Agency employs area and project officers, who do similar work. The Countryside Commission employ professional staff, mostly in an advisory or administrative capacity, but do not directly manage any land. The Countryside Commission for Wales has a similar role but includes the management of land. Other government bodies such as the Natural Environment Research Council offer opportunities for scientists in environmental research.

In the voluntary sector, many organizations provide opportunities for management, scientific research, advice, education and interpretation in the field of countryside conservation. The National Trust employs advisers, with technical and support staff, as well as estate wardens and a range of administrative and marketing staff. The National Trust for Scotland employs a small number of rangers, naturalists and specialist advisers – all science graduates. There are also a few openings with local and regional wildlife or nature conservation trusts, such as the network of Groundwork Trusts, the RSPB, Council for Protection of Rural England and other voluntary and charitable organizations.

There are a few opportunities with private companies and consultancies for conservation officers and advisers.

NATURE CONSERVATION: WAR

PAY AND CONDITIONS
Starting salaries range from £12,500 to £15,000 and may rise to over £25,000. In theory most officers work a 37- to 40-hour week, Monday to Friday, but a good deal of flexibility is expected and there may be frequent evening meetings or weekend work.

PROSPECTS
The statutory bodies provide a career structure leading up through senior scientific or administrative grades. Charitable and voluntary organizations offer less structured career prospects. It is often necessary to move around the country to gain experience and promotion.

Qualified and experienced conservation officers may become advisers with the National Trust, wildlife or conservation trusts, or other organizations such as the Farming and Wildlife Advisory Group.

RELATED OCCUPATIONS
Forest officer, horticultural scientist, landscape architect, town planner, estate manager, land agent, research scientist, leisure centre manager, ecologist, environmental consultant.

FURTHER INFORMATION AND READING
Please see article 2. COUNTRYSIDE RANGER/WARDEN.

2. COUNTRYSIDE RANGER/WARDEN (WAR)

THE WORK
Rangers and wardens look after the countryside for the benefit of its wildlife and of the people who visit and use it. The main elements in the work are advice and information, environmental education, liaison, conservation and day-to-day maintenance. The duties vary from one place to another and the job titles may be interchangeable but, in general, rangers have more dealings with the public, wardens with practical conservation.

Rangers help people to enjoy the countryside and to respect and care for it without causing damage or inconveniencing other users. They advise visitors where to go and what to look for, and they answer the public's questions about the area and its wildlife. Many will be involved in environmental education – working with the public in formal and informal settings such as talking to school or community groups, to encourage learning about the environment. They may organize guided walks. At weekends and holiday times they may be based at an information centre or car park. They also patrol the area looking for signs of damage and, in a firm but tactful manner, try to prevent people causing it. The aim is prevention by persuasion but, if necessary, they may need to report problems to the police.

Rangers are the link between the land-owning authorities, visitors and the local community. They sort out disputes over rights of access and put up stiles and signposts to help walkers keep to the paths. They talk to farmers about conservation on their land – preserving hedgerows or stone barns, for example – and may suggest sources of grant aid to help with this.

Rangers also pass information back to their employer on their area's special needs. They monitor the number of cars, mountain bikers and others, the state of the footpaths and the need to repair damage, combat erosion or improve facilities. They also help with ecological surveys, recording animal and plant species, numbers of nesting birds, and so on, and the need for special measures to protect them. Surveys can be a major part of the work for wardens on estates and nature reserves.

Both wardens and rangers may carry out practical maintenance work. This includes fencing, drainage, litter picking, path repair and the management of woodland by pruning, scrub clearance and tree planting. They usually carry out a good deal of the heavy work themselves and may also supervise estate workers and volunteers.

Wildlife rangers with Forest Enterprise are responsible for protecting plantations, creating areas for wildlife conservation, supervising sporting activities and assisting visitors.

Keeping records and reporting incidents entails a varying amount of paperwork. Some rangers and wardens are responsible for part of a budget; planning and costing products such as footpath maintenance or tree planting, and choosing equipment and materials for the job.

Rangers and wardens are trained in first aid, and they help to deal with emergencies such as fire, flood or mountain rescue.

WORK ENVIRONMENT
Rangers and wardens work outdoors most of the time, whatever the weather. Their areas vary widely – a stretch of long-distance footpath, a patch of woodland or wetland, a country park, a regional park or a range of hills.

SKILLS AND INTERESTS
Rangers and wardens need a good understanding of the needs of the countryside and of its users. The work calls for commitment to the conservation of the natural heritage and the ability to communicate this commitment to others, through environmental education and interpretation.

They should be able to explain matters clearly and simply to all sorts of groups and individuals, ranging from schoolchildren and picnickers to ecologists, birdwatchers and farmers. Tact and diplomacy are required in preventing trouble and solving disputes.

Rangers and wardens should be fit and strong and keen to work outdoors in all weathers. Practical skills such as hedge-laying or chainsaw operation are useful. In watching and caring for wildlife, patience and good powers of observation are required. They must be competent on a range of health and safety issues and have a first aid qualification.

Rangers and wardens should be responsible, self-reliant and able to work on their own initiative, often alone though sometimes in teams of two or three. They should also be competent to lead groups of walkers or naturalists and to take charge of voluntary workers.

ENTRY REQUIREMENTS
Formal academic qualifications are not always required for the job of ranger or warden. However, with the fierce competition for jobs, most new entrants hold qualifications ranging from an appropriate BTEC/SQA diploma or

NATURE CONSERVATION: WAR

NVQ/SVQ Level 3 award, a degree or postgraduate qualifications. All have prior practical experience.

Experience in related employment such as estate work or forestry is a great advantage. Commitment to natural heritage conservation is essential; as evidence, employers look for voluntary work, or experience as a part-time ranger or warden.

For many posts there is a minimum age of 21 years.

A countryside management course can provide a good background for work as a ranger or warden. Courses leading to nationally recognized qualifications at all levels are available at many institutions. They may be studied full-time, part-time or by distance learning.

Suitable courses include:

GNVQ in Land and Environment, and City and Guilds in Recreation; Care and Conservation – no formal academic qualifications are needed, although individual institutions may set entry requirements;

BTEC/SQA National Diploma/Certificate in Conservation; Land Use and Recreation; Countryside Skills; Countryside Management – no formal academic qualifications are required for SQA national courses. For BTEC national awards the normal entry requirements are four GCSEs/S grades (A–C/1–3), or Intermediate GNVQ/GSVQ Level II, or equivalent;

BTEC/SQA Higher National Diploma/Certificate in Countryside Recreation; Conservation Management; Rural Resources Management; Leisure Management – entry is usually with one A level/two H grades with four GCSEs/S grades, or a relevant BTEC national award, or equivalent.

The National Trust runs a three-year careership scheme for young people in Countryside Management or Amenity Horticulture, combining work experience with study for NVQ Level 3.

TRAINING

In-service training is organized by employers. A typical training programme for rangers covers: the role of the ranger; map-reading and moorland navigation; countryside safety including rescue, fire-fighting and first aid; the role of volunteers in conservation; local knowledge; radio communication; law in the countryside, communication skills, including interpretation and environmental education, visitor and recreation management.

Short external courses are also provided. These are organized by the Countryside Management Association, the Scottish Countryside Rangers' Association, the National Parks' Staff Association and colleges of agriculture and horticulture. Many of the courses are sponsored by the national agencies and are held at colleges and field study centres throughout the UK. Topics range from dry-stone walling to countryside interpretation and staff management.

The British Trust for Conservation Volunteers (BTCV) and the Scottish Wildlife Trust (SWT) run six-/twelve-month training courses in conservation skills, as well as short courses for trainees and volunteers. Courses are also run by the Field Studies Council.

NVQs/SVQs in Environmental Conservation are available at Levels 2 and 3.

LATE ENTRY

Most full-time rangers and wardens are appointed in their mid-twenties or later, after experience of related jobs. Upper age limits are not usually imposed, provided applicants are fit and strong.

There may be specific training opportunities directed at adults available in some areas for this type of work. Candidates may have to satisfy certain conditions to be eligible. Contact your local Jobcentre, careers service or TEC/LEC for details.

OPPORTUNITIES

Numbers of full-time rangers and wardens are small – under 1,000 – and growing only slowly. They are supplemented by many more part-time and seasonal assistants and by volunteers. Vacancies everywhere are few and over-subscribed and are usually filled by those with part-time or voluntary experience.

The largest employers of rangers are the countryside, planning and leisure departments of local authorities, and the national and regional parks. Forest Enterprise employs about 300 wildlife rangers, who are recruited from its own forest workers.

English Nature and Scottish Natural Heritage employ site managers and wardens in small numbers to run their National Nature Reserves. There are a few opportunities for wardens and rangers on private estates. The National Trust, Royal Society for the Protection of Birds, wildlife trusts and other charitable organizations occasionally offer paid work for wardens, as well as opportunities for volunteers.

The British Trust for Conservation Volunteers and many local groups also organize voluntary work in countryside conservation. This provides valuable experience and helps applicants test the depth of their own commitment to the work.

Vacancies are advertised in the national and local press and journals such as *New Scientist*.

PAY AND CONDITIONS

Pay varies widely, starting from between £7,158 to £10,000, rising with experience to £18,800 or more.

In the National Trust, local government and other statutory bodies the hours are officially 37 to 40 a week, but in practice they are often long and irregular and involve some weekend work.

Part-time or seasonal work is often available.

PROSPECTS

The statutory authorities and major charitable organizations such as the National Trust provide a career structure with promotion through senior grades to area, chief and district ranger or head warden. In smaller charitable and voluntary organizations, there is less scope for advancement. Promotion depends mainly on experience and opportunity.

For those seeking to become conservation officers or countryside managers, it can be helpful to gain qualifications such as an advanced diploma or a master's degree. These are available by full-time, part-time or distance study in a range of environmental and management subjects, such as ecology, environmental

NATURE CONSERVATION: WAR

management or countryside recreation management. Gaining NVQs/SVQs is helpful in seeking advancement.

RELATED OCCUPATIONS

Forester, estate worker, gamekeeper, fish farm manager, farm worker, landscape gardener.

FURTHER INFORMATION

British Trust for Conservation Volunteers*, 36 Saint Mary's Street, Wallingford, Oxon OX10 0EU, 01491 839766

The Countryside Commission*, John Dower House, Crescent Place, Cheltenham, Glos GL50 3RA, 01242 521381, www.countryside.gov.uk

Countryside Management Association*, c/o Centre for Environmental Interpretation, Manchester Metropolitan University, St Augustines, Lower Chatham Street, Manchester M15 6BY, 0161 247 1067

English Nature*, Northminster House, Peterborough PE1 1UA, 01733 455100, www.english-nature.org.uk

Environment Agency*, Rio House, Waterside Drive, Aztec West, Almondsbury, Bristol BS12 4UD, 01454 624400, www.environment-agency.gov.uk

The Environment Council*, 212 High Holborn, London WC1V 7VW, 0171 836 2626, www.greenchannel.com/tec

Wildlife Trusts National Office*, The Green, Witham Park, Waterside South, Lincoln LN2 7JR, 01522 544400, www.wildlifetrust.org.uk

Scottish Conservation Projects Trust*, Balallan House, 24 Allan Park, Stirling FK8 2QG, 01786 479697

Scottish Natural Heritage*, Battleby, Redgorton, Perth PH1 3EW, 01738 627921

LANTRA National Training Organisation, National Agricultural Centre, Stoneleigh, Kenilworth, Warwickshire CV8 2LG, 01203 696996

FURTHER READING

Leaflets/booklets are available from the addresses marked*.

Working in Environmental Services – COIC

Careers in Environmental Conservation – Kogan Page

The Environmental Careers Handbook – Institution of Environmental Scientists

Careers in Conservation – RSPB

Careers in the Environment – The Environment Council

Council Directory of Environmental Courses – The Environment Council

In the careers library classified under WAR.

GROUP Y – TRANSPORT

1. **AIRLINE PILOT CLCI:YAB**
2. **AIR CABIN CREW CLCI:YAB**
3. **AIRCRAFT MAINTENANCE ENGINEER CLCI:YAB/RAC**
4. **AIR TRAFFIC CONTROLLER CLCI:YAB**

BACKGROUND INFORMATION

The articles in this section refer essentially to employment in UK airlines. There are around 30 of these companies flying aircraft in and out of the UK. Other employment is with smaller firms such as air taxi companies or, in the case of maintenance engineers, with aircraft and component manufacturers.

Airlines or their agents employ many other types of staff than the ones described in the following articles – in airline security, airline lounges, in baggage handling, check-in facilities and passenger services, flight catering, and 'slot' allocation at Heathrow and Gatwick.

A great number of other jobs at airports are provided by employers other than airlines. These employers include BAA plc, HM Customs and Excise, Home Office Immigration officials, airport police forces, Department of the Environment, Transport and the Regions, and concessionaires appointed by BAA plc for car hire, parking, catering etc.

Air traffic controllers, employed by National Air Traffic Services (a joint Civil Aviation Authority (CAA) and Ministry of Defence organization) work at main control centres and at airports in the UK.

1. AIRLINE PILOT (YAB)

THE WORK

Pilots fly aircraft on long- and short-haul flights. Duties begin one hour before take-off when pilots check pre-flight plans. These define the route to be taken and height maintained, and include meteorological information. Pilots do complex calculations of take-off and landing weights, and they have to work out the fuel needed from distance travelled and height and weight to be maintained. Pilots also check that equipment and instruments are functioning properly and that noise regulations for take-off and landing are observed. Their work includes briefing the crew and supervising loading and refuelling. Initial contact is then made with air traffic control, who advise the pilot on take-off.

Pilots need to be able to understand and interpret the data presented to them on instruments and controls and they use computers in their calculations. Take-off and landing are the most complicated aspects of a flight, but pilots may have to make adjustments as necessary during flights and have to use their skills continuously, checking instruments for malfunction even while the plane is on automatic pilot.

They maintain contact with air traffic controls and cabin crew throughout the flight and speak at intervals to passengers, giving them information over the public address system on cruising speed and height and details of ground areas they are flying over, as well as warnings of turbulence and difficult weather conditions. They may also leave the flight deck to speak to passengers.

Duties are shared usually with one co-pilot, occasionally two on long-haul, but responsibility for the aircraft and its safety rests finally with the pilot.

After landing, when the aircraft has been taxied to its final position, the pilot shuts down the engines and writes a flight report, noting any problems or instrument difficulties.

WORK ENVIRONMENT

Flight decks, where pilots spend long hours in a seated position, are typically very confined spaces.

Delays because of weather or other difficulties, along with 24-hour schedules, mean irregular working hours and periods spent overseas in a hotel or airport. There are strict rules over the number of hours pilots may work without a rest period, but because they are flying unsocial hours they can experience jet lag, particularly on long-haul schedules, and may return on scheduled flights as passengers.

SKILLS AND INTERESTS

The work of pilots involves great responsibility both for aircraft and for the safety of passengers and crew. They need to be self-confident and at ease working with other people.

Pilots have to be reliable, calm and level-headed, able to take charge in an emergency and have good clear communication skills both within the team on board and with air traffic control. The ability to inspire confidence in both passengers and air crew is very important.

Good practical and co-ordination skills are needed along with technical skills and understanding. Written English must be of a good standard for report writing.

Good health and fitness are vital; it is tested on application and at regular intervals throughout a pilot's career.

ENTRY REQUIREMENTS

A commercial pilot's licence (CPL) with instrument rating (IR), awarded by the Civil Aviation Authority (CAA), is needed to fly aircraft registered in the UK 'for hire or reward'. To become the commander of an airliner requires an Airline Transport Pilot's Licence (Aeroplane) – ATPL(A).

There are currently moves to have a common European licensing structure and it is likely that all members of an airliner's flight deck crew will be required to pass the ATPL ground exams. For this reason, few UK airlines now accept the CPL with IR, without passes in the ATPL ground exams.

There are a number of different ways of obtaining the standard to acquire the CPL and ATPL, and entry requirements depend on the method used:

1. Full or partial sponsorship and training by airlines normally requires a minimum of five GCSEs/S grades (A–C/1–3) (seven for British Airways) including English, maths and a science with two A levels/three H grades preferably in maths and physics. Advanced GNVQ/GSVQ Level III and BTEC/SQA national awards are also acceptable, preferably in a relevant area, such as science or engineering.

2. Private residential training schools use entry standards that are recommended by the CAA. These are five GCSEs/S grades (A–C/1–3) including English, maths and a science that includes a substantial content of physics. Applicants with alternative qualifications, eg GNVQ/GSVQ and BTEC/SQA awards, are considered on their merits and will need to satisfy the training schools

that they have a sufficient level of English, maths and science to benefit from training. This is a very expensive method of training, costing upwards of £50,000.

3. Training as a pilot with one of the Armed Forces (entry requirements similar to above) and taking a conversion, or abridged, course for qualification for commercial pilot.

4. Gaining a private pilot's licence (PPL) and 700 hours' flying experience, perhaps by working as an instructor, to be eligible to sit the written and practical tests for the CPL and ATPL ground exams. This also is an expensive route though it can be taken over a little longer period. The expense can be reduced by a 'self-improver' route that combines a series of training courses with flying experience of approximately 250 hours. The PPL route may be affected by the introduction of a European licensing system.

Individual airlines have additional requirements which vary but all of them include good eyesight (that may include glasses but must reach a certain standard), normal colour vision, good hearing and physical fitness.

Age requirements are usually between 18 and 24 years for training (26 years for graduates). For previously experienced pilots, age requirements vary and entry depends on individual qualifications and experience.

Airlines have height restrictions – for British Airways, for example, it is between 1.58 metres (5 feet 2 inches) and 1.91 metres (6 feet 3 inches).

British airlines also require that applicants have the unrestricted right to live and work in the UK and be able to obtain a passport allowing unrestricted access worldwide.

TRAINING

Training may take place full-time on a residential basis at a college of air training, or part-time via approved flying schools.

Would-be pilots have to obtain one or more levels and categories of licence that permit them to fly aircraft – from command of smaller aircraft (or as co-pilot in larger ones) to the highest category, which is the ATPL, allowing pilots to be in charge of the wide-bodied jets – but see notes under ENTRY REQUIREMENTS for likely changes.

Residential courses are available at Oxford Air Training School (Oxford Airport), British Aerospace Flying College Ltd, (Prestwick Airport), and Cabair College of Air Training (Cranfield Aerodrome, Bedford)

Training lasts up to 15 months and provides training to full ATPL standard for sponsored and private students. Students finish with a CPL/IR with 'frozen' ATPL, which means that, when they reach the minimum age (21) and hours (1,500) requirements, their licence is automatically upgraded to ATPL.

Practical training includes flying in single and twin-engined aircraft and in simulators. There is a high technical subject content including avionics, aerodynamics navigation, meteorology, aircraft design and aviation law.

For people who already have some flying experience, shorter courses are available. They first need to be assessed by the CAA (who charge a fee), which gives details of the requirements that need to be met by doing an abridged course.

After completing training via one of the above methods, pilots with full ATPL standard train as co-pilots with an airline before being eligible for promotion to pilot.

The slightly cheaper method of training privately via a PPL, outlined under ENTRY REQUIREMENTS above, can be followed by short courses to obtain the ATPL. Some pilots gain flying experience at schools in the USA, where fees are cheaper, but CAA standards must still be met on return to the UK to be eligible to fly aircraft here (preference is usually given to UK-trained pilots).

Conversion courses are open to ex-Armed Forces pilots to train to ATPL standard.

Training continues throughout the career of a pilot as new aircraft and instruments are introduced and new type and instrument ratings need to be added to their licence. They also take regular refresher courses.

LATE ENTRY

Trainee pilots are normally aged between 18 and 24 years (26 years for graduates). British Airways recruits trainees between 18 and 28 years. For conversion courses, pilots may be aged up to 35 years.

OPPORTUNITIES

The majority, around 3,000, of civil airline pilots are employed by British Airways. The airline recruits a small number of cadet pilots but competition is intense, with about 40 applicants for each vacancy. Recruitment depends to a great extent on expansion of business and the purchase of more aircraft.

The fact that larger aircraft are being used, though, means fewer pilots for more passengers, and this also affects expansion of recruitment.

PAY AND CONDITIONS

The basic salary range for commercial pilots is around £30,000. A new captain begins at £48,700. Average captain's pay is between £55,000 and £61,000. All salary scales increase each year. In addition, expenses are paid and travel permits are granted.

PROSPECTS

Pilots usually begin as co-pilots or second officers, though military-trained pilots may well begin as first officers. Promotion is often based on the types of aircraft the pilot flies, with the highest pay going to captains of wide-bodied jets, but some airlines accord promotion, regardless of aircraft type, from second officer to first officer to captain.

After captain, promotion is to chief pilot, or some may move into management or training, some combining chief pilot with training duties and/or administrative positions.

Pilots tend to stay with the airline that employs them, though at times airlines may take experienced pilots from small companies. This is because moving from one company to another means starting at the bottom again, before being able to gain promotion to higher posts and higher pay.

RELATED OCCUPATIONS

Pilot: Armed Forces, pilot: air taxi company, RAF officer, RN officer, merchant navy officer, air traffic controller.

CIVIL AVIATION: YAB/RAC

FURTHER INFORMATION AND READING
Please see article 4. AIR TRAFFIC CONTROLLER.

2. AIR CABIN CREW (YAB)

THE WORK

Air cabin crew look after the welfare, comfort and safety of passengers travelling in aircraft. They attend a pre-flight briefing at the report centre at least one hour before take-off, which deals with the special needs of passengers, business information and matters of safety. They board at least half an hour before take-off and check the emergency equipment is in order, the aircraft and cloakrooms are tidy, and seat pocket information is in place. They also check that sufficient meals and drinks are available for the number of passengers and put away the catering trays.

Having welcomed passengers on board and shown them to their seats, they check that doors are closed and seat belts fastened. Before take-off they demonstrate the use of emergency equipment and point out exit doors, and notify the pilot when they are ready for take-off.

During the flight they serve meals and drinks. Meals are usually pre-packed and may need heating. On some flights cabin crew sell duty-free goods such as alcohol, perfume and tobacco. This work is usually done in pairs in certain sections of the cabin, the work being allocated by the chief stewardess or steward. They make announcements on behalf of the pilot and again check that safety belts are fastened.

During their work they may have to deal with emergencies, such as the ill-health of passengers, and must be able to administer first aid. In case of flight emergencies they have to immediately apply the safety drills they learned in training and help passengers from the aircraft before leaving themselves.

When the flight is over they check stocks of duty-free goods and complete account sheets showing balance of cash and stock so that new stock can be ordered.

WORK ENVIRONMENT

The working environment is cramped and often very warm. Cabin crew spend a lot of time on their feet. Long-haul flights involve spending periods away from home and some involve crossing time zones with the possibility of jet lag.

SKILLS AND INTERESTS

Cabin crew require a neat appearance. They need to be in good health and have stamina. Agility and a good sense of balance are needed, both for working in confined spaces and also for emergency procedure practice.

This work suits responsible, confident people who are good at dealing with all types of passengers. They require a polite, pleasant and tactful manner with the ability to put people at ease.

Common sense and calmness, together with the ability to react quickly in the case of emergencies, is needed.

Crew members need to be able to work in a team. A clear speaking voice is essential and good written English is required for writing reports.

They need to be numerate since they have to balance accounts and deal with a variety of currencies on a flight. Punctuality is very important.

ENTRY REQUIREMENTS

Each airline has different requirements. They all, though, expect a good standard of education, usually some GCSEs/S grades (A–C/1–3), often including English and maths. Airlines do not necessarily require a qualification in a foreign language but most insist on applicants being able to hold a conversation in a foreign language related to the routes on which the airline flies. British Airways, for example, requires applicants to be skilled in one of 26 specified languages.

The most essential requirements are the right personality, a good standard of health and smart personal appearance – applications need to be supported by a recent full-length photograph. Weight is expected to be in proportion to height and minimum height requirement is usually 1.57 metres (5 feet 2 inches) to 1.62 metres (5 feet 4 inches). Minimum age for entry to employment varies between airlines, but is usually 19–20 years.

Experience of working with members of the public or in the caring field is important, for example, nursing, teaching, catering, travel agency or airport work. Applicants are normally required to be able to swim.

Some companies permit glasses or contact lenses to be worn up to an unaided vision standard. Some companies require good colour vision. A medical certificate of fitness is required to fly world-wide.

Female staff have to wear a hairstyle suitable for the uniform hat. Males are not normally permitted to wear beards, although moustaches may be allowed.

Applicants must be in possession of a British passport or be able to obtain one before employment. Passports should allow applicants unrestricted access to the areas serviced by the particular airline.

Living within easy travelling distance of the airport with reliable transport is also a requirement.

TRAINING

Individual airlines provide their own training which normally takes between three to six weeks. It is usually held in an airline environment which includes a mock-up aircraft cabin. Practical and written tests are taken at various stages of the training, which includes study of food and drink service and galley management, currency exchange, customs and immigration regulations and documentation, first aid and medical training, safety and survival, care of special passengers, personal hygiene and grooming.

Methods of training include lectures, visits, demonstrations, discussions, films, slides and energetic emergency procedure practice.

On completion of initial training, entrants have a probationary period of between six months and a year. This consists of on-the-job training under the supervision of experienced cabin crew.

Crew also re-train in safety and emergency procedures for each type of aircraft they work in.

Some colleges provide the Foundation Certificate for Cabin Crew.

CIVIL AVIATION: YAB/RAC

LATE ENTRY

The upper age limit for entry is usually 28 to 35 years.

OPPORTUNITIES

Competition for employment is intense, with some airlines receiving as many as 25,000 or more enquiries each year. As a result, airlines rarely have to advertise.

Airlines that do a lot of charter work to holiday destinations may recruit people on a seasonal basis in a temporary capacity initially. They may then be offered permanent work if suitable positions arise. British Airways employs support cabin crew who work part-time.

Opportunities for work with foreign airlines is usually dependent on being able to converse fluently in the language of the country and being able to conduct an interview and training in that language. Some countries, such as the Gulf states, recruit British nationals.

Some airlines run training schemes for young people that include cabin services department training. Places available are, however, extremely limited. Trainees may gain permanent employment with the airline afterwards, or be helped to find alternative employment in the travel industry.

PAY AND CONDITIONS

These vary according to the employing airline.

Basic pay on entry is £8,336 per annum. This is increased by payments of allowances for unsocial hours or for overseas work. Cabin crew can expect to earn between £12,000 and £14,000 (allowances will vary according to fleet allocation) in their first year of employment. There are additional allowances, eg for being able to speak foreign languages, and commission may be paid on the sale of duty-free goods.

Shift patterns can be very irregular as airlines fly 24 hours a day. Within Europe, duties have a typical pattern of four to six days on duty with two to four days off, and each day's duty may include several short-haul flights. On long-haul flights, the system is different and may include rest periods abroad and time off on return. In addition, stand-bys are worked.

Subsidized travel is available, and payments for periods spent away from home.

PROSPECTS

These vary according to the employing airline. In some, promotion is automatic through seniority grades, while with others it is dependent on a more senior member of staff leaving. Promotion is also to senior steward/stewardess, called the 'Number One', who decides which sections of the plane the others work in. Promotion can also entail moving on to work in the first-class section of the plane.

Employment as air cabin crew is not as short term as it once was, with staff staying longer, into their late fifties on some airlines.

Opportunities may exist to move to another airline or into other work such as ground duties, administration and training and recruitment.

RELATED OCCUPATIONS

Ship steward/stewardess, waiter/waitress, hotel receptionist, resort representative, travel courier, travel agency consultant/clerk.

FURTHER INFORMATION AND READING

Please see article 4. AIR TRAFFIC CONTROLLER.

3. AIRCRAFT MAINTENANCE ENGINEER (YAB/RAC)

THE WORK

Aircraft maintenance engineers in civil aviation work normally specialize in mechanical or avionic engineering. Mechanical engineers service and overhaul engines and airframes. Avionics engineers specialize in the maintenance of instruments, electrical and electronic equipment, automatic pilot, navigation, radar and radio/communications equipment.

Both types of engineer carry out routine maintenance on the ground during aircraft turnaround at airports, and respond to reports from air crew of any difficulties experienced during flights, repairing and making corrections. They also do maintenance and overhaul of aircraft in hangars and workshops when an aircraft is due for its regular inspection and checks.

The work involves using hand and power tools for replacement of parts and the treatment of corrosion, checking of tyres, brakes, instruments, wheel flaps etc – any parts affecting the safety of the aircraft. Safety equipment is also checked. They complete worksheets for checks made and these are certified by themselves if they are licensed to do so, or by a qualified supervisor.

Engineers work as part of a very organized and highly efficient team and, particularly during turnarounds, they work at speed and under pressure. Work is normally carried out under supervision, though this depends on the categories of licence the engineer is qualified in.

Flight engineers are still carried in a few aircraft, such as the DC10, Tristar and some B747 models. They work on the flight deck during long-hauls and are responsible for the correct functioning of systems and equipment, liaising with ground staff when on the ground. Developments with the newer wide-bodied aircraft, though, have meant the use of computers in flight decks allowing only two-person crews of pilot and co-pilot, so the job of flight engineer is gradually disappearing.

WORK ENVIRONMENT

Aircraft maintenance engineers work in airports on the apron during turnaround, working in all types of weather conditions and at height in exposed conditions. On routine overhauls and checks they work indoors in workshops and hangars.

Work is normally carried out at the home airport. Aircraft maintenance engineers with seniority and experience sometimes work overseas, supervising the work of contracted foreign crew who do checks on the employing airline's aircraft.

Inside the aircraft, the work is carried out in often cramped and confined conditions, requiring bending in awkward positions.

Flight engineers work in the confined spaces of flight decks.

CIVIL AVIATION: YAB/RAC

Maintenance engineers normally wear overalls and safety equipment such as eye protectors, harnesses and ear defenders as necessary. Flight engineers wear a uniform similar to that of pilots.

SKILLS AND INTERESTS

All aircraft maintenance engineers must have a strong sense of responsibility since the safety of the aircraft and passengers depends on them to a large degree. All aircraft engineers need manual, technical and mechanical aptitude. Different areas of work require varying degrees of fine manual skills, good powers of analysis and the ability to read drawings.

Since aircraft have to be serviced in a short time, engineers have to be able to work at speed yet still be accurate. They must work well as members of a team.

They must have normal colour vision and a good head for heights. Physical fitness and agility for working in confined and cramped conditions are also required.

ENTRY REQUIREMENTS

Modern Apprenticeships

Major airlines and independent aircraft maintenance organizations may offer Modern Apprenticeships (part of the Skillseekers Initiative in Scotland). The recommended entry requirement is a minimum of three GCSEs/S grades (A–C/1–3) including English, maths and physics or combined science that includes physics. A practical subject such as CDT is very useful.

Full-time college courses

City and Guilds 2590 Aeronautical Engineering Competencies courses have varying entry requirements. They range from no specific qualifications but aptitude for science and calculations, to two GCSEs/S grades (A–C/1–3) including maths or a science subject.

Brunel College of Art and Technology's Foundation Certificate in Aeronautical Maintenance Engineering requires a minimum of three GCSEs/S grades (A–C/1–3) including English, maths and physics or combined science that includes physics; or BTEC First Diploma in Engineering; or a BTEC national diploma; or Intermediate GNVQ/GSVQ Level II in Engineering.

BTEC National Diploma in Engineering (Aerospace) or Aeronautical Maintenance Engineering or Aerospace Studies usually requires a minimum of four GCSEs/S grades (A–C/1–3) including English, maths and a science that includes physics; or a BTEC first award in engineering; or appropriate SQA national certificate modules; or Intermediate GNVQ/GSVQ Level II in Engineering.

Oxford Air Training School, a fee-paying college, requires a good secondary education standard with a minimum age of $17\frac{1}{2}$ on entry, for its aircraft maintenance engineering course.

The above outlines entry requirements for training places. It is possible to work in aircraft engineering without these qualifications and gain experience on the job, but employers usually require the minimum qualifications described above or experience in other areas of engineering.

Aircraft maintenance engineers must have normal colour vision and may be expected to pass a medical examination.

TRAINING

Training for aircraft maintenance engineers is normally via industry-recognized apprenticeships and college courses. This is because of the need for engineers to reach certain licence standards to be able to certify their own and others' work. The courses bring students to the level needed to take the necessary examinations for licences.

Training other than that outlined under ENTRY REQUIREMENTS is obtained via employment and experience on the job, and licences can be applied for after gaining experience and technical knowledge at work.

Pre-entry

City and Guilds 2590 Aeronautical Competencies courses are offered full-time for two years by several colleges and provide a basis of knowledge required for an NVQ in Aircraft Maintenance Engineering Level 3.

Brunel College of Art and Technology's one year full-time Foundation Certificate in Aeronautical Maintenance Engineering can lead to entry to the BTEC Higher National Diploma in Aeroplanes and Engines Maintenance Engineering, or Avionics Maintenance, and/or to the CAA maintenance engineering programme.

BTEC national diploma courses (two years, full-time) may be attended as a student or as an employee sponsored by an employer. Courses are designed to meet the educational and technical requirements for aircraft maintenance engineers. They are offered at several colleges and can lead to entry into work and further study at higher national certificate level or to entry into higher education for a higher national diploma or degree. These courses also provide a basis of knowledge required for the NVQ in Aircraft Maintenance Engineering at Level 3. It is possible that these courses will be phased out when Advanced GNVQ in Engineering and additional specialist aeronautical units are introduced.

Oxford Air Training School offers a twelve-month course leading to basic mechanic standard, then several courses that take between two-and-a-half to three years to complete for the CAA Aircraft Maintenance Engineer Licence.

On entry

Basic engineering training is usually carried out by employers in the aeronautical industry supported by release to an air training college or specialist aeronautical training provider.

The course of study followed depends on GCSE/S grade results. Entrants with four GCSEs/S grades (A–C/1–3) usually follow a BTEC National Certificate in Aerospace Engineering, while others follow the City and Guilds 2590 course.

NVQs/SVQs in Aircraft Engineering Maintenance are available at Levels 2 and 3.

Those on Modern Apprenticeships (part of the Skillseekers Initiative in Scotland) work towards one of several NVQs/SVQs at Level 3. There is no set length of time for Modern Apprenticeship training but it is likely to be at least three years. Contact your local careers office or TEC/LEC for details.

Licences are issued at present in various categories, such as Airframe, Engine, Avionic and Radio, and are divided into two parts: Licence Without Type Rating (LWTR), which shows basic knowledge but does not grant certification privileges, and Type Rating (TR), which include certification privileges in respect of certain light aircraft and their systems.

In addition to having experience and/or formal training, applicants must be at least 20 years before applying for LWTR and at least 21 years for TR. It is general practice that trainees follow an initial two years' training, then a further two years' experience is required to reach licence application standard. Applicants for licences have to show at least three years' experience relating to the maintenance of operating aircraft, and have to pay the appropriate fees.

Maintenance of large aircraft is undertaken by CAA-approved organizations who confer on their own engineers certain certification privileges. Those engineers must successfully complete a CAA-approved course (appropriate to Type) and be holders of an appropriate LWTR before being granted a Company Approval certificate that allows them to certify work.

The Aviation Training Association publishes Open Tech materials that enable aircraft maintenance engineers to prepare through distance learning for the LWTR, the Aeronautical Maintenance Certificate (AMC), and acquire the technical knowledge necessary for an NVQ/SVQ in Aircraft Engineering Maintenance (Mechanical and Avionic) at Level 3.

Part-time and short courses are available for people with a basic mechanical or electrical/electronic engineering background with little or no experience of civil aviation maintenance. There are also revision courses for those with experience but little or no training.

NB: The existing licence system is due to change to a European licence system some time from 1999. That will affect the information in this section on licensing.

LATE ENTRY

Upper age limits for apprenticeships are set by individual employers but college courses are available at all ages.

Employment opportunities may be available to those with a basic mechanical or electrical/electronic background.

OPPORTUNITIES

Most aircraft maintenance engineers are employed by airlines or independent aircraft maintenance engineering companies. Competition for training places is quite intense. Companies restrict entrants to those living within a certain radius of where they are based.

Other opportunities are in work for companies that do contract work for airlines, in air taxi companies, and flying clubs. Aircraft manufacturers who do work on the maintenance of aircraft also employ aircraft maintenance engineers, as do component workshops, where licences are not needed.

The possibilities of finding work abroad are diminishing as countries increasingly show preference for their own nationals, but the UK Maintenance Engineers' Licence is accepted by all countries signatory to the International Civil Aviation Authority. It is occasionally possible to work overseas for the home airline overseeing foreign contract workers on aircraft turnaround overseas.

Flight engineers are usually now recruited from ground engineering trades or the RAF, as demand for their services has diminished. Developments with newer wide-bodied jets have resulted in two-person air crews of pilot and co-pilot only.

PAY AND CONDITIONS

Aircraft maintenance engineers without licences earn between £15,000 and £19,500. Licensed technicians earn around £18,500 to £19,500. There are additional payments for the possession of CAA licences as well as overtime, shift and unsocial hours allowances. Salaries are set to amounts agreed with the engineering unions.

PROSPECTS

Promotion for aircraft maintenance engineers is to supervisory positions. Engineers holding a Licence with Type Rating or a Company Approval Certificate are at an advantage in seeking promotion.

Exams are available to qualify for flight engineer work but, as the need for this work has decreased, so have the opportunities for promotion via this route.

Work in aircraft design work and aeronautical engineering is confined to those who are able to extend their qualifications to a Higher National Diploma in Aeronautical Engineering.

RELATED OCCUPATIONS

Aircraft maintenance engineer: Armed Forces, motor vehicle mechanic, auto-electrician, engineer.

FURTHER INFORMATION AND READING

Please see article 4. AIR TRAFFIC CONTROLLER.

4. AIR TRAFFIC CONTROLLER (YAB)

THE WORK

Air traffic controllers (ATCOs) are responsible for keeping the aircraft under their control separated safely from each other, both in the air and on the ground. They work either at en-route centres (area control) or airports (aerodrome/approach control). They use VHF radio to issue instructions, advice and information to pilots in order to maintain a safe, orderly and rapid flow of air traffic. ATCOs keep close watch over the aircraft either visually (aerodrome) or by radar (approach/area control). Sophisticated computers are used to keep up-to-date information and help the overall air traffic situation.

Area control

This is provided at the two Area Control Centres (ACC), based at West Drayton, near Heathrow, and at the Scottish and Oceanic Control Centre at Prestwick. There is a further sub-centre based at Manchester Airport. These centres provide air traffic services within their designated area to all aircraft flying in controlled airspace in the UK and across the North Atlantic. (Not all airspace is controlled, to allow for such as pleasure and military flying.)

Control is maintained by taking into account vertical and horizontal distances between aircraft and using such factors as aircraft performance, requested routings and the effects of weather (for example, strong winds) on airspeed, aircraft headings etc.

Approach control

Approach controllers guide aircraft and organize the order in which they take off or land. They keep moving aircraft separate, either by using radar, or, if radar is not available,

CIVIL AVIATION: YAB/RAC

by a procedural control based on aircraft estimates and performance. They organize aircraft into the most rapid order for landing, or, if there are delays, place aircraft into a holding pattern clear of the departure path.

Aerodrome control

Controllers at aerodromes ensure aircraft taxi safely, taking their turn in an orderly manner from their parking stands to the runways, and vehicles are kept clear. The controllers are responsible for separating aircraft and instructing them to take-off or land as rapidly and efficiently as possible. At major airports, this task is divided into Air Control and Ground Movement Control (GMC).

WORK ENVIRONMENT

In area and approach control, ATCOs work in rooms with low levels of lighting to enable them to see clearly the information relayed to them on radar screens. Daylight-viewing radar, however, is increasingly being used. They do not have visual contact with the aircraft themselves.

Aerodrome controllers work in a control tower that has a 360-degree view of the surrounding area, thereby allowing them visual contact with aircraft.

Most ATCOs work in a seated position and wear headphones. Work, particularly at peak periods, can be intense – at Heathrow, for example, aircraft land and take off at a rate of two a minute.

SKILLS AND INTERESTS

The work requires the capacity for intense concentration and a very strong sense of responsibility. ATCOs need to be able to respond quickly and efficiently at all times, particularly in emergencies. They need to be decisive and have a calm, unruffled method of working. A high standard of physical fitness is required, including good colour vision, eyesight and hearing and a clear speaking voice.

As controllers normally work in the same team, gaining rapport with each other, ability in and liking for team work is very important. Technical aptitude is also important, because of the complex radar and computer systems used. The ability to deal with figure work and calculations is also important.

ENTRY REQUIREMENTS

Entry requirements for the necessary training depend on the employer. Most ATCOs are employed by National Air Traffic Services Limited (NATS) whose requirements for student entry are as follows:

– aged at least 18 and under 27 years on the date of application; and

– five GCSEs/S grades (A–C/1–3) including English and maths. As further evidence of academic ability, applicants should have completed a period of post-GCSE/S grade education, such as two A levels/three H grades, or a BTEC/SQA national course, or Advanced GNVQ/GSVQ Level III; or

– candidates with previous relevant aviation radar experience are required to have five GCSEs/S grades (A–C/1–3) including English and maths, but may be accepted without further examination passes.

ATCOs employed by NATS must be eligible to work in the UK; they need security clearance before starting work.

The other employers of ATCOs in civil aviation vary in their requirements, some only employing experienced personnel. Others usually recruit entrants aged between 18 and 21 years and expect five GCSEs/S grades (A–C/1–3) including English, maths and a science. Applicants with alternative qualifications, eg GNVQ/GSVQ, are considered on their merits.

A good standard of fitness is necessary, with normal colour vision, good eyesight and hearing and no speech defects. ATCOs have to pass regular medical tests.

All ATCOs have to obtain Civil Aviation Authority (CAA) licences to do their work.

TRAINING

NATS Student Air Traffic Controller Scheme

The training consists of courses of study followed by practical training lasting 74 weeks. Most of the courses are run at Bournemouth International Airport at the NATS College of Air Traffic Control. Practical training is on simulators at the college followed by live training at operational units throughout the UK. The courses include subjects such as aviation studies, telecommunications, navigation, meteorology, and radar and non-radar elements of aerodrome approach and area control. Examinations have to be passed at various stages in order to continue training.

Trainees study for the award of CAA licences, three of which are needed to qualify and are normally obtained during the course. The type of licence obtained depends on whether the student is due to go to an area centre or an airport.

Licences have to be validated for the place of work by completing a period of supervised duty before the ATCO is permitted to control aircraft solo. Other courses are available to experienced ATCOs, such as automatic data processing, technical appreciation and instructor training.

Other airports and local authority entry

Training is through courses at the College of Air Traffic Control at Bournemouth International Airport or other approved air traffic control training establishment. This is supplemented by on-the-job training, before beginning operational work.

NVQs/SVQs in air traffic control are being developed.

LATE ENTRY

The age restrictions outlined under ENTRY REQUIREMENTS apply.

OPPORTUNITIES

The majority of UK air traffic controllers are employed by NATS, which is a joint CAA/Ministry of Defence organization employing some 1,500 ATCOs. They work at BAA airports and certain other airports, and at the main area centres at West Drayton and Prestwick. The airport air traffic services are at Aberdeen, Belfast, Birmingham, Cardiff, Edinburgh, Farnborough, Gatwick, Glasgow, Heathrow, London City, Manchester, Stansted and Sumburgh. Although a preference can be expressed, ATCOs may be posted wherever needed.

Currently more ATCOs are needed as air traffic increases and new ATC systems are introduced. Recruitment is likely to be at a rate of over 90 student entrants a year over the next few years at least.

Air traffic controllers are also employed at private and local authority owned airports and at private airfields.

There are some opportunities in Commonwealth and other English-speaking countries, but these countries have their own licensing requirements and are increasingly employing their own nationals.

PAY AND CONDITIONS

Student air traffic controllers with NATS earn £15,149 on appointment and £15,906 on successful completion of radar rating. Trainee air traffic controllers earn £22,814 on appointment rising to £25,904 plus an accommodation allowance. On appointment as ATCO the annual salary is £29,236/£31,056 (depending on unit) rising to over £39,000, with prospects to over £51,000 for the most responsible positions. These figures include an unsocial hours payment for those working shifts.

Air traffic control services operate 24 hours a day and most ATCOs do a 40-hour week with eight-hour shift periods, spending two hours maximum sitting at a radar screen followed by half-hour breaks (longer at busy periods). The week usually includes night, early morning and late afternoon shifts, as well as bank holidays and weekends.

PROSPECTS

Promotion after training in NATS is by a grade system from ATCO 3 to ATCO 2 and then to ATCO 1, depending on the units at which ATCOs are stationed and their level of responsibility. Beyond grade 1, promotion is to management and planning. Additional training is provided at the College of Air Training for specific posts such as instructing.

RELATED OCCUPATIONS

Air traffic control officer (Armed Forces), airline pilot, airline flight operations assistant, coastguard, merchant navy officer.

FURTHER INFORMATION

Aviation Training Association*, Dralda House, Crendon Street, High Wycombe, Bucks HP13 6LS, 01494 445262, www.pavilion.co.uk/westdean

Recruitment and Selection*, Meadowbank, British Airways, PO Box 59, Hounslow, Middlesex TW5 9X, 0181 564 1450

Oxford Air Training School, CSE Aviation Ltd, Oxford Airport, Kidlington, Oxford OX5 1RA, 01865 841234, www.cse-aviation.com

Civil Aviation Authority*, Recruitment Services, Room T820, CAA House, 45–59 Kingsway, London WC2B 6TE, 0171 832 6696

Engineering Licensing Department, Civil Aviation Authority, Safety Regulation Group, Aviation House, South Area, Gatwick, West Sussex, RH6 0YR, 01923 573607

General Aviation Manufacturers and Trades Association Ltd, 19 Church Street, Brill, Aylesbury, Bucks HP18 9TG, 01844 238020

Monarch Aircraft Engineering Training, Prospect Way, London Luton Airport, Luton, Beds LU2 9QH, 01582 418668

National Air Traffic Services Ltd (NATS)*, Recruitment T1213, CAA House, 45–49 Kingsway, London WC2B 6TE, 0171 832 5555

FURTHER READING

Leaflets/booklets are available from the addresses marked*.

Working in Transport and Distribution – COIC

Flight International Directory Part 1 UK and Ireland – Flight International Directories

Periodicals: Flight International – Reed Business Publishing

In the careers library classified under YAB/RAC.

ROAD TRANSPORT: YAD

1. **ROAD TRANSPORT MANAGER CLCI:YAD**
2. **BUS/COACH DRIVER CLCI:YAD**
3. **BUS CONDUCTOR CLCI:YAD**
4. **TAXI/PRIVATE HIRE VEHICLE DRIVER CLCI:YAD**
5. **LGV DRIVER CLCI:YAD**
6. **CAR/VAN DRIVER CLCI:YAD**
7. **DRIVING INSTRUCTOR CLCI:YAD**

BACKGROUND INFORMATION

As many people in large cities rely on public transport to reach their places of work, most industries and businesses in the UK are dependent on a smoothly flowing passenger transport system.

Road passenger traffic consists largely of local public transport, coach companies running scheduled services between major towns and cities, holiday tour operators, and companies offering private coach hire.

Road haulage and delivery are carried out by operators that may be single-vehicle businesses or companies owning fleets of 1,000 vehicles. The road haulage industry is one of the most important service industries in the country: 85% to 90% of the nation's goods are carried by road in about 425,000 large goods vehicles.

1. ROAD TRANSPORT MANAGER (YAD)

THE WORK

The road transport manager's job is to maximize the use of resources, both people and vehicles. In some small firms the transport manager is also a driver, and in solo operations is owner-driver or, effectively, driver-manager.

There are two sectors of the road goods transport industry: the 'own account' sector – firms that transport their own goods; and the 'hire or reward' sector – firms that exist in order to transport goods for other people. A similar division exists in the bus and coach sector.

The main responsibility of transport managers is to plan the work schedules of drivers and vehicles. In road haulage, they arrange a vehicle, driver and delivery date for each load, make sure that every vehicle travels full, and try to find a load for the return journey as it is not economic to have lorries travelling empty. Plans are entered on large diary sheets. Transport managers calculate whether a load will fit into a vehicle without breaking the weight regulations, and whether it can be delivered on time without breaking laws either on drivers' working hours or on the distance travelled by a vehicle since its last service, and ensure the safe operation of the vehicle and business. Many firms use computers for such calculations.

Costing is an important part of the work; prices have to be competitive enough to attract customers but high enough to cover costs and make a profit. When customers ask for an estimate over the phone, the transport manager has to think quickly.

Route planning calls for knowledge of the road system, shipping, docks, tipping sites, overnight parking, and drivers' accommodation facilities etc. The transport manager works out the safest and shortest route to the destination, taking into account such hazards as low bridges and extensive road works.

They also ensure maintenance and repairs are carried out effectively at the scheduled times.

There is a considerable amount of paperwork: invoices, delivery notes, shipping documents etc. In addition the transport manager must follow up customers' complaints and cope with emergencies, such as accidents and breakdowns. There is also an element of personnel work; the transport manager must brief drivers, answer their questions, handle their complaints, delegate work and make sure the office runs smoothly.

There are a great many laws and regulations relating to the road haulage industry, and it is the transport manager's responsibility to see that none of these are broken, and at the same time that the best use is made of drivers and vehicles. In particular, they must ensure their drivers are aware of the current regulations regarding tachographs, drivers' hours and over-loading. They are responsible for preventing and removing any malpractices.

While all this falls within the responsibility of the transport manager, in larger firms the detailed work is carried out by clerical staff or junior managers whom the transport manager supervises.

WORK ENVIRONMENT

The transport manager spends most of the day in the traffic office, part of it in the yard with the drivers, and part in the workshop with maintenance staff.

SKILLS AND INTERESTS

Transport managers come into contact with all sorts of people: lorry drivers, mechanics, maintenance staff and customers. They will have some dealings with the police, the Department of the Environment, Transport and the Regions, the Licensing Authority, trade unions and employers' associations, and they have to be able to communicate with all these people, on the telephone, face to face and in writing.

Excellent organizational skills are required for planning and scheduling work. Computer literacy and mathematical ability are needed for route scheduling, expenditure control etc. An understanding of relevant legislation is essential. Foreign languages may be an advantage.

Transport managers should be practical and tough but flexible in outlook and not given to worrying. They must be able to think and act quickly and work under pressure. Tolerance and a sense of humour are needed to deal with disgruntled drivers, complaining customers and difficult situations. Transport managers must be accurate when doing cost calculations as mistakes can prove expensive. They have to take responsibility for their own actions; when anything goes wrong they are in the front line.

ENTRY REQUIREMENTS

Transport managers often hold a driving licence for the class of vehicle for which they are responsible. EU legislation requires all transport managers from both national and international firms to hold a Certificate of Professional Competence (CPC).

Many transport managers start their careers as drivers or clerks and work their way up, but direct entry to a one- to two-year management training scheme normally requires a minimum of five GCSEs/S grades (A–C/1–3), including English and maths, with two A level/three H grades. The

ROAD TRANSPORT: YAD

Chartered Institute of Transport recommends that A level/H grade subjects include economics or geography. Many management trainees have degrees or BTEC/SQA higher national certificates/diplomas.

TRAINING

Management training is primarily on the job, working alongside and assisting experienced managers in a series of different departments, possibly with short courses at training centres in specialist aspects.

Training may include assessment for NVQ/SVQ in Supervisory Management at Level 3 and/or in Management at Level 4, to standards set by the Confederation of Passenger Transport UK (CPT UK) and the Road Haulage and Distribution Training Council (RHDTC). This training may form a part of a Modern Apprenticeship.

In addition, practising managers of 'hire or reward' and passenger transport firms require a Certificate of Professional Competence (CPC). This can be achieved by passing an examination administered by the Royal Society of Arts (RSA) or the Institute of Transport Administration (IoTA), or by obtaining the Chartered Institute of Transport (CIT) Certificate in Transport.

Membership of the professional bodies mentioned above is achieved by passing or gaining exemption from their examinations. Holders of relevant degrees or BTEC/SQA higher national certificates or diplomas (in Transport Management, Transport Operations, for example) may gain full or part exemption. Further details are available from the CIT or IoTA.

Courses for the CPC are available via correspondence or at local colleges or other training establishments – a list of centres is available from the RSA or IoTA.

Postgraduate qualifications in transport are also available.

LATE ENTRY

There is no age limit for entry, though entry to management trainee schemes is normally after university or college. Entry may be possible from driving and clerical jobs into supervisory or junior manager posts. A relevant BTEC/SQA award or degree may assist promotion prospects.

OPPORTUNITIES

All firms in the haulage sector have a nominated transport manager. In smaller companies these duties will be handled by a manager who also has other responsibilities.

Contract haulage has increased in recent years while own-account operators have declined, as large companies have come to realize that it is more economic to contract out these services.

PAY AND CONDITIONS

Pay is negotiated by individuals and therefore varies from firm to firm. Rates of pay are likely to be higher in the 'own account' sector. Transport managers earn salaries broadly equivalent to other managerial posts demanding similar qualifications or experience. Most earn in the region of £15,000 to £25,000. Many transport managers earn additional payments for unsocial hours. These shift allowances can often be considerable.

Shift work and long/irregular hours are common.

PROSPECTS

In small firms promotion is unlikely but in large organizations it is possible to progress to responsibility for several branches or depots in an area or region, and from there to national transport manager. A move into general management may then be possible.

RELATED OCCUPATIONS

Distribution manager, warehouse manager, freight forwarder, LGV driver, vehicle maintenance manager, traffic clerk,

FURTHER INFORMATION

Chartered Institute of Transport*, 80 Portland Place, London W1N 4DP, 0171 467 9425, www.citrans.org.uk

Institute of Transport Administration*, 32 Palmerston Road, Southampton SO14 1LL, 01703 631380

Road Haulage and Distribution Training Council (RHDTC)*, 14 Warren Yard, Warren Farm Office Village, Stratford Road, Milton Keynes, MK12 5NW, 01908 313360

RSA Examinations Board, Westwood Way, Coventry CV4 8HS, 01203 470033

FURTHER READING

Leaflets/booklets are available from each address marked*.

The Transport Manager's and Operators' Handbook – Kogan Page

Working in Transport and Distribution – COIC

Transport and Distribution – AGCAS

Careers on the Move – CIT

Careers in Road Haulage and Distribution – RHDTC

Periodicals:Transport Management (the IoTA bi-monthly journal); Motor Transport, Commercial Transport Magazine (IPC Transport Press Journals)

In the careers library classified under YAD.

2. BUS/COACH DRIVER (YAD)

THE WORK

The duties carried out by the bus or coach driver depend on the type of service being offered.

Local bus services are the most common type of bus driving. Some London services and a few other companies offer a crewed service but most now favour one-person operation (OPO), ie one person driving and collecting fares.

Long-distance and excursion services – there are four different areas of work, and individual drivers may be involved in all four:

Long-distance express services – this type of driving has longer distances between stops and may include some motorway driving. Drivers have to move passengers' suitcases into and out of the boot of the coach when passengers embark or leave at a main stopping point. There is a network of these routes across the country. There may be shorter, express inter-city services between

ROAD TRANSPORT: YAD

large towns and cities within an area.

Private hire/day excursions include trips to the countryside, exhibitions, sports events, the seaside etc. The driver has to start at a particular time and location and arrive at a particular time at the destination. Full-day excursions are likely to involve day and evening work. Drivers must be careful not to exceed the legal number of hours they may drive without a break. Long periods of waiting may occur on reaching their destination.

Regular contract bookings – the coach and driver are hired by an organization to follow the same route, usually both morning and evening, picking up and setting down particular passengers (as opposed to the general public). These may be schoolchildren, factory workers, nurses etc.

Holiday tours – a driver may be away from home for long periods. The driver follows the main routes that the organization or employer has planned out but, within this, has some authority to make minor changes due to traffic hold-ups, unexpected hazards etc. This work involves responsibilities that are in addition to the usual ones of passenger (and pedestrian) safety. A serious mechanical breakdown could involve having the coach repaired, hiring another coach or arranging for alternative accommodation for the passengers if it is not possible to get them to the planned destination.

WORK ENVIRONMENT

Driving in a large town or city, with heavy traffic and many pedestrians, is very different from the slower pace of country routes. The driver of a crewed bus has a very different environment from the driver of an OPO bus who has to deal much more with passengers. All drivers must cope with driving safely under varying conditions and in all types of weather.

Local bus services. Town and city bus drivers, whose routes include the majority of local bus services, negotiate a route through heavy traffic and the pollution caused by traffic exhaust fumes.

Private hire and excursion services may involve driving in the city, countryside, or to the seaside. It is often necessary to wait around for several hours for passengers to return to the vehicle.

Holiday tours require much more involvement with the passengers. If the tour is to a foreign country, a driver has to cope with a different language as well as any problems that may occur. Changes of route, due to road conditions or other hazards, pose more problems if the country is not well known to the driver. He/she can spend long periods away from home.

The wearing of a uniform is usually compulsory. As much of the driver's time is spent sitting at the controls, modern buses and coaches usually have well-designed seats for maximum comfort.

SKILLS AND INTERESTS

Bus and coach drivers need to be skilled at driving in all conditions and on all types of roads. They need to be patient and calm with the ability to maintain concentration. Bus and coach drivers need to be honest and reliable. They should also be punctual and able to work unsupervised. Good communication skills are equally essential as is a pleasant manner when working with the public. Numeracy skills are needed for those taking fares and giving change. Coach drivers require good map-reading skills and, for those working with tourists, historical and general knowledge is useful.

ENTRY REQUIREMENTS

Most bus or coach operators do not require any formal academic qualifications. Organizations may give basic arithmetical tests to applicants to check that would-be employees would have no problems giving change or adding up the day's takings. Some also assess driving skills prior to specialist training. A full clean car driving licence is essential. Employers may also look for a few years' experience of driving and of working with people, eg as a shop assistant.

The minimum age for the PCV driving test is 18 years. To obtain a PCV licence, drivers are also required to pass a medical and eyesight examination which needs to be re-taken after the age of 45. People suffering from certain medical conditions may not be accepted.

All bus and coach drivers must hold a Passenger Carrying Vehicle (PCV) licence. Some firms, however, may prefer entrants who already hold a PCV licence. The minimum age for the PCV test is 18 years and is effectively the minimum age for entry but some companies may set their own age requirement.

PCV drivers under 21 years are restricted to local bus services. It is sometimes possible to join a company as a conductor and progress to driving.

TRAINING

A bus driver is required, by law, to have a PCV (Passenger Carrying Vehicle) licence. Private training and an examination is available at the individual's expense. It might also be possible to be trained by the employing firm. Consult *Yellow Pages* for private training organizations running courses for the PCV licence and approach local bus/coach companies to check whether they offer training

If accepted for driver training, a trainee spends some time in a training school, receiving tuition in a classroom, and on and off the road. For firms running one-person operated buses or coaches, training in handling passengers, dealing with fares and tickets etc may precede or accompany driver training.

Initial practice in manoeuvring takes place off the road but this is followed by a period spent practising manoeuvring on a variety of actual routes, accompanied by a trainer. The period of time spent on driver training depends on the quickness and ability of the trainee but is usually around ten to fifteen days. When trainees are considered ready they take a theory and practical PCV test.

When they have obtained a PCV licence, bus drivers are given a period of route-learning.

There is also an industry qualification. NVQs/SVQs in Transporting Passengers by Road are available at Level 2, with a Level 3 qualification also available for long-distance coach drivers who have additional responsibilities of dealing with hotels, tourist attractions etc.

LATE ENTRY

Some companies specify an upper age limit of between 50 and 60 years, but many employers accept people up to retirement age as long as they are fit enough to cope with the demands of the job and pass a medical. Experience of driving a minibus or van helps when applying for jobs.

ROAD TRANSPORT: YAD

OPPORTUNITIES

Bus and coach services are run by companies that tend to specialize in one of the areas outlined. Openings vary from region to region.

Self-employment is possible. As well as the capital requirement to buy a coach or bus, an Operators Licence is required for which there are certain qualifications.

PAY AND CONDITIONS

Wages vary from company to company and depends on the location and type of driving involved.

Shift work is often necessary, involving work on any day of the week from early until late.

Saturday and Sunday work is built into the basic schedule and overtime work is generally available. Pay rates sometimes vary according to the shift involved.

PROSPECTS

Possible career progression for a bus driver is to gain promotion to a supervisor. Some work on general traffic duties and ticket checking, whilst others are part of the garage supervisory staff. Others work in radio-control rooms. This could lead to eventual promotion as a manager. Prospects of advancement vary in many companies, as avenues for promotion can be limited.

Bus drivers may also take a sideways step and transfer to clerical work, progressing to managerial and administrative positions within a bus organization. Most large bus companies give vacancy information to all their employees. It may also be possible to train to become a bus and coach driving instructor. An NVQ/SVQ in Bus and Coach Driving Instruction is available at Level 3.

Some drivers move from bus work into driving for holiday tour groups or day trip operators.

RELATED OCCUPATIONS

LGV driver, car/van driver, roundsman/woman, removal man/woman, taxi/private hire vehicle driver.

FURTHER INFORMATION AND READING

Please see article 3. BUS CONDUCTOR.

3. BUS CONDUCTOR (YAD)

THE WORK

Bus conductors collect fares, issue tickets and check bus passes. They deal with passengers' questions, advising them when they have reached their destination and directing them around the district. They also provide help with customers' baggage, such as loading and unloading pushchairs and heavy shopping onto the bus.

Conductors must ensure the safety of their passengers at all times by limiting the number of passengers standing, controlling children etc. They ensure the bus does not pull away before passengers get on and off; the conductor signals to the driver to start off from bus stops.

Some paperwork is involved, such as recording the fares, referring to tables to check fares and times of buses, logging the length of journey and any incidents, such as writing brief accident reports when necessary. They count, bag and balance the money taken with the number of tickets issued.

WORK ENVIRONMENT

Buses and coaches are fairly comfortable but can be very cold on winter mornings and uncomfortably hot in summer. Conductors may also have to cope with the smell of traffic fumes.

The work can be physically demanding. Periods of very hectic work (such as rush hours) are often interspersed with periods of relative quiet. Conductors may have to wait to change buses and routes in all weathers.

SKILLS AND INTERESTS

Conductors need to be reliable and punctual, neat and tidy in appearance and willing to wear a uniform. They should have good communication skills and must be polite and patient when dealing with all members of the public. A friendly and cheerful nature is helpful. They should be able to do basic arithmetic, take fares and give change. Conductors need to work well without supervision and be able to work as part of a team with the driver. Conductors must also be fit and active as the job involves a large amount of standing, walking, and on most buses, climbing stairs.

ENTRY REQUIREMENTS

Applicants should normally be over 18 years, although younger people may be accepted by companies running special training schemes. No minimum academic qualifications are required. Most bus companies set tests, including spoken English and arithmetic/cash handling. Some firms prefer applicants to live near the garage where they are based. It is sometimes in the candidate's favour to have a driving licence or be learning to drive. Experience in work dealing with the public such as waiter/waitress or shop assistant may help as well.

Some bus companies specify a maximum height of 1.83 metres (six feet). Wearers of contact lenses and those with certain medical conditions may not be accepted for entry. All bus companies require candidates to pass a medical.

TRAINING

Conductors usually train for approximately two weeks but this varies from company to company.

Training covers all conductor duties, for example: reading fare tables; operating ticket machines; keeping records of tickets issued; cashing up; company regulations; safety; and customer care. A period of time is usually spent on route-learning and working with a crew under the supervision of an experienced conductor. Some companies give trainees a test at the end of their training; others rely on an assessment by the supervisor.

NVQs/SVQs in Transporting Passengers by Road - Support Services, are available at Level 2.

LATE ENTRY

There is usually no upper age limit for entry. Many companies accept or prefer mature applicants, providing they are fit, healthy and have the required personal qualities such as self-confidence and good communication skills.

ROAD TRANSPORT: YAD

OPPORTUNITIES
Limited opportunities exist with bus companies, almost all in London. Many companies have now switched to one-person operated (driver-only) buses.

PAY AND CONDITIONS
Wages vary from company to company and may depend on the location.

Shift work is often necessary involving work on any day of the week from early until late.

Saturday and Sunday work is built into the basic schedule and overtime work is generally available. Pay rates vary according to the shift involved.

PROSPECTS
Some conductors enter training to become Passenger Carrying Vehicle (PCV) drivers, once they are familiar with their company's services, routes and fare system. This opens up other career paths.

Conductors who are promoted to supervisor or controller level, work on schedules or routes. A few people move to work for private coach companies as stewards and stewardesses.

RELATED OCCUPATIONS
Train driver, taxi/private hire vehicle driver, station assistant, bus/coach driver.

FURTHER INFORMATION
See local telephone directories and *Yellow Pages* for addresses of local bus and coach companies.

TRANSFED*, Regency House, 43 High Street, Rickmansworth, Herts WD3 1ET, 01923 896607

FURTHER READING
Leaflets/booklets are available from the address marked*.

Working in Transport and Distribution – COIC

In the careers library classified under YAD.

4. TAXI/PRIVATE HIRE VEHICLE DRIVER (YAD)

THE WORK
Taxi and private hire drivers carry passengers to their destinations in return for payment.

Taxi drivers must hold a special licence (see TRAINING). They may stand at a designated taxi rank, or ply for hire, ie drive around looking for passengers.

Most drivers assist passengers and load luggage, then start the sealed fare meter (rented and maintained by large companies) to show the cost of the journey. They are responsible for driving the customer by the most direct or convenient route – this can be enforced by law.

They collect the fare from the customer when the journey is over, and change is given if appropriate.

All drivers perform minor emergency repairs and keep their taxis clean, inside and out. They are responsible for the car being in a roadworthy condition.

Private hire vehicles carry out similar duties but are not allowed to stand at taxi ranks or ply for hire.

Customers contact taxi hire agencies, who then contact drivers using two-way radios.

WORK ENVIRONMENT
Most time is spent in the cab or car, with limited space and long periods of sitting. Helping customers with luggage involves bending, lifting and carrying. There may be fumes from traffic.

SKILLS AND INTERESTS
Taxi/private hire drivers must be competent drivers, who remain alert and are able to concentrate. They need to be able to drive carefully in all conditions – bad weather, heavy traffic etc. They must be honest and trustworthy. Patience and the ability to deal with people tactfully are needed. Some mechanical knowledge is useful to undertake emergency repairs, though most use garage services. Basic numeracy skills are needed to give correct change to customers and complete tax returns.

Good health and eyesight are essential: taxi drivers have to go for regular health checks.

ENTRY REQUIREMENTS
Taxi drivers – no formal educational qualifications are required but a full, clean driving licence is needed. Applicants must obtain a special licence from their local authority, or, in London, from the Public Carriage Office (PCO). To hold this, they must be over 21 years but applications may be considered from those over 20 years and 3 months. They must also pass a medical. All applicants need a good knowledge of their area and may have to take a test.

In London, candidates must pass the 'Knowledge of London' test before they are issued with a licence.

Recent criminal convictions or serious traffic convictions are a bar to obtaining a cab driver's licence, although this may not apply if a reasonable number of years has elapsed without further incident.

Private hire vehicle drivers – do not require a special licence in all local authorities. However, some impose their own regulations, such as set tests and medicals. These may be the same as for taxi drivers and the licence may allow them to drive both types of car.

TRAINING
Taxi drivers must undertake training to gain their licence. This is most difficult in London where they must do 'the Knowledge'. For those aiming to work as a taxi driver in central London or at Heathrow Airport, they must do the 'All London' test. Suitable candidates are issued with a Blue Book which lists 400 'runs' within a six-mile radius of Charing Cross, which they must learn. This is usually done by riding a moped or cycling round London making notes. This can take up to four years but is possible in 18 to 24 months. Some private schools offer coaching in preparing for the test; students working in small groups can learn faster. When learner taxi drivers are sure that they know all routes, street names and places of interest required, they must pass the Knowledge of London test – a number of 15-minute oral examinations conducted by a Knowledge of London Examiner at the PCO, and a driving test.

ROAD TRANSPORT: YAD

If successful, they receive a licence and the green badge allowing them to ply or stand for hire anywhere within the Metropolitan and City of London police areas (a total of 786 square miles).

Another option is to study for a suburban licence covering one of 16 'sectors' outside the central London area. For a licence and a 'yellow badge', drivers must learn 30 runs and pass a knowledge test. This is possible in six to twelve months. Yellow badge drivers can ply for hire within their licensed area and are allowed to take passengers outside the area. However, they are not allowed to pick up passengers outside their sector.

Outside of London, most local authorities set their own tests of local knowledge, usually with a stringent driving test, before awarding licences.

Private hire drivers do not need a special licence in all local authorities. Some authorities, however, have the same requirements as for taxi drivers.

NVQ/SVQs at Levels 1, 2 and 3 should be available soon, suitable for new entrants, experienced drivers and for those planning to become taxi/private hire operators.

LATE ENTRY

There is no upper age limit for entry, and adult entry is common for taxi and private hire driving. Previous experience of driving work can be helpful.

OPPORTUNITIES

Licensed taxi drivers and private hire vehicle drivers are self-employed. They may be an owner-driver, a journeyman/woman (hires the cab from a fleet operator) or a flat operator (rents the cab from the owner).

The largest number of taxi drivers work in London and are governed by the Public Carriage Office. Other taxi drivers are granted their licence by the local authority. Opportunities occur throughout the country, but there is likely to be more demand in towns and cities.

PAY AND CONDITIONS

Earnings are entirely dependent on fares taken; owner-drivers generally earn more than journeymen/women. Licensing authorities control the maximum fares charged by taxi drivers, except in London where the tariff is set by the Government. Most private hire agencies use the same rates, to be competitive.

Taxi drivers can work long and irregular hours; there is no legal limit on the time they spend driving. They are only restricted when, as journeymen/women, they are working a double shift with another driver and must return to change over. Peak periods are morning and evening, between which times drivers may be out for 18 hours, although not all of this will be spent driving.

PROSPECTS

There is no promotion ladder; journeymen/women often work towards becoming owner-drivers, possibly with the long-term aim of owning a fleet of vehicles.

RELATED OCCUPATIONS

LGV driver, chauffeur/chauffeuse, car/van driver, bus/coach driver, roundsman/woman.

FURTHER INFORMATION

Licensed Taxi Drivers Association, 9–11 Woodfield Road, London W9 2BA, 0171 286 1046/7

Metropolitan Police Service, Public Carriage Office*, 15 Penton Street, London N1 9PU, 0171 230 1631

Private Hire, Hackney Carriage and Chauffeur ITO, c/o 14 Widdrington Terrace, North Shields, Tyne and Wear NE29 0BZ, 0191 258 1955

FURTHER READING

Leaflets/booklets are available from the address marked*. In the careers library classified under YAD.

5. LGV DRIVER (YAD)

THE WORK

Large goods vehicle (LGV) drivers (formerly heavy goods vehicle drivers) collect, transport and deliver goods. LGVs are divided into two categories, according to the weight and the type of vehicle: an LGV licence with category C entitlement qualifies the holder to drive rigid vehicles over 7.5 tonnes; an LGV licence with category C and E qualifies the holder to drive articulated lorries and lorries pulling a trailer.

Drivers may have to clean, refuel, load and unload their lorries; the load has to be secured with ropes and covered with special waterproof sheeting. This can be heavy, dirty, and wet work, and protective clothing is usually provided. Drivers are solely responsible for the safety of their loads; they must be able to deal with leakages, accidents and mechanical faults. Some drivers specialize in transporting dangerous loads, such as petrol, chemicals and nuclear waste.

Drivers may plan their own routes, aiming for the quickest and most economical. Those who work for small firms or are self-employed may have to find their own loads for the return journey.

Drivers must know, understand and obey the many regulations relating to their vehicles, eg weight and load-distribution rules, special speed limits. A tachograph in the lorry cab records the number of hours spent driving, resting, doing other work such as loading and unloading, the speed of the vehicle and the distance travelled.

Drivers are also likely to deal with documents such as customers' invoices and delivery notes.

WORK ENVIRONMENT

Modern lorry cabs can be very comfortable, with insulation, heating and air-conditioning. Some lorries have sleeping bunks, and even cookers and fridges, for long-distance trips. Some LGV drivers travel to overseas destinations. Much time is spent alone. Loading and unloading usually takes place out of doors.

SKILLS AND INTERESTS

LGV drivers must enjoy driving, have good driving ability and be physically fit. They require patience and a tolerant attitude to other road users. It is also important to be able to maintain concentration for long periods while driving. Drivers must be happy to spend most of their working hours alone. They need a responsible attitude and must be

ROAD TRANSPORT: YAD

able to work without supervision. They should be careful and security- and safety-conscious; the loads carried by lorries are valuable and some can be potentially dangerous. Loading and unloading can involve lifting and carrying heavy items. Drivers need to be polite to customers and must be able to complete the necessary paperwork.

ENTRY REQUIREMENTS

Drivers must be literate and numerate; they must hold the appropriate LGV licence (see TRAINING), and possess a good driving record. Some firms recruit only drivers over the age of 25 for insurance reasons. The LGV test includes a medical; good eyesight and good colour vision are necessary. Candidates must normally be at least 21 years old.

However, the LGV Young Driver Scheme has been re-introduced. Entry to this can be at 16–18 years. There are no educational requirements, but successful applicants are likely to have a few GCSEs/S grades (C/3 or above), preferably including maths and English, to indicate they can cope with NVQ/SVQ Level 2. They have to meet the same medical requirements as older drivers.

Modern Apprenticeships (part of the Skillseekers Initiative in Scotland) are also available, which may include LGV driver training. Applicants should have three GCSEs/S grades (C/3 or above) in maths, English and one other subject, or Intermediate GNVQ/GSVQ Level II, or equivalent, in order to display ability to complete the Apprenticeship and achieve NVQ/SVQ Level 3.

TRAINING

The LGV licence is divided into three categories: category C1 entitles the holder to drive vehicles over 3.5 tonnes, category C entitles the holder to drive rigid vehicles over 7.5 tonnes, and category C and E, which entitles the holder to drive articulated lorries and lorries pulling a trailer. Firms may train their own drivers, use a group training association, or use the LGV sections of private driving schools. Courses last one to three weeks, depending on the category of vehicle. In addition to driving skills and knowledge, they may also cover simple mechanics, loading, and securing loads. The test consists of manoeuvring the vehicle in a confined space, 25 miles of road driving and the completion of the LGV theory test.

Trainees on the Young Driver's Scheme will normally obtain a car/van driving (Category B) licence at 17 years and gain an LGV rigid vehicle licence at 18 years. This allows them to work as an unaccompanied driver on revenue-earning activities for their employer. After two years of satisfactory monitored experience, they may start training to drive an articulated lorry on a provisional C and E licence. They are assessed towards NVQ/SVQ in Transporting Goods by Road at Level 2. On completing the scheme at 21 years, they receive a Young Large Goods Vehicle Driver Certificate.

Modern Apprentices specializing in driving are expected to undertake NVQ/SVQ Level 2 in Organizing Road Transport Operations and Transporting Goods by Road, plus some units from the Storage and Organizing Road Transport Operations, followed by a Level 3 qualification. On completion, an Apprenticeship Certificate is awarded by the Road Haulage and Distribution Training Council (RHDTC). Apprenticeships are expected to take two and a half to three years.

Experienced drivers may also be assessed for NVQ/SVQ qualifications.

It is possible to train for an LGV licence privately, at a specialist driving school, and take the test independently.

LATE ENTRY

Opportunities are available for adults in this type of work. Entrants must hold the appropriate LGV licence, and possess a good driving record. The majority of LGV drivers are over 25 years. Some insurance companies demand drivers are over 30 years, for example those driving hazardous chemicals.

Some people enter LGV driving work or training for it from employment in other jobs in the road haulage and distribution industries such as warehouse worker.

OPPORTUNITIES

Opportunities are available throughout the country and there are shortages of LGV drivers in many areas. However, competition for work is keen. Many LGV drivers are self-employed, owning and driving one vehicle. Some firms operate lorries to carry their own goods, but the main employers of LGV drivers are independent road haulage firms. Some firms specialize in transporting certain goods, such as livestock and chemicals.

PAY AND CONDITIONS

Wages vary according to the carrying capacity of the vehicle and the nature of its load. Average earnings based on a standard 40-hour week range from £10,000 to £15,000, depending on the area and class of driver. There are usually good opportunities to increase these figures through overtime.

Petroleum tanker drivers can earn £20,000 to £25,000 per year, although they need special training for the carriage of dangerous and hazardous goods.

LGV drivers work a basic 40-hour week that is governed by strict legal requirements. A driver must not drive for more than nine hours in a day. After four-and-a-half hours' driving, whether continuous or accumulated, drivers must take a break of 45 minutes. A driver must have a minimum daily rest of eleven consecutive hours. This may be reduced to nine hours not more than three times a week as long as the reduction is compensated by an equivalent rest before the end of the following week.

A subsistence allowance for reimbursement of any overnight expenses incurred is paid tax-free.

PROSPECTS

Drivers who show management potential may become supervisors or move into managerial positions in larger firms. Many aspire to having their own vehicle, becoming self-employed and ultimately owning their own haulage firm. Some firms in the international haulage business offer good prospects.

RELATED OCCUPATIONS, FURTHER INFORMATION AND READING

Please see article 6. CAR/VAN DRIVER.

ROAD TRANSPORT: YAD

6. CAR/VAN DRIVER (YAD)

THE WORK

A tremendous variety of work is available; a detailed job description depends on the employer and the goods. The majority of van drivers deliver goods from one destination to another. Distribution begins with a manufacturer delivering bulk goods to a warehouse or wholesaler by rail and/or LGV. From there, smaller amounts of mixed goods are transported to retail outlets by light commercial delivery van drivers (vehicles between 3.5 and 7.5 tonnes). A tachograph in these vehicles records the numbers of hours spent driving, resting, carrying out other work such as loading and unloading, the speed of the vehicle and the distance travelled.

Delivery van drivers may load their vans following order sheets, plan their routes, unload the correct goods and obtain a receipt from the customer. They may be expected to help set up the goods (furniture, for example) to the customer's requirements. They may also be known as **merchandisers**. The size and weight of goods can vary enormously, from bouquets of flowers to grand pianos. Some drivers may be expected to contact their employer at least once a day. Some work in a small familiar area – within a 15-mile radius of base, for example – others go much further afield. Drivers in private security firms are given unarmed (and sometimes armed) combat training.

Van sales drivers are responsible for sales as well as delivery. Those in the wholesale trade usually have an area in which they visit all customers and potential customers, taking orders and delivering goods. In many cases they are responsible for deciding how much of a certain item they need to carry. They may also be expected to canvass for new customers and advise both them and existing customers on new lines and special promotions. Milk, bread, fish, grocery, butchery and greengrocery are the major areas in which light commercial van sales drivers work. They also work in fast food: vans carrying fish and chips, hot dogs, baked potatoes, ice-cream etc travel round certain areas, stopping frequently to sell, for example in housing estates or the lay-bys of large trunk roads.

Many drivers in door-to-door retail sales are self-employed; others start by buying a franchise from a company which then trains them, sells them the necessary equipment (ice-cream making equipment, for example) and advertises for them.

Chauffeurs/chauffeuses are employed by private households or by large companies to drive people rather than goods. In private households, they may drive their employer to and from work, to social functions, and their employers' children to school. In companies they are used to take senior managers to meetings, rail stations and airports etc.

WORK ENVIRONMENT

The main workplace is the van's cab; drivers must drive safely in changing traffic and road conditions, in varying light conditions and in all weathers. There is often variety in the premises visited and the routes taken during deliveries.

SKILLS AND INTERESTS

Drivers require good driving skills and the ability to concentrate for long periods. They must be able to work to a schedule and cope with delays, emergencies etc. It is useful for drivers to be able to carry out minor repairs on their vehicles. Drivers must be honest, reliable and punctual. They should be able to work alone and unsupervised, although some drivers have assistants. Drivers require a good knowledge of the local area and those making longer trips should be able to follow a map.

Good communication skills are needed for dealing with customers. Van drivers selling goods require sales ability and numeracy skills for handling cash. Those who load and unload goods need to be physically fit.

ENTRY REQUIREMENTS

Formal academic qualifications are not normally required. Employers look for reasonable reading, writing and arithmetic, and may set simple tests. A clean car driving licence is necessary. People of 21 years or, in some cases, over 25 years are preferred for insurance reasons. Some employers look for several years' driving experience, and value applicants whose previous work has involved dealing with people.

Employers operating light goods vehicles in category C1 on distribution work may offer Modern Apprenticeships (part of the Skillseekers Initiative in Scotland) that include driver training. Applicants may require three GCSEs/S grades (C/3) in maths, English and one other subject, or Intermediate GNVQ/GSVQ Level II, or equivalent, in order to display ability to complete the apprenticeship and achieve NVQ/SVQ Level 3.

TRAINING

Until recently the category B car driving licence covered vehicles up to 7.5 tonnes. Now it is necessary to pass an additional test for a category C1 licence in order to drive light goods vehicles between 3.5 and 7.5 tonnes gross. Applicants must be 18 years.

For driving work involving cars and small vans, there is little, if any, formal training. Any prior experience of distribution work is therefore useful for younger applicants. Drivers are taught the job and the route by experienced drivers or supervisors in anything from two days to a few weeks. Classroom sessions may teach routines of completing report forms, dealing with cash payments, and company policy. Drivers of vans and light goods vehicles can be assessed for NVQs/SVQs in Road Haulage and Distribution at Levels 1 and 2.

Modern Apprenticeships (part of the Skillseekers Initiative in Scotland) incorporate training and work experience in non-driving aspects of distribution as well as driving tuition. These apprentices are expected to undertake NVQ/SVQ units in Storage and in Organizing Road Transport Operations at Level 2, before completing units in Transporting Goods by Road. They go on to take units in Supervisory Management at Level 3. On completion, a Modern Apprenticeship Certificate is awarded by the Road Haulage and Distribution Training Council (RHDTC). Apprenticeships are expected to take three to four years.

Experienced drivers and trainee drivers may also be assessed for NVQ/SVQ qualifications.

ROAD TRANSPORT: YAD

It is possible to train for a C1 licence privately, at a specialist driving school, and take the test independently.

Chauffeurs/chauffeuses may receive special training in the care and maintenance of cars such as Rolls Royces and Bentleys. They may also be trained in anti-terrorist driving techniques.

LATE ENTRY

Many van driving jobs are open only to adults with the appropriate licence, and adult entry is usual. Almost any sort of driving and/or retail experience is useful. See ENTRY REQUIREMENTS.

Some people enter delivery/distribution driving work or training for it from employment in other jobs in these companies, such as warehouse worker or lift truck driver.

OPPORTUNITIES

Many manufacturing and service companies have their own delivery vans and employ their own drivers – eg dairies, bakers, private security companies, large department stores, large retail operations and wholesale suppliers. Some companies specialize in delivery work for other businesses, individuals etc. The Post Office employs van drivers to transport parcels and mail. There are opportunities for self-employment and for operation on a franchise basis.

Work is usually centred in and around large towns and cities. The distribution of goods is a major industry, and job prospects are fair.

Chauffeurs/chauffeuses are employed by private individuals, companies and government departments. Posts with private individuals may require additional skills such as gardening or valeting. Sometimes joint posts are available for couples.

It is possible, though rare, to be a self-employed chauffeur/chauffeuse.

PAY AND CONDITIONS

Wages vary from around £150 to £245 a week, depending on the work and the responsibility involved.

Hours vary, but a 40- to 48-hour week is average. Some firms operate a piecework system, allowing employees to finish work when they have completed the jobs allocated to them. Overtime is often available; weekend deliveries may be necessary. Some companies offer part-time work. Some jobs, such as milk delivery, mean a very early start and weekend work.

Chauffeurs/chauffeuses with private households often live in. They are usually expected to wear uniform and may have to work unsocial hours including evenings and weekends.

PROSPECTS

There is no direct promotion ladder; drivers may transfer to clerical jobs within the same company, or become transport supervisors in larger companies.

RELATED OCCUPATIONS

Taxi/private hire vehicle driver, bus/coach driver, large goods vehicle (LGV) driver.

FURTHER INFORMATION

Consult the *Yellow Pages* for addresses of possible employers.

Road Haulage and Distribution Training Council (RHDTC)*, 14 Warren Yard, Warren Farm Office Village, Stratford Road, Milton Keynes, MK12 5NW, 01908 313360

FURTHER READING

Leaflets/booklets are available from the address marked*.
Working in Transport and Distribution – COIC
In the careers library classified under YAD.

7. DRIVING INSTRUCTOR (YAD)

BACKGROUND INFORMATION

The road transport industry, with some 24 million motor vehicles (almost 20 million private cars), offers a vast field of work for professional instructors. Most start off by working for driving schools but eventually run their own businesses. There are also jobs training passenger carrying or large goods vehicle drivers mainly with the larger transport firms. There are approximately 33,000 approved driving instructors, and over 36 million driving licence holders in the UK.

THE WORK

Driving instructors are responsible for training people in vehicle handling and knowledge of the Highway Code to a sufficiently high standard to pass the driving test and theory test, and beyond. This is usually done by giving the learner driver a series of driving lessons, each lasting about an hour. The average person requires about 35 lessons before taking the 'L' driving test, depending on age and learning ability of the pupil. One driving instructor may coach from six to nine clients a day. Other instructors teach by using intensive methods, such as a five- to ten-day full-time courses, not only for the basic licence, but also to advanced levels.

A lesson usually consists of practical instruction in the car with the instructor sitting beside the pupil.

Instructors explain to the pupil how to use each control correctly. They often demonstrate the skills or procedures. As the pupil's skills improve, instructors give fewer instructions, leaving the pupil to make decisions.

Instructors use dual controls as a safety aid, to prevent danger or damage.

Instructors need to pre-plan routes for each lesson in order to avoid or incorporate specific road conditions according to the student's ability and progress. Instructors are fully responsible for the safety of their pupil, the vehicle and other road users during the period of the lesson.

In addition to practical driving skills, instruction is also given in road craft, including a knowledge of the Highway Code. This can be done by discussing with the pupil specific situations and how to react to them.

Sketch maps and diagrams are used as illustration. The pupil's knowledge is continually checked by the instructor, who must keep a close watch on the pupil's response and reactions while driving. Gradually the pupil learns to read, and react properly to, the signals and movements of other road users.

Some instructors also provide classroom instruction, for groups of pupils, with the help of visual aids, for the separate theory test.

Instructors need a basic knowledge of car mechanics in order to explain the working of car systems, eg the gears.

When the pupil is sufficiently trained, an application for a test date is made. The driving test itself is conducted by a driving examiner.

Instructors have to carry out a certain amount of paperwork, although some franchise driving schools employ clerical staff to deal with most of the administrative functions. Most self-employed instructors have some form of office support to answer the telephone and book lessons.

Driving instructors keep a daily record showing payments received and lessons given and receipts issued etc. They also keep records on the progress of each student, noting down strengths and weaknesses, progress, routes used etc.

Specialist instruction. Some driving schools also offer other forms of instruction, depending on the experience and ability of their instructors, such as tuition for experienced drivers in advanced and high-performance driving. Other schools offer private tuition for passenger carrying vehicle and commercial or large goods vehicle driving (though large passenger and commercial transport organizations have their own PCV/LGV instructors).

Some companies may ask driving schools to 'assess' commercial drivers before taking them on as employees. An increasing number of driver training centres also offer NVQ/SVQ assessment services.

WORK ENVIRONMENT

The majority of a driving instructor's time is spent on the road, in the tuition vehicle. Lessons take place in all but the most severe weather conditions. Hot weather can cause discomfort to both instructor and pupil, particularly when driving in cities and in heavy traffic.

SKILLS AND INTERESTS

As driving can be stressful, it is important to be both patient and even-tempered when teaching pupils with different levels of skill and temperament. Instructors need to be able to gain and build up the confidence of their pupils. They need to give clear and concise instructions to the learner.

The ability to explain procedures and techniques in straightforward and understandable terms is also important. Skills in assessment are required as the instructor needs to identify the pupil's strengths and weaknesses. The safety of the pupil, vehicle and other road users during the lesson is the instructor's responsibility, so it is important to be alert and act responsibly. Some knowledge of the mechanics of a motor vehicle is useful.

ENTRY REQUIREMENTS

No academic qualifications are required. To give driving instruction (for money) in a car, a candidate must be registered with the Driving Standards Agency (an agency of the Department of the Environment, Transport and the Regions) as an Approved Driving Instructor (ADI) or licensed trainee. Applicants must:

– have held a full British car driving licence for at least four years out of the six years preceding the date of application;

– have no motoring convictions of any kind (five or more penalty points can debar you but the Registrar may disregard offences that happened a long time ago);

– have no criminal convictions of any kind;

– provide two referees to attest to your good behaviour and suitability;

– pass the 'Register' qualifying examinations.

The minimum age is 21 years. Many driving schools prefer people over 25 years, as the insurance premiums are lower.

Specialist driving instructors are normally recruited by driving schools after individuals obtain professional qualifications. Some employers in the road haulage or bus and coach sectors select their instructors from among their experienced drivers and give them appropriate training either within the company or at a specialist training establishment.

TRAINING

The Register of Approved Driving Instructors and the licensing scheme for trainee instructors are administered by the Driving Standards Agency of the Department of the Environment, Transport and the Regions.

In order to be registered as an ADI, it is necessary to pass the Register Qualifying Examination. This is in three parts: a written test; a practical test of driving ability; and a practical test of ability to instruct. Each part must be passed before the next can be taken. Qualification must be achieved within two years, following the successful completion of the Part 1 written test.

Applicants may sit the exam independently, but many take training, normally at their own expense. Courses are run by specialist training establishments or by driving schools. Intensive courses last between one and three weeks. The exact nature, content, and standards of courses vary, so details should be carefully checked. The Driving Instructors Association's *Recommended Training Establishment Directory*, created by the industry and the DSA, lists approved training establishments.

Of 18,000 people who take the exams each year only about 3,000 are successful. For those who pass each exam first time, the fees, plus registration, total £374.

The **trainee licensing scheme** is open to those who have passed the first two parts of the Register Qualifying Examination (the written test and the practical test of driving ability). The trainee licence, which is valid for six months, allows the holder to instruct for payment without being registered as an ADI. Trainee licence holders are usually employed by a driving school, which must provide at least 40 hours' practical instruction, given by a qualified ADI. During the first three months that the licence is held, trainees must be under the direct personal supervision of an ADI for at least 20 per cent of the time they spend instructing pupils. The licence fee is £100.

It is not necessary to participate in the trainee licensing scheme in order to pass Part 3 of the Register Qualifying Examination.

ADI registration. On successfully passing all parts of the Register Qualifying Examination, the name of the applicant is entered on the ADI register and an official certificate of registration is issued. This must be displayed on the tutor's car. The registration must be renewed every four years. When required by the ADI Registrar, instructors must undergo a test of continued ability and fitness to give instruction. An instructor's name can be

ROAD TRANSPORT: YAD

removed from the register if the required standards are not met.

Professional qualification. The Associated Examining Board in conjunction with the Driving Instructors' Association have developed a professional qualification for all driving instructors entitled the Diploma in Driving Instruction, aimed at improving the status and standard of professional instruction. There are no formal entry qualifications. The DIA have also developed a BSc/BA degree in Driver Education, which is offered by Middlesex University, for which the Diploma constitutes the entry qualification. Further details are available from the DIA.

Specialist instruction. There is no compulsory registration for these instructors, though, for the LGV field, RTITB Services does hold a register of approved instructors which is recognized by the industry. Employers send experienced lorry or bus/coach drivers on driving instructor training courses at specialist training establishments or train them internally.

NVQ/SVQ in Driving Instruction at Level 3 is available for instructors in all licence categories – car, motor-cycle, bus/coach and road haulage.

LATE ENTRY

All entrants are adults; it is very rare for anyone under 23 years to enter this field and illegal for those under 21.

OPPORTUNITIES

There are currently some 33,000 approved driving instructors and about 1,500 licensed trainees in Great Britain, although not all ADIs operate. There are no restrictions on how many driving instructors can operate in an area and competition for business may be intense.

Many instructors begin by working with a franchised car driving school – there are many schools in each town and city throughout Great Britain. Some schools, such as The British School of Motoring, offer a franchise system for their instructors – the instructors are self-employed, but pupils and their cars are provided by the school in return for payment of a franchise fee. They may also provide help in the form of initial training, documentation and administration services.

Some specialist instructors, such as passenger carrying and large goods vehicle instructors, are employed by large transport and passenger vehicle companies in their own training schools, or work for training associations. The police, fire brigade, ambulance service and the Armed Forces also have their own driving instructors.

PAY AND CONDITIONS

A well-established instructor can currently expect to earn from about £8,000 to £20,000 (a large proportion work part-time). Out of this they must pay their car costs and business running expenses. Their net income is usually between £5,000 and £12,500.

Instructors need to work whenever clients are available: at any time during the week including weekends.

Most instructors are self-employed. It is possible, by only having a small number of pupils, to work part-time, but the actual hours worked are still dictated by the pupils' needs and tend to be in the evenings or at weekends.

PROSPECTS

The main progression is into self-employment, after having saved up enough capital to buy a dual control car and other initial expenses. The chances of becoming self-employed and successful vary from area to area. Some areas are over-subscribed with instructors, making it sometimes necessary to move home to become established. Initially there may be a loss of earnings before a reputation is built up.

It is estimated that there is only enough business for half of the 33,000 driving instructors on the Register if they all work full-time. However, many work part-time, and 2,000 to 3,000 ADIs leave the Register each year as 3,000 more come on.

Some instructors progress to become senior instructors, assistant managers and managers with their employing school. If there is a shortage of instructors, managers may continue to take pupil drivers as well as administer the office.

The Driving Standards Agency occasionally recruit experienced driving instructors as driving examiners. Examiners must be at least 26 years, with experience of working with the public in a position of authority. They must have held a licence for six years without a serious motoring conviction, and have wide experience of driving in the last three years including knowledge of motoring and road traffic problems and trends, elementary knowledge of transport law, and some experience of large goods or passenger carrying vehicle driving and/or motorcycles. Acceptance is by competitive examination, interview and driving test, plus a four-week course followed by a special test. Full details are available from the Driving Standards Agency.

RELATED OCCUPATIONS

Driving examiner, training officer, motorcycle instructor.

FURTHER INFORMATION

Driving Instructors' Association (DIA)*, Safety House, Beddington Farm Road, Croydon, Surrey CR0 4XZ, 0181 666 3333

Driving Standards Agency (DSA)*, Stanley House, Talbot Street, Nottingham NG1 5GU, 0115 901 2500

Bus and Coach Training Ltd - TRANSFED*, Regency House, 43 High Street, Rickmansworth, Herts WD3 1ET, 01923 896607

Road Haulage and Distribution Training Council (RHDTC)*, 14 Warren Yard, Warren Farm Office Village, Stratford Road, Milton Keynes, MK12 5NW, 01908 313360

RTITB Services Ltd*, CENTREX Training and Conference Centre, High Ercall, Shropshire TF6 6RB, 01923 777777

or in Scotland: RTITB Services, Hardie Road, Deans, Livingston, West Lothian EH54 8AR, 01506 497777

British Motorcycle Federation, 129 Seaforth Avenue, Motspur Park, New Malden, Surrey KT3 6JU, 0181 942 7914

FURTHER READING

Leaflets/booklets are available from the addresses marked*.

Working in Transport and Distribution – COIC

The Driving Instructor's Manual – DIA

ROAD TRANSPORT: YAD

So You Want to be A Driving Instructor – DIA

Your Road to Becoming an Approved Driving Instructor – DSA

In the careers library classified under YAD.

RAIL TRANSPORT: YAF

1. **TRAIN DRIVER CLCI:YAF**
2. **STATION ASSISTANT CLCI:YAF**
3. **TRACK/OVERHEAD LINE WORKER CLCI:YAF**
4. **SIGNALLING TECHNICIAN CLCI:YAF/RAL**
5. **RAILWAY FITTER/ELECTRICIAN CLCI:YAF/RAB/RAK**

BACKGROUND INFORMATION

Until April 1994 the railway industry was administered by British Rail, a single, government-owned company. It was then privatised and, as a result, the industry experienced massive organizational change. It now consists of many companies but employs considerably fewer staff overall. The industry is still undergoing substantial change, with some companies having merged or been taken over, while others are restructuring and many are re-thinking their policies and practices. One of the effects of these changes is that many employers are seeking to redeploy existing staff when vacancies arise. This is making it more difficult to enter the railway industry.

Railtrack owns almost all Britain's railway infrastructure, including track, signalling, bridges, tunnels, stations and depots. It provides access to its track and estates for use by train operators. It also manages timetables, train planning and signalling, and maintains the infrastructure.

There are 25 Train Operating Companies (TOCs), which are responsible for operating passenger train services in the UK, and a few companies responsible for transporting freight. In addition, Eurostar – a trinational Belgian/British/French company – provides passenger services through the Channel Tunnel to Brussels and Paris.

Infrastructure Maintenance Companies (IMCs) maintain signals, track and overhead lines on behalf of Railtrack, while Racal-BRT is responsible for telecommunications.

This article covers some specialist jobs unique to the railway industry. As in other industries, however, companies that employ specialist staff also employ a range of managers, administrators and specialists in such areas as computing, property, law and finance.

1. TRAIN DRIVER (YAF)

THE WORK

Train drivers drive diesel or electric trains that transport passengers and goods. Drivers work through set procedures before starting the train, to make sure that everything is in working order and safe to drive.

They move the train off at a set signal. They are then responsible for controlling the speed of the train, driving it smoothly and with particular care on gradients and bends. They obey speed limits, signals and set procedures for stopping and starting for passengers and freight.

Drivers have detailed knowledge of their usual routes including track layout, speed limits to be applied at , eg, junctions, curved tracks and gradients, and the location of signal boxes, stations and level crossings. They are also aware of what conditions to expect on the track in different weather conditions. In addition, they have to observe any temporary speed restrictions they may have been advised of before the journey.

Drivers try to keep to timetables but must observe signalling instructions and driving conditions that may make punctual arrival impossible.

Drivers are responsible for keeping a constant watch out for people, such as railway maintenance staff, or obstructions on the line, and acting accordingly. This may mean slowing or stopping the train or sounding a warning. If they see any incident on the track they stop the train, get out and investigate. If any engine or track fault occurs, drivers are responsible for assessing the seriousness of the situation and deciding whether to continue the journey. Drivers are able to communicate with control centres by using a radio link in their cab. They keep a record of each journey and report any incidents or engine defects.

An increasing number of trains are now driver-only. In such cases drivers may be responsible for remotely opening doors, making announcements and for passenger safety.

At the end of a journey, drivers immobilize their trains.

WORK ENVIRONMENT

Drivers mostly work alone. They spend much of their time seated in a cab at the front of a train. Cabs are small, tend to be noisy and may be draughty. The cabs in more modern trains, though, are more comfortable. Some drivers regularly drive long distances, while others drive shorter distances on suburban services.

There is some outdoor work when checking the safety of the train and track. This can be dirty and takes place in all weather conditions, including the cold and wet.

Eurostar drivers occasionally spend a night in a hotel in Brussels or Paris.

Drivers wear a uniform provided by their employers.

SKILLS AND INTERESTS

Train drivers must be very safety conscious and prepared to obey safety systems at all times. They need quick reactions, sound judgement and to be capable of making rapid decisions in emergency situations.

Much of drivers' work is routine and monotonous. They therefore need stamina and good powers of concentration to stay alert all the time.

It is helpful if drivers have some mechanical ability to be able to understand how the engine and cab equipment work and to help them identify minor faults.

Good memory is essential for remembering details such as signals, permitted speeds at different sections of track and stopping requirements at different stations.

Drivers must be reliable and punctual, as it is important they arrive at work on time. Willingness to work shifts is important.

The railway industry is concerned with customer care. When dealing with passengers, therefore, drivers must be courteous, pleasant and helpful. A smart appearance is important.

They should be capable of working on their own without direct supervision but also as a member of a team.

Drivers must be willing to adhere to a strict drugs and alcohol policy.

RAIL TRANSPORT: YAF

ENTRY REQUIREMENTS

There are no set entry requirements, each employer having its own recruitment policy. Most employers set an aptitude test that usually includes basic English, maths and mechanical skills, powers of concentration and observation, together with the ability to react quickly and accurately to adverse situations. Some employers recruit drivers from existing staff, while others recruit direct into driver training. Minimum age on entry to driver training varies between 18 and 21 years, although most employers prefer entrants of at least 21 years.

Train driving Modern Apprenticeships (Skillseekers Initiative in Scotland) for young people are currently under consideration.

Drivers must be physically fit, in good health and able to pass a medical examination; this includes tests for alcohol and drug abuse. Good hearing, good eyesight and normal colour vision are required.

Eurostar recruits people with at least five years' experience of driving high-speed main-line trains. Applicants have to pass aptitude and personality tests, a strict medical and assessments of their ability to learn the French language and the complex rules required to drive international high-speed trains.

TRAINING

The length of time taken on training drivers varies between companies but may take approximately 16 months. Training includes rules and regulations, traction knowledge (the mechanics of different train systems), route knowledge, train schedules, personal track safety, fire prevention and fire fighting, first aid, communication and customer care, and actual practical handling of locomotion. Drivers may work towards NVQ/SVQ Rail Transport – Driving at Level 2.

Not all employers train their own drivers, as some of the smaller companies do not have the resources to do so. Millennium Drivers has been formed by ASLEF (Associated Society of Locomotive Engineers and Firemen) and the Virgin Rail Group and has training centres in Crewe, London and Glasgow. They are used by some TOCs to train new drivers and to re-train existing drivers when required.

Eurostar drivers follow a one-year course of classroom training, which includes training on a simulator. During their training they also learn French to a high level and spend some time staying with French families.

LATE ENTRY

There is no standard upper age limit for entry to train driving. Most companies, though, set their own upper age limit of 45 to 50.

OPPORTUNITIES

Train drivers are employed by Train Operating Companies (TOCs), freight companies and Eurostar. The number of train drivers has decreased considerably since the reorganization of the rail system and the privatization of British Rail. There are currently just over 12,000 drivers.

Vacancies arise from time to time but some companies give preference to existing staff who wish to train for driving, rather than recruit from outside. It is estimated that 4,000 new drivers will be needed over the next five years.

PAY AND CONDITIONS

There are no national pay scales but drivers employed by most companies earn a basic salary of at least £20,000 a year. Eurostar drivers earn a basic salary of £30,030 a year. Employers provide free uniforms.

The basic working week varies but drivers work an average of 41-42 hours a week. They work shifts that include bank holidays, weekends and nights.

PROSPECTS

Drivers may seek promotion to supervisory and managerial work. They may also become inspectors.

RELATED OCCUPATIONS

Bus/coach driver, LGV driver, station assistant, bus conductor,

FURTHER INFORMATION AND READING

Please see article 5. RAILWAY FITTER/ELECTRICIAN.

2. STATION ASSISTANT (YAF)

THE WORK

Station assistants are responsible for a range of activities in and around railway stations. They may have different job titles depending on their employing company. Some companies call them platform staff, Railtrack have staff facilities assistants, while Eurostar have customer services team members. Duties vary but include some or all of the following.

Station assistants help to make sure trains leave on time. They do this by ensuring all passengers are safely aboard, then closing the train doors and signalling that the train may depart.

Assistants help some customers with their luggage. They also help disabled passengers to board trains and find their seats. They answer customers' queries about the times of train arrivals and departures, train connections and facilities at the station. They operate information boards and are responsible for making customers aware of any changes in train times or platforms. They display posters and timetables and make announcements over the public address system.

Assistants check tickets as customers arrive at platforms and, in some stations, collect tickets as customers leave. They are responsible for loading and unloading parcels and freight to and from trains.

Some assistants clean platform and waiting areas and keep them tidy, while some use equipment to clean carriages in station yards.

Station assistants may use hand or motorized trolleys to take parcels, post bags and goods to and from trains. Some drive courtesy vehicles to transport customers who have difficulty walking.

WORK ENVIRONMENT

Station assistants work both indoors and outdoors. Much of their work outdoors, though, is usually under cover but can be cold at times. Work involves standing, walking, lifting and carrying.

RAIL TRANSPORT: YAF

Employers provide station assistants with a uniform and also with protective clothing for cleaning duties.

SKILLS AND INTERESTS

Station assistants should enjoy providing a service to the public, as customer care is central to their work. They should be self-confident and approachable. They must be pleasant and polite in all their dealings with customers, not least with customers who may be frustrated and awkward as a result of train delays.

Assistants need a clear speaking voice and be able to communicate with all kinds of people.

Station assistants need to understand their company's services and regulations. They must be familiar with timetables and be able to use them to advise customers on, for example, connecting services.

Passenger safety is an important part of station assistants' work. They need to accept this responsibility and be aware of emergency procedures. They should be able to react calmly and decisively should an emergency situation arise.

Punctuality and reliability are important. Station assistants work as part of a team but must also be capable of working on their own initiative and of making decisions. Their work can be very busy at peak times but slow during off-peak times. They should be capable of coping with both situations.

Station assistants ought to have a smart appearance and be physically fit for lifting and carrying.

ENTRY REQUIREMENTS

Some Train Operating Companies (TOCs) require a minimum of four GCSEs/S grades (A–C/1–3). Other TOCs and Railtrack have no set academic requirements for entry but require a good general education and a reasonable standard of arithmetic and spoken English. They usually set literacy and numeracy selection tests. Employers requiring four GCSEs/S grades (A–C/1–3) may consider applicants with Intermediate GNVQ/GSVQ Level II. Applicants to Eurostar need a knowledge of French.

Applicants must be physically fit with good hearing, good eyesight and normal colour vision. They have to pass a medical examination, which includes tests for drug and alcohol abuse. There is no set minimum age on entry although many TOCs prefer entrants to be at least 18 years. Previous experience of work with the public is valuable.

National Traineeships for young people are under consideration. Employers will have their own entry requirements and selection procedures.

TRAINING

Railtrack and the TOCs both run short introductory training courses in their training centres. They normally include health and safety, knowledge of railway operations, emergency contingency plans and customer care. Training is then given in the workplace by experienced staff. Some employers encourage station assistants to work towards NVQ/SVQ Rail Transport (Passenger Services) at Level 2 or NVQ/SVQ Customer Service at Levels 2 and 3.

With National Traineeships, trainees will work towards NVQ/SVQ Rail Transport (Passenger Services) Level 2. Training will not be for a set length of time but is likely to last around two years. Contact local careers offices for information on National Traineeships.

LATE ENTRY

Entry is more common for adults than for school-/college-leavers, as maturity and previous experience of working with the public are valued by employers. There is no upper age limit for entry.

OPPORTUNITIES

Station assistants work at the 2,500 stations throughout Great Britain. Railtrack employs station assistants at the fourteen major stations it manages – Birmingham New Street, Edinburgh Waverley, Gatwick Airport, Glasgow Central, Leeds, Manchester Piccadilly, and – in London – Euston, Liverpool Street, Charing Cross, King's Cross, London Bridge, Paddington, Victoria and Waterloo. Station assistants at all other stations are employed by TOCs.

The number of station assistants has decreased since the reorganization of the rail system and the privatization of British Rail. Vacancies are not plentiful but arise from time to time. Some employers, though, prefer to fill vacancies from existing staff if possible and only recruit from outside if they cannot fill vacancies internally.

PAY AND CONDITIONS

There are no set pay scales but most station assistants earn between £8,500 and £9,500 a year, which can be increased with overtime and allowances to over £10,000 a year.

Station assistants work a basic week of approximately 39 hours. They work shifts on a rota to cover early mornings, evenings, weekends and bank holidays. At stations that operate 24 hours a day shifts include night work. Overtime is common.

PROSPECTS

Station assistants employed by Railtrack or TOCs may be promoted to supervisory or managerial positions. In major stations they may specialize in train information or train announcements. Those employed by TOCs may apply to be trained by their employer as a driver.

RELATED OCCUPATIONS

Train driver, bus/coach driver, bus conductor, hotel porter, airport baggage handler.

FURTHER INFORMATION AND READING

Please see article 5. RAILWAY FITTER/ELECTRICIAN.

3. TRACK/OVERHEAD LINE WORKER (YAF)

THE WORK

Track workers build new railway track and maintain the existing track and surrounding areas. Work differs between employers and between staff but can include some or all of the following.

RAIL TRANSPORT: YAF

Track workers are responsible for laying new track (the 'permanent way'). This involves digging, shovelling ballast (gravel used as a bed for railway lines), laying sleepers and bolting rails to the sleepers. They also deal with worn or damaged track, removing the faulty sections and replacing them with new track. In addition, track workers are responsible for building and maintaining drainage systems, bridges and other crossings, and controlling the growth of vegetation near the track.

An important part of their work involves track workers in making regular inspections of existing track and equipment. They are responsible for identifying and reporting any damage or undue wear, in order that maintenance and repair work may be carried out.

Overhead line workers install, modify, renew and maintain the electrical power lines above the railway track. Working in teams under the supervision of a senior, they put up structures and install wires. They also carry out any renewals or modifications that may be needed to existing lines.

Overhead line workers are responsible for the maintenance and repair of the overhead line and associated equipment. This involves regular inspections to check for faults. Faults may also be reported, eg when damaged by bad weather, in which case workers must locate the fault and diagnose the cause before completing repairs.

Attention to safety is critical. When working on a section of line, workers isolate that section from the power supply. All their work must meet set industry standards.

Track and overhead line workers use a range of machinery, heavy power tools and hand tools.

WORK ENVIRONMENT

Track and overhead line workers work outdoors in all weather conditions. Work can be cold, dirty and wet. It is physically very strenuous work and involves standing, bending, lifting, carrying and digging. Overhead line workers work at heights.

Track and overhead line workers travel from their base to the location of their installation or maintenance work, which, in some cases, can be a considerable distance. They wear protective clothing, headgear and footwear, which is provided by their employers.

SKILLS AND INTERESTS

Track and overhead line workers should like working with their hands and have some mechanical aptitude. They need to be capable of learning basic engineering skills, including the use of hand tools and power tools. Track workers also need to develop building skills, such as basic carpentry and cement mixing. Overhead line workers need to develop electrical skills and be able to use a range of tools skilfully and quickly. They must be careful and exact in their work and patient when trying to locate and diagnose faults.

A responsible attitude to safety is essential, as the railway environment is potentially dangerous. Track and overhead line workers work in teams, so they must be capable of working well as part of a team.

Willingness to work outdoors in all weather conditions, including wet and cold, is important. Strength and physical fitness are required. Track workers in particular need strength and stamina to cope with digging and heavy lifting.

Overhead line workers must have a good head for heights, as they may work up to twelve metres above the ground.

All workers must be willing to adhere to their employers' drugs and alcohol policy.

ENTRY REQUIREMENTS

There are no minimum qualifications for entry. Employers require applicants to have a good general education and many will test for a reasonable standard of reading, writing and numeracy. The minimum age on entry at present is normally 18 years.

Applicants must have good hearing, good eyesight and normal colour vision. They must pass a medical examination that includes tests for drug and alcohol abuse.

Modern Apprenticeships (Skillseekers Initiative in Scotland) for young people are being introduced in 1998. Employers will have their own entry requirements but they are likely to be similar to those at present.

National Traineeships for young people are under consideration. Entry requirements will be at the discretion of individual employers but are likely to include the need to pass an aptitude test.

TRAINING

Employers organize induction training for all entrants. This includes health and safety, railway drugs and alcohol policy, the company's organization and business objectives, fire prevention and fire fighting, railway environment, communications and customers, basic first aid, personal track safety and local depot induction. After induction, track and overhead line workers are trained on-the-job by experienced staff.

Modern Apprentices are trained by their employers, with some attendance at college or a training centre. Track workers work towards NVQ/SVQ Rail Transport Engineering Maintenance (Permanent Way) Levels 2 and 3, while overhead line workers work towards NVQ/SVQ Rail Transport Engineering Maintenance (Electrification) *or* (Plant) at Levels 2 and 3. Modern Apprenticeship training is not for a set length of time but is likely to last at least three years.

National Trainees will be trained in a similar way to Modern Apprentices but to the relevant NVQ/SVQ Level 2. Training will normally take around two years. Contact local careers offices for information on Modern Apprenticeships and National Traineeships.

All track and overhead line workers may work towards NVQ/SVQ Rail Transport Engineering Maintenance (Permanent Way) *or* (Electrification) *or* (Plant) at Levels 2 and 3.

LATE ENTRY

There are no upper age limits for entry to track or overhead line work. As the work is very strenuous, though, older applicants must be fit, able to pass the medical examination and capable of coping with the physical nature of the work.

OPPORTUNITIES

Track and overhead line workers are employed by Infrastructure Maintenance Companies (IMCs). Some IMCs employ both track and overhead line workers, while

RAIL TRANSPORT: YAF

others employ just one type. Track workers are employed throughout the UK, while overhead line workers are employed in most areas, the exceptions being those areas without electrification, such as the West Country, Wales and the North of Scotland.

The number of track and overhead line workers has decreased since the reorganization of the railway system and the privatization of British Rail. Vacancies are not plentiful. When vacancies do arise, some IMCs prefer to fill them from existing staff if possible, only recruiting externally if that does not prove possible.

PAY AND CONDITIONS

There are no set pay scales. Wages vary between employers but most track and overhead line workers earn just under £200 a week, which is increased by overtime payments.

Track and overhead line work takes place seven days a week. The basic working week is 39 hours, worked in shifts that include nights, weekends and bank holidays. Night and weekend work is important as it causes least disruption to rail services. Employers provide protective clothing, headgear and footwear.

PROSPECTS

Track and line workers can progress through a grade structure. They may become supervisors and some progress to management positions. They may change their type of work by applying for vacancies within their employing company or with other employers in the railway industry.

RELATED OCCUPATIONS

Road worker, construction operative, civil engineering operative, gas distribution worker, electricity distribution worker, welder, telephone technician.

FURTHER INFORMATION AND READING

Please see article 5. RAILWAY FITTER/ELECTRICIAN.

4. SIGNALLING TECHNICIAN (YAF/RAL)

THE WORK

Signalling technicians install, maintain and replace the signalling equipment used to control the movement of trains. The work involves electronic, light-current and mechanical engineering.

Technicians construct and fit new signalling equipment and cables. They also spend much of their time servicing, checking and adjusting equipment used in:

– railway signals;

– control systems that operate track equipment;

– control panels in equipment used to control train movements;

– track circuits, which detect the position of each train on the line;

– point machines that switch trains from one line to another.

Technicians diagnose and repair faults on all the equipment. They may be responsible for a section of the track and lead maintenance gangs.

Technicians usually work in small teams. They use a range of tools and testing equipment and keep records on work they have done.

WORK ENVIRONMENT

Most signals apparatus runs alongside the railway track, so signalling technicians spend most of their time outdoors. They travel from their base to the location of the work, which, in some cases, can be a considerable distance.

They work in all weather conditions, including cold and wet. Their work involves standing, bending, digging and lifting and is often at heights. They wear overalls and protective clothing and equipment, which is provided by their employers.

SKILLS AND INTERESTS

Signalling technicians should be interested in technology. They need good hand skills for using tools, test equipment, wires and components. They ought to have ability in maths in order to make calculations. They should be able to understand technical designs and drawings.

Patience and a logical approach are required, both for fault finding and to conduct step-by-step maintenance procedures. Accuracy is important, as is good attention to detail. Technicians need to be able to work quickly and concentrate for long periods. Problem solving skills are important, as is the ability to use initiative.

Technicians need to be fit, active and have stamina, as some of their work takes place in difficult conditions. They must be capable of working in confined spaces, at heights and in uncomfortable weather conditions. They must be willing to work shifts.

Technicians should be able to work well in a team. Good communication skills are required when talking and listening to colleagues. Accurate record-keeping is necessary.

The railway environment is dangerous, so technicians must be very safety conscious and able to understand and follow instructions and regulations. Willingness to comply with their company's drugs and alcohol policy is essential.

ENTRY REQUIREMENTS

There are no set entry requirements. Individual companies each have their own requirements but those recruiting apprentices usually ask for a minimum of four GCSEs/S grades (A–C/1–3), including English, maths and science. Relevant Intermediate GNVQs/GSVQs II, such as engineering, may be accepted.

Modern Apprenticeships (Skillseekers initiative in Scotland) for young people are being introduced in 1998. Employers will have their own entry requirements but they are likely to be as above.

National Traineeships are under consideration. Entry requirements will be at the discretion of individual employers but are likely to include the need to pass an aptitude test.

Some employers also recruit adults with relevant experience and/or qualifications, such as in electronic engineering.

All applicants must have good hearing, good eyesight and normal colour vision. They must pass a medical examination that normally includes tests for drug and alcohol abuse.

RAIL TRANSPORT: YAF

TRAINING

Employers organize induction training for all entrants. This includes health and safety, railway drugs and alcohol policy, the company's organization and business objectives, fire prevention and fire fighting, railway environment, communications and customers, basic first aid, personal track safety and local depot induction. After induction, technicians receive job-specific training and normally attend college on a block release basis to work towards NVQ/SVQ Rail Transport Engineering Maintenance (Signal Fault Finding) Levels 2 and 3.

Modern Apprentices are trained by their employers, with attendance at college. They work towards NVQ/SVQ Rail Transport Engineering Maintenance (Signal Fault Finding) Levels 2 and 3. Modern Apprenticeship training is not for a set length of time but is likely to last at least three years.

National Trainees will be trained in a similar way to Modern Apprentices but to NVQ/SVQ Level 2. Training will normally take around two years. Contact local careers offices for information on Modern Apprenticeships and National Traineeships.

LATE ENTRY

Modern Apprenticeships and National Traineeships are for young people but there is no upper age limit for entry by adults with relevant experience and/or qualifications. It is very difficult for other adults to enter this type of work. Older applicants must be fit and able to cope with the demands of shift working outdoors in all weather conditions.

OPPORTUNITIES

Signalling technicians are employed by Infrastructure Maintenance Companies (IMCs) throughout the UK. The number of signalling technicians has decreased since the reorganization of the railway system and the privatization of British Rail. The updating of existing signalling systems allowed by advanced technology has meant that this decrease has not, however, been as severe as for other types of work within the industry.

PAY AND CONDITIONS

There are no national pay scales and employers set their own rates of pay. Fully trained signalling technicians tend to earn between £10,000 and £18,000 a year.

Technicians work a basic week of 37 hours in shifts that includes evenings, nights, weekends and bank holidays.

PROSPECTS

Technicians can progress through a grade structure. They may become supervisors and can advance to management positions. It can be possible to progress to work involving design, testing or commissioning of signalling systems.

RELATED OCCUPATIONS

Electronics technician, computer service engineer, electrician, telephone technician, track/overhead line worker, electronics engineer.

FURTHER INFORMATION AND READING

Please see article 5. RAILWAY FITTER/ELECTRICIAN.

5. RAILWAY FITTER/ELECTRICIAN (YAF/RAB/RAK)

THE WORK

Railway fitters and electricians maintain and repair locomotives, passenger coaches and wagons. They also maintain, service and repair equipment such as boilers, pumps, cranes and lifts, together with power supplies.

Fitters and electricians conduct maintenance procedures on a regular basis. Maintenance examinations involve working through step-by-step procedures and include testing and checking units to see if there are any mechanical, electrical or electronic faults.

When fitters and electricians identify faults or have faulty units referred to them, they diagnose the problem and are responsible for necessary repairs. This may involve removing faulty components and replacing them. They may need to refer to manuals and circuit diagrams. When the repair has been completed they test the unit to make sure that it is safe and reliable and meets the company's quality and safety rules and regulations.

Fitters and electricians use a variety of specialist hand and power tools, test devices and heavy lifting gear. They keep records on all maintenance and repair work they carry out.

Fitters and electricians are helped by unskilled staff, who undertake more routine work, such as cleaning, labouring and heavy lifting.

WORK ENVIRONMENT

Fitters and electricians normally work indoors in workshops where units are brought for servicing or repair. Some work outdoors in sidings. Work involves standing, kneeling, bending and heavy lifting, and can be oily and dirty. They wear protective clothing provided by their employers.

SKILLS AND INTERESTS

Fitters and electricians need good hand skills for handling tools, test equipment, wires and components. They should have good writing skills. Ability in maths and physics is required in order to understand technical drawings and calculate formulae. Computer literacy is helpful.

Patience and a logical approach are necessary, both for fault finding and to conduct step-by-step maintenance procedures. They should be able to follow manuals and read instrument and computer displays.

Fitters and electricians must be very safety conscious. Their work, involving as it does machinery and electricity, is potentially hazardous and the safety of passengers depends on their working conscientiously and thoroughly.

They should be capable of working to tight time schedules. They must be able to work equally well in a team and on their own with the minimum of supervision. Willingness to work shifts is necessary.

Fitters and electricians need to be physically fit, agile and capable of heavy lifting. They must be willing to comply with their company's drugs and alcohol policy.

ENTRY REQUIREMENTS

There are no set entry requirements. Individual companies each have their own requirements but those recruiting apprentices usually ask for some GCSEs/S grades

RAIL TRANSPORT: YAF

(A–C/1–3), including English, maths and science. Relevant Intermediate GNVQs/GSVQs Level II, such as in engineering, may be accepted.

Modern Apprenticeships (Skillseekers Initiative in Scotland) for young people are being introduced in 1998. Employers will have their own entry requirements but they are likely to be as above.

National Traineeships are under consideration. Entry requirements will be at the discretion of individual employers but are likely to include the need to pass an aptitude test.

Employers also recruit qualified fitters and electricians from outside the railway industry.

All applicants must have good hearing, good eyesight and normal colour vision. They must pass a medical examination that normally includes tests for drug and alcohol abuse.

TRAINING

Employers organize induction training for all entrants. This includes health and safety, railway drugs and alcohol policy, the company's organization and business objectives, fire prevention and fire fighting, railway environment, communications and customers, basic first aid, personal track safety and local depot induction. After induction, fitters and electricians begin traction and systems training and may work towards NVQ/SVQ Rail Transport Engineering Maintenance (Traction and Rolling Stock) Levels 2 and 3.

Modern Apprentices are trained by their employers, with some attendance at college or a training centre. They work towards NVQ/SVQ Rail Transport Engineering Maintenance (Traction and Rolling Stock) Levels 2 and 3. Modern Apprenticeship training is not for a set length of time but is likely to last at least three years.

National Trainees will be trained in a similar way to Modern Apprentices but to NVQ/SVQ Level 2. Training will normally take around two years. Contact local careers offices for information on Modern Apprenticeships and National Traineeships.

LATE ENTRY

Modern Apprenticeships and National Traineeships are for young people but there is no upper age limit for entry by qualified fitters and electricians from outside the railway industry. It is very difficult for other adults to enter this type of work.

OPPORTUNITIES

Fitters and electricians work for Train Operating Companies (TOCs), Infrastructure Maintenance Companies (IMCs) – fitters only – and freight companies throughout the UK. The number of fitters and electricians has decreased since the reorganization of the railway system and the privatization of British Rail. Vacancies arise from time to time but some companies prefer to recruit trained fitters and electricians from outside the railway industry. There have been few apprenticeship openings for school-/college-leavers but these are now on the increase.

PAY AND CONDITIONS

Fitters and electricians work a basic week of 37 hours. That usually includes day shifts, night shifts, weekend and bank holiday working.

There are no set pay scales, employers having their own rates of pay. Fully trained fitters and electricians tend to earn between £16,000 and £21,000 a year.

PROSPECTS

Promotion is to supervisory or management positions.

RELATED OCCUPATIONS

Maintenance fitter, welder, auto-electrician, heating and ventilation fitter, telephone technician, mechanical engineering worker.

FURTHER INFORMATION

Rail Industry Training Council Ltd., Africa House, 64/78 Kingsway, London WC2B 6AH, 0171 320 0436

Railtrack, Railtrack House, Euston Square, London NW1 2EE, 0171 557 8000, http://www.railtrack.co.uk

FURTHER READING

Working In Transport and Distribution – COIC

Rail Industry Yearbook (includes addresses of Train Operating Companies, freight companies and Infrastructure Maintenance Companies).

In the careers library classified under: YAF; RAB; RAK; RAL

MERCHANT NAVY: YAL

1. **MERCHANT NAVY DECK OFFICER CLCI:YAL**
2. **MERCHANT NAVY ENGINEERING OFFICER CLCI:YAL**
3. **MERCHANT NAVY DUAL CERTIFICATE OFFICER CLCI:YAL**
4. **MERCHANT NAVY RATING CLCI:YAL**

BACKGROUND INFORMATION

The majority of merchant ships today either transport various types of cargo or provide support services to the Royal Navy and to drilling platforms and rigs. The Merchant Navy also includes tugs and many other specialist vessels. Apart from ferries and around 30 luxury cruise liners, very few merchant ships carry passengers.

Patterns of work vary widely. Coastal companies tend to undertake short voyages, the longest lasting about twelve weeks at a time. Longer voyages are made by ocean-going carriers, such as container ships going to Australia and New Zealand or tankers that transport cargo to ports in every corner of the world.

The Merchant Navy fleet has become smaller in recent years, mainly due to the introduction of larger ships staffed by smaller crews. In the 1970s it is estimated that for every giant container ship which was launched, seven conventional ships were scrapped. For some years job opportunities were poor, but this is changing. The Chamber of Shipping states that great opportunities are opening up for British shipping.

These articles describe the work of deck, dual certificate and engineering officers and ratings – the ship's workforce. Crew opportunities may not be as good as for officers, as many UK shipping companies have traditionally employed foreign crews. However, this situation is now changing, and in many areas the ratio of British to overseas ratings is becoming more even.

At one time the Merchant Navy was exclusively male, but women are now recruited at all levels and compete on equal terms with men. Women currently form around two to three per cent of the total workforce.

1. MERCHANT NAVY DECK OFFICER (YAL)

THE WORK

Deck officers are responsible for the safe navigation of the vessel while at sea and, when in port, for the safe and efficient loading or discharging of the cargo. Very often the cargo is stowed in large containers, which are lifted onto and off the deck by crane. If the cargo is in bulk, it is stowed in tanks or holds and discharged through pipelines and hose, or by other mechanical means.

Deck officers supervise the crew when they are engaged in such tasks as general maintenance work, cargo tank or hold cleaning and preparation work and mooring operations. If supplying a platform or a rig, the vessel does not tie up but is manoeuvred to keep it close alongside.

At sea, each officer usually takes responsibility for two 'watches' – four-hour periods of bridge duty – in every 24 hours. Watch-keeping officers navigate a course (previously decided by the captain), check the vessel's position periodically, and alter course to allow for the effects of tides and currents. They must, while on watch, remain aware of other ships, of weather conditions, and of any hazards to navigation. Although there are sophisticated navigational aids, deck officers must be able to navigate without them in case systems fail.

When not on the bridge, deck officers have other duties, such as checking safety and firefighting equipment, and making sure that all deck gear is working properly. In addition, there is always a certain amount of paperwork, including the correction of navigational charts. Most of the ship's legal and commercial business is looked after by senior deck officers.

WORK ENVIRONMENT

Deck officers, as their title implies, spend much of their time on deck, though on a modern ship the bridge itself, with all the navigational equipment, is protected from the elements.

On all ships, except some ferries, the ship is the crew's home as well as workplace. On large ships, officers have their own cabins with bathroom facilities and, when off duty, they usually have the use of a swimming pool, a library, videos, table tennis, darts and a bar for socializing. On smaller ships facilities are more limited.

A cruise ship gives officers a chance to mix with many different people, and the social facilities and meals are those of a first-class hotel. But there are only about 30 cruise ships out of a total trading fleet of more than 600.

SKILLS AND INTERESTS

Shipping companies look for self-reliant people who have demonstrated some capacity for leadership. They must be prepared to work long and unsocial hours, often with little or no time ashore.

Deck officers need mathematical ability for navigation. They also must have an understanding of engineering and scientific principles to enable them to cope with cargo handling, ship stability requirements and high-technology bridge equipment. They must be people who enjoy responsibility, and are capable of responding quickly to any emergency that may arise.

Except on ferries, they work and live in close proximity to the same people, perhaps for months on end, so they must be tolerant and sociable. A sense of humour is a great help.

ENTRY REQUIREMENTS

The normal entry age range is 16 to 19_ years at the time of joining, though there is more flexibility than in the past. Anyone planning a degree course before applying for training should consider this age range carefully as they may find themselves too old on graduation. Older applicants, up to the age of 25, are occasionally considered.

Candidates must be of good general health and physique and have to pass a stringent medical. Deck officers must have near perfect eyesight without glasses, and no defects of colour vision, in order to pass the DETR (Department of the Environment, Transport and the Regions) eyesight test.

Suitable candidates are normally employed as cadets by a shipping company or training group capable of organizing all aspects of training, both at college and at sea.

People with three GCSEs/S grades (A–C/1–3) including maths and physics with preferably a language, can apply for training for the Short Sea Restricted Licence that is

MERCHANT NAVY: YAL

operated within the European trading area.

The minimum educational requirements laid down by most shipping companies operating ships world-wide are GCSEs/S grades (A–C/1–3), or equivalent, in at least five subjects, including physics, maths and a subject involving the use of English. It should be noted that entry is highly competitive, and applicants with better qualifications than the minimum will enjoy an advantage.

Holders of A levels/H grades or equivalent qualifications may enter accelerated training schemes, which can be completed within three years.

TRAINING

For a 16- to 19-year-old with the required GCSEs/S grades, a cadetship is split between time at sea and time at college, and lasts three to four years, sitting the professional and ancillary examinations required for a Class 4 or Class 3 Certificate of Competency. Those with A levels/H grades may complete the course in three years, gaining a Class 3 Certificate of Competency.

Patterns of training vary according to the specific programme being followed. The following is fairly typical. Training begins with a four-week residential induction course held at a nautical college. This course prepares cadets for life at sea and covers safety, shipboard familiarization, the organization of a ship's company, health, hygiene and an outline of the structure of the Merchant Navy. Cadets also receive a record book which incorporates tasks and projects to be carried out throughout training.

The first period at sea usually lasts about ten months, normally in two voyages, with leave in between. During this time cadets learn basic seamanship and carry out practical tasks, helping the workforce. They also follow a correspondence course set by the college to which they are attached for the duration of the training period.

The next phase of training, at college, is mainly academic, introducing the cadet to professional subjects such as chart work and meteorology. During the second period at sea, cadets take on more responsibility and, towards the end, keep four-hour watches on the bridge under supervision.

After the examinations they return to sea to complete outstanding sea-time, and understudy the officer of the watch both at sea and in port. The training period finishes on completion of the sea-time required for the issue of the Class 3 Certificate. Cadets can then be considered for promotion to third officer.

The programme for deck officer trainees with slightly lower academic qualifications lasts about three to three-and-a-half years. It comprises periods at college and at sea, broadly covering the same areas of training as described above for cadets. A minimum of 20 months' sea-time must be completed and sea service is often performed in a rating capacity. The programme leads to a Class 4 or Class 3 Certificate of Competency in exactly the same way as above.

Much of the training organized by the Merchant Navy Training Board is carried out at colleges based in Gravesend, South Shields, Southampton, Glasgow and Fleetwood.

The Merchant Navy has introduced a system of qualifications based on NVQs/SVQs. It is envisaged that this system of training and assessment, in combination with oral examinations, will become the only route to gaining Certificates of Competency. NVQs/SVQs in Merchant Vessel Operations are currently available at Levels 2, 3 and 4.

LATE ENTRY

Adult entry as a deck officer is very rare except for former Royal Navy officers. In addition, some shipping companies sponsor deck ratings with the relevant academic qualifications on the Class 4 supplementary training scheme. The scheme includes extra studies in navigation and chartwork, a correspondence course and college modules, and leads to a Class 4 or Class 3 Certificate. Successful ratings can then qualify as watch-keeping officers.

OPPORTUNITIES

Britain's Merchant Fleet provides employment for about 18,000 deck and engineering officers and there is recruitment at present.

Employers vary tremendously and so do the ships they own and operate. There are 47 shipping companies currently recruiting. Their fleets range from a fleet of owned and chartered tankers to specialized vessels that support offshore exploration and production activities. The latest ships in container transportation are some 37,200 tonnes dead weight and carry cargo all around the world.

In contrast, there are vessels operating mainly in the European trading area, accounting for nearly one-third of the British Merchant Navy. The vessels include a variety of sizes and types but are generally smaller than ships sailing world-wide. Some can pass beneath road and rail bridges, and sail up rivers and canals to ports up to 200 miles from the sea.

PAY AND CONDITIONS

Pay for deck officers varies with the company and the type of trade in which it engages. Officers may work about five months and then take two months' leave. Over two years, the annual salary could then average out at around the following figures: third officer – £19,000 to £21,000; second officer – £21,000 to £23,000; chief officer – £25,000 to £29,000; master – £32,000 to £40,000.

Cadets earn from £4,000, depending on the employing company. Food and accommodation are provided, and travel expenses are also met by the employer.

A ship operates 24 hours a day, seven days a week. On a large ship, deck officers are normally on watch for four hours, with eight hours off before the next watch. Watch systems may be different on smaller ships. Tours of duty vary between several months and a few weeks, and are followed by leave periods which also vary depending on how long someone has been away. Crews do not stay together, or necessarily return to the same ship, although the captain and the chief engineer may be attached to a particular ship for about two years.

PROSPECTS

Present prospects are excellent, with all opportunities being open to both men and women.

Promotion depends on a combination of length of service and merit. To reach the most senior positions, drive and determination are essential. Officers must also obtain the relevant Certificate of Competency awarded by the Maritime and Coastguard Agency.

Class 3 and 4 Certificates equip someone as a watch-keeping officer on any ship anywhere in the world. Class 5 is the watch-keeping certificate for a ship of limited size in the European trading area. The Class 2 Certificate is the minimum qualification for a chief officer (most hold Class 1), and the Class 1 Certificate is for a master of any ship, anywhere in the world. Holders of any of the Certificates 2, 3, 4 and 5 may obtain a command endorsement enabling them to take command of a smaller ship in the European trading area.

Deck officers can also study for the Extra-Master's Certificate or a degree in nautical studies.

Experienced officers often find their skills in demand ashore, in administrative posts with shipping and oil companies, with dock and harbour boards, and in other posts where sea experience is relevant. Some master mariners go on to become pilots.

RELATED OCCUPATIONS

Coastguard, harbourmaster, marine engineer, Royal Navy officer, Royal Navy rating, telecommunications engineer, electronics engineer, ship's pilot, marine surveyor.

FURTHER INFORMATION AND READING

Please see article 4. MERCHANT NAVY RATING.

2. MERCHANT NAVY ENGINEERING OFFICER (YAL)

THE WORK

The ship's engineers have responsibility for the care and maintenance of the entire ship, and the operation of the ship's engine room. This holds the main engine, boilers, pumps, fuel systems, hydraulic systems, and the ship's electrical generating plant and distribution system.

Power requirements vary according to whether the ship is in port or at sea. However, a tanker may need as much power to drive the pumps as it does to move through the sea. This power must be available whenever it is needed. Some ships are powered by diesel engines, while others have turbines.

The latest ships have a good deal of electronic control and automation. On such ships the engine room is not continuously staffed; a panel of alarm and monitoring systems is connected up to the engineers' accommodation and to the bridge. As a result, engineers can often work a fairly normal day, from 9am to 5pm, but if there is an emergency they must turn out at a moment's notice.

The job is still a very practical one, and engineers spend most of the day in boiler suits. Junior officers up to the level of third engineer are mainly working with their hands, and to some extent supervising engine-room ratings. Even chief engineers spend about a quarter of their time in practical tasks. If any part of a ship's systems fails, it must be dismantled, assessed, repaired, reassembled and put back into operation. Sometimes spare parts have to be manufactured on board. In general, however, crews today are too small to execute major repairs, and all modern ships now have back-up systems, which can be switched in if one of the main systems fails.

WORK ENVIRONMENT

Engineering officers share the same facilities as deck officers and the general environment is the same. However, the main workplace for engineers is the engine room, which can be hot, noisy and, to some extent, dirty. Engineers are also involved in the maintenance of deck machinery, whatever the weather. The environment in which they work has improved considerably in recent years with the increase in automation. However, their job is demanding and they often have to work in far from ideal locations – for instance, maintaining and repairing equipment in confined spaces or in refrigerated areas.

SKILLS AND INTERESTS

Engineering officers must be practical and resourceful people with an aptitude for maths and physics – they must acquire a thorough knowledge of diesel engines, steam turbines, boilers, electrical power generation and circuits, electronics and systems engineering. Manual dexterity is necessary; much of the work involves the servicing and repair of equipment. They must enjoy solving problems, and be flexible enough to adapt to advances in technology and working practices.

Like deck officers, they need to be able to get on well with others, having qualities of leadership and communication skills.

ENTRY REQUIREMENTS

For normal age of entry, please see article 1. MERCHANT NAVY DECK OFFICER.

Candidates must be of good general health and physique and pass a thorough medical. They must have a reasonable standard of sight in both eyes, with or without spectacles.

The minimum educational requirements are normally four GCSEs/S grades (A–C/1–3), or equivalent. These must include maths, physics and a subject involving the use of English.

An alternative method of entry is to have completed at least three years' Department of Transport approved engineering craft practice training, or the Engineering Training Authority's modular system of training for engineering craft workers.

TRAINING

The training takes three to four years (three years for A level/H grade entrants, where the length of sea service is the same but the college time shorter). Patterns of training vary somewhat according to the specific programme being followed. The programme outlined below is typical.

The first year is spent in a residential marine college, concentrating mainly on the academic side of engineering. Subjects include applied mechanics, applied heat, engineering drawing and marine electrotechnology. Cadets also receive practical training in fitting, machining and welding. Towards the end of the year they complete the standard Merchant Navy sea-survival course and a basic firefighting course.

The second year is spent at sea – usually in two voyages with a period of leave in between – gaining shipboard experience under instruction from the ship's engineer officers. Cadets have to carry out a number of operational and maintenance tasks and projects set in their record book. They also follow a correspondence course.

MERCHANT NAVY: YAL

The final phase of training involves a further two years at college (one year for A level/H grade entrants). The course leads to the BTEC Higher National Diploma or SQA Higher National Certificate in Marine Engineering, and a DETR (Department of the Environment, Transport and the Regions) Class 4 (Engineering) Certificate of Competency. These complete the cadetship and qualify the students as watch-keeping officers. (Success in the higher national diploma will give students maximum exemptions in the DETR's examinations for Class 2 and Class 1 Certificates.)

The programme for engineer officer trainees entering with lower academic qualifications lasts three years, at college and sea, leading to a Class 4 Certificate of Competency and the written part of Class 3.

The programme for people with previous craft experience lasts about nine months, during which a minimum of six months' sea-time must be completed. Trainees are employed in the capacity of assistant engineer while training, and may obtain the Class 4 Certificate of Competency.

The Merchant Navy has introduced a system of qualifications based on NVQs/SVQs. It is envisaged that this system of training and assessment, combined with oral examinations, will become the only route to gaining Certificates of Competency. NVQs/SVQs in Merchant Vessel Operations are currently available at Levels 2, 3 and 4.

LATE ENTRY

As described in ENTRY REQUIREMENTS, it is possible for people who have trained in engineering skills to join the Merchant Navy. No age requirements are specified. It is also possible, though unusual, for candidates with relevant qualifications to take a degree in marine engineering, and then go to sea and obtain their Certificates of Competency.

OPPORTUNITIES

Opportunities for both men and women to train as engineer officers are good, provided they meet the required standards. Please see article 1. MERCHANT NAVY DECK OFFICER for details.

PAY AND CONDITIONS

Pay varies with the company and the type of trade. Officers may work for around five months and then take two months' leave. Over two years the annual salary could then average out at: junior or fourth engineer – £19,000 to £21,000; third engineer – £21,000 to £25,000; second engineer – £24,000 to £29,000; and chief engineer – £29,000 to £36,000.

Cadets earn from £4,000, depending on the employing company. Food and accommodation are provided, and travel expenses are also met by the employer.

On some ships engineer officers work watch systems in the engine space, and have other duties to perform when off watch. On modern ships with highly automated engine rooms, engineers may be on duty during daytime hours only. However, the ship has to be maintained 24 hours a day, seven days a week, and engineers are always on call for emergencies. They may revert to watch-keeping duties when the vessel is approaching land or is in a crowded seaway.

The length of time they spend on board depends on the type of ship on which they work. Leave varies, according to company and rank. Chief engineers can spend three months on and three months off; other engineer officers do up to five months on and have two or three months off. Officers rarely return to the same ship's company or indeed to the same ship, apart from the chief engineer, who may be appointed to a particular ship for about two years.

PROSPECTS

Present prospects are excellent. On obtaining the DETR's Class 4 (Engineering) Certificate of Competency, cadets are ready to take up an appointment as a watch-keeping engineer officer. Promotion usually follows success in further professional examinations.

Engineering officers interested in obtaining higher academic qualifications can enter for the DETR's Extra First Class Certificate of Competency, or study for degrees in marine engineering at higher education institutions.

After some years at sea, the training and experience of engineer officers is so wide-ranging that they are welcome in both offshore and shore-based industries. They may expect to achieve managerial posts in production and process plants or in work with local authorities, hospitals, hotels or large industrial complexes. There is also the opportunity to become an engineer or fleet manager with a shipping company.

RELATED OCCUPATIONS

Please see article 1. MERCHANT NAVY DECK OFFICER.

FURTHER INFORMATION AND READING

Please see article 4. MERCHANT NAVY RATING.

3. MERCHANT NAVY DUAL CERTIFICATE OFFICER (YAL)

THE WORK

Traditional dividing lines between the deck and engineering branches are becoming less easily defined, and the role of the ship's officer is changing. This is a consequence of the increasing sophistication of navigational and mechanical equipment, together with the use of computers and electronic control and automation in modern ships. This process of change is expected to continue.

In response, the dual certification cadetship has been devised. Cadets who successfully complete the course gain qualifications as both deck and engineer officers. The duties of both have been described in the previous articles in this section.

WORK ENVIRONMENT

Please see article 1. MERCHANT NAVY DECK OFFICER and article 2. MERCHANT NAVY ENGINEERING OFFICER.

SKILLS AND INTERESTS

People wanting to study for this dual qualification need to be good all-rounders with an interest in the use of

MERCHANT NAVY: YAL

machinery and an aptitude for understanding mechanical and electronic principles. Flexibility is one of the prime requirements, for their responsibilities are wide-ranging.

Like any ship's officer, they must be prepared to accept responsibility at an early age and be able to supervise and direct the work of others. For other desirable personal qualities, see article 1. MERCHANT NAVY DECK OFFICER and article 2. MERCHANT NAVY ENGINEERING OFFICER.

ENTRY REQUIREMENTS

The preferred age of entry is up to a maximum of 19 years. Applicants must be of good general health and physique, and have to pass a stringent medical examination. They must have near-perfect eyesight without glasses and no defects of colour vision, in order to pass the DETR (Department of the Environment, Transport and the Regions) eyesight test.

The course is a demanding one. Candidates must have a minimum of five GCSEs/S grades (A–C/1–3), including maths, physics and a subject involving the use of English.

TRAINING

The training is almost equally divided between college and sea. It lasts about 18 months longer than the training for either deck or engineering cadetships. Patterns of training vary somewhat according to the specific programme being followed. The programme below is typical.

The first year is spent in a residential marine college, concentrating mainly on the academic side of deck officer and engineering work; subjects include applied mechanics, applied heat, engineering drawing and marine electrotechnology. Cadets also receive practical training in fitting, machining and welding. In addition, they take the standard Merchant Navy sea-survival course and a basic firefighting course. At the beginning of the summer holiday they have a six-week block of workshop practice.

The second year is spent at sea – normally on two voyages with a period of leave in between – gaining shipboard experience under instruction from the ship's deck and engineer officers.

Time is equally divided between deck and engine-room duties. Cadets are issued with two record books (one deck and one engine) in which are set out a number of operational and maintenance tasks and projects that must be completed. They also follow a correspondence course set by the college. Eight hours of study time is given each week, but cadets are expected to spend at least an equal amount of their own time in studying.

The third phase involves returning to college for 30 weeks for further study. This includes both engineering and deck subjects, such as chartwork, meteorology, stability, cargo work etc. At the end of the college phase, cadets should have completed all the academic work for their engineering qualifications, but they require more practical experience before they are eligible to hold a Class 4 (Engineering) Certificate of Competency.

For the fourth phase, cadets return to sea for about nine months, again working in both engine room and deck departments. During this time, however, they undertake duties with more responsibility, and their involvement with bridge watch-keeping steadily increases, under the supervision of one of the deck officers. Cadets also have further correspondence course exercises and more complex record-book tasks and reports to complete.

Returning to college for two terms, they sit the various examinations required for a Class 3 (Deck) Certificate of Competency.

The final phase of training consists of a further three or four months at sea, to complete the statutory minimum sea-time needed to validate the certificate.

On successful completion of the courses, candidates are also awarded a Higher National Diploma in Marine Technology. Having passed the examinations and fulfilled the statutory sea-time requirements, they are ready to take up an appointment as a watch-keeping deck or engineer officer.

The Merchant Navy has introduced a system of qualifications based on NVQs/SVQs. It is envisaged that this system of training and assessment, in combination with oral examinations, will become the only route to gaining Certificates of Competency.

NVQs/SVQs in Merchant Vessel Operations are currently available at Levels 2, 3 and 4.

LATE ENTRY

The scheme is only available to people up to $19\frac{1}{2}$ years. There is no late entry.

OPPORTUNITIES

A number of the larger shipping companies recruit men and women to train for this dual qualification. The number of vacancies is limited, however, and competition for places is intense. For general opportunities, please see article 1. MERCHANT NAVY DECK OFFICER.

PAY AND CONDITIONS

Please see article 1. MERCHANT NAVY DECK OFFICER and article 2. MERCHANT NAVY ENGINEERING OFFICER. These would be the same for the Deck/Engineer Officer, perhaps a little lower.

PROSPECTS

Once qualified, the dual-certificated officer may decide to specialize in one department or to progress up the ladder in both. Whichever course is chosen, qualification gives exemptions from some of the professional examinations in both departments. Openings ashore are as in article 1. MERCHANT NAVY DECK OFFICER.

RELATED OCCUPATIONS

Please see article 1. MERCHANT NAVY DECK OFFICER.

FURTHER INFORMATION AND READING

Please see article 4. MERCHANT NAVY RATING.

4. MERCHANT NAVY RATING (YAL)

THE WORK

There are three kinds of ratings: deck, engine room and catering. Some ships operate with general-purpose crews, and such ratings spend some time working in the engine room as well as on deck. Today, crews are smaller than they

MERCHANT NAVY: YAL

used to be, and equipment is far more sophisticated. As a result, ratings take on more responsibility than in the past and work with less supervision, and there are fewer job and training opportunities.

Deck rating

Work at sea varies very much with the type of ship but is predominantly manual – cleaning, sweeping, chipping off rust, polishing etc. With a big company like P & O Containers, the emphasis is on general shipboard maintenance, along with stacking and manoeuvring containers, checking their contents, taking fire prevention measures etc. On the other hand, in the Royal Fleet Auxiliary (RFA) there is probably a larger content of traditional seamanship – wire splicing, rope work, and operating lifting gear. RFA ratings form flight parties during helicopter operations; they are also trained to assist in the operation and maintenance of sophisticated replenishment equipment, and in nuclear, biological and chemical defence.

Whatever the ship, time may have to be spent preparing and painting the steelwork. When a ship carries cargo, tanks or holds have to be cleaned and inspected. Ratings also act as look-outs and helmsmen on the bridge. In port, they assist in the mooring of the ship, in the preparations for cargo operations and taking on board of stores, as well as in fire and security patrols.

Engine-room rating

Engine-room ratings are responsible for the day-to-day cleanliness of the engine room and for routine oiling, greasing and servicing of machinery. As they gain experience, they help officers to monitor and ensure the safe running of main plant and ancillary equipment. They also help to repair and maintain other machinery on board.

In some companies, the work of deck and engine-room ratings is combined into that of 'general-purpose' ratings, allowing more flexibility in the tasks that they can undertake.

Catering rating

The duties of junior catering ratings are normally: to clean accommodation areas and public rooms; to help the cook in the preparation of food; to clean galleys and cooking utensils; to help in the maintenance of fridges, freezers and hygiene in all food preparation and serving areas; to serve meals to officers and crew; and to load and stow the ship's consumable stores.

WORK ENVIRONMENT

For deck and engine-room ratings, please see article 1. MERCHANT NAVY DECK OFFICER. Catering ratings work under cover except when loading stores or taking part in safety drills. Galleys can be hot. On most ships ratings have single cabins with adjacent toilet facilities, and off-duty facilities are good.

SKILLS AND INTERESTS

Shipping companies look primarily for some indication of an interest in a seafaring career, perhaps as a member of the sea cadets. Applicants need to be mature people, with a sense of responsibility, a willingness to leave home for long periods, and an ability to get on with others.

With the reduced size of crews, everyone's contribution matters and they must be able to work without constant supervision on what are often quite technical tasks. For most tasks a high degree of manual dexterity is necessary. Flexibility is required, too, particularly on smaller ships where divisions between the different jobs are sometimes blurred.

ENTRY REQUIREMENTS

All trainee ratings must be sponsored by a shipping company or training group. There are no specific age or qualification requirements for entry; these are determined by individual shipping companies. However, most applicants are between 16 and 19 years, and GCSEs/S grades (A–E/1–5) in maths and English are preferred.

To join a company as a Supplementary Scheme trainee, candidates must have, or expect to get, a minimum of three GCSEs/S grades (A–C/1–3) or equivalent, in maths, physics and a subject showing the use of English.

All candidates must be of good physique and health. Eyesight requirements are the same as for MERCHANT NAVY DECK OFFICER (please see article 1), though perfect colour vision is not required.

TRAINING

Rating training takes place at the nautical colleges at Glasgow, Gravesend, South Shields, Fleetwood and Southampton. There are three separate fully residential courses for junior ratings, all of which include a significant emphasis on health and safety. Every trainee rating takes the Merchant Navy Training Board Stage I Firefighting course, a first aid course, the DETR (Department of the Environment, Transport and the Regions) Personal (Wet Drill) Survival Course, and a recognized course leading to the DETR examination for the Certificate of Proficiency in Survival Craft. Successful trainees receive a Test Certificate at the end of all courses. All trainees – deck, engine-room and catering – spend a week at sea on board a training vessel. Formal instruction is limited to Monday to Friday, and a variety of extracurricular activities is available.

Deck and general-purpose rating

This 13-week course includes the DETR Efficient Deck Hand Certificate examination. It includes instruction in the use of hand tools and power tools, shipboard maintenance, bridge familiarization, engine-room machinery familiarization, rope and wire work, derricks and lifting gear, tanker safety, and general ship knowledge. Successful trainees gain remission of sea service, and are required to serve at sea as junior deck ratings for only two months before promotion.

Junior engine-room rating

Again, this is a 13-week course. Junior engine-room ratings complete much of the work undertaken by the deck trainee, but also receive instruction in a ship's main propulsion machinery and basic electrical equipment. Most of the instruction and work is of a practical nature and includes instruction on the safety precautions to be taken when using machinery. The course also includes an introduction to workshop practice.

Catering rating

This eleven-week course is designed to prepare ratings for work in either the main galley or as stewards. In addition to the safety training already described, there is instruction in basic cookery, food service and housekeeping, nutrition, personal hygiene and food hygiene.

MERCHANT NAVY: YAL

The Supplementary Scheme

Supplementary Scheme trainees attend a nautical training college and follow the same course as that taken by junior deck ratings. They also have additional classes to revise basic educational subjects such as maths, and to introduce them to chartwork and navigation.

Two periods of seagoing training follow, usually with leave between. During this sea phase, trainees must follow a correspondence course and gain practical experience.

The third phase – one academic term – is college-based, studying a range of academic subjects, and this is followed by another seagoing phase. A further correspondence course and record book work are undertaken, and trainees are given instruction about officers' duties and bridge watch-keeping. After a minimum of 26 months at sea, trainees return to college for two academic terms, leading to the examination for the DETR Class 4 Certificate of Competency (or Class 3, depending on progress). Ratings may then apply for a vacancy as a third officer.

The Merchant Navy has introduced a system of qualifications based on NVQs/SVQs. It is envisaged that this system of training and assessment, in combination with oral examinations, will become the only route to gaining Certificates of Competency. NVQs/SVQs in Merchant Vessel Operations are currently available at Levels 2, 3 and 4.

LATE ENTRY

Late entry is unusual, except for engine-room ratings with recognized engineering qualifications in maritime-related subjects obtained ashore.

OPPORTUNITIES

Individual shipping companies recruit their own ratings. Some companies employ British officers but use foreign crew to man the ship, so job opportunities for trainee ratings do not arise as frequently as for cadets. Some school-leavers who join as ratings have a chance to train as officers while working as part of the crew; this is known as the Supplementary Scheme. For details, please see ENTRY REQUIREMENTS and TRAINING.

For a description of different types of employer, please see article 1. MERCHANT NAVY DECK OFFICER.

PAY AND CONDITIONS

The weekly rate is based on a 40-hour week, but the average overtime worked by a seaman grade 1A on a foreign-going ship is over 25 hours a week. The average weekly pay would probably be around £200 to £300 a week. Many shipping companies pay a salary that consolidates the average overtime worked.

For conditions, please see article 1. MERCHANT NAVY DECK OFFICER.

PROSPECTS

During the first six to twelve months of sea service, promotion depends on length of service and age. After that, it depends on qualifications held, on service, and on ability. Deck ratings and engine-room ratings can advance to petty officer and chief petty officer. After about a year at sea, catering ratings can opt to become stewards, and ultimately advance to chief steward; or, with study for additional qualifications, they may become cook, then chief cook. Catering officers on passenger carrying vessels are usually promoted from catering ratings, though there are very few such posts.

RELATED OCCUPATIONS

Royal Navy rating, chef/cook, motor vehicle mechanic, maintenance fitter, Merchant Navy deck officer, Merchant Navy engineering officer.

FURTHER INFORMATION

Chamber of Shipping, Merchant Navy Officer Careers, Carthusian Court, 12 Carthusian Street, London EC1M 6EZ, 0171 417 8400

North West Kent College*, Gravesend, Kent DA12 2HR, 01322 225471

Ship Safe Training Group Ltd*, 2nd Floor, 135 High Street, Rochester, Kent ME1 1EW, 01634 405252

FURTHER READING

Leaflets/booklets are available from the addresses marked*.

Working in Transport and Distribution – COIC

In the careers library classified under YAL.

MATERIALS HANDLING AND DELIVERY: YAT

1. WAREHOUSE WORKER CLCI:YAT
2. LIFT TRUCK OPERATOR CLCI:YAT

1. WAREHOUSE WORKER (YAT)

BACKGROUND INFORMATION

Warehouses receive, store and send out all kinds of raw materials and manufactured goods. Items may pass through several different warehouses before sale or export, moving around in bulk or singly. The types of work and the numbers of people employed depend on the goods stored and the size of the warehouse; one or two people may do all the tasks described below, or there may be several employees, each with a specialized job.

THE WORK

Warehouse workers are involved in receiving, storing and sending out goods from warehouses.

Checking goods in and out. Goods arrive either from another department, as finished goods for dispatch, or from outside, as parts to be stored and used within the firm, such as fresh foods or component parts for engineering. The warehouse worker carefully checks everything that comes in and signs the delivery forms when everything is accounted for. This can be a long job, causing congestion if more than one lorry arrives at the same time. Warehouse workers may unload and stack goods by hand or may use trolleys and lift trucks (some warehouses employ full-time lift truck drivers to move heavy goods). It may be necessary to check dates for the use of goods and stack them accordingly. Supervisors and department managers arrange storage locations.

Order picking/assembling. Items that have been ordered, either by customers or by other departments of the firm, must be picked out. Order pickers/assemblers work from order sheets given out at the beginning of the day. Paperwork is involved in noting inconsistencies in orders, checking the state of stocks and re-ordering if necessary. To reach goods, workers often have to walk, stretch, bend and use ladders.

Packing. Assembled orders are prepared for posting or transporting in the smallest, safest, lightest packages possible. Goods may have to be checked for faults before dispatch.

Storekeeping. This may include counter work – selling parts to customers or to people in the trade – which involves taking money, dealing with cheques and debit and credit cards, and giving advice on a wide range of items of stock. Most store departments have computerized record systems; store staff may use computer terminals or refer to print-outs to check availability of parts.

WORK ENVIRONMENT

Warehouses are found throughout the UK, eg in mail-order firms, hospitals, supermarkets and manufacturing industries of all kinds. Warehouses are often large and airy; they can be cold in winter. Some (for perishable foods, for example) are refrigerated and staff must wear protective clothing. Warehouse workers are exposed to all weathers when accepting deliveries or loading lorries.

SKILLS AND INTERESTS

Warehouse workers need to be able to carry out basic figure work to check deliveries. They also require neat handwriting for marking orders.

Computers are used in many warehouses, to check goods in and out and to monitor stock levels. Workers should be adaptable and willing to learn how to use new technology.

Honesty is essential; a good memory is an asset. Warehouse workers should also be neat, tidy and safety conscious, especially when stacking and storing goods and moving them from heights. Stacking and storing goods requires the ability to judge space.

Some workers operate lift trucks to move large or heavy goods.

ENTRY REQUIREMENTS

No academic entry qualifications are usually required; however, entrants must be able to read and write clearly and carry out basic figure work. Keyboard skills are also an advantage.

The physical ability to lift and carry goods may be necessary in some jobs.

Entry may be via specific training schemes for young people.

TRAINING

Training is usually given on the job, given by experienced warehouse workers.

Training opportunities for young people, including Modern Apprenticeships (part of the Skillseekers Initiative in Scotland) may be available. These offer a trainee position with an employer leading to at least an NVQ/SVQ Level 3 and may include additional units in Key Skills (Core Skills in Scotland). Contact your local careers office, Jobcentre, TEC or LEC for details.

NVQs/SVQs in Distribution and Warehouse Operations are available at Levels 2, 3 and 4.

LATE ENTRY

There is no upper age limit for entry; many employers prefer adult entrants.

There may be specific training opportunities directed at adults available in some areas for this type of work. Candidates may have to satisfy certain conditions to be eligible. Contact your local Jobcentre, careers office or TEC/LEC for details.

OPPORTUNITIES

There are vacancies in many types of warehouses throughout the UK. Employers include supermarkets, hospitals, engineering and textile firms, colleges, offices, garages and DIY stores. They are located both in towns and on industrial estates. In large warehouses, workers are more likely to specialize in tasks such as storekeeping and order picking.

PAY AND CONDITIONS

Wages vary and there are often bonus schemes on top of the basic pay, which ranges from around £190 to £260 a week. Overtime rates can also increase wages.

MATERIALS HANDLING AND DELIVERY: YAT

Warehouse staff work around 40 hours a week. Some do shifts, involving early morning, late night or Saturday work. Overtime work is often available and it may also be possible to work part-time.

PROSPECTS

There may be opportunities for promotion with some employers. Warehouse workers may move into different types of warehouse work such as full-time lift truck driving.

Those with ability and experience may progress to supervisory posts, in charge of a number of workers. It is possible to move into warehouse management. NVQs/SVQs are available for managers in Wholesaling, Warehousing and Stores at Levels 3 and 4.

RELATED OCCUPATIONS

Lift truck operator, storekeeper, packer, warehouse manager, motor vehicle parts person.

FURTHER INFORMATION

Institute of Logistics, Supply-Chain Centre, Earlstrees Court, Earlstrees road, Corby, Northants, NN17 4AX, 01536 740100, www.institute-of-logistics.org.uk

United Kingdom Warehousing Association, Walter House, 418–422 Strand, London WC2R 0PT, 0171 836 5522

FURTHER READING

In the careers library classified under YAT.

2. LIFT TRUCK OPERATOR (YAT)

BACKGROUND INFORMATION

Most factories and warehouses dealing with goods employ at least one person to operate a lift truck. There are many different types of lift truck, from small conventional front- and side-loading lift-and-reach trucks to large industrial tractors, rough terrain and platform trucks, pedestrian-controlled and straddle-carriers. This article concentrates on the operation of conventional reach and counter-balanced lift trucks, operated by hand levers and foot controls, and powered by electricity, petrol, diesel or bottled gas.

On a standard counter-balanced lift truck the load is raised, carried and lowered outside the wheelbase of the truck with the weight of the load forward of the front axle. Reach trucks work the same way, but the load is carried within, or partially within, the wheelbase of the truck. A reach mast is extended to pick up the load and retracted to transport the load. The two projecting forks or lifting attachments used on both these types of lift truck are operated hydraulically.

THE WORK

Lift trucks are operated by one person and allow quick and easy transportation of heavy goods. Goods are loaded and unloaded from lorries, aircraft or vans and stacked on a level or at heights.

Loading, unloading and stacking. Before lifting the load, operators must know the rated capacity of the load and then make sure the truck is not overloaded or the load unstable.

Operators stack loose items or goods on pallet boards – open-sided platforms which hold the goods above the ground leaving space for the forks underneath. Storage space is costly and limited, so goods are often stored in high stacks. To stack, the operator approaches a stack with a load at ground level, then elevates the load to the required height, moves the truck slowly forward to position the load as required, and lowers the load onto the stack. Operators have to make sure they do not dislodge adjacent stacks or catch the load on any overhead obstacles. Having stacked the load safely the forks are slightly lowered until free of the load, and the truck is reversed clear.

Transporting. Operators have to drive accurately; space is limited in warehouses and factories, gangways are often only just wide enough for a truck's movements. Operators must be able to operate the truck in reverse, for example, when transporting a load down a slope or when travelling up inclines unladen. They must know the layout of the workplace, and be aware of any obstacles, such as lights, cables and support columns, and must remove any obstructions.

Safety. The operator must drive carefully, load the truck correctly, and make sure that the stack is secure. They have to give signals, warning horns etc.

Maintenance. Operators may be responsible for carrying out simple inspection and maintenance work on the truck, for example, charging the battery or refuelling. Routine daily checks must be made, and any defects must be reported to the service engineer.

Miscellaneous duties. Operators usually have to keep simple records, and must be able to follow worksheet instructions. They may also help load and unload trucks manually and perform other warehouse duties such as packing.

WORK ENVIRONMENT

Operators work both indoors, in a warehouse, and outside, in a goods yard or transporting goods to other sites. Some trucks have enclosed cabs which provide some protection against adverse weather, but outdoor work can still be cold and wet.

Operating lift trucks involves sitting for most of the day.

SKILLS AND INTERESTS

Lift truck operators must have a responsible attitude, and a patient and steady approach to their work; loading, unloading and stacking can take a long time. They must be able to follow safety rules and understand the importance of safe and careful operating.

Operators require good physical co-ordination to operate a truck and to be able to assess weights, distances etc. It may be necessary to follow written instructions, complete worksheets and keep records.

Lift truck operators must be able to co-operate with other members of staff.

ENTRY REQUIREMENTS

No formal educational qualifications are needed but there are recommended minimum age limits in some sectors of industry. In road haulage and distribution, the recommended minimum age is 17 years, and this is in line with the requirements of the Health and Safety Executive.

MATERIALS HANDLING AND DELIVERY: YAT

There is an approved code of practice covering operation and training. Applicants may have to pass a medical and an assessment test to determine their suitability for training. A driving licence is not required if a truck is used on works property only, but many employers may prefer candidates to hold one.

TRAINING

The Road Transport Industry Training and Business (RTITB) Services recommends that basic training should be provided for all lift truck operators, either by an RTITB-accredited in-house training scheme or a training scheme run by an RTITB-accredited commercial organization. Those run by commercial organizations – for example, lift truck manufacturers or specialist training companies – may take place in a training centre or on the employer's premises. Basic training courses usually last from one to five days, and involve theoretical and practical instruction and exercises. Subjects include an introduction to the truck, mounting and dismounting, steering techniques, using the controls, lifting and depositing, stacking and de-stacking, transporting, and working in confined areas. Trainees are also taught safe operating practices, engineering principles (counter-balance, stability, and so on), and truck maintenance procedures (inspection, refuelling etc). A certificate of basic training is awarded on successful completion of some courses. RTITB Services recommendations specify that all basic training should be carried out off the job by an RTITB-accredited training provider.

Basic training is usually followed by specific job and familiarization training, provided by the employer. Operators work under supervision after basic training until fully competent.

NVQs/SVQs in Lift Truck Operations at Level 2 are available and may be combined with Assisting in Road Haulage and Distribution Operations at Level 1 and Storing Goods for Distribution by Road at Level 2.

LATE ENTRY

Prospects for adult entry are quite good; employers often prefer adult applicants and look for a mature and responsible attitude. Some experience of work in warehouses or stores may be an advantage.

There may be specific training opportunities directed at adults available in some areas for this type of work. Candidates may have to satisfy certain conditions to be eligible. Contact your local Jobcentre, careers office or TEC/LEC for details.

OPPORTUNITIES

Lift truck operators work in factories, stores, warehouses, goods yards or heavy haulage depots. They may be employed in any industry dealing with heavy or bulky goods.

It is estimated that there are around 750,000 lift trucks in operation in Britain.

PAY AND CONDITIONS

Pay varies according to employer and hours worked. Generally operators can expect to receive average wages of around £290 a week. Additional payments may be made for shift and night work. Some employers have productivity bonus schemes which can raise earnings. Overtime rates are paid for extra hours.

Operators work hours to suit their employers. This can involve: standard day hours, Monday to Friday; shifts covering 24 hours; double day shifts; or permanent nights. Overtime may be available and may be required by some employers.

PROSPECTS

Promotion prospects are limited. Suitable and experienced operators may be selected to train as instructors; a number of companies are accredited by RTITB Services to offer specialist instructor training courses. Courses feature an independently conducted test and examination, success in which leads to registration on the National Register of Approved Instructors/Examiners maintained by Road Transport Industry Training and Business Services, and the award of a RTITB certificate of registration. The registration is valid for five years and may be renewed after re-examination of the instructor. Some operators progress by moving to other related jobs – for example, as supervisors in warehousing or dispatch.

RELATED OCCUPATIONS

Warehouse worker, car/van driver, LGV driver, construction plant operator.

FURTHER INFORMATION

RTITB Services*, CENTREX Training and Conference Centre, High Ercall, Telford, Shropshire TF6 6RB, 01952 777777

or in Scotland: RTITB Services, Hardie Road, Deans, Livingston, West Lothian EH54 8AR 01506 497777

FURTHER READING

Leaflets/booklets are available from the address marked*.

In the careers library classified under YAT.

POSTAL WORK: YAT/CAM

1. POSTMAN/WOMAN CLCI:YAT/CAM

BACKGROUND INFORMATION

The Post Office provides postal and retail services to the public and business community. It is among the top 30 businesses in the UK, with a turnover of more than five billion pounds, and one of the country's largest employers, with over 190,000 employees. The Post Office is organized into five main businesses.

Royal Mail is responsible for the collection, sorting and delivery of letters in the UK and overseas. It delivers over 70 million letters a day in the UK and is the largest part of the Post Office.

Parcelforce collects, sorts and delivers parcels to business customers and private individuals; both nationally and to/from the United Kingdom.

The Post Office's delivery work means it has an extensive transport network, including road, rail and air.

Post Office Counters Ltd operates around 20,000 Crown, franchise and sub-post offices. Apart from postage items, TV and other licences and passport applications are available in these retail outlets, as well as a variety of financial services.

The Post Office Group Centre offers headquarters services across the business, such as specialist finance, planning, legal services, welfare, purchasing, public relations and training and development.

Subscription Services Ltd is a wholly owned subsidiary including the TV Licence Records Office.

The government has announced a review of the Post Office which may affect its structure and opportunities within it in the near future. At present, apart from the jobs of postman/postwoman and counter clerk, each Post Office business offers a variety of opportunities for specialist managers (sometimes recruited at graduate level) in such fields as finance, personnel, marketing, operations, engineering, transport, estates management and information technology. Candidates are recruited to specific jobs, for which they must have the appropriate specialist expertise or potential.

1. POSTMAN/WOMAN (YAT/CAM)

THE WORK

Postmen/women collect, sort and deliver mail to homes and workplaces. Their work covers every stage of the journey of letters and small packets from sender to receiver.

Postmen/women collect mail from pillar-boxes, businesses and post offices, transporting mail by van to sorting offices. Mail is sorted there for despatch to its destination, into towns, cities, counties and countries. Although unusual-sized letters have to be sorted by hand, increasingly sorting is done by high speed machines which read the postcode and sort automatically. Items without postcode, or with postcodes the machine cannot read are re-routed to have their destination typed manually.

Next, the mail moves through a vast transport network, including road, rail and air. Postmen/women work at stations, airports and road depots loading and unloading mailbags. Others drive a variety of vehicles including vans and large goods vehicles, and some sort mail on travelling post offices (trains that have sorting offices).

Postmen/women then sort incoming mail by areas and roads, and deliver it by van, bicycle or on foot.

Parcelforce has its own network of sorting and delivery offices where staff work as parcel handlers, sorters and drivers. Like Royal Mail postmen/women, their work also involves collection, sorting, transporting and final delivery. Parcelforce sorting is highly automated, so very little sorting is done by hand.

WORK ENVIRONMENT

Making postal collections and deliveries is outdoor work. It has to be done in all weather conditions: working in the summer heat can be as difficult as working in the rain, or in the winter cold and ice. Delivery and collection rounds in some country areas involve a great deal of driving.

Sorting all the incoming and outgoing mail, and preparing mail for machine sorting are indoor jobs. Sorting offices are large and very busy places. Automatic sorting equipment can be very noisy.

Some jobs involve high physical demands, lifting and carrying, while others are mainly sedentary, working at a keyboard for example.

SKILLS AND INTERESTS

Postmen/women have a responsible job: to ensure the safe delivery of all mail. They must be honest and trustworthy. They often have direct contact with customers, either collecting or delivering, and must be comfortable with this personal contact. The ability to read addresses and carry out clerical tasks is required, eg re-sorting and redirecting mail.

While carrying out sorting duties, postmen/women need to be able to work accurately, quickly and carefully. They must also work as part of a team. Sorting mail ready for final delivery on a 'walk' needs a good memory and detailed local knowledge.

Postmen/women need to be fit and active; postbags are heavy at the start of a round, and the work can involve a great deal of walking. They also need to be able to work on their own, as well as in a team, and to be both reliable and adaptable.

ENTRY REQUIREMENTS

There are no formal academic qualifications required for entry as a postman/woman with Royal Mail, or as a parcel handler and sorter with Parcelforce.

Selection is by aptitude test and interview. The aptitude test is based on some of the skills used in the day-to-day work of postmen/women, such as checking for errors in lists of names and addresses.

Postmen/women may also be required to attend a medical examination. For some jobs, applicants must be willing to ride a bicycle.

TRAINING

New entrants at postman/woman grade with Royal Mail attend a variety of off-the-job short courses introducing them to their various duties during their first two weeks. Most of the basic delivery and sorting skills are taught on the job by more experienced colleagues. Further courses are given as staff take on more senior duties.

New entrants with Parcelforce attend an introductory

POSTAL WORK: YAT/CAM

course, and then work alongside experienced staff while they learn the basic skills. All new entrants also have the opportunity to attend off-the-job training courses at regional training schools. Courses lead to the City and Guilds Certificate in Parcel Distribution. There is also further on-the-job training during the first year.

Parcelforce collection, sorting and distribution staff can work towards the Certificate in Parcel Distribution awarded by City and Guilds. Staff over the age of 21 with a driving licence may apply for Large Goods Vehicles (Category C1) driver training.

LATE ENTRY

Adult entry is common. Entry for older candidates is by successfully completing the short test and passing the interview. There may be a medical examination.

OPPORTUNITIES

The majority of Royal Mail's staff work as postmen/women in the delivery offices and local sorting offices. Parcelforce has its own network of sorting and delivery centres.

At present, opportunities to join Royal Mail are limited and are expected to remain so for some time to come. The number of postmen and postwomen is falling, so recruitment has stopped in some cases and is restricted to temporary contracts in others. Competition for jobs can be strong. Christmas is usually a very busy period for Royal Mail and extra postmen/women are often employed for the festive season, as well as in the summer peak holiday period.

Parcelforce has increased the number of staff employed as collection and delivery staff and drivers, while reducing its administrative staff. Opportunities for depot staff and drivers are likely to remain steady.

PAY AND CONDITIONS

Royal Mail. The basic rate of pay for a postman/postwoman at 16 years is £118.65 a week, rising to £186.40 a week at 18 years. The basic rate of pay for adult recruits is £186.40 a week, rising to a maximum of £194.81 a week. Higher-grade postmen/women and supervisors are paid on a different scale.

There is a bonus scheme, linked to the performance of each sorting delivery office. This leads to minimum additional payments after twelve months' satisfactory service.

The business is moving towards a fixed shift with an emphasis on team working. Shifts start at 5am or 6am, 1.30pm and 9pm or 10pm. The early shift generally prepares and makes the morning deliveries of mail, while the late shift normally collects and sorts mail and the night shift sorts and despatches it. Some Sunday work is required.

An allowance is paid for unsocial hours. There are additional payments for Saturday working, for overtime and for driving.

Postmen/women get four weeks' holiday a year, rising to five weeks a year after 30 years' service. This is in addition to two-and-a-half 'occasional' days.

Other benefits include free uniform, subsidized meals and a contributory pension scheme.

Parcelforce. The basic rate of pay is £124.46 week. The basic rate for adult recruits is £177.68 a week rising to a maximum of £185.61. There is a bonus scheme at sorting offices linked to group performance, whilst at delivery offices bonus payments depend on the performance of each driver.

Most staff work Monday to Friday. Holiday entitlement is four weeks a year.

PROSPECTS

Postmen/women recruited at 18 years or over work on trial for the first six months. After one year of satisfactory service, promotion is possible to higher-grade postman/women, with greater responsibility, such as operating the range of automatic sorting equipment, or directly to management positions. Mobility is an advantage. At Parcelforce, staff can progress from Level 1 (recruitment grade) to Level 5 or directly to a supervisory post.

RELATED OCCUPATIONS

Post office counter clerk, warehouse worker, mail order clerk, car/van driver, messenger, courier, despatch rider, station assistant.

FURTHER INFORMATION

For more information, contact your local delivery office. Addresses are in the local phone book, or available from the nearest post office.

FURTHER READING

In the careers library classified under YAT; CAM.

DIVING: YAZ

DIVER CLCI:YAZ

BACKGROUND INFORMATION

Diving in itself is not a career; it should instead be considered as a vehicle to enable a person to carry out a job underwater instead of on land. Some divers dive full-time, others such as marine scientists may dive as part of their work. There are a number of different types of divers: commercial divers who work inland, inshore and offshore; police underwater search divers; Royal Navy divers; recreational diving instructors; and some marine scientists and nautical archaeologists. Occasionally divers are needed for film and television work.

THE WORK

Commercial diving is divided into two areas:

Inshore diving – this covers up to twelve miles from the coastline plus inland diving in harbours, reservoirs, rivers, canals, fish farms and lakes. Inshore and inland work is basically civil and structural engineering but underwater. Divers can be involved in port, harbour, reservoir and bridge inspection, construction and repair, construction of new sewage outfalls and lock gate inspection. They also carry out remedial work in lakes, rivers, reservoirs, canals etc. Where existing structures are to be removed they may demolish them with explosives. Divers build the structures and inspect them during and after construction for any faults. After structures are completed they regularly inspect and maintain them. Fish farms are another area needing divers, and here their work could include, for instance, sorting out nets or recovering dead fish. In ports, divers may also be used for such tasks as untangling ropes from a ship's propeller.

Offshore diving – includes the exploration and exploitation of sub-sea oil and gas resources all over the world. Divers work from ships or oil platforms and their work includes being involved in laying and maintaining pipelines and lines for communication systems. This may involve using specialized equipment to dig trenches on the sea bed, laying and connecting the pipes, which may involve welding. They carry out construction and maintenance work on oil platforms and rigs and inspect the structures for corrosion either by eye, by underwater cameras or by non-destructive testing equipment such as ultrasonics. They clear marine growth from the parts of rigs and platforms under the sea and carry out repairs.

Police underwater search divers – search for stolen property both in and out of the water. They also search for and recover bodies from lakes, canals, reservoirs, rivers, sewers, drains and cesspits. In many cases there is little or no visibility, and divers carry out their searches purely by feeling. They also deal with corpses on land where decomposition has taken place and breathing apparatus has to be worn. In the case of VIPs visiting an area, they carry out underwater security searches for explosives. Another part of their work is assisting customs and excise officers by searching the hulls of ships for drugs. There is not usually enough work for underwater search teams to dive full-time, so they also work in support groups carrying out general police duties.

Royal Navy divers – there are three types of divers in the Royal Navy, but all begin their careers in another specialization. Ship's divers or diving officers are based on board every ship in the Fleet and, although not full-time divers, they may be called upon at any time to check the ship's hull for limpet mines, carry out simple underwater maintenance tasks, or search for equipment lost over the side in harbour. Ship's divers in the Fleet Air Arm may volunteer to become search-and-rescue (SAR) divers. Usually working from helicopters, they are trained to rescue people trapped in capsized vessels or crashed aircraft, or from coastal cliff faces. Divers work within the Royal Marines as part of the Special Boat service.

Ship's divers and diving officers in the Fleet may volunteer to become full-time clearance divers. These divers are trained in all aspects of air and mixed-gas diving, some becoming saturation qualified. They are also trained to use all underwater tools and camera equipment and carry out bomb and mine disposal, search open water, for lost aircraft, for instance, and carry out underwater engineering and battle damage repair. Clearance divers are based either on mine countermeasures vessels or in specialized teams ashore.

Marine scientists – divers may be from any discipline needing to research underwater, including biologists, chemists, geologists and geographers. Their work is concerned with scientific data collection and observation. Depending on their discipline they could be testing oceanographic equipment or studying sea life – both plants and fish – looking at distribution patterns of various forms of sea life and examining the effects of pollution.

Nautical archaeologists – like the marine scientists, most nautical archaeologists do not dive full-time, although a small number do. Their work includes surveying vessels that have sunk. Normally they gather data and then protect the vessel from any threat. In exceptional cases, such as the *Mary Rose*, they are involved in recovering the vessel and bringing it onto land. They also survey any settlements that are now underwater.

All of these divers work in teams of about four or five. One diver is under water, the others are on the surface. One of the team looks after the submerged diver and communicates with them – this may be through a series of pulls on a rope attached to the diver or by voice through a communication line. Another diver is ready as a standby in case of emergency, and the fourth is preparing to dive. In addition there is a diving supervisor who controls the diving operation.

Recreational diving instructors – teach snorkelling and scuba diving to both children and adults. They teach both the theory – physics and physiology – and the practice of scuba diving – diving in buddy pairs, using and caring for equipment, the underwater environment, underwater navigation, and how to prevent problems and get out of trouble.

Film and television work – very occasionally divers are needed for this type of work. Camera work is done by experienced camera crews who also have the relevant diving qualifications. The underwater actors may be stunt men/women who are qualified divers, or in some cases commercial divers may be used.

All divers wear specialized equipment, which varies depending on the type of diving. It includes protective suits – these may be dry suits or, in the case of offshore diving, suits through which warm water is pumped. Divers wear fins on their feet or, in some cases, weighted boots. Some have full face masks; others wear helmets. Their breathing supply may be from cylinders strapped to their backs, or in many cases it is supplied by pipe from the surface. They also operate from diving bells.

DIVING: YAZ

WORK ENVIRONMENT

Commercial divers – offshore diving contractors are mainly based in Aberdeen and Great Yarmouth, and also in the Middle East and South East Asia. Offshore divers, when diving, live on board ships and on oil platforms, in Britain and abroad. They are often required to take up a job at very short notice, and may be away from home for considerable periods of time. Inshore divers travel from their homes to wherever in the country they are needed, and stay there for the duration of the contract which is often only a couple of days.

The waters they dive in are usually dark and, in some cases, can be cold in spite of protective clothing. Although divers are part of a team, once underwater they are often on their own. Some offshore divers work from diving bells, which can be cramped. Divers involved in deep work may be required to live in compression chambers for up to four weeks at a time.

Police underwater search divers dive in lakes, rivers, canals, reservoirs, drains and cesspits. They are based with one police authority and have to travel to anywhere within their area. They may also have to travel to neighbouring authorities who do not have an underwater search unit.

Recreational diving instructors usually work in a rather more pleasant environment, in swimming pools and suitable diving waters in the UK and abroad.

Marine scientists and archaeologists' environment depends on where they are working. Some of their work may be in warm clear waters. Their work can involve travel both in Britain and abroad.

Royal Navy divers are based at inshore establishments, here and abroad, and on board ship. They may be required to dive in any conditions at any time of the day or night.

SKILLS AND INTERESTS

Firstly, divers must be comfortable and confident in the water. It is vital that they can work as part of a team – the lives of divers depend on others in their team. They also have to be comfortable working on their own underwater with just a communication line to a supervisor on the surface. They should be physically fit. All divers need to be very safety conscious; they also have to be able to keep calm and act quickly in emergencies. Police divers in particular need to be very painstaking and methodical in carrying out searches.

ENTRY REQUIREMENTS

Commercial divers must have the appropriate Health and Safety Executive (HSE) approved qualifications or equivalent qualifications from overseas for the job they wish to do. There are no specific academic entry requirements for diving schools, although those who have no previous relevant qualifications or experience – such as engineering or construction work, welding, photography, mechanics fitting, plumbing or electrical work – may find it extremely difficult to get work. All applicants for diving schools undergo a medical and need to be fit and able to swim. Also, most have a commercial diving aptitude test which includes checks in maths and English, a swimming test, manual dexterity, and a shallow re-compression chamber dive.

Police underwater search divers join as police constables. After two years' probation, they can then apply to join an underwater search unit. Applicants must be physically fit and be able to swim. All applicants are interviewed to determine their suitability for this work. Please see the article POLICE CONSTABLE (MAB).

Royal Navy divers – there is no direct entry into this specialization; divers transfer from other branches. Please see ROYAL NAVY articles (BAB).

Recreational diving instructors – all paid recreational diving instructors in the UK must hold a certificate of training that complies with the industry Approved Codes of Practice (ACOPs) and recognized by the Health and Safety Executive. There are a number of good training schools; lists of addresses can be obtained from the HSE and from the governing body of the British Sub-Aqua Club (BSAC).

To start an instructor's course, applicants have to be able to swim, be fit to scuba dive and to hold relevant diving qualifications, such as BSAC's sports diver and dive leader qualifications, or PADI's open water diver, advanced open water diver, rescue diver and dive master qualifications.

Marine scientists and archaeologists require a degree, often a PhD in the appropriate discipline, plus appropriate HSE approved diving qualifications. Many take up diving whilst at university and already have a relevant sports diving qualification.

TRAINING

The main qualifications for professional divers are those issued by the Health and Safety Executive based on the three standards of commercial diving competence: SCUBA Diving; Surface Supplied Diving; Closed bell Diving. The HSE also recognizes similar, government controlled qualifications issued by other countries.

With the exception of police and Armed Forces divers, there may be government funding available for others to finance their own training.

Most courses leading to HSE qualifications cost between £1,200 and £7,500 plus accommodation for the duration of the course. A small number of academic institutions may finance marine scientists through their diving training. Recreational instructors also finance their own training, although this is more in the region of a couple of hundred pounds.

There are four HSE **commercial diving** courses:

HSE Part 4 (professional scuba diver). This is a three-and-a-half-week to four-week course which costs about £1,200. Holders are qualified to use underwater breathing apparatus, breathing air to a maximum depth of 50 metres (167 feet).

HSE Part 3 (inshore air diver). This is a four- to six-week course costing about £2,000. Holders are qualified to use scuba and surface-supplied equipment, breathing air to a maximum depth of 50 metres (167 feet), for operations not connected with offshore installations.

HSE Part 2 (mixed gas diver). Before taking this course, divers must first have held HSE Part 1 for twelve months and had considerable commercial experience. Divers are qualified to operate from closed diving bells using gas mixtures other than air, to depths over 50 metres (167 feet). The course lasts three weeks and costs about £7,500.

HSE Part 1. This is a ten-week course costing about £4,000. Scuba divers are qualified to use surface-supplied equipment, a wet bell and certain tools, breathing air or nitrox mixture to a maximum of 50 metres (167 feet).

DIVING: YAZ

These four courses vary but most cover diving medicine and physics, elementary seamanship and small boat handling, use of diving equipment, operation and maintenance of hand tools and legislation.

Police underwater search divers are trained at one of the two police diving schools in Glasgow or Newcastle. They undergo an eight-week course leading to HSE Part 3.

Royal Navy divers must start as ship's divers. Training involves a four-week course using compressed air equipment and learning how to perform elementary underwater tasks. They may then expect to spend at least two years on a ship or submarine as part of a team, honing their skills and gaining experience.

A ship's diver in the Fleet Air Arm may then volunteer to become a search-and-rescue (SAR) diver. This involves further training to become familiar with the operation of helicopters and additional diving training to acquire SAR skills.

Other ship's divers, if they enjoy diving and would like to become one of the RN's professional divers, may then apply to become clearance divers. If they are officers they do an intensive course (of approximately nine months), specializing in both mine warfare and clearance diving. Ratings do a basic course to qualify as able seaman (divers) and further advancement courses at each stage of their careers. Many RN qualifications are recognized by the HSE.

Recreational diving instructors – courses cover all aspects of diving instruction, both theoretical and practical, and include an examination. UK qualifications are generally well respected in overseas dive locations. Check for local regulations.

Marine scientists – usually have to finance their own training, and most go up to HSE Scuba Diver.

LATE ENTRY

There are no maximum age limits for divers, although they must be physically fit and undergo a medical examination every year. Entry and training are as described above.

OPPORTUNITIES

Most commercial divers work for firms of diving contractors, on short-term contracts. The need for divers has been decreasing over recent years – one of the reasons being the use of remotely operated vehicles (ROVs) which can do some of the tasks previously done by divers. Both offshore and inshore divers live anywhere in the country but must be prepared to travel anywhere in the world.

Police underwater search divers are usually based with one police authority; however, not all authorities have an underwater search unit and they may have to travel to neighbouring areas without one. There are not many police divers – an underwater search unit covering a large geographical area may have as few as nine divers.

Recreational diving instructors – this is the one area where opportunities are increasing, as more people today are interested in learning to dive. In particular, there are increasing opportunities abroad in diving holiday centres. Entry into this work is extremely competitive and would-be divers are advised to get as much relevant experience and training as possible. Work is not highly paid and is often seasonal.

PAY AND CONDITIONS

Inshore divers earn between £35 and £100 a day. Offshore divers may earn from £130 to £210 a day. All commercial divers work on contracts. Offshore contracts may last about two to four weeks. If it is a long-term contract then there may be teams of divers working one month on and one month off; however, during their time off they are not paid. Inshore divers tend to do small contracts of as little as one or two days each.

Hours vary depending on the type of diving – offshore divers usually work shifts of twelve hours on, twelve hours off. Police and Royal Navy divers work shifts but are on call 24 hours a day, seven days a week.

PROSPECTS

In commercial diving, as divers gain experience they can achieve more pay. The normal promotion route is from diver to diving supervisor in charge of a team of divers. Divers wanting promotion or the better paid jobs usually take further courses to qualify them as: underwater inspectors – trained to carry out underwater visual inspections and operate video and still cameras; or diver medics – trained to give emergency assistance to a casualty and carry out first aid under medical guidance. Divers with considerable experience may also take HSE mixed gas diver which opens up the possibility of deep and saturation diving at considerably more pay.

For those with the necessary qualifications and experience it may be possible to work as a HM Inspector of Health and Safety.

RELATED OCCUPATIONS

Training instructor, sports coach, teacher, RN rating.

FURTHER INFORMATION

Diving Policy, Health and Safety Executive*, 4th Floor South, Rose Court, 2 Southwark Bridge, London SE1 9HS, 0171 717 6592

Society for Underwater Technology*, 76 Mark Lane, London EC3R 7JN, 0171 481 0750

Nautical Archaeological Society, c/o 19 College Road, HM Naval Base, Portsmouth PO1 3LJ, 01705 818419

The British Sub-Aqua Club, Telfords Quay, Ellesmere Port, South Wirral, Cheshire L65 4FY, 0151 350 6200, www.bsac.com

PADI International Ltd, Unit 7, St Phillips Central, Albert Road, St Phillips, Bristol BS2 0PD, 0117 300 7310

Individual diving schools – details from *Yellow Pages*.

FURTHER READING

Leaflets/booklets are available from the addresses marked*.

Working in Outdoor Jobs–COIC

In the careers library classified under YAZ.

INDEX

Note: this index is in word-by-word order (eg 'Air Loadmaster' is listed before 'Aircraft Engineer'); link-words (such as 'and' / 'in' / 'of') are also ignored.

AA Patrolperson, 468–469
Abattoir Worker, 506
Above-water Operator Mechanic (RN), 8
Access Scaffolder, 571
Account Executive (advertising), **400**, **402**
Account Planner (advertising), **400**, **402**
Accountancy, **361–368**
Accountant
    in Armed Forces, 6, 16, 22–23
    in Civil Service, 33, 35, 36, 364, 365
    Financial, 361, 363
    Industry and Commerce, **363–364**
    in local authorities, 364, 365
    Management, 361, 363
    in NHS, 43, 364, 365
    Private/Public Practice, **361–363**
    Public Sector, 43, **364–366**
Accounting Technician, **366–368**
Accounts Clerk, 9, 19, 26, 61
Accounts Commission Accountant, 365
Actor, **153–156**
Actuary, 33, 35, 36, **387–388**
Acupuncturist, **295**, **296**, 297
Administration, Business, Clerical and Management, **29–92**
Administrative staff, **61–63**
    Agricultural, 57
    in Armed Forces, 5–6, 9, 11, 13, 16, 22–23, 26
    Civil Service, **30–32**
    Local Authority, **39–42**
    in NHS, 45
Administrator
    Bank Branch, 369
    Business, 48–49
    Civil Service, 30
    Computer Database, **72–74**
    Health Service, 43
    Local Authority, **39–40**
Admissions Clerk (NHS), 45
Advertising, **400–404**
    Account Executive, **400**, **402**
    Account Planner, **400**, **402**
    Copywriter, **401**, **402**
    Media Executive, **400–401**, **402**
    Photographer, 102
Advocate/Barrister, 16, 37, **331–334**
Advocates' Clerk, 338, 339
Aerobics Instructor, 166, 178
Aerodrome Controller, 652
Aeronautical Engineer, 16, 462
Aerospace Systems Operator (RAF), 25
Aerosystems Engineer, 22
Aesthetician, 234
African Dance Performer, 162, 164
Afro-Caribbean Hairdresser, 239
Agricultural Blacksmith, 549
Agricultural Development and Advisory Service (ADAS) staff, 603, 611
Agricultural Engineer, 462
Agricultural (Farm) Secretary, 57, 58, 59
Agricultural Inspector, 91

    see also Health and Safety Inspector
Agricultural Vehicle Tyre Fitter, 412
Agriculture, 602–608
Air Cabin Crew (civil aviation), **648–649**
Air Corps (Army) Officer/Soldier, 15, 19
Air Despatcher (Armed Forces), 19
Air Electronics Operator (RAF), 25
Air Engineer (Armed Forces), 5, 25
Air ground crew (Armed Forces), 19, 25
Air Loadmaster, 25
Air Traffic Controller
    Armed Forces, 5, 22, 25
    Civil Aviation, 646, **651–653**
Air Transport, **646–653**
Aircraft Engineer (Armed Forces), 22, 25
Aircraft Handler (Fleet Air Arm), 9
Aircraft Maintenance Engineer (civil aviation), **649–651**
Aircraft Mechanic/Technician (Armed Forces), 8, 19, 25
Airline Pilot, **646–647**
Airline Steward/Stewardess, **648–649**
Airman/Airwoman (RAF), 25–28
Airport jobs, 356, 646
Alternative/Complementary Medicine, **295–299**
Amateur Sports Coach/Instructor, 166
Ambulance Care Assistant, 292, 293
Ambulance Control Room Assistant, 292, 293
Ambulance Paramedic, 292, 293
Ambulance Person, **292–294**
Ambulance Technician, 292, 293
Ambulance Work, **292–294**
Amenity horticultural staff, 609, 610
Ammunition Technician (Armed Forces), 19
Anaesthetist, 248
Analyst
    Chemical, 434
    Investment, 389, **391–393**
Analyst Programmer/Software Engineer, **68–70**
Analyst/Designer (information systems), **66–68**
Ancient Monuments Inspector, 141, 143
Animal-Related Jobs, **621–640**
Animal Technical Assistant (Armed Forces), 20
Animal Welfare, **626–627**
    Kennel Worker, 629, 630
    RSPCA/SSPCA Inspector, **626–627**
    veterinary staff, 621, 623, 624
Animals, Plants and Nature, **602–645**
Approach Controller (civil aviation), 651–652
Arable Farm Worker, 604
Archaeologist, **141–144**
    Nautical, 685, 686
Architect, 33, 35, **552–554**
    Landscape Architect, **587–588**
Architectural Blacksmith, 549
Architectural Technician, 554
Architectural Technologist, **554–556**
Area Air Traffic Controller, 651
Armed Forces, **5–28**
    Accountant, 6, 16, 22–23
    Ambulance Person, 294
    Catering Manager/Officer, 6, 16, 22, 206, 208
    catering staff, 6, 9, 13, 19, 26
    Chaplain, 6, 15, 23
    Civil Engineer, 596
    Clerk, 9, 13, 19
    dental staff, 9, 20, 26, 263, 265
    Dentist, 6, 16, 23, 260

INDEX

Doctor, 6, 16, 23, 247, 248
Driver, 13, 19, 25
Engineer, 5, 15, 16
Kennel Worker, 20, 630
Lecturer, 16, 117
legal staff, 16, 23, 336
Maintenance Fitter, 8, 13, 19, 25, 482
Medical Laboratory Technician, 20, 291, 434
medical staff, 6, 9, 16, 20, 23, 25–26, 247, 248, 251, 253
Motor Vehicle Mechanic, 13, 19, 25, 468
Musician, 13, 20, 26, 157, 158, 159
nursing staff, 6, 16, 20, 23, 251, 253
PE/PT Instructor, 11, 13, 16, 23, 27, 168
Photographer, 26, 104
Physiological Measurement Technician, 20, 291
Physiotherapist, 20
Radiographer, 20, 26, 281
Social Worker, 307
Teacher, 16, 110, 112
veterinary staff, 16, 20, 621, 623
see also Army; Naval Service; Royal Air Force
Armoured Vehicle Crewman/Driver/Officer, 15, 19
Armourer, 13
Army, 15–21
Non-commissioned Officer/Private, **19–21**
Officer, **15–19**
Army Air Corps (AAC) Officer/Soldier, 15, 19
Aromatherapist, **295, 296, 297**
Art and Design, 93–106
Art Director (film/TV), 181
Art Editor, 127
Art Gallery Keeper, **129–131**
Art Gallery and Museum Work, 129–133
Articulated Lorry Driver, 659
Artificer (Armed Forces), 8
Artillery Officer/Soldier, 15, 19
Artist/Illustrator, 13, 93, **95–96**
Artistic Blacksmith, 540
Arts, Performing, 153–165
Assault Engineer (Armed Forces), 13
Assembler (Light Industry), 493, 498, **500–501**
Assistant (film) Director, 181, **186–189**
Auctioneer/Valuer, 589, 591
Audio Typist, 61
Audiology Medical Technical Officer, 289–290
Audit Commission Accountant, 365
Auditor (Accountant), 361, 363
Author, Technical, **124–126**
Auto-Electrician, 472
Avionics Engineer, 649
Avionics Technician (Armed Forces), 19, 25

Backtenders (papermaking), 539
Baker, 410, **503–505**
Baking and Confectionery, 503–505
Ballet Dancer, 162, 164
Ballroom Dancer, 162, 164
Bandsman/woman (Armed Forces), 13, 20, 26, 157, 158, 159
Bank Economist, 449, 450
Bank of England staff, 369, 371, 449, 450
Bank Manager, **369–371**
Bank Officer, **371–373**
Banking and Building Society Work, 369–373
Barber, 239
Barman/woman, **224–226**
Barrister/Advocate, 16, 37, **331–334**

Barristers' Clerk, **337–339**
Basketball Player (professional), 170, 173
Beaterman/woman (papermaking), 539
Beautician, 234
Canine/Dog, 631
Beauty Consultant, 234
Beauty Therapist, **234–236**
Bell Hop (hotel), 221
Bench Glassblower, 510
Bench Joiner, 562
Bespoke Tailor, 521
Bi/multilingual Secretary, 57, 58, 59
Bioengineering Technician, 289
Biologist, 434, 459
Biomedical Scientist, 434, **437–439**
Biotechnologist, 434
Blacksmith, 19, **549–551**
Blind-Children Teacher, 113, 114
Blood Transfusion Service staff, 438, 439
Blue Cross staff, 623, 624
Blues Musician, 156, 158
Boarding Kennel Manager/Worker, 624, 630
Boarding School Teacher, 108, 111
Book Editor, 127
Book publishing staff, 127
Bookbinder, **544–546**
Book-keeping Clerk, 61
Boom Operator (film/TV sound), 192, 193
Boxer (professional), 171, 173
Branch Manager
Bank/Building Society, 369
Retail, 405
Brass Band Musician, 156
Breeding Kennel Manager/Worker, 624, 630
Brewer, **508–509**
Bricklayer, **561–562**
British Airports Authority (BAA) jobs, 356, 646
British Airways staff, 647, 648
British Antarctic Survey staff, 457
British Council opportunities, 110, 117, 151
British Geological Survey staff, 452
British Rail (BR): *see* Railtrack; Railway...; Station...; Train...
British School of Motoring Instructor, 664
British Transport Policeman/woman, 346
Broadcast Journalist, 121
Broadcasting/Film/Theatre, 181–195
Broker
Insurance Broker, 374, **376–378**
Stockbroker, 389, **390–391**
Broker Consultant (insurance), 378
Brokers' Clerk, 381
Bugler (Armed Forces), 13
Building/Construction Operative, **575–577**
Building and Construction Trades, 561–574
Building Services, 582–586
Building Services Engineer/Technician, **582–584**
Building Society and Bank Work, 369–373
Building Society Customer Service Assistant, **371–373**
Building Society Manager, **369–371**
Building Surveyor, 590, 591
Building Technician, 558
Building Technology and Management, 557–560
Building Trade Blacksmith, 549
Burglary-and-Theft (insurance) Surveyor, 382
Bursar, 208
Bus Conductor, **657–658**

INDEX

Bus Driver, **655–657**
Business Administrator, 48–49
Business, Clerical and Management (and Administration), **29–92**
Business Connect/Link/Shop, advice from, 2
Business Equipment Service Engineer, **483–485**
Business Interpreter, 145
Butcher, 410, **415–416**, 506
Buyer, **428–430**
    Building, 557
    Retail, 428
Buying, Selling and Related Services, **394–433**

Cabaret/Club Performer, 155, 158, 164
Cabin Crew (civil aviation), **648–649**
Cabinet Maker, **528–529**
Café Cook, 210
Café Service Assistant, 215
Call-Order Cook, 210
Camera Operator (film/TV), 181, **189–192**, 685
Canine Beautician, 631
Canoeing Instructor, 168
Canteen Counter Assistant, 215
Car Mechanic, 467
Car Tyre/Exhaust Fitter, 412
Car/Van Driver, 32, **661–662**
Cardiologist (doctor), 247
Cardiology Medical Technical Officer, 290
Care Assistant, **256–259**, 292, 293, **309–311**
Careers Adviser, **318–320**
Careers Assistant, 319
Careers Service support staff, 319
Carpenter/Joiner, 19, **562–563**
Carpet-layer, 563
Cartographic staff, 13, 25, 33, 35, 36
Cash Till Operator, 410, 413
Cash-in-Transit Operative, 357, 358
Cashier, 372, 413
Caster (foundry), 533
Catering Butcher, 506
Catering, Hospitality and Other Services, **204–244**
Catering Manager/Officer, **206–208**
    in Armed Forces, 6, 16, 22, 206, 208
Catering staff, **204–222**
    in Armed Forces, 9, 13, 19, 26
    in Merchant Navy, 678
Ceramic Materials Scientist/Technologist, 442
Certified Accountant, 36, 362
Cervical Cytology Screener, 438
Chairman/Servitor (glass industry), 510
Chambers' Director (legal), 337
Channel Navigation Information Service (CNIS) Officer, 359
Chaplain (Armed Forces), 6, 15, 23
Chartered Accountant, 36, 362
Chartered Engineer, 462, 463, 464, 465, 582, 583, 594, 595
Chartered Psychologist, 326
Chartered Secretary, **48–49**
Chartered Statistician, 447
Chartered Surveyor, 589, 591
Chat Show Researcher, 184
Chauffeur/Chauffeuse, 661
Checkout Operator (supermarket), 410
Chef de Partie, 210
Chef de Rang (Waiter), 214
Chef/Cook, **210–212**
    in Armed Forces, 9, 13, 19, 26
Chemical Engineer, 462, 465

Chemical Industry Plumber, 569, 570
Chemical Metallurgist, 443
Chemical Pathologist, 248
Chemical Plant Process Operator, **547–548**
Chemist, 434, 456, 459
    Pharmacist, 269–271
Cheque Processing Officer (banking), 372
Children's (Holiday) Representative, 202
Children's Home Care Assistant, 309
Children's Nurse, 250
Children's Theatre Performer, 155
Chiropodist, **284–286**
Chiropractor, **295**, **296**, **297**
Choreographer, 164
Church Chorister/Musician/Organist, 156, 158
Church of England (C of E) Religious Studies Teacher, 109
CID Constable, 345
Circus Performer, 164
Civil Aviation, **646–653**
Civil Engineer, 37, 462, **594–597**
Civil Engineering/Construction Operative, 575
Civil Service, **29–38**
    Accountant, 33, 35, 36, 364, 365, 366
    Actuary, 33, 35, 36, 387
    administrative staff, **30–32**
    Archaeologist, 141, 143
    Architect, 33, 35, 553
    Architectural Technologist, 556
    Barrister/Advocate, 34, 35, 37, 331, 333, 334
    Building Services Engineer/Technician, 583
    cartographic staff, 33, 35, 36
    Catering Manager, 208
    Civil Engineer, 37, 596
    Coastguard Officer, 359, 360
    computing staff, 33, 35, 36
    Dietitian, 287
    Diplomatic Service staff, 33, 35, 36
    Economist, 33, 35, 37, 449, 450
    Engineer/Engineering Technician, 33, 35, 37
    Food Scientist/Technologist, 440
    Forensic Scientist, 460, 461
    forestry staff, 588, 616, 617, 618, 619
    Health and Safety Inspector, 34, 35, 37
    Immigration Service staff, 34, 35, 37
    Information/Press Officer, 34, 35, 37, 424
    Legal Executive, 340
    Librarian, 34, 36, 37, **134–136**
    Linguist, 34, 36, 37
    Materials Scientist/Metallurgist, 445
    Medical Laboratory Scientist, 434, 437, 438
    Meteorologist, 454, 455
    museum staff, 34, 36, 37
    Oceanographer, 457
    Patent Examiner/Officer, 34, 36, 37
    Photographer, 34, 36, 104
    planning support staff, 601
    Plumber, 570
    Probation Officer, 312
    Psychologist, 34, 36, 37, 327
    Publicity Officer, 34, 35, 424
    Research Officer, 34, 36, 37
    Scientist, 34, 36, 37, 434, 436, 437, 445
    Security Guard/Officer, 32, 358
    Social Researcher, 397
    Social Worker, 307
    Solicitor, 335, 336, 337

INDEX

specialist staff, **33–38**
Statistician, 34, 36, 37, 447, 448
support staff, **32–33**
Surveyor, 34, 36, 37, 590, 592
Tax Inspector, 35, 36, 37
Town Planner, 599
Veterinary Surgeon, 621, 622
Claims Clerk (insurance), 381
Claims Official (insurance), 374, **379–381**
Clapper-Loader (films), 189
Classical Ballet Dancer, 162, 164
Classical Musician, 156, 157, 158
Cleaning Services, 32, **230–233**
Clerical and Management (and Administration and Business), **29–92**
Clerk, **61–63**
    Armed Forces, 9, 13, 26
    Bank, 371
    Bank/Building Society, 371
    Barristers'/Advocates', 337–339
    Civil Service, 30
    Insurance, 374, **381–382**
    Local Authority, **40–42**
    Medical Records, **45–47**
    Post Office Counter, 683
    Travel Agency, **197–199**
Clerk Typist, 61
Climbing Instructor, 168
Clinical Chemist, 438
Clinical Coding Clerk (NHS), 45
Clinical Engineering Medical Technical Officer, 289
Clinical Instrumentation Medical Technical Officer, 289
Clinical Psychologist, 326, 327
Cloth Spreader/Cutter, **524–525**
Clothing/Fashion Designer, **98–99**
Clothing Industry, **521–527**
Clothing Presser, **526–527**
Coach
    Sports, **166–169**
    see also Instructor
Coach Courier, 199
Coach Driver, **655–657**
Coastguard Officer, **359–360**
Coating machineman/woman (papermaking), 539
Coffee Shop Service Assistant, 215
College Lecturer, **115–120**, 141, 143, 435, 441, 450, 588, 596
College Librarian, 134
Colouring/Tinting (hair) Technician, 240
Combat Medical Technician (Armed Forces), 20
Comedy Performer, 155
Commando troops, 13
    see also Royal Marines
Commerce and Industry Accountant, **363–364**
Commerce and Industry Economist, 449, 450
Commercial Dental Technician, 267
Commercial horticultural staff, 609, 610
Commercial Property Surveyor, 589
Commercial Theatre Actor, 155
Commis Chef, 210
Commis Waiter, 214
Commissioning Editor (book publishing), 127
Commonwealth War Graves Commission Horticulturist, 611
Communication-Impaired-Children Teacher, 113
Communications Systems Analyst (RAF), 25
Communications Technician, in Armed Forces, 8
Communications/Electronics Engineer (RAF), 22

Community Dance Performer, 164
Community Dental Service staff, 260, 262, 263, 265, 267
Community Dietitian, 286
Community Education Worker, 168, **323–325**
Community Health Care Assistant, 257
Community Interpreter, 145
Community Midwife, 252
Community Nurse, 250, 253–254
Community Orthoptist, 276, 277
Community Pharmacist, 269
Community Pharmacy Technician, 271
Community Physiotherapist, 279
Community Social Worker, 306
Community Theatre Performer, 155
Community (and Youth) Worker, 168, **323–325**
Compaction Plant Operator (building/construction), 577
Company Secretary, 48
Complementary/Alternative Medicine, **295–299**
Composer (music), 156, 158
Computer Aided Transcription (CAT) Writer, 341
Computer Work
    in Armed Forces, 19, 26
    in banks/building societies, 372
    in Civil Service, 33, 35, 36
Concierge (Head Porter in hotel), 221
Concreter, 575
Conductor
    Bus, **657–658**
    Orchestral, 158
Confectionery and Baking, **503–505**
Conference Interpreter, 145
Conjurer, 155
Conservation/Countryside Officer, **641–643**
Conservation and Nature, **641–645**
Conservator/Restorer, **131–133**, 549
Construction (and Building) Trades, **561–574**
Construction and Land Services, **552–601**
Construction Manager, 558, 594
Construction Operative, **575–577**
Construction Plant Operator, **577–578**
Construction Plant Tyre Fitter, 412
Construction Work (other than Building), **575–578**
Consultant
    Actuarial, 387
    Beauty, 234, **236–238**
    Civil Engineer, 596
    Economist, 449, 450
    Employment Agency, **321–322**
    Environmental/Oceanography, 457
    Food Science, 440, 442
    Forensic Science, 460
    Horticultural, 611
    Insurance Broker, 378
    Management, 361, 448, 449, 450
    Materials Science/Metallurgy, 445
    Medical/Surgical (hospital doctor), 247, 248
    Meteorologist, 455
    Public Relations, 423
    Recruitment/Selection, 50
    Travel, **197–199**
Consumer Affairs Adviser, 227
Consumer Protection, **85–86**
Consumer Research Executive, 396
Consumer Research Interviewer, 398
Contemporary Dance Performer, 162, 164
Contract Catering Manager, 208

INDEX

Control Engineer, 462
Control Room Assistant (Ambulance Service), 292, 293
Controller
    Air Traffic, 5, 22, 25, **651–653**
    Production, 493
    Quality, 493, **496–498**
    Retail, 405
Conveyancer, 334–335, 339, 340
Cook: *see* Chef/Cook
Copy Typist, 61
Copy-Editor (book publishing), 127
Copywriter (advertising), **401, 402**
Coremaker/Moulder (foundry), **535–536**
Corporate Finance Adviser, 361, 369
Cosmetics Sales Staff, 236
Costume Designer (films/theatre/TV), 99, 181
Counselling Psychologist, 326, 327
Counter Clerk
    Post Office, 683
    Travel Agency, 197
Counter Service Assistant (catering), **215–217**
Country and Western Dancer, 162
Country and Western Musician, 156
Countryside/Conservation Officer, **641–643**
Countryside Ranger/Warden, **643–645**
Courier, 19, 357
Court Interpreter, 145
Court Reporter, 341
Court Usher/Officer, **343–344**
Couture Dressmaker, 521
Couture (Fashion) Designer, 98
Couture Fashion Model, 431
Craft Baker, 503
Craft-based Designer, 96, 97
Craftsperson
    and Designer, 96
    Engineering, 462, 463
    Foundry, 534–536
    Furniture, 528–532
    Glassmaking, 510
    Heating and Ventilating, 584–586
Crane Operator (building/construction), 577
Cricketer (professional), 170, 172
Criminal Justice Social Worker, 312
Criminological Psychologist, 37, 326, 327
Crop Picker, 611
Crown Prosecution Service staff, 34, 35, 331, 333, 334, 335, 336
Cruise-ship jobs, 164, 236, 239, 240
Cultural Activities, 121–152
Curator, Museum, **129–131**, 143, 452
Current Affairs Programme Researcher, 184
Customer Care Assistant (retail), 407
Customer Service Adviser/Assistant/Manager/Officer
    Bank/Building Society, **371–373**
    fuel/energy industries, 227
    Retail, 405
Cutter, Cloth, **524–525**
Cutterman/woman (papermaking), 539
Cycling Professional, 170, 173
Cytologist, 438

Dance-in-Education Performer, 164
Dance/Movement Therapist, 164
Dance Notator/Reconstructor, 164
Dance Studio Manager, 175
Dance Teacher, 164

Dancer, **162–165**
Darts Player (professional), 171, 173
Data Processing: *see* Computer...; Information Systems...
Database Administrator, **72–74**
Day Excursion Bus/Coach Driver, 656
Deaf-Children Teacher, 113, 114
Deck Officer (Merchant Navy), **673–675**
Deck Rating (Merchant Navy), 678
Decorative Blacksmith, 549
Decorator
    Glassware, 510
    and Painter, **566–567**
Dedicated Day Transport (ambulance) Person, 292
Defence Fire Service Officer, 356
Delicatessen Counter Worker, 410
Delivery Van Driver, 661
Demonstrator, Retail Store, **408–410**
Dental Hygienist, 9, 20, **264–266**
Dental Nurse, **262–264**
Dental Support Specialist (Armed Forces), 20
Dental Surgery Assistant (Armed Forces), 9, 26
    see also Dental Nurse
Dental Technician, 20, 26, **266–268**
Dentist, **260–262**
    in Armed Forces, 6, 16, 23, 260
Dentistry, 260–268
Dentist's Receptionist, 262
Department Manager (retail), 405
Dermatologist (doctor), 247
Derrickman (oil drilling), 478
Design (and Art), 93–106
Design Engineer, 462, 493, 594
Designer
    Architectural/Building, 552, 554, 557
    Clothing/Fashion, 93, **98–99**
    Craft-based, 96, 97
    Glassware, 510
    Graphic, **93–95**
    Industrial, 96, 97
    Interior, 93, **100–101**
    Interior Landscape, 609
    Landscape, 587
    Textile, 93, **99–100**
    Three-Dimensional, 93, **96–98**, 552, 554
    Two-Dimensional, 93
Designer/Craft Worker, 96, 510
Desk Editor (book publishing), 127
Desktop Publishing (DTP) Operator, 541
Detective, 345
    in Armed Forces, 16, 23
Development Engineer, 462, 493
Development Food Scientist/Technologist, 440
Development Metallurgist/Materials Scientist/Technologist, 443
Development Surveyor, 589, 590, 592
Diagnostic Radiographer, 281
Dietitian, **286–288**
Diplomatic Service staff, 33, 35, 36
Direct Selling (insurance) Representative, 378
Director (films/radio/TV), 181
Director of Photography (films), 189
Disco Dancer, 162
Dispenser: *see* Pharmacy Technician
Dispensing Optician, 273, **274–276**
Display Designer, 100
Display Person (retail), **419–421**
District Nurse, **253–254**

INDEX

Diver, **685–687**
    Police Underwater Search, 345, 685, 686, 687
    Royal Navy, 5, 7, 8, 685, 686, 687
Diving, **685–687**
Diving Instructor, 685, 686
Doctor
    in Armed Forces, 6, 16, 23, 247, 248
    General Practitioner, **245–247**
    Homoeopathic, 297
    Hospital, **247–249**
Documentary Researcher (film/TV), 184
Dog Groomer, **631–632**
Dog Handler, 26, 345, 357
Dog Trainer, **628–629**
Domestic Appliance Service Engineer, **485–487**
Domestic Services Manager, 208
Door-to-door Retail Van Sales Driver, 661
Doorman/woman (hotel), 221
Double Glazing Fitter, 565
Drain Laying Operative, 575
Dramatic Arts, 153–156
Draughtsman/Woman, 19
Dressmaker, **521–522**
Driller, Oil/Gas Well, 478
Driver
    in Armed Forces, 13, 19, 25
    Bus/Coach, **655–657**
    Car/Van, **661–662**
    in Civil Service, 32
    Construction Plant, 577
    Farm Vehicle, 604
    Large Goods Vehicle, **659–660**
    Post Office/Royal Mail/Parcelforce Van/Lorry, 662
    Refuse Collection Vehicle, 231
    Security Van, 357, 358, 661
    Taxi/Private Hire Vehicle, **658–659**
    Train, **666–667**
Driving Instructor, **662–665**
Driving Standards Agency Examiner, 664
Dryerman/woman (papermaking), 539
Dual Certificate Officer (Merchant Navy), **676–677**
Dubbing Mixer (films/TV), 193
Dumper Truck Driver, 577
Dustbin Collector, 231–233
Dyehouse Operative, 519
Dyeing Technician (textiles), 516

Earth Sciences, **452–458**
Earth-moving Plant Operator, 577
ECG (electrocardiography) Medical Technical Officer, 290
Economist, 33, 35, 37, **449–451**
    Home Economist, **227–229**
Editor, **127–128**
    Book, 127
    Newspaper/Magazine, 127
    Picture (film/TV/video), 181, 189
    Sound (film/radio/TV), 181, 193
Editorial Manager/Director, 127
Editorial Photographer, 102
Education: *see* Lecturer; Teacher
Educational Dance Performer, 164
Educational Officer (Armed Forces), 16, 23
Educational Psychologist, 326, 327
Educational Theatre Performer, 155
EEG (electroencephalography) Medical Technical Officer, 290
Effluent Operative (paper manufacture), 539

Electrical Engineer, 16, 37, 462
Electrical Fitter, 462, 481
Electrical and Mechanical Servicing, **481–487**
Electrician, **472–474**
    Motor Vehicle, 19, 467, 472
    Railway, **671–672**
Electricity Power Generation/Supply Electrician, 472
Electronic Warfare Operator Mechanic (RN), 8
Electronics Engineer, 16, 37, 462
Electronics Fitter, 481
Embalmer, **242–244**
Employee Services Manager/Officer, 50
Employment Agency Consultant/Interviewer, **321–322**
Employment Assistant (Careers Assistant), 319
Engineer, **462–466**
    Aeronautical, 16, 462
    Aerosystems, 22
    Agricultural, 462
    Aircraft Maintenance, **649–651**
    in Armed Forces, 5, 15, 16
    Avionics, 649
    Building Services, **582–584**
    Business Equipment Service, **483–485**
    Chartered, 462, 463, 464, 465, 582, 583, 594, 595
    Chemical, 462, 465
    Civil, 37, 462, **594–597**
    in Civil Service, 33, 35, 37
    Communications, 22
    Computer Network, **70–72**
    Control, 462
    Design, 462, 493, 594
    Development, 462, 493
    Domestic Appliance/Gas Service, **485–487**
    Electrical/Electronics, 22, 37, 462
    Highway, 37, 594
    Incorporated, 462, 463, 464, 465, 582, 583, 594, 595
    Information Systems, 462
    Manufacturing, 443, 462, 493
    Marine, 462
    Materials, 462
    Mechanical, 16, 462, 649
    Mining, 462
    Municipal, 594
    Nuclear, 462
    Production, 462
    Research, 462, 493
    Software, **68–70**
    Structural, 462, 594
    System, 462
    Telecoms, 475
    Traffic, 594
    Water, 594
Engineering, **462–492**
Engineering Blacksmith, 549
Engineering Craftsman/woman, 462, 463
Engineering Geologist, 452
Engineering Officer
    Armed Forces, 5, 15, 16
    Merchant Navy, **675–676**
Engineering Operator, 462, 463–464
Engineering Surveyor (insurance), 382
Engineering Technician, 462, 463, 464, 465, 582, 583, 594, 595
    in Armed Forces, 8, 25
    in Civil Service, 33, 35, 37
Engine-Room Rating (Merchant Navy), 678
England and Wales

INDEX

Accountant, 362
Barrister, 331, 332, 333
College Lecturer, 116, 117, 119
Countryside/Conservation Officer/Warden, 641, 643, 644
Court Usher, 343
Craft Baker, 504
Environmental Health Officer, 87, 88
Firefighter/Fire Officer, 354, 355
Forensic Scientist, 459–460, 461
Health Service Manager, 44
Legal Executive, **339–341**
Nursery Nurse, 315
Orthotist/Prosthetist, 301
Physiotherapist, 279
Police Constable, 345, 346
Print Finisher/Bookbinder, 545
Prison staff, 349, 350, 351, 352
Probation Officer, 312
School Teacher, **107–110**, 160
Shorthand Writer/Reporter (legal), 341, 342, 343
Solicitor, 335, 336
Special Educational Needs Teacher, 114
Youth/Community Worker, 168, 324
see also under job titles (when there are no specific regional requirements)
English (as Foreign/Second Language) Teacher, 16, **149–152**
Entertainment and Leisure, 153–203
Environmental Health Officer, **87–89**
Environmental Health Technician, 20, 26
Environmental horticultural staff, 609
Environmental Scientist, 434, 452
Equestrian Rider, 171, 173
Equity Salesperson, **390–391**
Estate Agency Surveyor, 589–590
Estate Manager, 589
Estates Officer (Armed Forces), 23
Estimator, Building, 557, 590
Eurostar Customer Services Team Member, 667
Eurostar Train Driver, 666
Excavator Operator (construction industry), 577
Executive Officer (Civil Service), 30
Executive Research Interviewer, 398
Executive Search/Selection Consultant, 321
Executive Secretary, **55–56**
Executry Practitioner (legal), 334, 339, 340
Exhaust/Tyre Fitter, **412–413**
Exhibition Designer, 100
Exhibition Display Person, 419
Export Clerk, 61
Export Marketing Manager, 394
Express Bus/Coach Driver, 655–656

Fabrication Engineering, 488–492, 549
Fabricator/Plater (heavy engineering), **488–490**
Factory Inspector, 91
   see also Health and Safety Inspector
Falsework Scaffolder, 571–572
Family Court Welfare Officer, 312
Family Doctor (GP), 245–247
Farm Manager, **602–604**
Farm Secretary, 57, 58, 59
Farm Shop Sales Assistant, 611
Farm Work, 602–608
Farm Worker, **604–605**
Farrier, 549
Fashion/Clothing Designer, **98–99**

Fashion Model, **431–433**
Fashion Photographer, 102
Fast-Food Outlet Cook, 210
Fast-Food Outlet Food Service Assistant, 214
Fast-Food Outlet Manager, 206
Fast-Food Van Sales Driver, 661
Features Editor (newspapers), 127
Felt-Roofer, 571
Fettler (foundry), 533
Fibre Recovery Attendant (paper manufacture), 539
Fibrous Plasterer, 567
Field Archaeologist, 141
Field Service Engineer, 481
   Business Equipment, 483
   Domestic Appliance, 485
   Gas Appliance, 485
Field Social Worker, **306–308**
Fighter Controller (Armed Forces), 5, 22
Filing Clerk, 45, 61
Film Actor, 155, 685
Film Assistant Director, 181, **186–189**
Film Cameraman/woman, 181, 189, 685
Film Director, 181
Film Editor, 189
Film Producer, 181
Film Production Coordinator/Manager, 181, 182
Film Researcher, 181, 184
Film Scenery/Set Designer, 181
Film Sound Recordist, 181, 192–193
Film/Theatre/Broadcasting, 181–195
Finance and Related Work, 361–393
Financial Accountant, 361, 363
Financial Administrator (Chartered Secretary), 48
Financial Adviser, 361, 374, **378–379**
Financial Manager (NHS), 43
Finisher
   Furniture, 531
   Glassmaking, 510
   Manufacturing/Production, 498
   Printing, **544–546**
Firefighter/Fire Officer, 26, **354–356**, 618
Fire-and-Perils (insurance) Surveyor, 382
Fish Farm Worker, 606
Fish Farmer, **605–608**
Fitness (and Health) Instructor, 166, 167–168
Fitter
   Electrical, 462, 481
   Heating and Ventilating, **584–586**
   Maintenance, **481–483**
   Mechanical, 19, 462
   Railway, **671–672**
   Shop, 562
   Tyre/Exhaust, **412–413**
Fleet Air Arm
   Diver, 685, 687
   Naval Airman, 9
   Pilot, 5
Flight Engineer, 649, 651
Flight Operations Officer (RAF), 22
Floor Layer, **563–565**, 567
Floor Manager (TV), 181, **186–189**
Floor/Wall Tiler, **573–574**
Florist, **417–419**
Focus Puller (films), 189
Folk Dancer, 162
Folk Musician, 156

INDEX

Food Scientist/Technologist/Technician, 434, **439–442**
Food Service Assistant, **213–215**
Footballer (professional), 169–170, 172
Forecourt Attendant, **413–415**
Forensic Photographer, 102
Forensic Psychologist, 326, 327
Forensic Scientist, **459–461**
Forensic Social Worker, 307
Forest Officer/Manager, 569, **616–618**
Forest Worker/Ranger, **618–620**
Forestry, 616–620
Forestry Commission staff, 588, 616, 617, 618, 619
Formwork Construction Operative, 575
Formwork Joiner, 562
Formwork Scaffolder, 571–572
Foundry Coremaker/Moulder, **535–536**
Foundry Industry, 533–536
Foundry Patternmaker, **534–535**
Foundry Worker, **533–534**
Franchise operator, 2, 240, 664
Fraud Squad Police Officer, 345
Freelance...: *see individual jobs*
French Polisher, **531–532**
Fringe Theatre Actor, 155
Fund Manager, **391–393**
Funeral Director, **242–244**
Furnace Operator (foundry), 533
Furniture Crafts, 528–532
Further-Education Lecturer, **115–118**

Gaelic-speaking Camera/Sound Operator/Technician, 191
Gaelic-speaking Teacher, 112
Garden Centre Manager, 610
Garden Centre Sales Assistant, 611
Gardener, 611
Gas Industry Plumber, 569, 570
Gas and Oil Production and Drilling, 478–480
Gas and Oil Production staff, 479
Gas Service Engineer, **485–487**
Gastroenterology Medical Technical Officer, 290
General Assistant (retail), 407
General Practice Dental Hygienist, 265
General Practice Dental Nurse, 262
General Practice Dental Technician, 267
General Practice Dentist, 260
General Practice Manager, 59
General Practice Photographer, 102
General Practice Receptionist, 64–65
General Practice Surveyor, 589–590, 592
General Practice Veterinary Surgeon, 621, 622
General Practitioner (GP/Family Doctor), **245–247**
Geochemist, 452
Geologist, **452–454**, 456
Geophysicist, 452, 456
Geriatrician (doctor), 247
Glass Bender, 510
Glassblower, 510
Glasshouse Worker, 611
Glassmaker Craftsman/woman, **510–512**
Glassware Decorator, 510
Glazier, **565–566**
Golf Professional, 167, 170, 173
Goods-In Checker, 680
Government Actuary's Department staff, 33, 35, 36, 387
Government Departments: *see* Civil Service
Government Economic Service staff, 33, 35, 449, 450

Government Information Service staff, 34, 35, 424
Government Legal Service staff, 34, 35–36, 37, 333
Government Statistical Service staff, 447, 448
Governor, Prison, **349–351**
Grams Operator (TV sound), 193
Graphic Designer, **93–95**
Greyhound Kennel Worker, 630
Grinder (foundry), 533
Groom (horse), **632–635**
Groomer (dog), **631–632**
Groundsman/woman, **614–615**
Guide Dog Mobility Instructor, **628–629**
Guide Dog Trainer, **628–629**
Guide Dogs for the Blind Association
    Instructor/Trainer, **628–629**
    Kennel Worker, 629
Gun Fitter (Armed Forces), 19
Gunner (Armed Forces), 19
Gymnasium Manager, 175
Gynaecologist (doctor), 248

Haematologist, 438
Hairdresser, **239–241**
Halal Butcher, 416
Hall Porter (hotel), 221
Handicapped-Children Teacher, 113
Harvest Worker, 611
Hat Designer, 98
Head Chef, 210
Head Porter (hotel), 221
Head Waiter, 214
Health Care Assistant, 20, **256–259**
Health and Fitness Instructor, 166, 167–168
Health and Medical Services, 245–305
Health Psychologist, 326
Health Receptionist, 45
Health and Safety, 87–92
    Adviser, **89–91**
    Inspector, 34, 35, 37, **91–92**
Health Service Management, 43–47
Health Service Manager, **43–45**
Health Visitor, **254–255**
Hearing-Impaired-Children Teacher, 113, 114
Heating and Ventilating Fitter/Welder, **584–586**
Heavy-Industry Metal Fabricator/Plater, 488–490
Heavy-Vehicle Driver, 659
Heavy-Vehicle Driving Instructor, 662
Heavy-Vehicle Mechanic, 467
Heavy-Vehicle Tyre/Exhaust Fitter, 412
Heavy-Weapons Officer/Specialist (RM), 11, 13
Helicopter Pilot (Armed Forces), 5, 11, 15, 22
Help Desk Operator (IT), **78–80**
Herbalist, **295**, **297**
HGV: *see* Heavy-Vehicle...; Large Goods Vehicle...
High Street Bank staff, 368
Higher-Education Lecturer, **118–120**, 141, 143, 260, 287, 441, 450, 588
Highway Engineer, 37, 594
Histopathologist, 248, 438
Historic Buildings Inspector, 141, 143
Holiday Tour Coach Driver, 656
Holiday Tour Manager, **200–201**
Home Care Organizer, 227
Home Economist, **227–229**
Homoeopath, **295–296**, **297**
Horse Groom, **632–635**

INDEX

Horse Racing Jockey, 171, 173
Horse Riding Instructor, **635–638**
Horticultural Manager, **609–611**
Horticultural Therapist, 609, 611
Horticultural Worker, **611–613**
Horticulture, **609–613**
Hospital Catering Manager, 208
Hospital Cook, 210
Hospital Dental Service staff, 260, 263, 265, 267
Hospital Dietitian, 286
Hospital Doctor, **247–249**
Hospital Domestic Services Manager, 208
Hospital Eye Service staff, 274, 276, 277
Hospital Health Care Assistant/Nursing Auxilary, 256, 257
Hospital Manager, 43–45
Hospital Medical Records Clerk, 45–47
Hospital Midwife, 252
Hospital Nurse, 250
Hospital Operating Department Practitioner, 303–305
Hospital Pharmacist, 269
Hospital Pharmacy Technician, 271
Hospital Physiotherapist, 279
Hospital Porter, **302–303**
Hospitality, Catering and Other Services, **204–244**
Hotel Manager, **204–206**
Hotel Porter, **221–222**
Hotel Receptionist, **217–219**
Hotel Reservations Clerk, 61
Hotel Restaurant Manager, 206
Hotel Room Attendant, **219–220**
Hotel Services Manager (NHS), 43
House Model, 431
House Officer (hospital doctor), 247
Household Cavalry Officer/Soldier, 15, 19
Housekeeper/Housekeeping Manager, **208–210**
Housing Officer/Manager, **579–581**
Human Resources, **50–54**
    Clerk, 19, 26, 61
    Manager/Officer, 43, **50–52**
Hunt Kennel Worker, 629, 630
Hunt Stable Groom, 634
Hydrogeologist, 452
Hydrographic Surveyor, 5
Hygienist, Dental, 9, 20, **264–266**

Ice Dancer, 164
Illustrator/Artist, 13, 93, **95–96**
Immigration Service staff, 34, 35, 37
Immunologist, 438
Incorporated Engineer, 462, 463, 464, 465, 582, 583, 594, 595
Independent Financial Adviser, 378
Independent School Teacher, 108, 112
Indexer (of books), 127
Industrial Dentist, 260
Industrial Designer, 96, 97
Industrial Dietitian, 287
Industrial Pharmacist, 269
Industrial Pharmacy Technician, 271
Industrial Photographer, 102
Industrial Physiotherapist, 279
Industrial Relations Manager/Officer, 50
Industrial Research Executive, 396
Industry and Commerce Accountant, **363–364**
Industry and Commerce Economist, 449, 450
Infant School Teacher, 107, 111, 159
Infantry Officer/Soldier, 15

Information Assistant, **136–138**
Information and Library Work, **134–140**
Information Manager/Librarian, 34, 36, 37, **134–136**
Information Officer (Civil Service), 34, 35, 37
Information Scientist, **138–140**
Information Systems Engineer, 462
Information Technology (IT), **66–80**
    Adviser, 361
    Database Administrator, **72–74**
    Help Desk Operator, **78–80**
    Multimedia Specialist, **76–78**
    Network Engineer, **70–72**
    Software Engineer/Analyst Programmer, **68–70**
    Specialist (in commerce/industry/public sector), 43
    Systems Analyst/Designer, **66–68**
    Systems Integrator, **66–68**
    Webmaster, **74–76**
Innkeeper: *see* Publican/Licensee
Inshore Diver, 685, 686, 687
Insolvency Administrator, 361
Inspection Winderman/woman (papermaking), 539
Inspector
    Health & Safety, 34, 35, 37, **91–92**
    Insurance Claims, 380
    Insurance (sales), 378
    Tax, 35, 36, 37
Installation Building Services Technician, 582
Installation Electrician, 472
Installation Plumber, 568
Instant Muscle, advice from, 3, 4
Institute/Business Administration, **48–49**
Institutional Investment Analyst, 389, 391, 392
In-store Baker, 410, 503
Instructor
    Diving, 685, 686
    Driving, **662–665**
    Health and Fitness, 166
    Horse Riding, **635–638**
    Outdoor Pursuits, 168
    Physical Education/Training, 11, 13, 16, 23, 26
    Sports, **166–169**
Instrument Fitter/Technician, 19, 481
Insurance Actuary, 374, 387
Insurance Broker, 374, **376–378**
Insurance Claims Official, 374, **379–381**
Insurance Clerk, 374, **381–382**
Insurance Loss Adjuster, 374, **383–384**
Insurance Salesman/woman, 378
Insurance Surveyor, 374, **382–383**
Insurance Underwriter, **374–376**
Insurance Work, **374–386**
Intelligence (Armed Forces) work, 11, 15, 22, 25
Interior Designer, 93, **100–101**
Interior Landscape Designer, 609
Internal Auditor (Accountant), 363
Internet Webmaster, 74–76
Interpreter, **145–147**
Interviewer
    Employment Agency, **321–322**
    Market Research, **397–399**
Investment Adviser, 369, 389, 390
Investment Analyst, 389, **391–393**
Investment Banker, 369, 371
Invoicing Clerk, 61
Ireland, Accountant, 362

INDEX

Jazz Musician, 156, 158
JCB Operator, 577
Jockey, 171, 173
Joiner/Carpenter, 19, **562–563**
Journalism and Technical Writing, 121–126
Journalist, **121–124**, 611
    and Photographer, 102
Judge (legal), 334
Juggler, 155
Junior School Teacher, 107–108, 111, 159
Justice's Clerk, 334

Keep Fit Instructor, 166, 168, 178
Keeper
    Art Gallery, **129–131**
    Zoo, **638–640**
Kennel Worker, 20, **629–631**
Kerb Laying Operative, 575
Key Grip (films), 189
Keyboard Operator (printing industry), 541
Kitchen Assistant, **212–213**
Knitting Operative, 519
Knitwear Designer, 98
Knock-Out Operator (foundry), 533
Kosher Butcher, 416

Laboratory Technician, 20, 26, 434, 539
Land (and Construction) Services, 552–601
Land Management (and Surveying), 589–593
Landing Craft Officer/Specialist (RM), 11, 13
Landscape Architect/Designer, **587–588**
Language Teacher, 16, **149–152**
Language/Speech Therapist, **283–284**
Languages, 145–152
Large Goods Vehicle (LGV) Driver, **659–660**, 683
Large Goods Vehicle (LGV) Driving Instructor, 662, 663, 664
Large Goods Vehicle (LGV) Mechanic, 467
Large Goods Vehicle (LGV) Tyre/Exhaust Fitter, 412
Laser Medical Technical Officer, 289
Lathe Operator (glassmaking), 510
Law and Related Work, 331–344
Lawyer, 331–337
    in Civil Service, 34, 35–36, 37, 331, 333, 334, 335, 336, 337
    see also Advocate; Barrister; Solicitor
Learning Disability Nurse, 250
Learning-Difficulty-Children Teacher, 113, 114
Leather Technologist, **513–515**
Lecturer
    Further-Education/Tertiary-College, **115–118**, 435, 441, 450
    Higher-Education, **118–120**, 141, 143, 260, 287, 441, 450, 588, 621
Legal Adviser (Chartered Secretary), 48
Legal Assistant (Scotland), 339, 340
Legal Executive, **339–341**
Legal Officer (Armed Forces), 16, 23
Legal Psychologist, 326, 327
Legal Secretary, 57, 58, 59
Leisure (and Entertainment), 153–203
Leisure (and Sports), 166–180
Leisure/Sports Centre Assistant, **178–180**
Leisure/Sports Centre Manager, **175–178**
Lending Account Manager (banking), 369
LGV: *see* Large Goods Vehicle...
Liability-and-Accident (insurance) Surveyor, 382
Liaison Interpreter, 145
Librarian/Information Manager, 34, 36, 37, **134–136**

Library/Information Assistant, **136–138**
Library and Information Work, 134–140
Licensed Retailing, 223–226
Licensee/Publican, **223–224**
Life Assurance Actuary, 387
Life (assurance sales) Inspector, 378
Lift Truck Operator, 533, 681
Light-Industry Assembler, 493, 498, **500–501**
Light-Industry Sheet Metal Worker, 488–490
Light-Vehicle Delivery Driver, 661
Light-Vehicle Mechanic, 467
Light-Vehicle Tyre/Exhaust Fitter, 412
Lighting Cameraman/woman (films), 189
Lighting Designer/Technician (concerts/theatre), 181, 190
Lingerie Designer, 98
Linguist, 15, 34, 36, 37
    and Secretary, 57, 58, 59
Linoleum (floor-covering) Layer, 563
Livery Stable Groom, 634
Livestock Farm Worker, 604
Lloyd's Broker, 376, 377
Lloyd's Underwriter, 374–375, 376
Loans Officer (banking), 372
Local Enterprise Agencies/Trusts, advice from, 2
Local Government, 39–42
    Accountant, 364, 365, 366
    Administrator, **39–40**
    Archaeologist, 141, 143
    Architect, 553
    Architectural Technologist, 556
    Barrister/Advocate, 333
    Building Services Engineer/Technician, 583
    Care Assistant, 311
    Catering Manager, 208
    Civil Engineer, 596
    Clerical/Administrative Assistant, **40–42**
    Economist, 450
    Environmental Health Officer, **87–88**
    Firefighter, 354–355
    Groundsman/woman, 615
    horticultural staff, 609, 610, 612
    Housing Officer/Manager, 579, 580
    Landscape Architect, 588
    Legal Executive, 340
    Librarian/Information Manager, **134–136**
    Library/Information Assistant, **136–138**
    Occupational Therapist, 283
    Parking Attendant, 347, 348
    planning support staff, 601
    Plumber, 570
    Psychologist, 327
    Public Relations Officer, 424
    Security Guard/Officer, 358
    Social Researcher, 397
    Social Worker, 306, 307, 308, 309
    Solicitor, 335, 336, 337
    Surveyor, 590, 592
    Tourist Information Centre Assistant, **196–197**
    Town Planner, 599
    Trading Standards Officer, **85–86**, 227
    Veterinary Surgeon, 622–623
    Youth/Community Worker, 324
Long-Distance Bus/Coach Driver, 655–656
Lorry Driver, 659–660
Loss Adjuster (insurance), 374, **383–384**
Luggage Porter, 221

INDEX

Macer/Court Officer, **343–344**
Machine Operator
    Bakery, 503
    Engineering, 462
    Farming, 604
    Foundry, 533
    Papermaking, 539
    Plastics Processing, 537
    Printing, **543–544**
    Production, 498
    Sewing, **525–526**
Magazine Editor, 127
Magazine Journalist, 121
Magazine Model, 431
Magistrates' Court Service staff, 334, 336, 344
Mail Order Catalogue Model, 431
Maintenance Electrician, 472
Maintenance Fitter, **481–483**
Maintenance/repair
    aircraft, 8, 25
    in Armed Forces, 8, 13, 19, 25, 482
    electrical and mechanical servicing, 472, 481–487
    motor vehicle, 13, 19, 25, 467
    plastering, 567
    plumbing, 568–569
    shoes, 421–422
    telecoms, 475
Maitre Chef de Cuisine (Executive Chef), 210
Make-up Person, 234
Management Accountant, 361, 363
Management (and Administration, Business and Clerical), 29–92
Management Consultant, 361, 448, 449, 450
Management Services, 81–84, 435
Manager's Assistant (banking), 372
Manicurist, 234
Manufacturing Engineer, 443, 462, 493
Manufacturing Industries, 493–551
Marine Biologist, 456, 685
Marine Chemist, 456, 685
Marine Engineer, 462
Marine Engineer Officer (RN), 5
Marine Engineering Fitter/Mechanic (Armed Forces), 8, 19
Marine Geographer/Geologist, 456, 685
Marine Physicist, 456
Marine Plumber, 569
Marine Resource Management Surveyor, 589, 590
Marine Scientist, 456, 685, 686
Marines: *see* Royal Marines (RM)
Market Maker/Trader (Stock Exchange), **389–390**
Market Research Executive, **396–397**
Market Research Interviewer, **397–399**
Marketing Manager, **394–396**
Marketing Work, 394–399
Massage Therapist, 234
Mastic Asphalter, 571
Materials Engineer, 442, 462
Materials Handling and Delivery, 680–682
Materials Scientist/Technologist, 434, **442–445**
Mathematician, 434
Mathematics, Sciences and Related Work, 434–461
Maxillo-facial Surgeon, 260
Meat Hygiene Service staff, 622, 623
Meat Industry, 506–507
Meat Inspector, 416, 507
Meat Process Worker, **506–507**
Mechanic
    Aircraft (Armed Forces), 19, 25
    Marine Engineering (Armed Forces), 8, 19
    Motor Vehicle, 13, 19, 25
Mechanical and Electrical Servicing, 481–487
Mechanical Engineer, 16, 462, 649
Mechanical Fitter, 19, 462
Media Executive (Advertising), **400–401**, **402**
Medical Assistant (Armed Forces), 9, 26
Medical Employment Agency Interviewer, 321
Medical (and Health) Services, 245–305
Medical Herbalist, 295, 297
Medical Illustrator, 95
Medical Laboratory Assistant (MLA), 438
Medical Laboratory Scientific Officer (MLSO), 434, 437, 438, 439
Medical Officer (Armed Forces), 6, 16, 23, 247, 248
Medical Photographer, 102, 103
Medical Physics Technologist, 289
Medical Receptionist, 64–65
Medical Records Clerk, **45–47**
Medical Secretary, 56, 57, 58, 59
Medical Technical Officer (MTO), **289–291**
Medical Technician (Armed Forces), 9, 20, 291, 434
Medicine and Surgery, 245–249
Mental Health Nurse, 20, 26, 250
Mental Health Officer (Social Worker), 307
Merchandiser (van driver), 661
Merchant Banker, 369
Merchant Navy, 673–679
    Deck Officer, **673–675**
    Dual Certificate Officer, **676–677**
    Engineering Officer, **675–676**
    Rating, **677–679**
Messenger (Civil Service/legal), 32, 337
Metal Worker, 488–490
Metallurgist, 434, **439–442**
Metalsmith (in Armed Forces), 19
    see also Blacksmith
Meteorologist, 19, **454–455**
Microbiologist, 434, 437
Midwife, **252–253**
Military Bandsman/Musician, 13, 20, 26, 157, 158, 159
Military Policeman/woman, 16, 19, 23, 26
Mime Artiste, 155
Mine Warfare and Clearance Diving Officer (RN), 5, 685
Mine Warfare Operator Mechanic (RN), 8
Minerals Surveyor, 589, 590, 592
Mining Engineer, 462
Mobile Security Officer, 357, 358
Mobility Instructor (guide dog), **628–629**
Model, Fashion/Photographic, **431–433**
Motor Mechanic, 13, 19, 25, **467–469**
Motor Sports Professional, 171, 173
Motorcycle Mechanic/Technician, 467
Moulder/Coremaker (foundry), **535–536**
Mountain Leader, 11, 13, 167
Mountaineering Instructor, 168
Mounted Policeman/woman, 345
Movement/Dance Therapist, 164
Movements Controller/Officer/Operator (Armed Forces), 16, 19, 22, 26
Multilingual Secretary, 57, 58, 59
Multimedia Specialist (IT), **76–78**
Municipal Engineer, 594
Museum Archaeologist, 141, 143
Museum and Art Gallery Work, 34, 36, 37, **129–133**

699

INDEX

Museum Curator, **129–131**, 143, 452
Music Teacher, 111, **159–162**
Musical Theatre Performer, 155, 158, 164
Musician, **156–159**
    in Armed Forces, 13, 20, 26, 157, 158, 159

Nanny, 316
National Audit Office Accountant, 365, 366
National Canine Defence League (NCDL) Kennel Worker, 630
National Health Service (NHS)
    Accountant/Financial Manager, 43, 364, 365
    Alternative/Complementary Medicine Practitioner, 298
    Ambulance Person, 294
    Catering Manager, 208
    Chiropodist, 285–286
    Clerk, 45–47
    dental staff, 262, 263, 265, 267
    Dentist, 262
    Dietitian, 286–287
    Doctor, 247–249
    Health Care Assistant, 258
    Hospital Porter, 303
    Hotel Services Manager, 43
    Human Resources Manager, 43
    Librarian, 134
    Manager, 43–45
    Medical Laboratory Scientific Officer, 434, 436, 437, 438, 439
    Medical Records Clerk, 45–47
    Medical Technical Officer, 291
    Midwife, 253
    Nurse, 251, 253–254
    Occupational Therapist, 283
    Operating Department Practitioner, 304
    Optometrist, 274
    Orthoptist, 277
    Orthotist/Prosthetist, 301
    Pharmacist, 269, 270
    Pharmacy Technician, 272
    Physiotherapist, 279, 280
    Plumber, 570
    Psychologist, 327
    Purchasing/Supply Manager, 43
    Radiographer, 281–282
    Speech/Language Therapist, 284
    Volunteer Manager, 329
National Hunt Jockey, 171
National Trust
    Archaeologist, 141, 143
    Conservation Officer, 642
    Conservator/Restorer, 132
    Countryside Warden, 643
    horticultural staff, 609
Nature (and Animals and Plants), **602–645**
Nature Conservation, 618, **641–645**
Naturopath, **296**, **297**, **298**
Nautical Archaeologist, 685, 686
Naval Airman, 9
Naval Chaplain, 6
Naval Service, **5–14**
Naval Stores Supply Officer, 6
Navigator (Armed Forces/Merchant Navy), 22, 673
Navy: *see* Merchant Navy; Royal Navy
Navy Personal and Family Service Social Worker, 307
Network Engineer, **70–72**
Neurologist (doctor), 247
Neurophysiology Medical Technical Officer, 290

Neurosurgeon, 247
Newspaper Editor, 127
Newspaper Journalist/Reporter, 121
Newspaper Photographer, 102, 103
Night-Club/Cabaret Performer, 155, 158, 164
Non-Commissioned Officer (NCO - in Armed Forces), 19–21
Northern Ireland
    Audit Office Accountant, 365
    Environmental Health Officer, 87
    Health Service Manager, 44
    Police Constable, 346
Notator/Reconstructor (dance), 164
NSPCC Social Worker, 306, 307
Nuclear Engineer, 462
Nuclear Medicine Medical Technical Officer, 289
Nurse
    in Armed Forces, 6, 16, 20, 23, 26, 251
    Community, 250–252, 253–254
    Dental, **262–264**
    District, **253–254**
    Hospital, 250–252
    Nursery, **315–317**
    Occupational Health, **255–256**
    in Prison Service, 251
    Registered, **250–252**
    Veterinary, 621, **623–625**
Nursery Nurse, **315–317**
Nursery Teacher, 107, 111, 159
Nursery Worker (Horticultural), 611, 618
Nursing Auxiliary, **256–259**
Nursing and Auxiliary Work, **250–259**
Nursing Employment Agency Interviewer, 321
Nutritionist, 286, 287

Obstetrician (doctor), 248
Occupational Dental Hygienist, 265
Occupational Health Nurse, **255–256**
Occupational Physiotherapist, 279
Occupational Psychologist, 326, 327
Occupational Therapist, **282–283**
Oceanographer, **456–458**
Office Manager, 48
Office Work, **29–92**
Offshore Diver, 685, 686, 687
Offshore Oil/Gas Drilling/Production Worker, 478
Oil Exploration/Production Geologist, 452
Oil and Gas Production and Drilling, **478–480**
Oil and Gas Production staff, 479
Oncologist (doctor), 248
Opera Dancer, 164
Opera Singer, 156, 158
Operating Department Practitioner, **303–305**
Operating Theatre Technician (Armed Forces), 20
Operational Researcher, **81–82**
Operator Mechanic (RN), 8
Ophthalmic Optician, **273–274**
Ophthalmics, **273–278**
Optician
    Dispensing, 273, **274–276**
    Ophthalmic, **273–274**
Optometrist, **273–274**
Oral Surgeon, 260
Orchestral Musician, 156, 158
Order Picker/Assembler, 680
Ordnance Survey staff, 33
Organist, 158

INDEX

Organization and Methods (O&M) Officer, **83–84**
Originator (printing industry), **541–543**
Orthodontist, 260
Orthopaedic Surgeon, 247
Orthoptist, 273, **276–278**
Orthotist, **300–301**
Osteopath, **296**, **297**, **298**
Outdoor Pursuits Instructor, 168
Outerwear Designer, 98
Outpatient Nursing Auxiliary, 257
Outpatient Receptionist, 45
Outside Broadcast (TV) staff, 190, 193
Overhead Line/Track Worker (railways), **668–670**
Overseas Development Administration (ODA) opportunities, 119, 151, 455, 553, 611, 623

Packer (Production/Warehouse), 493, 498, **501–502**, 680
Paediatrician (children's doctor), 247
Painter, 469, **566–567**
　　see also Artist
Pantomine Performer, 155, 164
Paper Manufacturing Worker, **539–540**
Paper Technologist, 442
Paper Tester, 539
Parachute Regiment Soldier, 19
Paramedic, 292, 293
　　in Armed Forces, 9, 20
Parcelforce staff, 683, 684
Parking Attendant, 347, 348
Passenger Carrying Vehicle (PCV) Driver, 656
Passenger Carrying Vehicle (PCV) Driving Instructor, 662, 663, 664
Passenger Carrying Vehicle (PCV) Tyre/Exhaust Fitter, 412
Patent Examiner/Officer, 34, 36, 37
Pathologist, 248
Pattern Cutter/Grader (clothing), **522–524**
Pattern Maker (foundry), **534–535**
Paving Slab Laying Operative, 575
Pay Office Clerk, 61
Pay Officer (Armed Forces), 6, 16, 22–23
PCV: *see* Bus...; Coach...; Passenger Carrying Vehicle...
PE: *see* Physical Education/Training...
Pedicurist, 234
People's Dispensary for Sick Animals (PDSA) staff, 623, 624
Performing Arts, **153–165**
Perming Technician, 240
Personal Assistant/Secretary, 6, 32, **55–56**, 181
Personnel/Human Resources Clerk, 19, 26, 61
Personnel/Human Resources Manager/Officer, **50–52**
　　in Armed Forces, 6, 11, 16, 23
　　in NHS, 43
Petrol Pump Attendant, 413
Petroleum Operator (Armed Forces), 19
Pharmacist, **269–271**
Pharmacy Technician, 20, **271–272**
Pharmacy Work, **269–272**
Phlebotomist, 438
Photocopier Operator, 32
Photographer, 25, 34, 36, **102–105**
Photographic interpretation staff (Armed Forces), 13, 15, 22, 25
Photographic Model, 431
Photographic Technician, 102, **105–106**
Photography, **102–106**
Photography Director (films), 189
Photo-journalist, 102
Physical Education/Training Instructor/Teacher, 11, 13, 16, 23, 26, 111, 168
Physical Metallurgist, 443
Physician (doctor), 247
Physicist, 434, 456
Physiological Measurement Technician/Technologist, 20, 289–290, 291
Physiotherapist, 20, **279–280**
Phytotherapist, 295
Pianist, 156, 158
Picture Editor
　　Books/Magazines/Newspapers, 127
　　Films/TV, 181
Piling Operative, 575
Pilot
　　Airline (Civil Aviation), **646–647**
　　Armed Forces, 5, 11, 15, 22
Pipe Laying Operative, 575
Planner
　　Building, 557–558
　　Printing, 541
　　Production, 493
　　Town, **598–600**
Planning and Development Surveyor, 589, 590, 592
Plant Operator
　　Armed Forces, 19
　　Building/Construction, **577–578**
　　Farming, 604
Plants and Nature (and Animals), **602–645**
Plasterer, **567–568**
Plastic Surgeon, 247
Plastics Process Operative, **537–538**
Plastics Technologist, 442
Platemaker (printing), 541
Plater/Fabricator (heavy engineering), **488–490**
Platoon Weapons Specialist (RM), 13
Plumber, **568–570**
Podiatrist, **284–286**
Police Constable, **345–347**
Police Photographer, 102
Police Underwater Search Diver, 345, 685, 686, 687
Policeman/woman, 345–347
　　in Armed Forces, 16, 19, 23, 26
Polisher (furniture), 531
Political Editor (newspapers), 127
Political Researcher, 396
Polo Stable Groom, 634
Polymer Scientist/Technologist, 442
Pony Trekking Centre Groom/Leader, 634, 637
Pop Group Road Manager, 190
Pop Musician, 156, 158
Porter
　　Hospital, **302–303**
　　Hotel, **221–222**
Post Office Counter Clerk, 683
Postal Work, 16, 19, **683–684**
Postman/woman, **683–684**
Poultry Processing Worker, 506
Practice Manager
　　Barristers' Chambers, 337
　　GP Surgery, 59
　　law firm, 339
Press Agency Journalist, 121
Press Officer, 34, 35, 423
Press Photographer, 102, 103
Presser (clothing), **526–527**
Primary School Teacher, 107–108, 111, 159

701

INDEX

Prince's Scottish Youth Business Trust, advice from, 2, 4
Prince's Youth Business Trust, advice from, 2, 4
Princess Mary's Royal Air Force Nursing Service (PMRAFNS)
    Nurse/Officer, 23, 26
Print Finisher, **544–546**
Print Originator, **541–543**
Printing Industry, **541–546**
Printing Machine Operator, 543
Prison Governor, **349–351**
Prison Officer, **351–353**
Prison Service, **349–353**
    Lecturer, 117
    Nurse, 251
    Psychologist, 326, 327
Private (in Army), 19–21
Private Hire Vehicle Driver, **658–659**
Private Practice Accountant, **361–363**
Private Practice Veterinary Surgeon, 621, 622
Probation and Aftercare, **312–314**
Probation Officer, **312–314**
    in Scotland, 306, 312, 313
Process Development Food Scientist/Technologist, 440
Process Manager (brewing), 508
Process Metallurgist, 443
Process Operative
    Chemical Plant, **547–548**
    Papermaking, **539–540**
    Plastics, **537–538**
Processing Clerk/Officer (banking/insurance), 372, 381
Procurator Fiscal Service staff (Scotland), 336
Procurement Officer, 428
Producer (films/radio/TV), 181
Product Development Food Scientist/Technologist, 440
Product Development Manager (marketing), 394
Production Assistant (films/radio/TV), **182–184**
Production Controller/Planner, 493
Production Electrician, 472
Production Engineer, 462
Production Manager, 440, 443, 493
Production Scientist/Technician, 435, 440, 443
Production Supervisor, 494
Production Worker, 493, **498–500**
    Gas/Oil Industry, 479
    Glassmaking, 510
Professional Builder, **557–560**
Professional Engineer: see Chartered Engineer; Incorporated Engineer
Professional Sports Coach, 166, 167
Professional Sportsman/woman, **169–175**
Project Manager
    Construction Industry, 462, 552, 558, 594
    Manufacturing Industry, 462
Proofreader, 127, 541
Property Management Services Surveyor, 589
Prosthetist, **300–301**
Protective (and Security) Services, **345–348**
Provost Officer (Armed Forces), 16, 23
PSV: see Bus...; Coach...; Passenger-Carrying Vehicle...
Psychiatric Nurse: see Mental...Nurse
Psychiatric Nursing Assistant, 256, 257
Psychiatrist, 248
Psychologist, 34, 36, 37, **326–328**
Psychotherapist, 248
PT: see Physical Education/Training...
Pub Barman/woman, 224–226
Public Health Laboratory Service Biomedical Scientist, 438, 439

Public Practice Accountant, 361–363
Public Relations Officer, **423–424**
Public Sector Accountant, 36, 43, **364–366**
Public Service Interpreter, 145
Public Service Vehicle: see Bus...; Coach...; Passenger-Carrying Vehicle...
Publican/Licensee, **223–224**
Publicity Officer (Civil Service), 34, 35
Publishing, **127–128**
    Book, 127
    Magazine/Newspaper, 121, 127
Pulpman/woman (papermaking), 539
Puppeteer, 155
Puppy Walker (guide dog), 628
Purchasing Officer, 43, **428–430**

Quality control/assurance staff, 440, 443, 446, 493, 539
Quality Controller/Tester, 493, **496–498**
Quantity Surveyor, 557, 590, 592
Quarantine Kennel Worker, 630
Quarries Inspector, 91
    see also Health and Safety Inspector
Queen Alexandra's Royal Army Nursing Corps (QARANC)
    Nurse/Officer, 16, 20
Queen Alexandra's Royal Naval Nursing Service (QARNNS)
    Officer, **5–8**
Queen's Counsel (QC), 334

RAC Patrolperson, 468–469
Racehorse Jockey, 171, 173
Radar Operator, 19
Radar Technician, 19
Radiation Protection Medical Technical Officer, 289
Radio Actor, 155
Radio Journalist/Reporter, 121
Radio Production Assistant, 182
Radio Research Assistant, 184
Radio Studio Manager, 187, 193
Radiographer, 20, 26, **280–282**
Radiologist (doctor), 248
Radiotherapy Medical Technical Officer, 289
RAF: see Royal Air Force
RAF Regiment Officer/Airman(/woman), 22, 26
Rail Transport, **666–672**
Railway Fitter/Electrician, **671–672**
Railway Signalling Technician, **670–671**
Railway Station Assistant, **667–668**
Railway Track/Overhead Line Worker, **668–670**
Railwayman/woman (Armed Forces), 19
Rally Driver, 171, 173
Ranger
    Countryside, **643–645**
    Forest, **618–620**
Rating
    Merchant Navy, **677–679**
    Royal Navy, 8–11
Receptionist, 45, **63–65**
    Dentist's Receptionist, 262
    Hotel Receptionist, **217–219**
Reconstructor/Notator (dance), 164
Recreational Diving Instructor, 685, 686
Recruitment/Selection Consultant/Manager, 50, 321
Reelerman/woman (papermaking), 539
Reflexologist, **296**, **297**, **298**
Refuse Collector, **231–233**
Registered Nurse, 20, **250–252**

INDEX

Registrar (hospital doctor), 247, 248
Rehabilitation Engineering Medical Technical Officer, 289
Religious Studies Teacher, 109
Renal Dialysis Medical Technical Officer, 289
Repair Work: *see* Maintenance/repair
Repertory Actor, 155
Reporter
    Court (legal), 341
    News, 121
Representative
    Insurance, 378
    Resort/Tour, 196, **201–203**
    Sales, **425**, **426**
Reprographics Operator, 32
Research Dietitian, 286
Research Engineer, 462, 493
Research Food Scientist, **439–440**
Research Horticulturist, 611
Research Materials Scientist, 443
Research Meteorologist, 454
Research Officer (Civil Service), 34, 36, 37
Research Scientist, 34, 36, 434, 435
Research Veterinary Surgeon, 621, 622
Researcher (film/radio/TV), 181, **184–186**
Residential Home Care Assistant, 309, 310, 311
Residential Social Worker, **308–309**
Resort Representative, 196, **201–203**
Respiratory Physiology Medical Technical Officer, 290
Restaurant Manager, **206–208**
Restorer/Conservator, **131–133**, 549
Retail bank staff, 369
Retail Butcher, 410, **415–416**
Retail Distribution, **405–422**
    Food Scientist/Technologist, 440
Retail Pharmacist, 269
Retail Pharmacy Technician, 271
Retail Sales Manager, 405
Retail Sales Representative, 425
Retail Store Demonstrator, 408
Reuters (Press Agency) Journalist, 121
Riding Holiday Groom/Instructor, 634, 637
Riding Instructor (horse), **635–638**
Riding School Groom, 634
Rifleman (Armed Forces), 13, 19
Rig Superintendent (gas/oil drilling), 479
Risk Manager, 374, **385–386**
River Policeman/woman, 345
Road Transport, **654–665**
    Manager, **654–655**
Roadworks Operative, 575
Rock Musician, 156, 158
Roman Catholic School Teacher, 109, 110
Roof Glazier, 565
Roofer, **570–571**
Room Attendant (hotel), **219–220**
Roughneck (gas/oil drilling), 478
Roustabout (gas/oil drilling), 478
Royal Air Force (RAF), **22–28**
    Airman/woman, **25–28**
    Officer, **22–25**
Royal Armoured Corps Officer/Soldier, 15, 19
Royal Army Veterinary Corps Officer/Soldier, 16, 20, 621, 623
Royal Artillery Officer/Soldier, 15, 19
Royal Corps of Signals Officer/Soldier, 15, 19
Royal Electrical and Mechanical Engineers (REME) Officer/Soldier, 16, 19

Royal Engineers Corps Officer/Soldier, 15, 19
Royal Logistics Corps Officer/Soldier, 16, 19
Royal Mail Driver, 662, 683
Royal Mail Postman/woman, 683–684
Royal Marines (RM), 5, **11–14**
    Diver, 685
    Officer, **11–12**
    other ranks, **13–14**
Royal Navy (RN)
    Diver, 5, 8, 685, 686, 687
    Officer, **5–8**
    Rating, **8–11**
Royal Society for the Prevention of Cruelty to Animals (RSPCA)
    Inspector, **626–627**
    Kennel Worker, 630
    veterinary staff, 623, 624
RSPB Countryside Officer/Ranger/Warden, 644
Rugby Player (professional), 170, 172–173
Rural Practice Surveyor, 589

Safety (and health), **87–92**
Sailor: *see* Seaman
Sales Assistant (retail), 407, 611
    see also Store Assistant
Sales Clerk, 61
Sales Manager, **425**, **426**
Sales Representative, **425**, **426**
Salesman/woman
    Cosmetics, 236
    Insurance, 378
    Stocks and Shares, 389, **390–391**
    Van Sales Driver, 661
SAS Officer (Army), 15
Scaffolder, **571–572**
Scan Operator (printing), 541
Scenery/Set Designer (films/theatre/TV), 100, 181
School Catering Manager, 208
School Cook, 210
School Librarian, 134
School Teacher
    in England and Wales, **107–110**, 160
    in Scotland, **110–113**, 160
    Special Educational Needs Teacher, **113–115**
    see also Teacher
Science Teacher, 435
Sciences, Mathematics and Related Work, **434–461**
Scientific Glassblower, 510
Scientific Illustrator, 95
Scientific Photographer, 102
Scientific Technician, 34, 36, 37, **434–437**
Scientist
    Biomedical, 434, **437–439**
    in Civil Service, 34, 36, 37, 434, 436, 437
    Food, 434, **439–442**
    Forensic, **459–461**
    Materials, 434, **442–445**
Scotland
    Accountant, 362
    Advocate, 331, 332, 333
    Advocates' Clerk, 338, 339
    Animal Welfare Inspector, **626–627**
    Banker, 371
    Butcher, 416
    College Lecturer, 116, 117, 119
    Community Education Worker, 168, **323–325**

703

INDEX

Countryside/Conservation Officer/Warden, 641, 643, 644
Court Officer/Macer, 343
Craft Baker, 504
Environmental Health Officer, 87, 88
Firefighter/Fire Officer, 354, 355
Forensic Scientist, 460, 461
Hairdresser, 241
Health Service Manager, 44
Legal Assistant, 339, 340
Music Teacher, 160
Nursery Nurse, 315
Orthotist/Prosthetist, 301
Physiotherapist, 279
Police Constable, 345, 346
Print Finisher/Bookbinder, 545
Prison staff, 349, 350, 351, 352
Probation Officer/Criminal Justice Social Worker, 306, 312, 313
School Teacher, **110–113**, 160
Shorthand Writer/Reporter (legal), 341, 342, 343
Social Worker, 307, 312
Solicitor, 336
Special Educational Needs Teacher, 114
see also under job titles (when there are no specific regional requirements)

Scottish Society for the Prevention of Cruelty to Animals (SSPCA) Inspector, **626–627**
Script Co-ordinator (TV), 182
Sea Transport, **673–679**
Seaman/woman
   in Armed Forces, 8, 19
     Merchant Navy, 677–679
Search and Rescue (SAR) Co-ordinator, 359
Search and Rescue (SAR) Diver, 685, 687
Secondary School Teacher, 108, 111, 159
Secretarial/Secretariat Officer (Armed Forces), 6, 22
Secretarial Work, **55–60**
Secretary
   in Armed Forces, 9
   in Civil Service, 32
   Company/Chartered, **48–49**
   Executive/PA, **55–56**
   Specialist, **56–60**
   TV Production, 182
Security Glass Fitter, 565
Security Guard/Officer, **357–358**
   in Armed Forces, 16, 23, 26
   in Civil Service, 32, 358
Security and Protective Services, **345–348**
Security Van Driver, 357, 358, 661
Selection/Recruitment Consultant/Manager, 50, 321
Self-employment, **1–4**
   see also individual jobs
Self-Service Counter Assistant, 215
Self-Service Petrol Station Attendant, 413–414
Selling and Buying and Related Services, **394–433**
Senior House Officer (hospital doctor), 247, 248
Senior Secretary, 55
Service Electrician, 472
Service Engineer/Technician
    Business Equipment, 483–485
    Domestic/Gas Appliance, 485–487
Servitor/Chairman (glass industry), 510
Session Musician, 158
Sewing Machinist, **525–526**
Sheet Metal Worker, **488–490**, 549

Sheeter/Cladder (roof/wall), 571
Shelf Filler (supermarket), 410
Shell *Live*WIRE, advice from, 2, 4
Sheriff (judge in Scotland), 334
Shift Supervisor (Production), 493
Shipbuilding Fabricator/Plater, 488, 489
Shipbuilding Industry Plumber, 569, 570
Shipwright, 19
Shoe Repairer, **421–422**
Shop: *see* Store...
Shopfitter, 562
Short-Order Cook, 210
Shorthand Writer/Reporter (legal), **341–343**
Signaller (Armed Forces), 13
Signalling Technician (railways), **670–671**
Signals Officer (Armed Forces), 11
Silver-Service Waiter/Waitress, 214
Singer, 156, 158
Site Engineer, 594
Site Manager (building/construction), 558, 594
Sites and Monuments Record (SMR) Officer, 141
Slater/Tiler, 570
Slaughterman/woman, 506
Snack Bar Cook, 210
Snack Bar Service Assistant, 215
Snooker Player (professional), 171, 173
Soccer Player (professional), 169–170, 172
Social and Related Services, **306–330**
Social Research Executive, 396, 397
Social Research Interviewer, 398
Social Sciences Research Officer, 34
Social Work, **306–311**
Social Worker
   Field Worker, **306–308**
   Residential Worker, **308–309**
Software Engineer/Analyst Programmer, **68–70**
Soldier (Army), 19–21
Soldiers', Sailors' and Airmen's Families Association (SSAFA) Social Worker, 307
Solicitor, 16, 37, **334–337**
Solo Musician/Singer, 156, 158
Sonar Operator Mechanic (RN), 8
Sound Editor (film/radio/TV), 181
Sound Technician/Operator (film/radio/theatre/TV), 181, **192–195**
Sous Chef (Under-Chef), 210
South Asian Dance Performer, 162, 164
Spatial Designer, 93
Special Air Service (SAS) Officer, 15
Special Boat Service (SBS) Officer/Diver, 11, 685
Special Branch Police Officer, 345
Special Educational Needs Teacher, **113–115**
Special Investigation Branch (SIB) Officer, 16
Specialist Secretary, **56–60**
Speech and Language Therapist, **283–284**
Speedway Rider (professional), 170, 173
Sports Coach/Instructor, **166–169**
Sports Editor (newspapers), 127
Sports and Leisure, **166–180**
Sports/Leisure Centre Assistant, **178–180**
Sports/Leisure Centre Manager, **175–178**
Sports Physiotherapist, 279
Sportsman/woman, Professional, **169–175**
Spreader/Cutter (clothing), **524–525**
Squash Courts Manager, 175
Staff Officer (Armed Forces), 5–6, 11, 16

INDEX

Stage Manager (theatre), 181, **186–189**
State Veterinary Service staff, 621, 622
Station Assistant (railways), **667–668**
Statistical Clerk (NHS), 45
Statistician, 34, 36, 37, 43, **446–448**
Steel Reinforcement Bender/Fixer, 575
Steward/Stewardess
    Airline, 648–649
    in Armed Forces, 9
Stipendiary Magistrate, 334
Stock Exchange, **389–393**
    Actuary, 387
Stockbroker, 389, **390–391**
Stockbrokers' Investment Analyst, 389, 391, 392
Stockroom Worker (retail), 410
Store Assistant (retail), **407–408**
Store Demonstrator (retail), **408–410**
Store Manager (retail), **405–407**
Storekeeper, 9, 32, 680
Stores Officer (Armed Forces), 6, 16
Structural Engineer, 462, 594
Studio Manager (radio), 187, 193
Stunt Performer, 155, 685
Stylist (Hairdressing), 239
Sub-Editor, 127
Submarine Officer (RN), 5
Submarine Rating (RN), 9
Summer Show Performer, 155
Supermarket Worker, **410–411**
Supplies Manager/Officer, 43, 428
    in Armed Forces, 5–6, 16, 22
Supplies staff (Armed Forces), 9, 19, 26
Support Worker (Care Assistant), 309
Surgeon, 247, 260
    Veterinary, 16, **621–623**
Surgery and Medicine, **245–249**
Survey Recorder Operator Mechanic (RN), 8
Surveying and Land Management, **589–593**
Surveyor, **589–593**
    in Armed Forces, 5, 19
    in Civil Service, 34, 36, 37
    Geological, 452
    Insurance, 374, **382–383**
    Quantity, 557, 590, 592
Survival equipment staff (Armed Forces), 9, 25
Swimming Pool Attendant, 178
Swimming Pool Manager, 175
Swimming Teacher, 167
Swimwear Designer, 98
System Engineer, 462
Systems Analyst (Armed Forces), 25
Systems Analyst/Designer (information systems), **66–68**

Tailor, **521–522**
Tank Crewman (Army), 19
Tax Inspector, 35, 36, 37
Taxation Adviser, 361, 369
Taxi Driver, **658–659**
Teacher
    in Armed Forces, 16, 110, 112
    Dance, 164
    in England and Wales, **107–110**
    English as Foreign/Second Language, 16, **149–152**
    Hairdressing, 241
    Home Economics, 227
    Music, 111, **159–162**
    Nursery, 107, 111
    Physical Education, 111, 168
    Primary School, 107–108, 111, 159
    Science, 435
    in Scotland, **110–113**
    Secondary School, 108, 111, 159
    Special Educational Needs, **113–115**
    Swimming, 167
    Technology/Technological Education, 107, 110, 111
Teaching, **107–120**
Technical Author, **124–126**
Technical Brewer, **508–509**
Technical Illustrator, 95
Technical Sales Representative, 425
Technical Supply Officer (RAF), 22
Technical Surveyor, 589, 591
Technical Writing (and Journalism), **121–126**
Technician
    Accounting, **366–368**
    Ambulance, 292, 293
    Archaeological, 141, 143
    Architectural, 554
    Audio-Visual, 181
    Building, 558
    Building Services, **582–584**
    Civil Engineering, 594, 595
    Communications (Armed Forces), 8, 19
    Dental, 20, 26, **266–268**
    Dyeing (textiles), **517–519**
    Engineering, 8, 25, 33, 35, 37, 462, 463, 464, 465, 582, 583, 594, 595
    Environmental Health, 20, 26
    Food Science, **439–442**
    Forensic, 460
    Hair Colouring/Perming, 240
    Laboratory, 20, 26, 434
    Materials Science, 443
    Medical, 9, 20
    Medical Physics/Science, 289, 434
    Motor Vehicle, **467–469**
    Operating Theatre, 20
    Paper Testing, 539
    Pharmacy, 20, **271–272**
    Photographic, 102, **105–106**
    Physiological Measurement, 20, 289–290, 291
    Scientific, 34, 36, 37, **434–437**
    Signalling (railways), **670–671**
    Sound (film/radio/theatre/TV), 181, **192–195**
    Telecoms, 13, 19, 25, **475–477**
    Textile, **516–517**
    Textile Dyeing, **517–519**
    Theatre/Concert Lighting, 190
    Town Planning, **600–601**
    Vehicle Body Repair, 470
    Video Production, 181
Technologist
    Architectural, **554–556**
    Food, 434, **439–442**
    Leather, **513–515**
    Materials, 434, **442–445**
Technology/Technological Education Teacher, 107, 110, 111
Telecoms Engineer, 475
Telecoms Operator (Armed Forces), 19, 25
Telecoms Technician, **475–477**
    Armed Forces, 13, 19, 25
Telephonist, 32

INDEX

Television Actor, 155, 685
Television Camera Operator, 181, 189–190, 685
Television Floor Manager, 181, **186–189**
Television Journalist/Reporter, 121
Television Production Assistant, 181
Television Researcher, 181, 184
Television Scenery/Set Designer, 100
Television Sound Technician/Operator, 193
Tennis Player (professional), 170–171, 173
Tertiary College Lecturer, **115–118**
Tester/Quality Controller, 493, **496–498**, 539
Textile Designer, 93, **99–100**
Textile Dyeing Technician, **517–519**
Textile Operative, **519–520**
Textile Technician, **516–517**
Textiles, 516–520
Theatre/Broadcasting/Film, 181–195
Theatre Lighting Designer/Technician, 181, 190
Theatre Production Assistant, 182–183
Theatre Researcher, 184
Theatre Scenery/Set Designer, 100, 181
Theatre Sound Designer/Engineer/Technician, 181, 193
Theatre Stage Manager, 181, **186–189**
Theatre-in-Education Performer, 155
Theatrical Costume Designer, 99, 181
Therapeutic Radiographer, 281
Therapist
    Alternative/Complementary Medicine, 295–299
    Beauty Therapist, **234–236**
    Dance/Movement Therapist, 164
    Horticultural Therapist, 609, 611
    Occupational Therapist, 282–283
    Physiotherapist, 20, **278–280**
    Psychotherapist, 248
    Speech/Language Therapist, **283–284**
Therapy and Treatment, 279–288
Three-Dimensional Designer, 93, **96–98**, 552, 554
Tiler
    Floor/Wall, **573–574**
    Roof, 570
Toolpusher (gas/oil drilling), 478
Tour Coach Driver, 656
Tour Manager, **200–201**
Tourism and Travel, 196–203
Tourist Information Centre (TIC) Assistant, **196–197**
Town Planner, **598–600**
Town Planning, 598–601
Town Planning Technician/Support Staff, **600–601**
Track/Overhead Line Worker (railways), **668–670**
Tractor Driver, 604
Trading Standards Officer, **85–86**, 227
Traffic Engineer, 594
Traffic Policeman/woman, 345
Traffic Warden, **347–348**
Train Driver, **666–667**
Training and Enterprise Councils (TECs), advice from, 2
Training Manager/Officer, 50, **52–54**
    in Armed Forces, 5, 16, 23
Training Video Actor, 155
Transfer Courier (travel), 199
Translator, 34, 36, **147–149**
Transport, 646–687
Transport Manager, **654–655**
Transport movements staff (Armed Forces), 16, 19, 22, 26
Transport Reservations Clerk, 61
Travel Agency Clerk, 196, **197–199**

Travel Booking Clerk, 61
Travel Consultant, **197–199**
Travel Courier, 196, **199–200**
Travel and Tourism, 196–203
Treatment and Therapy, 279–288
Trekking Centre Groom/Leader, 634, 637
Tropical Medicine Doctor, 247
Truck Driver
    Construction Plant, 577
    see also Lorry Driver
TV: *see* Television...
Two-Dimensional Designer, 93
    see also Artist; Graphic...; Textile Designer
Typesetter, 541
Typist, 32, 55, 61
Tyre/Exhaust Fitter, **412–413**

UKAEA Police Constable, 346
Ultrasound Medical Technical Officer, 289
Under-Chef, 210
Undertaker, 242–244
Underwater Operator Mechanic (RN), 8
Underwater Search (Police) Diver, 345
Underwriter (insurance), **374–376**
Underwriting Clerk, 381
Unisex Hairdresser, 239, 240
University Lecturer, 118, 141, 143, 260, 441, 450, 596, 621, 622
University Librarian, 134
Upholsterer, **529–531**

Valuer/Auctioneer, 589, 591
Van Driver, **661–662**, 683
Van Sales Driver, 661
Variety Show Performer, 155, 162, 164
Vehicle Body Repairer, **469–471**
Vehicle Electrician, 19, 467, 472
Vehicle Maintenance, 467–471
Vehicle Mechanic/Technician, 13, 19, 25, **467–469**
Ventilating (and Heating) Fitter/Welder, **584–586**
Verbatim Reporter, 341
Veterinary Nurse, 621, **623–625**
Veterinary Surgeon, 16, **621–623**
Veterinary Work, 621–625
Video Actor, 155
Video Cameraman/woman, 190
Video Editor, 189
Video Sound Recordist, 193
Vinyl (floor-covering) Layer, 563
Virologist, 438
Vision-Impaired-Children Teacher, 113, 114
Voluntary Help Organizer, 329
Voluntary Service Overseas opportunities
    Accountant, 366
    Ambulance Person, 294
    Dentist, 262
    Horticulturist, 611
    Midwife, 253
    Teacher, 110, 119, 151
Volunteer Manager, **329–330**

Wages Clerk, 61
Waiter/Waitress, 213
Wales
    Health Service Manager, 44
    see also England and Wales; Welsh-speaking...
Wall/Floor Tiler, **573–574**

INDEX

Wallpaper Hanger, 566
Ward (health care) Assistant (NHS), 257
Warden
    Countryside, **643–645**
    Traffic, **347–348**
Warehouse Worker, 410, **680–681**
Warfare Officer (RN), 5
Watch-keeping Officer (Merchant Navy), 673
Water Engineer, 594
Weapon Engineer Officer (RN), 5
Weapons Specialist (RM), 13
Weapons Training Officer (RM), 11
Weather Forecaster, 454
Weaving Operative, 519
Weaving Technician, 516
Webmaster, **74–76**
Weight Lifting/Training Instructor, 166, 167, 178
Welder, **490–492**, 549, **584–586**
Welsh-speaking Camera/Sound Operator/Technician, 191
Welsh-speaking Teacher, 109
Wig-Fitter, 239
Wildlife Ranger, 643
Winderman/woman (papermaking), 539
Window Cleaner, **230–231**
Window Dresser (retail), 419
Window Fixer (Glazier), 565
Winter Sports/Holiday Representative, 202
Wood Floor Layer, 563
Word Processor Operator, 55, 61, 341
Work Study Officer, **83–84**
Workshop Fitter, 481
Workshop Joiner, 562
Workshop Service Engineer, 483, 485
Writer
    Copywriter (advertising), **401**, **402**
    Home Economics, 227
    Publicity/Public Relations, 34, 35, 423
    Technical, 124–126
    see also Journalist

Youth and Community Worker, 168, **323–325**

Zoo Keeper, **638–640**
Zoologist, 434

Index compiled by Paul Nash, Registered Indexer

OCCUPATIONS

STOP PRESS

For the first time, Occupations '99 is being piloted in a CD-Rom version.

The CD-Rom contains <u>all</u> the information included in the Occupations book with search facilities.

Please check minimum system specification requirements (see below) before placing your order.

There will be an evaluation card with the CD-Rom which will help with the future development of Occupations.

N.B. Occupations '99 on CD-Rom can <u>only</u> be ordered using the freepost order form below.

OCCUPATIONS '99

Minimum system specification: Windows 3.11® or Windows® 95, Pentium® or 486, 8Mb of Ram, SVGA monitor, 4 x CD-Rom drive speed or faster.

I/We would like to order Occupations '99 on CD-Rom at a cost of £16.50 (incl. VAT, postage and packing).

PHOTOCOPIES AND FAXED ORDERS ARE NOT ACCEPTABLE.

If you have any queries about the CD-Rom please telephone COIC on 0181 957 5030

Name..
Organisation ....
Address ....
....
....

OCCUPATIONS '99 CD ROM
COIC
FREEPOST SEA2853
PO BOX 298 A
THAMES DITTON
SURREY
KT7 0BR